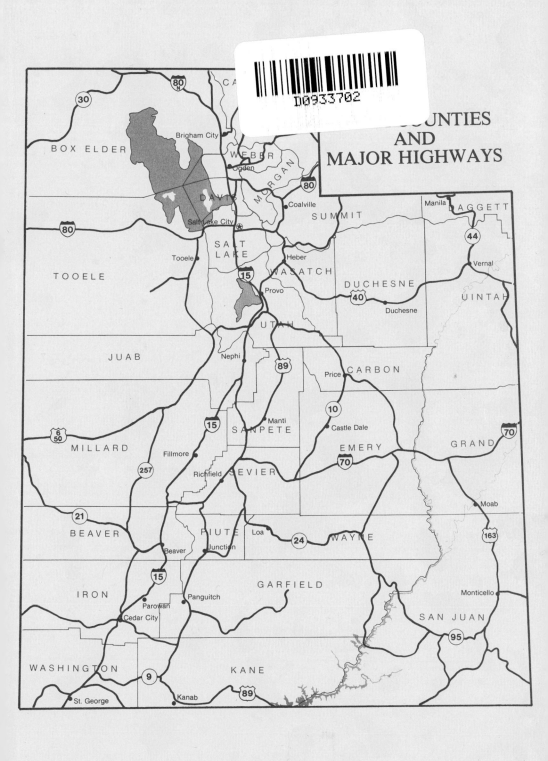

...UNTIES
AND
MAJOR HIGHWAYS

Publication of this volume
was made possible by financial contributions to
Utah: A Guide to the State Foundation
by the following benefactors:

Zeke and Kay Dumke
George and Gene Hatch
Herbert I. and Elsa B. Michael Foundation
Joseph and Evelyn Rosenblatt
Obert and Grace Tanner
Sam and Lila Weller

Utah Arts Council

Utah State Capitol.

Utah

A GUIDE TO THE STATE

Revised and Enlarged

by

Ward J. Roylance

Consulting Editor

Eugene E. Campbell

Sponsored by the Utah Arts Council
Published by UTAH: A GUIDE TO THE STATE Foundation
Salt Lake City, Utah
1982

WARD J. ROYLANCE is the author of more than 40 informational and educational publications on Utah. Holder of a graduate degree from the University of Utah, he has produced teaching materials on the subject of Utah for use in the state's schools, as well as popular guidebooks and state informational publications. For a number of years Mr. Roylance was employed by the Utah Tourist and Publicity Council (now the Utah Travel Council), where he was in charge of research and publications.

EUGENE E. CAMPBELL is professor emeritus of history at Brigham Young University. Dr. Campbell has published numerous articles on Mormon and Western history; has coauthored a college text on United States history as well as other volumes of history; and was associate editor of *Utah's History,* a college text published by Brigham Young University.

MARGARET D. LESTER, picture editor, is a professional librarian and picture source specialist. After a period with the Salt Lake City Public Library system, Mrs. Lester became Curator of Photographic Collections for the Utah State Historical Society, a position in which she served for more than 20 years.

First edition published in 1941
Revised edition published in 1982

First edition published under the auspices of
Utah State Institute of Fine Arts
Federal Works Agency
Work Projects Administration
First edition copyright 1941 by Utah State Institute of Fine Arts

Revised edition sponsored by
Utah Arts Council
Ruth Draper, Director
An agency of Utah Department of Community and Economic Development
Publication of revised edition financed by
Utah: A Guide to the State Foundation

ISBN 0-91470-23-7
Library of Congress Catalog Card No. 82-50370

Contents

Part 2. Touring Utah's Highways and Sideroads

Foreword
to the First Edition

Did you know that Theodore Roosevelt once took a bath beneath Rainbow Bridge; that Leland Stanford, when he swung on the "Golden Spike," missed; that Samuel Untermyer, trust-busting attorney, received the largest fee ever paid a lawyer for bringing about a merger of the Utah Copper Company with eastern interests; that Utah, a desert State, has a "sea serpent" story; that many of the "wisest" men a century ago predicted disaster for Mormon colonization of Utah under the direction of the Church President, Brigham Young?

Solid information interwoven with many a fascinating true story fills the pages of this book, written to make available to people without and within the State the facts about Utah—its places, its resources, its people. Complete coverage, accuracy, and readability was the three-fold goal. The large measure of success attained should make this book invaluable to schools, libraries, students, and casual readers alike.

Fully as significant, the Utah Guide supplies a glowing example of how reservoirs of unemployed labor and talent may be used to furnish the power for unique achievements that are valuable socially, artistically, and economically.

GAIL MARTIN
Chairman, Utah State Institute
of Fine Arts

June 1, 1940

Preface
to the First Edition

When Lansford W. Hastings wrote his *Emigrant's Guide to Oregon and California,* published at Cincinnati, Ohio, in 1845, urging use of the "Hastings Cutoff" across the Salt Desert to California, he produced the first guide book to treat even partially the present area of Utah. Hastings' book recommended a wagon route that could be traversed with difficulty on horseback, but it led wagon travelers, such as the Donner party, to tragedy. This guide to the Utah of 1941 is more conservative. One of a series prepared especially for automobile travelers on hard roads in the forty-eight States, it warns the traveler of rough stretches, quicksands, and waterless deserts. Lesser-known areas, reached only on shoe or saddle leather, are treated cautiously and factually, without the Hastings bravado.

The collective author has striven for accuracy, but in sifting thousands of facts from fifteen million words of field material, has no doubt fallen short in many instances. Where error is observed, we should appreciate substantiated corrections, looking toward the possibility of a future edition. This book has, indeed, a collective author. Local, county, State, and Federal agencies, transportation firms, commercial associations, motor clubs, newspapers, travel agencies, and hundreds of individuals have been of assistance in furnishing and checking material. Educational institutions —the University of Utah, Utah State Agricultural College, Brigham Young University, and others—have helped liberally in special fields. Librarians have been generous with their facilities, including Alvin Smith, L. D. S. Church librarian; Miss Julia T. Lynch, librarian, and Miss Johanna Sprague, former librarian, of the Salt Lake City Public Library; and Professor Esther Nelson, librarian of the University of Utah. Dozens of technical consultants have given their time and special knowledge in reading and correcting manuscript; space permits listing only a limited number of them in the Appendices.

In preparation of the text, too, the author was collective. The Utah Writers' Project takes pride in its cooperation with other projects: The Utah Art Project prepared art work and maps; William Wallace Ashby, Jr., executed the head pieces and Robert M. Jones the tail pieces. The Utah Historical Records Survey opened its files for much historical data, and aided the Writers' Project in preparation of the History essay, the Chronology, and the Selected Reading List. The Utah Adult Education Project provided the services of N. Field Winn for writing the articles on Geography and Climate, Geology, and Natural Resources and Conservation. Kenneth Borg, of the WPA Division of Operations, prepared the article on Irrigation.

Special thanks are due Mr. John M. Mills of Ogden and Mr. A. William Lund, assistant historian of the Church of Jesus Christ of Latter-day Saints, both of whom read the completed manuscript, corrected errors, and added essential material.

Maurice L. Howe, former State and regional director, and Charles K. Madsen, former State Supervisor, are responsible for gathering most of the factual matter presented in this book, and final work on the guide was done with the editorial co-operation of Darel McConkey of the WPA Writers' Program.

Population figures used are preliminary 1940 reports by the Census Bureau, subject to slight correction after issuance in 1941 of final figures.

DALE L. MORGAN
State Supervisor

Foreword

The original edition of *Utah: A Guide to the State* was a landmark publication, both as a model guidebook and as a model of good writing. It was among the best of the state guides put out with federal assistance during the Great Depression, and some of the best writers in the state at that time contributed to its success. Forty years have now gone by, and during that time new national and state parks have been created and a whole network of interstate highways has been built; cities have grown and times have changed. Because of these changes, almost everyone acquainted with the old guidebook has wished for a new edition that would bring the facts up to date while capturing those qualities that made the first edition so impressive.

Though many may have wished for an updated Utah guidebook, one person took steps to bring it about. Sam Weller, on his own initiative and out of his own pocket, retained the services of Ward Roylance to begin the work of revision. News of this activity reached Ruth Draper, Director of the Utah Arts Council, which, under the official title of the Utah State Institute of Fine Arts, had been the sponsor and holder of the copyright of the first edition. On 27 November 1978, Mrs. Draper brought together a group of people interested in promoting a new edition of the guidebook. Present at that meeting were Sam Weller, Ward Roylance, Edward L. Hart, chairman of the Literary Committee of the Utah Arts Council, Everett Cooley of the University of Utah, and representatives of a number of state agencies: Development Services, the Travel Council, Natural Resources, Industrial Promotion, and others. The group agreed that a republication of the guide was feasible and highly desirable.

It became apparent that an independent foundation was needed so that there would be a single agency responsible for handling the arrangements for revision and republication of the Utah guidebook; consequently, an organizational meeting was held on 15 July 1980 at which articles of incorporation were adopted for "Utah: A Guide to the State Foundation." The Foundation was established to function as a nonprofit corporation to receive and expend funds for the sole purpose of bringing into being and publishing a guidebook to the State of Utah. Edward L. Hart was elected chairman of the Board of Trustees, with Ruth Draper as director and Terrie Buhler as assistant director and secretary-treasurer. Other members of the Board were Reed T. Searle, Walter G. Smith, JoAnn Freed, Dennis Smith, and Lloyd Bliss; subsequently, Reed T. Searle resigned from the Board and Dale Carpenter and William B. Smart were added to it.

The Utah Guide Foundation purchased from Mr. Weller his investment in the revision work already done by Mr. Roylance and worked out an agreement and a schedule with Mr. Roylance for the completion of the rewriting and updating of the guidebook. The services of Eugene E. Campbell were retained as consulting editor of the projected book, with Mary Ann Payne to be copy editor. Early in 1981 Keith Montague became a technical consultant on the layout and design of the guidebook and Margaret Lester undertook the selection and handling of photographs and maps. Dr. Campbell, Mr. Montague, and Mrs. Lester all contributed time and professional skills far beyond any expectation of compensation, as did Anthony L. Rampton, who, throughout the whole course of the project, freely performed legal services for the Foundation, including drawing up the articles of incorporation and the various contracts required.

Work on the guidebook had proceeded sufficiently by April 1981 that basic decisions regarding design and size could be made, enabling the Foundation to request the submission of bids for the production of the book to a number of reputable printers. A subcommittee headed by JoAnn Freed studied the bids and recommended a choice to the Board, which accepted the recommendation and began immediately, through the Director, to effect the arrangements for the physical production of the guidebook.

Up to this point, funds for writing, editing, and technical assistance had been largely provided by the Utah Arts Council and the Utah Travel Council. Funds for the manufacture of the book: typesetting, printing, and binding, were far beyond the reach of the agencies that had nurtured the work through its gestation and had brought it to the point of birth. In an age of governmental belt-tightening, it was clearly perceived that private donors would have to be relied upon for the substantial sum of around $55,000 needed to make the guidebook a quality product of which the state and its people could be proud. Though no firm promises of contributions had been made by the autumn of 1981, the price of paper was about to go up, and the Foundation realized that if the cost was to be kept at the level of the bid a commitment to publish had to be made. It was; the necessary paper was purchased by the printer and the typesetting began. There could be no turning back.

The Foundation had believed from the start that public-minded benefactors would come forward to underwrite the remaining costs of the guidebook as soon as its significance was made known. That belief proved to be well founded. Early in January 1982 a generous sum of $10,000 each was donated by Zeke and Kay Dumke, George and Gene Hatch, the Herbert I. and Elsa B. Michael Foundation, Joseph and Evelyn Rosenblatt, and Obert and Grace Tanner. Sam Weller demonstrated commitment at the end as he had at the beginning when he and his wife Lila provided a gift of $5,000.

Funds accruing to the Foundation from the sale of the guidebook will be managed for the sole purpose of republishing it when a new edition is needed. Forty years have gone by since the appearance of the first edition. A revision probably should have been made sooner. It is the hope of everyone involved that the machinery is now in place to make the keeping in print of an up-to-date guidebook a self-perpetuating reality.

EDWARD L. HART
Chairman of the Board
Utah. A Guide to the State
Foundation

Preface

Moreso even than the 1941 edition, this volume has a collective author. If it were possible to identify all the observers, scholars, and compilers who were responsible basically for much of what is contained in this volume—and from whom I borrowed, knowingly or unknowingly—a mere listing of names would occupy many pages.

Dale L. Morgan, State Supervisor of the Utah Writers' Project which produced the 1941 edition of this guidebook, wrote in his Preface that thousands of facts were sifted from fifteen million words of field material in the preparation of that work. Even such an enormous quantity of research material, however, does not compare with what has been received by Utah archives in the four decades since 1940, or with the thousands of published titles on Utah subjects that have appeared since that date.

There is no claim, of course, that the author of the present work has found it possible to consult more than a fraction of the sources available for reference. However, this volume assuredly is the result of a sifting process, as was the 1941 edition—a personal sifting that has been underway not only during nearly four years of intensive research and writing immediately preceding the appearance of this guidebook, but during the prior thirty years as well. Throughout that period I have been involved in a serious love affair with Utah, to paraphrase Wallace Stegner, who once wrote about his love affair with Heber Valley. Those years have involved repeated travel to most parts of the state, observation, study, writing, photographic recording, and nearly eight years of employment with the Utah Tourist and Publicity Council, predecessor of the Utah Travel Council. Inevitably, my personal attitudes and convictions have become a part of this book; it is sincerely hoped, however, that these have not interfered with factual accuracy.

Whereas the former edition placed notable emphasis on history, this work places greater emphasis on geography, especially in the tour section, at the same time not neglecting historical, social, cultural, and economic factors. The book is a digest, a synopsis, and a synthesis of important facts, relationships, and concepts. It is concerned with generalities rather than minutiae. Therefore, it is not likely to be a research source for specialists. What will most gratify its creators is popular acceptance by the public as an enlightening *introduction* to Utah, and as a foundation from which to launch more detailed study.

I undertook the task of revising the 1941 edition in 1978, at the urging of Sam Weller, Salt Lake City businessman, Utah enthusiast, and bibliophile. Both were aware that the years following 1941 have been among the most eventful and momentous periods in Utah's history, but neither of us foresaw the magnitude of revision that would be required in updating and correcting the original book. The most recent four decades have witnessed change as profound as any in the state's history. Because of the limitations of space it became necessary to delete or abbreviate much of the first edition's content in order that material of more immediate interest to present-day readers could be added. Those who revere the old book will find many of its immortal passages reproduced in the new; and for the most part these are clearly identified. However, much of worth in the 1941 edition could not be included here. The new edition must be considered a *complement* to the first edition and not a replacement. Both works have independent value in their own right.

By far the greater part of this volume has been written since 1978. Most of the tour section is new; where quotations from the 1941 edition are used in that section, they are identified as such. Exceptions to this rule are portions of Tour No. 3 and descriptions of the older national parks and monuments, which have become composites of old and new. Part 1 (Utah's Background) represents a mixture of the old and new, though the greater part has been rewritten. Where portions of the 1941 edition were still applicable, those were retained in Part 1 with only moderate change. Examples are Plant Life, Animal Life, Indians and Archeology, and History before statehood. Latest available statistical sources were consulted, including the 1980 census. In a few cases I quoted verbatim, without attribution, from other of my published works. It is regretted that the admirable *Atlas of Utah* (Weber State College/Brigham Young University) was not available as a reference until the final months of manuscript preparation, but it did provide welcome assistance in later stages.

The section on The Arts is a cooperative product representing not only the research and interpretations of authors of new and old editions, but also those of current staff and consultants of the Utah Arts Council. That section is greatly indebted to the 1941 edition for history of The Arts to 1940. In this connection it should be noted that excerpts from the earlier book are not always identified as such. The Arts section, therefore, is truly an amalgam of new and old and represents the work of many authors.

Dr. Eugene L. Campbell, consulting editor, corrected and modified the first edition's account of 19th century history, in the process making a sincere effort to retain the outstanding literary and scholastic portions of the original. Dr. Campbell also revised several other history passages, including certain historical accounts in the tour section, and tendered valuable suggestions for a revision of the section on the Mormons in the Religion chapter.

The entire manuscript was read by Dr. Campbell, who proffered numerous suggestions for improvement. Dr. Campbell not only served as consulting editor; he was a wise adviser and friend who provided assistance and encouragement beyond the call of formal duty. A large portion of the manuscript also was read by Mary Ann Payne, by personnel of the Utah Travel Council, and by Dr. Dale J. Stevens, Professor of Geography at Brigham Young University, who likewise suggested corrections and beneficial changes. F. A. Barnes and S. George Ellsworth were kind enough to read Tours 11 and 1, respectively, and proffer suggestions. Various chapters and sections also were reviewed by subject specialists, chambers of commerce, government agencies, industries, universities, and others from whom information had been solicited. The contributions of all are acknowledged with deep appreciation.

Tour maps were adapted for the book by the author, from maps originally prepared by him for Wheelright Lithographing Company. Max Wheelwright generously made them available for modification. Special appreciation is extended to the following photographic sources for providing, without charge or at nominal cost, many of the illustrations used in this volume: U. S. Bureau of Reclamation, Utah Travel Council, Utah State Historical Society, Utah Division of Wildlife Resources, Utah Department of Transportation, Salt Lake Valley Convention and Visitors Bureau, S. George Ellsworth, and Union Pacific Railroad. Even commercial photographers were reasonable with their fees; among these should be mentioned F. A. Barnes, L. V. and Ruth McNeely, and Rell G. Francis (who provided G. E. Anderson photographs). A number of illustration gaps were filled, through necessity, with photographs by the author. Unfortunately, while satisfactory as color originals, these have lost a degree of sharpness during conversion to black-and-white. Any picture editor will verify the scarcity of quality black-and-white photographs, particularly of natural scenes; this scarcity was a serious problem in illustrating the tour section. Lastly, I must not fail to acknowledge the contribution of the Utah Outdoor Recreation Agency, which provided several of the full-page Utah maps appearing in the volume.

In his Foreword, Dr. Hart mentioned the contributions of Keith Montague, art consultant; Margaret Lester, picture editor; and Mary Ann Payne, copy editor. To his appreciation I append my own. All are experts in their respective fields, and they provided invaluable suggestions for layout, photo quality, and literary correctness. If this work does not reflect their standards, I must accept responsibility, for the reason that final decisions as to page layout, choice of illustrations and maps, content, and written expression were mine.

As noted above, and by Dr. Hart, Sam Weller provided the initial impetus for this work, with encouragement also from Dr. Everett L. Cooley of the Marriott Library, University of Utah. The book itself speaks my thanks to them. Ruth Draper, director of the Utah Arts Council, accepted the burden of preparation in mid-passage. Her gracious and able direction, and that of committee members who devoted uncounted volunteer hours to supervision and encouragement, merit the appreciation of every reader who finds this book of value. Without the contribution of financial sponsors, of course, there would be no book. Their names appear elsewhere, and I add here an expression of personal appreciation. Personnel of Publishers Press and Accu-Type also deserve commendation. To all those mentioned—and any others who might have been inadvertently omitted—I extend my heartfelt thanks.

The anonymous writers of the 1941 edition have had my gratitude and admiration for forty years. The volume they produced has become dog-eared from use, and their words inspired my dawning realization of Utah's uniqueness. Choosing which of their passages to retain or which to delete in this revision has been a most difficult and unpleasant task. I pray their understanding.

Responsibility for accuracy, of course, rests finally with the author. This I accept, but with trepidation and a plea for understanding if error is discovered. Several thousand sources have been consulted, evaluated, abbreviated, and paraphrased; in such a process, mistakes are inevitable. These I sincerely regret. It is hardly necessary to add that constructive criticism will be welcomed, and to ask that error be brought to the attention of the Utah Arts Council.

Last does not signify least: I cannot fail to acknowledge with deepest gratitude the contribution of my dear companion Gloria, who shared the burdens of the past four years but always revived flagging spirits with her unfailing faith and enthusiasm.

WARD J. ROYLANCE

April 1982

Facts at a Glance

Physical Facts

Area (1980) - Land   82,073 square miles
             Water   2,826 square miles

             Total   84,899 square miles   (Rank in U.S. - 11)

Maximum length of state - 345 miles from north to south
Average width of state - 275 miles from east to west
Highest point - Kings Peak in the Uinta Mountains, 13,528 feet above sea level
Lowest point - Beaver Dam Wash on Utah-Arizona border, about 2,200 feet above sea level
Highest recorded temperature - 116 degrees F. (St. George 1892)
Lowest recorded temperature - minus 50 degrees F. (Woodruff 1899 and Strawberry 1913)

Economic Facts

Most important economic activities -
    Government . . . Manufacturing . . . Trade and Services (including Travel/Recreation) . . . Mining . . . Construction

Most valuable products -
    Petroleum . . . Coal . . . Copper . . . Steel . . . Electronics . . . Machinery and Transportation Equipment (including missiles/rockets) . . . Livestock . . . Food

Civilian labor force (1981) - 640,000

Per capita income (1980) - $7,485 (46th among states, 79% of national average)

Population Facts

Population (1980) - 1,461,037
White 1,382,550
American Indians - Eskimos 19,256
Asian and Pacific Islands. 15,076
Black 9,225

Largest cities -

Salt Lake City	163,033	Bountiful	32,877
Provo	73,907	Logan	26,844
Ogden	64,407	West Jordan	26,794
Orem	52,399	Murray	25,750
Sandy	51,022	Layton	22,862

Counties of Utah

County	County Seat	Land Area (square miles)	1970	1980	Pop. per sq. mile of land area 1980*
Beaver	Beaver	2,584	3,800	4,378	2
Box Elder	Brigham City	5,603	28,129	33,222	6
Cache	Logan	1,174	42,331	57,176	48
Carbon	Price	1,476	15,647	22,179	15
Daggett	Manila	682	666	769	1
Davis	Farmington	297	99,028	146,540	490
Duchesne	Duchesne	3,255	7,299	12,565	4
Emery	Castle Dale	4,439	5,137	11,451	3
Garfield	Panguitch	5,158	3,157	3,673	1
Grand	Moab	3,682	6,688	8,241	2
Iron	Parowan	3,300	12,177	17,349	5
Juab	Nephi	3,412	4,574	5,530	2
Kane	Kanab	3,904	2,421	4,024	1
Millard	Fillmore	6,793	6,988	8,970	1
Morgan	Morgan	603	3,983	4,917	8
Piute	Junction	754	1,164	1,329	2
Rich	Randolph	1,023	1,615	2,100	2
Salt Lake	Salt Lake City	764	458,607	619,066	800
San Juan	Monticello	7,707	9,606	12,253	2
Sanpete	Manti	1,597	10,976	14,620	7
Sevier	Richfield	1,929	10,103	14,727	7
Summit	Coalville	1,849	5,879	10,198	5
Tooele	Tooele	6,923	21,545	26,033	4
Uintah	Vernal	4,487	12,684	20,506	5
Utah	Provo	2,014	137,776	218,106	109
Wasatch	Heber City	1,191	5,863	8,523	7
Washington	St. George	2,427	13,669	26,065	11
Wayne	Loa	2,486	1,483	1,911	1
Weber	Ogden	581	126,278	144,616	250
			1,059,273	1,461,037	18

*Rounded off for simplicity

Important Dates

1776 Fathers Dominguez and Escalante made first comprehensive exploration of Utah.

1824 General William H. Ashley's trappers entered Utah.

1825 Ashley explored Green River. First trappers' rendezvous held on Henrys Fork.

1830 Book of Mormon published. Mormon Church organized at Fayette, New York.

1841 Bartleson-Bidwell party, enroute to California, brought first emigrant wagons across Utah.

1843 Captain John C. Fremont explored northern Great Salt Lake; returned following year.

1844 Joseph and Hyrum Smith shot to death by mob at Carthage, Illinois.

1846 Harlan-Young and Donner-Reed emigrant parties broke wagon trails across Utah.
Mormons began migration from Nauvoo. Mormon Battalion entered U.S. Army.

1847 First companies of Mormon pioneers arrived in Great Salt Lake Valley. Brigham Young named president of Mormon Church.

1848 Treaty of Guadaloupe Hidalgo ended war with Mexico; Utah area passed under United States sovereignty. First pioneer crops harvested.

1849 Gold rush brought thousands west, many through Great Salt Lake City. Constitution adopted for Provisional State of Deseret.

1850 Congress created Territory of Utah. *Deseret News* began publication.

1851 Brigham Young took oath of office as governor of Utah Territory.

1852 Plural marriage proclaimed to world as Mormon doctrinal tenet.

1853 Ground broken for Mormon Temple in Great Salt Lake City.

1854 Grasshopper infestations began, to continue for several years.

1856 Hand-cart migrations across the plains began, continuing until 1860.

1857 Government ordered an army to quell "rebellion" in Utah; army was forced into winter quarters near Fort Bridger. Mountain Meadows massacre occurred.

1858 "Utah War" ended; troops settled at Camp Floyd.

1860 Pony Express commenced east and west operations through Utah.

1861 Overland Telegraph completed. Camp Floyd abandoned by federal troops.

1862 Salt Lake Theater dedicated. Camp Douglas founded.

1865 Ute Black Hawk war began, continuing until 1868.

1867 Grasshopper onslaughts renewed. Tabernacle completed in Salt Lake City.

1869 Union Pacific and Central Pacific railroads met at Promontory.

1872 First smelting and refining commenced in Salt Lake Valley.

1874 United Order established. Poland anti-polygamy bill passed by Congress.

1875 Brigham Young Academy founded; became university in 1903.

1877 Brigham Young died. St. George LDS Temple completed.

1880 Electric lighting instituted, followed shortly by first telephone system.

1882 Congress passed anti-polygamy Edmunds Law, disfranchising polygamists.

1883 Denver & Rio Grande Western Railroad completed between Denver and Salt Lake City.

1884 Prosecutions commenced under the Edmunds Law.

1887 Congress passed Edmunds-Tucker Act. John Taylor died, succeeded as president of Mormon Church 1889 by Wilford Woodruff.

1890 Utah State Agricultural College opened. Wilford Woodruff issued manifesto. Free school system established. Population 210,779.

1893 Mormon Temple dedicated in Salt Lake City. Amnesty granted to polygamists.

1896 Utah admitted as 45th state, January 4. First autos arrived in Utah.

1898 Park City destroyed in disastrous fire. Wilford Woodruff died, succeeded by Lorenzo Snow.

1900 Population 276,749. Explosion at Winter Quarters coal mine killed 200.

1901 Lorenzo Snow died, succeeded by Joseph F. Smith as Mormon Church president.

1903 Reed Smoot elected U.S. Senator, beginning 30 year Senate career. Lucin Cutoff completed across Great Salt Lake. Utah Copper Co. organized.

1905 Railroad completed between Salt Lake City and southern California.

1911 Strawberry Reservoir completed, first large reclamation project in Utah.

1915 State Capitol completed.

1917 Utah mustered men and capital for World War I. Prohibition laws took effect.

1918 Armistice signed. Joseph F. Smith died, succeeded by Heber J. Grant.

1920 Population 449,396.

1922 KSL radio station began broadcasting in Salt Lake City.

1926 Commercial airlines began operations in Utah. Ironton plant opened.

1928 Bryce Canyon National Park established.

1930 Population 507,847. Centennial of Mormon Church organization.

1933 Utah ratified prohibition repeal amendment.

1940 Population 550,310. Utah State Symphony Orchestra founded. Wendover Air Force Base established; enlarged 1942 and 1943. Construction began at Hill Field.

1941 Japanese attack on Pearl Harbor marked entrance of U.S. into World War II.

1942 Numerous military installations opened or were under construction in Utah.

1944 Geneva Steel Works completed, began operations.

1945 World War II ended. Heber J. Grant died, succeeded as president of Mormon Church by George Albert Smith.

1947 Utah Centennial Celebration. Pioneer Monument dedicated. Maurice Abravanel engaged as music director of Utah Symphony.

1948 KDYL (later KCPX) became Utah's first television station.

1950 Population 688,862. Korean War began. Wallace Bennett began 24-year Senate career.

1951 George Albert Smith died, succeeded as Mormon Church president by David O. McKay.

1952 Charles A. Steen discovered "Mi Vida" uranium deposit in San Juan County.

1954 Weber State College moved to new campus. First television broadcast in color.

1955 Utah's missile industry was born.

1956 Colorado River Storage Project authorized. Aneth Oil Field discovered. Construction began at Glen Canyon damsite.

1959 Multi-million dollar missile contracts awarded to Utah firms.

1960 Population 890,627. Ground was broken for Thiokol rocket plant.

1963 Glen Canyon Dam completed. Flaming Gorge Dam completed.

1964 Canyonlands National Park established.

1965 Craig Breedlove attained speed of 601 mph at Bonneville Salt Flats.

1968 More than 6,000 sheep died in Skull Valley, apparently of nerve gas poisoning.

1969 State Board of Higher Education created by legislature.

1970 Population 1,059,273. David O. McKay died, succeeded as Mormon Church president by Joseph Fielding Smith.

1971 Arches and Capitol Reef national parks established (formerly national monuments).

1972 Joseph Fielding Smith died, succeeded as Mormon Church president by Harold B. Lee.

1973 Harold B. Lee died, succeeded by Spencer W. Kimball.

1977 Scott M. Matheson (D) became 12th governor of Utah.

1978 Mormon Church president announced revelation opening Mormon priesthood to worthy men of all races.

1980 Population 1,461,037. Provo surpassed Ogden as second largest city.

1981 Construction began on Intermountain Power Project.

UTAH: A GUIDE TO THE STATE

Part 1

UTAH'S BACKGROUND

Contemporary Scene

The 1941 edition of this guidebook was noted for passages of stirring grace, and no section of that volume was more eloquent than its introductory chapter entitled the Contemporary Scene. There the anonymous author attempted to define those elusive qualities that contributed to Utah's uniqueness: its "cross-grained" history, the peculiarities of its dominating religious faith, the conservatism of its social fabric, its characteristic symbolisms, and the universal consciousness of earth among its residents. A masterful writer today would find it no small task to surpass that brief description in succinctness and appropriate phraseology, and indeed a number of its passages merit the immortality of repetition. Unfortunately, one example of length must suffice:

The Mormon habitat has always been a vortex of legend and lie. Even today, as the State settled down to gray hairs, there lingers something wonderful and outrageous about Utah, a flavor of the mysterious and strange. Many still journey to Utah to see a Mormon.

Even if there had been no background of Joseph Smith, Angel Moroni, and the Book of Mormon, Utahns would have been incomprehensible, misunderstood and lied about, because they set down in the book of Western history the most stubbornly cross-grained chapter it contains. All the conventions of Western life in Utah went haywire. Only late, and briefly, did Utahns turn feverish, like their neighbors, with get-rich-quickness. Wars of cattle baron and homesteader dissolved at Utah's borders, because farmers had come first to the creeks. Lynch law wandered into the bishops' courts to sit in the back pews and watch, bemused, the quiet sanity of theological justice. Immaculate woman and scarlet woman together lifted their petticoats to take flight before family migrations and polygamy. Utah has always had a way of doing things different. The rest of the country has never quite got over it.

Much of that pioneer distinctiveness survives in Utah life, although the forces of twentieth century civilization have shaped Utah into patterns of conformance, so that there are fewer outward stigmata to a Utahn, and somewhat less wild speculation about him. Most visitors now betray no disappointment at finding Mormons hornless.

1941 edition

The Contemporary Scene of recent times bears only fragmentary likeness to the Contemporary Scene of forty years ago. The Mormon flavor that was predominant in earlier days, so vividly described in the 1941 edition, no longer is as easy to discern. It would not be as accurate today as it was then to claim that "Utahn" is regarded as synonymous with "Mormon," or that "the stamp of a pioneer culture is everywhere manifest," particularly in the richest and oldest-settled area. The log and adobe houses so reverently pictured in the first edition and fairly abundant then, are not so apparent today.

It can still be claimed with qualification that "in the outlands most nearly survives the old Mormon society." Even in the outlands, however, traditional ways have been modified. Developments since the 1940s have brought newcomers by the thousands to the hinterlands, for a transient if not always permanent stay: to the Uinta Basin, Grand and San Juan counties, western Millard County, and eastern Garfield County, for example. Washington County has become a four-season vacationland and retirement community, and even rural Rich and Summit counties are being invaded by oil developers. Few if any undiluted bastions of old-time Mormonism remain in Utah. The automobile, paved roads, television, radio, tourist and recreational travel, the summer-home trend, growing population, in-migration, energy development—all have had a part in transforming not only the rural areas but the urban as well, from the provincial, slow-paced, past-oriented Utah of 1940 to a much different society today.

Yet there are kernels of description in the 1941 edition that might fittingly be applied to the Utah of today. Speaking of smaller towns, "If houses could not stand as monuments to a culture, trees, gardens, and sheer greenness could." Luxuriant greenness still marks the scattered oases where people live in this essentially arid state.

"The cities themselves, almost universally set four-square to the directions, reflect an ideal of spacious and noble planning. Exigencies of one kind and another have invaded the grand sweep of pioneer planning, but nothing is more quickly remarkable to visitors than the breadth and straightness of the streets, the width of the sidewalks, and the length of blocks in Utah cities. And all the cities are tree-grown, comfortable with homes and lawns and gardens and flowering shrubs." This description of Utah 1940 would be accurate today with respect to the older districts of larger cities. Urban sprawl, however, has profoundly modified the basic four-square character of the larger cities since 1940, in their outskirts if not in their cores. Diagonal boulevards and freeways now give rapid and direct access to the suburbs. Streets in newer residential areas are more likely to curve and wind than to follow a straight line, and numbered street names are the exception in newer districts.

Suburban and industrial sprawl had only begun in 1940. Since that time it has climbed the foothills to the highest levels of prehistoric Lake Bonneville, spread across the valley floors, and created metropolitan complexes where pastoral landscapes formerly blended with the outskirts of modest cities and towns. In the five-county area between Brigham City on the north to Payson-Santaquin on the south, the population tripled in forty years from 360,000 in 1940 to 1,160,000 in 1980. About 65 per cent of the state's population resided in those counties in 1940; the proportion had grown to 80 per cent in 1980.

"'Utahn' is regarded as almost synonymous with 'Mormon', although there have always been those who would quarrel fiercely with this assumption. Although the total Church membership ('Church' meaning always the Church) numbers perhaps only three-fifths of the population, the particular quality of Utah life is almost wholly Mormon. Whatever there is of substance to the 'gentile' influence represents, if native to Utah, a reaction to

Mormon culture rather than anything distinctive in its own right.'' These allegations certainly are less true today than they might have been in 1940, and even then their accuracy was questionable. "Good" Mormons (meaning active) probably number about half the state's population, and the significant non-Mormon segment would vehemently deny that "the particular quality of Utah life is almost wholly Mormon." It is true that "No smoking" is the rule in enclosed public places; that liquor is strictly controlled by the state; that a greater proportion of the population attend religious services on Sunday, probably, than elsewhere in the nation; and that there is less tobacco smoking and alcohol consumption than in other states. To the sophisticated traveler, however, these traits hardly set Utah apart as markedly peculiar. It might effectively be argued, in fact, that the well-traveled observer would detect only a few notable singularities of outward appearance and behavior between the people of Utah's larger cities and those of other northern cities of the United States. To be sure, close analysis of individual lifestyles undoubtedly would reveal differences, but those would hardly be apparent to the casual observer. Perhaps the most obvious difference between Utah and places of more cosmopolitan cultural mix is the uniformity of race in this state, there being in Utah an overwhelming preponderance of Caucasians of northern European origin. Some claim that Utah stands apart in the physical beauty of its youth, and of its younger women in particular.

It is a common complaint that Mormon religious strictures have created a staid, placid, restrictive social environment, where the sidewalks are rolled up at dusk and there is a dearth of vivacity. While it cannot be denied that Utah communities after dark hardly qualify as "swinging" places, evening cultural events and night-life opportunities are not absent, and it is doubtful whether Utah differs greatly in these respects from cultures of like population in other places. The central commercial districts of many American cities, including those in Utah, expire after business hours, primarily because only transient hotel and motel guests reside in them. This situation is beginning gradually to change, in Salt Lake City at least, as condominium apartments are built in the downtown area and commercial structures are converted to residential use.

Outward appearances aside, it must be admitted that subtle Mormon influences color many aspects of Utah life. The extent of these influences in particular cases may be (and often is) the subject of debate. Whatever that influence may be, seldom do Mormons take positions *en bloc*. When such a large portion of the total population is comprised of inactive Mormons or non-Mormons, it probably belabors an old whipping horse to assert inordinate Mormon influence except in specific cases where such influence can be shown.

In 1940, Utah's neighborliness was *"often remarked by visitors; here the years tell their own tale, for outlanders frequently, in early days, were viewed with a chill and suspicious eye.''* Visitors still remark about the open friendliness and courtesy of the majority of Utahns who serve their commercial needs. Nevertheless, judging by rather frequent letters to the editors of major newspapers, at least a few non-Mormon residents are embittered by what they perceive as a lack of either friendliness or neighborliness in Utah. It can be argued, of course, that this complaint is common in any society, regardless of religious constituency, and that it is everywhere prevalent in rural as well as urban areas.

"The State is also too close to its pioneer beginnings for the social amenities to come with entire grace. Art has been backward, and literature and music have been subordinated to religious ends." While Utah may yet be considered a cultural backwater in certain quarters (and in fact many of its own people have not completely shed a traditional sense of provincial inferiority, curiously tempered in some Utahns with a degree of self-righteous arrogance), there is no justifiable reason why Utahns should not take pride in their genuine social and cultural achievements. *"Probably there is a greater cosmopolitan leavening to Utah society, urban and rural, than anywhere in the country. . . ."* If that was true 40 years ago, it is not less so today. *"Education has been a pride of Utahns, who point to one of the highest literacy ratings in the country, but the State has not been sufficiently rich either economically or socially to attract from outside the mature, reflective minds that enrich popular living."* That observation of 1941 may have some validity today, but certainly not to the same extent, as attested by the state's admirable educational, cultural, and recreational assets and attainments. It is doubtful if any other society of equal numbers can claim a richer heritage in this respect than Utah, as described in the chapters that follow.

"In Utahns there is universally a consciousness of the earth, in part because of the recency of its pioneering, but principally because Utah is an uncertainly subdued land." Surely, among Utahns, there is a consciousness of nature, if for no other reason than its overwhelming omnipresence. And yet it must be admitted that Utahns are far from being unanimous in their opinions as to how their small part of the world should be developed or not developed. It is likely that the majority have no well-informed or considered opinions on that subject. Expediency, economic or otherwise, has been the customary criterion for development. Recent years have brought individual and official questioning of the traditional uses of land and other natural resources, a questioning rarely seen in the past except with respect to federal holdings. As a society, Utahns seem not to perceive their state as a place having distinctive and even unique natural qualities—qualities that deserve the most serious assessment and appraisal before transforming uses are permitted. Many Utahns, in fact, are adamant—as were their ancestors—in insisting that any use is preferable to purely scenic or wilderness status; and even on official and professional levels minimal attention has been given to esthetic compatibility as an element worthy of consideration in determining uses of land. This tendency alone would indicate that Utah lags behind cultures of greater age or sophistication where land is treated with respect and economic factors are not the sole determinants of use.

As with land, so have other resources been regarded in the past. Only in the most recent decades, for the most part, has unrestricted development been questioned. Serious environmental problems remain unresolved or only partially ameliorated, and new ones become apparent almost daily. Collectively, Utahns have no idealized concept of what they would like their environment to be, or what it should be. Specific goals there are, but broad, generalized, idealized societal and environmental goals are lacking.

"In Salt Lake City, in Ogden and Provo and Logan, the immensity of the State is circumscribed, and the world is as near as the front page of the daily newspapers. Yet the quiet hills bespeak something alien and impermanent to this urban reality of steel and stone, aspirin and cashiers' registers. One can almost start out of a dream to see these things perished and the land returned to the hills—green-gray with sage or tawny with dry June grass under the blue-drifting smoke of Indian campfires." Curiously enough, these words may be the stuff of prophecy. The Wasatch Fault is always a foreboding threat to "this urban reality," as is the very nature of the state's single most important economic activity, namely federal defense. Granted that no part of the world would be safe sanctuary in the event of nuclear conflict, Utah is particularly vulnerable in that three-fourths of the population reside within 50 miles of a number of inviting military targets.

In this connection it might be noted that the leaders of the dominant church recently opposed placement of the MX missile in Utah and Nevada on the grounds that "Our fathers came to this western area to establish a base from which to carry the gospel of peace to the peoples of the earth. It is ironic, and a denial of the very essence of that gospel, that in this same general area there should be constructed a mammoth weapons system potentially capable of destroying much of civilization. . . ." That statement did not refer to the state's existing military industry, but it might have been applied as aptly to the sobering reality that tens of thousands of Utahns have been employed for decades in the manufacture, storage, distribution, or maintenance of nuclear, chemical, biological, and conventional weapons —a greater proportion of the labor force, perhaps, than is engaged in similar work in any other state.

"In the red deserts are Utah's scenic and scientific marvels . . . Mormon pioneers, cowboys, and sheepherders have looked upon marvels of natural color to see them as 'piles of rocks' that couldn't sprout a kernel or feed a beast." The red deserts are Utah's truly unique natural endowment, not matched anyplace else in the world. Utahns are gratified that the state possess more national parks than any other state except California. All of these are in the red-rock country. On the other hand, the great majority of Utahns do not realize that these parks are only isolated segments of a larger region that displays natural phenomena of comparable if not surpassing wonder. In other words, they do not realize that nearly all of eastern and southern Utah is *unique* in its topography and geology. Unquestionably this uniqueness would be recognized in a more mature, less youthful culture. It is a truism that non-residents are more appreciative of Utah's natural heritage than residents, and it is probably true, with respect to scenery and other recreational assets, that non-native entrepreneurs recognize both ethereal and commercial values more readily than native Utahns.

"Utah's deserts wait still, wrapped in multicolored serenity, for their full measure of appreciation. It is fitting that the worthless dry deserts . . . should begin, profitably for Utah, to instill in popular consciousness some other definition of the State than Mormonism, for the richer land has been pressed almost to its uttermost by the Mormon struggle with the earth. . . ."

Utah's deserts are hardly worthless, of course. They are mined for minerals and underground water, grazed by livestock, utilized for military testing, admired by tourists, and hiked by nature lovers. Industrialists propose to use them for power plants, strip mines and dams, and the largest man-made lake in the state is nestled in a superlative desert. Deserts may well be Utah's future in unimagined ways, as the "worthless" Great Salt Lake of 1941 is now one of the state's most productive mines. If Utahns fail to comprehend the worth of their deserts—and especially their red-rock deserts of the east and south, owned almost entirely by the federal government—this recognition will be forced upon them by others, perhaps after shameful and irremediable mutilation.

"The fertility of the land has been outstripped by the fertility of the people. The sons and daughters born so strangely stalwart from the loins of Eastern and European converts who left urban homes to wrestle with unfamiliar Utah deserts, today are migrating from the State, bringing their strength, their vigor, and their eager ambition to the great cities of either coast. They go like a lifeblood, from wounds that Utah hopes one day to close.'' Those wounds have been closing from the days of World War II, soon after the 1941 edition appeared, as economic opportunities have enabled more youths to remain in their native state, have invited expatriates to return, and have attracted non-natives by the thousands to make their homes in Utah.

It goes without saying that Utahns are not the sole arbiters of their destiny. Utah is largely an economic colony of out-of-state financial interests, and two-thirds of its land is owned by the federal government. It is influenced by national and international trends that are beyond the control of its people—even if its people could think with a single mind and act with a single purpose. Nevertheless, it is exciting to imagine the civilization that could arise from this choice land if Utahns collectively could gain a vision of their culture's *possibilities* and an ideal of *what should be!* Physical resources beyond measure, an inspirational environment, remarkable educational attainments, religious idealism, an enviable culture and historical heritage, an honest and responsive governmental system, and a stable economic foundation: these are Utah's rich endowments, and they should make it a superior state. If they have not done so, an elusive something is lacking. Could this missing factor be *collective aspirations?*

Natural Scene

The State is immense and varied, almost beyond belief. The band of irrigated green, west of the Wasatch Mountains, extends from north central Utah southward, curving gently west to a corner with Arizona and Nevada. West of this band is the gray-green Great Salt Lake, gray desert, and peaked mountains. Eastward is the red desert country of the Colorado Plateau, yellowing as it approaches the Uinta Mountains on the north, ever reddening as it extends southward and eastward to the Arizona and Colorado lines—a country of flat-topped mountains and violent color. These dessicated gray and red deserts, and these mountains, represent more than 90 per cent of Utah. The tremendous weight of the land lies upon everything. The mountains climb into the skies; the deserts ache with sheer empty immensity. Utah is many things at once: Utah is green-carpeted vales lying peacefully under the shadow of the Wasatch; Utah is a wide solitude of rolling dry valleys, with hills marching beyond hills to blue horizons; Utah is unearthly white desert; Utah is tall snow-crowned mountains; Utah is blue lakes; Utah is canyon and plateau wonderfully fragrant with pines.

1941 edition

Heber Valley, Deer Creek Reservoir and the Wasatch Range, looking west. Mount Timpanogos is on the right, Cascade Mountain on the left.

BUREAU OF RECLAMATION (STAN RASMUSSEN)

Natural Setting

TOPOGRAPHY

Within an area of nearly 85,000 square miles, about 3,000 of which are water surface, Utah presents an irregular and diversified topography.

Lofty mountains roll northward and eastward into Idaho, Wyoming and Colorado; undulating, multicolored plateaus sweep southward into Arizona; vast basins, arid ranges, and deserts of salt and alkali stretch westward across the Nevada line.

Formally, Utah is divided into three distinctive topographic regions or provinces, as shown on the accompanying map. They are the Rocky Mountains in the north; the Colorado Plateau, also known as the Colorado Plateaus, in the east and southeast; and the Basin and Range Province on the west.

These major provinces, so vast they encompass numerous states, are further divided into subprovinces or sections which differ from each other both scenically and geographically. For example, Utah's part of the Rocky Mountains province consists of two very different mountain ranges: the Uintas and the Wasatch. The Colorado Plateau in Utah is comprised of Canyonlands, the High Plateaus, Tavaputs Plateau, and the Uinta Basin. Divisions of the Basin and Range Province are technical rather than scenically obvious, but they are apparent to travelers familiar with the region. That part of this province within Utah and most of Nevada is known as the Great Basin.

Formal divisions aside, the most striking feature of Utah's topography is the mountainous spine that extends from north to south along the center of the state. This is formed by the Wasatch Range in the north and continuing plateau highlands to the south, dividing the state roughly into two approximately equal sections. One of the highest summits in the Wasatch, Mount Timpanogos near Provo, reaches an altitude of 11,750 feet. Mount Nebo, at the range's southernmost point, is even higher at 11,877 feet. A sister peak to the north of Mount Nebo has an altitude of 11,928 feet, and other summits in the range exceed 11,000 feet.

A series of parallel high plateaus alternating with valleys continues southward from the Wasatch Range into Arizona. These plateaus are as lofty as the Wasatch, though not as rugged. Their chief characteristic is an overwhelming massiveness, unrelieved for the most part by prominent peaks; this massiveness belies the impressive height of their tabular summits. As a distinct sub-region of the great Colorado Plateau Province, they are referred to as the High Plateaus.

Along this mountainous central spine of Wasatch Range and High Plateaus, at the spine's western base and in its interior valleys, Utah's pioneer settlers established most of the state's communities. About 90 per

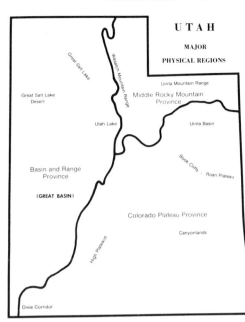

Glen Canyon Country *(left),* showing Lake
Powell and Navajo Mountain.

cent of Utah's people continue to reside there today. This forbidding rampart, so difficult to traverse and so cold in winter, proved beneficent in many ways. Bleeding the passing storms, it captured the precious water so vital for civilization. Canyons and slopes proved to be a treasurehouse of minerals and a grazing ground for livestock. Forests gave timber and food. And the giant mountain mass served to protect the region, much of the time, from frigid arctic air and the violence of tornadoes and hurricanes, moderating the climate to more livable extremes.

Extending eastward from the Wasatch, across much of northeastern Utah, are the east-west trending Uinta Mountains, where Kings Peak, the highest point in the state, rises to an elevation of 13,528 feet. Densely forested beneath an irregular backbone of barren crests and glaciated ridges, the Uintas are relative wilderness, a land of myriad lakes, including Flaming Gorge Reservoir, one of the region's largest artificial bodies of water.

South of the Uinta Range is Uinta Basin, a rugged valley bordered by sloping mesa lands rising gradually southward to 10,000-foot summits of the canyon-gashed Tavaputs Plateau. The Uinta Basin, a stern land of severe climate, resisted white settlement for 30 years after the Mormon pioneers arrived in Salt Lake Valley. It was long considered a wasteland fit only as a reservation for Indians. Living conditions have improved gradually for its residents with development of water, agricultural land, forests, mineral deposits, and recreational assets such as lakes, rivers, and Dinosaur National Monument.

The Canyonlands division of the Colorado Plateau, known generally as southeastern Utah, is an immense broken land extending over nearly a fourth of the state's surface. Most of this multicolored region is too rugged and dry for agricultural use except livestock grazing, and only a small part has enduring settlements. The *Deseret News* for September 11, 1861, described the territory adjacent to the Green River as "one vast 'contiguity of waste' and measureably valueless, excepting for nomadic purposes, hunting grounds for Indians, and to hold the world together."

Nevertheless, southeastern Utah is hardly valueless, for its streams have cut steep-walled gorges hundreds or thousands of feet deep, and the forces of erosion have strewn the landscape with startling and fantastic geological formations. The result is a rocky wonderland known the world over for its strange shapes and rainbow coloring.

The Great Basin, a part of the Basin and Range Province—including all of Utah west of the Wasatch-High Plateaus spine—is a geographic region enclosed by highlands and having no surface drainage to the ocean. The greater part of the province in Utah at one time was the bed of glacier-age Lake Bonneville. The Basin in Utah is characterized by arid valleys, extensive salt flats or dry lake beds, and rugged north-south trending mountain ranges. The scattered ranges rise like islands out of the drab monotony of the intervening basin valleys or flat deserts. Near the Nevada line is an unearthly white, salty wasteland, 4,000 square miles of almost completely level dry lake bottom known as the Great Salt Lake Desert.

Lowest depressions in the Basin are occupied by Great Salt Lake in the north, Bonneville Salt Flats of Great Salt Lake Desert in the west, Utah Lake in central Utah, and Sevier Playa in the southwest. Utah Lake is the largest natural body of fresh water in the state, and Great Salt Lake is the largest inland body of salt water in the Western Hemisphere, measuring approximately 75 miles in length and 50 miles in width. It has no outlet but is fed by a number of streams. *See Great Salt Lake in Tour No. 3.*

DRAINAGE AREAS

Utah drainage areas may be divided into three sections. The northwest corner of the state drains through the Raft River country into the Snake River. The remaining drainage is divided between the Great Basin and the Colorado River system.

Large areas in eastern Utah, together with most of the southern plateaus, drain through the Green River and other tributaries into the Colorado River and thence into the Gulf of California, an arm of the Pacific Ocean. The major exception to this pattern is the intensively utilized Sevier River, which drains the interior High Plateaus, flowing northward and then westward into the Great Basin, discharging what little free-flowing water remains (if any) into Sevier Dry Lake.

In northern Utah, the most important stream is Bear River, which originates in the western Uinta Mountains of Utah, flows across a corner of Wyoming, back into Utah, then loops into Wyoming and Idaho before discharging its waters into Bear River Bay of Great Salt Lake. Smaller streams cut through the Wasatch Mountains to find their way into Utah Lake or

Great Salt Lake. Among these are the Little Bear, Ogden, Weber, American Fork, Provo and Spanish Fork rivers.

CLIMATE AND WEATHER

Weather forecasters admit how difficult it is to predict tomorrow's weather, or next week's. "Changeable," "variable," and "unpredictable" are common descriptions of weather in the Temperate Zone. Because of its location and physical characteristics, Utah experiences some of the most changeable, variable, and unpredictable weather of any state.

In Utah as elsewhere, weather and climate are caused by the sun, characteristics of the earth and its movements, the atmosphere, and land and water features. Basically, the state's climate and weather are determined by its position on the surface of the planet, in the northern hemisphere at about 40 degrees latitude, almost halfway between the equator and north pole. This position gives Utah four approximately equal seasons, "temperate" or intermediate temperatures (not as hot as if it were farther south, not as cold as if it were farther north), and changing lengths of day and night.

Earth's atmospheric peculiarities dramatically affect Utah's climate and weather. Air masses flow between the tropics and the arctic, and in seem-

Bear Lake and grain fields *(left)*.

Snowpack at Alta in the high Wasatch *(below)*.

L. V. McNEELY

WARD ROYLANCE

ingly all directions. Most frequently, Utah and the intermountain region experience movements of air masses from west to east, these movements related to high-level jet stream flows. Additionally, southern Utah is affected — during hot summer months in particular — by moist air moving northward from the Gulf of Mexico; and the entire state may be affected by summer storms from the southwest. The path of these great flowing air masses or storms may be influenced by more-or-less stationary pressure systems (pockets of warm air or cold air) which can change the direction of storm paths. At times, storms may approach Utah simultaneously from the southeast, southwest, and northwest; at other times a storm may approach from only one direction. Much of the time storms are carried around Utah, missing the state entirely. And, of course, storms often pass across the state without dropping much if any moisture enroute.

Also helping to make weather so variable and changeable in Utah are its land and water features, and those of nearby states. Smaller local features may not have much effect on the movement of tremendous air masses from the poles, tropics and oceans, but they do influence what effect these air masses will have on a local area.

Mountains capture more rain and snow than lowland areas. Clouds must be cooled before they drop their moisture, and this cooling results from the upward movement of moisture-bearing air as it rises in its passage over higher elevations. Rain and snow fall in greatest amount on the mountain slope facing the moisture source, leaving lesser amounts for the opposite slope and areas beyond. In other words, a mountain may "bleed" clouds of their moisture. This is what happens throughout the western United States, and therefore mountains are important factors in the weather patterns of Utah.

In particular, the Cascade and Sierra Nevada mountain ranges of the Pacific coast, and the Rockies on the east, have a great effect on Utah's rain and snow patterns. Most importantly, the western ranges act as a barrier to moisture from the Pacific. And the Rockies help to funnel cool air from the north into the Great Plains and Mississippi Basin during both winter and summer. When northern air masses meet warm air from the Gulf of Mexico, they may result in blizzards, thunderstorms, and tornadoes. But Utah, being shielded by the Rockies, is largely protected from that type of severe weather.

Mountains, deserts and lakes within the state's boundaries also affect local climates. Higher elevations along the Wasatch-High Plateaus spine and in the Uinta Mountains receive more precipitation in both summer and winter than mountains in other parts of the state; at the same time, they serve to prevent Pacific moisture from falling on areas to the east. Certain areas in southern Utah receive moisture from summer storms coming from the Gulf of Mexico; these storms, coming from the southeast, are not blocked by the central mountains. Utah's deserts, both in the west and east, are among America's dryest because of persistent high air pressure and because they lie in the rainshadow of high mountains, not only those of the Pacific states but also mountains within Utah itself.

Finally, Utah's climate is influenced to an important extent by its elevation above sea level, and by differences in latitude from south to north. In general, the higher the elevation and the latitude, the cooler the average temperature. To illustrate: Salt Lake City, in northern Utah at 4,200 feet altitude, has a cooler average temperature than St. George in the extreme south at 2,900 feet altitude.

Of the 50 states, only Nevada receives a smaller amount of annual precipitation (snow and rain) than Utah's 13 inches, making Utah the second-dryest state in the union. Statistically this may be so; however, Utah is favored with regard to water beyond mere statistics. Its topography provides numerous sites for the storage of water. Much of the precipitation it receives is in the form of snow, which lends itself to use over a period of time. Abundant mountain terrain also stores water. Utah's groundwater reserves have not been exploited, or even explored, to the extent of certain other western states.

Some Utahns complain about a severe climate that is uncomfortably hot in summer, extremely cold in winter. Instead, they should congratulate themselves. Most of the world's people live in hotter or colder, more humid, wetter, or more arid parts of the world, enduring more severe rainstorms, hailstorms, tornadoes, hurricanes, and blizzards than Utahns ever encounter.

Climatic divisions. The state is divided climatically into seven divisions, each of which differs somewhat in climate. The southwestern corner, or Dixie, resembles southern Nevada and southern Arizona in having a fairly warm to hot climate (61 degrees annual average). Average temperatures of the other six regions vary between 43 degrees in the Uinta Basin to 51 degrees in the southeast corner. On an average, statewide, the temperature drops to the freezing level on 139 days of the year.

Utah's annual precipitation totals about 13 inches for the entire state. However, between the various climatic divisions it varies considerably, from 8 inches in the Uinta Basin to 19 inches in the Northern Mountains (Wasatch and Uinta ranges). Half of the precipitation in this latter region comes in the form of winter snow between November and March. Average snowfall for the state as a whole is 56 inches per year, more than many of Utah's neighboring states receive.

The Wasatch Front, where 80 per cent of the state's people reside, receives about 16 inches of precipitation during the year. This narrow oasis along the western base of the high Wasatch Range is nearly 200 miles long and only 10 to 15 miles wide. Because storms from the west drop much of their moisture on the nearby mountains and foothills, the populated areas here receive more rain and snow than communities elsewhere in the state. Parts of western Utah, the Uinta Basin, and the southeast corner receive less than 8 inches of precipitation during the year. The average relative humidity for Salt Lake City is 46 per cent, highest of any large city in the Four Corners states or Nevada. This is due mainly to its location near Great Salt Lake and nearby forested mountains.

WARD ROYLANCE

BUREAU OF RECLAMATION

Sanpete Valley and Mount Nebo from the Wasatch Plateau *(left)*.

Goosenecks of the San Juan River *(above)*.

The Needles, Canyonlands National Park *(below)*.

F. A. BARNES

Geology

The man-made history of Utah is but a letter in the latest "syllable of recorded time." The geologic history of Utah is a story of mighty rivers and deserts and mountains, of simple protoplasmic things in the dark ooze of ancient seas, and of their struggle through millions of years toward consciousness and light.

1941 edition

Utah's geologic history extends back to the beginning of earth itself, more than four billion years ago. But the first half of this history, in Utah, is a sealed book — still buried and not available for scrutiny. Older Precambrian rocks having an age of more than two billion years are exposed in several parts of Utah, while rocks of more youthful Precambrian age have been identified in numerous localities throughout the state. However, most of the rocks we see today are younger than Precambrian; not being so ancient, their origins are more easily ascertained. (Precambrian denotes geologic age of more than 600 million years.)

People who travel about Utah with an observant eye rapidly become aware of the state's extraordinary display of rocks, flaunted in all their bare-bones aspects, obscured only here and there by soil, vegetation or the works of mankind. All over the state, tens of thousands of feet of earth's crust have been exposed in vivid cross-section and seemingly in every possible manifestation, the result of deformation and erosion on a grand scale. Perhaps no other part of the planet, of comparable size, can match Utah's conglomeration of greatly diversified rock types as displayed in such a wide range of structural and topographic phenomena. The state's prismatic earth colors are an added bonus. This geologic diversity sets Utah apart as a most distinctive region, moreso than any other characteristic.

A ROCK FOUNDATION

The rocks we see today in the mountainsides and canyon walls, in the faces of cliffs, and in the jutting brows of ridges and ledges, had their origin (as rocks) many millions of years ago — or most of them did. Younger materials would probably not yet be rock, which requires pressure, heat, chemical action, time, or any combination of such for creation. They would be, instead, substances such as sand, mud, gravel or clay — or even lava or ash, which can form from molten magma issuing from the earth's interior. These latter are abundant throughout Utah. Eventually they are likely to become rock, or ingredients of rock, in the future. So the rocky landscape we view is but a momentary stage in the seemingly endless cycle of building up and tearing down of earth's crust. Here in Utah it is possible to inspect and study, in wonderful detail, the cyclical processes of crustal transformation through myriad stop-watch stages. The entire state is a matchless textbook of geological subject-matter that has intrigued students since pioneer days and is likely to fascinate ever more laymen with the passage of time.

WATER: THE KEY CONCEPT

If there is one concept above all others to keep in mind, when viewing the wonders of Utah's rocks, that is: Water has been involved in the form-ing of most of the rocks we see—not only the massive, bedded rock layers (strata) that assault the eye in mountains and cliffs, but also smaller debris consisting of boulders, cobbles, sand and gravel, etc., that litter the landscape. This concept is not difficult to understand when watching the turbulent waters of a flash flood in the red-rock desert, or the raging torrent of a mountain stream during spring runoff. But how could water have helped to create the 7,000 feet of rock in the face of Mount Timpanogos, or the thousands of feet of rock in a Carbon County escarpment? How, in fact, could water have much effect on the rocks of western Utah and the red deserts of the southeast, when these regions are true deserts with only a few inches of rain and snow each year?

The explanation is simple but also complex. It involves many factors that influence the actions of water, including uncounted climate changes . . . the shifting of earth's poles and equator . . . the breaking up of conti-nents . . . the ebb and tide of oceans . . . the uplifting and wearing down of myriad topographic features as well as entire regions . . . the birth, growth and demise of lakes and streams . . . all taking place over a time span of millions of years. In other words, the water patterns of today represent but a fleeting interlude in the ever-changing cycles of nature. Utah's rain and snow fall, and its drainage systems, differ from those of a few million, a few thousand, or perhaps even a few hundred years ago. For the most part, the ingredients which comprise Utah's massive beds of sedimentary rock were laid down in ancient oceans, lakes, swamps, marshes, or by ancient streams. This was ages ago, insofar as consolidated rock is concerned, though valley deposits in western Utah and the Uinta Basin, for example, and loose sand of the red-rock country, are more recent products of erosion.

In its entirety or in part, the area known as Utah was ocean bottom almost continually from Precambrian times to the late Cretaceous period of only 70 million years ago or so—at which time, in eastern Utah, the final ocean invasion gave way to long-lived lakes, some of enormous size. The time involved here, when oceans dominated Utah in part or in whole, is really incomprehensible to us. A billion years? 600 million years? Compare this vast water-related span with the few tens of millions of years that have elapsed since the last ocean pulled away. And even during this most recent ocean-free period, Utah has been the scene of great lakes, the advance and retreat of glaciers, and dramatic changes in climate.

In the ocean depths, along the shore, in tideland flats and deltas—or in marshes, swamps and lakes—sediments, bones, plants, and other debris settled and were buried. Through heat, pressure, and other processes these eventually became sandstone, limestone, siltstone, shale, mudstone, clay— or, in the case of organic matter they turned into coal, fossils, crude oil, natural gas, oil shale, gilsonite, etc. Landlocked seas and lakes, their water evaporating slowly as the climate changed, concentrated and deposited minerals dumped into them by streams. These include the potash and other salts of Great Salt Lake, the salt domes of southeastern Utah, and other places.

So water, above all other agents, was responsible for the original deposition of materials that form most of Utah's rocks. It was originally responsible as well, to a significant degree, for breaking down, transporting, and sorting the materials which comprise this rock — as it is largely responsible for sculpturing, breaking down, transporting and sorting the materials derived from the rock that crumbles before our eyes. Water, in the form of glacial ice, carved Utah's highest peaks and deepest mountain gorges. So it might truthfully be said — somewhat ironically, since Utah is such a thirsty state — that water is the ultimate architect of its choicest natural wonders. In water were laid the sediments that comprise so many of the rocks of today's landscape, and water has been their principal sculptor since. Nevertheless, despite its important role in the crustal drama of building up and tearing down, water has hardly been the sole factor at work, or even the chief reason for Utah's geologic uniqueness.

In fact, Utah's most unusual geologic status is due to a remarkable combination of past and present environments, perhaps unparalleled in the world. Over the ages this one small sector has witnessed an incredibly diversified panorama of changing environments — not only those having to do with water, but also tremendous deserts (in which were laid down thousands of feet of dune sands); mountain ranges, many of them long-since eroded to the core; volcanoes and fissures from which spewed lava and ash to cover an enormous area; upwelling magma that created curious mountain ranges; and crustal faulting, folding, uplifting and downdropping of awesome magnitude and confusing complexity.

Confluence of the Green and Colorado Rivers in Canyonlands National Park, looking south into Cataract Canyon.

F. A. BARNES

OTHER AGENTS OF CHANGE

Water is aided in its work by such agents as gravity, wind, chemicals, cold and heat, plants and animals. Gravity causes water to flow downhill, cutting as it moves, and transporting enormous volumes of material. As Utah's altitude has increased through regional uplift, water and other erosional agents have worked ceaselessly to lower its elevations. Gravity carries downward the blocks and smaller particles broken from rock faces by weathering. Wind helps to sculpture through abrasion, and it transports light-weight debris. Chemicals combine with water and other agents to disintegrate hard rock. Cold turns water to ice, and in this form water exerts irresistible pressure to fracture and crumble rock. Heat may have similar results. Plants alter rocks and soil in various ways, as do animals. In this latter category we include mankind, and it is hardly possible to enumerate the ways in which this species has influenced the landscape.

When land is near sea level or below, often there is little erosion; and if Utah had continued to remain at that altitude—where it was situated for ages—there would be no resemblance to the landscape of today. Today's topography is a result of uplift and crustal deformation, which in turn activated the various agents of erosion mentioned above. Utah's landscape is one of highs and lows, with a maximum relief (the difference between lowest and highest elevations) of 11,000 feet or so. Undoubtedly the movement of crustal plates and deeply buried magma are the foremost factors. These have caused tensions of compression and stretching, lifting mountains and dropping valleys, forming folds and faults, stimulating volcanic action (both extrusive and intrusive), fracturing the crust. Utah's landscape abounds with phenomena resulting from this type of crustal deformation, which has occurred periodically (or, in cases, continually and imperceptibly) since the most ancient of eras. However, the most noticeable examples are the result of crustal activity taking place during the past 70 million years, and in many cases much more recently.

THE WASATCH LINE

On a relief map of Utah, a major feature which strikes the eye forcefully is the mountainous spine that extends from north to south through the center of the state. This spine is formed primarily by the Wasatch Range/Bear River Plateau in the north and a chain of high plateaus in the south. Though the individual components of this alpine backbone differ from each other in technical respects, when taken together they form a major boundary known as the *Wasatch Line.* This giant uplift is 400 miles long within Utah but is much longer than that when traced to north and south outside the state. In our time it serves as a drainage divide between the Great Basin (interior drainage) and Colorado Plateau (ocean drainage). Together with the Uintas, it captures most of the rain and snow that fall on the state, and the great majority of Utah's people live along its western front.

West of the Wasatch Line, erosion is wearing down the highlands and filling in the valleys. Erosion also wears down the highlands east of the Wasatch Line, but streams there carry much of the debris out of Utah to the ocean. West of the line, most rocks are of drab and somber hue, contrasting markedly with the vivid and varicolored rocks of the east. Rocks in the western mountains, for the most part, were originally laid down as sediments in oceans that covered western Utah and Nevada almost unceasingly for 400 million years or more, until Jurassic times of 150 million years ago or thereabouts. Since Jurassic times there has been no marine (ocean) sedimentation in the west. This is in contrast to eastern Utah, where open seas continued for another 70 million years or so. In this region, marine conditions were accompanied and followed by tens of millions of years of amazingly diversified environments such as shorelands, marshes and swamps, tidal plains, sandy deserts, flood plains, stream deltas, stagnant basins, and enormous fresh-water lakes. Western Utah, and the central spine itself, have witnessed much more extensive igneous and faulting activity than the Colorado Plateau to the east, with the result that most of Utah's metallic minerals — products of such activity — are found in those areas. In contrast, the Colorado Plateau has experienced igneous activity of a different sort that left relatively meager metallic minerals. The Plateau's ancient environments were such, however, that certain other minerals are more plentiful there than they appear to be in the west.

In the west, the earth's crust has been fractured and folded to a much greater extent than it has in the east. Rock formations of the west are dramatically tilted and convoluted. Those of the east, in large measure, remain relatively horizontal. And finally — as is most vividly apparent to the viewer — erosion has sculptured the rocks of eastern Utah into an assortment of unusual designs with which the west cannot compare.

This list of geological differences between western and eastern Utah, separated by the Wasatch Line, could be lengthened. There is no need to do that here, other than to mention that the line corresponds generally with that zone of crustal instability known as the Sevier Orogenic (mountain-building) Belt, a part of the much more extensive Overthrust Belt. Apparently related to the movements of continental and oceanic plates, the Overthrust Belt has been the scene of mountain building and volcanic activity of tremendous magnitude, extending over vast periods of time. In particular it was the locale of a giant chain of mountains, thousands of miles long, that began rising in Triassic times of about 200 million years ago and survived as highlands for 100 million years or more. These mountains were the source of much of the sedimentary rock laid down in eastern Utah during this period, visible today in the grand cliff-faces of Carbon and Emery counties. In recent years the belt has been the subject of intensive geophysical exploration and drilling activity, and with discovery of new oil fields in Wyoming and northern Utah it promises to become one of the nation's important petroleum sites. Because of complex structure of its distorted rock formations, however, drilling is exceptionally difficult and expensive.

TODAY'S LANDSCAPE

The landscape features of today — their visible forms if not the materials from which they are made — are youthful on a geologic time-scale. Mountains have come and gone over the ages. The Uintas are Utah's oldest mountains still recognizable as such. They began to rise about 60 million years ago, coincident with the sinking of huge lake basins to the north and south. Several other less extensive uplifts in southeastern Utah were rising about the same time. Their greatly eroded remnants are known today as the San Rafael Swell, Circle Cliffs/Waterpocket Fold, and Monument Upwarp. The Henry, Abajo and La Sal mountains—formed by igneous intrusion—were created over a period ranging from about 48 to 24 million years ago (the Henrys being the oldest, the La Sals the youngest). Part of this period, between about 35 to 19 million years ago, also witnessed tremendous volcanic activity, with ash and lava covering tens of thousands of square miles in western Utah and the southern plateaus. Though extensively eroded, this igneous material is still dramatically evident, particularly in the High Plateaus of central Utah where it forms tabular summit caps and impressive cliffs.

Of much more youthful age are the black basalt lava flows and volcanic cones and craters of southern and western Utah, which range from less than a thousand to a million years or so in age. Some of these, notably in Millard County, are related to Lake Bonneville (*see below*). The rugged mountains of western Utah's Great Basin, as well as the state's central spine, are relatively youthful. Largely, they have been created during the most recent 10 or 15 million years; and in fact they may be said to be growing even today as crustal stresses and fracturing continue their inexorable processes. Earthquakes are the most apparent evidence of this, but geologists note other signs.

Erosion has been attacking Utah's uplifts since they first began to rise, though its pace has fluctuated. Through most of the region's geologic history, it was at or near sea level. Not until five or ten million years ago was western America lifted *en masse* to a mile or so above sea level, a change apparently related to the movement of crustal plates. As elevation increased, erosion accelerated. In a comparatively brief period, erosion removed tens of thousands of feet of rock that had taken eons to lay down. Its effects are most evident in the Colorado Plateau, where debris has been removed from the scene; but erosion is continuing as well in the west, where debris fills the basins and valleys to great depth. The pace of erosion is cyclical or intermittent, of course, being influenced by a variety of factors. Undoubtedly it proceeded rapidly during wet stages of the several ice ages that have occurred during the past million years or so—the most recent only 10 to 25 thousand years ago. In fact, it is likely that a considerable part of the shaping of small forms, cutting of canyons, and recession of cliffs in the Colorado Plateau is the work of accelerated erosion in very recent millennia. The direct results of glaciation are apparent in the Uinta and Wasatch mountains, and in the higher mountains and plateaus of the south. Hundreds of Utah's alpine lakes are remnants of the latest ice age.

EVIDENCES OF ANCIENT LIFE

The rocks of Utah contain fossil evidences of animals and plants that have existed in the region since the Cambrian period of 500 to 600 million years ago. Many of these are on display in the state's excellent natural history museums. The 1941 edition described some of the earlier life forms as follows:

UTAH TRAVEL COUNCIL

WARD ROYLANCE

Rocks of the Wasatch Mountains were laid down in ancient oceans, long before the age of dinosaurs.

Seas of the Paleozoic era advanced into Utah and retreated again many times, and each advancing sea brought with it strange new forms of life. At the beginning of the Paleozoic time the little crab-like trilobite, seldom more than three inches long, was the king of beasts. As the era lengthened into millions of years, gastropods, brachiopods, cephalopods, horn corals, and even higher types of fish appeared. Huge ferns and dense forest growths lined the waterways, and sprawling vertebrates swam in the oceans and crawled awkwardly on the shores. Exposure of Paleozoic rocks is widespread throughout Utah — particularly in the Wasatch, in the Uintas, in the basin ranges, and in the high plateaus of the south. Although vertebrate fossils of the Palezoic era are comparatively rare in the State, there is an abundance of invertebrate forms. Fossilized trilobites may be found by the thousands near Antelope Springs west of Delta. Protruding from the canyon walls, or lying in the slide-rock of the Wasatch Range, there are many fossilized specimens of corals, sea lilies, snails, clams, mussels, and similar forms. Fossil shellfish are also numerous in the Uinta Mountains, in various parts of the Great Basin, and in south central Utah.

The major part of the Great Basin was above water in Mesozoic time, and the eroded sediments were carried east and south into what is now the plateau region. Mesozoic rocks, therefore, are confined largely to the eastern and southern parts of the State; buried within them is fossil evidence of the slow progression of life. In Mesozoic waters the shellfish continued to evolve; on Mesozoic landscapes lived the first dinosaurs, birds, and mammals, and the first hardwood trees. During this period in geologic history, large areas in northern Arizona and southern Utah were covered by flood plains upon which meandering rivers and streams left stranded a great number of logs. Later deposition covered them with mud and sand, and waters bearing silica, manganese, and iron filtered through the ancient flood plains and replaced the vegetable material of the tree trunks with stone. At Capitol Reef National [Park], Zion National Park, and near Escalante, Kanab, and St. George there is petrified wood estimated to be more than a hundred million years old. [Petrified wood is probably the State's most widespread and abundant fossil.]

Excavations in the Uinta Basin near Jensen since 1909 have uncovered a veritable graveyard of dinosaur bones, and the site has been set aside as a national monument. In this region long ago was a flood plain across which streams meandered. Upon the banks of these rivers and in the surrounding marshes the great reptiles lived. Some of them, preying upon smaller dinosaurs, became masters of their primitive world; others, feeding upon water plants, attained a length of a hundred feet and a weight of thirty-five or forty tons. When these mighty reptiles died, their carcasses were borne away by floods and deposited on a bar, where the drifting sediments, covering them hardened into stone. The Jensen quarry (*see Dinosaur National Monument*) has yielded hundred of dinosaur bones. Among them are the back and leg bones of the herbivorous brontosaurus and diplodocus; the bones of a flesh-eating allosaurus; and the complete skeleton of an immense brontosaurus, a hundred feet long and twenty feet high.

Long after the dinosaurs were buried on the old river bar, masses of vegetable material accumulating on the margin of shallow seas were covered with sand and finally transformed by pressure into the extensive coal deposits of Carbon and Emery counties. Although no dinosaur bones have been found in this region, the sandstone above the coal beds still records the fact that no less than eight varieties of dinosaurs walked across the mud flats more than sixty million years ago. One huge beast left footprints which indicate that he took fifteen-foot strides, and another, apparently because he slipped in peaty mud, made an impression approximately four and a half feet long and two and a half feet across.

Since that was written, the Cleveland-Lloyd dinosaur quarry has been developed in Emery County (*see Tour No. 10*), adding to Utah's stature as the world's richest source of Jurassic dinosaur fossils. The dinosaur age was followed by that of mammals, and fossil remains of numerous mammals of ancient times have been found. Cenozoic deposits of the Uinta Basin, for example, have produced fossils of wolves, deer, cats, ancestral camels and horses, ancestral rhinos, mastodons, pigs, and mammal species that are now extinct. Fossils of fish and insects also have been found. Farther west, and of later date, the deposits of Lake Bonneville contain the remains of fresh-water snails, fishes, mammoth, musk ox, camel, horse, deer, mountain sheep, giant bear, and wildcat.

LAKE BONNEVILLE AND GLACIERS

Much has been learned and published about the geologic history of Lake Bonneville and its predecessor lakes in the past 40 years. Nevertheless, the account of the ancient lake that appeared in the 1941 edition remains a remarkably accurate description:

Among the geologic phenomena of late Cenozoic times in the Great Basin, perhaps most interesting to the layman is the evidence that an ancient lake once covered the greater part of Utah and extended into Idaho and Nevada. This huge body of water, known to geologists as Lake Bonneville, is thought to have originated during the last ice age, more than fifty thousand years ago, and to have endured [until about 10,000 years ago]. At its maximum the lake was 1,050 feet deep, 145 miles wide, and 346 miles long. Rolling hills, abrupt cliffs, and water-filled canyons formed an irregular shore line, and low mountains rising above the water studded the surface with islands. Contemporaneous with Lake Bonneville were more than seventy smaller lakes, which occupied minor depressions in the Great Basin.

Pre-Bonneville time was characterized by alternating lakes and deserts. The lake which immediately preceded Bonneville was probably little more than a brine pond in the midst of a vast wasteland. With the beginning of Bonneville time, however, the climate began to change. Cold wet years were more frequent, and evaporation was reduced. The level of the lake rose with the wet years, and though intermittent periods of drought prevented a constant rise, the trend was always upward. Approximately 1,000 feet above the present surface of Great Salt Lake the waters came to a halt and for a long time remained stationary. Pounding incessantly against their enclosing shores, the waves eventually carved out a shelf, in some places 1,500 feet wide. This shelf, known as the Bonneville Terrace, is today plainly visible on the north face of the Traverse Mountain about 18 miles south of Salt Lake City. It appears also on the north slope of the Oquirrh Range not far from Saltair, on Antelope Island, and on the mountains near Wendover.

The lake remained at the Bonneville level for a long time. Then, continuing its upward movement, the water reached Red Rock Pass in northern Cache Valley, and, through this lowest point in the rim of the basin, overflowed into the Snake and Columbia river systems. The Red Rock outlet carried the water through a loose gravel formation which was cut away so rapidly that within a comparatively few years the lake dropped 375 feet. When the outflowing water encountered a resistant limestone at the base of the gravel, the lake level again became constant and remained so until the Provo, largest of all Lake Bonneville terraces, was formed. Near Salt Lake City the Provo terrace appears at the foot of Ensign Peak and at Fort Douglas. Recognizable also in many other parts of the Great Basin, it stands in bold relief on the west side of the Wasatch and Oquirrh Mountains.

At the end of the Provo epoch the lake again resumed its downward course. After forming several intermediate terraces, the water dropped to a point approximately 300 feet above the present level of Great Salt Lake. Here for perhaps more than 1,000 years the waves ate into the jagged shoreline until they had produced the Stansbury Terrace, third in size and importance. In many places the record of the lake at the Stansbury level has been destroyed by erosion, but the terrace may still be seen from the Salt Lake-Ogden highway between the Municipal Baths and Becks Hot Springs (*see Tour 1c*). Between the Stansbury level and that of Great Salt Lake the waters of Bonneville left a great many small terraces, many of which appear today on the mountains at the north end of the present lake. More than fifty terraces, each recording a stage in the history of Lake Bonneville, have been recognized at various places within the Great Basin.

During the rise and fall of the ancient lake, streams flowing out of the mountains built deltas at the mouths of canyons. Many such deltas were formed while the lake stood at the Bonneville level, but nearly all of them were washed away and their sands and gravels reconsolidated into deltas on the Provo and other lower levels. Perhaps the most important remaining delta of the Bonneville stage is in Ogden Valley, where the village of Huntsville stands. At the Provo stage six major deltas — the Ogden, the Weber, the Logan, the Bear, the Provo, and the Sevier were built. In addition, many smaller deltas were scattered along the Wasatch from Santaquin to Brigham City. Much of the finest agricultural land in the State is of deltaic construction.

Sand and gravel bars formed by the action of longshore currents are further evidence of constructive forces at work in the old lake. Notable among these are the Stockton Bar at the north end of Rush Valley in Tooele County and the bar at Jordan Narrows near the Salt Lake-Utah County line. These embankments effectively separated Rush Lake and Utah Lake from the parent body of water. Rush, Utah, and Great Salt Lakes are thought to be present-day remnants of Lake Bonneville. Near Wendover, where Bonneville waters once covered the land, great flats extend westward into Nevada.

[It is probable that Lake Bonneville teemed with fish and invertebrate forms. Their existence is evidenced by the discovery of gastropod and fish remains in lake deposits. The story of other] vertebrate life in the Bonneville area is more nearly complete, for commercial removal of gravel along the base of the Wasatch Mountains has resulted in many enlightening discoveries. Along the shores of the old lake thousands of years ago roamed the hulking mammoth, the ponderous musk ox, and the predecessors of the modern camel and horse. Some of these creatures, attracted by water and abundant vegetation, wandered out on the deltas and sank in treacherous swamplands bordering the lake. Others were overcome by stronger beasts, and spring floods scattered their bones through gravel deposits at the water's edge. Although animals peculiar to glacial climates were common during the Provo stage of Bonneville history, they did not disappear entirely with the receding lake. In 1928 a post-Bonneville lava cave near Fillmore yielded the skull of a camel, apparently taken into the cave by some ancient carnivore.

At least twice during the latest ages of Cenozoic time ice accumulating in mountain basins scraped a path down Utah canyons. The southern plateaus record the story of slowly moving ice; the Uinta Mountains (*see High Uintas Primitive Area*) contain [hundreds] of glacial lakes; and in the Wasatch Range there are perhaps fifty glaciated canyons, as well as numerous lakes, hanging valleys, and huge amphitheater-like cirques. In Big Cottonwood Canyon the glacier moved down from the mountains, cutting a typical U-shaped path. Midway down the canyon, however, its progress was arrested by a narrowing channel and a mass of ice flowing in from the south. In Little Cottonwood the ice flow extended the full length of the canyon and pushed far out into Lake Bonneville. In Bell Canyon, south of Little Cottonwood, the shifting ice left well defined terminal and lateral moraines. All three canyons are strewn with the polished and grooved boulders characteristic of a glaciated landscape.

Regarding the lake's overflow at Red Rock Pass, mentioned above, scientists are not in agreement as to the actual date of this event. It may have occurred as recently as 18,000 years ago, or even later. Evidence shows that the flood was a natural catastrophe; it has been estimated that its volume exceeded by several times that of the Amazon River. The discharge may have continued, at an inconstant rate, for 300 years.

The giant body of water known as Lake Bonneville was only the latest and largest stage of fluctuating lake cycles in the Bonneville Basin during the past 70,000 to 100,000 years. According to geologist Roger B. Morrison, there were "probably at least ten sizeable lake cycles [rises and falls]" during this period, these cycles being collectively known as Lake Bonneville. "These late Pleistocene lake oscillations were preceded by at least two earlier periods when lake levels generally were high, in middle Pleistocene time [about half a million years ago]; the shorelines at the times of these cycles and the deposits then laid down are nearly everywhere now buried beneath younger sediments. Still earlier lakes existed in this region in Tertiary time [millions of years ago], but their record is exceedingly vague." *See also Great Salt Lake.*

Plant Life

Utah, because of its irregular up-and-down topography and latitudinal location, has six plant zones ranging upward from the Lower Sonoran, which covers the southwest desert lowlands, to the Arctic-Alpine, which extends above the timberline on the mountain summits. Between these, in ascending order, are the Upper Sonoran, the Transition, the Canadian, and the Hudsonian zones. Accompanying variations in temperature, altitude, and soil have encouraged the growth of nearly every type of plant ordinarily found between Alaska and Mexico. Botanists have recognized more than 4,000 species.

The Lower Sonoran zone in Utah is limited principally to the semitropical region of southwestern Utah, covering approximately 500 square miles adjacent to the Virgin River and its tributaries. The altitude here is less than 3,000 feet and the climate is warm and dry.

Because figs, pomegranates, cotton, and similar crops can be successfully grown here, this region has become known as "Utah's Dixie." The natural flora includes creosote bushes (also known as chaparrel), screwpod mesquite, and several species of cacti and sword plants. The screwpod mesquite is a peculiar shrub that grows in the dry, sandy soil of desert canyons. It bears numerous spirally-twisted pods containing ten to twenty beanlike seeds, from which the Indians formerly made a coarse grade of flour.

In this section also grows the strange Joshua tree, an arborescent yucca found only in the southwestern part of the United States. The plant has an unusual tufted appearance, entirely different from that of any other tree or shrub in Utah. Its leaves, bristling on large, clumsy branches, are sharply pointed and bayonetlike. The Biblical name, Joshua, was bestowed by Mormon pioneers, who likened the upturned limbs to arms lifted in prayer.

Growing profusely along the lower streams and washes of southern Utah are dense thickets of tamarix or tamarisk, also called salt cedar, an odd shrubby plant with small scaly leaves and feathery pink flowers. The tamarisk is not native to the United States; in many places it is considered a serious pest.

Nearly all of the Great Basin valleys and Colorado Plateau Province come within the Upper Sonoran zone, ranging in altitude from about 4,000 to nearly 7,000 feet (varying somewhat according to locality). Characteristic plants of this zone are sagebrush and other low-growing plants adapted to arid and semi-arid conditions. Considered an excellent indicator of good soil, sagebrush grows best in fertile, well-drained ground free from alkali. Much of Utah's prosperous agricultural belt, extending north-south along the foothills of the Wasatch Mountains, occupies land from which sagebrush has been cleared. In the alkaline soil of the lower desert areas, sagebrush gives way to shadscale, greasewood, and forage plants that provide

winter range for sheep and cattle. Alfalfa and sugar beets, both alkali toler-
ants, are the crops most successfully grown in this type of soil. Certain
extreme forms of saltbushes grow where alkali is too abundant to permit the
growth of anything else. Rabbitbrush, which displays colorful golden
flowers, also is a common plant of this zone. The zone's higher elevations
are characterized by thousands of square miles of pygmy evergreens, Utah's
most common trees, more specifically known as junipers and pinyon pines.

Forests. Native trees of Utah nearly all grow in mountainous regions,
ranging upward from the Upper Sonoran zone, and only about a score
occur in considerable numbers. Among them is the blue spruce, a symmetri-
cally shaped evergreen, blue-green in foliage, selected in 1933 as the state
tree. It grows most commonly near mountain streams and lakes, at an altitude of approximately 8,000 feet. In swamplands it is often yellow-green
and is sometimes called "water spruce." The wood is brittle and splinters
too easily to make desirable timber, but it is popular as an ornamental tree.
The Engelmann spruce, often miscalled "white pine," is a native of the high
mountain regions and one of the small group of forest trees that survive
near the timberline. It is an excellent timber tree, but frequently unprofitable for lumbering because of its inaccessible habitat.

Four species of pine are common in Utah. The ponderosa pine, generally known as yellow pine, grows in the mountains, mostly in southern
Utah and the Uinta Mountains, at the approximate level of the blue spruce.
It is rapid-growing, attains a height of 100 to 150 feet, and is a very important source of pine lumber in the intermountain region. Closely associated
with the ponderosa in the Uintas is the lodgepole pine, a tall slender tree
used by the Indians in the construction of their lodges. From this custom it
derived its most accepted name, though it has nearly a dozen others.
Because this pine is long and straight, it is particularly adapted for telephone poles, house logs, mine props, and railroad ties. Its amazing aptitude
for reseeding makes it a valuable asset in conservation and reforestation.
The cones protect its seeds against forest fires, and thousands of sprouts
quickly cover burnt areas, sometimes so densely as to result in
overcrowding. The gnarled and stunted limber pine grows on rocky ridges
and other inhospitable sites. This eccentric tree, which usually grows singly,
is apparently equal to the conquest of the most miserly mountain soil, but
its warped wood is of no commercial value. The pinyon pine, small and
round-topped, is found in foothill areas over much of the state. Its gnarled
wood is of little value, but the seeds are edible, and great quantities of "pine
nuts" are gathered for the market, principally by Indians. Pinyon pines and
junipers (below) tend to grow together in a community known collectively
as pygmy evergreens. These attractive little trees cover thousands of square
miles of foothills, low mountains, mesas and plateaus at elevations of about
5,000 to 7,000 feet.

Three species of junipers, known locally as cedars, are found in Utah.
The Rocky Mountain red cedar grows in scattered stands on rocky hillsides.
It is generally too small and crooked for commercial use, though short
lengths are sometimes sawed for cedar chests. One of these trees, the
Juniper Jardine in Logan Canyon, is one of the oldest trees in the inter-
mountain region. The One-seeded and Utah cedars grow, with the pinyon

Slopes of the La Sal Mountains support plant life zones from the Upper Sonoran to Arctic-Alpine. Several zones can be distinguished in this view.

pine, on hot dry foothills. The wood of the Utah cedar, by virtue of its resistance to decay, is much used for fence posts. The one-seed variety, so called because its cones contain only one seed each, is a multi-topped tree with many trunks, none of them suitable for post wood.

Of the firs, the alpine and white are the only true varieties in the state. The alpine fir, known in Utah as "white balsam," is a native of mountain highlands. Its wood is used in rough construction work. The white fir, bearing the contradictory local name of "black balsam," is found at lower elevations. It yields a fair quality of tasteless and odorless wood, adapted for butter and cheese containers. Because of its accessibility, quantities of white fir are used for general farm purposes. The Douglas fir, locally called "red pine," is actually neither fir nor pine, but spruce. Botanists differentiate this variety from true firs because its cones fall from the tree whole. Although it does not attain as great size in Utah as in Washington and Oregon, the Douglas fir is one of the state's most valuable timber trees. Its strong tough wood is particularly useful for heavy construction.

One of the commonest mountain trees is the aspen, popularly called the "quaking asp"; the characteristic shimmering action of its leaves in the slightest movement of air is caused by the fact that aspen leaves have flat stems. Male and female flowers are borne on separate trees, and since female trees are rare, aspens seldom grow from seeds. New trees usually sprout from underground roots of older trees, hence aspens generally grow in dense groves. The trees, however, require plenty of light, for they cannot live even in their own shade.

Bordering the canyon streams are a number of species of shrubs which ordinarily do not reach the size of trees. Among them are red birch, mountain alder, hawthorn, and several varieties of willows. The wood of the willows, being soft and flexible, is used by Indians in basket-weaving. Hillsides are covered with dense thickets of maple, scrub oak, chokecherry, service berry, and mountain mahogany. Also called "buck brush," the latter, related to the true mahogany, is of value as a browsing brush for deer, and straighter specimens were used by pioneers for cabinet work. Its wood is one of the few kinds that will not float. Of the maples, the dwarf is the commonest Utah species. This shrubby tree is an outstanding feature of the mountain scenery at all times, but particularly in the autumn, when the first touch of frost turns its foliage into a blaze of brilliant color. The big-tooth maple, a hardwood variety, grows to larger size, and in some of the national forests is more than a foot in diameter and more than fifty feet high. The box elder, for which one of the northern counties was named, is another variety of maple common along the water courses. The sweet sap of this tree was sometimes used for syrup in pioneer days, but it has an undesirable attraction for insects, especially a black-and-red-winged plant bug with the objectionable habit of wintering in houses. Chokecherry often forms extensive growths on canyon slopes. It has showy white flowers that bloom in May and June. The fruit is edible and quantities of it are gathered for jellies and wines. Service (or "sarvis") berries, which are also edible, are sometimes dried by the Indians and mixed with meat to make pemmican.

Growing along streams, from low to medium elevations, are several species of cottonwood. Like the aspen, they are members of the poplar family. The green of these trees was a welcome sight to early explorers, for it frequently marked the end of a weary desert journey. Great numbers have been transplanted from their native areas to near-by settlements, and many small communities are visible for miles because of green cottonwoods lining the streets.

More than 4,000 kinds of smaller plants are represented in the state. In most sections many species grow together, but in certain areas a few varieties, or sometimes plants of a single species, usurp extensive tracts. This monopolizing characteristic is particularly noticeable during the flowering season when the blooms of certain plants form a blanket of color: the yellow of docks and dandelions, the blue of mertensia and lupine, or the pink of sweet-williams and wild roses.

Utah's floral emblem, the sego-lily, is found in parts of the state. This plant, known also as Spanish mariposa (butterfly), is a west American bulbous herb with long-leaved, grayish green, grasslike foliage. It blooms in May and June, and has a flower consisting of three dainty white petals, delicately tinted with yellow, brown, and purple around the golden nectar glands. In southern Utah, possibly on account of some ingredient in the soil, the flower is frequently orchidlike in color. During periods of food shortage in early pioneer days, the bulb of the sego-lily was an important item of food. Friendly Indians explained that the sego roots were good to eat, and thereafter entire families were often busy digging on the hillsides, returning at night with buckets or sacks filled with bulbs.

In the blooming season, ranging from April to September, Utah's wild flowers offer a constantly changing display. They grow in canyons, mountains and on the deserts. Indian paintbrush grows in sagebrush country, where its spikes of bloom, in various shades of bright red or orange, are conspicuous against the background of gray vegetation. The dogtooth violet, with its bright yellow flowers, grows in rich mountain soil, and is one of the first to appear after the snow melts. Then come the trumpet-shaped blossoms of blue or red pentstemon, the grapelike purple clusters of monkshood, the delicate pink bells of mallow, the five-petaled flowers of pink or white geranium, the inverted blue blossoms of the shootingstar, the waxy red flowers of the prickly pear, the tiny white flowers of false Solomon's-seal, yellow clusters of Senecio and Oregon grape, pink sweetpeas and sweet-williams, small purple iris, blue and yellow violets, pale pink hollyhocks, scarlet monkeyflowers, and innumerable others. In autumn, dry pigweeds and Russian thistles break away from their roots and become "tumbleweeds," rolled by the wind until they pile up against fences or other obstructions.

To early pioneers, the value of wild plants was more than esthetic. Dandelion roots and prickly pears were used in concocting home remedies. Cattails were dried and stuffed into cushions and mattresses. Dry weeds and bushes made serviceable brooms. Roots, berries, and leaves of various plants were ground and boiled for dyes. Dandelion leaves were eaten, as were thistle roots and sego-lily bulbs. Chokecherries, service berries, wild currants, and berries from Oregon grape were made into jams and jellies. Chewing gum was prepared from milkweed juices, and in the spring the inner bark of cottonwood trees was sometimes scraped into a white pulpy mass which the early settlers called "cottonwood ice cream."

The pioneers, however, did not undervalue the beauty of plants. Nearly every home had its garden of flowers, some grown from seed carried across the plains, others transplanted from the mountains. Going to the canyons for wood, men frequently returned with a plant for the garden. Sometimes the watering of these gardens was a tiresome problem, many of the women finding it necessary to carry water from ditches and wells. Native and exotic trees were planted along the streets, and scattered Utah cities and towns soon gained the appearance of oases in the desert. Among the varieties introduced by the settlers were the American elm, umbrella elm, honey locust, black locust, sycamore, catalpa, acacia, ailanthus, horsechestnut, weeping willow, linden, hickory, mulberry, black walnut, and several species of poplar and maple.

Only three plants at all common in the state are poisonous to touch. These are poison ivy, poison oak, and stinging nettle *(Urtica)*. Poison ivy and poison oak, both species of poison sumac, exude a volatile oil that causes painful inflammation of the skin. Poison ivy and poison oak grow throughout the state, principally on hillsides. The two species are characterized by leaflets in groups of three, glossy on top and fuzzy underneath. Poison ivy is a vinelike plant that spreads over the ground, while poison oak grows in the form of a bush or shrub, and has notched oaklike leaves that color attractively in autumn. Stinging nettle, which borders nearly every stream in the state, is similar in appearance to catnip, peppermint, and spearmint. Contact with it results in an unpleasant stinging sensation; the effect is painful, but usually of short duration and rarely serious.

Utah's wildlife include snowy egret, pronghorn antelope, and great white pelican *(left, top to bottom)*, seagulls *(above)*, and mule deer *(below)*.

Animal Life

The mule deer, ranging principally in forest, mountain and foothill areas, but also in the valleys, is Utah's most numerous big game animal. Named for its long, mule-like ears, this creature is graceful and elusive, having choice meat and often a magnificent spread of horns. Mule deer increase rapidly where conditions are favorable. If not harvested by hunting, overpopulation develops serious problems.

Pronghorn antelope are found in a number of areas throughout the state: west of Great Salt Lake, in southwestern Utah, in south-central Utah, and in the northeastern corner of the state, for example. Elk, the state animal, is now rather plentiful (37,000 permits were issued in 1979). Elk herds range not only the national forests but other lands as well. Hunted to extinction early in the century, elk were reintroduced in 1912. Desert bighorn sheep are found in the rugged, craggy badlands of the Colorado River-Lake Powell region, and in Zion National Park. Rocky Mountain bighorn were recently introduced to the Mount Nebo area from Wyoming. Moose are thriving on the north slope of the Uinta Range. A herd of buffalo (bison) has occupied Antelope Island in Great Salt Lake for many years, and what is reputed to be the only wild, free-roaming population of buffalo in the lower 48 states ranges the Burr Desert-Henry Mountains area south of Hanksville.

The grizzly bear, the "Ole Ephraim" of the mountain men, is apparently extinct in the state. Black bears, once fairly common in the back country, are much less so today; only 28 were taken in 1979. Mountain lions or cougars are not as numerous as in past years, but they are present in parts of the state, as are bobcats. Since the extinction of the wolf and restrictions on use of poison bait, the coyote has spread into all sections of the state. Cunning and intelligent enough to merit their place in Indian mythology, they hold their own against traps, poison, and guns, and are a bane to stockmen.

The most numerous fur-bearing animals are weasel, muskrat, beaver, badger, skunk, marten, fox, and ringtail cat. Almost trapped to extinction in former days, beaver no longer are rare. The badger is valued for its fur and for control of destructive rodents; shaving brushes made from badger fur were guaranteed for a lifetime. In addition to the common striped skunk, Utah has a spotted skunk which first came to the notice of scientists in 1906. Utah has several kinds of foxes, including the red, the gray, and the kit fox. The gray fox was first described in 1852 from specimens taken in the Wasatch Mountains and purchased by Captain Howard Stansbury. It ranges through the mountains of Utah, Colorado, and Wyoming. Sporadic trapping of furbearers is carried on throughout the state, but most furs come from commercial fur farms.

Jack rabbits (long-eared, long-legged hares) are very abundant, as evidenced by the mangled remains of thousands on the state's highways. Cottontail rabbits also are plentiful in some areas, and snowshoe rabbits are present. Northern Utah is included in the range of the Idaho pygmy rabbit, a peculiar little animal with a small head, short broad ears, and a very short tail. It runs without leaping, feeds at night, and hides by day. In 1905 the pika or rock rabbit was found in the Beaver (Tushar) Mountains at an altitude of 10,000 feet and first described scientifically. This little animal, only about five inches long, is nearest of kin to the rabbits. Grayish brown in color, it has no tail, and utters a peculiar bleat unlike that of any other animal. Living in the Uinta, Wasatch, Tushar, La Sal, and other highlands, it cuts and stores "hay" for the winter. Its Asiatic and African counterpart is the little hyrax, of an ancient order of ungulates related to the elephant.

Utah has a species of prairie dog *(Cynomys parvidens)* that is peculiar to the state. First introduced to science in 1905, when a specimen from Buckskin Valley was described, it ranges through the mountain valleys of the Sevier River in southern Utah. Like other animals of its kind, it lives in villages and subsists on vegetation. White-tailed prairie dogs are found in eastern and southeastern Utah, and the Zuni prairie dog ranges southeast of the Colorado River.

Utah has many other kinds of rodents. The tree squirrel or chickaree is common throughout timbered regions. The flying squirrel, which glides through the air with the help of sailing membranes, inhabits dense coniferous forests of the Uinta and Wasatch ranges. A desert squirrel inhabits the sparsely vegetated Great Salt Lake Desert. Several races of pocket gophers are common in fertile valleys and on mountain slopes to an elevation of 10,000 feet. Utah also has a plenitude of pack or trade rats, which visit houses and camps and carry off miscellaneous small articles, usually leaving some kind of token in exchange. Kangaroo rats, of several forms, have long hind legs for jumping and a long tail for balancing, with small forelegs and forefeet. Marmots or groundhogs are common in the state. Foresters consider the porcupine a pest, because it often girdles trees.

Ducks are the most numerous game birds in Utah, coming through the state on migratory bird flyways by the hundreds of thousands. Ten or more species of surface feeding ducks include the mallard, gadwall, baldpate, American pintail, three kinds of teal, the shoveller, and the rare wood duck. Diving ducks include the redhead, ring-necked, canvasback, greater scaup, American goldeneye, Barrow goldeneye, and bufflehead. Among numerous other waterbirds are the grebe, egret, bittern, ibis, Canada goose, whistling swan, and tern.

The great blue heron, three feet high, is the tallest water bird in the Great Basin. The little marsh wren, in addition to its real nest fastened to tules in marshy places, builds three or more false nests to confuse its enemies. The seagull—Utah's state bird—is a resident of islands in Great Salt Lake, legally protected and held in reverence by the people because of its historic intervention against the crickets in 1848 and other early years. One of the most appealing scenes in Utah is to see a flock of seagulls, 700 miles from the ocean, following plows in the spring, picking up insects or worms from the furrows. In spite of local regard for them, gulls prey on young ducklings, pelicans, pheasants, and other birds, as well as their eggs,

Golden eagle *(right).*

Red foxes *(below).*

UTAH WILDLIFE RESOURCES

and have made inroads on cherries and other fruits. One of the largest colonies of the great white pelican, a diminishing species, is in Great Salt Lake. These majestic birds sometimes fly 100 miles or more from the rookery for their food.

The ring-necked pheasant is among the most numerous of Utah's game birds. Other upland game birds include sage hen, ruffed grouse, blue grouse, Gambel's quail, California quail, mourning dove, Hungarian and chukar partridge. Merriam's turkey is found in southern and eastern Utah.

Among the predatory birds, the bald and golden eagles are largest; they are found in outlying mountains and valleys. Hawks are numerous, and there are many kinds of owls, including the great horned owl, the western horned owl, and the western screech owl. The burrowing owl, slightly larger than a robin, is common throughout Utah in open flat country. This owl usually lives in abandoned prairie dog holes, but may occupy other burrows.

Four subspecies of birds were first described from Utah specimens: the Treganza heron, a resident of islands in Great Salt Lake; the Utah horned lark, a sweet songster; the Utah red-winged blackbird, quite common in the state; and the gray titmouse, a woodland songbird. A common songster in residential areas is the house finch. The magpie, an impressive black and white bird, is common throughout the state. The cedar jay, or "camp robber," a noisy thief, lives in wooded mountain areas. Other jays are prevalent. Ravens and vultures are widespread. Among Utah's many other birds might be listed the finch, swallow, blackbird, woodpecker or flicker, bluebird, starling, sparrow, warbler, meadowlark, and water ouzel.

It is said that there were eighteen native genera of fishes in Utah before the introduction of others by white settlers. The streams and lakes of pioneer Utah were filled with cutthroat trout. Isolation led to the development of mutants, with variations in color and size. Bear Lake had a type of blue-nosed trout and Utah Lake another variety; both are almost extinct. Other native fishes are whitefish, suckers, chubs, minnows (Colorado River "minnows" sometimes weigh up to thirty pounds), bullheads, dace, cisco, and squawfish. Irrigation, diversion of water, drought, and excessive fishing greatly depleted native trout in Utah waters. About 1885, carp, catfish and bass were introduced into streams and lakes; they are common today. Yellow perch were introduced during 1930-31. Today there are 12 state and one federal fish hatcheries rearing and distributing millions of fish in Utah waters each year. Designated game fish in 1980 were: trout (rainbow, cutthroat, German brown, brook, mackinaw, golden), Kokanee salmon, arctic grayling, Bonneville cisco, all bass species, channel and bullhead catfish, bluegill, crappie, walleye, northern pike, whitefish, and yellow perch.

The sidewinder, a pygmy rattler that occurs in the southern part of the state, rarely attains a maximum length of two feet. The name well describes its odd sidewise progression. There are a few other types of rattlesnakes, the gopher snake, several species of garter snakes, and several types of whiptail or racer snakes. Lizards are common all over the state, the maximum in size being the rarely-found poisonous Gila monster. The desert horned toad, really a spiny lizard, is common. The desert tortoise, nine inches in length, is found in the extreme southwestern corner of the state, but its numbers in Utah appear to be declining. Among the amphibia, Utah has toads and frogs common to the Rocky Mountain region, and the tiger salamander or waterdog, three to ten inches long, in lowland marshes and high mountain ponds.

Of the insects, the so-called Mormon cricket is recalled for its terrible invasions, which are told in many old diaries and reminiscences, and occur frequently in contemporary prints. It has been variously called "the frightful bug," "the black Philistine," and "a cross between the spider and the buffalo." Incursions of crickets and grasshoppers clear the countryside of every green thing, and cars sometimes skid from the roads because of them. Utah also has the pestiferous mosquito, and the wood tick, dangerous as a carrier of Rocky Mountain spotted fever.

The ultra-briny waters of Great Salt Lake are inhabited only by the brine shrimp, a miniscule member of the crab family, and by the brine fly, which passes its larval stage in the lake. It is a small insect, similar in general to the housefly. The brine shrimp is a primitive form of crustacean, closest living kin to Cambrian fossil trilobites.

Land, Air and Water

Land, air and water were not treated as separate subjects in the 1941 edition. At that time they were not of pressing concern to the public at large. The state's population then was little more than a third that of 1980, and the urbanized lands of today were much less densely settled then, with fewer land-related problems. Air quality was not a matter of serious concern for most people. And water, being in adequate supply for the majority of Utahns, at least in the cities, was not a subject for general conversation—except, perhaps, after a flood or during a dry spell. Sidewalk drinking fountains burbled day and night, and clear, cold water racing through city gutters was a matter of tourist curiosity.

Since that time, relative unconcern has given way to countless meetings, studies, reports and regulations; litigation and compacts between states, regions and the national government; and myriad regulatory and advisory bodies—all having to do with the ownership and use of Utah's land, the quality of its air, and the rights to develop, control, and use its water resources. No longer are land, air and water taken for granted. The truth has become apparent to all: While Utah is a large state with millions of acres of land, desirable land is neither plentiful nor conveniently suitable for use.

Land, air and water: natural resources typified by the Uinta Mountains. The Uintas also provide timber, wildlife, minerals, and an environment for recreation.
BUREAU OF RECLAMATION (STAN RASMUSSEN)

Air—pure and seemingly inexhaustible a few decades ago—has become polluted and a hazard to health at certain times and places. And water has become precious as never before.

LAND

In round numbers, Utah's surface area totals about 54,300,000 acres (84,916 square miles). Water occupies about 1,805,000 acres (2,820 square miles) of this area. While this is an enormous expanse, larger than some countries, it amounts to only about one-sixth of one per cent of the world's land area. Ten states of the union are larger.

Most of Utah's land is too mountainous, too rugged, too rocky, too sandy, too salty, or too arid for other than marginal agricultural use. This unsuitability for agriculture, in fact, is probably the most important reason why so much of Utah's land remains in federal ownership. Had it been otherwise, much more of the state's land is likely to have passed into private ownership during the 19th century. Today, the federal government retains title to approximately two-thirds (64 per cent) of Utah's land. About a fourth is in private ownership, with the remainder—about 11 per cent— being held as Indian trust lands or by state and local governments. In other words, only a quarter of the state's land is subject to state and local taxes. Only Alaska and Nevada contain a larger proportion of federal lands than Utah.

Of the approximately 52,000,000 acres of land in Utah, about 16,000,000 acres are utilized for some form of agriculture. By far the greater part of this agricultural land is used almost solely for livestock grazing; only about 2,000,000 acres are devoted to the growing of irrigated or non-irrigated crops. In other words, only four per cent of the state's land produces food crops purposefully grown for human or animal consumption—although several million additional acres are considered arable if irrigation water could be made available. Even the meager portion devoted to crop production is beset by serious problems of erosion, excess or insufficient water, unfavorable soil conditions, and unfavorable climate. Conservation surveys indicate that more than half the state's cropland is in need of treatment for those problems. Added to these physical deficiencies is Utah's accelerated population growth, urbanization and industrialization, which are rapidly devouring prime croplands throughout much of the state— especially along the fertile Wasatch Front. It is evident that Utah faces worrisome dilemmas respecting its scarcest and most valuable land. (See 1941 edition for historical background of homesteading in Utah.)

Within the state, land ownership varies considerably according to counties. For example, Box Elder County possesses by far the largest share of private land, amounting to about half the county's total area. No other county even approaches Box Elder in acreage of private land. Others with fairly large private holdings include Duchesne, Iron, Summit, Millard, and Utah counties. In proportion to total county area, Wayne and Kane counties have the smallest ratios of private land—only six per cent for each. Tooele, Millard, San Juan and Garfield counties contain the largest acreages of federal land—nearly 3,000,000 acres or more in each county. Federal land comprises from 80 to 90 per cent of the area of these counties:

Daggett, Emery, Garfield, Grand, Kane, Tooele and Wayne. Several other counties rank not far behind.

Federal Land. The United States Bureau of Land Management is the administrative landlord of slightly more than 22,000,000 acres in Utah, or about 40 per cent of the state's land area. Its holdings are known as *public lands.* Other federal agencies with major holdings include—in rounded numbers—the Forest Service (8,000,000 acres); Department of Defense (1,800,000 acres); and National Park Service (2,000,000 acres). These holdings include national parks and monuments, national recreation areas, national forests, wilderness and primitive areas, and military installations. Considerable water is included, as in Lake Powell and Flaming Gorge reservoir. Examples of Defense establishments are Hill Air Force Base, Dugway Proving Ground, Tooele Army Depot, and Defense Depot Ogden.

For the most part, federal land administered by the Bureau of Land Management and Forest Service is available for public multiple-use. That is, unless specifically restricted, it is used for varied purposes such as grazing, timber cutting, mining, hunting and fishing, winter sports, and other types of recreation. Public use of national parks, wilderness and primitive areas, is rigidly controlled; and even moreso, of course, at military installations.

Grazing on BLM and Forest Service land is controlled through a system of permits. Mining, timber cutting, hunting and fishing—even such recreational activities as skiing and use of off-road vehicles—are subject to regulations. Boating in national park (and state park) areas is regulated. (These areas, it might be noted, include most of the important boating streams and lakes in Utah.) Users of certain developed recreation areas are subject to fees. Even rock collectors on federal land must observe regulations.

While federal land is not taxed directly by local and state governments, in significant respects it does serve as an economic base for the state. Federal agencies provide employment for thousands of Utah people. Federal recreation areas and forests are visited by millions of out-of-state visitors each year, who bring "foreign" money into the state. The federal government spends millions of dollars within Utah for administration and development of federal holdings, and a percentage of income received from grazing, mining and other commercial activities on federal land is shared with the state and county governments. This amounts to several million dollars each year. In other ways, also, federal land is beneficial to Utah's people.

Nevertheless, there is not unanimous citizen support for such extensive federal involvement in land holdings. Recent years have seen the reactivation of a long-lived and controversial protest movement, in Utah and several other western states, directed against federal control of such a large proportion of western land.

About 2,000,000 acres of land are held in trust by the federal government for Indian tribes, notably on Ute, Navajo, and Paiute reservations.

State and Local Government Land. The State of Utah, through several divisions such as State Lands and State Wildlife Resources, holds title to more than 3,500,000 acres. At the granting of statehood, Utah was awarded four sections of land from each township—or lieu lands if specified sections were already occupied—to be used for the benefit of schools. From this Common School Grant and other grants the state eventually received, or was entitled to, more than 7,000,000 acres. A portion of this has not yet been transferred from the federal government. Several million acres have been sold or otherwise disposed of by the state, reducing its total holdings. Land controlled by the State Lands Division is administered largely for the benefit of schools, being leased for various commercial purposes such as grazing and mining, or being devoted to official state use, or in certain cases being transferred to private ownership. Outright sale is much less common than in former years. Additionally, some thousands of acres are administered by the Wildlife Resources Division as habitat for birds and other animals. A minor acreage—perhaps 300,000 acres or less—is controlled by cities, towns and villages.

Private Land. Of the 13,000,000 acres (approximate) of privately-owned land in Utah, by far the greater part is devoted to some form of agriculture: to irrigated or non-irrigated cropland, pasture, rangeland or timberland. Irrigated cropland amounts to only one-tenth or so of all private land; the remainder is utilized for grazing, or as homesites or commercial sites, or for timber production, mining and railroad operations, investment purposes, etc. The total amount of private land in Utah is growing very slowly since government policy of recent years has not favored relinquishment to private ownership.

Utah was affected adversely by uncontrolled land speculation of the 1960s and early 1970s, though not, apparently, to the same extent as some neighboring states. Nevertheless, sale of undeveloped rural land remains a public concern. Thousands of acres of land with questionable value for occupancy or investment have been sold to unsuspecting purchasers. This speculative land is scattered widely throughout the state, from the barren flats of the northwest and southwest to the red-rocks of the southeast, and from the mountains of the north to those of the south. Many buyers learn to their distress that water is not available on-site, or even nearby; that their holdings are miles from the nearest town; that costs of development far outweigh any advantages; and that the chance of resale is negligible.

AIR

Utah's air quality is affected by nature in diverse ways. This has been the case since pioneers arrived. Pahvant Valley, for example, is notorious for dust storms that may reduce visibility to near zero. Salt Lake Valley is subject to strong winds that carry fine dust from the western desert. When precipitated by rain, the dust turns to a coating of mud. Dust and sand storms also afflict other parts of the state. Fog is a bother and a hazard during winter inversions, notably in the vicinity of Great Salt Lake and Utah Lake. Even vegetation may influence air quality, as asthma sufferers will testify.

To these natural occurrences—which are unpleasant if not always harmful—have been added air pollutants generated by human activity. The burning of coal has been the cause of air pollution since early days of settlement. Older residents remember with distaste its pervasive black residue. But coal has not been the principal household fuel for decades, in the Wasatch Front area at least, though it has continued in industrial use to the present day.

Industrial pollution has been of serious concern for many years, despite the majority of people having accepted it passively as a necessary part of economic life. It is a matter for conjecture whether the general public would still continue to accept industrial air pollution if government had not intervened. Copper smelting operations near Magna and steel manufacturing in Utah Valley have been the most visible sources of industrial air pollution for decades. Oil refining in Davis County has added contaminants to the air, as have gypsum processing in Sevier Valley, open pit mining, coal-fired powerplants, and other industrial activities throughout the state. It must be noted that emissions from these sources have been reduced considerably in recent years.

Vehicle emissions remain a major source of contamination in the Wasatch Front, where most of the state's people live. Despite technological advances that control emissions of individual vehicles, vehicles grow in number as the population increases. The result is a problem of utmost seriousness to residents of the urbanized valleys where weather inversions are wont to trap a hazardous mixture of stagnant air and contaminants from many sources. The severity of this situation was emphasized during the winter of 1980-81, when winter storms failed to appear and the people of the Wasatch Front were subjected to almost two months of contaminated fog. Possible solutions include the reduction of pollutants, stabilization or reduction of vehicular use, and the slowing of population growth. It seems probable that these goals will not be realized before further critical situations occur.

Utah's air quality also is affected by out-of-state sources. Pollutants from the west coast are carried into and across Utah by prevailing winds. The Lake Powell area receives contaminants from the Navajo powerplant near Page, Arizona. The fear of atmospheric pollution roused indignation —mostly outside the state—when plans were announced for the giant Kaiparowits electric generating project in southern Utah. Another major generating plant, the Intermountain Power Project, found it necessary to change sites from Wayne County to Millard County when the Secretary of the Interior determined that its emissions would adversely affect air quality in Capitol Reef National Park. More recently, the problem of air quality delayed construction of the proposed Warner Valley generating plant near St. George and influenced decisions regarding the open-pit mining of coal near Bryce Canyon National Park.

Still other sources of actual and potential air pollution are military programs. During the 1950s, winds carried radiation from the atomic testing site in southern Nevada northward into Utah, allegedly afflicting residents of southern Utah with cancer, as well as injuring or killing livestock. Damages resulting from this episode are still in litigation. In 1968, 6,500 sheep died in Tooele County near Dugway Proving Ground, where open-air experiments with chemical weapons were underway. Damages were paid by the federal government; however, it refused to admit responsibility. Most recently, the Department of Defense moved a number of nerve gas bombs from Colorado to Tooele Army Depot, transferring public fears from that state to Utah.

In 1967 the state legislature adopted an Air Conservation Act and placed administration with the Division of Health. The act provides that policy be determined by an Air Conservation Committee and the State Board of Health. Funding is provided by federal and state governments. Under the program, "Standards, rules, regulations and policies have been officially adopted pertaining to open burning, visible emissions, particulate emissions, sulfur content of fuels, emissions of sulfur compounds, automobile emissions and requirements for review and approval of potential air pollution sources prior to construction." Under the act, air quality control regions have been established, as well as a network of surveillance stations to monitor levels of pollutants throughout the state. A pollution alert system warns of major pollution sources, and the Bureau of Air Quality has authority to control sources that are in violation of stipulated levels, as well as to review and approve or disapprove plans for any facility that might create sources of air pollution.

WATER

Nature rarely provides water just where Utah's people need it most, in the quality and quantity they would like. Water determines where they can place their settlements and farms and industries, where they can graze their livestock, what kinds of industries they may engage in, what forms their recreation might take, and so on. And water, of course, is of critical importance to plants and wildlife, for it determines their types and distribution.

Yet *usable* water is among the scarcest of Utah's natural resources. The term *usable* is accented because an enormous amount of water falls on the state every year. That is, even though the *average* annual total for Utah is only about 13 inches, if this were spread evenly over the surface of the state and did not sink into the ground, run off, or evaporate, Utah would be flooded by more than a foot of water. The truth is, of course, that none of these conditions exist in actuality. Precipitation varies greatly by region, from 5 inches or less in the western deserts to a maximum of 60 inches at Alta in the Wasatch Range. In fact, about half the state receives 10 inches or less during an average year. Most water is lost before Utah people can use it. And most precipitation falls where or when it is not needed the most, or where soil and climate conditions are not favorable to human activities.

Water appearing as runoff in Utah's streams amounts to only 15 per cent or so of the quantity that falls on the state—a ratio that is much less than that for the nation as a whole. Most of the remainder is lost to immediate human use through evaporation, transpiration by plants, or sinking into the ground. And much of the runoff water that is collected in reservoirs is eventually lost through these processes. Some non-stream water, of course, is utilized for dry-farming and by native plants—such as timber trees—that are beneficial to mankind. And a portion of the water that sinks into the ground is available for consumptive use by drilling wells and pumping water to the surface. The fact remains, however, that there is tremendous "waste" of water, insofar as utilization of available water is concerned

Water and its control are illustrated by these views of Upper Provo River Falls *(right)*, new addition to Lower Enterprise Dam in 1926 *(top left)*, and Willard Bay Reservoir *(next above)*. *Photos courtesy U.S. Bureau of Reclamation.*

This is a handicap and a formidable challenge to the state's collective ingenuity. More than any other factor, perhaps, it promises to circumscribe growth and development.

Water yield. Other than what is received *on site* from rainfall and snowfall, most of Utah's usable water is provided by streams. By far the largest streams in the state are the Green and Colorado rivers. Ironically, hardly any of their mainstream water is consumed within the state. These rivers flow in deep canyons through some of the least-populated, most arid, most rugged areas of Utah. And seasonal flooding, before the era of huge mainstream dams, prevented efficient utilization for agriculture even in the few arable valleys along their courses in Utah.

Utah takes its Colorado River water entitlement—or that part it is able to use (somewhat less than full entitlement at present)—by diverting water from tributaries of the main rivers. The most productive of these drain the south slope of the Uinta Mountains and the Uinta Basin, producing nearly a fourth of total runoff in the state. These streams are partially utilized in the Uinta Basin. Also, water from several of these streams is being partially diverted—or will in the future be diverted—across the drainage divide into the populated valleys of the Great Basin. Other tributaries of the main river system include the White, Price, San Rafael, Fremont, Escalante, San Juan, and Virgin. The San Juan passes through such rugged, arid terrain that it is little used within Utah. This is the case, also, with the White. However, both streams are valuable sources of industrial water, at least potentially. Water of the remaining tributaries is utilized in their headwaters, but only partially; much is lost before it reaches the main rivers or mainstream lakes.

To date, water used by the great majority of Utah's people comes from Great Basin streams: the Bear, Ogden, Weber, Cottonwood, Jordan, Provo, Spanish Fork, Salt, Sevier, Beaver, Coal and other smaller streams. These streams water the best agricultural lands in Utah—the area of first settlement and densest population. Comparing total runoff and population, however, there is serious inequity of water distribution. That is, Great Basin runoff produces little more than half of the state's runoff, yet more than 90 per cent of Utah's population resides in the Great Basin drainage area. This is the primary reason for transmountain diversion from the Uinta Basin. Diversion of water between hydrologic basins within the Great Basin also is being practiced to an extent and is likely to be expanded in the future.

Another source of water is underground reservoirs. Ground water has been tapped by wells since pioneer days and is an important source in certain areas. However, though several tens of thousands of wells produce water in Utah, many known and probable ground-water reservoirs are under-utilized. In fact, so little is known about some of these reservoirs that it is not possible to estimate very accurately their capacity, potential annual yield, or recharge characteristics. In respects, ground water is one of the state's least-known natural resources.

Many hundreds of natural lakes are distributed widely throughout the state. The majority of these are of minor size and are located in mountain regions, which limits the primary functions of most natural lakes to water storage, a degree of stream control, and recreation. Great Salt Lake, of course, is the largest natural lake in Utah. This huge lake also is a valuable source of minerals, an important recreation and wildlife resource, and a minor influence on climate. Utah Lake and Bear Lake are the largest natural fresh-water lakes, serving numerous useful functions. Others of fair size are Fish, Navajo, and Panguitch lakes. A number of small natural lakes have been adapted as more efficient storage reservoirs by damming and other modifications; in the process, many if not most have been enlarged beyond their original capacity. Additionally, a great many artificial reservoirs have been created where natural lakes did not formerly exist. The result is that more than 200 natural and man-made bodies of water now provide water for agriculture, industry, culinary, and recreational use; many of these also generate electic power. The largest of all—Lake Powell and Flaming Gorge Reservoir—do not contribute water directly to Utah consumers but serve rather to regulate fluctuating flow of the Green and Colorado rivers, generate electric power, and provide public recreation.

Water control and development. Most precipitation (rain and snow) falls onto or near the mountains instead of in the valleys or on the deserts and plains. This is fortunate from the standpoint of water control, for mountains store great amounts of water and release it in quantities that can be regulated by dams and reservoirs. From the highlands flow countless springs and brooks, which combine to form creeks and small rivers—or lakes—and finally a number of larger streams that drain the state.

Nearly all of Utah's major streams are controlled, at least to an extent, by dams and reservoirs. In few other states have people devoted so much thought, toil, engineering skill, and money toward making full use of streamflow. From the first days of settlement in 1847, when water from City Creek was diverted for irrigation, survival and growth depended on the ability to control the water supply. Control would not be of such crucial importance were it not for several characteristics of Utah's water supply: (1) Streamflow is not consistent throughout the year but is highest during spring months, dropping to low levels during months when farming needs are greatest; (2) Some streams are subject to intermittent flooding; (3) Many streams flow in entrenched channels and their water must be diverted to agricultural lands. Only by constructing dams, reservoirs, canals, ditches, pipe systems, and other controls can these characteristics be modified. Epic tales of efforts to tame Utah's streams are legion. Some are recounted or mentioned elsewhere in this volume. To a significant degree, Utah's history since non-Indian settlement is based on water and the herculean efforts expended in controlling it.

Lakes and dams usually are only elements in complex water-development systems that may incorporate canals, ditches, diversion dams, conduits, pipeline systems, treatment plants, and other costly facilities. A great many individuals, business firms, cooperative groups, and government agencies have been responsible over the years for the development of Utah's water resources. Organizations range in type from local cooperatives (which total more than 1,000) to regional associations, and from a variety of community-state agencies to numerous federal agencies. Privately financed water developments are legion.

Among diverse state agencies having to do with water, the Water Resources Division and Board of Water Resources, Water Rights Division (State Engineer), and Water Pollution Control Board are comprehensively involved. On a federal level, the U. S. Bureau of Reclamation has sponsored, constructed, or been cooperatively involved with the largest single water projects in the state's history. These include multiple segments of the Upper Colorado River Storage Project (Flaming Gorge and Glen Canyon dams as well as Uinta Basin projects) . . . Weber River Project . . . Weber Basin Project . . . Strawberry Valley Project . . . Provo River Project . . . and Central Utah Project (also involving the Uinta Basin). Some of these projects are described in the tour section. In cost, these projects total hundreds of millions of dollars, or many times the investment of state and local agencies. Also involved to an extent in water control and development are numerous other federal agencies, including the Soil Conservation Service, Fish and Wildlife Service, U. S. Geological Survey, Bureau of Land Management, and Corps of Engineers.

The first 90 years of water control, irrigation, and homesteading were described in the 1941 edition of the guidebook on pages 105 to 111—a detailed treatment that is too lengthy for inclusion here. Readers having an interest in those subjects will find that background summary of value.

Mineral Resources

Utah ranks high among states in value and diversity of minerals taken from the earth. As detailed in the chapter on **Mining,** which appears under **The Economic Scene** elsewhere in this volume, the value of minerals *actually mined* in Utah since 1870 totals some 20 billion dollars. The potential value of minerals which are known to exist in Utah but have not yet been mined cannot even be estimated, of course. Thorough exploration and evaluation await a favorable economic climate for perhaps the majority of Utah's minerals. But it can be claimed, in the words of a government publication, that "Utah's diversity of available mineral products in useful quantities is probably equaled by few other comparable-sized areas in the world."

With some exceptions, only a minor fraction of Utah's minerals have been mined on a large scale—or at least to an extent that has lowered their known reserves significantly. For example, though much of the higher grade, most accessible copper ore in the Oquirrh Range has been exhausted by open-pit mining, reserves of ore still remain in the vicinity to be recovered with modified techniques. A somewhat similar situation exists with regard to iron ore. Economics plays a very important role in determining which minerals will be developed, and to what extent. This is illustrated by oil exploration and drilling in the Overthrust Belt of northern Utah and in the Uinta Basin, where oil is being found in quantity, but only at great depth and after expenditures that would have been prohibitive only a few years ago.

The Great Salt Lake was recognized for a century as a repository of enormous quantities of valuable minerals—but only after decades of experimentation and at great financial cost is it proving economically feasible to extract those minerals. Utah's known coal deposits total billions of tons. Unfortunately, most of this coal is underground, relatively expensive to mine, and far away from the largest potential markets. After years of costly technological experimentation, it appears that oil may soon be produced in meaningful quantity from oil shale. These and other barriers to utilization of Utah's minerals are discussed at more length in the chapter on **Mining.**

Despite the formidable obstacles that must be surmounted before minerals are produced, Utah does possess incalculable quantities of minerals of varied types. Deposits of alunite and beryllium are believed to be among the largest in the world. Hydrocarbon minerals such as crude oil, natural gas, gilsonite, ozokerite, bituminous sandstone and limestone (tar sands), oil shale, and coal are remarkably abundant—probably moreso that the most optimistic estimates. Estimates of potential reserves soar into the billions of tons and barrels. Copper is found throughout the state, and rich new uranium deposits are being discovered periodically. There are large reserves of potash and phosphate rock, while remaining lead and zinc deposits may amount to as much as all past production. The saline minerals of Great Salt Lake are a resource of tremendous worth. Limestone, dolomite, building stone, sand and gravel, silica, volcanic aggregates, clays, and gypsum are present in quantities beyond estimate. The quantity of gold and silver not yet mined is unknown, of course, but undoubtedly it is very significant. All the minerals listed here have been produced in volume in the past or promise impressive future production.

The list of Utah's useful minerals could be extended for several pages. One source estimates that more than 200 useful minerals are found within the state. Some of these, of course, are found only in trace quantities, and others are in larger deposits but are of poor quality. It remains for the future to determine actual quantity and market value of many Utah minerals.

Molybdenum should be included with minerals of major economic importance. This has been produced for years at the Bingham copper mine and elsewhere in quantity. Also of economic note are gemstones, fluorspar, vanadium, cement, antimony, tungsten, sulfur, diatomite, arsenic, manganese, and mercury. Helium is a controlled mineral that has been little disturbed as yet. Still other minerals that have been produced in varying quantities are boron, aragonite, barite, and calcite. Even guano has been found in limited commercial quantity. Titanium and rare earth minerals such as thorium are present but have been little utilized as yet.

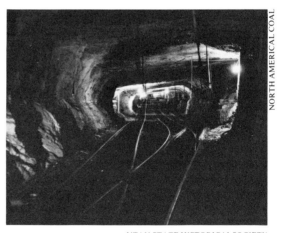

NORTH AMERICAN COAL

Billions of tons of bituminous coal and salt remain untouched by mining.

UTAH STATE HISTORICAL SOCIETY

Human history is commemorated by the Dominguez-Escalante Monument in Spanish Fork *(left)*, painting of a pioneer encampment along the Mormon Trail, the work of Samuel Jepperson *(above),* and the Ether Blanchard farm in Mapleton, 1902 *(below)*.

Historical Scene

Petroglyph panel at the mouth of Smith Fork, now inundated by Lake Powell.

Indians and Archeology

Native Americans comprise only about one per cent of Utah's population. However, in most parts of the state—excepting the Uinta Basin and San Juan corner—the ratio of Indians to persons of other racial backgrounds is much less even than that state average indicates. So it is easy for the majority to have little active awareness of this minority, who once possessed the entire region but were banished to the least desirable locations soon after white settlers arrived. Their history since pioneer days has been a saga largely of injustice, neglect and deprivation. Even today, with exceptions, Utah's Indian population remains a disadvantaged minority.

By far the largest Indian groups in Utah are the Ute and Navajo tribes, most of whom reside on tribal reservations or nearby. Their cultures are described in Tours No. 6 and 11, respectively. Numbering somewhat less as tribal groups are Paiutes, Gosiutes, and Shoshoni other than the Gosiute. Also resident in Utah are many non-native Indians, including students from other states. Numerous Indians of full or mixed blood have become assimilated into the general culture—to greater or lesser degree—living and working away from formal reservations.

In the 1941 edition it was stated that "Utah Indians have retained little of their original culture." If that questionable generality contained a germ of truth 40 years ago, it is even more accurate today. In 1940 the state's Indians were "engaged for the most part in agriculture and stock raising." It is doubtful that this statement applies as well today. Economic influences of recent decades have drastically altered the means of livelihood and customary lifestyles of Utah's Indians, even on reservations. Sheep production has declined greatly, while crop and cattle production have increased in certain areas. Mineral royalties and industrial employment, as well as income from various government and tribal programs, have raised the common standard of living to much higher levels than in 1940. For the majority, reservation housing, dress and food resemble those of the general culture, and most reservation children attend school. Still, serious problems remain, as described in the tour section.

The 1941 edition had little to say about the plight of Utah's Indians during the 75 years between the Black Hawk War and 1940. Indeed, no detailed history has been written about that period, or the years since, with special reference to Utah Indians—other than several works on the Utes of the Uinta Basin. Floyd A. O'Neil, writing in *The Peoples of Utah,* described the banished Utes: "Confined on reservations, no longer free to range over the mountains and deserts of their lands in the incessant quest for food, the hard-pressed Utes never completely forgot how they were supposed to live, who they were, and where they came from. The elders handed this knowledge down to them in family tepees, during tribal ceremonies, and in the everyday practice of religion and acknowledgment of their myths." Life on the Uinta reservation and smaller Paiute and Gosiute reserves to the west was one of incessant hardship. "The white settlers were never satisfied with the Indian land given them," O'Neil wrote. ". . . The Indians continued to be dispossessed in all areas of life: property, education, and employment. The old saying 'the only good Indian is a dead one' dogged Indians throughout their poverty-blighted lives. During the Great Depression they were refused WPA work. Their children were neglected in schools, their culture arrogantly dismissed. Struggling to keep their pride in being Indian, they have tenaciously held on to their culture and their religion." While O'Neil referred here to the Ute, Paiute and Gosiute, his remarks apply as well to the fate of the Navajo. Only during the past 10 or 20 years have the majority of Utah's Indians begun to enjoy a standard of living approaching that of mainstream society.

A valuable historical and cultural description of Utah's Indians of the 19th century, prior to removal to reservations, appeared in the 1941 edition as follows:

Utah Indians may be classified into three larger tribes: the Ute, the Paiute, and the Shoshoni, who include the Gosiute (or Goshute), though such a grouping is based only on similarities of language and culture and not on the existence of a central government or formal organization. In the early historic period the eastern and central portions of the State were claimed by eight bands of the Ute. Though they moved about to some extent, each occupied a fairly definite area. The Timpanoguts lived near Utah Lake; the Uintas and Kosunats in the Uintah Basin; the Yampas in the vicinity of the Green and Grand rivers; the Pahvants near Kanosh; the Seuvarits in Castle Valley; the San Pits in San Pete Valley; the Pavogogwunsings in Sevier County; and the Paiutes or Water Utes in southeastern San Juan County. Other bands of this group were found in an area extending east into Colorado and south into New Mexico. Eight bands of Paiute lived in the southwestern counties, including Beaver, Piute, Garfield, and southern San Juan. The Beaver band dwelt in southern Beaver and northern Iron counties; the Kaiparowits on and around the Kaiparowits Plateau; the Gunlock band in western Washington County; the Cedar in southeastern Iron County; the St. George band in southern Washington County; the Kaibab in southwestern Kane County; the Uinkaret in eastern Washington County; and the Panguitch in western Garfield and southern Piute Counties. There were other Paiute bands to the south and west. To the west and north of Utah Lake lay the Shoshoni country. At least four bands of Gosiutes lived at Deep Creek in western Juab County; at Skull Valley in central Tooele County; at Snake Creek in northwestern Millard County; and at Trout Creek in central Juab County. In western Box Elder County lived the Tubaduka (Pine Nut Eaters). To the east of these lived the Hukundukka and the Kamuduka (Jack Rabbit Eaters), while Cache and Rich Counties were occupied by the Pangwiduka (Fish Eaters). The Weber Utes lived on the east shore of Great Salt Lake. In addition to these permanent residents, bands of transient mounted Shoshoni from Idaho and Wyoming spent part of their time in northern Utah.

There was no great differentiation in mode of life among the Indians of Utah. Economic dependence was largely upon wild vegetable products and the smaller mammals. Except among the Ute and mounted Shoshoni larger animals were seldom hunted. Clothing was meager and poorly made in the southwest, but the Plains influence produced clothing of better quality in the north. Conical pole lodges covered with grass or brush were the usual type of dwelling, though skin tepees were in use among the Ute and mounted Shoshoni.

The greater part of the Utah Indian's time was spent in food-getting. The Ute, who obtained Spanish horses at a very early date, made good use of them in pursuing the buffalo which, before the nineteenth century, roamed as far west as northern California. Deer and antelope were lured or driven over precipices or into V-shaped enclosures where they were easily killed by arrows; antelope were also taken by "surrounds." Dogs were used, to some extent, by the Paiute for hunting deer and mountain sheep. Rabbits were driven into areas enclosed by long nets in which they became entangled. Several types of digging sticks were in use by the Paiute and Gosiutes for unearthing small rodents. Snares, including a type of deadfall, were also used. Although individual stalking with the bow and arrow was probably important, greater dependence was placed on traps, snares, and communal hunts. The sinewbacked bow, made of wood or mountain sheep horn, was perhaps the most effective weapon on the hunt. Ants and grasshoppers were a part of the Paiute and Shoshoni diet. Ants were obtained by scooping up the earth from ant hills and separating the ants from the earth by shaking in a basket somewhat after the manner of panning gold. Grasshoppers, driven into shallow pits, were gathered, dried, ground into meal, and used in a type of biscuit.

Although the western Utah bands depended to a very large extent on vegetable foods, agriculture is known to have been practiced by only one group, the Kaibab. Corn and squash were raised with the aid of irrigation. Even among this group, however, wild food products were the main staples. The leaves and stems of many plants were boiled and eaten. Various types of grass seeds were gathered and ground into meal on flat stones. Pine nuts, roasted for immediate use and stored raw for winter consumption, were an important article of diet. Annual expeditions into the hills were made by some groups to obtain great quantities of these nuts. Among the other plant products were sunflower seeds, sego-lily bulbs, camas roots, service-berries, yucca pods, cactus pears, and arrowroot leaves. The various types of meal were made into porridges or mixed with dried berries and baked in ashes. The meat of the larger animals was broiled or cut into strips and dried. Small animals were baked in ashes in their own skins. Most boiling and cooking was in waterproof baskets with the aid of heated stones.

Perhaps the most universal article of clothing in Utah was the rabbitskin blanket, made of long strips of skin with the hair on. The strips were twisted into fur ropes, which were woven into a heavy blanket or cape. Robes of deer and elk skin were also used. Among all Shoshoni, a semi-tailored garment of Plains style was worn when-ever materials for their manufacture were available. The men wore shirts and leggings, and ankle length dresses were worn by the women. In warm weather a breechclout or shredded bark kilt was the only garment of both sexes. Footgear was a hard-soled three-piece moccasin or a two-piece moccasin of knee or ankle length. A basketry hat was worn by Ute and Paiute women. Moccasins, when obtainable, and sandals of woven joss weed, were the common types of footwear. The most important garment of the Gosiutes was a rabbit-skin cape which was drawn about the neck with a cord. Moccasins and leggings were uncommon among them.

Dwellings were of poor quality. The Paiutes lived in lodges constructed on a framework of three cedar poles set up in tripod fashion. Two sides of this structure were covered with secondary poles and thatch, while the third, which always faced away from the prevailing winds, was left open. Villages were small and usually con-sisted of scattered dwellings. The Gosiutes were without lodges, in the strict sense of the word, but lived in circular windbreaks of brush without a roof. Perhaps the best habitations in Utah were the conical skin tepees of the Ute and mounted Shoshoni. Even these, however, were not as well made as the lodges of the Plains tribes to the east. They were constructed of ten to fifteen poles forming a cone about fifteen feet in height and thirteen or fourteen feet in diameter at the base. A skin cover was placed around this framework and staked to the ground, and a skin lining completed the structure. Among the Ute, a thatched dwelling of more or less rectangular outline was also used.

Basketry was an important minor industry. A great variety of forms were made by the coiled and twined techniques. A pitch-covered bottle with a globular body and constricted neck was used for carrying liquids on long treks into the desert for wild seeds. Other forms were winnowing trays, conical burden baskets, and cradles.

It is not surprising that little information regarding the social organization and religion of the Utah Indians has survived. Scientific reconstruction began too late to provide a complete picture. However, certain determinations have been made which give an insight into their life. The foot Indians of western Utah seem to have lacked centralized authority: the concept of "chief" apparently developed after contact with the whites. The mounted Shoshoni, Ute, and probably some Paiute had strong native chiefs, and pre-white bands. The foot Shoshoni, Gosiute, and possibly a few groups of Ute and Paiute had no chiefs or bands whatsoever. The Paiute bands are known to have had leaders who directed the rabbit hunts, and the Gosiute and other Shoshoni had hunt and dance leaders and antelope charmers; in other activities these officers had no authority. In historic times, however, a number of Ute bands were united under the able chief, Ouray. Although the poorer, horseless groups of Shoshoni seem to have been without leaders, one of the transient mounted bands of Wyoming, which spent a part of its time in northern Utah, was governed by the noted Washakie. There was no type of clan organization. The only divisions among some were the family and village, and among others the band. Polygyny (the state of having several wives) was practiced by those economically capable of it and polyandry (the condition of having plural husbands) existed among some groups. In historic times the Ute carried on an extensive slave traffic. Children were obtained by barter or by force from poorer bands of Paiutes and exchanged with the Navahos and Mexicans to the south for blankets and other articles. Certain Paiute bands were almost depopulated by this traffic.

Religion in Utah was underlain by a general animistic belief in the spirit personalities of animals and plants. The Ute worshipped a bi-sexual deity, the He-She, represented by the sun; this power was the creator of all things. There were a number of animal gods, chief among them being Coyote. Many legends were associated with the feats of these creatures, and the Ute made every effort to win their favor. The religion of the Paiute and Shoshoni was probably very much like that of the Ute. The *shaman,* or medicine man, was an important personage. Perhaps his most important function was performed in the care of the sick, to whom he ministered by driving out the spirit-cause of the illness. Among the Ute and Paiute one type of "doctor" trusted entirely to the supernatural while another used physical restoratives.

Burial was usually in a rock crevice or excavation. The corpse, with a number of his personal possessions, was placed in the branch-covered grave over which a small cairn was sometimes raised. Funeral arrangements and ceremonial mourning were carried on by female relatives. Men did not even attend the funeral; their important function was to destroy the dead person's property. The Gosiute and other Shoshoni sometimes practiced a form of aquatic burial in which the corpse was placed in a spring and weighted down with stones; usually, however, the rock crevice was used.

Paiute residents of Kanosh Indian Reservation, about the turn of the century.

G. E. ANDERSON

The Bear Dance, held each April at Whiterocks, is perhaps most characteristic of the Ute. Men and women participate, and the dance, which lasts several days, is the occasion for much courting. The Back and Forth Dance, derived from the Bear Dance, was adopted by the Gosiute and other Shoshoni. The Ute Sun Dance is an acquisition from the Plains by way of the Idaho and Wyoming Shoshoni. Its purpose is to acquire shamanistic powers, or relief from physical ills. The singing and dancing take place in a lodge consisting of a brush wall built around a central pole. The ceremony lasts four days, during which participants abstain from food and water and remain in the lodge. In former times the Ute had a number of other dances which provided a large part of their socialized amusement. Among them were the Lame Dance, the Dragging Feet Dance, the Women's Dance, the Double Dance, and others. Gambling games were a common form of recreation. Horse racing and other strenuous sports were engaged in by young men.

Most Utah Indians showed little of the warlike nature displayed by Plains tribes to the east. They were, to borrow Bernard DeVoto's characterization, "the technologically unemployed, victims of the competitive Indian society which had forced them to the badlands"; the density of population varied from one person to five square miles in the better hunting country east of the Wasatch Mountains to an extreme in the arid western deserts of one person to thirty-five square miles. Padre Escalante found them "gentle and affable," willing to receive his presents, and, so he thought, his preachings.

The attitude of the Mormons toward the Indians, or "Lamanites," generally was friendly. The Indians differentiated between "Mericats," or Americans, and "Mormonee," as Brigham Young shows in his letter of September 12, 1857, to Indian Commissioner James W. Denver: "Whenever the citizens of this Territory travel the roads, they are in the habit of giving the Indians food, tobacco and a few other presents." Among the things he "most respectfully suggested to be done" was "that travellers omit their infamous practice of shooting them down when they happen to see one." He added: "I have proven that it is far cheaper to feed and clothe the Indians than to fight them," which was a recapitulation of what he had written Commissioner Manypenny in April, 1856: "One fourth part of the money annually expended in fighting the Indians . . . rightly expended in peaceful operations, would not only leave thousands of Indians to cultivate the soil, cause them to raise their own subsistence, but maintain almost, if not entire peaceful relations with them."

The conflict between whites and Indians was not without "some show of justice" on the part of the Indians, as Brigham Young admitted in his report to Commissioner Manypenny. The land was parceled out among the tribal groups long before white men came. There was a centuries-old ceremony involved in passing from the land of one group to that of another, as William R. Palmer points out in his article on Paiute government in the April, 1929, issue of the *Utah Historical Quarterly*. White men ignored this ritual, either because they had no knowledge of it or because they felt, in their superiority, no need to observe it. Mr. Palmer further shows in his treatment of Paiute homelands, printed in the July, 1933, *Utah Historical Quarterly,* that the settlers of southern Utah occupied precisely the grounds set aside for various tribal units. There was not much economic land in Utah, and when one Indian group was forced out it had to enter the lands of another for subsistence. This caused conflict between groups, but they often joined against the common invader.

It is surprising on the whole that the history of Utah's Indian wars is not longer than it is. The killing of Captain J. W. Gunnison and members of his party by Pahvant Indians in 1853 was in retaliation for the fatal shooting of Chief Moshoquop's father by emigrants to California. The Walker War of 1853-54 was precipitated by the occupation of Indian lands by white people, and would probably have been more serious except for the restraining influence of the Ute war chief, Sowiette *(see Provo).* For years the killing of a number of white travelers at Mountain Meadows in 1857 was thought to be entirely the work of Paiute Indians, but subsequent evidence indicated that, though involved, they were not the instigators. A Mormon, John D. Lee, was executed in 1877, after conviction in a Federal court for his part in the crime. . . . Shoshoni resistance to white settlement was crushed when six hundred Indians were surrounded and [several hundred] killed by Federal soldiers in January, 1863. . . . The Black Hawk War of 1865-68 (a Ute conflict, not to be confused with the Illinois Black Hawk War in 1827-31), was waged over the same question of white preemption of hunting grounds, and had the same sort of ending. In 1879 the Indian agent, N. C. Meeker, and others were killed at the White River Agency in western Colorado by Ute Indians who objected to maltreatment and to having soldiers on the reservation. The outbreak was quickly subdued, mainly because of the peaceful attitude of Chief Ouray, and the Utes were afterward moved to reservations. . . . The three men who left Major J. W. Powell's Colorado River expedition in 1869 were killed by Shivwits Indians. There were Navaho raids in southwestern Utah in the sixties and seventies, and trouble with Paiutes and Utes in the San Juan area in the eighties and nineties. . . . As late as 1921 there was a lesser Paiute uprising in the San Juan country, which terminated when the leader, "Old Posey," was fatally wounded. . . . Between 1861, when the Uintah Basin was set aside for Indian use by President Lincoln, and 1929, when the Kanosh reservation was established, Indians within the State were settled on reservations.

ARCHEOLOGY: THE ANCIENT ONES

Utah is a treasure-house of antiquities, particularly those relating to cultures which flourished for a thousand years or so prior to 1300 A.D. Many of these can be viewed today, in place, as rock or mud dwellings, storage cists or caches, and defense structures, mostly in varied stages of ruin. Some have been excavated and others restored; still others have been rebuilt or copied as museum replicas; many have been vandalized. Among Utah's antiquities, also, are countless "rock writings" or rock art, scattered around the state—petroglyphs and pictographs of varying age and origin. A third category includes artifacts of prehistoric and early historic cultures, gathered by private and official collectors since arrival of the whites. Much of this cultural heritage is described in the tour section and in the Appendix.

The 1941 edition contained a summary of Utah's prehistoric peoples and the archeological heritage they left behind. This appears below, with modification. Before that volume appeared, the region's major sites had been excavated and the principal cultural features determined. The mosaic of prehistory envisioned in 1940 is largely accurate today in its basic outline, hardly requiring more than moderate corrections plus the addition of myriad touch-up details. Important work during the past 40 years includes the systematic study of prehistoric sites near Great Salt Lake and Parowan, the Glen Canyon and Flaming Gorge areas, Alkali Ridge and Montezuma Canyon, White Canyon, Kaiparowits Plateau, Canyonlands National Park, Nine Mile Canyon, Castle Valley-San Rafael Swell, Coombs Site at Boulder (Anasazi Village State Historical Monument), and others. A number of new, revised or expanded publications on the prehistory of Utah and neighboring states also appeared during this period.

BUREAU OF RECLAMATION (MEL DAVIS)

Navajo sheepherder with his flock in Monument Valley. Livestock raising, a long-time tribal activity on the Navajo Indian Reservation, has declined in importance in recent decades.

Many centuries before the dawn of the Christian Era, roving bands of Old World hunters were already crossing the ice-bound waters of Bering Strait to the uninhabited North American continent. Some of these early groups undoubtedly reached the Southwest, for, in such localities as Folsom, New Mexico, Gypsum Cave, Nevada, and the Lindenmeier site in Colorado, their chipped points and other artifacts have been found in association with the bones of prehistoric bison, camels, sloths, mastodons, and other animals. These early comers did not possess a highly developed culture. They knew the arts of stone chipping and fire making and, possibly, used spears propelled by the *atlatl* (a notched stick used to increase the velocity of a hurled spear), employed bone awls for piercing and sewing skins, and owned domesticated dogs. They had no pottery or agriculture; nor did they, as far as is known, have any form of permanent habitation other than natural caves.

The earlier inhabitants of Utah were probably a group comparable in most respects with those whose artifacts are found in other parts of the Southwest. . . .

Caves along the shore line of Great Salt Lake's predecessor, Lake Bonneville, have yielded objects the antiquity of which extends back [as early as ten thousand years ago], although they were not necessarily left by the first human inhabitants of Utah. Flint points, knives, bone awls, and flint scrapers attest the presence of primitive hunters.

About the time of Christ, the inhabitants of the San Juan, Paria, Virgin, and Kanab river valleys began to raise corn. This marked the beginning of the long development of a culture known as the *Anasazi* (Navaho, the Ancients), which was distributed over northern Arizona and New Mexico, southwestern Colorado, southern Utah and Nevada, and southeastern California. The earlier phase of the Anasazi is called Basketmaker and the later Pueblo, which developed without a break into the period of the modern Pueblo peoples of Arizona and New Mexico.

The development of agriculture imposed a semi-sedentary mode of existence upon the people who practiced it. From this period of their history comes [much of] the first accurate knowledge of the dwellers of southern Utah and other parts of the [Colorado River] basin. Permanent houses seem not yet to have come into use, but excavated in the floors of caves are found slab-lined bins, sometimes with a superstructure of pole and adobe construction. These apparently served as storage places for grain and occasionally as burial places for the dead. These people made coiled baskets, twined woven bags, ropes, woven sandals and robes, game snares, and long nets for catching small animals. The men probably wore small loin cloths while the women wore short apron-like skirts. Weapons were curved clubs, stone knives, and spears propelled by *atlatls*. The bow was unknown. Agriculture was carried on with wooden digging sticks. Pottery, in the form of crude, unfired, undecorated vessels reinforced with cedar bast (strong woody fiber obtained from tree bark), was attempted. This period was characterized by a rather simple culture. Although the Basketmakers understood agriculture, they still depended to a large extent upon wild vegetable foods and products of the chase. . . .

As time passed the people of the Southwest improved their mode of life. The storage cists (used especially for sacred utensils) were enlarged and improved until they took the form of semi-subterranean dwelling places. These pit houses and slab houses, as they are called, were constructed in excavations from one to five feet in depth. Sometimes four posts were set up at some distance inside the pit and their tops connected by horizontal beams. Slanting walls of pole and adobe construction connected the beams with the periphery of the pit. The flat roof of the same construction was provided with a smoke hole which, in some houses, also served as an entrance. The completed dwelling, having perhaps also a side entrance, must have looked somewhat like a small mound of earth. In other types of house the roof was a simple cone of pole and adobe construction with the base extending to the edge of the pit. The other important development in this period, designated as Basketmaker III or as Modified Basketmaker, was in the ceramic arts. These were improved with the invention of fired pottery sometimes painted with crude black designs on a gray background.

The people of the Basketmaker culture complex were short in stature and slender in build, with rather delicate features and long narrow heads. The end of the Basketmaker periods [witnessed the introduction of a cradle board which resulted in short, broad heads, artificially flattened behind. . . . Eventually the older, long-headed characteristic ceased to exist. About this time] the bow and arrow and grooved axe came into use. Cotton (for woven clothing) and several new varieties of corn were introduced. The turkey was domesticated; turkey skin, cut into strips, was woven into robes. Pottery technique improved in style and execution. In addition to plain and black-on-white vessels, jars were made in a manner that gave a banded appearance to the neck of the finished product. The semi-subterranean dwelling had shallow pits with free-standing walls of pole and adobe construction. . . . It is known as Pueblo I or Developmental Pueblo. It is best represented in Arizona, New Mexico, and Colorado, and probably dated from about [700] to 900 A.D., or a little later in southern Utah. [In Utah this cultural stage is represented in Montezuma Canyon, Edge of the Cedars, Grand Gulch, and other sites.]

Intensive cultivation of corn, beans, and squash provided food in such vast amounts that the Pueblo people were able to build substantial permanent villages. They developed flat-roofed masonry houses containing several contiguous rooms, some of which were used for living quarters, while other provided storage space. They were usually laid out in the form of a rectangle partially enclosed. A central court containing a semi-subterranean room that preserved certain features of the old Basketmaker houses was the prototype of the modern Pueblo ceremonial chamber or *kiva* (assembly chamber built under or in the Pueblo houses and used for religious purposes). Pottery was made with black designs on a true white or red background.

Cooking vessels were made with corrugated surfaces; structural coils of clay were pinched at intervals and not afterwards smoothed over. Crops were cultivated with simple agricultural tools, among which the digging stick was still the most important. This period, dating from about 900 to [1100] A.D., known as Pueblo II, is strongly represented in southern Utah. . . .

Somewhere around 1000 to 1100 A.D. there was a tendency on the part of dwellers in the small masonry houses of the San Juan valley to gather in large terraced pueblos of three or four stories. The dawn of the period known as Pueblo III or Great Pueblo produced large cliff dwellings similar to Mesa Verde's Cliff Palace in Colorado, great valley pueblos such as Pueblo Bonita in New Mexico, and large open-air villages in southeastern Utah. This concentration generated great cultural advances and specializations. Pottery was improved, each center producing a particular type. Fields were tilled, often at a distance from dwellings.

These Indian towns reached a cultural level unsurpassed at any other period in their history, and then . . . were gradually abandoned. First the northern centers and later those of the south were deserted until by the end of Pueblo III, about 1300 A.D., the villages in the San Juan Valley and Utah in general were abandoned. The culture continued in other parts of the Southwest and passed through two subsequent periods: Pueblo IV or Regressive Pueblo, extending from 1300 to 1700 A.D.; and Pueblo V or Historic Pueblo, extending from 1700 A.D. to the present. The modern descendants of these people can be seen today at the Hopi towns in Arizona and Zuni, Acoma, and the Rio Grande pueblos of New Mexico. It is possible to date these periods with some degree of exactness through study of the annual rings in timbers found within the ruins.

[*Editor's note:* Why the numerous Anasazi and Fremont peoples abandoned their habitations and farms in the 13th century remains a matter of speculation. One favored explanation is that a severe drought during the latter part of that century—indicated by tree ring analysis—would have made untenable a culture dependent on agriculture and forced an outward migration. In recent years many archeologists have come to the conclusion that drought alone was not responsible, though it probably was a significant cause that aggravated other contributing factors. Additional explanations include (1) pressure from nomadic peoples, as mentioned above; (2) damage to the ecology over a long period of time, worsening the effects of drought; (3) disease, aggravated by the malnutrition which must have accompanied drought; (4) dissension among the Anasazi and Fremont people themselves; and (5) increased population. Still another possibility, based on evidence, is that a climatic change shifted moisture from winter to summer months, bringing disastrous floods that washed away tillable land and crops in the valleys and canyon bottoms. It may well be that all these factors, working in combination, contributed to abandonment of the region.]

During the development of the Basketmaker-Pueblo sequence in southern Utah and adjoining States the larger part of Utah was inhabited by groups that lived in the northern hinterland of the progressive and comparatively highly cultured southern areas; from these they received their greatest stimulus. Since Basketmaker times cultural infiltrations have been diffused through central and northern Utah from the south. Certain ideas were more popular than others and moved more rapidly, producing strange combinations of comparatively recent traits practiced side by side with others that had been long discontinued in the focal area. This amalgamation of chronologically distinct southern traits, together with new adaptations and local inventions, produced a culture in Utah that can only be understood in terms of the Basketmaker—Pueblo sequence to the south.

The area in eastern Utah between the mouth of the San Juan River and the Uintah Basin acquired a culture that was basically Basketmaker but had such Pueblo ideas as the bow and arrow; at first, the people built shallow-pit lodges with pole and adobe roofs and a little later erected stone houses with free-standing walls. Cliff structures are common in this area, consisting mostly of small buildings on high ledges. Some are dwellings, while others are so small that they have given rise to the idea that they were inhabited by pygmies. Actually they were used as granaries. Truncated pyramidal pole and adobe structures have been found perched on high and narrow pinnacles many hundreds of feet above the valley floors. Similar dwellings are found near agricultural lands in the canyon bottoms, and slab-lined storage cists occur frequently.

[*Editor's note:* Outlying cultures north and west of the Colorado River in Utah— with several exceptions such as the Anasazi site at Boulder, and sites in the Paria- Virgin River area—are classified generally as Fremont cultures, as opposed to the Anasazi (Pueblo) culture of the San Juan-Four Corners region. Fremont cultures developed along the Fremont and San Rafael river systems, in Sevier Valley, in the Uinta Basin-Nine Mile region, and in the Great Basin northward from the Cedar City area to Great Salt Lake. Segments of the Fremont flourished at varying times and over varying periods from about 400 A.D. to 1300 A.D., disintegrating at ap- proximately the same time as that of the Anasazi.]

The people to the west of the Wasatch Mountains and north of Provo depended to a great extent upon hunting. The common type of habitation was a pit-house somewhat like that of northeastern Utah and that used by the Pueblo I people of southwestern Colorado. Pottery was poorer than in most other areas and only a small portion of the food bowls were decorated. Western Utah south of Provo and north of the Colorado Plateau was characterized by a stronger agriculture complex than the northern country. The type dwelling was an adobe-walled structure, usually with two to twenty rooms, and was built somewhat after the manner of the Pueblo II masonry houses of southern Utah. Pottery was similar to that of the south, but had characteristics of its own. A large group was distributed about the shores of Great

Poncho House Ruin, Navajo Indian Reservation.

UTAH STATE HISTORICAL SOCIETY

Salt Lake and somewhat to the south. They were a hunting and pottery-making people and preceded the Shoshoni, who occupied the area in historic times. . . .

Petroglyphs and pictographs represent an important class of antiquities of wide distribution in Utah. The former are pecked or scratched on rock surfaces, and the latter are painted. An abundance of smooth stones in the mountains encouraged the development of these art forms. West of the Wasatch Mountains the designs usually consist of crude human figures, mountain sheep, deer, and various geometric figures. Throughout the Colorado drainage basin, especially near Vernal, there are groups of large ornamental figures, some pecked and others painted in red, yellow, brown, black, and white. Among them are the finest examples in the United States. . . . A great many of them were, quite possibly, of a ceremonial nature, while others may have been inscribed for amusement. In a few cases there seems to have been an attempt to portray scenes of hunting, dancing, or war.

Aboriginal antiquities visible in Utah may be divided into two general classes: the minor elements of material culture, which can be viewed in museums; and the major antiquities, including cliff dwellings, mounds, glyphs, and other remains, which can only be seen *in situ*. . . . The arid climate of the Southwest has preserved many elements of the material culture, such as desiccated human remains, sandals, baskets, wooden implements, fur and feather blankets, corn, and other vegetable products. Beautiful examples of the ceramic wares of the ancient peoples are in great abundance, while the complete series of stone implements ranging from the largest *metates* (corn grinders) to the smallest arrow points illustrate the material equipment of every phase of life.

The best and most extensive major antiquities are concentrated in the southern part of the State, in regions closest to the focal area. However, a number of large and important groups of ruins are found farther north. Among these, perhaps, the structures in Nine Mile Canyon are most easily reached *(see Tour 10)*. Here, perched in every available crevice of the towering cliffs, are the most northerly examples of the cliff-dwelling type of architecture. Small, stone, tower-like structures occupy difficult ledges and commanding ridges. High above the canyon floor on the tops of narrow stone pinnacles are the remains of ancient living quarters. Numerous mounds on the canyon bottoms mark the sites of primitive villages. [Myriad rock surfaces are] covered with examples of some of the finest glyphs in the West. Other important glyphs and masonry structures are near Vernal *(see Tour 6)*.

There are countless ruins in the southern and eastern counties. Near Blanding, Bluff, and Mexican Hat *(see Tour 11)*, are large clusters of cliff dwellings, and on the mesas many open-air masonry structures exist as mounds. There is, perhaps, more to be seen in this area than in any other part of the State. In the Hovenweep National Monument are several large groups of ruins of a specialized architectural type *(see Hovenweep National Monument)*. East of Mexican Hat is a large cliff ruin known as Poncho House, interesting for its size and because it illustrates the Pueblo III type of cliff architecture. Other sites, reached by boat, are along the Colorado, Green, and San Juan rivers. Most of the remains that once existed in western Utah have been plowed under, and little of importance or interest survives in that section. [Caves near Great Salt Lake were] occupied by prehistoric peoples.

In visiting prehistoric sites the layman should remember that these ruins, often insignificant in appearance, represent valuable scientific material; any digging or disturbance of the site may cause irreparable loss to science. All archeological material in Utah is protected by . . . law and any excavation or other destruction by unauthorized persons entails a fine or prison, or both.

Among Utah's most interesting archeological sites—structures and rock writings—are the following, described in the respective tours:

Newspaper Rock State Historical Monument, Grand Gulch Primitive

Area, Edge of the Cedar Museum, Poncho House Ruin *(Tour No. 11)*
Anasazi Village State Historical Monument *(Tour No. 9)*
Nine Mile Canyon and San Rafael Swell *(Tour No. 10)*
Dry Fork Canyon *(Tour No. 6)*
Parowan Gap and Parowan-Paragonah Excavations *(Tour No. 8)*
Canyonlands National Park (Needles and Barrier Canyon)
Capitol Reef National Park
Dinosaur National Monument
Hovenweep National Monument
Natural Bridges National Monument

Archeological collections and displays of note include the Utah Natural History Museum, Salt Lake City . . . Prehistoric Museum in Price . . . Southern Utah State College, Cedar City . . . Emery County Museum, Castle Dale . . . Moab Museum, Moab . . . Edge of the Cedars Museum, Blanding . . . Dinosaur Natural History Museum, Vernal . . . Old State House Museum, Fillmore . . . Anasazi Village State Historical Monument, Boulder.

The 1941 edition only hinted at the tremendous losses of antiquities which have occurred since whites arrived in the Four Corners states. One comment, for example, was this: "Most of the remains that once existed in western Utah have been plowed under, and little of importance or interest survives in that section." Almost identical situations prevailed (or still prevail to a sad extent) in other parts of Utah—in Dixie, the Uinta Basin, Fremont River Valley, Sevier Valley, the San Juan corner, Castle Valley, etc. Irreparable damage has come not merely from agriculture but also from unauthorized excavation, chaining, and deliberate vandalism. Myriad petroglyphs and pictographs have been mutilated. And more prehistoric artifacts have been gathered and dispersed by private collectors, perhaps, than are now possessed by museums. Such losses continue, despite federal and state prohibitions. In 1979 David B. Madsen, State Archeologist, stated that there were some 27,000 archeological sites on record in his office. He estimated that these represented fewer than half of the potentially identifiable sites in Utah. In his opinion, as many sites may have been destroyed since whites arrived in the state as now remain.

Petroglyphs, Horseshoe Canyon, Canyonlands Park.

PARKER HAMILTON

Chief Kanosh, leader of the Pavants *(above)*.

Brigham Young in the 1850s *(left)*.

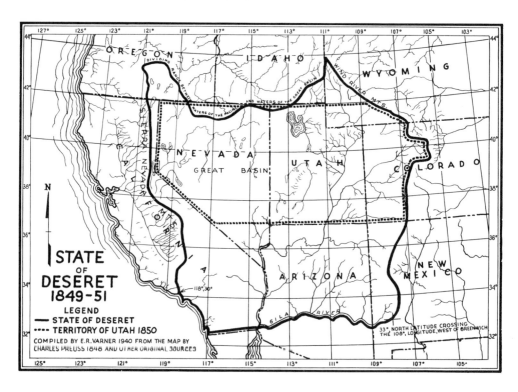

STATE
OF
DESERET
1849-51
LEGEND
—— STATE OF DESERET
•••• TERRITORY OF UTAH 1850
COMPILED BY E.R. VARNER 1940 FROM THE MAP BY
CHARLES PREUSS 1848 AND OTHER ORIGINAL SOURCES

History: Before Statehood

As a concise yet substantial and pithy summary of Utah's history from the days of Spanish exploration to the gaining of statehood in 1896, the History chapter of the 1941 edition of this guide has probably not been surpassed. The work, apparently, of Dale L. Morgan, state supervisor of the Writers' Program which produced the original volume, the History chapter was remarkably inclusive of significant events and surprisingly free of factual error and notable bias. It remains an instructive pleasure to read.

Those qualities alone would be justification for reproducing the greater part of that chapter, verbatim, in this revised edition. Yet it was not possible to do so without modification. The 40 intervening years have brought new historical findings, reappraisals, and interpretations that differ in respects from Morgan's. These have been integrated with the major part of the original work, and the composite product appears below without special notation as to where changes were made. It is hoped that the resultant chapter retains the distinctive vitality of the original.

The blue waters of the Gulf of Mexico rippling above their scuttled ships, the *conquistadores* of Hernando Cortez mounted their horses and turned to the heights of Mexico. That was in 1519. Twenty-one years later, and two thousand miles northwest, a detachment of *conquistadores* stood on the brink of the Grand Canyon of the Colorado. Led by Captain Garcia Lopez de Cardenas, they had reached this great river by a twenty-day march through the Painted Desert of Arizona, and for several days had vainly sought a means of descent down the precipitous canyon walls. The bright river five thousand feet below was unreachable, and their water ran low; at last Cardenas turned back toward Zuni. The exact route followed by Cardenas is not clear. Some historians have held that the Spaniards reached the Colorado somewhere on the southern rim of Glen Canyon, a little northeast of the point where the river crosses into Arizona from southern Utah. Others disagree. What is important, however, is not where Cardenas went but what he reported. By his verdict the northern desert lands were damned. Although Coronado, Cardenas' leader, remained at Zuni almost another year, he looked no more to the north, and no expedition of any importance entered Utah for 236 years.

Venturesome New Mexicans before 1776 penetrated the canyons of the Colorado in Utah. A 1642 inscription in Glen Canyon has yet to be explained, and there are legends among the Indians of southern Utah that their ancestors were forced by New Mexicans to work old lead mines in that region. Recently discovered documents reveal that New Mexican traders were in the vicinity of Moab as early as 1765; but it was the Escalante expedition of 1776 which first gave Europeans a true idea of the Utah region.

On July 29, 1776, when the ink was hardly dry on the American Declaration of Independence, Father Silvestre Velez de Escalante and Father Francisco Atanasio Dominguez left Santa Fe, New Mexico, in search of a direct route to Monterey, California. Accompanied by a small party of Spanish soldiers and Indian retainers, the Franciscan priests made their way up through what is now western Colorado and turned west along the southern flank of the Uinta Mountains, entering the Utah region near the junction of White River with the present state line. They crossed the Green River, which they called the San Buenaventura, and pressed westward along the Duchesne and Strawberry rivers, emerging in September into Utah Valley, via Spanish Fork Canyon. They stayed three days with the timid and inoffensive "Yuta" Indians dwelling on the shores of the lake. *(See Tour No. 5.)* Although told of a great salt lake to the north, they were insufficiently curious to investigate. Autumn was drawing on, and promising to return and establish a mission among the Yutas, the priests turned southward. Nowhere did they find word or sign of a promising route to California. In early October, encamped on Beaver River, they abandoned the effort to reach Monterey. Members of the party were so disaffected by this decision that another council was held, all to be bound by the solicited decision of God. "Concluding our prayers, we cast lots, and it came out in favor of Cosnina [New Mexico]. We all accepted this, thanks be to God, willingly and joyfully." This reaction, recorded by the padres, is understandable since they were convinced that death by exposure or starvation faced them had the lot casting favored Monterey. In fact, they seemed so certain the decision would be "Cosnina" that one wonders just how the lots were cast. *(See Tour No. 8.)*

Crossing the Virgin River near the site of St. George, the Spaniards wandered for two weeks in the badlands to the east, seeking a place to cross the Colorado River. At last they located a ford, and by carving stone steps in the canyon walls, were enabled to cross at "Padre Creek," so named in 1937 when it was shown that Escalante had forded the river here rather than at the so-called Crossing of the Fathers a mile west. From this point on the Colorado, the fathers and their company proceeded directly to Zuni and Santa Fe. *(See Tour No. 9B.)*

Trading expeditions between Santa Fe and Utah Lake soon resulted in a well-defined route since known as "the Old Spanish Trail." This route seems at first to have followed that of Escalante, but variant roads presently were found to the south and the long northern trail through the Uinta Basin was less frequently used. The Indians of central Utah, through intercourse with Escalante's party and obscure expeditions such as that in 1805 of Manual Mestas and in 1813 of Mauricio Arze and Lagos Garcia, picked up some smatterings of Christian belief, but also, and less reputably, acquired the idea of slave-trading; lesser tribes were subject to slaving raids by stronger neighbors, and, on occasion, sold their own children into slavery.

It was not Spanish intercourse in the south, however, but British and Anglo-American trapping enterprise in the north, which opened the Utah region. Returning from their epochal trip to the Pacific in 1806, Lewis and Clark met fur traders pushing out of St. Louis in their track. John Jacob

Astor established his unfortunate Astoria on the Columbia River in 1811-12. This venture may have resulted in the first white entrance into the Great Basin from the north, since four men, detached from the overland Astorian expedition in 1811, wandered hundreds of miles until meeting a return party of Astorians in 1812; they may have reached Bear River, and even Great Salt Lake. They were followed in 1819 by British trappers, who named Bear River and entered Cache Valley.

More years passed before the fur trappers entered the transmontane country. In the west the Hudson's Bay Company thrust eastward along the Columbia and Snake; in the east American trappers fought with Blackfeet and Aricaras on the Missouri, and then, headed by General William H. Ashley's parties, abandoned the Missouri for the broad highway of the Platte and Sweetwater, in 1823-24 penetrating to the lofty plains of Wyoming and, through South Pass, crossing the Continental Divide.

Ashley abandoned river transportation and permanent posts for horse-and-pack-train transportation, inaugurating annual rendezvous at designated points. Not a country of rivers, except for its turbulent mountain creeks and the appallingly-canyoned Green-Colorado, Utah could only have been looted of its furs by such a system. Ashley's men in the fall of 1824 came as far west as Cache Valley. Led by William Sublette, a party wintered on the Bear River, and wagers laid among the trappers resulted in the exploration by young Jim Bridger which ended in the discovery of Great Salt Lake *(see Great Salt Lake)*. Bridger was barely in time for the honor; indeed, it is disputed whether Etienne Provost may not already have looked out upon the broad waters of the lake, and claims have been made for Jedediah S. Smith and Peter Skene Ogden. Smith visited the Hudson's Bay post on Flathead Lake in Montana, pushing southward in late December in company with Ogden. They separated on the Bear River, Smith ascending and Ogden descending, the latter coming into Utah in May 1825 to give his name to Ogdens Hole and Ogden River. Trappers converged on Great Salt Lake from the north and northeast, but were halted by forbidding deserts beyond the lake.

Ashley himself was hard upon the heels of his men; in April, 1825, he embarked on the "Spanish" (Green) River in a voyage of exploration almost as far as the present town of Green River before turning back on horses purchased from the "Eutau" Indians. This canyon country Ashley found as appalling as Cardenas had found that of the Colorado: "The river is bounded by lofty mountains heaped together in the greatest disorder, exhibiting a surface as barren as can be imagined." Returning, Ashley circled the Uintas *(see High Uintas Primitive Area),* on his way to the rendezvous up Henrys Fork. In 1826 Ashley sold out his interests to Jedediah S. Smith, William L. Sublette, and David E. Jackson.

A young man hardly past his twenty-eighth birthday, a Methodist Yankee reputed to carry rifle in one hand and Bible in the other, Smith at once set out with seventeen men on an expedition of discovery. After making a detour to contact a Ute chieftain in the Carbon County area, Smith pushed straight south. Arriving at the Colorado, he turned west through the desert, reaching the San Gabriel Mission in November, 1826.

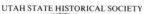

Etienne Provost, from Castonguay's *Les Voyageurs (above left).*

James Bridger in later years *(above).*

Jedediah S. Smith *(left)*

John Charles Fremont *(below).*

He met with a cold reception, but was finally permitted to purchase supplies on condition that he return the way he came. He traveled inland only far enough to give the impression of compliance, then swung northward along the western flank of the Sierra Nevada Mountains. He wintered on the Stanislaus River and in the spring crossed the lofty Sierras. Smith's journey northeastward across central Nevada and the Salt Desert was one of great hardship *(see Tour No. 4A)*.

He arrived at the Bear Lake rendezvous in July, being saluted by the wheeled cannon Ashley had sent to the trappers. Ten days later, with a company of eighteen men and two Indian women, he set out for California again, never to return to Utah. The young explorer, killed in 1831 on the Cimarron River, knew the Utah and adjacent area as no one else knew it for decades after him.

Envious of Ashley and his successors, the American Fur Company in 1830 extended its operations to the intermountain country, and competition between this firm, the already established Rocky Mountain Fur Company, and the powerful Hudson's Bay Company, for a decade was a wild, unscrupulous rivalry in which the Indians often were robbed and debauched by whiskey. William Wolfskill, in 1830-31, leading a party of trappers out of Santa Fe, pushed the Spanish Trail on to southern California from central Utah; though his route was not followed too closely by subsequent trading expeditions, he showed that intercourse between the two Mexican outposts was feasible by the northern overland route. Trapping of beaver remained profitable only until 1840, when the bottom fell out of the market for beaver fur. From 1825 to 1840, yearly rendezvous of the mountain men were held at various points in Utah, Idaho, and Wyoming. Wild and uproarious celebrations, they were punctuated by wholehearted drunkenness and fights with fists, knife, and gun. With aching heads and empty pockets, company and free trappers annually left the gatherings, their hankering for "civilization" satisfied in a few riotous days.

In 1832 Captain B. L. E. Bonneville, on leave of absence from the United States army, came west with an expedition that has puzzled historians ever since. Bonneville never entered Utah but was fortunate in falling into the hands of a great writer, and, through the medium of Washington Irving's account of his travels, named Great Salt Lake for himself. History rejected that verdict, but the power of publicity is such that Bonneville's name subsequently was given the Pleistocene lake that had covered much of the Great Basin *(see Geology)*.

Ashley sent a wheeled cannon to Bear Lake in 1827; Thomas Fitzpatrick took a wagon train to the Wind River Mountains in 1830; and Bonneville's wagons were brought across the Continental Divide in 1832 to Green River. It now became clear that the "boat" of the West was to be the "prairie schooner" drawn by horses, mules, or oxen. Dr. Marcus Whitman brought emigrant wagons to the Horse Creek, Wyoming, rendezvous of 1836. Obstinately determined to carry his wagons through to Oregon, Whitman had to abandon them west of Fort Hall, but the hour of the emigrant was at hand; in 1843 wagons traveled all the way to the Willamette Valley, and a year later climbed the passes of the Sierra Nevada and descended triumphantly into central California. The Oregon Trail, the "Great Medicine Road," was a highroad by 1840.

The trapping business was doomed. The few remaining trappers were settling down at isolated points in the mountains, or establishing fixed posts. In 1833, Kit Carson established a trading post at the confluence of the Green and White rivers, in the Uinta Basin. Four years later Antoine Robidoux also built his fort in the Uinta Basin, near the confluence of the Uinta and Duchesne rivers. About the same time, Philip Thompson and William Craig built "Fort Davy Crockett" in Browns Hole. This post was named for the famous Texan killed at the Alamo the previous year, but trappers more familiarly called it "Fort Misery" and described it as "the meanest fort in the West."

The trapper age had not ended before an emigrant party, bound for California, turned south from the barely established Oregon Trail and blazed a new pathway across northern Utah. This small group of 33 known as the Bartleson-Bidwell Company passed through Cache Valley and across the deserts north of Great Salt Lake in 1841. The group reached California safely, despite having to abandon their wagons enroute. Their difficult trail across Utah was never adopted by other emigrant parties, but most of their route in Nevada and California was followed in later years by countless thousands.

John C. Fremont, enroute to Oregon in the late summer of 1843, made a side trip into Great Salt Lake Valley from the north *(see Great Salt Lake)*. Ignorant of the trappers who had circumnavigated the lake when he was a boy in knee-breeches, Fremont imagined himself the first to venture on the salt waters. Fremont was never the great discoverer he was called, for in his significant explorations he had been anticipated almost everywhere by the trappers, but he produced scientific reports and maps of the West at the moment that the rising tide of empire demanded them; the times and the man came together, and Fremont won a lasting reputation. He went on to Oregon and California, and in the spring of 1844 came up through Utah as far as Utah Lake. He thought it the southern extension of Great Salt Lake, and could not understand why it was fresh. He had failed to calculate the elevation of Utah Lake, which is 300 feet higher than the Great Salt Lake, and he did not see the Jordan River connecting the two lakes, since he went east by way of Spanish Fork Canyon, the Uinta Basin and Browns Hole.

While Fremont was in the Salt Lake Valley during the summer of 1843, Jim Bridger was establishing his famous outpost on Blacks Fork of the Green River—the first fort to be established in the West designed to take advantage of the emigrant trade. Three years later, Miles Goodyear, anticipating the flood of emigrants that would use the shortest route to California through the Wasatch Mountains, built Fort Buenaventura near the confluence of the Weber and Ogden rivers, a full year before the Mormons chose Salt Lake Valley for their base settlement.

By 1846 the western migration had increased to flood proportions. Lansford W. Hastings, enthusiastic over settlement possibilities in California, actively encouraged a number of emigrant parties to follow his "cutoff" through Salt Lake Valley and across the Great Salt Lake Desert, a route traversed the previous year by Fremont and Carson and earlier in 1846 by Hastings himself on horseback. Hastings was successful in persuading several parties to follow his new route. Among these were the Bryant-Russell, Harlan Young, Lienhard and Donner parties. All had great difficulty breaking new wagon roads through the Wasatch Mountains and across the Salt Desert, but only the Donner experience ended in tragedy. *(See Tour No. 4A.)*

As the dust settled into the wagon-tracks of the Donners, the first era of white association with the Utah region was closed. *Conquistadores, padres,* Indian traders, trappers, explorers, and Pacific emigrants were transient shadows on the land. The destiny of Utah lay in the hands of a people who had never seen the country, and who, during the winter of 1846, were encamped 12,000 strong at Council Bluffs and along the Iowa plains, wretchedly waiting for spring. After sixteen tumultuous years in the midwestern states, the Mormons were in flight to the Rocky Mountains.

MORMON BEGINNINGS

Mormonism had its beginning in an atmosphere of super-naturalism, millennialism, and religious revivalism that characterized the "burned-over" district of western New York during the first decades of the 19th century. Joseph Smith, Jr., the founder and prophet of the religion, when in his early teens claimed to have experienced a series of heavenly visions beginning about 1820 in the vicinity of Palmyra, New York. In the first visitation, God the Father and His Son, Jesus Christ, informed the youth that there was no true church of Christ upon the earth, that he should join none of them. Other visions revealed the location of golden plates buried in a hill near his home on which were written the records and religious experiences of the ancient inhabitants of America, including a visit of the Christ to the American continent after His resurrection. After obtaining these plates, and some spectacle-like instruments to aid in the translation of the record, Joseph Smith, with the help of several scribes, produced the Book of Mormon, which he claimed to be an inspired translation of the golden plates. The book was published in 1830 and became a most effective missionary tool in the hands of the young prophet and his converts. Joseph also claimed to have received the Aaronic and Melchizedek priesthoods at the hands of heavenly messengers with the authority to re-establish the true Church of Christ, which was officially organized on April 6, 1830, at Fayette, New York. Three years later the phrase Latter-day Saints was added, reflecting the belief in the imminence of Christ's second coming and the end of the present age. Thus Mormonism began as a restoration of primitive Christianity with a strong eschatological and millennial flavor.

Such a story was not received without a good deal of skepticism and ridicule. Explanations ranged all the way from that of a conscious deceiver to more elaborate psychological theories of self-deception and paranoia. But his claim that he was a living prophet having authority to reestablish the true Church and possessing new scripture satisfied the needs of some of those who had been disoriented by the religious diversity that characterized 19th century Amcrica.

Early converts included Smith's father and mother and other members of his family, as well as other relatives and close friends. The first missionary call came in the fall of 1830 when four young converts were sent to take the glad tidings to the Indians. They stopped off at Kirtland, Ohio (near Cleveland) and succeeded in converting Sidney Rigdon, a popular preacher who had recently aided in the organization of Disciples of Christ, but who was then at odds with Alexander Campbell over communitarianism. Rigdon's conversion led many others to join, and soon some of these converts invited Joseph Smith to leave New York and join their community in Kirtland, which he did in February 1831. The missionaries continued their journey to the Indians, finally locating in Independence, Jackson County, Missouri, on the western borders of the United States. The Ohio and Missouri centers of Mormonism began to grow simultaneously, especially after Joseph Smith designated Jackson County, Missouri to be the site of the New Jerusalem and called on the Saints to build a temple there in preparation for the second coming of Christ and His millennial reign. Mormons still anticipate "going back to Jackson County."

Difficulties with older settlers in Jackson County, including differences over slavery as well as Mormon political solidarity, large land acquisitions, and millennial predictions, led to the forced expulsion of the Mormons from Jackson County to neighboring Clay County in 1833, and a more peaceable move from Clay County in 1835. Caldwell County in north-central Missouri became the center of Mormon activity until 1838, when all Mormons were ordered to leave the state under threat of extermination.

During this same period the Kirtland group was expanding, but some unfortunate land speculations and banking schemes resulted in internal dissension. Joseph Smith and other Church leaders were forced to flee Kirtland in January 1838, leaving a sizable portion of the congregation in a state of apostasy. The faithful joined the Missouri group in Far West, Caldwell County, only to become involved with the political and social differences that led to the governor's extermination order in 1838. At this time Joseph Smith was arrested and ordered to be executed by the state militia, but was saved when a militia general refused to obey the order. He was imprisoned, however, along with several close associates.

The Mormons, numbering several thousand at this time, moved eastward. They crossed the Mississippi River at Quincy, Illinois, and remained there a few weeks until the spring of 1839, when Joseph Smith escaped from the Missouri prison and led his followers up the river to Commerce, Illinois. There he established a new city-state on a broad bend of the Mississippi and named it Nauvoo, a Hebrew word meaning "the beautiful."

Despite difficulties and persecutions, the Church continued to attract new converts, especially in industrially-depressed England, where a mission had been established in 1837. Preaching not only the need for conversion but also the duty to "gather to Zion," Mormon missionaries sent hundreds of converts to help make Nauvoo one of the largest cities in Illinois; later, thousands more were sent to aid in colonizing the Great Basin.

Peace and prosperity in Nauvoo were short lived, however. The beginning of the secret practice of plural marriage by Joseph Smith and other

Church leaders led to internal dissension, while political difficulties, militarism, economic solidarity, and religious fanaticism resulted in continued opposition by their non-Mormon neighbors. The destruction of an opposition press in Nauvoo led to the arrest and murder, by a mob, of Joseph Smith and his brother Hyrum in June 1844. When the community continued to thrive, despite the loss of their prophet, irate Illinois neighbors demanded that the Mormons leave the region.

Now under the leadership of senior apostle Brigham Young, the Mormons determined to colonize an area where they would be the first settlers, thus assuring their right to practice their unique social and religious beliefs. The decision was made to settle somewhere in the Rocky Mountains, and the Saints began to move westward across Iowa on February 4, 1846. On that same day, 238 Mormons sailed out of New York Harbor on the ship *Brooklyn,* bound for California by way of the tip of South America and the Hawaiian Islands. Under the leadership of Samuel Brannan, the *Brooklyn* Saints were colonizing the San Francisco Bay area an entire year before Brigham Young's pioneer company settled in Salt Lake Valley.

Brigham Young, the guiding genius of the Church during its migration and in Utah, was born in Whitingham, Vermont, in 1801. He joined Joseph Smith in 1832, and was made a charter member of the Quorum of the Twelve (Apostles) in 1835. A man of enormous energy and great vision, he has come to be recognized as one of the major figures in western history.

In Mormon tradition, Brigham Young knew from vision, before leaving Nauvoo, that he should locate in Great Salt Lake Valley. Historically, his decision was determined by reading the published reports of Fremont and other travelers, and by special considerations affecting the Mormons as a group. Oregon, already peopled by many emigrant Missourians, seems to have attracted Young at no time. He gave some consideration to Vancouver Island, more especially for the English emigrants. But it was the Great Basin, so named by Fremont, that seized upon his imagination. As early as 1845 he had specifically mentioned Great Salt Lake Valley, the outstanding topographical feature of the Basin, and all through the early months of 1846 he talked about the Basin.

The Mormon migration to the Great Basin was delayed by the offer of the United States government to enlist a battalion of 500 Mormon men in the army, to aid in the conquest of California. War had been declared on Mexico while the Mormons were crossing Iowa. General Stephen W. Kearney, of the Army of the West, was authorized to "receive into service as volunteers a few hundred of the Mormons who are now on their way to California, with a view to conciliate them, attach them to our country, and prevent them from taking part against us." This action on the part of the President of the United States was meant to be a favor, for there were more volunteers than the army could accept, and he had no real need for the Mormon soldiers. Although Brigham Young said that he "would rather have undertaken to raise two thousand men a year ago in twenty-four hours than one hundred in one week now," the Mormon leader realized that there would be many advantages from such a voluntary enlistment and actively aided in recruiting the members of the Mormon Battalion.

It is unfortunate that the belief became prevalent among the Mormons that the call of the Battalion was an act of persecution by the federal government and that only the loyal response by Battalion members saved the Church from destruction. This belief was emphasized at the first reunion of the Battalion when the members chose as their theme "A Ram in the Thicket," comparing themselves to the sacrificial Ram of the Abraham and Isaac story in the Old Testament.

Most of the women and children, and approximately 150 of the men who were unable to continue the march because of sickness, were sent to the upper reaches of the Arkansas River at present-day Pueblo, Colorado, where they spent the winter of 1846-47 with a small contingent of Saints from Mississippi. These Mississippi Mormons had made their way to Fort Laramie during the summer of 1846, expecting to join the Mormon migration to the Great Basin. When they learned that the movement had been postponed until the following year, they sought a place to spend the winter. A fur trapper named John Renshaw told them of some fur trappers' cabins near the headwaters of the Arkansas River and suggested they spend the winter there. Communication of this information to the Battalion led to the sending of three sick detachments, most of the women and all of the children who were accompanying the Mormon soldiers, to the Pueblo community. Eventually this community totaled 287 Mormons, some of whom met Brigham Young's advance party at Fort Laramie in June 1847 and accompanied it to Salt Lake Valley. The Battalion's sick detachments, accompanied by the wives, children, and remaining Mississippi Saints, marched into the valley on July 29.

Brigham Young had brought the main body of Mormons to the banks of the Missouri River at Council Bluffs, Iowa, where the Mormon Battalion was recruited. A community was then established at Winter Quarters on the Nebraska side of the river, where the Saints struggled to survive and to prepare for the journey to Salt Lake Valley in 1847. The advance company, consisting of 143 men, three women, and two children, traveled north of the Platte River to Fort Laramie. They then followed the Oregon Trail to Fort Bridger, and the Donner Trail through the Wasatch Mountains, entering Salt Lake Valley by way of Emigration Canyon. Orson Pratt and Erastus Snow were the first to enter the valley, on July 21, followed by a small group on July 22. The greater part of the company arrived on the 23rd, while Brigham Young—who had been ill with "mountain fever"—and a few friends entered on July 24. Ever since, July 24 has been Pioneer Day, Utah's special holiday.

MORMON SETTLEMENT: THE FIRST DECADE

Plowing began July 23, the day before Young's arrival, and the waters of City Creek were turned out of their bed to irrigate the land. It was necessary to hasten if anything was to be grown this year, and a harvest would be important, for Parley P. Pratt and John Taylor were bringing westward more than 1,500 colonists who expected to winter in the valley. Some Battalion members appeared from the west in October, having been mustered out in California on July 16, but the greater part of the Battalion stayed in California, and some members, working at Sutters Mill near the

Wagon train emigration as remembered by W. H. Jackson.

One of the earliest views of Great Salt Lake City, sketched by Frederick J. Piercy in 1851.

site of Sacramento, participated in the discovery of gold the next year. Notwithstanding the need for a harvest, exploring parties were dispatched north to Cache Valley, west to Tooele Valley, and south to Utah Valley. Exploration, however, only served to convince the Mormons that they had already found their place of settlement. In August, Brigham Young and others returned to their families at Winter Quarters, having, in George A. Smith's words, "broke, watered, planted, and sowed upwards of 100 acres with various kinds of seeds; nearly stockaded with adobies one public square (ten acres)," and built "one line of log cabins in stockade."

The colonists were not permitted to scatter out over the land. Cooperative practices and thinking, which had characterized Mormon life in the Midwest, had led to an emphasis upon the group, and the nature of that group life made possible exploitation of the arid lands and the creation of a desert civilization. As with most Mormon colonies in later years, the 1847 settlers gathered in a fort, not only for protection against Indians but because such a communal settlement allowed for valid social life and religious activities. The settlers lived close together, and went out to a distance to farm their lands. It is one of the great triumphs of the Mormon Church that it not only surmounted the problems of an arid land, which forced settlers to scatter widely over a large area, but made those problems of isolation and tremendous distances contribute to the power and coherence of its social organization.

The first laws in the region, issued as decrees by Brigham Young on July 25, 1847, related to land ownership and conservation of resources. Land, Young said, was neither to be bought nor sold; it was to be apportioned to the settlers, and if they were to hold it, they must take industrious care of it. He also decreed community ownership of water and timber resources. The Mormons, neither then nor thereafter, were much concerned with formal law; in general, broad principles were laid down, and the people were governed to a considerable extent according to the moral codes and social relationships developed within the Church. No attempt was made until 1849 to establish a formal civil government, though civil laws were passed by the High Council in December, 1847, with legislation against vagrancy, disorderliness, theft and arson, adultery, and misconduct in general. There was no need for civil government, since Church government was functioning effectively. The land they occupied still belonged to Mexico, and was not ceded to the United States until after signing of the treaty of Guadaloupe Hidalgo in 1848.

In accordance with instructions given by Young before his departure, the High Council in November bought out Goodyear's interests on the Weber River. When Young, who in December, 1847, had become officially designated as President of the Church, returned from Winter Quarters in September, 1848, the Utah region lay ready for systematic colonization. Already, indeed, Goodyear's property had become transformed to "Brownsville," and some settlers had located in Davis County between Salt Lake City and Ogden.

Colonization of the desert was possible because Mormons were convinced of the need to establish a physical Kingdom in preparation for

Christ's second coming. "Faith through works" was the keynote to Mormon living. Men starved on sego-lily bulbs and thistle greens, on hawks, owls, and crows, while they stayed stubbornly with the land. They were working out their salvation on earth. They clung together because they had to; they succored one another because they could depend only upon themselves. Not all of the Saints were saints; often there were rascals among them; often their suspicion of the gentiles made them socially difficult; often as a people they were unbearably self-righteous. Had the Mormons aimed less high, however, and achieved less greatly, their shortcomings would have been less emphasized.

Brigham Young's efficient colonization of the arid mountain valleys was remarkable for its success and for the social discipline that resulted in success. Church members were "called" as for a mission. Groups were carefully selected to include blacksmiths, tanners, millers, carpenters—perhaps also a doctor, though for the most part the frontier settlements depended upon midwives and amateur doctors. Everyone, actually or potentially, was a farmer. A president would be named for the group, and on a designated date it would gather its property into wagons and set out, perhaps to the valley of the Sevier, perhaps to "Dixie," perhaps even to Idaho's Salmon River, or Nevada's Carson Valley. Arriving on the site of settlement, sometimes selected in advance by Brigham Young, as Fillmore was, the colonists would build a fort, then irrigation ditches, fence farm lands, and raise log or adobe houses. Major missions departed in midwinter, and crops were put in as soon as spring opened. Often newly arrived immigrants were incorporated into such colonizing missions, but the backbone was supplied by experienced settlers who had dwelt longer in Utah. A man who proved himself might suddenly be called to forsake the few comforts he had wrested from the desert for a new struggle with a barren untilled land. Sometimes he might feel that death was preferable to another uprooting, but almost invariably the "called" man obeyed, for he was contributing to the "upbuilding of the Kingdom"; he was laying up glories in heaven by his work on earth.

The late-sown crops of 1847 were scant, but the colonists planted several thousand acres of winter wheat. John Steele recorded in his journal in the spring of 1848, "Our wheat, corn, beans and peas are all up and looking grand and grass is 6 inches high. Sunday, June 4th, there is great excitement in camp. There has come a frost which took, beans, corn and wheat and nearly every thing, and to help make the disaster complete the crickets came by the thousands of tons, and the cry is now raised, 'we can not live here, away to California,' and the faith of many were shaken. . . ." However, by June 9 the valley leaders were able to report that "gulls have come in large flocks from the lake and sweep the crickets as they go; it seems the hand of the Lord is in our favor." Patriarch John Smith remembered that the gulls came every morning for about three weeks and then terminated their visits, although there were still crickets in the fields. In his report to Brigham Young, who was leading another large group of Mormon emigrants to Salt Lake Valley, Smith suggested that frost, drought, lack of fencing, and irrigation problems, as well as the cricket attack, were all factors in determining the success of the crops. The gulls were helping to solve the cricket menace "along with our own efforts" but could not aid in solving the other problems. Nevertheless, the gulls had made a difference and continued to do so in the years following. Little wonder that the Church commissioned Brigham Young's sculptor grandson, Mahonri M. Young, to execute the graceful Seagull Monument on Temple Square, and that the gull has been designated the state bird of Utah.

Crickets and late frosts were only a single feature of the Mormons' environmental adjustment. Their first houses were built, on the advice of Sam Brannan, after the California manner—flat-roofed adobe,—but the water gathered on the roofs and reduced some of the houses to mud puddles; then the Mormons built houses to withstand the storms. They lived thousands of miles from manufacturers and supplies; what they did not have, they went without or made themselves. Tanners made shoes, shirts, and breeches along with harness and saddles; expeditions were sent back along the emigrant trails to recover metal from discarded wagons, to be re-worked into tools and plowshares; native clays were made into pottery; lumber, laboriously hauled from the canyons, was utilized for a thousand things, from wooden shoes to boats.

In December, 1848, the Mormons wrote a memorial to Congress for creation of a territorial government. This memorial, bearing 2,270 signatures, and said to have been twenty-two feet long, was sent east the following May, but by that time the Mormons had undertaken to create a provisional government. A constitution was drafted in early March, and officers for the "State of Deseret" were elected in Great Salt Lake City. Brigham Young was named governor, Heber C. Kimball lieutenant-governor and justice of the supreme court, and Willard Richards secretary of state; the Mormons simply installed the First Presidency of the Church in the leading civil offices. The first session of the legislature was held in July, 1849, but no legislation was passed until the second session. The State of Deseret, named for a Book of Mormon word interpreted as meaning "honey bee," included within its proposed boundaries virtually all of what is now Utah and Nevada, the greater part of Arizona, and portions of Idaho, Wyoming, Colorado, Oregon, and New Mexico, as well as a strip of seacoast in southern California including San Diego and San Pedro near Los Angeles. One of the few physical reminders of the State of Deseret is an inscribed stone, donated by the provisional government, and still to be seen inside the Washington Monument in the nation's capital.

The legislature sent delegate Almon W. Babbitt to the east with a petition to Congress for admission as a state. Babbitt was joined by the bearer of the territorial petition, Dr. John M. Bernhisel, but their request for statehood was lost in the Compromise of 1850, by which California was to be admitted as a state, and New Mexico and Utah admitted as territories. Bitter argument between slavery and abolitionist partisans held up dispo-sition of the territory acquired from Mexico and it was not until September, 1850, Congress having become frightened by the necessity of doing some-thing, that proposals of the compromise committee were substantially adopted. The Mormon name of "Deseret" was held to be repulsive, and the territory was named Utah, to the chagrin of those who thought that "Utah" was descriptive only of a "dirty, insect-infested, grasshopper-eating tribe of

Indians.'' The Territory of Utah extended north and south from the Oregon (now the Idaho) line to the New Mexico (now the Arizona) line, and east and west from the summit of the Rockies through what is now central Wyoming and Colorado to the Sierra Nevada Mountains.

The Mormons had left civilization to avoid its abominations, but they had fled directly in the path of empire. In January 1848, James W. Marshall picked up the first gold in Sutter's mill races—uncovered, ironically, by six Mormon Battalion dischargees. The first overland gold-seekers arrived in Great Salt Lake Valley in June, 1849. Almost all of them were in need of provisions and fresh horses when they arrived at the Mormon oasis. Many of them had brought stores of merchandise—clothing, tools, manufactured goods—which they sacrificed ruthlessly for fresh livestock and crops. Priceless goods were offered to amazed Mormons at far less than cost. The Lord had provided for His own.

But the Mormons must have agricultural self-sufficiency if they were to survive. Gold was a convenience, but food and livestock, iron and coal, were necessities. Moreover, Mormon isolation must be maintained. Young forbade prospecting for precious metals in Utah, and rebuked those who would have gone to dig gold in California. "Gold," he thundered from the pulpit, "is for paving streets. The business of a Saint is to stay at home and make his fields green." Members of the Church in California left the gold fields without regret.

The "kingdom" began to build in Utah. Settlements spread down the mountain valleys south from Great Salt Lake City. Fort Utah was built near the site of Provo in 1849; the walls of Manti arose soon after in Sanpete Valley and by the end of 1850 George A. Smith was enroute south to settle Little Salt Lake Valley. But "building" did not proceed without harassment from without. In the summer of 1851 the officials named to territorial office by President Fillmore appeared from the east. Fillmore had been gracious to the Mormons; he had named Young governor of the new territory, and other Mormons to the office of marshal, attorney, and associate justice. But the non-Mormon appointees, including the territorial secretary, chief justice, and associate justice arrived to find that Young had completed a census of the territory, apportioned representation for the territorial legislature, and set a date for elections. The general assembly had formally dissolved the State of Deseret, and Young had assumed office as territorial governor, upon receiving word of his nomination through eastern newspapers brought from California.

Unfortunately for the hope that the Mormons would get on amicably in their new relation to the United States, the gentile federal officials were the first in a long line of scoundrels, fanatics, and well-meaning but ineffectual men who thoroughly exasperated the Mormons, who in turn thoroughly exasperated the rest of the nation. Invited to address the general conference of the Church in September, 1851, Associate Justice Perry D. Brocchus exhorted the Mormons to be true to the government, and then alluded to the as yet officially unadmitted practice of polygamy, strongly admonishing the Mormon women to be virtuous. An uproar ensued. Brigham Young hushed the audience and turned on Brocchus. The United States government had not, he said, earned the esteem of the Mormons when it stood idly by during the persecutions visited on the Mormons in Missouri and Illinois. It was an insult for such corrupt individuals as Brocchus to come before the Latter-day Saints as authorities on morality and virtue. "I love the constitution and government of the United States, but not the damned rascals that administer the government," he was quoted as saying.

A further source of irritation soon appeared. Broughton D. Harris, secretary of the territory, was dissatisfied because strict legal forms had not been followed in apportioning representation to the territorial legislature. A new census should be taken, and everything done over, but Brigham Young was not disposed to comply. Having completed a census of Utah's 11,380 inhabitants, he saw no need to do it over. Lemuel G. Brandebury, chief justice of the courts, sided with Brocchus and Harris. Hastily the territorial legislature was summoned, and an attempt was made by legal means to restrain Harris from leaving the territory with its papers and funds. Brocchus and Brandebury, meeting as the supreme court despite the fact that no legal session could be held until the time and place was designated by Governor Young, sustained Harris, and the three officials turned their backs on Utah, taking funds designated for the territorial legislature with them.

On the day following their departure, Brigham Young sent President Fillmore a letter detailing his actions as governor and criticizing the runaway officials. He asserted that "No people exist who are more friendly to the government of the United States than the people of this Territory. The constitution they revere and the laws they seek to honor. . . ." This letter, together with Representative Bernhisel's able defense of the Mormons, helped to counteract the very negative report given in the House of Representatives by Justice Brocchus. However, there was no denying the practice of polygamy, since the returning officials had observed the numerous wives of the Church leaders. Before the next group of officeholders arrived, the Mormons had publicly announced plural marriage as a fundamental tenet of Church doctrine.

The doctrine of polygamy (more correctly, polygyny, inasmuch as polygamy signifies "many marriages" rather than "many wives") was first put in written form in the revelation issued by Joseph Smith to Church leaders at Nauvoo in 1843. It is evident, however, that the doctrine had been advanced in some form as far back as 1831, in Kirtland. Persistent rumors of unorthodox marriage ideas and practices accompanied the Mormons throughout their migrations, and while these rumors were incorrect enough to be denied by Church authorities, the concept of plural marriage was developing and Joseph Smith may have begun the practice as early as 1835. Officially, the practice began in 1841 when Louisa Beaman was sealed to Joseph Smith by Joseph B. Noble. Soon afterward, when the Twelve Apostles returned from England, the Mormon prophet taught the principle to them and a few other close associates, and commanded them to enter into the practice.

The doctrine was one of the factors that led to the murder of Joseph Smith in 1844, but after his death the practice slowly expanded as the Nauvoo Temple was dedicated, and as the Mormons left Nauvoo and made their way west to Utah. In fact, the looseness of family ties during the

Exodus seemed to promote plural marriage as a means of solving social problems. Forced by circumstances to make a public announcement of the doctrine and practice in 1852, the Mormon apostle Orson Pratt defended it as a religious principle based on a revelation to their prophet, but he also pointed out that it was sanctioned by the Bible and four-fifths of the world's population. When practiced correctly, it helped to solve many social problems by giving every woman the right to be a wife and mother, and eliminating prostitution. Brigham Young did not hesitate to "call" men to marry widows or immigrant girls, and let it be known that preference for positions in Church leadership ranks would go to those who practiced plural marriage.

Nevertheless, only about a tenth of the eligible men entered into the practice, and of these only a third took more than one extra wife. Sociologist Kimball Young estimated that more than half of the marriages he studied could be classified as highly successful, with 23 per cent having considerable conflict. Marriages based on religious conviction or social needs seemed to have been more successful than those based on romantic love, and records of more than 1,700 divorce certificates issued by Brigham Young are evidence that many of the Saints were not ready to live the "principle." Lack of standards or behavior norms contributed to many problems and misunderstandings that might have been solved if a few generations had practiced polygamy under more stable conditions. Given such circumstances, the number of marriage failures should not be surprising, but the fact that so many were successful in developing happy marriage relationships and in producing fine families should command both wonder and respect.

Polygamy was a gathering storm, but for twenty years the Mormons occupied themselves with more immediate concerns. The dispossession of Indians from their lands inevitably led to embitterment among the aborigines, and though the Mormons endeavored to induce the Indians to settle down along with their white brothers, and were more humane than settlers elsewhere on the western frontier, the Indians were unable to adapt themselves at once to a new manner of living. The lands east of the Wasatch Mountains were at first ignored by the Mormons, and the economy of the Utes was not greatly disturbed, but the best lands of the Paiutes and Gosiutes were soon occupied by Mormon settlements. Indians were reduced to beggary or to intermittent theft and warfare. The important troubles of the white colonists, however, came at the hands of the powerful Utes, more particularly in the Walker "War" of 1853 and the Black Hawk War of 1865-68. Only twelve colonists lost their lives in the Walker conflict, but there was considerable loss of time and property. A tragic event that accompanied the Indian difficulties of 1853 was the massacre of Captain John W. Gunnison and seven men, engaged on a federal railroad survey. The murder of Gunnison near Sevier Lake was to revenge the killing of a Pahvant Indian by non-Mormon emigrants a few days before. The Pahvants fell on Gunnison's party at dawn; four men escaped and reached the rest of Gunnison's command.

The Ute Black Hawk War, Utah's last major Indian conflict, broke out in 1865, and until 1868 intermittent, desperate warfare was carried on between marauding Utes and the settlers of central Utah. More than fifty Mormon settlers were slain, and immense quantities of livestock lost, while many of the southern settlements for a time were abandoned. Economic losses of the settlers were estimated in excess of a million dollars, but despite the fact that the militia served for more than two years without pay, Congress declined to reimburse Utah settlers. The Utes finally quieted down, the greater part of the tribe not having participated in the war, and were settled, for the most part, on the reservation in the Uinta Basin.

Removal of the Indians seemed necessary as the Mormon immigrants continued to come to the new Zion in increasing numbers. Ten large hand-cart companies made their way to Utah between 1856 and 1860 as the anxious desire of many poorer English converts to migrate to Zion induced Church authorities, in the autumn of 1855, to issue an epistle to the Saints: "The Lord, through his prophet, says of the poor, 'Let them come on foot, with hand-carts or wheelbarrows; let them gird up their loins, and walk through, and nothing shall hinder them.'"But the thousand-mile trek across the plains, pulling or pushing heavy hand-carts, the women, the aged, and small children alike walking the entire distance, resulted in many immigrants being buried by the wayside. The first three companies of hand-cart migrations, in 1856, were quite successful; but the Willie and Martin companies were caught by October snows along the Sweetwater River in Wyoming and more than 200 perished—one of the major tragedies in the history of the American West.

The constant slow irritations of Mormon-federal relations, and the continued stream of anti-Mormon stories circulated in the east, determined President Pierce, in 1854, not to nominate Brigham Young as governor of Utah Territory for a second term. Lieutenant Colonel E. J. Steptoe, who wintered at Great Salt Lake City in 1853-54, was chosen as his successor but declined the honor. Pierce failed to appoint another successor, leaving Brigham Young in office without a definite term. Within a year, Mormon relations with the federal government thoroughly disintegrated. A new attempt to obtain statehood in 1856 was fruitless. Almon W. Babbitt, territorial secretary and Mormon apostate, was killed by Indians in Wyoming, and again Mormon critics were positive that the sinister hand of the Saints was in the deed. The relations with the "foreign" judiciary continued to be cancerous. The Saints thoroughly resented being ruled by outsiders with whom they had nothing in common, and who too often revealed themselves as rascals. Nor were they always on their best behavior; in conflict with a group of Mormon lawyers, Justice George P. Stiles, an ex-Mormon, had his office raided and certain of his personal papers burned. Early in 1857 Stiles returned to Washington to report, in effect, that the Mormons were in a state of rebellion. W. W. Drummond, colleague of Stiles, was even more exasperating to the Saints; he refused to recognize the decision of the probate courts, which in Utah had an extraordinarily extended jurisdiction; he bluntly disposed of the whole body of Utah law as having been "founded in ignorance"; his despotic behavior on the bench looked no better to the Saints when it was discovered that he had abandoned his family in the east, and that the woman whom he had brought to Utah as his wife, and whom he was accustomed to seat beside him on the bench, was in fact a harlot.

Returning east via California, Drummond reported that the Mormons regarded Brigham Young as sole authority in matters of government, and that they did not consider the laws of Congress binding; that the Church maintained a secret organization which took the lives and properties of those who questioned the authority of the Church; that Mormons had willfully burned the records of the Supreme Court; that federal officials were daily subjected to public abuse and slander; that Young abused his privilege of pardon and was guilty of instructing juries whom and whom not to indict; that Gunnison had been killed by Indians at the instigation of the Church; and that Babbitt had been killed at the express order of Brigham Young.

In view of the fact that the Republican National Convention, as a part of its 1856 platform, had termed polygamy and slavery "the twin relics of barbarism," that the Democratic Stephen A. Douglas, once a Mormon friend, had denounced Mormonism as "the loathsome ulcer of the body politic," and that the authorities in Washington were anxious to divert public attention to something other than the continuous strife over slavery, such charges could not expect sober consideration and investigation. The Mormons were characterized as being in open rebellion; President Buchanan issued an order terminating Brigham Young's governorship and directed General W. S. Harney to proceed to Utah with sizable units of the army to install and protect the new governor. On the invitation of Brigham Young, many of the people and most of the leaders were gathered at Silver Lake (Brighton) in Big Cottonwood Canyon, for the tenth anniversary of the arrival of the pioneers in Salt Lake Valley. To this gathering the ominous news was brought. In 1847 Brigham Young had declared, "Give us ten years of peace and we will ask no odds of the United States." The ten years were up.

THE "UTAH WAR"

Young and the Saints unshrinkingly faced the prospect of conflict. For years they had felt that the forces of Satan would be unleashed upon the Lord's elect. With the crisis upon them they made preparations for defense. Brigham Young declared martial law in the territory; to the Mormon colonies on the Salmon River, in Carson Valley, and in southern California, he issued orders to gather in Zion. The Utah militia (the Nauvoo Legion) began drilling, and Lot Smith, with a company of scouts, was ordered to the eastern plains to harass the government columns. To Captain Van Vliet, who interviewed him in behalf of the army on September 1857, Young said grimly, "We do not want to fight the United States, but if they drive us to it, we shall do the best we can; and I will tell you, as the Lord lives, we shall come off conquerors. . . . We have three years' provisions on hand, which we will cache, and then take to the mountains and bid defiance to all the powers of the government."

He was threatening a permanent guerilla warfare. That the threat was not an idle one was demonstrated by the success of Lot Smith, who had been dispatched to hamstring government wagon trains. Smith burned almost all available forage between South Pass and Fort Bridger; he cut off the advance army supply trains and burned them; swinging behind the main column of the Utah Expedition, he burned several more supply trains. In his entire campaign less than fifty shots were fired, and not a single man was killed, but his tactics forced the federal troops into winter quarters near Fort Bridger, 300 miles short of their objective. The precipitous walls of Echo Canyon were fortified by the Mormon troops, but it was lack of provisions and the onset of winter that enforced the decision to winter at Camp Scott on Black's Fork.

During September of this year, before the troops had settled down for the winter, the Mountain Meadows Massacre occurred in southern Utah *(see Tour 8)*. Fear and hatred aroused by the approach of the troops was a major element contributing to the commission of that crime.

General Harney, when ordered to Utah with his troops, had loudly declared, "I will winter in the valley or in hell." He wintered in Kansas, and the command was given to Colonel (brevetted Brigadier General) Albert Sidney Johnston, who later fought brilliantly for the South. Johnston joined his troops in November, and with them eked out a miserable winter near Fort Bridger, waiting for spring. But the tide of affairs had now taken another direction in the east. Captain Van Vliet reached Washington in November with his report of the interview with Brigham Young, and of the Mormon "scorched earth" policy. This, with an outbreak of scandal in connection with army contracts, gave public opinion a new perspective on affairs in Utah. The whole idea of the Utah Expedition began to be sharply criticized in the press, where it was frequently termed "Buchanan's Blunder." Several million dollars had been and were being expended, and more sober consideration was given to just what was being accomplished with all this expense.

With an acute sense of political timing, Colonel Thomas L. Kane, a Philadelphian who had proved himself a staunch Mormon friend, interviewed Buchanan about a possible solution of the Utah difficulty; Buchanan evidently made no official commitments, but Kane packed his bags and departed for Utah via Panama and southern California. He arrived in Great Salt Lake City in February, 1858, and after conferring with the Mormon authorities, made a difficult journey to Camp Scott, where he arrived March 12. Johnston received him coldly, but Alfred Cumming, named the previous July to succeed Young as governor, gave him a gracious reception, and was so impressed with him and his pacific proposals that he agreed to accompany Kane back to Great Salt Lake City, where the Mormon leader received Cumming with official deference. But if Cumming was governor in name, Brigham remained governor in fact, and however federal officials might come and go, to the end of his life Brigham Young's was the word by which the Mormons were guided. Young had, Cumming discovered, no faith in the troops and new officials. Despite his pledges of protection, the dismayed governor found the Mormons busy with preparations to flee the troops, and little disposed to give ear to reassurances. The idea of fighting the army had been given over, but now it had been determined that the people would enter upon a new migration. It was not exactly clear where they would go—rumors of Sonora and the South Sea islands were most current among the people; only Young knew that he had sent out an exploring expedition which he hoped would locate, somewhere in the desert wilds south of Great Salt Lake Valley, new oases where the Mormons might live in peace.

In late April and early May, the people began an active exodus. All the settlements north of Utah Valley, where they gathered, were abandoned; there remained behind only a few men in each settlement, to fire the houses and crops if the exodus should definitely be decided upon. Dismayed, Cumming watched the progress of "The Move." But from Brigham Young he won the assurance that if the troops did not molest the people, nor settle near them, the Saints would return. Cumming went back to Camp Scott in mid-May to report that the Mormons acknowledged his authority, and that many stories circulated about them were false. A few days after his arrival peace commissioners arrived from the east, bearing a proclamation of pardon which President Buchanan, bowing to the change in popular clamor, had issued on April 6. The commissioners and Cumming went to Great Salt Lake City, where they conferred with Young, Heber C. Kimball, and Daniel H. Wells, the first presidency of the Church. The Mormons were offended at being "pardoned" for "rebellion" they declined to admit, but granted that they had burned army supply trains and stampeded army cattle; for these acts they accepted the pardon. They also declared their desire to live in peace under the constitution and laws of the United States. This constituted sufficient compromise, and Johnston was notified of the successful outcome of negotiations. Johnston replied with a proclamation assuring the Mormons that all would be protected in person, rights, and the peaceful pursuit of their vocations. This proclamation was published with a declaration from Cumming that federal and territorial laws were to be strictly obeyed. Johnston left Camp Scott with his troops, and late in June marched through the silent, deserted streets of Great Salt Lake City. He crossed the Jordan River, marched south, and located west of Utah Lake in Cedar Valley. The Mormons waited upon events a few days, but since the soldiery showed itself pacific, turned their faces homeward in July.

Establishment of troops at Camp Floyd was, for the Mormons, a mixed evil. The camp-followers of Johnston's army transplanted themselves to Great Salt Lake City, and gambling, theft, drunkenness, and murder signalized the arrival of "civilization" among the Saints. Yet farmers were able to sell surplus foodstuffs and livestock at prices previously undreamed of, while manufactured goods of all kinds fell into their hands at absurdly low prices. Eastern speculators and contractors had licked up the greater part of the rich gravy attending the Utah Expedition, but the scattered drops that fell in Utah amazed the people. The army remained in Utah three years, until the outbreak of the Civil War, but was reduced considerably by mid-1860. Through most of those years there was imminent possibility of clashes between troops and people, each holding the other in contempt. Establishment of *Valley Tan,* first gentile newspaper in Utah, in 1858, did nothing to cement relations, since frontier editors had vigorous ideas as to how newspapers should be run.

AFTER THE "WAR"

The arrival of Johnston's Army was significant of the breakdown of Mormon isolation. However the Saints had kept to themselves with the statement that "we are a peculiar people," their location athwart the high-roads of American empire made inevitable constant adjustments to the current of American life. The soldiery was followed by the Pony Express, which began operations through Great Salt Lake City in April, 1860. Two stage lines had preceded the wild-riding horsemen, but neither had succeeded in maintaining anything like a schedule, especially in winter. The Pony Express brought Great Salt Lake City within seven days of the national capital, with semi-weekly service; the riders were hip-hurrahed east and west until completion of the Overland Telegraph in October, 1861, in Great Salt Lake City.

"The Move" had thoroughly shaken up the people; some remained in the south, while those who returned to their homes in the north sometimes were accompanied by southern settlers. Utah's population was forever in a state of ferment, men migrating or being "called" constantly from one part of the territory to another, so that they had roots in many places and knew many people; a thoroughly homogeneous culture resulted from this constant intermixing of the settlers, who were further confirmed in their identity with the Church by continual service in its behalf.

The Utah War and the move south ended the initial phase of Mormon colonization of the Great Basin. The outlying colonists in California, Nevada, Idaho and Wyoming had been recalled and the colonies abandoned as far as the Church was concerned. The new colonization policy stressed filling in the occupied valleys and extending settlement to Utah's Dixie and the Muddy River areas on the south, and along the Bear River and Bear Lake areas on the north. Cache Valley, which had been settled briefly in 1856, was dotted with settlements during the 1860s. Logan became the valley's chief settlement. Approximately 150 communities were established during the decade between 1859 and 1869; the peak year, 1864, witnessed the settlement of 30 communities. The Cotton Mission, which resulted in the founding of St. George and other settlements in the Virgin River Valley, had an especially colorful history, producing not only cotton and Dixie wine but a number of outstanding writers to tell its story. An attempt to settle the Uinta Basin was defeated through an adverse report by scouts *(see Natural Setting)* and through use of the region as an Indian reservation. The desolate lands east of the Colorado and Green rivers were not attractive to colonists so long as less arid lands were unoccupied.

This intensification of colonization was accompanied by a paring of Utah to its present-day dimensions. In 1861, after years of agitation, citizens of western Utah succeeded in persuading Congress to organize the Territory of Nevada, and all of Utah west of 116 degrees west longitude was lost to the new territory. By a somewhat disgraceful political deal Nevada was made a state soon after its creation as a territory; Utah lost two more degrees of longitude to Nevada, in 1862 and 1866. At the same time lands were carved off on the east, the creation of Colorado Territory in 1861 cutting off all the country between the summits of the Rockies and 109 degrees west of Greenwich. The final slice of Utah was taken in 1868, to complete the rectangle created as Wyoming. Though Utah in later years argued for more territory, notably for the "Arizona strip" north of the Grand Canyon of the Colorado, the boundaries of 1868 were not again altered.

Coalville in 1869, illustrating settlement pattern of fenced lots, corrals, log buildings, log fences, broad right-of-way. Note telegraph poles.

Early street scene.

The Civil War impacted spectacularly upon Mormon society. Here was fulfillment of the prophecy made by Joseph Smith in 1832, that civil war should break out in South Carolina, and that war should be poured out upon all nations. Surely the day of the Lord was at hand. Hardly three weeks before the attack on Fort Sumter in 1861, Brigham Young declared to a congregation in Great Salt Lake City, "The whole government is gone; it is as weak as water."

Hoping to benefit from this disarray, the Saints drew up their third constitution for a "State of Deseret," elected a governor (Brigham Young) and a legislature, and dispatched to Congress a memorial seeking admission to the Union. Congress, instead, passed a new law aimed directly at the practice of polygamy, and the federal government so far suspected Utah's loyalty as to detail Colonel Patrick Edward Connor, with 300 California-Nevada volunteers, to duty in Utah—ostensibly to protect the overland mail and telegraph. But Connor was convinced that his main duty was to keep the "disloyal" Mormons under surveillance. He refused to be quartered at Camp Floyd, establishing his camp on the bench above Great Salt Lake City in October, 1862, his cannon within range of Brigham Young's residence.

The legislature of the "State of Deseret" met in 1862 despite failure of Congress to recognize the Mormon state; the members met this and every succeeding year until 1870, a total of nine sessions, yearly passing, for the State of Deseret, the same legislation they had passed while sitting as the territorial legislature, so that, in Brigham Young's words, "everything [might] be in readiness when Congress [should] recognize our State organization, and to save confusion and trouble when the transition from a territorial condition to that of a state [should] have been fully accomplished."

General Connor, who disliked Mormon authoritarianism, sought some means of inducing sufficient gentile migration into Utah to equalize or dominate the vote. Agriculture was no solution; the Mormons already held virtually all the land which would offer a living, as well as much that would not. In the mining industry, however, he saw potentialities. The Church had stifled mining initiative except in the development of iron, lead, and coal deposits. Precious metals lay untouched—if they could be found. Connor gave his men leave to prospect the hills, where they found sizable deposits of gold, silver, copper and other metals in the Oquirrh and Wasatch mountains. He organized the first mining district in the territory in 1863, and wrote its mining code, thus earning his reputation as the father of Utah mining. His efforts to stimulate the mining industry bore no real fruit until the seventies; meanwhile the Mormons spoke sarcastically of the "poor, miserable Diggers" inhabiting the bench above the Mormon capital. But gentile business men took firmer root in Great Salt Lake City.

On May 10, 1869, the transcontinental railroad was completed at Promontory Summit *(see Tour No. 2, Transportation, and Golden Spike National Historic Site)*. This railroad had been dreamed about in 1850, and as early as 1852 the Mormons had memorialized Congress for its construction. The United States government for almost a decade kept surveying parties in the field, with the new emphasis on communication with California, but until the outbreak of the Civil War there was no active progress.

Governor Alfred Cumming *(above left)*. Heber C. Kimball, Mormon leader *(above right)*. George Q. Cannon, Mormon leader *(below left)*. General Patrick E. Connor, founder of Fort Douglas *(below right)*.

In 1862 Lincoln authorized the construction of a transcontinental railroad, and the following year work was launched by the Union Pacific and Central Pacific companies. The enterprise slowly gathered momentum, and by 1868 the two companies had graded into Utah. The Union Pacific built its grades down Echo and Weber Canyons to Ogden, and thence around the northern end of Great Salt Lake, but Ogden subsequently was made the junction city. When it became apparent that the transcontinental road would miss Great Salt Lake City (renamed Salt Lake City in 1868), Brigham Young organized a company to build a trunk line between the Mormon capital and Ogden, the last rail of the Utah Central being placed at Salt Lake City on January 10, 1870.

The immediate effect of the railroad was to break down once and forever the physical isolation of the Mormons, but the destruction of isolation in space promptly led to a new stress on isolation in spirit. The nature of the Mormon group life gave shape to the economic struggle. The ideal of co-operation, as also of consecration of property for co-operative ends, had become ingrained in Utah life. As the railroad neared Utah in 1868, Mormon leaders, in recognition of the success of co-operative stores, tanneries, and mills, organized a major commercial concern, Zion's Co-operative Mercantile Institution, more familiarly called ZCMI. Pressure was immediate upon gentile entrepreneurs, for the Saints were expected to trade with their own store rather than with outsiders, who were regarded as mere profiteers. Mormon leaders tired of seeing the Saints placed under the economic thumb of gentile merchants and virtually drove them to the wall; they were saved only by completion of the railroad, which enabled them to compete on even terms with ZCMI. Although no all-seeing eye of God, or legend "Holiness to the Lord," was engraved over their doors, a bargain is a bargain, and the gentiles survived the lean months until the mining industry awoke at the magic touch of rail transportation.

The Church now had to contend with a revolt in its ranks, of fateful social and political implications. Schisms before 1869 were not new to Brigham Young, though the removal to Utah had stilled many disruptive movements; in 1852 the public announcement of polygamy caused an uninfluential and unfruitful schism led by Gladden Bishop. A more spectacular apostasy was that of the Morrisites in 1861-62, when a self-proclaimed prophet, announcing the immediacy of the Millennium, was able to attract almost a thousand converts from the Mormon fold in the South Weber and Davis areas. The Godbeite rebellion of 1867-69 was a more formidable development. At the heart of the movement were the wealthy and influential William S. Godbe and Elias L. T. Harrison, who in 1869 were expelled from the Church for advocating, among other things, development of the mining industry. Essentially the conflict was between first and second generations in the Church, a struggle between the philosophy of aloofness and that of fraternization with gentiles; more directly, the established Church authority was challenged in its right to speak solely for the Mormon people—the Godbeites did not question Mormon doctrine but simply accepted it as a beginning step to the much higher religious experience of Spiritualism.

In the political field, a coalition of Godbeites with followers of Colonel (now General) Connor led to the organization of the Liberal Party. At its first organization in 1870 at Corinne, the Liberal Party was primarily a reform organization, but extremist elements subsequently gained full control, and when the Godbeites withdrew, the Liberal Party became bitterly anti-Mormon, its voice for many years being the *Salt Lake Tribune.* Previously no political parties had existed in Utah, candidates for public office being named by Church leaders and "sustained" by the populace in periodical plebiscites. The Mormon organization now, however, assumed the name of People's Party and continued to control politics in Utah for the next twenty years with some minor exceptions.

While Mormon exploration and colonization were following their orderly, purposeful course, exploration of a different nature was proceeding in remote parts of the territory, largely untouched as yet by settlement. Interest in the possibilities of a transcontinental railroad resulted in a survey expedition by Captain J. W. Gunnison and Lt. E. G. Beckwith during 1853-54. Captain J. H. Simpson in 1859 led an exploring and surveying party westward from Camp Floyd. In the same year, a scientific expedition commanded by Captain J. N. Macomb explored southeastern Utah from Santa Fe, failing in their attempt to reach the confluence of the Green and Colorado rivers.

The late 1860s and the 1870s witnessed explorations and scientific surveys by professionals. Known by the names of their leaders, the most notable of these were the following: Clarence King, the Uinta Mountains and northern Utah, 1868-71 . . . Major John Wesley Powell, canyons of the Green and Colorado rivers in 1869 and 1871, and systematic surveys of northeastern, southern and central Utah during most of the 1870s . . . Captain George M. Wheeler, surveys of much of the state during the years 1871-79 . . . and Professor F. V. Hayden, surveys of southeastern and northeastern Utah in 1874-77.

Government surveying party in the Uinta Mountains, 1870s.

UTAH STATE HISTORICAL SOCIETY

THE ISSUE OVER POLYGAMY

The struggle over polygamy took particular shape after 1870. Previously it had been a moral more than a political issue, and except for the dead-letter Anti-Polygamy Act of 1862, the Saints had been pretty much left to themselves. Moral indignation in the east unquestionably influenced the refusal of Congress to admit Deseret into the Union, and was responsible for the niggardly appropriations by Congress for the territory, the disposal of land, and for the fact that no land titles in Utah were granted by the federal government until 1869. The Radical Republican Congress, bent on reconstructing the South, was also determined to "reconstruct" the Mormons. Polygamy was to be crushed. Two bills to that end were introduced into Congress in 1869-70. In substance they would have abolished trial by jury in cases arising under the 1862 law, transferred appointment of territorial officers to the governor, made the governor auditor of Church funds and properties, given the judiciary right to seize any building for its needs, and transferred direction of jails and prisons from the legislature to the governor. Both bills were voted down by southern legislators, who had tasted carpet-bag rule, but they were significant of the thinking Washington did about Utah during the next two decades. The federal government was searching for political expedients to get at polygamy and the Mormons.

The Mormons had troubles with federal governors, but their most desperate struggles were with the judiciary. One of the most formidable federal judges was James B. McKean, a Grant appointee of 1871. McKean was exemplary in his private life, a fine scholar, and a man of high principles. His principles, however, he was willing to sacrifice for the ends to be attained. He set aside the territorial law governing selection of jurors by lot from the taxpayers' lists, and transferred selection to the U. S. marshal. With the handpicked grand jury thus obtained, he set about scuttling the Mormons. In 1871, his grand jury had indicted Brigham Young for "lewd and lascivious cohabitation," McKean flatly declaring, "The case at the bar is called the people versus Brigham Young, [but] its real title is Federal Authority versus Polygamic Theocracy." Young was forced to make a trip through snow and cold from his winter home in St. George in order to appear at the trial, and when his bail was set at $500,000, even General Connor protested and offered to help furnish bail. The Mormon leader was put on house arrest for 120 days and required to pay his guard ten dollars per day. However, before the case came to trial, the United States Supreme Court reversed the Englebrecht decision, ruling that McKean's court had exceeded its authority. Young, along with many others, was released.

McKean's willingness to sacrifice strict legality for anti-Mormon ends is evidenced by his decision in 1873 when Ann Eliza Webb Young, who later wrote *Wife No. 19,* sued for divorce and alimony. The federal government did not acknowledge the validity of polygamic marriage, and there could be no civil divorce where there had been no civil marriage, least of all alimony; notwithstanding these contradictions, McKean assessed Young with court and lawyer fees and ordered him to pay alimony at the rate of $500 per month. When Young refused to pay and appealed the case, McKean found him in contempt of court, fined him, and imprisoned him for twenty-four

Lehi Co-op, 1888.

hours. The case was decided in Young's favor just a few months before his death.

McKean was replaced in 1875, but he had given the Mormons a frightening view of their helplessness before autocratically inclined federal officers. The fourth effort, in 1872, to attain statehood was a desperate reaction to oppressive federal administration. The memorial for state government was ignored, and the Poland Act of 1874 voided the extended jurisdiction of the Mormon probate courts, where polygamists previously had been assured a sympathetic hearing at the hands of fellow religionists. The courts thus were given over completely to the federal judiciary, and effective prosecution of polygamists was made possible.

This attack from without, together with the success of Mormon co-operatives, and perhaps the depression following the panic of 1873, was influential in the effort of 1874 to reestablish the United Order. Principles of "consecration" and of "stewardship" had characterized Mormon social thinking since 1831. After a series of revelations issued by Joseph Smith, Church members had lived for a time in what was variously known as the "United Firm," "Order of Enoch," or "United Order."

The United Order was an effort by a local group to attain self-sufficiency and a favorable balance of trade. If the Saints lived frugally, bought nothing from without, and produced an exportable surplus, they might, in Brigham Young's view, become a rich people. Moreover, by uniting their individual means, the Saints might evade mortgaging themselves to outside capital. The United Order was also a religious reaffirmation. Applicants for membership frequently were required to renew their covenants by baptism, and religion strongly influenced all that was done. Several different types of Orders were attempted, including a joint-

stock arrangement at Brigham City; over a hundred agricultural cooperatives, known as the St. George type; and several completely communitarian
settlements such as Orderville. Urban centers cooperated with projects on a
ward basis. Brigham City and Orderville were probably the most successful,
lasting fifteen and ten years respectively; but most of the agricultural orders
failed within a year, primarily because of internal dissension. Federal prosecution of polygamists was also a factor that led to the dissolution of some
Orders. Ultimate re-establishment of the United Order is still taught as an
essential Church doctrine, but the date is placed in some indefinite future
when the people shall have proved themselves worthy.

BRIGHAM YOUNG'S DEATH TO STATEHOOD

Brigham Young's death occurred on August 29, 1877, in the Lion House
in Salt Lake City. The Saints were stunned and the entire nation took note
of the death. For thirty-three years he had been the Mormon colossus, a
giant who bestrode the Mormon universe and who symbolized Mormonism
for the world. The Lion of the Lord had led the Saints to an empire, built it
with them, fought for it with them. By some he had been hated; by more he
had been loved. Thousands of his people he knew and called by name. He
had been so dominant a figure that many believed Mormonism must
collapse with his death.

With Young the Church lost its last great personal leader, but if there
was no dominant personality to succeed him, there were able men trained in
a hard school of experience, who have led the Church since 1877. Young's
death was followed by an "apostolic interregnum" of three years and the
accession of John Taylor to the presidency of the Church. The people in
Utah were occupied with economic concerns—with dry-farming possibilities, with mining, and with the growth of the livestock industry. Political
battles between Liberal and People's parties grew yearly more spectacular.

Struggle in the eighties centered fiercely and conclusively about
polygamy, which was in actuality the lever, if not the object to be moved.
Enemies of the Mormons wanted to shatter the temporal power of the
Church, to break down its economic, social, and political domination of
Utah, but there is no doubt that they were sincere in their distaste of
polygamy.

In 1882 Congress passed the Edmunds Act, designated to implement the
Anti-Polygamy Act of 1862 and the Poland Act of 1874. It defined
polygamy as a felony, punishable by fine not exceeding $500, and by
imprisonment not exceeding five years. To evade the difficulty of proving
Church marriages, it defined polygamous living (unlawful cohabitation,
within or without the marriage relation, with more than one woman) as a
misdemeanor, punishable by a fine not exceeding $300, by imprisonment
not exceeding six months, or both. It excluded all found guilty of either
offense from the right to vote and hold office. It declared vacant all elective
and registration offices in Utah, providing for a commission of five men to
supervise registration of voters, conduct of elections, eligibility of voters,
counting of votes, and issuance of certificates to elected candidates.
Between 1882 and 1884 the Utah Commission disfranchised some 12,000
voters, utilizing a test oath which required the prospective voter to swear

that he was not a polygamist, bigamist, or guilty of unlawful cohabitation, or in sympathy with these practices. The people of Utah made another effort for statehood in 1882, the first under the name of Utah, but the effort was fruitless.

Chief Justice Charles S. Zane, arriving in 1884, convicted Rudger Clawson, subsequently a member of the Quorum of the Twelve, of polygamy under the Edmunds Act, and sentenced him to four years in the penitentiary. The appeal to the Supreme Court was lost. With this case under their belts, federal authorities began intensive prosecutions. Mormons were peremptorily excused from jury service if they declined to deny the doctrine of polygamy; wives and minors were permitted, even forced, to testify against husbands and fathers. Prosecution centered about the misdemeanor clause of the Edmunds Act. Federal officials devised a system of indictment for separate offenses, so that sentences might by pyramided even to life imprisonment.

Six terrible years ensued for the polygamists. Church leaders almost uniformly had embraced polygamy as a test of their faith. The most prominent leaders were forced into hiding. Brandishing warrants, United States deputies broke into homes at the dead of night on "polgy hunts." It went hard with the "cohabs" who were caught. However, imprisoned men were considered martyrs and often were met by the town band upon their release, and parties were held in their honor. Congress put even more savage teeth in the laws against polygamists with the Edmunds-Tucker Act of 1887: the L.D.S. Church was disincorporated and most of its property confiscated; female suffrage was abolished; the Perpetual Emigration Company was abolished; the Utah Commission was continued in office, and a test oath was required of citizens who would vote, hold elective office, or serve on juries. The Church was already in financial stress; this last blow all but bankrupted it. Congress was memorialized again in 1887 for a State government, the proposed constitution expressly prohibiting polygamy, but Congress had no intention of giving up its power over Utah while the struggle over polygamy endured, and the warfare continued until 1890.

By that year the leadership of the Church once again had changed hands, John Taylor having died while in hiding in 1887. Acting for the Church, the new president, Wilford Woodruff, in September, 1890, published a manifesto advising members of the Church to abstain from the practice of polygamy. In October the manifesto was ratified at a general conference, and the Saints officially abandoned polygamy as an essential Church doctrine. This crucial decision was not taken without bitterness among the Church membership, or skepticism among the gentiles. Many of those who had suffered for polygamy doubted the power of man to set aside the decree of God, and in the ensuing ninety years there have been undercurrents of polygamic thinking, some within Church ranks (the extent of which is difficult to assess), much more visibly among offshoot branches that are not recognized by the main body of the Church. Many gentiles were unable to conceive that Mormonism in a few decades would become as wholly monogamic as Methodism; in their view the Church had made a shabby deal to save itself from extermination. Chief Justice Zane, however, accepted the pronouncement of Woodruff at face value. Further punitive legislation pending in Congress was abandoned, and the President of the United States, after a period of waiting, pardoned all polygamists, and restored their civil rights.

Developments within the territory gave promise, between 1887 and 1890, of better days for Utah. Gentile business men began to desert the radical anti-Mormons. The Mormon People's Party, in 1889 offered four places on its Salt Lake City ticket to prominent gentiles in a gesture of reconciliation, and the fusionist party easily carried the election. In Salt Lake City, a Chamber of Commerce was organized which made a point of ignoring creedal differences. The immediate effect of the capitulation to federal pressure was to deliver populous centers, politically, into gentile hands. The Liberals carried Ogden in 1889, and the next year took Salt Lake City. They embarked on a program of spending for municipal improvements. The People's Party officeholders had tended to over-conservatism in expenditures for public improvements; the Liberals had less hesitancy about bonding cities for waterworks, sewers, and other appurtenances of urban civilization. The Liberal ascendancy also bore fruit in the schools, an 1890 act of the territorial legislature establishing public schools throughout the territory for the first time. Centralization of education on a non-sectarian basis emphasized the separation of church and state. As though to offer an earnest proof of their continued sincerity, the Mormons abandoned the People's Party, Church leaders advising the people, in 1891, to affiliate with the Democratic and Republican parties. Reluctant to abandon its hard-won victory, and perhaps distrustful of Mormon trickery, the Liberal party maintained its organization two years longer.

Joseph L. Rawlins, elected to Congress in 1892, introduced an enabling act for Utah, and a bill providing for the return of escheated Mormon Church property. Both bills carried; Caleb W. West, governor during the last phase of the polygamic struggle, recommended statehood in his annual report for 1893. The Enabling Act was signed by President Cleveland the following July.

Broom Hotel, Washington Boulevard in Ogden, about 1888.

UTAH STATE HISTORICAL SOCIETY

Cedar City Main Street, about the turn of the century.

Eureka Branch, D&RGW Railroad, in the 1890s.

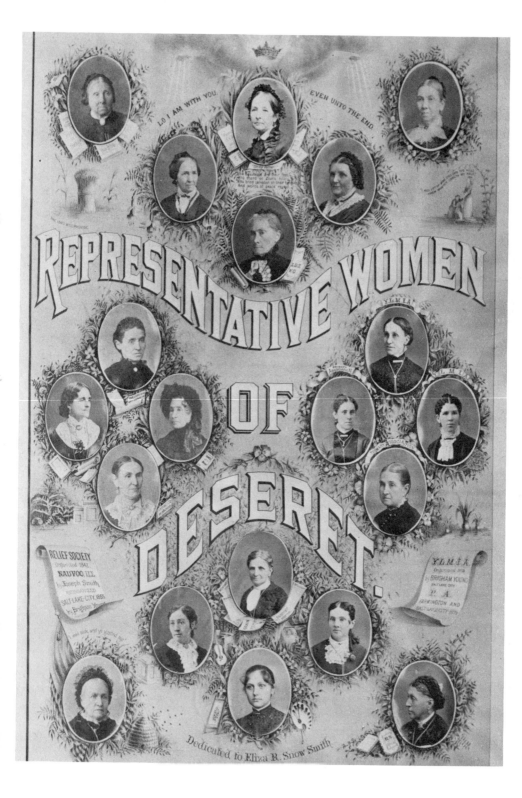

REPRESENTATIVE WOMEN OF DESERET.

Dedicated to Eliza R. Snow Smith.

History: Statehood to the Present

Utah's seventh constitutional convention met in Salt Lake City in March, 1895. Real debate ensued only on two points. The long quarrel over female suffrage ended with giving the vote to women—an unusual concession at that time. The second dealt with polygamy. The Enabling Act explicitly required that polygamous marriage should be forever prohibited, but the problem arose as to whether those who had already contracted polygamous marriage should be permitted to continue living in polygamy, or whether polygamous living itself should be prohibited. The more humane alternative was adopted. The constitution was ratified by the people of Utah in the autumn of 1895, when State officers were elected, headed by Heber M. Wells, first Governor of the State of Utah. On January 4, 1896, President Cleveland proclaimed Utah as the 45th State of the Union, and two days later its officers were inaugurated.

1941 edition

Spectacular conflicts with the rest of the nation had tended to obscure the substantial social and economic development that had occurred in Utah prior to the gaining of statehood. Completion of the transcontinental railroad in 1869 revolutionized Utah economically. Prices of manufactured goods fell, and those of agricultural products rose greatly; the railroad had much to do with the failure of the United Order in 1874; it doomed irrigation-raised cotton in "Dixie" and discouraged native manufactures. Opening of the mines, however, was contingent on transportation, and boom developments in the Wasatch, Oquirrh, Tintic, Frisco, and other areas owed much to the railroads. In turn, opening of mines was influential in expansion of the railroads through much of Utah and other western states *(see Transportation)*. For example, construction of the Denver & Rio Grande Western coincided with the first real development of country east of the Wasatch Mountains. The railroad ran through the richest coal sector in Utah, and exploitation of the Carbon-Emery mines followed quickly. Between 1881 and 1883 the D&RGW graded west into Utah from Colorado, and by 1883 it had 386 miles of narrow-gauge road in Utah. In 1890 this company changed to standard gauge, and an affiliate, the Western Pacific, in 1908-10 built a road to San Francisco from Salt Lake City.

The railroads were built just as western livestock began to acquire importance. Mormon pioneers had brought livestock of every kind, but their ideas on animal husbandry were those of the east and midwest. Environmental conditions led to changed handling of herds, from farm to range technique, but the real stimulus for livestock in the west followed introduction of Texas ranching practices on the Wyoming plains. Construction of railroads and the spread of great herds into the desert adjacent to the Colorado River made raising of sheep and cattle an important factor in Utah economy by statehood. The dying glow of the frontier lit eastern and southern Utah through the final years of the century. Indians ceased to be a serious military problem after the Black Hawk War, though existence of the Uinta reservation, largest in Utah, slowed white settlement of much of the Uinta Basin until 1905 *(see Tour No. 6)*.

By 1896 the most desirable lands had been occupied—some of them for decades— and abuse through overgrazing was becoming more evident. Intensive logging and wood gathering had cleared the mountain slopes in many areas. The growing rural population—now comprising several generations— was finding it increasingly difficult to survive on the state's limited farmlands and in its rural communities. By 1896 almost 40 per cent of Utah's 240,000 people resided in urban areas, compared with only 23 per cent in 1880, and the migration of native Utahns to other states was beginning a trend that was to last for 40 or 50 years. Mining, construction, manufacturing, and commerce had become major components of the economy. There were 1,400 miles of railroad and about 550 manufacturing establishments in the state by 1895, electricity was a servant, and telephones were a reality.

STATEHOOD TO WORLD WAR I

The two decades between the achievement of statehood and America's involvement in World War I are a dark age for most contemporary Utahns. Anyone born at the close of that period, if still living, would now be more than 60 years of age, and those who participated as adults in the events of those years would now have passed their 80th milestone. The lack of understanding and appreciation of that period of Utah's history—insofar as modern generations are concerned—may be attributed at least partially to the lack of concise, interesting, organized, widely disseminated information. More importantly, perhaps—though that era witnessed stirring episodes of human drama—it is too close in time to the present and therefore does not possess the halo of pioneer romance that makes the more distant past so exciting. *Continued on page 103.*

Springville in 1900.

G. E. ANDERSON

David Eccles.

William Jennings

GIANTS IN THOSE DAYS
Leaders of Finance and Industry

Great personal fortunes had been made by 1896, or were in process of accumulation. Though the majority of these were the result of mining, others came from cattle, merchandising, and other activities—or a combination of several. A biographical sampling appears below to illustrate the 19th century maxim that hard work reaps rich rewards. Brigham Young may have been the wealthiest person in Utah in 1877, the year of his death. Others were amassing wealth by that time, also, though most of the greatest fortunes were to come in the decades before and after the turn of the century, the result of large-scale mining, banking, agriculture, lumbering, and merchandising.

Park City's metal mines laid the foundation for fortunes of Thomas Kearns, David Keith, A. B. Emery and his widow the "Silver Queen," John J. Daly, and John Judge. The copper ores of Bingham brought wealth to Daniel C. Jackling, Enos A. Wall, and Samuel Newhouse. Jesse Knight gained a fortune from the silver and lead of Tintic and the coal of Carbon County. Mines in Utah, Nevada, and Wyoming brought wealth to William S. Godbe.

Mining also was a factor in the accumulation of the Eccles, Walker, and Jennings fortunes, though financial activities of different nature were primary in the careers of those capitalists. There were others who achieved wealth in the decades immediately before and after statehood, among them Thomas Weir, Fred J. Kiesel, John Q. Packard, A. W. McCune, W. S. McCornick, S. H. Auerbach, Elizabeth Bonnemort, and Albert F. Holden. According to O. N. Malmquist, writing in *The First 100 Years; A History of the Salt Lake Tribune,* the New York World Almanac in 1902 listed the names of 19 Utah millionaires, at the same time noting "that probably a dozen more could be added to the list." In proportion to total population this was a remarkable showing for Utah.

ELIZABETH DUNLOP FERGUSON BONNEMORT was the state's wealthy and cultured Sheep Queen. As described in Margaret D. Lester's *Brigham Street,* Elizabeth and her first husband James Ferguson homesteaded at Ibapah in the 1870s and

1880s, accumulating land and sheep, and raising four daughters in a cultivated though frontier atmosphere. After Ferguson died in 1883, Elizabeth married Edward Bonnemort, a cattleman. "The combination of Ferguson sheep, the Bonnemort cattle, and the joint acreage made a highly successful venture. The Bonnemorts continued to live at the ranch house [in Ibapah], which they equipped with handsome Victorian furniture, fine rugs, draperies, and kerosene ceiling lamps with colored bowls and crystal prisms. . . ." In 1889 the Bonnemorts moved to Salt Lake City, where they built a handsome residence on Brigham Street (South Temple), furnished it lavishly, and entertained generously. Elizabeth became a civic and social leader, interested in the arts, and traveled widely. She died in 1914.

THOMAS D. DEE (1844-1905). A financial associate of David Eccles in Ogden, Dee was born in Wales and came to Utah in 1860 with his parents. During an active business and public career extending over some 40 years Dee served as assessor, collector, justice of the peace, alderman and councilman, as well as a member of the state board of equalization. As a businessman, Dee was involved as an officer or promoter in lumber firms, railroads, and various sugar companies that eventually were absorbed by Amalgamated Sugar Company. He was president of Ogden Rapid Transit Company, Ogden Water Works Company, Utah Canning Company, Ogden Furniture and Carpet Company, Dee-Stanford Shoe Company, Utah Construction Company, and Ogden Pressed Brick & Tile Company. In his honor, after his death, his family erected the Thomas D. Dee Memorial Hospital and nurses' home. Dee also became known as the "father of the Ogden public school system" through 25 years of service as a school trustee and ten years as president of the Board of Education. In addition he was active in his church for many years as Sunday School superintendent and bishop's counselor.

DAVID ECCLES (1849-1912), a native of Scotland, came to Utah with his parents in 1863. As a young man he worked as a coal miner, freighter and logger, gradually acquiring sawmills, a planing mill, and a retail lumberyard in Utah. Eventually, in the 1890s, his lumber interests expanded to the Mount Hood area in Oregon, where he built two railroads. He was instrumental in the organization of a number of sugar companies in Utah, Idaho and Oregon, eventually consolidated into the Amalgamated Sugar Company of Ogden, and was a founder of the Utah Construction Company. Among other firms with which he was associated: coal mines, street car companies, land and stock companies, condensed milk company, implement companies, and 20 banking institutions. At one time, it was said, he was president and director of 16 industrial corporations and director in 20 others, and among banking institutions he held the presidency of seven and was a director of four others.

WILLIAM GODBE (1833-1902) was born in England and came to Utah in 1851 as a youth. He soon gained wealth as a commercial agent and merchant, freighting goods to the territory from eastern points before arrival of the railroad. Originally a Mormon of prominence, Godbe disagreed with church leaders on certain matters, including the development of mineral resources, and was excommunicated. He was a co-founder of the Godbeite movement and of the *Mormon Tribune,* later the *Salt Lake Tribune,* spending much of his fortune on this enterprise before withdrawing in 1873. Thereafter until his death he was active in the development of mines, mills, and smelters in Utah, Nevada and Wyoming. Between 1857 and 1884, according to Bancroft's *History of Utah,* Godbe had crossed the Atlantic 21 times and the plains more than 50 times; 24 plains crossings were made prior to the coming of the railroad. In addition to these travels were several trips to California by different routes. As a sailor, in his youth, Godbe visited Greece, Turkey, Africa, Brazil, and a number of European countries.

DANIEL C. JACKLING was a resident of Utah for only 20 years, but during that brief time he laid the foundations of wealth for himself and the Utah Copper Company. A college-trained metallurgist, Jackling came from Colorado to Mercur in 1896 to build and operate a metallurgical works. Shortly thereafter he became interested in the low-grade copper ores of Bingham Canyon. Jackling's instrumental role in development of these ores is told in Tour No. 3. A brief summary of his career appeared in *Kennescope* issue of February 1976: "For five years he tried to build interest in developing Bingham Canyon deposits, but his plans were so 'radical' they met only with scorn. Not until 1903 did he obtain financial backing that resulted in formation of Utah Copper Company. . . . Between 1904 and 1942, Jackling was director, general manager, managing director, vice president and president of various mining and metallurgical companies including Utah Copper. . . . He held presidencies in 15 major companies. . . . He received highest honors of the mining and metallurgical world and a number of honorary scholastic degrees. . . ." Among the firms for which he served as an officer or director were copper, gold and oil companies, a steamship line, railroads, banks, and Utah Power and Light Company, of which he was president.

WILLIAM JENNINGS (1823-1886), born in England, came to Utah in 1852. Jennings became wealthy by engaging in large-scale merchandising in Salt Lake City as well as other commercial activities. He began his career on a small scale as a butcher and seller of goods, added a tannery and expanded into leather manufacturing. He supplied poles for the Overland Telegraph, grain for the Overland Mail, and entered the banking and brokerage fields. For a time he bought and sold gold dust in large quantities. Jennings helped to organize two railroads, raised thoroughbred cattle and financed farms, wool and flour mills, mines, smelters, canals, and other enterprises. When he died in 1886 after serving as mayor of Salt Lake City, Jennings was one of Utah's wealthiest citizens, a Mormon in good standing in his church.

THOMAS KEARNS (1862-1918), a native of Canada, became one of the wealthiest of Utah's mining magnates, an owner of the *Salt Lake Tribune,* one of the new

Elizabeth Dunlop Ferguson Bonnemort *(right). Photo courtesy of Margaret Lester.*

Joseph R. Walker, merchant, banker, developer of western mines *(below).*

UTAH STATE HISTORICAL SOCIETY

state's first United States senators, and builder of an imposing mansion that now serves as the governor's residence. Coming to Utah in 1883 as a young man, Kearns worked as a miner in Park City. Studying geology and mineralogy at night, he prospected during his remaining spare time. In 1890 he and others leased the Mayflower Mine, soon struck a million-dollar lode, and in 1892 purchased the Silver King claims that paid more than ten million dollars in dividends during the next 15 years alone. David Keith, a mining foreman, became a lifelong friend and partner of Kearns during this period; they gained wealth together and died within six months of each other in 1918. Kearns was elected United States Senator by the state legislature in 1901, serving one term. The same year he and Keith purchased the *Salt Lake Tribune*. His ornate French Renaissance mansion, built in 1904 on South Temple (Brigham) Street, was given to the state by his widow in 1939 and now serves as the governor's residence. Director of banks, builder of railroads and other enterprises, Kearns was known for his public service and philanthropies.

JESSE KNIGHT (1848-1921) of Provo was reputed to be the largest tithepayer in the Mormon Church for a period of years after the turn of the century. Coming to Utah in 1850 with his widowed mother, Jesse was an ambitious worker even in youth. After his marriage in 1869, while living on a ranch near Payson he and his young sons prospected the Tintic hills and located valuable claims; one of these later became the rich Humbug mine, foundation of the town of Knightsville, which flourished during the first two decades of this century. During the same period Knight also developed other Tintic claims, including productive mines near Silver City where he built a smelter, electric plant, railroad, mill, as well as housing and facilities for Knight employees and their families. Near Helper he developed coal mines in Spring Canyon. There the stable company town of Spring Canyon prospered for 30 or 40 years, from 1912 until some time after World War II. Knight's mining towns were distinguished not only for their schools, churches, and substantial homes, but for their lack of saloons and gambling halls.

In addition to 20-odd mining companies, "Uncle Jesse" Knight developed a portion of the sugar industry in Utah and Alberta, Canada; irrigation systems in Utah Valley; electric power plants and railroads; the Provo Woolen Mill; banks; ranches; and other enterprises. He was revered for his benevolence, and his philanthropy enriched not only Brigham Young University but many other institutions and individuals as well.

Mineral wealth built many buildings in Salt Lake City.

UTAH STATE HISTORICAL SOCIETY

These early decades of statehood were years of stabilization, consolidation, and integration. Mormon-Gentile confrontations continued to abate, and ecclesiastical influence on economic, social, and political life was less apparent at the end of the period than at the beginning. The migration from rural to urban areas proceeded, as did migration from Utah to other states. And foreign control of Utah's natural resources as well as its economy continued an inexorable advance. This period also marks the halfway point in Utah's history between settlement in 1847 and publication of this revised volume.

The Spanish-American War, which broke out in 1898, demonstrated the changes in popular Utah feeling since the Civil War. The Mormons took very little part in the internecine conflict, but for the war with Spain Utah supplied three batteries of light artillery and two troops of cavalry, volunteers seeing active service in Cuba and the Philippines.

Three major echoes of the long struggle with the United States featured the next dozen years. Brigham H. Roberts, a ranking Mormon and a polygamist, was elected to Congress in 1898. His opponents made campaign issues of his church connections, and his participation in polygamy, and a petition protesting his seating, signed by upwards of a million citizens, was sent to Congress. The House voted not to admit him, necessitating a special election in 1900, when he was succeeded by William H. King, who later was elected to the Senate and until 1940 was a junior and senior senator from Utah. Democrats dominated early elections, but in 1900 the Republicans carried the general election and assumed a dominance virtually unbroken, despite several Democratic governors, until the Roosevelt upheaval of 1932, when the state became decisively Democratic. Reed Smoot, an apostle of the Mormon Church, was elected to the Senate in 1903, and another violent struggle began. Smoot fought almost four years for his seat, and won, serving until 1932 and becoming dean of the Senate.

The Smoot case reverberated locally and nationally. Locally a new anti-Mormon party was organized in 1904. The central plank of the "American Party" was unalterable opposition to Mormon ecclesiasticism in politics, and a determination to break the Mormon influence over the public schools. The American Party carried Salt Lake City in 1905 and 1907, but after a decisive Salt Lake City beating in 1911 disappeared from the political scene. Of more consequence to the church was the muckraking period in American journalism, which swung into full stride at the time of the Smoot hearings. For a number of years national magazines depicted Mormons as polygamous, treasonable, and alien, and as a monstrous oligarchy sucking at the financial life blood of the west. Much damage was done the church by this onslaught.

Despite nationwide financial crises in the 1890s and early 1900s, mining remained in good or reasonably good health. This was the period when mines of the intermountain region were creating millionaires. (Total mineral production in the state to 1915 is estimated at 750 million dollars.) The low-grade ores at Bingham Canyon came into their own during this early period of statehood; within 15 years of its incorporation in 1903, Utah Copper Company had built or acquired a great industrial complex that included many miles of railroads, a tramway, mills, more than 50 locomotives, and several dozen steam shovels. By 1917, according to one source, the open-pit mine had already produced ore valued at more than 100 million dollars, had paid dividends of 76 million dollars, and was employing more than 4,000 workers. Smelting, the state's single most important industry in 1940, made its major development after 1910. After that year, with adequate and inexpensive power available and large reserves of coal and fluxing material near at hand, large smelters were built in Salt Lake Valley and at Tooele, and the mines sold their products in Utah. The tremendous demands for non-ferrous raw metals made by the United States and foreign powers during World War I launched the mining and smelting industry on a period of development that continued to 1929, when a peak was reached that was not surpassed until World War II. For a time Salt Lake and Tooele valleys comprised the largest smelting center in the world. This expansion, as well as growth in other large industries in Utah, was financed largely by out-of-state capital. Utah by then was an economic colony.

The physical appearance of Utah's cities and towns was altered dramatically within a decade or two after the gaining of statehood. Thousands of older homes and commercial buildings, built in the first decades after settlement, were replaced by new structures. Utah's first "skyscrapers" appeared on the scene. Wealth from mines, trade, banking, and other lucrative enterprises built imposing mansions as well as bank buildings, office buildings, hotels, and other commercial structures. The State Capitol was completed in 1916, and numerous other government buildings were built. City streets—far from being fully paved by World War I—served as rights of way for horse-drawn vehicles, tracked trolleys, pedestrians, and a growing number of automobiles. For several decades they also resembled forests, with myriad wooden poles supporting a bewildering tangle of electric and telephone wires. Yet the spirit of beautification was not without influence. Many of the structures from that era are treasured today for their distinctive styling and exceptional craftsmanship.

State government was preoccupied with tax equalization, education, working conditions, revenue measures, highways, and other problems of an evolving culture, an expanding population, increasing urbanization, and growing industrialization. Hundreds of public schools as well as college and university buildings were constructed during this period. Many of these are still in use. The arrival of automobiles demanded better roads and federal sharing of costs. By 1919 the state boasted 133 miles of hard-surface roads, 836 miles of graveled roads, and 948 miles of graded roads.

Writing in *Utah's History* (Brigham Young University, 1978), Thomas Alexander devoted 40 pages to developments of this period. "After 1900 the efforts of the Republican-dominated state government to come to grips with problems caused by urbanism and industrialism increased, even as the two socioeconomic phenomena became more characteristic of the state," he wrote. "During the first two decades of the twentieth century the state population grew from 276,749 to 449,396 (sixty-nine percent), but Salt Lake City and Ogden doubled in size, and by 1920 almost half the Utah population was living in cities." Passed by the legislature were laws having to do with food purity, mine safety, regulation of professions and banking, child labor, employment of women, minimum wage and pensions, regulation of public utilities, workmens compensation, recognition of labor unions, taxation, and convict labor. Also a product of this era (1917) was prohibition of manufacture, sale, and use of alcoholic beverages, as well as provisions for initiative and referendum, corrupt political practices, water rights, and irrigation.

"The image of Utah that emerges from a study of these first years of statehood is at variance with the commonly held myths about the state's political history," wrote Alexander. "Far from trailing other states, Utah generally stood in the first third of states of the Union in the passage of social legislation regulating conditions of work in dangerous occupations. Utahns moved quickly to deal with the conservation of natural resources, especially timber and water, and to adopt pure food legislation. The state also adopted progressive laws in the area of political reform. In the one area of utility regulation, however, Utah lagged far behind other states and the myth appears to have been based in part on this factor."

Development of dry farming techniques and federal actions during this period, or slightly before, opened new sections of the state to homesteading and farming, at approximately the same time that the establishment of the national forests system (1905) closed the state's mountainous areas—or the greater part of them—to indiscriminate timbering and grazing abuse. By 1915 there were twelve national forests in Utah, embracing eight million acres. New or expanded agricultural settlements were made in the desert near Huntington in Emery County, at Widtsoe in Garfield County, in the Delta area, in Sevier Valley at Clarion, and in the central Uinta Basin, which previously had been reserved as a Ute Indian reservation. New coal mining communities began to flourish at Hiawatha and vicinity, at Sunny-

Reed Smoot, United States Senator from Utah 1903-1932.

side, and at Spring Canyon and other coal fields near Helper. Other mining settlements were revived or founded in Park Valley, at Kimberly and Gold Hill, in the Tintic area (Knightsville, Mammoth, Silver City, etc.), and elsewhere.

Agriculture prospered, for the most part. The sugar beet industry was launched in the 1890s; by 1919 Utah ranked high among all states in number of sugar factories and production of beet sugar, with factories in Lehi, Ogden, Logan, Payson, Lewiston, Garland, and Gunnison, among other places. Cattle and sheep raising remained profitable, the bases for a large meatpacking, leather and wool industry. Orchard fruits, dairy products, and alfalfa joined wheat and feed grains as valuable agricultural products. Garden crops provided the foundation for a number of new canneries. Food processing, with changed emphases, has continued to be an important industry to the present day.

Manufacturing, much of it based on agriculture and mining, employed 6,000 workers in 1899 and 26,000 in 1919, while the number of manufacturing establishments increased from 575 to 1,035 in the same period. The number of banks more than doubled, while deposits multiplied ten times during those 20 years. The state's economy in general became more complex as population expanded and agriculture, mining, trade and manufacturing changed their traditional character, encouraging the growth of satellite industries such as construction, insurance, and specialized financial services. Rapid growth in the development of public utilities also occurred during this period of the state's history, among them the electrification of urban areas, growth in telephone use, and construction of passenger railroads within and between larger cities. Commercial entertainment (theaters, dance halls, bathing resorts, amusement parks, etc.) also flourished in this age when motion pictures, radio, and television were either unknown or barely in their infancy. Commercial airplane travel was still several years in the future, and automobiles had yet to become commonplace, when World War I pulled the United States into a community of nations.

The attaining of statehood and prosperity bolstered self-confidence and animated a spirit of boosterism. Though the glories of Utah's landscape were to remain unsung for yet a time (with a few exceptions), promoters had been praising the mineral, agricultural, homesteading, and commercial possibilities in Utah—or in parts of the territory and state. After statehood was attained, in the years between 1897 and 1915, the legislature appropriated funds for official state participation in commemorative and industrial expositions at Nashville, Tennessee . . . St. Louis, Missouri . . . Portland, Oregon . . . Norfolk, Virginia . . . Seattle, Washington . . . Chicago, San Francisco, and San Diego. During this period four national monuments were established in the state: Natural Bridges, 1908 . . . Mukuntuweap, 1909 (name changed to Zion in 1918) . . . Rainbow Bridge, 1910 . . . and Dinosaur, 1915.

By 1917, when the United States entered the war against Germany, Utah had been a miniature United Nations for 70 years. The great majority of original pioneers were natives of the United States and Canada, but they were joined by thousands of Mormon converts from northern Europe—

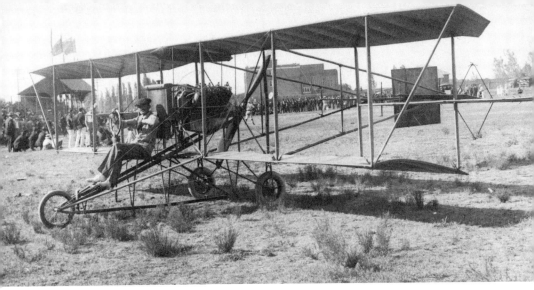

T. T. Maroney and his flying machine at Payson, 1916. *G. E. Anderson photo.*

from Great Britain and Scandinavia, Switzerland and Germany—and by non-Mormon Irish, Chinese, Mexicans and Mexican-Americans, Japanese, and immigrants from southern and western Europe. A fourth of Utah's people were foreign-born in 1890 and 1900. This proportion began declining after the turn of the century as older generations passed from the scene and new immigration slowed.

Four state governors held office during this period: Heber M. Wells (R) 1896-1905 . . . John C. Cutler (R) 1905-1909 . . . William Spry (R) 1909-1917 . . . and Simon Bamberger (D) 1917-1921. Wells, Cutler and Spry were of Mormon background; Bamberger was a member of a prominent Jewish family. Governor Cutler's career serves to illustrate the interlocking and increasingly complex business relationships of the time that influenced the economic destiny of the state. He was president of Cutler Brothers and Company, operators of Provo Woolen Mills, and a director or officer of Utah-Idaho Sugar Company, Utah Power and Light Company, Utah Hotel Company, Beneficial Life Insurance Company, Home Fire Insurance Company, Deseret Savings Bank, Monroe State Bank, Bank of Garland, Deseret National Bank, and First National Bank of Murray.

"The rapprochement of Mormon Utah and Gentile United States" was sealed by World War I, according to the 1941 edition. On April 6, 1917, Congress declared war against the Imperial German Government. Two months later occurred the first registration of all able-bodied men in the United States between the ages of 21 and 30 years. In Utah, 42,000 men were registered, and more than 11,000 were drafted for active duty. Added to these, nearly 13,000 volunteers brought to 24,000 the number of men who served in the armed forces from Utah. A regiment of artillery from Utah was trained and sent to France; as a unit, this regiment did not see action, but some of its individual members, transferred to other units, fought at the Somme. An ambulance corps and a field hospital, trained in Utah, saw action, as did the 91st Division, which included many Utah men. According to Warrum's *History of Utah Since Statehood,* "The Ninety-first division was the organization that saved the day for the allied forces at the Argonne Forest. The men of this division were all drafted men, but their action at Argonne Forest demonstrated that conscripts can be depended upon as well as volunteers to uphold the honor of their country.'' More than 700 Utah men died in service. Of these, some 220 lost their lives as a result of combat. The people of Utah subscribed to Liberty Bonds in the amount of nearly 73 million dollars, donated other funds, and spent countless hours in otherwise supporting the war effort.

The signing of the Armistice on November 11, 1918, marked the symbolic threshold of a new era in Utah as in the nation.

Bingham Canyon soldiers, World War I.

FROM WORLD WAR I TO WORLD WAR II

The 23 years between the end of World War I and America's entrance into World War II (November 1918 to December 1941) were years of economic trial for many Utahns, particularly those engaged in mining, manufacturing and agriculture. The first war had brought prosperity; its aftermath saw long-term or temporary decline in the price of mineral and farm products. This slump continued for three or four years in the mining industry, during the early 1920s, affecting nearly all minerals and causing many mines and smelters to close at least for a time. Crop prices plunged drastically in the early 1920s, not to recover fully until the 1940s. In manufacturing, an industry based largely on mining and agricultural products, firms dropped from a total of 1,035 in 1919 to 645 in 1921. The number of workers fell during the same period from more than 20,000 to 13,000. Hundreds of plants closed permanently, others only temporarily, but not until the 1940s did firms and employees in manufacturing again match the numbers that prevailed in 1919. Government revenue fell and unemployment rose before a gradual economic improvement became noticeable about 1923.

Even Utah's population stagnated during the decades between the wars. In 1920 the census recorded 449,396 inhabitants. In 1940, 20 years later, the total was only 550,310, reflecting an increase of 101,000 during those 20 years—a gain of only one per cent per year on average, or one of the lowest population increases in the state's history. Out-migration of native-born Utahns continued, as did the flow from rural to urban areas. In 1930, for the first time, rural residents comprised fewer than half of the state's population.

The decade of the 1920s was not entirely bleak, of course. An economic upswing became apparent about 1923. Despite low mineral prices for several years following the war, total value of mine production rose to 100 million dollars in 1925 and 115 million dollars in 1929, compared with only 64 million dollars in 1919. In *Utah's History,* Thomas Alexander wrote:

> Some sectors of the economy were not seriously affected by the depression [of the 1920s]. The dawning automobile age produced both business stimuli and social changes during the 1920s. . . . Aviation and radio industries also began to affect the state. . . . Electric energy consumption increased from 471 to 858 million kilowatt-hours from 1920 to 1929 (only to fall back to the 1920 level four years later). At the close of the war less than one farm in ten had electrical service; by 1930 fifty-five and a half percent, chiefly located along the Wasatch Front, were so provided. . . . In spite of the relatively high price of building materials and high interest rates, the volume of new construction was hardly affected by the postwar depression. Apparently the demand for buildings had become so acute during the wartime curtailment of nonmilitary construction that demand was now great in spite of cost. . . . Another bright spot in the economic picture was the revival—or reestablishment—of an iron industry. Columbia Steel Company developed a pig iron plant at Ironton, located between Provo and Springville.

The majority of Utahns voted for Harding, Coolidge, and Hoover, all Republicans, during the 1920s. Two governors were elected: Charles R. Mabey (R) for one term (1920-24) and George H. Dern (D) for two terms (1924-1932). Senators William H. King (D) and Reed Smoot (R) continued to represent the state in the United States Senate during the entire decade, while Republicans dominated the state legislature between 1921 and 1931. "Although basically conservative," wrote F. Ross Peterson in *Utah's History,* "Utah voters are difficult to classify and they repeatedly defy descriptions and pollsters' prognostications." Yet their ballot performance in the 1920s was understandable. Democrats had controlled the presidency and the state legislature during the deepening depression of the early 1920s. That was their misfortune, as it was the Republican misfortune to control the presidency and state legislature when the Great Depression struck a decade later. In either case, the party in control was an easily identifiable target for blame and retribution.

Several more national monuments and a national park were established during this period: Zion National Park, 1919 (formerly Zion National Monument) . . . Timpanogos Cave National Monument, 1922 . . . Hovenweep National Monument, 1923 . . . Arches National Monument, 1929. Cedar Breaks National Monument was established in 1933.

The Great Depression

"The depression bore severely upon Utah," stated the 1941 edition, continuing as follows:

Collapse of the mining industry, the backbone of Utah economy, was especially serious. During the early years of the depression, one person out of every four in the State received relief. This high percentage of unemployed fluctuated with business revivals and recessions, but remained fairly constant through the years 1933-40. Self-help efforts like the National Development Association, which preceded direct Federal welfare, accomplished little. The Church Welfare program, initiated by the Mormon Church to aid needy members . . . proved of local utility and . . . won considerable publicity but . . . accomplished nothing toward solving the larger problems of labor and relief.

Written before the Depression had ended, the 1941 edition went on to describe Utah's economic difficulties: how it was no longer possible to spread out into new lands, how irrigation costs were "out of all proportion to the returns brought by crops in open market," and how "in the intricately developed capitalistic business economy" it was not "usually possible for individuals or groups to create a business with shoestring capital." Other difficulties included high freight rates, distance from markets, small farms, "a birth rate out of all proportion to [the state's] capacity to absorb the increase," and out-migration of youths educated at high cost.

The Great Depression was described at greater length by John F. Bluth and Wayne K. Hinton in *Utah's History.* "Full recovery from the 1920-21 depression had not been achieved," they wrote, and Utah was affected more severely than most other states. Agriculture "was none too healthy" in 1930; the number of workers employed in manufacturing had declined; a disproportionate number of workers were engaged in service activities; and relative *per capita* income had declined. "These were years of human distress and unrest, of rejuvenation of the labor movement, and of startling political upsets—manifestations that Utah had indeed been Americanized and was becoming quite typical of the United States in general and urban states in particular."

By 1931 Utah's *per capita* income fell to 71.5 per cent of the national average and was only 80 per cent in 1933. "At the depth of the depression, 61,500 persons—35.8 percent of Utah's work force—were unemployed, while comparable thousands on farms and ranches faced foreclosures and market prices that did not recover production costs." In 1934 one out of five Utahns was on public relief. By 1935 a fourth of the state's population was receiving public assistance; and in that year nearly half of all state spending was devoted to welfare. During the Depression, wrote Bluth and Hinton, "About seven dollars were spent by the federal government in Utah for each dollar that was sent to Washington in taxes."

State and local efforts to ameliorate economic distress during early Depression years were not adequate. Federal assistance commenced in 1932 and by March 1933 "almost one-third of Utah's population was receiving some form of government aid." Subsequent years saw the creation of the Federal Emergency Relief Administration, State Advisory Committee on Public Welfare and Emergency Relief, National Industrial Recovery Act,

Utah Industrial Recovery Act, Civil Works Administration, National Youth Administration, Civilian Conservation Corps, Utah Emergency Relief Administration, Public Works Administration, Works Progress Administration, Utah Department of Public Welfare, a national Social Security program, a Mormon Church Security Plan, and other federal, state, local, and private assistance programs. A much higher ratio of workers in Utah were employed on WPA, CCC, NYA, and PWA projects than in most other states.

A number of federal programs launched during this period—known collectively as the New Deal—have continued to the present day in modified form. They were successful to an extent in ameliorating some of the most severe economic problems of the Great Depression. However, as stated by Bluth and Hinton, "complete recovery did not come until World War II brought the American economy back to full employment."

The 1930s introduced a much more favorable environment for labor unions, liberal social and reform legislation, the repeal of prohibition, a swing to political control by the Democratic Party, and a pronounced growth in federal spending and influence within Utah that has continued, with modifications in specific programs, through the intervening years.

S. GEORGE ELLSWORTH

Much reclamation and conservation work was performed during the Depression years.

U.S. FOREST SERVICE

WORLD WAR II TO THE PRESENT

The most recent four decades in Utah's history have been momentous indeed. Nearly a million people have been added to the state's population, many of them immigrants or natives returning from other places. New developments not even dreamed of by writers of the 1941 edition have affected seemingly every aspect of life in the Beehive State. Since 1940 the nation has been involved in three foreign wars, far surpassing in their influence on Utah and Utahns any previous conflicts. During World War II the economy began a process of growth and transformation that shows scant signs of abating, and concentration of the population into a tight urban enclave has continued its long-time advance. Most significant of all trends, perhaps, is the inexorable "Americanization" and "universalization" of Utah—the cultural and economic leveling that began soon after settlement but which has speeded its pace of common acculturation in recent decades, accelerated by such factors as television, commonplace air travel, renewed in-migration, economic interdependence, and the phenomenal internationalism of the Mormon Church. These changes and others mentioned throughout this volume have resulted in a present-day Utah that would hardly be recognized by the authors of the 1941 edition.

World War II and the 1940s

Even before the Japanese attack on Pearl Harbor in December 1941, America's national defense program was affecting Utah. The armed forces were expanding before 1941. Construction began at Hill Field and Wendover Air Force Base in 1940 and at Utah General Depot and Remington Arms Plant in 1941. Operations at Ogden Arsenal were expanded at that time. The year 1942 saw the beginning of operations or construction at Kearns Army Air Base, Dugway Proving Ground, Tooele Ordnance Depot, Deseret Chemical Depot. Bushnell General Hospital, Clearfield Naval Supply Depot, Topaz War Relocation Center, and Geneva Steel Works. Fort Douglas became headquarters for the Ninth Service Command and the site of additional important military operations. The Utah Oil refinery was expanded at government expense, and other war-related plants were built, either directly by the government or on the basis of military contracts. Among these were a brick refractory at Lehi, a radio tube plant in Salt Lake City, a parachute company in Manti, and an alunite mill in Salt Lake City. Between 1942 and the end of the war in 1945, hundreds of millions of dollars were spent by the federal government in land acquisition, construction, maintenance, staffing, and operations of these defense-related installations in Utah.

For five years these federal defense activities impacted directly and profoundly on Utah, and in fact their repercussions have never ceased. Not only was the declining rate of growth in population reversed, but all measures of economic health were improved. Agriculture flourished, as did trade, manufacturing, construction, mining, banking, etc. Total personal income in Utah rose from less than 300 million dollars in 1940 to more than 700 million dollars in 1943. *Per capita* income surpassed the national average for the first and almost the only time in 1943.

While the roles and ownership of a number of war-related bases, plants, and installations changed after the war, most were to become permanent components of the state's economy. Hill Field became Hill Air Force Base, Utah's largest employer. Tooele Ordnance Depot became Tooele Army Depot with an expanded role. Ogden Arsenal was absorbed by Hill Air Force Base and Deseret Chemical Depot by Tooele Army Depot. Utah General Depot and Dugway Proving Ground continue to function as viable military installations, as does Fort Douglas in a greatly reduced capacity. Remington Arms Plant and Clearfield Naval Supply Depot were converted to commercial use. Geneva Works was purchased by United States Steel Corporation. Bushnell General Hospital became the Intermountain Indian School, and the land, utilities, and some of the buildings of Kearns Air Base provided the foundation for the community of Kearns. Only Wendover Air Force Base and Topaz War Relocation Center exist more as memories than physical entities. Also, many of the houses built during those years of population growth are still in use.

Many of the workers and military personnel who came to Utah during World War II remained in or returned to the state after the war, contributing to the net gain of 138,000 people during the 1940s. This was an increase of 25 per cent for the decade—to that time the largest numerical increase in the state's history and the largest percentage increase in 40 years. The majority of these new residents located in the urban Wasatch Front and in Tooele County, where the preponderance of defense installations and new industries were situated, continuing an urbanization trend that had been evident for some time.

Geneva Steel Works in Orem was built by the federal government during World War II. *Photo courtesy S. George Ellsworth.*

Since 1950

Since 1950 the population has doubled, from 688,862 in 1950 to 1,461,037 in 1980. Much of this growth in people has resulted from or been the cause of growth and other changes in the economy, housing, educational system, cultural attributes, government, etc.—all of which are discussed elsewhere in this volume. A detailed discussion of the history of these three decades is beyond the scope of this book, if for no other reason than that so much of its content reflects developments of recent times. However, a summary of important trends will be useful to the reader. . . .

If any single influence of recent times may be said to have determined the course of Utah's destiny beyond that of any other, that influence surely has been Government. Not only did Government employ the largest number of workers until recently (it was surpassed in 1977 by Trade), but its operations affect every other industry group either directly or indirectly. The tremendous expansion of governmental activities in the years since the Great Depression has profoundly affected Utah in many ways.

Defense installations of the federal government have employed several tens of thousands of Utahns continually since World War II, largely supporting the economies of Weber, Davis and Tooele counties, and being significant influences on the urbanization of the state. Indirectly, federal government has provided the financial base for the missile-rocket manufacturing operations of Thiokol and Hercules, and for a good part of the state's electronics industry. The missile and electronics industries came to Utah in the 1950s and continue to the present day, their operations and work forces fluctuating with changes in military, space, and commercial market needs.

Federal and state governments also have supported the economy and influenced life in Utah with massive building projects, such as the interstate highway system, reclamation projects, school buildings, and diverse other public works. Interstate highway construction costing hundreds of millions of dollars has been underway for 20 years or more and will not be completed for many more. Reclamation projects of recent decades, costing well over a billion dollars, include the Glen Canyon and Flaming Gorge, Weber River, and Central Utah projects. Hundreds of public schools have been built since World War II, as well as scores of new buildings on campuses of the state's colleges and universities. Also, government at all levels has required the addition of numerous new office buildings since the 1940s.

Tourism and recreation have been systematically encouraged and stimulated by government since World War II. On a state level, Utah's recreational advantages have been advertised since 1941 by a state agency now known (after several name changes) as the Utah Travel Council. Through the efforts of this agency, complemented by those of local chambers of commerce, regional travel councils, and convention bureaus—in combination spending millions of dollars every year for advertising and promotion —travel/recreation/conventions have become one of Utah's foremost industries. The federal government has been involved in Utah recreation since the first national parks, monuments and forests were established in the early 1900s, not only spending large sums on recreational facilities in those areas but also on facilities connected with water projects. A number of new national parks and national recreation areas have been created and considerable upgrading of facilities accomplished since World War II, primarily in the 1960s and early 1970s. Several wildlife refuges also are supported by the federal government. The state, through its Division of Parks and Recreation, has established and developed scores of state park areas since the late 1950s, while the State Division of Wildlife Resources contributes to recreation through management of game species and wildlife habitats.

Also instrumental in building Utah's economy is the state's Division of Industrial Promotion, which has functioned since the mid-1960s in providing information and guidance to business firms that might be considering a move to Utah or expansion within the state. Both federal and state governments have initiated programs of assistance to the arts, Utah's program dating from 1899 (first in the nation) and the national government's from more recent times. These have had incalculable influence on the quality of life of Utah's people, as described in The Arts section. Not to be neglected, in conclusion, is mention of the enormous governmental expenditures in the medical-health field. Together, federal and state governments now spend great sums in support of hospitals, nursing facilities, doctors, and insurance programs, the result being an unprecedented expansion in these categories. This growth is largely a product of the 1960s and 1970s.

Government activities, of course, have not been solely responsible for the state's development since World War II, although they have provided, directly or indirectly, the financial foundation for much of the growth in manufacturing, construction, transportation, trade, finance, and services that has transpired since 1940. Without the catalytic stimulation of government expenditures it is conjectural what the condition of the state would be at this time. For example, even the uranium booms of the 1950s and 1970s would not have been possible without the injection of large doses of federal money in the form of price support, road construction, etc. Utah's mining and manufacturing industries would have been much the poorer if the federal government had not built Geneva Steel Works during World War II,

Waste disposal is only one among many serious environmental problems facing government as Utah's population grows.

U.S. BUREAU OF RECLAMATION

Recreation takes many forms. In recent years
it has become Big Business.

an enterprise that utilized Utah iron for 30 years and Utah coal for an even longer period.

Privately-financed mining has continued its invaluable contribution to the state's economy through the intervening years, changing emphasis from time to time. Kennecott spent hundreds of millions of dollars in new plants and equipment during the 1960s and 1970s. The ascent of petroleum and natural gas began in earnest with the discovery of the Greater Aneth Field in 1956, and though production in that field gradually lessened, new discoveries in the Uinta Basin, Overthrust zone, and elsewhere have kept total production high. Coal mining has been undergoing a revival in recent years that surpasses anything seen in the past, while massive infusions of capital during the 1960s and 1970s have succeeded in reaping the mineral rewards of Great Salt Lake.

As population, industry, and travel have grown, so have air facilities, the business community, communications, services, and housing. The growth of the travel/recreation/convention segment has resulted in the appearance of convention-sports centers and many new hotels and motels throughout the state, in addition to affiliated services and major resort developments at Park City, Snowbird, etc. For the most part these are products of the 1960s and 1970s. The business community has expanded not only in dollar volume but physically as well, sprawling horizontally in new business-industrial parks and malls, and vertically in numerous high-rise buildings. This dramatic physical expansion has occurred most notably in the past two decades.

Hardly of minor significance is the growth of the Mormon Church. While the church's numbers have not increased proportionately within the state as greatly as without, its worldwide expansion in recent years has resulted in an explosion of operations activity and new construction in Utah. These are described in the Religion section.

At this writing, as noted elsewhere, Utah stands at a crossroads of sorts. The serious economic recession that besets not only the United States but other countries of the world, while its effects have not yet been felt in Utah to the same extent as in many other places, does pose an ominous threat. Increased expenditures for national defense promise a viable future for Utah's military installations, thus providing a stable economic base of sorts, but the private sector is subject to the same adverse influences (inflation, high interest rates, unemployment, business stagnation, etc.) that face private enterprise throughout the nation. Two of the largest employers, Geneva Works and Kennecott, have recently effected massive layoffs of workers, while Utah Power and Light Company has announced cancellation of plans to build a fourth generating unit in Emery County. Even the future of the oil shale industry in the Uinta Basin, so bright a year ago, has become clouded once more with reductions in the federal budget. All these are causes for concern.

It is not possible to anticipate tomorrow. That limitation is amply illustrated by the pessimistic analysis of Utah's future that appeared in the final paragraphs of the History chapter in the 1941 edition, written just prior to America's involvement in World War II.

WHEELER MACHINERY CO.

Numerous industrial parks and expansive commercial buildings are being added rapidly to the urban landscape *(above)*.

SNOWBIRD RESORT

Snowbird resort, representing commercial recreation, is a development of the 1970s.

Economic Scene

Downtown Salt Lake City, financial heart of Utah and the Intermountain West.

To an observer, looking casually at the visible economic scene, today's Utah would not differ too obviously from other parts of the United States. This is the case particularly in the state's urban areas. There is the ordinary bustle of traffic and commercial activity. New construction projects are apparent in all directions, and the sounds of machines—of cars and trucks, planes and trains, industrial and construction equipment—are heard throughout the land. Urban Utah has joined the metropolitan mainstream of the nation, and economic differences are more apparent statistically than visually. There are, and always have been, differences—but these change from time to time, in relative importance and significance.

Utah's economy of today bears slight resemblance to that of a hundred years ago. For that matter, the state's economy differs dramatically from the "Industry and Commerce" described in the book's first edition of 1941, when Utah was barely recovering from effects of the Depression. At that time agriculture, mining and manufacturing based on natural resources were of relatively greater importance than now. Tourism and the recreation industry were in their infancy. In 1941 there was barely a hint of the tremendous economic impacts from military and civil programs of the federal government, beginning with World War II, which were to transform the state's economic base *(see Government, this chapter)*. Transportation and communication have changed in profound ways. The population has more than doubled, bringing attendant growth in trade, construction, services, and the financial segment. And during those intervening decades the economic roles of federal, state and local governments expanded to an unprecedented level, not only in Utah but in the nation as a whole.

Utilizing the standard industrial classification of recent years, Utah's diverse economic activities at the present time may be categorized into the following major industry groups, which apply not only to Utah but to other states as well and make statistical comparisons possible:

Agriculture
Manufacturing
Mining
Contract construction
Transportation, Communication, Public Utilities
Trade, Wholesale and Retail
Finance, Insurance, Real Estate
Services
Government: Federal, State, Local

These industries may be compared statistically on various bases: that is, according to number of employees and percentage of total work force, total wages and salaries paid, average of individual wages paid, sales volume, value added by manufacture, profits, etc. They may be compared also on the basis of "absolute" importance, but this is an exercise in cultural and personal values.

Perhaps the most meaningful comparison for these pages is the number of employees in each industry. Non-agricultural employment increased from about 130,000 workers in 1940 (24 per cent of the population) to nearly 600,000 in 1980 (about 40 per cent of the population). These workers were employed in various industries as follows:

Non-Agricultural Employment - 1980

(Ranked from high to low)

Government (including public schools and colleges)
	Federal	38,000	
	State	34,000	
	Local	56,000	128,000

Services (including religions)	105,000
Retail Trade	100,000
Manufacturing	93,000
Wholesale Trade	36,000
Transportation, Communication, Utilities	36,000
Contract Construction	35,000
Finance, Insurance, Real Estate	27,000
Mining	18,000

With respect to employment, Utah resembles the national average in some ways but is dissimilar in others. For example, manufacturing in the nation as a whole employs more than a fourth of the non-agricultural labor force; in Utah manufacturing employs only a sixth of the labor force. Government employs a higher proportion of workers in Utah (about 23 per cent) than in the nation as a whole (less than 20 per cent). Mining has much more impact in Utah, in terms of employment, than in the nation. Insofar as the remaining industries are concerned, Utah resembles the national average very closely; in fact the similarity is remarkable, indicating that Utah's economic patterns no longer are as peculiarly its own as formerly. Utah appears to have been swept into the consuming Americanization flood-tide, economically as well as otherwise; and while it may not have lost its special identity completely, there is ample reason to assume that this great assimilation process is an ongoing one.

Basically, Utah's economy has been determined or influenced by factors such as the following:

a. **Physical Geography,** including climate, remoteness from markets and sources of supply, land characteristics, land ownership, natural resources, etc. For example, climate affects all aspects of life including the economic. With particular respect to the economy, it severely limits the amount of available water. A physical location far from markets and supply sources has necessitated long-distance transport (involving added time and expense). Topography and land ownership, as well as the scarcity of water, influence land use and the siting of communities, industries and buildings. And natural resources have determined to an extent the state's primary industries and quality of life—moreso in the past, no doubt, than more recently.

b. **People and Cultural Factors,** including birthrate, concentration of population, migration, education and training, income levels, unionization vs. right-to-work laws, and even personal aspirations *(see Attitudes below).* A few examples will suffice:

Utah's birthrate, which tends to be among the highest of any state, results in comparatively large families and a large proportion of young people in the total population. Among the economic results of these factors are a low *per capita* income that ranks Utah among the lowest states in this category; comparatively high educational costs; and an unemployment-underemployment problem with regard to younger workers. The level of *per capita* income also is related to the number of working mothers.

The concentration of Utah's population—the crowding of 80 per cent of the people into four Wasatch Front counties—has profound economic implications. Many of these are obvious. It is apparent that these counties are the centers of industry and commerce, offer the most desirable jobs, and display the most costly homes and other outward signs of relative affluence.

C. **TRENDS AND EXTERNAL INFLUENCES.** Utah resembles other places in being subject to external influences. Evidence points to its economic sensitivity in this respect. Only during the first two decades of settlement were Utahns relatively self-sufficient, and even then they were not completely so. With the development of a national and international economy based on complex interdependency, all parts of the nation and the world have become hostage to external influences of diverse sorts. Depression, recession, financial "panics," metal prices and demands, wars, freight rates—all have widespread repercussions, wherever they occur. Certainly this has been the case with Utah.

Mining is a prime illustration. Had it not been for out-of-state capital and out-of-state markets, it is likely that few Utah minerals would have been mined in quantity. Utah construction firms which operate in many states and countries are another. Utah financial institutions serve the entire intermountain region, as do many of its retail and wholesale establishments. Utah warehouses are important regional transshipment centers, and the Salt Lake City International Airport services passengers and freight bound to and from all parts of the world. Were it not for federal military and defense programs, Utah's economy would be much poorer. Federal resource, highway, and social programs are vital to the state's economic wellbeing. And millions of tourists from other places make Utah's travel industry a major element of the overall economy.

Most of Utah's largest manufacturers depend on out-of-state and international markets for a significant part of their sales. Many of these, in fact, are divisions of multi-unit national or international firms. During the past century or more the general Utah economy has been dependent on external capital to a marked extent, including ownership and/or control of its largest enterprises by national or overseas corporations. Examples are legion, beginning with pioneer merchants and freighters . . . Union Pacific and Central Pacific Railroads . . . English financial involvement (however minor) in early Utah mining and cattle ranching . . . and out-of-state capitalization of the largest mining operations from earliest times to the present. It is hardly an exaggeration to observe that, with few notable exceptions, any Utah business enterprise or economic operation of large size—particularly those having national or international ramifications—either were established in Utah as branch operations of national firms or the federal government, or if founded as Utah firms that prospered to an exceptional degree, were eventually absorbed by out-of-state economic interests.

In the mining industry, for example, so much capital is required for exploration, development, mining, processing and marketing of minerals having potential markets outside of Utah (copper, petroleum, coal, iron, silver, uranium, potash, salts, cement, etc.) that only corporations having access to capital on a massive scale can afford to become involved. This has been the case traditionally, from earliest years. As Utah has become more industrialized in recent decades, the major manufacturing operations tend to be branches of national firms. Dozens of examples could be cited, including United States Steel Corporation. Many flourishing Utah-born enterprises have been acquired by out-of-state entities, among them Christensen Diamond Products, Ireco Chemicals, Ajax Presses, and Eimco. The same situation prevails to a notable extent in trade, and less so in finance, construction, services and agriculture. Utah's large-volume food outlets nearly all are members of national or regional chains. A number of financial institutions are controlled by out-of-state interests. Many of the better hotels and motels are chain or franchise operations. Even agriculture (and Utah has not been ideally suited for mass agribusiness) is being affected: for example, the purchase of Deseret Livestock Company, the state's largest such operation, by Hong Kong interests.

It goes almost without saying that firms involved in transportation, communications, and public utilities within the state—with relatively few exceptions—are owned or economically controlled by out-of-state financial interests. Finally, note should be made of one of Utah's foremost industries in terms of employment and total economic impact, namely the federal government, whose final economic decisions are made outside the state.

Having economic undertones are the attitudes of Utahns toward work, and the kinds of work they prefer . . . what they desire and support in the way of education and training . . . their attitudes toward unionization . . . the standard of living and wages they are willing to accept . . . their attitudes toward in-migration, cultural and racial minorities. The list could be extended. Also of importance are attitudes of non-Utahns toward Utah. Does Utah have a favorable image in the minds of industrialists considering the location of a new plant, and in the minds of their employees who might have to move to Utah? There is evidence of a poor Utah image in respects, though this may be improving. Does Utah have a positive image in the minds of prospective tourists or conventioneers? Perhaps no simple answer is appropriate here, but certainly Utah is not regarded as a destination state by the vast majority of travelers, who pass through after only a brief stay.

Private and government programs having the goal of influencing attitudes cost millions of dollars every year. These can be summed up as advertising and promotion. With regard to attracting new industries to Utah and increasing the number of visitors, there is little question that these programs are effective to a degree. But the exact extent of their influence is debatable, because of broad economic and cultural trends that operate independently of local efforts and cannot be directly related to those efforts.

PERSONAL INCOME

In the consideration of personal income in Utah, one comparison has remained strikingly consistent year after year, decade after decade. That is: Utah's *per capita* personal income remains far below the national average, and near the bottom among its sister mountain states. Even more surprising, perhaps, is the fact that the ratio of discrepancy has changed but little since 1940. At that time Utah's *per capita* income was 18 per cent below the national average; 40 years later the comparable percentage is only slightly lower.

Reasons for Utah's unflattering standing in this respect are several. Most often cited as a contributory factor is the large size of Utah's average family—somewhat larger than the national average, resulting in a statistical and actual lessening of *per capita* income. Comparing much more favorably with the national average are the state's family and household incomes.

A second reason for Utah's poor standing in *per capita* income is the relative dearth of high-paying industries such as manufacturing. Other cited causes are a low level of unionization; the youth and/or inexperience of many workers; and Utah's long-standing image as a "cheap labor" state.

Not only does Utah compare unfavorably with other states in *per capita* income. The same discrepancy occurs within the state, between regions, as a concomitant of the extreme concentration of population, industry and the financial community in general. It is not surprising that, with few exceptions, the highest incomes are found in the area of the Wasatch Front, where most of the state's people live and where the most remunerative economic opportunities are found. Notable exceptions to this are the sparsely populated mining counties of Carbon, Emery and Grand, where high mining and construction wages raise the *per capita* averages.

About 80 per cent of personal income in Utah comes in the form of wages and salaries, with most of the remainder as proprietors' income, property income and transfer payments. Non-agricultural industry is responsible for more than 90 per cent of all personal income. It is revealing to compare industry groups according to their income contribution. The following list ranks these groups in the approximate order of personal income they contributed in a recent year to the state's economy *(ranked in order from the highest contribution to lowest):* (1) Trade, (2) Manufacturing, (3) Services, (4) State and Local Government, (5) Federal Government, (6) Transportation-Communication-Public Utilities, (7) Construction, (8) Mining, and (9) Finance-Insurance-Real Estate.

Utah's Economy in Historical Perspective
(excerpted from the 1941 edition)

Gristmills and sawmills were Utah's first industrial "plants." They appeared rapidly, though not without a certain deliberate orderliness, following arrival of the Mormons in 1847, and tanneries, carding, spinning, and weaving mills followed close behind. . . .

Captain Howard Stansbury found in 1850 that the Mormons had a woolen factory, a pottery, and plans for a beet sugar factory, and adds that it was their policy "to provide for their own wants by their own skill . . . and to dispense, as much as possible, with the products of the labour of others." How well they succeeded is attested by a list of prizes granted by the Deseret Agricultural Society in 1860 for home-produced plows, cultivators, drills, rakes, shovels, washing machines, spinning wheels, reapers, threshers, corn shellers, steam engines, lathes, well pumps, shoes, saddles, harnesses, wool and cotton fabrics of all kinds, furniture, rifles (made from crowbars), revolving pistols, knives, wrought nails, glassware, wine, soap, landscapes and bird's-eye views of Salt Lake City, transparent blinds, and sculpture. . . . Such a list of local production for a colony just thirteen years removed from its beginnings in a desert wilderness is impressive. The products had a certain rugged crudity, for they were designed to fill an immediate and functional need rather than a polished and decorative niche. Flour from the early gristmills, for example, had about the texture of corn meal, but was not wanting in nutrition value. Leather made in Salt Lake Valley, one traveler noted, compared favorably with the product of English tanneries; it came to be known as "valley tan" in distinction to imported stocks, and the expression was for a time applied to all home products. The label fell into disrepute after its application to "home grown" whisky, which Mark Twain said was "made of imported fire and brimstone." . . .

The presence of Johnston's Army at Camp Floyd during the years 1858 and 1859, and troops quartered at Fort Douglas after [1862], gave Utah settlers their first substantial market. Products were sold high and bought low from the government, and for a time things "prospered exceedingly." Completion of the transcontinental railway in 1869 was hailed as a kind of final bulwark to prosperity. . . . The railroad was, however, not an unmixed commercial blessing. It gave Utah an outlet for low-grade ores, for beef, and for wool, but destroyed many small industrial enterprises; eastern manufacturers could put their goods on Utah markets more cheaply than they could be produced at home. The ideal of self-sufficient isolation, which the Saints very nearly achieved, slid away along the shining rails. Imports increased 800 per cent, and so did exports. In 1870 Utah was buying farm machinery, dry goods, clothing, groceries, lumber and other building materials, and leather goods; it was selling gold, silver, lead, copper, beef, wool, hides, pelts, furs, and tallow. The business of tanning, because it had to import extracts of tanbark, was replaced by the shipment of hides; the silk, linen, and cotton industries were driven into bankruptcy before they had well started; Utah timber, in many cases too remote to be profitably cut, was replaced with outside stock; iron foundries, for which high hopes had been entertained, met lethal competition in eastern machine factories.

Between 1870 and 1890, Utah industry marked time. Industrial beginnings were made in the period, but Utahns had not the necessary capital to develop them, and Mormon-Federal antagonism in polygamy and other matters made eastern capital wary. . . . Twentieth-century industrial Utah began taking definite shape about 1880 . . . after publication of the Woodruff Manifesto in 1890 and the subsequent return of escheated Church property, the Mormons, who then comprised some 80 per cent of the total population, settled themselves to develop what they had.

Canning, a logical process for a region blessed with prolific truck-garden soil and distant markets, began in 1886, when a man and his wife hand-soldered and -packed tomatoes and fruits in a home plant at Ogden. New companies added peas, beans, beets, pickles, sauerkraut, fruits, catsup, and milk to the list of canned foods, and by 1932 about 20,000 acres were devoted to canning crops. By 1937 the industry was the State's fourth most important, with an annual pack worth seven million dollars. Beet sugar manufacture, first attempted in 1853 on Temple Block, Great Salt Lake City, and the subject of much subsequent experiment, was not commercially successful until [1891], when a plant was operated at Lehi. The industry had sixteen major factories in 1940, with a combined annual production of about ten million dollars worth of sugar. . . .

Flour milling assumed commercial significance about 1890, when the practice of grading wheat was introduced. In the following decade the development of dry-farm wheat provided Utah millers with raw material to make flour for export. Utah in 1940 had sixty-five flour mills in operation, with a combined output of about $12,000,000 worth of flour and $3,000,000 worth of livestock feeds. . . .

The textile industry has perhaps undergone more vicissitudes than any other single field of Utah manufacture. The urgent pioneer need for clothing led to an expansion of textile manufacture that could not, as a profit and loss business, survive. Silk, cotton, and flax processing were almost completely abandoned by Utah mills after 1880. The climate was not well suited to growth of raw materials, and the textile industry in New England could put finished goods on the Utah market more cheaply than Utah plants. Wool, however, offered possibilities and after 1890 was Utah's major textile. The Provo Woolen Mills, founded in 1858, was for many years the largest maker of woolen fabrics west of the Mississippi. The industry suffered heavily in the early depression years after 1929, and many of the mills, including the Provo company, closed and did not reopen. After 1935, a few new mills and several old ones opened or expanded, and by 1937 there were thirty-four in the State. . . .

Cheap and fast motor-truck transportation opened Pacific Coast markets to Utah dairymen and poultrymen during the 1920s. About 1924 they began the practice of co-operative marketing, and since that date have steadily pushed to the front of the State's agricultural industries. . . .

Smelting, Utah's single most important industry [in 1940], made its major development since 1910. Between 1870 and 1900, the richest mines operated their own stamp mills and shipped concentrated ores out of the State for reduction. After 1910, with adequate and inexpensive power available, and large reserves of coal and fluxing material near at hand, smelters were built in Salt Lake Valley and at Tooele, and the mines sold their products in Utah. The tremendous demands for non-ferrous raw metals made by the United States and foreign powers during the World War of 1914-18 launched the industry on a period of development which culminated in the peak year of 1929, when Utah's mineral production was valued at $112,989,000. In the depression years that succeeded 1929, smelting was hit harder than any of Utah's industries.

Agriculture

Symbolically, the first act of the Mormon pioneers, when they entered the valley of Great Salt Lake in 1847, was to plow the soil. This was described by Thomas Bullock as a "fertile, pliable loam with fine gravel." While plowing and planting were proceeding, some of the men built a dam across City Creek, "so as to irrigate our plowed land." Occasionally a plow was broken, but others continued until sizable plots were overturned and planted before the water was diverted from City Creek to irrigate rather than soften the land. Thus began the process that was to transform the fertile oases in the Great Basin into productive farming communities.

The system of Mormon settlement, in agricultural villages and communities, brought farmers in from their acres each evening, where they could "swap" experiences and theories with their neighbors. This system has not materially changed; Utah farmers still are preeminently community dwellers, with social, economic and religious life centered around communities.

During the first decades of settlement, agriculture was Utah's major industry, since most communities survived largely on what they produced. There was comparatively little trade with the outside world because of isolation, and mining did not come into its own before the 1870s. Utah's

A rural scene in 1898: the Christian Otteson children, Huntington, Emery County.

people, for the most part, were farmers and stockraisers. From plants and animals they obtained their food and meager cash incomes—in short, the major part of their livelihood.

Most of the irrigable land was under cultivation at the close of the last century, and the farms, never large, were subdivided among large families which faced the problem of making a small farm of 20 acres or less support a family. The trend since the 1940s has been away from numerous small farms toward fewer farms of much larger size.

Gradually, with regional and national interdependence, better transportation, urbanization, and a more sophisticated economy, agriculture's comparative importance in Utah has lessened. Today it ranks in economic value behind such industries as manufacturing, tourism, trade, mining and government. In today's world there is a complicated network of food interchange between countries and areas. Few if any places are self-sufficient. Yet agriculture remains an economic factor of vital importance in Utah. Its influence extends far beyond mere number of employees or value of farm marketings.

There remain some 13,000 farms in Utah. These amount to only half the number existing when the first edition of this book was published in 1941; nevertheless, total farm acreage has increased considerably since then. About a fifth of the state's total land area now is devoted to some form of agriculture—three times as much as in 1900. The average farm has increased steadily in size since early days of settlement, from 30 acres in 1870 to 900 acres or more at present, while the total number of farms has decreased from a high of 31,000 in 1935 to about 13,000 today.

These farms produce an annual income of more than $400 million, an impressive figure for a state of limited population and comparatively little farmland. Utah's farm acreage is less than half that of New Mexico, less than a third of Arizona's or Colorado's. In average size its farms are the intermountain region's smallest. Yet they are intensively cultivated and irrigated, and thus are very productive. About a tenth of the state's agricultural land produces harvest crops, and nearly all of this is irrigated land. By far the largest part of remaining farmland is unimproved range, used primarily for livestock grazing.

Utah's principal agricultural products—listed in rough order of market value—are cattle and sheep, milk, turkeys, hay, barley and wheat. The most productive counties are Box Elder, Utah, Cache, Weber, Sanpete, Millard, and Salt Lake. Until recent years, when unfavorable market conditions forced their abandonment, sugarbeets were a major crop—one example of how shifting trends influence agriculture in Utah as elsewhere. The relative importance of farm products changes with time.

The high value ranking of livestock is related directly to Utah's topography and climate, the scarcity of irrigation water and rainfall. Cattle and sheep have been major agricultural products since pioneer days. Millions of acres of foothills, mountain slopes and valleys serve as grazing range, their native forage plants dependent on the weather, while irrigated fields produce animal food for winter months. Accounting for more than half of the market value of all agricultural products are cattle, sheep, hogs, and their products. Some of Utah's most important crops are related to the livestock industry, including alfalfa hay, barley, oats, and feed corn. Poultry in general and turkeys in particular are significant farm products. Turkey farming has become "big business" in parts of the state, primarily in Sanpete and Sevier counties, where several million turkeys are raised and processed each year.

Important crops other than those related to livestock include wheat, potatoes, soybeans, alfalfa seed, sugarbeet seed, vegetables, and berries. Orchards produce commercial quantities of apples, cherries, apricots, pears, peaches and plums. Said the 1941 edition:

> Dry farming, commonly practiced throughout the arid West, began in Utah in 1863. "A group of Utah farmers," says *Bulletin 282* of the Utah Agricultural Experiment Station, "found their farm lands, which had for years been irrigated with water from Malad Creek near Bear River City, so impregnated with alkali that growth of crops was impossible. In desperation they plowed and seeded the dry land above the canal. The ripened dry-farm grain which they harvested in the fall . . . was almost as much a gift of heaven to these transplanted, old-world Mormon converts as manna to the children of Israel." For years after this successful if somewhat desperate experiment, many doubted that crops could be grown without irrigation. David Broadhead, who owned a farm near Nephi, testified in court in the middle 1880's that "of course wheat can be raised without irrigation," and was indicted for perjury. Broadhead went back to his farm, hung up a sign, "PERJURY FARM," and for many years was one of the biggest growers of dry-land wheat in the State.

Cattle, both range and milk cows, total nearly a million head with a capital value of several hundred million dollars. The U.S. Forest Service and Bureau of Land Management grant permits for the grazing of many of

Cattle, sheep, and livestock feed crops are the most important components of the state's agriculture industry.

BUREAU OF RECLAMATION (STAN RASMUSSEN)   FARM SECURITY ADMINISTRATION (JOHN VACHON)

these animals on public lands. Cattle are admitted to the forests (the higher areas) in May or June. Locally this is called "putting the cows on the mountain," where they graze until the latter part of October. Then they are "brought off the mountain" and yard-fed, or they are grazed on cut-over grain and alfalfa fields or on public lands at lower elevations. Dairy cows are kept mainly in feed lots, and primarily in northern counties.

Horses on farms have long been on the wane, having been replaced as work animals by machinery. The tendency is to have better breeds of horses for show and as riding animals. Some fine draft animals are shown at state and county fairs, and many people keep blooded horses for riding and breeding.

About half a million sheep graze over much of the land that will not support cattle. These amount to only a fourth of the sheep in Utah in 1940; in contrast, cattle are increasing. Sheep growers have faced serious problems in Utah, including reduced grazing allotments on public lands, losses from predators, adverse market conditions, competition, etc.

Irrigation. The historical background of irrigation and water rights was treated extensively in the 1941 edition *(see pages 105-111 of that volume).* It is sufficient to comment here that irrigation (the artificial provision of water to crops) is vital to the successful growing of many food crops as well as fruit orchards in Utah. Certain crops—among them wheat, beans, barley, oats, seed alfalfa, corn, rye, and potatoes—can be and have been grown without irrigation water. However, relatively few locations in the state are suited for this type of farming, and even where harvests are possible with rainfall as the sole source of water, they are more bountiful where supplemental irrigation water is provided.

Irrigated row crops, a common sight in rural areas, are becoming less common in urban valleys.

BUREAU OF RECLAMATION (MEL DAVIS)

A migrant worker picks apples in Utah Valley *(left)*.

Spray irrigation has had a revolutionary impact on agriculture in the state *(below)*.

Since this photograph was taken in 1940, grain harvesting has been transformed by new types of machinery *(bottom)*.

BUREAU OF RECLAMATION *(MEL DAVIS)*

SALT LAKE VALLEY CONVENTION BUREAU

FARM SECURITY ADMINISTRATION (RUSSELL LEE)

The old and new are contrasted in these pictures: Copper mining at Bingham in 1907 *(above, left)* and in the 1970s *(above, right)*. Coal mining operations at Winter Quarters about 1886 *(below, left)* and at Castlegate in the 1960s *(below, right)*. Precious metals mining is illustrated *(bottom)* by a view taken at the Deer Trail Mine near Marysvale in 1917.

Mining

(see also *Mineral Resources*)

World's Record Shaft Crew of Walter Fitch, Jr. Company.
Shaft and Tunnel Contractors 427.5 feet in 31 Days in the
Water Lily Shaft of the Chief Consolidated Mining Company
Tintic District, Eureka, Utah. July 15 to August 15·1921

Said the 1941 edition, "Utah ranked 15th in the production of metals in the United States and fourth among the western states. Behind that bald statement lies nearly eighty years of adventure, romance, tragedy, bitterness, poverty, sudden wealth, and equally sudden failure." The history of mining in Utah—now lengthened to 120 years or more—is replete with myriad tales reflecting the poignancy of such human experiences. Some of those tales are recounted in this volume. More appeared in the 1941 edition but have not been reprinted here. Countless others, of course, are scattered through the pages of history books, biographies, and unpublished manuscripts.

Directly or indirectly, mining has been a crucial element in Utah's economy from the earliest years of settlement. Coal, iron and lead were mined soon after the Mormon pioneers first arrived. Gold was brought from California by members of the Mormon Battalion, and Gold Rush Argonauts traded much-needed equipment and supplies to the early Utah settlers. Beginning with the late 1860s, metal and coal mining brought thousands of non-Mormons to Utah, resulting in the founding of numerous new communities and creating an industry that has continued to rank among the state's vital economic pillars.

Utah's geological heritage has provided the state with a truly remarkable bonanza of minerals. It is said that almost all useful minerals can be found within the state—perhaps 200 of them. But this is a mixed blessing at best, for Utah's minerals often are difficult to mine and/or to process . . . may be present only in uneconomic quantities . . . may require excessive capital to develop . . . are too far from potential markets for consideration . . . or otherwise are not competitive. Hundreds of millions of dollars have been spent in exploring for Utah minerals and developing technologies for their mining, processing and refining. Many of these millions have failed to return a profit. Most frustrating of all, perhaps, is the mining industry's extreme sensitivity to influences of benumbing variety: to market prices and fluctuating demands, to quantity and quality of ore reserves, to competition from other sources and other materials, to transportation costs, labor costs, production costs, technological changes, financial trends, government regulations, environmental controls, and so on. All these factors and more plague the mining industry and make it a less than dependable economic factor, at least on a local basis. (It must be admitted that the same factors, or most of them, afflict other industries to greater or lesser degree.)

Nevertheless, on an average, mining consistently has contributed many millions of dollars annually to Utah's economy for more than a hundred years. Since the book's first edition of 1941 it has provided employment for an average of about 13,000 miners every year, ranging from a low of 10,000 to 16,000 or more in recent years. The value of minerals produced since 1870 totals some 20 billion dollars, a major part of which has filtered through the state's economy in the form of wages, purchases, construction, taxes and other in-state costs of production.

Yet, though total mineral production keeps rising year after year in value (first surpassing a billion dollars annually in 1976), Utah's relative share of the national total is somewhat less today than it was in 1940.

In terms both of employment and value of minerals produced, copper has added most to Utah's economy over an extended period. Since 1950, for example, value of Utah's copper production has exceeded six billion dollars, nearly all of this from Kennecott's Utah Copper Division operations. Most of Utah's gold production is a by-product of Kennecott copper mining, having a total value since 1950 of about 600 million dollars.

Petroleum (crude oil) ranks next to copper in long-range production value, totaling more than three billion dollars since 1950. Coal production totaled about two billion dollars in value for that period; iron and uranium about 500 million dollars each; and silver about 300 million dollars. These have been Utah's top-ranking minerals on the basis of long-term production values.

Significant changes in relative standings are occurring in recent years. Crude oil surpassed copper in total value in 1975, for the first time; coal did so a year or two later. Production of both these minerals, as well as uranium, promises to increase at a more rapid rate than that of copper. Somewhat offsetting gains in other categories, iron ore production from

Crude oil, in value, is the leading mineral in Utah. Oil is known to exist in many parts of the state but has been produced mainly in San Juan County, the Uinta Basin, and Summit County.

Utah has declined steadily, gradually being replaced by Wyoming ore at the Geneva Works in Orem. Crude oil and natural gas values now comprise about a third of total state mineral production. Needless to say, such ratios change over the years.

Lead and zinc have been important minerals since the 1870s and continue in that role to an extent, but market factors have tended to discourage their production at consistent levels. Since the last lead-zinc smelter closed about a decade ago these ores have been shipped out of state for processing.

Salt production is increasing year by year, mainly from the brines of Great Salt Lake. Potash and phosphate are mined in quantity, as are lime, clays, pumice, stone, and beryl ore. Finally, sand and gravel—unromantic as this group's image may be—is a statistical giant, accounting for annual production of more than ten million tons with a value of perhaps 20 million dollars. Of all Utah minerals, sand and gravel may have the most varied uses.

Copper. *(See Tour No. 3 for details of Kennecott operations.)* Copper production in 1940 was 232,000 tons. In the four decades since then it rose to a high of 297,000 tons in 1969, but the trend since then has been downward to levels far below those of 40 years ago. At one time, during the 1950s, Utah accounted for nearly one-third of the nation's copper production. This proportion has dropped considerably in recent decades. Monetary figures, of course, have remained high, but this is more a function of the declining value of the dollar than of real production.

Accountable for this decline are several factors, including market competition (primarily from foreign imports), unfavorable prices and the working-out of richer ore bodies at the Bingham mine. The latter problem may be alleviated to a degree by new technologies such as leaching. In 1974 Anaconca Copper began developing a new underground mine and concentrating mill at Carr Fork, on the west side of the Oquirrh Mountains. At full operation this 200 million dollar Anaconda complex is expected to produce about a fourth as much ore as Kennecott, or about 10,000 tons per day. The ore at Carr Fork is several times richer in copper content than Bingham ores.

Petroleum and natural gas. Production of crude oil and natural gas was negligible in Utah prior to the 1950s. Then in 1954 and 1959 the flow of natural gas increased dramatically, and in 1958 the trickle of crude oil became a flood, jumping from four million barrels in 1957 to 25 million in 1958. These increases were due primarily to development of the Greater Aneth oil and gas field in southeastern Utah, and in the 30 years since then this giant field has produced more than 700 million barrels of oil, or about 40 per cent of the state's production during those years.

Oil production gradually declined from a high of 40 million barrels in 1959 to a low of 23 million barrels in 1970-71 (natural gas peaked in 1964); since then oil production has been fluctuating on a rising trend with the development of new fields in the Uinta Basin and, most recently, of the promising Overthrust Belt field of Summit County. Explorations in Great Salt Lake show that oil and natural gas are present there in quantity; however, the oil's peculiar characteristics will require new technologies for economic production.

Natural gas production fluctuated between three and seven million cubic feet between 1940 and 1953; jumped to a plateau of 17 to 19 million cubic feet from 1954 to 1958; then soared to 39 million cubic feet in 1959. Gas production has exceeded that amount ever since, with a high of 80 million cubic feet in 1964. Natural gas comes from a number of counties, including San Juan, Grand, Uintah, Daggett, Carbon, Duchesne, Emery and Summit.

Coal. Coal has been mined in quantity in Utah since the 1880s, passing the million-ton annual mark in about 1900. Production reached peaks of more than seven million tons per year during the 1940s, then declined steadily to a low of four million tons in 1967. Since then production has climbed to more than ten million tons every year. Even with this impressive gain, Utah produces little more than one per cent of the nation's tonnage.

Largest users of Utah coal are Geneva Steel Works and coal-fired power plants of Utah Power and Light Company in Emery County. When this power complex is fully completed it is expected to burn four to five million tons of coal every year. An even larger consumer, several years hence, will be the huge Intermountain Power Project in western Utah, requiring up to ten million tons annually. Most of the state's coal has come from mines in Emery and Carbon counties.

Despite the state's enormous wealth of bituminous coal, prospects for more than modest production gains in the future are not entirely bright. To paraphrase one authority, there is a "simply incredible" oversupply of coal in the west, with a corresponding increase in demand nowhere in sight. Tentative plans have been announced for large-scale mining of coal from deposits on the Kaiparowits Plateau and near Alton in Kane County. The future of these projects is uncertain, however. Gasification use also is a growth potential for the future.

Manufacturing

As noted in the 1941 edition, manufacturing based on agriculture and natural resources had been very significant in the state's economy to that time. That situation has continued to the present day, though with changed emphases. Among the manufacturing activities described in 1941 were the production of hydroelectric power, canning of agricultural products (fruits, vegetables, milk), dairying, sugar and sugar products, flour milling and baking, textiles (primarily wool), smelting, machinery and printing. Of all those listed, only the latter two were not related to agriculture or natural resources. Utah-produced sugar has declined since the first edition until it is practically non-existent today.

In the nation as a whole, more than a fifth of all workers are employed in some type of manufacturing enterprise. Manufacturing on a national scale employs more workers than any other industry. Thirty times as many people are employed in manufacturing as in mining. So it is obvious that manufacturing is a vital part of the nation's economic life.

Manufacturing in the 19th century was very labor intensive, as illustrated by this view of the Jex Broom Factory in Spanish Fork, taken in 1896.

G. E. ANDERSON

This has not been quite the case in Utah, though not for lack of desire or effort expended in trying to lure manufacturing enterprises to the state. Promotional efforts of latter years have been responsible to an extent for the migration into Utah of diversified new manufacturing activities, which have been heartily welcomed by the majority of residents. Still, it appears that manufacturing as an industry accounts for a smaller *proportional share* of Utah's total employment than it did 20 years ago. (It should be noted, however, than in *actual numbers* manufacturing employment has increased five-fold since the first edition of 1941, thus illustrating that statistics can be confusing.)

Utah's population is extremely urbanized or concentrated into the Wasatch Front; so, also, is its manufacturing industry. Ninety per cent of manufacturing employment is within 50 miles of Salt Lake City. This includes the Geneva steel complex at Orem; Kennecott milling-smelting-refining center; petroleum refineries; nearly all of the state's electronics firms; Hercules missile center; and several mineral extraction industries of Great Salt Lake. Within this complex are numerous other manufacturing enterprises related to the mineral processing activities named above: for example, fabricated metal products, machinery, transportation equipment, chemicals and allied products. To a greater extent than elsewhere in the nation, perhaps, the mineral-related industries of Utah have been developed into an intricate relationship of mining and processing, from raw materials in the ground to finished products for the consumer market.

The manufacture of food products continues to be a major industry in Utah, as does lumber-related manufacturing. These resource-based activities, together with those founded on Utah's minerals, account for nearly half the state's total manufacturing employment and involve perhaps 60 per cent of all manufacturing firms.

In terms of mere figures alone, Utah's manufacturing industry is imposing. The annual payrolls of more than 2,000 manufacturing concerns total more than a billion dollars. And the value added by manufacturing totals several billion dollars, or more than twice the industry's payroll.

Supreme among Utah's manufacturing establishments in all measures of scale are Kennecott's Utah Copper Division operations, and United States Steel's Geneva Works. The former has been a leader of industry and mining for 70 years or more; the latter has been in the forefront of Utah industry since it was built by the federal government during World War II. Both operations involve mining and minerals processing, the latter falling technically in the category of manufacturing. Both employ several thousand workers in their multi-faceted activities, generally utilizing Utah minerals except for Wyoming iron ore and some Colorado coal. The copper, steel, gold, etc. which result from their operations are exported, for the most part, but a significant quantity is utilized in Utah-based manufacturing and construction—for fabricated metal products, machinery, transportation equipment, etc. Also based on minerals are more than a hundred firms utilizing the state's stone and clay deposits, included among which are gypsum and cement. Both of these are mined and processed on a massive scale. Gypsum, for example, is mined and manufactured into wallboard and other products by two plants at Sigurd. Cement has been produced in

WARD ROYLANCE

Provo Woolen Mills during the 1890s *(above)*. Textile manufacturing no longer is the important industry it was in the past.

Oil refinery in Davis County *(left)*, one of several in that vicinity.

Air view of Thiokol's manufacturing and administration areas west of Brigham City *(below)*. Thiokol manufactures solid fuel motors for military missiles and boosters for space rockets.

THIOKOL

The processing of metals is Utah's largest manufacturing activity. Shown here is Kennecott's Magna copper concentrator *(left)* and a segment of U. S. Steel's Geneva Works near Orem *(below, left)*.

Timber production has been an important economic activity since pioneer days. The sawmill below produced railroad ties in the Scofield area, late 19th century.

volume in Salt Lake City and at Devils Slide in Weber Canyon, for decades; and in 1980 plans were announced by Martin Marietta Corporation for a huge new cement plant costing almost 70 million dollars, near Leamington.

Oil refiners and the processors of gilsonite, phosphate, potash, salts and numerous other minerals also base their operations to a varying extent on Utah's minerals. More than 200 firms are involved in this latter group, employing more than 5,000 workers. Related to minerals are the operations of Ireco Chemicals of West Jordan, founded in 1957 by Utah scientist Melvin Cook and now the world's largest single supplier of slurry explosives and their technology to an international market.

Several hundred firms are engaged in the processing of foods and related products. Employing about 10,000 workers, these companies utilize an important part of the state's agricultural production such as vegetables, fruits, grains, cattle, sheep, hogs, turkeys and chickens, milk, eggs, wool and hides. Their operations include canning, bottling, baking, flour milling, meat packing, animal byproducts, milk and cheese processing, potato chip manufacturing, and sugar refining. Moroni Feed and Processing Company in Moroni, for example, is believed to conduct the largest turkey operation in the United States.

While many large mineral processing operations tend to be located in the Wasatch Front area—for reasons of transportation, labor force and other factors—those based on agriculture are not concentrated in any one location to such a degree but are scattered throughout the state, more or less according to markets and sources of supply. This is the case as well with lumber and wood manufacturers; apparel manufacturers; printing and publishing; and smaller firms in other fields.

Somewhat surprisingly, more individual firms are involved in printing and publishing than any other segment of the manufacturing industry. Most of these tend to be operations of modest size, having fewer than 25 employees, and they are distributed widely throughout the state. A number, however, are impressive operations with several hundred employees. Included in this latter group would be Deseret News Publishing Company, Newspaper Agency Corporation, Ogden Standard-Examiner, Paragon Press, Publishers Press, Moore Business Forms, Rocky Mountain Bank Note Company, Mountain States Bindery, Meridian Publishing Company, Bookcraft, Freeman's Institute, Salt Lake Tribune, and others.

The activities of about 200 firms are related to lumber and wood, ranging from the cutting of timber to planing, milling, and construction of cabinets, furniture, and myriad other wood products. Logging and sawmill-planing mill operations are dispersed widely throughout the state, close to sources of supply; in contrast, other wood-related operations follow the general trend of Wasatch Front concentration.

Among the state's largest employers are a growing number of firms engaged in electronics-based manufacturing—a "clean" industrial activity considered especially desirable by communities in which such firms are located. A partial listing of larger firms would include Sperry Univac, which manufactures computers and other high-technology electronic products; Montek Division of E-Systems, specializing in navigational aids and flight controls; Collins Telecommunications; Litton Systems; Evans & Sutherland Computer Corporation; National Semiconductor Corporation; Varian Associates, Eimac Division; Applied Digital Data Systems; and Signetics Corporation. Other firms are engaged in the manufacture of electrical machinery and equipment, bringing the total number of electrical-electronics manufacturing firms in Utah to about 100.

Nearly 200 other firms manufacture non-electrical machinery and transportation equipment. Among these are some of Utah's largest manufacturers: Envirotech Corporation, Eimco Division; Kenway Engineering; Beehive Machinery; McGraw-Edison Company; Hobart Manufacturing; Trane Company; White Trucks; Boeing Company; Entwistle Company, Roadrunner Division; Rancho Trailers; and Jetway Equipment. Eimco, born in Utah some years ago, is a manufacturer of industrial equipment and machinery having varied applications. Among these products are heavy machines for mining. Eimco is reputed to be Utah's largest exporter to foreign countries with worldwide sales exceeding a hundred million dollars.

Manufacturers of professional and scientific instruments number about 100, including Deseret Pharmaceutical Company (more than 1,000 employees) and Sorenson Research Company (more than 500). O. C. Tanner Inc. is a jewelry manufacturer of national stature. Also deserving of note is Christensen Diamond Products Inc., manufacturer of industrial and petroleum products including a major part of diamond drilling bit supply for the world's petroleum industry.

In a special category of transportation equipment are Hercules Inc. (Bacchus Works) and Thiokol Inc. (Wasatch Division), which have engaged for two decades in research, development and production of solid-propellant missile motors. Combined employment of these firms exceeds 6,000 at times. Often working jointly, Hercules and Thiokol developed and produced more than 2,000 motors for the Minuteman ICBM. Also they worked jointly on the Poseidon missile and currently are joined in production of all three motors for the Trident missile. Recent assignments include research and development on the MX missile motor and production of solid-propellant boosters for NASA's space shuttle. Hercules also produces in Utah an unusual graphite fiber named magnamite (from nearby Magna) which has numerous industrial applications.

Mention should be made of Utah's textile mill and apparel industry, which has grown significantly since 1940, at least in respects. According to the first edition there were more than 30 textile and clothing mills in the state in 1937 "with an aggregate output of clothing, blankets, and other woolen fabrics worth $3,800,000, a figure which has continued to 1940 with but small variation." Four decades later there were more than 100 such establishments employing nearly 10,000 workers. The majority of these are clothing manufacturers of modest size, many of them distributed widely around the state in smaller communities which can meet the industry's requirements as to labor supply, salary scales, siting needs, etc. Unfortunately, the mortality rate of firms in the very competitive clothing field is relatively high.

Trade

An accurate estimate of the cash volume of pioneer industry in Utah is difficult, because almost all commercial transactions were conducted by barter, by the due-bill system, or with script issued by the Mormon tithing house. H. H. Bancroft in his *History of Utah* estimates that the entire cash capital of the Mormons in Utah in 1848 did not exceed $3,000. The merchants Livingston and Kinkead, who opened the first store in Great Salt Lake City in 1849, expected it would take five years to dispose of a $20,000 stock. Some cash income from forage, horses, cattle, and farm produce, was created by passage through Utah of gold seekers and colonists to the Pacific Coast but in general they, as the Mormons, came west with equipment, not money. Great Salt Lake City issued script and attempted to mint gold coins in 1849, but abandoned both projects when it was discovered that script was discounted and the coins had too much gold in them. In one sense the Mormons were fortunate: a man might make his farm yield all he needed to eat, and he could "swap cabbages for yarn" at the local carding mill, or establish credits at the tithing house and draw on them as he needed. Tithing was paid in produce too, and a well-to-do farmer might have an abundance of home-made comforts, but he might conduct his business for a twelve month without a dollar passing through his strong box. Such lean cash reserves as the Mormons possessed could not long survive if they were invested in imported "luxuries" such as sugar at forty cents to a dollar a pound and calico at seventy-five cents a yard. Accordingly, Brigham Young and other Mormon leaders kept a weather eye on imports, and tried to reduce them by establishment of home manufactures. Pack and wagon-freight exports to adjoining territories were also encouraged.

1941 edition

Store in Hanksville, about 1960.

UTAH BOARD OF EDUCATION

The distribution industry, or retail and wholesale trade, is a major component of the state's economy, employing about a fourth of all workers. Wages and salaries from trade account for about one-seventh of total personal income in the state; and this disparate ratio correctly indicates that average wages paid in trade rank lower than any other industrial group except services. In fact, average wages in trade are less than half of those in mining and little more than half the average wage in manufacturing or construction.

For purposes of economic reporting the trade category is divided into wholesale and retail trade, with wholesale trade employing about a third as many workers as the retail segment. Since the book's first edition in 1941, employment in trade has multiplied four times as compared with little more than doubling in the total population.

Retail trade. In that Utahns resemble other Americans in buying habits, trade patterns in Utah conform fairly closely to national averages. In this industry category, perhaps, Utah exhibits its national mainstream tendencies to a greater extent than in other industrial groupings. Marked trends of varying sorts are apparent—and some are noted below—but these, for the most part, are not unique to Utah.

The economic effects of retail trade are widely dispersed around the state, bearing a significant relationship to population distribution. However, it is apparent that this is not a one-to-one relationship, reflecting the known tendency of buyers in outlying rural areas to make some of their purchases in the urbanized Wasatch Front counties— which have a higher proportion of the state's total retail sales than mere population and larger incomes would warrant.

Noteworthy trends in retail merchandising apply not only to Utah but to other states as well. There are questions about Utah's role as an innovator in merchandising. Traditionally it has been a follower rather than a leader, though this role undoubtedly is changing. Among the trends of recent years might be mentioned the following: (1) the development of shopping malls, both in the suburbs and central cities; (2) disappearance of small independent food stores, particularly in larger cities, with a concurrent growth of affiliated and chain grocers, not only in numbers but also in sales volume; (3) marked growth in both sales volume and number of employees for the average retail establishment; (4) phenomenal growth in restaurant patronage and in the number of eating places, including franchised food outlets; (5) growth of absentee ownership of retail outlets in general, and franchise-chain outlets in particular; (6) declining numbers of independent gasoline service stations and auto mechanics; (7) changes in downtown shopping patterns in the larger cities. It should be noted, finally, that food stores and eating establishments now employ almost half of all workers involved in retail trade.

Wholesale trade. Wholesale trade approximates retail trade in total sales (several billion dollars annually), though employees number only a third as many. Whereas retail sales are made primarily to residents, tourists and shoppers from adjoining states (in particular Wyoming, Idaho and eastern Nevada), wholesale trade involves a much larger geographical area: not only Utah and the intermountain west, but in fact the entire world in cases where export of Utah-manufactured goods is involved.

Formerly, exports from Utah to foreign countries did not comprise a major part of wholesale sales, accounting for less than ten per cent of the total. In more recent years, however, foreign sales have been increasing at a steady rate and now amount to several hundred million dollars annually. Utah-produced machinery (for mining in particular), petroleum drilling equipment, medical supplies and equipment, electronic and computer equipment, all are being exported to foreign countries.

A major grocery wholesaler of distinctly Utah origin is Associated Food Stores, a cooperative enterprise owned by some 700 member retailers in six intermountain states. Founded in 1940, Associated ranks among the ten largest food groups in the nation.

A relatively new development in trade is Utah's freeport and foreign trade status. Under the state's liberal freeport law, certain goods, wares and merchandise are exempt from *ad valorem* taxation. Included are goods in transit, those prepared in Utah for out-of-state sale, and merchandise inventories of retailers, wholesalers or manufacturers meant for sale or processing within the state. These provisions are a decided inducement for wholesalers and manufacturers to utilize Utah warehousing facilities for transshipment of merchandise, as well as for other merchants and manufacturers to locate in Utah. Though Utah is not unique in having freeport tax provisions, it does have decided advantages of geographic location

Freeport Center at Clearfield is the state's first and largest freeport distribution center.

TRIAD UTAH

Salt Lake International Center dates from 1975. The 900-acre business park adjoins the Salt Lake International Airport and already houses about 60 different firms.

and excellent transportation. That is, northern Utah is roughly equidistant (800 miles or less) from all major population centers between the Pacific coast and the Great Plains, and from the Canadian to the Mexican borders. About 70 major truck lines, numerous major airlines, four major railroads, and a network of highways link the Wasatch Front with the rest of the nation, offering one-day transport service in many cases to markets in this distribution radius.

The designation of Salt Lake City as a port of entry for the U. S. Customs Office, in 1969, also has been a boon to Utah industry—not only in expediting the flow of goods but also in making possible, depending on circumstances, the postponement or avoidance of customs duties. In 1977 a foreign trade zone was established near the city's International Airport. This zone permits the storage, inspection, assembling and/or manufacturing of foreign goods, its advantage being the reduction or deferral of customs duties.

As a result of its freeport provisions, port of entry and foreign trade zone, Utah is witnessing a growth in its warehousing industry. Of special note in this regard is the Clearfield Freeport Center, which utilizes the site and many buildings of the former Clearfield Naval Supply Depot to serve more than a hundred firms with warehousing, manufacturing, and shipping facilities. Of more recent vintage is the Salt Lake International Center, a development of the 1970s and 1980s, located west of the International Airport. The center is designed, among several functions, to house and service light industry with office and warehouse space, as well as being the site of Utah's foreign trade zone. Initial tenants include First Security Corporation's operations and computer center, a Hilton Inn, Skaggs Warehouse, Beehive International, and many other business firms.

Recreation and Tourism

More leisure time . . . More available money for recreation . . . Faster and less expensive transportation . . . A large and growing choice of recreational opportunities: These are part of life for the majority of Utahns today, as they are for most Americans. Combined with Utah's recreational wealth, they have made Recreation and Tourism a major industry in the state.

In this book's first edition of 40 years ago, it was stated that "Although the tourist is no novelty in Utah, recreation as a significant economic factor is a comparatively recent development." At that time the annual income from recreational traffic (tourism) was about $12,000,000. Today the income from tourism amounts to several hundred million dollars every year. Recreation in general must generate hundreds of millions of dollars more. Tourism and recreation jointly have become one of the state's foremost industries.

Flaming Gorge National Recreation Area.

BUREAU OF RECLAMATION (MEL DAVIS)

The first edition's chapter on Recreation emphasized the following activities as most worthy of description: hunting, fishing, winter sports, boating, hiking, riding and packing. Since then, though all of those activities continue in popularity, recreational tastes and trends have changed somewhat.

Utahns still favor outdoor activities, and there may be validity in the statement that "Utah people are said to be the greatest campers and pic-nickers in the world." Today, as then, "on hot summer evenings or week-ends it is customary to toss a camp or picnic outfit in the family car [or camper] and go where canyon breezes blow, or where increased altitude provides relief from the heat."

Utah's natural scene continues to provide an important base for the state's most popular recreational activities. Among them, camping and pleasure driving rank at the top, followed in rough order by the following: fishing, hiking, skiing, hunting, golfing, boating, horseback riding, bicycling, picnicking, swimming and trailbiking. But recreation in this age is much more complex than even that lengthy list suggests. Recreation comprises myriad activities, nearly all of which involve money to a degree, and they are important as a part of both economic and personal life.

Pleasure driving, for example, requires expenditures for a vehicle and fuel, and probably for a camera and film as well. Camping requires vehicle, fuel, equipment and food. Skiing may involve transportation, outlays for special clothing and equipment, expenditures for lifts, lodging and training. Fishing and hunting necessitate equipment, licenses, and transportation. Recreational expenses are a familiar fact of life.

In a technical sense, recreation should hardly by considered a distinct economic activity, inasmuch as it is only one element in such broad economic categories as Trade, Manufacturing, Transportation, Services and Government—and, for that matter, only one facet of the Arts and Communications. Nevertheless, recreation is such an important aspect of living in Utah, economically and otherwise, that it warrants special treatment.

TOURISM. When people travel away from home for recreation or vacation, they are tourists. In that sense, Utahns traveling in their own state for those purposes are tourists. Ordinarily, however, a tourist is thought of as someone from another state or country. The distinction is not always meaningful; whatever their origin, tourists spend money for fuel, food, lodging, entertainment, and other goods or services.

Travel in general, including tourism, is a vital segment of Utah's economy. It is estimated that more than ten million non-resident visitors spend in excess of $400,000,000 in the state every year, in addition to many millions spent by Utah residents touring their own state. (There is a distinction between travelers and tourists. Travelers may travel for many reasons, among which are sightseeing, business affairs, conventions and meetings, skiing, family visiting, hunting and fishing, etc. Tourists are travelers who travel for recreation or vacation purposes. In Utah, non-resident tourists comprise about 70 per cent of all non-resident travelers.)

For more than 30 years state government has conducted a systematic program of advertising Utah's attractions outside the state, trying to lure greater numbers of tourists for longer periods of time. At present the State Travel Division disburses about two million dollars each year for advertising, publicity, publications, and other promotional expenses, in addition to impressive amounts spent by local chambers of commerce, convention bureaus, regional travel councils, commercial enterprises, and industry groups.

There is no question that tourist visitation and expenditure totals are increasing every year, but it is not possible to tell with exactness how much of the increase is due to promotion as compared with the influence of general travel and recreational trends. The average length of stay by tourists (less than two days) appears to be increasing; nevertheless, Utah is not yet considered a destination by most visitors. There are more than a few reasons for this, some of which are conjectural.

Utah's tourist offerings are both natural and cultural. The state was settled for religious reasons, and its cultural-religious heritage is of interest to most visitors. For example, Mormon Temple Square in Salt Lake City is the prime single tourist attraction in the state. The list of specific attractions that hold interest for residents and non-residents alike is impressive. These are described in Part II. Visitation totals increase yearly, and for the first time—in some parts of the state—the question arises: How much is too much? That question will become more persistent, especially as regards attractions in and near urbanized centers. Answers will be no easier in Utah than elsewhere.

National Park Service areas in the state attract more than seven million visitors each year. These 14 areas encompass more than two million acres. The majority are remote from large centers of population and can hardly be said to suffer from over-visitation, except perhaps with respect to improved campgrounds at certain times. Several parks, however—notably Zion National Park, Timpanogos Cave National Monument, and Glen Canyon National Recreation Area—have real problems of visitor control. Attendance at Utah's state park areas is growing even more rapidly than at the national park areas. In 1978, for the first time, attendance at state park areas surpassed that of national park areas. About half the 40-odd state areas are devoted to water-based recreation, a fourth are scenic and nature areas, and another fourth are historical and museum areas.

Wasatch and Uinta national forests extend for 150 miles along the Wasatch Range and nearby mountains, adjoining the densely populated Wasatch Front, and over much of the Uinta Mountains. Used for camping, picnicking, skiing, sightseeing, and a multitude of other recreational activities, as well as being a crucial watershed, these forests are among the most intensively utilized of all national forests in the country. Management problems, already worrisome, undoubtedly will become more severe in coming years.

Utah's varied landscape invites pleasure driving. At the same time its vastness can be discouraging, and even frightening. Distance between towns and special points of interest may be tiring. A definite negative factor is the lack of destination resorts as accents to the scenery. The majority of tourists prefer a variety of activities and conveniences as spicing on the scenic cake,

BUREAU OF RECLAMATION

Fishing at Deer Creek
Reservoir *(left)*.

Picnicking in Logan Canyon
(below, left).

Professional basketball,
featuring the Utah Jazz, in the
Salt Palace Arena *(below)*.

SALT LAKE VALLEY CONVENTION BUREAU   UTAH TRAVEL COUNCIL

and the paucity of multi-faceted recreational facilities in Utah's outlying areas detracts from potential income and from the state's image as a recreational destination.

Despite its reputation as an arid state, Utah is blessed with thousands of miles of fishing streams and hundreds of lakes, some of them huge bodies of water but most of modest size. Government agencies, primarily the Utah Division of Wildlife Resources, help to keep these waters stocked with about 20 different game fish types, and the state is noted for comparatively good fishing. Fishing pressures are heavy and increasing, however. It becomes difficult to keep waters adequately stocked, even in areas that formerly were isolated. The phenomenal growth in ownership of truck campers, motor homes, and vacation trailers is one of the primary reasons for this, as these vehicles transport not only residents of the urbanized Wasatch Front, but myriad non-residents as well, to the hinterlands.

Utah's varied terrain offers habitat for a wide variety of animals and birds, many of which are classified as game species. Both hunters and game are protected by regulations, and the expense of licenses and special fees remains moderate though growing.

Skiing and Winter Sports. Despite an annual precipitation that is among the nation's lowest, Utah has a world reputation for the skiing quality of its winter snow. Not only are mountain snow depths sufficient for ideal skiing, normally there is enough snow for skiing between November and April or May, depending on location—in other words, a remarkably long season of five or six months. Terrain is varied enough for every degree of expertise, and the best snow areas, with a few exceptions, are conveniently situated with respect to centers of population. But even those advantages are not all. What gives Utah special distinction is the unique texture of its "powder snow," dry and fluffy, superlative as a skiing medium.

These attributes have been recognized since the first Utah skiers took to the hills. Yet it was the 1920s and 1930s before serious development of lodges, lifts and jumps began. Since those relatively primitive developments, national and world trends in winter sports, combined with Utah promotional efforts, have resulted in an annual business volume of more than $100,000,000 from the state's ski industry. In Little Cottonwood Canyon, Alta now has six chairlifts and four tows; nearby Snowbird features an aerial tramway and five chairlifts. In Big Cottonwood Canyon to the north, Brighton and Solitude areas offer seven chairlifts and a number of tows. Park City and Park West, across the mountains to the east, have expanded into winter-summer resorts of major proportions, with golf course, myriad lodges and condominiums, an authentic western mining town, dozens of restaurants and night spots, gondola tramway, more than a dozen chairlifts, and a hundred ski runs.

East of Ogden are Nordic Valley, Snow Basin and Powder Mountain, all developed ski areas. East of Logan is Beaver Mountain; east of Provo-Orem is Sundance; east of Beaver, Mt. Holly; near Cedar City and Parowan, Brian Head Resort. And near Provo is planned the Heritage Mountain development, to cost tens of millions of dollars and featuring several villages, shops, restaurants, lodging, cable railcar, lifts, 70 ski runs, 46 miles of trails, etc. Whether or not Heritage Mountain becomes a reality to any degree approaching the magnitude envisioned by its planners, the scope of their vision indicates what is possible for Wasatch Mountains development in years to come.

Needless to say, the still blossoming winter sports industry is welcomed not only by resort operators but also by Utah's urban business community, in particular that segment catering to visitors. Previously, tourism was a summer boom-or-bust affair; now, with skiing and conventions, it is an all-year industry for motels, hotels and restaurants, or at least those in strategic locations. And it has been a boon for airlines.

Residents and out-of-state visitors alike are responsible for Utah's ski industry. Together they account for several million skier days on the slopes each year. From the standpoint of expenditures, however, promotion is directed mainly at non-resident visitors, for they remain longer at the resorts and spend more freely than local residents.

Transportation

Streams and rivers were Utah's first trailmakers. Unimportant in themselves for navigation, they carved valleys that were used by the buffalo, possibly America's greatest road engineer, as avenues for herd migration. Early Utah Indians followed the buffalo, a source of food and shelter as well as a trail-blazer. Before white men introduced horses, the Indians traveled on bare or moccasined feet, and women were the usual beasts of burden. Some Indians, east and north of the Wasatch Range, tied their belongings together and secured the bundle to two poles, which were fastened at one end to a dog and left to drag on the ground at the other. With this crude device, known as a travois, the load was pulled along the trails that were ultimately followed by railroads and automobile roads. Father Escalante, who brought a pack train through Utah in 1776, is the first known traveler to use horses in the present State. Ashley's cannon *(see History)* was, ironically, the first vehicle to leave the print of wheels on Utah land.

The first pioneer wagon caravan to cross Utah was the Bartleson-Bidwell train of 1841 *(see History)*. Six years later, thousands of Mormon pioneers began the long trek westward into Utah. They traveled in covered wagons and kept accurate accounts of their journey. . . .

As a result of unprecedented demand for supplies and military stores during the

Street scene in downtown Salt Lake City, before the advent of the automobile.

gold rush of 1849-50, overland freighting companies were organized. Although Utah men engaged in the freighting business, the most important firm of the 1850's was that of Russell, Majors, and Waddell, whose principal office was in Leavenworth, Kansas. At one time this company owned 75,000 oxen and more than 6,000 prairie schooners. The freight caravans usually consisted of about twenty-five wagons, each wagon drawn by six yoke of oxen and carrying approximately 5,000 pounds. . . .

Passenger service, however, was slow, cumbersome, and erratic. Travelers who came by ox team required several months to cross the plains, and mail to the frontier grew old in transit. Utah, created a Territory in 1850, did not receive full details until January of the following year. By 1851, however, stage coaches were making regular trips from Independence and St. Joseph to Great Salt Lake City, and soon afterward to Sacramento. The stage coaches, light vehicles drawn by six fast horses, accommodated fourteen passengers, with mail, express, and about twenty-five pounds of baggage for each person. To insure speed, horses were changed frequently at stations along the route. At first thirty days were necessary for the journey from St. Joseph to Great Salt Lake City, but ultimately the time was reduced to eighteen days. Coach fare varied from $150 to $180, and during the Civil War it reached an all-time high of $350. While the overland coaches were operating in the country west of the Missouri River, smaller stage lines were carrying passengers, mail and express between scattered towns in Utah. The necessity for travel within the Territory resulted in the building of roads, bridges, and ferries, nearly all maintained by tolls.

A great many Mormon immigrants, however, were too poor to travel by wagon train or stagecoach. Church authorities devised a new plan for migration, by hand-carts. Every traveler was limited to seventeen pounds of luggage, and every able-bodied person was expected to pull a hand-cart. The plan went into effect in the spring of 1856. Between then and 1861 nearly 4,000 persons crossed the plains with the hand-cart companies. . . .

In 1860 the freighting firm of Russell, Majors, and Waddell organized the Pony Express to carry mail from St. Joseph to Sacramento. The firm provided 500 fast horses and employed more than 200 men. Stations were established at intervals, and 80 of the lightest men were selected as riders. The first rider left Sacramento on April 3, and arrived in Salt Lake City on April 7, where he met another rider who arrived six days after leaving St. Joseph. The route through Utah from east to west, entered through Echo and Weber Canyons, ran southwest to Salt Lake City, thence skirted the southern end of Great Salt Lake and the Salt Desert, reaching the Nevada line west of present Ibapah. The Pony Express continued to carry the mail until 1861, when the Overland Telegraph provided faster and more effective communication. In 1867 the Deseret Telegraph Company began operating a line between Great Salt Lake City and St. George, and later in the same year the service was extended into Idaho. The company operated independently until it was absorbed by Western Union in 1900.

For many years residents of the Great Basin had discussed the feasibility of a rail-road, and in 1852 the Territorial legislature approved a memorial to Congress asking for the establishment of rail service. On May 10, 1869, the golden spike ceremony marking completion of the [first transcontinental railroad] was held at Promontory. . . . *(See Golden Spike National Historic Site.)*

Brigham Young, disappointed when he learned that the two railroads forming the transcontinental line would not meet in Salt Lake City, set out to build branch roads within the State. The Utah Central Railway from Salt Lake City to Ogden was completed in 1870, the Utah Southern from Salt Lake City to Draper in 1871 (and an extension south to Milford by 1880), and the Utah Northern from Ogden to Logan in 1873 and to Silver Bow, Montana, in 1880. The Utah Central and the Utah Northern now form part of the Oregon Short Line (affiliated with Union Pacific), which connects Salt Lake City with Montana points.

Although the first railroads served large areas in Utah, the mountainous regions were still dependent upon more primitive transportation. About 1869, ore produced by the Emma Mine at Alta was "rawhided" to the mouth of Little Cottonwood Canyon. The process of "rawhiding" consisted of loading ore into green skins and using horses to drag it down to the nearest road, where it could be transferred to ox-drawn wagons and hauled to the railroad terminal at Ogden.

The development of mining, however, soon resulted in the extension of rail service to the mountains. One of the first ore-hauling lines was completed in 1880, when the Utah Eastern Railway established a line from Coalville to Park City. In 1883 the Denver and Rio Grande began operating between Salt Lake City and Grand Junction, Colorado; in 1903 the Southern Pacific built the Lucin Cutoff *(see Great Salt Lake)* across Great Salt Lake; and in 1905 southern California was linked to Utah by the San Pedro, Los Angeles, and Salt Lake Railroad.

1941 edition

Electric railways appeared in Utah toward the close of the last century, and there were, in 1940, four interurban lines operating in the central and northern parts of the state. From Salt Lake City electric trains traveled northward to Ogden, Logan, and Preston, Idaho; southward to Provo and Payson; and westward to Magna and Garfield. Within a decade or so following World War II, however, these electric railways had ceased operations.

In 1940, when the book's first edition was written, Utah was served by four major railway systems: the Union Pacific, the Southern Pacific, the Western Pacific, and the Denver & Rio Grande Western (now the Rio Grande Railroad). These interstate railways still are the major rail systems in Utah, supplemented within the state by the following Class II railroads: Utah Railway, Carbon County Railroad, Tooele Valley Railway, and Salt Lake, Garfield and Western Railway.

Since 1940 significant changes have occurred in the railway industry.

Union Pacific rail yards in Ogden, a vital link in the nation's railroad system.

UNION PACIFIC RAILROAD

Steam locomotives have been replaced by diesel engines. The famed wood-pile trestle across Great Salt Lake was replaced by a rockfill causeway. Employees in the industry dropped from a total of 15,000 during World War II to hardly more than 5,000 today; at the same time, annual freight tonnage has changed relatively little since the war years, totaling only a third more in recent years than it did some 30 years before.

The most notable change in railway transportation in Utah, as throughout much of the nation, has been the almost complete cessation of passenger traffic. With the exception of limited Amtrak service, no passengers are carried in Utah by rail. The reasons for this are complex, but they include growth and increased popularity of competitive forms of transportation, such as air, private automobile and bus travel, combined with curtailment of passenger service by the railroads because of economic reasons.

Motor Vehicles and Highways

Since 1900, when the first gasoline automobile in Utah bumped over the rough roads between Ogden and Salt Lake City, there has been increasing emphasis on highway building and improvements. A concrete road, the first of its kind in the State, was built from Tremonton to Garland in 1912; it was eight feet wide and three miles long. What might be termed the first modern highway in Utah was the Salt Lake City to Ogden road, portions of which were paved in 1915 by convict labor. The highway across the Salt Desert, built in 1925, used a new principle in highway engineering. . . . In 1940, six Federal highways traversed the State, and a network of graded roads gave access to small towns and recreation areas. As an outgrowth of highway improvement, truck and bus transportation developed rapidly in Utah. In 1910 trucks began hauling goods to and from mountainous districts not served by rail. A decade later many of the mining companies were transporting ore in fleets of large trucks. About 1913 the moving and transfer companies were born, and in a few years were offering serious competition to the railroads.

(1941 edition)

Development of Utah's highway system and growth in the number of vehicles using its roads are as responsible as any other factor for the immense number of changes that have occurred in Utah since this book's first edition of 1941. Total road mileage almost doubled in that period, to almost 50,000 miles today. Passenger cars increased from 126,000 in 1941 to about 700,000 today. Trucks and buses increased nearly 15-fold; trailers and semitrailers jumped from less than 1,000 in 1941 to about 100,000 today. In total, the number of all registered motor vehicles soared from 154,000 in 1941 to more than a million in only 35 years or so—almost as many vehicles as there are people.

Local roads account for slightly more than half of Utah's total road mileage; the remainder are state and federal roads. Nearly half of all roads are surfaced. During the 1960s and 1970s, construction of the interstate highway system required hundreds of millions of dollars. For example, between 1965 and 1977 alone, more than a billion dollars were spent for construction and maintenance by the Utah Highway Division. About 900 miles of interstate highways are within the state's borders.

The commercial trucking and warehousing industry in Utah employs some 10,000 workers in about 500 firms. About 40 large interstate motor freight carriers operate terminals in the state, and several national bus lines provide passenger service.

Following national trends, Utah's urban mass transit systems declined drastically in ridership after World War II. In Salt Lake Valley, ridership dropped from 33 million in 1946 to only four million in 1969. Only during the past decade or so, under stimulation of public funding, has ridership increased significantly. Though progress has been encouraging, serious problems remain.

Mention should be made of several other types of motorized vehicles. Though used for recreation rather than commercial passenger transport, these are becoming increasingly popular in Utah as elsewhere. They include snowmobiles, trailbikes and motorcycles, and four-wheel-drive vehicles. More than 60,000 motorcycles and almost 20,000 snowmobiles are registered in Utah. The number of four-wheel-drive (off-road) vehicles must be surmised, but unquestionably they are very numerous. While these vehicles are popular, especially in the case of their owners, they have created problems for land agencies, property owners, and people who resent some of their characteristics. These special problems have not all been solved.

Air Transportation

With the advent of the airplane, the Salt Lake airport assumed a focal position as the chief junction point in the intermountain area. In 1920, when travel by air was in its infancy, the Federal government routed its first national airmail line through Salt Lake City. Commercial planes began to transport passengers to and from Utah in 1926, and by 1940 the business had grown to a schedule of thirty planes a day. *(1941 edition)*

The growth of air transport since those early days of flying has been no less than astounding. World War II served as a tremendous catalyst to flying. Thousands of Utahns served in the Army Air Force. Hill Air Force Base and Wendover Air Base were established, and Great Salt Lake Desert was utilized as a bombing range. Gradually, after the war, airplanes became a common mode of travel for increasing numbers of travelers. Today, more than 2,000 Utahns own private aircraft, a dozen or so commercial firms carry air passengers, several thousand workers are directly employed in air transportation, and the state boasts more than 50 improved airports and heliports.

The Salt Lake City Municipal Airport has developed into the Salt Lake City International Airport, a regional commercial air center for five states, ranked among the nation's top 50 airports for volume of air freight and air express. Every year, millions of passengers embark or debark at its terminals, their numbers growing steadily. At least eight national and regional carriers serve the airport, providing direct flights to cities in every direction. In addition to major airlines, the industry is served by several commuter airlines of moderate size, as well as a number of smaller flight services around the state.

Pipelines

Not ordinarily considered when discussing transportation, pipelines do carry an enormous volume of "freight" such as crude oil, natural gas, refined petroleum products, and water; and it may well be that in the future they will carry coal in the form of slurry.

In Utah, pipelines carry natural gas and crude oil from fields in Utah, Wyoming and Colorado to refineries in North Salt Lake and Woods Cross, as well as from Utah wells to other states. Gasoline and fuel oil are transported from Utah refineries to the Pacific Northwest, and into Utah from Wyoming. Numerous firms are involved in the pipeline industry.

At this writing, a pipeline costing hundreds of millions of dollars is being planned from Wyoming through Utah to California. Another of similar magnitude is being planned from northern Utah to Nebraska.

Water Transport (Boating)

Water transportation has never been important in arid Utah, but its history is peculiar. Attempts have been made to operate freight and passenger boats on Great Salt Lake, but its heavy, briny waters usually pound boats to pieces *(see Great Salt Lake)*. It has been traversed by explorers in bull boats and by Fremont's patent rubber boat, but it remains a unique and intractable body of water, traveled by a relatively few pleasure craft. *(1941 edition)*

Utah's rivers do not lend themselves to navigation on a massive scale, but thousands of explorers, scientists, and thrill-seekers have journeyed down the swift, cliff-walled Green and Colorado rivers. Tourist adventure trips can be arranged today on parts of these rivers and on the San Juan. Lake Powell has replaced the Colorado River in Glen Canyon, and Flaming Gorge Reservoir the waters of Green River for many miles. More than a few people still mourn these developments. Yet it cannot be denied that tens of thousands now boat these lakes every year where only hundreds traversed the rivers they supplanted.

Commercial boating has become "big business" on these huge lakes, as well as elsewhere in Utah—not always in the form of passenger traffic. While commercial passenger transport is confined mainly to the rivers and Lake Powell, boat rentals, marina and boating services involve large amounts of money at numerous locations around the state, including Bear Lake, Utah Lake, Great Salt Lake, Lake Powell, Flaming Gorge Reservoir, and other popular boating sites. More than 40,000 private boats are registered in the state; how many people they transport each year can only be conjectured.

Electric power generators in Glen Canyon Dam.

Communications and Utilities
(See also Communications Media in the Cultural Scene)

As an economic category, and as discussed here, communications includes radio and television (the electronic media) and telephones. Logically this group should include printed media and the postal system as well; however, economic reporting classifies publishing as a manufacturing industry and government postal workers are included under Federal Government. Utilities include electric power, natural gas, and sanitary services.

Together, communications and utilities employ about 14,000 workers in Utah, or almost as many as mining. Both industries are less labor-intensive than most others; that is, labor costs are relatively small compared with revenues, which amount to hundreds of millions of dollars each year.

Communications

In 1940 there were eight radio stations in Utah. Forty years later there were more than 50 commercial AM and FM radio stations and another 15 non-commercial FM stations operated by local schools, colleges, universities, etc. Television was only a dream in 1940, but by 1980 there were four commercial television stations, two non-commercial educational stations, and several cable television systems in the state. Utah's radio and television broadcasts are received clearly in nearby states, and in fact are relied upon by a significant part of the population in Utah, eastern Nevada, western Colorado, most of Idaho, and much of Wyoming and Montana.

Income from advertising is the main source of revenue for commercial stations. It can be assumed that at least the commercial television network stations operate at a profit, though it is said that a number of radio stations are not so fortunate. Advertising revenue in the nation as a whole amounts to more than eight billion dollars annually for television (three commercial networks and 714 stations), while national radio revenue exceeds three billion dollars (about 5,700 stations).

Station revenue and expenditures, of course, represent only a part of the enormous amount of money associated with electronic media. Also to be considered is the cost of purchasing the hundreds of thousands of television and radio sets owned by Utahns; the cost of cable hookups and service fees; the cost of repair and maintenance of equipment; etc. Recent years have seen the introduction of costly home video recorder/playbacks and electronic entertainment devices. It need hardly be added that purchase costs of this equipment and necessary accessories are considerable.

Telephone service is an accepted fact of life for almost every Utahn, as evidenced by approximately 500,000 telephones in service in the state. It is estimated that 98 per cent of all households in Utah are equipped with a telephone. About 96 per cent of these are owned and serviced by Mountain

Bell, a unit of the giant Bell system. A dozen other telephone companies of moderate size provide telephone service in scattered rural areas such as the Uinta Basin, Summit and Daggett counties, Sanpete County, Box Elder County, Kamas-Woodland, southwestern Utah, Moab, and the Navajo Indian Reservation. Statistics reveal that nearly two billion telephone calls originate in the state each year, and that Mountain Bell has spent more than 100 million dollars annually for expansion and improvements in recent years.

Utilities

By far the largest privately-owned utilities in Utah are Mountain Fuel Supply Company and Utah Power and Light Company. These firms provide natural gas and electric power to the majority of the private homes as well as business establishments and industrial plants. About 6,000 workers are employed in the state by utilities, a figure only slightly less than that for communications.

More than 80 per cent of electric power produced in Utah is generated by privately-owned facilities, the remainder by municipalities, federal government, and other public-ownership facilities. More electricity is generated by fuel-powered plants than by water-powered installations. Production of electric power in the state has more than doubled in the past decade, and sales amount to many hundreds of millions of dollars each year. Industrial users are responsible for about 40 per cent of the total power use; residential users consume about 30 per cent; and commercial and other users are responsible for the remainder.

Many of the state's streams are utilized for the generating of hydro-electric power, some of them more or less directly and others after damming. Flaming Gorge Dam contains the largest hydroelectric generating system in the state; Glen Canyon Dam, just across the Utah line in Arizona, is even larger. A portion of the electric power from these dams is utilized in Utah,

Waiting for the mail in Santaquin 1893.

G. E. ANDERSON

and most communities in the state are dependent at least partially on stream-generated power. However, streams cannot produce sufficient electric power for the state's needs, and more is generated by gas- and coal-fired plants than by water. The largest complex of coal-fired power plants in the state is near Huntington and Castle Dale in Emery County *(see Tour No. 10)*, while the largest coal-fired generating plant in the free world, the Intermountain Power Project, is now under construction near Delta *(see Tour No. 4)*. Proposals for coal-fired power plants have been environmentally controversial in recent years; in this regard, see discussion of the proposed Kaiparowits Power Plant in Tour No. 9. Kennecott produces its own power in a plant at Magna. There are no nuclear plants in the state.

Mountain Fuel Supply Company and several smaller firms supply natural gas to more than 380,000 customers in Utah through a system of gas mains totaling more than 7,000 miles. Revenues amounted to about 230 million dollars in 1979. On a national scale, total sales of natural gas increased from two billion dollars in 1960 to 39 billion dollars in 1979.

Construction of dams, highways, water systems, power plants, and buildings is among the greatly varied economic activities of government. Shown here is construction of Glen Canyon Dam.

Government as an Economic Activity

Government in Utah surpasses all other economic activities in its influence. Not only does government collect and spend enormous sums of money: it has a far-reaching effect on the lives of people and fortunes of business. It is a rare citizen who cannot attest, from personal experience, to the impact of government.

Through taxation, government redistributes a significant part of the nation's wealth and income. Nationally, government expenditures in 1979 amounted to more than 35 per cent of the gross national product. Annual expenditures in that year were 52 times greater than they were 77 years earlier—after adjusting for decrease in the value of the dollar—or 500 times greater in terms of current dollars. The proportion of government expenditures to gross national product rose from 7 per cent in 1902 to 35 per cent in 1979. In that latter year, government expenditures amounted to $3,800 for every man, woman and child in the nation.

Government obtains most of its funds, of course, from taxation. Utahns paid more than $3.3 billion dollars in federal, state and local taxes in 1979, or 38 per cent of the state's total personal income. About two-thirds of this was collected by the federal government, the remaining third by state and local governments. For all levels of government collectively, income taxes (individual and corporate) are the most important source of revenue, amounting to 40 per cent of the total. Social security taxes, sales and excise taxes, and property tax follow in relative importance. Also contributing to the grand total are utility revenue, retirement and unemployment funds, and miscellaneous revenues, charges and fees. Income taxes provide the largest share of revenue for the federal government. Sales and income taxes contribute 43 per cent of state government revenue. Local governments rely on property tax and state aid for more than two-thirds of their income.

Money taken by the government from its citizens is returned in the form of services, grants, employment, income payments, etc. The federal government, for example, spends more than half its income for national defense and income security. State government spends more than 40 per cent of its income for education, with high expenditures also for social welfare and highways. Local governments spend nearly 60 per cent of their income for education. Government's role in the economic life of Utah is highly visible in some respects, not so apparent in others. Among the most visible activities of government are the public schools, as well as state-supported colleges, universities and technical schools, which require government expenditues totaling about a billion dollars per year. These schools represent one of the largest employment groups in Utah with approximately 40,000 employees. In Salt Lake City the Federal Building, State Capitol, and City-County complex are prominent structures, the state's most dominant symbols of government involvement in seemingly every aspect of economic life.

More than a fifth of all non-agricultural workers in Utah (one in 11 residents) were employed by government in 1980. This proportion, which is relatively high, places Utah near the top among states in that respect; fewer than half a dozen states had a higher ratio of government workers compared with non-government workers. Such a ranking is due to Utah's large number of federal employees and workers in education—somewhat greater in comparison with population than in most other states. However, if Utah is compared with other states on the basis of *non-educational employment* by state and local governments, its relative position drops considerably.

In 1980 all units of government employed a total of more than 129,000 persons in Utah. Local government units employed more than 40 per cent of these, the majority of whom were public school teachers. Employment by local units of government multiplied several times between 1950 and 1980, reaching almost 57,000 in 1980. State employees now approach those of federal government in total numbers, a growth trend that has been increasing for several decades. In 1950, for example, state employment totaled about 8,000. In 1980 it exceeded 33,000. Federal employment, in contrast, has remained fairly stable in recent years.

In Utah there is one government employee for every 11 residents. Stated differently, government employees comprise 9 per cent of the state's population. This statewide proportion differs somewhat between counties, although most adhere rather closely to the state norm. Salt Lake County, for example, with 40 per cent of the state's population, has 40 per cent of the government workers. In contrast, Davis, Tooele, and Daggett counties have a much higher proportion of government workers than do other counties—a difference due almost entirely to unusually high federal employment in those counties.

The single largest federal employer in Utah is Hill Air Force Base, where approximately half of Utah's federal employees work. Several thousand other federal defense workers are employed at Tooele Army Depot, Defense Depot Ogden, Fort Douglas, Dugway Proving Ground, and elsewhere. The Internal Revenue Service is a major employer in Ogden. In many rural counties, the Departments of Interior and Agriculture are among the largest employers. On a state level, institutions of higher education form the largest employing category, with nearly 15,000 full-time-equivalent employees in 1980. No other state operation even approaches this employment figure. More than 3,000 persons (full-time-equivalent) are employed by state Social Services activities and about 2,000 in Transportation activities. Other state functions employ fewer than 1,000 workers in each category.

Public school teachers and other education workers comprise the largest category of local government employment, as stated above. These totaled more than 20,000 in 1978. Roads and highways, hospitals and health, police and fire protection, sanitation, utilities, parks and recreation, and general administration employ most of the remaining workers in local government operations.

Federal government finance. Each year the federal government returns more money to Utah than is collected in federal taxes from the state. In this

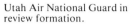

Utah Air National Guard in review formation.

M/SGT ELGIE CAMPBELL

Dedication of the Hite Bridge on U-95, a state highway, in June 1966.

BUREAU OF RECLAMATION (MEL DAVIS)

respect Utah is not unique—about 30 other states also receive a greater number of dollars from the federal government than they contribute in federal taxes. Utah ranked 10th among all states in 1979 with respect to the amount received: that is, $1.29 in federal expenditures compared with $1 paid in federal taxes. This imbalance is due to several factors, including the large amount of land owned by the federal government in Utah, which requires significant federal expenditures for administration and development. Another contributing factor is the number of large defense installations in the state. Still another is the relative youthfulness of the population (most children do not pay federal taxes).

Nearly a third of total federal expenditures in Utah in 1979 were defense-related. These amounted to more than 800 million dollars. Another one-fourth was in the form of income security payments (Social Security, retirement, unemployment compensation, public assistance), which amounted to more than 700 million dollars. Spending on natural resources (parks, forests, public lands, water development, etc.) totaled nearly 400 million dollars. Veterans benefits, aid to education, health, and miscellaneous federal programs accounted for the balance.

Who are the recipients of federal dollars in Utah, disbursed through more than 600 federal programs? First, there are more than 30,000 federal employees, each of whom receives a salary and other benefits. About one in ten Utahns receives old-age, survivors, disability or health insurance payments directly from the federal government. Some thousands also receive unemployment compensation, veterans compensation, and educational benefits from the federal government. In addition, thousands of Utahns receive federal money indirectly from state and local programs funded partly by federal grants. (Federal aid to state and local governments in Utah totaled more than 570 million dollars in 1980, awarded for numerous purposes, including the following: employment and training; natural resources conservation; payments in lieu of taxes; historical preservation; environmental programs; educational programs; health, medical and social services; public works; community services; food, nutrition, sanitation, and agricultural programs; public housing; arts; highways; airports; mass transportation; and general revenue sharing.)

Every segment of the general economy is affected, to greater or lesser degree, by federal expenditures—which have been the equivalent in recent years of about a third of total personal income in the state. For example, federal outlays for construction directly affect the building trades and construction industry. Federal purchasing affects trade and manufacturing. Federal operations have direct financial impact on transportation, communication, utilities, finance, insurance, real estate, services, etc. And, of course, federal salaries and income payments filter throughout the entire economy.

State government finance. The budget for the State of Utah totaled about 1.7 billion dollars in fiscal year 1981-82. Revenue to cover this budget was received from a variety of sources, including general sales tax, income taxes, federal grants, motor fuel tax, unemployment tax, license taxes, fees and sales, and other revenue sources. In terms of relative importance, federal grants, income taxes, and sales tax were by far the largest income producers, accounting for nearly three-fourths of state government revenue.

State aid to public schools and state support of higher education are the largest expenditure categories in the state budget. Together they consume more than 40 per cent of the state revenue. Public welfare and highways also require large expenditures, amounting to about a fourth of the budget.

Local government finance. County and municipal governments as well as school districts and special districts, comprise this category. Total local government revenue in 1980 approximated a billion dollars and was received primarily from property tax, sales tax, miscellaneous charges and fees, or in the form of aid from state and federal government. The largest category was state aid for local schools, amounting to more than 300 million dollars. Property taxes contributed more than a fourth of all local revenue, and federal funds slightly less than one-tenth.

Local governments devote more than half their total budgets to education. In descending order of cost, other programs include police and fire protection, roads and streets, parks and recreation, and sewerage and sanitation. Among less costly programs are interest on debt, general control and administration, airports and transportation, corrections, buildings, libraries, and public welfare.

Other Economic Activities

This category of diversified economic activities includes Contract Construction; Finance, Insurance and Real Estate; Services and Miscellaneous. Together they employ about 170,000 workers, or nearly a third of all non-agricultural employees in the state.

Contract Construction

Contract construction is a major industry, and in formal economic comparisons it is shown as a separate industrial classification. In 1981 the industry employed an average of nearly 30,000 workers in three categories: Residential, Nonresidential, Public Works and Utilities. Salaries and wages of construction workers add a half-billion dollars or more each year to the state's personal income.

Current valuation of all construction in 1981 exceeded a billion dollars. For the previous ten years (1971-80) total construction value exceeded seven billion dollars in 1980 dollars, or four billion dollars in terms of inflation-corrected 1970 dollars.

More than 163,000 residential dwelling units were built in Utah during the years 1970-1980, the great majority of them single-family units. Residential construction reached its all-time peak in 1977, when about 23,000 dwelling units were built. Since that time residential building has declined every year, undergoing in 1981 what has been termed the "worst slump for the housing industry since the end of World War II." In this respect Utah resembles other states as the nation's housing industry has become the victim of inflated building costs and prohibitive interest rates. Among the results of this trend: the inability of people of middle or lower incomes to purchase single-family dwellings . . . a marked drop in mortgage loans and a rise in repossessions . . . concern over the solvency of many savings and loan associations . . . a stagnant real estate market with respect to houses . . . a high rate of home-builder mortality . . . and increased unemployment in the building crafts. Another result is the growing popularity of condominiums, in particular those units of moderate size and cost.

Nonresidential construction, including public works and utilities, ordinarily accounts for less than half of all construction value. In 1980, however, because of the decline in home-building, it surpassed residential construction for the first time in many years. Nonresidential construction totaled about 450 million dollars in 1981, the lowest total in four years. Of this, slightly more than 100 million dollars was for public works and utilities. (In this connection, it should be noted that the value of the 1980 dollar was less than half the comparable value of the 1970 dollar.)

A number of major nonresidential construction projects of the 1960s and 1970s are described in The Arts section (Architecture). At the risk of repeating, it is well to list here a few of the more noteworthy projects: Campuses at Brigham Young University, University of Utah, Utah State University, Weber State College, and other institutions of higher learning, as well as new public school buildings . . . downtown redevelopment in Salt Lake City and Ogden . . . new hospitals . . . new industrial and research parks . . . new terminals at the Salt Lake City International Airport . . . uranium mills in San Juan and Garfield counties . . . Martin-Marietta cement plant near Leamington . . . new hotels, Salt Palace and Bicentennial Arts Center in Salt Lake City . . . Kennecott smelter . . . new local, state, and federal government buildings, particularly in Salt Lake City.

Public works and utilities construction includes progress on the interstate highway system . . . the Central Utah water project . . . Great Salt Lake shore development . . . Emery County power generating plants (Utah Power and Light Company) . . . and construction now beginning on the Intermountain Power Project near Delta as well as the Deseret generating plant near Bonanza.

Governor Scott Matheson breaking ground for new construction, Great Salt Lake Marina.

DIVISION OF PARKS AND RECREATION

Bank at Milford about the turn-of-the-century.

Finance, Insurance and Real Estate

Nearly 30,000 people are employed in Utah's banking, credit, lending, financial, real estate, and insurance activities. These workers handle and, to greater or lesser degree, control a large portion of the funds generated by all other economic categories.

In 1980, in Utah, there were some 76 commercial banks (with more than 250 branches), 16 savings and loan associations, and a large number of mutual savings banks, credit unions, federal loan banks, consumer credit firms, securities and investment firms, insurance companies and agents, real estate firms and agents. Deposits of commercial banks amounted to four billion dollars in 1981 while savings deposits totaled another three billion dollars. Bank loans amounted to more than three billion dollars and bank assets approached seven billion dollars.

According to the 1941 edition, "the firm of Hooper, Eldridge, and Company, Utah's first financial house, opened its doors [in 1869] and matured two years later into the Bank of Deseret, with a capital of $100,000 and Brigham Young as president. Walker Brothers bank incorporated the next year, and within ten years the Territory had twelve private and five national banks with an aggregate exchange business between twelve and fifteen millions of dollars.'' Prior to the coming of the railroad, cash capital was scarce, as described in the 1941 edition and quoted on page 143 of this volume. A more detailed and comprehensive history of banking in the state can be found in *Atlas of Utah* (Weber State College/Brigham Young University 1981), to which interested readers are referred. Banking facilities were not regulated by the territory until 1888, after nearly 40 banks had opened and closed. Between 1888 and 1920 more than 200 banks were chartered, reorganized, or closed their doors. A banking depression between 1921 and 1933 caused a decline of 64 banks—more than half of the previous total. Legislation in the 1930s resulted in a growth of branch banking. The dramatic growth of bank assets, multiplying more than ten times between 1950 and 1980, must be attributed in part to devaluation of the dollar, though expansion of the economy and increased population are responsible to a more significant extent.

Formerly healthy and thriving, savings and loan associations have experienced serious adversities in recent years as the result of soaring housing costs and high interest rates, which have caused a decline in mortgage lending; occurring at the same time is a drastic outflow of savings into higher-yield investments.

The state's largest financial institution is First Security Corporation, which controls 13 banks (150 banking offices) and a number of subsidiary companies involved in mortgages, leasing, insurance, securities, etc. In 1981 the corporation claimed assets of more than four billion dollars and employed nearly 5,000 people. First Security Bank of Utah, NA, headquartered in Ogden, is the corporation's leading bank, and also the largest in Utah, with resources totaling nearly two billion dollars in 1980. First Security Bank is followed closely by Zions First National Bank (1.4 billion dollars). Others having resources of great magnitude are First Interstate Bank of Utah (formerly Walker Bank and Trust Company), Commercial Security Bank, Valley Bank and Trust Company, Continental Bank and Trust, and Tracy Collins Bank and Trust, all with resources in excess of 200 million dollars. The First Interstate banking system, whose name replaced that of Walker Bank and Trust in 1981, has 900 banking offices in 11 western states.

Individually or otherwise, Utahns in 1979 paid premiums on more than two million insurance policies, representing a face value of 17 billion dollars. Benefit payments amounted to 139 million dollars in 1979.

Services and Miscellaneous

Despite its "catch-all" nature, this economic category supports more than 100,000 employees, or one in every six non-agricultural workers in the state. Under this classification, for reporting purposes, are placed Medical and Health Services (25,000 employees), Personal and Business Services (24,000), Private Education (9,400), Hotels and Motels (7,000), Amusements (7,000), Membership Organizations (11,000), and Other (10,000 employees who provide repair, engineering, legal, architectural, and miscellaneous services).

Cultural Scene

Sports fans crowd the Marriott Center, Brigham Young University.

GARY TOM

Paiute Indians: Looking to a brighter future.

Population and Peoples

Utah's population in 1980 was 1,461,037, or 400,000 more than the population of 1970. This gain of 38 per cent was one of the highest percentage gains of any state, and the increase of 400,000 far exceeded that of any other ten-year period in the state's history. In fact, it almost equalled the state's total population of 1920. (In 1940, when the first edition of this volume was written, Utah's population numbered 550,310.) If the same *percentage* of gain were to continue through the 1980s, the state's population in 1990 would be about two million. This is not likely to happen, though it is conceivable. However, even if the gain of the 1970s (400,000) were added in each of the next two decades, Utah's population in 1990 will be about 1,900,000 and in 2000 it should approach 2,300,000. If this conservative increase does occur, Salt Lake Valley might realistically expect a population in the year 2000 of nearly a million inhabitants.

Readers interested in statistical trends and comparisons having to do with population and vital characteristics are referred to the *Atlas of Utah* (Weber State College/Brigham Young University 1981), which devotes many pages to an analysis of these factors. Only generalities can be discussed here.

As anyone familiar with Utah is aware, the bulk of the population resides along the Wasatch Front, that long, narrow oasis at the western base of the Wasatch Range. The most urbanized part of this oasis extends for about 110 miles, from Ogden (Weber Valley) on the north to Payson-Santaquin (Utah Valley) on the south, with Salt Lake Valley and the Davis strip between. Within this four-county area, in 1980, resided 1,129,000 people, or 77 per cent of the state's population. This percentage differed very little from that of 1970. Stated differently, 82 per cent of Utah's people lived within 60 miles of Salt Lake City in 1980.

The state's greatest gain in *numbers* between 1970 and 1980 came in this urban core. On the other hand, the largest *percentage* gains occurred in Emery (123%), Washington (91%), Summit (74%), Duchesne (72%), Kane (66%), and Uintah (62%) counties. All of these exceeded the urban front's fastest-growing county (Utah County, 58%) in percentage gain, though certainly not in absolute numbers. The decade of the 1970s was especially significant for rapid growth of the majority of rural counties, ten of which exceeded the state average in percentage rate of growth. With few exceptions, all areas of Utah have grown in population since 1940. Exceptions include Beaver, Garfield, Juab, Millard, Piute, Sanpete, and Wayne, all in the center of the state. Though increasing gradually in recent decades, those counties still remain below 1940 in population. Sevier County is the principal exception to that rule in central Utah, but it will soon be joined by Millard and possibly Sanpete.

The growth of rural counties during the 1970s was symptomatic of general demographic trends on a national level: for example, movement to less congested areas from city cores. In Utah it was also a result of economic developments within the state, as for example construction of large coal-fired power plants and accelerated coal mining in Emery County . . . development of hydrocarbon resources in Uintah and Duchesne counties . . . growth of the Park City recreation-residential complex in Summit County . . . and Washington County's in-migration of retirees and others attracted by its mild climate and scenery. Utah County's high rate of population increase is attributable in part to its phenomenal birth rate, which ranks highest in both the state and nation.

The state's ranking in total population rises slightly with each census. A larger share of Utah's people live in metropolitan areas than the people of most other states; at the same time, the density of population (people per square mile) in Utah's two metropolitan areas (Salt Lake City-Ogden and Provo-Orem) is among the lowest in the nation. As a state, Utah's population density is less than a third that of the nation as a whole, and only about eight states are less densely populated.

Characteristics of the population

Among numerous population characteristics which are measured statistically to enable comparison are: size of households, birth and death rates, marriage and divorce rates, age and sex characteristics, racial divisions, and *per capita* income. Income is discussed in the Economic Scene, and other categories can only be examined cursorily here. As suggested, interested readers are referred to the *Atlas of Utah* for detailed treatment of these topics.

Utah's population is distinctive in several respects. Children and youths under 18 comprise a larger part of the population, and those over 65 years of age account for a smaller proportion, than is the case with most other states. The median age in 1980 (24 years) compared with a national median of 30, ranking Utah lowest in this category.

Utah's birth rate is the highest in the nation (nearly twice the national average and 50 per cent higher than the world rate). It has retained this relative ranking among states, with slight variation, for decades. At the same time, its death rate has been among the lowest for decades. Utah ranks low among all states in incidence of deaths from heart disease, strokes, and certain cancers (lung, throat, mouth, and colon in particular).

The marriage rate in Utah has been higher than the national average since the last century, excepting only a few years between the late 1940s and early 1960s. The divorce rate also is greater than the national average, a relative position maintained by Utah nearly constantly since the 19th century. Both in Utah and the nation, the divorce rate has increased steadily over the years, being nearly six times greater in 1980 than it was in 1900 (Utah) and more than that in the nation as a whole. Utah's abortion rate is only a fourth or a fifth that of the nation as a whole. The median duration of marriage at time of divorce in Utah has hovered near five years for several decades, well below the national median of six and one-half to seven years. As many as half of all first-time marriages involve a teen-ager, and in

Days of '47 Parade, Salt Lake City.

certain rural counties this proportion may rise to more than 70 per cent. In Utah as nationally, the more youthful the age at marriage, the greater the chance of early divorce, and a significant proportion of teen-age brides are pregnant at the time of marriage.

Racial and ethnic characteristics

Utahns predominantly are of the white race. In 1980 about 94.5 per cent of the population appeared on the census as white, and much the greater part of these were of northern European-Yankee-southern white origin. The next largest racial group in 1980 was the Asian-Pacific Island group, which comprised about two per cent of the population, if the members of that group who were included in the "Other" category are considered. American Indians accounted for more than one per cent, while blacks were the smallest group of all with less than one per cent.

Foreign-born residents comprise only about one-tenth of the population, a much smaller part, comparatively, than the national average. This was not always the case, of course: a hundred years ago as many as a third of Utah's people were of foreign birth. Mormon converts of earlier territorial days came primarily from the eastern United States and Canada, Great Britain, and Scandinavian countries, joined later by converts from German-speaking countries, Switzerland, and the Netherlands. Jews arrived in the 1850s, growing in numbers as circumstances permitted. After 1869 the development of mining and railroads encouraged the influx of non-Mormon immigrants of Irish, Chinese, Italian, and Mexican-Mexican American origin, all of whom were in the state before statehood. The years from 1880 to 1920 in particular witnessed the arrival of thousands of non-Mormon immigrants from Italy, Japan, Greece, Yugoslavia, Mexico, and the Middle East, who found work on the railroads, in the coal mines of Carbon County, and in the mines and mills of Salt Lake and Tooele counties. This type of work, for many, was only a step toward other occupations in business, agriculture, the professions, etc. *The Peoples of Utah*

(Utah State Historical Society, 1976) is the most comprehensive treatment of this subject. Immigration laws after World War I diminished the flow of migration if they did not stop it, but new residents from other parts of the world continue to arrive in Utah, to study at universities or to establish themselves permanently.

Residents of Spanish-speaking origin numbered at least 60,000 in 1980. The majority of these were of Mexican or Mexican-American background, commonly known as Chicanos. Salt Lake County was the residence for half of this group in 1980, with the major part of the remainder in other urban counties. American Indians numbered 19,256 in 1980. More than a fourth of these (5,600) resided in San Juan County and 4,324 in Salt Lake County. Other concentrations were found in Box Elder (1,294), Uintah (1,952), and Utah (1,879). Navajos and Utes are the state's largest Indian groups.

Blacks numbered only 9,225 in 1980, or .06 per cent of the total population. Very few states have a smaller proportion of blacks in their population than Utah; the national average is about 12 per cent. Blacks were among the earliest settlers of Utah and have been represented in the population since 1847. However, their numbers were always small until World War II opened greater employment opportunities. Of minority groups, their numbers are increasing at the slowest rate, hardly exceeding the state average during the 1970s. More than 90 per cent of blacks reside in Davis, Salt Lake and Weber counties, where the majority of black wage-earners are employed by the federal government.

Throughout the nation and the world, minorities have special problems. Prejudice takes many forms, and in Utah it has not always been of a religious or ethnic nature. Ethnic minorities in particular have been confined to certain types of work . . . have been restricted in inter-racial, inter-cultural, and inter-denominational social relationships, including marriage . . . have been subjected to inferior education, health care, housing, and economic opportunities . . . and have had little or no direct representation in governmental decision-making processes. These problems and others have confronted ethnic minorities in Utah, in greater or lesser degree, since they first arrived. While certain problems have been ameliorated, others have shown scant improvement. Chicanos still point to unequal or deficient educational and economic opportunities, and their confinement to areas of inferior housing. The same complaints are voiced by blacks, Indians, and many of Asian origin. Only a few representatives of minority ethnic groups serve on police forces, as judges, on school boards, in the legislature, or in other important governmental positions. A survey of blacks in Salt Lake County, conducted in 1976, revealed that the majority felt a high level of social isolation, were less satisfied with life as a whole than whites, believed that they were discriminated against in employment, and felt that the Mormon Church had a negative influence on economic, social and political opportunities for blacks in Salt Lake City. The same survey showed that the median household income for blacks was much less than that for whites, and that the black rate of unemployment was double that for whites. It is likely that similar surveys for Indians, Chicanos, and certain Asian minority groups would have comparable results in many of the categories studied in the survey of blacks.

Religion

While it should not be asserted as a generalization that religion has been the dominant factor in the overall history of Utah since 1847, or even that it is a dominating influence in the everyday lives of the majority of its people today, it seems reasonable to claim that religion was the most important influence on the state's history during the 19th century, and that this influence permeates today's society in subtle and not-so-subtle ways.

Only on superficial levels are the manifold influences of religion apparent to the eye and capable of being measured, as for example in the extent of church membership, attendance at services, and the number of church buildings in a community. Based on those indices alone, Utahns are surely the most religious people in the nation. According to the *Atlas of Utah* (Weber State College/Brigham Young University 1981), a 1973 survey indicated that more than 80 per cent of the state's residents were members of a religious organization—a higher proportion than existed in any other state, and far above the national average of 50 per cent. It is hardly necessary to add that the majority of these church members were Mormons, adherents of the Church of Jesus Christ of Latter-day Saints. The survey did not, of course, measure the degree of faith among church members and the influence of religion upon their behavior.

Religion was part of life for Utah's native residents long before arrival of white settlers. This is evidenced, in the case of prehistoric Pueblo Indians, by kivas, artifacts, and rock art that apparently were ceremonial in nature. Indians of later ages had religious beliefs which were noted in print by whites. Some of these are described sketchily on page 53, and interested readers may supplement that summary with numerous in-depth studies.

Christianity came to the Utah region in 1776 with the Franciscan friars Dominguez and Escalante *(see History),* but their religious influence was slight or nil, as was that of explorers, trappers, traders, and emigrants who immediately preceded the Mormon settlers of 1847. Mormon settlement was a religious movement, and colonization of Utah during the succeeding 20 or 25 years, with hardly an exception, was an extension of that movement. While attempts to convert Mormons from their faith began as early as the 1870s, their numbers have been lessened to a far greater degree by apostasy and discontent within church ranks than by proselyting of other faiths, while natural increase and missionary labors have expanded Mormon membership rolls far beyond the numbers of the 19th century.

Other denominations paid little attention to Utah during the first two decades after 1847 because so few non-Mormons resided in the territory. Catholic priests officiated at Camp Floyd and Camp Douglas in early years, but their activities did not extend to the general population. Jewish businessmen arrived in the 1850s but offered no religious threat to the prevailing church; and this was the case as well with transients and settlers of other faiths during early decades. Not until the transcontinental railroad was completed at Promontory in 1869, mining development commenced in earnest, and Corinne began its brief career as a non-Mormon nucleus did the number of Gentiles in the territory encourage other denominations to support pastors, missionaries, and teachers in Utah. Mormons always maintained a numerical superiority, despite the arrival of thousands of non-Mormons in the 1870s and 1880s as the Utah economy evolved from its traditional orientation toward agriculture into an economy of more diversified facets.

It may be assumed that most non-Mormons in early-day Utah were religiously unaffiliated or inactive, because records of non-Mormon churches do not indicate great numbers of members/communicants during those years. Nevertheless, non-Mormon denominations did become active, beginning essentially in 1869. From approximately 1,000 in 1870, non-Mormon church membership increased steadily to some 100,000 in 1971, the latest year for which reliable figures are available. During that same period membership of the Mormon Church in Utah increased from approximately 85,000 to 789,000. The decade since 1971, of course, has increased both categories. According to the Mormon Church, its membership in Utah at the end of 1980 totaled 985,000, or 69 per cent of the state's population. This proportion was slightly less than the 72 per cent of 1971.

Active antagonism did not prevail between all non-Mormon denominational groups and Mormons. Roman Catholics, though they were among the first non-Mormons to arrive in Utah, devoted little effort to proselyting, concentrating instead on serving the spiritual needs of Catholics and establishing a system of schools, hospitals, and an orphanage. The Episcopal Church devoted most of its means and efforts to churches, schools, hospitals, and missions, though at times it was more active than the Catholic Church in attempting to convert Mormons. The Jews have been a nonproselyting group.

In a chapter entitled "The Churches in the Territory," appearing in the volume *Utah's History* (Brigham Young University, 1978), T. Edgar Lyon and Glen M. Leonard stated the following:

> The Presbyterians, Methodists, Congregationalists, Baptists, Lutherans, and members of the Church of Christ were the chief evangelical Christian bodies that operated in Utah during its territorial period. . . . The evangelical groups entered Utah to organize missions directed toward converting the "deluded" Mormons from what they sincerely believed to be a non-Christian religion. They soon discovered, however, that conversion of adult Mormons was almost impossible, for most of the Mormons had previously been converted from the evangelical Christian denominations. . . .

> It was obvious to the evangelical churches that the "Mormon Problem" must be attacked in another manner. Given the character of Utah's common schools, the children might be saved by providing a true Christian education for the Mormon youth, fewer than one-half of whom were enrolled in and were irregularly attending schools which might be operating for as few as three months a year. If free schools were established with a nine-month course of study and with certified denominational teachers from outside Utah, the evangelical church members thought that the more intelligent Mormon youth would flock to their classes. Along with the

standard curriculum, biblical, moral, and Christian education would be provided. . . .

With this conviction, the evangelical churches turned to schools as their primary mission tool. By the time most of the mission schools closed near the end of the century, the sponsors claimed a cumulative total of more than 50,000 Mormon enrollments.

The momentum behind early evangelical efforts was maintained into the 1890s by nationwide anti-Mormon, anti-polygamy fervor, which gradually waned as the polygamy issue subsided, as the need for church schools was negated by the establishment of public schools, as it became clear that missionary success did not justify the costs, and by the attainment of statehood. As described by Lyon and Leonard:

For the evangelical Protestant churches the years from 1890 to 1910 were . . . a period of contracting activity. . . . The smaller schools were abandoned and with them the small churches and preaching stations were closed. . . .

The evangelical churches manifested a continuing determination to fight the Mormon Church in the period following statehood. Their Utah leadership was instrumental in the successful fight against seating B. H. Roberts in the United States House of Representatives and in the unsuccessful effort to keep Reed Smoot out of the United States Senate.

In terms of service to their own membership, these Protestant churches were going through a transition period from denominational rivalry to a shared solution. Earlier attempts had been made to produce cooperation among them, but as the century opened they were still trying to maintain three and four competitive congregations in small Mormon towns where the combined gentile population wasn't enough to effectively support even one Protestant church. Not until 1915 did these Utah churches form the Home Missions Council to sponsor the community church concept. This technique has enabled the evangelical churches to maintain congregations in many of the small Utah towns that they could not have served by competing for members.

At the close of the period under discussion [1896] some noticeable changes had taken place in the religious climate of Utah. . . . In contrast to the situation a half century earlier . . . [non-Mormon churches] were firmly grounded, some having become self-supporting and no longer mere missions of their respective national organizations. Their members were actively participating in the social, economic, political, and religious life of their communities. They were to be found cooperating with the Mormons in civic endeavors, moral problems, and community projects.

Roman Catholic Church

Roman Catholics in Utah totaled about 50,000 in 1971, a figure that exceeded the combined total for all other non-Mormon denominations in the state. As noted, Catholics came to Utah with the Dominguez-Escalante expedition of 1776 but did not return in a religious guise until 1859, when a Catholic priest served the spiritual needs of Irish and German troops at Camp Floyd. Another priest came to Camp Douglas in 1864, followed a year later by Father Edward Kelly, who celebrated the first Christmas mass in Salt Lake City in 1866. Prior to 1869, when the ceremony at Promontory ended the pioneer era in Utah, it is recorded that "Catholics in Utah were transient and poor," and not very numerous. Activities of the Catholic Church began in earnest at Corinne in 1869-70, as did those of several other denominations. Corinne, being the Gentile capital, was a base from which non-Mormon churches probed outward, gaining footholds in other places before eventually abandoning Corinne as it declined.

St. Mary Magdalene, the first Catholic church in Utah, was built in 1871 in Salt Lake City. St. Mary's Academy—the "largest and most elegant educational establishment in the Territory"—opened in 1875, its studentbody consisting largely of Mormons and other non-Catholics. The history of Catholicism in Utah has been marked by the opening of numerous schools, among them the Sacred Heart Academy in Ogden (1878-1938), St. Joseph's High School in Ogden, All Hallows College for young men (1885-1918), Judge Memorial High School, St. Mary's Academy and College, Cathedral School, Bishop Glass School, Cosgriff Memorial School, St. Olaf's School, and schools in Price, Park City, Tintic, etc. (A number of these schools have closed during intervening years.) The church also is noted for its establishment and support, among other philanthropies, of Holy Cross Hospital, an early hospital at Silver Reef, and St. Ann's Orphanage in Salt Lake City. Newman student centers at University of Utah and Utah State University promote Catholic activities. *See Cathedral of the Madeleine, Tour No. 3.*

Episcopal Chuch

Numbering almost 7,000 in 1971, Episcopalians are one of the largest non-Mormon church groups in Utah, and also one of the oldest. The first non-Mormon church building was erected by Episcopalians at Corinne in 1869, and one of the most venerable religious edifices in the state—St. Mark's Cathedral in Salt Lake City—was erected in 1870-71. While the Episcopal Church has actively proselyted in Utah, it has been more active in establishing schools, churches, St. Mark's Hospital (1872), and Mount Olivet Cemetery (1877). Individually and as a religious body, Episcopalians have been seriously concerned with community affairs and social problems. St. Mark's School for boys was established in 1869 and Rowland Hall School for girls in 1881; these schools, now combined and still operating, earned an enviable reputation over the years. Episcopal churches have functioned, at one time or another, in Salt Lake City, Ogden, Provo, Springville, Eureka, Park City, Vernal, Moab, and other places. Since the 1950s new missions have been established in Price, Moab, Brigham City, Clearfield, Holladay, Bountiful, Tooele, etc. The church was particularly active with missionary work on the Ute reservation around the turn of the century, and since the early 1940s has supported the Episcopal Mission at Bluff founded by the Reverend H. Baxter Liebler. The church has also supported student residences near universities and academies, though most of its day schools were closed by the 1890s as public schools developed.

Presbyterian Church

As noted above by Lyon and Leonard, the Presbyterians were numbered among the Evangelical Christian churches which placed early emphasis on converting Mormons through an extensive system of mission schools. They "began their first missionary work in Utah in 1869 at Corinne," wrote Lyon and Leonard. "Two years later a church was established in Salt Lake City. By the close of the territorial period, twenty-five years later, twelve churches and forty-nine schools had been in operation in Utah, although not all of them had functioned at the same time. As many as sixty-five imported teachers and nineteen missionary-ministers had worked in the Presbyterian missions among the Mormons at one time. More than a million dollars had been invested in their educational-missionary effort."

Presbyterians numbered 6,563 in 1971, ranking as one of the four largest non-Mormon church groups in the state. According to the *Atlas of Utah,* almost 80 per cent are concentrated in Salt Lake and Weber counties. Westminster College in Salt Lake City and Wasatch Academy in Mount Pleasant have received the church's support since their founding.

Baptist Churches

The American and Southern Baptist conventions (11,100 members in 1971) together rank as the third largest church group in Utah, behind the Mormon and Roman Catholic churches, and also as the largest Protestant group in the nation. First organized in 1881 in Ogden, and claiming a comparatively small membership in the territory and state during the 1880s and 1890s, the Baptists were maintaining four schools and nine churches by 1896. In 1971 they were widely dispersed around the state in 24 of the 29 counties.

Methodist Church

Methodists were among the most active of the missionary-education groups in territorial days, beginning their activities in Corinne in 1869. In the mid-1890s they reported 26 schools and 41 churches or preaching stations, and a membership of 1,440. By 1971 their numbers had grown to 6,000, with most residing along the Wasatch Front.

Congregational Church

Though numbering only 635 in 1971, in Utah, the Congregationalists were active evangelists during territorial years, joining other Protestant groups in establishing mission schools. At the height of this effort 28 schools and 48 teachers "were serving the missionary effort," according to the *Atlas of Utah.* "About fifteen congregations had been established, presided over by ten pastors in 1893. Expenditures were in excess of $625,000."

Other religious groups

Those religious groups described above were the most active and influential in pre-statehood days. Since that time organized religion has had a declining influence on the temporal fortunes of the state, at least overtly. It must be admitted, of course, that *individuals* of different religious or non-religious persuasions have had incalculable influence on the state's affairs, as have organized bodies exercising collective power through individual members. In this regard, minority religious groups such as the Greek Orthodox Church and Jewish bodies certainly have been influential in non-religious affairs because of the civic and business prominence of many of their adherents. Utah hardly differs from other parts of the nation, or the world, in this respect. Two dozen denominations were listed in the *Atlas of Utah* (Religion chapter). These included most of the leading Christian denominations of the United States. In addition to those the state certainly numbers among its people adherents of numerous other churches, cults, and religious beliefs, including Buddhists, Hindus, Moslems, native Americans, and adherents of various modern esoteric religious movements.

THE MORMON CHURCH (Church of Jesus Christ of Latter-day Saints)

Mormon influences on Utah are noted throughout this volume. Utah has been known as the Mormon stronghold for more than 130 years, and in fact Mormonism and Utah are virtually synonymous for millions of people. This commonly accepted equivalence is a cause of distress for many non-Mormons in Utah. Yet the widespread acceptance of that concept is understandable, since Utah was settled by Mormons, the greater part of its people have retained membership ties with the Mormon Church since 1847, and church headquarters are in Salt Lake City. As Rome is connected in the world mind with Roman Catholicism, Mecca and Medina with Islam, and Jerusalem with Judaism and Christianity, so Utah and Salt Lake City represent Mormonism in the minds of millions.

This is not to suggest, of course, that Mormonism compares on a scale of magnitude or antiquity with those great religious movements, for in age it is very youthful and its adherents barely number five million. Yet it is said to be the only denomination born on American soil that has developed into a world church, and its message is preached in more than 40 languages and 80 nations by more than 30,000 full-time missionaries. In United States membership it ranks among the 12 largest religious bodies in the country.

About seven in ten Utahns claim membership in the Mormon Church; however, fewer than one in five Mormons reside in Utah. Mormonism has become an international faith, and nearly half of all Mormons are citizens of countries outside the United States.

Only rarely does the Mormon Church exert its influence overtly in matters of governmental or social policies affecting the citizenry at large. Occasionally it will let its official position be known in behalf of, or in opposition to, a policy on which its leadership feels strongly, as in the matter of supporting the nation's war effort, in opposition to basing the MX missile system in Utah and Nevada, in opposition to the Equal Rights Amendment and government support of abortion, and other matters. Official church stands are avoided on most public matters within the state, and in fact are seldom required because Mormons, by their very numbers, exercise considerable power at all levels of governmental decision making and are individually familiar with hierarchic opinion.

The geographical distribution of Mormons in Utah and the United States is discussed and graphically illustrated in *Atlas of Utah.* The terms culture region, core, domain, sphere, and emerging Mormon centers are used there to denote Mormon influence as measured by population density and intensity of ecclesiastical organization. It is not surprising to Utahns and westerners that the Mormon culture region embraces not only Utah but parts of contiguous states on all sides, as well as sizable Mormon clusters in a number of other western states. The Mormon *core* extends along the Wasatch Front from Logan-Brigham City on the north to Utah Valley in the south. The Mormon *domain,* which differs from the core primarily in having less density of population, encompasses almost the entire State of Utah and about a third of the State of Idaho, as well as the borders of surrounding states. The Mormon *sphere* is somewhat more encompassing, extending northward from Utah-Idaho in a narrow band into Oregon and

Washington, and from Utah-Colorado southward into Arizona and New Mexico. *Emerging Mormon centers* are concentrated in California, Oregon and Washington, but there are numerous other centers around the country. In round numbers in 1980 there were 985,000 Mormons in Utah, 405,000 in California, 240,000 in Idaho, 138,000 in Arizona, 105,000 in Washington, and 74,000 in Oregon. In the nation as a whole, there were nearly three million members of the church.

Mormon Doctrine

Mormon doctrine is based on the Bible, the Book of Mormon, the *Doctrine and Covenants,* and the *Pearl of Great Price.* The Book of Mormon is chiefly a history of ancient peoples. The *Doctrine and Covenants* is a compilation of the revelations received by Joseph Smith and others. These revelations laid down one by one nearly every article of faith and creed that the Mormons live by. The *Articles of Faith,* a condensation of Mormon gospel which Joseph wrote in answer to a request from a gentile, give Mormonism in a nutshell. Abridged, they are as follows: Mormons believe in God, in Jesus, and in the Holy Ghost; they believe that man will be punished for his own sins and not for Adam's; that mankind can be saved through the atonement of Christ and by obedience to the gospel. The gospel includes . . . a belief in repentance, in baptism, and in the laying on of hands for the gift of the Holy Ghost. Mormons believe in the same organization that existed in the "primitive church": namely, in apostles, prophets, pastors, etc.; they believe in the gift of tongues, in prophecy, spiritual healing, visions; they believe the Bible to be (so far as it is translated correctly) the word of God, and the Book of Mormon also; they believe in the literal gathering of Israel, in the restoration of the Ten Tribes, in the building of Zion upon this continent, and in the reigning of Jesus personally upon this planet for a thousand years. Perhaps their most famous article of faith is the thirteenth: "We believe in being honest, true, chaste, benevolent, virtuous, and in doing good to all men; indeed we may say that we follow the admonition of Paul: 'We believe all things, we hope all things,' we have endured many things, and hope to be able to endure all things. If there is anything virtuous, lovely, or of good report or praiseworthy we seek after these things." The *Pearl of Great Price,* purporting to be a translation of certain writings of Moses and Abraham, is a practical day-by-day guide to healthful and righteous living.

On the whole, Mormon doctrine is simple and practical. It believes in baptism by complete immersion for the remission of sins; in righteousness, which under some of the leaders approached the sternness and self-denial taught by the famous New England divines; in serious contemplation of this life as a preparation for the next; and . . . in the holiness of the human body as an instrument created and endowed by God. It was this reverence for the human body that produced the "Word of Wisdom"—those stern prohibitions against the use of alcohol, tea, coffee, tobacco, and all foods, beverages and habits which impair efficiency and health. For the gentile—a word used by Mormons to designate non-Mormons—nothing in Mormonism is more striking than the emphasis placed on health, and on the saint's duty to keep his body and mind healthy and clean. In Mormonism cleanliness has always been and still is next to godliness—and when their doctrine speaks of cleanliness, it means inside and outside. . . .

Children are christened in the Church when a few weeks old; at the age of eight the child is baptized, and is usually confirmed as a member the next day. At the age of twelve boys enter the [Aaronic] priesthood—but priesthood in Mormonism does not mean what it means in other churches. The highest members in Mormonism are not distinguished by official robes or gowns; it is a democratic church in this, that even the humblest [male] lay member has the privilege of priesthood, and in dress is indistinguishable from his apostles and prophet.

The priesthood is an avenue of spiritual authority, with many temporal obligations. The Aaronic Priesthood, embracing deacons, teachers, and priests, is concerned chiefly with temporal welfare. The Melchizedek Priesthood, embracing elders, seventies, and high priests, is concerned chiefly with spiritual welfare. The temporal and the spiritual, however, are closely integrated and mutually supporting. . . . [At approximately age] 19 a man is eligible to the Melchizedek Priesthood in which the younger members give unction to the sick, or baptize converts and the young; serve as missionaries; ordain officeholders in the lower priesthood; and anoint ill persons with consecrated oil. Certain groups of male adults are known as "seventies" or as "minute men": they serve in the mission field and teach the gospel at home and abroad. Thus, deacons become teachers, teachers become priests, priests become elders, elders become members of the seventies, and the seventies advance to high priests. Women never hold a priesthood, but share in the blessings of priesthood with their husbands.

1941 edition

While the excerpt above is an excellent summary of many church beliefs, it omits mention of some of the principal teachings and practices that led other Christian churches to oppose Mormonism as an anti-Christian system. Among these is the concept of eternal marriage, which includes plural marriage. When practised, plural marriage resulted in prosecution, persecution, and widespread unfavorable publicity. The Mormon practice of building temples where they perform sacred ordinances for both the living and the dead was not mentioned, even though it is a most important aspect of Mormon religious life. Mormon emphasis on genealogical research is a concomitant of temples, for it is necessary to identify the deceased by name, family relationship, and vital data before proxy ordinances can be performed in temples. *(See Tour No. 3 for detailed discussion of genealogical program.)*

Lack of detail in the Articles of Faith tends to make Mormon doctrine resemble the doctrines of other Christian churches more than it does in reality. Few Christians would disagree with the first article, which simply states that "We believe in God, the Eternal Father; and in His Son, Jesus Christ; and in the Holy Ghost." That bare statement does not reveal the Mormon belief that God is a resurrected, glorified man, who once was in a state similar to that of imperfect mortal men, and that men can progress to become as God is now. There are other differences, as with regard to continuing revelation, the mission of Jesus the Christ, the nature of the Holy Ghost, interpretations of scripture, and many other basic beliefs.

Church Organization

Ecclesiastical organization. The church is presided over by a group of men known as the General Authorities. At the top is the President and two counselors, who form a quorum known as the First Presidency. The President is considered to be God's representative on earth. He is chosen by the Quorum of the Twelve Apostles, who have always selected as President the senior member of the Quorum who has served longest without interruption. This Quorum is equal to the First Presidency in authority and is assisted in its world-wide duties by the First Quorum of Seventy, comprised of a Presidency and numerous members. In charge of temporal affairs is the three-member Presiding Bishopric.

Assisting this top echelon of authorities with supervision and administration of church organization are more than 200 regional representatives, a large headquarters staff, hundreds of mission officials, several thousand officials of stakes, and many thousands of ward officials (bishops, counselors, clerks, etc.). By far the greater number of ecclesiastical officials are laymen who work without remuneration; full-time authorities and staff workers, of course, are paid. Many women are involved in women's organizations, as staff workers, and as missionaries, but inasmuch as they do not bear the priesthood they do not hold ecclesiastical positions.

The basic, grassroots division of membership organization is the ward and branch, which correspond roughly to congregations or parishes in other Christian churches. Wards may consist of from 100 to 500 members, and when they become too large they are divided. Several wards comprise a stake. In 1980 there were some 1,200 stakes and about 9,500 wards or independent branches throughout the church. Where membership is not concentrated enough to form stakes and wards, members are organized into missions and branches. In 1980 there were nearly 200 missions and more than 2,000 mission branches in the church.

Mormons consider Sunday to be a holy day and members are urged to confine Sunday activities to church meetings, devotion, and family togetherness. Recreation in the popular sense is not deemed appropriate as a Sunday activity. Needless to say, that is an ideal not always observed. Prior to 1980 good Mormons were said to be the most "meetinged" church people in the world, with willing members attending three or four meetings on Sundays and others during the week. A new schedule inaugurated in 1980 consolidated the majority of meetings into a three-hour time block on Sunday. However, good members also involve themselves in scout work, laboring on church farms and welfare projects, performing visiting and teaching assignments, and otherwise keeping occupied with church duties. Good and faithful members pay a tithing of ten per cent of their increase, usually interpreted as gross income, plus additional contributions for the poor (fast offerings), ward or branch budget, construction costs of temples and other church buildings, missionary contributions, and special assessments.

Administrative organization. Prior to World War II, Mormons took pride in the assertion that the church's administrative-membership infrastructure was equal in efficiency to that of the German military machine. While that comparison is no longer appreciated, church efficiency certainly has not declined. Mormons are said to be the most efficient record keepers in history, and a large bureaucracy is the result. An immense building program requires a large staff of architects, draftsmen, purchasing agents, and traveling supervisors. The missionary program involves not only missionaries but a host of travel agents, language teachers, public relations and audiovisual specialists, mission personnel, and administrators. Commercial and welfare enterprises employ thousands of workers. Church publications require editors, writers, photographers, artists, and printers. The Genealogical and Historical departments employ hundreds of catalogers, buyers, microfilm technicians, and attendants. A vast system of schools and seminaries is staffed by thousands of teachers. All these activities require the services of a large legal staff. In short, activities of the Mormon Church undoubtedly represent the largest non-commercial, non-government industry in the state.

Church Programs

While all church programs cannot be described, mention should be made of temples, education, welfare, and the phenomenal missionary program. The church's genealogical program is described in Tour No. 3, as is Temple Square, and the Tabernacle Choir is discussed under The Arts (Music). Church contributions to painting, sculpture, music, theater, and dance also are discussed in The Arts section. Utah temples and other Mormon points of interest are described in the tour section.

Temples. Temples are used for sacred ordinances and are open only to Mormons in good standing. Ordinances performed in Mormon temples include marriages for the living and the dead and baptisms on behalf of the dead. In 1982 there were 21 operating temples: seven in Utah, seven in other states, and seven in other countries. Seven additional temples were under construction.

Education. The Mormon Church educational system operates in nearly 60 countries. In addition to Brigham Young University in Provo *(see Tour No. 5),* Ricks College in Idaho, BYU's Hawaii campus, and LDS Business College in Salt Lake City, the church supports numerous seminaries and institutes of religion—which offer religious education to high school and college-university students—as well as schools in more than a dozen foreign countries. Educational materials are available in 20 languages. Special education, including literacy training and continuing education courses, is made available to church members.

Welfare services. The church welfare program provides job placement assistance, emergency subsistence help, food and commodity production on church farms and in bishops storehouses. A social services program assists members in the amelioration of social and emotional problems, and welfare missionaries are dispatched to help improve health and agricultural practices among members in developing countries. The Deseret Industries thrift-store program, which refurbishes and sells used items, provides employment for many elderly and handicapped members.

Missionary program. The Mormon missionary system has been functioning since the beginning of the church in 1830, with elders being sent out in twos with a commission to "call the world to repentance," to baptize by immersion in the name of Jesus Christ, to confirm members, to bestow the gift of the Holy Ghost, and to heal through faith. In early years they traveled without purse or script, being dependent upon local generosity for food, clothing, and shelter. Today, missionaries and their families bear the greater part of missionary expense. Every member is expected to be a missionary, whether at home or abroad, and young people in particular are urged to spend two years or more as missionaries in any part of the world to which they might be assigned. Predominantly a program for young men, beginning at age 19, about 20 per cent of the missionary force now is made up of young women and increasingly of retired persons. At present the

Mormon missionary program involves more than 30,000 full-time missionaries who serve in some 80 countries, teaching in nearly 50 languages. Mormon works are translated into 15 new languages every year, and a million copies of the Book of Mormon are distributed each year. Missionaries in recent decades have had considerable success in Mexico, Central America, and South America, where membership now totals about 600,000. Though conversions in Great Britain and continental Europe have slowed, missionary efforts in Asia, particularly Korea and the Philippines, are meeting with success. As many as 200,000 new converts have been baptized into the church in each of several recent years.

Mormon missionary work is not all of the door-to-door, street corner variety. Temple Square in Salt Lake City is a mission, and historic sites such as Nauvoo attract investigators. Broadcasts of Mormon conferences are directed as much to non-Mormons as to Mormons, and broadcasts and concerts of the Tabernacle Choir are effective missionary activities. The church obtains names of prospective investigators from sources such as world fair exhibits, advertisements in national publications *(e.g. Readers Digest),* referrals, and literature distribution. A professional public relations staff complements the missionary effort.

Changes and challenges

The church observed its sesquicentennial (150th anniversary) in 1980. Could Mormon pioneers of 1847 observe their church today, they would note profound differences—not too many changes in scriptural doctrine but certainly important modifications in doctrinal emphasis and dramatic transformation in other respects. Polygamy, of course, was officially abandoned in 1890, and the long-standing prohibition against holding of the priesthood by blacks was removed in June 1978. This event was crucial to Mormonism becoming a universal church. Apostasy and schism, significant problems of the 19th century, perhaps are not as bothersome today as apathy and inactivity among members, or as serious as differences of opinion concerning women's rights, abortion, family size and birth control, liquor by the drink, the authenticity of certain scriptural and historical claims, and other controversial matters. A degree of resentment of hierarchical authority is present today as it has been since church beginnings. Also, certainly, the Mormon Church is beset by the same adaptational dilemmas and difficulties that perplex all religious bodies whose codes of belief and conduct—based on more or less rigid ethical and moral foundations—conflict with widespread attitudes and customs of the matrix society. Urbanization, industrialization, racial intermingling, heresy versus orthodoxy, liberalism versus conservatism, loosening of behavioral standards, the decline of belief in God, the weakening of family ties—all of these are causes of church concern and the subject of exhortation.

Mention should also be made of the organizational adaptations and doctrinal stresses engendered by the church's phenomenal growth and emergence as an international denomination. These stresses are certain to modify Mormonism as it changes from a staid religious body preoccupied with its American-European origins and sphere of influence into a universal religion with evolving doctrinal emphases.

Class and teacher, Molen School, Emery County 1907 *(left)*.

School activity in Scofield about 1900 *(below). G. E. Anderson photo courtesy Brigham Young University Library.*

Education

Utahns have long prided themselves for possessing one of the best educational systems in the nation. They point to the high ratio of students as compared with population . . . pupil achievement on comparative tests . . . the number of high school and college graduates . . . and so on. There is reason for self-congratulation. Utah's educational attainments *are* enviable, and there is no question that the state's taxpayers contribute a greater share of their personal income to the support of public education than those of most other states. While giving due credit, however, it must be stated that Utah's public education system faces problems of great seriousness and is being criticized for alleged deficiencies. Lavor Chaffin, who retired from the *Deseret News* in 1981 after 30 years as education writer and education editor of that paper, summed up his impressions as follows:

> How good is Utah education? How does it measure up when compared with schools in other states and around the world? After 30 years of observation and several changes of attitude on the question, I believe Utah education is better than the people of Utah realistically should expect, but that it is not nearly as good as it ought to be. . . . Utah and the United States face a new challenge that is certain to change the role of the schools. . . . spectacular changes in transportation and communication have created a worldwide community. The children we educate in Utah now must not only be able to compete with students in the next state and across the nation, but with those around the world as well.

Historical Background

A peaked military tent was Utah's first schoolhouse, and Mary J. Dilworth, 17, a Mormon of Quaker descent, the first teacher of a day school that opened in October, 1847, some three months after the vanguard of Mormon emigrants pitched camp in Salt Lake Valley. She had thirty scholars of assorted ages, a Noah Webster speller, half a dozen Lindly Murray readers, one arithmetic book, and a Bible. The following spring, Hannah Holbrook opened a similar school somewhere near the site of Bountiful, and though they are but indifferently recorded, other schools appeared in almost all of the settlements during the next two years. They seem to have been run on a haphazard basis, whenever the exigencies of plowing, weather, and house building would permit. . . .

In 1850, the *Deseret News* announced with considerable pride that "Elder Woodruff has arrived with two tons of school books," and in the same year the legislative assembly of the Provisional State of Deseret empowered the city councils of the already numerous Mormon settlements to "establish, support, and regulate" common schools. This law, ratified without change by the Territorial legislature, seems to have been tentatively aimed at a free school system supported by local tax levies, and many villages did, in the first flush of civic pride, attempt to support their schools wholly by tax. Ogden, for example, voted such a tax, but the assessor and collector reported at the end of 1852 that the city had been unable to collect the money, "owing to the scarcity of it." Other communities found themselves in the same predicament, and, for a time at least, the public school system of Utah was forced to operate on a tuition basis. It was not until 1866 that the first free school was established at American Fork. The villagers in most cases had no more money for tuitions than for taxes, and early teachers were more accustomed to trundle wages home in barrows than to carry them in their pockets. Nevertheless, a schoolhouse was usually among the first considerations of new communities, and the legislature passed compulsory attendance laws as early as 1852. Minor apprentices must be sent to school at least three months out of the year, and this was also the case for indentured Indians between the ages of seven and sixteen.

The legislature of 1850 passed also an ordinance incorporating the "University of Deseret," and placed control of it in the hands of a chancellor and board of twelve regents. . . . This paragon of universities opened in the parlor of John Pack's adobe cabin, November, 1850, under the name of Parent School. The *Deseret News* for the same month said that the object of the school was "to qualify teachers for the district or ward schools." . . . The legislature of 1851 appropriated $5,000 for the university—from an empty treasury—hopefully memorialized Congress for a like sum in 1854, and became discouraged. The Parent School was abandoned in 1855, and the university was suffered to lapse into nominal existence until 1867.

Common schools (which loosely comprised the grammar grades) were more fortunate. By 1854, there were 226 of them in Utah Territory, about 13,000 scholars, and three hundred-odd teachers, not a few of whom were of the Ichabod Crane stamp. The *Deseret News* (still championing the cause of education) in that year observed that it was "high time to turn a little attention, and means toward hiring good teachers at fair salaries and prompt pay." . . .

In outlying regions, school seldom "kept" more than six months of the year, and three months would probably come closer to the average. During the first three decades after settlement of Utah, the city council of many a town went on record as being unalterably opposed to "female" teachers. One Mr. Chadwick, pioneer schoolmaster of Eureka, "always carried a six shooter in his pocket when in the school room," according to I. E. Diehl's manuscript, *Tintic*. The ubiquitous Burton owned Mormon education to be "peculiar. . . . At fifteen a boy can use a whip, an axe, or a hoe—he does not like the plow—to perfection. He sits a bare-backed horse like a Centaur, handles his bowie-knife skillfully, never misses a mark with his revolver. . . . With regards to book-work, there is no difficulty to obtain in Great Salt Lake City that 'mediocrity of knowledge between learning and ignorance' which distinguished the grammar schools of the Western Islands in the days of Samuel Johnson. . . . Everyone learns to read and write," though the Mormons had discovered that "the time of school drudgery may profitably be abridged. A boy, they say, will learn all that his memory can carry during three hours of book-work, and the rest had far better be spent in air, exercise, and handicraft." Burton concludes that the purpose behind Mormon education was "to rear a swarm of healthy working bees. The social hive has as yet no room for drones, book-worms, and gentlemen."

Public school support until 1874 came wholly from local taxes—"local" being almost universally coextensive with "town"—and from tuitions, but between 1874 and 1878, the legislature made regular appropriations of lump sums to be apportioned on a school-age per capita basis among the various districts, and in 1878 inaugurated a Territorial tax for a permanent school fund. Generous land grants, both Territorial and Federal, had been made for the public school system between 1850 and 1870, but it was not until after 1870 that title to Utah lands began to be granted. The meager income obtained from taxing a people without any cash, and from tuitions paid in produce, besides barely affording to support a teacher for three or four months at best, would not permit construction of schoolhouses unless they served as community meeting places. The Territorial superintendent of common schools reported in 1857 that there were "log school houses in most of the settlements, most of which had slab seats, some of which had very long legs, doing a double duty among the rising and risen generations." The ward or community chapel of the Mormon Church frequently served as a school on weekdays, a town hall on election days, and a meeting house on Sundays. The quality of instruction in such schools, plus the inadvertent creeping in of doctrine in communities where the school and the Church were scarcely to be distinguished, led in the 1870's to establishment of a number of denominational schools. Completion of the transcontinental railway in 1869 brought to Utah a substantial non-Mormon population which was in no way disposed to have its children reared in "Mormon dominated" schools. Moreover, Mormon-Gentile antagonism was rapidly approaching crescendo, and there were those among the critics of Mormonism who felt that the most effective method of undermining the Mormon position was through education. Denominational schools grew so rapidly that in 1888 the Territorial commissioner of schools reported (almost with alarm) a total of 99 such institutions, of which but six were Mormon. In 1894 there were 113 of them; the Mormons in the meantime "having bestirred themselves," had 26, the Congregationalists 33, the Presbyterians 33, and the Methodists 21, the rest being distributed among Catholics, Lutherans, Baptists, and Episcopalians.

Many private schools had appeared during the earliest days, especially in Salt Lake City. As early as 1852 the Polysophical Society offered high school courses, with gymnastics and military training for young men and music and drawing for young ladies. Orson Pratt's Science School was especially remarkable because it taught college courses. Such schools were in the main ephemeral, seldom lasting more than a year or two, while the denominational schools of the 1870's and 1880's were established on a more or less permanent basis. Moreover, the denominational schools had nine- and ten-month school terms, and the best instruction they could obtain. They began at common school levels, but soon pushed into preparatory school work, and were undoubtedly instrumental in forcing development of colleges. The public school system had not, as late as 1884, any high schools. . . .

Whether the denominational schools had a direct bearing on Utah colleges or not, the University of Deseret was revived in 1867 and placed under Dr. John R. Park two years later. In 1869 Dr. Park established a normal department and a training school and though until 1890 most of the University students were on high school levels, the schools of law, medicine, education, and mining followed rapidly. In 1892, the name was changed to University of Utah and in 1900 the institution was moved to its present site on the broad East Bench of Salt Lake City. In 1875, the Mormon Church "called" Dr. Karl G. Maeser to establish Brigham Young Academy (renamed Brigham Young University in 1903) at Provo. The school originally granted teachers' certificates for one year's work, later gave two-year normal certificates and the degree of Bachelor of Pedagogy on completion of four years' work. In the 1890's, William K. Reid of Sanpete reported that his county had a "great many very good teachers and a few bad ones." Most of the early teachers were graduates of Brigham Young Academy or the University of Utah. Utah was turning out its own teachers. In 1875, also, the Presbyterian Church founded the Salt Lake Collegiate Institute, which subsequently became Westminster College, and in the same year the Catholic Church established Saint Mary's Academy in Salt Lake City. In the 1880's the Mormon Church founded Brigham Young College at Logan. In the midst of all this college-making, the Morrill Act of 1862 bore fruit, and the Utah State Agricultural College was established at Logan as a land-grant school.

The presence of many institutions of higher learning seems to have had a reciprocal effect on the lower levels. The comprehensive school law of 1890 made all common schools free. . . . The constitutional convention of 1895 engaged itself with a prolonged quibble over the status of high schools. . . .

In 1910 the State legislature voted a special tax for support of high schools, and the following year authorized counties to "consolidate" for high school purposes. In 1930, encouraged by a generous State fund and by consolidation of districts, the high school system could show an enrollment of almost 81 percent of high school-age students, as against a national average of 57.3 per cent. Breakdown of secondary education into a junior-senior high school organization began somewhat timidly in 1908. . . . Except for a brief "reaction against reactionism" in the universities during the decade before [World War I] and an occasional flare-up of sectarian antagonism, the progress of education in Utah has been consistent since 1910. . . . Custodial schools for deaf, blind, feeble-minded, and delinquent minors have been established since the turn of the century. . . . In 1930, the State legislature established an equalization fund which in 1940 had done much toward standardization of public schools. . . . The uniform school fund, set aside by the legislature in 1937 and 1939, further equalizes educational opportunity in the State.

1941 edition

In subsequent years the state legislature greatly modified the "equalization" and "uniform school funds" financing programs mentioned above, and in fact has changed school programs and the school system in many ways since 1940. Legislation in 1947 established minimum standards for a basic school program in all districts and provided for a uniform property levy. If revenue from this levy was insufficient to provide the basic program, the state would make up the difference. Excess revenue in wealthier districts was placed in a uniform school fund. This program was revised in 1973, resulting in the largest increase in state support ever provided at one time. In 1972 a comprehensive building assistance program was established, following a series of less encompassing measures. This program has since been amended. In 1959 the Coordinating Council for Higher Education was established, then replaced in 1969 by a State Board of Higher Education which was soon renamed the State Board of Regents.

Considering the nation as a whole, about a sixth of all government revenue is devoted to public education. Insofar as Utah's state government is concerned, education's share of the state budget exceeds 40 per cent, with two-thirds of this being expended for aid to local schools and the remaining third being devoted to support of higher education. In 1980-81, for example, more than a billion dollars was spent by state and local governments for the education of 355,000 students in public schools and 61,000 students in public colleges, universities, and technical colleges. Additional millions were spent by private schools and colleges. State and local governments employ about 25,000 teachers, faculty members, administrators, and staff workers in public education.

Organization of Education

Basically, education in Utah may be divided into (1) education supported by public funds (public education) and (2) education supported by private funds (private education).

Public education. Public education receives financial support from every level of government including the federal. It is controlled and administered, however, by local school districts and state government, working cooperatively but with differing powers and authority. Elementary and secondary public schools are operated and administered by 40 local school districts, 22 of which coincide with counties, 13 with parts of counties, and five with larger cities. Local school district policies are determined by local boards of education, members of which are elected. These boards appoint district officers, including a superintendent of schools, who is responsible for school administration and operation. In 1980 there were 619 public day schools in the state, including 396 elementary and 21 middle schools, 172 junior-senior high schools, and 30 special schools.

Granite School District in Salt Lake County is the state's largest district, enrolling about a fifth of all public school pupils. No other district approaches Granite in enrollment. Granite is followed in enrollment by Jordan, Davis, Salt Lake City, Alpine, Weber, and Nebo. In 1979 school expenditures ranged from a low of $1,500 per student (Jordan) to $3,500 (Daggett); the state average was about $1,900. Figures and rankings are only indicative; they change from time to time, influenced by inflation, population movements, etc.

General control of basic educational policies and activities for public schools is vested in a State Board of Education, comprised of 11 members. This board provides leadership, advisory services, and basic administrative policies for the public schools, appoints a State Superintendent of Public Instruction, and—among other multitudinous functions—establishes teacher certification standards, supervises administration of technical colleges and vocational centers, and appoints the director of Special Education and members of the State Course of Study and State Textbook com-

UNIVERSITY OF UTAH

mittees. At the present time there is a degree of uncertainty and controversy between the State Board of Education and the State Board of Regents as to control of the state's technical colleges, vocational centers, and skills centers.

Public colleges, universities, and technical colleges. According to the Utah Foundation, "Utah spends a relatively higher proportion of its income for higher education than most states in the nation. In many years Utah surpasses all other states in this regard. The proportion of personal income devoted to public higher education in Utah is more than double the national average. Utah also is one of the leading states in the nation in the proportion of its total population and of its college age population that are enrolled in institutions of higher learning within the state."

Colleges and universities are subject to the authority of the State Board of Regents, comprised of 16 citizens who are appointed by the governor with the consent of the Senate. The board appoints a staff and a Commissioner for Higher Education to act as its executive officer. Among its duties: establishment of roles and courses of study for each institution, approval of changes in curricula, review of institutional budget requests, and preparation of a combined appropriations request. Public institutions of higher learning are: University of Utah in Salt Lake City . . . Utah State University in Logan . . . Weber State College in Ogden . . . Southern Utah State College in Cedar City . . . College of Eastern Utah in Price . . . Snow College in Ephraim . . . Dixie College in St. George . . . Utah Technical College in Salt Lake City . . . and Utah Technical College in Provo and Orem. *See the respective tours for descriptions of these schools.* In 1981 the combined enrollment at public colleges and universities was in excess of 60,000 and their total budget amounted to more than 150 million dollars.

Private education. With some exceptions, private schools in Utah are affiliated with religious denominations, or were so affiliated at one time. Brigham Young University in Provo, which has the largest student enrollment in the state, is affiliated with the Mormon Church *(see Tour No. 5)*. Westminster College in Salt Lake City is a nondenominational school, supported by several religious bodies *(see Tour No. 3)*. About 30 private elementary or high schools, or combined elementary-high schools, were operating in the state in 1980; the majority of these were affiliated with or supported by a religious denomination. A number have been in existence for many years, among them Wasatch Academy in Mount Pleasant and Rowland Hall-St. Mark's in Salt Lake City—both of which were born more than 100 years ago—as well as Judge Memorial and J. E. Cosgriff schools in Salt Lake City. Combined enrollment of these private elementary and high schools in 1980 totaled about 4,500. In addition to those, mention must be made of LDS Business College, Henager Business College, and other specialized schools which offer instruction in business, television repair, computers, barbering and hairdressing, nursing, and other fields.

Strengths and Weaknesses

"Utah is the leadership state in education in the nation, and thus the leading jurisdiction in the world," Dr. Clark Kerr is reported to have told University of Utah graduates in 1974. Dr. Kerr at the time was chairman of

John R. Park, University of Utah.   Karl G. Maeser, Brigham Young University.

the Carnegie Council on Policy Studies in Higher Education. "Utah stands first in the percentage of the total population age three to 34 enrolled in school. Utah stands first in the percentage of the total population enrolled in school at every age level except ages 16-17. Utah stands first in the average years of school completed for all of its citizens age 25 and older. Utah stands high in the in-migration to its institutions of higher education. Utah, overall, has been to the United States . . . a model for educational development, a rich source for leadership."

Dr. Kerr was referring to statistical rankings of that time, and the state has continued to rank near the top, if not always at the top, in *quantitative* comparisons, if not quite so favorably in *qualitative* factors. For example, in 1980 it ranked second among states in the number of school-age children per 100 adults age 21 and over; at the same time it led all states in public school enrollment as a percentage of total enrollment and was sixth in public school enrollment as a percentage of school-age population. Few states make a greater financial commitment in terms of the percentage of personal income devoted to public education.

Such figures are cause for concern as well as pride. The state's high birth rate (highest in the nation) has given it more children compared with total population than any other state, requiring greater proportional expenditures for their education. Despite its admirable financial effort, Utah ranks very low among states in actual dollars spent per pupil, and its teachers have the largest pupil loads in the nation. Somewhat offsetting this heavy pupil load is the state's mid-point ranking in teacher salaries.

Concerning quality of education, Lavor Chaffin wrote in 1982: ". . . Utah has above-average homes and socioeconomic stability, and fewer disadvantaged minorities, ghettos and other problems, yet, through the years, children in Utah schools have tested only about average. Worse, the longer they stay in school, the lower they test against the national average." Admittedly this statement is a generalization, and data for more than superficial comparison are lacking. Utah pupils do compare well with national norms in certain subjects at certain levels, if not so well in all. Comparative scores in high school math and English have dropped since the 1960s, stimulating criticism from colleges and universities to the effect that entering freshmen are not adequately prepared in basic subjects.

While Utah's students apparently do not compare unfavorably with their peers in other states in academic achievement, the same cannot be said about their scholastic abilities—and those of their American peers—when selected abilities are compared with certain other countries. The school year is 180 days in Utah and the majority of other states, whereas it is 225 in Japan, 220 in Russia, and in a number of other countries is longer than it is in the United States. Of these 180 days in school, perhaps as few as 100 are devoted to serious study in academic subjects. It is commonly known that not only the majority of students in Utah, but those throughout the nation as well, are deficient in their mastery of mathematics, science, English, foreign languages, and even the arts. The causes for this deficiency can be attributed more to educational and societal philosophies and values than simply to student dereliction.

Among a host of other problems faced by school systems in Utah: teacher dissatisfaction with pupil loads, salaries, and emotional stress . . . rapidly growing enrollments and costs without commensurate revenue . . . refusal of several local districts to permit leeway levies for schools . . . complaints from ethnic minorities about alleged educational discrimination . . . drastic reductions in federal aid . . . and criticisms that schools are not preparing students for college, for vocations, for "life," etc. Another problem of potential future significance is the claim by women's groups that Utah lags behind most other states in the professional involvement of women in school administration. Also colleges and universities insist that legislated budgets are not adequate for growing enrollments and rising costs.

Educational Trends

Inertia is a cause for frustration in education as in other mass cultural activities. Change occurs slowly and often painfully. The problems described above undoubtedly will receive attention if not immediate solution. Trends and innovations that may hardly be discernible today are bound to influence education of the future. For example, computers promise significant impact on learning, as do new audiovisual devices and psychological findings. School architecture is changing. Pressures (not all of which will have positive results) are being exerted toward lengthening or modifying the traditional school year, shortening the school week and lengthening the day, utilizing school facilities more fully, and otherwise modifying educational programs and schedules. There appears to be increasing public criticism of "permissive" curricula and "frills," and definitely there are swelling tides of opinion regarding the desirability of more intensive preparation in subjects such as mathematics, writing and English skills, natural sciences, economics, foreign languages, and even history, social sciences, and fine arts.

Communications Media
(See also Communications and Utilities in the Economic Scene)

Utahns are generally conceded to possess an admirable level of literacy and an active interest in and awareness of the world around them. How these attainments compare with other parts of the world can hardly be measured objectively in all respects, and Utah's comparative ranking on the culture scale is significantly a matter of personal opinion. It cannot be denied, however, that if ignorance abounds it is not for lack of the media of communications. Knowledge is there for the learning, with few or no restrictions.

In the context of this chapter, communications media include printed materials and the electronic media (television and radio). Cinema also is a communications medium; this is treated in The Arts. A corresponding chapter in the 1941 edition, entitled *Press and Radio,* discussed briefly the historical background of newspaper and magazine publishing in the state. That chapter devoted a paragraph to the status of radio broadcasting, then less than 20 years old.

Printed Media

The printed media group is a comprehensive category embracing newspapers, periodicals, books, brochures, pamphlets, flyers, and anything else of a printed nature. Associated with these materials, of course, are libraries, publishers, and sales-distribution outlets.

Publishers and printers. There is statistical indication that Utah is extraordinarily well endowed with publishers and printers. As stated in the chapter on Manufacturing, "more individual firms are involved in printing

High-speed newspaper press, Ogden Standard-Examiner.

OGDEN STANDARD-EXAMINER

and publishing than any other segment of the manufacturing industry."
Listed in the 1980 *Directory of Utah Manufacturers* are 49 newspaper publishers and printers, 11 periodical publishers, 21 book publishers, and 21
miscellaneous publishers, in addition to 132 commercial printers and 39
other firms associated closely with the printing-publishing industry.

With regard to book publishing, LaVarr Webb wrote in the *Deseret
News* (May 12, 1979), "The elusive great Utah novel has yet to be written,
and when it is, plenty of publishers will be waiting to snap it up. The Utah
publishing business is booming, and more and more publishers are looking
seriously at fiction . . . Utah publishing is becoming more diversified, less
regional in nature . . . And it appears that the competitive, hard-to-crack
LDS-related publishing field is beginning to open up." Webb's survey of a
dozen multi-title publishers determined that about 170 new titles are published in the state each year.

The largest publishing entity in the state, and one of the largest in the
west, is undoubtedly the Church of Jesus Christ of Latter-day Saints, or
Mormon Church. Several years ago the church-owned Deseret News Press,
one of the major commercial printers and publishers in the state, ceased
commercial operations and now devotes its production capability to church-
related work. In addition to three magazines having a combined circulation
of nearly 900,000 *(see below)*, the church publishes—mostly in Utah—the
Church News and *Deseret News (see below)*, curriculum materials, missionary literature, foreign editions of church literature, church scripture in
enormous volume, public relations materials, and other printed material
commensurate with a membership-proselyting organization of large magnitude.

Newspapers. At the present time Utah supports six daily newspapers
having a paid circulation of nearly 300,000, namely *Salt Lake Tribune,
Deseret News, Ogden Standard-Examiner, Provo Daily Herald, Logan
Herald-Journal,* and *Color Country Spectrum.* On a *per capita* basis, this
circulation is somewhat below the national average. In addition to the
dailies there are about 48 commercial weekly newspapers and several daily
college-university papers in the state. Surpassing the paid dailies and
weeklies in circulation are representatives of a new publishing phenomenon,
the free local or regional "zoned" editions, delivered by carrier or mail,
dependent on advertising for revenue but containing news and features of
special interest to local readers. Several of these are issued by the major
newspaper publishers. Another trend of recent years is the consolidation of
ownership of weekly newspapers. It is estimated that three-fourths of
Utah's weeklies now are published by multiple-ownership chains. Technological change has resulted in the elimination of hot-metal type and the
utilization of more advanced methods of typesetting and printing. While
Utah's newspapers appear to be financially healthy, at least on the surface,
publishers are concerned about the inroads of the electronic media, which
compete with news, entertainment and advertising. Another of their concerns at this time is the potential adverse impact of cable television.

The newspaper of largest circulation published in Utah is the *LDS
Church News,* a weekly which observed its 50th anniversary in 1981. This
Mormon paper claims a circulation of 250,000.

Readers are referred to the 1940 edition (pages 149-152) for a historical discussion of journalism in Utah. Beginning in 1850, when the *Deseret News* began publication, some 500 newspapers "had come and gone in Utah" by 1940. Eight newspapers "succumbed to the inevitable" for every one that was in existence in 1940. "Salt Lake City received the name 'Journalistic Cemetery', and pessimistic editors more than once called Ogden the 'Graveyard of Western Journalism'." The *Salt Lake Tribune* began publication in 1870 as the *Mormon Tribune,* dropping the word Mormon the following year. "Of the 585 papers which have appeared at one time or another in Utah very few have persisted," said the 1941 edition, going on to state that there were 65 newspapers in the state in 1940, seven of which were dailies. As noted above, the number has declined by about a dozen in the 40 years since.

Periodicals. The magazine of largest circulation published within the state undoubtedly is *The Ensign* (circulation nearly 500,000), published by the Mormon Church. This is followed by two other Mormon periodicals, *The New Era* (circulation about 180,000) and *The Friend* (circulation about 200,000). Compared to these, other periodicals originating in Utah are modest in circulation. The majority appeal to specialized readerships: for example, the *Utah Architect, Utah Bar Journal, Utah Educational Review,* and *Intermountain Contractor. Utah Holiday Magazine* and *Mountainwest Magazine* appeal to a general urban readership market. *Sunstone: A Quarterly Journal* is of interest to Mormon readers, while *Expression,* a new periodical, is directed to those having an artistic bent. The mortality rate of periodicals is high, as verified by library periodical files, which list more defunct titles than those still surviving.

Publications distribution. The major retail book-sales outlets in the state, located in Salt Lake City, include Sam Weller's Zion Book Store, Deseret Book Company, and B. Dalton. Numerous others are scattered throughout the state, only a few devoted solely to the sale of books. Magazine Shop, for example, specializes in periodicals and paperbound books, while many firms sell not only books but souvenirs, recordings, offices supplies and stationery as well. Every college and university is equipped with a bookstore. A great many books are sold on newsstands, in drugstores and food markets. These tend to be popular titles in paper bindings.

Libraries. Libraries in Utah probably number in the vicinity of a thousand. The majority of these are associated with schools—somewhat more than 600—and are utilized by more than 400,000 students. They range from modest libraries in elementary schools to the great repositories at University of Utah and Brigham Young University, which number in the millions of volumes and are, with the genealogical and historical libraries of the Mormon Church, the largest libraries in the state. Many business firms, government agencies, and military installations also support libraries, as do the various religious denominations.

There are 55 municipal and county public libraries in the state, which operated on a total budget of about 12 million dollars (a *per capita* cost of about $8.50) in 1980. In that year those libraries circulated in excess of nine million items. The services of county and municipal libraries are complemented by a fleet of more than 20 traveling bookmobiles, which visit nearly every outlying community in the state on a regular schedule. With the exception of Salt Lake County, which has its own program, bookmobiles are supported cooperatively by the various counties and the state. Assistance of various kinds is provided to local and county libraries by the Utah State Library, which has a staff of specialists. Among State Library functions: special services for the blind and physically handicapped (braille books, talking books, books on tape, large print books, and cassette books, as well as a radio reading service). This special services division also is utilized by 16 other western states.

Television and radio

As described in the Communications and Utilities section (Economic Scene chapter), Utah is served by more than 50 commercial AM and FM radio stations, 15 non-commercial FM stations, four commercial television stations, two non-commercial educational television stations, and several cable television systems, all operating in the state. In addition, of course, Utah listeners and viewers have access, through network and cable systems, to uncounted other broadcast sources, connecting the state with the rest of the world and hastening its common acculturation.

It is an accepted fact that Americans spend much more time looking at the television screen or listening to radio than reading the printed page. Utahns probably differ but slightly from the national norm in this respect. Since 1940, as noted elsewhere in this volume, Utah has come to resemble other states in diverse ways—in the characteristics of its economy, its recreational habits, its culinary preferences, social mores, educational attainments, and in other respects. Chief among the factors responsible for this subtle and non-so-subtle "Americanization" have been radio and television, in addition to cinema, national magazines, and other mass influences.

KSL, the first radio station in the state, made its initial broadcast in 1922. KDYL (now KCPX) followed shortly afterward, or as some claim, about the same time. There were eight radio stations in the state in 1940; by 1953 the number had more than doubled to 19 stations; and at the present time there are nearly 70. Radio has changed dramatically in content and function. The greater part of commercial radio time today is devoted to music, news, "talk" and advertising; rarely is it utilized for voice drama as it was in 1940. Radio is also used by police and fire agencies, airplanes and air controllers, hospitals, transportation firms, natural resource agencies, etc. Many enthusiasts are radio "hams" or communicate with each other on citizen bands (CB).

According to the *Atlas of Utah,* "Commercial television was inaugurated in Utah on April 15, 1948, when KTVX (Channel 4) went on the air. KSL-TV (Channel 5) followed in 1949 and KUTV (Channel 2) in 1954. The state's only UHF station, KSTU-TV (Channel 20), began operations in 1978. The first color television broadcast was transmitted into the state from the Tournament of Roses in Pasadena, California, in 1954." In 1981 a number of firms made application to the FCC for rights to channel 13, last on the commercial VHF dial.

The Arts

The arts in Utah are youthful and dynamic. They are supported by a heritage brief in historical time and by a heritage capable of bringing them to a full flowering. The realities of pioneering, scratching out a living in a hostile land, naivete and lack of training, devotion to a religion which required much of its people's leisure time—these placed limits on attitudes conducive to artistic brilliance during the early days of statehood.

In the early days of Utah's history, the Mormon Church was in need of architects and painters to build and beautify, and of singers, actors, and musicians to entertain. This need was a boon to the arts, and the Mormon Church deserves high credit for the commissions and opportunities it has given to artists. Utah would have been a different place without that support.

In spite of the overall lack of opportunities for an aspiring artist afforded by a pioneering society, there were ameliorating forces at work. One of these was a philosophy of the Mormon Church, that the purpose of life is to obtain joy, and that great joy is obtained through development of each person's talents. Even in the earliest settlements there were likely to be opportunities for the performing artist in music, drama, and "elocution." Some Mormon converts from foreign countries settled together in ethnic concentrations, such as Scandinavians in Sanpete County and Swiss in Midway, where they fostered arts and crafts from their homelands. Non-Mormon immigrants, attracted by opportunities in mining, railroading, agriculture, etc., brought with them the enriching arts and cultures of Greece, Italy, the Orient, Hispanic countries, and other places.

A third condition that has contributed to Utah's artistic awareness is its location. Simply because Utah lies astride transportation routes that cross the country, traveling artists from the earliest days have stopped to perform in the state. Their warm reception here contributed to the reputation of Utah as a place that *must* be visited by touring artists or groups of artists.

It should be recognized, however, that Utah has had a relatively short history and that a work ethic born of pioneer necessity still colors the belief

Acknowledgment: At the request of the Utah Arts Council, authorities in various art categories were gracious enough to examine the draft manuscript for this section, each reading that part devoted to his or her field of expertise, correcting, suggesting changes, or in cases making extensive revision. In appreciation, their names are listed here, with the express qualification that they should not be held responsible for error, for the reason that subsequent editing may have inadvertently distorted their intent: Peter Goss and Ray Kingston (Architecture) . . . Arley Curtz and Dorothy Bearnson (Crafts) . . . Lloyd Bliss and Elizabeth Hayes (Dance) . . . Chris Montague (Film and Video) . . . Hal Cannon (Folk Art) . . . Edward L. Hart (Literature) . . . Lowell Durham and Conrad Harrison (Music) . . . Dan Burke and Robert Olpin (Painting) . . . Dennis Smith (Sculpture) . . . and Keith Engar (Theater). Hal Cannon, Conrad Harrison, Edward L. Hart, Elizabeth Hayes, Chris Montague, and Robert Olpin in particular made extensive and time-consuming revisions of their respective portions of the original draft.

of many people who see any effort for anything other than survival as dispensable. To be sure, pioneer crafts that had utility were emphasized by the Mormon cultivation of the family unit; and this emphasis on the home-making arts has helped to produce some genuine fiber artists and quilt designers.

In addition to the overcoming of utilitarian attitudes, artists in Utah have faced other real challenges. Extremes in the topography, color, and nature of the land have been difficult elements for artists to interpret. Physical isolation from larger centers of population and culture has resulted, at least in the past, in a degree of artistic provincialism, individualism, and independence. Not necessarily bad in themselves, these qualities have often been accompanied by self-consciousness and doubt.

In surveying prospects for the arts in the state, we must take an optimistic overall position. Every difficulty is matched with opportunity. Artists in the state have been fortunate in having access to a high quality of instruction in the public schools and institutions of higher learning. Most Utahns traditionally have assigned a high place to education in their thinking; one important reason for this attitude is the Mormon belief that "The glory of God is intelligence." Finally, the concentration of the population along the Wasatch Front has made possible cities of a size capable of supporting symphony orchestras, art museums, art fairs, theaters, exhibitions, and all the other appurtenances necessary to create an atmosphere in which the individual artistic talent can thrive. In this respect, Utah possesses a gift not shared by all sister states. Utah artists are growing in numbers and in the quality of their work. Performing groups and individual artists in every discipline today rank favorably with their counterparts throughout the nation.

The status and nature of the arts in Utah have been transformed since the 1941 edition. Indeed, this has been the situation across the nation. An artistic renaissance has occurred throughout the land. In Utah the transformation has been unprecedented in scope and intensity, particularly during the past 15 or 20 years. Certain musical and dance groups based in Utah have gained national, and a measure of international, renown. Government financial support for the arts has increased to levels undreamed of only a few years ago. Public interest and participation are phenomenal.

A great many talented sons and daughters have been forced to leave the state to gain recognition. Though many of these return when the chance arises, it is likely that Utah has been a net exporter of artistic talent. As a nurturing nest, the state is too small to contain all its fledglings. However that may be, enough talent remains within the state to make it exceptionally rich in artistic offerings and creative potential.

Artists (speaking here in an inclusive sense, not only of painters and sculptors) are the most individualistic of persons. The creative impulse may surface even in adverse environments. For full flowering, however, there seems to be a need for encouragement in the form of patronage or other support. Encouragement in Utah, as elsewhere, has come partially from the private sector as well as various levels of government (including the Utah Arts Council) and the Mormon Church. These are discussed below.

SUPPORTERS OF THE ARTS

1. GOVERNMENT AND THE ARTS

Except in the form of limited school instruction, architecture, geographic photography and painting, scientific writing, etc., government was not a supporter of Utah arts during the first 50 years or so following settlement. Government in territorial Utah was more preoccupied with survival. Support of the arts, such as it was, was left largely to the private and religious sectors. This neglect was not due entirely to scarcity of revenue. It was the result as well of the individual and cultural philosophy that government should not be involved in all aspects of life.

Nevertheless, three years after statehood was acquired, the state legislature did create the Utah Arts Institute, direct ancestor of the present-day Utah Arts Council *(see below)*. This action established a precedent: The Utah arts agency was the first such state agency in the nation, though it languished almost without funding for many years. Despite its meager budget for half a century or more, the Institute did manage to encourage the arts (primarily painting) through annual exhibits and the purchase of prize-winning works, which at the same time formed a valuable state art collection.

During Depression years of the 1930s and early 1940s, prior to America's entry into World War II, the arts were stimulated by the federal Work Projects Administration (WPA). Programs were developed to employ painters, writers and musicians. Said the 1941 edition: "Creation of the WPA Art Project in 1935 enabled young and progressive artists to remain in the State, and, under the leadership of State Director Elzy J. Bird, has given widespread stimulus to art in Utah, through its exhibits and the painting of murals for communities that could not otherwise have afforded them."

The Utah Arts Institute was reorganized and renamed by the legislature in 1937, becoming the Utah State Institute of Fine Arts. A year later the Utah State Art Center opened in 1938 at 59 South State in Salt Lake City in cooperation with the WPA art program. It provided space for exhibits, weekly radio dramatizations from the lives of great artists, musical programs, public affairs forums, lectures, workshops, extension services, and classroom instruction. Again quoting from the 1941 edition, ". . . at the end of the first year (November, 1939), more than 75,000 persons had visited the galleries and attended lectures, musicales, and forums, while 2,000 students had enrolled in art classes. Branch centers were launched by the Utah Art Project at Provo, Helper, and Price. . . ."

Though it was closed in 1943, during World War II, the Art Center provided a foundation of ideas and experience which proved invaluable for future developments.

The WPA music program resulted in the creation of a symphony orchestra, forerunner of the Utah Symphony Orchestra of today. And writers of the WPA Federal Writers' Program created the popular volume *Utah: A Guide to the State,* published in 1941, the result of exhaustive research and some exemplary writing. The Writers' Program also inventoried county archives and produced a number of useful reference publications.

Before, during, and after the WPA period, a bright if brief interlude in the history of Utah arts, government has provided sporadic employment for artists in various fields. Public buildings such as the State Capitol and Salt Lake City and County Building were coveted architectural plums. Public officials have been immortalized by portrait painters. Murals have been placed on walls and ceilings of public buildings, notably the Capitol, where painted works decorate the dome, Senate chamber, Gold Room, and other sites. In Price, the Municipal Building is distinguished by a historical mural painted by native son Lynn Fausett. Another of Fausett's works is the Pioneer Mural in the visitor center at Pioneer Trail State Park in Salt Lake City; a portion of the cost of this work was contributed by businessman Leon Harman. Public funds also partially paid for sculptor Mahonri Young's Pioneer Monument nearby.

Among the most significant programs through which government supports the arts today are: The Utah Arts Council, schools, fairs, festivals, libraries, art centers, museums, and the National Endowments for the Arts and Humanities.

Utah Arts Council

The lineal descendant of the Utah Arts Institute, established in 1899 by the state legislature, today's Arts Council is the primary agency through which state and national government monies are funneled to stimulate and encourage the arts. The Arts Council distributes funds appropriated directly for the arts by both the state and the National Endowment for the Arts. It acts as a state coordinator and advisor, having an awareness of varied programs that might be underway at any given time around the state, assisting with professional help where needed and providing financial aid on a matching basis to more than 100 arts organizations across the state.

The Arts Council also conducts programs of its own, for which it provides the major funding. Overall the Council serves as a catalyst and pollinator, stimulating the creative seeds that sprout throughout the state.

The Utah Arts Council is comprised of 13 members, appointed by the governor with approval of the Senate. Membership consists of five business or professional people, in addition to eight members who are professionally involved with the arts and who represent literature, architecture, painting, sculpture, music, theater, crafts and dance. Council programs are administered by a full-time director and a small staff. Prior to 1966, during the 67 years after its establishment, the Council had no paid staff. In December 1966, when Wilburn C. West was appointed as the first full-time salaried director, the agency had "no office, no staff, a meager budget—and great hopes for the future." At that time the Institute provided token aid to five artistic organizations. By 1974, when West retired, 50 organizations were being assisted by the Council. Ruth R. Draper has served as director since 1974. Excerpts from a history of the Council, written by Mrs. Draper in 1981, appear below:

Three years after statehood, in 1899, the Utah Arts Institute was created by the Legislature to "advance the arts in all their phases." The Arts Institute (the agency today called the Utah Arts Council) was mandated to hold a competition/exhibition for Utah artists each year and to

Alice Merrill Horne introduced the bill creating the Utah Art Institute in 1899 and served as the institute's first chair.

purchase the "best of show" for the state. That mandate has been faithfully adhered to over the years, and consequently the state today has a valuable collection representing Utah's finest artists. The visual arts dominated the Institute's activities through the first 30 years of this century. There was no agency staff. Volunteer board members appointed by the governors, assisted by many interested volunteer citizens, with continuing financial support regularly appropriated by the Legislature, kept the arts activities flourishing, which added an important sustaining element to the lives of Utah citizens. . . .

Almost 200 years after the birth of this nation, in 1965, legislation creating the National Endowment for the Arts was finally signed into law. That federal legislation stipulated that 20 per cent of the monies appropriated by Congress to the Endowment would be distributed to the 50 states and territories, provided an agency was established within the state to administer the funds. Utah was ready, its agency established over half a century earlier. For the first time, a salaried director and secretary were provided to carry out the policies and plans of the board. At that same time, revision in the Executive Branch of state government put the arts agency into a Department of Development Services and called it the Division of Fine Arts. [The name was changed to Utah Arts Council in 1978.]

Great strides for the arts in Utah followed. With block grant funding assistance from the Endowment available to pool with the state's appropriated amounts, with the economy healthy and with the interest of citizens increasing, the agency was able to assist more arts groups. . . . which made arts programming available to communities across the state. Programs were developed to place professional artists in school settings, to assist communities to sponsor professional and semi-professional performances providing a cultural series for outlying areas, and visual arts exhibitions were made available to schools and communities across the state.

As the nation turned its attention toward celebrating its 200th birthday in 1976, and with leadership from philanthropist O.C. Tanner, Utahns reaffirmed their commitment to the arts by assigning a large percentage of Utah's Bicentennial funding to the building of the Bicentennial Arts Center Complex. The complex includes the beautifully renovated Capitol Theater, fastidiously restored to the grandeur of its original Renaissance decor, now the home for Ballet West, the Utah Opera, Ririe-Woodbury Dance Co. and Repertory Dance Theatre. Originally named the Orpheum when built in 1913, it played road-show attractions in vaudeville and legitimate theater. The elegant Salt Lake Art Center houses galleries, classrooms and library space, museum shop and a sculpture court. Symphony Hall, a combination of blonde hardwood, massive expanses of tempered glass, 24-karat gold leaf and acoustical excellence, is the permanent home of the Utah Symphony and completes the arts complex designed by the architectural firm of Fowler, Ferguson, Kingston and Ruben, Inc. In addition, the Legislature purchased and renovated the old James R. Glendinning home at 617 East South Temple, Salt Lake City, for a permanent office and gallery for the Utah Arts Council.

Public Schools

Government support of the arts has taken many forms. One of the most far-reaching has been the teaching of the arts in public schools, colleges and universities. The influence of this form of public support for the arts is, of course, incalculable. Through the schools, public or private, at one time or another, nearly all citizens are exposed to the arts. It is largely in the schools that artistic talent is discovered and encouraged. In the schools, those with talent and enthusiasm are enabled to infect others. Many of Utah's most gifted and creative artists have served as teachers of others.

Some of Utah's educational institutions have become repositories of valuable art collections, or have been instrumental in forming such collections. Among these is the Springville High School, which gathered a collection that later formed a nucleus for the Springville Museum of Art. Other high schools throughout the state have considerable collections of art. Colleges and universities are the primary training centers for serious students of the arts. All of them support permanent exhibits of the visual arts. These public institutions also support programs of music, dance, theater, literature, architecture, design, etc., which continue to produce some of Utah's most talented artists and performers.

Fairs and Festivals

The Utah State Fair, county fairs, and festivals of various kinds have played important roles in fostering the visual and performing arts. In fact, for many artists, fairs and festivals afford the primary channels of public exposure. Government, of course, does not fully subsidize all of these activities, but it does bolster them with some money and services.

Harris Fine Arts Center, Brigham Young University

Among the most popular attractions of state and county fairs are exhibits of crafts, paintings, sculpture, and photography. Prize-winning art works, purchased by the Utah State Fair over the years, have become a part of the state's valued art collection. Arts festivals, such as the Utah Arts Festival in Salt Lake City and the Park City Arts Festival, attract enormous crowds to view exhibits, make purchases, and enjoy dance and music. A number of the most popular of Utah's fairs and festivals are listed elsewhere in this volume *(see Calendar of Events)*.

Libraries

Libraries are influential in supporting and advancing the arts. They disseminate information and provide experience through printed works as well as audiovisual materials such as films, prints, records, and tapes. Libraries provide exhibit space and help to advertise happenings in the art world. Many libraries have auditoriums, meeting rooms, and facilities for audiovisual presentations, available for public use. In these ways and others, government provides invaluable services to the arts through public libraries.

Art Centers and Museums

At least partially through public funding, Utahns support a number of visual art centers, museums, and performing arts centers.

2. THE MORMON CHURCH

Since pioneer days the Mormon Church has provided support to a great number of Utah's artists, to painters, sculptors, architects, artisans, dramatic performers, and musicians. Painters have been commissioned to create murals in temples, meetinghouses, and visitor centers. Sculptors have created monuments and statues. Architects and craftsmen have built a multitude of religious structures of sometimes exotic and unusual design.

Writers have found creative outlets in church-owned newspapers and church-oriented books and magazines. Mormons with musical, dramatic and dance talents have found expression through the years in church cultural and religious activities. Among the most widely recognized of these are the broadcasts, concerts, and recordings of the Mormon Tabernacle Choir; yet this notable choir is only the most distinguished among hundreds, perhaps thousands, of musical groups formed by members of the church.

Dance has been one of the most popular activities in church-directed recreation, particularly in the Mutual Improvement program of former years. As recently as the 1960s local competition winners from many states were brought to Salt Lake City to participate in extravaganzas involving thousands of dancers—among the largest dance festivals ever held. Music and dance festivals of more modest scale, involving several hundred participants, continue to be sponsored by the church on a local and regional basis. At Brigham Young University large numbers of students receive training and experience in radio, television, filmmaking, music, dance, drama, and other arts. BYU's campus contains outstanding museums of art, as well as several theaters. And the campus itself is a remarkable study in diversified architectural styles. This list of church-related cultural and artistic activities could be extended.

3. THE PRIVATE SECTOR

This category is so diversified, with so many nuances of influence on the arts in Utah, that justice cannot even be approached in these pages. Readers are referred to the 1941 edition and other sources for fuller treatment. Embraced by this category are literally thousands of arts-minded citizens of the state, working individually and collectively for the cultural betterment of society. Alone or in association, individuals have been responsible for art programs in schools, in museums and art centers, in theaters and symphony halls, in festivals and fairs. Those with means assisted struggling artists. The gifted taught others with evident talent. Churches other than the Mormons built attractive buildings, made them beautiful with stained glass and other works of art, encouraged their members in cultural ways. Philanthropists have contributed funds for education and training, purchased works of art, donated collections, helped to defray the costs of art centers and museums.

Ever since the Deseret Academy of Fine Arts was established in 1863, artists have joined together for mutual support, education, constructive criticism, cooperative exhibits, or publication of members' works. Contemporary painters are represented by groups such as the Associated Utah Artists, Utah Watercolor Society, Kaysville Art Club, and Ogden Palette Club. Writers support several membership groups (see Literature). Craftsmen, filmmakers, and other artists also associate in membership groups. On community, county, and regional levels, there are citizen arts councils, products of recent years, involving individuals, private organizations, and government, supported by private and public funding, with technical assistance from various agencies. Among their functions is sponsorship of arts and crafts exhibits, workshops, dance and theatre performances, and musical concerts.

Private or quasi-official organizations also are responsible for most of

Utah's festivals and celebrations, as well as many of its museums and public galleries. Note must be made also, of commercial galleries and private schools in Utah, which are indispensable for the encouragement of the arts.

One of the most interesting groups to be formed in recent years, perhaps a trend setter and innovator, is the artist's cooperative known as North Mountain, located at Alpine in Utah Valley. Founded by a small group of professional artists, some of whom were residents of Alpine and fellow members of the faculty at Brigham Young University, North Mountain was organized formally during the early 1970s. Activities have included summer seminars, a community newsletter, and an exhibit of members' works at the Salt Lake Art Center in 1980. Several of the founders have congregated in a new planned unit development near Alpine, known as Bull River, where they have been joined by other artists and nonartists. An open-air sculpture park is being developed, and space has been set aside for an art center. The founders of North Mountain were: Michael Graves, designer-art director; Neil Hadlock, sculptor-painter; Joseph Linton, architect; John Marshall, industrial designer; Marvin Payne, composer-singer-painter; Frank Riggs, sculptor-environmental designer; Dennis Smith, sculptor-poet; Gary Smith, painter-illustrator-muralist; and Trevor Southey, painter.

THE VISUAL ARTS

The visual arts include painting, sculpture, photography, and film-making. Painting and sculpture were treated in detail in the 1941 edition. At that time, photography and filmmaking were not unanimously regarded as arts, though photography was discussed in the earlier edition as a graphic art. Even today professional opinion is divided concerning their position among the arts. Crafts, design, and folk art are considered in this section as visual arts. Architecture is treated in a separate classification.

PAINTING

The history of painting in Utah to 1940 was admirably summarized in the 1941 edition. A substantial part of that summary provides a basis for historical discussion in these pages, though with organizational changes and certain other clarifying modifications. Deserving of appreciation in this respect is Dr. Robert S. Olpin of the University of Utah, eminent art historian, who revised the 1941 edition's art section and provided biographical and critical notes concerning painters and graphic artists of more recent times.

Prehistoric Indians were Utah's first painters, of course. As described on page 158 of the 1941 edition, cliff-faces and ceremonial chambers "were decorated with markings that range from elaborate paintings of ceremonial scenes to crude drawings scratched in the rock with a sharp stone." Occasionally, "the paintings attained heroic proportions . . . with hour-glass figures and triangular heads." A voluminous literature has developed on the subject of Indian rock art, providing much greater detail than is contained in the 1941 edition. *See also chapter on Indians and Archeology.*

With the arrival of the Mormon pioneers into Salt Lake Valley in 1847, another stage was fostered in the development of Utah painting.

By 1855 Brigham Young was recommending that foreign missionaries address special emphasis to the conversion of skilled artisans and architects. C. C. A. Christensen (1831-1912), a Danish convert, painted panoramic views of incidents and places along the trail from Nauvoo to Great Salt Lake City. His charming *Mormon Historical Panorama* was painted on a 3,000-foot continuous scroll comprised of 24 different scenes, 22 of which have been separated and are now part of Brigham Young University's art collection. Between 1860 and 1863, three painters, George Martin Ottinger (1833-1917), Danquart Weggeland (1827-1918), and John Tullidge (1826-1899), were brought to Utah and employed at painting scenery for the Salt Lake Theater, and later, murals for the ceremonial chambers of Mormon temples. These three men, though they came from New York, Norway, and England, respectively, had all matured in the same general tradition. Ottinger received his scant instruction under teachers imbued with the precepts of the Hudson River School of Landscape. His work is labored, literal, and usually quite static, but his enthusiasm for legendary subjects (drawn from the Book of Mormon and from the fabulous histories of the Incas current in his day) keeps local interest in him fresh and usually stirs the curiosity of those who have not known his paintings before. His two contemporaries, though they had not Ottinger's literary interest, were perhaps the more competent craftsmen. Both were literalists in the manner of the painters of the Dusseldorf Academy in Germany. Weggeland, later called "The Father of Utah Art," was one of the major influences on a second generation of Utah painters. Tullidge capped his career by painting in LDS Temples at St. George, Logan, and Manti.

Another creative spirit of Utah's earliest pictorial development was Harry Squires (1850-1928), who grew up in Salt Lake City after arriving in Utah as an infant in 1853. Squires became a self-trained local printer of starkly hard, but often effectively composed primitive landscape works.

Many other pioneer landscape efforts in Utah were essentially representative of the "Rocky Mountain School." Talented Deseret settlers including Alfred Lambourne, H. L. A. Culmer, and George Beard admirably apprehended the hugeness of western American nature and painted typical panoramic landscape scenes.

Alfred Lambourne (1850-1926) came to Utah from Missouri in 1856. He studied with Weggeland and Tullidge, graduated to scene painting for the Salt Lake Theater, and near the middle of his life abandoned painting for a literary career. During his short period of production he devoted himself almost exclusively to painting pictures of the Wasatch Mountains and Great Salt Lake, two segments of the Utah scene for which he had a passion. Culmer (1854-1914) was a businessman to whom painting was a Sunday avocation, yet with the assistance of Lambourne he became one of the best known of Utah's painters. He fell early under the influence of Thomas Moran, and in his mature work adopted a frankly imitative style. Moran painted several pictures in Utah, most of which now hang in the Library of Congress, Washington, D.C.

Beard (1855-1944) immigrated to Utah from England in 1868. Another "jack-of-all-trades," this self-taught artist not only developed a naively precise landscape style in painting, but served his settlement as pioneer

Barrier Canyon petroglyphs,
Canyonlands National Park
(above).

LeConte Stewart, painter *(right)*.

doctor and nurse, school trustee, store keeper, and finally as a state legislator in Salt Lake in 1896 where he helped design the official state seal.

Painters of this early period were hampered by a lack of organized exhibits and public interest. Paintings were normally shown in jewelers' shops, department stores, and recreation halls, where space was restricted and the lighting poor. About 1869, the Deseret Agricultural and Manufacturing Society, forerunner of the State Fair, was persuaded to exhibit and to award medals for paintings as well as Durham bulls, insuring at least one comprehensive annual show. In the 1870s the universities began to include art instruction in their courses; previously the Salt Lake Polysophical Society announced classes in drawing "for young ladies," declining to make such provision for young men. In general the people of the territory were too engrossed in the endless struggle with their lands to give the arts more than a cursory (and somewhat suspicious) glance.

John Hafen (1856-1910), regarded by many as Utah's finest landscapist, came to the territory from Switzerland in 1862. He studied under Weggeland and Ottinger, and in 1890 was sent abroad by the Mormon Church, with Lorus Pratt, J. B. Fairbanks, and Edwin Evans, to prepare himself for commissions in Mormon temples. In France, Hafen came under the influence of Corot, with whom he was already identified by disposition, and there perfected the sensitive approach to nature which is characteristic of his work. Almost every major collection of paintings in the state boasts a Hafen, the most comprehensive group being in the Springville Museum, which owns *The Quaking Aspens,* considered by Hafen his best work. John B. Fairbanks (1855-1940), though he is well loved for his glowing harvest-scapes, has been sometimes eclipsed by the achievements of his two sons, Avard, sculptor, and J. Leo, painter. Edwin Evans (1860-1946), soon after his return from Europe during the nineties, became chairman of the Art Department at the University of Utah and continued as its head for twenty-five years. He was perhaps the first teacher in Utah to break with the methods of the Academie Julian and insist that his students be allowed to develop naturally. His own painting derives its chief charm from solid space and form relationships as well as rich and varied textural effects.

James T. Harwood (1860-1940) preceded Hafen to France by about two years. Harwood was a teacher directly or indirectly to many of Utah's finest painters. From 1905 he exhibited regularly at the Paris Spring Salon, was a contributor to many American shows, and he was known on the Continent as one of the most adept moderns in colored etching. His *Preparation for the Dinner,* which hangs at the University of Utah, is a representative early piece; in his late years he adopted the pointellistic brush technique of the impressionists without the pure palette, which imparted to his landscapes an atmospheric quality much prized by his buyers.

John W. Clawson (1858-1936), who made his home alternately in California and Utah, was known throughout the intermountain region for his richly colored portraits, several of which hang in the collection of Brigham Young University and in the Capitol. Mary Teasdel (1863-1937) was the first Utah woman to be accepted in the Paris Spring Salon. Lee Greene Richards (1878-1950), though he helped paint the murals for the Utah State

Capitol, will probably be best remembered for his portraits, several of which hang in the Capitol. His *Portrait of a Violinist,* in the collection of Brigham Young University, is generally conceded to be his best work.

Alma Brockerman Wright (1875-1952), teacher and art chairman at the University of Utah, was a painter of standard though competent landscape scenes and had developed a rather admirable "Whistlerian" portrait style in his early years.

Donald Beauregard (1885-1914), noted for his scenes of Indian life, died while painting murals depicting the life of Saint Francis in the Santa Fe (New Mexico) Museum. Mabel Frazer (1887-   ), teacher at the University of Utah for 33 years, has been one of Utah's most versatile, productive and revered artists. LeConte Stewart (1891-   ), head of the University of Utah Art Department from 1938 to 1956 and the first of Utah's recognized painters to turn his back uncompromisingly on sentimental landscape, belongs in point of time with this group of painters, though he has steadfastly refused to study in any but American schools. Lawrence Squires (1887-1928) is remembered for his etchings as well as his paintings. E. H. Eastmond (1876-1936), former head of the Brigham Young University Art Department, was a sensitive master of the monotype.

Bent F. Larson (1882-   ), Brigham Young University's long-time art chairman from 1936 to 1953, has been one of the most thoughtful craftsmen among Utah painters. His earlier landscapes in oil, usually low in key and quite subtle, strongly reflect his French masters; his pictures of western life produced after 1930 were more boldly painted. Ranch Kimball, businessman and painter, whose *Man Manicures Mountains* was hung in the National Exhibition of American Art, and Waldo Midgley, known for his water colors and portraits, are other Utah painters who broke with tradition and adventured in new fields. Dean Fausett, younger brother of Lynn—both sons of pioneer parents in the Carbon County coal fields—has won national recognition as a muralist and portraitist. Other artists who attained prominence in the period before and after World War II include Cornelius and Rose Howard Salisbury, Orson D. Campbell, Florence Ware, Caroline Parry, Joseph A. F. Everett, Milton Wassmer, Henri Moser, and John H. Stansfield. Calvin Fletcher (1882-1963), chairman of the Art Department of Utah State University from 1906 to 1947, led a small group in experimenting with cubistic forms, bringing Mrs. Irene Fletcher, George Smith Dibble, Mary Farnham, and H. Reuben Reynolds into prominence.

Creation of the WPA Art Project in 1935 enabled young and progressive artists to remain in the state, and, under the leadership of State Director Elzy J. Bird, gave widespread stimulus to the visual arts in Utah through exhibits and the painting of murals for communities that could not otherwise have afforded them.

The influence of the painters named above will continue to be felt for generations to come. The styles of many would be classified today as traditional, conservative, realistic, representational, objective, or academic, as compared with modern, nonobjective, abstract, nonrepresentational, impressionistic, expressionistic, or surrealistic styles that have gained in popularity in this century. Yet it would be inaccurate and unjust to place all of these earlier painters in strict style categories, for all were originals, some experimented with different styles and techniques, and many changed their stylistic preferences with time.

It is much more difficult today than it was in 1940 to select in a brief outline those artists who are "best qualified" to represent Utah painting. Artistic expressions are in a state of experimental flux that may be unprecedented, not only in painting but in other art disciplines as well. As never before, laymen search for subtle meanings and messages in art, and artists experiment with diverse forms of expression. Also, with a renaissance now fulminating in creative circles, there is such a multitude of talented artists that critical choice can hardly be more than subjective opinion.

Several of the painters mentioned above continue to the present day, gaining enhanced distinction and adding lustre to the arts in Utah. Still active is LeConte Stewart, often called the dean of Utah landscape artists. George S. Dibble, who taught for many years at the University of Utah and elsewhere, is a master watercolorist and has been a long-time art critic for the *Salt Lake Tribune*. Dean Fausett, while a Utahn more by nativity than residence (he has lived in the east during most of his working life), has received much recognition for his murals, landscapes, and portraits of distinguished subjects. Neglected in the earlier volume were painters who deserve ranking with many of those whose names were listed. Among others, these include Frank I. S. Zimbeaux (1861-1935), a talented Pennsylvanian who made his home in Utah during the final decade of his life . . . Willis Adams (1854-1932), prolific painter and photographer of Park City . . . George Henry Taggart, a rather sophisticated portrait specialist and tonal impressionist figure/landscape painter . . . Alice Merrill Horne, painter and more importantly an early Utah "visual arts activist" who was instrumental in the establishment by legislative act of the Utah Art Institute, known today as the Utah Arts Council . . . Dorothy van Stipriaan Luiscius, arts librarian for years in Salt Lake City, who was a sensitive, well-educated, and gifted painter . . . and Francis Horspool (1871-1951), who undoubtedly was Utah's most distinctive and productive primitive artist.

Through the years, Utah's public schools and institutions of higher learning have trained and been the career bases or professional springboards of many of the state's most talented and productive visual artists. For example, Utah State University (formerly Utah State Agricultural College) nurtured such outstanding teacher-painters as the late Calvin Fletcher and H. Reuben "Harry" Reynolds. Everett Thorpe, Harrison T. Groutage, and Gaell Lindstrom are presently instructors in USU's art department. Thorpe is an impressive talent now known for both his earlier dynamic regionalist/realist/expressionist style and for the locally courageous abstract expressionism of his Hans Hofmann-influenced maturity; Groutage concentrates on romantic landscapes of Cache Valley; and Lindstrom is considered a dedicated realist painter.

The arts staff of Weber State College has included Farrell R. Collett, who founded the art department and retired in 1976 after 37 years of teaching. Though Collett is admired for his paintings of wildlife and animals, he is accomplished as well in portraits, landscapes, and sculpture. Among other noted teacher-artists at Weber State College are Dale Bryner, one of the great virtuoso performers in Utah in terms of the drawing of the human figure; Richard Van Wagoner, the present chairman of the Weber State College art program and a painter who works in the "photo-realist" style to express the "good life" of Utah's suburban north; and Charles A. Groberg.

Staff members from Southern Utah State College have gained recognition for their creativity, including Thomas A. Leek, noted for his masterful depictions of the red-rock country; Glen Dale Anderson; and Robert L. Gerring. A number of the state's best-known painters trained or taught at SUSC before transferring to professional life or the art staffs of other schools.

Elaine Michelsen, for many years chairman of the Art Department at Westminster College, was the first woman to hold such a position in the state. A master of varied techniques and a prolific creator, Professor Michelsen has been the recipient of numerous awards and honors. C. Don Doxey, a teacher at Westminster, also is noted as a painter.

A number of Utah's most distinguished artists have been affiliated with the University of Utah's Department of Art at one time or another. Among these were many whose names appear in the 1941 edition—for example, Edwin Evans, Florence Ware, Maud Hardman, LeConte Stewart, George S. Dibble, A. B. Wright, and Lee Greene Richards. In the decades since, many other members of the university arts staff have gained prominence, some being acknowledged as leaders in the introduction of avante-garde, contemporary, often controversial styles and techniques. V. Douglas Snow, a member of the arts faculty since 1954, has been a dominant force in Utah in terms of a painterly direction away from "realistic" form. Having a rich background of training, Snow has received numerous awards. Among the best known of his many works are murals in the Salt Lake City Public Library and Pioneer Memorial Theatre at the University of Utah. Edward D. Maryon, a distinguished painter of landscapes in oil and watercolor, served as Dean of the University's College of Fine Arts for 17 years (1964-1981). The late Alvin Gittins, perhaps the state's most respected painter of portraits in recent years, taught at the university for more than three decades. A native of England, Gittins had been a resident of Utah since the mid-1940s; numbered among his portrait subjects are many persons of national and international stature. Still another former teacher at the university is Arnold Friberg, long-time Utah resident who has gained renown as a versatile illustrator, portraitist, and creator of monumental paintings of religious and historical subjects. Frank Anthony "Tony" Smith, a teacher of painting (and a sculptor), developed a distinctive abstract style that has been the subject of more than a few critical reviews in recent years and the substance for animated discussion wherever his works are shown. The terms "illusion" and "paradox" are commonly used in attempting to describe Smith's treatment of subject. Three more recent additions to the art faculty are Paul Davis, Roger "Sam" Wilson, and Anton "Tony" Rasmussen. Davis is one of the most imaginative and talented figurative painters working in Utah. Wilson, painter and printmaker, is noted for his stylistic use of "trompe l'oeil." Rasmussen displays his style in a mural of southern Utah's red-rock country at the Salt Lake International Airport.

Brigham Young University has nurtured more than a few notable painters, as well as artists of other disciplines. Painters of earlier years included Elbert H. Eastmond and B. F. Larsen. In recent years the growth of BYU's art program has been especially successful in developing independent talents, among whom are Robert L. Marshall, painter and present chairman of the Art Department . . . William F. Whitaker, Jr., a figure painter who often uses the Wild West as subject matter . . . Gary L. Rosine, a talented semi-abstractionist painter who has provided strong individual statements in paint within a largely realistic community of artists . . . Gary E. Smith, perhaps the most interesting young Utah artist specifically concerned with Mormon themes expressed in painting . . . and Trevor Southey, a convert to the Mormon faith who, like Smith, is an innovator in the treatment of Mormon subject matter. Smith and Southey are among the cofounders of the North Mountain artists' cooperative in Alpine, described above.

As an active teaching institution, the Salt Lake Art Center (begun as the Salt Lake Art Barn), has numbered among its faculty many artists of outstanding talent and distinction. For example, Michael R. Cannon, who served on the faculty for 18 years (1942-1960), specialized in restrained still life subjects that exhibited characteristic and convincing qualities of sharply apprehended light. Don Olsen, on the other hand, developed from an earlier form of brutal and painterly symbolic expressionism to an absolutely mind-clearing and joyful precision geometry. Lee Deffebach, another painter of exciting expressionist abstractions, continues her thoughtful experimentation with the finely felt color-field fusions of paint and canvas. Olsen and Deffebach in the 1960s would share with Doug Snow of the University of Utah staff a dominance of the local scene in terms of a painterly direction away from realistic form. Earl M. Jones, representing a "traditional" approach to painting, has established himself as one of Utah's most effective figure/landscape painters. Denis Phillips, co-owner of Phillips Gallery with his wife Bonnie, is a gifted painter of both abstract and realistic works; Bonnie Phillips is a respected painter as well. The versatile David Sucec also is an Art Center instructor at this time.

In discussing the Salt Lake Art Center it should be noted that James L. Haseltine, the Center's director from 1961 to 1967, authored one of the most useful of published works concerning the general development of Utah art. The volume was entitled *100 Years of Utah Painting.*

There have been, and are now, hundreds of other Utah painters of extraordinary talent. Space allows the listing of only a few additional names. Stephen R. Beck, for example, like Tony Smith forsakes the brush and consistently converts nature into a wholly clean-hewn world via an essential simplicity and orientation to hard edge. Approaching "purist" form, Beck's work has represented a halfway point between realism and absolute geometric balances on canvas.

Deserving of special mention are the masterful religious murals in the North Visitors Center on Temple Square in Salt Lake City. Strikingly forceful in their depictions of episodes from sacred texts, these murals are viewed by throngs of visitors to the Mormon center. They are the work of several exceptionally gifted painters, among whom are Harry Anderson, originator of a number of the Biblical scenes; Grant Romney Clawson, who repainted and enlarged Anderson's originals; Kenneth Riley; Alexander Rosenfeld; and John Scott.

Paul Salisbury, nephew of Cornelius, has gained note as a painter of western scenes and animals. Louis Heinzman is a popular and successful painter of western landscapes and European subjects. Lynn Griffin of Escalante is a self-taught painter of western subjects. The late Stanford E. Samuelson was a prolific painter of murals, portraits, landscapes, still life, and theater scenery. L. Goff Dowding of Bountiful is a respected graphic designer, painter, and art teacher, specializing in western subjects; LaMyra Dowding, his wife, is a talented painter in her own right. Elva Malin's landscapes are considered exceptional. Posthumous recognition should be given to Ernest Untermann, Sr., the remarkable painter of the Uinta Basin, whose studies of prehistoric life forms and ancient landscapes adorn the walls of the Dinosaur Museum of Natural History in Vernal. In the last years of a long life, Untermann created some of the most original art in Utah.

Among other Utah painters of distinct talent—many of whom are young in years and can be expected to gain increased recognition in the future—might be mentioned Sharon Shepherd, Ken Baxter, Kathryn Wilson, Ron Clayton, Chad Smith, Sam Collett, Maureen O. Ure, Bonnie Sucec, Ralph Schofield, and Ed Dolinger.

SCULPTURE

Introducing the discussion of sculpture in the 1941 edition was the statement that "In point of excellence, it is probably in the field of plastic art that Utah has contributed most." While artists in other disciplines might argue that assertion, it is certainly a fact that sculpture has become a prominent force in Utah art. According to sculptor Dennis Smith, "The number of public commissions has skyrocketed in the past five years. Works of sculpture are a refreshing addition to the urban landscape. Architects are designing sculpture into their buildings, to add a human dimension to the simple forms of contemporary architecture. Public and private interest and awareness of sculpture have increased to a level never before experienced."

The careers and works of a number of distinguished Utah sculptors were described in the 1941 edition, to which readers are referred for more detail than appears below:

Mahonri Young, a grandson of Brigham Young, fellow of the Arts and Letters Society and of the National Academy . . . is among the most prominent of contemporary American sculptors. . . . His sculpture is realistic, and, though not imitative, is somewhat in the manner of Meunier, the Belgian. . . . Young, though he has maintained his studio in New York City for many years, has returned to Utah at intervals to execute commissions, among them the Sea Gull Monument . . . and the excellent life-size statues of Joseph and Hyrum Smith, all in Temple Square, Salt Lake City. In 1939 Young was commissioned to design and execute an ambitious monument to the Mormon pioneers of 1847, to be placed at the mouth of Emigration Canyon, overlooking Salt Lake City. . . .

Cyrus E. Dallin, best known for his often-reproduced Indian equestrian statues, *The Appeal to the Great Spirit, The Medicine Man,* and *The Signal of Peace,* was born in Springville, Utah, and did his first modeling there with coarse native clays. In 1882, in competition with many of the finest sculptors in America, he was com-

Mahonri M. Young, sculptor, and Seagull Monument on Temple Square, one of his many works.

Avard Fairbanks in his studio.

UTAH ARTS COUNCIL

Dinosaur group at Prehistoric Museum, Price—Gary Prazen, sculptor *(above)*.

Sculpture work by Dennis Smith, Western Airlines Terminal, Salt Lake City *(left)*.

missioned to execute the statue of Paul Revere [in Boston]. . . . His enthusiasm for native subjects, especially the Indian, has not been without influence in the contemporary tendency of American artists to depict American topics. The best known of his statues in Utah [is a bronze copy of Massasoit on the grounds of the State Capitol, which is a duplicate of the original bronze Massasoit on Coles Hill, Massachusetts, overlooking Plymouth Bay].

Avard Fairbanks received his preliminary instruction from his father, John B. Fairbanks, and while still very young was granted a special scholarship to the Art Student League in New York City as a reward for his group study, *Fighting Panthers.* He entered the Ecole des Beaux Arts at seventeen, and was in 1940 professor of sculpture at the University of Michigan. . . . Other Utah sculptors of prominence are Millard F. Malin, whose best-known work, the Sugar House Monument in Salt Lake City, has received much comment for the structural honesty of its two heroic figures; Torlief Knaphus, executor of the Constitution Monument in Salt Lake City, the Hill Cumorah Monument (a Mormon shrine) in New York State, and the hand-cart pioneer group [on Temple Square]; and Maurice Brooks, best known for his portrait busts [and for Mormon Church commissions].

1941 edition

The careers of these outstanding artists are treated in depth in references such as Olpin's *Dictionary of Utah Art.* Young lived for ten years following dedication of This is the Place Monument in Salt Lake City, in 1947, for which he had created 74 figures in bronze. Dallin lived until 1944. Knaphus worked in Mormon temples in Idaho, Canada, and Arizona, and taught at University of Utah and Brigham Young University. Malin and Brooks also continued to work for years following their mention in the 1941 edition. Avard Fairbanks returned to Utah in 1946 as the first dean of the School of Fine Arts at the University of Utah, where he remained as a teacher until

1965. Examples of his work in Utah include *The Young Lincoln* (Marriott Library, University of Utah), *Daniel Jackling* (State Capitol), *Mother and Child* (Springville), and working models in the Fairview Museum. Both Ortho Fairbanks, brother of Avard, and Justin Fairbanks, Avard's son, have added lustre to the family name as noted sculptural artists and teachers.

Gaining prominence and acclaim in recent decades, not only within the state but regionally and nationally as well, are a number of sculptor-teachers from Utah's colleges and universities. Franz M. Johansen, for example, has taught at Brigham Young University since 1956, during that period creating many notable works. Since the same year, Angelo Caravaglia has been a teacher at University of Utah, garnering awards and professional eminence as a leader in the contemporary figurative idiom. His works include a relief at the Mountain Bell offices and a garden sculpture in the atrium of the Public Library, both in Salt Lake City. The faculty of Brigham Young University includes Warren B. Wilson and Dallas J. Anderson. A Utah native, Wilson is known for his rough-hewn figures in wood and for abstract ceramic sculpture. Anderson studied in Norway and Denmark. Olpin describes him as a "master carver in stone"; his remarkable symbolic grouping of alabaster stones, known as Gilgal—east of Bryce Canyon—is described in Tour No. 9C. Weber State College claims at least two talented sculptors, James McBeth and David Cox, who are mentioned also under Crafts—McBeth for "a strong jewelry program" and Cox as "an accomplished stoneware artist and ceramic sculptor." Larry Elsner of Utah State University is an acknowledged master of sculpture and ceramics; his name also appears under Crafts.

The most noted of Utah's independent sculptors, not already mentioned, include the following *(named in alphabetical order):* Clark Bronson, a master of animal modeling who has gained national recognition for his work. . . . Ed Fraughton, well known for western images (frontier and Indian). Among his many works are the heroic Mormon Battalion Monument in San Diego and bronze sculptures in the Mormon Pioneer Memorial Park in Salt Lake City *(see Tour No. 3).* . . . Neil Hadlock, formerly a university teacher, founder of Wasatch Bronzeworks and a sculptor of large minimalist forms. *Fayette,* a Hadlock work, approximately 25 feet in height, stands at the I-15/Provo Canyon interchange. . . . Florence Hansen, who worked with Dennis Smith *(below)* in creating the Relief Society garden park in Nauvoo. . . . Richard Johnston, a teacher at University of Utah and creator of "exquisitely crafted . . . abstract sculpture" (Olpin). Johnston has exhibited widely. . . . Raymond Jonas, who "deals with organic carved forms in a very profound manner." . . . Frank Nackos of Payson, who has exhibited throughout the west. A painted steel sculpture by Nackos marks the entrance to the Valtek complex in Springville. . . . Frank Riggs, who has created several large-scale works, among them *Tree Forms* (Salt Lake City Parks) and *Uinta* on Exchange Place. . . . Jo Roper, sculptor of the stone relief on the exterior of the Salt Lake City Public Library, "a fine example of the marriage that can occur between sculpture and architecture." . . . Dennis Smith, a versatile sculptor, co-founder of North Mountain in Alpine and a creator of the *Monument to*

Women sculpture park at Nauvoo, Illinois, commissioned by the Relief Society of the Mormon Church. Duplicates of three works from the park are on display in the plaza east of Temple Square, while other works can be seen in Salt Lake City on 3rd South between Main and State *(The Doll and the Dare),* at business offices, Western Airlines Terminal, Utah Department of Transportation, etc. . . . Trevor Southey, a well-known painter, the creator of a sculptor entitled *Healing* in the main entrance of the University Medical Center in Salt Lake City, "a metaphysical statement exploring the relationships of the strong and the vulnerable." . . . Grant Speed, a "loose realist" sculptor of Wild West forms whose work is recognized as some of the finest of its type and is found in major collections of western art.

GRAPHICS

The graphic arts have always played an important role in the development of Utah's visual arts. From photography and filmmaking to printmaking and commercial design, many prominent artists have emerged in this category.

Photography

Perhaps the nearest approach to a graphic art in the early days of Utah was the work of a hardy band of photographers who undertook to supply the curious East with views of the Plains, Rocky Mountains, Mormons, Indians, and whatever else that was strange or romantic in the West. Apparently the first man to lug daguerreotype equipment into Utah Territory was M. Cannon, who had a photographic gallery in Salt Lake City as early as 1850. The original plates made by John Wesley Jones, who daguerreotyped his way from Missouri to California after 1851, have all been lost, but several pencil sketches made from them, including a view of Great Salt Lake City in 1853, have been preserved in eastern museums. Jones was closely followed by S. N. Carvalho and C. C. Mills, both significant figures in the history of American photography, and in 1860 by C. R. Savage. Savage obviated the difficulties of transporting the heavy equipment of the day (a photographer's outfit during the 1850's weighed something more than 200 pounds) by setting up a gallery in Great Salt Lake City, which he used as a base for forays into the mountains and Indian country. His pictures are rated as classic by collectors . . . During the 1870's E. O. Beaman, Clement Powell, and Jack Hillers, photographers to one or another of Major John Wesley Powell's Colorado River expeditions, made a fine collection of photographs, some of which were published in 1939 by the Smithsonian Institution.

1941 edition

Savage still occupies a position of eminence as a pioneer of Utah photography, as described in the 1941 edition. Since 1941, however, the pantheon of photographic artists of bygone years has welcomed others whose work has been "discovered" during the ensuing years. Perhaps foremost among these is George Edward Anderson (1860-1928), a middle-era photographer who recorded the features and costumes of thousands of Utahns, not only in the studio but in their homes, on their porches, and at work. Based for many years in Springville, Anderson specialized in scenes of central Utah before and after the turn of the century. His negatives, many of which survived after years of neglect, are a priceless pictorial legacy. Deserving mention also was Anderson's contemporary, Willis Adams of Park City (later of Salt Lake City), who gained recognition not only as a recorder of people and places in Park City but also as an able and original painter. His brother, Charles Adams, served for years as a commercial photographer in Ogden. The Utah State Historical Society recently acquired the photographic negatives of J. George Midgley, who specialized in rural and landscape scenes, printing by the Bromoil transfer process.

These artists, of course, were only a few among the photographers who have recorded on film the landscape, people, and changing scene of Utah. The majority are immortalized by their works rather than their names. Utah's newspapers and electronic media have nurtured a multitude of talented photographers, many of whom have received honors for their work. Ralph T. Clark and Craig Law (Utah State University) and John Telford, Joseph Marotta, and Craig Pozzi (University of Utah) exemplify those photographic artists who share their talents and skill through teaching. Nelson Wadsworth (Brigham Young University) and H. Reuben Reynolds, now deceased (Utah State University), also represent this distinguished teaching fraternity. Utah can boast a number of very able commercial photographers. For example, the late Hal Rumel occupied a position of eminence among this group, being a masterful technician as well as a sensitive artist in such diverse fields as portraiture, aerial, industrial, and landscape photography. Among well-known living artists in commercial photography might be listed Borge Anderson, Richard Burton, Don and Gary Blair, Frank Jensen, and Bill Shipler.

Film and Video

As early as 1922 Utah was a "discovery" of the Hollywood film factories (in a Tom Mix western) and for 50 years southern Utah was one of the most frequently-used backlots of the film industry. Literally hundreds of films and television episodes were set against the state's remarkable landscapes. Images selected by John Ford, Cecil B. DeMille, George Stevens and many others helped to make Utah scenes emblematic of the vanished past. With time, however, the diminished public interest in the western genre had stemmed the tide of those welcome producers entering the state with their production caravans, and by the early 1970s the volume of out-of-state productions in Utah had dropped sharply.

In 1978, the Media Production Studio of Brigham Young University celebrated 25 years of continuous production, a period during which several hundred varying-length motion pictures were produced at that studio. This installation is one of the most elaborate and most productive of its kind in Utah. Originally established to produce films for use in varied programs of the Mormon Church and the university, the studio later broadened its market scope by producing films for non-Mormon clients. Founder of the studio was Wetzel O. "Judge" Whitaker, assisted by his brother Scott.

Since the 1970s, the University of Utah has also produced some fine individual filmmakers through training in film production in the Department of Art.

Markets for local television commercials and for promotional, educational and industrial films, created a cadre of small format film producers during the 1960s and 1970s; and federal government-contracted film and

Utah has been the filming scene for scores of outdoor movies.

audiovisual work occasionally stimulated small production units in Salt Lake City and other Utah cities.

A resurgence of film and television production activity began in the late 1970s as a number of new facilities and services were developed. Sunn Classic Pictures (later Taft International Pictures), a prolific producer of mostly family-oriented product for theatrical and television release, employs as many as 300 Utahns. The highly respected Osmond Studio, completed in Orem in 1977, is host to ongoing production for network television and theatrical markets. Skaggs Telecommunications Services and Bonneville Productions (together with their affiliate Video West) are becoming important video producers.

Returning to Utah from bases in California, Lyman Dayton *(Seven Alone, Baker's Hawk, Against a Crooked Sky)* and Kieth Merrill *(Great American Cowboy, Takedown, Harry's War, Windwalker)* each produced or directed theatrical release feature films in his home state.

A critical ingredient in the general resurgence is the Utah Film Development office, a state agency charged with attracting film and television production and with representing industry interests under the guidance of John Earle. With good success in renewing the state's relations with the California production community, the agency also was instrumental in founding the Utah/US Film Festival, said to be the most ambitious event of its kind ever held in the west outside Hollywood. The first festival was held in September 1978, the second in October 1979—both in Salt Lake City—and the third and fourth in January 1981 and 1982 at Park City. By 1981 the name had been changed to the United States Film and Video Festival in Utah. Features of the festival include competition showings and judging of feature films produced by independent filmmakers . . . seminars and programs involving prominent actors, directors, producers, cinematographers, and other film personages . . . award ceremonies . . . and public screenings of notable films. According to participants, the Utah festival is having a significant impact on the nation's film industry by bringing together persons representing the diverse elements of the film and video industry, developing new audiences, and providing encouragement, critical appraisal, technical advice, and economic assistance to independent producers.

Actor-producer-director Robert Redford, a resident of the state, has steered several film projects to Utah, among them *Butch Cassidy and the Sundance Kid, Jeremiah Johnson,* and *Electric Horseman.* Encouraged by the success of the Utah Film and Video Festival he and others moved to establish the Sundance Film and Video Institute in August 1980 with Sterling VanWagenen (past Festival director) as executive director. Located at the Sundance Resort, its goals are the discovery and development of new talent in the film industry and the identification of industry problems and their resolution.

The Utah Media Center, created in 1979, has focused on programs aimed at promoting film and video as media arts. Among its goals: educating children and the public about film and video, sponsoring exciting film/video events not readily available in the area, and assisting and supporting independent area media artists. The center arranges the distribution of special film/video packages to schools and groups throughout the region, supports a filmmaker-in-residence program in public schools, hosts a visiting film/video artist series, and sponsors film festivals and premieres. It has also organized a weekly exhibition program of quality feature films not generally available in this area. Facilities, personnel and programs of the center are available to the public, to the film industry, and to students. The Utah Media Center is supported by the Utah Arts Council and the Salt Lake Art Center, where the media center is located.

Printmaking

The success of printmaking as an art in Utah in recent years is due largely to the efforts of a small group of talented and dedicated artists. For example, three instructors at Utah State University, Moishe Smith, Adrian Van Suchtelen, and Marion Hyde, are noted for their skill and artistic expression in the medium of printmaking. Smith, a well-known realistic intaglio printmaker, has widespread representation in collections. Van Suchtelen is a figurative/semi-abstract printmaker who works both in relief and intaglio. Hyde—a printmaker, painter and sculptor—works as a realistic stylist in woodcut and wood engraving.

Brigham Young University has also produced three printmakers of distinction. Wulf Barsch, whose prints are of abstract composition, has exhibited locally, nationally, and world-wide. Trevor Southey, noted also as a painter, works in intaglio with figurative images which often represent Mormon subject matter in an innovative way. Michael Clane Graves, former graphic designer for Deseret Book, is an effective printmaker working in an abstract style.

Two instructors at the University of Utah who have made notable contribution to the art of printmaking are Robert Kleinschmidt and Margret Carde. Kleinschmidt tends to pursue a theme through nuance after nuance to create statements in prints that one must search out to enjoy. Carde's work very frequently expresses fragile textile-like patterns.

Other talented printmakers presently working in Utah include Marilyn Miller, Royden Card, Alex Bigney, and John Belingheri.

Commercial Design

With regard to commercial design, the 1941 edition stated that "Three of [Mahonri] Young's Salt Lake students have achieved national prominence as commercial artists: William Crawford of Provo (who signs himself Galbreith), illustrator for the *New Yorker, Esquire,* and other magazines; Hal Burrows, illustrator of the former *Life* and *Judge;* and John Held, Jr., creator of the now passe flapper girl cartoons."

This category, and others, are only superficially valid as means of classifying artists. John Held, Jr., mentioned above, for example, gained fame primarily as an illustrator and cartoonist; but he was a sculptor, ceramicist, writer, dancer, and singer, among other attributes. Jack Sears was exceptionally talented as a cartoonist, painter, illustrator, commercial artist, and teacher of techniques at the University of Utah. So it is with more than a few contemporary graphic and design artists. Among these, for example, was Verla Birrell, for many years a dynamic teacher of interior design at the University of Utah. Birrell was a painter, interior designer, textile designer, poetess, and historian, not to mention being credited with several "firsts": first to teach silk screen in Utah; first to teach spatial and mobile 3-D art here; first in the U.S. to design, construct and frame a linoleum mosaic. She also initiated the teaching of industrial design, plastic design, pottery, sculpture, and mural painting classes at Brigham Young University.

Recent additions in this category are the busy illustrator, Glen L. Edwards of Utah State University, and the *Deseret News* cartoonist, Calvin Grondahl. Others, perhaps equally as worthy, could be listed if space permitted. Among the most respected and versatile of the state's commercial designers are Ted Nagata, Keith Eddington, Keith Montague, Richard Bailey, Richard Scopes, F. McRay Magleby, Glade Christensen, and Ray Morales.

CRAFTS AND FOLK ART

A historical summary of Utah crafts appears in the 1941 edition. Several pages are devoted to Indian arts and crafts, beginning with prehistoric cultures, and several more pages describe cowboy and pioneer crafts. Craftwork of bygone eras, including pioneer handiwork, appears in museums throughout the state, is treasured in countless homes, or is sometimes available for purchase in commercial shops.

Interest in ceramics, fiber arts, jewelry-making, glassblowing, and other expressions in the area of the crafts has been coincident and indeed part of the blossoming of creativity in painting, sculpture, photography, and other visual arts—a trend that has developed phenomenally during the past several decades. Prior to 1960, art exhibitions in Utah were not open to craft people. Schools, colleges, universities, and art centers have responded to the surge of creativity and activity in the crafts, and in many instances represent a nucleus of interest and participation by professionals and amateurs alike.

A distinguished leader in the field of craft instruction and encouragement, Mrs. A. L. (Glenn) Beeley, was mentioned in the 1941 edition. She is remembered also as the founder and first director of Pioneer Craft House, which is active at 3271 S. 500 East in Salt Lake City.

Delbert W. Smedley, who served for years as supervisor of art for Granite School District, was another influential individual in the encouragement of the crafts. There are many others working today who deserve mention. Among these, Dorothy Bearnson—on the faculty of the University of Utah since 1946—has earned a reputation as a skilled ceramic artist, particularly in working with glazes. She has been instrumental in teaching ceramics as an art form to a large number of students. Also at the University of Utah is David Roy Pendell, a leader in exhibit and organizational activities, and a teacher of kiln technology (among other subjects). Pendell is skilled in working with ceramics, wood, metals, and other materials. Other University of Utah teachers, Gayle Weyher and Gail Della Piana, specialize in fabric design and weaving. At Utah State University, Larry Elsner is a sensitive potter, sculptor, and teacher who has exhibited widely. Under the guidance of James McBeth, a strong jewelry program has been developed at Weber State College. David Cox, also at WSC, has built a reputation as an accomplished stoneware artist and ceramic sculptor. Kay Kuzminsky, who developed a ceramics program at Westminster College, is known for her outstanding porcelain and raku work. Warren Wilson at Brigham Young University has recently completed a lengthy series of Primitive Pottery Workshops in Utah's back country and is the author of a book on the subject of primitive pottery. Kevin Frazier started the ceramics program at Utah Technical College in Salt Lake City, was one of the founders of Salt Lake Independent Potters, and is noted for his artistry in porcelain, stoneware, raku, and low fire work.

Many crafts people are affiliated with art centers or work independently. Milt Beens, for example, started the pottery and built the first downdraft kiln at the old Salt Lake Art Barn. Lee Dillon operates a successful ceramic program at the Salt Lake Art Center. Jane Hartford is a fine weaver and textile artisan. Roger Davis set up the pottery at the Bountiful Art Center. Known for his humorous duck series and copper red porcelains, Davis has been a teacher and now operates a studio in Alpine. Other teacher-entrepreneurs include John and Diane Shaw, owners of the North Salt Lake Pottery, who are known for the excellence of their stoneware. Jim Stewart is reputed to be the first studio potter in Utah to make a living from the sale of his work. Stewart also has taught at University of Utah. Utah's roster of pioneering ceramic entrepreneurs also includes Joseph and Lee Bennion, who operate the Horseshoe Mountain Pottery in Spring City.

Joseph Bennion of Spring City, potter.

Ronnie Sharp, willow furniture maker.

Viewing displays at a craft exhibit.

Elbert H. Porter, a sculptor who studied and worked with Avard Fairbanks, became skilled in the field of plastic resin and fiberglass. Porter devoted years to creating a group of full-size models of prehistoric dinosaurs. After temporary stops enroute, these monster sculptures now reside at Dinosaur Natural History Museum in Vernal.

Craft organizations include Utah Designer Craftsmen, Mary Meigs Atwater Weavers Guild, and Salt Lake Independent Potters. Utah Designer Craftsmen was founded in 1960 and has sponsored a number of exhibits featuring a comprehensive variety of crafts.

The products of Utah's craft artists may be viewed and purchased in commercial galleries—some specifically devoted to the crafts (for example, Stone Age Crafts Gallery in Salt Lake City)—and in public art centers, museums, and at fairs and festivals. The Utah Arts Festival and Park City Art Festival feature scores of craftsmen and artisans, working in myriad areas, utilizing a wide range of materials. It is difficult to detect a distinctive Utah style in contemporary crafts. Handmade items in clay, metal, wood, glass, leather and other materials are sometimes universal in design and execution, though the strong individual stamp of the artist becomes recognizable to those who follow the crafts carefully. Copper souvenirs are popular with tourists, and Indian handicrafts (not always genuine) are stocks in trade for many gift shops. Throughout the state, the individual craftsperson continues to produce fine works of utilitarian nature blended with esthetic sensitivity, for sale to tourists and residents alike.

Folk Art

"Folklife is what identifies us," according to Hal Cannon, folk arts coordinator for the Utah Arts Council. "It's our common culture which embraces everything that is traditional, handmade and artful. You can find folk art in the songs we sing, the houses we build, the food we set at our tables—folk arts are simply defined as the tools of our lives." Additionally, "Folk art is the art of the common man . . . it is usually conservative and reflects the traditions of several generations . . . it is rarely viewed as art, even by the artist himself . . . and is representative of the typical working class and their values, morals, and traditions."

Indications of increasing interest in Folk Art are the establishment or revival of historical and cultural museums and exhibits throughout the state—the relocation of the Sons of Utah Pioneers' Pioneer Village Museum to Lagoon, the establishment of "living historical farms" such as Man and His Bread Museum (Logan) and Wheeler Historical Farm (Salt Lake City).

Many of the same pioneer crafts which were noted in the earlier edition of this book have continued during the intervening years. Quilting in Utah is still a major Mormon social pastime which has been undaunted by the coming and going of quilting fads. Utah graveyards not only tell a history of the state but display extraordinary carved headstones which symbolize the pioneer aesthetic. Vernal is still Utah's center for saddlery and the making of the nation's standard in saddletrees—at the Standard Saddletree Company, Since the early days, Mormons have excelled in the making and eating of sweets. Northern Utah boasts local chocolate and ice cream manufacturers who bring the sweet to an art. In fact, Snelgrove's Ice

Cream, Utah's most famous, has offered a beehive-shaped ice cream treat for the last forty years.

That beehive ice cream, along with 200 other crafted versions of the state's official symbol, were recently gathered by the Utah Arts Council for an exhibit, first in the Salt Lake Art Center and then at the Renwick Gallery, National Museum of American Art, Smithsonian Institution, in Washington, D.C. A book from this collection was issued in 1981 by the University of Utah Press entitled *The Grand Beehive.*

Begun in those early days when Brigham Young sent Charles Lowell Walker to the Dixie Mission (St. George) for his ability as a poet and song-writer, poetry, storytelling and song writing continue today in the southern part of our state. Over 1200 songs and poems of Charles Lowell Walker not only helped our pioneers through those hard, hot days but planted the seed for a distinctive local musical tradition which still blooms today. It is a rare occasion when the private traditions of the people of Utah's Dixie display their unique folklife heritage. Yearly, some gather for the Southern Utah Folklife Festival at Zion National Park early in September. Southern Paiute people bring their folk artistry to the festival. The Paiute culture is one which is as subtle and illusive as the life they have eked out of western Utah's dry expanse.

The Navajos in the southeast and the Utes in the northeast each have their distinctive traditional arts which are also shared at powwows, Indian fairs and rodeos.

Not only does Utah boast a pioneer and Indian folk art indigenous to the state, but through the last decades Utah has been blessed with a more eclectic population of Hispanic Americans with their own dance, music and crafts. More recently, the Salt Lake area has lured a large number of South Sea Islanders to the state with their beautiful choral singing and dance. And recently from Southeast Asia we have a sizable population of refugees, bringing with them great artistry such as Hmong embroidery and Kouei basketry. Utah is not the homogeneous population that it is usually stereo-typed to be. The innumerable cuisines in the food arts, which are offered in Salt Lake City and other areas of the state and featured at the Utah Arts Festival, indicate our spice is indeed varied in Utah.

A small part of this folk artistry has been preserved and documented by two generations of Utah folklorists. Austin and Alta Fife, Lester Hubbard and Thomas Cheney have recorded and published folk art from the time of the first edition of the Utah Guide. Today, Jan Brunvard, William Wilson, Tom Carter, Richard Poulsen, Margaret Brady and Hal Cannon have con-tinued in this pursuit. Among recent works can be found a general guide to Utah's traditional art: *Utah Folk Art: A Catalog of Material Culture* (BYU Press), sponsored by the Utah Arts Council.

PERFORMING ARTS

Whatever attention the outside world pays to Utah, credit for a measure of that attention is due to Utah's most remarkable Performing Arts. The Mormon Tabernacle Choir has tuned countless ears to the choir's weekly radio and television broadcasts for 50 years; countless others have heard it on records or in personal concerts. Lovers of symphonic music in many states and foreign lands are familiar with the Utah Symphony Orchestra through concerts and recordings. And dance fans in places far and wide have thrilled to Ballet West, Repertory Dance Theatre, Ririe-Woodbury, and other Utah-based groups.

These are the touring giants, of course, representative not only of a state but rather of a vast region, a culture, and a world church, though they are based in Utah and are products largely of the state. Utah's performing arts cup "runneth over" with individual talent, evident as solo artists or in groups both large and small, ephemeral or long-lived, renowned or little known, amateur or having the professional expertise of hoary years. There is talent in the state, beyond assessment. It is sad, however, that even here—where opportunities for stage experience are plentiful for a culture of such limited population—even the most gifted artists often must earn their livelihoods in other pursuits.

THEATER (THEATRE)

The first play produced in Utah was either *Robert Macaire* or *The Triumph of Innocence*. It was presented "with the aid of a little homemade scenery, a brass band, and considerable fanfare" in the old Bowery on Temple Square by the Musical and Dramatic Association. The year was 1851; the Salt Lake colony was four years old. Two years later the pioneer stock company changed its name to Deseret Dramatic Association—having dispensed with the band by this time—and the following year moved its homemade scenery into Social Hall. The Hall was less commodious than the Bowery, but more comfortable, and it had a permanent stage. . . . In 1858, Sergeant R. C. White organized a dramatic company among the soldiers stationed at Camp Floyd and built a theater there of "pine boards and canvas—principally canvas." His scenery was painted with beet juice, mustard, and other commissary delicacies. . . . The Mechanics Dramatic Association, organized by "Phil" Margetts at Great Salt Lake City, had a more permanent influence. The association began producing plays in 1859 at Bowring's Theater—which is to say, in the unfinished living room of Harry Bowring's home, but the first theater to be designated as such in Utah. The playhouse was intimate, about 18 by 40 feet, of which the stage occupied one third—the families of Brigham Young and Heber C. Kimball (about 90 in all) filled it to capacity. After attending a performance at this theater in 1860 Young announced his intention [to build] a "real one." . . .

Brigham Young's "real one," the Salt Lake Theater, was begun in 1861 and dedicated to use (after the custom of the Mormons) the following year. From 1862 until 1928 the record of this playhouse was [a major part of the] history of the theater in Utah. Makeshift theaters, and, later, "opera houses" (the term was applied indiscriminately to ramshackle false fronts, converted public buildings, and the gory show palaces of the 1890's) appeared here and there through the Territory. . . . However, all these enterprises suffered from amateurism, from transience, and from modest income. The Salt Lake Theater alone remained a regular playhouse with professional standards.

(Note: There seem to be no rigid guidelines governing the spellings "theater" and "theatre." Either is correct, according to the dictionary. The profession itself prefers "theatre," while the press generally adheres to "theater." At the risk of confusing the reader, "theater" is used in these pages except where the other spelling appears in proper names or quotations.)

The Salt Lake Theater building was, at the time of its construction, and for many years thereafter, the most imposing structure in the Territory. Both the Church and Young's private exchequer were at low points, but the theater was a community enterprise and laborers worked for tickets, for orders on the Tithing House, and often for nothing at all. . . . The theater was opened to the public March 8, 1862, with a double-header, *Pride of the Market* and *State Secrets.* The precedent set then was . . . followed for many years—a performance at the theater consisted of a drama and a farce separated by an olio. Many Utahns came great distances to attend and they would have their fill of play-acting before returning to the outlands. . . . About 1880 complete companies began to be booked from New York agents. The stock company was abandoned, and the big names in American theater of the time began to appear regularly on the Salt Lake Theater billboards. . . . The Walker Opera House, built in 1882, crippled the Salt Lake Theater for a time by securing superior bookings. However, the theater's managers "persuaded" booking agencies to divide evenly between the two theaters, and in 1891 the opera house burned down.

1941 edition

The 1941 edition also devoted a lengthy paragraph to Maude Adams, born in Utah and revered as the state's most famous early-day thespian despite her few years of residence here.

Immediately following World War I, the cinema gradually drove Utah's legitimate theaters toward insolvency. In 1928 the Salt Lake Theatre was razed to make way for a telephone exchange. Legitimate theatrical activity then shifted to little theater groups, to high schools and colleges, and to occasional road shows.

Contemporary Utah is rich in offerings of live theater, theatrical facilities, and talented performers. Every college and university campus contains a theater or auditorium, used for live performances. Most if not all of the hundreds of Mormon stake houses, and many ward houses, are equipped with recreational halls and stages. The same situation prevails with respect to non-Mormon church buildings, and with the majority of public and private schools. All of these, of course, are in addition to commercial theaters, dinner theaters, and touring theatrical artists from other places. Theatrical training is a part of the curriculum of colleges and universities in the state, and in many of the high schools. Even elementary school pupils may receive instruction and stage experience. Church recreation programs provide experience in dramatics for myriad thespians and supporting casts.

University of Utah has been associated with theater in Utah since that school's beginnings. Maud May Babcock, who was to teach there for 47 years, arrived in 1892 at the urging of her friend Susa Young Gates. A most versatile person, Professor Babcock taught oratory, speech, and physical education. As Raye Price wrote in "Utah's Leading Ladies of the Arts" *(Utah Historical Quarterly,* Winter 1970), "Maud May Babcock received many honors. She was a guest director for the Washington Square and Provincetown Players (1916); organized the first University Little Theater west of the Mississippi (1917); was largely responsible for the University of Utah being among the first to offer undergraduate classes in dramatic production; was charter member, national president, and honorary member of several professional associations. . . ." She founded the university's departments of Communications and Theatre, and a college (Health, Physical

Education and Recreation). The Babcock Theatre, in the Pioneer Memorial Theatre, was named in her honor. Lila Eccles Brimhall, a Babcock student and protege, taught at the university for 31 years (1929-1960), becoming known as the first lady of Utah theater and being the first inductee of the Hall of Fame at Pioneer Memorial Theatre. Dr. C. Lowell Lees was for many years director of the University of Utah Theatre and was the moving force behind the construction of Pioneer Memorial Theatre. Lees Main Stage is named in his honor. Completed in 1962, the theater currently presents a subscription series of six plays and musicals attended by 100,000 patrons. Under the direction of Dr. Keith M. Engar, the theater has become known for its presentation of musical comedy with visiting stars and professional casts.

Cedar City's Utah Shakespearean Festival presents three Shakespeare plays in repertory on the stage of the Adams Memorial Theatre, a replica of an Elizabethan playhouse. Fred Adams is the producing director of the Festival. The company is made up primarily of college students and professionals from around the country. The Festival season extends from July into August. *See Tour No. 8.*

In Logan, the Old Lyric Repertory Company has presented stage entertainment during summer months since the mid-1960s. Under the direction of Vosco Call, the company performs at the Old Lyric Theatre. Promised Valley Playhouse is a community theater operated by the Mormon Church. Housed in a delightfully restored vaudeville-movie theater at 132 South State in Salt Lake City, the Playhouse offers family entertainment such as musical theater that has proved popular on Broadway. The Playhouse also is the stage every summer for the traditional *Promised Valley* summer musical, which played in 1981 for the 15th consecutive year.

Summer theater presentations are held at Sundance Resort in Provo Canyon, and melodrama at Kanab and Park City, among other places. The Lagoon Opera House features musical theater. By no means is this an exhaustive list of summer theatrical events. Theater continues through the year, of course, with high schools, colleges, universities, and independent theaters staging numerous events. Among currently active independent groups are Theatre 138 in Salt Lake City, which presents a variety of productions from new plays to traditional operettas; the Salt Lake Acting Company, which presents avant-garde plays; Walk-Ons, Inc., which produces plays at Shire West Theater; the elegantly restored Capitol Theater, which presents professional road-show attractions; and the Villa Playhouse Theatre in Springville, which produces popular plays and musicals.

A summer laboratory theater for playwrights is sponsored at Sundance by the Utah Arts Council in partnership with the Sundance Institute. The program is designed to assist playwrights to develop their skills and projects in an environment where ideas and concepts can be explored in depth. Playwrights, are given the opportunity to work in collaboration with a variety of distinguished theater professionals, a process which has been successfully developed for the Institute's film program.

The Rural Arts Consortium, sponsored by the Utah Arts Council, makes touring theatrical productions available to communities around the

Capitol Theater *(above)*.

Utah Shakespearean Festival,
Southern Utah State College,
Cedar City *(right)*.

state. Drama, comedy, and musical theater are offered variously by college and university companies and by professional theater companies in an effort to bring quality theater to communities throughout the state.

In 1978 the Utah Arts Council estimated that at least a thousand Utahns were involved in some form of theater. Many of these participate in Community Theater, "a popular creative outlet for townspeople who have never lost interest in the theater experience they might have received in high school or college"—or those without experience but desirous of expressing themselves in new ways. Numerous community arts groups are involved with theater, including Castle Valley Community Theatre . . . Weber State Alumni Community Theatre . . . and community theater activities in other localities.

DANCE

Professional or theater dance as a performing art is a relatively new phenomenon in Utah. Dance was ignored as a category of The Arts in the 1941 edition of this guide. That is understandable when it is realized that professional ballet and modern dance companies are products largely of the last few decades, at least in this state.

Social dancing, of course, has been a popular pastime in Utah since the earliest days of settlement. In fact, ensemble music was played primarily as accompaniment for dancing and group singing. Every community with means rapidly endowed itself with a social hall, which might consist originally of a temporarily converted school building or even the local meetinghouse. Dancing has been a foundation stone of Mormon recreational programs since the church's beginnings, developing for a time into elaborate competitions and exhibition festivals; and though emphasis might have been on partner and group dancing, countless individuals became proficient dancers. It goes without saying that the popularity of dancing has continued to the present day, though participation has waxed and waned in cycles, and dancing styles have changed over the years. Ballroom dancing's popularity extended into the 1960s, in its heyday resulting in such grand expanses as the vast dance floors at Saltair and Coconut Grove (later The Terrace). Changing tastes caused the demise of these huge ballrooms. The disco trend of recent years involves far fewer dancers than the ballroom era of former times.

Dance as an art, for the majority of people today, is a spectator activity. Few are virile enough, or possess the required time, talent, and determination to become proficient in ballet, modern dance, or serious folk dancing—the most popular dance art forms of today. So professional dance is theater, involving a few hundred trained dancers at most, and many of these find it necessary to leave Utah in furtherance of their careers. Utah does nurture a number of remarkably fine dance groups, but even these have positions for only a relative few of the many who have talent and desire to perform.

Role of the University of Utah

Although the church was an ardent supporter of dance at the amateur, experiential level, it was the University of Utah that became the fountainhead for the development of professional dance as a fine art form. Possibly as a result of lingering remnant of religious disapproval in many other parts of the United States, dance as theater art form was slow in developing. Few American dance companies had received national attention and acceptance outside of New York City until the mid-thirties. It is not surprising, then, that no mention was made of dance as a theater art in the 1941 edition of the guide.

Soon after the arrival of Maud May Babcock in 1892, to establish the theater and women's physical education programs of the University of Utah, dance was introduced into the university curriculum. The first mention of dance in a university catalog was to be found in 1906. Public performances called "dance dramas" involved the presentation of stories through gesture and dance. These were presented out-of-doors in various campus settings. The first such dance drama for which there is evidence was "Snow White," directed by Georgia Borg Johnson. With the arrival of Myrtle Clancy Knudson in 1929, a dance performing group called "Orchesis" was organized under her aegis and performances were moved indoors. The first Orchesis dance drama, presented in 1931, inaugurated the opening of the recently completed Kingsbury Hall. Although still called dance dramas, the Orchesis programs now consisted of a series of short, un-related dances. Choreographic responsibility was shared by Mrs. Knudson with the students. Among these students was a young woman by the name of Virginia Tanner.

Upon Mrs. Knudson's resignation in 1940, Elizabeth Hayes was appoin-ted director of Modern Dance at the University of Utah, a role that she would continue to occupy until 1978. Her first endeavor was to build an educated Salt Lake City dance audience. For several years after her arrival, the annual Orchesis performance was presented in the form of a demon-stration-concert in which a portion of the program was devoted to a lecture-demonstration designed to increase audience discernment and under-standing of dance choreography. During the decade of the 1940s attendance at the dance concerts grew from approximately 500 to 3,000 people.

With the establishment of the modern dance major program at the Uni-versity of Utah in 1948, opportunity was provided for the training of specialized dance teachers and eventually professional dancers. Physical education teachers at East High School supported Elizabeth Hayes in per-suading the Board of Education to hire the first dance specialist in Utah public schools. Other secondary schools were quick to follow the lead of East High School, and Utah became one of the first states in the nation to employ dance specialists in most of its major urban high schools and to offer secondary school certification for dance specialists. Among the first specialists to develop dance programs in the high schools were Emma Lou Warren, Joan Kingston and Connie Jo Hepworth.

The year 1951 saw the addition of Joan Woodbury to the university modern dance faculty, followed soon by the appointment of Shirley Ririe. A talented musician, Maurine Dewsnup, who served the department from 1942 to 1974, composed much of the music for the faculty choreography. Responsibility for directing the annual Orchesis dance concert (which until 1953 constituted practically the only dance theater event in Salt Lake City of local origin) was for some years shared by Elizabeth Hayes and the two new dance faculty. Joan Woodbury and Shirley Ririe eventually assumed full responsibility for the concerts as the administrative demands of a growing department increased.

During the ensuing years, various new faces have been added to the modern dance faculty, each making unique contributions to dance in Utah. Among these are two that deserve special mention. Loabelle Mangelson, as organizer and director of the Modern Dance Department's Performing Dance Company established in 1979, has brought honor and recognition to Utah with the company tour of Great Britain and Europe in 1980, and invited appearances at the Los Angeles Bicentennial Celebration and at the Kennedy Center as a winner in the first American College Dance Festival competition in 1981. Anne Riordan's teaching of dance to the mentally handicapped, the award winning film of her work, the many workshops she has conducted, and the deeply moving performances of her "Sunshine Dance Group" have also received nation-wide praise and attention.

Graduates of the Modern Dance Department have provided the major portion of the dance personnel for the professional modern dance companies in Utah as well as for the Bill Evans Company in Seattle and the San Francisco Moving Company, directed by Rhonda Martyn, another Utah graduate. The Modern Dance Department unquestionably ranks among the most highly respected in the nation.

Ballet

The responsibility for teaching of ballet had for many years been carried on in Utah through commercial dance studios. By 1940 at least three important people were teaching ballet of reputable quality, laying the foundation for further developments. These were Mrs. Sophie Reed of Ogden, Jean Renee and Peter Christensen of Salt Lake City. Uncle "Pete," as he was affectionately known, directed the Le Crist School of Dance and had the added distinction of being the uncle of the famous Christensen brothers Lew, Harold and Willam.

In 1951, C. Lowell Lees, chairman of University of Utah Department of Speech and director of the University Theatre, needed a choreographer to assist with his theater productions and to help stage the big summer musicals that were presented annually in the University of Utah Stadium. Willam Christensen, who was at the time co-director of the San Francisco Ballet, was invited to become a member of the Department of Speech and accepted the position of professor of Ballet. While he fulfilled his assigned duties admirably, Bill Christensen had dreams of his own. In 1954, he established a ballet major in the College of Fine Arts, the first of its kind in any American university. Aware of the fact that professional dancers must begin their training early, Willam Christensen, soon after his arrival, inaugurated a program of ballet classes for children through the university's Division of Continuing Education. Thus, through this program, hundreds of youthful dancers have benefited from excellent ballet training and many have been launched on their professional careers. In 1966, the university administration decided to create the Department of Ballet and Modern Dance, with Gordon Paxman as chairman, Willam Christensen as director of Ballet, and Elizabeth Hayes as director of Modern Dance. A number of outstanding ballet faculty have contributed to the growth and fine reputation of the department. Among these have been Mattlyn Gavers, Bene Arnold and the late Yurek Lazowski, and Toni Landers (Marks), a prima ballerina from the Royal Danish Ballet, who now teaches the advanced students.

Christensen has maintained a relationship with the university for 30 years as a teacher or advisor, and has received numerous professional and civic honors.

Ballet West

Closest to Willam Christensen's heart was his University Ballet Theatre. The company gave its first performance in Kingsbury Hall in 1953. To augment this young company during its growing years, guest soloists were often imported from the San Francisco and New York City ballet companies until eventually talented young dancers within the company were sufficiently trained to assume these roles. Some of these company soloists whom Salt Lake City audiences will certainly remember are: Janice James, Tom Ruud, Barbara Hamlin, Jay Jolley, Bart Cook, Victoria Morgan, Ed Farley and Tauna Hunter.

The annual *Nutcracker Ballet* was inaugurated by Willam Christensen in 1954. It has become an annual yuletide tradition and involves a large complement of dancers and the Utah Symphony. In 1963 the University Ballet

Ballet West: *Pipe Dreams* with Tauna Hunter.

BALLET WEST

Theatre, now sponsored by the community of Salt Lake City, became known as the Utah Civic Ballet, a name that was changed to Ballet West in 1968.

The Utah Ballet Society assumed the responsibility of sponsoring the company's performing seasons and providing funds for that purpose. In addition, a sizable Ford Foundation grant was pledged to aid the company program.

In 1976 Bruce Marks was selected as co-artistic director of the company, and upon Willam Christensen's retirement in 1978, he became sole artistic director. Prior to coming to Utah, Bruce Marks had been a principal dancer with American Ballet Theatre and Royal Danish Ballet. Since his accession as artistic director, choreographer, and administrator, Marks has retained association with the University of Utah ballet program. In 1981 he became chairman of the Dance Advisory Panel of the National Endowment for the Arts. Willam Christensen, after his retirement from Ballet West, became director of the Christensen Ballet Academy, a junior company affiliated with Ballet West.

Ballet West is now one of the nation's leading professional ballet companies, generally ranked by critics among the dozen most prestigious of dancing companies—of which there are more than 2,000 in the nation. Its full tour schedule includes communities in Utah and surrounding states as well as major cities in America, Europe, and the Far East. In 1980 the company performed at City Center in New York City.

Although Ballet West is probably the best known and receives the most support of the companies in Utah, the state is fortunate in being the home of several other companies of excellent reputation. In 1953, a group of five young choreographers—Joan Woodbury, Shirley Ririe, Bob Blake, Juan Valenzuela and Jan Day—banded together to form a semiprofessional dance company which they called "Choreodancers," Later, others were invited to join the company. Although its life span was brief, the young company became the harbinger of succeeding professional companies and the forerunner of the first Ririe-Woodbury Dance Company created in the late 1960s and officially incorporated in 1971. Its purpose was to provide performing opportunities for the company members and to bring theater dance to Utah communities.

Children's Dance Theatre

Shortly before 1940, the late Virginia Tanner (Bennett) had established in Salt Lake City a school of creative dance for children. Studying and teaching dance for most of her life, "Miss Virginia" developed a philosophy and a technique for teaching dance to children that gained her national acclaim. As an outgrowth of her school, she created her Children's Dance Theatre which in 1953 was invited to appear at Jacob's Pillow in Massachusetts, The Connecticut College Summer School of Dance, and at New York University's summer camp.

In 1960, after teaching for many years at the Old McCune School of Music, and later above a bowling alley in downtown Salt Lake City, Virginia Tanner became affiliated with the University of Utah, where she served as director of the creative dance program of the University's Division of Continuing Education until her death in 1979. Since Mrs. Tanner's death, the school and dance theatre have continued under the leadership of Mary Ann Lee.

Utah Repertory Dance Theatre

Because of the exciting work being done by the Children's Dance Theatre, the University of Utah Dance Department, and the Ririe-Woodbury Dance Company, a much larger Rockefeller Grant was awarded to the university in Virginia Tanner's name for the establishment of a resident, professional modern dance company to become known as the (Utah) Repertory Dance Theatre. Company members were drawn from University of Utah modern dance students and graduates. Joan Woodbury was appointed artistic director. Guest choreographers were brought to Salt Lake City to augment the company repertory. A roster of choreographers included, among others, such names as Jose Limon, John Butler, Glen Tetley, Geoffrey Holder, Donald McKayle and Anna Sokolow. After two years, direction of RDT passed from Joan Woodbury to a committee of three company members—Linda Smith, Kay Clark and Bill Evans, who then served as its co-directors. Unique to the company has been its democratic form of governance and artistic planning that relies heavily upon group consensus. One of its major accomplishments to date has grown out of a need for people to understand and appreciate the history of dance in America. As a consequence, the company has endeavored to become a repository of choreographic works of numerous major American artists. In a recent concert, company members narrate and perform an historical panorama of authentic dance choreography from Isadora Duncan to Doris Humphrey. This concert, entitled "The Early Years of Modern Dance," has been performed in many places including the Riverside Church in New York City and the Smithsonian Institution in Washington, D.C. In its 15 years, Repertory Dance Theatre has been adopted by its host city and has become a company of national stature. The company today, with Linda Smith and Kay Clark acting as co-artistic directors, performs and teaches in numerous communities with the National Endowment for the Arts' "Artist-in-Schools" program. Many of its members have graduated to other important dance roles throughout the nation, among whom have been Tim Wengard, who left to become principal male dancer of the Martha Graham Company, and Bill Evans whose own company in Seattle has received national acclaim.

Ririe-Woodbury Dance Company

With the establishment of the Dance Touring Program and the Artist-in-the-Schools residency programs by the National Endowment for the Arts in 1969-70, Virginia Tanner was chosen director of the dance portion of the nationwide project, a role that she relinquished the following year to Shirley Ririe. It immediately became apparent that there was a critical need for quality dance companies that could present a repertory of dances appealing to people of all ages within a community, including elementary school children, and whose company members were skilled as teachers as well as dancers. The recently revived Ririe-Woodbury Dance Company decided to fill the need. Under the co-direction of Joan Woodbury and Shirley Ririe this versatile dance group had become known for its innovative, experimental approach to modern dance. The ensemble works in conceptual areas in dance that run through all the arts, encompassing "a combination of warmth, humor, and abandon in space." While the directors are the principal choreographers for the company, works of other dance artists have also been commissioned for their repertory. The company has achieved a reputation, nationally and internationally, especially in the world of dance for children. Their touring schedule has included places as far away as South Africa where they represented United States dance at an international congress. By 1980, the company had become known as "the most traveled dance company in the country," providing one third of the National Endowment Artist-in-the-Schools dance residencies. When at home, the company performs at the Capitol Theatre. Both Shirley Ririe and Joan Woodbury continue to teach part-time as full professors at the University of Utah.

Although not directly connected with Ririe-Woodbury Dance Company, several other Utahns have also actively participated in fulfilling national residencies in the Artist-in-the-Schools Program. Some of these include Joan Kingston, Connie Jo Hepworth, Loabelle Mangelson, Dee Winterton, Pat Debenham, Anne Cannon and Mary Anne Lee.

Ethnic Dance

While the University of Utah has been the leader among Utah institutions of higher learning in the areas of ballet and modern dance, Brigham Young University, true to Mormon church tradition, has placed emphasis upon social and recreational dance forms. Folk dance classes are crowded with hundreds of students. From among these students, teams of highly skilled performers who can execute difficult ethnic dances with technical skill and theatrical finesse are selected annually. Under the direction of Mary Bee Jensen, the International Folk Dancers each year present in the BYU Marriott Center a stunning performance of authentically costumed dances from around the world. The Folk Dancers also tour constantly and perform to standing ovations. In summer, a small select unit is chosen to represent America in dance festivals throughout the world, including behind the Iron Curtain, winning prizes and accolades on every occasion. An "exhibition" social dance group, called the BYU Ballroom Dancers, has also toured abroad and received international recognition for its performing abilities.

A discussion of dance at BYU would not be complete without a mention of Dee Winterton, who served for a number of years as director of the modern dance and ballet programs at BYU and during the summers directed the weekly theatrical production at Sundance, owned and operated by Robert Redford. Presently Dee Winterton directs the "Young Ambassadors," the BYU traveling variety show.

Ethnic dance in Utah is certainly not limited to the university scene. There are many lively ethnic groups that delight in performing the dances of their former homelands, sharing their cultural heritage with the general public.

MUSIC

A history of music in Utah must begin with the state's native inhabitants, long before whites arrived. "The music of the Indian is scarcely known outside his race," said the 1941 edition, perhaps because it is so alien to white ears. If that is the case, it is not for lack of opportunities to hear such music. Indian music may be purchased on recordings and listened to at dance ceremonies of the Utes as well as Navajo festivals in the Four Corners region.

Music of the white culture in Utah had its beginnings with the Mormon pioneers, who brought their band, choir, and songs to a new home on the edge of an arid desert. Before coming to Utah, the Mormons had established music as an important part of their culture. In Nauvoo they organized what might have been America's first university-level music department in 1841. The Nauvoo Band, a small orchestra, provided martial music for the Nauvoo Legion and music for other functions. With such a musical foundation, it is not surprising that music played a more important part in community cultural life than any other art. As described in the 1941 edition:

It was a humble music, inclined to hymns, ballads, sentimental songs, reels, and, where instruments were available, to martial airs; but it was a folk music gathered, as were the rank and file of the Church, from every State in the Union and from half the countries of Europe. The Mormons played or sang with very little restraint; indeed, their authorities encouraged them to do so and the Church sponsored singing and dancing—they had no dour Puritan taste for rote singing nor terror of mixed dancing. "There were musical instruments," says Bancroft, "in every company of Mormons that crossed the plains." And, however remote, there was rarely a community that grew up in the days of the Territory that did not boast, besides its choir, a quadrille band or "squeeze box," and fiddles—in prosperous sections the band would include a bass viol, clarinet, flute, and trombone, but no drums. In outlying towns the quadrille bands persisted until the widespread advent of radio, when they were gradually replaced by small "woefully rhythmical" jazz bands. . . .

In the cattle country, cowboy ballads, cow lullabies, and trail songs continue to be the cowhands' chief relief from loneliness. . . . In the sheep country there is seldom a camp that has not at least one instrumentalist. Banjos, harmonicas, and guitars are the preferred instruments.

Mormon religious music lies mainly in the province of hymns, and though the Mormons borrowed heavily from the hymnal literature of other denominations, they themselves composed many excellent works. However, in keeping with their self-reliance and the objectivity of their religious views, much of their hymn book does not, in a strict sense, belong to the genre at all, being odes to the Great Basin Zion, exhortations to courage, or snatches of doctrine put to music. . . . The beginnings of more serious music in Utah are rooted in the Salt Lake Musical and Dramatic Association and the Salt Lake Tabernacle Choir, both organized in the early 1850's at the express order of Brigham Young. Out of the former grew the Salt Lake Theater, which in its heyday between 1870 and 1900 billed the finest musical artists in America, and maintained its own company of "command" performers (it was Young's custom to "call" singers as well as settlers) who produced light operas not markedly inferior to those of visiting professional companies. . . .

1941 edition

Mormon hymns, the Tabernacle Choir, the annual Messiah oratorio, opera, and symphony—all had their beginnings years ago. Music as a part of life has amplified its role enormously in recent decades, as a result primarily of cinema, radio, television, and recordings—media which place unbelievable musical variety (and volume) within the reach of all. Never before in history has music been such an important part of life for so many people, particularly the young. In fact, it may be more difficult in places to avoid the sound of music than to be exposed to it. The abundance of musical offerings facing today's Utahns is almost overwhelming, making the choice of concert no easy matter.

While it cannot be claimed that symphonic or choir music is the preference of the majority of Utah's people (and in this respect they probably do not differ markedly from residents of other states), it is this type of music that has done the most to build the state's musical reputation. Foremost among the musical groups that have focused national and international attention on Utah are the Mormon Tabernacle Choir and the Utah Symphony.

Choral music

Symphonic or choir music has done the most to build the state's musical reputation, and because it was first on the scene and has maintained its position as a leader in choral music, the Salt Lake Tabernacle Choir provides an unbroken connection between pioneer beginnings and the present day.

In its infancy so small it needed no conductor, the choir first sang for a church conference in the bowery on Temple Square in August 1847, 29 days after the first pioneer company arrived. Under John Parry and subsequent conductors, during the 1850s and 1860s, the choir expanded and became a permanent musical component of Temple Square. In October 1857 it was joined by Joseph Ridges' first pipe organ, brought from Australia, and in October 1867 by the first organ in the new domed Tabernacle, its home from that day to the present. *See also Tour No. 3 (Temple Square).*

The choir's directors and the Tabernacle organists have occupied positions of eminence in their fields, and in the regard of Utahns generally. In addition to those early conductors, who preceded the days of the present Tabernacle, the impressive roster includes George E. P. Careless, Evan Stephens, Anthony C. Lund, J. Spencer Cornwall, Richard P. Condie, Jay E. Welch and Jerold D. Ottley. Albert J. Southwick also served as acting director for a short period prior to Cornwall's appointment.

Organists have included Joseph J. Daynes, John J. McClelland, Edward P. Kimball, Tracy Y. Cannon, Frank W. Asper, Alexander Schreiner, Wade N. Stephens, Robert Cundick, John Longhurst and Roy M. Darley.

Since its modest beginnings the choir has expanded to more than 350 singers, all of them unpaid volunteers, having a repertory of several hundred works. The choir has broadcast weekly on national network radio since 1929, and on network television in later years. It has recorded more than 50 record albums, most of them appearing under the Columbia label. The choir performs at all general conferences of the Mormon Church in the Tabernacle and has performed in numerous major cities of the nation as well as European countries, Canada, Mexico, Japan and Brazil. It has sung at the inaugurations of presidents Lyndon Johnson, Richard Nixon and

Mormon Tabernacle Choir in the Great Tabernacle, Salt Lake City.

Ronald Reagan, and has performed in the White House in Washington, D.C., for other presidents as well.

While the choir stands as the largest, oldest and most renowned, it is only one of Utah's numerous choral groups, many of which have flourished for years. More people, undoubtedly, have been involved in choral music through the years than any other form of musical expression.

The Oratorio Society of Utah, founded as the Salt Lake Oratorio Society in 1914 by Squire Coop, the first professor of music at the University of Utah, has performed Handel's "Messiah" in the Tabernacle during the Yuletide Season for 65 years, missing only the World War II years, 1942-44. Among major performing institutions in the state, only the Tabernacle Choir is older.

Coop conducted the "Messiah" at the Empress Theater and the Salt Lake Theater respectively on New Year's Day in 1915 and 1916, after which the production was taken to the Tabernacle, where it has remained to this day. After Coop moved to California in 1922, a tradition of engaging guest conductors ensued. Preparing the massive chorus, sometimes as many as 450 singers, since Coop left, have been Lisle Bradford, David Shand, Jay Welch and, for the past two decades or so, John Marlowe Nielson.

Other choral organizations have come and gone, but some remain on the scene today. During the 1940s, H. Frederick Davis presented his Salt Lake Philharmonic Choir in an annual series of concerts, which included what are considered the first performances in Utah of Bach's B Minor Mass and the Missa Solemnis of Beethoven.

College-related choruses of note have performed with excellence over the years. Squire Coop's first "Messiah" performance, an abbreviated version, was by his University Choral Society in 1910. In more recent years the Utah Chorale, originated on the University of Utah campus under John Marlowe Nielson for volunteer singers throughout the region, has become the principal choral unit of the Utah Symphony Orchestra. For several years it has been under Newell Weight, who transferred to the state school some years ago from Brigham Young University, where his A Capella Choir had gained wide attention.

Nielson went on to organize Pro Musica, an ensemble which annually presents a series of concerts featuring music from the Baroque and Renaissance periods.

Also making its mark on the choral front has been the Mormon Youth Chorus and Symphony, originated by Jay Welch while an assistant conductor of the Tabernacle Choir. The group has flourished under other capable leadership, while Welch, once head of the Music Department at the University of Utah, after a short stint as conductor of the Tabernacle Choir, organized the Jay Welch Chorale in 1978. This 300-voice chorus continues to receive high praise from listeners and critics.

A Capella choirs have long been popular in the schools of the state, both on a secondary and college level, many of them achieving a high degree of excellence. Typical in the past have been Salt Lake City's East High School choirs of Lisle Bradford and South High a capella groups under Armont Willardsen. Using singers from his high school choirs as a nucleus, Willardsen founded the Salt Lake Symphonic Choir in 1949 and conducted it for 27 years before relinquishing the baton. The singers traveled widely throughout the United States and Canada on concert tours and continue today to present concerts both in Utah and on tour.

For many years, male glee clubs were numerous on community and school levels. Salt Lake City's Orpheus Club was organized in the 1890s under Anton Pedersen and performed for 60 years. The Swanee Singers formed another early glee club, coming on in the early 1900s. The club remains today as the Beehive Chorus. Others over the state include the Imperial Glee Club in Logan, Mark Robinson's chorus in Ogden, the Mendelssohn singers, and others. The various ensembles once formed the Associated Male Glee Clubs of Utah and joined in several concerts in the Tabernacle, during which they presented noted singers such as Beniamino Gigli, the famous Italian tenor, in 1938.

Equally prominent have been the women's choruses. Founded about 1930 by Les Goates, the Symphony Singers performed for several decades under his baton and featured, among others, Blanche Christensen, soprano, and the young accompanist, Grant Johannessen, as soloists. Another women's chorus of note, The Schubert Singers, has presented annual spring concerts since its founding in 1933.

Another long-standing choral group dealing purely with liturgical music is the Cathedral of the Madeleine Choir with its fine organ. Among many others are the Calvary Church Choir, Faith Temple Choir, and Utah Travelers Gospel Singers.

The Bountiful Sweet Adelines, Clearfield Job Corps Center Choir, The Wasatch Children (a 21-voice children's choir), and the Utah Barber Shop Chorus are only a few of unnumbered other choral groups, including hundreds of church choirs and smaller ensembles such as barbershop quartets, who make music throughout the state. At one point—in 1960—the Evans Brothers Quartet of Salt Lake City reached the pinnacle of the Barber Shop world by winning first place International medalist honors in the Society for Preservation of Barber Shop Quartet Singing in America.

Opera

Before organization of the present-day Utah Opera Company, opera in the state had a sporadic existence, more so even than the Utah Symphony Orchestra in its beginnings. Early performances were presented in the Salt Lake Theater and in the Walker Opera House. George D. Pyper, general manager of the Salt Lake Theater to the time it was demolished in 1929, was heard as a soloist with choral organizations and in opera as well. Pyper was a strong promoter of opera as a regular feature at the theater.

Two grandchildren of President Brigham Young—Emma Lucy and B. Cecil Gates—pioneered the cause of opera in Utah, as described in the 1941 edition:

Between the years 1918 and 1923, they organized, managed, directed and took leading roles in Lucy Gates Grand Opera Company productions. Emma Lucy Gates (Mrs. A. E. Bowen), coloratura soprano, had received intensive training in Germany, where she sang leading roles in the Royal German Opera before the World War. Her brother, B. Cecil Gates, had studied conducting. Though having achieved marked artistic and popular success, the Lucy Gates Grand Opera Company had to cease activity, and its founders assumed a sizeable deficit. Between productions, Emma Lucy Gates carried on with her concert and stage career, touring America.

The brother-sister team returned in the late 1920s to revive the opera company for one final production including Mascagni's "Cavalleria Rusticana" and the "Sextette" and "Mad Scene" from Donizetti's *Lucia de Lammermoor*. John Summerhays, Margaret Anderson, and A. J. Southwick were among Utah singers who joined Emma Lucy Gates in the cast. B.

Utah Opera Company performance, 1981.

MARK WAGNER

Cecil Gates, in addition to his conducting, was acclaimed as a composer of widely sung anthems, cantatas and songs.

Attempts to present opera on a civic and community basis were many, among them several seasons of production by Carlos Alexander. The most lasting and successful, both as to excellence and popularity, was the production of summer opera in Stadium Bowl at the University of Utah. The initial production, during Utah's centennial celebration in 1947, was *Promised Valley*. Crawford Gates, a descendant of Brigham Young, wrote the music and Arnold Sundgaard the lyrics. Jay Blackton came from New York City to conduct. Future productions, encouraged by success of the first, were under direction of Maurice Abravanel. Eventually other light operas and musicals were presented along with an opera each summer, featuring Beverly Sills, Robert Rounseville, Kitty Carlisle, and other stars.

Opera was again revived in Utah during the 1970s through the dedicated efforts of opera devotees and musicians. Foremost among these was Glade Peterson, who returned to his native state after gaining operatic eminence in the east and in Europe. Peterson was instrumental in forming the Utah Opera Company, starring as a vocal lead in its productions at Pioneer Memorial Theatre and Capitol Theatre. Another Utah singer of exceptional ability, Robert Peterson, returned to his native state some years ago after a successful career in leading roles in New York City Broadway musicals. Since then he has devoted his versatile talents—not only in music but in promotion and administration as well—to furthering popular acceptance of musical theater in Utah.

Although outstanding singers have been imported for leading roles in Utah Opera productions, none has been more impressive than Utah's JoAnn Ottley, wife of Jerrold Ottley, conductor of the Tabernacle Choir. Mrs. Ottley also is a soloist with the choir and has appeared with the Utah Symphony in oratorio productions, as has Cohleen Bischoff, a dramatic soprano of note.

Instrumental music

The internationally acclaimed Utah Symphony Orchestra, developed to its point of excellence under the baton of Maurice Abravanel, is the crowning achievement in the long history of instrumental ensemble production in the state. The century or more leading to that achievement, however, is crowded with the appearance of bands, orchestras, and small ensembles in concerts, parades and various other functions.

Almost as soon as the pioneers arrived in Salt Lake Valley in 1847, the Nauvoo Band under William Pitt supplied music to build their spirits. For some time Pitt's band was the principal means of musical entertainment, serving as a brass band and an orchestra.

Important to early instrumental groups was the construction in 1852 of the Social Hall and in 1862 the Salt Lake Theater, across the street from each other on State Street. The Social Hall was designed for dancing, concerts, theatrical events and choir rehearsals. The theater was given high priority by Brigham Young as a new home for the concert and theater arts. Among the first to make use of the two facilities was a band and church orchestra.

The Salt Lake Theater orchestra and the Walker Opera House orchestra of 1892 supplied the core of the first symphony orchestra in Utah. Playing under the baton of Anton Pedersen, this orchestra of 32 pieces and two zithers rehearsed at the Social Hall and performed in the Salt Lake Theater on May 17. Pedersen was born in Norway and soon became a dominant figure on the music scene after arriving in Utah. He conducted male glee clubs, organized and conducted a women's orchestra, was an organist and composer, played the piano, baritone horn, viola, violin and clarinet, besides directing music affairs for the All Hallows College in Salt Lake City.

The symphony was revived in 1904 under 24-year-old Arthur Shepherd, a youthful prodigy from Idaho who left for New England in 1909, later becoming conductor of the Cleveland Orchestra and winning international acclaim as a composer. John J. McClellan conducted until 1911, when the orchestra disbanded, to be revived in 1913 under Professor Pedersen. After the death of Anton Pedersen in 1914, conductors included Arthur P. Freber, Charles Shepherd, and Albert Shepherd, who helped the orchestra through a fitful existence before it became a WPA orchestra under Reginald Beales in 1935. Said the 1941 edition, "Using the WPA Orchestra as a nucleus, augmented by other professional musicians, the Utah State Symphony Orchestra Association, a department of the Utah State Institute of Fine Arts, gave its first concert May 8, 1940, with Hans Heniot, young American, as guest conductor. Artistic and financial outcome of this first venture give rise to the hope that Utah may at last possess a symphony orchestra." Heniot was also responsible for a fine military band at the Kearns Air Base during World War II. Beales was given credit in the 1941 edition for carrying symphonic music to "a new audience of 50,000 school children, besides many others who never before had heard" such music. The 1941 edition went on to state that "Concert audiences have increased in leaps and bounds since 1930. More amateur orchestras and bands exist in Utah than ever before."

Though World War II intervened, the words in the 1941 edition were prophetic: the state symphony began playing professionally in 1946, with Werner Janssen, who commuted from his home in Hollywood for rehearsals and concerts, conducting the modern Utah Symphony in its first season.

During the summer of the Centennial year of 1947, Maurice Abravanel was engaged as conductor of the Utah Symphony Orchestra. After 32 years at the helm, in April, 1979, the revered maestro announced his retirement as music director and conductor. Between 1947 and 1976 he had not missed one of the orchestra's 3,000 concerts. Ill health rather than age alone (76 years) influenced his decision to step down. During those 32 years, Abravanel was the one person most responsible for building Utah's state symphony into a full-time 80-member group honored throughout the music world. The orchestra traveled more than 200,000 miles during his tenure, made nearly a hundred recordings, toured in many states, traveled overseas four times, and expanded its annual concert season to 52 weeks. During the 1977-78 season, 338,000 people attended the symphony's concerts, including thousands of young people in public schools of five states.

Early in his Utah career, Abravanel started taking the orchestra to the public schools of the state, both secondary and elementary, a move that was recognized in Time Magazine and the New York Times, among other noted publications. He carried on the practice to the great benefit of school children throughout the state.

During the "Abravanel years" the symphony performed all subscription concerts in the Tabernacle, moving to the new Symphony Hall on September 12, 1979, following his retirement, for the 1979-80 season. Varujan Kojian, chosen as Abravanel's successor, is a gifted artist who has not yet had time to imprint the marks of his own individuality, but who obviously is leading the orchestra into a new era. In May, 1981, the symphony traveled to Europe on its fifth international tour, performing 14 concerts in five countries. Critical praise was generous, reinforcing the symphony's reputation as one of the nation's finest orchestras.

The 1941 edition also acknowledged other musical activities of the 1940 period:

The achievements of the Brigham Young University orchestra at Provo, under the direction of Professor LeRoy J. Robertson, winner of the Society of American Composers' award, have earned the acclaim of professional musicians. The State's three universities and the McCune School of Music and Fine Arts (owned and operated by the Church) stress the importance of music; through their work with bands and orchestras, they are building audiences for the future. The Church Music Committee's program, under the direction of Tracy Y. Cannon, is providing a

Maestro Maurice Abravanel.

UTAH SYMPHONY

service, unique in the annals of American music, by holding Church music institutes and training annually several thousand amateur organists and choristers.

Thus, in brief outline, were laid the foundations of instrumental music in Utah. On these foundations were built the training programs of hundreds of public schools, colleges, universities, commercial schools, churches and private teachers in Utah. Instrumental ensembles are far more numerous (if church choirs are excepted) than choral groups or vocal soloists—or so an examination of musical event listings would indicate. In fact, more than 70 different instrumental groups performed on stages of the Utah Arts Festival in 1980, playing seemingly every type of music from contemporary rock to symphonic classical, as well as folk music of other cultures. A mere listing of a few of these groups is indicative of the vast range of instrumental offerings available in the state in 1980: Cow Jazz . . . Easy Winners Dixie . . . Fertile Dirt Band . . . Bebop Band . . . Latin Night . . . Linke Hebrew Group . . . Mainstream Jazz Quartet . . . Nova String Quartet . . . Salt Lake Chamber Ensemble . . . Shupe Family Fiddlers . . . Old Time String Band . . . Woodwind Quintet . . . Brass Ensemble . . . Bluegrass Band . . . Salt Lake Municipal Band . . . Harmonica Band . . . Tongan Sounds . . . Utah Chamber Orchestra . . . Utah Symphony . . . and Utah Youth Orchestra. To these should be added the Deseret String Band, which specializes in folk music and is known to Utahns far and wide through its appearances on Rural Consortium tours. Also, there are community orchestras, such as the Utah Valley Symphony, and instrumental ensembles at Utah State, Weber State, the University of Utah, and Brigham Young University, the latter claiming honors for its String Quartet. Small

Varujan Kojian conducting the Utah Symphony.

UTAH SYMPHONY

ensembles, many comprised of symphony players, for a number of years have brought a new appreciation for music and insight into musical instruments through the Young Artists program.

Despite the popularity of contemporary "pop" music, there are sufficient Utahns who appreciate more traditional instrumentation to support a number of symphony and smaller ensemble orchestras. Among these must be mentioned the University of Utah Symphony . . . Utah Symphony Chamber Orchestra . . . Utah Valley Symphony . . . Brigham Young University Philharmonic . . . Brigham Young University and the University of Utah Chamber Orchestras . . . Utah Youth Symphony (founded in 1959 by Robert Lentz) . . . Westminster College Community Symphony (100 pieces) . . . and Murray Symphony Orchestra. Smaller ensembles include the University of Utah's Early Music Ensemble, which performs medieval, renaissance and baroque music, and the University's Symphony Band, Faculty String Quartet, and Percussion Ensemble. The Salt Lake Chamber Winds and Salt Lake Chamber Ensemble also must be noted as being representative of other groups having definite merit.

Recitals on the great Tabernacle Organ have become pleasant memories for countless visitors to Temple Square. At St. Mark's Cathedral, Clay Christiansen also provides organ concerts during the noon hours; his New Year's Eve program of Bach music has become an institution after six years. The Chamber Music Society of Salt Lake City, the Salt Lake Jazz Society, and others sponsor concerts of outstanding local and touring musicians.

Best known of all Utah pianists is Grant Johannesen, who has performed professionally since 1944 and has received numerous awards, prizes and honors. Johannesen has appeared on tour with America's leading orchestras, and in Europe and Russia; and though residing in the east, he returns to Utah often for appearances. President of the Cleveland Institute of Music, Johannesen has been commended by Virgil Thomson for his "profound, dignified music making" and is described as "a superior musician, one of the finest of American pianists."

The name of LeRoy J. Robertson of Brigham Young University and the University of Utah deserves repetition, for he is the greatest of Utah's symphonic composers. Ardean Watts served well during his long and energetic service as associate conductor of the Utah Symphony, artistic director of the Utah Opera Company, University of Utah professor of music, and musical associate of Ballet West.

Crawford Gates is another Utah composer and conductor of note. He premiered some of his own works as conductor of the Utah Symphony Orchestra and with Robertson arranged better known Mormon hymns for symphony orchestra and for choir and orchestra presentation. Gates was for several years a member of the music staff at Brigham Young University before moving on to further exploits at midwestern universities.

Other Utah pianists have achieved mention for excellence in the concert field, among them Reid Nibley. Earlier keyboard artists included Charles Shepherd, Becky Almond, and William Peterson.

The list of musicians could be extended, not only of talented native musicians but of adopted Utahns who honor the state with their art. Daniel

L. Martino is a member of this second category. Former chairman of the Utah Arts Council, Martino is a "nationally known researcher, musicologist, conductor, educator and composer." He has been associated with music at Brigham Young University, Ogden City Schools and at Weber State College, as well as music reviewer, guest conductor, author of several books, composer of original scores, and active member of numerous organizations.

Popular music and musical entertainment

It need hardly be noted that popular, contemporary music appeals to the great majority of Utah's youth, as attested by sold-out houses at the Salt Palace, the University of Utah Special Events Center, Brigham Young University, and other large auditoriuims when big-name stars come to the state. Summer rock festivals may attract thousands of young people, whereas performances of more conservative and traditional music may attract a few hundred listeners—or even fewer, as some conservative ensembles have discovered to their dismay. Recordings of "serious" music, of course, do not even approach those of popular, contemporary music in sales; in fact, such recordings may not even be available in many record shops. Utahns probably do not differ markedly from other audiences of the nation in their musical tastes, or at least that is likely the case with youth.

Eugene Jelesnik is an adopted son who has added significantly to the music experience of Utahns. Trained as a concert violinist, Jelesnik moved to Utah in 1945. During succeeding years this versatile artist has been—-among other activities—a radio music director, orchestra conductor, impresario (arranging for appearances of celebrity artists), and encourager of amateur talent. Jelesnik also has been an indefatigible national advisor for USO and producer of numerous USO shows for American troops in three wars.

One of the best-known vocalists having a Utah origin was the late James Haun, known professionally as Rouvaun. Trained in serious music, Haun gained a measure of fame as a singer in Las Vegas, on concert tours, and through recordings, before his death at an early age. For many fans he was "Utah's Caruso or Lanza." Finally, though listed last in this discussion of Utah music, the Osmond family are very far from least with respect to talent in musical entertainment and public recognition on a national and international scale. For nearly 20 years members of this family, as a group or individually, have performed on television, in films, and on recordings, as well as on stages around the world. In the process they have become identified in the public mind with Utah and their church.

LITERATURE

Utah has a proud and impressive tradition in the art of writing. Names such as Bernard DeVoto, Vardis Fisher, and Phyllis McGinley spring to mind from the immediate past to mingle with the names of people still writing: Wallace Stegner, Brewster Ghiselin, Virginia Sorensen, and a host of others. As a locale, Utah has also attracted great writers ever since the beginnings of Mormon settlement in 1847. The crossroads location and the seeming strangeness of Mormon religious beliefs attracted such diverse writers as Mark Twain, Sir Arthur Conan Doyle, Sir Richard Francis Burton, and Zane Grey. Some of these, notably Mark Twain and Sir Richard Burton, actually visited Utah and left their impressions of the land and people, whereas Sir Arthur Conan Doyle relied solely on the lurid accounts of hostile witnesses in laying a background for one of his stories, *A Study in Scarlet.*

During the first half-century after Utah's settlement, survival was necessarily of first importance; and during that period works of imaginative literature were rare but not entirely absent. The most impressive writing done during the early period, however, took the form of simple but heroic journals, biography and autobiography, and theological discussion.

The preponderance of Utah literature during the first 60 or 70 years after settlement was related to Mormons or Mormonism, though certainly not all. Much of this was religious, by writers such as Brigham Young, Orson and Parley P. Pratt, Joseph F. Smith, and John A. Widtsoe, or historical by such Mormon writers as Brigham H. Roberts. Of the many "home literature" efforts printed during those years, mainly in LDS magazines, the few survivors include pieces of Eliza R. Snow's poetry which are now Mormon hymns. One of Nephi Anderson's early novels has been reprinted recently as more of a curiosity than anything else. The 1941 edition treats this subject in greater detail.

Much literature about Utah during early years was "exposure" type if written outside Utah or biographical if written inside the state. The materials of Mormonism offered a fertile field, and although a number of writers attempted to use the setting, it was Maurine Whipple who first treated the polygamy story with both sympathy and truth when she was awarded a Houghton Mifflin Fellowship in 1938 to complete her novel *The Giant Joshua.* Virginia Sorensen followed in 1942 with *A Little Lower Than the Angels.*

In his essay *Mormonism and Literature,* William Mulder wrote:

It is not without significance that Mormonism, beginning with a book, had to make its appeal to a literate following. The proselyte had to be able to read. The Saints, be it remembered, equipped their ideal community not only with a temple and a bishop's storehouse, but with a printing press, and they appointed not only elders and bishops and teachers as their ministering officers, but an official printer to the Church. Even Winter Quarters had a press where was struck off what is believed to be the first printing west of the Mississippi, an epistle from the Twelve to the scattered Saints. And a people uprooted, on the move across Iowa and the great plains, carried Webster's blue-backed speller with them and heard their youngsters diligently recite their lessons in the dust of rolling wagons. Once established in Salt Lake Valley, they made an urgent request for a federal appropriation of $5,000 for a territorial library; and within short years they were promoting lyceums, a Polysophical Society, a Deseret Dramatic Association, a Universal Scientific Society, a Library Association, and an Academy of Art.

It is not without significance that Joseph Smith himself, whether viewed as the divinely inspired translator or as a transcendental genius, was the product of a literate background, both in terms of an average New England schooling with its available village culture and of his own family, particularly the maternal side: his grandfather Solomon Mack had published in chapbook form a highly readable spiritual autobiography. It is not surprising that around the Prophet's millennial standard gathered school teachers and college graduates, men as gifted as Oliver Cowdery and Willard Richards, the Pratt brothers—Parley and Orson, Orson Spencer, John Taylor, William Phelps, Lorenzo Snow, and his talented sister Eliza, persuasive orators and fluent writers who founded and edited capable periodicals like the *Millennial Star* in England, the *Messenger and Advocate* in Kirtland, the *Evening and Morning Star* in Independence, *The Mormon* in New York, *The Seer* in Washington, the *Luminary* in St. Louis, the *Nauvoo Neighbor* and the *Times and Seasons* in Nauvoo, and the *Frontier Guardian* in Kanesville—some of them brilliant, all of them fearless and eloquent.

The section devoted to literature in the 1941 edition was only five pages in length. Despite its brevity, it remains a useful interpretation of the history and status of Utah literature to that time:

The literature of Utah, like that of other frontier States, is marked rather by volume than by literary distinction, and is valuable chiefly as a part of the historical record of a time and an area. The published accounts of early explorers, trappers, scouts, leaders of Government expeditions, and homeseekers who crossed the Great Plains in covered wagons have the vividness of untutored and experimental writing. They are supplemented by a vast store of unpublished material, chiefly letters and diaries, that completed, if somewhat crudely, the impressive picture of a desert region transformed into a fertile land. Consciously literary pioneer works—whether poetry, fiction, biography, history, or literary criticism—were a curious mixture of old traditions and new and vigorous forces. The verse of Parley Pratt, one of the early Mormon apostles, for instance, is an imitation of Pope mingled with the spirit of the early West.

There is a more important, and too infrequently emphasized, aspect of the early literature of Utah and other western States. Life on physical frontiers has always been hard and earnest. There is little time or place for social amenities and cultural refinements. It is not surprising, therefore, and it is perhaps inevitable, that the children and grandchildren of pioneers should react against the lives of their forebears. On the physical frontier there is too much hardship, too much hunger and cold, for its offspring to remember it with kindness. They have almost invariably tried to shut it out, to remember only that which is pleasant to remember. And so the stories and verse about it are for the most part stories and poems about clouds and sunsets and peaks, lucid stream and burgeoned shrubs, golden valleys and tapestried skies. There are stories and poems about men compounded almost entirely of courage and tenderness, women of patience and vision, and children of wide-eyed and appealing wonder. Almost never is there a description of the shacks and huts and cabins in which pioneers lived; of the crude tools with which they labored; of the galling physical and emotional hardships which they endured.

In 1776 Silvestre Velez de Escalante, a Catholic priest, made an exploratory journey from Santa Fe toward Monterey, crossing through the region that was to become Utah. His accurate observations, recorded in his diary, are of value as the impressions of the first white man to enter the region. Some fifty years later, fur traders and trappers, following buffalo trails through the Rockies, added their casual journals to the knowledge of this little-known land. The "experiences" of James Beckwourth in the 1820's found their way into book form as *The Life and Adventures of James P. Beckwourth*. In the next two decades, the personal journals of Osborne Russell, Jedediah Strong Smith, James Clyman, and Peter Skene Ogden were set down and eventually published.

Washington Irving's *Adventures of Captain Bonneville* (1837), based on the unpublished journals of an explorer, made up in popular interest what it lacked in historical accuracy. Widely and eagerly read a short time later were the reports of John Charles Fremont, who visited Great Salt Lake on his way to the Pacific Coast in 1843. Thousands of copies of his report of this expedition of 1843-44 were absorbed by a public intensely curious about the Salt Lake region. In the fifties S. N. Carvalho made capital of this widespread interest in *Incidents of Travel and Adventure in the Far West with Colonel Fremont.* Not so well known are the Government report of Captain Howard Stansbury and the *History of the Mormons* by Lieutenant J. W. Gunnison. Among the most interesting of the explorers' accounts were those of Major J. W. Powell and F. S. Dellenbaugh, who between 1869 and 1873 made several hazardous boat journeys down the Colorado. Powell, who led the expeditions, tells his dramatic and popular story in *First Through the Grand Canyon;* the result of Dellenbaugh's experience and research was *The Romance of the Colorado River.* Among the finest of government reports are those of Clarence Edward Dutton, which have literary values rarely found in government annals.

Pioneer ways and hardships are reported in such books as the *Autobiography of Parley P. Pratt,* an early Mormon leader; *Life of a Pioneer,* by James S. Brown, a California gold-seeker; *Reminiscences of Alexander Toponce,* by an early-day freighter of that name; *Forty Years Among the Indians,* by Daniel W. Jones; *The White Indian Boy* (or *Uncle Nick Among the Shoshones*), by E. N. Wilson and Howard R. Driggs; and *Pioneering the West,* by Howard R. Egan.

1941 edition

Little has been written about literature in Utah for the years since 1941, during which there has been literary output of imposing quantity by Utah writers or by non-Utahns writing about Utah subjects. Evaluation for this latter period could hardly be as succinct as in 1941, not only because of the great quantity of literature produced during the past 40 years but also because of the broader diversity of subject matter being treated in latter years, as well as changing literary standards and styles. It is probable that as many works have been published on Utah during the years since 1941 as appeared prior to that time. Population increase alone could explain this apparent trend, though that surely is not the sole reason.

As treated here, "Utah literature" encompasses published work on every subject and in all forms of literary expression. The category is not (and cannot be) limited to the works of native Utahns or to the subjects of Utah and Mormonism for the simple reason that many writers on those subjects were not born in Utah, or if born in Utah did not confine their works to Utah-Mormon subjects.

If descriptions of the vicissitudes of life in early years are lacking in the writings of many of those who experienced them, that cannot be said about the writings of those who have followed. Publications of the Daughters of the Utah Pioneers are filled with descriptions of the lifestyles of pioneers and hardships endured by them. The late Kate B. Carter, guiding light of the DUP for years, was the author of many historical works and edited the writings of hundreds of others. Juanita Brooks has gained eminence and honors as the author, co-author, or editor of volumes on Utah history and biography, including *The Mountain Meadows Massacre, John Doyle Lee, On the Mormon Frontier: The Diary of Hosea Stout 1844-1861,* and *Not by Bread Alone.* The Utah State Historical Society has published a great many articles about life in early Utah, in the *Utah Historical Quarterly* and in separate titles. Since 1941, Mormon writers by the score—in histories and biographies—have chronicled the details of Utah life in early days.

Many excellent historical works on Utah-Mormon history have been published since 1941. A large number of journals, letters, and other primary source materials have become available for research in recent decades, making possible the re-evaluation of certain aspects of history.

Among historical titles of special significance that have appeared since 1941 are: Bernard DeVoto's prizewinning trilogy of western expansion: *The Year of Decision, 1846, Across the Wide Missouri,* and *The Course of Empire* . . . Charles S. Peterson, *Utah: A Bicentennial History* . . . Richard D. Poll and others, *Utah's History* (Brigham Young University) . . . LeRoy and Ann Hafen's monumental ten-volume series on the Mountain Men and Fur Trade of the Far West . . . William H. Goetzman's works on scientific exploration in the west . . . Wallace Stegner's *The Gathering of Zion: Story of the Mormon Trail* and *Beyond the Hundredth Meridian,* a study of John Wesley Powell and his surveys . . . and an excellent series of publications by the Utah State Historical Society, having to do with exploration of the Colorado River and southern Utah by the Powell Survey. Dale L. Morgan produced an extraordinary library of historical writings of commendable quality, including *The Great Salt Lake, The Humboldt, Jedediah Smith and the Opening of the West,* and *The West of William L. Ashley.*

Leonard J. Arrington, a prolific and versatile author of works on history, is one of the most respected Utah historian-writers of the present time. Besides those already named, the list of important history writers of recent decades would include Thomas G. Alexander . . . Gustive O. Larson . . . George Ellsworth . . Eugene E. Campbell . . . David E. Miller . . . C. Gregory Crampton . . . Glen M. Leonard . . . Don D. Walker . . . and James B. Allen. Crampton's *Standing Up Country* and *The Land of Living Rock* are visually impressive works on the history and physical setting of southern Utah and northern Arizona. Jesse D. Jennings, S. Lyman Tyler, and Floyd O'Neil have authored a number of works on the history and cultures of Utah's Indians, while Helen Z. Papanikolas has gained a distinguished reputation as an authority on the subject of non-Indian ethnic minorities in Utah. E. Richard Hart is a recognized authority on Zuni Indian history and culture.

In the specialized field of historical fiction having a Utah-Mormon background, many writers have been active. The best-known works in this category have dealt with life in the Mormon mileau. Several volumes of this nature were mentioned in the 1941 edition, among them Maurine Whipple's *The Giant Joshua* and Vardis Fisher's *Children of God.* These novels, published more than 40 years ago, retain positions on the roster of the most noteworthy Utah fiction; no works of more recent age have received a comparable outpouring of critical acclaim. Jean Woodman's *Glory Spent,* Lorene Pearson's *The Harvest Waits,* and Richard P. Scowcroft's *Children of the Covenant* are among numerous other fictional works having a Mormon theme. Worthy of notation, also, are Virginia Sorensen's *A Little Lower Than the Angels, On This Star,* and *The House Next Door.* Bela Petsco's *Nothing Very Important* (1979) fictionalizes the experiences of a Mormon missionary. Among the successful biographical works of recent years has been Edward and Andrew Kimball's biography of Spencer W. Kimball.

Frank C. Robertson, a native of Idaho and long-time resident of Utah, may be the state's most prolific and well-known writer of fiction. By the mid-1960s Robertson had written more than 150 books and more than a thousand short stories, most with a western motif. Oba A. Robertson, his brother, also authored many fictional works. Jonreed Lauritzen wrote several popular fictional works that appeared between 1943 and 1951, set in southern Utah, northern Arizona, and New Mexico.

Wallace E. Stegner lived in Salt Lake City as a young man, attended University of Utah, taught at that institution, and has maintained strong Utah ties. Stegner embarked on his writing career during the 1930s and has gained literary eminence on a national scale with a continuing flow of novels, historic and biographical works, and articles. Many of his works have a western or Utah setting. Among Stegner's better known works are *Big Rock Candy Mountain, Mormon Country, On a Darkling Plain, Fire and Ice, Joe Hill, Beyond the Hundredth Meridian, The Gathering of Zion, Angle of Repose,* and *The Uneasy Chair.*

Fawn M. Brodie, a Utah native and history teacher who died in 1981, gained repute as a writer of psycho-biography. *No Man Knows My History,* her controversial biography of Joseph Smith the Mormon prophet, was published by Knopf in 1945. Mrs. Brodie's other works include biographical studies of Sir Richard F. Burton, Thaddeus Stevens, Thomas Jefferson, and Richard Nixon. Norman Mailer's *Executioner's Song,* winner of the Pulitzer Prize in 1980, has literary connotations for Utah because its subject was Gary Gilmore, notorious murderer executed at the Utah State Prison.

Still another productive writer of history and fiction, much of it on Utah-Mormon subjects, is Paul D. Bailey of Westernlore Press in Los Angeles. An editor and publisher, born in Utah, Bailey has authored more than 20 books, including novels and biographical-historical works on Samuel Brannan, Jacob Hamblin, and Walkara. Howard R. Driggs, an educator, was the author of numerous works on Utah-western history and Mormonism, many of them for young people. The late Olive W. Burt was another indefatigable author who published more than 50 books, hundreds of magazine articles and newspaper features, more than 100 poems, a number of plays, and a great many short stories. Samuel W. Taylor, a Utah native and Hollywood screenwriter, has authored volumes of fiction, biography, cultural description, and reminiscences, as well as short stories and articles. Utah events and personages are featured in many of these, as in *Heaven Knows Why, Rocky Mountain Empire,* and *Family Kingdom.*

Rodello Hunter was the author of several volumes of personal memoirs that became popular sellers during the 1960s and 1970s, including *A House of Many Rooms* (1965) and *Daughter of Zion* (1970). Albert R. Lyman chronicled the history of southeastern Utah and his own life in a number of fictional and factual works, and Pearl Baker authored *Robbers Roost Recollections* and *The Wild Bunch at Robbers Roost* as well as biographical studies of river-runner Bert Loper and flyer Jim Hurst. This list of Utah's writers of history and biography, both popular and serious, could be extended. Additional names are contained in the reading list.

The field of descriptive travel, landscape and nature writing, apart from poetry, involves more than a few writers, though not as many, perhaps, as certain other literary specialties. Edward Abbey, author of novels, essays, and articles, merits a position here because of Utah-related titles such as *Desert Solitaire, The Monkey-Wrench Gang,* and *Slickrock.* Ward Roylance has authored travel and informational publications for the state as well as commercial travel titles and educational materials for schools. F. A. Barnes is the author of numerous travel articles and guide publications on southern and eastern Utah. The husband and wife team of the late G. E. and B. R. Untermann, geologists and curators of the Dinosaur Natural History Museum in Vernal, published numerous books, articles and maps interpreting the Uinta-Dinosaur region. Other geologists since 1941 have combined scientific discourse and creative writing in works such as Donald L. Baars's geological studies of Canyonlands National Park and the San Juan River . . . W. Lee Stokes's many geological writings . . . Herbert E. Gregory's geological and geographical descriptions of southern Utah, published as professional papers of the U.S. Geological Survey . . . and S. W. Lohman's geologic stories of Arches and Canyonlands national parks. *Down the Grand Staircase* by Paul F. Geerlings typifies an expanding category of visually striking books in color which are the team-products of writer, photographer (who might also be the writer), graphic artist, and publisher—often with less emphasis on the written word than on pictorial, graphic and design elements.

C. W. McCullough, Claire W. Noall, and Vesta P. Crawford were notable among the group of travel writers who featured Utah subjects in newspapers during the 1940s and 1950s. All three were productive in other literary fields as well. Mrs. Crawford, for example, was one-time editor of the *Relief Society Magazine* and authored more than 2,000 articles, poems, stories, and other writings. McCullough wrote fiction, history, verse, and features on travel, agriculture and mining. Mrs. Noall's range embraced fiction and nonfiction, prose, and poetry. *Windsinger,* Gary Smith's pioneering "poetic and pictorial odyssey about America and her people," combines the printed word, illustrations, and recorded music.

It is unfortunate that only the briefest mention can be made of Utah's very talented creative writers. Alice Morrey Bailey is an award-winning author of poetry, fiction, biography, etc., in addition to notable work in the visual arts, music, and playwriting. Clarice Short, professor of English at the University of Utah, is an eminent poet and author. Marba C. Josephson is a magazine editor, poet and author . . . Anna Prince Redd, a poet, author and playwright . . . Mabel Harmer, author of thousands of stories for children and adults, magazine articles, plays, and more than a dozen books . . . and Emma Lou Thayne is poet, teacher, and novelist (e.g. *Never Past the Gate*).

Among other talented writers of recent times who should be mentioned are the following, listed in alphabetical order: Elouise Bell, Gale Boyd, Mary L. Bradford, Marilyn M. Brown, Ann Cannon, Wayne Carver, Dennis Clark, Marden Clark, Paul Cracroft, Richard Cracroft, Joyce Ellen Davis, Richard Ellsworth, Paul Fisher, Edward Geary, Randall Hall, Herbert Harker, John S. Harris, Bruce Jorgensen, Arthur Henry King,

Rozanne Knudson, Eileen Gibbons Kump, Neal Lambert, Lael Littke, Karen Lynn, Vernice Wineera Pere, Dian Elizabeth Saderup, Charles Tate, Jr., Ray B. West, Jr., and William A. Wilson.

Phyllis McGinley was described in the 1941 edition as "Utah's best known poet." A resident of Utah, in fact, for only a few years during the 1920s, Ms. McGinley authored many volumes of verse as well as children's books, received the Pulitzer Prize for poetry in 1961, and was awarded many other honors. Utah has an enviable reputation as being the nurturing nest for a host of distinguished poets. The list of best-read Utah poets at this time would include Brewster Ghiselin, Edward L. Hart, Clinton F. Larsen, Edward Lueders, Veneta Nielsen, and Emma Lou Thayne. Deseret News critic and poet, Jerry Johnston, wrote in 1979 of Hart's *To Utah* book of poems: "If Utah were to appoint a Poet Laureate, these are likely the poems he would write."

Other poets who must be mentioned: Carlton Culmsee . . . Charles R. Mabey . . . Harrison R. Merrill . . . Geraldine Pratt . . . Lael Hill . . . Berta Christensen . . . Max Golightly . . . Carol Lynn Pearson . . . Ora Pate Stewart . . . Edward Tuttle . . . Kathryn Kay . . . Bonnie Howe Behunin . . . Alfred Osmond . . . LeRoy Meagher . . . Frank M. Decaria . . . and May Swenson, an expatriate Utahn who is a poet of national note. Edward G. Leuders, professor of English at University of Utah for years after 1966, has been honored as one of the nation's leading contemporary poets. Clinton F. Larsen, professor at Brigham Young University and director of its writers conference, has published several volumes of poetry and plays.

The most honored of Utah poets is Brewster Ghiselin. Professor Ghiselin taught at the University of Utah for more than 30 years, founded that school's writers conference, served as poetry editor of *Rocky Mountain Review,* and received numerous awards and prizes for his verse. He has also authored books, articles, stories, and essays. Edward L. Hart, professor of English at Brigham Young University, is noted not only for distinguished verse *(see above)* but for essays, fiction, biography, and varied other writings as well.

Promising young poets include Ken L. Brewer, Orson Scott Card, Patricia Hart, Stephen Ruffus, Sherod Santos, and Linda Sillitoe.

Representative of the state's legion of gifted newspaper writers, who must be included in any serious consideration of the literary scene, are the following: Clifton Jolley, Jerry Johnston, O. N. Malmquist, Maxine Martz, Hack Miller, John Mooney, Douglas Parker, Dorothy O. Rea, Harold Schindler, and Dan Valentine. Schindler also is the author of the acclaimed biography *Orrin Porter Rockwell: Man of God, Son of Thunder,* while O. N. Malmquist wrote *The First 100 Years: A History of the Salt Lake Tribune 1871-1971.*

Barbara Williams has authored more than 35 books (primarily juveniles) since 1965, in addition to many stories, plays, and poems. The professional specialty of Lela Wadsworth has been the mystery novel for juveniles, and Lorraine Henroid also has published books for juveniles. Blaine Yorgason is the author of two popular works of fiction: *Charlie's Monument* and

Windwalker. Claire Huffaker, a Utah native, is probably the state's most prolific screenwriter and television scriptwriter. The late Scott Whitaker was another highly regarded screenwriter. Among Utah's other playwrights and screenwriters are Ken Jenks, Janice Dixon, Helen Ratcliffe, Claire Whitaker Peterson, and David Kranes.

This brief account should not close without mention of Whit Burnett, Utah expatriate who with his wife founded *Story* magazine about 1930 and continued as editor for more than 30 years. This publication, devoted to the short story, is credited with bolstering the careers of many famous writers. Franklin S. Forsberg, another Utah native, served at various times during the period of the 1940s as publisher of *Mademoiselle, Charm, Yank,* and *Liberty.* Bernard DeVoto, a native of Ogden, mentioned in the 1941 edition and also above as an author of historical works, gained a national reputation not only for his important works on western history but also for his novels, essays, and works of criticism. Harold Ross, another Utahn, was well known as the long-time editor of *New Yorker* magazine.

Utah writers are encouraged and assisted in their creative endeavors by various agencies and organizations, including the League of Utah Writers, the Utah State Poetry Society, and state branches of the National Federation of American Pen Women. Among their special activities is an annual Writers' Roundup (League of Utah Writers), which features a keynote speaker of national reputation. The Utah State Poetry Society sponsors annual awards competitions and publishes a series of poetry anthologies entitled *Utah Sings,* with new volumes appearing every ten years. Writers' workshops also are sponsored by universities and colleges.

State and national assistance to writers is coordinated by the Utah Arts Council, which helps provide funding for the development of literary talent. The council cosponsors events such as the annual Statewide Junior Creative Writing Competition, Poets-in-the-Schools Project, and the annual State Playwriting Conference, sponsored in conjunction with Sundance Institute, which aids budding playwrights with rehearsals, critiques, revision assistance, and performance workshops. Since the 1950s the council also has sponsored an annual Statewide Creative Writing Contest. Entries in eight literary categories are judged and prizes awarded. Three years ago a publication prize was initiated, and each year the Arts Council assists in the publication of a work of literature that has significance for the state but which, without assistance, might not have been published. Among winners of these contests in the 1970s and 1980s are four writers who have been published nationally and are gaining recognition: novelists Elizabeth Lane and Patricia Hart (Molen), and children's literature authors Barbara Williams and Gloria Skurzynski.

Considering the amount and quality of literature produced by Utah writers since the pioneer settlement of 1847, it takes no great prescience to predict that current trends will continue, that the quality and quantity of output will increase, and that Utah has indeed a bright literary future.

ARCHITECTURE

Utah seems not to be associated in the public mind with distinctive archi-

Presentation of Utah Arts Council creative writing award by Norma Matheson, 1981.

tecture, excepting perhaps the several Mormon temples, the great tabernacle in Salt Lake City, or the State Capitol. This is regrettable, since the state does exhibit a remarkably broad spectrum of architectural styles reflecting not only the changing preferences of time but the influences of diversified cultures, religions, ethnic backgrounds, economic conditions, and natural setting.

Nevertheless, it must be admitted that, with respect to architecture, many if not most of Utah's communities are non-distinctive. This is not to say that the state's cities and towns do not rank favorably in architecture with others in the west. However, compared with places where people have lived for a much longer time—for example, in the east or midwest, or in Europe—Utah's architecture appears to be floundering in a state of undirected flux, experimentation, and immaturity, with little indication of an emerging regional identity. In fact, not until 1981 did Salt Lake City even consider architectural compatibility as a desirable element of zoning and planning.

Writing in the *Deseret News* (October 25, 1979), Sylvia Kronstadt cited observations about Utah's architecture by professional architects. Referring to Salt Lake City in particular, there was some consensus that local building design—for the most part—is mundane, standardized, repetitious, bland, cheerless, drab, and dull. Primarily because of economic factors, "beauty, comfort, and harmony with surroundings are subsumed" and "a sameness, a standardized, cheap approach to building is reflected throughout the city." The same criticisms might accurately be applied throughout the state.

Economic factors, it goes almost without saying, have been largely responsible for architectural design since settlers first arrived, though cultural-ethnic-religious background and esthetic sensitivity (or lack of it) have been influential as well.

And yet, without denying the validity of criticism, Utah is far from lacking architectural originality, variety, beauty, and distinction. If it has not discovered (or rediscovered) a regional or cultural identity in architecture, this may be due—as it is in other growing places throughout the world —simply to rapid and uncontrolled change. At one time, in fact, it could be claimed that Utah *did* have a regional identity, with respect not only to architecture but to other cultural factors as well. Today, Utah's more remarkable buildings are visitor attractions, competing with culture and the natural landscape for attention. Only a sampling of those that existed in pioneer times still remain, especially in Salt Lake City and other growing areas. Thousands of antique buildings have been replaced by structures of newer vintage and, in cases, perhaps less grace, while other thousands have collapsed or are in advanced stages of deterioration. Enough venerable buildings have survived, however, to add a definite accent of human interest and romantic nostalgia to the overpowering natural scene.

It is likely that few other western states exhibit as broad a variety of architectural styles as Utah—styles representing not only Indian cultures but also the greatly diversified ethnic-religious-cultural backgrounds and changing fashion choices of non-Indian settlers since the 1840s. These settlers came from many states of the east as well as from numerous foreign countries, bringing with them architectural traditions peculiar to their regions of origin. Utah's 19th century architecture was influenced by settlers from New England, the midwest, and the south, as well as from many countries of Europe. Religion and local availability of construction materials also were important influences on architecture for decades after settlement. Logs, rocks and adobe *(see below)* were used initially, followed by cut stone, bricks, milled wood, stucco, concrete, etc. All these materials are represented in extant structures today throughout the state, components of a remarkable conglomeration of architectural styles. Hundreds of distinctive buildings are listed on state and national historic registers, and many are noted in the various tours.

Natural Architecture

Wrote Richard F. Burton in 1860, as quoted in the 1941 edition: "An American artist might extract from such scenery as . . . Echo Kanyon, a system of architecture as original and as national as Egypt ever borrowed from her sandstone ledges or the North of Europe from the solemn depths of her fir forests."

Sir Richard never viewed the unique natural architecture of southern and eastern Utah, though he would have recognized shades of structural similarity to the natural architecture of Egypt and the Middle East, with which he was familiar. Architecturally suggestive elements assault the eye and imagination, particularly throughout the Colorado Plateau province. Architectural concepts are displayed in cliffs and countless sculptured forms, and are suggested in their very names: Factory Butte, Cathedral Valley, Church Rock, Great White Throne, Temple of Sinawava, Temple Mountain, Castle Valley, Wall Street, Capitol Dome, Fisher Towers, Monument Valley. . . . The list could be extended. Those relatively few natural forms to which names have been applied represent only a fractional part of the numberless forms and designs, created in rock by nature, that suggest architectural concepts originating in the mind—and perhaps elements not yet recognized.

This region has been known to the western world for little more than a hundred years (parts of it for less), and its esthetics—so strange in respects, unfamiliar to most artists and without exact counterpart—has had no formal study by architects, artists, or philosophers. It is interesting to speculate as to whether the natural artistry of the red-rock country, as it becomes better known and evaluated, might gradually add new dimensions to human art and architecture.

Indian Architecture

Native inhabitants of Utah lived in an assortment of habitations, depending on culture and environment. These ranged from brush wickiups to pit houses roofed with sod or brush, and from wigwams or tepees made of hides to Navajo hogans and the even more ancient rock and mud structures of the Fremont and Anasazi *(see Indians and Archeology for details)*. Contrary to popular opinion, the majority of early Indians did not live in cliff dwellings; but the common dwelling, built of fragile wood, mud, or skins, did not survive to modern times. Even rock structures, if not built in protected overhangs, eventually collapsed. Excavation and reconstruction of these buildings today are time-consuming and costly.

The 1941 edition, in the Architecture and Indians sections, contains a description of cliff-dweller architecture which would apply to only a few ruins in Utah because large cave-pueblo communities were not common in the state. Multi-family cave dwellings in Utah are found primarily at Hovenweep, Poncho House, Montezuma Canyon, Grand Gulch, White Canyon, Westwater Canyon, and several other sites in southeastern Utah. Elsewhere, cave sites were modest, serving as dwelling places for small groups or for food caches. Ruins of cliff-cave structures can be seen at numerous sites in the southern and eastern part of the state, with reconstruction serving as the basis for museums at Anasazi Village (Boulder) and Edge of the Cedars (Blanding). *See Indians and Archeology.*

"The modern inheritors of the mesa country [the Navajos] have profited nothing from the examples left them," said the 1941 edition. They "build a kind of fixed tepee, called *hogan,* of cedar posts set in the ground, brought together at the top, and made weathertight with a thatchwork of mud and twigs. The desert winds, in their ceaseless moving of sands, cover them sometimes until they are indistinguishable from the mounds that accrete about sagebrush and chaparral." The majority of Navajos no longer use the hogan as a principal residence, preferring conventional dwellings introduced by the whites. This is the case as well with the Ute, Paiute, and Goshute.

THE BUILT ENVIRONMENT FROM WHITE SETTLEMENT TO 1940
(modified excerpts from the 1941 edition)

Miles Goodyear, trader to the Indians, built a cabin of logs and a stockade on the present site of Ogden about 1844. The log-cabin architectural tradition, brought west from the rainy eastern frontier by Mormon pioneers in 1847, very early encountered proponents of the adobe house. The first of these was Sam Brannan, who had lately passed through California; he said 'dobe houses could be built, and well in a week. Necessity for immediate housing, and the relative availability of materials, led to a wedding of the two structural forms in the original Pioneer Fort, constructed of adobe and logs. Soil for adobe bricks existed everywhere, but green fir timber had to be hauled tediously from distant canyons.

A majority of colonists turned to "mud 'n' straw" adobe, moulded in bricks a foot and a half long, hardened in the sun, and laid in walls two or three feet thick. It was not always a happy material. Consider the plaint of the old-timer from St. George, whose house "riz right up outa the mud she stood on, 'n' when it rained, oozed right back down again." But, with a proper mixture of straw, or manure, if straw were lacking, and adequate drying and a bit of "fixin'" now and then when the bricks were in place, it could be made to endure indefinitely. The earliest adobe homes were cabins one or two rooms wide. If a man found time, the house might boast a porch across the front and a timber lean-to aft. The cornice was narrow and simple in outline, and the roof was quite flat. The rectangular plan was retained in later 'dobe homes (they were easiest and cheapest to construct and simplest to heat), but with four or six rooms on the first floor, and a dormer-windowed second story added. Roofs except the makeshifts of the first season in a settlement, were usually common gable and shingled. The floors were, as often as not, the dirt the house was built over.

Though the Mormons turned to adobe as a grim necessity, and not without protest, it has splendid building properties. Adobe clay is a good insulator, and the blocks, though not as durable as modern fired bricks, are easier to make and with care will last about as long.

About 1853, Brigham Young let contracts for an official residence for the Mormon Church president, a Church Office, and a private residence, all to be built in Great Salt Lake City on what is now South Temple Street. They were designed by William Ward and Truman O. Angell, the first practicing architects in the Territory, excepting of course, Young himself, who in his capacity of final authority for all things Mormon, had some positive (and workable) notions of his own about construction. They were built of the ubiquitous adobe, laid in walls three feet thick over foundations of hewn stone, the interiors whitewashed and the exteriors plastered. *See Tour No. 3 for further description.*

The Salt Lake Temple, which took forty years to complete, was also commissioned to Angell early in the 1850s; and in 1863 William Folsom and Henry Grow began to build a tabernacle with a seating capacity of five thousand. Folsom and Grow raised an egg-shaped dome above a series of stone buttresses, using rawhide and thole pins in lieu of nails. Grow was a bridge builder, and he constructed the tabernacle on the Remington principle of the arched truss.

After his success in designing the tabernacle, Folsom was given the commission for the Manti temple. This was modeled on the temple the Mormons were forced to abandon in Kirtland, Ohio, which in turn was an enlarged version of the typical New England "meeting house." It is rectangular in plan, with pyramidal-roofed square bell towers at the front. Construction was of stone, vermilion-hued sandstone in St. George and limestone at Manti, which was quarried by the crudest of methods. The blocks were cut along natural cleavages by the Egyptian method of drilling holes into which pegs were driven and wetted, the stone splitting when the pegs swelled. The temple at Logan, designed by Angell, though of the same basic design, has from the darkness of its stone and its octagonal corner towers the gloomy aspect of a Norman castle. Of all their buildings, however, the Mormons take greatest pride in the Salt Lake Temple, built tediously and carefully of native granite. Though sternly rectangular in plan as the others, its east and west ends are heightened by a system of ascending pyramidal towers, which, if not strictly Gothic, give much the same impression of vertical aspiration as the products of Gothic architects. Lesser buildings belonging to the early period of Utah architecture include the Mormon tabernacles at Logan and Brigham City, and the chapels built in almost every community possess the naive charm of straightforward building with native materials. The Old State House at Fillmore, in design, consisted of an elaborate system of Greek Revival wings about a central Moorish dome, but limitation of the territorial treasury reduced the actual building to one austere wing. Of the low-walled forts that in early days were everywhere in the territory, the best remaining examples are the crumbling mud walls of Fort Deseret *(see Tour 4),* and the perfectly preserved Cove Fort *(see Tour 4),* whose houses have but three walls, the fourth being the fort wall itself.

The penetration of Utah by railroads in 1869, with the attendant mine boom, had a profound effect on the whole social structure of the territory, an effect that was nowhere more marked than in its architecture. Between 1847 and 1870, homes had gradually grown more spacious, more comfortable, without, however, altering the basic design or freeing them from the pioneer simplicities. In many towns, such as Pleasant Grove, commodious old dormitories rear themselves somewhat grimly above the more modest dwellings, with unadorned entrances in the exact middle of the front, windows broken into small panes (since it was easier to freight small pieces of glass by wagon), and interiors of unfinished pine. If an occasional home had a bit of scrollwork about the porch or stoop, or a patch of paneling carved freehand inside, it was simply done. The railroad altered all that. The anonymous author of *Art in Utah,* published in twelve immense folio volumes in Chicago (1896), said: "The air had cleared wonderfully in Utah. . . . The house of adobe has become but a relic of the past; it is superseded by the artistic home of pressed brick or stone." Utah was within seven days of the Atlantic seaboard, freight rates were shattered, and the people of the Great Basin had nothing to restrain them from imitating an East which was, in its turn, imitating with all its might the gaudy extravagances of the Second French Empire. Mansard roofs replaced the honest gable; cornices and porches were larded with floriated machine-cut brackets; turrets, towers, and bay windows broke the old rectangularity. By 1880 the moneyed portion of Utah had entered fully into the age of the "Queen Anne" and mail-order-house gingerbread. The residential districts of Salt Lake City, Ogden, Logan, and Provo were still, in 1940, tolerably well supplied with these pretentious and uncomplicated houses. Commercial and public architecture was generally more restrained. The tabernacles of Ogden and Provo, the Brigham Young University Administration Building, and the Utah State Agricultural College Administration Building, though they have the broken facade, the towers, and the turrets of the times, have retreated into ivy coverings, and groves of trees have grown high about them. The Cathedral of the Madeleine in Salt Lake City (built much later, however), is a combination Romanesque and Gothic style, while the First Presbyterian Church next door is English Gothic. Business districts of the larger towns sport an occasional turret, but in general the Gothic influence was minimal.

In the 1890s Richardsonian Romanesque was introduced into Utah in the Salt Lake City and County Building, a complex of pillared upper-story windows, corner towers, pinnacles, arches, pilasters, erected in gray sandstone. The venerable old building was almost shaken apart during the gentle earthquake of 1934, but it was reinforced, its east and west halves bolted together, and continued in 1940 staunchly to serve as the outstanding example of Romanesque in Utah. The Executive (Kearns)

Mansion in Salt Lake City is an example of the elaborate chateauesque style in residential construction.

After 1900, Utah followed the rest of the Nation in a return to "classic architecture"—a renaissance expressed principally in public buildings such as the State Capitol, the City and County Building at Provo, and the Maeser Memorial Building at Brigham Young University. The Hotel Utah in Salt Lake City, built in 1911, is of the ornate French-Classical style. Residence design wandered from craftsman bungalows to Colonial Revival, exhibiting the general taste for classicism in an occasional home, as the lovely Peyton residence in Salt Lake City, or creating designs garnered from the whole background of Utah architecture, as the old David Eccles home in Ogden. About 1900, home builders discovered the bungalow, which completely dominated small residence architecture in the state until the late 1920s. Examples of it, in its worst and best forms, appear in every community.

Since the depression began in 1929 there seems to have been a revival of Colonial straightforwardness. The direct design of industrial buildings, office buildings, and apartment houses, having crept into schools, government buildings, and even into churches, has its counterpart in a residential architecture. The cottage, as well as the less extreme forms of California and modified New England Colonial houses, have appeared since 1935 with increasing frequency. The Ogden City and County Building is an admirable adaptation of stepped back skyscraper structure to the modest needs of a western community. Mormon and other church chapels constructed during the 1930s incorporated the block forms and horizontal movements of concrete and steel construction, though they were content to do without the more extreme styles that attached themselves to this material.

In the mining towns and regional commercial centers, Utah's indulgence in the old "false front" commercial buildings can still be seen. Copperton, in Bingham Canyon, is a livable "company town," planned by post-war architects. Two of its houses are experiments in the use of copper in home construction; the roof, walls, and partitions are of sheet copper.

The four decades since 1940 have brought profound change in architecture, both technologically and stylistically, and the buildings that have appeared since then bear scant resemblance to those of the past century—or even to those of the 1920s and 1930s. Only recently has there been an

attempt on the part of some cities to evaluate the architecture of the past 50 years, and it appears that Utah's architecture has followed trends set in other parts of the country. However, according to Peter L. Goss, post-World War II designs of the late 1940s and early 1950s were "pale imitations of the sources that inspired them, and this continued to occur even as late as the 1960s. . . . Several factors contribute to this situation: Economics, the general level of design talent, and a lack of good out-of-state competition for the stimulation of better design." Readers are referred to Professor Goss's article in the *Utah Historical Quarterly* (Summer 1975) for more comprehensive details about architectural trends and styles in Utah. The same issue contains an excellent treatise on religious architecture of the Mormon Church, as well as articles about the architecture of Spring City, Beaver, and Willard.

Contemporary architecture is strikingly evident throughout Utah, of course—more apparent because of sheer volume than architecture of the 19th and early 20th centuries. Exceptions to this situation are rural towns, villages and farms, where change has been slow to occur; but even there the old is rapidly giving way to the new as older structures (unless they have distinct historical and architectural value) are replaced by contemporary buildings. The most obvious result of this flood-change to modernity is an architectural "leveling" or "mass Americanization" of the state. With some exceptions, only the older buildings serve to provide the state with an element of architectural originality. In general, glass towers and glass-faced houses in Utah differ little, if at all, from myriad counterparts throughout the nation. This can be said as accurately of contemporary shopping malls, grocery stores, government buildings, commercial buildings, industrial parks, mobile home parks, suburban housing developments, etc.

Fortunately, certain contemporary structures do stand apart as examples of creative originality. Readers may judge the extent of such originality for themselves; even architects do not always agree. Examples of contemporary architecture are legion throughout the state, of course, but the most imposing clusters would certainly include the following: The modern campuses of Brigham Young University, University of Utah, Weber State College, and Utah State University, the products largely of construction during the past 20 years or so . . . University of Utah's Research Park . . . the business centers of Salt Lake City and Ogden, now in a process of dramatic transformation . . . Utah Technical College in Orem . . . Snowbird Resort in Little Cottonwood Canyon . . . numerous shopping centers . . . and new industrial parks in Salt Lake Valley, west of the city (for example, Salt Lake International Center). Not to be neglected in such a listing are industrial structures such as the vast Thiokol complex west of Brigham City . . . the Hercules complex at Bacchus . . . Kennecott's new smelter and stack at Garfield . . . and even the grand assemblage of buildings at Hill Air Force Base. The state's most expensive, imaginative, and elaborate contemporary homes are found on the mountain slopes overlooking Salt Lake City, Ogden, and Provo. In Salt Lake City, the new Symphony Hall-Art Center complex is noteworthy. The Mormon Church Office Building, east of Temple Square, is regarded by many as the most distinctive high-rise building in the state. Trolley Square has combined the

Devereaux House, Salt Lake City *(above).*
Kearns Mansion, Salt Lake City *(next below).*
Samuel Allen residence, Provo, 1898
(bottom).

Enos Wall residence, Salt Lake City *(above).*
Officers quarters, Fort Douglas *(next below).*
John E. Dooly residence, Salt Lake City
(bottom).

old and new in an assemblage never before seen in Utah. Also of architectural interest is the developing complex of government-commercial-residential buildings near the Salt Lake City and County Building.

The 1960s and 1970s brought a marked awareness of the architectural heritage descended from the 19th century and early years of the 20th century. Owners of many exceptional older buildings are choosing to restore, preserve, and utilize rather than to replace. This change in attitude came barely in time to retain a part of the man-made charm of the state and nation.

The recognition of value in the old certainly has not been limited to Utah. In fact, it is probable that the demolition-replacement trend would have continued across the nation had it not been for congressional passage of the National Historic Preservation Act in 1966. This helped to bring profound change to the preservation-restoration scene. Among its direct and indirect results: involvement of state government and grass-roots organizations, increased public awareness of the nation's historic and architectural heritage, changing attitudes with respect to the worth of older structures, the inventorying of distinctive historic buildings and sites, the creation of historic districts within the state, and financial-advisory assistance with preservation and restoration. An advisory committee on Historic and Cultural Sites was appointed by the governor, and a state Historic Preservation Office was affiliated with the Utah State Historical Society to coordinate government programs, including funding. Another important development was the creation of the Utah Heritage Foundation to represent the private sector in identifying worthy sites and encouraging preservation-restoration.

Those who savor the old and unusual in pre-modern architecture can still whet their appetites in Manti, Ephraim, and Spring City *(Tour No. 7)* . . . Dixie and Beaver *(Tour No. 8)* . . . Cache Valley *(Tour No. 1)* . . . Park City and Utah Valley *(Tour No. 5)* . . . Willard, Farmington, and Kaysville *(Tour No. 2)* . . . Eureka *(Tour No. 4)* . . . Bluff *(Tour No. 11)* . . . . Kanab, Panguitch, and Escalante *(Tour No. 9)* . . . Monroe *(Tour No. 7)* . . . Spring Canyon and Hiawatha *(Tour No. 10)* . . . Pioneer Village at Lagoon *(Tour No. 2)* . . . Old Deseret Village in Salt Lake City *(Tour No. 3)* . . . and E. South Temple Street in Salt Lake City *(Tour No. 3)*. These are some of the best of the "living museums" in Utah, though certainly not all.

UTAH: A GUIDE TO THE STATE

Part 2

TOURING UTAH'S HIGHWAYS AND SIDEROADS

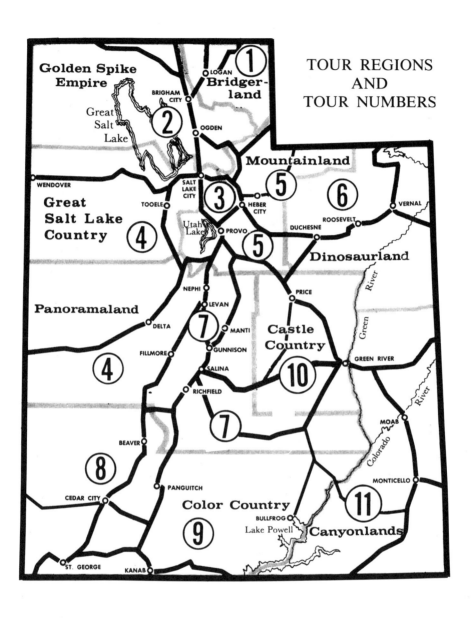

TOUR REGIONS
AND
TOUR NUMBERS

Part 2
Tour Section

Utah

A GUIDE TO THE STATE

Revised and Enlarged

by

Ward J. Roylance

Consulting Editor

Eugene E. Campbell

Sponsored by the Utah Arts Council
Published by UTAH: A GUIDE TO THE STATE Foundation
Salt Lake City, Utah
1982

WARD J. ROYLANCE is the author of more than 40 informational and educational publications on Utah. Holder of a graduate degree from the University of Utah, he has produced teaching materials on the subject of Utah for use in the state's schools, as well as popular guidebooks and state informational publications. For a number of years Mr. Roylance was employed by the Utah Tourist and Publicity Council (now the Utah Travel Council), where he was in charge of research and publications.

EUGENE E. CAMPBELL is professor emeritus of history at Brigham Young University. Dr. Campbell has published numerous articles on Mormon and Western history; has coauthored a college text on United States history as well as other volumes of history; and was associate editor of *Utah's History,* a college text published by Brigham Young University.

MARGARET D. LESTER, picture editor, is a professional librarian and picture source specialist. After a period with the Salt Lake City Public Library system, Mrs. Lester became Curator of Photographic Collections for the Utah State Historical Society, a position in which she served for more than 20 years.

First edition published in 1941
Revised edition published in 1982

First edition published under the auspices of
Utah State Institute of Fine Arts
Federal Works Agency
Work Projects Administration
First edition copyright 1941 by Utah State Institute of Fine Arts

Revised edition sponsored by
Utah Arts Council
Ruth Draper, Director
An agency of Utah Department of Community and Economic Development
Publication of revised edition financed by
Utah: A Guide to the State Foundation

Copyright 1982 by Utah Arts Council

Manufactured in the United States of America

ISBN 0-91470-23-7 (Part 2)
Library of Congress Catalog Card No. 82-50370

Contents: Part 2

Part 2. Touring Utah's Highways and Sideroads

Introduction to the Tour Section

Part 2, which follows, describes the 11 varied travel regions of Utah. In treatment of typography and content it resembles the 1941 edition. However, it differs from that work in that travel regions of this volume coincide with those delineated by the Utah Travel Council, whereas the former volume arranged tours by highways. Each travel region exhibits distinctive historical, cultural, geographical, or geological characteristics.

In the former edition considerable emphasis was placed on history and cultural anecdotes. These added an intriguing flavor which, unfortunately, is not so plentiful an ingredient in this revised volume. The forty years between editions saw many changes in Utah, making it necessary to delete or abbreviate much of the old to make room for the new. Also, the author's personal leanings resulted in more emphasis being placed on physical attributes (architecture, topography, geology), which can be seen with the eye, than on the ephemeral (historical) background of a place. At the same time, history has not been entirely neglected.

With regard to attractions which are open only during specific hours and in certain seasons—as in the case of museums, parks, etc.—this volume differs from many guidebooks in that such transient information has not been included. Details of that type are constantly changing, and current information may be easily obtained from the Utah Travel Council and other information sources on request. So, also, tour descriptions do not include information concerning accommodations and services. Utah is very much a part of the travel age, and even in rural areas there are motels, restaurants, stores, and auto services in nearly every town of any size. Visitors needing to know the availability of services in any particular locale may obtain current information from a number of sources *(see page 277).*

Of necessity, maps in this volume have been designed for general orientation. Page size did not permit inclusion of small detail. Users of this book should obtain a detailed state highway map, or equip themselves with comprehensive regional maps issued by the Utah Travel Council, or purchase topographic maps from the U. S. Geological Survey. The U. S. Forest Service also issues detailed maps. Serious students also are advised to consult other published works having to do with specific areas or points of interest.

This volume contains detail enough to satisfy the majority of travelers. Readers should be aware, however, that hundreds of sources totaling thousands of pages were digested and abbreviated in the compilation of this tour section. This verifies that almost infinite detail is available from other sources for those who have need of such.

Seasons and Climate

Utah's position on the globe has provided it with four seasons, approximately as follows: Winter (December 20 to March 20) . . . Spring (March 20 to June 20) . . . Summer (June 20 to September 20) . . . and Fall (September 20 to December 20). Summer months are hottest, winter months are the coldest, spring and fall the most moderate. Traditionally, the majority of tourists visit Utah during summer months, between early June and Labor Day, when most families with school-age children take their vacations. Temperatures are warm and even hot in this season. More recent times show signs of change in these travel habits, with many tourists choosing spring and fall months and others coming in mid-winter for skiing. In other words, Utah is becoming an all-season vacationland, although attractions in the hinterlands still see very few visitors between October and March.

Temperature varies from place to place and season to season. Example: in the urban north, summer temperatures (July and August) commonly reach 95 to 100 degrees F. in the day, dropping some 30 degrees at night. They are even higher in St. George (lowest and warmest city in the state). In mid-winter, temperatures in the northern cities normally are in the 30s or 40s in daytime and always below freezing at night. The deserts of eastern and western Utah approximate these temperatures. Humidity is low throughout the state, being highest near Great Salt Lake, Lake Powell, and in the mountains.

Utah is arid or semi-arid in most locations except the high mountains, where snow may be present from late October to June and rain may be plentiful during summer afternoons. Ski season often (but not always) begins in November and extends into April or May. Snow conditions are consistently good for skiing in January, February and March.

Summer months are likely to bring thundershowers to much of the state. Ordinarily these are of brief duration, but they bring welcome relief from heat. In rocky areas of the south and east, summer storms may result in flash flooding. During that season visitors are cautioned to stay out of narrow stream channels when storms threaten in the vicinity or upstream.

Even in summer, in most parts of the state, nights are likely to be cool. Visitors should be prepared with jacket or sweater at all seasons. "Well-advised tenderfeet keep shirt collars buttoned and sleeves rolled down, for the desert and high mountain sun burns unmercifully." That advice from the 1941 edition may not appeal to today's young people, who prefer dark tans, but it is a word to the wise for all.

Even residents are not aware that winter months can be delightful in the red-rock country. Snow melts rapidly on warm rocks and seldom is a hindrance to travel, on foot or in vehicles, except possibly in January and early February. Sunny days may be more pleasant in mid-winter than in summer. Also, for the imaginative photographer, white snow and red rock blend in superb combination not seen at other times of year.

Sources for Additional Information

Principal source for travel information—

Utah Travel Council, Council Hall—Capitol Hill (3rd North and State), Salt Lake City, Utah 84114

Official information center and clearinghouse for travel and recreational information publications issued by the Council, chambers of commerce, regional travel councils, resorts, commercial firms

Regional travel councils

Bridgerland, 52 W. 2nd North, Logan, Utah 84321

Canyonlands, Moab, Utah 84532 or Monticello, Utah 84535

Castle Country, Price, Utah 84501

Color Country, Cedar City, Utah 84720

Dinosaurland, Vernal, Utah 84078

Golden Spike Empire, Union Depot, Ogden, Utah 84401

Mountainland, 160 E. Center, Provo, Uth 84601

Panoramaland, Richfield, Utah 84701

Salt Lake Valley Convention & Visitors Bureau, Salt Palace (Suite 200), Salt Lake City, Utah 84101

Utah State government offices

Arts Council, 617 E. South Temple, Salt Lake City, Utah 84102

Geological and Mineralogical Survey, 606 Blackhawk Way (University of Utah Research Park), Salt Lake City, Utah 84108

History Division, 300 Rio Grande Street, Salt Lake City, Utah 84101

Industrial Development Division, 165 S. West Temple, Salt Lake City, Utah 84101

Park and Recreation Division, 1636 W. North Temple, Salt Lake City, Utah 84116

Wildlife Resources Division, 1596 W. North Temple, Salt Lake City, Utah 84116

Federal offices

U. S. Bureau of Reclamation, Federal Building, 125 S. State, Salt Lake City, Utah 84138—information on water-recreation projects

U. S. Bureau of Land Management, University Club Building, 136 E. South Temple, Salt Lake City, Utah 84111—information and publications

U. S. Geological Survey, Public Inquiries Office, Federal Building, 125 S. State, Salt Lake City, Utah 84138—maps, publications

U. S. National Park Service (Utah State Office), Federal Building, 125 S. State, Salt Lake City, Utah 84138—information and publications.

Also contact individual national parks: see tour section for addresses.

National Forests:

Regional Forester, U. S. Forest Service, 324 - 25th St., Ogden, Utah 84401

Supervisor, Ashley National Forest, 437 E. Main, Vernal, Utah 84078

Supervisor, Dixie National Forest, 500 S. Main, Cedar City, Utah 84720

Supervisor, Fishlake National Forest, 170 N. Main, Richfield, Utah 84701

Supervisor, Manti-LaSal National Forest, 350 E. Main, Price, Utah 84501

Supervisor, Uinta National Forest, 88 W. 1st North, Provo, Utah 84601

Supervisor, Wasatch-Cache National Forest, 4438 Federal Building, 125 S. State, Salt Lake City, Utah 84138

Supervisor, Sawtooth National Forest, 1525 Addison Avenue East, Twin Falls, Idaho 83301

Events

Daily newspapers and other publications such as *Utah Holiday Magazine* describe myriad events taking place continually in Utah. The Utah Travel Council distributes comprehensive monthly and annual listings without charge. Following is an abbreviated list of events that normally are scheduled every year. Exact dates vary from year to year and therefore are not shown.

Winter (January-February-March)

Indoor sporting events: basketball, wrestling, ice hockey, gymnastics, swimming . . . cultural events: theater, music, travel lectures, dance, etc. . . . museum and gallery exhibits . . . skiing, snowmobiling, dog sled racing, competition skiing . . . sports, travel, home and boat shows . . . winter carnivals (Park City, Snowbird) . . . feeding of the elk at Hardware Ranch . . . cisco fishing at Bear Lake

Spring (April-May-June)

Opening of Lagoon and Saratoga resorts . . . symphony concerts . . . art exhibits . . . ski events . . . first rodeos of the season . . . gem and mineral shows

April—Mormon General Conference, Salt Lake City
   National Art Exhibit, Springville Museum of Art
   Annual Jeep Safari, Moab
   Annual Concert, Salt Lake Symphonic Choir

May—Golden Spike Ceremony, Promontory (May 10)
   Smithfield Health Days
   Richmond Black and White Days
   Millard County Junior Livestock Show, Delta
   Intercollegiate Rodeo, Logan (USU)
   May Day, Mendon
   Gemboree, Price

June—Regular fishing season opens
   Mineralogical Society of Utah annual show, Murray
   Art City Days, Springville
   Utah Pageant of the Arts, American Fork
   Summer Festival, Orem
   Utah Arts Festival, Salt Lake City
   Morgala Rodeo, Morgan
   Strawberry Days, Pleasant Grove

Summer (July-August-September)

Summer festivals of art and music . . . rodeos and parades in many communities (especially on July 4 and July 24) . . . tennis and golf tournaments, other outdoor sports activities

July—Independence Day celebrations, many communities
  Shrine Circus, Salt Lake City
  Ute Stampede, Nephi
  Western Art and Antique Fair, Ogden
  Mormon Miracle Pageant, Manti
  Utah Shakespearean Festival, Cedar City (SUSC)
  Festival of the American West, Logan (USU)
  July 24 Pioneer Day and Week—parades and other events, many
    communities
  Days of '47 Celebration, Salt Lake City
  Pioneer Days Celebration, Ogden

August—County Fairs and Homecoming Days, many communities
  Park City Arts Festival
  Swiss Days, Midway
  Golden Onion Days, Payson

September—County Fairs, many communities
  Peach Days and Art Festival, Brigham City
  Hydroplane races, Willard Bay
  Utah State Fair, Salt Lake City
  Softball and golf tournaments, various communities
  Cache Valley Threshing Bee, Logan
  Dixie Roundup, St. George
  Greek Festival, Salt Lake City
  Melon Day Celebration, Green River
  Bonneville Nationals Speed Trials, Bonneville Salt Flats
  Gem and Mineral Show, Tooele

Fall (October-November-December)

Cultural season begins: music, dance, drama events . . . indoor sports season begins . . . ski season begins (late November or December)

October—Fall color season (late September-early October)
  First snowfall (late October in mountains)
  General Conference, Mormon Church, Salt Lake City
  Oktoberfest, Snowbird
  Regular deer hunting season opens

November—Golden Spike National Livestock Show, Ogden
  Christmas Parades, Ogden and Salt Lake City
  Opening of ski resorts (late November)

December—Christmas events—parades, shows, concerts, tree lighting
  Christmas lights on Temple Square, Salt Lake City
  Festival of Trees, Salt Lake City
  "The Messiah" annual production, Salt Lake City, St. George, and
    other communities

Travel Tips

Photography

Intensity of light and clarity of atmosphere (away from the urban Wasatch Front with its degraded air) should be considered by photographers. It is generally advisable to underexpose slightly, particularly on water, where snow is present, or in the red-rock country where reflected light tends to wash out colors if shot even at what is customarily normal exposure. Bear in mind at all times that richer, slightly underexposed color is preferable to weaker, overexposed color. It is a wise rule, also, to carry more film than one expects to use. Film may not always be available in rural or remote areas, and if available may not be the desired size or type; invariably, also, it is more expensive there than in cities. Take care to protect cameras, lenses and film from dust, sand and heat.

Insect and animal pests

The most troublesome insects likely to be encountered in Utah are flies, mosquitoes, gnats and ants. Not much can be done about flies in the outdoors except to carry a swatter. Mosquitoes and gnats can be discouraged with chemical repellents and appropriate clothing (long sleeves, collars and hats). In warmer months gnats may be very distressing in both the dry desert and on the shores of Great Salt Lake. Their poison can cause painful itching and welts. Mosquitoes are common in mountain country and marshy areas. Most ants are small and harmless; however, in a few areas they may be large and bothersome. Tarantulas inhabit some desert areas, as do scorpions. Rattlesnakes also are present and should be watched for, though they are not common in most parts of the state and certainly are not as prevalent as in many states. Wood ticks only rarely are infectious (Rocky Mountain spotted fever), but travelers in brushy terrain should be alert for their presence. The application of kerosene, gasoline, or a hot match to the body of an embedded tick normally suffices to bring it out of the skin. A snakebite kit is recommended as first-aid equipment for backcountry foot travel.

Poisonous Plants

Three-leafed poison ivy, with foliage bearing an irritating oil, occurs throughout the state except in deserts. If infected, wash exposed parts with strong soap and warm water; calamine lotion or sugar of lead are good counteractives after irritation sets in. Lupine, growing on mountain slopes and foothills, has poisonous foliage; treat similarly to poison ivy. Stinging nettle, irritating but non-poisonous, occurs among thick growths in canyons and along rivers; sting is eased by vaseline or cold cream. Many plants are poisonous if ingested.

OFF-HIGHWAY TRAVEL

It is always a good rule to inquire locally before attempting an unpaved road with which you are not familiar, especially in isolated areas. Avoid traveling alone. Advise others of your anticipated route and how long you expect to be gone. Unpaved roads may deteriorate rapidly if not regularly maintained. Avoid driving on unpaved roads when they are wet; not only does this damage the road, but it may be dangerous for drivers. Make a habit of "Keeping far right" on hills and curves, especially on narrow, winding roads. Few roads in Utah do not carry at least some traffic each day, and head-on collisions even at moderate speed can be fatal.

Certain areas are closed to motorized vehicles, particularly in national forests, parks, and some BLM areas. If you plan off-highway travel in such areas, obtain applicable "Off-Road Vehicle Travel Plan" maps. Such maps, as well as information concerning off-road vehicle areas and snow-mobile trails, are available from state and federal agencies. *See Sources for Additional Information.*

—Avoid loose sand. Loose sand can stop even four-wheel-drive vehicles.
—Check firmness and depth of fords, mud and suspicious soil, on foot, or with sticks, before entering with your vehicle. A minute of checking may save hours of hard shovel work.
—If your vehicle breaks down, remain near it. Raise hood and trunk lid to denote "help needed." Set signal fires (smoky in daytime, bright at night); three fires in a triangle denote "help needed." Keep out of direct sun if possible and cover the head. If you must leave vehicle, leave a note telling direction you are taking and time you left.
—If water is limited, keep your mouth closed. Do not talk, do not eat, do not smoke, do not drink alcohol, and do not take salt. If you must drink local water from ponds, streams, tanks, etc., treat chemically or boil if at all possible.
—To avoid poisonous creatures, put your hands or feet only where your eyes can see.

Vehicle checklist

Full tank
Engine and transmission oil levels
Good tires
Sound radiator hoses

Good battery, fully charged
Good engine belts
Correct tire pressure

Equipment checklist

Drinking water (at least one gallon of water per person per day)
Extra water for vehicle and emergencies
Extra gasoline, motor oil, transmission oil
Spare tire, tools, jack, lug wrench, fan belt, tow rope or chain, jumper cables

First-aid kit, snakebite kit
Food for several days
Blankets, warm clothing, hat
Flashlight and/or lantern
Shovel, axe
Matches, newspapers, firewood, camp stove
Detailed map of area

Selected Reading List

The published literature on Utah amounts to many thousands of books, magazine and newspaper articles, pamphlets, brochures, flyers, maps, and other printed matter. In addition to these are a multitude of unpublished dissertations and theses, and a great wealth of manuscripts, diaries, records, and other primary source materials. With respect to Mormonism alone, more than 10,000 items are listed in *A Mormon Bibliography 1830-1930* (Chad J. Flake, editor) and about 3,000 items are described in *Guide to Mormon Diaries and Autobiographies* (Davis Bitton, editor).

The following list of published works, numbering about 120 titles, is but a miniscule sampling of what is available in print on the subject of Utah and the Mormons. Most items can probably be found in larger Utah libraries. The 1941 edition of this guidebook included a Selected Reading List of some 240 titles, the majority of which do not appear below and therefore may be considered supplemental to the titles in this revised edition. Bibliographical listings of value to students also appear in other works, some of which are listed below under Bibliographies.

Many governmental, promotional, commercial, and private agencies distribute printed materials of an informational nature. Much of this is available without charge or for a nominal fee, at agencies listed above under Sources for Additional Information.

Abbreviations used in the Reading List —

BYU	— Brigham Young University	UGMS	— Utah Geological & Mineralogical Survey
DN	— Deseret News Press		
DUP	— Daughters of Utah Pioneers	UHQ	— Utah Historical Quarterly
ed	— editor	USHS	— Utah State Historical Society
et al	— and others	USU	— Utah State University
GPO	— Government Printing Office	UTC	— Utah Travel Council
LA	— Los Angeles	UU	— University of Utah
NHA	— Natural History Association	WPA	— Work Projects Administration (Utah Writers' Project)
NY	— New York City		
SLC	— Salt Lake City		
SUP	— Sons of the Utah Pioneers	WSC	— Weber State College
U	— University		

BIBLIOGRAPHIES

Bitton, Davis (ed). *Guide to Mormon Diaries and Autobiographies.* Provo, BYU, 1977.

Flake, Chad J. (ed). *A Mormon Bibliography 1830-1930: Books, Pamphlets, Periodicals, Broadsides Relating to the First Century of Mormonism* (10,145 items). SLC, UU, 1972.

Tyler, S. Lyman. *The Ute People: A Bibliographical Checklist.* Provo, BYU, 1964.

Lengthy bibliographies also appear in the following books—

Allen, James B. and Leonard, Glen M. *The Story of the Latter-day Saints.* Salt Lake City, Deseret Book, 1976.

Arrington, Leonard J. *Great Basin Kingdom: Economic History of the Latter-day Saints, 1830-1900.* Lincoln, U of Nebraska, 1966 (reprint).

Arrington, Leonard J. and Bitton, Davis. *The Mormon Experience.* NY, Random House, 1979.

Crampton, C. Gregory. *Land of Living Rock: The Grand Canyon and the High Plateaus: Arizona, Utah, Nevada.* NY, Knopf, 1972.

Crampton, C. Gregory. *Standing Up Country: The Canyon Lands of Utah and Arizona.* NY, Knopf, 1964.

Greer, Deon and Wahlquist, Wayne et al. *Atlas of Utah.* WSC-BYU, 1982.

Poll, Richard D. et al. *Utah's History.* Provo, BYU, 1978.

WPA. *Utah: A Guide to the State.* NY, Hastings House, 1941.

THE STATE — GENERAL

Deseret News. *Deseret 1776-1976: A Bicentennial Illustrated History of Utah.* SLC, DN, 1975.

Ellsworth, S. George. *Utah's Heritage.* SLC, Peregrine Smith, 1972. A textbook.

Greer, Deon and Wahlquist, Wayne et al. *Atlas of Utah.* WSC-BYU, 1982.

Peterson, Charles S. *Utah: A Bicentennial History.* NY, Norton, 1977.

Poll, Richard D. et al. *Utah's History.* Provo, BYU, 1978.

Sutton, Wain (ed). *Utah: A Centennial History.* NY, Lewis, 1949 (3 vols)

HISTORY

General

Bancroft, Hubert H. *History of Utah.* San Francisco, History Co., 1890.

Daughters of the Utah Pioneers, Salt Lake City.
Heart Throbs of the West, 1939-1951 (12 volumes)
Our Pioneer Heritage, 1958-1975 (18 volumes)
Treasures of Pioneer History, 1952-1957 (6 volumes)

Greer, Deon and Wahlquist, Wayne et al. *Atlas of Utah.* WSC-BYU, 1982.

Morgan, Dale L. *The Great Salt Lake.* Indianapolis, Bobbs-Merrill, 1947.

Morgan, Dale L. (ed). *Overland in 1846: Diaries and Letters of the California-Oregon Trail.* Georgetown, Calif., Talisman, 1963.

Neff, Andrew L. *History of Utah 1847-1869.* SLC, DN, 1940.

Whitney, Orson F. *History of Utah.* SLC, Cannon, 1892-1904 (4 vols).

Trappers and Traders

Chittenden, Hiram M. *American Fur Trade of the Far West.* NY, Harper, 1902 (3 vols). Reissued 1936 with additional material.

DeVoto, Bernard. *Across the Wide Missouri.* Boston, Houghton, 1947 + .

Hafen, LeRoy R. (ed). *The Mountain Men and the Fur Trade of the Far West* (Far West Series, 10 volumes). Glendale, Clark, 1954 + .

Morgan, Dale L. *Jedediah Smith and the Opening of the West.* Indianapolis, Bobbs, 1953 + .

Explorations and Surveys

Bartlett, Richard A. *Great Surveys of the American West.* Norman, U of Oklahoma, 1962.

Chavez, Fray Angelica and Warner, Ted J. (eds). *The Dominguez-Escalante Journal* (English and Spanish texts and field work notes). Provo, BYU, 1976.

Cline, Gloria G. *Exploring the Great Basin.* Norman, U of Oklahoma, 1963.

Hafen, LeRoy R. and Ann W. *Old Spanish Trail: Santa Fe to Los Angeles.* Glendale, Clark, 1954.

Powell, John W. *Exploration of the Colorado River and Its Canyons.* New York, Dover, 1961 (reprint of *Canyons of the Colorado,* originally published in 1895).

Stegner, Wallace. *Beyond the Hundredth Meridian: John Wesley Powell and the Second Opening of the West.* Boston, Houghton, 1954.

Utah State Historical Society. "The Exploration of the Colorado River and the High Plateaus of Utah by the Second Powell Expedition of 1871-72." UHQ, Vols 16-17, 1948-1949.

The Mormons

Allen, James B. and Leonard, Glen M. *The Story of the Latter-day Saints.* SLC, Deseret Book, 1976.

Arrington, Leonard J. and Bitton, Davis. *The Mormon Experience.* NY, Random House, 1979.

Larson, Gustive O. *Prelude to the Kingdom: Mormon Desert Conquest.* Francestown, N. H., Marshall Jones, 1947.

Mulder, William and Mortensen, A. Russell (eds). *Among the Mormons: Historic Accounts by Contemporary Observers.* NY, Knopf, 1958.

O'Dea, Thomas F. *The Mormons.* Chicago, U of Chicago, 1957 +.

Roberts, Brigham H. (ed). *History of the Church.* SLC, DN, 1902-1932. 7 volumes.

Smith, Joseph Fielding. *Essentials in Church History,* SLC, Deseret Book, 1973.

Stegner, Wallace. *The Gathering of Zion: Story of the Mormon Trail.* NY, McGraw, 1964.

Biography

Binns, Archie. *Peter Skene Ogden, Fur Trader.* Portland, Binford, 1967.

Brodie, Fawn. *No Man Knows My History* (biography of Joseph Smith). NY, Knopf, 1945.

Brooks, Juanita (ed). *On the Mormon Frontier: The Diary of Hosea Stout, 1844-1861.* SLC, UU and USHS, 1964 (2 vols)

Brooks, Juanita. *John Doyle Lee: Zealot, Pioneer Builder, Scapegoat.* Glendale, Clark, 1961 (rev. 1972).

Esshom, Frank E. (ed). *Pioneers and Prominent Men of Utah.* SLC, 1913 (reprint 1966).

Evans, John Henry. *Joseph Smith, an American Prophet.* NY, Macmillan, 1933.

Jenson, Andrew. *Latter-day Saint Biographical Encyclopedia.* SLC, Jenson, 1901-1936 (4 vols). Reprint Western Epics 1971.

Local, County and Regional History

Brooks, Juanita. *The Mountain Meadows Massacre.* Stanford, Stanford U, 1950.

Crampton, C. Gregory. *Land of Living Rock: The Grand Canyon and the High Plateaus: Arizona, Utah, Nevada.* NY, Knopf, 1972.

Crampton, C. Gregory. *Standing Up Country: The Canyon Lands of Utah and Arizona.* NY, Knopf, 1964.

Hunter, Milton R. (comp.). *Beneath Ben Lomond's Peak: History of Weber County 1824-1900.* SLC, DN, 1945.

Larson, Andrew Karl. *I Was Called to Dixie: The Virgin River Basin; Unique Experiences in Mormon Pioneering.* SLC, DN, 1961.

Lester, Margaret D. *Brigham Street* (Salt Lake City). SLC, USHS, 1979.

Miller, David E. *Hole-in-the-Rock: An Epic in the Colonization of the Great American West.* SLC, UU, 1966.

Reid, H. Lorenzo. *Dixie of the Desert: Exploration and Settlement* (southwestern Utah). Springdale, Zion NHA, 1964.

Ricks, Joel E. and Cooley, Everett L. (eds). *The History of a Valley: Cache Valley, Utah-Idaho.* Logan, Cache Valley Centennial Commission, 1956.

Tanner, Faun M. *The Far Country: A Regional History of Moab and La Sal, Utah.* SLC, Olympus, 1976.

Daughters of the Utah Pioneers—County Chapters (more than 20 volumes—this is only a sampling):

Builders of Uintah: A Centennial History of Uintah County, 1872 to 1947. Springville, Art City, 1947.

Golden Nuggets of Pioneer Days: A History of Garfield County. Panguitch, Garfield County News, 1949.

History of Box Elder County. Box Elder County DUP, 1947.

History of Tooele County. Tooele County DUP, 1961.

Milestones of Millard: 100 Years of History of Millard County. Springville, Art City, 1951.

Rainbow Views: A History of Wayne County. Springville, Art City, 1953 and 1977.

Tales of a Triumphant People: A History of Salt Lake County, 1847-1900. SLC, Stevens & Wallis, 1947. Name index by USHS 1977.

NATURAL SCENE

Abbey, Edward. *Desert Solitaire: A Season in the Wilderness.* NY, McGraw, 1968.

Greer, Deon and Wahlquist, Wayne et al. *Atlas of Utah.* WSC-BYU, 1982.

Gwynn, J. Wallace (ed). *Great Salt Lake: A Scientific, Historical and Economic Overview.* SLC, UGMS, 1980 (Bull. 116).

Geology and Mineral Resources

Baars, Donald L. *Red Rock Country: The Geological History of the Colorado Plateau.* NY, Natural History Press, 1972.

Barnes, F. A. *Canyon Country Geology for the Layman and Rockhound.* SLC, Wasatch, 1978.

Dutton, Clarence E. *Report on the Geology of the High Plateaus of Utah* (with separate atlas). Washington, GPO, 1880.

Hintze, Lehi F. *Geologic History of Utah.* Provo, BYU, 1973.

Lohman, S. W. *The Geologic Story of Canyonlands National Park.* Washington, GPO, 1974 (USGS Bull. 1327).

Utah Geological and Mineralogical Survey. *Geology of Salt Lake County.* SLC, UGMS, 1964 (Bull. 69)

ECONOMIC SCENE

Arrington, Leonard J. *Great Basin Kingdom: An Economic History of the Latter-day Saints, 1830-1900.* Cambridge, Harvard U, 1958 (reprint 1966).

Athearn, Robert G. *Rebel of the Rockies: A History of the Denver & Rio Grande Western Railroad.* New Haven, Yale U, 1962.

Bureau of Economic & Business Research. *Utah! Facts.* SLC, Utah Industrial Promotion Division, 1978.

Bureau of Economic & Business Research. *Utah Statistical Abstract.* SLC, UU, 1979 + .

Greer, Deon and Wahlquist, Wayne et al. *Atlas of Utah.* WSC-BYU, 1982.

Stucki, Roland. *Commercial Banking in Utah, 1847-1966.* SLC, UU (BEBR), 1967.

U. S. Bureau of the Census. *Statistical Abstract of the United States.* Washington, GPO, 1980 + .

CULTURAL SCENE

General and Miscellaneous

Ashton, Wendell J. *Voice in the West: Biography of a Pioneer Newspaper.* NY, Duell, 1950.

Greer, Deon and Wahlquist, Wayne et al. *Atlas of Utah.* WSC-BYU, 1982.

Malmquist, O. N. *The First 100 Years: A History of the Salt Lake Tribune 1871-1971.* SLC, USHS, 1971.

Utah Foundation. *State and Local Government in Utah.* SLC, author, 1979 + .

Utah Foundation. *Statistical Review of Government in Utah.* SLC, author, 1980 + .

Peoples and Groups

Barnes, F. A. *Canyon Country Prehistoric Indians: Their Cultures, Ruins, Artifacts, and Rock Art.* SLC, Wasatch, 1979.

Brooks, Juanita. *The History of the Jews in Utah and Idaho.* SLC, Western Epics, 1973.

Gilpin, Laura. *The Enduring Navaho.* Austin, U of Texas, 1968.

Jennings, Jesse D. *Prehistory of Utah and the Eastern Great Basin.* SLC, UU, 1978.

Lyman, June and Denver, Norma (comp). *Ute People: An Historical Study.* SLC, UU, 1970.

Mayer, Vicente V. (ed). *Utah: A Hispanic History.* SLC, UU, 1975.

Papanikolas, Helen Z. (ed). *The Peoples of Utah.* SLC, USHS, 1976.

Utah State Historical Society. *Indians of Utah.* Special issue UHQ Vol. 39 No. 2, 1971.

Mormon Doctrine, Beliefs, and Characteristics

Publications in this field—even of recent date—are extremely numerous. A visit to the Deseret Book Store in Salt Lake City, a sales outlet of the Mormon Church, makes evident the abundance of theological and historical material published under auspices of the church or with its blessing. Many books are written by general authorities or officials of the church. In addition, of course, many items on the subject of Mormon theology continue to be published by non-Mormons.

The Arts

Goeldner, Paul. *Utah Catalog: Historic American Buildings Survey,* SLC, Utah Heritage Foundation, 1969.

Haseltine, James L. *100 Years of Utah Painting: Selected Works from the 1840's to the 1950's.* SLC, Salt Lake Art Center, 1965.

Horne, Alice M. *Devotees and Their Shrines.* SLC, DN, 1914.

Olpin, Robert S. *Dictionary of Utah Art.* SLC, Salt Lake Art Center, 1980.

Parish Publishing Co. *Art Work of Utah.* Chicago, author, 1896 (2 vols.).

Utah State Historical Society. *Toward an Architectural Tradition.* Special issue UHQ Vol. 43 No. 3, 1975.

Wadsworth, Nelson B. *Through Camera Eyes* (early Utah photographers). Provo, BYU, 1975.

Literature (Imaginative or Creative Writing)

See Literature section of chapter on The Arts for discussion of Utah writers and description of their works. Literary works—delimited here to poetry, fictional prose, poetry, scriptwriting, creative journalism, essays, and related types of creative writing—have been produced by myriad Utahns on a vast array of topics or by non-Utahns on the subject of Utah.

DESCRIPTION AND TRAVEL

Arizona Highways Magazine (many articles on Utah)

Barnes, F. A. Canyon Country Guide Series (various titles: *Canyon Country Scenic Roads . . . Canyon Country Exploring . . . Canyon Country Hiking and Natural History . . . Canyon Country Off-Road Vehicle Trails* in six titles . . . *Canyon Country Camping . . . Canyon Country Geology for the Layman and Rockhound).* SLC, Wasatch Publishers, 1979 + .

Muench, David and Wixom, Hartt. *Utah* (descriptive pictorial). Portland, Belding, 1973.

Ratcliffe, Bill and Welsh, Stanley S. *Utah II* (descriptive pictorial). Portland, Graphic Arts, 1981.

Utah State Historical Society. *Utah's Parks and Scenic Wonders.* Special travel Issue, UHQ Vol. 26 No. 3, 1958.

Museums and Exhibits

(The majority of these museums and exhibits are mentioned in the respective tours.)

ART MUSEUMS AND EXHIBITS
(Art is also featured in many of the museums listed under other categories.)

Bountiful	Bountiful Art Center	2175 S. Main
Brigham City	Brigham City Museum—Gallery	24 N. 3rd West
Cannonville	Gilgal Monument *(see Tour 9)*	
Cedar City	Southern Utah State College	
	Braithwaite Fine Arts Gallery	
	Adams Memorial Theatre	
Logan	Alliance for the Varied Arts	300 N. and 400 East
	Utah State University	
	Art Gallery (Fine Arts Center)	
Ogden	Eccles Community Art Center	2580 Jefferson
	Union Depot—Art Gallery	25th and Wall
	Weber State College Art Gallery	3750 Harrison
Park City	Kimball Art Center	Main Street
Price	College of Eastern Utah	
	Art Gallery	451 E. 4th North
Provo	Brigham Young University	
	Harris Fine Arts Center	
St. George	Dixie College	
	Fine Arts Building	225 S. 7th East
	Southwestern Utah Arts Center	90 S. Main
Salt Lake City	Bicentennial Art Center	
	Capitol Theatre (Performing Arts)	46 W. 2nd South
	Salt Lake Art Center	20 S. West Temple
	Symphony Hall	Corner South Temple and West Temple
	Cathedral of the Madeleine	Corner South Temple and B St.
	Gilgal (religious sculpture)	749 E. 5th South
	Glendenning Gallery (Utah Arts Council)	617 E. South Temple
	Mormon Temple Square	
	Pioneer Craft House	3271 S. 5th East
	Pioneer Trail State Park (mural and monument)	2600 E. Sunnyside (850 South)
	State Capitol	300 N. State
	Tracy Avery Atrium Gallery	Salt Lake Public Library, 209 E. 5th South
	Utah Museum of Fine Art	University of Utah
Springville	Springville Museum of Art	126 E. 4th South
Vernal	Little Gallery of Arts	225 E. Main (County Library)

SCIENCE—NATURAL HISTORY—INDUSTRIAL MUSEUMS
AND EXHIBITS
(Many of these also feature Art, History and Culture)

Abbreviations: NHS - National Historic Site   NRS - National Recreation Area
         NM   National Monument   SHM - State Historical Monument
         NP   - National Park   SP   - State Park

Utah State Waterfowl Management Areas—there are numerous such areas in the state, the majority located on the shores of Great Salt Lake. Open to the public.

Arches National Park	Visitor Center	
Bingham Copper Mine	Visitor Center (overlook)	Bingham Canyon
Brigham City	Bear River Migratory Bird Refuge State Information Center (I-15)	
Bryce Canyon NP	Visitor Center-Museum	
Capitol Reef NP	Visitor Center-Museum	
Cedar Breaks NM	Visitor Center-Museum	
Cleveland	Cleveland-Lloyd Dinosaur Quarry	
Dead Horse Point State Park	Visitor Center-Museum	Moab
Dinosaur NM	Visitor Center-Museum-Quarry	Jensen
Echo	State Information Center (I-80)	Echo Canyon
Farmington	Lagoon Resort (zoo)	
Fish Springs	Fish Springs National Wildlife Refuge	
Flaming Gorge NRA	Flaming Gorge Dam-Visitor Center	
Hyrum	Hardware Ranch (elk habitat)	Blacksmith Fork Canyon
Kanab	Moqui Caverns (rocks and minerals)	Kanab Canyon
Lehi	Hutchings Museum of Natural History	678 N. 2nd West
Loa	Inglesby Collection (rocks-minerals)	County Courthouse
Logan	Intermountain Herbarium	Utah State University
	Willow Park Zoo	
Natural Bridges NM	Visitor Center-Museum	
Ogden	Union Depot	25th and Wall
	Browning Firearms Museum	
	Browning-Kimball Auto Museum	
	Railroad Hall of Fame and Museum	
	Weber State College	3750 Harrison Blvd.
	Natural History Museum	
	Ott Planetarium	
Ouray	Ouray National Wildlife Refuge	
Price	Prehistoric Museum	City Hall
Provo	Brigham Young University	
	Monte L. Bean Life Science Museum	
	Summerhays Planetarium	
	Museum of Archeology and Ethnology	
	Earth Science Museum	
St. George	State Information Center	I-15 (3 miles south)
Salt Lake City	Children's Museum of Utah	840 N. 3rd West
	Hansen Planetarium	15 S. State
	Hogle Zoological Garden	2600 E. Sunnyside (850 South)

	Mormon Welfare Square	751 W. 7th South
	Tracy Aviary	Liberty Park
	Utah State Arboretum	University of Utah
	Utah Museum of Natural History	University of Utah
	Westminster College (rocks-minerals)	1800 S. 13th East
	Wheeler Historic Farm	6351 S. 9th East
Smithfield	Cache Valley Swiss Cheese Factory	
Timpanogos Cave		
NM	Visitor Center-Museum	
Vernal	Dinosaur Natural History Museum	235 E. Main
Zion National Park	Visitor Center-Museum	

HISTORY—CULTURE—RELIGION MUSEUMS AND EXHIBITS
(DUP = Daughters of Utah Pioneers)

American Fork	DUP Museum	60 E. Main
Beaver	Old Court House Museum	190 E. Center
Blanding	Edge of the Cedars Museum	660 W. 4th North
	Hucks Museum and Trading Post	South Highway
Boulder	Anasazi Indian Village SHM	
Canyonlands	Horseshoe (Barrier) Canyon Rock Art	
Nat'l Park	Numerous other prehistoric culture sites	
Castle Dale	Emery County Museum	
Cedar City	Iron Mission SHM	North Main
	Old Rock Church and Museum	1st East and Center
	Southern Utah State College	
	William R. Palmer Indian Museum	
Deseret	Old Fort Deseret SHM	South Highway
Ephraim	Numerous 19th century buildings	
Eureka	Tintic Mining Museum	Old Railroad Depot
Fairfield	Stagecoach Inn and Camp Floyd SHM	
Fairview	Fairview Museum of History and Art	85 N. 1st East
Farmington	Quaint rock buildings	
	Lagoon—Pioneer Village	
Fillmore	Territorial Statehouse	City Park
Fort Duchesne	Ute Tribal Museum	Bottle Hollow Resort
Golden Spike NHS	Visitor Center-Museum	
Grand Gulch	Prehistoric Indian structures	
Grantsville	Donner-Reed Memorial Museum	97 N. Cooley
Heber City	Railroad Museum and Pioneer Village	
Helper	Mining Museum	
Hinckley	American Art Center	
Hovenweep NM	Prehistoric Indian structures	
Kanab	Heritage House Museum	14 E. 1st South
Logan	DUP Museum and Relic Hall	52 W. 2nd North
	Man and His Bread Museum and	
	Jensen Living Historical Farm	US 89 south of Logan
Manti	Mormon Temple Visitor Center	
Moab	Moab Museum	118 E. Center
Monticello	Monticello Museum	Library Building
Monument Valley	Navajo Tribal Park	
Mt. Pleasant	Old Pioneer Museum	150 S. State
Newspaper Rock		
SHM	Indian rock art	Indian Creek Canyon
Nine Mile Canyon	Prehistoric Indian rock art/ruins	North of Wellington

Ogden	Union Depot (see under Science Museums above)	
	Fort Buenaventura SHM	West 24th Street
	Mormon Temple-Tabernacle	Washington/21st
	Miles Goodyear Cabin and DUP Museum	Temple-Tabernacle Square
Orderville	DUP Museum	
Panguitch	DUP Museum	100 E. Center
Park City	Old Town (vintage mining town)	
Pleasant Grove	DUP Museum	53 S. 1st East
Provo	McCurdy Historical Doll Museum	246 N. 1st East
	Mormon Temple Visitor Center	
	Pioneer Museum and Pioneer Cabin	5th W./6th N.
Richfield	DUP Relic Hall	340 W. 5th North
St. George	Brigham Young's Winter Home	200 N. 1st West
	Mormon Temple Visitor Center	
	DUP Museum (McQuarrie Memorial)	133 N. 1st East
Salt Lake City	Beehive House	67 E. South Temple
	Council Hall	3rd North and State
	Executive (Kearns) Mansion	603 E. South Temple
	Fort Douglas Military Museum	Fort Douglas
	International Peace Gardens	1000 S. 9th West
	Liberty Park (Chase Home and Pioneer Grist Mill)	9th to 13th South, 5th to 6th East
	Memory Grove (war memorials)	City Creek Canyon
	Mormon Museum of Church History and Art	Corner West Temple and South Temple
	Mormon Pioneer Memorial Park and Brigham Young Grave	1st Avenue east of State
	Ottinger Hall	233 Canyon Road
	Pioneer Memorial Museum	300 N. Main
	Pioneer Trail State Park—	
	Old Deseret Village, Pioneer Monument, Pioneer Mural	2600 E. Sunnyside (850 South)
	Temple Square and Visitors Centers	
	Utah State Historical Society—	
	Peoples of Utah/History Museum	300 Rio Grande
	White Memorial Chapel	3rd North east of State
Santa Clara	Jacob Hamblin Home	
Spanish Fork	DUP Museum	
Spring City	Vintage architecture	
Springdale	Pioneer Museum	
Springville	DUP Museum	175 N. Main
Tooele	DUP Museum	47 E. Vine
Vernal	DUP Museum	500 W. 2nd South
	Leo Thorne Indian Museum	18 W. Main

GREAT SALT LAKE

Great Salt Lake, Utah's unique inland sea, has been called exciting and disappointing, magnificent and desolate, sublime and fearful, grand and bleak. Its temper and appearance change with the season, the weather, the time of day. Its size varies from year to year and from season to season. Roughly, the lake is 80 miles long and 35 miles wide. The largest lake in the United States west of the Mississippi, in area if not in volume, it is more noted for its salt content than for its size.

The saline content of Great Salt Lake is about four to eight times that of the ocean, depending on its water fluctuations. Its water contains an estimated four and a half billion tons of various salts, which give the water great buoyancy and bitterness. Most of this mineral content is common salt or sodium chloride. Horace Greeley wrote in 1859, "You can no more sink in it than in a clay bank."

A description of the lake is difficult because of the constantly changing water level. In 1925 the water came within a few feet of the highway; five years later it dropped to a low level, receding nearly a mile from the road and leaving the Saltair beach pavilion high and dry. When the water is low, the view from the highway reveals comparatively little of the lake. Barren salt flats occupy the foreground, and the lake is visible as a thin horizontal line of water in the distance. The surrounding land is little higher than the lake itself, and a good view can only be obtained from an elevation.

By day, the lake is impressive chiefly because of its size. Far across its surface, the dull gray-green of the water fades imperceptibly into the horizon. Here and there the bright rays of the sun are caught in the sails of occasional small boats. Gulls fly overhead. At sunset the lake awakens with brilliant reflections.

Saltair Resort and Great Salt Lake, about 1950.

UTAH TRAVEL COUNCIL

Only about two dozen forms of life exist in Great Salt Lake, the majority of these being rather primitive and too small for easy observation.

As described by Dr. Angus M. Woodbury:

> The Great Salt Lake, with its saline content approaching saturation, presents a hostile environment to most living organisms. . . . The principal food-makers of the lake are blue-green algae. . . . These are undoubtedly the food base for very limited fauna . . . which can withstand immersion in the water of the lake. . . . Of the visible forms, the brine shrimp . . . and two brine flies . . . are common inhabitants of the lake . . . these arthropods have been enabled to multiply with little or no molestation to the limit of the food supply. . . .

The lake's brine flies are pests, though considerable effort has gone into controlling them near visitor areas. Not only are the flies themselves bothersome at times because of their swarming numbers, but their larva—developing near the shore in the lake's water—are responsible at certain times and places for a most unpleasant stench.

Great Salt Lake is the remnant of a much larger body of water. At its largest and deepest stage, perhaps 18,000 years ago, this ancestor of Great Salt Lake—known as Lake Bonneville *(see Geology)*—was a fresh-water giant that filled the valleys of western Utah during much of the most recent Ice Age. The lake had numerous static levels of varying duration, some of them lasting long enough to wear distinctive bench marks into the mountainsides. Today's lake, only 30 feet or so at its deepest, is but a suggestion of its great predecessor, which at one time was almost as large as Lake Michigan and a thousand feet deep.

Since 1851 a continuous record of the annual rise and fall of the lake has been kept by various agencies. Since that pioneer date the water level has varied 20 feet. Such variations affect the shoreline and size of the lake tremendously. Because of the gradual slope of the lake bottom, it is estimated that a ten-foot change in water level covers or uncovers several hundred square miles of lake bed. The water was highest and the lake largest in 1873, when it occupied an area of 2,200 square miles. The water was lowest and the lake smallest in 1963, when its surface level was about 20 feet lower than the 1873 level and its surface area was only 900 square miles or so.

Greatest measured depth was 48 feet in 1873; a hundred years later, at the lake's shallowest, the maximum depth was only 26 feet. Average depth in recent years is about 13 to 15 feet. Despite its fluctuations in historic times, there seems to be no scientific reason to believe that the lake will either dry up completely or inundate the works of modern humankind.

Great Salt Lake, as compared with other lakes of similar size, has been sailed by few large boats. All boats ride high in its dense waters. Though calm in fair weather, a sudden storm can quickly transform the lake into a surging mass of heavy wild waves. The *Timely Gull*, launched by Brigham Young in 1854, was destroyed four years later in a gale. A three-decked stern-wheel steamboat, the *City of Corinne*, was launched in 1872 to haul ores from Lake Point to Corinne. The boat reached Corinne by sailing 20 miles up the Bear River, but in 1874 the level of the lake began to fall, and the river became unnavigable. For a few years thereafter the steamer was used as a passenger boat. Other large boats sailed for brief periods on the lake, but most were wrecked by storms.

Thousands of smaller boats have sailed the lake, their numbers limited more by the lack of suitable marina facilities than by the lake itself, which offers exciting recreation possibilities for sailing craft and motorized boats alike. Because of the danger of sudden storms and choppy water, very small boats such as canoes and rowboats are especially hazardous. A genuine respect for the lake, and a knowledge of its peculiar moods and physical characteristics (including the corrosive effects of its brine) should be first on the list of requirements for boaters on Great Salt Lake.

HISTORICAL BACKGROUND

Discovery of Great Salt Lake is ordinarily credited to Jim Bridger, early mountaineer. Sir Richard F. Burton, in his *City of the Saints,* wrote that "the early Canadian *voyageurs* . . . recounted to wondering strangers its fearful submarine noises, its dark and sudden storms, and the terrible maelstrom in its centre, which, funnel-like, descended into the bowels of the earth." There was also a belief that Great Lake Lake was connected subterraneously with the Pacific Ocean.

While camped near Utah Lake in 1776, Father Escalante was informed by friendly Indians of a salt lake a short distance north: "The other lake that joins this one, occupies, as we are told, many leagues, and its waters are very harmful and very salty; the Timpanois assured us that anyone who moistened any part of the body with it would at once feel the part bathed greatly inflamed."

During the winter of 1824-25, Jim Bridger, while trapping on Bear River, discovered the lake as the result of a bet on the probable course of the river. According to a popular but perhaps inaccurate account, Bridger went down the river in a "bull boat," and arrived at Bear River Bay, northeastern arm of Great Salt Lake. Taking a drink of the water, he spat it out with the ejaculation, "Hell, we are on the shore of the Pacific!" This misconception was dispelled a year later when James Clyman and three others, searching for beaver streams, "circumambulated" the lake in round "bull boats" made of buffalo skins; they reported that the great body of water had no outlet.

In September, 1843, Captain John C. Fremont visited Fremont Island in "a frail batteau of gum cloth distended with air." He found that, "Roughly evaporated over the fire, the five gallons of water yielded fourteen pints of very fine-grained and very white salt, of which the whole lake may be regarded as a saturated solution."

In 1849, Captain Howard Stansbury, of the U. S. Army, came west to make a detailed survey of Great Salt Lake and the surrounding country. His view of the lake from Promontory Point was disappointing: "The stillness of the grave seemed to pervade the air and water; and, excepting here and there a solitary wild-duck floating motionless on the bosom of the lake, not a living thing was to be seen. . . . The bleak and naked shores [were] without a single tree to relieve the eye." Stansbury skirted the lake, "being the first party of white men that ever succeeded in making the entire circuit of the lake by land."

GREAT SALT LAKE ISLANDS

Great Salt Lake contains approximately ten islands, the exact number varying with the level of the lake. When the water is low, many islands become peninsulas, connected with the mainland; when the water is high the lake contains two large islands—Antelope and Stansbury—and nine or more islets.

The lake's islands have served at various times as nesting sites for seagulls, pelicans, cormorants, terns and blue herons—even for falcons, ravens and rock wrens. Their use for this purpose changes with conditions: for example, at periods of high water all the islands offer sanctuary from coyotes and other predators, while low water levels make some of the islands accessible to predators. Humans are always a danger, especially during nesting season when their presence is disturbing;

and cases are known where people have destroyed thousands of birds for the sheer "fun" of it.

Antelope Island is a prominent landmark mass in the southern part of the lake, rising to summits of more than 2,000 feet above the water surface. Largest island in the lake, it measures about 15 miles in length, 5½ miles in width, and has an area of approximately 23,000 acres. It was purchased in its entirety by the State of Utah in 1981, and a master plan is now being prepared for its use as a recreation area. *(See also Tour No. 2.)*

Osborne Russell, a trapper, who was on the shore of Great Salt Lake in 1841, was the first to mention the fluctuating level of the lake. He talked with an old Indian chief, who "could recollect when buffalo passed from the mainland to the island without swimming. The depth of the water was increasing, and the buffalo had long since left the shore of the lake." The island was named by Captain John C. Fremont when he visited the lake for the second time, in 1845.

Possessing several springs of fresh water, the island became known as Church Island about 1849, when the Mormon Church began to use it as a herding ground. Since then countless horses, cattle, sheep and bison have grazed there. Brigham Young frequently visited the island, and sometimes entertained guests with programs that ranged from bathing to bronco-busting. Wild horses were captured, broken, and taken to the mainland for use on farms.

When Captain Howard Stansbury made his survey of Great Salt Lake in 1850, he used Antelope Island as the base for much of his work. "Like all the other islands in the lake," he writes, "it consists of a long rocky eminence, ranging from north to south, rising abruptly from the water, and attaining an elevation of about three thousand feet above the lake."

On Antelope Island once lived, with his wife and children, George Frary, who knew the lake perhaps better than anyone. Fifty years of his life were spent in building boats to sail and explore the inland sea. Frary's wife died and was buried on the island in 1897, but Frary remained for many years thereafter. He assisted in making the first soundings for the Lucin Cutoff *(see below)* and his daughter was a passenger, in 1903, on the first scheduled train that crossed the lake.

Antelope have disappeared from the island—the last were seen in 1870—but buffalo again graze the rugged slopes. They are not native, but descendants of a dozen head placed on the island in 1892 by William Glasmann, Ogden publisher. The herd once numbered more than 300, but during the 1920s it was reduced by hunting and has never since reached that population.

Fremont Island, in the east central part of the lake, is 5 miles long, 2 miles wide, and has an area of 2,945 acres. Stansbury named it for Captain John C. Fremont, who had called it Disappointment Island. Fremont describes it as "simply a rocky hill, on which there is neither water nor trees of any kind."

When Stansbury visited Fremont Island in 1850, "Search was made for the cover to the object-end of Fremont's telescope, which he had left on the summit of the island, but it could not be found." Later it was found by a local rancher. The island has been used for stock grazing since early days of settlement, and in the late 19th century it was the home of the Wenner family.

Gunnison Island, in the northwestern part of the lake, is less than a mile long and has an area of only 163 acres. It was named for Lt. John W. Gunnison, chief assistant to Captain Howard Stansbury in his survey of the lake.

In 1886-87 Alfred Lambourne, Utah artist and writer, preempted a homestead on Gunnison Island, where he lived for fourteen months. Out of this hermit existence came his illustrated book, *Our Inland Sea,* and many of his best paintings. "From my father," he writes, "I have inherited these—a love for an island and a love for a vine," and he planted a vineyard. With the eye of a poet Lambourne observed the seasonal aspects of the lake and its surroundings. In winter "the distant mountain heights smoke in the dawn like tired horses, or the sun rises like a disc of copper, ruddy through the spindrift brine.'' Of summer he exclaims, ''O, the glare of the light upon the waters of the Inland Sea! Like polished steel gleams the briny surface; and across it, the sun's path is like that same steel at molten heat.'' In autumn, ''A mighty drowsiness is on the land. The Harvest-Moon—the Indian's Moon of Falling Leaves—has supplanted the Moons of Fire. . . . Haze-enwrapped are the distant Wasatch; through deepening shades of saddened violet, the Onaqui lapse into melancholia. The western headlands, the jutting promontories, appear as if cut from dim, orange crepe, or maroon-colored velvet. Wistful and vague stand the peaked islands, and shell-like is the gleam of the far-stretched brine.''

Guano-gatherers were on the island at the same time as Lambourne, but efforts to market bird guano, or manure, deposits on the island were never commercially successful.

Bird (or Hat) Island, in the southwestern part of the lake, is less than a quarter mile in diameter and has an area of only 22 acres. ''Merely a pile of granitic conglomerate,'' it is, nevertheless, inhabited by birds, principally seagulls. The safety of isolation must have prompted birds to nest here, for there is no food on the island itself, nor in the surrounding salt water. The gulls are scavengers, content to eat whatever they can find.

Egg Island, north of Antelope, and **White Rock,** west of Antelope, are also occupied by gulls.

Carrington Island, in the southwestern part of the lake, is a circular isle, slightly more than 2 miles in diameter, with an area of 1,767 acres. It was named by Captain Stansbury for Albert Carrington, a Mormon (later an apostle) who assisted with the 1850 survey. The summit, Stansbury reports, ''consisted of ledges of excellent roofing slate.'' During the 1930s an attempt at homesteading was made by Charles Stoddard and his family, and after World War II the island was used as a practice target range by military aircraft.

Mud Island, 8 miles northeast of Fremont Island, is an island only when the lake is low. At other times it is merely a sandbar, with an area of approximately 600 acres. Stansbury found ''A belt of soft, black mud, more than knee-deep . . . between the water and the hard, rocky beach, [which] seemed to be impregnated with all the villainous smells which nature's laboratory was capable of producing.''

Stansbury Island, in the southwestern part of the lake, has not actually been an island since the 1870s, when Great Salt Lake was at its highest recorded level. For decades it has been connected with the mainland, and is more accurately a peninsula. Nevertheless, the ''island,'' capped by rugged mountains rising 2,400 feet, is described as being 11½ miles long, 5½ miles wide, and 22,314 acres in area. It was named for Captain Howard Stansbury by officers of his party, during the survey of the lake in 1850. *(Also see Tour No. 4A.)*

Strongs Knob, in the west central part of the lake, is connected with the mainland except when the lake is high. It is geologically a part of Strongknob Mountain, from which it takes its name, and has an area of 703 acres.

Dolphin Island and **Cub Island** are the two northern-most islands in the lake. Both are small and barren. When the water is low, Dolphin is connected with the mainland, and Cub is a part of Gunnison.

MINERALS

The tremendous potential worth of the lake's minerals has long been recognized. Salt has been removed since pioneer days, and the extraction of common salt by evaporation remains a profitable enterprise today, engaged in by several firms scattered near the lake's shores.

Common salt (sodium chloride), though the lake's most plentiful mineral, is not necessarily its most valuable. Ordinary salt is easily obtainable around the world, and therefore this product has never become one of the state's foremost mineral exports. In contrast, the enormous economic potential of more valuable salts in the lake's brines has enticed developers for years. During the past decade or two, several firms have spent two hundred million dollars or more in perfecting the complex techniques required for extracting the lake's various brine minerals. In recent years they appear to be successful, both technically and economically, in producing large quantities of magnesium, lithium and potassium through a process of solar evaporation, chemical treatment, furnace refining and electrolytic separation.

In the forefront of these efforts have been Great Salt Lake Minerals, which operates facilities on Bear River Bay *(see Tour No. 2)* and AMAX Inc., (successor to NL Industries), which operates facilities west of Stansbury Island *(see Tour No. 4A)*. In connection with the brine operations, acrimonious debate and legal complications have resulted from the Southern Pacific causeway, which divided the lake into north and south segments. Critics charge that the causeway prevents circulation of brine between north and south, resulting in more concentration of salts in the northern arm and less in the south. The result, it is claimed, is an economic advantage to the firm utilizing brine from the northern segment (Great Salt Lake Minerals), but a marked disadvantage to firms along the south shore.

Oil and natural gas: Petroleum seeps in the lake's northern arm near Rozel apparently were known by the Indians, who are said to have utilized the "asphaltum" for medicinal purposes. According to the book's original edition (page 124) these seeps were known by whites since about 1880. In 1940, three companies were operating wells in the district. However, though fluid at the bottom of the well, the material becomes thick and sluggish as it rises and cools. Because of this characteristic, which prevented a commercial flow, earlier efforts at large-scale production did not succeed. During the late 1970s, increasing production of oil and gas in the Overthrust Belt brought renewed interest in Great Salt Lake as a source of such minerals. Between 1978 and 1980, Amoco Production Company spent more than 50 million dollars in drilling 15 prospect wells in the lake bed—one of them more than 12,000 feet deep. Though hydrocarbons were found in three of the wells, the oil was of poor quality. It is possible that the solution of technical problems will see meaningful production in future years.

RECREATION ON THE LAKE

Great Salt Lake has been popular for bathing since the first month of Mormon settlement in 1847. Its briny water, almost saturated with salt, prevents sinking; and though diving is not advisable because the water is caustic to the eyes, throat, and nose, passive floating and non-splash swimming are pleasant and exhilarating.

During the past hundred years or so, numerous resorts have catered to the public. All have been located on the south shore, about 15 miles from Salt Lake City. Among them have been Black Rock, Saltair, Garfield Beach, Lake Shore, Sunset Beach, Sand Pebble Beach, and Silver Sands Beach. All except the latter had closed by 1972. The most recent is Great Salt Lake State Park (Saltair Beach). *See below.* Salt Lake County Boat Harbor also served a useful purpose for many years as the lake's only marina. The old harbor complex was replaced in 1980-81 with a new **South Shore Marina** costing in excess of one million dollars. The new marina includes more than 250 boat slips, facilities for Great Salt Lake Yacht Club, and commercial services. Lake tours are offered from the marina aboard a 35-foot hydrofoil.

These beach resorts offered a variety of activities in addition to bathing. There were picnic facilities, refreshment and concession stands, playgrounds, and dance pavilions. Some offered boat excursions and even boat dining. Fine sand was hauled in for better beaches. But all were beset by fluctuating water levels, brine flies, bad odors, and other problems. Recent years have brought fresh piped water and plans for a sewage disposal system. In 1980, visitors to the lake numbered almost two million.

Most elaborate of all the lake's resorts was **Saltair,** built in the 1890s on more than 2,000 wooden piles. For nearly six decades it was Utah's glamorous Lady of the Lake, renowned for its giant roller coaster, huge dance floor (largest in America in its day), and flamboyant architecture. Visitors arrived by train, as many as 10,000 in a single day. Bathers could drop from the pier directly into the lake during the resort's heyday. There were numerous entertainment concessions, including a large funhouse.

Few resorts ever encountered or survived the disasters faced by Saltair. It was destroyed by fire in 1925 and rebuilt; fire attacked again in 1939 and 1951. Violent winds and waves caused extensive damage. When the lake level dropped, leaving the resort high and dry, bathers were transported to the water. Bathhouses were moved. An artificial lagoon was created. But changing trends in recreation, coupled with the lake's continued decline and destructive winds, finally closed the resort in 1959. Abandoned, vandalized, a sad vestige of past glory, the resort stood until 1970 when a final fire destroyed it completely.

Great Salt Lake State Park includes two districts, one at *Saltair Beach* on the south shore, another on the northern tip of *Antelope Island:*

Saltair Beach, 16 m. west of Salt Lake City, includes the site of old Saltair Resort and extends to Black Rock. More than four miles of continuous beach offers salt-water bathing, open showers, restrooms, refreshments, picnic and camping areas. The park's master plan calls for a visitor center, expanded marina facilities, improved beaches, additional picnic and camping facilities with natural shade, facilities for off-road vehicle and trailbike activities, an improved road system, amusement park, restaurants, shops, and other commercial facilities.

This master plan took an important step toward realization in 1981 when the state issued a long-term lease to a commercial enterprise for construction and operation of a new resort on the south shore, located about one mile south of the site of old Saltair. Now underway is construction on a 36,000-square-foot building to house retail shops and other visitor facilities. Its ornate five-story facade is being designed to resemble that of the original Saltair. Among recreational offerings will be a water slide, tube sled, swimming pool, bumper boats, dune buggy rentals for use on a beach track. Also proposed is a scenic railroad between Saltair Beach and Antelope Island. Development will occupy several years and is expected to cost as much as five million dollars.

See Tour No. 2 for additional details concerning Antelope Island.

SOUTHERN PACIFIC TRESTLE AND CAUSEWAY

The transcontinental railroad through Utah, first completed at Promontory in 1869, had the disadvantage of a circuitous detour north of the lake for many miles, and also of severe grades and curves where it crossed the Promontory Range. As described on page 487 of the book's original edition, Southern Pacific Railroad resolved this problem by construction of the Lucin Cutoff (pronounced Lu-SIN). Begun in 1902 and completed in 1903, the Cutoff "extends 102 miles between Ogden and Lucin and includes [12 miles of wood trestle and 13 miles of rock fill] across Great Salt Lake. The Cutoff replaced the longer railroad route around the north end of the lake, shortening the distance by 44 miles and eliminating numerous curves and grades. Construction required one and a half years of work by three thousand men, cost more than eight million dollars, and used hundreds of trainloads of rock and the timber from 38,000 trees" for that many piles!

This famed trestle served to carry countless Southern Pacific trains across the lake for more than 50 years. Maintenance costs were excessive, however, and there was always the danger of fire—a threat realized in 1956 when more than 600 feet of trestle actually burned. The result of these difficulties was replacement of the old wood trestle by a new rock fill railbed paralleling the trestle 1500 feet to the north, an engineering achievement of major proportions. The very statistics are sobering: Four years of actual construction . . . 50 million dollars in total cost . . . dredging of 16 million cubic yards of soft sediment from the bed of the lake to form a trench . . . excavating, conveying and dumping of 45½ million cubic yards of rock, sand and gravel to fill the trench and build a railbed embankment reaching from below lake bottom to above the water surface, in places more than 50 feet high and from 175 to 600 feet wide at the bottom, 38 feet wide at the top.

To accomplish this colossal task of earth-moving and placement, it was necessary to establish a construction camp at Little Valley near Promontory Point, with facilities adequate for a peak population of more than a thousand. A harbor and shipping channel were dredged. A belt conveyor, the world's largest at that time, was built to carry up to 4,000 tons of rock per hour or 80,000 tons in a single day. Eleven special barges were constructed at distant points and shipped in sections to Little Valley for assembly; a fleet of tugboats arrived in like fashion.

Huge trucks and shovels moved rocks from quarry to conveyor belt. The large bottom-dump barges were positioned over the correct spot, then emptied by remote control. Smaller barges, used for hauling to locations near the water surface, were emptied by tractors. In addition to the barges, hauling was done by trucks and side-dump rail cars. Finally came track laying and signals, and the causeway was officially opened for rail traffic in July 1959.

Utah State Parks

The State of Utah has developed more than 40 parks, historic monuments, museums, beaches, marinas, and other water recreation areas. Nearly all of these are described in the tour section. There are user fees at many of these areas, particularly where services are provided (for example, campgrounds, boat marinas, developed exhibits, bathing facilities, etc.). Additional details may be obtained from the Utah Travel Council, Council Hall/Capitol Hill, Salt Lake City, Utah 84114 . . . State Division of Parks and Recreation, 1636 W. North Temple, Salt Lake City, Utah 84116 . . . or from numerous visitor information centers *(see Sources for Additional Information)*. Because recreational facilities on Great Salt Lake are being developed by the State Division of Parks and Recreation, Great Salt Lake is described in detail in the preceding pages.

Key to abbreviations — SB: State Beach   SHM: State Historical
                          SP: State Park   Monument
                          SR: State Reserve   SRA: State Recreation Area

State Park Area	See Tour No.	State Park Area	See Tour No.
Historic and Museum Areas		*Water Recreation Areas*	
Anasazi Indian Village SHM	9	Bear Lake SRA	1
Camp Floyd and Stagecoach Inn SHM	4	Deer Creek Lake SRA	5
Danger Cave SHM	4	East Canyon Lake SRA	2
Dinosaur Natural History State Museum	6	Green River SRA	10
Edge of the Cedars SHM	11	Gunlock Lake SRA	8
Fort Buenaventura SHM	2	Huntington Lake SRA	10
Fort Deseret SHM	4	Hyrum Lake SRA	1
Iron Mission SHM	8	Jordan River State Parkway	3
Newspaper Rock SHM	11	Lost Creek Lake SB	2
Pioneer Trail State Park	3	Millsite Lake SB	10
Territorial Statehouse SHM	4	Minersville Lake SRA	8
Scenic and Nature Areas		Otter Creek Lake SB	7
		Palisade Lake SRA	7
Bonneville Salt Flats SR	4	Piute Lake SRA	7
Coral Pink Sand Dunes SR	9	Rockport Lake SRA	5
Dead Horse Point State Park	11	Scofield Lake SRA	10
Escalante Petrified Forest SR	9	Starvation Lake SRA	6
Goblin Valley SR	10	Steinaker Lake SRA	6
Goosenecks of the San Juan SR	11	Utah Lake State Park	5
Great Salt Lake State Park		Willard Bay SRA	2
Antelope Island District	2	Yuba Lake SRA	4
Saltair Beach District	3		
Kodachrome Basin SR	9		
Monument Valley SR	11		
Snow Canyon SP	8		
Wasatch Mountain State Park	5		

National Forests

National forests in Utah occupy nearly all the highest mountains and total approximately eight million acres, or about a sixth of the state. This is an enormous area—more than some eastern states—yet it is smaller than the national forest acreage in every other western state except Nevada.

Utah's national forests are used for a variety of purposes: watershed protection and management, timber, recreation, wildlife habitat, grazing, and mining. The primary reason for their existence, originally at least, was protection of watersheds from grazing abuse, over-logging, fires, etc. These are still important objectives. Large numbers of sheep and cattle are summer-grazed on national forest lands, and up to 74 million board feet of timber have been cut in the state's national forests in some years. A significant proportion of Utah's richest coal lands are on national forests.

By far the greatest share of rain and snow falls in the mountains and therefore on national forests. Major streams originating in Utah have their sources in national forests, and hundreds of natural lakes are located in national forests, as are a number of large and small reservoirs.

So, too, are most improved campgrounds, developed picnic areas, and ski resorts. The Forest Service has established several thousand individual camp and picnic units in several hundred different locations. A number of these are mentioned in the tour section.

National forests provide habitat for much if not all of the state's wildlife (many animals live in the lowlands or foothills). Deer, elk and moose prefer forests at least part of the time, as do bear, cougar, bobcat, and many other animals. Big game hunting, for the most part, takes place on national forests. Streams and lakes of the national forests are home for cool-water fish such as rainbow and brown trout. Utah's forest streams commonly are swift and rather small.

Comprising Utah's national forests are hundreds of plant species, ranging from wildflowers and small shrubs to brush, pygmy evergreens (pinyon pine and juniper), quaking aspen, and large evergreens such as Douglas fir, ponderosa pine, lodgepole pine, blue spruce, and Engelmann spruce. *See Plant Life.*

The state's national forests and approximate number of acres in each:

Ashley	1,300,000	Uinta	800,000
Dixie	1,900,000	Wasatch-Cache	1,300,000
Fishlake	1,400,000	Sawtooth	70,000
Manti-LaSal	1,200,000	Caribou	7,000

While off-road vehicles are permitted in many national forest areas, on established roads, other areas are closed to motorized vehicles.

Mormon Temple, Logan

Sailboating, Willard Bay

Pioneer Village, Lagoon

Avocet, Bear River Refuge

Mormon Tabernacle, Brigham City

Skiing in the Wasatch Mountains

Lagoon Amusement Park

Symphony Hall, Salt Lake City

State Capitol, Salt Lake Valley, and Wasatch Mountains

Pioneer Monument, Salt Lake City

Dancers, Ballet West

Mormon Temple Square, Salt Lake City

Wasatch Mountains near Alta

Wasatch Mountain State Park

Mount Timpanogos

Cathedral of the Madeleine, Salt Lake City

Blue Lake, Uinta Mountains

Flaming Gorge Lake from Red Canyon Overlook

Dead Horse Point

Double Arch, Arches National Park

Moab Valley from Poison Spider Rim

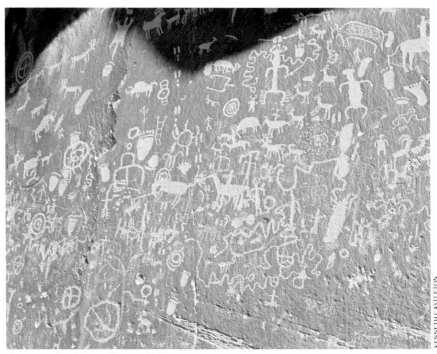

Newspaper Rock State Historical Monument

Angel Arch, Canyonlands National Park

Rainbow Bridge National Monument

Boating a side canyon of Lake Powell

Torrey and Thousand Lake Mountain

Paria Valley and Table Cliff Plateau

Bryce Canyon National Park

Cedar Breaks National Monument

Joshua trees

Temples and River: Zion National Park

Pine Valley Mountains

National Park Areas

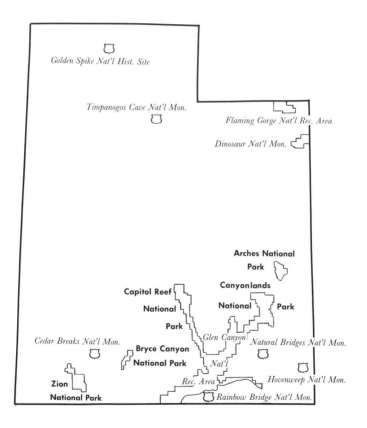

Golden Spike Nat'l Hist. Site

Timpanogos Cave Nat'l Mon.

Flaming Gorge Nat'l Rec. Area

Dinosaur Nat'l Mon.

Arches National
Park

Canyonlands

Capitol Reef

National   National   Park

Park

Cedar Breaks Nat'l Mon.   Glen Canyon   Natural Bridges Nat'l Mon.

Bryce Canyon

National Park   Nat'l

Zion   Rec. Area   Hovenweep Nat'l Mon.

National Park   Rainbow Bridge Nat'l Mon.

F. A. BARNES

Delicate Arch.

ARCHES NATIONAL PARK

Highway Approach: Visitor Center and Park entrance, 5 miles north of Moab via US Highway 163.

Season: Open all year.

Administrative Office: Superintendent, Canyonlands National Park, Moab, Utah 84532.

Information: Visitor Center at Park entrance, 5 miles north of Moab.

Accommodations and Facilities: Accommodations in Moab (none at Park). Park campground at Devils Garden, 18 m. from Visitor Center.

Transportation: Private car.

Communications: Public telephone at Visitor Center and in Moab. Post office in Moab.

Climate, Clothing, Equipment: Elevation of the Park is 4,000 to 5,000 feet. Mostly arid with summer showers; winter snowfalls seldom exceed 4 inches or last more than a day. Daily temperature range, however is large: hot days in summer, cool evenings; cold in winter. Warm clothing the year round is advisable for evening wear. For daytime, except in winter, light rugged clothing. Hats with chin straps are advisable. Rubber soles helpful for climbing "slickrock," but oxfords are an abomination in sand. Carry drinking water.

Recreation: Photography, hiking, climbing. Nightly campfire talks at campground. Naturalist-led hikes. One of the finest areas in Utah for photography of erosional curiosities.

Warnings and Regulations: Usual Park regulations. Do not destroy property, carve initials, or remove artifacts, plants or other natural objects. Stay on trails. Carry drinking water. Backcountry hikers should inform rangers about plans.

Admission: National Park fee area.

Arches National Park lies in the redrock country, north of Moab, between the Colorado River and US 163. It is a region of desert sandstone, of deep and tortuous canyons, and its thin, multicolored topsoil supports grasses, many shrubs, and occasional patches of pinyon pine and juniper. Southward the pyramided La Sal Mountains rear, alien blue, from the valley floor, and the high peaks may show snow the year around. Northward are the Book Cliffs of Tavaputs Plateau, but eastward and westward the desert rolls out interminably, with a deceptive levelness. Squat hillocks of sand or slickrock conceal gorges hundreds of feet deep, their sheer or overhanging crests revealed only from the rim. Many of the canyons have sweetwater springs in them, and patches of meadow in sandy alluvium,

In the Park proper, the wind has carved massive rock into forms that, even in a region noted for spectacular erosion, are remarkable. Here are arches and windows through solid stone, from a size that can scarcely be crawled through to immense spans that would accommodate a troop of cavalry; monoliths measured in hundreds of tons balanced on fragile, decaying bases; chimneys, deep caves, and high, thin, sculptured walls or "fins" of salmon-hued rock. There are arches in all stages, from caves not yet cut through, to towering spans that have fallen, their buttresses pointing skyward. Although the terms "arch" and "bridge" are, in keeping with western informality, used somewhat loosely by Grand County people, there is a difference between them. A bridge occurs as the effect of stream erosion *(see Natural Bridges National Monument)*, and it spans a stream course. An arch (or window) occurs where there is no stream course, and is in the main the product of weathering. Actually, of course, a combination of factors—such as the composition and characteristics of various rocks, fractures, plants, chemicals, and other natural processes—are involved in the creation of bridges, arches, and other erosional features. A recent survey of arches and windows in the Park indicates that there are more than 100 arches and other openings of three feet or larger—or about 60 openings of at least ten feet in any one direction.

The rock in Arches National Park was laid down as sediment in ancient seas, streams and lakes, or as windblown sand. All of the arches and windows in the Park are in the Entrada sandstone, a wind-formed rock that ranges in color from white to salmon, pink and red. The Entrada, because its cementing material is readily dissolved and because the quartz grains which make up its main bulk are small and uniform in size, weathers easily into massive round-edged ledges, low configured domes, spool-shaped monuments, and hourglass forms that, wearing through at the waist, topple the upper half or leave it in precarious balance. In the Arches, many of the rock layers have been fractured by a criss-cross of cracks or joints, mostly from ten to 20 feet apart. Rain water, seeping through, has carried with it the cementing material and small grains of sand, enlarged the cracks and crevasses and gorges, and left immense upright slabs or "fins" of pink and orange sandstone standing between. The wind, driving crumbled sand, has found weak spots and pecked windows through, chiseled out pinnacles, and chipped the contours of a stubborn piece of stone into life forms and ragged battlements.

The whole area is rich in desert flora, especially in the canyon bottoms. Pinyon pine, desert ash, and juniper are the only trees found in abundance, but brush, cacti, and grasses are everywhere. Coyote, western red fox, Great Basin skunk, Colorado cottontail, jack rabbit, chipmunk, gopher, pack rat, porcupine, and mule deer are present. Birds are numerous, with the smaller species predominating, though golden eagles, ravens, and red-tailed hawks are frequently seen.

Historical background. Enterprising cattlemen moved into the environs of Moab in the 1870s, and were ranging the whole countryside by 1885. Many of the canyons now in the Park afforded good range, and since it was legend among cowboys that the frugal Mormons never lost a cow if she could be followed, it is not unreasonable to assume that the intricacies of the canyons were well known to them—as well as to non-Mormon stockmen.

More than a few individuals and agencies were involved during the 1920s with encouraging establishment of the first Arches National Monument. Alexander Ringhoffer, a prospector, urged the passenger manager of the Denver and Rio Grande Railroad to visit a part of the area; he in turn recommended National Monument status to the National Park Service.

Professor L. M. Gould, an eastern geologist, had visited the area and also used his influence toward the same end. The National Park Service agreed, arranged for surveys, and finally was successful in having two sections, totaling 4,520 acres, proclaimed a National Monument by President Herbert Hoover in 1929.

During the 1930s, the Moab Lions Club worked actively for enlargement of the Monument and improvement of roads and facilities. Dr. J. W. Williams and L. L. "Bish" Taylor of the *Moab Times-Independent* were among a number of enthusiastic local boosters, Dr. Williams eventually becoming known as the "Father of the Arches." The efforts of these citizens, and the work of others, resulted in expansion of the Monument in 1938—by proclamation of President Franklin D. Roosevelt—to a total area of 33,680 acres. Some work on roads and facilities ensued, but not until the Mission 66 program of the 1950s and 1960s was a new paved entrance road completed (1958), water system at headquarters developed (1959), and new Visitor Center completed (1962). These improvements as well as others took place during the superintendency of Bates Wilson, who occupied that position from 1949 to 1972. The Monument was greatly enlarged in 1969 and became a national park in 1971, with an area of more than 70,000 acres. Annual visitation grew from 2,500 in 1940 to 290,000 in 1980.

SEEING THE PARK

Arches National Park has six somewhat distinct sections, each different in geologic interest and scenery. They are, in the order seen from the main scenic drive: **(1) Courthouse Towers, (2) The Windows, (3) Delicate Arch, (4) Fiery Furnace, (5) Devils Garden, and (6) Klondike Bluffs.**

The scenic drive is an excellent paved road which switchbacks up a steep cliff from the Visitor Center and affords spectacular high-level views of Moab Canyon, the Colorado River, Moab Valley, and the La Sal Mountains.

1. **COURTHOUSE TOWERS** (2 m. from Visitor Center). The Courthouse Towers section lies in a system of broken cliffs, ledges and free-standing monuments. Its principal feature is **Park Avenue,** a rocky lane whose walls resemble a row of tall buildings. The one-mile downhill trail through Park Avenue offers no difficult climbs but leads along the base of a continuous slab of Entrada and Navajo sandstone from 150 to 300 feet high, perfectly vertical and intricately eroded. Among the more spectacular forms are **Egyptian Queen** and **Sausage Rock,** the latter a balanced and symmetrical pinnacle some 40 feet high. Northward the trail works through wind-carved piles to **Unjoined Rock,** an undercut block of stone 20 feet thick, which overlooks the canyon from its wall 300 feet above, and to the **Three Gossips,** who take form at the top of a fin 400 feet high and no more than 50 feet thick at the base. Here also is **The Organ,** a V-shaped fin, knife-thin at the top, and hundreds of feet high.

2. **THE WINDOWS** (9 m. from Visitor Center). The Windows section is an eroded crest of ruddy Entrada sandstone. From the highway north of Moab its battlemented contour, half mosque, half feudal castle, dominates the skyline, and patches of blue show clearly through two of its arches. The

scenic drive, after the manner of desert roads, seems to thread uncertainly through hillocks, washes and around outcroppings of sandstone bedrock, affording a chance to observe that the desert is much maligned, that it is full of green things and has even an occasional patch of grass. **Balanced Rock,** eight miles from the Visitor Center, consists of a 200-foot pinnacle of hard stone that has survived erosion, and atop it a 50-foot balanced block of even harder stone, its edges extending precariously past its base.

Near Balanced Rock, a three-mile branch drive (right) leads past a vantage point from which Delicate Arch and Devils Garden can be seen to the northeast, then on to the **Garden of Eden.** There are **Adam and Eve,** cleanly sculptured and complete even to the apple, with Adam holding the fruit to take the first bite. Nearby, on a 250-foot pinnacle, **Eagle Rock** surveys the business with aquiline unconcern. The road continues past intricate crossbedded slopes of Navajo sandstone and the **Cove of Caves,** an amphitheater whose wind-pocked walls return echoes that double back on themselves. It ends at several parking areas half surrounded by fantastic erosional forms. On the north is **Double Arch,** sometimes known as the "jughandles." Here, two massive arcs of streaked salmon-pink stone swing outward and downward from the common abutment of **Windows Reef.** The larger extends 165 feet from reef to base, and towers 156 feet above the debris below. The smaller, though not by any means dwarfed by its companion, probably is no more than high enough to shelter a three- or four-story building. From Double Arch, foot trails lead by a sculptured butte, where **Satan** uncovers ominous tushes in Mephistophelean approval of the doings of Adam and Eve, and a **Parade of Elephants** marches in echelon, trunk to rump.

A short distance south of Double Arch, near the parking area, is **South Window,** 66 feet high and 105 feet long, and hard by, its companion, **North Window,** of like size. Both are less smoothly sculptured than Double Arch, but both are imposing in size and regularity, and frame imposing desert vistas. **Turret Arch,** last major formation in The Windows area, is so named because the rock protrusion in which it is found terminates in a great spear-headed tower. The arch itself is shaped something like an immense keyhole and is accompanied by a smaller window.

3. **DELICATE ARCH** (14 m. from Visitor Center). Beyond Balanced Rock a branch of the main drive leads 2 m. east into **Salt Wash,** to **Wolfe Ranch cabin.** In Delicate Arch section there is but one arch of any consequence, yet it is probably the most popular section with return visitors. Wolfe Ranch cabin is a specimen of the frontier log-and-mud-chink architecture almost completely identified with the ground on which it stands. From the cabin, the west buttress of **Delicate Arch** is visible against the skyline. A 1½-mile foot trail (strenuous) begins in the canyon bottom, ascends from it after a quarter of a mile, and climbs across slickrock to the top of the canyon wall. Below, in a shallow depression, its sides rising like those of an irregular saucer, is a platform that rises almost as high as the walls, and atop it, alone and sharp against the sky, is Delicate Arch. Descent into the bowl and the climb up the platform is slow but not dangerous. The slickrock is truly "slick," and when it catches the slanted rays of the sun in its sculptured whorls, it spatters the light almost as flint does. The arch's opening (33 feet wide, 45 feet high) can be made to serve

splendidly as a frame for the La Sal Mountains and for the Colorado River country between. Delicate Arch also can be viewed across a deep gorge, at a distance, by hiking up a ridge from the end of the side road one mile beyond the cabin.

4. **FIERY FURNACE** (viewpoint 14 m. from Visitor Center). This extremely broken terrain is viewed from a parking area about 2½ m. along the scenic drive from the Delicate Arch turnoff. It is a labyrinth of great fins and pinnacles, separated by narrow slots. Guided hikes are conducted in summer. Persons wishing to enter this maze unaccompanied by a ranger should consult with Park personnel in advance.

5. **DEVILS GARDEN** (end of road is 18 m. from Visitor Center). **Devils Garden,** which contains the majority of the Park's arches and windows, is the largest and most complex section of the Park. It extends along a continuous sandstone ridge (the east slope of Salt Valley Anticline), eroded into jungles of upright fins, huge amphitheaters with sinuous interconnecting passageways, and wind-gnarled monoliths. Small parks with sweetwater springs are secreted here and there, surrounded by vertical slabs of sandstone, and sometimes joined to natural "slickrock" corrals that were used by cattlemen at branding time. It is distinctly a region for hikers, but it is hardly possible to get lost in it because "you have to come out the way you go in."

Northward from end-of-road parking area, the foot trail winds in a cliff-lined notch and across slickrock ledges for several miles, passing numerous arches on the way. **Pine Tree Arch,** half a mile beyond **Arch-in-the-Making,** has an opening 46 feet wide and 48 feet high, and takes its name from a hardy pine that grows immediately beneath it. **Hole-in-the-Wall,** another half mile northward, is high in the cliff face and commands a wide sweep of desert, a kind of Gargantuan peephole. **Landscape Arch,** at the end of the improved trail a mile from the parking area, is perhaps the most spectacular formation in Devils Garden. Its slender ribbon of banded black and salmon stone, only a few feet in thickness, has a length of 291 feet and is 118 feet above the canyon floor. It is believed to be the longest natural span in the world. There are those, seeing it and the warm-hued desert vista it frames, who are content to turn back without further exploration. Others push on through scored corridors, past **Wall, Navajo,** and **Partition** arches, to **Double-O Arch,** 2½ m. from trailhead, a pair of windows arranged in double-deck—as if to keep alive an appetite jaded by mere single windows. There are numerous other arches in the broken country beyond.

6. **KLONDIKE BLUFFS.** Reached by unpaved side road from the main scenic drive in Devils Garden, the Klondike Bluffs section is the least visited portion of the Park. Cowboys reported that it was impossible to get a horse more than 50 feet into the area anywhere, but a good foot trail leads to two points of interest. The Bluffs are a jungle of salmon-hued sandstone, not very large in area but endless in variation. One sculptured butte discloses **Joseph Smith,** the Mormon prophet, at the moment of his discovery of the Golden Plates, from which he translated the Book of Mormon. Into another butte the wind has carved beautifully symmetrical **Tower Arch,** one of the most striking erosional forms in the Park.

Pinnacle Wall, Bryce Canyon National Park.

BRYCE CANYON NATIONAL PARK

Highway Approach: Via State 12, turning east from US 89 seven miles south of Panguitch.

Season: Open all year. Road south of Inspiration Point usually closed by snow November-April. Bryce Canyon Lodge open May 30-September 30. Cabin camp and cafeteria open about May 15-Oct. 20. National park campground open about May 15-Oct. 30; longer if weather permits; use fee. Commercial facilities adjacent to Park are open all year.

Administrative Offices: Superintendent, Bryce Canyon National Park, Utah 84717. Information obtainable from rangers or museum-visitor center.

Admission: Admission fee is charged.

Saddle Horses and Guides: Horses are available within the Park at a modest fee. Saddle horse trips along the Peek-a-Boo Loop Trail may be arranged.

Airplane Service: Bryce Canyon Airport, three miles from park entrance.

Accommodations and Services Within the Park: Lodge, inn, restaurant, store, cabins, service station. *Outside the Park,* near entrance station: motels, restaurants, stores, service stations. Services also at Panguitch, Hatch, other nearby towns.

Climate, Clothing and Equipment: Cool to chilly evenings, days may be quite warm; dress accordingly. In winter, low temperatures and high winds, too cold for winter camping. Shops in Park or vicinity carry camera supplies, groceries, curios and Indian handicrafts. Bring camera, comfortable clothes and hiking shoes.

Medical Service: Registered nurse at Lodge. Dentist, physicians and hospital at Panguitch.

Warnings and Regulations: Snow tires recommended in winter, carry chains for safety. In early spring, trails may be slightly washed out before repairs are made. Drive carefully, especially at intersections and viewpoints. Parking permitted in designated areas only. Picnicking permitted only in picnic areas. Picking of flowers or defacing trees and rocks strictly prohibited.

Recreation: Museum-visitor center provides exhibits, audiovisual program, publications, schedule of programs and hikes. Naturalist-conducted hikes are featured several times daily during warmer months; also illustrated lectures, evening nature walks, star programs, animal and plant study, entertainment programs by Park personnel.

Communication: Post office and telephone at Bryce Canyon Lodge.

Bryce Canyon National Park is really not a canyon, but a series of "breaks" in fourteen enormous amphitheaters extending down a thousand feet through the pink and white limestones of the Paunsaugunt Plateau. Neither the English, nor perhaps any other language, is sensitive and various enough in distinctions of form and color to give more than an obtuse characterization of this amazing area. The best Paiute Indians could do was to call the area *Unka timpe-wa-wince-pock-ich,* which means "red-rocks-standing-like-men-in-a-bowl-shaped-canyon." In regard to colors, it is said that sixty tints have been recognized; and in regard to form, it can be said that almost every conceivable shape can be found in the myriad fantastic figures. Bryce Canyon is popular with tourists, accommodating well over 600,000 each year.

The entire park area, plus some thirty miles of the Pink Cliffs, can be seen from Rainbow Point at the southern end of the Park. In addition, there are magnificent views across the "land of purple sage" to Navajo Mountain, 80 miles to the east, and to the Kaibab Plateau and Trumbull Mountain to the south, the latter 99 miles distant. The Kaiparowits Plateau, one of the least visited areas of Utah, is to the east and southeast.

Although chiefly known for its scenic and geological interest, Bryce has fairly abundant wildlife, of which the most common large animal is the mule deer. Bobcat tracks and signs of mountain lion are frequently observed after rain or snow. Small animals such as porcupine, yellowbellied marmot, chipmunk, and golden mantled ground squirrel, are seen in abundance. Bird life includes crossbills, Clark nutcrackers, jays, and many other birds.

Bryce is entered at the rim with trails leading to the floor, in contrast to Zion, which is entered from the floor. The Rim Road at Bryce, called the most colorful 20 miles in the world, is a misnomer because only in a very few places does it approach the rim, but parking places are provided and numerous short hikes can be taken to the rim at the north and south ends of the Park. All the trails are relatively short and of moderate grade.

Predominant forms in Bryce are pinnacles, spires and temples; predominant colors are red, pink and cream. The first adjectives that come to mind are possibly grotesque, bizarre, and beautiful. Like Cedar Breaks, the Bryce and other amphitheaters can be regarded as the workshops of ancient sculptors of gigantic size and ambition, who were defeated by the splendor of their craftsmanship and left it unfinished; or as great tubes of paint that have exuded from the canyon floors and solidified; as the ruins of an ancient city; or as the graphic representation of a magnificently insane mind.

At first glance Bryce seems to be rampantly Gothic, as compared to the Grecian architecture of Zion. It is Gothic in its unrestrained profusion of decoration, its apparent allegory and symbolism, its world of monsters and grotesque beasts which fill the capitals, grin from gargoyles and corbels, and look across the parapets. Less obviously, it also is Gothic in its roofless interiors, which are forests of slender stone piers, engaged like pilasters or detached like columns. That Zion is classic and Bryce wildly romantic is clear at a glance. But close study demands more than a similitude with the Gothic. In the overwhelming picture of gorgeous ruins, the larger structures often bear striking resemblances to cathedrals, to castles and temples; and among the smaller ones are lions couchant, gargoyles, dragons, idols and heathen gods, limboes and purgatories and torture chambers, nave and architrave, pagoda and pantheon and mosque.

Close and prolonged study disabuses the mind of Gothic likeness, except in the general and panoramic aspect, and finds more definite similarities with the architecture of other peoples and times. The Egyptian is more apt, for here are the monstrous figures in the Great Temple of Ipsambul or Amen-Ra, and there are ancient subterranean grotto temples with the earth-roof cleared away. The Wall of Windows more than faintly resembles the Basilica of Constantine. The final appraisal comes to this, that in these amphitheaters are types of all periods and kinds of architecture from the most savage to the most civilized. A Roman entablature or a Doric column may be neighbor to the ruins of a Coptic church or a pagan altar. A Romanesque column stands in the foreground of a cliff dwelling or a rococo wall. Perhaps the adjective that most fully sums up the area is megalithic; for here indeed are thousands of monuments made up of great stones; and here is cromlech and menhir, trilithon and cyclolith, of remarkable perfection.

In coloring, not least astonishing are the changes that come with the changes in light. This is especially so on a cloudy day, when the sun alternately appears and disappears. A group of monuments may in one moment be a dull orange and in the next a brilliant yellow. A sullen red statue of a heathen god becomes almost vermilion; golden dunes flash as if a carload of diamonds had been scattered upon them; and a shrouded wall stands forth in blinding glory. The colors not only shift in tints with morning, noon or evening sun, or after dusk; the shapes grow and diminish in size, become invested with new meanings and symbolisms. By moonlight, deep shadows set brilliant white spires aglow with a light that is almost phosphorescent. When the morning sun lights up the canyon, it resembles a huge bowl of glowing embers.

Fifty-odd million years of geological history is covered in the book of the rocks at Bryce, tracing the earth's history since the Cretaceous Period, or Reptile Age. Not least astonishing is the fact that the story goes on today; older forms are crumbling, new ones appear. The rim of the canyon is receding at a rate that undermines trees, some of which cling precariously with roots exposed. At times, Bryce was covered by the sea; at times, broad rivers flowed across it, at still other times it was swept by hot desert winds. A great block of the Pink Cliffs was raised from near sea level to a high altitude, steepening the pitch of the streams, causing them to flow and erode more rapidly. Running water, frost and rain, ground water and chemical agencies active through eons carried billions of tons of ground-up rock to the Colorado.

The Paiutes say in a legend that Bryce was built as a city for the people of Coyote—the birds, animals, lizards, and those that looked like humankind. The Coyote people displeased Coyote because they worked too long beautifying their city. Coyote was angry, and he turned over the paints they were using, and he turned the people all to stone. They are still standing there, stone rows of them. And their faces are painted with the war paint they were using when Coyote was angry and threw it in their faces.

The Kanarra Cattle Company and several sheepmen used the plateau adjacent to Bryce for grazing in the early seventies, but the first permanent settler was Ebenezer Bryce, pioneer cattleman, who took up a homestead in the fall of 1875. When asked about the canyon to which Bryce had given his name, he made the classic remark, "Well, it's a hell of a place to lose a cow."

The earliest written description of Bryce was by T. C. Bailey, U. S. Deputy Surveyor, in 1876: "There are thousands of red, white, purple and vermilion rocks, of all sizes, resembling sentinels on the Walls of Castles;

monks and priests with their robes, attendants, cathedrals and congregations. There are deep caverns and rooms resembling ruins of prisons,
Castles, Churches, with their guarded walls, battlements, spires and
steeples, niches and recesses, presenting the wildest and most wonderful
scene that the eye of man ever beheld, in fact it is one of the wonders of the
world." Bailey "lost" two days at Bryce Canyon, looking for his large
meerschaum pipe, which was usually chained to him. The hunt was unsuccessful, but the pipe turned up several years later.

Ruben C. Syrett purchased 160 acres of land adjacent to Bryce in 1916,
and made homestead entry on another 160 acres within the present park. In
the spring of 1920, after he received patent for his homestead, he built a
small lodge and cabins near Sunset Point and began entertaining tourists.
The same year he was made the first postmaster of Bryce Canyon. Water
was hauled for three miles to the camp. In the fall of 1923 the Utah Parks
Company purchased his improvements, and the following year he opened
Rubys Inn.

Established in 1928, Bryce Canyon National Park was greatly enlarged
in 1931 to its present size. The Rim Road was completed in 1934. Not until it
was extensively advertised in the early 1930s by the Union Pacific Railroad,
which built lodges and provided transportation, did Bryce become widely
known, even within the state.

ROADS, TRAILS AND VIEWS

State 12 branches eastward from US 89 at a point 7 miles south of Panguitch *(see Tour No. 9A)*. Fourteen miles east of this point, State 12 makes
a junction with State 22. Turning south at this junction, the highway enters
the Park. at 3 m. from the junction is the entrance station.

Trails and Conducted Hikes: All trails from rim to lower elevations are
safe but may be strenuous. Horseback trips are made daily during the
summer to **Peek-a-boo Canyon.** By far the most popular trips are by foot.
Most popular conducted hike is the **Navajo Loop Hike,** which begins twice
daily at Sunset Point, descends 520 feet, and follows the Navajo Loop trail
for 1½ m. from start to finish. *Strenuous.* Of interest at close range on this
trip are Wall Street, the Temple of Osiris, Thor's Hammer, and The Pope.
The climb out of (or into) **Wall Street,** over what the guide calls 35 zags and
34 zigs, is alone worth the trip.

Fairyland, a huge amphitheater, is most beautiful in early morning light.
Fancy can run riot here and still be at a loss, but the character of the area
can be suggested by saying that it is a three-dimensional Arabian Nights. In
the foreground are walls and columns, rose-colored below and with cream
colored capitals; in the center is a huge crumbling monument that looks like
a thousand tons of disintegrating copper; and beyond to the right and left
are acres of ruins. They stand in barbarously eroded abutments and
terraces, their gaunt and wind-beaten skeletons softened by the play of
sunlight upon the deep rose and red, and yellow and gold, of the stone.

Park Headquarters has in its vicinity a public campground, restaurant,
cabins, store, visitor center and Bryce Canyon Lodge. The **Rim Road** leads
south, but there are well-marked turn-offs to the principal views, parking
spaces, and short trails to the rim.

From **Sunrise Point,** on the trail east of the lodge, the eastern view reveals a gently rolling landscape that looks like fields of spun gold. Its structures are more massive than those of Fairyland; the great walls, saturated with red, are in sharp contrast with monuments that seem to be of white chalk. The sculpturing here is more gigantic, is less barbarous, though there are many lean shafts, emaciated bulkheads, and weirdly lacquered crags. In the foreground the erosion is more spectacularly purposeless than on the far side, where huge castles need only windows and doors to be complete. Binoculars show that portions of the roofs have fallen in, staircases and mezzanine floors are crumbling, vestibules are too rugged for human occupancy, and corridors have lost most of their vaulted ceiling, but the excellent stucco of the walls is intact. Some of the roof fragments seem to be elaborately adorned with cupolas and steeples, but the walls below have a chaste restraint.

Sunset Point, half a mile south of Sunrise Point, offers a broader panorama. The immediate foreground of Sunrise Point is a series of massive welded structures, with great segmented columns of yellow and orange rising to a garden of ragged spires on the left, and to orchid and pale-rose pediments on the right. The columns support capitals that look like solidified cream. Directly below Sunset Point is Thor's Hammer. On the right, the chasm is full of ruins. Down below is **Wall Street,** a long, narrow corridor, and on the right of it are acres of brilliant upthrusts, like a field of stalagmites known as Silent City. Just to the left, the well-preserved ruins of a castle embody a half-dozen savage architectural motifs and cap them all with three colossal columns. The walls here are honeycombed as if bees as large as dragons had worked in them for ages.

Beyond, to left and right, the forms approach the Grecian, with more severe lines, leaner columns, and more austere buttresses. The far view is deceptive; when brought close with binoculars, this area is a menagerie of statuary, idols of men and beasts standing on picturesquely extravagant pyramids and escarpments. In the far left center is **Fairy Castle.** For some, the forms much more closely resemble a cemetery, with a magnificent mausoleum in the center, flanked on either side by rows of white headstones.

Inspiration Point, a mile south, offers a most comprehensive and overwhelming view. On the right is the Wall of Windows; below it is an area of old-rose battlements, adorned with rows of pale mauve spires, and far beyond is the cavernous southern wall reaching from the floor to the rim. Most spectacular is the view toward Sunrise Point—for here is Bryce in all its barbarous glory. The first impression may be of a mountainside of thousands of segmented columns; the second of countless joined monuments standing row on row from the floor of the canyon to the rim; but the third and most satisfying summary is of all the finest cycloliths of ancient times, brought to this amphitheater to be preserved unto posterity.

The Rim Road proceeds southward to other views including **Bryce Point,** atop a thrilling sheer-walled peninsula, which affords one of the Park's choicest panoramas of the great amphitheater. Beyond the turnoff to Bryce Point, the main road leads to **Rainbow Point, Paria View,** and **Bryce Natural Bridge,** a ragged arch in yellow and orange and gold.

Aerial view of Upheaval Dome in Canyonlands National Park *(foreground)*, looking south across the cliffs and buttes of the Junction Country. *For other views of the park, see page 16 (The Needles), page 19 (Confluence), page 715 (canyons of lower Green River), and Color Section (Angel Arch).*

CANYONLANDS NATIONAL PARK

Highway Approaches:

Island in the Sky (North District) — State Highways 313 and 279 from US Highway 163 near Moab. Paved to Park boundary; unpaved within Park.

Needles (South District)—State Highway 211 from US Highway 163, 13 miles north of Monticello. Limited system of improved roads within Park.

Maze (West District)—Unnumbered dirt road from State Highway 24, 20 miles north of Hanksville (Temple Mountain Junction); or unnumbered dirt road from State Highway 95 near Dirty Devil Bridge at Lake Powell.

Season: Open all year.

Administrative Office: Superintendent, Canyonlands National Park, Moab, Utah 84532.

Information: Superintendent's Office, Moab; Visitor Center, Arches National Park, Moab; or ranger stations in each district.

Accommodations and Facilities: Limited camping and picnicking facilities within Park. Motels, restaurants, stores, vehicle rentals, supplies and services at Moab, Monticello-Blanding, and Hanksville. Limited facilities, supplies and services may be available at Canyonlands Resort near The Needles; inquire locally or from Park headquarters.

Transportation: Private car or boat. Aerial scenic flights, vehicle and boating tours may be arranged locally or with operators outside the local area.

Communications: Public telephone and mail service at nearby communities. Emergency radio service at ranger stations.

Climate, Clothing and Equipment: Open all year. Spring and fall are the most pleasant months for hiking and exploring. Park elevation ranges from 4,000 feet at river level to 5,000 feet at intermediate levels (White Rim, Maze, Needles) to 6,000- 7,000 feet on the mesa tops (Island in the Sky-Cedar Mesa). Climate resembles that at Arches: mostly arid with light annual rainfall and snowfall, except during summer months (July-August-early September) when thundershowers of short duration are common. Winter snowfall seldom exceeds a few inches, but during the coldest months snow may remain on the ground for several weeks. Daily temperature range is large with hot days, cool nights; cold in winter. Jackets or wraps advised for evening wear in summer; warmer clothing in winter. For daytime, except in winter, wear light rugged clothing including durable shoes and broadbrimmed hats with chin straps. Carry drinking water. Insect repellent is advisable in summer. Backcountry travelers should take special precautions: make certain vehicles are in good condition; carry tools, spare tire, shovel, extra gasoline and water, food, suitable clothing and bedding, first-aid kit, matches, cooking fuel (firewood cannot be collected in Park).

Recreation: Photography, hiking, climbing, boating, exploration, off-road vehicle travel, camping, study of nature-archeology-geology, tours by air-boat-vehicle.

Warnings and Regulations: Usual park regulations. Do not damage or destroy antiquities or other property, carve initials or remove artifacts, plants or other natural objects. Stay on designated trails and roads. Carry drinking water. Backcountry hiking and boating permits required.

If there is one single most overwhelming characteristic of **Canyonlands National Park,** that characteristic is **BARE ROCK:** naked rock exposed in the steep walls of innumerable washes, canyons and gorges . . . naked rock flaunted in the faces of hundreds of miles of cliffs . . . bare rock, only here and there concealed by sand and a sparse covering of vegetation, stretching away as corrugated flats and mesa tops . . . naked rock sculptured into an infinitude of entrancing shapes, their sheer numbers bewildering, variety of form alone causing disbelief.

No other spot, perhaps, displays so much bare rock in such incredible erosional diversity. John Wesley Powell, who traversed the Canyonlands region by boat in 1869 and 1871, verbally portrayed its essence. Speaking of the view from a canyon rim near the junction of the Green and Colorado, he wrote:

> . . . we emerge from the fissure, out on the summit of rock. And what a world of grandeur is spread before us! Below is the canyon, through which the Colorado runs. We can trace its course for miles, and at points catch glimpses of the river. From the northwest comes the Green, in a narrow, winding gorge. From the northeast comes the Grand, through a canyon that seems bottomless from where we stand. Away to the west are lines of cliffs and ledges of rock—not such ledges as you may have seen where the quarry-man splits his blocks, but ledges from which the gods might quarry mountains . . . and not such cliffs as you may have seen where the swallow builds its nest, but cliffs where the soaring eagle is lost to view ere he reaches the summit. Between us and the distant cliffs are the strangely carved and pinnacled rocks of the *Toom'-pin wu-near' Tu-weap'* [Land of Standing Rock] . . . Wherever we look there is but a wilderness of rocks; deep gorges, where the rivers are lost below cliffs and towers and pinnacles; and ten thousand strangely carved forms in every direction; and beyond them, mountains blending with the clouds.

These, then, are the elements of Canyonlands: a chaotic wilderness of rock displayed in cliffs and ledges, canyons and gorges; erosional complexity; and grandeur of scale. Added to these is vivid color: primarily a full range of reds and browns, interspersed with off-whites, yellow, green, purple, and subtler tints, all sufficient to challenge any painter's palette. The result is a landscape of unique spectacle.

Canyonlands National Park was created in 1964 as the first national park in eight years, then enlarged in 1971. Its 337,000 acres (more than 500 square miles) incorporate the rugged Junction Country, that wilderness of rock where the Colorado and Green rivers join in a chasm more than a thousand feet deep. So forbidding is this terrain that it has always defied easy overland travel. It may well be that the vertical surface of the Park approaches its horizontal surface in extent.

One result of this extreme ruggedness is that the three districts of the Park—though visible in overview from a high-flying plane or, less comprehensively, from several promontories—are so effectively cut off from each other by gorges and cliffs that many miles of circuitous travel are required for visiting them individually. For example, someone wishing to visit both The Needles and Maze districts—which are physically separated only by Cataract Canyon—must drive from 200 to 300 miles from one area before reaching the other. Similarly, Island in the Sky is separated from the Needles by more than 100 miles of road, though they are only ten airline miles apart.

Natural History. Canyonlands National Park is desert in the technical sense that annual precipitation places it in that category. Much of it—particularly the intermediate flats and rims—does resemble the stereotyped desert of sand and bare rock; sparse brush, cacti and desert flowers; dry stream channels (most of the time); and little apparent water. Yet the Park's higher reaches and its riverbanks are lush with vegetation. Pygmy evergreens (pinyon pines and junipers) and a variety of moisture-conserving shrubs and flowers are the typical plants of higher elevations at 6,000 feet or more. At an altitude of 4,000 feet, the river banks and floodplains provide ample moisture for a great variety of plants, including cottonwoods and other broadleaf trees, numerous kinds of shrubs and bushes, willows, and tamarisk.

Animals and insects are present, though the latter are more evident and bothersome at all elevations. Flies and no-see-um "gnats" are pests in warmer months. Lizards are common, rattlesnakes rare. Jackrabbits are often seen. The following is excerpted from an official description of the Park:

> The isolation of high mesas and deep canyons, and obstacles like broad rivers and sheer cliffs affect the distribution of plants and animals just as they affect man's movements in the area . . . The desertlands look desolate and empty but are very much occupied by plant and animal life. Bighorn sheep, mule deer, cougars, bobcats, coyotes, foxes, and pronghorn are present, as well as rodents in great variety and numbers, various kinds of other small mammals, and some reptiles. Along the rivers are beaver, shorebirds, ducks, and other wetland animals.
>
> Birdlife in Canyonlands is especially diverse because of the wide range of habitats. Totally different conditions may occur within very short distances, and birdwatchers find a rich variety of species throughout the year.

SEEING THE PARK

Because of the Park's extreme ruggedness and the great travel distances involved, any individual is likely to tour only one or two of its districts during any one visit. This is the main reason for describing the various districts separately.

1. ISLAND IN THE SKY (North District). *See also Tour No. 11A.* Island in the Sky is a high triangular peninsula contained between the Green and Colorado rivers, in the acute angle formed by their convergence. The summit of the Island is a series of rolling flats at about 6,000 feet altitude, but these flats are gashed by yawning gorges, and the Island is bounded on east and west by great red cliffs—those magnificent palisades known as the **Orange or Wingate Cliffs,** which are almost uniformly perpendicular for 400 feet or so above their sloping talus base. The serpentine course of soaring red cliffs around Island in the Sky is at least 70 miles in length; elsewhere throughout the Park they total several hundred more.

The cliff-ringed Island is based on a broad intermediate terrace known as the **White Rim,** a thousand feet below the Island's crest and itself a thousand feet above the rivers, entrenched in gorges beneath the White Rim. The Island in the Sky district, then, is comprised of two principal divisions: Island in the Sky peninsula or mesa, and the White Rim terrace. The rivers are considered a separate district *(see below).*

(a) **Island in the Sky,** from its high rim, provides some of the Park's most stirring panoramic overviews, similar in emotional impact to those from Dead Horse Point, Canyon Rims *(see Tours No. 11A and 11C),* and cliff-top vantage points to the west, but differing in the details that may be seen. Views of breathtaking magnitude are obtainable all along the rim (short hikes often required); however, Green River Overlook, Murphy's Point Overlook, and Grand View Point are the most popular and in respects the most dramatic. **Green River and Murphy's Point overlooks** give high-level panoramas of the Park's Maze district, the broad basin of Green River, and the White Rim, with the river itself appearing here and there within its green-fringed inner gorge. From **Grand View Point,** on the southernmost tip of the Island, the heart of Inner Canyonlands spreads away beneath the feet in a sublime vision. Though the point is not high enough to give more than tantalizing hints of the Park's erosional intricacy (an airplane is required for the full impact of that), it does afford an orientation of sorts—an introduction to the Park's surface personality, a visual, emotional and geological banquet. The rivers cannot be seen—they are too deeply confined—but their general courses can be traced toward their confluence in a jumble of cliffs, canyons, ledges and standing rocks. Great buttes rise in every direction, and the weird sandstone forest of **The Needles** assaults the eye only a few miles away toward the south. Immediately below the point is **Monument Basin,** gouged out from the White Rim in multiple pockets, filled with a profusion of dark brown skyscrapers, hundreds of feet high, their erosional delicacy, fragility and perfect balance challenging belief. A short foot trail leads east from the point to Grand View Overlook, providing a variation of the view from the main parking area.

Even a smattering of geological understanding is worthwhile in appreciating the view from Grand View Point, as well as those from other promontories around the Junction Country. These overlooks are near the upper levels of the Glen Canyon group of cliff-forming sedimentary rocks—the Navajo, Kayenta and Wingate formations—so typical of this region, laid down in the Jurassic-Triassic periods of 175 to 200 million years ago. Rocks younger than these, such as the Entrada formation (common in Arches National Park), rise here and there from the flats atop the cliffs. Older rocks of Triassic, Permian and Pennsylvanian age descend in steps beneath the sheer face of the Orange Cliffs, formed primarily by the Wingate sandstone, perhaps the most imposing physical feature of the Park. Earth's layered crust rolls away from the base of the cliffs, naked and skeletal, the structural secrets of a hundred million years exposed to the eye.

Grand View Point is reached by maintained road leading 22 miles from its junction with State 313 (28 miles from US 163). Several miles north of the point, a short sideroad forks west for 1½ mile to **Murphy's Point Overlook,** on the rim overlooking lower Green River Canyon and the Maze-Standing Rocks country beyond. About six miles south of the junction with State 313, an unpaved sideroad forks east, in four miles dropping a thousand feet down the cliff-face in tight, steep switchbacks to the White Rim road *(see below).* This notorious corkscrew drive is known as the **Shafer Trail,** one of the most hair-raising stretches of road in Utah. Near the Shafer Trail turnoff is the Park's district ranger station (temporary), situated at **The Neck,** a natural causeway joining Island in the Sky to the "mainland" on the north. **The Neck** is a narrow ridge between two rapidly-deepening gorges: Taylor Canyon of Green River on the west and South Fork of Shafer Canyon (Colorado River) on the east. About six miles south of **The Neck** a sideroad forks west to **Green River Overlook** and **Upheaval Dome** (5 m. from junction), the latter a geological phenomenon without exact counterpart in Utah. Best seen from the air, Upheaval Dome is a circular, crater-like depression with a perpendicular inner wall of Wingate sandstone, and above this a concentric outer wall of light-colored Navajo sandstone. Apparently it is the eroded remnant of a salt-related uplift of ancient times.

(b) **The White Rim** is a broad, incised but relatively level shelf or terrace midway in elevation between Island in the Sky and the rivers. It is formed from the light-colored White Rim sandstone, a member of the Cutler formation of Permian age. The White Rim serves as a platform for the surpentine Orange (Wingate) Cliffs. Into it are sunk the inner gorges of the Green and Colorado rivers, as well as tributary channels and "hanging valleys" such as Monument Basin. This intermediate position on the Park's Grand Staircase features views extending both upward and downward. The rim is traversed by a fairweather dirt road known as the **White Rim Trail,** suitable only for off-road vehicles including those with four-wheel drive. Up to 100 miles or more in length, the trail winds sinuously over slickrock, through sand and across packed sediments, into and out of washes, heading gorges and surmounting precipitous cliffs. Travelers should carry drinking water, firewood or stove fuel, gasoline, food, etc., scheduling two or three days for maximum enjoyment of the route. Travelers are cautioned to register in advance with Park rangers and to observe Park regulations.

2. **THE RIVERS.** More than 90 miles of river are included within the Park: 46 miles of the lower Green, 30 miles of the upper Colorado, and 15 miles of the main Colorado in Cataract Canyon below the confluence. These stretches of river carry hundreds of recreational boating craft every year, through gorges that have few equals for scenic grandeur. With one exception (The Slide), the rivers upstream from Cataract Canyon are rapid-free, allowing leisurely floating with the current, or powerboat travel at almost any desired speed, subject to the limitations of driftwood and seasonal low water.

Visitors who travel the rivers view the Park from its lowest level, as in the Grand Canyon, with cliffs and ledges looming as much as 2,000 to 3,000 feet overhead or high in the distance. But many river miles in Canyonlands are expansive, unconfined miles, with panoramic vistas to stir the soul and excite the artistic urge. It can hardly be claimed that river perspectives excel those at higher levels of the Park, but they certainly are different, adding a dimension of unique esthetics not obtainable in many other national parks.

Canyonlands boating parties embark variously at Green River, Moab, Potash, or the mouth of Mineral Canyon. The majority of rafting parties, for example, launch at a site near the Potash mine downriver from Moab. Most powerboaters travel the 183 miles between Green River and Moab, a distance of 118 miles on the Green and 65 miles on the Colorado, during the

Friendship Cruise—heretofore scheduled every Memorial Day weekend but now facing an uncertain future. *(See Tour No. 10D.)* Other powerboaters put in at Potash or Moab or Green River, and a few at Mineral Canyon. Powerboating is restricted in both season and locality by water level, which usually is adequate only during spring runoff (May-June). If in doubt, inquire at Park. Floaters traverse the rivers on rubber rafts, or in kayaks or canoes, while commercial outfitters provide diversified tour offerings—such as guides and pontoon rafts for the exhilarating traverse of upper Cataract Canyon's 20-odd rapids. (There were more than 50 distinct rapids in the canyon before rising Lake Powell completed inundation of the canyon's lower 27 miles in 1980.)

During historic times the rivers have been the stage for much of the Park area's human history. Vehicle roads were almost nonexistent before the 1940s, when the four-wheel-drive jeep came onto the scene. Therefore, except for travel on foot or horseback, the rivers were the only convenient arteries of transportation until about 40 years ago. As described in Tour No. 10D, the Green has carried an impressive volume of small boats, beginning (so far as known) with D. Julien in 1836 and John W. Powell's first expedition in 1869. The Colorado below Moab was used less frequently than the Green as an entrance to Cataract Canyon and the lower Colorado, though it did witness oil-rig freighting and perhaps as much local boating traffic. Before the development of small and powerful outboard engines in this century it was an arduous and hazardous undertaking to travel between Moab and Green River on the rivers, because of the long upstream journey required on at least one river leg above the junction. Most river travelers of earlier years continued on downstream through Cataract Canyon or perished in the attempt.

3. **THE NEEDLES (South District).** *See Tour 11C for description of entrance highway.* By any measure of esthetics and geography, The Needles is one of the remarkable areas of the world. Admittedly, the Canyonlands region does not have a monopoly on magnificent canyons and cliffs, rivers and red-rock overlooks, though it is likely that no combination of such features excels the mosaic of Canyonlands National Park. But there is only one Needles, so geologically distinctive and scenically marvelous that the area can only be called unique. The name is appropriate, for sharp-pointed spires are the best-known representation of The Needles; yet there is much more to the district than those splendid erosional forms. The district was described first in print by Professor J. S. Newberry of the Macomb Expedition of 1859, and soon thereafter by Major Powell, who applied the Indian name *Toom'-pin wu-near' Tu-weap'* (Land of Standing Rock) to the general area of the Junction Country—"ten thousand strangely carved forms in every direction. . . ." *(see full quotation at beginning of this chapter).*

Gothic spires there are, but Gothic is only one of myriad resemblances to human art and architecture in The Needles, where a seeming infinitude of three-dimensional design is on exhibit. Considered as a unit with the Salt Creek and Maze systems, The Needles may well represent the most splendid concentration of intricately sculpted rock forms on earth.

The Needles proper is a zone of crustal faulting and fracturing. It includes a series of closely spaced, parallel, north-south trending fault lines, between some of which graben valleys have formed—that is, depressions caused by down-dropping of the valley floor, leaving steep-sided ridges between the valleys. These ridges of banded sandstone in turn are fractured at right angles to the valleys, resulting in a surface of close-knit, crisscross jointing. This faulting and fracturing was caused in ages past by underground movement of salt, a phenomenon responsible for many of the Park area's unusual geological features, such as anticlines, synclines, gypsum plugs, and even Upheaval Dome. Subsequently, multiple agents of erosion have taken advantage of crustal weakness represented by intricate jointing and the interbedding of different rock types to create the fantastic sculptures that we see today.

Whereas The Needles are remarkable for their complex small-form erosion, spires and pinnacles, linear fault-line lanes, and open parks ringed by sawtooth standing rocks, the adjoining **Salt Creek-Horse Canyon area**—not being so influenced by faulting and jointing, but being composed of the same rocks—displays erosional artistry that is similar to that of The Needles but yet is different. From the ground, differences are not too noticeable, but comparing the two areas from the air makes them apparent: forms and lines of The Needles are sharper, more abrupt, somewhat more angular, while those of Salt Creek-Horse Canyon are more softly contoured, with gentler angles and ridges that tend to roundness. Canyons of the latter form a meandering, many-tentacled labyrinth, with delightful, spacious parks in its higher southern reaches.

The Needles-Salt Creek district is terrain for discovery on foot or with four-wheel-drive. Its numberless recesses invite exploratory probing. Before the area became a Park it was cowboy country—perhaps the wildest cattle range in America—and since then there has been a minimum of development on roads and trails. **Elephant Hill,** bulldozed by cattlemen in the 1940s, remains a challenge to jeeps. **Salt Creek** and **Horse canyons** still are entered along their streambeds, intermittently wet or impassable, depending on weather. And roads through the graben valleys to **Confluence Overlook, Chesler Park** and **Beef Basin,** or into **Lavender** and **Davis canyons,** remain primitive and suited only for four-wheel-drive vehicles. Only the main access road to the entrance station at Squaw Butte (State 211) is paved, as well as short spurs to Squaw Flat Campground and Big Spring Canyon. In other words, almost the entire district is near-wilderness, and is likely to remain so, accessible only by off-road vehicles or foot.

Of special scenic interest are the area's many natural arches, several of which are among the most distinctive in Utah. Chief among these are **Angel** and **Druid** arches. The district also displays some remarkable Indian antiquies (ruins and rock art). **Cave Spring** is an authentic cowboy camp.

4. **THE MAZE DISTRICT** including **The Maze, Land of Standing Rocks, The Fins,** and **Horseshoe Canyon.** *(Carry all supplies including water, food, extra gasoline, cooking fuel. For safety, travel in caravans of at least two vehicles or hiking parties of at least two persons.)* The Maze District consists of 60,000 acres of extremely rugged terrain west of the con-

fluence of the rivers. For nearly a hundred years—from the time of Major Powell—this area was known generally as the **Land of Standing Rocks.** Since establishment of the Park, this inclusive term has been gradually replaced by more specific names such as the Maze, the Fins, the Standing Rocks, the Doll House, etc.—distinctive features within the area formerly known as the Land of Standing Rocks. Today the west district is referred to by the National Park Service as the Maze District.

In coloring and erosional design the Maze District bears resemblance to the Park's other two districts across the rivers, yet only in a general way, for in details it differs. It is wilder, more remote, more difficult to reach.

Except for Horseshoe Canyon, which is a detached unit, features of the Maze District are clustered together on an intermediate terrace between river gorges on the east and the Orange Cliffs rampart on the west. They can be seen in panorama from the upper edge of the Orange Cliffs; indeed, the views from these aerial heights rank in sheer spectacle with those high-level views on the east. The overview points are approached from U24 *(see Tour No. 7B)*—or from Green River—over 60 miles or more of rough, sandy road. The descent from cliff-top to lower elevations via the steep switchbacks of **Flint Trail** matches the thrills of Island in the Sky's hair-raising Shafer Trail.

Another main access road winds a tortuous path north from State 95 just east of where the highway crosses Lake Powell at the Dirty Devil Bridge. It parallels Narrow and Cataract canyons, which can be viewed from their rims by short cross-country drives or hikes. Spur "roads" within the district are suited only for rugged vehicles of the four-wheel-drive type, or for trail bikes, though pickup trucks with two-wheel-drive and high clearance might negotiate most of them without undue difficulty. One spur leads north from the bottom of **Flint Trail** through Elaterite Basin to the Millard Canyon Benches and the bottoms of Green River. A branch of this spur leads to the **Maze Overlook** *(17 miles from Flint Trail).* Maze Overlook and other rim vantage points in the vicinity provide sweeping panoramas of the Junction Country's wilderness of rock, as well as intimate glimpses downward into the bewildering Maze labyrinth of steep-walled, narrow, many-fingered box canyons—complexly eroded tributaries of the Green, beautifully colored and containing little water except in periods of storm.

Another spur—even rougher than that leading to Maze Overlook—leads north from the junction near Sunset Pass (Water Hole Flat) to the **Fins, Lizard Rock, Totem Pole,** and the **Doll House,** where it deadends about 20 miles from the junction. This spur penetrates a compact tangle of amazingly varied erosional forms ranging from giant parallel fins and natural arches resembling those in Arches National Park, to skyscraping pinnacles reminiscent of those in Monument Basin, to a fairyland of dainty sculptures suggestive of The Needles. Foot trails lead to **Pete's Mesa** overlooking the heart of the Maze canyons; down to the Maze itself; and to **Spanish Bottom** of the Colorado River. Other hiking and scrambling possibilities are limited only by time, desire and expertise. Though traversed by Indians, outlaws and stockmen—and possibly even by travelers deviating from the Old Spanish Trail this area was not entered by wheeled vehicles until 1957, after construction of mineral exploration roads to its outskirts made vehicle access possible. It was first described as a tour destination in *Westways* and *Desert* magazines in the fall of that same year.

Horseshoe Canyon, though far from the Park proper, was included as a unit of Canyonlands National Park because it contains some of the nation's priceless examples of prehistoric Indian rock art (rock writings). Known also as **Barrier Canyon,** Horseshoe is a huge cliff-walled gorge, tributary to the Green and so long, wide and deep that it may—at some distant time in the past—have been the channel of a major stream. Today it contains running water only intermittently, though springs permit livestock operations. The following appeared in the 1941 edition:

> Barrier Canyon, locally known as Horseshoe Canyon, is a meandering gorge that works northward to the Green River from highlands west of the Orange Cliffs and Horse Thief Pasture Mesa. Its head is in Robbers Roost *(see Tour 7a)* and the canyon once served as an avenue by which fleeing outlaws reached their badlands refuge. Entry into the canyon is possible only at widely spaced intervals —in the area of the paintings there is but one horse trail into the gorge for ten miles in either direction. The walls rise sheer from three to five hundred feet above the canyon floor—massive bulwarks that scale off flecks of buff and magenta sandstone as large as houses. Near the bases, where water has worn the cliffs smooth or where cleavages have left flat facets, a prehistoric race carved and painted naive representations of its people and the things they did. The carved designs (petroglyphs) are small, from six inches to two feet high, and were apparently made by pecking into the soft sandstone with a piece of flint. They represent men, sheep, deer, antelope, and, apparently, dogs, accompanied by undecipherable symbols with lines as uncertain as twentieth-century doodles. The paintings are more restrained in subject matter—they depict men, animals, and hands. They are predominantly red, and are made of iron ore dyes with animal fat for a binding medium. The most imposing of these murals is about three miles up-canyon from the point of entry. Here, the figures are as much as nine feet high, and are occasionally bedecked with ceremonial regalia. In the summer and fall of 1940, the Utah Art Project reproduced these murals on canvas for an exhibition in the Museum of American Art, New York City, in the late winter and early spring of 1940-41.

The mural reproductions mentioned above have since appeared in other exhibitions around the country and now reside permanently (in sections) in the Prehistoric Museum in Price and the Utah Museum of Natural History in Salt Lake City.

The **Grand Gallery,** noted only briefly above, extends along the cliff face for about 80 feet and contains more than 50 human figures, nearly half of which are life-size or larger. The canyon's rock art was long believed to be the work of Fremont Indians, with an age of 700 years or more. This has been regarded with skepticism in recent years. The origin, age and purpose of the pictographs and petroglyphs really are not known.

Horseshoe Canyon may be entered from the west (by trail) or the east, from Hans Flat Ranger Station, by four-wheel-drive road and/or trail. The 20-mile fairweather road from Hans Flat—very rough and sandy—descends in sharp switchbacks to the canyon bottom and thence a short distance to a camping area (end of road). From there the Grand Gallery requires an up-canyon hike of nearly two miles. *Carry all supplies including water, food and cooking fuel.*

Shinob Canyon, Capitol Reef National Park.

Cathedrals of Cathedral Valley, Capitol Reef National Park.

CAPITOL REEF NATIONAL PARK

Highway Approach: State Highway 24 (paved, open all year).

Season: Park and highway open all year. Trails and unpaved side roads may be closed for short periods during rains or in midwinter.

Administrative Offices: Visitor Center and headquarters are at Fruita within the Park. Address: Superintendent, Capitol Reef National Park, Torrey, Utah 84775.

Accommodations: Nearest motels in Torrey vicinity, 10 miles west. Restaurants, stores, gasoline at Torrey. Motels and services also at Bicknell, Loa, Hanksville. No services or accommodations within Park; camp and picnic areas only; film and publications at Visitor Center.

Transportation: Private auto or charter bus. Commercial guide and tour service available at Rimrock Motel, Torrey.

Climate: Four distinct seasons. Climate is influenced by altitude (5,000 to 7,000 feet within Park; up to 11,000 feet in nearby highlands). Most moderate months are May, June, September, October. Temperature may reach 100 degrees F. in summer (June-July-August) with cool evenings. Winters are cold. Expect rain showers in spring and August-September. Insects may be bothersome during hot season; be prepared with insect repellent.

Clothing and Equipment: Carry food and supplies; none available in Park (except limited film). Wear suitable outdoor clothing, comfortable hiking shoes. Light jacket advisable for summer evening wear; warmer clothing for winter, spring and fall.

Medical and Dental Service: Public medical clinic, dentist in Bicknell. Nearest hospital in Richfield.

Communications: Public telephones in Park and nearby towns. Post office: Torrey, Utah 84775.

Recreation: Hiking, climbing, photography, sightseeing, camping, picnicking, wildlife observation. Naturalist tours and lectures. Exhibits and orientation film at Visitor Center. Bathing in Fremont River. Fishing, hunting, camping, exploring in adjoining forests and red-rock wilderness.

Warnings and Regulations: In case of cloudburst or heavy rain, *get out of dry washes immediately!* This warning applies even if storm appears miles away in headwaters area. Be careful in climbing—rocks may be slippery, footholds none too sure. Be absolutely certain you can retreat if way ahead is blocked. Check mechanical condition of car and tires before off-highway trips; carry plenty of fuel, oil, water, food, spare tire, tools, etc. Always carry water on hikes of more than an hour. Register with Park personnel for backcountry camping permits. Do not gather or cut native wood for a fire. Do not remove artifacts, plant life, petrified wood or rock samples.

Capitol Reef National Park features splendid erosive forms—grand cliffs, goblin rocks, carved pinnacles, stone arches, great butte-forms and deep gorges. It combines the fantasy of Bryce and the grandeur of Zion national parks, with more variety of color than either, and is larger than both combined (378 square miles). It also contains archeological and historic resources.

The Park's vivid colors run in streamers, bands, and layers, both vertically and horizontally. There are blues and greens in broad stripes, and purple, orchid and lavender give remarkable softness to the rock walls. Every primary color is visible in any of several different formations, but shades of red and white predominate. Indians of the Four Corners region are reputed to have called such prismatic displays the "Sleeping Rainbow."

The Park's colors, of course, are related to its varied rock types. Many natural areas exhibit rocks of only a few types, often obscured by vegetation or soil, whereas Capitol Reef displays bare rocks of great variety in an assortment of vivid colors. The Park's sparsely veiled rocks assault the eye not in gentle undulations but in massive frontal exposures.

Capitol Reef, which gives its name to the entire Park—though it is but a segment of the whole—fits a definition used in the West for an upthrust ridge with a cliff face. A part of the Waterpocket Fold, the reef stands high above its surroundings and has been a formidable barrier to travel. White domes of Navajo sandstone, topping reddish Wingate sandstone cliffs, resemble the domes of various Capitol buildings. Hence the name. The Waterpocket Fold received its name from numerous natural pockets or "tanks" that collect and hold runoff water.

Having a length of 75 miles, Capitol Reef National Park includes not only Capitol Reef itself but much of the remainder of the Waterpocket Fold, which stretches from Thousand Lake Mountain on the north almost to Lake Powell on the south—a total distance of approximately 100 miles. Despite its great length, the Park is relatively narrow—only five to ten miles wide in most places—yet its topography is so rugged that a mere statement of land area is deceptive. In fact, its area on a vertical scale might well exceed that on a horizontal scale.

Visible rocks of the Fold were laid down, for the most part, during the Jurassic and Triassic periods, about 150 to 225 million years ago. To the east and west of the Park, and in deep canyons within the Park, older and younger rocks are present. Originally laid down in layers, the older rocks were uplifted and bent (flexed) along a north-south axis some 60 or 70 million years ago. At that time the rocks now exposed in today's Park were overlain with thousands of feet of younger strata. Since then, most of the younger rocks have been removed by erosional processes, and the older rocks—now exposed—are being affected by the same processes.

History. Archeologically, the Park and its environs are rich, though early settlers collected and disposed of large quantities of baskets, pottery, weapons, sandals, and even skeletal remains. Some of these were displayed for years in personal museums, for example in the collections of Ephraim P. Pectol and Charles D. Lee of Torrey, but most were dispersed over the years. Prehistoric peoples known as the Fremont Indians carved petroglyphs and painted pictographs on cliff walls of the region. The Fremonts were contemporaries of Anasazi cultures of the Four Corners region. Both disappeared about 1300 A.D. It is believed by many archeologists that the Anasazi migrated south to the Hopi mesas and Rio Grande Valley. What happened to the Fremonts is more uncertain, but it is possible that they were the ancestors of today's Utes and Southern Paiutes.

During the 1870s, Mormon pioneers established settlements in upper valleys on the river which Major John W. Powell first called the Dirty Devil and later renamed the Fremont. The Fruita area was settled in 1878 by Franklin D. Young. Other settlers followed, homesteading every likely spot. E. P. Pectol of Torrey, becoming interested in the "Wayne Wonderland" as a potential park area in 1910, induced a photographer to make the first pictures. Joseph H. Hickman, a local teacher and a member of the state legislature, convinced that body to set aside 160 acres at Fruita as a park. Dr. J. E. Broaddus, writer and lecturer of Salt Lake City, did much to publicize the region, as did others. In 1933 Mr. Pectol was elected to the legislature and memoralized Wayne Wonderland to Congress as a national park. In 1937 the Capitol Reef area was set apart as a National Monument by presidential proclamation, largely as a result of efforts by Pectol, Dr. Broaddus, and Dr. A. L. Inglesby of Fruita. During the 1960s, after creation of Lake Powell brought national attention to the Canyonlands region, the Monument area was greatly expanded to include most of the southern and northern extensions of the Waterpocket Fold. In 1971 the Monument's boundaries were changed again and it was designated a national park.

Plants and Animals. Desert and semi-desert plants grow plentifully in the Park. In late April, May, and June, several dozen varieties of hardy desert wildflowers are in bloom. Several varieties of cacti continue in flower through most of the summer. Among numerous other forms of plant life reported from the Park and vicinity are juniper, desert primrose, red, yellow, and green cactus roses, Indian paintbrush, Spanish bayonet (yucca), desert geraniums, sagebrush, and prickly pear. Areas that seem barren often have sagebrush, rabbit brush, saltbush, greasewood, clumps of grass, and an occasional yucca.

While there are few rattlesnakes, bullsnakes and gartersnakes are plentiful in the Park. Small animal life includes field mice, cliff mice, "trade" rats—which usually leave something for everything they take, according to old-timers—ground squirrels, chipmunks, coyotes, and various lizards. Pinyon jays, sage sparrows, rock wrens, and sage thrashers are some of the birds found in the area.

DESCRIPTIONS OF PARK DISTRICTS

The Park can best be described by districts, each of which differs from the others in respects:

1. CENTRAL (CAPITOL REEF) DISTRICT

Encompassing the original Monument area, this district includes the cliff-face of Capitol Reef, the Visitor Center-Park Headquarters, the site of old Fruita community, fruit orchards, the former Floral-Sleeping Rainbow Ranch, and ancient Indian rock art. Here, too, are all the Park's improved hiking trails; its most renowned canyons; its only paved highway; and the Capitol Reef Scenic Drive.

Between Torrey and Caineville, a distance of 30 miles, State Highway 24 parallels the face of Capitol Reef for a distance, winds beside the Fremont River where it has cut through the Reef in a splendid canyon, and penetrates Utah's Painted Desert east of the Park. *See description in Tour No. 7B.* Most visitors view the Park from this paved road. For visual impact, this 30-mile drive ranks among the best in Utah.

South of the Visitor Center, the Park's Scenic Drive southward along the multicolored face of Capitol Reef gives access to the site of old Fruita, the picnic area, campground, Grand Wash, Capitol Gorge, and Pleasant Creek. Improved trails are accessible from this drive. Also within the Central District are the deep gorges of Fremont River, Sulphur Creek, and Pleasant Creek where they cut through Miner's Mountain.

Points of interest along the Scenic Drive South of Visitor Center:

This road served for 80 years as the main highway through the Reef. It is unpaved but well graded and maintained. For short periods, when wet or snowpacked, it may be closed. *Mileages are distances from Visitor Center.*

Visitor Center-Park Headquarters, an attractive structure of native rock. Information desk, publications, exhibits, orientation film, restrooms.

Site of Fruita community (0-1 mile), the Park residential area and site of a former hamlet dating from about 1880. Early residents planted hundreds of fruit trees here in the valley formed by Sulphur Creek and Fremont River. The orchards are being preserved by the National Park Service, though nearly all the original buildings have been removed. Orchard fruits include apples, pears, peaches, apricots, cherries and plums.

Main Campground (1.4 miles). Tables, firestands, restrooms with running water. From this vicinity trails lead to **Fremont River Overlook** (2.5 miles round trip), a scenic viewpoint about 800 feet above the valley floor, and **Cohab Canyon.** The trail to Cohab Canyon zigzags up a steep slope into a narrow, weirdly eroded gash in the rim of a cliff overlooking Fruita and the campground. The canyon's name is an abbreviation of "cohabitation," a reference to Mormon polygamists of the last century who are said to have used the canyon to avoid federal officers. The hike to the canyon and return totals about two miles.

Grand Wash (3.5 miles), left, marked by a yawning gap in the cliff. A dirt road *(closed in wet weather)* gives access to the first mile or so of this beautiful gorge. Visible to the left after entering Grand Wash are excavations in the rocks at the base of the cliff, marking the Oyler Mine where small quantities of uranium ore were removed in earlier times. A mile down the wash, a red cliff rises (L) perpendicularly hundreds of feet from the road, like the wall of a giant's house. Left of this cliff, and about 400 feet above the floor of the wash, is the second largest natural arch in the Park, usually missed unless pointed out. This is **Cassidy Arch,** which can be reached by improved foot trail (3.5 miles round-trip) from the parking area in Grand Wash. **Singing Rock,** 1.0 m., is an arched grotto in the wall of the wash (R), 600 feet high and 400 feet across. The grotto, which has unusual acoustical properties, was used for dedication ceremonies at the opening of the Monument in 1937. **Shinob Canyon,** a deep, narrow, deadend gorge, forks south in this vicinity. In Shinob Canyon are several interesting natural arches. At 1.2 m. is the end-of-road parking area, from which trails lead to Cassidy Arch *(above),* Frying Pan Trail, and the **Grand Wash Narrows.** The Narrows trail leads to **The Narrows** (1.3 m.) and eventually (2¼ m.) to State Highway 24 in the Fremont River Canyon. The cliffs reach overhead for hundreds of feet; in one place they are 500 feet high and only 20 feet apart.

Capitol Gorge (8 miles) is entered between widely separated portals—castellated formations set high on sloping purple bases, their summits a thousand feet or so above the canyon floor. The gorge is walled by red and cream-colored cliffs, hundreds of feet high, with a tremendous variety of monoliths, pinnacles, and rock tapestry, all magnificently colored.

Until 1962, State 24 passed through Capitol Gorge. Cloudbursts, rushing off the non-porous landscape, sometimes raced through the gorge, tumbling boulders weighing tons. Highway maintenance here was always costly and troublesome. Today, the road ends at a parking area 2 m. from the main Scenic Drive; from there a trail leads a mile or so farther, through the Narrows, to Fremont Indian petroglyphs and the Pioneer Register, where early white travelers inscribed their names. At the east end of the Narrows are natural tanks (L) in the rock.

Another trail from the Capitol Gorge parking area climbs the north wall to the base of **Golden Throne,** a golden-hued dome, one of several huge sandstone monoliths on the crest of Capitol Reef. The trail is fairly strenuous (2 miles each way) but repays exertion with a high-level display of dramatic rock erosion.

South of the Capitol Gorge turnoff, the main road continues to **Pleasant Creek Canyon,** through which a trail passes east to meet the Waterpocket Fold road near Notom. A fairweather road continues beyond Pleasant Creek to Tantalus Basin, Lower Bown's Reservoir, and junction with the Grover-Boulder highway *(see Tour No. 7B).*

Major Points of Interest on State 24

West of Visitor Center

Chimney Rock (3 miles), a lofty spire of layered Moenkopi rock capped by a block of Shinarump sandstone. From a parking area near the spire's base a fairly strenuous improved trail (3.5 m. round-trip) climbs to the top of a ridge above Chimney Rock, giving choice panoramic views of Capitol Reef for 20 miles as it curves in a great semicircle from west to south. From this trail an unimproved route leads to the awesome lower reaches of Spring Canyon, the Park's longest, emerging at the Fremont River 4 m. east of the Visitor Center.

Goosenecks Overlook and Panorama Point (2.7 miles). A short side road leads 1 m. from the highway to Goosenecks parking area. From there, a short trail climbs to the upper rim of **Sulphur Creek Canyon** where it winds around in curving "goosenecks." The canyon is about 800 feet deep here, the view is a thrill. **Panorama Point,** only a few hundred yards from the highway along the Goosenecks road, provides a full-circle panorama of Capitol Reef's face, Torrey Breaks, Thousand Lake Mountain, the swell of Miner's Mountain, Aquarius Plateau, and peaks of the Henry Mountains.

East of Visitor Center

Historic Fruita Schoolhouse (1m.), restored wood structure built in 1896.

Fruit Orchards (1 to 2 m.), planted by pioneer settlers and their descendants, now maintained by the Park. Mule deer may be seen here at dusk, grazing among the trees. Occasionally they become the prey of cougar in the orchards.

Prehistoric Indian Rock Art (1.1 m.), on face of cliff to the north. Nearly a thousand years ago this area was occupied by the Fremont Indians, whose culture somewhat resembled that of the contemporary Anasazi of the Four Corners region. Other similar sites are found along perennial water courses in the Park.

Trailhead and Parking Turnoff (2 m.). Capitol Dome looms in a curve of the canyon to the east. Cohab Canyon Trail is across the highway. From the parking area an improved trail leads 1 m. to **Hickman Natural Bridge,** largest natural span in the Park, measuring 133 feet from rim to rim, 125 feet above the streambed. A spur trail leads 2 m. from the parking area along the steep slope of the Waterpocket Fold to **Rim Overlook,** a cliff-edge viewpoint nearly a thousand feet above the Fremont River.

2. NORTH DISTRICT

Known generally as **Cathedral Valley** for its most-visited natural features, this district includes or adjoins other points that are less renowned but still remarkable in their own right.

Cathedral Valley is an extensive area lying east of the Waterpocket Fold where it emerges from Thousand Lake Mountain. The "valley" consists of many miles of beautifully sculptured cliffs and several groups of lofty buttes that bear idealized resemblance to cathedral spires. Unique and majestic in design, these cathedral buttes rise hundreds of precipitous feet above the valley floor.

In addition to buttes and cliffs, the Cathedral Valley area contains curious and impressive igneous features (dikes and sills), a cylindrical pit known as **Gypsum Sinkhole,** and a large mound of selenite crystals known as **Glass Mountain.**

Visible from higher points is **South Desert,** a strikingly scenic, arid basin east of the Waterpocket Fold. South Desert features sculptured cliffs and buttes resembling those in Cathedral Valley to the north. Westward, corrugated slopes of the Fold unite with Thousand Lake Mountain. Little known, these slopes are a wild area of deep canyons and impressive butteforms; one section bears the apt name "Paradise." Hikers can approach on dirt roads from Torrey or Fremont.

South Desert is a challenge for hikers. So, too, are Deep Creek and its tributary, Water Canyon, exceptionally deep and rugged gorges in the slopes of the Fold. Anyone intending to hike this country should confer and register in advance with Park rangers.

The Cathedral Valley area can be reached by high-clearance vehicles on fairweather dirt roads, leading from several directions as follows: (1) From State 24 at River Ford, 12 miles east of the Visitor Center (28 miles into Cathedral Junction); (2) from State 24 at Caineville, 19 miles east of Visitor Center (21 miles to Cathedral Junction); (3) from State 24 at Loa, about 25 miles to Cathedral Valley via Fremont, passing over a high shoulder of Thousand Lake Mountain; and (4) from State 10-Interstate 70. *See also Tour No. 7B.*

3. SOUTH DISTRICT

The Park's South District is comprised of the long, narrow spine of **Waterpocket Fold** south of Capitol Reef. The Fold here is naked rock, painted in shades of red and white, rising as much as two thousand feet above its eastern base. Its convoluted rock is a tangle of marvelous erosional forms: cliffs and slopes of every degree of incline . . . canyons and chasms . . . buttes and numberless smaller forms.

Wilderness and natural beauty are the appeals of this district, as with the North District. Water must be carried, as well as food and all supplies. Cloistered canyons and slickrock slopes invite the hiker and scrambler.

The area is accessible by fairweather graded dirt road that parallels the eastern base of the Fold between State 24 on the north (9 miles east of the Visitor Center) and Bullfrog Marina on Lake Powell to the south. This road gives access also to the Henry Mountains and Circle Cliffs. Short hikes from the road lead to canyon recesses and undulating slickrock slopes.

Canyons of the Fold range from one to a dozen or more miles in length. The short canyons are suitable for day hikes. Some are extremely narrow in places with overhanging walls, mere slots gouged out of stone. In this southern district, too, are the Park's largest "tanks" or waterpockets . . . natural arches such as Peek-a-boo and Brimhall . . . Red Slide, an impressive product of a recent ice age . . . and notorious **Burr Trail** road, an unpaved switchback route ascending/descending the steep wall of the Fold.

Grand Gulch (Hall's Creek Canyon), which parallels the Fold south of Burr Trail to Lake Powell, is about 30 miles long, a truly wild sanctuary for adventuresome backpackers. **Lower Muley Twist Canyon,** accessible from the top of the Burr Trail, is a favorite hiking route. An exceptionally scenic gorge, the canyon is 12 miles long, but those who hike its full length must walk another five miles to the nearest parking area (plus another four miles back to trailhead). However, those desiring a shorter route may leave the canyon after four miles, hiking about two miles from that point to The Post parking area.

A northern extension of Lower Muley is **Upper Muley Twist Canyon,** which heads a mile west of the former. The first three miles of this narrow, rugged, exotic gorge may be traversed by high-clearance vehicles; the final six miles, however, are for hikers only. A number of natural arches appear along the way. From the end-of-the-road parking area, a primitive trail leads about half a mile through sand and over slickrock slopes to **Strike Valley Overlook** on the crest of the Fold. From this point, a thousand feet or so above the floor of Hall's Creek Valley, the eye sweeps in half-circle overview across the upturned edges of rock layers formed over a hundred million years of oceans, swamps, rivers, lakes, tidal plains, deltas and sandy deserts. Across the eastern horizon, peaks of the Henrys loom high above a colorful, chaotic landscape. The view is one of Utah's choice spectacles.

West of the Muley Twist canyons is **Circle Cliffs,** a giant amphitheater ringed by inward-facing ramparts whose rocks display many brilliant hues. *See Tour No. 9.*

Hickman Bridge, Capitol Reef National Park.

Cedar Breaks National Monument

CEDAR BREAKS NATIONAL MONUMENT

Highway Approaches: 20.4 miles east of Cedar City via State 14 to junction with State 143; 26.8 miles west of Long Valley Junction (on US 89) via State 14 to junction with State 143; or approximately 20 miles south from Parowan on State 143.

Speed Limits: 35 mph maximum within Monument.

Season: Memorial Day to Nov. 1; viewpoints closed by snow in winter and until late spring.

Administrative Offices: Administered jointly with Zion National Park. Address of Superintendent: Cedar Breaks National Monument, Cedar City, Utah 84720. Information at Visitor Center.

Admission: Free.

Medical and Dental Services: Cedar City and Parowan.

Accommodations and Facilities: Public campground with water, fireplaces and restrooms in Monument and at Forest Service camps nearby. Accommodations and services at Cedar City and Parowan; limited selection at Brian Head Resort.

Transportation: No public transportation.

Climate, Clothing, Equipment: Nights cool, days may be warm; sudden temperature changes due to altitude (10,300 feet). Stout hiking shoes and outdoor clothing. Bring camera with extra color film. Binoculars useful.

Communications: Public telephone at Visitor Center.

Recreation: Hiking, fishing nearby. Hunting in season adjacent to Monument. Photography, ranger-naturalist lectures, campfires, self-guided and naturalist-guided trails. Visitor Center with exhibits on plants, animals, geology.

Warnings and Regulations: Usual regulations applying to National Parks and Monuments. Roads from Cedar City and Parowan to the Monument climb more than 4,000 feet in 20 miles; steep switchbacks in places.

Cedar Breaks National Monument, set aside by presidential proclamation in 1933, covers 6,154 acres in the high Markagunt Plateau. It is a vast amphitheater, almost a half-mile deep and two miles from rim to rim, enclosing several semicircular basins. Its walls are furrowed, eroded and broken into massive colored ridges radiating from the center (fitting the western definition of breaks—an abrupt, broken, and deeply eroded canyon or amphitheater), and painted like the wheel of a gigantic circus wagon.

Although Cedar Breaks is cut from the same geological formation as Bryce, it is 2,000 feet higher. The cliffs are white or orange at the top, breaking into deep rose and coral. The Pink Cliffs here have a thickness of nearly 2,000 feet and innumerable warm shades of red predominate. Color, which caused the Indians to name Cedar Breaks, "circle-of-painted-cliffs," is the chief feature of the Monument. It blazes with reds, is sultry with yellows, blinds with sun-reflecting whites, is drenched with molten golds and orange, and in the shadows, as they lengthen toward evening, it is deep purple and cool blue.

In the alpine country surrounding the Breaks is an expansive forest free from underbrush, lush with mountain meadows and grassy parks, streams and lakes where big trout wait. An unpaved but maintained road leads to the summit of volcanic Brian Head, 11,315 feet, highest in the southwestern corner of Utah. From its observation station, a sweeping view encompasses the country surrounding Zion and Bryce, country draining to the Colorado and Great Basin, and reaching out to the seared Nevada desert. Brian Head Resort is nearby. Large Engelmann spruce predominate in the typical timberline forest cover on the rim, which includes fir, limber pine, and bristlecone pine, and farther down the mountain is the white-boled quaking aspen. One large bristlecone on the rim is estimated to be about 1,600 years old. From mid-July to mid-August alpine flowers garland the mountain around the Breaks—penstemon, lupine, bluebells, enormous white starlike columbines, and the vivid blues of fringed gentian and larkspur. Bird life is more common than in other Utah parks and mule deer are often seen.

CEDAR BREAKS ROADS AND VIEWS

The usual entry to Cedar Breaks is by way of Cedar City or Parowan, turning eastward from Interstate Highway 15. It may also be approached by turning west from US 89 at Long Valley Junction and traveling across the high Markagunt Plateau on State 14 (see Tour No. 9). Northward from State 14 on State 143 the road passes through mountain meadows dotted with fir trees and enters Cedar Breaks National Monument, 3 miles from the junction. One mile farther, at **Point Supreme,** is **the Visitor Center.** The public campground is ½ mile from the Visitor Center.

At **Point Supreme,** Cedar Breaks is suddenly and magnificently present. It is hard to tell whether the brilliant coloring of the Breaks or its grotesque sculpturing is the more remarkable. In the former, forty-seven tints have been counted by an artist; and in the latter, though the variety is less astonishing than in Bryce, the formations nevertheless run the gamut from cathedrals to tombstones. For those who gaze into this enormous basin, the physical aspects suggest a multitude of similes. It is surprising to find a natural amphitheater so huge and at the same time so perfect. As one gazes down upon the hundreds of columns and towers, balconies and pinnacles, arches, gateways and standing walls, it is not difficult to pretend that an ancient civilization, with an architectural taste for the Gothic, was once crowded into this huge bowl.

One can fancy that some prehistoric sculptor of gigantic size had his workshop in the Breaks and set out to carve from forty-seven tints in stone. Of insatiable ambition and undirected purpose, he left nothing finished, nor perhaps even fully realized what he was trying to do.

From Point Supreme, the maintained Wasatch Ramparts foot trail leads two miles along the rim toward the west, affording thrilling views into the great amphitheater. The trail passes through forests and open meadows, giving access to a stand of bristlecone pine on Spectra Point.

Two other points of vantage are worthwhile: **Sunset View** at 1.5 m. north of Visitor Center (25-yard walk L. to edge of break), and **Chessmen Overlook** (2 miles further) which involves a walk of 2/5 mile to the rim; a short trail leads also to a stand of bristlecone and limber pine on the ridge.

For the fullest appreciation, the amphitheater should be viewed at sunset, when the thousands of formations stand gloriously desolate in their ruins.

DINOSAUR NATIONAL MONUMENT

Highway Approaches: Quarry Visitor Center is 7 miles north of US 40 and Jensen, Utah, via paved State 149. Monument Headquarters, Superintendent, and entrance to Harpers Corner Scenic Drive, 2 miles east of Dinosaur, Colorado.

Season: Quarry Visitor Center open daily all year (except Thanksgiving, Christmas, and New Year's Day). Backcountry roads are usually closed during winter months (October-November to April) and after heavy rains. Boating is most enjoyable during warmer months from May to September (June-July are ideal). The Yampa can seldom be run after August 1 and may be closed even sooner by low water. Winters are cold, summers fairly hot, spring and fall are cool to warm.

Admission to Quarry: Free.

Administrative Offices: Rangers and information, Quarry Visitor Center, Jensen, Utah 84035. Superintendent and Monument Headquarters, Dinosaur, Colorado 81610.

Accommodations and Services: No lodging or commercial services in Monument. Vernal, Rangely and Craig are nearest communities with comprehensive services, supplies and lodging. Limited services and supplies are available at Jensen, Dinosaur, and smaller communities along US 40. Two improved campgrounds are beside Green River near Quarry Visitor Center: Split Mountain (open all year) and Green River (most spacious and shady).

Transportation: Private car or boat. Bus and air service to Vernal and Craig; bus service to Jensen; Dinosaur, Colorado; and other communities on US 40.

Clothing and Equipment: Wear appropriate sports or outdoor clothing, depending on season *(see above)*. Coat or jacket desirable for evening or high-country wear, even in summer. Wear suitable shoes for hiking. Bring camera and color film. When driving backcountry roads, carry water, spare fuel, spare tire, tools, food, first-aid kit, etc. Boaters are subject to strict requirements regarding equipment.

Medical and Dental Services: Nearest services are at Vernal, 20 m. from Quarry Visitor Center. Also Rangely and Craig.

Dinosaur fossils in relief, Quarry Visitor Center.

UTAH TRAVEL COUNCIL

Recreational Activities: Sightseeing, study of nature and geology, boating, camping, fishing, photography, hiking, scenic touring.

Guides: Boating tour services (guides and boats) available in Vernal. Write Superintendent for list of outfitters.

Warnings and Regulations: Observe all National Park Service regulations within Monument. Permits and campground reservations must be obtained in advance for private boating, which is subject to strict regulations and requirements. Write Superintendent for details.

Dinosaur National Monument is most noted for its rich deposits of fossilized dinosaur bones. In fact, the Monument was originally established and named in recognition of these evidences of ancient life. Its fossils are a national treasure, indeed, and they attract myriad visitors every year to view the Quarry Visitor Center's fascinating exhibits.

Yet the Monument of today includes more than the quarry. First established in 1915, its size was increased in 1938 from the original 80 acres to more than 200,000 acres (326 square miles), incorporating not only the quarry but also a rugged wilderness to the north and east. Here at the east end of the Uinta Mountains, the Green and Yampa rivers have carved splendid canyons. Those of the Green (Lodore, Whirlpool and Split Mountain) are among the deepest and most awesome along its 700-mile length, and they contain some of its most challenging rapids. The Yampa's canyon, though not as deep, is remarkable for sinuosity, delicate coloring, and erosional beauty. Visitors to the Monument may enjoy this canyon scenery not only from bird's-eye viewpoints along the rim, but from water level as well, by boating the rivers. The entire Monument is a geologic spectacle, where weathering, faulting, folding, and uplift have deformed and sculptured the earth's rainbow crust, creating in the process an astonishing landscape.

1. **THE VISITOR CENTER AND QUARRY.** Overlooking Green River where it emerges from the gaping mouth of Split Mountain Gorge, built flush against the tilting ledge where the dinosaur fossils are embedded, is a striking glass structure that completely encloses the face of the dinosaur quarry. Attached to it is a circular building containing offices and information counter. This is the Quarry Visitor Center of the Monument, located 7 miles north of Jensen and US 40 via paved State 149.

The Visitor Center was opened in 1958, in recent years attracting so many visitors that mass transit is required during the summertime from a parking area some distance away. Of most interest, of course, is the quarry itself—a high, long, sloping rectangular sandstone face, which some 140 million years ago was a sandy bar or delta of a Jurassic river. This bar or delta was the burial site for myriad creatures of the time (mostly dinosaurs) whose bodies apparently floated downstream and were collected there. Softer parts disintegrated and skeletal material became buried and preserved in sand. During the ages since then the bar was covered with thousands of feet of younger sediments, the bones gradually being "petrified" or fossilized and the sand turning to rock. Earth movements uplifted and tilted the rock layers, and erosion exposed some of the ancient burial ground to the view of modern-day scientists. For some years after discovery of the deposit in 1909, excavation was carried on by various institutions *(see below)* and thousands of bones were removed. Today, however, the fossil bones are left in place in the ledge as they are uncovered by careful chiseling. Only enough matrix rock is removed to outline each bone in distinct relief, and the result is a fascinating, vivid exhibit of a dinosaur graveyard as it appeared 140 million years ago.

An abundance of interpretive displays complement the quarry face, telling an illustrated story of ancient life and clarifying the monument's geology. Through a window, visitors may watch technicians at work in the laboratory. Attendants are on duty to answer questions, and publications are available for purchase. Open daily all year except Thanksgiving, Christmas and New Year's Day.

The following background information appeared in the 1941 edition:

The region surrounding the quarry is the epitome of barrenness and desolation—a vast waste scarred by innumerable washes and strewn with dingy yellow-gray mounds of disintegrating stone. Isolated buttes rise abruptly out of the valleys, and naked hills hunch against the skyline like silhouettes of prehistoric monsters. South of the quarry the Green River creeps sluggishly across the desert floor toward Desolation Canyon, and to the east a series of broken upturned ledges in pastel shakes of red, gray, and brown merge into the shattered pile of rocks that forms Split Mountain.

Northeastern Utah was not always a desert highland. More than 100 million years ago, probably in the Jurassic period of Mesozoic time, the site of Dinosaur Monument was an area of low relief, where a river with its tributary streams flowed northward through a broad valley. In some places ox-bow lakes and pools green with scum marked abandoned stream channels, and occasional shallow lagoons flooded the valley floor. The waters teemed with crocodiles, fishes, and amphibians, while . . . reeds, ferns, grasses and trees grew in luxuriant profusion. . . . insects swarmed above the marshes; strange [flying] reptiles spread their leathery wings and flapped across the sky. . . . small primitive mammals roamed the higher ground. The Mesozoic era, however, was an age of reptiles. In every favorable habitat throughout the world, the dinosaurs were supreme. They developed in amazing variety, until there were no less than 5,000 distinct species.

In 1908 the Carnegie Museum of Pittsburgh, Pennsylvania, sent Dr. Earl Douglass into the Uintah Basin to search for fossil mammals. During this expedition ranchers called his attention to dinosaur bones protruding from a bluff near the Green River, and the following year he returned to make a systematic search for reptilian fossils. According to a newspaper account, "a ledge of sandstone which contained scattering bones was followed down one side of a canyon or ravine and up the next hill. On arriving at the top of the hill the hunter was startled by seeing a series of articulated joints of a huge animal weathered out in relief on the face of the sandstone ledge." The exposed bones were part of the tail of a large dinosaur, and quarrying operations revealed the [almost] complete skeleton of a brontosaurus.

[From the time of this discovery in August 1909 until 1923 the Carnegie Museum removed from the quarry 350 tons of bones, including parts of 300 dinosaur specimens representing 10 different species. Various institutions, including the Smithsonian and the University of Utah, continued the work. By 1940, 22 complete skeletons and thousands of individual bones had been found in the Monument, representing 10 species of dinosaurs, crocodiles, invertebrate forms, and plants. These fossils were sent to many important museums in the country. In 1924 Dr. Frederick J. Pack, then professor of geology at the University of

Utah, brought 19 wagons loaded with dinosaur fossils to Salt Lake City. As the caravan paused in one of the smaller towns, an inquisitive old woman asked Dr. Pack the age of the bones. When she received an answer in terms of millions of years, she was visibly annoyed. "But that can't be right," she said. "You told me the same thing last year."

The American Museum of Natural History became actively interested in the fossil deposits about 1931, and in 1934 the museum's curator of fossil reptiles, Dr. Barnum Brown, became consulting paleontologist for the Monument. Since 1933, when Dr. A. C. Boyle assumed the duties of custodian and resident geologist, the program of development at the quarry has been under the direction of the National Park Service. In 1934 about 100 transients were employed in cleaning out the old quarry and making various improvements. Between 1936 and 1940 the Monument was developed by WPA labor. After that time, until 1958, little work was done on the quarry face. The new visitor center was opened in 1958, and from that year to the present technicians have exposed nearly 1,450 bones, using only small hammers and chisels to chip away the matrix stone. In addition to other important discoveries during this period, a new species of extinct turtle was found in the late 1960s, and a very young dog-size Stegosaurus was found and mounted in the 1970s.]

Dinosaurs trod the earth for more than a hundred million years during the Triassic, Jurassic and Cretaceous periods of the Mesozoic era. The fossil remains at Dinosaur represent 10 of the dinosaur species that lived during a part of the Jurassic period, about midway through the dinosaur age. Among these were some of the largest and most interesting land animals of which we have knowledge. The quarry has yielded a nearly complete skeleton of the gigantic *Apatosaurus,* commonly known as the *Brontosaurus,* a huge plant eater more than 70 feet long. Even more plentiful have been the bones of *Diplodocus,* a less massive but even longer (84 feet) plant eater resembling the *Apatosaurus* in general form. Most fascinating of all, perhaps—at least to the general public—is the fearsome *Allosaurus,* a large carnivore that walked on two legs and displayed a set of frightful teeth. The remains of this strange creature are rare at Dinosaur but have been found in abundance at the Cleveland-Lloyd Dinosaur Quarry south of Price *(see Tour No. 10B).* Most numerous of all fossils have been those of *Stegosaurus,* the weird armored dinosaur having upright plates along its spine. Among other species represented by the quarry's fossils are *Dryosaurus, Camarasaurus, Barosaurus,* and *Camptosaurus*—altogether the skeletal material of more than 300 individual dinosaurs of 10 different species. The bones of more than 20 skeletons could be assembled as complete specimens after restoration of some missing parts. Models of several of the quarry's dinosaur types are on display at the Dinosaur Museum in Vernal *(see Tour No. 6).*

   2. **THE RIVERS.** Leaving Flaming Gorge National Recreation Area, the **Green River** passes through Browns Park. In Colorado, east of the Utah line, it enters Dinosaur National Monument. For the next 46 miles the river's course is within the Monument, and for most of that distance the river is confined in deep, narrow gorges. Traveling downstream within the Monument, the first and largest of these gorges is the **Canyon of Lodore,** so named by Major Powell's river explorers in 1869 because of its resemblance to poet Robert Southey's "The Cataract of Lodore":

. . . And thumping and plumping and bumping and jumping,
And dashing and flashing and splashing and clashing;
And so never ending, but always descending,
Sounds and motions for ever and ever are blending
All at once and o'er, with a mighty uproar,—
And this way the water comes down at Lodore.

River runners since the time of General Ashley's traverse of the canyon in 1825, when he "was forcibly struck with the gloom which spread over the countenances of my men," would agree with the appropriateness of Southey's description as applied to this stretch of river. Here are the worst rapids along the Green River, and the dark walls rise precipitously from the river for 2,000 to more than 3,000 feet. The canyon extends for about 19 miles, from the Gates of Lodore on the north to the mouth of the Yampa on the south, and for most of this distance it passes through very ancient rocks dating from Precambrian to Permian age—deposits representing a billion years or more. At **Echo Park,** marked by a sheer-walled sandstone monolith known as Steamboat Rock, the Green is joined by the **Yampa,** coming from the east.

The **Yampa,** known in early days as the Bear, heads in the White River Plateau of Colorado more than 100 miles from its confluence with the Green. The lower 46 miles of river are within Dinosaur National Monument. The Yampa's canyon is noted for the beauty and grandeur of its walls, which are colored in pleasing hues of red, gray, tan and white. Since the river's volume is similar to that of the Green, water is usually adequate for an early summer rafting season, and several rapids are severe enough to be dangerous. Geologically the river's terrain is interesting, displaying a number of different rock formations as well as monoclinal folds, erosional curiosities such as hoodoo pinnacles, glens, alcoves, and side canyons. Canyon walls immediately above the river are not as high as those in Lodore, but summits several miles away loom two to three thousand feet higher than the river. In its lower reaches the Yampa's channel is very sinuous, one series of bends requiring seven river miles to traverse an airline distance of only two. Several proposed damsites have been surveyed along the river within the Monument.

Downstream (west) from Echo Park, where the Green and Yampa merge, the combined rivers enter **Whirlpool Canyon.** Though this canyon is only 14 miles long, it is very deep (3,000 feet) with steep walls and exceptional geological exposures in ancient Paleozoic rocks similar to those of Lodore. Exiting from Whirlpool Canyon the river enters an open expanse of parks and islands, known appropriately as **Island Park** and **Rainbow Park,** colored in flamboyant Mesozoic hues and boasting relatively lush vegetation. This has been ranching country for a century or more and displays rustic evidences of long occupation. Here the Green meanders in a leisurely loop before entering Split Mountain Canyon. In the 7½-mile length of this spectacular gorge— which slices in twain the Split Mountain anticline, like a jagged gash from end to end through a loaf of bread—the river drops 147 feet. According to one writer this fast stretch "is the most exhilarating ride on the Green River." Paleozoic rocks form the walls, surmounted by striking erosional forms. At the mouth of the gorge the river slackens its pace and enters the Uinta Basin. Here, near the Quarry Visitor Center, a boat landing and campground have been developed on the west bank.

Boating the Rivers. Both the Green and Yampa within the Monument are extremely popular for boating. Trips of varying length, duration, water conditions, and scenic environment are possible. For example, trips offered by one commercial operator within the monument range from one day to six days. Split Mountain Canyon can be run in one day. The stretch from Echo Park (mouth of the Yampa) to the Split Mountain ramp and campground (26 m.) may occupy two or three days . . . the Green through Lodore to Split Mountain ramp and campground (44 to 61 m.), from four to six days . . . and the Yampa-Green from Lily Park or Deerlodge Park to Split Mountain ramp and campground (72 to 84 m.), from four to six days. These are unhurried schedules, floating with the current, allowing ample time for camping, hiking, swimming, fishing, exploring, and overland travel to put-in point.

Embarkation points within the Monument are located at (1) the **Gates of Lodore** *(ranger station, campground, ramp),* reached by circuitous improved roads from Utah, Colorado or Wyoming . . . (2) **Echo Park** at the mouth of the Yampa *(ranger station, campground, ramp),* reached from the Harpers Corner road . . . (3) **Deerlodge Park** *(ranger station, campground, ramp),* reached by improved road from US 40 in Colorado . . . and (4) **Rainbow Park** (campground, ramp), reached by a dirt road from Vernal or the Quarry area. Many boaters on the Green launch upstream from the Gates of Lodore, in the Flaming Gorge or Browns Park region. Doing this adds up to 45 miles of floating. Yampa boaters may choose to launch upstream at Lily Park instead of at Deerlodge Park, which adds 12 miles of river.

Whether boating with commercial groups or in private parties, boaters within the Monument must observe National Park Service regulations and requirements. These include, for private boaters, the obtaining of boating and camping permits in advance; whitewater boating experience; reliable boats; wearing of life preservers; carrying maps, first-aid kit, etc. Fishing, hunting and firearms regulations must be observed, as well as other park regulations. Information, permits and list of commercial outfitters can be obtained from the Superintendent, Dinosaur National Monument, Dinosaur, Colorado 81610.

3. **SEEING THE MONUMENT BY ROAD.** Though the dinosaur quarry and river canyons attract the majority of visitors to the Monument, a network of backcountry roads surrounds the Monument. Several of these penetrate its boundaries. Only one is paved, however—namely the scenic drive leading from Monument headquarters (2 m. east of Dinosaur, Colorado) to Harpers Corner Viewpoint, 31 m. *(below).* Other fairweather roads lead from Vernal to Rainbow Park and Island Park; to Jones Hole Fish Hatchery, from which a trail leads down-canyon to Green River; and to Browns Park upstream from Lodore Canyon. *See Tour No. 6.* These roads, closed in winter, provide splendid panoramic views and intimate closeups of

the colorful, corrugated Uinta-Dinosaur country. Still other roads, in Colorado, crisscross the heights of Blue Mountain and Douglas Mountain and along Yampa Bench, affording aerial glimpses across the haunting, surrealistic Dinosaur landscape. One of these, the **Harpers Corner Scenic Drive**—for views of sheer sublimity—ranks among the choicest in western America. It is generally open from April to late October, being closed by snow in winter months. The drive climbs more than 2,000 feet from the Monument headquarters on US 40 to the rolling summit of Blue Mountain (Yampa Plateau) at almost 8,000 feet altitude.

There, from several points, the drive looks down into an astonishing labyrinth of serpentine gorges, walled by magnificent cliffs, sculpted from the tumultous waves of massive highlands. The entire landscape is a jumble

Whirlpool Canyon and Green River, looking west from Harpers Corner Viewpoint, Dinosaur National Monument.

WARD ROYLANCE

of tortured rocks, deformed by uplifting, warping, tilting, and faulting, then laid bare and shaped by ages of erosion. Those with a geologic bent will note effects of several major faults in the area, which have offset rock formations by hundreds and thousands of feet. Visible in overview are Island Park, Whirlpool and Split Mountain canyons, the yawning abyss of Lodore, and miles of the sinuous Yampa gorge, sunk in a broad basin beneath Blue Mountain's brow. The climax view is from Harpers Corner itself, a lofty peninsula overlooking the confluence of the Green and Yampa. Great canyons radiate from the point in three directions: Whirlpool to the west, Lodore to the north, and Yampa (Bear) to the east. The Uinta uplift looms to the north and west. Harpers Corner Overlook is reached by a one-mile foot trail from the parking area, which is 31 m. from Monument headquarters.

From the main scenic drive, 6 m. from Harpers Corner, an unpaved road forks east to Echo Park at the confluence of the rivers (13 m.). An official publication describes this road: "The steep 13-mile grade into Echo Park from the Harpers Corner Road is one of the most rewarding back-road experiences. The road descends 2,000 feet through Sand and Pool Creek Canyons, past Indian petroglyphs and Whispering Cave, and into Echo Park, which is dominated by towering Steamboat Rock. There is a shady, primitive campground near the confluence of the Green and Yampa Rivers. *Travel trailers and other heavy vehicles should not be driven into Echo Park or to other remote areas because of sharp curves and steep grades.* In back-country camps, use only dead and down wood for campfires." A branch of this sideroad continues eastward across Yampa Bench, overlooking the inner gorge of Yampa River, connecting with US 40 at Elk Springs, 46 m. from the Scenic Drive junction. Travel on this Yampa Bench road is limited to four-wheel-drive vehicles. Because of soil conditions, *all backcountry roads are impassable when wet.*

PLANTS AND ANIMALS. Dinosaur National Monument resembles life-habitats of the Colorado Plateau to the south, being lower in altitude than the high Uintas to the west and main Rockies to the east. Typical groundcover away from the streams includes sagebrush, greasewood, grasses, shadscale, rabbitbrush, wildflowers, and other small plants. Pygmy evergreens (junipers and pinyon pine) are common at intermediate levels. Higher elevations may support stands of aspen, ponderosa pine, Douglas fir, and mountain mahogany. Where water is available, notably along stream channels, cottonwood, box elder, willow, tamarisk, alder and birch grow in luxuriant profusion. One of the largest trees in Utah, an enormous cottonwod measuring 26 feet in circumference, is found in Island Park on the Ruple Ranch.

According to an official description, "Deer, bobcats, and coyotes are found throughout the Monument. A considerable number of smaller mammals also live here. The rodents are well represented and include beavers, muskrats, porcupines, marmots, prairie dogs, and chipmunks. Two members of the rabbit family, cottontails and white-tailed jackrabbits, are often seen. Other mammals of the monument include mountain sheep (big-horn), badgers, mountain lions, foxes, weasels, minks, skunks, an

UTAH TRAVEL COUNCIL

Boating Green River in
Dinosaur National
Monument.

pack rats. Golden-mantled ground squirrels and whiptail lizards are numerous near the Visitor Center.'' Elk and black bear are seen rarely.

More than 80 species of birds have been recorded, including the wren, robin, warbler, swallow, swift, owl, hawk, magpie, raven, golden and bald eagle, turkey vulture, and the endangered peregrine falcon. Fish are limited in variety within the Monument. Catfish are present in the Green and Yampa. Humpback chub and Colorado squawfish, both listed as endangered species, are rare. Trout may be found in Jones Creek. Many years ago, Colorado squawfish, locally known as Colorado white salmon, reached six feet in length and 80 pounds in weight, but such specimens are rarely if ever noted today.

ANTIQUITIES. The Monument contains numerous archeological sites, ranging from petroglyphs and pictographs on the cliffs to caves, open village sites, rock shelters and chipping grounds. Many of these antiquities originated with the Fremont culture of 800 to 1,000 years ago, while others may date from 2,000 to 7,000 years ago, and still others are of uncertain age and origin. **Cub Creek archeological area,** 8 m. east of the Quarry, contains at least 30 known sites, including ''rockshelters, petroglyph panels, open habitation sites, and chipping stations.'' Ten sites in this district were excavated by the University of Colorado in 1965 and 1966. The **Jones Creek-Ely Creek archeological area,** near the Jones Hole Federal Fish Hatchery, contains campsites, granaries, rock shelters and chipping sites. **Deluge Shelter** in this district is believed to have been occupied as early as 5,000 years B.C., with more than a dozen stratigraphic levels indicating use of the shelter from that early date until the Fremont cultural era of A.D. 1150 or thereabouts. Other sites within the district seem to have been used by Indians as late as historic times, hardly more than a hundred years ago. Near the Island Park road, 19 miles from Vernal, the famed **McKee Springs petroglyphs** extend in a series along the cliff face. Attributed to the Fremont culture, this ancient art is considered to be some of the finest of its type in Utah. **Mantle's Cave** in Castle Park apparently was occupied by agricultural Indians between A.D. 400 and 800. In contrast, **Hells Midden** in the same vicinity seems to have been occupied first by Indians who lived by hunting and gathering, as early as 1500 B.C.

All Monument resources—whether natural or man-made—are protected by law, and therefore no collecting is allowed. Visitors are urged to respect all Monument features as priceless and irreplaceable elements of our national heritage.

Green River downstream from Flaming Gorge Dam.

Flaming Gorge Reservoir. *See also page 147.*

FLAMING GORGE
NATIONAL RECREATION AREA

Highway Approaches:
   From the south - State 44 and State 260 from Vernal and US 40
   From the north - Roads connecting with Green River, Rock Springs and Fort
      Bridger in Wyoming (Interstate Highway 80)

Season and Climate: Dam, visitor center, lake open all year. Four distinct seasons. Most pleasant season for camping and water recreation: May to September. Snow may create highway hazard or inconvenience from late October to March. Fishing permitted on the lake all year; fishing on streams according to state regulations. Most forest campgrounds and some visitor services open only from April-May to September-October. If in doubt, check with national recreation area offices or local chambers of commerce.

Accommodations and Visitor Facilities: Wide selection of lodging and supplies available outside the recreation area, at Vernal (US 40) and Wyoming communities (I-80). Within and near the recreation area, lodging is available at Manila, Flaming Gorge Lodge between the dam and Greendale Junction, Red Canyon Lodge near Red Canyon Visitor Center. Limited supplies and fuel available at Manila, Dutch John, lodges and marinas. Numerous public campgrounds within recreation area and in Ashley National Forest nearby *(see below).*

Fees: Expect to pay fees for camping, marina services, rentals, licenses.

Transportation: Bus and air service to Vernal and Wyoming communities, where rental vehicles may be available. Public airport at Dutch John. Boats, motors, fishing equipment, waterskis may be rented at marinas *(check in advance).* Commercial Green River float trips available.

Clothing and Equipment: Wear outdoor and recreation clothing suitable for season and activity. Carry jacket or sweater for cool nights in summer, warmer clothing at other times. Additional suggestions: sunglasses, sun lotion, chapstick, insect repellent, drinking water, food, maps, first-aid kits, plenty of color film. Boating regulations strictly enforced, including requirements for life preservers, spotters for waterskiing.

Medical and Dental Service: First-aid assistance at marinas or from rangers. Medical and dental service available only at Vernal and larger Wyoming communities. Remember: this is wild, remote country, far from city services. Prepare in advance, insofar as possible, for health needs.

Communications: Telephone service at Manila, Dutch John, lodges, visitor centers.

Warnings and Regulations: Be acquainted with and observe all applicable regulations, including those covering boating safety and camping. Flaming Gorge lake has special hazards such as cold and deep water, sudden strong winds, abrupt dropoffs, steep banks. Carry adequate fuel and supplies including drinking water.

Recreational Activities: Boating, fishing, waterskiing, swimming, sightseeing, camping and picnicking, exploring, hiking and backpacking, nature study, photography.

Naturalist Service and Information: Rangers and information at visitor centers and marinas. Information centers at the dam and Red Canyon Overlook provide seasonal orientation programs, exhibits, guided walks and self-guided tours, interpretive literature. Information also available from offices below.

Offices: Flaming Gorge National Recreation Area is a joint project of National Park Service (Department of the Interior) and U.S. Forest Service (Department of Agriculture) but is managed by the U.S. Forest Service through Ashley National Forest. Address: Supervisor, Ashley National Forest, Vernal, Utah 84078 or District Ranger, Box 157, Dutch John, Utah 84023. Dam operations are supervised by the U.S. Bureau of Reclamation, Box 278, Dutch John, Utah 84023. Rangers are on duty at visitor centers (dam and Red Canyon Overlook), marinas, and boating campgrounds.

Flaming Gorge National Recreation Area, in Utah and Wyoming, is a many-featured playground. Despite its remoteness from large centers of population and its youth (barely 20 years old), the area attracts throngs of visitors every year. The recreation area is centered on Flaming Gorge Lake or Reservoir, a deep, cold, man-made lake formed by Flaming Gorge Dam. The lake fills the entrenched channels of Green River for 91 miles, backing up behind the dam (in Utah) almost to the city of Green River in Wyoming. One of the largest fresh-water lakes in western America, Flaming Gorge Reservoir has an area of more than 66 square miles and a shoreline of 375 miles.

The lake provides a base for varied recreation such as powerboating, waterskiing, swimming and bathing, fishing from boats or shore, camping, and rafting. Furthermore, the terrain which surrounds it—ranging in topography from high forested mountains to semi-arid badlands, is the scene for even more varied activities. These include camping, hiking, hunting, stream fishing, the study of nature and geology, and scenic photography. Green River downstream from the dam flows clear and cold through the depths of Red Canyon, an ideal setting for stream fishing and float-boating. Mountain lakes and tributaries of the Green, within the recreation area, also invite the angler. Last, but hardly least, the entire region is a flamboyant geological exhibit of dramatic erosional features painted in vivid colors. Some of its canyons are indisputably grand, while examples of crustal deformation in the region approach the awesome.

HISTORICAL BACKGROUND. Until the 1950s this northeastern corner of Utah was relatively little known, being isolated and accessible only by rough, unpaved roads. As Don Brooks wrote in the *Salt Lake Tribune* (December 8, 1957), "Here in the great bend of the Green River where the stream sweeps east toward Colorado, Utah's outdoorsmen have supposed fondly that they had one of their last wilderness outposts. It was here . . . that they came in late fall to hunt wild horses, antelope, elk, deer and mountain lions. And each of their trips was linked to Utah's pioneer past, for this country at one time was the wilderness retreat of some of the state's boldest outlaws and some of its most intrepid settlers . . . Even in recent years a trip to this remote part of Utah was not always an easy one."

Fur trappers were in the area by 1825, boating Green River in the spring, then later that same year, on Henrys Fork, holding the first rendezvous of trappers, traders and Indians west of the main Rockies. Major Powell and his two exploring expeditions traveled down the Green in 1869 and again in 1871, applying names to many of its natural features—names by which they are known today. Among these is Flaming Gorge itself.

Soon after leaving the gate of Flaming Gorge, the Powell explorers faced the first of the frightful rapids they were to encounter much of the remaining distance on the rivers. They named Horseshoe Canyon, Kingfisher Creek-Park-Canyon, Beehive Point, Red Canyon, Ashley Falls, and Brown's Park (changing that name from Brown's Hole). Of Red Canyon, Powell wrote "The cliffs on either side are of red sandstone and stretch toward the heavens 2,500 feet. On this side the long, pine-clad slope is surmounted by perpendicular cliffs, with pines on their summits. The wall on the other side is bare rock from the water's edge up 2,000 feet, then slopes back, giving footing to pines and cedar. As the twilight deepens, the rocks grow dark and somber. . . ." He calculated the length of Red Canyon as 26 miles.

Boaters in uncounted numbers followed Powell down Green River in this area during the next 90 years, until dam construction stopped boating traffic in 1958 and replaced the rapids with a blue-green lake hundreds of feet deep. This corner of Utah never has supported more than a few hundred people at a time, agricultural land being scarce. Shortly after Powell's voyages, the few resident old-timers were joined by other settlers in greater numbers who relied primarily on livestock raising for their livelihood. Ranchers came to Browns Park and to Lucerne Valley, the site of Manila and Linwood, Daggett County's only communities before the establishment of Dutch John in 1957. According to the 1941 edition, **MANILA** (6,400 alt. 272 pop.) was

> a clean-swept town in Lucerne Valley, at the base of a flat-topped pink ridge running east and west along the Utah-Wyoming Line. The site was being surveyed in 1898 when Admiral Dewey captured the Philippine capital, and the town was named for that event. When Daggett County was created in 1918, Manila became the smallest county seat in the State. Daggett County, without a felony until 1938, got its first glimpse of a district jurist when Judge P. C. Evans came to Manila to hear an assault case.

Linwood in 1941 was "a group of weathered log buildings on **Henrys Fork,** five miles east of its confluence with the Green River." In its vicinity was held the first rendezvous of American fur traders in the summer of 1825. The site now lies beneath the lake's Lucerne Valley bay.

DUTCH JOHN (6,500 alt. 400 est. pop.), largest community in Daggett County, was born in 1957 and 1958, built by the U.S. Bureau of Reclamation to house officials and workers engaged in construction and operation of Flaming Gorge dam. Within the first year it boasted hundreds of permanent and temporary residences, warehouses, service station, hospital, school, office buildings, sewage disposal system, airport, postoffice, water system—and surrounding the town was a chain link fence to keep out the deer. Its site in a natural clearing was chosen partly because of its proximity to a natural gas line connecting the Four Corners region with the Pacific Northwest. For a time the new town was known informally as Flaming Gorge, the name Dutch John not being adopted until 1958 after a newspaper contest brought scores of name suggestions. (Dutch John was the long-time name of a low mountain to the north.) Months after adoption of the new name, mail was being received at the postoffice with addresses such as Long John, Uncle John, Brother John, or even Dutch Jack. During the peak of dam construction the town's residents numbered in the thousands. Dutch John did not have a direct, convenient road connection with Vernal until Cart Creek bridge was completed in 1959, two years after the town's founding. In the meantime—and even during dam construction—most materials were brought from Green River, Wyoming.

FLAMING GORGE DAM blocks Green River in Red Canyon. The dam is a thin-arch, gracefully tapering concrete structure, its crest rising 455 feet above the riverbed and 502 feet above the lowest point in its foundation. The dam's crest, which carries a two-lane road (State 260), is 1,180 feet in length—many times the 150-foot width of its base. Within the dam are three huge generators, together producing more than 100,000 kilowatts of electricity. The dam and powerhouse may be seen by means of self-guided tours, beginning from a visitor orientation center where information is available.

In 1958 a 30-million dollar prime contract for building of the dam and powerplant shell was awarded to a consortium of major contractors. Earth-moving began that same year, with roads, a thousand-foot diversion tunnel, keyway slots, and coffer dams preceding actual pouring of concrete. Almost a million cubic yards of concrete were used in the dam, poured gradually and steadily over a period of about two years, beginning in 1960. Cement was shipped from Devils Slide, Utah, and mixed on-site with aggregate from the dam vicinity. Water storage began in 1962 and the dam was completed the following year. By 1964 the powerplant was in full operation. Total cost of the Flaming Gorge project exceeded 60 million dollars.

WATER RECREATION. Flaming Gorge Reservoir and the Green River downstream from the dam form the recreation base for the majority of visitors. Fishing, boating, waterskiing, and swimming are the most popular activities. Though the lake no longer provides the phenomenal fish catches of early years, it still remains a productive locale—for trout in particular. Fishing is from shore as well as boats. Downstream from the dam, Green River flows through Red Canyon to Little Hole and Browns Park, a popular stretch for rafting and rod fishing *(no motors allowed)*.

Marinas and launching sites within the Utah section of the recreation area (from north to south): **Lucerne Valley,** accessible from Manila . . . **Antelope Flat,** accessible from Dutch John . . . **Sheep Creek Bay** . . . **Cedar Springs,** south shore near the dam . . . **Mustang Ridge** and **Spillway Boat Ramp,** north shore near the dam . . . **Little Hole,** downstream from the dam *(float boat launching)*. Campgrounds are attached to all of these boating sites except Sheep Creek Bay. Commercial services such as boat rentals, as well as beaches and picnic areas, are provided at the larger marinas. In addition there are boating campgrounds at several sites where launching/take-out are not feasible.

FOREST AND LAND-BASED RECREATION. Within Utah, the national recreation area is almost surrounded by Ashley National Forest. Though the mountainous terrain of this area is not the highest in the Uinta Range, summits do reach 8,000 and 9,000 feet in altitude. Most parts of the forest are heavily wooded with pygmy evergreens at lower levels, larger conifers and aspen in the higher reaches. The federal government has developed more than a dozen non-boating campgrounds in forested areas away from the lake, including several sites along State 260 between Greendale Junction and the dam. Still others are accessible from State 44 and the Sheep Creek loop road. These campgrounds are at altitudes ranging from 6,000 to 8,000 feet; facilities include toilets, tables, firepits, and drinking water. *Visitors are encouraged to obtain detailed maps and information from sources listed above, or from other sources—preferably in advance.*

POINTS OF INTEREST REACHED BY ROAD:

Greendale Junction (7,500 alt.), 39 m. north of Vernal at junction of State 44 and 260. Commercial services. In the Greendale vicinity, as part of a summer home, is one of the oldest log cabins in Utah. Known as "Uncle Jack Robinson's Cabin," the quaint building dates possibly to the 1830s when it was erected by a fur trapper-mountain man on Henrys Fork, a site now inundated by the lake. It was moved and restored by Keith Smith, the present owner. *Listed on state historic register. See Linwood above.*

Red Canyon Visitor Center and Overlook. Providing one of the more spectacular canyon vistas of Utah, this overlook is perched on the south rim of Red Canyon. The canyon is 1,500 feet deep here and the blue lake extends away in two directions. Exhibits of flora and fauna; ranger and information services. Forest Service campgrounds and commercial lodging are nearby. Overlook is 3 m. by paved road from State 44.

Swett Ranch (public) is 1 m. west of Greendale Junction. As described in its national historic register listing, "the Oscar Swett Homestead is a capsule of frontier life . . . operated by horse and man power for nearly sixty years. Most of life's necessities were produced on the ranchland and in the National Forest. The beautiful ranch provides an opportunity to preserve an example of homesteading life so important to America's frontier development and a vivid life example of man learning to live in harmony with nature in order to survive."

Sheep Creek-Hideout Canyon Overview is on State 44, about 9 m. south of Manila.

Sheep Creek Canyon Geological Area (U.S. Forest Service) is reached by loop road from State 44 south of Manila. The area features dramatic palisades in which the strata have been distorted into twisted convolutions by forces that uplifted the Uintas and created "an immense earth fracture, the Uinta Crest Fault." According to an official description, "The earth's crust on the south side of [the fault] was once thrust up over 15,000 feet. Along its northern line, however, there was little vertical movement. Instead the strata [were] bent up like the ruffled pages of a book—pages filled with geologic history. Sheep Creek originates south of the geological area in quartzite uplifts estimated to be 2½ billion years old. Among the canyon's interesting features are Sheep Creek Cave within its west wall, fossils of trilobites, marine crustaceans, gastropods, brachiopods, corals, sponges, and sea urchins—reminders that this land was once a part of the 'briny deep'. Tracks of crocodile-like reptiles are also found in the area, along with petrified wood." Within the area is an improved forest campground and picnic area, with others nearby. The present access road was the route of State 44 before rerouting of the highway at the time Flaming Gorge dam was built.

Boating a side canyon of Lake Powell.

GLEN CANYON
NATIONAL RECREATION AREA

See Tour No. 9B for details about Glen Canyon Dam, Bridge and Page.

Highway Approaches:
South end (Wahweap, Page and Lees Ferry)—US Highways 89 and Alt. 89
North end (Bullfrog, Hite, Hall's Crossing)—Utah Highways 24, 95, 276, 263
Unpaved roads give overland access to Hole-in-the-Rock, Escalante canyons, the Orange Cliffs and other benchland areas above the lake.

Season and Climate: Paved access roads, lodging and boating facilities are open all year. Backcountry roads normally are open all year but may be snowpacked or muddy at times; avoid during inclement weather. Winter temperatures may fall below freezing at night but snowfall is rarely heavy and winter days may be sunny and not too cold. Most pleasant season for boating and water sports: spring, summer and fall (May to October). Winds may be expected from February to September. Annual precipitation totals only 5 inches; wettest months are August and September. The lake's water temperature exceeds 60 degrees from May to November.

Accommodations and Visitor Facilities: Lodging and supplies available at highway access points such as Page, Kanab, Hanksville, Blanding, Green River, Mexican Hat, and at Lake Powell marina-resorts described in text. For marina-resort information, write individual marinas or Lake Powell Resorts & Marinas, P.O. Box 29040, Phoenix, AZ 85038.

Fees: Expect to pay fees for camping, marina services, tours, rentals, etc.

Transportation: Bus and scheduled air service to Page and several other towns in vicinity; consult Utah Travel Council or your travel agent for details. Commercial air, boat and vehicle tours are available from Page, some of the marina-resorts, and other points in lake vicinity; also charters and rentals. Landing strips at all marina-resorts and nearby towns. Several firms offer river boating expeditions from Lees Ferry, Green River, Moab, Bluff, Mexican Hat; inquire from area superintendent or Utah Travel Council.

Clothing and Equipment: Wear outdoor clothing suitable for season and activity. Hats with chin straps advised, especially in summer. Wear appropriate shoes; rubber soles are desirable. Carry jacket or sweater for cool nights in summer; dress warmly in winter. Other suggestions: sunglasses, skin lotion, chapstick, insect repellent, drinking water, food, tools, maps, first aid kits, plenty of color film.

Medical and Dental Service: First-aid assistance at marinas or from rangers. Limited medical and dental services at nearby towns. Remember: this is wild, remote country, far from big-city services. Prepare in advance, insofar as possible, for health needs.

Communications: Telephone, radio mail service at marina-resorts and nearby towns.

Warnings and Regulations: Be acquainted with and observe all applicable regulations, including those covering boating safety and camping. Lake Powell has special hazards such as sudden strong winds, submerged rocks, cold and very deep water, abrupt ledges and dropoffs, rockfalls, sheer-walled banks, and relatively few desirable campsites. Driftwood is a problem in places. Be familiar with these characteristics. Carry adequate fuel and supplies, keeping in mind that supply points are far apart. Do not drink lake water without purification.

Recreational Activities:

Lake Powell - Boating, waterskiing, swimming, fishing, nature study, sight-seeing and photography

Benchlands - Vehicle sightseeing, exploring, hiking and backpacking, camping, photography, nature study

Naturalist Service and Information: Rangers and information at marina-resorts. Official information center at Carl Hayden Visitor Center (Glen Canyon Dam). Campfire programs and interpretive activities at Wahweap.

Administration Office: Superintendent, Glen Canyon National Recreation Area, Box 1507, Page, AZ 86040. Dam operations are supervised by the U.S. Bureau of Reclamation, Box 1477, Page, AZ 86040.

Glen Canyon National Recreation Area, a unit of the National Park Service, comprises about 1,200,000 acres of extremely rugged terrain in southern Utah and northern Arizona. It is by far the largest national park area in Utah and one of the largest in the nation. The recreation area's formal boundaries were established by an act of Congress in 1972, though much of the area had been set aside by executive order in 1958 during construction of Glen Canyon Dam.

Measuring about 150 airline miles from north to south, Glen Canyon National Recreation Area includes within its boundaries all of the main channel of the Colorado River from Canyonlands National Park on the north almost to Grand Canyon National Park on the south. Arms extend far up the San Juan and Escalante river channels. Its northern extremity flanks Canyonlands National Park on the west, incorporating spectacular sections of the Orange Cliffs-Robbers Roost-Green River-Junction country. In actuality the recreation area forms one unit of a huge, integrated complex of national parks and other public lands devoted primarily to recreation. As shown vividly on a map, National Park Service areas alone form an almost unbroken 400-mile chain along the Colorado River system from Arches and Canyonlands national parks on the north through Glen Canyon National Recreation Area to Grand Canyon National Park on the south, with Capitol Reef National Park forming a long and narrow north-western extension.

From a natural and scenic standpoint the area is probably unique in the world, and of national park stature, but as a national recreation area it differs from national parks in that technically it is open to multiple use—that is, mining, grazing and other activities may be permitted. Recreation, however, is the primary use.

The area's central feature is Lake Powell, the great reservoir which backs up behind Glen Canyon Dam for nearly 200 meandering canyon miles. The lake is contained in the labyrinthine basin of the former Colorado River, extending northward from the dam into the lower reaches of Cataract Canyon. Here, over untold centuries, the Colorado and its tributaries incised a maze of profound gorges into solid sandstone, their lower walls perpendicular or overhanging, and often only a few feet apart, flaring out above into a weird realm of rounded fins and domes and knobs, buttes and spires, mesas and skyscraping cliffs. It is a region that ranks among the intricately rugged landscapes of our planet, and because of this corrugated topography the lake's shoreline is ten times as long as the length of its main body, or nearly 2,000 miles.

Glen Canyon, as the river's main channel was named by the Powell expeditions, was noted for 90 years as one of the loveliest of the Colorado's canyons. The river's flow here was relatively unimpeded by rapids. Every bend opened new vistas of natural beauty, of bare red rock sculptured into infinitely varied contours. Scores of side canyons opened into the main channel, most of them narrow and serpentine, containing flowing water only during runoff but harboring oases of vegetation and wildlife. For 70 years or so after the Powell expeditions of 1869 and 1871, only a few hundred boaters and gold miners became familiar with Glen Canyon's remote fastnesses. Then World War II brought the versatile rubber raft and a pervasive desire for adventure, and Glen Canyon—among other segments of the Colorado River system—witnessed an influx of recreation boaters. This heyday of travel through Glen Canyon lasted for little more then a decade, but during that brief period some thousands of modern river travelers experienced the canyon's unique charms. In 1963 water began backing up behind Glen Canyon Dam, gradually changing the free-flowing river to a static reservoir, flooding the maze of size canyons and drowning the myriad riverside beaches.

Today's travelers are fascinated by the strange landscape, but most do not realize that they see only the upper levels. The sheerest cliffs and narrowest chasms, vegetation and Indian antiquities and historical sites, nearly all the secluded grottoes, natural arches and standing rocks, and much of the erosional artistry, now lie mostly beneath the water.

Basically, Lake Powell was a trade-off in values. It is one unit of the Colorado River Storage Project, authorized in 1956, and the material results of this grandiose water and power engineering feat can be seen in the civilizations of southern California, Arizona, Nevada, Utah, Wyoming and Colorado. The recreation area itself is a result—and the lake, which has become a playground for millions, who enjoy what is still visible of the Glen Canyon landscape and do not miss what they never knew. What was lost by the flooding of Glen Canyon (at least temporarily, for the dam and lake will have short lives, even in human time) has been described by numerous writers, including Wallace Stegner in *Holiday Magazine* (May 1966). The best visual treatment of the canyon in its original state is *The Place No One Knew; Glen Canyon on the Colorado* (Sierra Club, 1963-). Edward Abbey, writing in *Slickrock* (Sierra Club, 1971), compared the original canyon with the present lake on the basis of values.

NATURAL SETTING. Glen Canyon and its environs are a part of the Canyonlands subdivision of the Colorado Plateau topographic province. Canyonlands, as its name signifies, is a region of canyons; but the mere name does not indicate the peculiar nature of these canyons, which are distinctive in more than a few respects. The region is a literal maze of entrenched drainage channels, cut into bare rock, and the diverse characteristics of this rock are such that the canyon walls are of every degree of slope but normally perpendicular or near-perpendicular in their lower reaches or as they pass through uplifts. The walls of some canyons may be only a few feet apart; in places it is not possible to squeeze between them, and they may overhang to block the sky from view. Only in their shallow upper reaches, or at their mouth, or where there might be a rare break in the rampart, is it possible to leave or enter some of these gorges, which may be cut a thousand feet deep into massive rock.

Most rocks of the recreation area were laid down during the Jurassic and Triassic periods of the Mesozoic era, dating about 150 to 225 million years ago. These form the walls of the major canyons and the lower benchlands throughout most of the area. To the north and south, even older rocks have been exposed. Younger rocks form the grand cliffs and mesas to the west, such as those in the Kaiparowits Plateau and Henry Mountains region. Relatively young igneous rocks cap the nearby High Plateaus, and igneous upwellings created the Henry Mountains during more recent Cretaceous and Tertiary times.

The immediate shoreline of Lake Powell for most of its length—the sheer cliffs of massive sandstone so notable for erosional tapestry and picturesque streaking of desert varnish, exhibiting rounded domes and mounds on their upper levels—is formed by Navajo sandstone of early Jurassic age. Navajo sandstone, for the most part, was laid down as dune sand in ancient deserts; its great thickness (hundreds, even thousands of feet), and the fact it is present throughout a vast region today, indicate the widespread, long-lasting nature of the original desert—which, incidentally, gave way at last to encroaching water. Because of its rich coloring (near-white to shades of red), the beauty of its textural designs, and its pleasing erosional personality of rounded contours and sheer cliffs, the Navajo is one of the region's most striking rock formations.

Lake Powell's maximum surface level is 3,700 feet above sea level or some 500 feet above the original river channel at Glen Canyon Dam. The lake is shallowest in Cataract Canyon. Topographic relief in the recreation area and nearby is extreme, varying from an altitude of about 3,000 feet at Lees Ferry to more than 10,000 feet in Navajo Mountain and the Henry Mountains. Changes in elevation are often very abrupt since cliff-faces mark the boundaries of canyons, plateaus, mesas and buttes. In general, the benchlands immediately surrounding the lake range from 4,500 to 6,000 feet in altitude.

Climate - Climatically the region is temperate and semi-arid, with well defined seasons. In the lake area, precipitation totals only 5 inches annually; a third of this falls in August and September as rain showers. The temperature range is great between seasons, and even between daytime and nighttime. Between late October and March there may be freezing temperatures at night. Daytime temperatures may reach more than 100 degrees in mid-summer (July and August), and the heat is stored and amplified by the rocks. Lake Powell modifies local weather to some extent with its water: that is, humidity in the lake area is somewhat higher than usual for this country, and the lake's water temperature does not fluctuate as air temperature does. Lake water ranges from about 45 degrees in January (coldest month) to 80 degrees in July and August, the hottest period.

Aerial view of lower Glen Canyon in 1968, showing Lake Powell at an intermediate level. Glen Canyon National Recreation Area.

Hikers in Davis Canyon, a tributary of the Escalante. Glen Canyon National Recreation Area.

Plants and Animals - Though Lake Powell is fairly rich in fish, its immediate shoreline is not a favorable habitat for vegetation or wildlife because of water fluctuations and lack of soil. Plants and animals are more likely to occur beyond the lake in the upper ends of canyons, on the benchlands and highlands. Aridity and scant soil do not make the recreation area an inviting terrain for organic life except in the case of relatively few specialized types. Pygmy evergreens (pinyon pine and juniper) are the most common trees of the region, forming an almost luxuriant cover in places. Where sufficient water is present along streambeds, cottonwoods, willows and tamarisk flourish. Cacti, wildflowers, grasses and small shrubs are fairly abundant. Animals include mule deer, bighorn sheep, antelope, coyote, badger, beaver, rodents, snakes, frogs and toads, insects and other creatures. Many of these are not likely to be seen or heard, but flies and stinging "gnats" can be troublesome and rattlesnakes, though rare, warrant caution. A herd of bison ranges the slopes of the Henry Mountains.

HISTORICAL BACKGROUND. Before dam construction began in the late 1950s, the Glen Canyon area had very few permanent inhabitants during historic times. It was too remote, too rugged, and agricultural lands too limited to attract settlers. Therefore the area's human background during historic times consists of relatively few episodes—but some of these were of epic dimensions, romantic and significant chapters in the history of the West.

Whites did not enter the region until 1776 *(see below)*. Prior to that time it was the domain of Utes, Navajos and Paiutes—perhaps a no-man's land —and before that, until about 1300 A.D., the home of Anasazi and Fremont Pueblo Indians. Archeologists from the University of Utah and Museum of Northern Arizona surveyed the Glen Canyon area over a period of years, beginning in 1956 under auspices of the National Park Service, studying and salvaging as many antiquities as possible before they were flooded by Lake Powell. They found that Pueblo Indians had used the area for centuries, leaving hundreds of structures (most of them small storage granaries) in every likely location, and marking their passage with "writings" on the rocks. Whether there ever had been communities of any size is conjectural; no remains of such were found away from the bottomlands, and if built along streamcourses they had long since washed away. Today most evidences of ancient occupation are beneath the lake.

This is the case with fabled Crossing of the Fathers (El Vado de los Padres). This ford of the Colorado River apparently had been used from time immemorial by Utes, Paiutes and Navajos—perhaps even by the Ancient Ones. Mormon settlers knew of it and called it the Old Ute Crossing. Jacob Hamblin, noted Mormon missionary to the Indians, crossed there in the 1850s and 1860s, and the ford as well as the country in which it was situated were well described by Edwin G. Woolley, adjutant of a Mormon militia party in pursuit of marauding Navajo Indians in the spring of 1869, several months before the first river appearance of Major Powell:

> . . . If the deserts of Arabia or Africa are any worse than this place we don't think we should like traveling in those countries . . . Whichever way we look we see red or white sand-stone mountains, except the slight glimpse of the Buckskin Mountains [Kaibab Plateau], and directly ahead, seeming close at hand, is the

snow covered Spanish Shank Mountain [Navajo Mountain], towering above all the other . . . Whichever way we look there is nothing but rock mountains, in fascinating shapes. It is rock around, rocks above, rocks beneath, rocks in chasms, rocks in towers, rocks in ridges, rocks everywhere; it is, in fact, all rock; what little sand there may be is decomposed rock. *(Woolley's journal, annotated by C. Gregory Crampton and David E. Miller, appears in UTAH HISTORICAL QUARTERLY XXIX April 1961.)*

But the Mormons had been preceded across the ford by the Dominguez-Escalante party from New Mexico, the first whites in Utah *(see History)*. Here at Glen Canyon in October and November 1776, this small group of explorers encountered the most formidable natural barrier on their entire journey. They had been informed of the ford by Indians, but like the Woolley party 93 years later they had difficulty locating it. After abortive attempts to cross the river at the mouth of the Paria (Lees Ferry), they spent anxious days exploring the broken country to the north. Finally on November 7 they succeeded in crossing the river at the ford which they called La Purisima Concepcion de la Virgen Santisima. Today it lies under more than 400 feet of water, marked by an imposing complex of landmark buttes.

The ford was used by New Mexicans in ensuing years until a new route (the Spanish Trail) was established to the north, and it was utilized by Jacob Hamblin and other Mormon missionaries before the first ferryboat was built at Lees Ferry in 1869. Thereafter it fell into disuse, Lees Ferry being the only Colorado River crossing for hundreds of miles until Marble Canyon bridge was opened nearby in 1929.

It is doubtful whether whites explored the entire length of Glen Canyon before 1869, when Major Powell's first exploring expedition passed through. This was a reconnaissance survey, and not until the second more scientific Powell expeditions of 1871-72 were formal maps drafted and numerous topographic names applied. It was the Powell survey which gave the name Glen Canyon, as described in Powell's report of 1875 entitled *The Exploration of the Colorado River*. The Powell survey also applied formal names to such area features as the Henry Mountains, Dirty Devil (Fremont) River, Orange Cliffs, Land of Standing Rocks, Cataract Canyon, Kaiparowits Plateau, and Escalante River.

More years elapsed before the canyon above Lees Ferry reverberated to the sound of human voices. In the winter of 1879-80 a large party of Mormon pioneers made an epic crossing of the river at Hole-in-the Rock, a slot in the cliff several miles south of the Escalante's mouth. This party established a settlement at Bluff in the state's southeastern corner *(see Tours No. 9 and 11)*, and for some years afterward there were fordings of the river at Hole-in-the-Rock and Hall's Crossing farther upstream. Neither of these crossings was ideal, however, and they were largely superseded by Dandy Crossing (Hite). Dandy Crossing *(see Tour No. 7B)* was founded by a prospector-gold miner named Cass Hite, whose findings of placer gold in Glen Canyon sparked a "rush" that involved some hundreds of miners between the mid-1880s and turn of the century—not only in Glen Canyon but also in the Henry Mountains and along the San Juan River. Heavy machinery was set up in Glen Canyon and that of the San Juan. Though herculean efforts were expended and some gold was found, the region never became a major gold producer.

These episodes and others are vividly portrayed by Dr. C. Gregory Crampton in *Standing Up Country* (Alfred A. Knopf and University of Utah Press 1964), the most comprehensive treatment of the Glen Canyon area.

Major Powell's expeditions were followed by a legion of adventurers and visionaries: Frank M. Brown and Robert B. Stanton, the Kolb brothers, Nate Galloway, Julius Stone, E. C. LaRue and government engineers and mappers, Bert Loper, Norman Nevills and others. Glen Canyon was only one segment of the entire river system, a gentle and lovely interlude between rapids, but during the 15 years or so before Lake Powell came into being it attracted many more boaters than other stretches of the river. Individually or in groups led by professional guides, thousands passed through the canyon to sample its natural and historical treasures. River guides moved on after Lake Powell came—to the rapids of the Green and upper Colorado, Cataract Canyon, Marble and Grand canyons, the San Juan River. Many were native Utahns, fascinated by the canyons, and through them thousands experienced Glen Canyon in its pristine state.

The uranium years of the 1940s and 1950s brought a network of fair-weather dirt roads (many of them now washed out), which opened the region to vehicle access. Key highways have been improved. Lake Powell, helicopters and small planes have made access much easier. Still, foot travel remains the only feasible means of becoming intimately familiar with much of the area. Despite the hordes of boat visitors and machine-borne sightseers, large parts of Glen Canyon National Recreation Area continue to be wild, a sanctuary for those willing and able to leave the beaten path.

LAKE POWELL AND WATER SPORTS

Lake Powell is one of the world's largest man-made reservoirs, with a seemingly endless shoreline and scores of intriguing side canyons that invite exploration. Hence its popularity with the vacationing public, who number several million every year.

The National Park Service has long planned numerous marina developments along the lakeshore. At this writing, only half a dozen or so are in operation, lack of funding having prevented the construction of more. The National Park Service provides public campgrounds, launching ramps and docking facilities, ranger and information services. Concessionaires operate stores, rentals, tours, lodging and eating facilities, and marina services. For rates, reservations and information contact individual marinas or Lake Powell Resorts and Marinas, P.O. Box 29040, Phoenix, Arizona 85038.

Marinas are located along the lake at approximately 50-mile intervals. All except Rainbow Bridge are land-based marinas accessible by paved highway; Rainbow Bridge is a floating facility of modest size. Generally speaking, each marina has certain advantages and disadvantages: for example, the northern marinas offer easier access from Utah's metropolitan areas, Colorado, the East and Midwest, northern California and the Pacific Northwest; Wahweap offers the most complete and varied facilities and services, and is closest to southern California, Las Vegas and Arizona. The southern lake is deeper and more expansive than the northern, which is relatively confined between high walls, but every section is scenically dramatic. A map should be consulted to determine which marina is nearest to specific points of interest.

MARINA DESCRIPTIONS FROM NORTH TO SOUTH ALONG THE LAKE *(see also Tours No. 9B and 7B)*

Hite Marina (address Hanksville, Utah 84734) reached via Utah Highway 95. East side of lake, several miles south of U95 and about 40 miles north of Bullfrog-Hall's Crossing. Houseboat and powerboat rentals, boat docking and storage, equipment and boat rentals, fishing charters, store, boat fuel and service, airstrip. Public campground and launch ramp. Hite Marina gives easiest access to lower Cataract and Narrows canyons, Dirty Devil canyon, White and Red canyons, and others in the Henry Mountains area.

Hall's Crossing Marina (Address Blanding, Utah 84511) reached via Utah Highways 95 and 263. East side of lake, 82 miles from Blanding, two miles from Bullfrog Marina across the lake. Boat and equipment rentals, boat tours and fishing charters, store and restaurant, boat fuel and service, docking and storage, airstrip. Public campground and launch ramp. Hall's Crossing Marina is the east-side equivalent of Bullfrog Marina with respect to point-of-interest access. The marinas are only two miles apart by water, 160 miles or so by road.

Bullfrog Marina and Resort (Address Hanksville, Utah 84734), 72 miles south of Hanksville via Utah Highways 95 and 276. Bullfrog is on the west side of the lake and in size is next to Wahweap, about 100 miles to the south. In some respects the site of Bullfrog-Hall's Crossing is more advantageous than that of Wahweap: being closer to the center of the lake, and equidistant from or closer to major points of interest, they are more convenient bases for exploration. For example, Bullfrog-Hall's Crossing are 35 miles from the mouth of the Escalante compared with Wahweap's 67; 44 miles from the San Juan (Wahweap is 58); and Rainbow Bridge lies almost exactly halfway between the sites.

Rainbow Bridge Marina (address c/o Wahweap Marina) is a modest floating facility near Rainbow Bridge, about 50 miles from either Wahweap or Bullfrog-Hall's Crossing. Limited services and supplies including fuel, store, restrooms.

Wahweap Marina (P.O. Box 1597, Page, Arizona 86040). *See also Tour No. 9B.* Overlooking Wahweap Bay, several miles from the dam. Accessible by US 89; scheduled bus and air service to Page. Commercial lodge and motel, dining, camper and trailer village, golf and tennis courts, houseboat and powerboat rentals, boat docking and storage, equipment rentals, fishing guides, scenic boat-vehicle-air tours, boat charter service, landing strip. Public campground and boat launch ramp, drinking water and toilets. Public campground at Wahweap fills early on summer and holiday weekends.

Wahweap Marina is about 100 miles from Bullfrog, 51 miles from Rainbow Bridge, 58 miles from San Juan River arm, and 67 miles from Escalante River arm.

Lees Ferry, on the Colorado River below the damsite, is the point of embarkation for boating expeditions through Marble Canyon and Grand Canyon. Boating facilities, ranger, campground; store and restaurant nearby. Write Superintendent of GCNRA for details.

WATER SPORTS

Boating, of course, is the most popular activity on Lake Powell. Thousands of private boats—powerboats, sailboats and houseboats—ply the lake. Houseboats, powerboats and fishing boats may be rented at the larger marinas. Many visitors take advantage of various sightseeing tours offered at several of the marinas. Some of these are combination tours involving boat, jeep and airplane.

Boating is hardly separable on Lake Powell from waterskiing and swimming. The lake is ideal for these activities. Many boaters spend more than one day on the lake, and in such cases camping and hiking are likely to be involved.

Fishing ranks next to boating and sightseeing in popularity. Lake Powell is renowned for its bass and catfish, some of large size, as well as walleye pike, brown and rainbow trout, northern pike and kokanee salmon. The river below Lees Ferry, with cooler water temperature than the lake's, yields large rainbow trout.

HIKING AND VEHICLE EXPLORING

Because Lake Powell is the heart of the recreation area, boating involves by far the majority of visitors. Nevertheless, parts of the area are suited only for land activities such as hiking, backpacking and vehicle exploring.

For example, the Escalante River canyon system is one of the most popular wilderness hiking areas in Utah. In the lower system, flooded by the lake, boaters may disembark and hike the main Escalante and side canyons. Land-based visitors approach the canyons from the town of Escalante *(see Tour No. 9C).* This magnificent system of entrenched meanders somewhat resembles the original Glen Canyon in physical characteristics, being a labyrinth of narrow gorges with vertical or overhanging walls, hundreds of feet deep near the main canyon. There are remarkable natural arches and bridges, and Indian antiquities, but of perhaps greatest appeal are the rare wilderness attributes of the canyons.

Not so well known is the recreation area's northern extension, which adjoins Canyonlands National Park on the west. Access to this remote region is by unpaved road from State 24 north of Hanksville, or south on another unpaved road from Green River. This part of the recreation area embraces a good deal of the fabled Robbers Roost country of Butch Cassidy fame and broken rimrock overlooking the fantastic Junction country. High points atop the vertical Orange Cliffs in this area provide some of western America's sublimest panoramas. *(See Tour No. 7B and Canyonlands National Park.)*

GOLDEN SPIKE NATIONAL HISTORIC SITE

Highway Approach: Visitor Center at Promontory Summit is 32 miles west of Brigham City via State Highway 83 and paved sideroad, or 32 miles west of Tremonton via State Highways 102-83 and paved sideroad.

Season: Visitor Center open daily all year. Locomotives on display daily May through September.

Administrative Office: At Promontory Summit. Address: Golden Spike National Historic Site, P.O. Box 394, Brigham City, Utah 84302.

Information: Visitor Center at Promontory Summit. Exhibits, information and publications, audiovisual program.

Accommodations and Facilities: Accommodations and services at Brigham City or Tremonton. Restrooms and drinking water at Visitor Center.

Communications: Telephone at Visitor Center.

Climate: Elevation of Promontory Summit is 4,900 feet. Climate is relatively arid with few rainshowers in warmer months and sparse snowfall in winter. Warm days, cool nights between mid-May and mid-October; cool or cold days and nights generally prevail at other times. The Historical Site is noted for strong winds.

Recreation: Viewing historic exhibits and authentic locomotive replicas; touring historic railroad sites; witnessing commemorative ceremonies.

Warnings and Regulations: National Park Service regulations apply. Do not damage property, carve initials, or remove artifacts, plants or other objects. Observe speed limits and drive carefully, especially along the old railroad grade. Fires are not permitted.

Golden Spike National Historic Site was authorized by Congress in 1965 to commemorate the spot where the nation's first transcontinental railroad was completed on May 10, 1869. Containing 2,200 acres, the Historic Site features a Visitor Center-Museum, working/operational replicas of the two steam locomotives involved in the Golden Spike ceremony of 1869, and approximately 15 miles of the old railroad right-of-way. The locomotives travel between an enginehouse and the Visitor Center, utilizing about 1.7 miles of track laid on the original railbed.

The story of the building of the transcontinental railroad and the driving of the Golden Spike at Promontory was told in the 1941 edition. A part of this account appears below. "Promontory had enjoyed its hour of glory," wrote Robert M. Utley in *Golden Spike* (National Park Service 1976), "but the town did not immediately die. The two companies [Union Pacific and Central Pacific] did not agree on a price for the Promontory-Ogden section until November 1869. For nearly a year Promontory served as the terminus, where passengers transferred from one railroad to the other. . . ." Utley's account continued as follows:

During the months that it served as the terminus, Promontory resembled the other boomtowns that had followed the Union Pacific across the country. A string of boxcars on a siding provided offices and living quarters for railroad employees. A row of tents, many with false board fronts, faced the railroad across a single dirt street. They housed hotels, lunch counters, saloons, gambling dens, a few stores and shops, and the nests of the "soiled doves." . . . Liquor sales boomed. Water was scarce. The nearest source was 6 miles away, and the railroads were forced to haul long strings of tank cars full of water to Promontory from springs 30 to 50 miles distant. . . . Promontory's life as a "hell on wheels" boomtown was a short but lively one. J. H. Beadle, editor of the *Utah Daily Reporter,* summed up its character when he wrote: ". . . it certainly was, for its size, morally nearest to the infernal regions of any town on the road!"

They drove the Spike and then they left.
The armies marched away.
A town grew up, a sickly thing,
Of gamblers, bars, and "doves."
For half a year the changing point,
And then it slowly died.

After the terminus was transferred to Ogden in early 1870, the Central Pacific built a station, water tank, and roundhouse for helper engines at Promontory. "Dry farming and successful artesian wells dug in the last years of the century revivified the region," said the 1941 edition, "but completion of the Lucin Cutoff across Great Salt Lake in [1904] robbed the town almost completely of its railroad importance. The Southern Pacific, successor to the C. P., for many years ran a weekly train along the old Golden Spike route. . . ." The company announced abandonment of regu-

Replicas of the Jupiter and No. 119 on display at the Visitor Center.

UTAH TRAVEL COUNCIL

larly scheduled train service in April 1940. Two years later, in 1942, during World War II, the 123 miles of rail between Corinne and Lucin were taken up and relaid at military depots in Utah and Nevada. This "Undriving of the Golden Spike" was described in the *Utah Historical Quarterly* (Winter 1969), a comprehensive issue devoted to the history of the transcontinental railroad. Southern Pacific Railroad erected a monument at Promontory in 1919, the half-century anniversary of the original Golden Spike driving. This monument served as the principal reminder of the site's historical significance until the Visitor Center was completed in 1969, Promontory's centennial year.

The centennial observance was marked by festivities in Utah communities and a ceremonial reenactment at Promontory attended by at least 12,000 visitors, many of whom came from other states. Since the original locomotives—Union Pacific's *No. 119* and Central Pacific's *Jupiter*—no longer existed, locomotives of contemporary vintage were borrowed from sources in Nevada and California, modified to resemble the originals, and transported to Promontory for the 1969 ceremonies. Two other engines were substituted for these during the years 1970 through 1978. Authentic working replicas of *No. 119* and *Jupiter,* the result of painstaking research and hand-crafting, were built in California between 1975 and 1979, then transported to Promontory by truck in that latter year. Costing nearly two million dollars, these replicas are on display and running at the Visitor Center during summer months.

ACTIVITIES AND EVENTS AT THE HISTORIC SITE

Events at the Historic Site include an annual reenactment of the Driving of the Last Spike on May 10, and an annual Railroader's Day in August. Developments are ongoing. In addition to interpretive signs, exhibits, films, and talks about the transcontinental railroad and steam locomotives, the Historic Site offers a self-guided tour along "The Promontory Trail." The trail is a 15-mile section of the original roadbed, along which can be seen impressive rock cuts, fills, grades, overlapping parallel grades of the two railroads, box culverts, and the area where Central Pacific workers laid ten miles of track in one day to set an unequalled record.

THE TRANSCONTINENTAL RAILROAD (excerpted from the 1941 edition)

On May 10, 1869, the golden spike ceremony marking completion of the road was held at Promontory. . . . That cold, sunny May day closed a spectacular chapter in American history. The Forty-Niners who crossed the continent the hard way, on foot, or horseback, astride tough, stringy mules, or behind the powerful shoulders of yoked oxen, set up an immediate clamor for a railroad. To that "golden-browed" demand the Federal government hearkened as it never had to the importunities of Asa Whitney, who between 1840 and 1850 haunted Washington with his plans for a Pacific railroad. Surveying parties were dispatched into the field, and the American West for a decade was criss-crossed by the tireless feet of topographical engineers. More than a commercial convenience, the Pacific Railroad was regarded as a military necessity, to bind the Pacific Coast to the Union. Construction work was kept at a standstill until outbreak of the Civil War by quarrels over the respective advantages of northern and southern routes, but Congress, in July, 1862, passed the Pacific Railroad Act, authorizing the Forty-Second Parallel route, to be subsidized by the Federal government. Builders were promised a right of way through the public domain; cash subsidies of $16,000 a mile on the plains and from $32,000 to $48,000 a mile through the mountains; free use of building materials from public lands; and every alternate, odd-numbered section of public land, checker-board fashion for 20 miles back on each side of the tracks.

The Union Pacific, in the East, and the Central Pacific, in California, organized to undertake the work. The C. P. bogged down in a morass of small difficulties and snaked its way eastward only by such stratagems as "moving" the Sierra Nevada twenty-five miles west to hasten the increase in bonus, while the U. P. drove a few rails west of Omaha and discontentedly wasted the months in search of more thorough ways to milk Congress. Despite new railroad legislation, the Pacific Rail-road until 1866 dragged out a miserable visionary existence. In that year, however, the U. P. rails began to move. Location parties, with a wary eye for Sioux scalp-hunters, marked the path, followed quickly by brawny construction gangs, which graded a hundred miles or more at a crack. Transportation problems were enor-mous. Supplies for a force amounting sometimes to 10,000 animals and as many humans had to be brought all the way from Omaha. . . .

The railroads were racing for wealth. In 1862 Congress had fixed the junction point at the California State line; in 1864 the junction was moved 150 miles east; in 1866, getting the spirit of the thing, Congress provided that the railroads might build until they met. Cash subsidies for every completed mile of track were an immediate windfall, and the land grants were of incalculable value. The Union Pacific graded as far west as Humboldt Wells, in central Nevada, while the Central Pacific graded as far east as Echo, Utah. At many points the two grades ran side by side. . . . Through the early spring of 1869, it began to look as though the Union Pacific had settled upon San Francisco as its terminus, while the Central Pacific seemed enamored of the Missouri River. Congress settled the argument in April, fixing Promontory as the point of junction. Tracklaying was finished May 2, and the stage was set for driving the final spikes. Special trains set out from east and west; the first, from California, arrived May 7 to find that the ceremony must be delayed some days; the dignitaries frowned out the train windows upon Promontory, "drenched and forlorn in a driving rain, its sodden streets an extensive mudhole, colored bunting hanging limp and dripping across the facades of its wooden shacks." Held up by floods, the U. P. special train did not arrive until Monday, May 10. . . .

For hours, in an icy wind, the celebrants waited. Two magnificent special trains were to have arrived from east and west to touch iron noses. Instead, battered con-struction trains rolled in loaded to bursting with pop-eyed graders, track-layers, and teamsters. The morning went by; noon passed, and the early afternoon hours—where was the Union Pacific special? Strong words began to pass among the on-lookers. At last the screech of the Union Pacific whistle was heard, and the special rolled into Promontory to the sound of ironical cheers. Out of it piled U. P. officials and guests, several companies of the 21st Infantry, and the Camp Douglas regi-mental band. The soldiers were mustered as police to force some semblance of order upon the crowd. A more motley five hundred than the Golden Spike audience could hardly have been gathered. . . .

Special ties and spikes had been prepared for the ceremony. A Nevada represen-tative presented a silver spike; from Arizona came a spike "ribbed with iron, clad in silver, and crowned with gold"; from Idaho and Montana, spikes of gold and silver. Most important of the ceremonial spikes was the "gold spike"—in reality not one spike but two, presented by David Hewes of San Francisco. While a nation listened, the telegraph operator tapped out the tale of proceedings. "We have got done pray-ing," he presently reported; "the spike is about to be presented." For an hour spikes were presented and received while the crowd shifted from one collective foot to the other. The spike driving, into a polished tie of California laurel, commenced at last.

Lest the spikes be flattened out by some honest blow, holes had been bored to receive the fabulous nails; for almost an hour distinguished guests hammered away with a silver maul. Finally the gold spike was placed, a telegraph line attached to it, and another to the silver hammer, so that the actual blows might ring out telegraphically to the nation. California's Governor Leland Stanford raised his hammer and swung a mighty blow. He missed the spike entirely, but the telegraph operator, a man of practical foresight, simulated the blow with his key and let tumult loose upon the cities of the country; fire bells, cannon, and factory whistles joined with the shouting human voices to signalize the linkage of a continent. At Promontory the two locomotives gingerly nozed their cowcatchers together. To the world the telegrapher tapped out a lean and beautiful message:

> The last rail is laid.
> The last spike is driven.
> The Pacific railroad is finished.

Stanford, Dodge, and the other dignitaries clambered into the Central Pacific special trains where, as Dodge records, "many speeches were made."

Behind the Union Pacific engine at Promontory lay 1,085.5 miles of track; behind the Central Pacific "iron horse" lay 690 miles. To bring its rails from Omaha to Promontory had cost the Union Pacific $90,000,000; with much the harder job in crossing the Sierras, it had cost the Central Pacific $75,000,000 to come from Sacramento to the junction. . . .

Golden Spike Ceremony, May 10, 1869.

F. A. BARNES

Ruin in Hovenweep National Monument.

HOVENWEEP NATIONAL MONUMENT

Highway Approach: From Utah—Turn east from US 163 at junction between Blanding and Bluff, drive 8 miles on paved State 262, then 15 to 20 miles on fair-weather dirt road to ruins in Monument. From Colorado—drive 40-odd miles west from Cortez on unnumbered gravel and dirt road. The Colorado approach road is better, but inquire at Mesa Verde National Park (303) 529-4469 as to road conditions.

Season: All year. Best in spring or fall.

Administrative Office: Superintendent, Mesa Verde National Park, Mesa Verde, Colorado 81330.

Admission: Free.

Accommodations: Campground at Monument. Rooms and meals at Cortez, Colorado; and at Bluff and Blanding, Utah.

Transportation: Private automobile only.

Climate, Clothing, and Equipment: Altitude at Hovenweep is about 5,000 feet. Nights are usually cool and days are hot during summer months. Wear light outdoor clothing in summer, and rugged shoes, with coat for summer evenings and colder months. Carry drinking water and suitable equipment for camping and hiking.

Warnings and Regulations: Usual regulations applying to national parks and monuments. Do not remove artifacts or vandalize dwellings. All trails are self-guided. To see all dwellings in Hovenweep requires at least a full day and a hike of about 12 miles.

Hovenweep National Monument, in the remote canyon country north of the San Juan River, straddling the Colorado-Utah line, was established by presidential proclamation in 1923 to extend Park Service protection to the ruins of a numerous prehistoric civilization. The reserve, though small—it is no larger than a middle-size farm by desert standards—contains four separate groups of buildings, perhaps suburbs of a single city, among which are several towers that are of great interest to archeologists. The Monument includes four large and several tributary canyons in the mesa between Montezuma and McElmo creeks, the principal ruins being in Ruin and Cajon canyons in Utah, and Hackberry and Keeley canyons in Colorado. Sage Plain, the mesa into which the canyons at Hovenweep are cut, is horizon-wide in all directions, broken only by the blue Abajos and the distant La Sal Mountains northward. Over it, sage grows everywhere, sometimes in thick stands from three to five feet high, interspersed with pinyon and scattered juniper. In the canyons, especially in those with springs, there are small parks, patches of meadow, and growths of cottonwood trees. It is difficult for many to believe that Hovenweep once supported a large population. Old-timers, however, point out that "Hovenweep" in the Ute Indian tongue (the "o" is long, as in "over") means "deserted valley," and often add "no wonder."

Padres Escalante and Dominguez passed by the region of the Hovenweep dwellings in 1776, discovered one ruin in what is now southwestern Colorado, damned it with a passing reference, and left it for W. H. Holmes and W. H. Jackson of the Hayden expedition to rediscover, together with others on McElmo Creek, an even century later. In 1879, Peter Shirts, a roving trapper who by repute had more experiences than furs at season's end, was camped at the mouth of Montezuma Creek, and a family named Mitchell was living at the mouth of McElmo Creek. Settlement of San Juan Valley by the Mormons in 1880 threw no new light, as far as known, on the ruins of Hovenweep, but stockmen who succeeded the farmers toward the end of that decade ranged the country from one end to the other. By 1910 the dwellings in Ruin and Cajon canyons were well-known landmarks, a few of them had been looted, and archeologists were interesting themselves in the tower structure at canyon heads. J. Walter Fewkes, chief of the Bureau of American Ethnology, published a comprehensive study of the Hovenweep ruins in the annual report of the Smithsonian Institution for 1923.

Ruin Canyon and its south fork, sometimes called **Square Tower Canyon,** contains the most numerous and important group of buildings in the Monument. The canyon heads about twelve miles north of the San Juan River and drains to it by way of McElmo Creek. Gregory speaks of Sage Plain as "deeply dissected by streamways that begin as canyons and continue as canyons all the way to the San Juan." Ruin Canyon fits this description; it appears without warning, 300 to 500 feet deep, and as sheer-walled as a sewer trench. It has no gradual beginning, but presents an abrupt drop from the mesa at its head. Along this ledge, in caves within the canyon wall, and along its base, are the prehistoric ruins. **Hovenweep House** stands at the cliff rim in the head of Square Tower Canyon. It was, in the times of its Pueblo builders, a large semicircular structure that housed perhaps fifty families, and included circular underground rooms (now called *kivas)* for priestly rites and a large D-shaped tower that rose from the middle of the house. Under the cliff below Hovenweep House are the remains of another large dwelling, and atop a pinnacle that rises from the canyon is Square Tower, the remarkable ruin from which the canyon takes its name. **Hovenweep Castle,** on the north rim of Square Tower Canyon, is the best preserved building in the Monument. It was built in two wings, not unlike the L-shaped feudal manors of Europe, and contained, besides sleeping and living chambers, several towers and underground ceremonial *kivas.* The walls of this building are massive affairs of rock and mud mortar, some of them still rising more than twenty feet. At the apex of the peninsula that separates the north and south forks of Ruin Canyon is another tower, which commands a splendid vista eastward over the main canyon, and below it, on the canyon floor, are several dwellings.

On the north rim of Ruin Canyon, a short walk from Hovenweep Castle, is the **Unit Type House,** a circular *kiva* surrounded by rectangular rooms. Down-canyon on the north rim are still other dwellings, among which is picturesque **Stronghold House.** The best preserved structures in Ruin Canyon are, however, on the south rim. **Eroded Boulder House,** perched atop a projecting rock much like Square Tower, is chiefly remarkable for its position, but the dwellings adjacent to it show clearly the method by which the Pueblos laid their mortar. **Twin Towers** occupy a platform at the cliff rim and are separated from the main body of the mesa by a deep cleft. The foundation of the larger tower is oval, that of the smaller, horseshoe-shaped; and walls of both are in a fair state of preservation.

Cajon Canyon, a few miles southwest of Ruin Canyon, contains one major ruin called **Cool Spring House** because the canyon below it flows with sweetwater. Hackberry and Keeley canyons, over the Colorado line a short hike eastward from Ruin Canyon, contain additional dwellings and towers, the most important of which are **Hackberry Castle** and **Horseshoe House.**

Of the folk who built the dwellings in Hovenweep very little is known beyond what has been gleaned from deserted houses and burial grounds. Archeologists agree that the houses have not been occupied in 700 years, perhaps longer, and Fewkes concludes that the origin of these sedentary aborigines in canyons of the San Juan probably antedates written history. They seem to have migrated from the north, for their progress southward through the Colorado Plateau toward the Rio Grande is marked by increasingly complex dwellings. When they first settled along the tributaries of the Colorado River in what is now Utah, they had not yet learned to build above ground nor to bake pottery. They lived in pit dwellings, cultivated corn, and worked river reeds into baskets to carry their possessions. The Basketmakers *(see Archeology and Indians)* in the security of their hidden gorges and scarcely accessible mesas began to build more enduringly, higher and higher above ground, became more dependent on their corn patches, and ultimately developed fixed communities, which archeologists call pueblos.

That the people of Hovenweep were skilled farmers at the peak of their civilization is evidenced by remains of check dams and irrigation ditches near their cornfields. Their pottery is of a high order, and the masonry of their adobe-cemented stone buildings shows skillful workmanship. They built as high as three stories and raftered each floor with cedar logs. The towers of Hovenweep have been variously explained as forts, storage bins (not unlike a twentieth-century grain elevator), observatories, lookout towers, and as temples for the performance of religious rites. Probably they were put to all these uses: several are in canyon bottoms where they have no view at all, others are built directly over subterranean *kivas,* which are known definitely to have been consecrated to religious ceremonies, others occupy strategic cliff-edge positions that seem to have been selected with an eye to defense. Fewkes suggests that since the Hovenweep Pueblos were an agricultural people, their towers may have been observatories from which planting time was determined by priestly observations of the sun's rising and setting. He adds that "a building from which aboriginal priests determined calendric events by solar observations very naturally became a room for sun worship." As to the *kivas,* which frequently appear beneath the towers, they were retained for the celebration of rites to the mother earth.

See Indians and Archeology chapter for discussion of possible reasons for disappearance of the ancient Pueblo peoples.

F. A. BARNES

Owachomo Bridge, Natural Bridges National Monument

Sipapu Bridge, Natural Bridges National Monument.

F. A. BARNES

NATURAL BRIDGES NATIONAL MONUMENT

Highway Approach: 38 miles west of Blanding on paved State 95.

Season: Open all year.

Administrative Offices: Canyonlands National Park, Moab, Utah 84532.

Accommodations: Motels at Blanding, Mexican Hat, Bluff, Monticello. Campground at Visitor Center.

Admission: Admission charge during summer. Off-season, free.

Transportation: Private automobile.

Climate, Clothing and Equipment: Summer temperatures may vary 50 degrees in a single day from hot days to cool nights. Low humidity; heat not oppressive. Cold nights in winter, though days may be pleasant. Snowfall in winter (November to March) seldom exceeds a few inches; however, roads may be snowpacked or slick for short periods. Wear outdoor clothing, including stout shoes for hiking. Bring camera, extra color film. Carry water, food, gasoline, and oil—only water is available at Monument.

Post Office: Blanding, Utah 84511.

Medical Service and Dentist: Doctor and dentist at Blanding. Nearest hospitals: Monticello (64 m.) and Monument Valley (66 m.).

Communication: Mobile telephone through Moab: (801) 259-0290 (emergency only).

Naturalist Service: Visitor Center open daily. Roving patrols six months of year.

Recreational Facilities: Hiking, climbing. Fishing, hunting in season in adjacent Manti-La Sal National Forest. Boating, fishing on Lake Powell.

Warnings and Regulations: Do not remove artifacts, wild flowers or other objects. Do not carve initials on rocks. Usual regulations applying to national monuments. Horses not allowed in Monument.

Natural Bridges National Monument is an area of spectacular erosive formations, its chief attractions being three immense water-carved bridges and a number of prehistoric cliff-dweller villages. Eastward, the green-wooded diagonal rise of Elk Ridge leans against the sky; in all other directions the unending red and dun of the plateau face rolls with deceptive and innocent smoothness toward the horizon; 40 miles westward the waters of Lake Powell lap the red walls of Glen Canyon, formerly the channel of the Colorado River. In the canyons of the Monument the dominant red of the plateau country is broken into endless gradations, from a metallic yellow where the sun glints, to deep and misty violet in the shadows, with streamers and blotches of lichen green.

The entire region between Blanding and Lake Powell is, in a sense, a single plateau, overlain by smaller plateaus that ascend and descend stepwise, or rear up as isolated buttes, or reach from horizon to horizon as immense mesas. The whole system is composed of sedimentary rock laid down in Triassic and Permian times and raised above the waters about the time of the dinosaurs. The forces which raised the plateaus tilted them gently, forming the essential features of the Colorado drainage system, and rain water, working oceanward through it, carved a meshwork of intricate cracks and cleavages, and enlarged the cracks to box-walled gorges and canyons sometimes as much as 2,500 feet deep. Where soft and hard beds of stone alternate in the canyon, the soft beds have been eroded out, leaving massive overhangs, caves, alcoves, fluted columns, and bridges. The meandering course of San Juan waterways often takes the form of great loops. The streams, throwing their force against the loop necks, in time cut through and leave islanded buttes beside the new course. Where the capstone is hard and the underlying beds soft, the water carves deep, overhung alcoves in the soft stuff, and eventually may punch completely through it in a narrow neck, leaving an island that is joined to the "mainland" by a bridge or capstone. Subsequent erosion of the new channel cuts it deeper without affecting the overspanning capstone, and a bridge such as the Sipapu is tediously formed.

Wild life and vegetation on the plateau are diverse. The igneous Abajo Mountains, 10 miles north of Blanding, have been driven up wedgewise through the plateau face to altitudes of 10,000 feet and they are heavily wooded, as is Elk Ridge, about half way between Blanding and the Monument. Desert shrubs, pinyon, and juniper subsist somewhat thinly in the coarse dry patches of soil on the plateau face, but in the well-watered canyons it is not uncommon to see pine, white fir, manzanita, and snowberry growing beside saltbush, chapparal, greasewood, and yucca. In Dark Canyon and Grand Gulch primitive areas nearby, bighorn sheep, mule deer, mountain lion, bobcat, bear, and beaver have been sighted. Several varieties of snakes are found in both alpine and desert regions of the plateaus, but poisonous species are rare in both places. Birds of the high mountains and those of the desert nest within a few miles of each other—magpies, mourning doves, pinyon jays, sage sparrows, canyon towhees, bluebirds, rock wrens, swallows, and chickadees are the most plentiful, though eagles, ravens, meadowlarks, cranes, finches, grouse, and water ouzels are sometimes seen.

In prehistoric times the plateau was occupied by Anasazi peoples, sometimes called Cliff Dwellers. White and Allen canyons and Grand Gulch have large clusters of houses (built sometimes of fitted stone, sometimes of adobe) that yield fine examples of pottery, and stone and bone implements; smaller communities have been found elsewhere in the area. Herbert E. Gregory, of the U.S. Geological Survey, was so moved by the remarkable preservation of the dwellings that he felt "the families have merely gone on a long visit." The Anasazi of this region, however, abandoned their dwellings at least 600 years ago, to be followed by Ute and Paiute Indians, whose descendants now occupy Allen Canyon. The first white visitors are anonymous. A few trappers may have traversed the country, but they left no record. In the 1880s, Cass Hite, a desert misanthrope whose name still graces a marina on Lake Powell, worked his way through this country, and according to historical gossip of San Juan oldtimers, brought back accounts of many wonders including three "whoppin'" natural bridges. About 1885, cattlemen began filtering into the Grand Gulch and Dark Canyon country, and some of them stayed. In 1895, cattleman Emery Knowles saw the bridges in White Canyon and later in the same year, James Scorup visited them. In 1903, Scorup guided Horace M. Long to his find, and in August 1904, W. W. Dyar published an account of their explorations in *Century*

Magazine. By 1908 the bridges were sufficiently well known to be set aside as a national monument, and in 1928 a road was "extended" from Blanding over Elk Ridge (Bear's Ears Buttes). This rough mountain route was replaced later by a paved highway at a lower level.

HIGHWAY ACCESS

State Highway 95 — Known as Utah's Bicentennial Highway because hard-surfacing was completed in 1976, the Bicentennial year, U-95 connects Blanding on the east with Hanksville on the west. The 133-mile link affords vehicle access to Natural Bridges, Lake Powell and its northern marinas, and numerous other scenic and recreational points that formerly were among the remotest parts of the nation. The present route, bypassing Elk Ridge at a lower level, was made possible by a notable engineering feat, namely that of cutting a road through the 800-foot face of Comb Ridge.

Points of interest along U-95 are described in tours No. 7 and No. 11.

State Highway 261 — The Monument can be reached from the south by way of U-261, a mostly paved link with U.S. Highway 163 near Mexican Hat. This highly scenic route gives access to Grand Gulch Primitive Area, Muley Point Overlook, Moki Dugway Switchbacks, Valley of the Gods, and Grand Goosenecks of the San Juan River. *See Tour No. 11 for details.*

SEEING THE BRIDGES

A paved access road leads 5 miles from U-95 to the Monument's **Visitor Center-Museum,** where visitors should examine exhibits and obtain information about the bridges, trails and Indian sites. From the Visitor Center an 8-mile loop road (one-way) links parking areas at the head of trails leading to the three bridges.

In earlier days the road ended near Owachomo Bridge, and it was necessary to hike long miles to the other two bridges. Now the paved loop road passes within a few hundred yards of all three bridges, beginning with Sipapu. Trails are short but in some cases steep, because the bridges are in canyons below the parking areas.

Sipapu Bridge, largest of the Monument's stone bridges and first along the scenic loop, measures 220 feet in height and has a span of 268 feet. Width of the arch is 31 feet, thickness 53 feet. The access trail involves a 600-foot descent on wooden ladders and steel stairs, but the climb is not difficult otherwise.

Sipapu Bridge is the most impressive of all. To Dyar, it seemed "a structure so magnificent, so symmetrical and beautiful in its proportions, as to suggest that nature, after completing the mighty structure of the Caroline, had trained herself for a finer and nobler form of architecture." Long, following Scorup's precedent, named the bridge for his wife, who was "very appropriately" christened Augusta. The name Sipapu was taken from Hopi legend and it refers to "the gateway through which the souls of men come from the underworld and finally return to it." The span of Sipapu would give egress to an army; the Capitol at Washington, D.C., could sit under it very nicely and have 50 feet to spare. Dyar estimated that the tallest Sequoia in Calaveras Grove, if planted under the bridge, would have thirty feet to grow before its tallest tip would brush the under side of the span.

Kachina Bridge, accessible from the second parking area, measures 210 feet in height with a span of 206 feet. Width across the arch is 44 feet, thickness 93 feet, making it the most massive of the three bridges. The trail descends about 600 feet with handrails in one section. Scorup stipulated as part of his agreement to Long for guiding him that he should be permitted to name one of the bridges for his wife. He chose this one, and called it Caroline. Government officials, in the proclamation establishing the Monument, substituted the name Kachina because prehistoric artwork on the bridge's abutment resembles the elaborate masks worn by Kachina spirits (Hopi). Kachina is the most massive of the three bridges, 107 feet thick at its narrowest place, and the stone of which it is composed is a deeper red. At the bridge a fork of the trail leads downstream about 200 yards to a scattered community of cliff dwellings and several excellent rock pictures. The scalloped walls of White Canyon vary in color from a warm pearl gray to brick red; at several points they widen, forming small parks, and as often they contract until the overhanging lip of the plateau above almost shuts out the sky. The canyon throughout its length is well watered and supports lush vegetation.

Owachomo Bridge, smallest and most fragile of the bridges, measures 106 feet in height with a span of 180 feet. Width across the arch is 27 feet, thickness 9 feet. The access trail, not too steep, descends only 300 feet.

Owachomo Bridge, 100 yards from the parking area by foot trail, was named Little Bridge by Long and Scorup, and renamed Edwin for a time. The word Little is appropriate only in comparison with the other two bridges. Owachomo, a Hopi word meaning "flat-rock mound," was chosen for a near-by promontory. The stone of Owachomo Bridge is light, a pale salmon pink, shot through laterally with vermilion streaks, and accented here and there by green and orange lichens. The "slickrock" canyon walls beneath and beyond it are "most voluptuously" whorled and as delicately colored as the bridge itself. By evening light the hard stone seems velvet soft, and it glows until the coyotes begin to howl. Almost beneath the bridge is a "tank" or pothole in the slickrock such as desert men cherish as sources of drinking water—this one, however, is commonly known as "Zeke's bathtub."

In earlier days, when the road ended at the Owachomo overlook, many visitors did not leave their cars and the camp tables at the end of the road. For those who wanted to see the other bridges, it was necessary to hike a nine-mile triangular trail.

In June 1980, near the Monument Visitor Center, was inaugurated what was believed to be the world's largest solar power generating system at that time. Designed by Massachusetts Institute of Technology, the system was built as a demonstration and experimental project of the National Park Service and Department of Energy. It provides electricity for the Visitor Center, residences, pump, water system, etc. The system consists of about 250,000 minute photoelectric cells arranged in 12 long rows of collector panels. Surplus power is stored in 28 huge batteries, with diesel generators providing backup power.

RAINBOW BRIDGE NATIONAL MONUMENT

Access: By boat on Lake Powell from Wahweap Marina, Arizona, 50 miles; or from marinas on the lake in Utah (Bullfrog, Halls Crossing, Hite), 45 to 85 miles.

Season: Weather permitting, the Monument may be reached at any time of year. Mid-summer is very hot, winter is cold.

Administrative Office: c/o Superintendent, Glen Canyon National Recreation Area, Box 1507, Page, Arizona 86040.

Nearest accommodations: Page, Arizona; Wahweap Marina, Arizona.

Transportation: Private, rental or charter boats; or boat tours from marinas on Lake Powell; also scenic air flights from Page.

Climate, Clothing and Equipment: Occasional severe winters, hot in summer. Wear suitable outdoor clothing; very limited walking is required, so clothing and equipment should be more appropriate for boating than for hiking.

Medical and Dental Service: Nearest medical services are many miles away by boat, at marinas or Page. First aid kits are advisable.

Recreation: Boating, fishing, water sports, hiking, rock climbing, photography, exploring, nature study.

Warnings and Regulations: Observe National Park Service rules and regulations; both Rainbow Bridge and Lake Powell are federal park areas.

Rainbow Bridge in its slickrock setting. Waters of Lake Powell are visible below, Navajo Mountain in distance. *See also Color Section.*

BUREAU OF RECLAMATION (V. JETLEY)

Rainbow Bridge National Monument, in southern Utah, is about 6 miles north of the Arizona line on an arm of Lake Powell, which backs up into Utah behind Glen Canyon Dam in Arizona *(see Glen Canyon National Recreation Area).* It includes 160 acres around the largest natural bridge yet discovered, and was set apart by President Taft as a Monument in 1910. The bridge is not accessible by car.

The Monument is in one of the most rugged areas of the United States. The Colorado River, a busy and efficient hydraulic excavator, made it impractical for roads to reach the region; and before Lake Powell made it comparatively easy to reach the bridge by boat, seeing it by land required a two-day pack trip northeast from lodges at the base of Navajo Mountain, or longer trips from Mexican Hat or Monument Valley. River boaters formerly visited the bridge by hiking up Forbidding and Bridge canyons from the Colorado River.

Navajo Mountain looms southeast of the bridge, more than 10,000 feet above the sea, but seeming much lower because of its rounded slopes. The Navajos avoid it, the dwelling place of their thunder god. The tops of plateaus, mesas, and mountains in the area around Rainbow Bridge are rounded; natives call them whalebacks and baldheads. To traverse such slanting surfaces is sometimes hazardous as scaling the perpendicular, since the rocks are best described by their familiar name—"slickrocks." Native horses and mules, and even Indian ponies, sometimes slide disastrously when taken off established trails. There is no soil, only finely pulverized sand and accumulated humus in the bottom of gorges. The shoes of the white man's horses ring on the smooth rocks or swish through the soft heavy sand, which pervades everything.

This is a country, as Irvin S. Cobb puts it, "where Old Marster stacked it up and scooped it out and shuffled it together again so violently, so completely and with such incredibly beautiful tonings, such inconceivably awesome results." The bare naked rocks blaze with blended colors; curves and outlines display stark massive strength. There is, in the country, a vivid eternal peace, vastness, and power. Intermingled with the serenity of solitude, yet causing no apprehension to the seasoned desert dweller, is the ever-present thirst menace of the region. Yet Bridge Canyon, spanned by Rainbow Bridge, before the invasion of Lake Powell was a lush green oasis, spattered with brilliant flowers.

Rainbow Bridge is in the Navajo country. In 1906, John Wetherill and his young bride drove rumbling freight wagons north from Kayenta, Arizona, to establish the first trading post in the region. This courageous woman grew to love the desert. To the Indians she was *Shema Yazi,* Little Mother. They told her their lore and tales of their wanderings in strange desert places. They brought her their troubles and their babies. Finally came Nashja, a Paiute, with a strange story. He had seen *Nageelid Nonnezoshi,* the-hole-in-the-rock-shaped-like-a-rainbow. And there was sweet water, and grass to feed many goats. But the trail was hard. Indian ponies, he said, could travel it, not white man's horses.

Mrs. Wetherill interested Professor Byron S. Cummings of the University of Utah in a trip to discover the great bridge. The expedition was made in 1909, with John Wetherill and Nashja-begay, son of Nashja, as guides, W. L. Douglass, surveyor of the U. S. General Land Office, and two student assistants. Douglass' story is that he had word of the bridge direct from the same Indian, and that the two expeditions, started separately, continued together. There was an acrimonious debate in after years as to whether Cummings or Douglass first saw the bridge. The question was quietly disposed of in 1927, when the Wetherills erected a bronze plaque at the bridge to Nashja-begay, "who first guided the white man to Nonnezoshi."

Professor Cummings published probably the first printed description of the bridge in a University of Utah pamphlet in 1910. He gave the dimensions of the gigantic red and yellow sandstone arch as 308 feet high and 275 feet between abutments. (Today's official dimensions: 309 feet high, 278 feet span, 33 feet wide.) The bridge was formed through the same process of undercutting by stream meanders, Cummings said, as that which resulted in the concentration of three giant bridges in White Canyon *(see Natural Bridges National Monument).* The professor likened the natural structure to an "enormous flying buttress" rather than a bridge, because of the form taken by the gracefully curved "arm of the cliff." On a bench almost beneath the bridge, Professor Cummings found fire-blackened rocks, indicating that prehistoric peoples had probably used the site as a shrine for building sacred fires. His imagination kindled at the thought, and he could visualize a firelit congregation of cliff-dwellers assembled in this awesomely beautiful spot, paying reverence to their pagan gods. Present-day Indians still regard the bridge with feelings of religious awe. C. A. Colville, who visited the arch late in 1909, led by a Paiute guide, Whitehorse-biga, relates that the Indian would not pass under the bridge because he had forgotten a prayer required by Paiute custom before such a venture could be safely made.

Theodore Roosevelt, guided by John Wetherill, visited Rainbow Bridge in 1913, and described it for *The Outlook* of October 11 that year. The season was apparently a wet one, for "T. R." found deep pools of water in the canyon under the bridge. The former President, hailing an opportunity for a bath after a hard, dry, desert journey, floated luxuriantly on his back in the water, with the great arch towering above him. To Roosevelt the bridge was a triumphal arch, greater in its lone majesty than any monument ever erected by a conquerer. When twilight came, the guides built a fire under one of the great buttresses, and the fire flared up now and then, illuminating the underside of the bridge. White men and Indian packers ate together, and afterward sat around the fire. The night was clear, and a full moon came up beneath the curve of the bridge. Roosevelt waked several times during the night and looked for a long time at the looming arch against the night sky.

Charles L. Bernheimer was so fascinated by the bridge that he made three trips to it in four years, each time accompanied by John Wetherill, and Zeke Johnson, custodian (1940) of the Natural Bridges National Monument. On each trip they sought a shorter and easier trail, and eventually found it. Bernheimer published his book, *Rainbow Bridge,* in 1926. To him the bridge was a unique and stupendous monument, with a lean and effective muscular strength. "Where the strain is greatest, its contour suggests the arm and shoulders of a trained athlete." Yet, as he pointed out, its size is such that the national Capitol at Washington, D.C., could be placed beneath it and have ample clearance above.

Since Lake Powell began to offer easy access by boat during the 1960s, Rainbow Bridge does not have the romance of days when it was remote and isolated, a difficult and magic goal to attain. Now it can be reached in several hours from the nearest marina, or seen from a fast-moving plane within minutes of takeoff. During the 50 years between its discovery and the advent of Glen Canyon Dam and Lake Powell, only a few thousand people had seen the bridge. Now it is visited by hundreds of thousands every year. Whether what was lost is balanced by what was gained is, of course, a matter of opinion.

The bridge now spans a shallow arm of the lake, backed up in the narrow inner canyon beneath the bridge. During the early 1970s this slender finger of water was the focus of national environmental attention and the subject of lawsuits in federal court. Plaintiffs claimed that legislation authorizing the Colorado River Storage Project, of which Lake Powell is an element, prohibited any dam or reservoir constructed under its provisions from being within any national park or monument. In addition, they argued, long-standing principles of "violation" of parks were involved, as well as the quality of wilderness and natural esthetics. Furthermore, there was (and is) serious concern about the future stability of the bridge when the rocks supporting its abutments become saturated with standing water.

From the government's point of view, it was mandatory that the lake's level be raised to 3,700 feet elevation, placing its waters beneath the bridge, if the dam's full effectiveness were to be realized. As is apparent today, arguments and challenges against raising the lake's water level were over-ridden.

Rainbow Bridge from the air *(lower center)*.

BUREAU OF RECLAMATION (A. E. TURNER)

TIMPANOGOS CAVE NATIONAL MONUMENT

Highway Approaches: 12 miles east of I-15 at Alpine exit (State 92); 8 miles north and east of American Fork on State 74, State 92; 9.6 miles north and east of Pleasant Grove on State 146 and State 92; 17.6 miles northwest of Wildwood on State 92.

Season: Cave open May through September with guide service available. Visitor Center with exhibit room and free 12-minute slide program open year around.

Admission: Entry to Monument area free. Fee for admission to cave with guide service (children under 16 free). Reservations required for groups of 10 or more.

Administrative Office: Superintendent at Monument headquarters, American Fork Canyon (address Rt. 2, Box 200, American Fork, Utah 84003).

Facilities: Picnic area with water, tables and fuel; a snack and gift shop available at Visitor Center, foot of trail to Timpanogos Cave. Campgrounds in U.S. Forest Service areas nearby.

Accommodations: Nearby communities.

Transportation: No public transportation.

Climate, Clothing and Equipment: Cold nights and cool days in summer; snow between November and April usually makes area too cold for winter camping or hiking. Hiking shoes for steep climb to cave, jacket to wear in cave, where temperature is 42 degrees; hiking or climbing togs for ascent of Mount Timpanogos and glacier. Film available at Visitor Center-gift shop.

Post Office: Pleasant Grove and American Fork.

Medical and Dental Service: Doctors and dentists at American Fork, Pleasant Grove, Lehi, Provo, Orem. Hospitals at American Fork, Provo. Directions to first aid stations at Visitor Center.

Speed Limit: Narrow asphalt road with sharp curves. Drive at posted limits.

Timpanogos Cave National Monument. *See also Color Section.*

UTAH TRAVEL COUNCIL

Warnings and Regulations: Do not damage natural objects within Monument. Do not touch formations in cave; acids from human body are deleterious to them. Do not appropriate, injure, deface, remove, or destroy any features of the Monument. Observe Forest Service regulations in surrounding areas.

Naturalist Service and Information: At Visitor Center.

Recreational Facilities: Well-equipped picnic and camp grounds, numerous hiking trails, trout-stocked stream, countless natural subjects for photography.

Timpanogos Cave National Monument, a 250-acre area containing Utah's outstanding scenic cavern, is on the precipitous northern slope of **Mount Timpanogos** in the Wasatch Range, and is reached by a trail up the south wall of **American Fork Canyon.** The Monument is in a small area, easily accessible from good roads and only a few miles from towns and accommodations. Crowded into a restricted section around it are scenic wonders and natural phenomena on a grandiose scale. The road that swings in a rough circle around the larger area of Mount Timpanogos is known as the **Alpine Scenic Drive** *(see Tour No. 5).* Along the drive are the limestone cave, a rugged canyon, a towering mountain, an outdoor summer school and theater, a tiny "glacier," and Sundance Resort.

The cave is approached, from the Visitor Center on the canyon floor, by a 1½-mile-long zigzag trail that climbs 1,065 feet up a steep mountainside. Tickets are purchased *(daily 8-4)* at the Monument Visitor Center. The well-advised visitor to the cave wears low-heeled hiking shoes (low heels are even more of a help coming down than going up), and carries a jacket to put on when he enters the cavern. A good, steady stride, with occasional stops at benches to get the second, third, and fourth wind, will take the climber to the cave in the average time of one hour. The ramp-like trail follows a naturally flower-bordered course up the spasmodically wooded steep slope. There is a pungent aroma of sun-warmed pine as the trail climbs higher, and signs warn against picking flowers or taking short cuts. Most people are not tempted to disobey the second injunction, for the near-perpendicular mountainside is covered with loose and flinty rocks that promise a quick, pants-warming descent, in addition to setting off a miniature landslide dangerous to those below.

The westward view, between the steep walls of American Fork Canyon, takes on a different character at every turn of the trail, as altitude and perspective change. Productive Utah Valley opens out beyond rugged canyon walls, its cultivated fields cut into geometric blocks of tilled and crop-greened land.

The rocks along the way are inconceivably old. Quartzite near the bottom of the canyon is of Cambrian age, containing little or no remains of fossil life. It is surmounted by a shaly strata, and all above that, on this trail, is limestone, mainly of Carboniferous age. Minute marine plant and animal life, including coral, can be found by a trained eye in this great bed of limestone, which extends upward for five thousand feet; it is marked by a sign at the lower edge. The limestone has been intricately cracked by terrestrial disturbances, and the cracks filled with white calcareous matter, similar to that of the cave formations. Survival of this exposed limestone mass is clearly owing to the arid climate; in a humid region, with plentiful water dashing upon and over it, dissolving and carrying away its soluble lime, the deposit would quickly, in a geologic sense, have been undermined, and more resistant rocks from above would have tumbled down to cover the outcrop.

As the trail climbs higher, portions of it can be seen below, cutting sharp M's and W's in the mountainside. High above, perched like a swallow's nest, is a little stone rest station, and a black-shadowed arch west of it indicates the cave entrance. Once the rest station is reached, there is only one more long ramp, through an arch in the trail, to the cool, man-made grotto where the visitors register, put on their jackets, and, with the guide, enter a wooden door into the cave.

Timpanogos Cave (6,730 alt.), half a mile long, is in reality three caves, connected by man-made tunnels. They are all part of the same geologic structure, a fissure along the lines of a fault that occurred probably in Eocene time, some fifty million years ago. It is thought that the fissure was washed out by waters of a stream corresponding to American Fork Creek, which in the succeeding epoch, the Miocene, began cutting American Fork Canyon. Deposits within the cavern—icicle-like stalactites, upthrust stalagmites, and the branched, oddly-angled helictites—are thought to have required the same time to grow as the cutting of American Fork Canyon. Once the stream bed was cut below the cavern-fissures, water was scarce, and dripped rather than flowed. As the calcium-saturated drops came slowly down, evaporating the while, they began to deposit limy material on the ceiling of the cave, the beginning of stalactites. Falling to the floor, they deposited other infinitesimal particles, and began to build stalagmites upward. In the course of time some of the stalactites and stalagmites joined, to form columns; others occur in the cave that have not yet joined. The "macaroni-like filigree" of helictites apparently formed where less moisture was present; they branched off in every direction, even forming complete circles, having left deposits where water was drawn out by capillary action and evaporated completely.

Hansen Cave, through which entrance is made, was discovered in 1887 by Martin Hansen, who then owned the land. The cave was almost completely stripped of formations, some of which were sold to curio-hunters, some of which were taken by chance visitors. This, like the other caverns, is ingeniously lighted by a system of indirect electric lights. The guide, who knows where the light switches are concealed, turns off a circuit behind and turns on another ahead, sometimes leaving visitors in absolute darkness for a moment, to give them a notion of the profound Stygian gloom. At such times, when there is a tendency to listen, the only sound that can be heard is the dripping of water. The way trends downward and eastward, the caverns passing through the mountain behind the stone rest station. An 85-foot arched tunnel, built by hand, leads to Middle Cave.

Middle Cave, discovered in 1922, in the course of penetrating Timpanogos Cave proper, is a narrow, winding channel with a high vaulted ceiling, sometimes reaching a height of 125 feet. When first entered, from the top, explorers let themselves down with ropes. One man fell and was injured, resting on a ledge until rescued. The top entrance was closed in the course of development, to prevent terrific drafts from outside. A series of winding passages, stairs, and grilled footways leads from one area in the cave to another. Here the formations are for the most part unspoiled, in colors that range from pure white through lemon yellow, ivory, coral, brown, and mauve. In an inaccessible portion of this cave are formations indicating a slight movement in the mountain, thousands of years past: Formation of a stalagmite, by dripping from a stalactite above, was abandoned, and a new stalagmite was begun three-quarters of an inch away.

Timpanogos Cave proper, connected to Middle Cave by a 190-foot man-made tunnel, reaches an area abounding in coloration, odd forms, and curious resemblances. There is a hidden lake, and hundreds of formations, configuring to the imagination of each person a different set of resemblances—the Dove's Nest, the Reclining Camel, Father Time's Jewel Box, Mother Earth's Lace Curtains, the Chocolate Fountain (well named), a seal, a dressed chicken, and scores of others. The "Heart of Timpanogos," bearing a remarkable likeness to the human vital organ, is illuminated from behind; variations in opacity give it a lifelike appearance. A thermometer in this cave has a constant all-year reading of 42 degrees. By means of doors it is kept the same throughout the caverns, to maintain the proper humidity, which gives color to formations and encourages continued deposition. There is more to see after the heart, more marvels of lighting, form, color, more likenesses pointed out by the guide, more of that vague loss of direction within a cave, more dripping of water. Finally there appears ahead and below a faint shining of blue light, as if the electrician had prepared a new and different set of glows and indirects. It is the sunlight, shining in around the wooden exit door. The eyes, accustomed to half a mile of yellow or red artificial light, refuse temporarily to accept all the colors of sunlight, and translate only the blue.

Timpanogos Cave was probably discovered as early as 1915 by "a group of Lehi people," who kept its whereabouts a secret, and attempted to lease a "mining claim" from the Forest Service, in order to develop it commercially. Official discovery of the cave is credited to Vearl J. Manwill, who told the story in the *American Fork Citizen* for April 28, 1939.

The Forest Service took the cavern under its protection, and a trail was built. Civic groups contributed to development of the cavern, and about 10,000 persons visited it the first year, 1922; in recent years 80,000 visitors tour the cave each year, with many more being turned away. Total visitation to the Monument area is several times that number each year.

For protection of the cave resource and high quality interpretation, tour group size is limited to 20. On Saturdays and holidays, tour space is filled by early afternoon and late arrivals cannot be accommodated.

The cave, 600 feet long when opened, was declared a National Monument the following year. A lighting system was installed in 1923-25, and replaced in 1939. A trail to Hansen Cave was completed in 1936; necessary tunneling was done, and beginning in 1938 the cavern trip was made, as now, through the three caves. No further extensions are known, but there is a persistent local rumor of another giant cavern in the vicinity.

ZION NATIONAL PARK

Highway Approaches: Main entrance, 1 mile north of Springdale on State 9. East entrance, 12 miles west of Mount Carmel Junction on State 9. Kolob Canyons, enter from I-15 at turnoff 2 miles south of New Harmony junction. Kolob Section, turn north from town of Virgin.

Season: Park Visitor Center and roads within Zion Canyon, as well as Mount Carmel Highway, open the entire year. Kolob Canyons road from I-15 is closed by snow during winter months, from (usually) early November to (usually) Easter weekend.

Administrative Office: Superintendent, Zion National Park, Springdale, Utah 84767.

Accommodations: Zion Lodge, open early May to mid-October. Park campgrounds open all year. All-year accommodations and services in Springdale, other nearby towns.

Admission: Fee area.

Transportation: Private automobile, commercial tours.

Climate, Clothing and Equipment: Sports clothing is appropriate; lightweight clothing is preferable during warm months. For hiking, serviceable shoes (not oxfords) should be worn. Water should be carried on some hikes (inquire at Zion Lodge or Park Visitor Center). Jackets needed for evenings during spring and fall, heavier clothing for winter.

Post Office: Zion Lodge or Zion National Park, Springdale, Utah 84767.

Medical and Dental Service: Cedar City, Hurricane, St. George, Kanab.

West Temple, Great West Wall, and highway switchbacks from overlook near Zion-Mount Carmel Tunnel.

UTAH TRAVEL COUNCIL

Communications: Public telephones at Zion Lodge, Visitor Center, campgrounds.

Speed Limits: Roads are posted; 20 m.p.h. is safe; 15 m.p.h. in campgrounds.

Warnings and Regulations: National Park Service regulations, conspicuously posted within the park, must be observed. Keep to posted trails except where off-trail hiking is permissible. Permit required for backcountry hiking. Permit not required for day hikes except for Virgin River Narrows. All overnight camping trips require a permit.

Naturalist Service and Information: Visitor Center and Museum at Park Headquarters. Naturalists conduct nature study walks and hikes daily, on variable schedule posted at Visitor Center, Zion Lodge, campgounds, and facilities in Springdale. Evening talks in summer at public campgrounds and Zion Lodge. No charge.

Recreation: Hiking, horseback riding, motor trips. Escorted mule trips to West Rim. Horse rides available from April through November (depending on weather). A tram operates in Zion Canyon during summer months.

Zion National Park, an area of 147,000 acres in southwestern Utah, is the best-known example of a deep, narrow, vertically-walled canyon readily accessible for observation. Through much of its course it is about as deep as wide, though in the Narrows it is 2,000 feet deep and less than 50 feet wide. The Park area is one of towering walls and steep slopes, which here and there recede into alcoves and amphitheaters, everywhere decorated by broad arches, pilasters, statues, balconies and towers. Beneath the white and red of the higher walls are the purple, pink, lilac, yellow, blue, and mauve shades in the most brilliant-colored rocks, and the colors shift constantly with the light and seasons. In winter, when the upper reaches are blanketed with snow, the lower walls are by contrast all the more brilliant; in autumn they are a gorgeous backdrop for the yellow and golden foliage of deciduous trees and shrubs on the canyon floor; and in the spring innumerable cascades plunge down the vast escarpments, some of them dropping a sheer thousand feet, colored by their burden of sand, each waterfall sometimes a different hue from its neighbor.

This is a realm of temples and cathedrals. Some of the names were bestowed by persons who were members of no church, but no other nomenclature would fit: Mountains of stone are called temples, patriarchs, Angels Landing, thrones, and cathedrals.

Visitors enter the Park on the floor of Zion Canyon, or descend to it from the East (Mount Carmel) Entrance. Most visitors are content with the grandeur that towers above them from the canyon floor. The relative few who climb to the east or west rim, or even to Angels Landing, get a vista of a far different kind. From the floor, the beholder is walled in by tremendous cliffs that rise half a mile in places. From the summits, he looks out over a breathtaking landscape of wondrous erosional forms and riotous colors.

The elevation at Zion Lodge is 4,275 feet. The main mountain tops are West Temple, 7,795 feet . . . East Temple, 7,110 feet . . . and the Great White Throne, 6,744 feet. These altitudes provide the Park with a cooler atmosphere in summer than the surrounding section of southern Utah. Compared with desert country roundabout, the streams and cascades, the trailing ferns and flowering plants, the pines and firs, make Zion a multi-colored oasis. Mule deer are sometimes seen in the evenings. Mountain lions, coyotes, and bobcats leave their tracks after rain or snow. Porcupines, marmots, chipmunks, and squirrels are present, as are several types of harmless lizards. Bird life includes the forms typical of areas having heavier rainfall as well as those indigenous to arid and semiarid country. Bighorn sheep have been seen most frequently in the Zion-Mount Carmel switchbacks area and across the river from the Visitor Center.

The sedimentary rocks exposed in Zion are assigned by geologists to the Triassic, Jurassic, and Cretaceous periods of the Mesozoic era. Many of the rocks were laid down by water as gravel, sand, mud and slimy ooze; however, the Park's most impressive rock—the Navajo sandstone that forms the sheer cliffs and great domes—was formed in ancient deserts as windblown sand. The original sediments were converted into solid rock by the weight of layers above them and by cementing lime, silica and iron. Though Zion's rocks were deposited during the "Age of Dinosaurs," only fossil tracks have been found here.

Today, Zion is an area of gorges, cliffs and mesas. From the hard surfaces, softer layers have been stripped by water and wind. The principal gorge, Zion Canyon, was cut by the North Fork of the Virgin River. Originally a shallow valley, it has become a narrow trench between towering walls, but the river follows the same meanders as it did millions of years ago. The stream, having nine times the fall of the Colorado River, carries out of the Park about 180 carloads of ground rock daily. Adding to the erosive process are rainfall, surface run-off spilling over the high rims, ground water emerging as springs, wind, frost, growing tree roots, which loosen great slabs, and chemical agencies that weaken the stone. Continuous sapping and undermining have developed alcoves, opened fissures, and spilled blocks from the cliffs upon the talus slopes below.

Long ago Zion was the home of a prehistoric people, cliff ruins having been discovered in the Park. These ancient people "farmed" near the creeks and rivers, raising corn, squash, and melons. Their dwellings, perched high above, like the nests of swallows, gave them protection from marauding enemies.

Zion Canyon was explored in 1858 by Nephi Johnson, a Mormon pioneer, who rode up the canyon as far as the present Zion Stadium. Three years later Joseph Black explored the region and led farmers and stockgrowers into the canyon, where their descendants tilled and grazed the land until it was proclaimed a national park. In 1872 Major John W. Powell visited the canyon and applied the Indian names, Mukuntuweap to the North Fork of the Virgin River (Zion Canyon), and Parunuweap to the East Fork. Indians refused to live in the canyon and were fearful of being overtaken by darkness there. This happily provided a sanctuary for the Mormons, who called their small settlement Little Zion. When Brigham Young told them it was not Zion at all, they called it, for a while, Not Zion.

A portion of the area was set aside as Mukuntuweap National Monument by President Taft in 1909. Nine years later the Monument was enlarged by President Wilson and the name changed to Zion. In 1919 the status was changed by act of Congress to that of a national park, and in

1931 the Park was enlarged. Zion National Monument, created in 1937, was made a part of the Park in 1956.

A. ZION CANYON ROADS, TRAILS AND VIEWS

(Note: Only brief trail descriptions are included here. Inquire at Visitor Center for full details.)

Visitors enter Zion Canyon by way of State Highway 9, which connects I-15 on the west with US 89 on the east. There are 35 miles of improved roads in the Park, including the 11.5 miles of Zion-Mount Carmel Highway within the Park boundaries. The main Zion Canyon scenic road, with several short branches to points of interest, runs north from Park Head-quarters-Visitor Center to the Temple of Sinawava. Closed-car travelers find it advantageous to make frequent stops, since the top of the car obscures the lofty tops and sheer walls. Approximately 26 miles of well-kept trails lead to sections of the Park not reached by roads. They can be used at all seasons, except those to the canyon rims, which are closed by snow in winter. A horseback trail leads to the west rim.

Roads, trails and features covered in this log are listed in order of distance from Park Headquarters—Visitor Center, moving north to the Temple of Sinawava.

Park Headquarters-Visitor Center, 0 m., in a canyon of nearly perpendicular cliff-walls, is surrounded on all sides by stupendous sandstone formations. Soaring skyward to the west is the highest point in the southern portion of the Park, **West Temple** (7,795 alt.), its great height belied by its mammoth proportions. The formation rises 3,805 feet above the canyon floor, and its sheer east face is like a smooth wall of veined marble. Across the canyon from it is **The Watchman,** with red dominating the orange and rust, green and rose; in design, it looks as if a dozen Gothic skyscrapers had been placed side by side, heated, and welded into one enormous cathedral. A 1-mile trail leads from South Campground to the edge of a cliff above the campground, giving an exciting view of The Watchman, West Temple, and Springdale.

Bridge Mountain, overlooking the Zion-Mount Carmel switchbacks from the south, is named for a "flying buttress" or natural bridge on its face—a slender arch of stone 156 feet in length. Even through powerful glasses, the bridge looks like a thread of rock that a man could put on his shoulder and carry away; its insignificant size against the wall emphasizes the colossal proportions of these monuments. Beyond Bridge Mountain to the north of the switchbacks is **East Temple,** its great size and exquisite coloring closely resembling **West Temple** across the canyon.

Across the main canyon (west) from **East Temple,** the superlative **Towers of the Virgin, The Beehives,** and **The Sentinel** combine with **West Temple** and **Mount Kinesava** to form the great amphitheater in which the Visitor Center is set. This **Great West Wall,** three miles long and from 3,000 to nearly 4,000 feet high, is regarded by many as the single most imposing feature in the Park. It is best viewed in panorama from the Zion-Mount Carmel switchbacks.

Zion Canyon becomes narrower beyond the gateway formed by **East Temple** and **The Sentinel.** Within a short distance the west wall is broken by the mouth of Birch Creek and the cool green **Court of the Patriarchs,** over which loom the **Three Patriarchs** themselves. Opposite is the **Mountain of the Sun,** catching the first golden rays of sunrise and the last brilliant colors of sunset. In an expansive wooded valley bottom in this vicinity, 3 m. from the Visitor Center, is **Zion Lodge** (lodging, meals, supplies, horseback trips, tram tours). The lodge is a focal point for several trails. **Sand Bench Trail** crosses the river from the lodge and follows the base of the west wall to **Court of the Patriarchs** and the foot of **The Sentinel** *(3.5 m. round-trip).* Horseback rides are available in summer for this trail. The **Emerald Pools Trail** begins at the lodge or Grotto Campground *(below);* from the lodge, it crosses the river on a footbridge and joins the West Rim Trail. **Emerald Pools** are small pockets of water formed by ribbon-like waterfalls that plunge hundreds of feet down the face of steep cliffs. Another trail formerly led from the lodge to the top of **Lady Mountain** *(now closed).* Hikers may also walk from the lodge to **Grotto Picnic Area,** ¾ m., and connect there with trails leading to **West Rim** and **Angels Landing** *(see below).*

Leaving Zion Lodge, the road continues up-canyon past **Great White Throne, Angels Landing,** and **Weeping Rock** to **Temple of Sinawava.** This is an area for viewing vividly colored waterfalls that appear immediately following a shower, or during spring runoff. Sometimes only a few minutes in duration, they are a thrilling sight while they last. As many as 30 have been counted from a single point. The water carries richly tinted silt and sand from the plateaus above, coloring the falls yellow, red, chocolate, orange, and even black. These waterfalls are the joy and aggravation of color photographers, who are tempted to wait, and pray for rain, until they occur.

At 4 m. from Visitor Center (**Grotto Picnic Area**), signs point the way to West Rim Trail, Angels Landing, Emerald Pools, and Court of the Patriarchs. **West Rim Trail,** oil-surfaced for the first mile, is a strenuous foot or horse trail of 13 miles round-trip to **West Rim Viewpoint.** It may be traveled farther if desired. The trail leaves the canyon floor at the foot of Angels Landing, and is benched along a precipitous ledge of the west wall for 600 feet into Refrigerator Canyon. Hewn into the face of the almost vertical cliffs, it winds through cool narrow gorges, and comes out on top of bare rock ledges. The trail zigzags up, nearly to the level of Angels Landing, and turns north, continuing over the colorful sandstone formation for two miles before making the final ascent to the rim. Coming out on top, 3,000 feet above the river, it extends along the rim to Potato Hollow on **Horse Pasture Plateau,** and beyond to **Lava Point.** From the rim there is a view of **Zion Canyon,** with all its startling color and strange forms, and into the broken wilderness of **Right Fork of North Creek.** Carry water, lunch. Mule rides available.

A sign at 5 m. points to **Weeping Rock** parking area, departure point for trails to East Rim and Weeping Rock. **East Rim Trail** involves a fairly strenuous 7-mile round trip for the full hike, leaving the canyon floor at the foot of **Cable Mountain** and ascending its north flank. There are wonderful views of Zion Canyon from various points on the trail, but the finest is reserved for the last—that from **Observation Point,** more than 2,000 feet above the canyon floor. From this point Kaibab Forest can be seen on the North Rim of Grand Canyon, far to the southeast; Cedar Mountain, in the Cedar Breaks country, looms on the northern horizon; and to the southwest is the Virgin River Valley and the settlements of Utah's Dixie, visible as far as St. George. Carry water, lunch. An easy, self-guiding trail leads from the parking area to **Weeping Rock.** Water seeping from the rocky walls moistens the soil to which cling cool green mosses and drooping ferns, intermingled with gay yellow columbines, purple shootingstars, and scarlet monkeyflowers. Also from the Weeping Rock parking area, a fairly strenuous trail leads 1 m. to the mouth of **Hidden Canyon,** a typical hanging valley.

Back on the main road, there is a good view of **The Organ** (L), and at 5.5 m. is a parking area with a choice view of the **Great White Throne** through the saddle between The Organ and Angels Landing. The **Great White Throne** (6,744 alt.) is the best known monolith in the Park. The summit of this gigantic truncated mass of white sandstone has been reached

Great White Throne overlooks Zion Canyon and Virgin River.

HAL RUMEL

numerous times, but climbers have been injured in attempting to scale its precipitous walls and the feat should be attempted only by experienced climbers. Directly opposite is **Angels Landing** (5,785 alt.), its dull red color in contrast to the white of the Throne. A trail from the Grotto picnic area leads to the summit of this peak, 2.5 m. from trailhead and 1,500 feet above. The trail affords an excellent bird's-eye view of Zion Canyon, but the last half mile is strenuous and best avoided by those who fear heights.

Leaving this viewpoint, the road and river make a great bend around the colossal **Organ,** a red spur projecting from Angels Landing. The road terminates at the **Temple of Sinawava,** 6.5 m. from Visitor Center, a truly spectacular amphitheater almost surrounded by sheer cliffs. The parking area is shaded by trees. *Restrooms, drinking water.* Here begins the hard-surfaced **Gateway to the Narrows Trail,** over which ranger-naturalists conduct parties daily. A trailside exhibit explains the geology and natural history of the area. Half a mile up is **Zion Stadium,** a walled-in alcove with wild flowers growing from crevices and clinging to the cliffs; on the canyon floor is a pool of cold lucid water. At **The Narrows,** a mile up the canyon from the parking area, the walls rise vertically for 2,000 feet but are only 50 feet apart at river level. At the end of the trail, those who would venture farther must wade along the river edge. *Permit required for Narrows hiking.*

Automobile tourists view the **Virgin River Narrows** here as a gateway. For downstream hikers, however, the Narrows in this vicinity mark the end of a strenuous but thrilling 12-mile hike for those descending the chasm from higher reaches of the Kolob Terrace. Details about this unique wilderness experience may be obtained from the Park Visitor Center. The Narrows (full length) are typically open from late June through early October, with weather conditions closely monitored by the Park; adverse conditions result in immediate closure. Upstream beyond the end of the trail, the Narrows are closed between early October and late June because high water may be dangerous and/or cold air and water might result in hypothermia.

B. ZION-MOUNT CARMEL HIGHWAY (STATE 9)

About half a mile north of the Visitor Center, the paved road forks: Zion Canyon scenic drive (preceding section) continues up-canyon to the left, State 9 switchbacks up the steep slope of cliff-walled **Pine Creek Canyon** to the right. Pulloffs at intervals allow dizzy views down into the main canyon and across to the stupendous west wall formed by West Temple, Towers of the Virgin, and The Sentinel. Beautifully colored **East Temple** looms above the road as it enters **Zion-Mount Carmel Tunnel,** where the road has been cut through solid rock for a mile. Windows in the sheer cliff give tantalizing glimpses of giant forms, but parking within the tunnel is not permitted as it once was. From a parking area at the tunnel's upper (east) end, a short self-guiding trail leads to an overview of Zion Canyon, Pine Creek Canyon, and the Great West Wall. Only a mile in length (round-trip), this **Canyon Overlook Trail** leads to a point directly above the **Great Arch of Zion.** The highway tunnel is a marvel of engineering; built during the 1920s, it was dedicated in July 1930.

East of the tunnel, State 9 winds sinuously for miles through a wondrous landscape of beautifully colored, gently contoured slickrock slopes, domes, cones, plateaus, and deep gorges. Forms are completely different from those seen in Zion Canyon. Gradually, near the Park's **East Entrance,** the terrain changes from bare, rounded rock to more open woodlands, with far-spreading vistas of mountains and cliffs.

C. KOLOB SECTION

The Kolob Section, formerly Zion National Monument, northwest of Zion Canyon, can be entered by road from two directions: (1) from Interstate Highway 15 near New Harmony (the *Finger Canyons*); and (2) north from State 9 at the town of Virgin.

The Kolob Section contains a portion of the Hurricane Fault, visible to the east of I-15 between Virgin River Valley and Cedar City *(see Tour No. 8).* The fault forms a bold, jagged escarpment in places, with an edge "as ragged and sharp as a ripsaw," having an elevation of more than 8,000 feet. The **Kolob Finger Canyons** are visible in impressive panorama from the vicinity of New Harmony. They can be seen in dramatic closeup from the paved Kolob park road *(closed in winter)* that forks east from I-15 two miles south of the New Harmony turnoff. The road climbs in switchbacks, ascending 1,300 feet in five miles to a spectacular viewpoint-parking area on the crest of Hurricane Fault, overlooking the yawning mouths of half a dozen sheer-walled, redrock gorges. These wild canyons offer delightful back-country hiking.

The other-worldly beauty of the **Kolob Terrace,** into which the canyons of Zion National Park have been sunk, undoubtedly prompted Mormon pioneers to name the area for the central sphere of the universe in Mormon "Book of Abraham" cosmology—Kolob, "the great one . . . nearest the throne of God," its revolution requiring a thousand years. Red cliffs rise abruptly from the canyon bottoms, breaking into a series of rugged canyons with walls 1,500 to 2,500 feet high. The most southerly canyon carries the waters of LaVerkin Creek, which flows south between Andersons Ranch and LaVerkin. Sparkling streams from the Kolob Terrace flow through some of the eastern canyons, covering the floors with a profusion of wild flowers and dense vegetation. However warmly these verdant canyons may welcome the visitor, once away from streams and familiar roads they can become less hospitable, being remote from towns or accommodations.

The second access road, from State 9 at Virgin, climbs from less than 4,000 feet at Virgin to more than 9,000 feet on the Markagunt Plateau near Cedar Breaks National Monument. Enroute, it traverses the broken **Kolob Terrace,** an intermediate platform into which the Park's canyons have been cut. The road involves steep climbs and hairpin turns but is paved for 18 miles, between Virgin and the north Park boundary. It affords a series of breathtaking views of Zion's temples, cliffs, mesas, buttes, knolls, lava cones and lava flows, and tremendous gorges. Views of West Temple and the Guardian Angels are particulary impressive.

From this road, hiking trails and unimproved routes lead to remote canyons and rims such as Hop Valley, Timber Top, Kolob Arch, and the Finger Canyons, all in the Kolob Section . . . Great West Canyon . . . North Creek . . . Wildcat Canyon . . . and West Rim Trail leading to Zion Canyon. At Lava Point there is a primitive campground.

Tour No. 1
BRIDGERLAND REGION
(Cache and Rich counties)

See Tour No. 2 for map of this region.

Bridgerland is Utah's north country, cold in winter, delightful in summer, an important breadbasket. Relatively compact in area, Bridgerland consists of Cache Valley, Bear River Range, Bear Lake, and Bear River Valley. The region combines pastoral landscape, city and town, wooded mountains, and one of the state's largest natural lakes. US 89 and US 91 are its main highways.

Its name a tribute to James Bridger and his fellow mountain-men of the 1820s and 1830s, Bridgerland is a transition zone of sorts between Utah's rugged Wasatch and arid Great Basin, and the semi-frontier north country of Wyoming, Idaho and Montana. Both Cache Valley and Bear Lake are physical links between Utah and Idaho, while Bear River ties those states to Wyoming. Culturally, too, this region is integrated with southern Idaho and to a lesser extent with Wyoming.

"Sartorial demands of beaver-hatted eastern dandies brought the first white men into Cache Valley in 1824," said the 1941 edition. That statement was incorrect in that Michel Bourdon of the British North West Company (traders and fur trappers) had visited Cache Valley earlier than that, in 1819, but it was American fur trappers, arriving in force in the fall of 1824, who remained in the area for several years and harvested the greater part of its rich crop of beaver pelts. The first party of American trappers to enter Cache Valley in 1824, under the leadership of John Weber, were employed by Ashley and Henry *(see History)*. Their numbers included some of the

Cache Valley.

UTAH TRAVEL COUNCIL

most renowned of all mountain men, among them James Bridger who followed the Bear River to its mouth and has since been considered the "discoverer" of Great Salt Lake. The following year a large party of British trappers led by Peter Skene Ogden came south from Montana, passing through Cache Valley into present-day Ogden Valley (Eden-Huntsville) and over the divide into Weber River Valley (Mountain Green). After an encounter there with American trappers he returned to the Snake River country. The Americans remained in the Cache Valley-Bear Lake region for several more years, holding an annual rendezvous in Cache Valley and two at Bear Lake. These early adventurers either named—or their own names were eventually applied to—such features as Great Salt Lake, Cache Valley, Bear River, Bear Lake, Ogden's Hole (Valley), Ogden, Weber River, Weber Valley, Weber County, and Bridgerland. "Because their number included a fair proportion of French-Canadian *voyageurs*," said the 1941 edition, "the Canuck name for fur deposits, or *caches,* was soon attached to the valley. James P. Beckwourth, a mulatto trapper, tells of *caching* seventy-five packs of beaver skins in 1825. . . ."

Permanent settlement did not come for more than 30 years after the trappers arrived. Even the Mormons avoided Cache Valley as a colonizing site for the first few years after they arrived in Salt Lake Valley, having lost much stock to its frigid winters. Finally, however, tentative beginnings were made at Wellsville (1856) and soon thereafter at other places in the valley. By 1860 thriving settlements had been established at Logan, Hyrum, Smithfield, Richmond, Mendon, Hyde Park, Providence, and Paradise; still others were added in subsequent years. Bear River Valley and Bear Lake Valley also were settled in the 1860s. As elsewhere in the pioneer west, early colonists endured severe privations, among them cold, hunger, poverty, and fear of Indian attack.

Tour No. 1A - Cache Valley (US 89-91)

Cache Valley is a pastoral basin, trending north-south, bordered by high ranges on its long sides and by low divides on either end. The valley measures about 50 miles in length and up to 15 miles or more in width. It is well watered by the Bear River and by tributary streams flowing primarily from the forested Bear River Range on the east. An extensive system of reservoirs, canals and wells has been developed for irrigation, and some thousands of acres are devoted to dry land farming of alfalfa, hay and grain. Cache Valley farms are among the most productive in either Utah or Idaho. Though these farms tend to be modest in size, compared with average farms in other parts of the region, they are fertile, efficiently managed, and produce a wide variety of livestock, grains, garden crops, and other products. Dairy cattle provide the milk for Utah's largest concentration of cheese factories, which are said to employ some 1,500 workers. The valley also supports a number of manufacturing firms of diverse nature, many of which are based on agriculture.

Entering Cache Valley from the south, US 89-91 climbs over a low divide (5,800 alt.) from Brigham City *(see Tour No. 2),* passing through a picturesque highland park overlooked by rocky peaks of the northern

Wasatch. Here is **Sherwood Hills,** a recreational resort offering sports facilities, dining, and lodging. The highway enters Cache Valley through **Wellsville Canyon,** near the mouth of which roads fork east and west.

Turn east from US 89-91 to Hyrum, Hyrum Lake State Recreation Area, Paradise and Avon. **HYRUM** (4,700 alt, 3,952 pop.) is the largest community in the south end of the valley, about six miles from Logan. A clean and pleasant city, Hyrum was settled in 1860 and named for Hyrum Smith, brother of the Mormon prophet Joseph Smith.

Old First Ward Meeting House (Mormon), 290 S. Center, was built in 1903-05 of red brick on a stone foundation and features a unique horseshoe balcony and carved woodwork. **Soren Hansen "Castle,"** 166 W. Main, was built in 1906-07 for Soren Hansen, a prominent local citizen. With many gables and an unusual three-story round tower, the Hansen home was large and ornate for its period and locale.

Hyrum Reservoir, formed by Hyrum Dam, impounds the water of Little Bear River flowing down from the Monte Cristo area. The dam is an earth and concrete structure, 540 feet across at the top and 101 feet high, completed in 1935 by the U.S. Bureau of Reclamation. On the shore of the 450-acre reservoir is **Hyrum Lake State Recreation Area,** a state park with developed camping, beach, and boating facilities. A historical marker near the dam denotes its location as the site of a fur-trapper cache.

Continue east from Hyrum to Blacksmith Fork Canyon, Bear River Range and Hardware Ranch. **Blacksmith Fork Canyon** is an impressive gash in the mountains with steep walls that loom several thousand feet on either side. Its stream is popular for fishing, and there are four developed camping and picnic areas (Cache National Forest) in the main canyon and its left-hand fork. **Hardware Ranch,** 16 miles east of Hyrum, is a working ranch operated by the State Division of Wildlife Resources primarily as a hay growing and feeding station for elk. The ranch occupies about 19,000

Hyrum Reservoir.

acres of rolling, brush-covered mountain terrain, with about 130 acres of irrigated meadow used for hay production. During the winter, deep snow in the high country encourages hundreds of elk to migrate to the ranch, where they feed on hay and on natural vegetation in the vicinity. Visitors are welcome all year to observe ranching and feeding operations; however, elk congregate in large numbers only in winter months, usually between December and March, when as many as 500 or 600 may gather at the ranch. Visitors may view the elk from a visitor center or enjoy a ride on a horse-drawn bobsled.

Turn south from Hyrum to **PARADISE** (542 pop.), 4 miles, and **AVON,** 6 miles, small towns at the south end of Cache Valley. Avon, the original site of Paradise, was settled in 1860; a few years later, worried over the threat of Indian attack, residents were advised to move to a more strategic location. Paradise Tithing Office, 28 N. Main, dates from the mid-1870s. In excellent condition, the building was built of red brick from one of the valley's first brickyards. South from Avon an improved but unpaved road crosses a low divide into Ogden Valley, giving access to Liberty, Eden, Huntsville and Pineview Reservoir *(see Tour No. 2).*

PROVIDENCE (4,600 alt, 2,675 pop.), a farming and residential community on the outskirts of Logan, was settled chiefly by Mormons of German and Swiss origin. Berries and fruits are important local crops and dry-farm wheat is grown on the slopes. The pioneer structures of log or adobe so apparent in 1941 are not so plentiful in the much larger, more modern city of today. **Edgewood Hall,** 325 S. 300 East, a private estate marked by a luxuriant growth of trees, dates from turn-of-the-century years when its first owner, Joseph A. Smith, built a 28-room mansion and started a plantation of trees. Born in England, Smith came to Utah in 1868, became a prominent citizen, an aboriculturist, and an avid reader. After his death the house burned to the ground. Financier Boyd Hatch, who purchased the estate in 1937, built a number of buildings in English Tudor style. The estate has been greatly reduced in extent but much of interest remains. For years it was operated as a dairy farm. *Private.* Edgewood Hall was described by David Cornwell in the *Salt Lake Tribune Magazine* issue of August 12, 1979.

From the west side of US 89-91, roads fork to Wellsville, Mendon, Newton, and other communities on the west side of Cache Valley.

WELLSVILLE (4,500 alt. 1,952 pop.) is a dairying, farming and residential community at the base of the Wellsville Mountains. The community was the first Mormon settlement in Cache Valley, being colonized in September 1856 by Peter Maughan, his family, and a few others from Tooele Valley. Maughan was known thereafter as the first pioneer of Cache Valley, becoming probate judge and presiding bishop. He directed the valley's colonization during the late 1850s and 1860s. Wrote J. Howard Maughan about the first party: "They were still in their wagons when the first snowfall came on September 26, and that night Mary Ann gave birth to the first white child born to the settlers of Cache Valley." The settlement was known as Maughan's Fort until 1913. Wellsville displays a number of distinctive early buildings.

WELLSVILLE MOUNTAINS loom above Wellsville and Mendon to summits of 9,356 feet in Wellsville Cone and 9,372 feet in Box Elder Peak. The mountains form the northernmost extension of the Wasatch Range proper, which terminates about ten miles north of Wellsville at Bear River Canyon. Only five miles wide in the area of maximum elevation, with an absolute rise of nearly 5,000 feet, the range is a topographic curiosity because of its narrow base combined with unusual height. Foot trails lead to its ridge from Mendon and Wellsville Canyon, affording dramatic panoramic views across parts of three states.

US 89-91 continues across the nearly level floor of Cache Valley to Logan, largest city in the state north of Ogden. *See Tour No. 1B.* Beside the highway, six miles south of Logan, is the joint **Ronald V. Jensen Historical Farm/Man and His Bread Museum,** projects of Utah State University. Occupying more than 100 acres of land, the farm-museum display thousands of farming artifacts of bygone years, including vintage tractors, threshing machines, wagons, plows, household items, etc. Many 19th century machines and implements are utilized or displayed on the historic farm, which functions as and resembles insofar as possible a working farm of that period, with horses, granary, smokehouse, root cellar, lambing shed, barn, hay derrick, 1875 farm house, and 1867 log house. The annual Cache Valley Threshing Bee is held at the farm each fall. *Open to the public; inquire locally for the schedule.*

In Logan is the junction of US 89 and US 91, US 89 forking east to Logan Canyon, Bear Lake, Idaho, and Wyoming *(see Tour No. 1C below),* while US 91 continues north to Preston, Pocatello, and other northern points.

North of Logan, US 91 passes through the open expanse of Cache Valley, paralleling the foothills of the Bear River Range. The valley is well filled with farms, towns, and residential suburbs for a mile or so on either side of the highway. Cache County grew 35 per cent in population between 1970 and 1980 and has doubled in the 40 years since 1940. Most of this growth has taken place in Logan and nearby communities. Beyond Bear River to the west, towns and individual dwellings continue to resemble in scattered dispersion the patterns of earlier years. Antiquity is yet apparent in the older, central parts of the first-settled communities, and away from the main highway, along which modern development dominates the scene. In the extent of roadside commercial and industrial development, US 91 between Logan and Smithfield now bears likeness to urbanized strips in the Wasatch Front area to the south.

SMITHFIELD (4,600 alt. 4,993 pop.) is the county's second city in size, having increased in population by 49 per cent between 1970 and 1980. It is a commercial and agricultural center, and also a bedroom community for Logan, only a ten-minute drive away.

The Del Monte (California Packing Company) plant in Smithfield was long one of the state's leading canneries. The main plant was built in 1919 by the Morgan Canning Company, which encouraged local farmers to plant peas and at one time handled the yield of several thousand acres. In the 1920s it was believed to be "the world's largest pea cannery," having a capacity of 25,000 cases of peas per day.

Turn east from Smithfield to **Smithfield Canyon** and Smithfield Canyon Forest Campground (Cache National Forest), 4 miles from town.

Turn west from Smithfield to **AMALGA** (pop. 323), 3 miles, site of **Cache Valley Cheese Factory,** which is reputed to be the largest maker of Swiss cheese in the world. The factory also produces a variety of other cheeses, and operations may be viewed on self-guided tours. Sales and gift shop. Cheesemaking is one of the valley's most important industries, conducted by some five large firms which utilize locally-produced milk. Amalga received its name from the Amalgamated Sugar Company, which operated a number of sugar factories in Utah and other western states for many years.

Continue west from Amalga on State 218 to **NEWTON** (4,500 alt. 623 pop.), an agricultural town, 10 miles from Smithfield, situated near the canyon-pass through which Bear River leaves Cache Valley. It was settled as a "new town" in 1869-70 by residents of Clarkston to the north.

Turn north from Newton to **Newton Reservoir,** an irrigation impoundment on Clarkston Creek that covers an area of 200 to 300 acres and irrigates some 2,000 acres of farmland in the vicinity. The original **Newton Dam** described in the 1941 edition was built of dirt and rocks, completed in 1886 after years of hard work and several failures. This dam may have been the first reservoir of substantial size in the nation to store water for irrigation. It was replaced during the 1940s by the present earthfill structure, 101 feet high and more than a thousand feet long, built by the federal government at a total cost of more than $700,000 (including canal system); half of this cost is being repaid by local water users.

Turn south from Newton via State 23 to junction with State 30, which connects Logan with Garland-Tremonton and I-15. Near Newton State 23 crosses Bear River not far upstream from **Cutler Dam,** which impounds Bear River and its Cache Valley tributaries in a large lake known as Cutler Reservoir. At the dam is a power plant and also the source of the West Side Canal, which supplies Bear River water to Box Elder farms. **Cutler Reservoir** occupies some 6,000 acres, extending behind the dam for eight or ten miles and creating a popular lake for boating as well as shallow marshes west of Logan where the Little Bear, Logan, and Blacksmith Fork rivers converge. At the hamlet of **BENSON,** 9 miles west of Logan, is a county park with picnic facilities, marina, boat ramp and dock. The marshes are habitat for myriad waterfowl.

Turn northwest from Newton via State 142 to **CLARKSTON** (4,900 alt. 562 pop.) at the foot of the steep, narrow ridge known as Clarkston Mountain. The 1941 edition stated that "a complete crop failure has never been reported" at Clarkston, and that "yields of thirty to forty bushels of hard wheat per acre are common, and those of fifty bushels are not unusual." The area produces dry-land alfalfa and grain crops for the most part. Settled in 1864, Clarkston received its name from Israel Clark, one of the original colonizers. In the local cemetery an 18-foot granite shaft marks the grave of **Martin Harris,** one of the three witnesses to the authenticity of the Book of Mormon who was buried there in 1875. Harris came to Utah at the age of 88 and died at 93. South of the cemetery but nearby is the **Martin Harris Memorial Amphitheater,** ground for which was broken in 1980.

Turn east from Clarkston via State 142 to Trenton and Richmond, passing through, in the words of *Deseret News* columnist Jerry Johnston, "a catalogue of green: pea-greens, sea-greens, jade and juniper. There's even emerald in the water wells." Much of this green is a result of the **West Cache canal system** which diverts water from Bear River near Preston, Idaho, and distributes it to farmlands in Idaho and the Cornish-Trenton-Amalga-Newton area of Utah.

RICHMOND (4,600 alt. 1,705 pop.) almost doubled its population between 1970 and 1980. In 1941, "Older houses stand in a close-knit group around the parked city square with its red-painted brick tabernacle. Farms lay on the slopes and valley floor, and, behind tree-shaded dwellings, are barns, corrals, and farm machinery." Visitors may judge for themselves how the Richmond of today resembles that of 40 years ago. Holstein cows were brought here in 1904 and thrived so well that Richmond won recognition as the state's Holstein center. Originated in 1913, the Richmond Holstein show was reputedly the first in the country and remains a popular spring event known as Black and White Days. For many years Richmond was the site of large creameries. The most important industry today is a huge Pepperidge Farm bakery that employs more than 500 people and utilizes local products. The 1941 edition described the town's early history in reminiscence that might be applied substantially to other Cache Valley communities:

Pleased with the lush grasses and adequate water, settlers built scattered log cabins, dugouts, and a log fort in 1859. A ditch was dug from a near-by stream and a dam placed in another to provide irrigation for the first year. The settlers built shingle, grist, carding, and molasses mills, and a horsepower sawmill was erected in 1860. A threshing machine with maple-wood cogs and cylinder was assembled, and Thomas Griffin, pioneer mechanic, constructed the first miniature steam engine in the State.

Turn west at Webster Junction, 4 miles north of Richmond, to **LEWISTON** (4,500 alt. 1,438 pop.), 2 miles, a prosperous farm and dairy community. Said the 1941 edition: "Platted on blocks one mile square when the townsite was settled in 1870, it has the largest spread of any incorporated city of equal population, covering twenty-four square miles." Local farmers grow a wide variety of crops in addition to dairying and livestock raising. In 1940 a sugar factory employed nearly 500 workers in season, but sugar beets no longer are the important crop they once were. Lewiston's early days were described in the 1941 edition.

A gray stone monument beside the highway, 1 mile south of the Utah-Idaho state line, commemorates the last major Indian battle in the vicinity of northern Utah. This was an encounter in late January 1863 (mid-winter) between a band of Shoshone-Bannock Indians and some 300 federal troops from newly-founded Camp Douglas in Salt Lake City, commanded by Colonel Patrick E. Connor. The battle took place near Bear River, at the mouth of Battle Creek, five miles north of Preston. It was prompted by harassment of overland travelers, settlers and miners by the Indians, whose traditional lands were rapidly being preempted by whites. Criticized later as a massacre and a dark stain on the history of the west, the battle was described in the 1941 edition:

It was sub-zero weather, deep snows submerged the trails, and seventy soldiers were disabled by frozen feet. The Indian camp was in a gorge twenty feet deep and forty feet wide. "I ordered the flanking party," Colonel Connor reported, "to advance down the ravine upon either side, which gave us the advantage of an enfilading fire and caused some of the Indians to give way and run toward the north end of the ravine. At this point I had a company stationed who shot them as they ran out. . . . Few tried to escape, however, but continued fighting with unyielding obstinacy . . . The most of those who did escape from the ravine were afterwards shot in attempting to swim the river." Firing ceased in four hours. Federal losses were 14 killed, 49 wounded. [Eight of the wounded later died.]

Accounts of native casualties vary. "We found 224 bodies on the field," Colonel Connor officially reported. A Cache Valley settler, William G. Smith, later said: "Instead of offering the Indians a chance to surrender, and be taken peaceably, General Connor issued a very cruel order to his men—'Take no prisoners, fight to the death; nits breed lice'." Colonel Connor paid handsome tribute to his troops for their intrepidity and fortitude. Two months later he was brevetted a brigadier-general.

US 91 crosses the state line 8 miles south of Preston, Idaho. Cache Valley terminates a few miles north of Preston, US 91 leaving the valley at a low divide known as **Red Rock Pass.** Some 18,000 years ago this area formed the rim of the Cache Valley Bay of glacial **Lake Bonneville** at its highest level. As the lake rose, geologists claim, its waters spilled over the rim into the Snake River drainage, carving a deepening channel (Red Rock Pass) and eventually, over a period of years, draining the immense lake to a much lower level before hard rock stopped the draining process. Geologic evidence in Idaho indicates that the resultant flood was catastrophic. *See Lake Bonneville in Geology section.*

BEAR RIVER, which enters Utah about 6 miles west of US 91, near Cornish, begins in the Uinta Mountains (Rocky Mountains) and empties into Great Salt Lake (Great Basin). It is said to be the largest stream in the western hemisphere that does not reach the ocean. The Bear is a very sinuous river, taking a 500-mile circuitous route through three states before terminating only 90 airline miles from its source. Along the way it is intensively utilized. The Bear is one of Utah's largest streams, its flow being exceeded only by the Green and Colorado. At its mouth, the Bear carries almost as much water as the Green River above Flaming Gorge Dam. About half this lower-end volume is contributed in Cache Valley by streams flowing from the Bear River Range. Some geologists believe that the Bear originally emptied into the Snake River but was diverted southward by lava flows into Lake Bonneville, causing that great body of water to rise to its highest level and eventually overflow at Red Rock Pass.

Tour No. 1B - Logan City

LOGAN (4,500 alt. 26,844 pop.), Cache County seat and the largest city in that part of the state, is built on the lowland and terraces of a north-reaching arm of prehistoric Lake Bonneville. Sheltering it on the east is the lofty Bear River Range, peaks of which reach 9,000 feet and more within a few miles of the range's base. The imposing mouth of Logan Canyon opens into the eastern outskirts of the city, immediately behind the campus of Utah State University.

Logan displays a not unpleasant mixture of the new and old, having retained much of the charm of venerable and distinguished age. At least this is the case in older, central parts of the city, where modernity has not changed the antique aspect to an unrecognizable extent. Logan's outskirts, however, are products of recent decades, and new developments are interspersed here and there among the old. In respects Logan is an interesting "living museum," its residents treasuring their historical heritage to the degree that indiscriminate change has not become the order of the day. Many of its older buildings have been preserved, and Center Street is listed in the National Register of Historic Places as a Historic District. Descriptions in the 1941 edition are still applicable: "The city is a pleasant residential community, its streets lined with trees. Lawns are numerous, and are kept green in summer by frequent watering. . . . Visible for miles from any approach in the valley, the Mormon Temple, with its twin gray towers, stands on an eastern terrace overlooking the tree-grown city. The square gray belfry of the Mormon Tabernacle rises above the trees in the downtown area; and to the northeast . . . is the bell tower of [Old Main]'' on the campus of the university. Here, from the edge of the hillside near Old Main, Logan and Cache Valley can be viewed in a breathtaking panorama.

Logan is an ideal representative of the American dream of free enterprise, its business roster listing the names of some 500 commercial operations within the city—surely an ample number for a community of Logan's size. Agriculture is a major industry in the county, with farm sales amounting to 40 million dollars or more each year; however, Utah State University is Logan's most important economic activity, as Brigham Young University is Provo's. The school's ten thousand students and large staff contribute millions of dollars to the local economy. Logan also is a regional commercial center, attracting consumers not only from Cache Valley but Box Elder County, southern Idaho, and western Wyoming as well. Though Wellsville was settled as Maughan's Fort in 1856, the Utah War discouraged further colonization until 1859, when Logan and other settlements were established. The following historical background is excerpted from the 1941 edition:

In 1859 the Mormons scraped a shallow irrigation canal from Logan River to farms in the town and made plans for irrigation of the valley. In the same year James Ellis and Benjamin Williams established the first sawmill, with a hand-operated whipsaw. During the succeeding decades, water power replaced hand labor, and sawmills, carding mills, and flour mills were built along the banks of streams. Hezekiah Thatcher opened a retail store for business, and Thomas Weir and Joel Ricks began tanning leather for "harness, saddles, shoes, britches, and shirts." The city was granted a charter and incorporated in 1866. The following year, telegraphic communications with Salt Lake City were completed.

In the early seventies, a watchmaker named Growe published a folio newspaper —half in Danish and half in English—and another watchmaker introduced photography. The public school was moved from its log cabins to a new stone building; the Episcopalians established a grammar school, the Presbyterians an academy, and the

Logan, Logan Canyon and Bear River Range. Utah State University can be seen at mouth of the canyon.

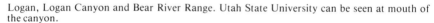

UTAH STATE UNIVERSITY

Mormons a college. The United Order, established by the Mormons in various parts of Utah and Arizona, as a communal form of living, was instituted in Logan about 1875. Harvests and produce were distributed on a basis of the amount of work contributed. The plan failed in a decade.

Mrs. Lydia Hamp Baker, whose family came to Logan from England in 1877, recalls in an interview that "the town was mostly willows in the early days." She worked at her trade of boot-closing, or sewing boot and shoe uppers by hand. The settlers slept in four poster cord beds, with rope stretched on the frame in lieu of springs. They burned willows for fuel, carried water from irrigation ditches for home use, and farmed exclusively with hand tools. Meat was scarce, and neighbors gave their peelings and table leavings to help fatten the nearest pig; when it was butchered they received "pig fry" for their investment—liver, fat, and a little pork. Indians begged from house to house, carrying their bundles of biscuits, sugar, and scraps to wigwams in the willows.

Completion of the Utah Northern Railroad from Ogden in 1874 gave Logan the outlet necessary for the development of native resources. But this advantage was mitigated by lack of capital and by Brigham Young's predilection for the fruits of the soil. Timber and farm produce were almost the sole exports of Logan for many years. Factories in and about the city were introduced for the most part after the turn of the century.

ATTRACTIONS IN LOGAN

(Many older buildings described below are listed on national and state historic registers.)

MORMON TEMPLE, 1st North and 2nd East, is maintained by the church for the administration of sacred ordinances, and is not open to the general public. The building, a castellated structure with octagonal corner towers surmounted by cupolas and massive buttresses, commands the city from the crest of an abrupt promontory two blocks east of Main Street. The walls, of rough-hewn limestone, are unrelieved by ornamentation, except mouldings of light sandstone at the story levels and on the cornices. Fenestration is simple, and the end towers, 170 and 165 feet high, are capped with unornamented cupolas. The level grounds and parking area east of the building are landscaped with trees and flower plots, on the west they slope down sharply from the building and are covered, in conformity with the severe character of the temple, by a wide sweep of lawn. *See Color Section.*

The temple was completed in 1884, seven years after Brigham Young selected the site and conducted ceremonies for breaking of ground in 1877. Its architect was Truman O. Angell, designer of the Salt Lake Temple. Church members labored on the building for seven years without wage, hauling timber and stone from Logan Canyon, and the church raised about $600,000 in the form of labor, merchandise and produce, and a relatively small amount of money. Extensive renovation and enlargement of its capacity, occurring between 1976 and 1979, cost nearly $8,000,000.

Both the temple, and the tabernacle *(below),* were described by Leonard J. Arrington and Melvin A. Larkin in the *Utah Historical Quarterly* (Summer 1973). The Mormons, they wrote, regarded the Logan temple as "a kind of private mountain—a corporeal embodiment of their ideals—a formidable defender of the Saints' way of life, symbolically guarding the church from the threats of the larger society around them. It was also a symbol of their reaching out to God—of their closeness to God—a place

Mormon Tabernacle in Logan *(left)* and 19th century rock house, Wellsville *(right)*. Distinctive early architecture is a Cache Valley asset.

where the Savior would come to dwell with them. In many respects the temple came to be regarded almost in a mystical sense. . . . To the twenty-five thousand persons who built it and labored on it 'without purse or scrip', it was a visual reminder of the omnipresence of eternity.'' Visitors are welcome at the temple's Visitor Center.

Mormon Tabernacle, Main and Center streets, a cupola-crowned structure of gray stone, is an excellent example of early Mormon architecture. The building, started in 1864, was not completed for many years, being dedicated in 1891 by church president Wilford Woodruff, seven years after completion of the temple. It seats about 1,500 and may be visited, when open, by the public.

Cache County Relic Hall (Daughters of Utah Pioneers) occupies the lower level of the modern Chamber of Commerce building at 52 W. 200 North. The museum displays pioneer relics and artifacts such as pioneer tools, clothing, furniture and furnishings, and art. Open during summer months.

Lyric Theater, 28 W. Center, was built in 1913, later restored by Utah State University for theatrical and musical productions . . . **David Eccles Home,** 250 W. Center, a stately edifice of brick and white stone, built in 1907 for financier David Eccles, since the 1940s used as a dormitory, sorority and fraternity house for USU students . . . **Lindquist Hall,** corner 1st East and 2nd North, salt-box structure built in 1868, used variously as city hall, high school, college, and residence . . . **Union Pacific Railroad Station,** 6th West and Center, built at the turn of the century, one of the finest remaining examples of its type in the state . . . **Old Cache County Courthouse,** 179 N. Main, built in 1882-83 by the local United Order . . . **St. John's Episcopal Church,** 83 E. 1st North, built in 1906 by the Episcopal Church, which had established a school and mission in Cache Valley in the 1870s . . . **Joseph Thatcher Home,** 164 S. 3rd West, built about 1862, an outstanding example of pioneer rock construction.

UTAH STATE UNIVERSITY overlooks Logan and Cache Valley from a bench at the mouth of Logan Canyon. Founded in 1888 by the territorial legislature to take advantage of a succession of federal "land-grant" acts which provided for support of agricultural colleges and experiment stations throughout the nation, it was known as the Agricultural College of Utah (AC) until 1929, then as Utah State Agricultural College (USAC) until the name was changed to Utah State University (USU) in 1957. The university embraces eight colleges, 44 departments of instruction, and some 600 courses of study. Enrollment totals more than 10,000. Students attend from all states and over 80 foreign countries; the majority are from Utah, but Idaho, California, Wyoming, Montana, and other western states are well represented.

"Utah State University has been able to retain some of its original appearance and mission," according to a university publication, "and to combine these with the most sophisticated and current elements of higher education and research. From the original 19th century buildings and trees associated with Old Main and the Quad to the sculptured gardens of the Tanner Fountain and Plaza and the modern designs of the new Life Span Learning buildings, Utah State blends the old and new in a pleasant and invigorating manner." Enrollment in 1940 was only a third the size of the present studentbody; most buildings on the campus have appeared since 1950.

The strong offerings in agriculture, natural resources, irrigation engineering, commerce and home economics that characterized Utah State from its earliest beginnings have been augmented by equally strong offerings in a broad spectrum of other disciplines.

Campus scene, Utah State University.

Among USU's programs of longest standing are its research and extension programs. USU was among the first institutions of higher learning in the intermountain area to have a research program, primarily devoted to agriculture for many years but now embracing nearly every department. The Agricultural and Engineering experiment stations were established in 1888 and 1918, respectively. Involved with some 150 research projects, the Agricultural Experiment Station operates 12 farms and associated research facilities around the state; its staff includes faculty members and students from many university departments as well as employees of the U. S. Department of Agriculture. The Engineering Experiment Station is financed by mineral lease funds and federal, state and industrial grants. Today Utah State is consistently among the top five or ten universities in the nation in attracting engineering research contracts and grants in relation to number of faculty members. The university has gained particular fame for its research in upper atmosphere studies, plant breeding, biology, energy development and other areas. USU's research program also involves centers, laboratories, bureaus, units, and institutes devoted to research in water resources, electro-dynamics, exceptional children, education, economics, ecology, outdoor recreation and tourism, fisheries, wildlife, land rehabilitation, forest sciences, computers, and other subjects.

Cooperative Extension Service—financed jointly by federal, state, and county governments—involves a system of county and area agents serving every county, as well as specialists in a number of subject fields. Information and assistance are provided to the citizenry to help solve problems, improve the home and community environment, and raise the standard of living.

International Programs and Studies involves faculty and students in cooperative research and as consultants to private industry, government agencies, and research groups abroad as well as in this country. USU personnel in recent years have provided technical assistance having to do with food, water resources development and management, education and other areas to numerous countries in Central and South America, Africa, and Asia.

Visitors are advised to tour the campus on foot and by auto, entering most conveniently from 400 North (US 89), or from 700 North via 800 East. **Old Main,** the administrative headquarters, is a venerable towered structure perched on the western edge of the campus, overlooking the city and valley. Other buildings of special note include the **Merrill Library and Learning Resources Center, Chase Fine Arts Center, Taggart Student Center,** focal point for student social and recreational life, the **Kellogg Life Span Learning Complex,** and the **Spectrum arena. Romney Stadium,** at the north end of the campus, was enlarged to 30,000 seats in 1980; this 10,000-seat enlargement is remarkable for the fact that it was built largely with donated labor, materials, equipment, services, and funds contributed for the most part by Cache Valley business firms, private citizens, students, faculty, and alumni.

Each year in late July and early August, USU's campus is visited by tens of thousands of visitors who come to participate in varied activities scheduled by the *Festival of the American West.* Among the festival's diversified offerings is a spectacular historical pageant entitled, "The West: America's Odyssey," held in the Spectrum arena, which combines dance, song, and mutli-media sight-and-sound effects. The Great West Fair features pioneer and Indian craft exhibits and food booths, a quilt show, western cookout, photo and art exhibit, and Frontier Street, a reconstruction of an early western commercial street.

Tour No. 1C - Logan Canyon, Bear Lake and Rich County

US 89 forks east from US 91 in the center of Logan, giving access to Utah State University and immediately thereafter entering the mouth of Logan Canyon. **LOGAN CANYON** is one of the longest mountain canyons in the state, extending for about 30 miles from its mouth to a summit pass on the Bear River Range at 7,800 feet. It provides a delightful alpine drive, being especially dramatic in late September when the reds and golds of autumn are at their height. Cache National Forest maintains nearly a score of improved camping-picnicking sites in the canyon—one of the greatest concentrations of such facilities in the state—and Logan River is a popular fishery where German brown trout weighing more than 20 and 30 pounds have been caught. A maze of hiking trails and unpaved forest roads criss-crosses the mountains on either side of the highway.

It is probable that the **BEAR RIVER RANGE** has been more thoroughly utilized—for recreation, grazing, and timbering—than any other mountain region in the state, with the possible exception of the Wasatch near Salt Lake City. For the most part the range is a gentle highland, away from the steep western front and grand precipices of Logan Canyon in its lower reaches; in fact, it is termed a plateau by geographers. The range is commonly considered a northeastern segment of the Wasatch, and only geographers or geologists would have cause to disagree. The greater part of the range north and east of Blacksmith Fork Canyon is included within Cache National Forest, with the exception of considerable private land in the headwaters of Logan River. Hikers are referred to forest maps or guidebooks such as *Cache Trails* (Mel Davis and Ann Schimpf) for trail and recreation details.

Points of interest reached from US 89 in Logan Canyon

Wind Caves (also known as Witches Castle, DeWitts Cave, Sun Dance Cave, or Devils Cave), are a series of eroded arches and rooms more than a thousand feet above the highway. Reached by 1-mile trail from DeWitt Campground, 5 miles from Logan.

Logan Cave is a two-story cavern about 2,000 feet in length, inhabited by bats and requiring a flashlight. *Not recommended for casual exploration.* The cave can be reached from Cottonwood Campground, about 15 miles from Logan.

Old Jardine Juniper, the largest known Rocky Mountain red cedar, is perched on a limestone ridge about 1,500 feet above the highway. Its age is estimated as 3,500 years, and the tree now supports only a few green branches on its warped and twisted, mostly hollow trunk. Old Jardine measures 27 feet in circumference and 45 feet in height. There is evidence that originally it may have been two trees. It can be reached by a steep climb of 1½ miles from Cottonwood Campground or a longer hike from Wood Camp Campground, two miles down-canyon. The tree was discovered in 1923 and named for William J. Jardine, USU alumnus who served as Secretary of Agriculture during the Hoover administration.

Old Ephraim's Grave is marked by an 11-foot shaft denoting the height of a giant grizzly bear killed at the site in 1923. It can be reached on unpaved forest road or foot trail via Temple Fork (junction about 16 miles from Logan) and is about 6 miles from the highway.

Tony Grove Lake is a secluded, scenic gem at 8,100 feet with forest campground, popular for fishing. About 5 miles from US 89 (junction 20 miles from Logan).

Beaver Mountain Ski Area is a developed resort on the summit of the mountains, about a mile north of US 89 from junction 26 miles east of Logan. Launched in 1939 by the Seeholzer family, which still operates it, Beaver Mountain is advertised as "one winter ski resort that's big enough to challenge the really good skier, and small enough to include people who've never skied at all." Skiers come from Sweetwater

Park of Bear Lake *(accommodations)* as well as Logan and more distant points. The resort features four lifts ranging from 1,300 to 4,600 feet in length and 350 to 1,600 feet vertical; 16 maintained trails, day lodge with cafeteria, ski shop and rentals, night skiing, ski school, ski patrol. Altitude 7,200 to 8,832 feet.

Limber Pine (Mountain Monarch) is reached by walking along a good 1-mile trail from parking area at Logan Canyon Summit (7,800 alt.), 29 miles from Logan. The ancient tree is thought to be about 500 years old and measures more than 24 feet in circumference and 44 feet in height. Until recent investigations raised some doubt, Limber Pine was thought to be 2,000 years old. In 1978, forestry professor Ronald M. Lanner of USU determined that it consisted of five trees which had grown together and that its age probably did not exceed 500 years. The self-guiding nature trail provides high-level views of Bear Lake and its environs.

Near Beaver Mountain, in January 1953, an airplane crash killed 40 passengers and crew members. Passengers were veterans of the Korean War. Their remains could not be removed until spring because of deep snow; during interim months the area was protected by a military guard.

Travelers from the west view **BEAR LAKE** in breathtaking panorama from a lookout point beside the highway, 30 miles from Logan and 10 miles from Garden City. A scenic spectacle because of its distinctive blue-green coloring and mountain setting, the lake is at an altitude of 5,900 feet. It lies equally in Utah and Idaho and measures about 21 miles in length by 7 miles in maximum width. Bear Lake is fed indirectly by Bear River and directly by numerous smaller streams and springs. Resorts, marinas, and houses are scattered along its shore and on the western mountain slopes, overlooking the fields of Garden City.

Bear Lake is estimated by geologists to be at least 28,000 years old. Until recent years its water was exceptionally clean. Between 1909 and 1918 canals and pumping stations were constructed at the north end of the lake by power companies to divert Bear River water into the lake during times of

Juniper Jardine *(right)*.

Fishing in Logan River *(below)*.

UTAH TRAVEL COUNCIL

high runoff and to pump water from the lake back into the river in periods of reduced flow. This converted the lake into a storage reservoir for water control, which was beneficial to downstream farmers and assured ample year-round water for power generation. However, the diversion has gradually altered the ecology of the lake, since the river contributes alien chemicals not originally found in the lake in such large quantities. Increased population and recreational use are adding pollutants as well. Bear Lake, as a result, is changing from cold water to warm water status and is showing signs of "premature aging" or eutrophication. Governmental and private interests are cooperating in studies and corrective measures in an attempt to slow or halt this deterioration.

Problems of over-use are compounded by the lake's rise in recreational popularity. Whereas Garden City-Laketown had a population of less than 1,000 in 1980, summer residents multiply that total four or five times, while transient recreationists number in the tens of thousands on busy weekends. Facilities are not adequate to handle the influx because a short season discourages private investment and the tax base has not been sufficient for construction of public facilities. Unsavory land speculation has not been absent from the scene. Officials anticipate future growth from ongoing exploration for oil and gas in the lake's vicinity, which is part of the Overthrust Belt.

GARDEN CITY (5,950 alt. 259 pop.) has multiple personalities, changing with season. It is a quiet hamlet in colder months. In warmer months it swarms with part-time residents and transient pleasure-seekers who come to boat, swim, waterski, fish, dive, or just relax. Law enforcement is a problem, even in winter, when there is a disturbing incidence of burglary and vandalism.

Garden City greatly expanded its area in the late 1970s with annexation of **Pickleville** to the south and land developments along the lake and on the slopes to the west. Current and proposed developments, both public and

Marina, Bear Lake State Recreation Area.

private, include a water and sewer system, many new homes, parks for campers and recreational vehicles, motel, lodge and restaurant, public park, and recreational facilities.

Garden City was settled by pioneers under the leadership of Charles Coulson Rich, Mormon apostle. Starting with two small cabins in 1864, the town acquired a flour mill, a sawmill, a blacksmith shop, a picker, carding machines, and looms. Later an irrigation canal was built, and the townsite was surveyed in 1877.

Bear Lake State Recreation Area, a mile north of Garden City, is a large breakwater marina developed by the State Division of Parks and Recreation. Its features include a visitor center, nearly 200 boat slips, a dry-storage area, camping and picnicking facilities, restrooms and showers, launching and docking facilities. Open May-September.

Rendezvous State Recreation Area at the south end of the lake, near Laketown, was developed in the late 1970s and early 1980s with water, utilities, and numerous units for camping and picnicking. Covering a 65-acre area, the park also includes a mile-long beach, boat launching ramp, and boat parking area.

LAKETOWN (6,000 alt, 271 pop.) is an agricultural community at the south end of Bear Lake, neighbor to a new state beach and a contemporary leisure-time development known as Sweetwater Park—both of which may portend further change for this bucolic rural area. Laketown was settled during the 1860s, having been a rendezvous site for fur trappers many years prior to that, in the late 1820s. In 1870, it is recorded, about 3,000 Indians camped in the vicinity, causing consternation among the settlers but departing peacefully for Wyoming.

BEAR RIVER VALLEY is a beautifully green and picturesque ranching district, its lands devoted primarily to the raising of cattle and sheep and the growing of feed crops such as alfalfa and barley. Except for passing cars, there is little evidence here of the recreational boom that afflicts Bear Lake Valley to the north. A number of local residents are employed in phosphate mining in the Crawford Mountains to the east.

Bear Lake recreation. *Utah Travel Council photos.*

RANDOLPH (6,300 alt. 659 pop.) is seat of Rich County, a trading center, and one of the most markedly rural towns in the state. "Randolph H. Stewart led the first group of settlers from St. Charles (now in Idaho) to the present site in 1870," said the 1941 edition. "The town was surveyed with a rope in the absence of a surveyor's chain, and Brigham Young personally organized the town in 1871, when he made a treaty with the Bannock Indians."

Rich County had a population of 2,100 in 1980, a 30 per cent increase in ten years but still one of the smallest county populations in the state. Traditionally, the county's economy has been based mainly on agriculture, with travel, recreation, construction, and trade in the Bear Lake region becoming more important in recent times. Phosphate and natural gas are the major mineral products. Petroleum holds promise for the future. Game birds, deer, elk, and fish are plentiful.

WOODRUFF (6,340 alt. 222 pop.), 10 miles south of Randolph, is a center for farms and ranches and the eastern terminus of State 39, which crosses the Bear River Range at Monte Cristo summit in its transmountain passage between Woodruff and Huntsville *(see Tour No. 2)*. The town was settled in the winter of 1870-71 and named for Wilford Woodruff, Mormon apostle and later church president. The lush meadows of Bear River Valley in this vicinity produce thousands of cattle. Woodruff's winter climate is one of the coldest in Utah, and even in summer it is relatively cool. A low of 50 degrees below zero was recorded in February 1899, a record that was almost equalled in 1939 and 1949.

UTAH TRAVEL COUNCIL

Tour No. 2
GOLDEN SPIKE EMPIRE
(Box Elder, Davis, Morgan, Weber counties)

Golden Spike Empire encompasses more than 8,000 square miles of northwestern Utah, stretching from the Wasatch Range across Great Salt Lake and its enormous flat basin. A land of startling topographic contrast, the region combines the rural and pastoral with congested metropolis. The majority of its people reside along the narrow Wasatch Front, from Bountiful on the south to Brigham City on the north.

This tour region extends 70 miles from south to north and up to 150 miles from east to west. Only the fertile Wasatch belt and Bear River Valley support more than a meager population. Elsewhere, people live on scattered ranches or in small towns, and thousands of square miles are virtually empty of human residents. Great Salt Lake itself occupies a fluctuating area of more than a thousand square miles. Between 1970 and 1980 the combined counties added 72,000 residents to their populations, increasing from 257,000 to 329,000, or a percentage gain of 28 per cent. The region's economy is broadly diversified, including large-scale and small-scale farming and ranching, transportation, trade, tourism, recreation, manufacturing, and defense.

Tour No. 2A - Brigham City and Box Elder County

BRIGHAM CITY (4,400 alt. 15,596 pop.), the county seat of Box Elder County, is on the fan-shaped alluvial delta of Box Elder Creek, at the base of the steep and rugged Wasatch Range. The range here is more than 9,000 feet high, or nearly a mile higher than the city. Brigham City is remarkable for its tree-shaded neatness; in fact, trees, the Mormon Tabernacle, and the great metal arch across Main Street symbolize the city for most visitors. For years it has received national beautification awards. Brigham City is noted as a center of fruit orchards and truck farms, and its economic position is enhanced by its being a commercial center for a far-spreading empire of farms, ranches, and livestock raisers. In recent times manufacturing has increased in importance.

Peaches were introduced here in 1855 and have become an important local product. Brigham City is known as the Peach City, the site of a traditional Peach Day celebration in September, held annually since early years of the century.

Brigham City was settled in 1851 as Box Elder, being renamed in 1856 for Brigham Young, who made his last public address here in 1877. The Brigham City Mercantile and Manufacturing Association, organized in 1864 by local leader Lorenzo Snow—a Mormon apostle and later president of the church—was a long-lived and largely successful experiment in cooperative community enterprise, becoming a model for United Order pro-

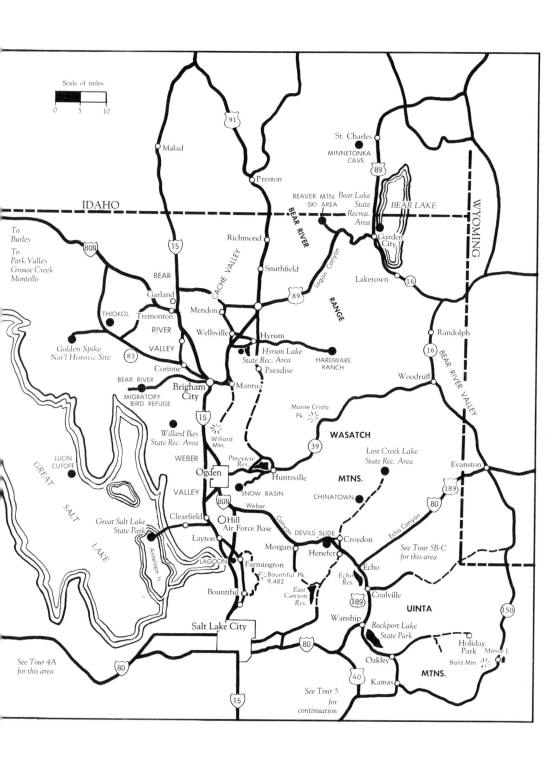

Scale of miles
0   5   10

To Burley
To Park Valley
Grouse Creek
Montello

IDAHO

WYOMING

91

Malad

St. Charles

MINNETONKA CAVE

89

BEAVER MTN. *Bear Lake State Recrea. Area*
SKI AREA

BEAR RIVER

BEAR LAKE

Preston

Richmond

CACHE VALLEY

Smithfield

89

Logan Canyon

RANGE

Garden City

Laketown

16

80N

15

BEAR

Garland

THIOKOL

Tremonton

RIVER

VALLEY

83

Mendon

Wellsville

Hyrum

Randolph

16

BEAR RIVER VALLEY

Golden Spike Nat'l Historic Site

Corinne

Hyrum Lake State Rec. Area
Paradise

HARDWARE RANCH

Woodruff

BEAR RIVER
MIGRATORY BIRD REFUGE

Brigham City

Mantua

Monte Cristo Pk.

WASATCH

LUCIN CUTOFF

15

Willard Bay State Rec. Area

Willard Mtn.

WEBER

39

Lost Creek Lake State Rec. Area

Evanston

GREAT

SALT

LAKE

Ogden

VALLEY

Pineview Res.

Huntsville

MTNS.

CHINATOWN

189

80

Echo Canyon

SNOW BASIN

Great Salt Lake State Park

Clearfield

80N

Weber

Canyon

DEVILS SLIDE

Croydon

See Tour 5B-C for this area

Hill Air Force Base

Layton

Morgan

Henefer

Antelope Is.

LAGOON

Farmington

Bountiful Pk. 9,482

Echo Res.

Echo

89

Bountiful

East Canyon Res.

Coalville

150

Salt Lake City

Wanship

Rockport Lake State Park

UINTA

Holiday Park

Mirror L.

80

Oakley

Bald Mtn.

See Tour 4A for this area

80

40

Kamas

MTNS.

15

See Tour 5 for continuation

grams established in other Mormon communities during the 1870s. Beginning with a cooperative store, the association gradually added a tannery, leather products department, woolen factory, thousands of sheep, cattle and hogs, sawmill and wood products factory, public works and construction departments, a flax farm in Mantua, blacksmith shop, and other enterprises to a total of 40 departments. Wages were paid to workers, mostly in merchandise or local products, and at one time 500 employees were on the rolls. Hundreds of people owned stock in the association; dividends were generous. In 1874 stockholders voted to join the church's newly established United Order. Thereafter a series of misfortunes dealt blows that eventually led to the association's abandonment: destruction of the wool factory by fire in 1877, a $10,000 assessment by the federal government in 1878 (later returned), loss of crops to drought and grasshoppers, and other troubles. Before 1880 all departments except the store had been transferred to private ownership, and by 1895 the store was bankrupt—partially as a result of the national depression of that period. The Brigham City Cooperative was described by Leonard J. Arrington in *Utah Historical Quarterly* (Summer 1965).

Attractions in Brigham City

Mormon Tabernacle (Box Elder Stake), on Main Street between 2nd and 3rd South, has been termed the most beautiful building in Utah. It is a striking edifice with Gothic arched doors and windows, massive tower, and 16 smaller steeples atop 16 brick buttresses. The present building of stone and brick dates from the 1890s when it was built to replace an earlier tabernacle destroyed by fire in 1896. Its interior features a fine pipe organ, ornamental plaster ceiling decorations, and a gallery supported by Doric columns. *Open during summer months for public tours. See Color Section.*

Intermountain Inter-Tribal School, established in January 1950, occupies the renovated and expanded physical plant of World War II's huge Bushnell General Hospital. The school is the largest Bureau of Indian Affairs residential school in the country, its coeducational studentbody numbering about 830 in 1981-82. At one time it offered programs for both elementary and high school students; today it is an accredited high school with a full academic curriculum and diversified vocational training program. Students represent more than 90 Indian tribes from every part of the country. Before 1973 the school specialized in the training of Navajo youth, in that year becoming an inter-tribal school. More than 5,000 students had received their high school diplomas from the school by 1981, the largest number (384) in 1971, since which time the studentbody and staff have declined and the school has been threatened with closure because of federal budget reductions.

Box Elder County Courthouse, Main and Forest (city center), a distinguished pillared edifice with clock in the dome, dating from the last century . . . **First Security Bank Building,** Main and Forest across from the Courthouse, was completed in 1891 as the Brigham City Co-op Store but served only a few years in that capacity . . . **Community Center-Museum-Art Gallery** in Brigham Young Square, Forest between 2nd and 3rd West . . . **Brigham City Railroad Depot,** a vintage gabled structure, 8th West and Forest .

1. Turn east from Brigham City on US 89-91, through Box Elder Canyon, to Mantua (5 miles), Cache Valley and Logan *(see Tour No. 1)*. Near **Mantua** is Box Elder County Park and forest campground, with facilities for camping, picnicking, etc. **Mantua Reservoir** is popular for fishing, boating, waterskiing, camping and picnicking.

Turn south from Mantua on an unpaved but improved road to Willard Basin and Inspiration Point, about 12 miles from Mantua. **Willard Basin, enclosed by steep** mountain walls thousands of feet high, marks the upper end of Willard Canyon's West Fork. Enclosing it on three sides are majestic ridges of the Wasatch. At 9,000 feet is a small picnic-camping area (Cache National Forest) with drinking water, toilets, tables. Open June-October. A small lake is nearby. Immediately beyond, the road switchbacks up the mountain to **Inspiration Point** (9,422 alt.), a dizzy aerie only three miles from the town of Willard. One mile of this distance is vertical. Seemingly the whole of northwestern Utah is spread out beneath the point in sublime panorama. Bear River Migratory Bird Refuge and Willard Bay can be seen in their entirety, as can Weber Valley and Ogden. Points in Idaho, Wyoming and Nevada are visible on a clear day, and much of Great Salt Lake is spread beneath the eye. From the point, Skyline Trail leads south and east along the Wasatch crest to **Willard Peak** (9,764 alt.) and **Ben Lomond** (9,712 alt.), continuing to North Ogden Canyon and beyond, terminating in Ogden Canyon at Wildwood. The last six miles of the road to Inspiration Point are not recommended for the timorous, as the road clings to high slopes, is sinuous and narrow, and may be rough. Passable only during summer months.

2. Turn north from Brigham City on State 69 to Honeyville, Dewey-ville, Collinston, Bear River Canyon, Malad Valley, and Cache Valley *(see Tour No. 1)*. **HONEYVILLE** (4,300 alt. 915 pop.) is a farming community, as are **DEWEYVILLE** (311 pop.) and **COLLINSTON.** Harper's Ward, a mile south of Honeyville, contains several beautiful, aged rock houses, listed on historic registers and considered to be among the finest in Utah. Looming high above Honeyville and Deweyville is the tremendous west face of the northern Wasatch, a rocky escarpment of forbidding aspect. East of Honeyville the great mountain wall rises 5,000 feet in two miles to the 9,300-foot summits of Wellsville Cone and Box Elder Peak. As noted in Tour No. 1 the Wasatch Range here is only five miles wide in its base. This narrow width combined with great height places this segment of the Wasatch in a special class among American mountains.

Crystal Springs, 2 miles north of Honeyville, is a tree-shaded resort surrounding a hot spring and a cold spring. Bathing, swimming, skating, camping, picnicking, refreshments.

3. Continue north from Brigham City via I-15 to Malad, Pocatello, Idaho Falls, and other northern points. In Utah I-15 traverses the valley of Malad River, which narrows as it approaches the Idaho line. The valley is a productive dry farming region of vast grain fields that sprawl across the rolling valley floor and far up its sides. Irrigated farming also is practiced. Crops include wheat and barley, alfalfa, potatoes, and vegetables. Cattle are an important product. The valley was used as a herd ground by Mormons during the 1850s and Malad City was settled in 1864.

PLYMOUTH (4,400 alt. 238 pop.) was settled in 1869 and has been an agricultural center in the years since. Nearby, between 1979 and 1980, Nucor Corporation built a new steel plant costing more than 30 million dollars. Shakedown operations began in 1981. The plant is designed to process steel scrap in electric furnaces, resulting steel being utilized for shaped steel products. In 1980-81 Nucor also began construction of plants near Brigham City for production of steel grinding balls and steel joists.

4. Turn northwest from Brigham City via I-15 and I-84/I-80N to Tremonton, Snowville, Idaho and the Pacific Northwest. **TREMONTON** (4,300 alt. 3,464 pop.) is the commercial capital of a widespread agricultural region. In its vicinity are thousands of acres of productive dry farms and irrigated farms, devoted to the raising of grain, alfalfa, etc. Tremonton was settled in 1888 and experienced a boom during the early 1900s when the townsite was laid out. Many residents commute to work at the Thiokol plant near Promontory, 20-odd miles away.

Turn north from Tremonton to **GARLAND** (4,340 alt. 1,405 pop.), 2 miles, a farming and residential community now joined to Tremonton by a residential strip. At one time Garland was an important sugar beet center, the site of a large sugar factory operated by Utah-Idaho Sugar Company. The plant was closed in 1979 because of declining profits and most beet growers converted to other crops.

Northwest of Tremonton, I-84/I-80N traverses a region of low hills and increasingly lofty mountains where expansive grain fields—many of them watered by sprinklers—follow the contours of the land. These fields gradually give way to the sparse ground cover that is so typical of arid western Utah where not cultivated.

Turn south on State 83 from junction 17 miles west of Tremonton to Thiokol and Golden Spike National Historic Site *(see No. 5 below)*.

SNOWVILLE (4,550 alt. 237 pop.), 37 miles west of Tremonton, is the center of Curlew Valley farming and dairying activities. It was settled by Idahoans and named for Lorenzo Snow, Mormon apostle and church president *(see Brigham City above)*. Some residents work at the Thiokol plant.

Turn south on an unpaved road, passing through Curlew Valley to **Locomotive Springs State Waterfowl Management Area,** 20 miles. This is an extensive marshland formed by Locomotive Springs, at the north tip of Great Salt Lake, popular for waterfowl shooting in season. An east-west road here follows the route of the abandoned transcontinental railroad, connecting Golden Spike National Historic Site on the east with Kelton and Lucin on the west. *See below.*

Turn west on State 42 from junction with I-84/I-80N, 3 miles west of Snowville, driving 15 miles to Curlew Junction. Turn south on State 30 to Park Valley and Nevada. This paved highway—76 miles from Curlew Junction to the Nevada line—is an adventure road through the vast expanse of scrub-covered desert that marks the bed of vanished Lake Bonneville. The highway skirts the foothills of impressively high and rugged **Raft River Mountains** (9,900 alt.) and **Grouse Creek Mountains** (9,000 alt.). Little is there to testify that this empty land once resounded to the cacophony of pioneer wagon trains, bawling cattle, and the whistle of chugging trains—that for 30 years or more between the 1840s and 1870s it was the route of uncounted travelers on their way to and from California. While the majority of overland travelers passed to the west and north of the mountains on the main Salt Lake Cutoff, many came this way. The first wagons to cross northern Utah pioneered the future route of the railroad. These belonged to the Bartleson-Bidwell emigrant train of 1841. Charles Kelly retraced their trail in an automobile some 90 years afterward and described the route in *Desert Magazine* (March 1946).

A spiderweb of fairweather roads gives access to recesses of the mountain country of Utah's northwest corner, forested in places and utilized for stock grazing and sporadic mining. High points provide inspirational views of the desert west of Great Salt Lake, its surface almost completely flat and devoid of vegetation to the south, higher and broken and less barren to the north, with scattered ranges here and there like islands in a sea. The area was described in the 1941 edition:

... in summer, the heat waves obscure the land like rippling water as the sun beats down on the baked, white clay flats. . . . **PARK VALLEY** (5,600 alt.) was settled by ranchers in 1869, the rich grass in the valleys supporting large herds of cattle, though scarcity of water always counterbalanced fertility of the soil. More lively days came with mining excitement in the late years of the century. A vein of gold was struck, and, as recalled by C. W. Goodliffe, early settler, for some time "everything was hustle and bustle. A small five-stamp mill was erected and money was turned out at the rate of $500 per day."

In 1914 a group of Russians moved in to colonize the valley, but successive years of drouth forced abandonment of their project in 1920. Sheep- and cattle-raising has become the chief source of income for settlers of the region. . . .

Stephen L. Carr in *The Historical Guide to Utah Ghost Towns* describes the glory days and decline of Park Valley, and also of Kelton and Promontory to the south. Kelton's experience with the earthquake of 1934 is told in the 1941 edition (page 364).

5. Turn west from Brigham City via State 83 to Corinne, Thiokol, and Golden Spike National Historic Site. **CORINNE** (4,230 alt. 512 pop.), known as the Burg on the Bear, "dreams in the sun, like an old man remembering his youth. The once roaring, fighting, hilarious rakehell town has little to show for its riotous past. A handful of houses, a few weather-stained business buildings, a church, and a school, are all that remain of a city of more than 2,000 people." So wrote the authors of the 1941 edition. Since then the Railroad Village Museum, its locomotives, and old Railroad Depot have been moved to Heber City *(see Tour No. 5),* after a period in Corinne. Still remaining: **Bank of Corinne,** Montana Street, a simple one-story frame and brick structure that was built in 1871. Serving as a bank until about 1875, the building was then used as City Hall from about 1890 to 1961 . . . **Methodist Church,** corner of Colorado and S. 6th Street, a quaint brick structure built in 1870 as one of the first (perhaps *the* first) non-Mormon church houses in Utah. Readers are referred to Brigham D. Madsen's *Corinne: The Gentile Capital of Utah* for a detailed study of Corinne's past; also see the 1941 edition.

West of Corinne, State 83 passes across flat, marshy former lake bed north of Bear River Bay. Salt Creek and Public Shooting Grounds water-fowl management areas are north and south of the highway, respectively. Terraces of prehistoric Lake Bonneville are prominent on the slopes of the hills near the highway and to the east, along the base of the Wasatch. At a junction 19 miles west of Corinne, State 83 swings north to Thiokol, Howell, and I-84/I-80N. A paved sideroad forks west from this junction to Golden Spike National Historic Site *(see National Parks section),* continuing westward beyond the Historic Site to Kelton and eventual junction with State 30 *(see No. 4 above).* Two miles west of junction with State 83 an improved road forks south from the Historic Site road, traversing a narrow strip between Bear River Migratory Bird Refuge and the Promontory Mountains to **Promontory Point,** the **Southern Pacific Railroad,** and the site of the former construction camp at **Little Valley,** active during building of the rock-fill causeway across Great Salt Lake. Visible to the east in Bear River Bay is the far-spreading expanse of dikes and ponds built by Great Salt Lake Minerals *(see Tour No. 2B below).* Distance from State 83 to Little Valley is 42 miles.

A short distance north of Golden Spike Junction, to the right of State 83 and stretching along the lower slopes of the Blue Springs Hills, the multicolored buildings of Thiokol's great Wasatch Division Plant gradually come into view, individually and in groups.

THIOKOL'S WASATCH DIVISION PLANT sprawls across thousands of acres of mountain slopes and valley about six miles northeast of Golden Spike National Historic Site *(see)*, some 27 miles west of Brigham City and an even shorter distance from Tremonton. Occupying more than a hundred brightly-colored buildings, Thiokol operates here a plant devoted primarily to research, development and manufacture of solid-propellant rocket motors. The plant is recognized as the largest such installation in the world.

The Wasatch Division plant dates initially from 1957, when construction began as part of America's response to Russian challenge in the fields of space and military rocketry. In the words of an anonymous writer, "Where once the stillness of the hills and small valleys was penetrated by the tooting whistles of early locomotives, the deeper, bigger voice of the new space age can often be heard." This thundering voice was heard by thousands of spectators during the late 1970s and early 1980s, when Thiokol tested seven full-scale motors for NASA's space shuttle vehicle. Measuring 12 feet in diameter by 125 feet in length, each motor developed two and one-half million pounds of average thrust. In practice, the enormous motors are jettisoned into the ocean after the first two minutes of flight, then recovered and returned to Thiokol for refurbishing and eventual reuse. It is anticipated that hundreds of these motors will be needed in future space firings.

Some of the plant's buildings and improvement of the access highway were funded by the Air Force, as has been the case with a number of the plant's major programs. Employment at the present time exceeds 4,000, making Thiokol the largest employer and leading taxpayer in Box Elder County.

The Wasatch Division has been involved in numerous programs during its relatively brief existence. Some of these have been cooperative projects involving (in Utah) not only Thiokol but also Hercules *(see Tour No. 3)*, Boeing, and Ogden Air Logistics Center at Hill Air Force Base. During the 1960s and early 1970s, the plant's most important mission was the development and manufacture of more than 2,000 first-stage and nearly 1,000 third-stage motors for the Minuteman intercontinental ballistic missile (ICBM). Missile components were assembled by Boeing at Air Force Plant 77, located at Hill Air Force Base. Thiokol is now developing the first-stage motor and ordnance work for Minuteman's successor, the MX. Thiokol and Hercules are now involved in a joint venture to produce the Navy's Trident missile propulsion system as they did for Trident's predecessor, the Poseidon. The Wasatch Division is engaged also in development of other missiles for the Navy.

Space shuttle booster motor in test stand, Thiokol's Wasatch Division. 125-foot-long motor consumed more than a million pounds of solid propellant in two-minute burn time.

THIOKOL WASATCH DIVISION

6. Turn west from Brigham City on a hard-surfaced road which traverses a region of flats and salt marshes rimming Great Salt Lake to the 65,000-acre **BEAR RIVER MIGRATORY BIRD REFUGE,** 15 miles, which occupies a land and water area at the delta of Bear River at an avian crossroads of two of the continent's major migratory waterfowl flyways. Visitors may gain a closeup view of the refuge from a 12-mile auto tour route. *Office open 8-4:30 every day all year except on weekends from January to March 15; auto tour route open same days until sunset. All visitors must register. Hunting, fishing. No gasoline available.*

The river's delta and its spreading marshes have long been a natural feeding ground for millions of birds that pause here on their flights from Alaska to South America or to and from the Mississippi Valley. In pioneer days waterfowl were so thick they blackened the sky. Commercial hunters of the nineties sold teal for $1 a dozen, mallard for $1.50 a dozen. George Mueller, Salt Lake City sportsman, recalled in the *Salt Lake Tribune* of April 21, 1940, that in 1894 he met a disconsolate hunter who "only got 325" in a day's bombardment.

On the gigantic "birdport" squadrons of birds of 200 species alight and take off in aerial symphonies of movement. About 60 species nest here. Among species that visit are the white-faced ibis, similar to the bird worshipped by ancient Egyptians; whistling swan; snowy egrets, nearly exterminated in the mauve decade for feminine plumage; the great blue heron and black-crowned night heron; and the marbled godwit. Other birds seen at the refuge include pelicans, snow goose, bald and golden eagles, marsh hawks, prairie falcons, long-billed curlew, and several species of ducks.

Because of habitat loss through drying of the marshes, and because of severe epidemics of botulism, the refuge was created in 1928 by Congress and placed under jurisdiction of the U. S. Biological Survey, now the U. S. Fish and Wildlife Service. Much of the construction was done by the CCC. In 1929 an extensive canal system was dug and water control structures installed. A dike was built around the outer rim of the swamp to impound the fresh waters of Bear River and keep out saline waters of Great Salt Lake. To the main bulkhead were attached four cross-dikes, dividing the 50,000-acre water area into five units. At the spillways, egrets, terns and pelicans gather to fish for suckers, chubs, carp and minnows. Besides feeding and nesting grounds, the refuge has a visitor center and administration building, service and storage buildings, and residences. A 100-foot observation tower affords a view of the entire area.

Extensive management programs are conducted at the refuge each year, primarily during the warm months, to improve habitat and to monitor nesting, wildlife populations, and results of new management programs. Research was conducted on botulism at the refuge for more than 40 years but no research is being conducted at this time.

7. Turn south from Brigham City to Ogden and Salt Lake City. I-15 crosses the flatlands west of the foothills and, being at a lower elevation, is rather restricted in expanse of view. This is the faster route. If speed is not required, the visitor is advised to drive US 89-91 through **Perry, Willard,** and **Pleasant View** to Ogden, and from Ogden south through the Davis County communities to Salt Lake City. This is the old foothill highway that connects the majority of original Wasatch Front communities. It provides a more intimate contact with historical and cultural points of interest.

South of Brigham City, US 89-91 is known as the **Golden Spike Fruit-way** because local fruits and vegetables are sold fresh in season from roadside stands. Though a distressing number of orchards and truck farms along the Wasatch Front have given way to the encroachment of other uses, enough remain to provide an abundance of home-grown orchard fruits (peaches, pears, apricots, apples, cherries, plums), berries, and garden vegetables. Utah produce, while not generally noted for large size, is remarkable for excellent taste.

WILLARD (4,300 alt. 1,241 pop.) perches on a foothill terrace overlooking Willard Bay and Bear River Bay of Great Salt Lake. The town in turn is over-shadowed by the incredibly rugged, rocky, precipitous face of the Wasatch, which soars more than 5,000 feet in less than two miles—something of a record, even along the steep Wasatch Front. **Inspiration Point** (9,422 alt.), on the very top of the range above Willard, provides a superlative overview of much of northern Utah. This point is reached from Mantua *(see No. 1 above)*.

Willard Canyon, heading beneath and behind Inspiration Point, is a gash through which disastrous floods poured in earlier times before upstream terracing and revegetation. Though no longer so evident, rock, adobe, brick and frame dwellings of frontier simplicity remain from the past century, built during the decades after settlement in 1851. Solid and utilitarian, many of these houses are still in use. Willard, in fact, is the rock-house showplace of northern Utah, as Beaver and Sanpete communities are of the south. The entire community is a registered Historic District.

Utah Hot Springs, 5 miles south of Willard beside the highway, features mineral water containing iron and salts, said to have curative properties. The springs emerge at a temperature of 144 degrees, at the rate of 750,000 gallons a day.

West of I-15 in this vicinity is **Willard Bay Reservoir,** a 15-square-mile fresh-water lake created by a 15-mile-long dike or dam. Part of the billion-dollar Weber Basin Project of the U. S. Bureau of Reclamation, the dam consists of a 29-foot-high dam, 25 feet wide, atop a massive pad (6 feet high) placed on the former lake bottom. Some 15 million cubic feet of earth and rock were used to build the dam during the years from 1958 to 1964, the first water from Weber River being turned in to the reservoir in November 1964. Willard Bay is a storage reservoir, receiving water from the Weber and Ogden rivers in winter and spring via an 11-mile canal from the Slaterville Diversion Dam, then feeding it back through the same canal during irrigation season. On the lake's shore is **Willard Bay State Recreation Area,** a major boating park with picnic and camping facilities, launching and dock facilities, boat rentals, and food concessions. Willard Bay is very popular for both power-boating and sailboating. Open April-October.

Tour No. 2B — Ogden and Weber County

Of all counties in the state, Weber most resembles Salt Lake County in being a sprawling mixture of rural and urban, agricultural and industrial, commercial and residential, private enterprise and government. Though the county's Mormon Church affiliation matches the state average in percentage, that percentage is much lower than Utah County's, and since the late 1860s the Weber area has been alternately a fomenting or relatively dormant stewpot of Mormon and non-Mormon tensions. In these respects, among others, Utah and Weber counties—on either side of Salt Lake County—have counterbalanced each other. From 1940 to 1970 and even before, the sister counties were remarkably comparable in population. Between 1970 and 1980, however—continuing a trend that was slightly discernible before 1970—Utah county spurted ahead of Weber for a gain of

58 per cent, compared with 15 per cent for Weber. During this period Provo became the state's second largest city for the first time while Ogden lost 5,000 residents and fell to third place. The county as a whole gained 18,000 inhabitants in this period, a percentage increase (15%) that was much less than that of many other counties, or for the state (38%). However, local planners and officials were not dismayed; this was a gratifying growth and problems of adjustment were less severe than they would have been with faster growth.

Practically the entire population of Weber County (145,000 in 1980) lives within 15 miles of downtown Ogden, including the people of Ogden Valley to the east and the flatlands to the west. It is an industrialized county, with numerous manufacturing plants, three industrial parks, several large shopping malls, and a bustling downtown commercial district. Agriculture also is important to the local economy, local farms producing sizable quantities of grain, hay, vegetables, and orchard fruits, as well as livestock. Ogden is a major importer and processor of livestock and farm produce. Grain elevators are local landmarks.

Ogden became the railroad Junction City in the 1870s, gaining then a financial base that has been of incalculable economic worth in the century since. Thousands of local people still are employed by the Union Pacific, Southern Pacific, and Denver & Rio Grande Western. Also, Ogden is an important crossroads for national highways (I-15, I-84, US 30-89-91-191), and it is equidistant or nearly so from major cities west of Denver. These strategic advantages were instrumental in selection of the Ogden-north Davis area for siting of the federal defense installations that have become keystones for the region's economy.

OGDEN (4,300 alt. 64,407 pop.), third largest city in Utah, is the principal railway center of the intermountain region. The city is built on the deltas of Ogden and Weber (pronounced Wee-ber) rivers, where these two streams once emptied into prehistoric Lake Bonneville. East and north of the city looms the massive bulk of the Wasatch Range, topped with snow from November to June or July. Extensive areas of prosperous farmland merge with the city's spreading suburbs.

The most marked feature of Ogden is the broad, straight vista of Washington Boulevard, main commercial thoroughfare, running north and south. The city's wide streets, planned in true Mormon geometrical style on the four cardinal directions, are bordered by trees. Vestiges of the old can still be seen, particularly along 25th Street, but central Ogden has been in a stage of transformation for several years, with individual buildings and even entire blocks being razed and replaced with malls, a Hilton Hotel, and other contemporary developments. As in Salt Lake City, most of Ogden's historical heritage—as evidenced by architecture—is no longer concentrated in a relatively tight core; what remains is dispersed and requires seeking out. Such effort is rewarding, for Ogden does possess both old and modern attractions of note, as described below.

"In early years Mormonism attracted many emigrants from England and northern Europe. Later, the industrial and agricultural growth of the region brought small groups of Mexicans, Japanese, Negroes, Chinese,

Italians, and Greeks, most of whom are engaged in railroad and farm work. . . . The dominant church is that of the Latter-day Saints, but other religious denominations, including Catholic, Protestant, Jewish, and Buddhist adherents, are well represented. Many business, fraternal, and charitable organizations draw membership from all sects; Ogden was one of the first Utah cities to overcome antipathy between Mormons and non-Mormons.'' That analysis of Ogden's ethnic and religious background, in the 1941 edition, has not changed. Considering size, Ogden is the most cosmopolitan city in the state, made even more so since 1941 by arrival of federal installations, which have attracted thousands of workers of diverse cultural and religious backgrounds from other states.

Ogden's historical background was described in the 1941 edition, which gave considerable attention to the trapper era. Only excerpts have been quoted below:

> After the coming of white men, the site of Ogden and its vicinity was an important rendezvous and wintering place for fur traders and trappers over a period of six or seven years. As such it was a focal point for explorations, and for trade rivalry between American fur companies and the British Hudson's Bay Company. . . . The [American] trappers spent the winter of 1825-26 at the present site of Ogden, living in skin tents. Many of them had taken Indian wives, and they settled down, ''healthy as bears,'' to a winter of eating, sleeping, yarn-spinning, and contests of strength. More than a thousand Shoshone Indians came down and camped around them. . . . Early in the spring four men, one of whom was James Clyman, set out in bullboats to ''circumambulate'' Great Salt Lake, to find beaver streams, and to determine whether it was an arm of the Pacific. . . . The summer rendezvous of 1826 on the

Ogden, Weber Valley, and Wasatch Mountains, looking east from the vicinity of Great Salt Lake. *U. S. Bureau of Reclamation photo.*

site of Ogden was a gala affair, after the arrival of General Ashley from St. Louis with 100 well-laden pack animals. . . . At that rendezvous General Ashley sold out his interests to Jedediah S. Smith, David E. Jackson (for whom Jackson's Hole, Wyoming, was named), and William L. Sublette. . . . The following winter the trappers spent on the site of Ogden, and the summer, or trade, rendezvous of 1827 was held on Bear Lake, near present Laketown. . . .

As the fur trade declined and the trappers showed a disposition to settle down, the site of Ogden continued to be an occasional camping place for Indians and trappers, until the arrival of Miles Goodyear (1817-49), a native of Connecticut, who built a cabin here in [1846. Goodyear] was the earliest white settler in Ogden, and probably the first in Utah to plant a garden. Coming west from present Kansas with the Whitman party in 1836, he assisted in pioneering an untried wagon road as far as Fort Hall, Idaho, out of which he worked as hunter, trapper, and trader until he had gained sufficient experience to open a trading post of his own. To the original cabin, intended for the use of Goodyear, his Indian wife, and their two children, was added a stockade for livestock and other cabins for his partners, one of whom was Jim Baker, noted mountain man. The arrival of the Mormons in 1847 induced him to sell out, claiming that he held a Mexican grant; existence of such a grant has not been found, but the Mormons probably considered it worth about $2,000 to establish a clear title to all of the Utah region. As for Goodyear, neighbors forty miles away at Great Salt Lake City made things too crowded, and he was glad to dispose of his "property." The purchase was made under the direction of the Mormon Church by Captain James Brown of the Mormon Battalion, who moved his family into the fort and with the aid of his sons planted five bushels of seed wheat and half a bushel of seed corn, brought from California. Butter and cheese made from the milk of cows and goats purchased from Goodyear gave rise to Ogden's first industry. . . .

Brigham Young came to the settlement of Brownsville, so named from Captain Brown's occupancy, late in 1849, and climbed a near-by hill "to view out a location for a town." The following year the townsite was surveyed and 100 families were sent by the Church leader to settle here. . . .

The most significant event in the history of Ogden was the coming of the railroad. In March, 1869, the first train steamed into the city. . . . In 1870, the year the Utah Central Railroad was completed to Salt Lake City, census returns showed that Ogden had doubled its previous decennial population of 1,463. Most of the newcomers were non-Mormons, and there quickly developed, in the early newspapers, and in the battle for political control of the city, a marked bitterness between Mormons and "gentiles." The Mormon Church, which had acquired the site of Ogden from Miles Goodyear, resented possible control by rough people brought in by the railroad.

Branch railroad lines were built in the seventies and eighties, connecting the transcontinental system with other settlements in Utah, Idaho, and Montana. . . . By 1880 the population had doubled again, bringing more non-Mormon settlers, and the acrimonious feeling between Church members and gentiles was reflected in the plain-spoken press of the period. . . . Between 1880 and 1900, Ogden boomed. Electrical service was extended to homes and factories; the telephone system, one of the first in the West, was established; the canning industry began; and a clothing factory was opened. An electric street railway system was installed, replacing horse-drawn cars. . . . The census of 1900 gave Ogden a population of 16,313.

In the early years of the twentieth century civic improvements were numerous and the feeling between Mormons and non-Mormons gradually improved. . . . Ogden is one of the largest distribution points for manufacturing, milling, canning, livestock, and agriculture in the intermountain West; it ranks third in the nation in the number of sheep received in its yards, and eleventh in cattle. The Union Stockyards is the largest shipping point for sheep and cattle west of Denver. . . .

Attractions in Ogden

Municipal Building and Municipal Gardens, Washington Boulevard between 25th and 26th streets, occupy an area of ten acres in the heart of the city. The mansarded old City Hall, built in 1888 and "decorated" with neon lights, was superseded in 1938 by the present ten-story City and County Building, erected with PWA funds and considered probably the finest example of Art Deco architecture in the state. The surrounding gardens are noted for botanical variety and beauty of landscaping; during the Christmas season they become a lighted, animated village.

Lower 25th Street Historic District, which includes several blocks in the vicinity of the Union Depot, (a part of the district), was formed to encourage restoration of a number of deteriorating vintage structures dating from the years 1875 to 1920. "This is an area rich with history and tradition," once the economic, social and cultural center of Ogden. As the age of railroad passenger travel declined after World War II, so did 25th Street. Restoration of the depot and redevelopment of the immediate environs prompted civic action on behalf of 25th Street.

Union Depot, 25th Street and Wall Avenue, was built in 1923-24 as replacement for a depot destroyed by fire in 1923. The present depot "was designed on a grand scale

Downtown Ogden *(below, left)*, Mormon Temple *(below, right)*, Union Depot *(bottom, left)*, and Bertha Eccles Community Art Center *(bottom, right)*.

OGDEN STANDARD-EXAMINER

UTAH TRAVEL COUNCIL

OGDEN STANDARD-EXAMINER

OGDEN STANDARD-EXAMINER

by John and Donald B. Parkinson of Los Angeles,'' states the National Register of Historic Places. ''The classic Spanish architecture of the building is seen in the vivid tile roof and rounded windows on the end gables. Inlaid brick designs, bright blue decorative mosaic tile, wood trusses with handhewn edges, and huge wrought iron chandeliers add to the beauty of this impressive monument to Ogden's role in the history of railroading. During World War II, more than 120 trains were served out of the depot daily.'' Still utilized as a depot for limited Amtrak passenger service, the station was acquired by the city in 1977 after years of negotiation. Renovated at a cost of two million dollars, the station was dedicated in 1978 as a civic center and museum—a living monument to Ogden's Golden Age of Steam. It houses the **Railroad Hall of Fame Museum** . . . the **John M. Browning Firearms Museum,** where models of guns invented by the Browning family, as well as the Browning workshop, are displayed . . . the **Browning-Kimball** collection of vintage automobiles . . . **Matthew S. Browning Theatre** . . . **Myra Powell Art Gallery** . . . **Grand Lobby,** the locale for public functions, Amtrak ticket office, and information desk of Golden Spike Empire, the regional travel agency . . . and gift shop.

Miles Goodyear Fort Buenaventura State Historical Monument, between the depot and Weber River to the west, across the railroad tracks, is a landscaped park containing a reconstruction of a log stockade (Fort Buenaventura) built in 1846 by trader Miles Goodyear, who sold it to Mormon pioneers in 1848. The monument was inaugurated in the late 1970s by the State Division of Parks and Recreation. At a cost of more than a million dollars it is being developed as a living history exhibit. Enter from 24th Street, turning south from the west end of viaduct, then east *(follow signs)*.

Ogden City Mall occupies a 30-acre site west of Washington between 24th and 22nd. The mall was built between 1979 and 1981 as a private-public redevelopment project, three blocks of older buildings being razed to make construction possible. Cost was estimated at 60 million dollars. The mall houses more than 120 stores, shops and restaurants in its 772,000 square feet of retail space. In the vicinity of the mall is a new 300-room Hilton Hotel, built between 1981 and 1982. Newgate Mall, a few blocks south, is another large construction project of the same period.

Mormon Temple-Tabernacle-Goodyear Cabin occupy a block between 21st and 22nd, fronting Washington Boulevard. A distinctive edifice of white cast stone, gold-anodized aluminum grillwork and segmented central spire (180 feet high), the temple was dedicated in January 1972. Measuring 220 feet by 184 feet, the temple contains 283 rooms on four floors and is identical in plan to the Provo Temple, dedicated one month later. Cost of each temple was approximately four million dollars. Used for sacred ordinance work, the temple is not open to the public, but the grounds and white steepled tabernacle to the south may be visited. A visitor center is located at the tabernacle. On the same block, to the west, is the Daughters of Utah Pioneers Museum-Relief Society Stake Meeting Hall. In Gothic style with walls of brick and a stone foundation, the quaint building dates from 1902 when it was dedicated as the first and only Relief Society Stake Hall in the Mormon Church. It was presented to the DUP in 1926. Adjoining the museum, under a canopy, is the quaint Miles Goodyear Cabin, oldest remaining non-Indian dwelling in the state. The cabin was built in 1846 of cottonwood logs and was moved to its present site by the DUP in 1928.

Episcopal Church of the Good Shepherd, 2374 Grant Avenue, is a Gothic stone edifice with pitched roof, buttresses, Tudor stained glass windows, and exposed wood rafters. Nostalgically reminiscent of aged Gothic churches of Europe, it is said to be the oldest church in Ogden in continuous use and is listed on the National Register of Historic Places. The church was consecrated in 1875.

Bertha Eccles Community Art Center, 2580 Jefferson Avenue, is an imposing 2½-story Richardsonian Romanesque style house of brick and red sandstone. It is characterized by round-arch windows, dormers, and cylindrical towers with conical roofs. Built in 1893 for James C. Armstrong, it was sold to David Eccles, noted financier, in 1896 and became the residence of his wife Bertha. Since then it has been a private and public social and cultural center, eventually becoming a civic center, now used for fine arts exhibitions, lectures, programs and instruction.

Internal Revenue Service Center, West 12th Street, processes federal tax returns from 14 western states. The center employs as many as 2,000 full-time workers and the same number of temporary seasonal workers.

Defense Depot Ogden occupies more than 1,000 acres north of 12th Street. Originating as the Utah General Depot prior to World War II, in 1940-41, and once covering 1,700 acres, the depot has served for 40 years as one of the largest military depots in the nation. During World War II it employed as many as 12,000 workers. At present it employs about 1,700 civilians in the handling of a great variety of military supplies and equipment. The depot's history to 1964 was told in *Utah Historical Quarterly* (Spring 1964).

WEBER STATE COLLEGE is Utah's largest state-supported four-year college, its enrollment of about 10,000 students roughly matching that of Utah State University in Logan. The college is situated on a spacious, 375-acre campus on the foothills of the Wasatch Mountains, overlooking Ogden and Weber Valley from the city's southeastern heights. It is accessible from Harrison Boulevard.

Expansion during the 1950s forced WSC to move from its former campus on Jefferson Avenue; the new campus is a modern complex of landscaped grounds and attractive buildings of harmonizing architectural styles and soothing, coordinated colors. The great majority of buildings are products of the 1960s and 1970s, representing expenditures in the tens of millions of dollars.

Campus, Weber State College. *Jeannie Young photo.*

Essentially a community college, WSC's studentbody nevertheless represents more than 40 states and many foreign countries. Baccalaureate degrees are awarded in seven schools, while associate degrees and two-year certificates are offered in vocational fields and health occupations. The college has been a four-year institution since 1959; its first senior class was graduated in 1964. Its origins date to 1889, when it was founded by the Mormon Church as a church academy. In 1933 the academy was transferred to the state, becoming Weber Junior College at that time.

"Our students aren't the only ones to benefit from the presence of the Weber State campus," states a college publication. "Numerous fine arts programs and other events are free to the public or are offered at minimal cost. Weber's theatre and musical programs offer a continuous high calibre of entertainment for area residents." Recently completed on a 45-acre site near the main campus is the 12,000-seat **Dee Events Center.** Resembling the popular concept of a flying saucer, the $12,000,000 center is used for college and community sports-cultural events. Theaters and auditorium of the **Val A. Browning Center for the Performing Arts** are the scene for cultural events such as ballet, symphony, concerts, lectures, and theatrical performances.

Also of interest to visitors are the **Stewart Library . . . Ott Planetarium . . . Natural History Museum** (Science Building) . . . and the **Stewart Carillon Tower,** the "voice" of the college. A hundred feet high, costing a quarter of a million dollars, the tower contains a clock on each of four faces; in its base is an electronic carillon of 183 bells. The carillon is one of numerous gifts to the college by Donnell B. and Elizabeth S. Stewart.

Turn west from Ogden on 12th Street to **Little Mountain Industrial Area,** 13 miles, adjoining Bear River Bay of Great Salt Lake and Southern Pacific's main line, developed by Southern Pacific for heavy industry. Among the park's tenants is **Western Zirconium Company,** a subsidiary of Westinghouse Electric, which manufactures cooling systems for water-cooled nuclear reactors. Another is **Great Salt Lake Minerals Company,** which has received considerable publicity for its efforts in utilizing solar evaporation in the mining of Great Salt Lake's minerals. Beginning in the 1960s the firm has experimented with diked ponds in Bear River Bay (to total 34,000 acres by 1984), pumping concentrated brine from the north end of the lake and "settling out" its mineral components through evaporation. Many problems have been encountered, among them dilution of brine by an ominous rise in the lake's level during the 1970s which stopped just short of breaching dikes and causing financial disaster. (This is a continuing concern to all salt firms on the lake.) Common salt is the most abundant product and the firm is now the largest salt marketer in the state. The most valuable product is potassium sulfate, a fertilizer compound. Others are magnesium chloride and sodium sulfate. Lithium has potential value. The firm has invested more than 50 million dollars in this area to date.

Turn east from Ogden via 12th Street and State 39 to **Ogden Canyon** and to **Ogden Valley,** a pastoral basin in the heart of the Wasatch. The road gives access to three ski resorts, Pineview Reservoir, numerous forest camp-sites, and continues across Monte Cristo Summit to Woodruff in Bear River Valley.

Ogden Canyon is a deep, narrow gash, just wide enough for the highway and the Ogden River. "The towering cliffs in the canyon, several thousand feet high, seem to block the way, but a passageway continually opens through vertical masses of pink quartzite. In the more eroded deposits of blue-gray limestone and sandstone, the canyon broadens into fertile glades. From the steep green-patched slopes, jagged monoliths lean far out over the road.'' Before construction of a toll road in the 1860s ''the canyon was impassable, except for an Indian trail high on the south wall.'' It is the site of numerous vacation retreats.

Turn north across Pineview Dam via State 162 to **EDEN** (4,950 alt.) and **LIBERTY** (5,100), hamlets on the North Fork of Ogden River. Between Eden and Liberty, on the slopes of the high Wasatch, is **Nordic Valley ski resort,** advertised as ''Ogden's most accessible ski area'' and noted for night skiing on lighted runs. Two double chair lifts, beginner to expert runs, day lodge, snack bar, ski shop, ski school.

North from Liberty an improved road *(closed in winter)* winds through low, rolling mountain country to Avon and Paradise in Cache Valley *(see Tour No. 1)*.

Turn north from Eden to **Patio Springs** resort and golf course, 2 miles. The road continues up-canyon to **Powder Mountain ski resort,** 8 miles from Eden on the topmost slopes of a 9,000-foot ridge marking the Cache-Weber county line. A relatively youthful resort, Powder Mountain features three high-capacity chair lifts and a surface tow, all interconnected but ''each lift on its own mountain.'' 600 to 1,300 feet vertical rise. Day lodges and overnight accommodations, ski shop, ski school, restaurant. Main lodge is located at the top of the resort. Numerous runs. As with other resorts in the vicinity, Powder Mountain owners have plans for impressive development.

Pineview Dam almost blocks the gateway to Ogden Valley, and **Pineview Reservoir** behind the dam occupies a large part of the valley floor. The many-fingered lake extends behind the dam for three or four miles in several directions, and on its banks Cache National Forest has developed half a dozen picnic and camping areas containing several hundred units, as well as ramps and docks. Pineview Dam was built in the 1930s and enlarged in 1957 by the Bureau of Reclamation to a height of 132 feet and a crest of 600 feet. It is an important element in the Weber Basin water project. Artesian wells beneath the lake are tapped by pipes for Ogden domestic use. The lake is very popular for boating, fishing and waterskiing.

Turn south from State 39, 3 miles west of Huntsville, to **Snow Basin ski resort,** largest and oldest in the Ogden area. Founded in 1939, the resort now features six lifts and more than 30 runs. Terrain is varied with runs for novice, intermediate, and expert. Altitude 6,400 to 8,800 feet. Day lodge, cafeteria, ski school, ski shop. The resort's new ownership includes developers of Vail, Colorado. Tentative plans, announced in 1981, call for addition of more lifts and development of a large area to the south with lodging, shops, and other amenities. Also being considered is access from Weber Canyon.

HUNTSVILLE (4,900 alt. 577 pop.), 3 miles from Ogden, is a rustic older village, founded in 1860 by Captain Jefferson Hunt, former member of the Mormon Battalion. Angus McKay Home, 141 S. 7600 East, is a two-story red sandstone house built in 1871-73 by Hugh McKay. David O. McKay Summer Home, 155 S. 7600 East, was built in 1870 for the grandfather of Mormon apostle and church president David O. McKay. President McKay was one of the most revered of church presidents, born in the house in 1873 and died in 1970 at the age of 96.

Abbey of Our Lady of the Holy Trinity (Trappist or Cistercian Monastery) occupies nearly 2,000 acres of agricultural land four miles southeast of Huntsville. The monastic community numbers some 30 to 40 monks, who operate an efficient modern farm that produces dairy and beef cattle, poultry, honey, etc. Visitors are welcome at the chapel and the greeting room, where the monastery's program is explained and local honey and bread may be purchased.

State 39 continues east and north of Huntsville, traversing the canyon of **Ogden River's South Fork,** along which Cache National Forest has developed seven camping and picnicking areas. The road forks 8 miles east of Huntsville. Turn right 2 miles to Weber County Memorial Park, Causey Dam and Causey Reservoir, and Skull Crack Forest Campground. **Causey Dam** is an earth-fill structure 200 feet high and 900 feet across the crest. It was built between 1962 and 1965 by the U.S. Bureau of Reclamation at a cost of four million dollars. **Causey Reservoir** stores water for use in the Huntsville-Eden-Liberty area. It is a unit of the Weber Basin project.

State 39 continues up **Beaver Creek** from Causey junction, gaining elevation gradually. (Higher reaches are closed in winter.) About 9 miles from Causey Junction a fairweather road forks north to Hardware Ranch (16 miles), passing through gently contoured, sparsely forested plateau country at about 7,000 feet. This area is popular for snowmobiling in winter. State 39 winds through groves of fluttering aspen and sharp-pointed fir as it passes **Monte Cristo Peak** on the right (9,148 alt.) and crosses the summit (9,008 alt.) "with magnificent views of distant mountains." **Monte Cristo campground** (8,400 alt.) is a large developed area with tables, water, toilets, playground, amphitheater, and natural arboretum. Beyond the campground State 39 descends the east slopes of Bear River Range through Walton Canyon to **Woodruff,** 60 miles from Ogden *(see Tour No. 1).*

Tour No. 2C - Weber River Canyon and Morgan County

I-84/I-80N, formerly US 30S, parallels Weber River and the Union Pacific railroad through Weber Canyon, an open gorge that slices through the Wasatch. The 1941 edition devotes a page to the historical background of **UINTAH** and **SOUTH WEBER,** hamlets in the canyon's broad mouth where it emerges from the mountains into Weber Valley. Weber Canyon was traversed in the summer of 1846 by the mounted Bryant-Russell party and shortly thereafter by the Harlan-Young and Lienhard wagon parties. The Harlan-Young experience in the rocky lower canyon was told in the 1941 edition.

MOUNTAIN GREEN (5,000 alt.), north of the highway, is a tranquil alcove almost surrounded by mountains and hills. Many newer dwellings have been built in the area in recent years. In 1964 the Browning Arms Company established a headquarters complex here with facilities for research and development. Mountain Green was the site of a confrontation between Hudson's Bay fur brigade leader Peter Skene Ogden and a group of American trappers in 1825, during which Ogden lost 23 men through desertion.

MORGAN (5,060 alt. 1,896 pop.) is the county seat of Morgan County, a commercial and residential center for a charmingly picturesque farming area. The grand 9,000-foot ridge of the main Wasatch forms the western horizon, with lower ranges and hills in all directions. Patchwork fields clothe the valley floor and extend onto the foothills. Morgan County is a dairying and livestock area, with barley, wheat and alfalfa being the main crops. Many residents commute to the Wasatch Front or Ideal cement plant or the Browning plant for work. At one time Morgan was noted for its fine peas and local cannery. In 1980 the county's population numbered 4,917, scattered throughout one of the smallest counties in the state.

Como Springs, a mile east of Morgan, is an aging resort known for its natural warm sulphur bathing water. In addition to a swimming pool, the resort features a motel, restaurant, picnic area, bowling and roller skating facilities.

Turn south from Morgan to **East Canyon Reservoir,** which is popular with Wasatch Front residents for boating and other water sports. The lake's shores have been developed as a state recreation area with ramps, picnic and camping sites, and concessions. The old **East Canyon dam** was replaced in the mid-1960s with a curving concrete structure measuring 250 feet. Before completion of the railroad in 1869, East Canyon served as a pioneer migration route to Salt Lake Valley. *See also Tours 3 and 5.*

Devils Slide, on the south side of the highway, 7 miles east of Morgan, is a natural rock formation resembling a playground chute, consisting of two parallel vertical limestone ridges 20 feet apart, standing about 40 feet above the canyonside.

Across the highway to the north is the cement plant of **Ideal Basic Industries.** Cement has been taken from this area since early years of the century. Several million barrels are produced annually, utilizing limestone as the primary raw material. Continue on this road to **CROYDEN,** a hamlet in the mouth of Lost Creek Canyon. Continue from Croyden on an improved road along Lost Creek Canyon to **Lost Creek Reservoir.** The lake is formed by a 220-foot high earth-fill dam built by the U. S. Bureau of Reclamation in the mid-1960s as part of the comprehensive Weber Basin project. It is the site of **Lost Creek Lake State Beach,** developed by the State Division of Parks and Recreation with picnic and camping facilities and boat ramp. The area is popular for fishing. Enroute, about 6 miles from Croyden, a sideroad forks east and gives access to **Chinatown,** described in the 1941 edition as "a natural amphitheater with vividly colored walls fifty feet high. Exquisitely carved natural rock formations occur here, shaped like Chinese pagodas, a huge ball in balance atop a supporting pillar, and Totem Pole Park—a group of eroded pillars resembling Indian totems."

East Canyon Reservoir. *Division of Parks & Recreation photo.*

HENEFER (5,350 alt.) is a farming and livestock community. In 1941 "a few gray log cabins" still stood among more recent structures. The road south of Henefer to East Canyon Reservoir and Salt Lake City marks the route of the Donner-Reed and Mormon pioneers of 1846 and 1847 respectively, and was used as a migration route for years afterward. Historic site markers are placed beside the road at intervals. The trail was first broken by the Donner-Reed party and followed by the Mormons a year later. Johnston's army came this way in 1858 and the route was used by the Overland Stage and Pony Express.

At Echo is the junction of I-84/I-80N and I-80, leading to Salt Lake City. I-80 traverses Echo Canyon enroute to and from Wyoming and the east. *See Tour No. 5.*

TOUR No. 2D - Davis County

Davis County has one of the smallest land areas of any county in the state but ranks third in total population, having surpassed Weber for that position in the 1970s. Davis also is the most densely settled county, after Salt Lake County, its people being confined to an area little more than 20 miles long and hardly 10 miles wide. Near Lagoon the county's waist is pinched to only three miles by Farmington Bay and the mountains.

Davis County combines diminishing agricultural lands with expanding residential, commercial and industrial areas. Between 1970 and 1980 its population increased by almost 50 per cent, from 99,028 to 146,540, the greatest numerical gain occurring in the northern half of the county. During the 40-year period between 1940 and 1980 its population multiplied nine times.

Hill Air Force Base is by far the largest employer, being a major contributor to the economy not only of Davis but of Weber and Morgan counties as well. While the county does have an additional base of industry and commerce, it relies heavily on Hill Air Force Base and satellite economic activities generated by that base.

The 1941 edition's description of Davis County communities is hardly recognizable 40 years later. **Clearfield:** "Irrigated alfalfa fields and acres of forage crop land crowd the highway and press close to the business district. Dirt roads branch off to residences, which are half-block to two blocks apart." **Layton:** "In addition to its stores and business houses, the town has a sugar factory, canning and packing plants, coal and lumber yards, and a flour mill." **Centerville:** "Hardly recognizable as a town, [Centerville] has business houses widely separated by farmlands. Orchards, interspersed with cottages and vegetable patches, cling to the foothills of the Wasatch. Bordering the highway are grain fields, truck gardens and retail fruit stands. Cherry season, in June, is hitch-hiking season on the highway between Centerville and Salt Lake City. The roadside is lined by youthful fruit-pickers eight to fourteen years old, who sit hopefully for hours, jerking vigorous thumbs at every passing car. Pickers' wages fluctuate from 25¢ to $2 (for an expert) per day, according to crops, prices, and the amount picked. . . ." **Bountiful:** "The business district is compacted alongside the highway. Primarily an agricultural center, Bountiful has several large greenhouses. . . .

Many workers commute from here to Salt Lake City, lending a semi-suburban character to the town.''

Anybody familiar with those places today will not recognize them as the same towns described in 1941. Such idyllic scenes may be present in Davis County 1982, particularly in the mid-county area around Farmington, which has not changed so greatly. However, the rustic certainly is not as common as it was in the past. Cherry growers—much less abundant today than in 1941—are fortunate to find pickers at any price, and $2 would be scorned as an hourly wage, let alone as pay for a hard day's work. Housing and commercial developments have absorbed thousands of acres of prime farmlands and orchards. With regard to Bountiful, many times more workers commute to Salt Lake City than in 1941, and in truth Bountiful may be considered a bedroom suburb of that large city only ten miles away to the south.

Sightseers interested in contrast between old and new are advised to drive the original main highway along the foothills between Ogden and Bountiful. Sidestreet driving is rewarded by glimpses of older houses, farms, and orchards, now the exception more than the rule. The county's communities include the following, shown with 1980 and 1940 populations. In all cases the larger figure is the 1980 population: Bountiful 32,877 (3,341) . . . Centerville 8,069 (670) . . . Clearfield 17,982 (799) . . . Farmington 4,691 (1,339) . . . Kaysville 9,811 (992) . . . Layton 22,862 (597).

Space permits mention of only a few of the county's points of interest:

HILL AIR FORCE BASE and its related activities, as an economic enterprise and considering the amount of public funds expended and number of employees, ranks only behind Utah state government in magnitude. About 20,000 civilian and military personnel are employed on the base, while expenditures exceed a billion dollars annually. The base's payroll alone, exclusive of other in-state expenditures, is indispensable to the economic well being of Weber County and northern Davis County, and in fact to that of the state.

Hill Air Force Base (HAFB) is a unit of the United States Air Force, and its operations are greatly diversified. A number of tenants with changing and varying missions are located on the base. Situated on a level bench or terrace at the mouth of Weber Canyon, the base occupies an area of some 6,600 acres between Interstate Highway 15 on the west and U.S. Highway 89 on the east. Physical facilities include more than 1,600 buildings, 112 miles of roads and 36 miles of railroad, more than a thousand vehicles, and an extensive system of runways and aprons. Its longest runway, capable of accommodating any military aircraft, is 13,500 feet in length. The largest of its many huge warehouses and hangars occupies 12½ acres under a single roof.

In addition to the main base, HAFB also has accountability and responsibility for nearly a million acres of federal land in the remote Great Salt Lake Desert of western Utah, as well as a testing site at Little Mountain.

The principal unit at HAFB is **Ogden Air Logistics Center (Ogden ALC),** one of five support centers of the Air Force Logistics Command in the United States. The center's formal area of support responsibility includes 56 Air Force activities in eleven western states and much of Canada; in practice, however, ''it supports virtually every United States Air Force installation around the world in one way or another.'' Support functions are many-faceted and complex, but they may be grouped under the major directorate categories of Maintenance, Distribution, Materiel Management, Contracting and Manufacturing, and Plans and Programs.

The Maintenance function, for example, employs about 6,800 people in the maintenance, repair and modernization of aircraft, missiles, training devices, photographic and navigation equipment, airmunitions, etc. In Distribution, more than 2,000 people are occupied in receiving, storing, packaging, issuing, and transporting Air Force materiel to customers around the world. Automated and computerized, the distribution function handles about 70,000 different small items, processes nearly 20 million pounds of air freight cargo each month, and transacts more than five million transactions each year. Value of materiel distributed from HAFB amounts to several billion dollars annually.

Materiel Management is charged with keeping aircraft, missiles and support systems at optimum levels of operational readiness. Contracting and Manufacturing purchases needed items, spending half a billion dollars every year with thousands of different contractors.

The base's most important responsibilities at this time include maintenance of aircraft such as the F-4 and F-16, the Minuteman and Titan ICBMs, Maverick air-to-ground missile and numerous essential commodities, plus logistics management responsibility for these, the new M-X under development and other missiles, weapons, training devices, and photographic equipment.

The 388th Tactical Fighter Wing arrived in 1976 and was soon thereafter equipped with the F-16 fighter; since then the wing has had the responsibility of training aircrews for this plane, from European nations as well as the United States, while the base has the assignment for worldwide management of the F-16. Also based at HAFB is the 508th Tactical Fighter Group, largest reserve unit in Utah, and the 6514th Test Squadron, which tests and evaluates unmanned vehicles. The 2952nd Combat Logistics Support Squadron provides maintenance, supply and transportation to Air Force units in 17 countries and the United States, primarily in support of the F-16 and F/RF-4 aircraft. Many other military organizations from several Air Force commands are tenants at Hill. These include the 1954th Radar Evaluation Squadron—one of a kind in the Air Force. Its mission is to optimize radar sensor configurations, quantify sensor system capabilities and monitor the development of new radar systems. The 40th Aerospace Rescue and Recovery Squadron, a Military Airlift Command tenant activated at Hill in 1978, flies Huey helicopters. It had saved 67 lives by mid-April 1981, most of them civilians lost or injured in the mountains.

Historical Background

The origins of Hill Air Force Base date to the late 1930s, when efforts of the Ogden Chamber of Commerce and other Utah boosters culminated successfully with Air Force designation of the site as Hill Field (1939). The first shovel of dirt was turned on January 12, 1940, followed by a period of construction that has hardly ceased, except temporarily. During World War II, when the base was utilized for maintenance, rehabilitation and storage of airplanes, materiel and equipment—as it has been through succeeding years—civilian employment reached 16,000 (1943), dropping to 8,100 civilians in 1945 and even further, to 3,600 civilians, in 1949. At that time the base's future was uncertain, but the Korean conflict, beginning in 1950, and acquisition of the adjacent Ogden Arsenal in 1955 helped assure its survival as a key military installation. Following the consolidation, which doubled Hill in size, the base became the airmunitions logistics manager for the Air Force.

Many types of aircraft have been either repaired, modified, serviced, or stored at HAFB during its 40 years of existence. A full list is too lengthy for inclusion here, but mention should be made of B-17, B-24, B-26, and B-29 bombers, as well as P-38, P-47 and P-61 fighters, during World War II and Korean War eras. The transition to jet aircraft occurred in the 1950s, when HAFB became a depot for servicing and modifying F-101 Voodoo, F-102 Delta, F-89 Scorpion, and other jet fighters. During the 1960s it was assigned logistics management for the F-110 tactical fighter aircraft,

Hill Air Force Base and surrounding communities. *Hill AFB photo.*

which later became the F-4. Logistics management and maintenance support for this fighter-bomber, used by many allied Air Forces, still are HAFB functions. In 1977, Hill became the logistics manager for the Air Force's new F-16 fighter, which remains one of its most prestigious management responsibilities.

The late 1950s brought the first of many missiles for repair; this was the Snark ICBM, and it arrived in November 1957. Little more than a year later HAFB was selected to be logistics manager of the Minuteman ICBM, then under development. Construction began in 1960 on Air Force Plant 77, sited on land once belonging to the Ogden Arsenal, which had been combined with HAFB in 1955. This plant was used during the 1960s and 1970s for assembly of Minuteman and Short Range Attack Missiles (SRAM) by Boeing, beginning in 1962. HAFB was assigned complete logistics management for the Minuteman in 1965, and the Titan workload was assigned in the same year.

In 1968 HAFB assumed responsibility for developing, operating and managing the Air Force Logistics Command Test Range in the Great Salt Lake Desert. The range became the Utah Test and Training Range in January 1979 and range operational management shifted to the Air Force Systems Command's 6545th Test Group at Hill. By the end of 1979 almost 21,000 people were employed at the base.

The 1970s witnessed the arrival—and in several cases the departure—of communication, airlift, Strategic Air Command, refueling, test, rescue and recovery, and fighter squadrons, groups, and detechments. One of these was a helicopter training and test wing, which qualified about 2,000 pilots and crew members in the operation of the Jolly Green Giant helicopters.

In late 1980, Hill Air Force base ended its fourth decade. The birthday was celebrated officially with an open house on May 9, 1981. Thousands of people from the surrounding area visited the installation and its many displays.

FREEPORT CENTER, Clearfield, is advertised as the "Manufacturing, Warehousing, and Distribution Hub of the West" and as "the largest distribution center in the United States." Congregated in a compact area measuring less than a square mile are more than a hundred industrial buildings utilized by scores of business firms for warehousing, manufacturing and distribution. Nearly half of these buildings are enormous structures measuring 200 by 600 feet. The center contains more than six million square feet of warehousing and manufacturing space, attractive to tenants because of the center's strategic location with respect to transportation (railroads, highways, airlines), central siting with respect to markets, Utah's liberal freeport law, labor costs and attitudes, and cultural environment.

The Freeport Center originated as the Clearfield Naval Supply Depot, built in 1942 and 1943 by the federal government at a cost of some 25 million dollars. During the height of World War II it employed 8,000 workers; its facilities included 191 buildings, 41 miles of railroad, and 24 miles of roads. By war's end half a million different items were stored at the depot, representing a value of nearly 600 million dollars. The depot continued an active but diminishing military role during most of the 1950s but was formally deactivated in 1961 and soon thereafter passed to private

F-16 Fighting Falcons at Hill Air Force Base.
Hill AFB photo.

Mormon chapel, Farmington.

WARD ROYLANCE

ownership. The depot's military history was described in *Utah Historical Quarterly* (Spring 1963).

GREAT SALT LAKE STATE PARK (Antelope Island) occupies the northern end of Antelope Island, 13 miles west of Clearfield via State 127 and a causeway. Developed by the State Division of Parks and Recreation, beginning in the 1960s, the park features picnic shelters, campground, boat marina, nature trails, bathing beach, and fresh-water showers. Observation overlooks provide inspirational views across the lake to north and west, and a tremendous visual sweep of the Wasatch Range for a hundred miles or more. Antelope Island was recently acquired in its entirety by the State of Utah and is being studied for its recreational potential. *See also Great Salt Lake, pages 291-298.*

BOUNTIFUL PEAK DRIVE is an aerial skyway that merits special ranking among roads for panoramic spectacle. The drive connects Farmington and Bountiful (it can be driven in either direction), climbing in switchbacks up the face of the Wasatch Range, overlooking in bird's-eye perspective the Davis urban strip, lake marshes, and the vast expanse of Great Salt Lake itself. Morgan Valley can be seen far below to the east. The road is not recommended for those who fear high places because it attains an elevation of 9,000 feet at Bountiful Peak—nearly 5,000 feet above the valley floor—and for much of its length it clings to steep slopes and is so narrow in places that two cars can only pass with difficulty. The Forest Service maintains two camping-picnic areas along the route. One-way distance between Farmington and Bountiful is about 16 miles. On the Farmington end the road passes through Farmington Canyon, a steep, narrow gorge. In Bountiful the drive is approached from 400 North and 1300 East.

LAGOON AMUSEMENT PARK AND PIONEER VILLAGE, beside I-15 and US 89 in Farmington, is an attractively landscaped, multi-featured entertainment resort. Considering its limited population market, Lagoon is all the more remarkable for the quality and diversity of its offerings. The resort dates from the 1890s, retaining its popularity through the years and expanding attractions and facilities greatly during the past decade or two. In addition to dozens of midway rides, games, and refreshment stands, the park features a huge swimming pool, lush landscaping, picnic facilities, miniature golfcourse, children's playground, a zoo and aviary, and a stadium. Entertainment events include musical shows, high-diving exhibitions, rodeos, and demolition derbies. **Pioneer Village** (Sons of Utah Pioneers) at Lagoon is a "living museum" of old-time transportation equipment and authentic 19th century buildings that house shops and valuable collections of guns, Indian relics, pioneer artifacts, etc. Among its aged buildings are a rock church, an early schoolhouse, and original houses furnished in period style. **Lagoon Opera House,** a charming Victorian edifice, features popular musicals. Adjoining the resort is a large commercial campground. *See Color Section for illustrations.*

HISTORIC ARCHITECTURE. Davis County boasts a number of vintage buildings dating from as far back as 1849. Many are listed on state and national historic registers. It is not possible to list more than a few, but careful observation while driving the foothill highway and side streets in Bountiful, Centerville, Farmington, and Kaysville in particular will be rewarded with discoveries of quaint adobe, rock, and frame structures that have survived from pioneer days. Of special note are the following: **Mormon Tabernacle,** Main and Center, Bountiful, completed in 1862 and revered as one of the state's outstanding early church buildings . . . **Mormon Rock Chapel,** 272 N. Main in Farmington, built of rock in 1861-63 and still in use . . . **Old Rock Mill,** N. Main in Farmington, erected by Mormon leader Willard Richards in 1849-50 as the first grist mill in Farmington, now a restaurant . . . the birthplace and later residence of Utah governor Henry H. Blood in Kaysville (9 S. 2nd West and 95 S. 3rd West respectively).

KEY TO TOUR NO. 3 TOURS

Tour No. 3
SALT LAKE VALLEY AND VICINITY
(Great Salt Lake Country—East)

SALT LAKE CITY (4,300 alt. 163,000 pop.), capital of Utah, is a metropolis of broad streets, the first of many Utah towns laid out by the first Mormon settlers foursquare with the compass, built on the floor and benches of vanished Lake Bonneville in a sheltered angle of the Wasatch Mountains. In 1940 the city's population was 150,000; in 1980 it was 163,000—an increase of less than ten per cent in 40 years. These figures, however, reveal little of what has actually transpired in the way of population growth in Salt Lake Valley during that period, for Salt Lake City proper—a tight enclave with formal boundaries that have changed little in many years—is only the core of a fast-growing metropolitan area that has tripled in population since 1940.

When the term Salt Lake City is used today, by most Utahns, it is meant as a reference to the metropolitan area, in the same way that the names Los Angeles and New York City are used, in a general rather than specific sense. That is the sense in which the name is used in this volume. The Salt Lake City metropolitan area, as considered here, is more or less coterminous with Salt Lake Valley and Salt Lake County. The county's population was 619,000 in 1980, while more than a million people resided within 50 miles of Salt Lake City's downtown center.

The capital of an arid state, Salt Lake City and its environs present the paradox of an exceptionally well-watered metropolis. Drinking fountains are present here and there, the valley's lawns are exceptionally well-flowered and well-turfed, and it is often necessary to detour exuberant sprinkler systems. Another paradox for a city 700 miles inland is the sight of seagulls flying overhead or waiting for handouts in public parks.

Visitors are usually taken to the tops of high buildings, to the State Capitol, or along the bench drives for a bird's-eye view of the valley. Sloping down from the foothills toward the lowest-lying center of the great valley, where the River Jordan flows, the city and its suburbs spread across the benches and valley floor. To the north are the capitol and the temple, the central business district, and the Mormon Church complex. State Street cleaves the populated area in a nearly straight line from the capitol to Draper, nearly 20 miles away. Commercial and industrial clusters and scattered residential areas add an urban accent to the outlying pastoral fringes, finally thinning at the southwestern and western outskirts. On the east stretches the majestic Wasatch Range, its heights rising in upward crescendo to the 11,000-plus feet of the Cottonwood peaks, blocking the horizon 20 miles to the south. Westward, in a north-south tangent, the Oquirrh Range stabs the sky. From the north end of this range wisps ascend from the great smelter stack at Garfield. To the west, across the valley's flat bottom, are mushrooming industrial centers, the runways of the International Airport, and the waters of Great Salt Lake, hidden from full view by the obstructing mountain slopes of Antelope Island.

Salt Lake City can trace its varied periods of growth by its architecture. The transitions are not always obvious, and little remains to represent the first few decades of settlement. Nevertheless, the directional expansions of the city and its suburbs are marked by changing architectural thought and trends.

During stages of architectural evolution, the city spread southward, and beyond Ninth South Street many an avenue might aptly be named "Bungalow Boulevard." Norman, English Colonial, Spanish Mission, New England Colonial, and other types occur in various additions especially on the lower East Bench. Areas once restricted, opened during the 1930s, reflect the trend toward modern architecture. Since World War II, and especially since 1960 or so, a booming population has resulted in an explosion of new construction of all types. The valley does exhibit numerous examples of praiseworthy construction *(see Architecture),* but these are in the minority, as they are elsewhere in the world.

Temple Square is the undisputed hub of tourist activities—it hosts several million visitors each year—and the streets around it are reserved during the tourist season for automobiles with foreign licenses. Temple Square is the site of the city's oldest scheduled mass gatherings, the spring and fall conferences of the Mormon Church, when downtown accommodations are crowded. Downtown traffic jams are common then, as they are after a symphony performance or a popular event at the Salt Palace.

HISTORY TO 1940

The history of Salt Lake City is almost inseparable from that of Utah, the city having been the capital in turn of the State of Deseret, Territory of Utah, and State of Utah, excepting several years during the 1850s. The major part of the city's story, consequently, is that of the state *(see History).* The quoted excerpts below are from the 1941 edition, with slight modification:

Brigham Young . . . was not looking for a land flowing with milk and honey. When Sam Brannan urged him to go on to California, the church leader is reported to have said, "Brannan, if there is a place on this earth that nobody else wants, that's the place I am hunting for." In the eyes of some of his followers, he had found it. To George Washington Brimhall and to Gilbert Belnap, both of whom came in 1850, the valley seemed "as nude of a wardrobe as the Indians themselves," and "a vast desert whose dry and parched soil seemed to bid defiance to the husbandman."

Soon after entering this "extensive scenery," the vanguard of the pioneers, on July 23, 1847, began to plow, "and the same afternoon built a dam to irrigate the soil." The following day Brigham Young came behind the main body of the pioneers: 143 men, 3 women, 2 children, 70 wagons, 1 boat, 1 cannon, 93 horses, 52 mules, 66 oxen, and 19 cows. . . .

Four days after their arrival, according to Wilford Woodruff's journal, Young called a council of the Quorum of the Twelve, and they "walked from the north camp to about the centre between the two creeks, when President Young waved his hand and said: 'Here is the forty acres for the Temple. The city can be laid out perfectly square. . .'." The quorum then decided that the blocks would contain ten acres each, that the streets would be 132 feet wide, and the sidewalks twenty feet wide. The following Sunday the first Bowery was built in Temple Square, and the next day Orson Pratt "commenced laying out the city, beginning with the Temple block."

By the time Captain Howard Stansbury came to the Great Basin to survey Great Salt Lake in 1849, he found that "A city has been laid out upon a magnificent scale, being nearly four miles in length and three in breadth. . . . Through the city itself flows an unfailing stream of pure, sweet water, which by an ingenious mode of irrigation, is made to traverse each side of every street . . . spreading life, verdure and beauty over what was heretofore a barren waste."

Brigham Young, with characteristic energy and leadership, authorized construction of a wall around the city and around Temple Square, partly as protection from the Indians and partly as a work-relief project. The temple foundation was started in 1853, and there was almost constant activity within Temple Square in succeeding years. Meantime, the California gold rush brought emigrants through Great Salt Lake City, and though the Mormons for the most part kept strictly to agriculture, trade with emigrants brought them a measure of prosperity. One transaction by Zodak Knapp Judd serves to present the picture: "I traded them two horses, for which I received three yoke of cattle, a good wagon, a sheet iron stove, a dozen shirts, a good silver watch and nearly a half barrel of pork and some mechanical tools."

During the so-called Utah War of 1857-58 *(see History),* when the United States government declared "a state of substantial rebellion" in Utah, the people of Great Salt Lake City joined a general movement southward. When the troops came through the city that summer day in 1858, as recorded by an army correspondent, "the utter silence of the streets was broken only by the music of the military bands, the monotonous tramp of the regiments, and the rattle of baggage wagons." George "Beefsteak" Harrison, a cook with Johnston's army, "said that Salt Lake was still as a cemetery when they marched in. He saw only two people, a man riding a sorrel mule and an old lady who peeped out of a window blind at the troops."

Great Salt Lake City became a Pony Express post in 1860, when the first riders came in from Sacramento and St. Joseph. Upon completion of the Pacific Telegraph line to Great Salt Lake City in 1861 Brigham Young sent the first eastbound message. . . . The Nevada-California Volunteers, under the leadership of Colonel P. E. Connor, marched through the city in 1862, surprised to find women and children out to greet them; they had heard rumors of rebellion in Utah.

The 1870s and early 1880s were railroad years, in the course of which Salt Lake City (the "Great" was dropped in 1868) was connected by rail to cities in each of the four cardinal directions.

Meantime, the Salt Lake Theater was opened in 1862, and took its place as the leading theatrical center of the intermountain west. The tabernacle was sufficiently completed to house the annual conference of the Mormon Church in 1867. Musical history was made in 1875, when Handel's *Messiah* was presented in the Salt Lake Theater. Building progressed meantime on the temple, its granite walls gradually rising tier after tier, and Temple Square was a scene of constant industry.

The death of Brigham Young in 1877 was a shocking event that drew 25,000 people to view the body of the great church leader as it lay in state in the flower-decked tabernacle. Music played on the tabernacle organ included *Brigham Young's Funeral March,* composed for the occasion by Joseph J. Daynes. The funeral address, by Daniel H. Wells, occupied probably less than a minute. "I have no desire or wish to multiply words," he said, "feeling that it is rather a time to mourn. Goodbye, Brother Brigham, until the morning of the resurrection day. . . ."

Young's death occurred just as political battles, initiated in 1870 by the formation of a non-Mormon Liberal Party, took on greater heat. For all their strenuous efforts, however, the Liberals could not carry the city until 1890, when the "manifesto" disavowing polygamy in the church ended the warfare in the city and territory over that issue *(see History).*

Building of the temple, which had been slow up to 1873, when a branch railroad line was run into Little Cottonwood Canyon to facilitate the moving of granite blocks, was speeded thereafter, and the capstone was placed at the time of the annual church conference in 1892. Andrew Jenson, Assistant Church Historian, writing in the *Utah Magazine* for September, 1936, relates that "over 40,000 people gathered within the confines of Temple Block, while other thousands, unable to find a place in the great square stood in the street or looked down from roofs or windows of adjoining buildings. This was the largest assembly of people ever known in Utah up to that time." Dedication, pending completion of the interior, was deferred to the following year.

Utah marked its semi-centennial, or "Golden Jubilee," with five days of celebration in the summer of 1897, opening with the unveiling of the Brigham Young Monument at Main and South Temple.

In the closing decades of the 19th century and those opening the 20th, Salt Lake City began to assume the physical characteristics it was to retain, relatively unchanged, until the years following World War II. Streets were paved, electric trolleys were installed, Eagle Gate was taken down and erected again at a higher level. The capitol was built, and many new business buildings were erected, including a number of high-rise structures. Up to 1928 streetcars served the city's transportation needs, and in that year the first trolley bus was installed. During the 1930s streetcars were gradually displaced by trolley and gasoline buses, and the last streetcar line was abolished in 1941.

SINCE 1940

The decades since 1940 have altered the face of Salt Lake City and its surrounding communities. Even the giant mountains that overlook the valley are hardly the same, insofar as they cannot be seen clearly on many days of the year because of air pollutants, and because of developments in the canyons and high on the mountain slopes. Though population of the city proper has not changed considerably since 1940, that of the county has more than tripled. The greater part of this increase occurred during the 1950s and 1970s.

In 1940 Salt Lake City was a quiet, almost sleepy provincial capital, still in the throes of the Great Depression. Many of its landmark buildings have been remodeled or replaced since then. The pioneer past is evidenced by little more than a few antique buildings, monuments, murals, and museum exhibits. Even the great Mormon temple, once a dominant feature of the city's skyline, is overshadowed by loftier structures. The State Capitol—built high on a bench where it was meant to be an inspiration from every vantage point—has become surrounded by a clutter of high-rise apartment buildings, office buildings, a residential subdivision, and restorations of historic edifices moved from their original sites. Main, State and other streets in the central business district have been redesigned with new sidewalks, planter boxes, trees, crosswalks, and lighting fixtures, not to mention the removal of overhead signs, the addition of many new buildings, the facelifting of others, and the closing of several streets. Not of minor significance is the development of the freeway system.

Residential areas have replaced farmlands in much of the valley, extending southward, and west across the Jordan River, as the eastern benchlands

East valley and Wasatch Mountains with University of Utah in foreground.

and foothills approach the saturation point of building. State Street, which formerly included numerous homes south of the central business district, has become an unbroken commercial strip extending for ten miles or more through Salt Lake City, South Salt Lake and Murray, to Midvale and beyond. Main Street, while not as long, has identical characteristics in certain areas. Whereas in the years before 1960, State Street was the principal north-south thoroughfare in the valley, Interstate Highways 15 and 215 now carry a volume of north-south traffic that would have been inconceivable for most people in earlier days. Interstate 80 has replaced 21st South and other east-west routes as the carrier of volume traffic in those directions.

Large industrial parks and square miles of commercial developments have sprouted across the valley. And automobile emissions, combined with other pollutants and atmospheric inversions, make the valley's air unfit for health at times. Yet it must be admitted that most younger and many older residents probably would not wish to revert to the past. Today's Salt Lake Valley, while it has lost much if not all of the distinctive historic, cultural, and architectural flavor of 1940, is in many respects a richer and more exciting place to live. It has become much more cosmopolitan. Recreational possibilities and cultural opportunities are incomparably greater than they were in 1940. For years the economic climate has ranked as one of the best among metropolitan areas, and the valley's population growth, in rate of increase, is one of the nation's highest. New residents and contemporary

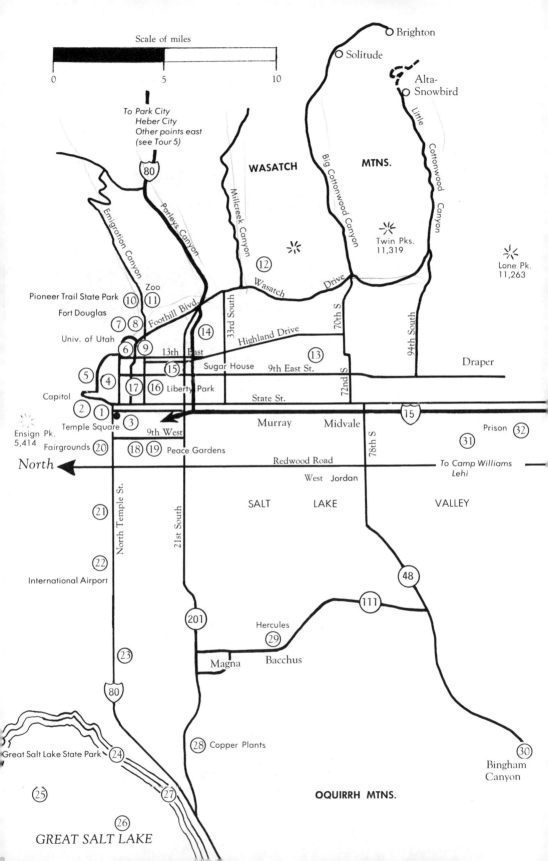

Scale of miles

0   5   10

○ Brighton

○ Solitude

Alta-
Snowbird

To Park City
Heber City
Other points east
(see Tour 5)

⑧⓿

WASATCH   MTNS.

Big Cottonwood Canyon

Little Cottonwood Canyon

Millcreek Canyon

Parleys Canyon

Emigration Canyon

Twin Pks.
11,319

Lone Pk.
11,263

Wasatch   Drive

⑫

Zoo

Pioneer Trail State Park ⑩ ⑪

Fort Douglas

⑦ ⑧

Foothill Blvd

33rd South

Highland Drive

70th S

94th South

Draper

Univ. of Utah

⑥ ⑨

13th East

⑭

Sugar House

⑤

④

⑮

9th East St.

⑬

Capitol

② ①

⑰ ⑯ Liberty Park

State St.

③

9th West

Murray   Midvale

15

Ensign Pk.
5,414

Fairgrounds ⑳

⑱ ⑲ Peace Gardens

72nd S

Prison ㉜

㉛

North

Redwood Road

78th S

To Camp Williams
Lehi

West Jordan

SALT   LAKE   VALLEY

㉑

North Temple St.

21st South

㉒

International Airport

48

111

㉓

201

Hercules

㉙

80

Magna   Bacchus

Great Salt Lake State Park ㉔

㉘ Copper Plants

㉕

㉗

30

㉖

Bingham
Canyon

GREAT SALT LAKE

OQUIRRH MTNS.

influences such as television and cinema have brought diversified cultural mores to the valley and state, changing traditional habits and ways of looking at things. Utah's youths have no reason to feel nostalgia for pioneer adobe and logs, Victorian architecture, or a slower pace of life. Even polluted air means less to them than to their elders, for they have known little else.

Still, people do not like traffic congestion . . . excessively high housing costs . . . noise . . . crowding . . . and dependence on intricate systems for their safety and livelihood. These are facts of life today for the valley's people. For better or worse, Salt Lake Valley has joined the urban American mainstream. The pace of population and economic growth seems to be accelerating rather than slackening. What the valley will be in another 20 years is hard to envision, but it is likely to be as different from the valley of today as today's valley differs from that of 1940.

KEY TO ATTRACTIONS
ON MAP

1. Mormon Church Complex—Temple Square
2. Capitol Hill—Memory Park
3. Central District
4. South Temple Street
5. The Avenues
6. University of Utah
7. University Medical Center
8. Fort Douglas
9. Veterans Administration Medical Center
10. Pioneer Trail State Park
11. Hogle Zoological Garden
12. Mount Olympus Residential Area
13. Wheeler Historic Farm
14. Sugar House Park (Old State Prison Site)
15. Westminster College
16. Liberty Park
17. Trolley Square
18. Mormon Welfare Square
19. International Peace Gardens
20. Utah State Fairgrounds—Jordan River
21. Litton—Sperry Univac—Municipal Airport
22. International Airport—International Center
23. Morton Salt Company
24. Great Salt Lake State Park
25. Antelope Island
26. Great Salt Lake *(Tour No. 3C)*
27. Commercial beaches—Black Rock
28. Copper smelter—refinery—concentrators
29. Bacchus Works, Hercules Inc.
30. Bingham Copper Mine
31. Jordan River Temple (Mormon)
32. Utah State Prison

POINTS OF INTEREST

Touring the city and valley. The incorporated area of Salt Lake City proper is irregular in outline and totals about 50 square miles in extent—a compact area measuring hardly more than seven miles from east to west or north to south. Salt Lake Valley is about 20 miles long (north to south) and slightly less than that from west to east. A system of freeways, boulevards, and other strategic roads gives convenient access to all parts of the valley, though traffic congestion at times is a problem here as in other large urban areas.

Most visitors content themselves with touring Temple Square and nearby attractions, as well as the State Capitol, less than half a mile away. This limitation of interest is a shame, for the entire valley contains a multitude of worthwhile attractions of diverse nature. In the following pages these attractions have been grouped according to location, in distinct areas or districts, an organization that assures the least amount of travel required to visit them. The valley is provided with a mass transit system of buses; these may be useful to visitors in certain cases, but walking is the most convenient way to see much of the central district, while private auto or Grayline sightseeing tours will be the preferred mode of travel for most visitors to outlying points. Maps, brochures, and visitor information are available at motels, hotels, the Salt Palace (Visitors Bureau), Utah Travel Council (300 North and State, across the street from the State Capitol), and in the lobby of the State Capitol, as well as other information centers.

TOUR NO. 3A — SALT LAKE CITY (CITY PROPER)

(1) MORMON CHURCH COMPLEX

The Mormon Church Complex includes Temple Square, the church administration block adjoining Temple Square on the east, and several points of interest nearby.

a. TEMPLE SQUARE

Open daily 8 A.M. (earlier in summer) to 11 P.M. No collections, no gratuities. Smoking not permitted.
Entrances: South Temple, North Temple, and West Temple.

Temple Square is considered the symbolic heart of worldwide Mormonism and is the most-visited point of interest in Utah. The square is a ten-acre city block enclosed by a fifteen-foot wall dating from the 1850s and entered through large wrought-metal gates which allow unrestricted viewing of the interior. The grounds are landscaped with trees, shrubs, winding walks, flower beds in seasonal display, and lush lawns. The square is dominated by the six-spired Temple of the Church of Jesus Christ of Latter-day Saints, on the east side, and the turtle-backed Tabernacle on the west. The Assembly Hall, two imposing visitor centers, and monuments present a cross-section of Mormon religious architecture, history and beliefs. More than a thousand employees and volunteers act as hosts and hostesses for the multitudes who annually visit the square. Tours and organ recitals are conducted frequently.

Visitors Centers. At the north and south gates are Visitors Centers designed to interpret Mormon theological beliefs and church history for the square's millions of visitors. North of the Tabernacle is the Visitors Center North, austere in design, which originally functioned briefly as a Temple Annex but was converted in 1966-67 into a Visitors Center. Visitors Center South, in the square's southeast corner, replaced the old Bureau of Information and Museum with a new building opened in 1978. Both centers are equipped with informational and interpretive displays such as dioramas, murals and graphics, guides and information, publications and library, as well as auditoriums in which films are shown.

Seagull Monument, east of the Assembly Hall, surrounded by a granite-rimmed pool, was erected in 1913 as a memorial to the gulls for saving crops of the pioneers during the cricket invasion of 1848. It was described in the 1941 edition:

> Mounted on a square granite base is a sixteen-foot Doric column, surmounted by a sphere upon which two gilded seagulls are alighting. Four excellent high-relief bronzes decorate the sides of the square base. The north plaque gives the name of the monument and shows two gulls in flight. That on the east presents a pioneer camp scene, with the head of an ox extending around the corner of the granite—a pleasing bit of sculptural unorthodoxy. The south plaque shows the advent of the gulls, and that on the west shows the subsequent harvest.

The story of opportune help by seagulls from the islands of Great Salt Lake is one of Utah's most favorite oft-told tales. Some consider the incident to have been a miracle.

ASSEMBLY HALL, in the southwest corner of the square, is a gray rough-cut granite structure with a forest of white spires thrusting above its steep roof. Seating about 2,000 on benches similar to those in the Tabernacle, the semi-Gothic building dates from 1877-82, when it was built as a meeting place for Salt Lake Stake. Architect was Obed Taylor; construction supervisor was Henry Grow, one of the designers and builders of the Tabernacle. The hall serves a wide variety of functions, from religious gatherings to musical concerts to funerals. From 1979 to 1981 a program of restoration added a basement, air-conditioning, a new organ, new roof, and replacement of some of the exterior wood.

The **TEMPLE** *(open only to Mormons in good standing),* facing east from the east-central section of the square, is a monumental six-spired gray granite edifice, representing more the inspiration and theologic functionalism of its founders than any one architectural style. The building is 186½ feet long and 118 feet wide, with walls 167½ feet high. The east center tower rises 210 feet, capped by the shining, trumpet-bearing statue of the angel Moroni, 12½ feet high. The statue, of hammered copper covered with gold leaf, is the work of Cyrus E. Dallin, Utah-born sculptor. It is anchored by a pendulous iron rod, extending into the spire beneath, where it is heavily weighted, allowing free movement of the figure in high winds. The six spires, three on the east and three on the west, with their varying heights, represent the two high priesthoods of the church. Those on the east signify the higher Melchizedek Priesthood, and those on the west, the highest rising 204 feet, symbolize the Aaronic Priesthood, each with its president and two counselors.

There are two large recessed portals at either end, seldom used except for high church officials or for special ceremonies. The heavy oaken doors each have three medallions, centered by the ubiquitous beehive. An iron fence surrounds the building, preventing a nearer approach than twenty or thirty feet by any but church members. The Temple is used exclusively by members of the church for such religious rites as baptisms for the living and dead, sealing ceremonies, and for marriages.

Conference crowds on Temple Square.

Construction of this $3,500,000 edifice was envisioned before the Mormon exodus from Illinois in 1846-47. Its plan was conceived by Brigham Young, and the details were worked out by Truman O. Angell, church architect. Ground was broken in 1853 and the first cornerstone was laid that year. Work was suspended in 1857, before the advent of General Johnston's army; Mormon workmen refilled the foundation and the grounds resembled a plowed field when the soldiery arrived. Some of the great stones were hauled, one at a time, by four-yoke ox-teams, from Little Cottonwood Canyon, 20 miles south. After the arrival of the railroad, a spur was built into the canyon in 1873. The walls were twenty feet high when Brigham Young died in 1877. Construction was completed and the Temple dedicated in 1893, forty years to a day after it was begun.

For a short time following the dedication the public was admitted to the richly appointed interior, but the building was soon closed to all except church members. Several church-approved publications, available commercially, describe and illustrate the Temple's interior and its religious functions.

The **TABERNACLE** *(open for public functions, organ recitals, or when accompanied by guide),* centering the west section of the square, is a mammoth oval auditorium seating about 8,000, 250 feet long and 150 feet wide, resembling the gray back of a huge tortoise. Unique and severe in design, it is a pioneer among structures employing the self-supported, vaulted type of roof, which was designed as an ellipsoid with a focal point at either end; this, together with the unbroken inner ceiling surface, accounts for the unusual acoustics of the building. A pin dropped at either focal point, when the building is quiet, can be heard at the opposite end, more than

Tabernacle interior. Mormon Tabernacle Choir and great organ at far end.

LDS CHURCH INFORMATION

200 feet away. Forty-four gray-painted buttresses of red sandstone mark the circumference of the building. Upon them rest giant wooden arches, ten feet thick, making a span of 150 feet, 80 feet high at the center. The timbers, still in perfect condition—the building was begun in 1864 and first used in 1867—are braced with lattice-like cross-members, fastened with wooden thole pins and rawhide thongs, since reinforced by nails. A gallery, 30 feet wide, extends around three sides of the interior. Of offset construction, separate from the Tabernacle walls, it is supported by columns, and there is a space of two and a half feet between gallery and wall.

The design of the Tabernacle is attributable to Brigham Young, and the plans were drawn and the building erected under the supervision of William H. Folsom and Henry Grow, a Pennsylvania bridge-builder, who employed the Remington lattice-truss method by which suspension bridges of the 1860s were built.

The **Great Pipe Organ,** at the west end, is known the country over through CBS network broadcasts every Sunday, with the 375-voice Tabernacle Choir. A mammoth structure, the organ was first constructed in 1867 with 700 pipes; since then it has been modified and greatly enlarged. Of the 51 pipes in its famed facade, patterned after the organ in the Boston Music Hall, only ten actually play; the others serve only for decoration. The facade pipes are said to be the only round wooden organ pipes in the world. They were made from specially selected white pine found in southern Utah. Today's organ includes 11,000 pipes of all sizes, shapes and configurations, ranging from 3/8 inch to 32 feet in length, powered by a 30-horsepower electric motor and blowers. The console features five manual keyboards, one pedal keyboard, and almost 200 stops. Organists generally consider it to be one of the finest instruments of its kind, one writer terming it "the Stradivarius of all organs." The great organ can be heard at recitals held weekdays at noon and Sundays at 4 p.m.; during summer months, additional recitals are held on certain days in the evening. The organ may be heard also at Tabernacle Choir rehearsals on Thursday at 7:30 p.m.; during the CBS radio Choir and Organ broadcast on Sunday mornings; and during certain religious services and musical events.

Spring and fall conferences of the Mormon Church are held in this auditorium, and it has been the scene of many civic and patriotic gatherings, including the appearances of United States presidents and other dignitaries. Nationally known symphony orchestras, instrumentalists, and singers have appeared here. For many years, until the opening of the new Symphony Hall in 1979, the Tabernacle was used by the Utah Symphony under Maestro Maurice Abravanel, for its concerts and practice.

b. Adjoining Temple Square

Museum of Church History and Art, corner of West Temple and North Temple (on the block west of Temple Square) is expected to open in 1983. Housing many of the collections formerly displayed in the old museum-visitor center on Temple Square (replaced by the South Visitors Center), the new museum is devoted to "telling the history of the Latter-day Saint people" and presenting "150 years of the church's cultural history." Featured are items relating to the martyrdom of Joseph and Hyrum Smith . . . the oldest house in Salt Lake City, built by Osmyn Deuel in 1847 and for many years a Temple Square curiosity . . . an original handcart . . . church-related objects from other countries . . . arts, crafts, photos, paintings . . . Indian antiquities . . . and artifacts connected with prominent church leaders.

Brigham Young Monument, centering the intersection of Main and South Temple streets, is a heroic bronze figure of the church leader, on a granite base. Seated at the base is the bronze figure of an Indian facing east, while the figure of a bearded trapper, in a similar pose, faces west. On the south face is a bronze bas-relief of a pioneer man, woman, and child. Another plaque, on the north face, lists the pioneers and equipment making up the main body of Mormon pioneers who arrived in Salt Lake Valley on July 24, 1847. The 25-foot monument, unveiled during the Utah Jubilee in 1897, was executed by Cyrus E. Dallin, Utah-born sculptor. In recent times, its location in the center of a busy traffic intersection has been the subject of sometimes bitter civic and official controversy, with many people demanding its removal, as many others indignant over such a proposal. The base has been reduced to accommodate heavy traffic in the intersection.

c. Church Administration Block (east of Temple Square)

Hotel Utah, on the northeast corner of Main and South Temple streets, is a distinguished hostelry of white terra-cotta brick, erected in 1911, expanded and extensively renovated in recent years. Owned by the Mormon Church, the ornate French Renaissance building is lavishly decorated with figure carvings, scrollwork, and a grandiose crystal chandelier in the lobby. Its cupola is topped with a beehive, the state emblem. A roof-garden restaurant affords a bird's-eye view of Temple Square and Salt Lake Valley and has garnered awards over the years for its fine cuisine.

Church Administration Building, 47 E. South Temple, is a granite structure of Greek Revival design, with fluted Ionic columns extending the full height of its four stories. Completed in 1917, the building houses the offices of church leaders. The lobby displays walls and stairway of polished marble.

Lion House *(closed to the public),* 63 E. South Temple, is a two-story cement-covered adobe structure with small-paned windows, shutters, tall chimneys, and a tile roof. The excerpts below are taken from the 1941 edition:

> East and west exposures are topped with ten steep-roofed gables. The house is named for the carved stone lion, executed by William Ward, pioneer craftsman, over the first floor portico, and is used as a social center and banquet hall by L. D. S. Church organizations. This building, because it housed some of Brigham Young's wives, has always been an object of great curiosity to visitors, who have

Brigham Young Monument and Mormon Temple.

UTAH TRAVEL COUNCIL

often stood outside and counted the gables, in the belief that each gable represented a wife's apartment. Brigham Young, who is credited by some authorities with twenty-six wives, offered no assistance in this guessing game. On the contrary, he seemed to take particular delight in keeping curious persons in suspense. Concerning family trips into the country, he once said, "You know what they say about me in the east; should I take my ninety wives and their children, with carriages and wagons enough to convey them, it would make such a vacuum here, and so many others would wish to go, that there would be no Salt Lake City. I think I will take a few of them, but I dare not take the whole, for if I did they would then know how many wives I have got, and that would not do."

The keeping of law and order in such a household as this must have been one of the Mormon leader's major projects. All reports indicate that he ruled his family with the same firm hand as he did his followers. He rose every morning at seven o'clock, went to his office next door, and spent the morning administering Church matters. At two o'clock he had dinner with his family at the Lion House, in the room now used as a cafeteria. Picnics and outings were usually planned at this time, including gay rides in the *Julia Dean Haynes,* a bobsled named for the noted actress. He maintained a sort of gymnasium for his children, using the equivalent of a present-day medicine ball for exercise. Good posture was encouraged among his daughters by making them wear wooden yokes to keep their shoulders back. In the afternoon he visited his wives individually, and at seven o'clock rang the prayer bell, calling his fifty-six children and their mothers into the room now used as a sitting room. Here, too, were held the family councils, including "juvenile court," at which differences between children were adjusted by the father-judge. The family then retired, if no social events were planned for the evening, the women with small children to bedrooms on the first floor, those with older children to the twenty bedrooms on the second floor. A daughter, Clarissa Young Spencer, has written charmingly of life in the Lion House in *One Who Was Valiant.*

For five years during the 1960s the Lion House underwent an extensive interior restoration, having as its objective the restoration of rooms and furnishings (except for bedrooms), approximately to their appearance during Brigham Young's lifetime. It is not a static museum, however, being used for church and community social and educational functions such as wedding receptions and meetings. A ground-floor restaurant caters to members and their guests.

Brigham Young's Office, 67 E. South Temple, is a small adobe structure between the Lion and Beehive houses, serving today as a visitor reception area for the Beehive House. Designed by Truman O. Angell and built in 1852, it has a one-story portico surmounted by iron grillwork and small-paned windows. A steep stairway behind a closet leads to the oval mezzanine, said to be the first in the west.

Beehive House, at the corner of South Temple and State, is the restored residence of Brigham Young. A two-story straw-colored adobe structure in Greek Revival Colonial style, the Beehive House was built in 1853-54. It has the distinction of being one of the oldest residences still extant in Utah, and is certainly the most elaborate building of its time in the state. Truman O. Angell, church architect and designer of the Mormon Temple in Salt Lake City, was its architect.

The Beehive House was described in the 1941 edition (pages 243-244). At that time it was serving as a home for young women and had undergone several remodelings since the death of President Young in 1877. Beginning in 1959 and continuing until 1961 the house was restored, under the direction of three prominent architects (grandsons of Brigham Young), to a condition resembling its appearance when occupied by the church president and one of his families. Since 1961 it has been open to the public for guided tours.

Quoting an official guidebook, "The Beehive House was designed to meet the varied needs of Brigham Young, second President of the Church and first governor of Deseret (later to become the Utah territory). It was to be an official mansion where the Mormon leader could receive and confer with other Church leaders and with state and federal dignitaries, as well as entertain prominent traveling visitors. But above all, the Beehive House was to be a home for his family." In actuality, only one of his families resided there at any one time, first (1854-1860) Mary Ann Angell Young, and next (1860-1888) Lucy Ann Decker Young with her seven children. Distinguished guests who were entertained by Brigham Young in the mansion included President U. S. Grant, General William T. Sherman, Ralph Waldo Emerson, Mark Twain, Jay Gould, and Horace Greeley.

After President Young's death in 1877, Lucy Ann continued to reside in the Beehive House until 1888, when she sold it to John W. Young, a son of Brigham Young. He remodeled the house to "mid-Victorian splendor," adding several rooms; subsequent owners also changed it, covering original walls and floors and otherwise modifying its character. Between 1893 and 1918 it served as the official residence of church presidents Lorenzo Snow and Joseph F. Smith, then becoming a home for girls.

There is much of interest in the house: Brigham Young's office and his bedroom . . . a 19th century kitchen . . . a store from which his families were supplied . . . a gracious sitting room and a grand parlor known as the Long Room . . . a formal dining room . . . bedrooms, children's playroom, family dining room, and pantry.

Free guided tours for the public, daily except Sundays.

Eagle Gate, spanning N. State St. at South Temple St., designates the former entrance to the private property of Brigham Young. The present gate, bearing little resemblance to its predecessors, was dedicated in November 1963 as a more functional replacement for an older, narrower gate that was severely damaged by a truck in 1960. The new gate was designed by architect George Cannon Young, a grandson of Brigham Young. Its copper eagle, patterned after the original model, is much larger, weighing two tons and having a wingspread of 20 feet. Pillars are 76 feet apart compared with 22 feet for the original gate, and base of the beehive is 36 feet above street level. Construction was a cooperative effort of state, city and Mormon Church.

The first Eagle Gate was erected in 1859 and for many years served as the only entrance to City Creek Canyon. It was described in the guide's first edition.

CHURCH OFFICE BUILDING, 50 E. North Temple, is the valley's tallest building (28 floors above ground, 3 levels below). Built over a three-year period between 1969 and 1972, the massive white structure houses nearly all auxiliary and departmental organizations of the Mormon Church. The central tower is flanked by two four-story wings, the west wing being occupied by the Genealogical Library *(see below)* and the east wing by the Church Historical Department. On the 26th floor is an observatory from which is obtained a spectacular circle view of the city, valley and mountains. *Open to the public on request at information desk in lobby.*

The building's statistical facts are impressive: 420 feet in height . . . underground parking for 1,400 cars . . . 21 elevators . . . 3,600 windows . . . nearly 700,000 square feet of office space. Many older buildings were razed to make room for the office building, expansive plaza, and the underground parking levels.

Genealogical Department Library, located in the Church Office Building (west wing), is recognized as "The genealogical treasure house of the world." Its vast collections of vital and biographical records from countries around the world are indisputably the most comprehensive to be found. Open to the public, the library's resources are utilized by thousands of visitors for research, many coming long distances solely for this purpose. For decades the church has been engaged in a systematic worldwide program of microfilming documents, books, and records useful for genealogical research, resulting in some million rolls of microfilm—the equivalent of nearly five million printed volumes of 300 pages each. These microfilms, as well as more than 170,000 printed volumes, more than six million family record sheets, and tens of millions of individual index cards, are available for public use. Computers are utilized increasingly for cataloging and indexing. Duplicate copies of the department's holdings are preserved in the **Granite Mountain Records Vault** in Little Cottonwood Canyon, where storage chambers cut into solid, unfractured granite assure their survival through cataclysm or catastrophe.

Plans were announced in 1980 for a new five-level Genealogical Library to be built within a few years on the block west of Temple Square, adjoining the new Church Museum.

The phenomenal interest of Mormons in genealogical research is a result of church belief in continuing family relationships after mortal death. These relationships involve not only those of husband and wife, parents and children, but of progenitors, descendants, and relatives of every degree. Mormon doctrine teaches that individual salvation in the fullest sense requires an acceptance of the gospel of Jesus Christ, if not in mortality then in afterlife. Acceptance must be symbolized by baptism by immersion, which may be performed in behalf of those on spirit planes by proxies in Mormon temples. Mormons believe that the gospel is taught in the afterlife as well as in mortality. If spirits accept its truth, the proxy baptisms and other ceremonies (including marriages for eternity), performed in Mormon temples for the dead, are as valid as if they had been performed before death. Hence the necessity for temples, and for genealogical records and the research required to establish individual names and vital information for identification. *See also Religion section.*

d. **Mormon Pioneer Memorial** and **Brigham Young's Cemetery** *(half a block east of State Street on 1st Avenue)*

These consist of a lawned park, surrounded by apartment buildings and shaded by trees, containing monuments, works of sculpture, and the grave of Brigham Young (1801-77), second president of the Mormon Church, leader of the Mormon pioneers who founded Utah in 1847, colonizer and territorial governor. Several of his wives and children also are buried here, among them the revered Eliza R. Snow (1804-1887), leader in women and youth organizations and composer of the favorite Mormon hymn, *O My Father.* Monuments include a heroic bronze and granite sculpture of a pioneer husband, wife and child in affectionate embrace, symbolizing "All is well," the work of Edward J. Fraughton; also a bronze bust of Brigham Young by Fraughton; a granite monument and plaques honoring William Clayton, writer of the hymn *Come, Come Ye Saints;* and a bronze plaque reciting the story of the pioneer trek to Utah.

(2) CAPITOL HILL, MARMALADE DISTRICT, MEMORY GROVE

Capitol Hill extends from North Temple on the south to Ensign Peak on the north, and from 2nd (200) West to City Creek Canyon (Memory Grove). The Hill district incorporates not only the capitol complex of state buildings and gardens but architectural specimens ranging from quaint and aged houses of pioneer vintage in the Marmalade District—which clings to the steep slopes west of the capitol—through a spectrum of styles representing every period from Victorian to contemporary modern. Many larger homes have been converted to apartments. In recent years, despite heated opposition, the character of the hill has been altered by the erection of high-rise apartments and the replacement of older buildings with new. The pace of change has been slowed by its classification as a Historic District and listing on the National Register of Historic Places.

a. North Main Street

McCune Mansion, 200 N. Main, is one of the stateliest of Utah's turn-of-the-century homes, rivaling the grandest of those on South Temple in ornateness and fine craftsmanship. Now occupied by private offices, the tile-roofed, towered edifice was built as a residence for Alfred W. and Elizabeth McCune, on a site formerly occupied by the homes of Robert N. Baskin and William Godbe, prominent men of 19th century affairs.

Pioneer Memorial Museum and Carriage House, 300 N. Main, immediately west of the State Capitol *(admission free),* was dedicated in 1950 as a replica of the old Salt Lake Theater. It is maintained by the Daughters of the Utah Pioneers (DUP) as one of Utah's finest historical museums and as headquarters of the DUP's National Society.

The museum's historical collections, numbering thousands of items on four floors, feature relics, artifacts, and craftwork from the early days of Utah, including displays of furnishings, furniture, clothing, and myriad artifacts having to do with 19th century transportation, industry, Indians, religious and military life, etc. Utah's largest doll exhibit is a special attraction. A two-story Carriage House, dedicated in 1973, displays antique wagons, coaches, a streetcar, buggies, and other vehicles, as well as old-time transportation equipment.

Marmalade District, so-called because of the names of some of its street (Apricot, Quince, etc.), is an area of older homes clinging to the steep hillside west of the State Capitol. Many homes in the district date from the last century, and some of these have special architectural and historical values. When razing of old and construction of new buildings are proposed, the district becomes a focus of acrimonious controversy. A number of the area's older homes have been restored as functional residences. **Thomas Quayle House,** 355 Quince St., is a quaint wood-frame structure that originally stood on West 4th South, where it was built during the 1880s. The house was moved to its present location in 1975 and restored to serve as headquarters of the Utah Heritage Foundation. **John Platts House,** 364 Quince St., is a modified cobblestone structure dating from the late 1850s.

b. South of the State Capitol

Council Hall, State and 3rd (300) North, across 3rd North from the capitol *(free admission; travel information),* is an attractive towered structure of brown stone and white painted wood, reminiscent of New England architecture. The building is a reconstruction of the historic building that served for 30 years as Salt Lake City Hall and early meeting place for the territorial legislature. The present structure dates from 1962-63 when its stones and other salvageable materials were moved from the original site at 120 E. 1st South, where the Federal Building now stands. Since that time it has served as a state information center and office of the State Travel Division. Its rooms contain furnishings of the building's early territorial period; some are open for public inspection.

White Community Memorial Chapel, across 3rd North from the State Capitol, just east of Council Hall, is a replica-reconstruction of a distinctive 19th century Mormon chapel. In general design it represents the old 18th Ward chapel, originally built in 1881 at 2nd Avenue and A Street, dismantled in 1973. The original chapel's steeple, window frames, and certain other construction materials were utilized in the reconstruction, which began in 1979. Dedication occurred in June 1980. Presented to the state by private sponsors, the chapel is used for civic and religious purposes; it also houses the Honors Library of Living History.

c. State Capitol Grounds

Mormon Battalion Monument, southeast of the capitol, is a mass of rose-pink granite, centered by the heroic bronze figure of a Battalion infantryman; from the prow of stone behind and above him emerges a symbolic woman's figure. In the concave sides of the granite mass, front and back, are high reliefs depicting scenes in the life of the Battalion, and on bronze plaques are listed the names of Battalion members. The work of Gilbert Riswald, Chicago sculptor, the monument was erected in 1927 to perpetuate the memory of the Mormons who enlisted for the United States in the Mexican War of 1846. *See History.*

The **STATE CAPITOL** overlooks the valley from the north end of State Street. It is a classically styled four-story edifice built on the lines of the National Capitol, and occupies a bench of the Wasatch foothills at the northern rim of the city, its magisterial air emphasized by its elevation 300 feet above the valley floor. It can be seen from nearly every approach to the city, but no longer without obstruction. Of Corinthian lineage, the capitol was designed by Richard K. A. Kletting, Salt Lake City architect. Though capped by the usual dome, it is articulated with spacious simplicity. Following the structural precedent of two wings, one for each branch of a bicameral legislature, it departs from the precedent in placing the House of Representatives in the west wing, the Senate in the north center, and the State Supreme Court in the east wing. Built of Utah granite on a rectangular plan, it is 404 feet long, 240 feet wide, and 285 feet high at the tip of the dome, which is covered with Utah copper. The south facade is broken only at the center by the customary monumental entrance leading up to a well-proportioned Corinthian portico.

Until 1912, when ground was broken for the present capitol, the legislature and high court of Utah had an orphaned existence. Meeting in the old Council House in Great Salt Lake City, the first territorial legislature of 1851 picked Fillmore as a central location for the state capital. Truman O. Angell, church architect, designed a three-winged, acorn-domed State House, the completed south wing of which was first occupied by the legislature in the session of 1855-56. The building was never finished, though the one wing still stands in Fillmore *(see Tour 4).* Finding the new capital too far removed from the center of population, the same legislature returned the government to Great Salt Lake City. Several subsequent legislatures trekked to Fillmore, 150 miles away, to fulfill legal requirements, but immediately adjourned to Great Salt Lake City. Sessions continued in the Council House until it burned in 1883, and one session was held in Social Hall. There was agitation for the erection of a capitol during the last years of territorial government, but the legislature continued to meet in the Old Courthouse until completion of the City and County Building in 1894, when it was occupied as capitol. Finally, in 1912, when $1,500,000 had been collected from inheritance taxes, authorization was given to start the building. The cornerstone was laid by Governor William Spry in 1914, and the edifice was completed the following year at a cost of $2,739,528.54.

The interior of the building is laid out with a spacious and rectangular dignity, departing from the usual formula of a rotunda under the dome; the plan conforms to this tradition only to the extent of a circle of opaque glass set in the floor. The great hall is flanked with smooth monolithic columns of gray Georgia marble, with Ionic capitals. The walls of the main floor are paneled with quartered marble, and guides point out such configurations as "the Persian rug," "the butterfly," "the hour-

State Capitol *(above)*.

Mormon Battalion Monument *(left)*.

Council Hall *(below)*.

glass," "the yawning lion," and "heels of two socks together," while "Santa Claus" is seen peering down from a column.

For decades the central spot under the dome was occupied by a bronze-painted plaster cast replica of Cyrus E. Dallin's heroic *Massasoit,* the original of which looks out over Plymouth Bay, Massachusetts. Some said that the capitol was built around Massasoit; at any rate the tall magnificent figure long dominated the view from any point within the three-story rectangular hall. In 1958 the plaster copy was removed and a bronze replica installed outside in front of the capitol, overlooking the valley.

In the pendentives, or arched triangles leading up to the dome, are four murals depicting phases in Utah's early history—the march of the Dominguez-Escalante expedition in 1776, in the southwest pendentive; Peter Skene Ogden, Hudson's Bay Company trader, in the northeast; John C. Fremont at Great Salt Lake in the northwest; and Brigham Young with an ox-drawn covered wagon, on the southeast.

The interior of the dome, 165 feet above the floor at its highest point, is decorated with a skyscape, and from its center hangs a 6,000 pound chandelier on a 7,000-pound chain that is 95 feet long. Giant semi-circular murals at each end of the long hall were done by Girard Hale and Richard White in 1917. The west mural depicts the arid Great Salt Lake Valley as it looked to the pioneers in 1847, and that on the east shows the green and fertile valley after it was cultivated by early settlers.

The **Gold Room** *(opened for display by guide),* on the southwest side of the main hall, is the State reception room, in which presidents and royal visitors have been received. It is a long rectangular room with a vaulted ceiling, liberally decorated with yellow metal. Capitol guides take pleasure in listing foreign-made furniture and decorations.

The skylit **House of Representatives** opens off the end of the stairway leading to the third floor at the west end of the building. It is reminiscent of the House in the National Capitol, with its clock- and flag-surmounted dias, but is built on a smaller scale, and the desks of the 60 members are in close-crowded rows. The **Senate Chamber,** on the north central side of the main hall, is similar in plan to the House, except that it is less crowded in accommodating 20-odd senators.

The fourth floor is occupied by offices of the state legislature, the legislative council, and other agencies. Featured on the first or lower floor are exhibits of Utah's 29 counties, their industrial, historical, cultural and recreational attributes, as well as Utah's national parks, forests, etc.

Adjoining the capitol on the north are the **State Office Building and Plaza,** completed in 1960 and dedicated in 1961 at a cost of five million dollars. The six-story office building, built of steel and precast concrete facing, houses primarily various operations of the highway, tax and public safety divisions. On the plaza are colorful flower gardens and a glass-walled, circular cafeteria building; below is a parking garage and a service station for state vehicles.

While the office building and plaza were under construction, the capitol itself was undergoing extensive modernization, a program costing nearly a million dollars. Panelled walls created new office space; new lighting was installed, as were automatic elevators and air conditioning.

d. Memory Grove Area *(enter from Canyon Road, which forks north from 2nd Avenue one-half block east of State and North Temple)*

Memory Grove, also known as Memory Park and Memory Grove Park, is a secluded, beautifully landscaped park on both sides of Canyon Road in City Creek Canyon, below the State Capitol. It is dedicated to Utah soldiers who lost their lives in America's wars and contains a number of monuments: a white marble pergola commemorating the 760 Utah soldiers who died in World War I . . . a memorial shaft erected by the 145th Artillery . . . a World War I cannon and an armored vehicle of later vintage . . . name plaques memorializing soldiers killed in World War II . . .

and a memorial bell tower. Overlooking the park is a meditation chapel of colored marble. Memorial House, beside the road, is used for public functions, wedding receptions, etc. Development of the park began in 1923.

(3) CENTRAL DISTRICT

With few exceptions, important attractions in the Central District are concentrated within a mile of Temple Square; therefore, walking is the most convenient and rewarding method of touring the heart of this district, perhaps with the occasional assistance of a bus, taxi, or private auto. For tour purposes, the district extends from 4th (400) West to 13th (1300) East and from the north foothills to 17th (1700) South.

The Central District was the first-settled part of the valley. It has long been the financial core of Utah, containing the tallest buildings, the largest concentration of retail stores, and the main offices of the largest banks. The district is the site of the Bicentennial Arts Complex, the Salt Palace, and a host of theaters, hotels, motels, and restaurants. It is the locale as well for federal, state, city, and county offices.

a. **Downtown Area** *(Main-State-West Temple streets from South Temple to 9th South)*

Recent decades have seen the replacement of many older buildings in this area and the facelifting of streets. Some of the newer buildings—products largely of the past two decades—are of striking originality and imposing dimensions. At such close range in time it is not possible, as yet, for Utahns to fully evaluate the architectural, esthetic, and personality changes that have transformed their capital city so rapidly. Accent to modernity is provided here and there by older structures, particularly on either side of Main Street.

The redevelopment of downtown Salt Lake City has been an inexorable, continuing process for a hundred years or so, with marked plateaus of inactivity and surges of replacement of old with new. John S. McCormick has provided details in a recent volume entitled *Salt Lake City: The Gathering Place.* High-rise buildings of more than two or three stories made their appearance in the 1880s and by 1912 the highest of all—the 16-story Walker Bank Building—had been completed. This remained Utah's tallest "skyscraper" for some 50 years. Unlike those of 19th century vintage, the majority of large buildings of the early 20th century are still in existence, among them the Deseret News Building (1902) . . . Utah Savings & Trust Building (1907) . . . Boston and Newhouse buildings (1910) . . . Kearns Building (1911) . . . Hotel Utah (1911) . . . Walker Bank Building (1912) . . . State Capitol (1915) . . . Newhouse Hotel (1915) . . . First Security, formerly Deseret National Bank (late teens) . . . Continental Bank and Tribune buildings (1924). A hiatus in construction, lasting several decades, followed during the Great Depression of the 1930s and war years of the 1940s, extending into the 1950s. The early 1960s witnessed a remarkable surge in construction: State Office Building . . . 17-story Kennecott Building . . . Joint City-County Metropolitan Hall of Justice and Jail . . . Federal Office Building . . . Prudential Federal Savings and Loan Building . . . Mormon Temple Annex . . . Salt Lake City Central Library . . . LDS Church Office Building . . . Salt Palace . . . and other notable structures. Another modern downtown renaissance, beginning in the 1970s, shows little sign of losing momentum. Completed projects of recent years include the ZCMI Center and Beneficial Life Tower . . . Crossroads Plaza and Commercial Security Tower . . . Bicentennial Arts Complex

. . . Marriott Hotel . . . and Mountain Bell Building. Completed or in process of construction are condominium towers, office buildings, and a Sheraton Hotel on Block 58 (bounded by 2nd and 3rd South, Main and West Temple). This block probably will see replacement of nearly all its old buildings.

Resembling Block 58 in extent of present and future development is Block 53, north of the City and County Building, where a new state office building is under construction and other structures have been completed or are in stages of planning. The venerable Newhouse Hotel (1915) is marked for demolition in 1982; a large Salt Palace expansion is underway; and other new buildings are under construction around the downtown district. Points of special interest include the following:

State Street (south from South Temple)

George T. Hansen Planetarium, 15 South State *(admission charge),* is an attraction made possible initially by a $400,000 gift from the G. T. Hansen Foundation, for purchase of the star projector. Building and funds were provided by the Salt Lake City Library Board and Salt Lake County Commission. The planetarium features an auditorium or star chamber, Space Science Library, Space Museum, Foucalt pendulum, black light mineral display, etc. For many years the building in which it is located was occupied by the city's Main Library, which moved to new quarters in 1964. The planetarium began operating in 1965.

Federal Office Building, corner of 1st South and State, an eight-story edifice with white facade, was completed in 1964 at a cost of more than six million dollars.

Promised Valley Playhouse, 132 S. State, is one of the most elegant theaters in the west, renovated by the Mormon Church for performances of church-theme and popular stage entertainment. An adjoining building houses offices, rehearsal and conference rooms, an experimental Little Theater, and a costume department where local church groups may rent costumes. First opened in 1905 as a vaudeville theater, it passed from vaudeville through the golden age of cinema as a movie palace known successively as the Orpheum, Wilkes, Roxy, Lake, and Lyric. The theater was purchased by the church in 1972, renovated, then renovated again in 1980-81.

Block 53, east of State between 3rd and 4th South, is being redeveloped by private capital as a city Redevelopment Agency project. The new Heber M. Wells State Office Building, costing seven million dollars, was completed in 1982.

Salt Lake City and County Building occupies a city block known as Washington Square, between 4th and 5th South, State and 2nd East. Modeled after the London City Hall, it is said, and completed in 1894, the many-turreted castle displays ornate Romanesque Revival features. Its central tower rises more than 300 feet. The interior has been modified extensively. Exterior restoration during the late 1970s and early 1980s required a spectacular maze of high scaffolding.

Buildings on the block to the east of Washington Square are occupied by city-county courts and jail, city police, and Salt Lake City Public Library. The greater part of the complex was built in the 1960s, with parking facilities and renovation in the 1970s.

Main Street (south from South Temple-Brigham Young Monument)

The most imposing structures here are the massive ZCMI and Crossroads shopping malls, on either side of Main Street between South Temple and 1st South. The 17-story Kennecott Building, dating from the mid-1960s—one of the first of the city's modern skyscrapers—occupies the corner across South Temple from Hotel Utah. A walking tour along Main Street reveals a melange of architectural styles dating from the 1890s or earlier. Though some of the older buildings display their

Downtown Salt Lake City (Central District). Mormon Church Administration Building on left, Temple Square in foreground. *Salt Lake Valley Convention Bureau photo.*

original facades, others have camouflaged their age with modern fronts. Development is ongoing, and the future of many older buildings is uncertain as new construction proceeds rapidly.

ZCMI Center is one of Utah's largest shopping malls, incorporating about 60 shops as well as ZCMI Department Store; it is surmounted by a 27-story office building known as Beneficial Life Tower and includes a 2,000-car parking garage.

ZCMI is an abbreviation for Zion's Cooperative Mercantile Institution, a church-owned operation dating from 1869. The distinctive Main Street cornice that graced ZCMI's facade for more than 90 years was refurbished, then reinstalled as an entrance to the new center.

Crossroads Plaza Center, across Main Street from ZCMI Center, was begun in 1978 after the demolition of many older structures. With a Main Street facade extending more than 400 feet, the center's retail area features open market stalls, inspired partially by Quincy Market in Boston, as well as retail stores. The 16-story tower is named for Commercial Security Bank. Cost of the new center is estimated at about 70 million dollars.

Three of the corners of **2nd South and Main** are occupied by banks. On the northeast corner is the Walker Bank Building (1912), for decades the tallest building in Utah. Walker Bank and Trust Company became a part of the First Interstate system in 1981, and the 15-story headquarters of First Interstate Bank of Utah is now under construction across the street. Continental Bank Building (1924) occupies the southwest corner, J. C. Penney Department Store the southeast corner.

Exchange Place, between 3rd and 4th South, separates the twin Boston and Newhouse buildings, built more than 70 years ago by wealthy mining magnate Samuel Newhouse. Now a mall in part, it is the site of the historic Salt Lake Stock and Mining Exchange Building (1909) and, across the street, Commercial Club Building and a small park. Exchange Place is the center of an aging cluster of significant buildings dating from the first decades of the century, a number of them financed or encouraged by Newhouse and other non-Mormon capitalists. These include, in addition to those mentioned: the Newhouse Hotel . . . Old Federal Building-Main Post Office . . . New York Hotel (Post Office Place) . . . New Grand Hotel . . . Judge Building . . . Felt Building. The Paris and Auerbach's department stores, owned by prominent Jewish mercantile families, recently ceased operations after many years in business. These were located on 3rd South (Broadway) between Main and State.

West Temple Street (south from South Temple Street)

West Temple bears only the vaguest resemblance to the same street of 1940. Fewer than half a dozen original buildings remain between South Temple and 4th South, their peers having been replaced by the Salt Palace-Arts complex, Arrow Press Square, new office buildings, and three new hotels.

Salt Palace, located on the west side of the street between 1st and 2nd South, is Utah's largest integrated sports, convention and exhibit complex. Construction was begun in 1963 after Salt Lake County voters approved a 17 million dollar bond issue for the center. Most distinctive feature of the Salt Palace is the arena's huge flat-topped circular tower or dome. More than 350 feet in diameter, its suspended roof is supported by a system of double steel cables, and when built was the largest roof of its type in the nation. In the arena's floor is a built-in ice rink measuring 85 by 200 feet and containing ten miles of pipe.

Appended to the arena—which can seat as many as 14,000 spectators—is a large exhibit hall (now being expanded), a theater, assembly hall, and meeting rooms. The Salt Palace functions as the state's most important convention center. In addition, since its opening in 1969, it has been utilized for concerts, circuses, exhibits, rodeos, tournaments, ice shows, public ice skating, hockey and basketball games, recreation and sports shows, and other civic and commercial functions. The Palace also has served as home court for the Salt Lake Golden Eagles (Western Hockey League), Utah Jazz (National Basketball Association), and former Utah Stars (American Basketball Association). In 1980, events at the Salt Palace were attended by nearly two million persons.

BICENTENNIAL ARTS CENTER consists of three distinctive structures devoted to music, the performing arts, and the visual arts. It is the result of a massive cooperative effort involving state, county, church, private citizens, foundations, Utah's Bicentennial Commission, and bonding. The center was completed during the late 1970s at a cost of about 20 million dollars.

Symphony Hall, overlooking an expansive plaza and fountain on the southwest corner of West Temple and South Temple, is the largest and most costly building in the complex (about ten million dollars). The hall was inaugurated in September 1979 with concerts by the Utah Symphony Orchestra. An austere facade of brick and glass hardly suggests the ornate interior where striking visual effects complement the remarkable quality of sound. A four-story lobby features a grand staircase and a huge glass wall measuring 135 feet in width, 43 feet in height. There are crystal chandeliers with 18,000 prisms, oak ceilings, sconces, an abundance of gold leaf and brass trim, and on the plaza an illuminated fountain. The fountain was the gift of philanthropist Obert C. Tanner who, as chairman of the state's Bicentennial Commission, had played a prominent role in planning and obtaining funding for the arts complex. Many of the hall's decorative features were the result of gifts totaling a million dollars or more. Seating 2,800, the concert hall was designed by Cyril M. Harris, noted acoustical authority. It resembles other well-known concert halls in being rectangular. The hall is encased in a thick plaster ceiling, oak walls, and hardwood floor.

Salt Lake Art Center adjoins Symphony Hall on the south and was dedicated in May 1979. In the form of a right angle triangle, with a sunken sculpture court and polished hardwood floors, the center contains more than 8,000 square feet of gallery space, including a two-story-high main gallery, a smaller exhibit gallery, and a collector's gallery for sale and rental works. A true community art center, the new structure replaced the Art Barn at 54 Finch Lane, which served as the Salt Lake Art Center for 48 years between 1931 and 1979.

The center emphasizes the visual arts: painting, sculpture, crafts, film/video, photography. It houses the Utah Media Center, a state funded operation that offers facilities and services in the fields of filmmaking, photography, audiovisual media, and communications. Classrooms, studios, and galleries support the center's teaching and creative programs; an auditorium serves for lectures and films, poetry readings, musical concerts, dance and drama presentations.

Capitol Theater (Bicentennial Center for the Performing Arts), 46 W. 2nd South, is the restored edition of one of the city's popular and flamboyant movie palaces. Originally opened in 1913 as the Orpheum Theater, it served for more than 60 years as an auditorium for cinema showings; during much of that time it was advertised by a soaring bridgework sign, a familiar local landmark, arching across the full width of 2nd South in front of the theater.

After a costly restoration under the direction of architect Stephen T. Baird, during which its original Italian Renaissance facade was revealed after being camouflaged for many years, the new theater witnessed performances by Ballet West and Repertory Dance Theatre in late 1978, with a grand opening in the spring of 1979. It is also used by Utah Opera Company and other performing groups. Seating is designed for comfort and unobstructed viewing of the large stage. These advantages, plus the strikingly ornate interior, hand-painted draperies, and crystal chandeliers, stimulated the comment by Bruce Marks, artistic director of Ballet West, that it is "the most beautiful theater between the east and west coasts . . . not a theater for now, but a theater of the future." Of special note is the theater's great Wurlitzer Pipe Organ, originally installed in 1927 and carefully restored for use today.

b. Central District (West)

This district, for tour purposes, may be said to extend west from Temple Square and the Salt Palace for about a mile, and south to the International Peace Gardens. For the most part it is an area of older buildings and uncertain personality, a mixture of residential, commercial, and industrial zoning. That part of the district in the vicinity of the Salt Palace and Temple Square is in the throes of redevelopment; within a few years, barring unforeseen influences, this area will be dramatically altered by new construction. Among planned developments are new apartment houses and condominiums, shops, theaters, parks, parking lots, and malls—even perhaps, a 40-story high-rise building.

Pioneer Park, a shaded oasis in a changing, aging commercial district, occupies a city block between 3rd and 4th South, 3rd and 4th West. Upon this spot Mormon settlers built their first fort and living quarters in 1847-48. Said the 1941 edition, "Brigham Young laid the foundation in August, 1847, and seventeen log and adobe houses were built during the winter of 1847-48. The first school in Utah was established in a tent on this site. Mary Jane Dilworth was the teacher, and her original class consisted of nine Mormon children. The area was made a public park in 1898. . . ." Various proposals for "higher" use of the park have been offered through the years. It is likely that the park will be a key element in the ongoing redevelopment of the area.

Denver & Rio Grande Railroad Depot, Utah State Historical Society (Division of State History). The Denver & Rio Grande Railroad Depot, 300 Rio Grande Street (400 West), forms a massive barricade across the west end of 300 South. An imposing structure containing elements of Renaissance Revival and Beau Arts classicism, the depot's central facade is composed of six large arched windows. After its completion in 1910 the depot served for many years as one of Salt Lake City's principal railroad stations. Following World War II railroad passenger service fell dramatically, and by the 1970s the depot no longer served the purpose for which it was built. In 1977 the depot was purchased by the State of Utah for $1.00. Since its purchase the building has undergone extensive renovation for occupancy by the Utah State Historical Society (Division of State History), which occurred in January 1981.

Other than the building itself, which is listed on the National Register of Historic Places, visitors will find of interest the research library, noted for its rich collection of historical photographs, manuscripts, books, documents and other materials relating to Utah, the Mormons, and the West . . . a developing state history museum . . . a book store which offers for sale Society publications and appropriate works from other publishers . . . the State Historic Preservation and State Antiquities offices, which include the State Archeologist and State Paleontologist.

Union Pacific Depot, facing east, blocks the west end of South Temple at 4th West. Reflecting the grandiose French Renaissance architectural style, the depot was completed in 1909. The huge waiting room is adorned with painted murals and stained glass windows depicting historic scenes. The depot is listed on the National Register of Historic Places and is a distinctive element in redevelopment plans for the district.

Devereaux House, 334 W. South Temple, near the Union Pacific Depot, is one of the oldest remaining mansions of Utah. Dating in part from 1857, it was built by William Staines, then later acquired and modified by William Jennings, wealthy merchant and Salt Lake City mayor. The mansion was a center of cultural and social affairs, including receptions for President Ulysses S. Grant, Secretary of State William E. Seward, generals Sheridan and Sherman. Since its glory days in the 19th century the edifice has seen varied uses and considerable neglect, most recently functioning as offices for a dealer in machinery. In 1978 the state legislature appropriated $750,000 for its restoration. Shortly thereafter much of its interior was gutted by fire. In 1981 a federal grant in the amount of 1.5 million dollars was approved for restoration and landscaping.

Triad Utah, developer of Salt Lake International Center and owner of considerable property in the vicinity of Devereaux House, has announced tentative plans for development of the area, to include parks, retail shops, hotel, theater, and other facilities.

Mormon Welfare Square, 751 W. 7th (700) South, visible from the freeway and marked by a high grain elevator, is the public showplace for the Mormon relief program. Visitors may join tour groups at Temple Square or phone Welfare Square for tour details. Tour points include the granaries, food processing facilities, and storehouses, and an explanation of the remarkable church welfare program that has assisted needy members since the Great Depression of the 1930s.

International Peace Garden in Jordan Park, 1060 S. 9th (900) West, might be described as a United Nations in landscaping. Beside the Jordan River, nationality groups of Utah have created individual gardens representative of their original homelands: Chinese, a pagoda . . . Swiss, a mountain chalet and miniature Matterhorn . . . Danish, antique oil street lamps, a mermaid beside a pool, a Viking mound . . . German, a massive wooden gate, fountain and linden tree . . . Lebanese, cedar trees and stone archway . . . Dutch, a windmill and flower garden . . . Japanese, stone lanterns and curved footbridge. Other gardens represent Sweden, England, the United States, Norway, etc.

c. Central District (North)

This part of the city extends somewhat indefinitely to the north of Temple Square and west of Capitol Hill. It has not yet been greatly affected by modern expansion and remains primarily a residential area of modest homes of intermediate age—that is, few are of pioneer vintage and few are younger than 40 years or so.

Children's Museum of Utah, 840 N. 3rd West, is now under development in the former Wasatch Springs Municipal Baths (Wasatch Plunge) building. Plans for the museum began in the late 1970s after the city decided to close the baths and sell the building. With transfer of the building by the city, assisted by a community development grant and donations, development was underway by 1980. Full development is expected to require three or four years and to cost nearly two million dollars. According to a historic register description, Wasatch Springs were discovered by Mormon pioneers on July 22, 1847, and "soon became a favorite bathing resort for travelers and residents. A bath house was built at the site as early as 1850, with several changes and alterations since that time. The present structure was completed in 1922."

d. Central District (The Avenues)

The Avenues comprise an expansive hillside district extending north of South Temple and east of State Street. Here the blocks are smaller than elsewhere in the city, and the address numbering system deviates from the valley's norm. Architecture is greatly diversified in style and period, ranging from random 19th century in the lower avenues to ultra-modern, ultra-expensive mansions on the higher foothills. Here, perhaps, in a compact area, is greater contrast and variety in residential architecture than any other place in Utah. Most buildings are private residences and apartment houses, but the area also contains Primary Children's Medical Center (Mormon), LDS Hospital, old Veterans Hospital, Shriners' Hospitals for Crippled Children, and the City Cemetery, where the majority of early-day pioneers are buried.

The Avenues Historic District encompasses the first-settled part of The Avenues. This area is bounded by 1st and 7th Avenues (south to north), Canyon Road-Memory Grove on the west and Virginia Street on the east. Containing more than 2,000 buildings having an age of 50 years or more, the historic district is listed on both state and national historic registers.

e. Central District (East)

In these pages, Central District (East) is that part of the city between State Street and 13th (1300) East, and from South Temple to 17th (1700) South. The district's uses and characteristics are very diversified, being as it is the locale of houses, apartment buildings, churches and cathedrals, schools, medical clinics, a hospital, and a growing number of businesses and professional offices. The district may well display a greater variety of architectural styles, representing different periods and functions, than any part of the state—though The Avenues may feature a wider range of residential architecture.

UTAH TRAVEL COUNCIL

Governor's Residence
(Kearns Mansion) *(above)*.

Utah State Fair *(above, right)*.

Trolley Square *(right)*.

Federal Building *(below)*.

Salt Lake City and County
Building, 1913
(below, right).

SALT LAKE VALLEY CONVENTION BUREAU

UTAH STATE HISTORICAL SOCIETY

SOUTH TEMPLE STREET, forming the south boundary of Temple Square, extends from the Union Pacific Railroad Depot on the west (400 West) to about 1400 East, where it dissolves into narrow, curving streets of the Federal Heights area. All north and south addresses in the valley are based on South Temple, which serves as the point of division, as Main Street divides east and west.

In respects, South Temple is the most historic and prestigious street in Utah, being the locale—at one time or another—for many of the state's distinguished citizens and business firms. In earlier days it bore the name *Brigham Street,* an appellation used by Margaret Lester as the title for a fascinating published history of the street and many of its prominent residents in bygone years. With few exceptions, the state's most imposing mansions of the turn-of-the-century era were located along South Temple or in its immediate vicinity. The majority no longer exist, though a few distinguished examples have been preserved, among them Brigham Young's Lion House and Beehive House, the Executive (Kearns) Mansion, and the Devereaux House—all described in these pages. Other survivors of notable architectural and historical interest include the striking European villa built by Enos A. Wall, wealthy mining magnate, now the home of LDS Business College (411 E. South Temple) . . . the majestic David Keith mansion, 529 E. South Temple, restored and occupied for years by Terracor Corporation . . . Daniel C. Jackling home, 731 E. South Temple (offices) . . . Matthew Walker mansion, 610 E. South Temple (offices) . . . Glendinning Home, 617 E. South Temple, dating probably from the 1870s and now serving as offices of the Utah Arts Council . . . and Joseph R. Walker Home, 1205 E. South Temple (private residence). Others also stand, on 100 South as well as South Temple, but those remaining provide only an intimation of the architectural splendor that once graced this "most beautiful thoroughfare between Denver and San Francisco."

Cathedral of the Madeleine, 331 E. South Temple (corner of South Temple and B streets), is a massive Roman Catholic edifice of brownish-gray sandstone in the Roman Gothic style. Built in the early 1900s, it is a splendid building, and its ornate twin towers, decorated with gargoyles, are a landmark. Inside the cathedral, pipes of the organ outline a huge circular rose window, comprised of individual sections that picture angels playing various musical instruments. This and other richly colored stained glass windows in the cathedral were done by the House of Zetter, Royal Bavarian Institute, Munich, Germany. Decorated columns reach upward to vaulted arches high above, and there are fine wood carvings and murals. In 1975 a major restoration program was inaugurated, during which the building was cleaned, the stonework restored, roof repaired, and a new lighting system installed to accent the beautiful interior artistry.

First Presbyterian Church, 347 E. South Temple, near Cathedral of the Madeleine, was completed in 1906. Built of red stone, the distinguished religious edifice displays a striking English Gothic Revival style. Architect W. E. Ware also designed the First Church of Christ, Scientist.

The **Executive Mansion (Kearns Mansion),** 603 E. South Temple, is a palatial three-story building of cream-colored oolitic limestone. French Renaissance in design, resembling a chateau, it flaunts conical corner towers, tall chimneys, and arched windows. The mansion was completed in 1902 at a cost of a quarter of a million dollars. Designed by architect Carl M. Neuhausen, it was built as a family residence for Senator Thomas Kearns, wealthy mining magnate and an owner of the *Salt Lake Tribune (see sketch in History section).* Senator Kearns died in 1918 but the mansion continued to serve as the Kearns home for several decades afterward. As originally built, it contained 36 rooms, ten fireplaces, 4½ bathrooms, a bowling alley, and a billiard room. Exterior limestone came from Sanpete County, granite from Wasatch Mountain quarries, marble from Italy and Africa, and woods from other countries.

In 1937 the mansion was presented to the state by Mrs. Jennie J. Kearns, the senator's widow. Soon thereafter it was occupied as an official residence by Governor Henry H. Blood, followed by governors Herbert B. Maw and J. Bracken Lee.

Between 1957 and 1977 the governors occupied a newer, contemporary residence at 1260 Fairfax Avenue. During this period the old mansion served as the home of the Utah State Historical Society. Exterior restoration was undertaken in 1973. In 1977, in preparation for the mansion's renewed function as the official residence of Governor Scott B. Matheson and succeeding governors, extensive interior remodeling and restoration began. In addition to refurnishing and restoration of woodwork, renovation included modernization of wiring, plumbing, insulation, heating and air conditioning, remodeling of the kitchen, and installation of an elevator. Supervision of interior decorating was provided as a public service by members of the Utah chapter, American Society of Interior Designers. Funds to cover expenses came from sale of the Fairfax residence, federal grants, and contributions from numerous donors and volunteers. Interior restoration was completed in 1980. Most of the mansion's first floor is reserved for public use, with private living quarters on the second floor. A large ballroom occupies the third (top) floor.

Other points in the east district

St. Mark's Episcopal Cathedral, 231 E. 1st South, is the oldest non-Mormon cathedral in Utah, dating from 1871 with later additions and modifications. The venerable church resembles the cathedrals of Europe with its transepts, nave, vestibule, cloisters, bell gable, Gothic arches, and stained glass windows. It is listed on the National Register of Historic Places.

Trolley Square occupies a city block between 6th and 7th East, 5th and 6th South, with the main entrance on 7th East. A private development, Trolley Square utilizes as its structural core a group of rustic brick buildings or "barns" that originally housed trolley cars and motor buses of the city's early public transport system. It was begun during the 1960s as a somewhat revolutionary commercial restoration, eventually becoming a popular shopping-entertainment center and a magnet for out-of-state visitors. The Square and contiguous developments feature a variety of restaurants, theaters, and shops in a picturesque "antique" environment of old brick and stone, wood timbers, stained glass, wood and brick walkways. Developers have recently announced tentative plans for a hotel and convention center.

Liberty Park occupies 110 acres, or the equivalent of eight city blocks and the 6th East right-of-way. It is bounded by 9th and 13th South, 5th and 7th East. Originally a part of Brigham Young's estate, the grounds were acquired by the city in 1880 and developed over the years with lawns, trees, flower beds, lake, bandstands and picnic facilities, swimming pool, tennis courts, playground, concession area (refreshments, merry-go-round, ferris wheel), aviary, etc. In 1979-80 a million-dollar program of development closed 6th East to traffic, dredged and reshaped the lake, built new bandstands, restored the outside of the Chase Mill, created a new Children's Garden, and upgraded the aviary facilities.

Tracy Aviary displays several hundred varieties of birds, including many water species. Most of these are on outdoor display in warmer months. Wilson Bird Pavilion, an enclosed octagonal structure, provides a controlled habitat for exotic birds and winter shelter for those not adapted to cold. The aviary originated as a gift to the city in 1938 by Mr. and Mrs. Russell L. Tracy; it was known for a time thereafter as Tracy's Aviaries.

Isaac Chase Mill is a gable-roofed gray adobe building. Said the 1941 edition, "Chase, who transported the millstones and irons across the plains by ox-team, built the mill in 1852. Free flour from this mill saved many lives in a famine winter of the fifties." Brigham Young became its owner by 1860. Some of the mill's original machinery remains. Under a canopy beside the mill is "one of the first log cabins built in Utah," erected in 1847. To the north, adjoining the greenhouse, is the Isaac Chase House, a two-story yellow adobe building erected in 1852.

Westminster College, 1840 S. 13th (1300) East, occupies a 27-acre campus centered by the distinctive four-story Converse Hall (1906), which houses administrative offices. The only private liberal arts college in the intermountain west, Westminster is an "interdenominational, co-educational, four-year, fully accredited liberal arts college." Enrollment in 1981 was 1,300 students, triple that of 20 years before. Westminster was founded in 1875 as the Salt Lake Collegiate Institute, an evangelical school established by the First Presbyterian Church. At the turn of the century the name was changed to Westminster. The first college class was admitted in 1897. Westminster became a senior college in 1944. Affiliated with several Protestant denominations, the college receives support from other churches as well.

(4) EAST BENCH

UNIVERSITY OF UTAH, the state's largest and oldest public institution of higher learning, sprawls across 1,500 acres of sloping benchland overlooking Salt Lake City and Salt Lake Valley. Much of its campus and some of its buildings were part of Fort Douglas at one time.

In 1940 the university occupied 153 acres and boasted an enrollment of some 4,000 students, taught by a faculty of 275. Enrollment boomed following World War II, passing 20,000 in 1971-72 and totaling more than 23,000 in 1981. Faculty numbers about 3,500 and staff nearly 8,000, giving the university the distinction of being one of the largest day-time communities in the state.

The university comprises 16 colleges and confers degrees in 64 different areas of study, including advanced degrees in medicine and law. A number of its colleges and schools are noted for excellence. In addition to its full-time educational program, the university provides adult and continuing education services to thousands of part-time students. It serves as a cultural and recreational center for myriad visitors (two million in 1980), who attend a variety of music concerts, lectures, theatrical and dance presentations, and sports events; many of them also visit the university's museums, libraries, arboretum, and beautifully landscaped campus.

The University of Utah was first established as the University of Deseret by the Provisional State of Deseret in 1850, and the first classes were held that year. It was chartered the following year but classes were suspended from 1851 to 1867 for want of funds. Reestablished as a commercial academy in 1867, it was reorganized by Dr. John R. Park two years later; normal, classical, and scientific curricula were introduced at that time. In 1884 the university was empowered to confer degrees, and engineering courses were inaugurated in 1891-92. The name was changed to University of Utah in 1892, and the itinerant university settled on the present site in 1900. In 1901 the school of mines was established by legislative enactment.

SPECIAL VISITOR ATTRACTIONS

Presidents' Circle and Vicinity *(Lower Campus, east end of 200 South)*

Utah Museum of Natural History, southeast corner of 200 South and University Street (1450 East), illustrates the anthropological, geological and biological story of Utah and the intermountain region in more than a hundred exhibits. Featured in five halls are dioramas of animals in their natural environment, illustrated displays on the history of mankind, reconstructions of prehistoric dwellings, and exhibits of fossilized plants and animals, including the mounted skeletons of dinosaurs and other strange creatures. Of special note is the superlative collection of rocks, minerals and gemstones in the Norton Hall of Minerals. The museum opened its doors in 1969; prior to that time the building housed the George Thomas Library. Gift shop. Guides provided for groups by prior arrangement. Open seven days a week. Modest admission charge.

State Arboretum of Utah consists of more than 7,000 trees dispersed around the campus, the majority in several major clusters. These trees represent more than 300 different species and hybrids. The arboretum's largest and oldest cluster is located on the central lawn of the Presidents' Circle and in the vicinity of the Museum of Natural History, the Park Building, and the greenhouse east of the Park Building. A walking tour guide pamphlet is available at university information centers.

John R. Park Memorial Building, at the east end of the circle, is a white, four-story edifice with monumental steps and a tall Ionic portico. Completed in 1914, the building was named in honor of Dr. John R. Park, prominent educator who guided the university during fledgling years of the last century. The Park Building has served since its dedication as the university's administrative headquarters. At varying times, in addition to offices, it also housed the bookstore, Museum of Fine Arts, an archeological museum (described in the 1941 edition), and the law school, psychology department, and art department.

Kingsbury Hall, north side of the Presidents' Circle, is a "three-story structure, built in 1930 [and] decorated after the Egyptian manner." This unpretentious building might well claim the distinction of being, next to the Mormon Tabernacle, the state's most versatile and best known cultural center. During its 50 years it has housed offices of speech, drama, and dance, among others, and its auditorium and stage have been the setting for thousands of dramatic, dance, and musical productions, as well as uncounted lectures, assemblies, convocations, travel shows, and other cultural events—not only for students but for the community at large.

University of Utah and Wasatch Mountains. *University of Utah photo.*

UTAH TRAVEL COUNCIL

Utah Museum of Natural History.   Campus scene.

North and northeast of Presidents' Circle are the ballet building, physics buildings, sorority and fraternity houses, military and naval science buildings, Kennecott Research Center, Merrill Engineering Building, and Mines and Mineral Engineering buildings.

South of Presidents' Circle and the Museum of Natural History is **Pioneer Memorial Theatre,** the state's official theatre, and various instructional buildings (law, history, dance, health, etc.), as well as Einar Nielsen Field House and Rice Stadium. Directly east of Presidents' Circle and the Park Building is the **A. Ray Olpin University Union,** a large glass-walled structure which serves as the center of student social activities. The building features food services, bowling alley, auditorium, dance hall, and other facilities. *Information desk.*

The **J. Willard Marriott Library** houses collections of books, periodicals, maps, and documents totaling nearly two million items. Collections of special note include government publications and United Nations documents, Western Americana and Rare Books, maps, and Middle East resource materials. The imposing fountain east of the library was a gift of O. C. Tanner, emeritus professor and philanthropist.

Utah Museum of Fine Arts, "the primary cultural resource for the visual arts in Utah," provides a varied exhibition program during the year. Its rich holdings cover a wide range of historical periods and styles. Exhibits are rotated from the museum's permanent collections as well as from other sources. The museum also prepares traveling exhibits and provides services such as tours for adult and school groups, gallery talks, and lectures. Its 420-seat auditorium is utilized for cultural functions.

Upper (East) Campus

The university's Upper (East) Campus, adjoining Fort Douglas, includes the four-building Physical Education Complex and the **Special Events Center,** a circular, domed, 15,000-seat arena that is used for public and university gatherings such as concerts, commencement exercises, and sporting events. Nearby, on the east, is the wooden, winged Annex building, built during World War II as a military administration center (Ninth Service Command) but utilized since that time for university instructional and administrative purposes.

The imposing **University Medical Center** has developed over the past several decades into the largest complex of its kind in the intermountain region. Centering on a newly completed hospital (1981), which replaced a hospital built in the 1960s (now utilized by the College of Medicine), the complex includes among its diversified facilities a seven-story medical education and research tower, Eccles Medical Science Library, College of Nursing Building, College of Pharmacy (Skaggs Hall), radiology laboratory, housing for medical center personnel and students, and facilities for cancer and artificial organ research. Buildings of the Utah State Department of Health also are located here.

A short distance from the main campus is the **University Research Park,** south of Fort Douglas and east of the Veterans Medical Center (accessible from Foothill Boulevard). Situated on 320 university-owned acres, the Research Park was inaugurated in 1971 to provide a fertile environment for high-technology research, development, and industry. A partnership between the university (trained personnel, computer center, research services, library) and private enterprise (financial resources and commercial expertise), the park has 27 tenants and 15 buildings at this time. The great majority of tenants involve university students and faculty as consultants or in research, and university-owned equipment is used for many projects.

FORT DOUGLAS (east on 500 South and South Campus Drive) has been an independent community on the city's outskirts for more than a century. In size and function it has changed greatly over the years; once controlling an area of many thousands of acres of benchland, canyon, and mountain slopes, the fort has diminished to only a few hundred acres today. No longer is it occupied by the regular army troops it hosted for many years. Tenants now are administrative and recruiting units of the various defense services, Army Reserve headquarters and operations, offices of other reserve units, a financial center, Dugway procurement, and additional federal offices.

The historic core of the fort remains fairly intact, a dignified reminder of bygone years, surrounded on three sides by the university's campus, Research Park, and Medical Center. Today, in the words of *Deseret News* writer Arnold Irvine, "War and bloodshed are just about the last things that come to mind amid the tranquil, park-like setting of Fort Douglas. The hustle and bustle of the city seem remote on the post's quiet, almost empty streets and walkways. The charming old stone and brick buildings exude history and proud tradition." The post's charm is that of graceful aging, distinctive styles of architecture, different ways of life, and the nostalgia of memory. Its history has been formed by generations of soldiers going to war or returning from war, or calling the post home during peacetime interludes. Its proud tradition is that of military order, service, and formality, symbolized by well-kept grounds, the parade field, the Victorian facades of officers' quarters, utilitarian barracks, and orderly alignment of buildings in formal rows and circles.

Fort Douglas was established as Camp Douglas in September-October 1862 by California-Nevada volunteers under the command of Colonel Patrick E. Connor. The ostensible purpose for its founding was protection of the overland mail during the Civil War, but federal officials including Connor were convinced that the Mormons required surveillance from a strategic post. The camp was named after Stephen A. Douglas, senator and Lincoln's opponent in the 1860 election. Temporary quarters were built by the troops when they arrived, and more permanent buildings the following year. In late January 1863, several months after their arrival in Utah, Connor's troops attacked a large party of Shoshone Indians on the Bear River in northern Cache Valley. Several hundred Indians, including many women and children, were killed in the encounter, which some historians term a massacre rather than a battle. Other skirmishes followed. Connor and some of his troops also became involved in prospecting for precious minerals and were instrumental in encouraging the eventual mining of some of the state's richest lodes. The post's name was changed to Fort Douglas in 1878.

The eventful history of Fort Douglas between 1862 and 1965 is detailed in the *Utah Historical Quarterly* (Fall 1965). It has been used through the years for varying functions: as a training base, as a fixed post for regular army troops, as a prisoner of war camp, as an induction and discharge center, as a base for military reserves, and as an administration and finance center for other defense installations. During World War II—the period of its greatest growth and importance—Fort Douglas served as headquarters for the Ninth Service Command, as a reception and separation center, as the site for a centralized finance office, and as a base for troop training, maintenance of ordnance and vehicles, etc. During subsequent years the fort has been reduced drastically in size, thousands of acres being transferred to the Forest Service, National Guard, University of Utah, Salt Lake City, Veterans Administration, Bureau of Mines, and Navy. Its continuance as an active installation has been in doubt several times, most recently in 1979-81 when the Army was considering plans to phase out most of its activities at the post by 1982. At least partly as a result of loud outcry by Utahns, including the state's congressional delegation, this decision was rescinded in 1981.

Visitors may explore the quiet roads and circles on self-guided tours. Those with serious curiosity are advised to obtain information and maps at the **Military Museum** *(follow signs),* which contains several rooms of fascinating exhibits on the military history of Utah. Buildings at the fort represent various periods and styles. Most buildings to the east and north of the museum, including the dignified quarters on Officers Circle (Quartermaster Victorian), date from the 1870s and 1880s. Many others on the post date from the turn of the century, and still others from the 1930s. Of special nostalgic interest is the old **Post Cemetery** *(approach via the University Research Park),* a tree-shaded sanctuary containing the graves of hundreds of soldiers and prisoners of war, including those of the fort's founder, Colonel Connor, and soldiers killed at the Battle of Bear River in 1863.

VETERANS ADMINISTRATION MEDICAL CENTER, 500 Foothill Boulevard (about 1700 East and 500 South), is an extensive complex of brick buildings serving as a major health care and research center. It was opened in 1952 as a center for treatment of neurological and psychiatric problems; since then its functions have vastly expanded to include medical, social and psychiatric treatment for thousands of in-patients and out-patients coming from several mountain states. In addition to treatment it serves as a teaching and research institution, cooperating with the University of Utah and other agencies in the training of medical students, dentists, psychologists, social workers, nurses, etc. At present the center includes a hospital with more than 400 beds as well as a nursing home unit and outpatient clinic.

PIONEER TRAIL STATE PARK, 2600 E. Sunnyside Avenue (850 South), at the mouth of Emigration Canyon across the road from Hogle Zoological Gardens, features the famed This is the Place Monument, Pioneer Mural, and Old Deseret Village. Occupying more than 500 acres of grassy foothill, overlooking the valley, the park is situated in the general area where the first group of Mormon pioneers emerged from the Wasatch Mountains in July 1847 and their leader, Brigham Young, reputedly uttered the immortal words "This is the right place. Drive on."

This is the Place Monument is a large work of granite and bronze, imposing in dimension but austere in form. The monument was dedicated on July 24, 1947, to commemorate arrival of Utah's first permanent settlers a hundred years earlier, as well as the explorers and trailblazers who preceded them. The project was conceived, promoted and erected by a state commission representing the principal religious faiths of Utah. Designer and sculptor was Mahonri M. Young, a Utah artist of national repute and a grandson of Brigham Young. Cost amounted to nearly half a million dollars.

Measuring 86 feet in length and 60 feet in height at the central figures, the monument displays as its most prominent features three bronze groupings. The largest figures, 12 feet high atop the central pylon, depict Mormon leaders Brigham Young, Heber C. Kimball and Wilford Woodruff. The north pylon features a group of trappers and fur traders, the most noted of that intrepid band of adventurers who preceded the Mormon pioneers by several decades. The south pylon depicts Utah's first white explorers, the Catholic Dominguez-Escalante party who traversed much of Utah in 1776 on an exploring expedition from New Mexico.

Bronze figures and plaques on the monument's west and east fronts commemorate important events and personages of 1847 and prior years.

The Pioneer Mural. Located in the visitor center to the monument's north is a three-wall mural depicting major episodes in the migratory trek of the Mormons from Nauvoo, Illinois, to Salt Lake Valley in 1846 and 1847. Remarkable for color, detail, and craftsmanship, the mural was completed in 1959 by the late Lynn Fausett, a Utah native who gained renown as a muralist and landscape painter.

Old Deseret Village is a "living museum" designed to teach about life in an early Utah community between 1847 and 1869, years which marked the pioneer era in Utah. An ongoing, long-term project that eventually will cost several million dollars, the village is expected to be one of the foremost of its kind. In its initial stages the village features a number of authentic early-day homes of adobe, log and frame construction, brought from various sites around the state. As the village develops, every facet of pioneer life will be represented, with a school, church house, industrial and commercial establishments, etc. The year 1980 witnessed completion and dedication of a replica of historic Old Social Hall, a pioneer social center which stood in downtown Salt Lake City between the 1850s and 1922.

HOGLE ZOOLOGICAL GARDEN *(admission charge, open all year),* 2600 Sunnyside Avenue (850 South), occupies about 50 acres at the mouth of Emigration Canyon where it emerges from the Wasatch Mountains, across Sunnyside Avenue from Pioneer Trail State Park. More than a thousand animals are on display, including African gorillas, giraffes, sea lions and seals, bears of several kinds, numerous big and little cats, elephants, reptiles, deer, rhinoceros and other animals including orangutans, monkeys and chimpanzees. Insofar as possible, animals are displayed in a natural environment, with separate buildings for cats, apes, giraffes, birds and small animals. The year 1980 saw completion of the Animal Giants Building, a house for elephants, rhinos, and large birds.

Perhaps the zoo's most famous inhabitant was Shasta the Liger, an unusual animal born in 1948 of a tigress mother and lion father. Shasta lived for 24 years, reaching a weight of more than 300 pounds, dying in 1972 at an age equivalent to that of a 120-year-old human.

Another Hogle Zoo inhabitant with more than local renown, described on page 254 of the guide's first edition, was Princess Alice, a 9,000-pound elephant.

TOUR NO. 3B — SALT LAKE VALLEY

(1) SOUTH VALLEY

Pioneer Craft House, 3271 S. 500 East, is an active school of craft arts as well as a museum of distinctive Utah crafts. Instruction is given in weaving, pottery, textiles, wood crafts, printing, puppetry, etc. Workshops and puppet shows are among varied activities of the Craft House, which features exhibit galleries, a puppet theater, arboretum, and sales facilities. A community enterprise, the Craft House owes its existence in large measure to long-time director Glenn (Mrs. Arthur L.) Beeley.

Wheeler Historic Farm, 6351 S. 900 East, is a "working" farm or museum of rural life operated by the Salt Lake County Recreation Department since 1976. The 75-acre farm was owned by the Wheeler family for about 80 years between the 1880s and 1960s. Formerly a dairy operation in the rural outskirts, today it is surrounded by the city's residential suburbs. Wheeler Farm is open to the public. It appeals especially to children, who may participate in or view butter churning, milking, hay-rides and wagon rides, farm chores, etc.

Jordan River Temple (Mormon), 10200 South and 1300 West in South Jordan, is a large white edifice with central tower and unusual design. Atop the 200-foot tower is a gilded statue of the Angel Moroni with trumpet. Devoted to the performance of sacred ordinances, the temple was dedicated in November 1981 after more than two years of construction. Completion followed in 1982. Prior to dedication it was opened for 35 days of public tours; visitors numbered 570,000. The temple was the first to be built in Salt Lake Valley since completion of the Salt Lake Temple in 1893. It is one of the largest of all Mormon temples and was built entirely with donated funds.

Utah State Prison, visible from I-15 as the highway ascends Point of the Mountain near Draper, is a complex of gray concrete buildings surrounded by a double row of wire fences. Four guard towers overlook the prison compound, which is lighted at night. Adjoining the fenced compound is the prison farm of 1,175 acres, on which minimum security prisoners work to produce hay, corn, cattle, pigs, milk and other products.

When the prison was first occupied in 1951, its maximum capacity was 600. Each inmate was quartered separately in individual cells. Despite expansion of facilities and the development of halfway programs, the prison is beset by serious over-crowding. In 1981 its population was about 1,000 at the prison, with others scattered about in community correction centers, county jails, federal prisons, and special programs.

Camp W. G. Williams Millitary Reservation straddles the Salt Lake-Utah county line between Jordan Narrows and foothills of the Oquirrh Mountains. Incorporating an area of more than 50 square miles, the reserve serves as a training base for units of the Utah National Guard. Also based at the camp is the Utah Military Academy, a National Guard officer-candidate school and non-commissioned officer academy.

(2) WEST VALLEY

Utah State Fairgrounds occupy a large expanse between 1000 West and Jordan River, north of North Temple Street. A cluster of exhibition build-ings, arena, stadium, lawns and gardens, the fairgrounds host not only the annual Utah State Fair in September but special events as well. The first state fair was held at this location in 1902. The majority of present buildings are old, and some are decrepit. In 1980 a long-range program of expansion, demolition, new construction, and overall upgrading was commenced.

Jordan River, about 1000-1500 West, flows from Utah Lake on the south to Great Salt Lake on the north, dropping 300 feet from the source to mouth in an airline distance of 35 miles. Named the "Western Jordan" by Mormon pioneers in 1847, for more than a hundred years thereafter the modest stream was an open drain for wastes of all kinds. Enforcement of strict sanitation laws in recent decades has transformed the stream to the point whcre it is now suitable for canoeing and other non-immersion recreation. Along the river for six miles north of 2100 South Street, the State Park & Recreation Division is developing a recreational parkway with litter-free banks, picnic area, trails and pathways, canoe docks, etc. Long-range plans envision a developed parkway along the entire length of the river.

In the vicinity of North Temple and 2200 West are two of Utah's oldest and largest electronics firms, **Litton Industries** and **Sperry Univac,** which established operations in the state during the 1950s. Litton manufactures guidance systems for aircraft, military weapons, and other applications, while Sperry Univac engages in diversified research, development, and manufacture of intricate electronics products such as computer systems, communication and guidance systems, weapon systems, etc. Employing about 3,000 workers, Sperry Univac has branch installations in North Salt Lake and Ephraim.

West of Sperry Univac is the city's **Municipal Airport,** which serves as operations base for the Utah Air National Guard, FAA, and general aviation. The old terminal/administration building, described in the 1941 edition, was demolished in the late 1970s and a number of hangers constructed for general aviation use. In 1941 the airport dispatched "thirty silvery 'mainliners' daily in five directions . . . It ranks third in the nation in the volume of airmail handled and seventh in number of transport passengers—88,656 in 1939. . . ." Volume of air traffic has increased phenomenally since then, presently amounting to more than four million passengers annually and more than a hundred scheduled departures daily. In 1959-60 a new terminal building was built to the west of the old airport runways, and runways were expanded to accommodate large jet airliners. The new airport became known as the **Salt Lake City International Airport.** Nearly 20 years later, between 1977 and the early 1980s, a new terminal building was added for occupation by Western Airlines, the No. 1 terminal remodeled, the road system upgraded, and other improvements made.

Adjoining the International Airport on the west is the **Salt Lake International Center,** an expansive business park which began operations in 1975. A project of Triad Utah, a development firm owned by Saudi Arabian entrepreneurs, the International Center occupies some 900 acres of former wasteland that is rapidly being transformed into parks, lakes, and ultramodern buildings. Full development is to occupy another five or ten years at a cost of several hundred million dollars.

South of US 40 (North Temple) and I-80, which is under construction at the present time, are scattered industrial and business parks, residential clusters, and commercial buildings, nearly all the products of recent years and the vanguard of fast-moving development that promises to overrun this open expanse of former lake bottom within a few years. Formerly considered the least desirable area for occupation, this northwestern corner of the valley—the last remaining open space of considerable size near the city —undoubtedly will see profound changes before many years elapse.

Morton Salt Company operates a large salt-processing complex located south of I-80 (US 40/North Temple), about five miles west of the International Airport. One of the largest and longest-lived (founded 1889) producers of common salt from brines of Great Salt Lake, Morton extracts salt by pumping brine from the lake into a vast series of ponds, where various minerals are precipitated through solar evaporation. Salt is harvested with special machines and trucks, then dried, crushed, screened, and otherwise processed for culinary, industrial, and agricultural use. Salt bearing the Royal Crystal name has been produced here since the 1920s.

Beyond the salt plant the highway soon curves southwest along the shore of **Great Salt Lake,** America's famed Inland Sea, one of the world's remarkable inland bodies of water. Along this shore have been located, over a period of 130 years, a number of resorts and marinas, nearly all of them transitory and ill-fated. Only in recent years has government entered the lake's recreational scene with adequate funds for the provision of fresh water, sewage disposal, insect control, beach development, etc. *See Great Salt Lake, pages 291-298.*

West of the South Shore beaches, I-80 continues to Wendover, Nevada, and California *(see Tour No. 4A).*

At the north tip of the Oquirrh Mountains, where that range abuts the lake, State 201 forks east from I-80. This important highway connects Salt Lake City with the **huge concentrators, smelter, and refinery** of Utah Copper Division, Kennecott Minerals Company. Looming skyward near the junction is the monumental stack of the **smelter.**

Tallest man-made structure in Utah, the 1,200-foot stack can be seen against the western horizon from much of Salt Lake Valley. It replaced two smaller stacks in 1978, being the most visible symbol of a program of the 1970s which essentially replaced the old smelter and allowed more efficient environmental controls. The smelter project's cost of 280 million dollars made it one of the costliest projects in Utah's industrial history. Smelting is a near-final stage in the processing of ore mined at the Bingham open-pit mine. Concentrates containing about 25 per cent copper are transported from the concentrating mills at Magna *(see below)* and processed at the smelter to a copper purity of 99.6 per cent. From the smelter this product is taken to the nearby refinery, where it is further processed. Dust and gas released during smelting are collected and treated, so that only very dilute materials are emitted from the stack. Sulfuric acid is the principal byproduct of the complex emission-control process.

Two miles east of the smelter, on a foothill terrace overlooking the lake, is Utah Copper Division's **electrolytic refinery.** Completed in 1950, the refinery produces about 20,000 tons of refined copper per month. Refined copper from the smelter is treated electrolytically here to a purity of 99.96 per cent and sold in marketable shapes. Annual production is more than 200,000 tons of refined copper.

In the cove between the refinery and the highway once existed the community of **GARFIELD,** which flourished as a company town from early years of the century until the mid-1950s, when its buildings were sold and removed or demolished.

Near the refinery, on the east, is the great **Magna industrial complex,** an imposing terraced maze of railroads, enormous buildings, and dikes. Located here are Utah Copper Division's **power plant** and **three huge mills** for crushing, grinding and concentrating the more than 100,000 tons of copper ore that are mined each day at the Bingham mine *(see below)*. The Magna and Arthur concentrators date from the first decade of this century, being modified and expanded numerous times since then. The Bonneville plant (crushing and grinding) was built during the 1960s. In 1979 the company announced that it was considering replacement of present mills during the 1980s.

Ore is hauled by train from the mine, 15 miles to the south. At the Magna complex it is crushed and pulverized in a series of crushers, rod mills, and ball mills to near-powder consistency. Now in slurry form, it is then processed in flotation cells where copper of 25 per cent purity—as well as other valuable minerals such as molybdenum—are obtained. Waste is deposited in a vast, dike-enclosed tailings pond north of the highway. This pond covers more than 5,000 acres and is estimated to contain 1.4 billion tons of material, deposited to a depth of 100 feet. Also in the vicinity of the concentrators is Utah Copper Division's power plant, which was built in the early 1940s and expanded in 1960. Costly emission controls were added several years ago. The plant's capacity is sufficient to supply a city of 350,000 with electric power.

MAGNA (4,300 alt. 14,050 pop.), a residential and business center, was founded in the early years of the century during construction of the copper mills. Many of its residents are employees or former employees of Kennecott and their families, though the majority no longer belong in that category. In 1940 the town's population was only 1,604; its most rapid growth occurred during the 1970s.

Turn east from Magna to West Valley City, Kearns, and other sprawling suburban communities and unincorporated county areas that are rapidly occupying this part of the valley.

KEARNS is a western suburb with distinct boundaries that are somewhat blurred in the public mind. Its staid residential and commercial personality gives no indication of its origins in 1942 as a military base. The area flourished during World War II years as **Kearns Air Base,** which became one of the state's largest communities for a brief period. Its history between 1942 and 1948 was told in the *Utah Historical Quarterly* (Spring 1966). The base served primarily as a basic training center for Air Force personnel in ground combat, gunnery, weapons use, etc., and at one time (1943) was the temporary home for 40,000 troops. At an estimated cost of 17 million dollars, the government built a complete utility system (water, electricity, paved streets, sewage treatment, railroad) and about a thousand buildings, including warehouses, barracks, theaters, recreational facilities, mess halls, railroad station, library, chapels, and a large hospital. After the war, in 1948, the 1200-acre townsite—complete with utilities and a few of the buildings—was sold to a New York firm for less than $300,000. Homebuilding on a mass scale, initially by a developer, soon followed. By 1950 Kearns numbered 2,100 civilian residents, and by 1960 the number had reached 17,000; the population does not appear separately in the 1980 census.

South of Magna, State 111 clings to the foothill base of the Oquirrh Mountains, overlooking the valley. **BACCHUS** in 1940 was a company town with a population of 225, "concentric in form, with homes separated by wide lawns and trees. It was created in 1913 by the Hercules Powder Company and its plant, with an annual capacity of 18,000,000 pounds of powder, employs approximately 90 men.'' The name Bacchus today refers more specifically to the Bacchus Works of Hercules Inc., a large industrial enterprise occupying 3,000 acres of land south of Magna.

Bacchus Works of Hercules Inc. (known before 1966 as Hercules Powder Company), remained a modest explosives plant for more than 40 years, until the late 1950s. In 1958 the firm's newly-created Chemical Propulsion Division began construction of a facility at Bacchus to develop the third-stage propulsion system (engine) for the Minuteman intercontinental ballistics missile. Subsequent years saw production of this engine by Hercules as well as development and production of Polaris A2 and A3 second stage, Poseidon C3 first and second stage, in a Joint Venture with Thiokol, and Trident I (C4) in the same Joint Venture. The Bacchus Works is developing MX third stage for the Air Force and Pershing II first and second stage for the Army. Bacchus is also the site for manufacture of graphite fiber, used in lightweight aircraft and aerospace structures, sporting goods, etc. At a large plant in Clearfield, Hercules manufactures filament-wound rocket motor cases and filament-wound tube sections for the MX handling, storage and launch canister, in addition to numerous other composite structures. Aerospace employment peaked during the missile heyday of the early 1960s at 6,000 but has stabilized in recent years at approximately 3,000.

Six miles south of Bacchus Junction, State 111 intersects State 48, the east-west highway connecting Bingham Canyon with Midvale. Turn west from this junction to Copperton, Bingham Canyon, and Bingham Copper Mine.

COPPERTON (5,600 alt.), at the mouth of Bingham Canyon, is today as it was in 1941 ''a model mining town with copper-shingled, copper-screened brick houses, [and] was built by operators of the Bingham mine. Its gardens and tree-shaded lawns contrast with barren hills roundabout.'' The company sold the homes to residents in the 1950s.

BINGHAM COPPER MINE has nearly engulfed Bingham Canyon and the site of the former community of that name. The mine is one unit in Utah's largest industrial enterprise, Kennecott Minerals Company's Utah Copper Division, which operates the mine as well as concentrating mills, smelter, and refinery at the north end of the Oquirrh Range *(see above)*. Nearly 7,000 workers (the number fluctuates) are employed in the vast mining and processing operations of Utah Copper Division. Control of Kennecott Corporation, the parent company, passed to Standard Oil of Ohio in 1981; in turn, Standard Oil is controlled by British Petroleum, one of the largest firms in the free world.

The Bingham mine is the world's oldest and largest open-pit copper mine, the largest single mining operation ever undertaken, and the largest man-made excavation. Since open-pit mining began in the early 1900s, more than 4.5 billion tons of earth have been removed; from this, more than 11.5 million tons of refined copper have been produced. To recover one ton of ore with a copper content averaging less than .6 of one per cent copper, it is necessary to remove as much as 3.5 tons of overburden or waste. The waste is discarded at this time on the terraced, light-colored slopes that are so apparent from the valley, while ore is shipped by rail to three concentrators near Magna, described above. About 10 per cent of the division's copper output comes from a leaching-precipitation system in the mouth of the canyon.

Bingham Copper Mine in winter.

Smelter stack, Kennecott Minerals Co. *(right)*.

Daniel C. Jackling, founder of Utah Copper Company *(below)*.

Statistics of the mine are staggering. More than 470,000 tons of material are moved *each day*. The mine employs about 2,600 people; detonates more than 50 tons of explosives every day; and utilizes about 60 electric and diesel-electric locomotives, 40 large electric shovels, and more than 90 huge dump trucks, the majority of which have capacity of 100 or 150 tons. The mine itself—a tremendous stepped amphi-theater—measures nearly 2.5 miles from rim to rim at the top and is about a half mile deep. Benches are 50 feet high. In 1940 the mining and stripping area measured 650 acres and the depth from the top level was 1,500 feet. Forty years later the excavation covered about 2,000 acres and operations had extended the depth to 2,600 feet.

Copper was not the original reason for mining interest in Bingham Canyon. The canyon was located by miners in 1863, but gold, silver and lead represented major production value until the 1890s. Enos A. Wall recognized its copper potential as early as 1887 and became the owner of a number of claims during the next decade. Samuel Newhouse and Thomas Weir, becoming enamored of the canyon's copper prospects in the 1890s, placed the first copper smelter in Utah into operation in 1899. This modest enterprise soon became a well-financed firm known as the Boston Con-solidated Mining Company, eventually acquired by Utah Copper in 1910. This period also witnessed the arrival of mining engineers Daniel C. Jackling and Robert C. Gemmell, whose tests confirmed the area's enormous copper deposits. A dynamic and visionary promoter and developer, Jackling was instrumental in forming the Utah Copper Company, consolidating diverse holdings, obtaining adequate capital, and supervising development of the unprecedented, large-scale mining and process-ing systems required for successful production of the low-grade Bingham ores. In 1906 the first Utah Copper steam shovels began operating in Bingham Canyon. These shovels stripped 100,000 tons of overburden each month, compared with three times that quantity of overburden *each day* in more recent years. Mills and smelter were constructed between 1905 and 1906. Jackling went on to a long and dis-tinguished career in other places but continued at the helm of Utah Copper Com-pany for 38 years. In 1936 Utah Copper Company was acquired by Kennecott Copper Corporation, and in 1947 its name was changed to Utah Copper Division. An expansion and modernization program costing 100 million dollars took place at the mine and processing plants during the 1960s.

The fascinating story of the town of **BINGHAM CANYON** is told in the 1941 edition, to which readers are referred for details of its history to 1940. In that year the town had a population of 2,957, but at one time it is said to have counted 5,000 residents. As the mine expanded, the town of Bingham died. First to go was **Copperfield** or Upper Bingham, connected with Bingham by a 7,000-foot tunnel which carried a one-lane road, sidewalk, and utility lines. Buildings were removed during the 1950s and Copper-field's final residents departed in 1958. In Bingham, the mining company purchased all private property over a period of years, and the town had finally disappeared by 1961.

Magna copper complex, Kennecott Minerals Co. *Utah State Historical Sociey photo.*

Wasatch Mountains, looking south. Big Cottonwood Canyon is in foreground.

TOUR NO. 3C — WASATCH MOUNTAINS AND CANYONS

THE MOUNTAINS

The Wasatch Range, with the southern High Plateaus, forms the eastern edge of the Basin and Range Province (Great Basin) in Utah. These imposing mountains surely rank among the most rugged and precipitous ranges in the 48 contiguous states, and also among those with the greatest absolute elevation, rising steeply in places from 6,000 to 7,000 feet from base to crest. The range is approximately 150 miles in length, extending in a formidable front from the canyon of Bear River in the north to Mount Nebo in the south. Contrasted with its length, width is rather narrow, not exceeding 20 miles at most and measuring somewhat less than that over most of the range's length.

With the Uintas, the Wasatch Range represents the Middle Rocky Mountains topographic province in Utah. It is an important playground for the million-plus people who live along its western front; even more important is its function as a critical watershed *(see Natural Scene)*. The highest peaks are in the southern part of the range, from the Cottonwood peaks of Salt Lake Valley (11,300 alt.) south to Mount Timpanogos (11,750 alt.) and Provo Peak (11,068 alt.), to the Mount Nebo massif (11,928 alt.).

Geologically, the Wasatch is a fascinating and complex mountain system. The greater part of its exposed rock—tilted and deformed in a confusing jumble—was originally laid down as ocean sediments over a period of time extending from about 90 million to more than a billion years ago. Exceptions are conglomerate deposits of more recent age and massive intrusions of granitic rock, appearing most dramatically in the lower end of Little Cottonwood Canyon and between Alta and Brighton.

Regional and local uplift have occurred since the last ocean departed, nearly 100 million years ago. The mountains of western Utah, including the Wasatch, apparently were formed in their early stages by a series of compressional pulses that fractured, uplifted and steepened the crustal blocks we know today as mountains. Where there was crustal resistance, younger (upper) rocks were overridden by older (lower) rocks in a process of "overthrusting"—a phenomenon apparent in the Wasatch, Oquirrh, Canyon, and other ranges. Also, a section of the Wasatch near Salt Lake City was influenced by the great Uinta Arch that formed the Uinta Range.

It is believed that the Wasatch Range we see today is essentially a product of the past 10 to 20 million years, the classic result of block faulting on a gigantic scale. Crustal compression in the past is credited with some of this work, but there is evidence that release from compression, or stretching of the crust, may be significant in recent ages. There is no doubt, however, that movement continues along the great Wasatch fault at the western base of the range, such movement being accompanied by earthquakes.

Glaciation has affected the Wasatch in three distinct stages during the past half million years or so. The latest stage, contemporaneous with the highest levels of Lake Bonneville, lasted from about 25,000 to 11,000 years ago. Glaciers formed along higher reaches of the Wasatch from Mill Creek Canyon southward into Utah Valley (*e.g.,* Mount Timpanogos and Provo Peak), and of course in the Uintas and on some of the high plateaus. Geologists calculate that 33 glaciers once occupied that part of the range within Salt Lake County. None of these remain. R. E. Marsell wrote in *Geology of Salt Lake County* (UGMS Bulletin 69):

> . . . as one approaches the loftier peaks and ridges to the southeast, the former presence of the glaciers is at once apparent, especially from the air. Instead of the narrow V-shaped valley bottoms and the broad, rounded ridges of the subdued, mature, stream-worn topography of Emigration and Parleys Canyons, for example, one finds deep, U-shaped valleys, flat-bottomed, with over-steepened walls and sharp knife-like bounding ridges that are typical of glacial topography. These glaciated valleys commence in crescent-shaped, cliff-walled basins called "cirques" that are often the sites of jewel-like mountain lakes. It is the sculpture by mountain glaciers that has produced the awe-inspiring, rugged beauty of the choicest mountain scenery, both in the loftier parts of the Wasatch Range and to even a greater degree in the Uinta Mountains.

Little Cottonwood Canyon and its south-wall tributaries contained the longest and largest of the ancient glaciers in the entire range, according to Marsell. At one time the main Little Cottonwood glacier was more than 14 miles long and 650 feet thick near its terminus. Glaciers also affected upper reaches of Big Cottonwood Canyon and several of its tributary canyons, as well as Mill Creek Canyon and short canyons along the mountain front. Moraines left by these glaciers are evident today.

THE CANYONS

Seven major canyons break the face of the Wasatch Range in Salt Lake Valley, as described below. These canyons drain a corrugated watershed that provides a large portion of the valley's culinary water. The greater part of the watershed is included in the Wasatch National Forest, which manages its uses for the public good, insofar as the law allows, and claims ownership of most of the watershed land. Lands of the national forest in the mountains east of Salt Lake Valley are the most heavily utilized by visitors of any national forest in the nation. "People pressure" is intense not only in summer but in winter as well, creating problems of land use, water purity, waste disposal, and abuse that are the bane of administrators at all levels of government.

Emigration Canyon is the route of paved U-65 (850 South), which climbs out of the canyon over Little Mountain (a popular area for tubing and sledding in winter), and—as the Pioneer Memorial Highway—follows the route of the Mormon-Donner pioneer trail over Big Mountain, past East Canyon Reservoir to junction with I-80N at Henefer, or alternately to Morgan *(see Tour No. 2)*. East Canyon Reservoir is the site of East Canyon Lake State Recreation Area, an important developed area for boating, waterskiing, fishing, camping and picnicking. On either side of the road at the mouth of Emigration Canyon are Pioneer Trail State Park and Hogle Zoological Garden *(see above)*.

Parleys Canyon was named for Parley P. Pratt, pioneer Mormon leader who developed a road through the canyon in 1849-50., connecting with the original trail in Mountain Dell, as an alternate to the difficult Emigration Canyon route. In its upper reaches the canyon is expansive and verdant, allowing far-spreading vistas of the Wasatch heartland: it narrows toward its mouth, emerging into Salt Lake Valley between steep cliffs and slopes. The canyon is the route of transcontinental highways I-80 and US 40; therefore, highway travelers from the east first view the great valley and the distant lake from the mouth of Parleys Canyon. *See also Tour No. 5.*

Big Cottonwood Canyon enters the valley through a magnificent gateway formed by steep walls that soar thousands of feet on either side. Between the canyon's mouth and road's-end in Brighton Basin, about 13 miles away, U-152 traverses a region of concentrated alpine grandeur that has few peers in the 48 "lower" states—at least when ease of access and proximity to a metropolitan area are considered. In places the canyon becomes the epitome of a gorge, hemmed in by giant cliffs and peaks. In spots the road climbs steeply in sharp bends, and in its upper reaches the canyon becomes a great basin ringed by majestic peaks and ridges.

Big Cottonwood Canyon is one of the most popular recreation areas for the valley's people, resulting in traffic congestion that may be frustrating at times. Wasatch National Forest has developed a number of sites for camping and picnicking; a spiderweb of foot trails gives access to mountain fastnesses; and facilities at Solitude and Brighton serve a multitude of skiers in winter. The canyon also contains numerous homes, the majority of which are utilized part-time.

Located in a basin at the upper end of the canyon, 25 miles from downtown Salt Lake City, **BRIGHTON** is a resort at 8,700 feet altitude. It was described in the 1941 edition as being "nestled in a bowl-like valley almost surrounded by craggy mountain peaks":

The buildings are log cabins, log hotels and inns, log stores, and a log post office. The inns remain open all year and skiers crowd the slopes and ski-lifts on weekends . . . Surrounding Brighton are Sunset Peak, Mount Majestic, Mount Wolverine, Mount Millicent, and other lesser peaks. Water melting from the snows of these peaks and running into the Brighton basin provide a major portion of Salt Lake City's culinary supply. Hiking trails radiate in all directions to numerous lakes, set in flower-sprinkled mountain meadows . . . On cold winter nights at this altitude it is sometimes possible to see the aurora borealis. . . .

Brighton is one of the state's oldest winter sports resorts. It does not have the national and international "charisma" of Alta-Snowbird and Park City because various factors have prevented development as a destination resort. However, it has remained popular through the years, particularly with local people. Facilities at Brighton Ski Bowl include the Mt. Majestic Lodge-Motel . . . Silver Fork Lodge . . . rental cabins . . . snack bar . . . ski shop . . . ski school . . . stores and eating facilities. There are four double chairlifts servicing 25 trails and runs; these lifts vary in length from 2,450 to 3,950 feet, with vertical rises of 425 to 1,120 feet (alt 8,730 to 10,255 feet). Average snowfall, 430 inches.

In snow-free months, drivers may travel the road over Guardsman's Pass (9,800 alt.) to Park City or Midway. Providing stirring panoramic views of mountains and valleys, this road was built by National Guard engineers and officially opened in 1958.

SOLITUDE RESORT, 2 miles down-canyon from Brighton, is developed with double and triple chairlifts (3,500 to 5,100 feet in length, 500 to 1,600 feet vertical rise), 19 trails, lodge (cafeteria, shops, lounge, bar, etc.), ski school, grooming machine. Altitude 8,000 to 9,800 feet. The resort first opened to the public in 1959.

Brighton Basin, Big Cottonwood Canyon.

WARD ROYLANCE

LITTLE COTTONWOOD CANYON is confined between tremendous walls formed by rows of high peaks on either side. The canyon is open and almost straight, a U-shaped gorge about 10 miles long. Its floor is steep, rising from 5,000 feet at its mouth to 8,100 at Snowbird, 8,500 at Alta, and even higher at Albion Basin. A number of peaks to the north, south and east exceed 11,000 feet. Lifts at Alta take skiers to 10,550 feet, at Snowbird to 11,000 feet, for vertical rises of 730 to 3,000 feet. Hiking trails give access to the high country, as do the resort lifts. Serious visitors are referred to detailed sources such as *Alta Canyon Guide,* edited by Dale Gilson—a comprehensive handbook—and the two-volume *Wasatch Trails* guidebooks published by Wasatch Mountain Club, available in local bookstores and sporting goods outlets.

Inside the canyon's mouth a short distance, markers indicate the location of the **Granite Mountain Record Vaults** and **temple granite quarry.** The vaults *(see above under Mormon Church Complex)* have been excavated from the steep north face of the canyon and are utilized to preserve genealogical and other records of the church. With more than 65,000 square feet of floor space at present, the vaults are large enough to store some five million rolls of microfilm, the equivalent of 25 million 300-page volumes. *Not open for public touring.*

Broken granite in the vicinity of the vaults was used as a source of quarry stone for the Mormon Temple in Salt Lake City, operations continuing for some 30 years between the 1860s and 1890s.

SNOWBIRD is a compact, all-season resort consisting of multi-story lodges, a resort center, five chairlifts (142 to 1,244 vertical feet), an aerial tramway, and other amenities. The tramway rises 2,900 vertical feet from Snowbird Center to the top of Hidden Peak (11,000 alt.). Snowbird is second only to Park City and Deer Valley (as planned) in range of services, being a popular destination for out-of-state vacationers and appealing especially, as does Alta, to intermediate and advanced skiers because of its challenging slopes and deep powder snow. Services include a number of restaurants, shops, bank, grocery store, helicopter excursions, ice skating, tennis courts, pharmacy, swimming pools, ski school, and post office. Gourmet dining and cultural events (festivals, institutes, concerts, etc.) attract visitors throughout the year.

Snowbird was born amid environmental controversy in the early 1970s, the result of years of planning by local ski enthusiast Ted Johnson and financing by wealthy Texan, Richard Bass. It is estimated that some 40 million dollars and ten years were invested in the resort before a profit was shown.

ALTA (8,500 alt.) is one of the oldest and probably the best known ski resort in Utah, insofar as name recognition is concerned. Situated in the upper end of Little Cottonwood Canyon, about 28 miles from downtown Salt Lake City and two miles from Snowbird, Alta claims to have "the best and most consistent snow conditions in the world—with depths of up to 15 feet in the spring." The dry powder snow of this area is said to be unsurpassed for skiing. Alta's ski terrain resembles that of nearby Snowbird in challenging the expertise of intermediate and advanced skiers; however, a fourth of its runs are classed as suitable for beginners. Not a formally integrated, one-owner resort, Alta is the site of independent lodges, condominiums, shops, and restaurants. The area is served by six double chairlifts, from 3,600 to 5,100 feet in length, giving vertical rises of 730 to 1,300 feet.

Alta was "a rip-roarin', rootin', shootin', mining camp" at one time, said the 1941 edition, which described its early history in more detail than the following excerpts indicate:

The men who entered the valley from Colonel Patrick E. Connor's army camp, came for one purpose—to locate minerals. They were sharp-eyed, hard, and boisterous. The name of the first discoverer is lost, but J. B. Woodman is credited with early development of the great Emma silver mine in 1865, a discovery that almost caused international complications. The Prince of Wales and the South Hecla were other early mines. Among them, they brought thousands of people streaming up the canyon between 1865 and 1873. Woodman and his partners, who are now unknown, nearly starved those first few years. They offered a fourth interest for $3,000 but found no takers. They finally "rawhided" the ore in green cowhides down the canyon to oxdrawn wagons, which took the ore to the railroad at Ogden, whence it was shipped to San Francisco. There the ore was transshipped to sailing vessels, and sent around Cape Horn to Wales. After all transportation and smelting charges were deducted, the partners received $180 a ton, testimony to the richness of the ore. . . .

The Gold Miner's Daughter and the Bucket of Blood, most notorious of the twenty-six saloons, were not only busy serving drinks and raking in money over the tables, but were well occupied mopping up after the 110 killings as they occurred within the hospitable swinging doors. The men were buried in a little cemetery at the base of Rustler Mountain. . . .

By 1872 Alta had reached its peak. More than a hundred buildings, some three stories high, were scattered over the flat; six of them were breweries. The population was 5,000.

Then came the "Crime of '73," as George Watson calls it. Congress demonetized silver. One by one the mines closed down, and the miners drifted out of the canyon. Those who hung on found that even nature was against them. Landslides and snowslides took more than 140 lives during the seventies. Between 1885 and 1940 the camp has produced fitfully. Alta came to life as a ski resort in 1937, when Salt Lake County provided year-round road equipment for the canyon.

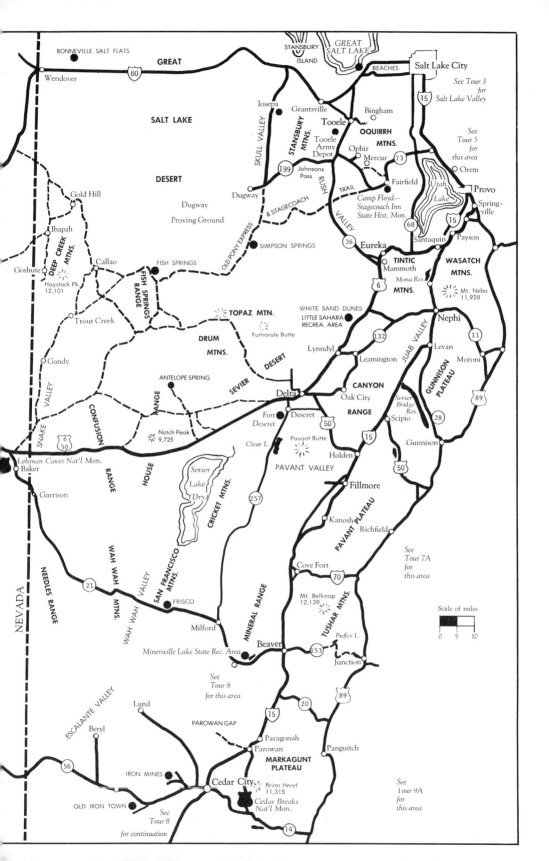

Tour No. 4
WESTERN UTAH

Seemingly endless valleys and mountain ranges—alternating in monotonous succession—march across western Utah and Nevada to the Sierra Nevada Range of California, 500 miles away. This arid and semi-arid region, where no streams reach the sea, is known as the Great Basin, or more technically the Basin and Range topographic province. In Utah it occupies a third of the state, extending westward from the mountainous spine formed by the Wasatch Range and the High Plateaus.

Tour No. 4A - GREAT SALT LAKE COUNTRY—WEST (Tooele County)

This tour region encompasses Tooele County, second largest in Utah—nearly 7,000 square miles of arid valleys, skeletal mountains, the bitter waters of Great Salt Lake, and the desolation of Great Salt Lake Desert. Here and there—in the valleys, the canyons, or the deserts—the forbidding land gives way to human oases. These seem out of place, startling in their unexpectedness. Some are but ghostly relics of bygone years, nostalgic reminders of the flow of time and change.

Tour No. 4A(1) - Interstate Highway 80 from Lake Point Junction to Wendover.

I-80, the Dwight D. Eisenhower Highway, crosses the entire length of Tooele County, a hundred miles of wide-open expanse. There are fewer curves and grades on this stretch of road than any other in Utah, one 50-mile segment east of Wendover being arrow-straight. For many motorists the highway provides two hours of unrelieved monotony. This is regrettable, for few places in Utah have been the stage for more dramatic human exploits, or boast a more interesting geological background—all within view of the highway. Those having an affection for unique landscapes will find this a weird and eerie world of peculiar charm. Along most of its route through Tooele County, I-80 passes across the exposed bed of ancient Lake Bonneville, predecessor of Great Salt Lake, hardly deviating more than a few feet—for 70 miles—from a sustained altitude of 4,230 feet above sea level.

At **Lake Point (Lakepoint)** the highway is confined to a narrow strip between the lake and precipitous slopes of the Oquirrh Mountains. In the vicinity are beach and boating resorts *(see Great Salt Lake),* and salt extraction works. Parking turnoffs permit viewing of the inland sea in its hypnotic immensity. At **Lake Point Junction,** I-80 diverges from state routes leading to Tooele and Grantsville *(see Tour No. 4A(2) below).* Tooele Valley borders the highway on the south, blue lake and barren flats on the north. For the entire distance to Wendover, highway and railroad are close companions.

At a junction 15 m. west of Lake Point Junction, State 138 (old US 40) forks south to Grantsville and the Stansbury Mountains *(see Tour No. 4A(2) below).*

One mile west of this point, turn north on an unpaved road to **Stansbury Island.** This rocky range is about 11 miles in length, more than 2,000 feet high, and is used primarily for grazing. In actuality the "island" is a peninsula and has not been a true island for a hundred years, since the lake reached its historic high level of 4,211 feet in 1873. At that time, for a short period, Stansbury Island was cut off from the mainland by shallow salt water. It was named, as were the Stansbury Mountains to the south, for Captain Howard Stansbury, Army engineer who headed the first scientific survey of the lake in 1850. **Sandy Beach,** on the east side of the island's northern tip, can be reached by steep, sandy road over a low saddle. Though remote, the beach is one of the finest on the lake. A bonus—worth the possibility of assault by swarms of tiny biting gnats—is the view, which encompasses a breathtaking sweep of blue water, Antelope Island, and the magnificent facade of the Wasatch Range, appearing from here as a tremendous front some 60 or 70 miles long. Summer visitors are advised to come prepared with long sleeves, head and face coverings, and insect repellent. Several years ago the lake's dangerous waves apparently caused the death of two young men who launched their boat at Sandy Beach but were unable to return to shore. Their bodies were found days later, far from the beach.

Visible from the north end of Stansbury Island is the brine pond system of **AMAX Inc.** Consisting of huge evaporation ponds, formed by miles of dikes in Stansbury Basin of Great Salt Lake, the system was developed during the 1970s to concentrate lake brines for extraction of magnesium and other minerals at AMAX's Rowley plant on the lake's west shore *(see below).* At the island's south end is another large pond system, that of the Lakepoint Salt Company, used for the production of common salt.

Visible to the south of I-80 in the vicinity of Stansbury Island turnoff are surface mine workings at the north end of the main Stansbury Range. Lime and limestone have been produced here in large quantity for many years, for use in copper smelting, roadbuilding, cement manufacturing, water

At **Timpie (Rowley) Junction,** 7 m. west of the Stansbury Island turnoff, sideroads fork in several directions.

Turn north to the imposing brine processing complex at **ROWLEY,** 12 m. Developed by NL Industries in the 1970s at a cost of more than 150 million dollars, the installation failed to return a profit and was sold in 1980 to AMAX Inc. for less than half that amount. Because of technical difficulties, NL did not attain its annual production goal of 45,000 tons of magnesium. The new owners, however, are confident that this target will be reached and exceeded. Magnesium and other minerals are extracted from the lake's brines through a multi-stage process, beginning with solar evaporation, then continuing with heating and evaporation with gas, chemical refinement, drying and purifying, and finally separation in electrolytic cells. Among resulting products are magnesium metal, chlorine, and calcium chloride. Basic to the concentrating process is a series of huge ponds, formed by dikes in the Stansbury Basin and covering an area of 54,000 acres. Here the several mineral components of the brine are precipitated at varying rates by solar evaporation. The most desirable minerals are then pumped into a five-segment holding pond having a capacity of 210 million gallons. Here the brine is stored for processing in the adjacent chemical processing facility. Magnesium, the most valuable product, is used principally as an aluminum alloy, as an intermediate to make other metals, in the iron and steel industry, and as a structural metal. Production of the Rowley plant ranks it as the No. 3 largest magnesium producer in the free world.

Timpie Springs State Waterfowl Management Area is accessible from Timpie Junction.

Turn south from Timpie (Rowley) Junction to Skull Valley, Iosepa, and Dugway Proving Ground. **SKULL VALLEY** is a broad basin cupped between the Stansbury Range on the east and Cedar Mountains on the west. Despite its forbidding aspect, the valley has long been a favored winter range for sheep. Perennial springs furnish water for ranching operations as well as meadows and marshes.

Skull Valley is a most unlikely site for a settlement of Polynesian natives—a successful farming and stockraising community which existed in the valley for nearly 30 years. The town of **IOSEPA** was situated on the Stansbury foothills 15 miles south of Timpie Junction. (Its name is the Hawaiian version of the name Joseph, pronounced variously as Yo-seh-puh or Yo-say-puh, applied in honor of Mormon Church president Joseph F. Smith, who had been a missionary in Hawaii as a young man.) According to Dennis Atkins in his manuscript entitled *A History of the Polynesian Colony at Iosepa,* Iosepa was founded in 1889 by the Iosepa Agriculture and Stock Company, a Utah corporation formed by the Mormon Church to purchase a ranch and livestock owned by John T. Rich, for the express purpose of Hawaiian settlement. Most of the company's stock was owned by the church and directors representing the church. Numbering about 50, the first body of settlers arrived on August 28, 1889, a day observed thereafter as Iosepa's Pioneer Day. A sawmill was soon purchased and lots surveyed; construction of homes began in September. In the center of town was a public square of 11 acres, and every lot was a corner lot having sufficient room for a home, garden, barn, and corral.

Colonists were entitled to purchase city lots (most apparently did not), to own livestock, and to homestead other lands, but the company retained title to most land and livestock. Workers received wages and purchased supplies from the company. Additional land was purchased over the years, bringing total holdings to more than 5,000 acres. Economic activities included raising of hay, oats, wheat, and barley, potatoes, garden vegetables, orchard fruits, flowers and trees. Sheep, cattle and hogs were raised, livestock was boarded for others, and feed was sold. In 1914 it was estimated that the population included 150 Hawaiians, Samoans, Tahitians, Portuguese, and South Sea Island whites. The following year the state sanitary inspector ranked Iosepa "as a whole the very highest in cleanliness, both in the streets and yards and in the interiors."

According to Atkins, the matter of leprosy has been overemphasized by writers. This disease afflicted only a few members—none sufficiently for hospitalization after the turn of the century. The colony was disbanded between 1915 and 1917, following the building of a Mormon temple in Hawaii; many of the town's residents returned to their former island homes. Holdings were sold in 1917 to Deseret Livestock Company for $150,000. Iosepa's cemetery is listed on the National Register of Historic Places. Only this wistful burial ground, some foundations and ranch buildings, a few trees and fire hydrants, mark Iosepa's site. *Privately owned; request permission locally before visiting.*

The ill-fated Donner-Reed pioneers camped near a spring in the vicinity of Iosepa in September 1846. There they cut grass and filled their water containers before continuing over Hastings Pass to the west, enroute to the Salt Desert beyond. One of the founders of Orr's Ranch, 16 m. south of Iosepa junction, was the late Dan Orr. Orr was fascinated by the Hastings-Donner trail; singly or accompanied by others he retraced much of the pioneer route across the Salt Desert, collecting relics along the way. Some of Orr's experiences were described by Charles Kelly in *Desert Magazine* (December 1946).

About 10 m. south of the Iosepa turnoff, the **SKULL VALLEY INDIAN RESERVATION** straddles the highway. As described in the 1941 edition, the reservation "consists of 18,640 acres of desert land set aside for the Gosiute Indians, who herd a few sheep, gather pine nuts, till small poverty-stricken farms, and rent part of their grazing land to ranchers." This area has been occupied by the Goshutes (Gosiutes) since prehistoric times, as a source of wild food before whites arrived, and of cultivated crops since the 1860s. See *Goshute Indian Reservation below.*

In this vicinity, in 1968, about 6,500 sheep died an unexplained death. Suspicion was directed at the nearby Dugway Proving Ground *(see below)*, where open-air testing of chemical warfare agents was alleged to have been underway at the time. Though never admitting direct responsibility, the federal government did eventually compensate owners of the sheep.

Skull Valley pinches to a narrow waist near the entrance to **Dugway Proving Ground.** Here the highway has gained elevation to 5,000 feet, permitting sweeping views across the desolate heart of Great Salt Lake Desert. At Dugway the Skull Valley road is joined by State 199, which connects with State 36 in Rush Valley south of Tooele *(see Tour No. 4A(2) below).* State 199 is usually preferred as the main access route to Dugway. Sixty years ago this road—then known as the Lincoln Highway—continued west from Dugway to Granite Mountain, then south to the Old Pony Express and Stage Trail near Black Rock. South of Dugway, the Skull Valley road (unpaved beyond the Dugway gate) leads 11 miles to the Old Pony Express and Stage Trail *(see Tour No. 4A(3) below).*

DUGWAY PROVING GROUND *(military reserve; access restricted)* occupies about 841,000 acres (1,300 square miles) of Tooele County. Much of the reservation consists of near-barren, low-lying desert, the bed of Lake Bonneville, but low mountains on the east and north—undisturbed for years by livestock grazing—are the habitat of pygmy evergreens, lush desert groundcover, and relatively abundant wildlife. Dugway's general mission is a matter of public knowledge. Yet remoteness, limited access, the secrecy attached to some of its works, and the fearsome nature of certain projects, have surrounded the Proving Ground with an aura of mystery—even of awe and dread.

Specifically, since its establishment some 40 years ago, Dugway's projects have included the development and testing of chemical mortars, incendiary and flame-throwing weapons, chemical and biological warfare agents (including toxic gases such as nerve gas). Other projects have included the development of protective clothing and equipment, and measures for defense, decontamination, neutralization, and detection. Dugway's work has not been limited to military weapons. It is involved as well in environmental and ecological research and development—for example, the study of animal and insect diseases, pollution abatement, and waste disposal. Sections of the Proving Ground also are utilized by the Air Force in its flight testing program.

Dugway Proving Ground was established in 1942 by the Army Chemical Warfare Service. Since then the installation has experienced status changes and fluctuating employment, being deactivated for several years following World War II and undergoing consolidation with Deseret Chemical Depot for a time. At present it is a unit of the Army Test and Evaluation Command. The installation consists of some 600 buildings, its facilities being valued at more than 240 million dollars. During the past decade employment has ranged between 1,000 and 2,000; about a third of these are military personnel. Most employees and their dependents reside in a central area known as English Village (Dugway postoffice). Though technically a government reservation with restricted public access, Dugway is a community whose residents are entitled (through court decree) to vote in elections. In 1981 its population numbered approximately 2,700. The town consists of military housing, more than 500 family housing units, two schools, shopping center, churches, movie theater, library, and health clinic. Other amenities include a golf course, bowling alley, gymnasium, and adult education center.

West of Timpie (Rowley) Junction, sideroads fork north at **DELLE** (6 m.) and **LOW PASS** (16 m.). These roads lead into and between the Lakeside and Grassy mountains, an area which provides browse for surprising numbers of sheep. The unpaved main road from Low Junction ends at Lakeside (30 m.), a siding at the west end of the Southern Pacific causeway across Great Salt Lake. Enroute, it passes through a portion of Hill Air Force Range:

Hill Air Force Range *(military reserve; restricted access)* is a military testing facility occupying more than 600 square miles of the Great Salt Lake Desert. The range is one unit of the vast Hill/Wendover/Dugway Range Complex, utilized by Department of Defense agencies for varied military programs. These programs include practice in aerial bombing, gunnery and rocketry; testing of explosives, munitions, and rocket motors; ordnance disposal; and testing of aircraft flight proficiency. Managed by the Air Force Systems Command, the complex also is used by various tactical Air Force groups for combat mission training, and for testing of the cruise missile. In its entirety, the three-unit complex occupies more than 2,600 square miles of Utah's western desert. In 1964 the Air Force dedicated a munitions and rocket test site at Lakeside, costing more than $7,000,000. The facility was designed primarily to test the Minuteman and other missiles. *See also Dugway Proving Ground, above, and Wendover Air Force Base, below.*

West of Low Pass the highway descends several hundred feet into the great basin known as **GREAT SALT LAKE DESERT.** Even on maps the desert appears white. This is an appropriate color, for much of the desert is composed of salt or light-colored sand or clay. The desert is the bed of prehistoric Lake Bonneville, the ancestor of Great Salt Lake—or, more accurately, a bay of that inland sea which became separated from Great Salt Lake by a low divide as the lake level declined. It is probable that the basin contained water in fairly recent times—only a few thousand years ago, perhaps. Cut off from major streams, this portion of Lake Bonneville evaporated completely, whereas Great Salt Lake has avoided the same fate because streams replenish what is lost by evaporation.

Great Salt Lake Desert west of Stansbury Island.

WARD ROYLANCE

Having an area of more than 4,000 square miles, Great Salt Lake Desert is one of the most desolate areas in the United States. Hundreds of square miles support no life of any kind. The desert is also one of the flattest land areas on the planet, most of its surface varying no more than 50 feet in elevation, and much of it being almost completely level. "On the edge of the desert brush and grass supply winter forage for thousands of sheep; in the heart of the desert nothing grows," said the 1941 edition. "With hardly a curve in more than 50 miles, the highway forms a black ribbon across the salt and alkali. Mirages are numerous. Small mountains seem like floating islands, with ends turned up like the toes of wooden shoes. In places the mountains appear to be upside down, with gigantic tunnels through them. Realistic water mirages are everywhere, and distances are tremendously deceptive." Even the curvature of the earth can be detected, it is said, from the Bonneville Salt Flats. I-80 was completed across the desert in the 1970s, paralleling the Western Pacific Railroad and occupying in places the route of US 40, its predecessor. Construction was a herculean feat. Since World War II the greater part of the desert has been reserved for military purposes and is closed to public access.

Before the coming of the railroad and highway in this century, this central part of the desert was a forbidding barrier to travel. Several of the more dramatic incidents of the 19th century were recounted in the 1941 edition:

> The first recorded crossing of the Salt Desert was made from west to east by Jedediah Strong Smith and two other fur trappers on their return from California in 1827. Their course was over the southern edge of the desert, but Smith's uncomplaining 137-word description of the trip indicates some of the difficulties: "After travelling twenty days from the east side of Mount Joseph, I struck the southwest corner of Great Salt Lake, travelling over a country completely barren and destitute of game. We frequently travelled without water, sometimes for two days over sandy deserts where there was no sign of vegetation, and when we found water in some of the rocky hills, we most generally found some Indians who appeared the most miserable of the human race, having nothing to subsist on (nor any clothing) except grass-seed, grasshoppers, etc. When we arrived at the Salt Lake, we had but one horse and one mule remaining, which were so feeble and poor that they could scarce carry the little camp equipage which I had along; the balance of my horses I was compelled to eat as they gave out."
>
> In 1833 Joseph Walker's detachment of Captain Benjamin L. E. Bonneville's party circled the northern edge of the desert en route from Wyoming to California. No other crossing was attempted until 1841, when the California-bound Bartleson wagon train skirted the north end of Great Salt Lake and cut over the northern part of the desert. . . .
>
> Captain John Charles Fremont, exploring the West for the United States Government in 1845, with Kit Carson as guide, charted a route over the desert from Skull Valley to Pilot Peak, 20 miles north of Wendover. Mounted on horseback, Fremont's party completed the trip with comparatively little difficulty. Failing to consider the slowness of heavy wagons, Fremont reported that the route was feasible.
>
> Lansford Warren Hastings, empire dreamer, occupies an important if infamous place in the history of the Salt Desert. Having led emigrant trains to Oregon and California in 1842 and 1843, Hastings apparently had an idea of conquering Pacific Coast territory and setting himself up as president. He returned

East in 1844 and prepared his *Emigrant's Guide to Oregon and California,* then organized a party to return with him to California. They followed the Oregon Trail to Fort Hall, Idaho, and then branched southwest to California. Seeking a shorter route, Hastings and a small party started eastward in 1846 with James Clyman, trapper, as a guide. Mounted on good horses, they took the route surveyed by Fremont and Carson, and completed the trip with no serious trouble, though Clyman wrote in his diary, "This is the most desolate country on the whole globe, there being not one spear of vegetation, and of course no kind of animal can subsist." Continuing to Fort Bridger, Wyoming, Hastings recommended the route to everyone he met.

At Fort Bridger, Hastings found four parties, totalling eighty wagons and including the parties of Samuel C. Young and George Harlan, who accepted his offer to guide them over the shorter desert trail. Hastings, however, had a penchant for trying new and uncharted routes. Deviating from the trail with which he was familiar, he attempted a new course between Fort Bridger and Great Salt Lake, and his party had great difficulties in crossing the Wasatch Mountains. Eventually, however, they emerged through Weber Canyon . . . bringing the first wagon to enter Salt Lake Valley by any route. Skirting the south end of Great Salt Lake and traversing Skull Valley, the company began the first crossing ever attempted by wagon over the center of the desert. The distance was greater than they had anticipated, and they found no water. Oxen dropped from exhaustion and wagons were left strewn along the trail. When the emigrants finally reached Pilot Peak, they hauled water and grass over the back trail to save stock and to bring in abandoned wagons. Many days were required to collect their possessions before they could continue to California.

A week or ten days behind the Hastings party came the Donner-Reed wagon train. The caravan spent two weeks trying to get through a canyon, then found the route impassable. Eventually they worked their way down Emigration Canyon into Salt Lake Valley. It was early September when the Donner-Reed party began its tragic trek over the Salt Desert. After two and a half days of travel without water, Reed volunteered to ride in search of a spring. He found no trace of water until he reached Pilot Peak, 30 miles ahead. Returning, he met the first of his party still 20 miles out. The oxen were falling one by one and being left on the desert. Wearied by five days and nights without sleep, Reed found his wagon mired down. Carrying their small children, he and his wife began the long walk across the wasteland. Meantime Jacob Donner reached Pilot Peak, watered his oxen and started back for the Reed family. He found them exhausted, resigned to death on the desert. Several wagons were abandoned and many cattle died, but the entire company survived. The delay, however, was costly. They reached the Sierra Nevadas too late to cross before winter, and became snowbound a hundred miles from Sutter's Fort. Many perished of starvation and exposure. Others survived by cooking and eating their boots, harness, and the flesh of dead members of the party. Of the eighty-seven emigrants who began the journey, only forty-four reached California.

Evidence of the Donner-Reed crossing is still preserved in the surface of the desert. Tracks made nearly a hundred years ago by wagons too heavy for the thin salt crust are still visible. The route of the Hastings Cutoff has been retraced and many articles left along the trail have been gathered. . . .

The experience of the Donner-Reed party discouraged further attempts to cross the desert until 1849, when Captain Howard Stansbury was sent by the Government to survey Great Salt Lake and the surrounding country. Circling the north end of the lake, he followed the Bartleson route across the desert to Pilot Peak. Here he rested a few days, and began a second desert crossing—eastward over the Hastings Cutoff to the southern end of the lake. He saw evidences of the

Donner-Reed journey—several wagons, a cart, skeletons of oxen, and discarded personal property. Stansbury's arrival at Salt Lake City completed the first circuit trip around Great Salt Lake. During the California gold rush of 1849-50, the desert route was again used by over-eager westbound travelers, and again wagons and oxen were abandoned along the trail.

In 1854 Lieutenant E. G. Beckwith was sent to Utah by the Government to make a survey for a railroad to the Pacific. Laying his course a little south of the old Cutoff, he found water at convenient intervals and made the trip without mishap. Building of the railroad was postponed, but the route was used for many years by wagon freighters. The Beckwith road had a steep grade over the Cedar Mountains, and Captain J. H. Simpson, another Government surveyor, came to Utah in 1859 to find a better route. His course led south through Tooele Valley and then west, crossing the desert farther south than previous roads. The Pony Express and the Overland Stage followed this route, and ruins of the old stone relay stations still exist at Fish Springs and Callao. *[See Tour No. 4A(3) below.]*

The next attempt to plan a route over the desert came in 1896, when William Randolph Hearst, chain newspaper publisher, decided, as a publicity stunt, to send a message by bicycle from his *San Francisco Examiner* to his *New York Journal.* William D. Rishel of Salt Lake City was delegated to map out a portion of the course. Rishel and C. A. Emise took a train to Lucin, Utah, where they unloaded their bicycles and started back to Salt Lake City, laying their trail over the desert around the south end of the lake. . . .

In 1903 the Southern Pacific Railroad built the Lucin Cutoff *(see Great Salt Lake)* across Great Salt Lake and the Salt Desert. In 1907 the Western Pacific Railroad laid its rails across the desert, closely following the Hastings Cutoff. Early attempts to build a highway over the desert were unsuccessful. . . .

Several miles east of Wendover, a road forks north to **Bonneville Salt Flats,** site of the famed **Bonneville Raceway (Speedway),** fastest automobile course in the world for many years.

The **Bonneville Salt Flats** are comprised of rock-hard salt, precipitated as Lake Bonneville evaporated. The area most suitable for racing measures about 10 by 15 miles and consists of hard salt of sufficient thickness to support heavy vehicles. During most of the year the salt is either under water or too moist for racing, but the summer sun evaporates the surface moisture, and usually the flats are in ideal condition by August and September. Said the 1941 edition, they look "very much like an immense lake of snow-covered ice . . . The remarkable qualities of this natural course [were] first shown in 1914, when Teddy Tetzleff, nationally-known race driver, set an unofficial world record of 141 miles an hour for a measured mile. In 1926 Utah's Ab Jenkins drove for 24 hours without relief, and broke almost every world speed record by traveling 2,710 miles at an average speed of 112 miles an hour." Jenkins returned in the 1930s to establish new records. Sir Malcolm Campbell exceeded 300 miles per hour (mph) in 1935, being the first person to reach that speed in an automobile. His record was broken in 1937 by Captain George Eyston's 311 mph. John Cobb set new world records in 1938, 1939 and 1947. Athol Graham, a Utahn, died in the crash of his *City of Salt Lake* in 1960, at 300 mph. That same year Donald Campbell of England survived a crash of his *Bluebird* at 365 mph. Cobb's record of 394 mph, set in 1947, was not officially surpassed until 1963, when Craig Breedlove—driving a three-wheeled jet racer—reached 428 mph in the one-way mile. Breedlove and Art Arfons competed in October 1964, "the greatest racing month in the speedway's history," when Breedlove attained a speed of 526 and Arfons 536 mph. The following year, in November 1965, Arfons and Breedlove competed once again. This time Arfons reached a top speed of 576 and Breedlove 601 mph, giving Breedlove the honor of being the first person to surpass 500 and 600

Walt Arfons' racer, Bonneville Salt Flats, 1965.

mph in an automobile. His 1965 record held until 1970, when Gary Gabelich reached 631 mph in the one-way mile, driving a rocket-powered racer. In 1979 Stan Barrett's rocket vehicle attained the speed of 639 mph. In the fall of 1981 a British team attempted to set official records exceeding this speed but were defeated by bad weather.

Though the world record speed runs receive more notoriety, because of their drama, the **Bonneville National Speed Trials** involve more participants on a regular basis. This annual event in September—billed as "The world's safest auto speed trials"—has attracted hundreds of participants and spectators every year for more than 30 years. Entrants try to set new records with a fascinating assortment of vehicles ranging from stock cars to antiques, as well as modified motorcycles and exotic vehicles of revolutionary design.

About 2 m. east of Wendover, visible to the south from I-80, are potash processing facilities of **Kaiser Chemicals and Aluminum Corporation.**

Potash and sodium chloride (salt) have been recovered from the brines of Bonneville Salt Flats since 1917. The Salt Flats proper—including the speedway area to the north—is a rather limited area which fluctuates in size from 110 to 160 square miles, depending on precipitation. In effect it is a "drainage sump" for the much larger Great Salt Lake Desert. As such, its subsurface brines are extremely concentrated and in places a hard salt pan has formed (at the speedway in particular). Kaiser collects brine through a hundred miles of deep trenches. This brine is fed into a large solar evaporation pond where potassium (potash) salts are concentrated, then further treated on-site by industrial processing. About 100,000 tons of potash are produced annually by the Bonneville operation and marketed primarily in the west. The Utah Salt Company plant nearby processes some of Kaiser's by-product salts for specialized uses.

WENDOVER (4,246 alt. 1,099 pop.) utilizes the Utah-Nevada state line as its western boundary of incorporation. (Only the Utah side of town is incorporated.) In 1941 Wendover was "a railroad town . . . The railroad roundhouse and the large yellow frame depot are conspicuous among the unpainted frame houses." Long ago these ceded prominence to motels, casinos, new houses, and the huge military structures of Wendover Air Force Base *(below)*. The first transcontinental telephone line was joined at Wendover in 1914.

Wendover was founded in 1907 as a railroad watering point during construction of the Western Pacific Railroad, serving as a terminal for a pipeline carrying water from Pilot Peak, 20 miles to the north. Not until after the highway was completed in 1925 did it become a travelers' oasis with service stations and lodging. A casino was added on the Nevada side in the 1930s. This evolved into today's elaborate State Line Hotel and Casino, joined in recent years by other such enterprises. Local boosters anticipate an unprecedented boom founded on gaming, casino entertainment, dining and lodging. Only the latter two activities are permitted on the Utah side of town.

Danger Cave, about 2 m. northeast of Wendover in the Silver Island Range, is an undeveloped State Historical Monument and is listed on the National Register of Historic Places. Utilized as a shelter by some of the most ancient peoples known to have lived in Utah, the cave was excavated during the 1950s by archeologists from the University of Utah under the direction of Professor Jesse D. Jennings. Danger Cave measures about 60 feet in width by 120 feet in length and originally contained a layer of refuse as much as 13 feet deep. According to its National Register description, Danger Cave "has been one of the key sites for understanding the prehistoric cultures of the desert West. Five strata of cultural occupation were present, beginning with Archaic material [estimated to be at least 10,000 years old.] The thousands of artifacts of chipped and ground stone, bone, horn, antler, wood, leather, cordage, basketry, and shell recovered from the Archaic levels were the basis for defining the Desert Archaic lifeway, a model of prehistory that has since influenced all scientific work done in the Western United States. . . ." After approximately A.D. 400 the site was used by Sevier culture peoples, who hunted buffalo and the abundant waterfowl found near the cave.

WENDOVER AIR FORCE BASE (AUXILIARY FIELD), now but a skeletal remnant of the huge military base that flourished here during World War II, sprawls south of the highway on the eastern outskirts of Wendover. During the early 1940s the base contained more than 600 buildings: barracks, houses, hospital, warehouses, hangars, shops, and everything else required for a self-contained community where nearly 20,000 civilian workers and military personnel lived. The base's history was summarized in the *Utah Historical Quarterly* (Fall 1963) by Leonard J. Arrington and Thomas G. Alexander, who termed it "The World's Largest Military Reserve." (At the height of operations the base encompassed some 3,500,000 acres.)

Wendover Air Force Base was born in 1940, prior to Pearl Harbor, as a result of Air Force program expansion. Until March 1942 it was a sub-post of Fort Douglas. During World War II it served as a base for the training of crews of heavy bombers. Crews were trained in bombing and gunnery, formation flying, navigation, target identification, and simulated combat. A city was built of salt for bombing practice. Lifelike battleship targets were constructed, as was a mobile machinegun range. One program, having the purpose of training fighter pilots to fly bombers, is said to have cost the lives of 121 men as a result of crashes. By late 1943 the base had a population of 17,500 military personnel and 2,000 civilian workers.

After the war ended in 1945 it became known that the base had been the training site for the bomber group that dropped atomic bombs on Hiroshima and Nagasaki. Though this training group comprised nearly 2,000 men, including FBI agents and military police, only the group commander is said to have had knowledge of its ultimate mission.

The base continued to be used sporadically as a site for bombing, rocketry, gunnery, missile recovery, and other training purposes. It was deactivated and declared surplus in 1948; reactivated; deactivated again in 1957; reactivated on a minor scale in 1961; and declared surplus again in 1962. In that year only 128 buildings remained of the original 668. For several years in the late 1960s and early 1970s, Wendover Base and the Salt Desert were considered as a potential site for a NASA spaceport, in connection with the space shuttle program. The base's facilities no longer are used by the military, except in emergencies, though much of the former training range is a part of the Hill/Wendover/Dugway Range Complex of the Department of Defense.

South of Wendover, between 1917 and 1939, the DEEP CREEK RAILROAD connected the mainline Western Pacific with mines at Gold Hill, as described in the 1941 edition.

Tour No. 4A(2) - From Lake Point Junction south through Tooele and Rush valleys

In the vicinity of Lake Point Junction a village flourished for 60 years or more. Settled in the mid-1850s by Peter Maughan and others (Maughan later was a prominent settler of Cache Valley), the community was long known as **E. T. City** in honor of Ezra Taft Benson, Mormon Church apostle who was a leader in the colonization of Tooele Valley.

At **Mills Junction,** 4 m. south of Lake Point Junction, State 138 (old US 40) forks west to Grantsville. **Adobe Rock** marks the junction. A historic landmark, Adobe Rock stands beside a route used since days of the fur trappers and Salt Desert pioneers. A spring nearby provided fresh water for campers. West of Mills Junction a short distance, beside the highway, is the **E. T. Benson Mill.** Dating from 1854, the antique gristmill was still in use as a flour mill in 1941 when the first edition of this guidebook appeared. It was referred to therein as Brigham Young's Gristmill. The Benson Mill is "one of the oldest buildings still standing in western Utah," according to its National Register description. "It was still in use in 1960 to grind feed for turkeys and cattle." Nearby, in 1941, was the **Utah Wool Pullery,** "a group of buildings in which nearly a million pounds of wool are pulled from pelts annually."

GRANTSVILLE (4,300 alt. 4,419 pop.) is a residential community that stretches along the highway for several miles. In 1941 it was "a typical rural Mormon community, deriving its livelihood from alfalfa, grain, sheep, and turkeys. Squat adobe houses built by the first settlers rub shoulders with later brick dwellings. Water is obtained from artesian wells." Since 1941 the population has multiplied four times and the economy depends to a lesser degree on agriculture. Many local people commute to work at Tooele Army Depot, Dugway Proving Ground, and AMAX's magnesium plant at Rowley. But Grantsville's pioneer heritage (it was settled in 1851) can be seen in older buildings and rural lanes, bordered by tall lombardy poplars.

The **Donner-Reed Memorial Museum,** 97 N. Cooley St., displays artifacts left by the Donner-Reed pioneers of 1846 along the route of their memorable trek through western Utah, in addition to other valuable historic relics and Indian artifacts. Open by arrangement.

Grantsville was the birthplace and boyhood home of J. Reuben Clark, Jr., counselor in the First Presidency of the Mormon Church and U.S. Ambassador to Mexico in 1930-32. President Clark kept a home in Grantsville in his later years.

Turn south from Grantsville 5 m. to **South Willow Canyon** in the Stansbury Mountains. A partially paved road climbs steeply through Wasatch National Forest to a parking and camping area at 7,800 feet (12 m. from Grantsville), from which a foot trail leads about 4 m. through pleasant glades and over rocky ledges to the top of **Deseret Peak** (11,031 alt.), highest point in the range. This lofty perch affords a circular panorama across the western desert, Great Salt Lake, and seemingly boundless valleys and mountain ranges in every direction. A small stream provides a modest fishing experience. South Willow Canyon contains four improved campgrounds of Wasatch National Forest.

State 36 continues south from Mills Junction to Tooele, passing through a wide-open expanse of dry farms and irrigated fields. The lofty Oquirrhs loom to the east, the even higher Stansbury Range to the west. A keen eye may detect the route of an aerial tramway rising from the valley floor near Mills Junction to the top of Coon Peak, 5,000 feet higher, where a television transmission station is located. The hamlet of **ERDA** dates from pioneer days of the 1850s. Built around Tule (Tuilia) Springs, it was known first as Rose Springs Fort, then Bates and Batesville. **STANSBURY PARK,** west of the highway, is one of Utah's first modern-day planned communities. Featuring expansive lawns, golf course, sailing lake, and recreation center, Stansbury Park is situated on 2,000 acres of landscaped valley bottom. The community was planned and financed by Terracor, a Utah development firm which had previously initiated development of Bloomington community near St. George. First phases were begun in the 1960s.

TOOELE (4,900 alt., 14,335 pop.) is the seat of Tooele County, situated in the high southern end of Tooele Valley, only 12 miles from Great Salt Lake but 700 feet higher. Its elevation affords a vista of lake, valley and mountains that is breathtaking. In Tooele reside more than half the population of the county, which is Utah's second largest with 6,923 square miles of area. The name is pronounced variously as Too-IL-uh or Too-EL-uh. Derivation of the name is uncertain and controversial. It may have originated from the Spanish *tule,* pronounced too-leh, for bulrushes in the valley's marshes, or from the name of a Gosiute chief, Tuilla. Of possible significance is the fact that the map of Captain Bonneville's expedition of 1837 bears the inscription "Too-el-i-can Indians," placed in a territory adjoining Shoshone country far to the northwest of what is known today as Tooele Valley.

Tooele was settled by Mormon pioneers in 1849 and today is a clean, attractive city with a busy main street and modern residential developments. A parked mall in the central business district is a product of recent years. Many residents depend for a livelihood on nearby Tooele Army Depot and Anaconda's Carr Fork mine *(see below).* Others commute long distances to work. Farming and stockraising are of relatively less importance today. The city's population is a cosmopolitan mix of nationality origins, due in part to its mining and smelting background and the proximity of large military installations. Because of rapid growth, Tooele's early origins are not as apparent as they were a few years ago. However, early structures do remain, as side-street driving will attest. The old **Tooele County Courthouse,** built in 1867, is a registered historic site, maintained by Daughters of the Utah Pioneers as a relic hall. Parks in the downtown area contain a pioneer log cabin and a steam locomotive of former days.

Turn northeast from Tooele to the former site of the great lead concentrator and smelter of International Smelting & Refining Company. This landmark was closed and dismantled in the early 1970s after nearly 60 years of production, being Utah's last remaining copper-lead-zinc smelter. Built in 1910, the huge smelter was still processing a million tons of ore annually in 1940. Ore was brought over the mountain from the Bingham Mine by aerial tramway. In this connection, the 1941 edition described one of Utah mining's most ambitious and visionary projects, the **Elton Tunnel.** The tunnel was never completed, and the water flow has been cut off by a cave-in, but excavation did result in discovery of ore bodies now being mined by Anaconda *(below)*.

At the old smelter site, 4 m. from Tooele in **Carr Fork,** Anaconda Company is now developing a new mining complex costing more than 200 million dollars. As the result of an extensive exploration program, Anaconda recently discovered rich mineral deposits several thousand feet below the surface. In the mid-1970s the company began sinking shafts and driving a system of tunnels. Production began in 1979. Reserves are estimated at some 60 million tons of ore containing relatively high grade copper (nearly two per cent), as well as molybdenum, gold and silver. Ore is hauled by truck and electric train from the mining face to an underground crusher, then lifted to the surface for additional crushing and concentrating. Anticipated mine production is 10,000 tons of ore daily.

Turn east from Tooele to **Middle Canyon,** a narrow, steep-walled gash in the Oquirrh Range. Paved for much of the distance, the road passes through wooded bottoms for a few miles, then rises swiftly in tight curves to **Butterfield Pass** (8,400 alt.), marking the divide between Tooele and Salt Lake valleys. (Trailers not permitted beyond Bingham Metals, 9 m. from Tooele.) The road forks at Butterfield Pass, the east spur descending Butterfield Canyon to Lark and Herriman. The

Middle Canyon near Tooele.

McNEIL STUDIO

north spur continues a steep and winding climb for another mile or two to **Sunset Peak (West Mountain) Overlook,** a parking area atop the Oquirrh summit ridge. From this 9,400-foot eyrie the view encompasses several thousand square miles of northern and western Utah—a breathtaking jumble of mountains, basins, valleys and lakes. Tooele Valley can be glimpsed to the west, with Salt Lake Valley and Salt Lake City sprawling in their entirety to the east, 5,000 feet below. On a clear day (rare in recent years) the whole magnificent front of the Wasatch Range can be traced for 150 miles, from one end to the other, from Mt. Nebo on the south to the range's northern terminus beyond Brigham City. Rivaling the natural scene in visual impact is the giant crater of **Bingham Copper Mine,** yawning beneath one's feet, a fantasy of geometric patterns and dimensional depth. Until provision of new overlooks in Bingham Canyon, the Sunset Peak viewpoint provides the best alternative for a bird's-eye perspective of the mine. Sunset Peak Overlook is about 15 miles from Tooele. *Avoid steeper sections of this road when there is danger of ice or snow!* National Guard engineers, with assistance from Tooele County, improved the upper road for auto traffic in 1958.

Turn southeast from Tooele to **Settlement Canyon,** a popular scenic drive and the site of **Legion Park,** a community recreation area. Picnicking, camping.

West of State 36, 3 m. south of Tooele, is the entrance to **TOOELE ARMY DEPOT,** a military installation and headquarters of a farflung depot complex known as TEAD. TEAD is Tooele County's largest employer, with nearly 4,000 workers. The Tooele Valley installation alone occupies 25,000 acres, and all of this can be seen from the highway in panoramic overview: orderly rows of soil-covered igloos and magazines, warehouses, shops, rail yards, administrative and housing complex, and hundreds of acres of open-air storage aprons. An additional 19,000 acres are in Rush Valley nearby (Depot South Area).

Tooele Army Depot was born during World War II. It was established in 1942 by the Army Ordnance Department as a back-up installation for depots in California. For the next 20 years it was known as Tooele Ordnance Depot. At present TEAD is a depot complex of seven locations in five states, one of 12 such installations of the Army Materiel Command within the United States. Its functions include Supply and Storage (ammunition, explosives, chemicals), Maintenance and Repair (2,000 different types of equipment such as automotive-construction-rail equipment, missile systems, armaments, combat vehicles), and Training. Maintenance shops alone occupy nearly a million square feet of area. Since its founding, TEAD's mission has expanded due to the consolidation and closing of depots in other western states. The depot now has command of smaller installations in Oregon, Colorado, New Mexico, and Arizona. Deseret Depot to the south *(see below),* now known as Depot South Area, was placed under TEAD's command in 1955. Another detached area is the Army's Rail and Generator Repair Shop at Hill Air Force Base.

A short distance south of the entrance to TEAD, another sideroad forks west to **Bauer,** where Combined Metal Reduction Company operated two mines (metallic ores) and a concentrating mill between 1923 and 1959. About 15,000 fruit trees were planted nearby to utilize water pumped from the mine workings. After closing of the mines, Combined Metals processed perlite from Nevada and fossil resins shipped from Carbon County. These resins—derived from coal waste fines—were used in the making of paints and varnishes, inks, adhesives, fabrics and chewing gum. The Bauer plant was destroyed by fire in 1980.

South of the TEAD and Bauer turnoffs, State 36 passes over a low divide between Tooele and Rush Valley. A flat-topped ridge to the west of the highway, known as **Stockton Bar** or the Great Bar, is an interesting geological curiosity. The bar is composed of sand and gravel and was created by waves of prehistoric Lake Bonneville during its highest stages. As the lake fell, the bar became a dike separating shallow Rush Valley Bay from the main lake to the north. Stockton Bar and prominent benches formed by waves on the mountain slopes of this vicinity are among the most vivid reminders of the great lake's existence in the not-too-distant past. **Rush Lake**—marked today by marshes in the valley bottom west of Stockton—is a remnant of a much larger body of water that once occupied Rush Valley. Rush Lake contained water and fish for years after white settlers arrived, for that reason being selected as the site of military camps by Lt. Colonel Steptoe in 1854 and Colonel Connor a few years later *(see below)*.

STOCKTON (5,100 alt. 437 pop.) is a rather nondescript residential village dating from the 1860s and 1870s, when several smelters were built to process ore from the area's mines. The first of these was constructed in 1864 by Colonel Patrick E. Connor, the "father of Utah mining," whose Fort Douglas soldiers discovered valuable ore deposits in the vicinity. The town was an outgrowth of Connor's Camp Relief, established in the early 1860s soon after he and his troops arrived in Utah. Camp Relief in turn was built on or near the site of Lt. Colonel Steptoe's encampment of 1854-55, near Rush Lake. Later, the lake's water was utilized for ore smelting.

St. John Junction, 5 m. south of Stockton, is a major fork. State 36 continues south from here to US 6 near Eureka *(see Tour No. 4B),* while State 73 turns southeast to Fairfield and Utah Valley, giving access to Ophir and Mercur *(see State 73 below).*

State 36 south from St. John Junction.

State 199 forks west from State 36 at a point 4 m. south of St. John Junction. This paved highway is the main route to **Dugway Proving Ground** *(see Tour No. 4A(1) above),* passing from Rush Valley to Skull Valley by way of Johnsons Pass, a natural divide between the Onaqui and Stansbury ranges. **CLOVER** and **ST. JOHN** are rustic farming hamlets in Rush Valley, taking irrigation water from Clover Creek. Clover was settled in the mid-1850s by Luke Johnson and others, and St. John in 1867 by former residents of Clover who were advised to move by church leaders. These rural villages, isolated from big cities, still display poignant reminders of Utah's early years in the form of aging 19th century structures. A log house in St. John, for example—owned by the Arthur family—dates from 1869 and is listed on a historic register. The area's population is hardly less today (about 350) than it was 100 years ago.

Sprawling across the valley slope to the east of State 36 is **Depot South** *(see State 73 below).* The main line of Union Pacific Railroad, connecting Salt Lake City with Los Angeles, parallels the highway through Rush Valley. East of the highway, 9 m. south of St. John Junction and near the south boundary of Deseret Depot, once existed a farming settlement known as **CENTRE** or **CENTER** and a remarkable establishment with the name **Ajax Underground Store.** The town disappeared long ago, and only an excavation in the ground marks the store's former location. Centre was settled in the early 1860s and once had a post office. The store was the work of William Ajax and his family, beginning modestly about 1870, then expanding with the growth of local mining, ranches and road traffic. What made the store unique was its underground location—11,000 square feet of floor space, excavated by hand, the soil-covered roof supported by cedar poles and the interior lighted by high south-facing windows. Lodging and food were available for both people and livestock, as well as a department-store selection of goods. By 1914 changing conditions forced the store to close, and within a few years it caught fire and collapsed.

Near Faust Station, 12 m. south of the junction with State 199, an unpaved but graded and maintained sideroad forks west toward the mountains. This is the famous **Old Pony Express and Stage Trail,** described in Tour No. 4A(3) below.

VERNON (181 pop.) is a farming village marked by the impressive two-story brick residence built for John C. Sharp in 1888 *(registered historic site)*. Vernon was settled in the early 1860s, some of its people earning wealth from cattle, sheep, large-scale farming, and mining claims. John C. Sharp, Mormon bishop of Vernon for 25 years, became prominent in Utah financial and business affairs. In 1900, it is estimated, 100,000 horses, cows and sheep ranged the area's mountains and valleys. As a consequence of overgrazing, much of the area became unproductive as grasslands and reverted to sagebrush. Dryland wheat farming was successful for a time, but eventually this was given up. Beginning in the 1940s, experiments at the **Benmore Soil Conservation Project** south of Vernon were successful in demonstrating how such overgrazed and marginal lands could be reclaimed for livestock by clearing unwanted vegetation, then reseeding with crested wheatgrass and controlling subsequent grazing. A native of the Russian steppes, crested wheatgrass was found to be an extraordinarily nutritious food for cattle.

State 73 from St. John Junction to Fairfield.

From its junction with State 36 south of Stockton, State 73 climbs Rush Valley's rising slope, which affords a stirring overview of that vast mountain-rimmed bowl and **Deseret Depot (Depot South Area),** below the highway to the west.

Occupying 19,000 acres—an area measuring five by six miles in extent— Deseret Depot was constructed in 1942-43 by the U.S. Army and given the name **Deseret Chemical Depot.** Thousands of workers quit their jobs during construction because of fierce dust and sand storms. A new town was built with housing and support facilities for a thousand people, and during World War II as many as a thousand workers were employed at the depot. The depot's mission then was the storage and shipment of chemical warfare materials, including poison gases, chemicals, and chemical ammunition. After that war it was deactivated. The Korean War in the 1950s brought reactivation and new construction. In 1955 the depot was assigned to Tooele Army Depot *(see above)* and is now known as the Depot South Area, having a primary function of ammunition storage and maintenance.

OPHIR (6,500 alt. 42 pop.) is nestled among lush creekside trees and shrubs in the bottom of Ophir Canyon, 3 m. from State 73. The pleasant little community of today gives only the slightest indication that it was a mining boomtown a hundred years ago. Though occupied houses are old, they are well kept; civic pride is evident. Many residents are retired or widowed; younger ones may commute to work in Tooele. The last mine closed in 1972 and a small store is the only business today. Several venerable rock buildings, a few tumbledown frame shacks, and the restored **Old City Hall and Fire Station** (1870) are nostalgic reminders of Ophir's glory days, which were described in the 1941 edition as follows:

> The town was named by Colonel Patrick E. Connor's soldiers for the fabulous mines of King Solomon. Ophir has risen from the sick bed so often, the very buildings seem bored with constant resurrection. The lop-sided, caved-in ruins lean on their elbows and complacently view the goings-on of each new strike. Frame structures of every period mark the dates of Ophir's revivals.
>
> Indians mined silver and gold for trinkets, and lead for bullets, in this little canyon. Connor's men, hearing of the Indian mine, staked the St. Louis Lode in the late 1860's. The strike touched off a boom. Miners and prospectors dashed into camp from Nevada and California, and soon the Pocatello, Velocipede, Wild Delirium, and Miner's Delight were located. Mack Gisborn, who made his stake at Mercur, built a toll road from Ophir to Stockton. Wagons hauled ore over this road and north to Lake Point, on Great Salt Lake, where it was boated to Corinne and the railroad. The usual "boomers" hurried into camp and threw up shacks. Saloons lined the street, interspersed with brothels and gambling dens. . . .

Ophir 1910.

UTAH STATE HISTORICAL SOCIETY

The mines at Ophir furnished Marcus Daly, Montana copper king, with his start to riches. Fired from the Emma Mine at Alta, Daly was hired by the Walker Brothers, Salt Lake City bankers, to work their property at Ophir. He staked the Zella claim for himself, and profits from that mine helped develop Anaconda Copper in Montana.

Ophir's ore contained relatively little gold but was rich in silver, lead and zinc. It is estimated that production value of these minerals between 1870 and 1970 totaled more than 40 million dollars. In 1981, Sperry Univac announced tentative plans to build a specialized electronics plant in Ophir Canyon, a proposal that sparked immediate opposition from local residents.

Ruined foundations, marking long-abandoned mining works, can be seen along the highway between Ophir Junction and the west access side-road leading to Mercur. This unpaved, fair-weather road to Mercur passes through the shallow canyon of Mercur Creek and emerges finally into a mountain-girt pocket where one of Utah's largest and most famous mining communities once existed. The main highway, State 73, continues to Fairfield and Utah Valley.

The site of **MERCUR** is marked primarily by mine shafts, dumps, a few tumble-down shacks, collapsing walls, and empty foundations. Above all, the imposing ruins of the great smelter complex known as the Golden Gate mill occupies a hilltop like an ancient temple. It would be impossible, from what remains, to visualize the city of 6,000 or more that flourished here about the turn of the century. Mercur's beginnings were described in the 1941 edition:

Mercur came to life in the late 1860's when Colonel Patrick E. Connor's soldiers discovered silver ore in the canyon, but early yields were disappointing. The Floyd Silver Mining Company optimistically put $700,000 into development of property that returned only $175,000. Mack Gisborn started the stampede, however, when he lifted $80,000 from his hole in the ground, the Carrie Steel. Silver seekers fought their way into the new camp in every kind of conveyance, and the stage companies ran six trips a day. News of the strike brought business men, gamblers, saloon keepers, and the usual camp parasites. Buildings sprang up along the gulch, and the new town was named Lewiston. Hotels and "hook shops" did a land office business, and if they missed extracting all of a miner's money, the saloons and gambling houses finished the job. A million dollars was taken out, but in 1880 the boom folded up and everybody left.

Arie Pinedo, a Bavarian prospector, drifted into the district in 1882 [1879?], and located the Mercur lode, a cinnabar or quicksilver deposit, which gave the town its present name. Assayers found gold in all samples, but the prospectors were unable to pan any of it. Pronouncing a curse on all assayers, the prospectors, including Pinedo, departed. In 1889 Joseph Smith rediscovered gold on the Pinedo claim. Smith "rawhided" *(see Transportation)* ore to the amalgamating mill at the bottom of the canyon, but no gold would come out. . . .

Colorado engineers [developed] the cyanide process in 1893 and Mercur hit the headlines again. . . .

About this time the railroad came, and by 1896 the population had jumped from 400 to 6,000. A move was made to incorporate the town on Statehood Day, January 6, 1896, but a fire swept the town, leaving little to incorporate. The "Hook Department" went into action. Water was scarce and the volunteer fire department used a long pole with a hook on the end, with which they dragged flaming shacks into the street and let them burn. In spite of the fire, however, the town was incorporated.

After the fire of 1896 Mercur was rebuilt and the Golden Gate mill was completed in 1898. The mill's builder was D. C. Jackling, who subsequently developed the open-pit copper mine at Bingham. By 1902 Mercur was a substantial community once more. According to Stephen L. Carr it supported two newspapers, "a fire department, a brass band, schools, a church, a large opera house, dance hall, dental office, saloons, restaurants . . . several grocery, dry, hardware and milliner stores, candy shops, livery stables, and a couple of good hotels." (These in addition to numerous houses.) Then, in June 1902, a fire started behind a lunch counter. "Less than two and a half hours later," Carr continued, "every business building in town was destroyed including all the stone ones. Fortunately most of the residential areas were spared as was the mill which continued working."

The Golden Gate mill operated between 1898 and 1913, by which latter year mining and milling had become unprofitable. Revivals brought production, mainly from the reworking of tailing dumps, but few substantial buildings. Though old tailings have been reworked and extensive exploratory drilling performed in the intervening years, Mercur remains a ghost town. Of interest is the fact that George H. Dern—governor of Utah (1924-30) and later Secretary of War in the administration of Franklin D. Roosevelt—was general manager of Consolidated Gold Mines Company (owner of the Mercur mill and mines) when everything closed in 1913. His father was president of the company. For years after 1913, as many as 600 old-timers met each year in festive reunion. By 1959, when the reunion was held in Salt Lake City, two-thirds of those present were widows, and attendance had dwindled to a hundred. Recent years have witnessed renewed activity at Mercur.

East and south of Mercur, the unpaved road climbs over a ridge and through Manning Canyon to a junction with State 73 near Fairfield. Old ore mill remains are visible along the road in the canyon, where a busy railroad once ran.

FAIRFIELD (4,900 alt.) is a farming village in the wide expanse of Cedar Valley, marked by aged cottonwood and poplar trees. The town's principal attractions, other than a picturesque old school building, are **Camp Floyd Military Cemetery, Old Stagecoach Inn,** and a reconstructed **Army Commissary Building.** These latter are State Historical Sites, open to the public, administered and maintained by the State Division of Parks and Recreation. The cemetery, one-half mile south of town, marks the former site of old Camp Floyd/Fort Crittenden. Markers memorialize the graves of 84 soldiers known to have been buried there; the markers were placed in 1960. **Old Stagecoach Inn** is a quaint two-story structure, built of frame and adobe, with upper and lower porches across the front. Built about 1857 by the John Carson family as a dwelling, it was soon converted to an inn known thereafter as the Carson Inn and Fairfield Hotel. The building functioned in that capacity until 1947. It was restored by the state in 1959. The old inn also served as a Pony Express station in 1860-61 and as a stagecoach stop for years after that. Insofar as possible the inn has been restored to its original condition. Furnishings, while not original to the inn, do resemble those commonly in use during its early years. The commissary building, across the street from the inn, is a restoration of a military building which stood on the site in the days of Camp Floyd.

CAMP FLOYD was established by the army of Colonel Albert Sydney Johnston immediately after its arrival in Utah in June 1858 *(see History)*. The army consisted of "some 3,500 officers, enlisted men and civilian employees—cavalry, artillery, infantry, supply trains, engineers, bands, and ambulance corps. There were 586 horses for the mounted units, 500 wagons and 3,000 mules''—in short, the ''largest troop concentration then in the United States—1,100 miles from its base, Fort Leavenworth, Kansas.'' More than 300 buildings were erected during the first summer at Fairfield, of stone, adobe and lumber.

''Overnight, Fairfield became one of those typical hell-roaring, wild places of the West, and with Camp Floyd, soon had a population of some 7,000 or more people. The population of Salt Lake City was then only 15,000 . . . Along with trades-people, artisans and mechanics, came a civilian riff-raff of saloon-keepers (there were 17 saloons in the town), gamblers, women, slickers, thieves and robbers—all attracted there by the Army payroll, which was about the only actual money in the Rocky Mountain West . . . A theatre was built and a military Dramatic Association was organized. Plays were given weekly and later daily . . . Dances and balls were frequent. And, of course, Frogtown, or 'Dobieville', as Fairfield was called, just over the creek, furnished other outlets for those who could obtain off-bounds passes. By 1860, the storm clouds of the Civil War were gathering. Many of the troops were ordered away from Camp Floyd in that year, and by fall only 10 com-panies of troops remained. General Johnston was ordered elsewhere, and Colonel Phillip St. George Cooke was sent to take command of the Post. He later changed its name to Fort Crittenden. On May 17, 1861 he was ordered back to Fort Leaven-worth with the 10 companies under his command, and on July 27, 1861, what re-mained of the Army of Utah departed. Some $4,000,000 of Army surplus was sold at auction for $100,000. The buildings were burned or otherwise razed. As the Army of Utah left Fort Crittenden, fuses touched off trails of powder that led to piles of arms and ammunition that had not been disposed of otherwise. The hell-roaring Fairfield blew out as suddenly as it had blown in. By September 2nd of that year only 18 families called Fairfield their home. . . .''

(Quoted material courtesy Utah Division of Parks & Recreation)

Old Stagecoach Inn, Fairfield.

WARD ROYLANCE

Tour No. 4A(3) - Old Pony Express and Stagecoach Trail from Fairfield to Utah-Nevada State Line

The **Old Pony Express and Stagecoach Trail** between Fairfield and the Utah-Nevada state line—a distance of about 154 miles—is an unpaved but maintained route, passable with ordinary automobiles when dry. (Several stretches in the Fish Springs-Callao area may be impassable when wet.) This spectacular stretch of road, considering its length, undoubtedly has changed the least in alignment and other characteristics, over the longest period of time, of any road in Utah. Travelers on this route find it easy to visualize pioneer travel of the 19th century, because the land remains much the same as it was 120 years ago when the route was surveyed by army troops. And because the land remains comparatively wild and unspoiled, forbidding and entrancing, the road is a trail of discovery and adventure for those who travel it the first time.

WARD ROYLANCE

Looking west across Great Salt Lake Desert from Black Rock Station.

Warning: Travelers should not expect to obtain food, gasoline, lodging or other services between Rush Valley and Wendover, a distance of 150 miles. Carry tools, food, water, spare tire, etc. Extra gas may be advisable. Stay on traveled roads for safety, as sand and mud are real hazards. Remember that historic sites are protected under federal and state law. Leave the land at least as undisturbed as you found it.

For most of its length, this route was one of the earliest to cross western Utah, having been used—in part—as early as the 1840s. The trail was used by Chorpenning's Jackass Mail in the 1850s, and by hordes of other travelers during that decade. It was formally surveyed in 1859, between Camp

Floyd and Genoa, Nevada, by an Army detachment under the command of Captain J. H. Simpson. Thereafter the route was followed by the Pony Express in 1860-61, by stagecoaches and other horsedrawn vehicles from 1860 into the 20th century, and by uncounted thousands of other travelers to the present day. It was also the route of the first transcontinental telegraph line between 1861 and 1869.

The sites of original Pony Express and stagecoach stations—or the majority of them—are marked today by stone monuments and plaques. Some have been vandalized. The U.S. Bureau of Land Management (BLM) has restored several ruins, recreated a station at Simpson Springs, and provided interpretive exhibits at several sites. *Mileages shown are distance from preceding station.*

West of Fairfield, the Old Trail forks from State 73 at Fivemile Pass (5 m. from Fairfield) and drops into Rush Valley, through which it passes for nearly 20 miles. **East Rush Valley Station,** 10 m. from Fairfield, is marked by a stone monument and plaque. **Faust Station** (9 m.), an important trail stop, is marked by a monument and BLM interpretive site at the trail's junction with State 36. These mark the general vicinity of Faust Ranch, named for Henry "Doc" Faust, who operated the ranch and station between about 1860 and 1870. As a young man, Faust carried mail between Utah and California along this route, operated the Pony Express station at Faust and served as a substitute rider. **Lookout Pass** or **Point Lookout** (8 m.) is marked by a monument and a small cemetery containing the remains of pet dogs owned by Horace and Libby Rockwell, who lived here for a time after 1870 or thereabouts. **Government Creek Station** (8 m.), marked by foundation ruins, was a telegraph station and is believed to have served as a Pony Express station.

Simpson Springs, also known as Simpson's Spring, was named for Captain J. H. Simpson, army engineer who surveyed the route in 1859. It has been an important rest stop since 1851 or before because of its plentiful water. A rock monument and plaque are beside the road, near the replica of a rock station building. Believed to be an accurate representation of the original station, the building was erected in 1974 by the Tooele Chapter of Future Farmers of America, in cooperation with BLM. BLM has developed a 14-unit campground near the fenced-off spring. *Open all year, pit toilets, no firewood; water available March-October.* Simpson Springs was the site of a CCC camp during the 1930s; remains of this camp can still be seen. Historical excavation of the old station site was conducted by BLM and Brigham Young University in 1974 and 1975. Located on the side of a hill, this area affords a sweeping panoramic view of Dugway Proving Ground, the western desert, and rugged island ranges.

Old River Bed Station (8 m.) was in the sandy channel of a prehistoric stream connecting the main body of Lake Bonneville to the north with Sevier Bay to the south. Since water seeks a common level, both bays should have had identical surface levels and there should not have been a "river" connecting them in this vicinity. The explanation, according to some geologists, is that the main lake—covering a much larger area than Sevier Bay—evaporated more rapidly and its level dropped faster than Sevier Bay,

Pony Express marker *(left)*, Deep Creek Mountains from Callao *(top)*, and Fish Springs *(above)*. *Ward Roylance photos.*

which therefore drained northward through the Old River Bed. The rock monument at River Bed site was built by CCC workers in 1939-40. Nothing remains of the original station. **Dugway Station** (10 m.), marked by a monument, was a dugout substation without water. **Black Rock Station** (14 m.), located beside a dark volcanic outcrop, was known also as Butte or Desert station. A vandalized monument marks the general site of the station, which no longer exists. The site provides a spectacular view of Great Salt Lake Desert, high ranges to the west, and skeletal Granite Mountain in Dugway Proving Ground to the north. Jedediah Smith crossed the salt basin to Granite Mountain in 1827, enroute from California to Great Salt Lake. Beckwith also traversed that desolate terrain in 1854. West of Black Rock, between 1913-27, the old trail served for some distance as the Lincoln Highway, which came in from the direction of Dugway and Johnsons Pass.

Fish Springs Station (10 m.) exists as a rock foundation in **FISH SPRINGS NATIONAL WILDLIFE REFUGE.** The refuge is a remarkable oasis in a fearsome desert and was established in 1959 to administer and improve some 18,000 acres of marshland surrounding about 75 freshwater springs. The marshes invite migrating waterbirds such as ducks, cranes, herons, avocets, curlews, and egrets, as well as myriad shorebirds. A permanent government complex is located at the refuge. *Visitors welcome.*

An area of hot springs, known as Little Yellowstone or Wilson's Health Resort, is near the road at the north end of Fish Springs Range. The springs are the result of hot mineral water flowing out from an underground fissure. Years ago a public-spirited citizen placed a sign on an old frame shack at the site, reading "welcome to all visitors. Come in and make self at home." Such hospitality obviously was abused by vandals. An old-fashioned bathtub in one of the springs attests the water's therapeutic properties. "Salt flowers"—globular incrustations of salt, caused by the evaporation of upwelling saline ground water—surround the springs. They are said to be especially colorful in June and July. *Warning: It is dangerous to leave the path in hot springs area because of thin surface crust.*

Boyd Station (14 m. from Fish Springs) is marked by the crumbling rock walls of the original Pony Express station, guarded by a protective fence. The interpretive exhibit was erected by BLM. The site of **WILLOW SPRINGS STATION** (8 m.) is in the quaint hamlet now known as **CALLAO.** Its exact location is uncertain. Callao, known as Willow Springs in pioneer days, lies between the 12,000-foot **Deep Creek Mountains** and the Great Salt Lake Desert. One of the most isolated communities in the state, Callao also was one of the least changed until recent decades. A maintained county road forks south from Callao to Trout Creek, Gandy, Eskdale, and US 6 *(see Tour No. 4B).*

North of Callao, the old trail passed through **Overland Canyon,** veering west from the present road at Sixmile Ranch, 4 m. from Callao. Three stations (Willow, Round, and Burnt) were located along this rough stretch of road between Callao and Ibapah (Deep Creek), but only the site of **Round Station** is definitely known and properly marked.

The present road skirts Montezuma Peak (7,368 alt.) along benches overlooking the salt desert, before entering **GOLD HILL,** 23 m. from Callao. According to a state travel publication, Gold Hill was born in 1892 and "saw a number of dramatic declines and revivals."

Mines for years produced commercial quantities of gold, silver, copper, bismuth, tungsten, arsenic, and other materials. The town boomed in 1917 when a railroad spur was finished south from Wendover, and its prosperity continued during World War I and for a few years after, when its arsenic deposits were exploited. Then mining production subsided and Gold Hill almost died. During World War II, its arsenic again was in demand, and the town boomed for a few years. But isolation, high transportation costs, and vagaries of the mineral market all combined to defeat the town, and Gold Hill became a ghost town almost overnight in 1945 when the arsenic market collapsed.

Some old buildings still remain, and a few residents still live in Gold Hill. Travelers may continue northwest from Gold Hill to US 93A and Wendover, or turn south to Clifton and Ibapah.

CLIFTON, a short distance south of Gold Hill, dates from the 1860s. It has experienced deaths and some rebirths, but none to match the heydays of Gold Hill. Few evidences of its existence remain except for crumbled ruins and abandoned mine workings. Stephen L. Carr's *Historical Guide to Utah Ghost Towns* summarizes the history of these two ghost towns. In 1981 plans were announced for a large-scale revival of mining in the area.

The old Express trail passed near Clifton to **IBAPAH,** formerly known as Deep Creek, and thence into Nevada. Located in Deep Creek Valley, flanked by lofty peaks of the **Deep Creek Range** *(Haystack Peak 12,101 alt.),* Ibapah today is a picturesque farming and ranching village, one of the most isolated in the state, notable for rusticity and Old West atmosphere. Here was the westernmost Pony Express and stage station within Utah's present boundaries, serving as a division headquarters. The station site is on private property. The main road continues west into Nevada, where it joins the Wendover-Ely highway.

A sideroad forks south from Ibapah to **Goshute,** 12 m., a cluster of modest homes in the **GOSHUTE (GOSIUTE) INDIAN RESERVATION.** *Public travel restricted.* Forage and water limitations prevent more than marginal operations in farming and livestock raising.

Related to the Shoshoni of Nevada and Idaho, the Goshutes of Deep Creek are descendants of hardy natives who roamed the arid valleys and mountains of western Utah for ages before whites arrived. Known as "diggers" in early literature, the Goshutes (more technically Gosiutes) were marvels of ecological adaptation, managing to survive in one of the west's least hospitable environments. When whites arrived, the Goshutes were utilizing about a hundred varieties of plants, including roots, seeds, and nuts of the pinyon pine. Insects, reptiles, fish, rabbits, birds, and rodents were used as food, supplemented by larger game when available. White settlement reduced the Goshutes to extreme levels of deprivation before farming and stockraising—radical departures from traditional customs—could be developed. Though intervening years have brought improved living conditions (gradually), the lot of the Goshutes has never been an enviable one. In 1962 the Indian Claims Commission ruled that the Goshutes, as well as other Shoshone and Bannock tribes, were entitled to compensation for loss of lands by white encroachment.

WARD ROYLANCE

Tour No. 4B - PANORAMALAND—WEST (Juab and Millard counties)

This tour features the Great Basin in Juab and Millard counties, from Utah Valley south to Cove Fort (via Interstate Highway 15) and from Santaquin west to Eureka, Delta, the Sevier Desert, and the Utah-Nevada state line (via US Highway 6). A land of far-spreading horizons, this is a region of exciting history, strange geology, and planned developments of staggering multitude—completely unforeseen only a few years ago. Historically, the greater part of its people have lived in towns strung like the links of a chain along the general route of I-15, which follows the mountain front with its life-giving streams. Exceptions to this rule have been Delta and nearby population centers dependent on the western Sevier River, as well as Eureka and a few other communities based less on irrigated agriculture and mainline highways than on mining, railroading, dryfarming, etc.

Tour No. 4B(1) - US Highway 6 from Santaquin west to Eureka, Delta, the Sevier Desert, and Nevada

From Santaquin, US 6 crosses the fertile lowlands of Goshen Valley, a southern offshoot of Utah Valley, through a pastoral scene of fruit orchards, farms, and the modest but prosperous-looking towns of Goshen and Elberta. Soon, however, the highway leaves the valley and climbs into the East Tintic Mountains, a stark landscape of rugged igneous highlands known familiarly as Tintic, more formally as the East Tintic Mining District. Evidences of extensive mining activity soon appear in the form of some modern, well-kept structures but more commonly as "old shafts, trenches, abandoned dumps, weatherbeaten camps, and prospecting holes." Mount Nebo looms majestic in the near distance.

EUREKA (6,400 alt. 670 pop.) remains one of Utah's most picturesque mining communities, though evidencing neglect, fluctuating fortunes, and an abundance of dilapidation. The 1941 edition's description of Eureka applies as well today:

> . . . wooden houses painted long ago, and squat brick buildings hug the narrow streets. In some sections of the town brick bungalows stand beside tumble-down, weather-beaten buildings. The dump of the Gemini mine—symbol of twofold prosperity in the past—almost pushes into the lobby of the leading hotel, and newer stores stand scornfully beside false-front structures of another day. There is an occasional tree, vividly green.

Since 1941, the general trend has been *down* in overall prosperity. No longer is the following description completely accurate; however, it does afford perspective:

> Constant blasting, deep underground, shakes the "jerry-built" houses. Beneath the streets, in tunnels and drifts that honeycomb the earth, miners stolidly tear the ground to pieces, taking out millions of dollars worth of gold, silver, copper and lead. Huge trucks roar through the streets, some carrying armed guards to protect the fabulously rich ore. Eureka, surrounded by ghosts of former mining camps, is the focal point in the Tintic district.

Millions of dollars have been spent since 1941 in trying to revitalize Tintic's mining industry, by Kennecott as well as other firms—probing for richer ores, applying new techniques of extraction and processing. Depressed market prices, rising costs of operation, poor grades of ore, processing and transportation costs, all have been obstacles to success. Nevertheless, several mines still remain in operation. In 1978 the Burgin lead-zinc-silver mine was closed after 14 years of operation, due to depressed market prices, high costs and low ore grades. The Burgin was Utah's last remaining lead-zinc mine. Many Eureka residents are now forced to commute long distances to work. The original Union Pacific Railroad depot has been converted into a fascinating **mining museum.** *Open to the public.*

Eureka and surrounding towns (a 64-square mile area) are listed on the National Register of Historic Places as a historic district because of "their value in the documentation of metal mining history, both on a state and national level. . . . Examples of residential (all types), commercial, institutional, and industrial structures, as well as ore dumps, railroad grades, and shafts and tunnels remain and function as an excellent means of interpreting the mining past. . . . Mining continues in Tintic, thus offering a rare view of past and present in one compact area."

The following excerpts are from the 1941 edition, which devotes considerable space to a recitation of anecdotes about Eureka's mining heydays. Interested readers are referred also to specialized publications such as Stephen L. Carr's *Historical Guide to Utah Ghost Towns* for detailed summaries of the history of such Tintic towns as Eureka, Mammoth, Silver City, Knightsville, Dividend and others.

The Tintic Valley was a favorite Indian campground long before the Mormons came. The grass grew high then, the springs and streams ran full, and game was plentiful. A minor Ute chieftain, Tintic, claiming all the land in Tintic Valley, bitterly resented invasion by white men and carried on guerilla warfare. His band was repeatedly pursued by the Territorial militia, but always managed to escape. . . . Stockmen, entering the valley in the early 1850's, saw only the lush grass and the bubbling springs. Before long, charcoal manufacturing was begun, forests were slaughtered, the watershed was ruined, the high grass disappeared, and sagebrush crept in from the desert. Soon only sheep could survive on the range.

Eureka, looking southwest, about 1923.

UTAH STATE HISTORICAL SOCIETY

With the discovery of a "funny looking" piece of rock by George Rust, cowboy, in 1869, the valley arrived at its destiny. For several years, however, the shouts of rich strikes at Park City, Alta, and in the Cottonwood Canyons drowned out the news of more quiet prospecting in the Tintic Mountains. Five men fought their way through a blizzard to locate the "Sun Beam" in December, 1870, the first registered claim in the valley. In January, 1871, another group of men located the "Black Dragon," and in the same month the "Corresser Lode," now known as the "Carisa," was discovered. By April Sunbeam ore was worth $500 a ton, Montana and Eureka ore $1,500 a ton, Mammoth ore $1,000 a ton, and the remaining thirteen mines ran down the scale to the Bull's Eye, which mined ore worth $86 a ton. . . .

By 1872 it was not uncommon for mines to ship ten-ton lots of ore assaying from $5,000 to $10,000. Specimens assaying 15,000 ounces of silver to the ton were sent to the Vienna Exposition in 1873. One fifty-ton lot from the Centennial Eureka netted the company $200,000, and the Grand Central, which was reopened in 1937, got $198,000 for a fifty-ton lot. In 1914, ore valued at $10,000 a carload was still being shipped from the district, and the year before the Colorado mine was shipping from a two-foot vein assaying 2,000 ounces of silver to the ton. Mining camps sprang up all over the mountains in the early 1870's, and Silver City, the first real camp, is described in Diehl's manuscript as having "a billiard saloon, blacksmith shop, grog hole, some tents, several drunks, a free fight, water some miles off, a hole down 90 feet hunting a spring without success, and any number of rich or imaginary rich lodes in the neighborhood. The owners are all poor, and the poor men work for them. By next spring the poor will be poorer."

Following the settlement of Silver City (1870), came Diamond (1870), Mammoth (1870), Ironton (1871), Homansville (1872), and Knightsville (1897). Silver City's population fell from 800 to almost zero when the mines reached water-level and the cost of pumping proved prohibitive. A new boom was started in 1908, when a smelter was built in Knightsville, but the plant ran only a few years. In 1940 the town had only a handful of people to keep its memory alive. The last house in Diamond, named for crystals found near by, was moved away in 1923, and all that remains of this once bustling camp of 900 persons is the cemetery, a few old mine dumps, and yawning holes that were once cellars. . . .

Wealth pouring out of the hills started an epidemic of "high-grading," which forced some of the mines to shut down. Miners sneaked rich ore out of the mines in their lunch buckets, up their noses, in special pockets in their overalls, and once a whole carload of exceedingly rich ore disappeared from the railroad station. Tracers were sent out, and the car—empty—was finally found in Mexico. The mystery was never solved. The Mammoth roughly estimated that it had lost $150,000 to "high-graders."

Mine "salting" was another little game played in the district. Sometimes the "salted" mine turned out to be a rich producer: The men who purchased the Wyoming mine from a Mr. Pease, were so pleased wih the rich ore in the shaft that they gave him $20,000 in cash, the remaining $2,000 to be paid within a week. Pease accepted the $20,000 and disappeared. The strangers built a mill, but found that Pease had dumped two carloads of rich ore from the Eureka Hill down the shaft. They were forced to use custom ores at the mill, but later uncovered a rich vein that brought them $1,000,000. Salting of mines sometimes worked the opposite way: A superintendent would open a rich vein, "salt" the vein with low grade ore, and report to the company that it was not worth developing. Later he would lease the mine and make his fortune. . . .

By 1910 most of the mines in the Tintic district were under the ownership of the Chief Consolidated Mining Company and the Tintic Standard, which controlled various mines, and in 1937 became one of the mines in Eureka Lily Consolidated.

By the 1920's, the mines of the Tintic district were all tapping deeper ores by means of perpendicular shafts, 2,000 feet deep or more. . . .

Figures in the *United States Bureau of Mines Yearbook* show that between 1869 and 1938 the Tintic District produced 2,394,527 ounces of gold, 244,532,264 ounces of silver, 229,422,014 pounds of copper, 1,748,854,741 pounds of lead, and 36,999,120 pounds of zinc all valued at $363,133,791.

The day of the small operator has passed, and the mines are under the control of large companies who can afford to sink deeper shafts, install pumping equipment, construct long tunnels, run underground railroads, and provide the other necessities of modern mining. Pines and the firs grow no longer on the hills, springs have ceased to tumble down the mountainside, and even the indomitable sagebrush is stunted and scant. . . .

West of Eureka, US 6 abruptly drops into **Tintic Valley** between the West and East Tintic mountain ranges, being joined there by State 36 which forks north to Rush Valley, Stockton and Tooele *(see Tour No. 4A)*. Near this junction a paved road leads 1 m. east to **MAMMOTH** (6,000 alt.), high on a steep mountain slope. Today's town bears scant resemblance to the large community of the glory days that prevailed between the 1870s and 1920s or thereabouts. Those years saw hundreds of residents, stores, hotels, saloons, etc., serving a number of mines and mills. In 1941 Mammoth's main street consisted "of a few bleached, false-fronted buildings. Residents live in decrepit plank shacks, some of them painted a dirty yellow, and dry barren hills close in upon the town. The Mammoth Mine, where most of the male population works, is one of the richest in the district." This mine continued sporadic operation during the 1940s and early 1950s, but then was closed until 1962, when New Park Mining Company invested considerable funds in a program of diamond drilling. Though successful in finding promising new ore bodies, other problems have prevented full production since then.

SILVER CITY (6,100 alt.) in 1941 was "a trading center for numerous small silver, gold, and lead mines in the district" but today is not even a respectable ghost town. Nothing but dumps and foundations remind today's visitor that here was a community numbering 800 residents in 1899 and 1,500 in 1908, a peak from which decline soon began. Said the 1941 edition:

> The Swansea mine was developed by William Hatfield, the first man in this region to extract ore below the water level; it produced nearly $700,000. Silver City was the boyhood home of George Sutherland, one-time Associate Justice of the United States Supreme Court.

After a disastrous fire in 1902, the town was rebuilt largely through the activities of Jesse Knight, wealthy Mormon mine owner and philanthropist, who developed mines, smelter, power plant and railroad, and built a number of new houses to replace those destroyed by fire. About the same time, Knight founded the community of Knightsville near Eureka, a company town known as "the only mining camp in the United States without a saloon."

About 14 m. south of Eureka, an unpaved road forks east and south into **Riley Canyon** of the East Tintic Mountains. A 3-mile drive along this road, then a half-mile hike up a dry streambed, bring one within view of

Paul Bunyan's Woodpile, overhead on a mountain slope. A geological curiosity, rare in Utah, the "woodpile" is a cluster of lava logs—lengths of igneous rock which in ages past crystallized into orderly columns having three to six sides. The columns measure about a foot in diameter and up to 15 feet in length.

At Jericho Junction, 19 m. south of Eureka, a marked sideroad leads west to White Sand Dunes and **LITTLE SAHARA RECREATION AREA,** a development of the U.S. Bureau of Land Management.

Here at Little Sahara is Utah's largest expanse of free-blowing dune sand, covering several hundred square miles, the state's single most popular area for off-road vehicle recreation (dune buggies, cycles and four-wheel-drive vehicles). The formal recreation area occupies 60,000 acres of the dune area. Visitors number in excess of 100,000 each year, many of whom come on the Easter weekend for vehicle recreation, picnicking, camping, hiking, sunbathing and nature study. Sand Mountain features a sand cliff hundreds of feet high, which provides an excellent site for competitive hill climbing. Racing (drag, cross country, hare n' hound) attracts numerous participants. Little Sahara is divided into special areas for nature study (Rockwell Natural Area), sandplay-picnicking-camping, and vehicle recreation. A new visitor center, opened in 1980, utilizes solar energy.

JERICHO, at the junction of US 6 and the main dunes access road, was a major sheep shearing center for many years. The 1941 edition described the center's shearing operation in interesting detail.

East from Jericho Junction a paved sideroad leads to State 132 and Nephi. *See Tour No. 4B(2) below.* US 6 continues south into the **SEVIER DESERT (PAHVANT VALLEY),** the vast sink of Sevier River and the flat bed of vanished Lake Bonneville. White Sand Dunes occupy a far-spreading area west of the highway.

White Sand Dunes
(Little Sahara Recreation Area).

Historic charcoal ovens
near Leamington.

LYNNDYL (4,800 alt. 90 pop.) is a rather nondescript farming center on the **SEVIER RIVER**. The mud-banked, lazy river in this vicinity is but a sorry reminder of the noble Sevier in its headwaters. Yet even here, near the end of its long journey from the High Plateaus, enough water remains to irrigate some thousands of acres of farms in Pahvant Valley. Little if any is allowed to enter the river's age-old destination, Sevier Lake, now but a near-dry playa. From Lynndyl, State 132 forks east to Leamington, a farming community, and Nephi. *See Tour No. 4B(2) below.*

Ten miles east of **LEAMINGTON** (113 pop.), construction began in 1980 on the huge **cement plant** of Martin Marietta Corporation, a national firm. Limestone, shale and silica are to be mined in the vicinity, with iron ore being shipped in as the fourth major ingredient. Plans call for a capacity of 600,000 tons of cement per year. Total cost of the completed project is estimated at more than 80 million dollars. Beside U132, 2 m. east of Leamington, are two **historic charcoal ovens,** built in 1885. Wood was cut in the mountains nearby and hauled by mule to the ovens; the charcoal was then freighted to Salt Lake City. South of Leamington, U125 leads to Oak City and Delta. **OAK CITY** (389 pop.) is a quaint, old-fashioned country town at the base of the rugged Canyon Range. Says the 1941 edition, Oak City's "quiet main street is lined with trees and flower gardens, and water flows along each side of the road." East of town a forest road climbs along the canyon of Oak Creek into the heart of the Canyon Range to a campground (Fishlake National Forest). **Canyon Range** is recognized by geologists as a vivid example of folding and overthrusting, an illustration of the results of the dramatic crustal deformation so apparent in the Basin and Range Province.

From US 6, 5 m. south of Lynndyl, a paved sideroad forks west. Known as the Brush Wellman road, this route connects the large Brush Wellman beryllium mill in the vicinity of the junction with the firm's beryllium mines some 50 miles west. Also beside this road, 8 m. west of US 6, is the site of the huge Intermountain Power Project *(below)*. The **Brush Wellman Mill** began operations in 1969, when it began processing bertrandite ore, rich in beryllium, from deposits in the Topaz Mountain area 50 miles away. Concentrates are shipped to Ohio for further processing and manufacture into a variety of industrial products. The mill also processes imported beryl ores and uranium byproducts. The Lynndyl mill was the first large-scale beryllium facility in the nation. By 1981 Brush Wellman had invested more than 30 million dollars in the local mill and mines.

The giant **INTERMOUNTAIN POWER PROJECT,** largest coal-fired power plant in the country if not the world, is under construction on a site 8 m. west of US 6 via the Brush Wellman road. Long planned, the huge installation was first proposed for siting in Wayne County, near Hanksville, but proximity of that site to Capitol Reef National Park forced relocation to Millard County in the late 1970s. The plant is the largest and most costly industrial complex ever proposed for Utah, designed to produce more than 3,000 megawatts of electric power from four 820-megawatt turbine-generators. Coal is to be hauled from mines up to 100 miles away, and as many as ten million tons will be required every year. About 45,000 acre-feet of water will be used each year, to be obtained from wells and Sevier River impoundment; rights to this water were purchased from more than 600 rights holders at a cost of some $84,000,000. Total cost of the project is estimated at more than eight billion dollars, including interest. Site preparation began in the fall of 1981, with peak construction expected in 1986-87. Power is to come on line between 1986 and 1989. The plant's sponsor, Intermountain Power Agency, is a cooperative with more than 30 members, including six California municipalities (Los Angeles and vicinity), who together will purchase 58 per cent of the power; Utah Power and Light Company; and 20-odd Utah municipalities. Opponents of the project have lodged suits in court to stop the project on grounds that it is illegal to divert Utah's agricultural water for California industrial use.

DELTA (4,600 alt. 1,930 pop.) is the commercial center of western Pahvant Valley, long a staid community of wide streets and modest homes. From its founding in 1907 until 1978 or so, life proceeded at an unhurried rural pace with hardly a hint of the transformation that was to come. Irrigated agriculture, stockraising, trade and mineral production furnished a fairly stable economic base. Then in the late 1970s, with little warning, the Delta-Lynndyl area was selected as the site for the great Intermountain Power Project after its sponsors' first site choice near Hanksville was rejected by the Secretary of the Interior *(see above)*. This development was followed shortly by announcement of plans for the enormous MX Missile project to be constructed in western Utah and Nevada *(as described below)*. The result has been profound change, as indicated by a growing population, a local building boom, soaring real estate prices, and the sale of agricultural water rights to non-agricultural users (notably Intermountain Power Project).

Delta's beginnings were summarized in the 1941 edition:

> The Great Pahvant Valley was condemned as wasteland in 1900, but five years later a group of Fillmore men purchased half interest in the Sevier River Reservoir, and 10,000 acres of land, to found a settlement on the Sevier River delta. Reasonably priced farms were parceled out, with one share of water for each acre. Town lots sold at $15 each. Plentiful water contributed to cultivation of many crops, especially alfalfa. Cleaning, grading, and marketing of alfalfa seed developed into an enormous business, and in 1940 nearly one-fourth of the alfalfa seed in the United States was produced in the Delta district.

Delta sugar factory about 1920.

Turn north from Delta and Hinckley to the farming clusters of Sutherland, Woodrow, Sugarville and Abraham. Known as the North Tract, this area is a flat, sparsely settled expanse of irrigated fields bordered by forbidding desert. The scattered dwellings and farm buildings hardly suggest that many years ago the district was teeming with hundreds of homesteaders enticed by low-cost land, plentiful canal water, and the dream of prosperity. Between about 1909 and 1930 several small communities grew, thrived and declined as new landholders arrived, developed sugar beet fields, built homes, became discouraged and moved away. People came from many states; most eventually moved away, many buildings being demolished or removed, small holdings being absorbed into larger farms. In **WOODROW,** several miles north of Sutherland, **Woodrow Hall** is one of the few notable structures of this period. A white frame building, the modest hall was built in 1916 by local settlers and used for dances, elections, meetings and church services. Now privately owned, the hall is a registered historic site.

Eight miles west of the paved highway leading to Sutherland and Sugarville, from junction several miles north of the Mormon chapel in Sutherland, **TOPAZ WAR RELOCATION CENTER** was constructed as an internment camp for persons of Japanese descent evacuated from the West Coast. Between 1942 and 1945, when it was closed, the camp housed about 9,000 evacuees. Topaz was one of ten camps in the nation devoted to this purpose during World War II. According to its National Register description, Topaz symbolizes "the extreme prejudice and war hysteria following the attack on Pearl Harbor." Its residents "lived in the barracks-type structures which were furnished from army stores. Residents made most of their own furniture. Dining, recreational, and sanitary facilities were shared. . . ." Stephen L. Carr in *Historical Guide to Utah Ghost Towns* summarized the camp's history in more detail: culinary water came from wells; the townsite was laid out in 42 blocks with wide streets; three to four families lived in a building; and the town's 600 or so buildings included a hospital, fire station, post office, library, theater, churches, schools, stores, and recreation halls. A fence with guard towers enclosed the camp's 20,000 acres. After the camp was closed, its facilities were sold and removed, and the land was sold. Physical evidence of its existence remains in the form of concrete foundation slabs, rubble, and the network of streets. Topaz is a registered historic site, marked by a monument of stone and concrete.

North and west from the area of irrigated lands, a spiderweb of roads—most of them unpaved—lead to mines, grazing ranges and rockhound areas. **SEVIER DESERT (Pahvant Valley)** is one of the largest of Utah's Great Basin valleys, occupying about 3,000 square miles. In fairly recent ages, geologically speaking—the latest only 15,000 or 20,000 years ago, perhaps—the valley served as one of glacier-fed Lake Bonneville's largest bays. As the climate changed and the lake shrank, the bay's water retreated southward into Sevier Lake; but at a higher stage it had drained north through the channel of Old River Bed into Lake Bonneville's main body (now Great Salt Lake Desert). The main access road, State 272, commonly known as the Brush Wellman road *(see above),* is paved; this route connects Brush Wellman's beryllium plant south of Lynndyl with the firm's mines in the Topaz Mountain area. An unpaved extension of that route proceeds north to the Old Pony Express Trail and Fish Springs *(see Tour No. 4A).* Other unpaved roads north and west from Delta lead to Hot Plug, Old River Bed, Dugway Pass, Drum Mountains, Fish Springs, Antelope Springs, and other points of special interest for rockhounds, geology students, and sightseers. **Hot Plug,** called by Frank Beckwith "a red mountain that smokes" and "the most beautiful object in Pahvant Valley," is a red and gray volcanic mass nearly 200 feet high and approximately the same distance in diameter. The vent of an ancient volcano, Hot Plug still conducts heat from the depths of the earth, creating visible mist when the air is cool. Nearby is a group of hot springs, containing water at a very high temperature, the basis for a local spa known as **Crater Springs Health Resort.**

Farther north, **Old River Bed** is a geological curiosity, its very name out of place in such an arid desert, far from any flowing stream. At one time—thousands of years ago—today's sandy valley bottom was a channel through which overflow waters from Sevier Bay of Lake Bonneville drained northward into the lake's main body until a lower, stabilized level was reached. Its ancient function as a water channel is plainly visible, even to the untrained eye. *See Tour No. 4A for geological explanation.* **Topaz Mountain,** a part of the Thomas Range, is well known to rock collectors as a fruitful source of topaz crystals. Though the surface has been exhaustively combed, weathering and excavating continually expose more crystals. The area is mined commercially; and one section has been reserved for amateur collectors. The Topaz Mountain area contains commercial deposits of bertrandite (beryllium) ore. Rich fluorspar ore was mined from Spors Mountain for years, notably by the Spor family of Delta, after whom the mountain was named. **Drum Mountains,** a low desert range, received its name because of weird subterranean noises sounding like blows on a drum; other sounds are heard, such as rumblings, thumps and grindings. Since the 1870s the Detroit Mining District in the Drum Mountains produced gold, silver, copper, manganese and other minerals, though on a sporadic basis. Today's ghost town of **JOY** was for many years a populated center for miners and ranchers.

US Highway 50 joins US 6 at Delta continuing into Nevada as joing US 6-50. At **HINCKLEY** (pop. 464), 5 m. west of Delta, paved State 257 forks south to Deseret, Clear Lake, Black Rock, and Milford.

State 257 passes through a wide-open expanse of flat desert. Pahvant Butte and other volcanic remnants can be seen to the east. The village of **DESERET** is the site of **Old Fort Deseret,** just south of town, marked by crumbling ruins of a defensive structure hastily built in 1865 by Mormon settlers *(state historical monument, registered historic site).* The remaining walls are but a portion of the original 550-foot-square fort, intended as protection of settlers against Indians. The fort was never used for its primary purpose. Men, women, and children participated in building the fort in less than ten days, constructing the foundation of lava rock and the walls of adobe clay strengthened with straw. Originally the walls were ten feet high, three feet thick at the base, and 1½ feet thick at the top. **Gunnison Massacre Monument,** about 5 m. west of Deseret and Hinckley near what remains of the Sevier River, marks the site of the massacre in October 1853 of Captain John W. Gunnison and seven members of his government exploring expedition. *Inquire locally for directions; the monument is not easy to find.* While engaged in a federal railroad survey, the Gunnison party were attacked at dawn by Pahvant Indians intent on avenging the death of one of their tribe who had been killed by non-Mormon emigrants (it is said) a short time before. The site is listed on the National Register of Historic Places. **Pahvant Butte,** 850 feet high, juts dramatically from the flat valley floor about 15 m. to the southeast of Deseret. An inactive volcano, Pahvant Butte (also known as Sugar Loaf Mountain) is the largest and most prominent crater of the Millard Volcanic Field *(see Tour No. 4B(2) below.)* Evidence points to its having been formed during Lake Bonneville times, with eruptions occurring deep under water and building a crater high enough to project above the lake's surface.

A few miles south of Deseret, west of the highway, flat-topped **Dunderberg Butte** is a striking reminder of the deep lake that once inundated the valley and planed off the butte's summit. A rock formation on the butte's northern flank is known as the **Great Stone Face** because of its resemblance to the profile of Joseph Smith, Mormon prophet. Not far away, **Clear Lake** is a state waterfowl management area. At the base of the **Cricket Mountains,** 31 m. south of Delta, near State 257 and the Union Pacific Railroad, construction began in 1979 on a multi-million-dollar plant for the manufacture of quick lime. Raw material (limestone) is mined several miles away in the Cricket Mountains. **Black Rock** a junction point on U257 to the south of this plant, is the locale of commercial obsidian deposits, which also attract collectors.

The Dominguez-Escalante exploring party traversed this region in October 1776, generally following the route of today's State 257 from Clear Lake on the north to Milford, and from there to Cedar City. *See Tour No. 8.* This segment of trail, about 70 miles in length, required 12 days because of marshy ground, snow, cold, loss of an Indian guide, and indecision about which route to travel. Though Monterey lay to the west, terrain forced a long detour to the south.

West of the Delta-Hinckley oasis, US 6-50 penetrates one of Utah's most forbidding deserts, a stark and thirsty land of far horizons. The unearthly white sink of **SEVIER DRY LAKE** appears as a white mirage to the south.

This blinding playa (dry lake bed) superficially resembles the salt flats of Great Salt Lake Desert, from which it differs in having a less substantial crust of salt over a deep layer of mud. In 1872, when first mapped, Sevier Lake had a water surface of 188 square miles, was about 28 miles in length and had a saline content of 9 per cent. Less than ten years later, due to diversion of Sevier River for irrigation, the lake was almost dry. Since then, though maps continue to indicate the 1872 shoreline, the "lake" has actually been little more than a dry lake bottom or salt flat; however, water does stand in part of the area at certain times. The series of 14 latticed "fences" visible on the lake bed are microwave reflecting barriers installed by American Telephone & Telegraph Company in 1967. Their vertical supports are 18-foot poles, lowered by helicopter into holes that were hand-dug through mud up to five feet thick.

Though seemingly a wasteland, this desert region of western Utah has been a favored winter grazing ground for livestock, mainly sheep by the thousands. Isolated ranches are scattered across the valleys and foothills, dependent on springs, wells and reservoirs for water. Also, somewhat surprisingly, there are marshes in some valley bottoms. One of history's worst winters in 1948-49 brought snowfall so deep that thousands of sheep and cattle died of cold and starvation.

THE MX MISSILE PROJECT. Between 1979 and 1981, the mammoth MX Project—perhaps the largest feat of construction ever conceived—was proposed by the Department of Defense for the valleys of western Utah and Nevada. In 1979 President Jimmy Carter approved the "racetrack" concept of basing the new MX intercontinental ballistics missile (ICBM), one of the nation's triad of land-air-sea nuclear weapons. This basing plan, favored by the Air Force, involved a vast complex of 200 clusters of reinforced concrete shelters (23 shelters in each cluster), scattered across 45,000 square miles of Utah and Nevada. One MX missile would be shuttled between the 23 shelters of each cluster on rails, transported by an enormous vehicle-launcher weighing a million pounds with its missile load.

Construction statistics alone were difficult to comprehend: 8,000 miles or more of new roads . . . 160,000 acres to be cleared for construction . . . twice the amount of concrete used in Hoover Dam . . . nearly two million tons of steel

. . . and as many as 60,000 workers during peak construction years of 1986-88. Estimates of total cost ranged from 34 to more than 100 billion dollars. In addition to the clusters there were to have been assembly and deployment areas, maintenance centers, area support centers, and main operating bases.

About a fourth of the planned missile clusters would be placed in the valleys of western Utah, the remainder in Nevada. Few valleys west of Eureka, Delta, and Beaver would be without at least one cluster; some valleys would contain as many as five clusters. Both Delta and the Milford area were considered as potential sites for area support centers, or as the locations for a main operating base.

No military proposal ever resulted in more publicity and agitated debate in Utah. Initially cautious when the project was first announced, as its implications became more apparent the majority of the state's population eventually took stands in opposition to the planned method of deployment, if not to the missile itself or to the policy of nuclear proliferation. Even the Mormon Church entered the fray in May 1981 with a statement of the First Presidency: "Our fathers came to this western area to establish a base from which to carry the gospel of peace to the peoples of the earth. It is ironic, and a denial of the very essence of that gospel, that in this same general area there should be constructed a mammoth weapons system potentially capable of destroying much of civilization. . . ."

Profound injury to a fragile environment . . . adverse impact on mineral prospecting, mining, water resources, livestock grazine, local quality of life . . . overwhelming problems of housing, education, and capital facilities . . . a severe "bust" following construction: fear of these consequences was voiced by numerous people. Also expressed was the fear that placing so much of the nation's offensive-deterrent capability in one area would make the region a potential nuclear target or "sponge," this having repercussions of inconceivable magnitude such as the annihilation of a large part of the world's population. Other arguments having to do with military implications also were proffered.

Supporters of the plan to deploy the missiles in Utah and Nevada mustered as arguments the topographic and geologic advantages of the region . . . its sparse population . . . the considerable economic benefits . . . and strategic advantages to the national defense.

As with the proposed Kaiparowits power project, which also occasioned years of study, media coverage, speculation and debate *(Tour No. 9),* announced plans for the MX missile deployment came to naught—at least for the immediate future. In late 1981, President Ronald Reagan abandoned the shell-game concept of basing in Utah and Nevada. Utah's future role, if any, remains indefinite at this writing.

From junctions 27 and 37 miles west of Hinckley, unpaved sideroads fork north from US 6-50 to Whirlwind Valley, and to the Drum and House mountain ranges.

Notch Peak in the House Range, looming above the highway at Skull Rock Pass, is a western landmark all the way from Delta, its notched silhouette dominating the skyline. Reputed to be the largest limestone monolith in Utah, the huge massif towers 5,000 feet above its base in White Valley to the west, reaching an altitude of 9,700 feet and presenting on the west a series of great precipices. The **House Range,** particularly its steep western face, displays a magnificent exposure of layered sedimentary rocks of very ancient Cambrian age, into which igneous material has intruded. Like the nearby Drum Mountains, Notch Peak is noted for weird underground noises. To the north of Notch Peak, the grand dome of **Swazey Peak** (9,700 alt.) marks an area famed as a fruitful source of fossil trilobites. As described in the 1941 edition, "a surveying party found well-preserved fossil trilobites around the peak in 1870."

Remains of the extinct beetlelike marine creatures of the middle Cambrian period, more than 430 million years old, were thickly strewn in tiny reefs of rocks. Perfect specimens ranged in size from one-sixteenth of an inch to two inches long. Scientists tried for more than fifty years to relocate the deposit, which was rediscovered by Frank Beckwith, Sr., of Delta, in 1927. Another deposit was subsequently found at Blue Knoll near Antelope Springs *(see below)*. More than 3,300 specimens, of different species, some of them extremely rare, were sent to the Smithsonian Institution.

Antelope Springs issues from the hillside above a CCC camp, at 23 m., on the main side road. Near here Arm Nay, early-day bad man, occupied a cave known as Robber's Roost. Part of the old corral, in which stolen livestock was kept, is still standing.

The **Confusion** and **Conger** ranges—relatively barren jumbles of warped strata and other geological curiosities—are the westernmost of Utah's mountains in this region. Along the Utah-Nevada border, the grand expanse of Snake Valley stretches for a hundred miles or so, its northern end emptying into Great Salt Lake Desert at Callao.

Despite its desolate appearance, **Snake Valley** supports scattered ranches and small agricultural settlements such as Gandy, Trout Creek, and Eskdale. Because of its isolation, the valley is home for unorthodox religious groups who find it possible to observe their tenets here in relative peace and obscurity. Among these are practitioners of plural marriage in the **Partoun** area, and members of the communal Order of Aaron, a Christian sect modeled after Hutterite communes of the mid-west, at **Eskdale.** "Modern-day Levites," the Order of Aaron was founded in 1942 by the late Maurice L. Glendinning. Eskdale was settled by members a few years later in the 1950s. Residents live in individual houses but join in community dining, which begins with scripture, song and prayer. There is no individual ownership of property. The community is largely self-supporting, operating a prosperous dairy farm as well as a bakery, laundry, orchard, and farms. Emphasis is placed on learning: children attend school from pre-kindergarten through grade 12, and graduates are encouraged to attend college. Labor is considered a religious obligation. Though small, fewer than 100, the community supports a 35-piece symphony orchestra and two choirs.

Near Gandy is **Crystal Cave,** also known as Crystal Ball Cave, which features an underground display said to rival or excel that of nearby Lehman Caves National Monument in Nevada. The cave is on private land but is available for tours by local arrangement.

US 6-50 crosses the Utah-Nevada line near Baker and **Lehman Caves National Monument** in Nevada, 67 m. east of Ely. Southward, State 21 wends its way through broad valleys and low mountain passes to Milford. *See Tour No. 4B(2) below.*

Tour No. 4B(2) - Interstate Highway 15/US Highway 91 from Santaquin Junction south to Cove Fort and junction with I-70

From Santaquin Junction southward the highway passes over a low ridge marking the drainage divide between Utah Valley and Juab Valley. The huge bulk of **Nebo massif** forms the eastern horizon for 20 miles, cresting in hoary, multiple summits near Mona, 7,000 precipitous feet higher than the valley at their base. One of these crests, Mt. Nebo proper, has an altitude of 11,877 feet; but an unnamed sister peak to the north, at 11,928 feet, is the highest summit in the Wasatch Range. The Nebo massif marks the southwestern terminus of the Rocky Mountain Province in Utah.

The small town of **MONA** (4,900 alt. 536 pop.), cradled near the center of the valley, has been bypassed by the highway. In the 1941 edition it was described as "remarkable for its late mornings—Mount Nebo, directly east . . . rises almost from Mona back yards, and withholds the sun for almost an hour after towns elsewhere in Utah have had their sunrise." Mona Reservoir extends along the valley floor to the north.

NEPHI (5,100 alt. 3,285 pop.) is the seat of Juab County and a regional commercial center. As late as the early 1980s it was one of the few cities along the route of I-15/US 91 in Utah not yet bypassed by the interstate highway; in 1981 as in 1941 "the highway is the town's main thoroughfare. . . ." Nephi's varied economy is based on highway traffic, farming, small manufacturing, trading and a little mining. A rubber-products plant has been an important economic factor for 35 years. Nephi's noted Ute Stampede, held every year in July for half a century, features a parade and a popular rodeo that attracts visitors from far and near. The following is from the 1941 edition:

> The city was settled in 1851, fortified with a moated wall, and named for the patriarch who in the Book of Mormon came with his family from Judea to the

Mount Nebo and Nephi from the southwest (January).

WARD ROYLANCE

Americas in the time of the Babylonian captivity. Nephi's most important early event was the making of peace between Brigham Young and Chief Walker (Ute, Wah-kar-ar, yellow), somewhere near the city in 1854. According to S. N. Carvalho, who was present, Young, accompanied by 50 mounted men and 100 wagon loads of curious settlers, came to Walker's camp. After a day of preliminary oratory and gifts, Walker began plaintively: "Sometimes Wakara take his young men and go far away to sell horses. When he is gone, Americats come kill his wife and children. Why no come fight when Wakara home?" But he concluded: "Wakara no want fight Mormonee. If Indian kill white man again, Wakara make Indian howl." There was consistent peace until 1865. After 1900, with development of dry-farm techniques, immense tracts in the hill country west of Nephi were put under cultivation, and the town grew as a shipping point for livestock and grain.

Part of the old Salt Creek Fort, dating from the 1850s, is preserved in the city park. The original fort, built of gravel, mud and straw, enclosed nine blocks with 12-foot walls. Architecture and history buffs are rewarded by examples of 19th century architecture ranging from log cabins through adobe, frame, brick and stone structures. Among the more imposing sites are: the 25-room **Whitmore Mansion** (1898-1900), 106 S. Main, a three-story edifice of brick and stone, restored in recent years by the Bendoski family, "built in Eastlake/Queen Anne style—with all the ornamentation, shingles, finials, moldings, carved panels, friezes, and balusters that characterize the style" (National Register description) . . . **Booth House,** 94 W. 300 South, late 19th century Victorian residence (National Register).

East from Nephi, State 132 winds through scenic Salt Creek Canyon to Fountain Green, Moroni and US 89 in Sanpete Valley *(see Tour No. 7A).* **Salt Creek Canyon** forms the boundary between the Rocky Mountain and Colorado Plateau provinces in Utah, a division more apparent to geologists than to laymen. Six miles east of Nephi a partially paved sideroad forks north from State 132 into Uinta National Forest and alpine heights of the Nebo massif. This is the **Nebo Loop Road,** described in *Tour No. 5,* a visually and emotionally stirring scenic drive which can be entered or terminated either here, or near Santaquin or in Payson. The **Bear Canyon-Cottonwood-Ponderosa forest campground complex** (Uinta National Forest), 11 m. and 12 m. from Nephi, is near this road *(tables, toilets, water, trailer spaces).* In the vicinity of the turnoff of Nebo Loop Road from State 132 is a picturesque alcove of eroded forms, corridors and chambers described by J. Cecil Alter in *Through the Heart of the Scenic West.* Alter applied the name **Temple of the Sand Pillars,** writing that Indian legend connected this area with Maple Canyon near Moroni *(see Tour No. 7A);* they avoided it as a dwelling place of ghostly figures.

West from Nephi, State 132 leads to Leamington and to US 6 at Lynndyl *(see Tour No. 4B(1) above).*

South of Nephi, I-15/US 91 skirts a sloping terrace known as **Levan Ridge.** Extending both north and south of Levan, this foothill terrace provides a bountiful harvest of dry-land (non-irrigated) grain. Only a few places in Utah are suitable for dry-land agriculture. Levan Ridge's suitability was discovered accidentally by a Nephi rancher, David Broadhead, who found during a drouth year in the 1880s that grain would grow without irrigation. Declaring this on a homestead application, he was indicted for perjury. Acquitted, Broadhead thereafter named his operation Perjury Farm, and in subsequent years the entire ridge became utilized for dry-land farming.

LEVAN (5,200 alt. 453 pop.) is a farming village at the junction of US 91 and State 28. Side streets still proffer nostalgic glimpses into Utah's small-town rural past, with tree-shaded yards and modest homes of varied styles, weary outbuildings and tottering fences, some a hundred years old or more. The impressive **Mormon chapel,** a registered historic site, dates from 1904. Built of cream white brick with stone foundation, the structure is distinctive for its unusually long rows of pews and large Gothic windows on the sides rather than the ends. Levan was the boyhood home of Willard E. Christiansen, later known as Matt Warner the outlaw. For some years during the 1880s and 1890s Warner was an associate of Butch Cassidy and Tom McCarty, both notorious bank and train robbers. In 1889, he participated with them in a lucrative bank robbery at Telluride, Colorado, and engaged in other robberies as well as cattle rustling. After serving a penitentiary term between 1896 and 1900, Warner went straight, eventually becoming city marshal and justice of the peace in Carbon County *(see Tour No. 10A).*

Near Levan is a large coal handling installation, opened in 1980, capable of loading 4,000 tons of coal per hour into a moving train of 85 coal cars, each having a capacity of 100 tons. The coal is brought to Levan by truck from mines in Salina Canyon, then carried by train and ship to the west coast and Japan.

Turn south from Levan via State 28 to Gunnison and US 89 in Sevier Valley, passing through an area of widespreading dry-farms with expansive Great Basin views. Sevier Bridge Reservoir is glimpsed enroute, filling the valley of Sevier River for many miles. State 28 carries a heavy volume of truck traffic, including mammoth trailers loaded with coal from Salina Canyon—destined for Levan *(above)*—and trucks piled high with plaster wallboard from the gypsum mills at Sigurd.

In 1941 the main north-south highway crossed Yuba Dam, which forms Sevier Bridge Reservoir on the Sevier River. Realignments in later years moved US 91/I-15 farther downstream, to the west. **Sevier Bridge Reservoir,** known more popularly as Yuba Dam Lake, is a fluctuating body of water which may extend 15 miles upstream at times. Near the dam, several miles from the highway, the State Division of Parks and Recreation maintains **YUBA LAKE STATE RECREATION AREA,** developed with facilities for camping and boating.

SCIPIO (5,300 alt. 257 pop.) is near the junction of I-15 and US 50. An agricultural town, Scipio has a pleasant location in Round Valley under the nestling peaks of the Canyon, Valley, and Pavant mountains. The area's hillsides and bottomlands support herds of livestock, fields of hay and grain. In 1866, a year after the Black Hawk Indian War had begun in central Utah, a large band of Black Hawk's warriors came into Round Valley, killed two men, and drove off about 500 head of cattle and horses. Soon afterwards several military detachments were in pursuit, making contact with the raiders at Gravelly Ford in Sevier County, where a battle ensued. Black Hawk was wounded in the battle, but apparently the stock was not recovered.

Turn south from Scipio Junction via US 50 to **Salina** and junction there with US 89 and I-70 *(see Tour No. 7A).* Enroute the highway passes through a sparsely settled countryside of scattered farms and rangelands.

West of Scipio Junction the highway surmounts **Scipio Pass,** a low divide between the rugged Canyon Range to the north and Pavant Range or Plateau to the south. At the summit of Scipio Pass a monument commemorates passage here in 1776 of the **Dominguez-Escalante expedition** *(see History).*

This small party of explorers consisted of a dozen Spaniards and New Mexicans, including the Franciscan fathers Dominguez and Escalante, cartographer Miera y Pacheco, and others who served as soldiers, servants and interpreters. Enroute they engaged Indians as guides. The expedition's purpose was to find a suitable northern route connecting Santa Fe, New Mexico, with the newly-founded Spanish settlement at Monterey, California. Leaving Santa Fe in late July, 1776, the party traveled far northward, skirting the forbidding canyon country, entering Utah near Vernal and eventually reaching Utah Valley and Utah Lake. Their route southward from Utah Valley to Scipio Pass is paralleled roughly by today's I-15/US 91. On September 29, 1776, near the present site of Levan, they encountered six friendly Indians, with whom they talked. Shortly thereafter they "met an old Indian of venerable appearance. He was alone in a little hut, and his beard was so thick and long that he looked like one of the hermits of Europe." On that same day they arrived at the Sevier River, a short distance downstream from today's Yuba Dam. Not being familiar with the stream, they assumed—not without serious doubts—that it was the San Buenaventura (Green River) which they had previously crossed near Vernal. Though they named it the Rio de Santa Ysabel, Miera showed the Sevier as an extension of the San Buenaventura on his map, thereby confusing mapmakers and travelers for the next half-century. While camped on the Sevier a number of Indians joined them, "wrapped in blankets made of the skins of rabbits and hares . . . These people here have much heavier beards than the Lagunas. . . . In features they look more like Spaniards than like the other Indians hitherto known in America . . . At this river and place of Santa Ysabel this tribe of bearded Indians begins." (The Sanpitch and Pahvant Utes or Paiutes of this area did grow beards and mustaches into historic times. Kanosh, chief of the Pahvants during the early Mormon period, wore a long mustache.) From the Sevier River the expedition continued south into Round Valley, where they camped on September 30, and on October 1 they crossed Scipio Pass into Pahvant Valley ("a vast plain surrounded by sierras"). There they had difficulty finding fresh water but were aided by local Indians, some of whom "had such long beards that they looked like Capuchin or Bethlemite fathers." To them as to the natives of Utah Valley the fathers taught their gospel and promised to return with more religious teachers. The route of the Dominguez-Escalante expedition in Pahvant Valley generally followed that of today's State Highway 257, described in Tour No. 4B(1) above.

I-15 drops from Scipio Pass into **Pahvant Valley,** the bed of ancient Lake Bonneville *(see tour above).* **Pahvant Butte,** the crater of an inactive volcano, juts from the floor of the valley—truly "a vast plain"—and extensive lava flows are scattered about. Father Escalante described the plain as "In most places . . . very short of pasturage and although two rivers enter it . . . we saw no place whatever suitable for settlement." Despite his negative assessment, Mormon pioneers of the 1850s and 1860s made the land blossom, not alone along the mountain front to the east but out in mid-valley as well. *(Pahvant also is spelled Pavant and Pah Vant, and in territorial days as Pauvan. It derives from the name of the native Indians, the Pah Vanduts or "water people.")*

HOLDEN (5,100 alt. 364 pop.), an agricultural village with pioneer origins, now marks the junction of I-15 with US 50. US 50 veers northwest to Delta and a junction there with US 6. According to the 1941 edition, Holden "seems to have been settled on the pioneer maxim that where sage grows well, crops will thrive. Sagebrush stands about Holden, especially to the north and west, are jungle-thick and sometimes grow higher than a man's head, but the water supply has strictly limited the extent of cultivation." West of Holden is an extensive area of white drift sand.

FILLMORE (5,100 alt. 2,083 pop.) is the seat of Millard County and the largest community along the highway between Nephi and Cedar City, a distance of nearly 200 miles. No longer is it the town of 40 years ago, when "'Levi's', five-gallon hats, and peg-heeled cow-punchers' boots are common habiliments" and "saddled cayuses hitched outside" were common sights along main street. Yet, though costumes and transportation have changed, Fillmore still remains a commercial center for a vast farming and livestock region.

Fillmore was named and designated as the seat of territorial government even before the town had been settled, namely in October 1851, when the townsite was personally selected by Governor Brigham Young and other dignitaries. The Pahvant Valley was chosen as the capital site because of its location in the approximate center of vast Utah Territory, which at that time extended about 800 miles from the Sierra Nevada on the west to the Rocky Mountains on the east, and some 400 miles from north to south. Colonization began immediately after site selection.

Territorial State House State Historical Monument (Old State House) is maintained by the State Division of Parks and Recreation as a museum and visitor center. A curious two-story, red stone structure in the central city park, the Old State House served as Utah's first territorial capitol, and is one of the very few public buildings of its age still extant in Utah. It was designed by Truman O. Angell, architect of the Mormon temple and tabernacle in Salt Lake City, and was intended to be a large domed structure with four wings in the form of a cross—grandiose enough to serve as the state house of an immense territory which at that time included not only present-day Utah but all of Nevada and parts of Colorado and Wyoming as well.

Old State House in Fillmore (Territorial State Historical Monument).

WARD ROYLANCE

However, only one wing—the present State House—was actually completed. This housed the Fifth Session of the territorial Legislature in December 1855. Only two brief sessions were held in the building thereafter, the Legislature adjourning from Fillmore to Salt Lake City for the remainder of its business. Reasons for this abandonment include refusal of the federal government to appropriate funds for completion of the building (due in part to strained Mormon-federal relations) . . . the lack of suitable accommodations in pioneer Fillmore . . . the difficulty of traveling between Salt Lake City and Fillmore in mid-winter, when legislative sessions were scheduled . . . and the overriding practicality of Salt Lake City as the more suitable seat of government.

Construction began in 1852, reaching a climax of frenzied activity by December 1855 when the Legislature met in Fillmore for the first time. The following year, in December 1856, it met in the State House only long enough to pass a resolution changing the seat of government to Great Salt Lake City, thereafter adjourning to that place. Due to legal misinterpretation and misunderstanding, it met once more in Fillmore, but only briefly and for the last time. This was in December 1858. In subsequent years the State House was used by local government offices, for school classes, dances, religious and public meetings, and even as a jail. Title was transferred from the federal government to Fillmore City in the 1890s, and to the state in 1927. During interim years it had deteriorated badly. After 1927 state funds were used for renovation, while the Daughters of the Utah Pioneers undertook the task of collecting museum materials and arranging them for exhibit. With support from numerous organizations and individuals, including Governor George H. Dern, the State House was opened and dedicated as a museum in July 1930. Over the next 30 years it was operated and supported largely by the Daughters of the Utah Pioneers, with modest financial aid from the state. Since 1957, when the building came under control of the State Park and Recreation Commission, more state funds have become available for personnel and maintenance. In general, the building itself is a state concern while the relics are the responsibility of the Daughters of the Utah Pioneers. These treasures— gathered over many years from countless donors—comprise one of Utah's most valuable historical collections. Included are pioneer furniture and furnishings, photographs, musical instruments, paintings and sculpture, and Indian artifacts. *Open daily.*

The story of Chief Kanosh and his Pahvant band *(see Kanosh below)* has been romanticized in a dramatic and musical pageant, held each August during Millard County Fair Days. Presented in the Old Capitol Amphitheater at Fillmore—a Bicentennial project—the pageant has been an annual affair since 1978.

Fillmore was the birthplace of many who attained prominence in later life. Among these was William H. King, a member of the United States Senate from 1917 to 1941 (four terms); his son David S. King, a congressional Representative; and Culbert A. Olson, one-time governor of California. Examples of noteworthy architecture abound in Fillmore, a number of sites remarkable enough for inclusion on national and state historic registers. Among them: (1) **Huntsman-Nielsen Home,** 155 W. Center, built in 1871-75 of red brick and sandstone, two-story in style described as "Early New England Colonial"; (2)**Edward Partridge Home,** stone 1871; (3) **Rock Schoolhouse,** northeast corner First South and First West, built in 1867.

Turn east from Fillmore to **Chalk Creek Canyon,** "a steep-walled ravine densely clad with cottonwood, maple, box elder, and oak brush." Fishlake National Forest maintains four developed picnic areas in the canyon.

On the flat valley floor west of Fillmore, Meadow, and Kanosh is an extensive area of diversified igneous phenomena, now dormant but active in fairly recent ages. Known as the **MILLARD VOLCANIC FIELD,** the area includes the grand volcanic crater of Pahvant Butte as well as less imposing craters, lava fields, hot springs and ice caves representing eruptions occurring over a long period of time. A Utah Travel Council publication describes them as follows:

Nearest to Fillmore (10 m. west) are the **Ice Spring craters,** surrounded by a large field of basaltic lava. Several miles south of this field is **Tabernacle Crater,** also surrounded by basalt. Several prominent volcanic buttes lie west of Kanosh, and a huge crater—**Pahvant (Pavant) Butte**— is situated in a broad valley some ten miles north of the Ice Spring lava field. South of Deseret is flat-topped **Dunderberg Butte,** which is probably the eroded remnant of a volcanic cone. North of the Millard volcanic field, in Juab County, is the famed **Hot Plug** or **Fumarole Butte** *[see Tour No. 4B(1) above].* There are also a number of less extensive lava fields in the area.

The Ice Spring craters are particularly noteworthy, consisting as they do of at least 12 colorful, overlapping, closely grouped craters. . . . Ask in Fillmore for road instructions. These volcanic fields and craters are easily reached by improved roads and are particularly interesting for hikers and photographers.

South of the Fillmore interchange, I-15 passes across the valley floor several miles west of the foothills where US 91, the former main highway, takes a more circuitous route through Meadow and Kanosh. West of Kanosh, at the south end of Pahvant Valley, I-15 bisects the imposing **Black Rock volcanic field.** Here a turnoff viewpoint provides far-spreading views across the vast valley, surrounded by or containing at least a dozen different mountain ranges, all of which can be seen from this one overview point.

KANOSH (5,100 alt. 435 pop.) is a small farming town that received its name from Indian chief Kanosh. Settled in 1859, Kanosh was known first as Corn Creek. Near here lived **Chief Kanosh** and his band of Pahvants, known variously throughout the years both as Utes and Paiutes. The distinction is too technical for these pages. A renegade group of Pahvants was responsible for the Gunnison Massacre of 1853 *(see Tour 4B(1) above),* but generally the band was friendly to whites in pioneer days. Kanosh was their leader during the early decades of Mormon colonization. Kanosh joined the Mormon Church in his later years and took as one of his wives an Indian girl by the name of Sally, who had been a maid in Brigham Young's home. Sally had learned the white man's ways during her years in the Young household, and it was a heavy cross for her to bear when she was forced to revert to the life offered by Kanosh. Local people say that she died not long after her marriage, of a broken heart. Eventually Kanosh forsook his old life to a degree, condescending to wear white man's clothes and live in a log house. He died in 1881 and was given a Mormon funeral with Christian burial in the Kanosh cemetery.

A photographic portrait of Kanosh reveals a dignified mien that would do justice to a Spanish don. More than a few intriguing tales have come down through history about this remarkable man. One recites how he refused to leave his house to greet Brigham Young in his carriage, insisting that protocol demanded that Brigham Young dismount and enter his home for the meeting. Another story tells of Betsikin, an older wife, who secretly murdered Mary, a newer and younger love. The crime was discovered and Betsikin was given several choices by her people as to how she should die. Choosing death by starvation, she was then isolated in a wigwam about one mile north of present-day Kanosh on the west side of the highway. There she remained in loneliness until slow death ended her misery. The notorious **Walker (Wakara),** about whom several books have been written, died on Meadow Creek in this vicinity in January 1855. He was buried in a secret grave in the cliffs east of

Meadow, with sacrificial ceremonies considered barbaric by white pioneers. An Indian boy and girl are said to have been buried alive nearby, and a number of horses were killed. Charles Kelly, who visited the site in this century, found the grave empty. He was told by local Indian guides that it had been robbed about 1909.

A number of Pahvants continue to reside at least now and then on the **KANOSH INDIAN RESERVATION** near Meadow and Kanosh. In 1954 a congressional bill terminated the tribal status of Utah's five Paiute bands: Kanosh, Koosharem, Shivwits, Cedar City, Indian Peaks. Sponsors of the bill believed that termination would speed integration of the Paiutes into non-Indian society. By the late 1970s, however, results were so unsatisfactory that leaders of the Paiutes, who number about 500, were urging restoration of the original status. Tribal status was restored in 1980, entitling Paiutes to assistance in education, job training, and other social services. Remaining tribal land, which had declined from 43,000 acres to 27,000 acres since 1954, was placed in trust.

South of Pahvant Valley the highway enters a rugged region of low, dark, volcanic hills wooded with pinyon pines and junipers—the latter a name hardly ever used by westerners, who prefer the term cedar. Massive slopes of the Tushar Range or Plateau soon come into view, looming high above Cove Fort.

COVE FORT (6,000 alt.) was a welcome waystation on the Salt Lake-Los Angeles road for a hundred years after it was built in 1867. For the past 10 or 15 years, however, it has been bypassed by most travelers, who glimpse it from a distance. I-15 and I-70 join in the vicinity of the old fort, which is near the western entrance to Clear Creek Canyon *(see Tour No. 7A)*. In 1941, Cove Fort consisted of "a barn, farmhouse, and service station facing the well-preserved Mormon fort, walled with volcanic rock." Little has changed since then. The old stone fort lies in a small valley under the dark peaks of Cove Mountain. Built in 1867 by Ira N. Hinckley for the Mormon Church, the fort is very well preserved with walls measuring 100 feet square and 13 feet high. It is said that the fort's construction cost the Church some $20,000; and though it never witnessed an actual Indian war, the fort served as a convenient stop for stages, mail riders, and thousands of travelers including the Brigham Young parties which journeyed south to Dixie every winter or so. *The fort is privately maintained as a museum; admission charge.*

East from Cove Fort Junction, I-70/State 4 winds through rugged terrain to a junction with US 89 at Sevier *(see Tour No. 7A)*. Construction on the interstate highway in this vicinity is not expected to be completed for some years. The superb white massifs of Belknap and Baldy peaks loom in startling majesty from one viewpoint, while intricately sculptured volcanic cliffs also help to make this stretch of highway one of Utah's most scenic drives.

A few miles south of Cove Fort, in the eastern foothills, is **SULPHUR-DALE,** the site of sulphur mining operations since the 1880s when sulphur was mined for use in gunpowder and sugar refining. Intermixed with sand and lapilli, the sulphur here has accumulated in large quantities around an ancient volcanic cone. Drilling operations have disclosed proved reserves of several million tons of sulphur-rich rock in the vicinity, leading to a million-dollar extraction facility in the 1950s. This proved unprofitable, however, and was sold. Other attempts at commercial production have been made.

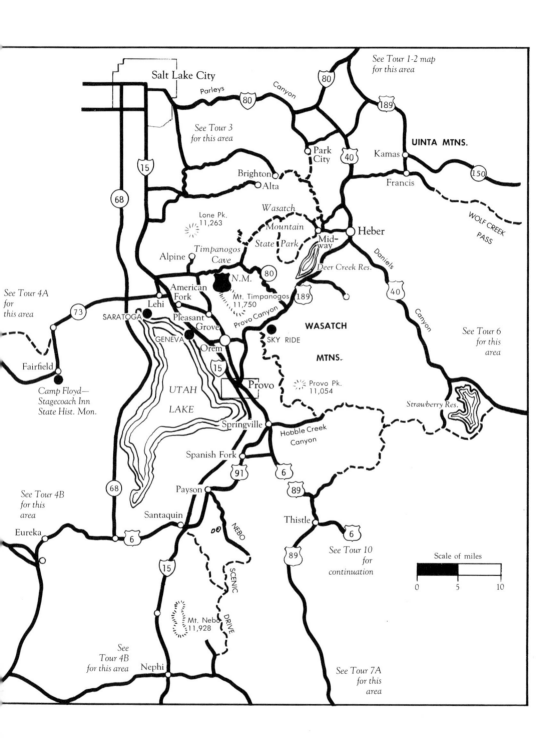

Salt Lake City

Parleys Canyon

See Tour 1-2 map
for this area

UINTA MTNS.

See Tour 3
for this area

Park City

Kamas

Francis

WOLF CREEK PASS

Brighton
Alta

Lone Pk.
11,263

Wasatch

Mountain

State Park

Midway

Heber

Timpanogos
Cave

Deer Creek Res.

Daniels

Alpine

N.M.

Mt. Timpanogos
11,750

American Fork

Lehi

SARATOGA

Pleasant Grove

GENEVA

Orem

Provo Canyon

WASATCH

SKY RIDE

MTNS.

See Tour 4A
for
this area

Fairfield

Camp Floyd—
Stagecoach Inn
State Hist. Mon.

UTAH LAKE

Provo

Provo Pk.
11,054

Strawberry Res.

See Tour 6
for this
area

Springville

Hobble Creek
Canyon

Spanish Fork

Payson

See Tour 4B
for this
area

Eureka

Santaquin

Thistle

NEBO

See Tour 10
for
continuation

Mt. Nebo
11,928

SCENIC DRIVE

See
Tour 4B
for this area

Nephi

See Tour 7A
for this
area

Scale of miles

0   5   10

Tour No. 5
MOUNTAINLANDS REGION
(Summit, Utah and Wasatch counties)

This tour region encompasses parts of Utah's two highest mountain ranges—the southern Wasatch and western Uinta—as well as Utah Valley, Heber Valley, and intermontane valleys of the Provo and Weber rivers. The main north-south artery through Utah Valley is Interstate Highway 15. Mountain valleys to the east are accessible via I-80, US 189, State 150, and several other roads.

Point of the Mountain is the popular name for the natural divide between Salt Lake and Utah valleys, a low barrier known technically as the Traverse Mountains. Formed of ancient rocks, upon which Lake Bonneville's currents deposited terraced spits of gravel, the **Traverse Mountains** are a geological link between the Wasatch and Oquirrh ranges. This link has been bisected by the **Jordan River,** which flows northward from Utah Valley through a channel known as the Jordan Narrows. No road follows the Jordan through the Narrows, but I-15 and State 68 flank the river on either side at higher elevations.

Said the 1941 edition: "The obvious parallel between the Utah river, which flows from fresh-water Utah Lake to salt-water Great Salt Lake, and

Utah Valley and Mount Timpanogos, looking east. Geneva Steel Works is in the middle distance, Pleasant Grove *(left)* and Orem *(right),* beyond.

the Jordan River of the Holy Land, which flows from fresh Galilee to the Dead Sea, impressed itself on Mormon explorers, who called the Utah river the 'Western Jordan'."

From Point of the Mountain, 500 feet above Utah Lake, highway travelers can view **Utah Valley** in its mountain-girt entirety. It is seen to be an enclosed basin of irregular shape, measuring about 40 miles from north to south and 15 miles from east to west, containing in its bottom the largest natural, fresh-water lake solely in Utah. On a clear and sparkling day it is easy to agree with Miera's appraisal of the valley in his 1777 report to the King of Spain, wherein he termed it "the most pleasing, beautiful, and fertile site in all New Spain." Mount Timpanogos dominates the eastern skyline with its immense flat-topped bulk, flanked by sister peaks that are hardly subordinate in alpine beauty. Mount Nebo, highest of all, looms apart on the southern horizon.

In 1941, when this volume's first edition appeared, Utah Valley was a tranquil vale with a population of some 60,000. Communities were separate and distinct, the majority of them strung out along US Highways 91-89. Agriculture was the most important industry. Brigham Young University enrolled about 2,800 students and Geneva Steel Works were only barely under consideration. The snowy summits of the giant peaks could be seen with crisp clarity during most days of the year.

Since those halcyon times the valley has been transformed. Its population has soared to more than 200,000, with no limit yet in sight. Some communities are distinguishable only by name, their formal boundaries absorbed by urban sprawl. Main Street no longer is the principal through-highway, and agriculture has become a secondary industry. The student enrollment of Brigham Young University approximates 29,000, or ten times that of 40 years ago. Having lived an industrial lifetime in 40 years, the great steel works at Geneva now approach a precarious old age. And, sad to say, the magnificent encircling peaks—and the valley itself—seldom can be seen with the pristine clarity that prevailed in 1941. *(In terms of population, Utah County is almost identical with Utah Valley. The county's population in 1980 was 217,281. As a standard metropolitan statistical area, it ranked 9th in the nation in rate of population growth during the 1970s.)*

Utah County possesses one of the densest concentrations of active and dedicated Mormons in the world. About 80 per cent of the county's population is listed on Mormon Church membership rolls, compared with a state average of 70 per cent. In significant ways the county is a living model of Mormon ideals and worldly achievement, on display for the closest scrutiny. Here, perhaps to a greater extent than elsewhere, Mormonism has found it possible to practice what it teaches with little adverse impact from outside influences. Visitors may judge the results from the county's visible indices of culture—its communities, homes, parks, schools, ecological balance, industry, dress, personal behavior, etc. Less obvious indicators, such as social relationships and mores, require more serious observation and study. Even the most enthusiastic boosters would not be unanimous in their praise, of course, but it would be difficult to deny that the county represents much that is considered good by the majority of Americans. One aspect of the local culture that becomes increasingly controversial is the county's astronomical birthrate of 40 births per 1,000 population—one of the highest birthrates of any locality in the nation, a third higher than the state average, and nearly three times that of the nation as a whole.

Mormons were the first whites to settle Utah Valley, in 1849, two years after their arrival in Salt Lake Valley. Long before that, however, the valley was visited by the Dominguez-Escalante expedition in 1776 *(see History)*. The New Mexican party entered the valley on September 23, departing several days later after a peaceful visit with the Indians. "The Timpanogotzis," wrote Escalante in his journal, "were so-called from the lake on which they live, which they call Timpanogo, and this is the special name of this lake. . . ." Many of the Indians displayed heavy beards. Escalante wrote enthusiastically of the valley's advantages for settlement: its spacious land, the lake which abounded in fish, geese, beaver and other animals, "plentiful firewood and timber, sheltered places, water and pasturage for raising cattle and horses." Travelers from New Mexico returned to the valley or its vicinity in subsequent years, as traders, trappers and slavers if not as missionaries and settlers. Among these was Etienne Provost (Provot), a French-Canadian trapper based at Taos, New Mexico. In 1824 Provost and a dozen or so other mountain men explored the Uinta Basin, followed Provo River to Utah Lake, and were attacked somewhere in the Wasatch region by Snake Indians. Seven of the party were killed. Provost returned to Utah with a larger party in 1825. Anglicized phonetically, his name eventually was applied to Provo River and Provo City, though the river was commonly known as the Timpanogos for years after Mormon settlement.

Provo was settled in 1849 as the first Mormon community in Utah Valley, and before 1850 had ended settlers were living on the sites—among others—of Lehi, Pleasant Grove, American Fork, Springville, and Payson. In short, the valley was settled within three years of Mormon arrival in Utah. During the years since then it has continued to rank as the state's second or third most populous valley.

Before establishment of the Geneva Steel Works during the early 1940s, Utah Valley was one of the state's most productive breadbaskets. In this respect it still occupies an important position, but not to the same extent. As population has grown, land formerly devoted to crops, orchards, and livestock has been converted to residential, industrial and commercial uses. Today, as an industry, agriculture in Utah County ranks far below manufacturing, trade, services (including private education), and government in the amount of money involved.

Manufacturing, services, and trade are the county's foremost industries, both in terms of total employment and personal income. Services (including private education) employ the most people, while manufacturing contributes the most personal income. Geneva Works of U.S. Steel Corporation, of course, is the single largest manufacturing industry, employing more than 5,000 workers. In addition to Geneva there are more than 200 other manufacturing plants in Utah County, producing a wide variety of products. Most of these are of modest size (under 50 employees), yet a number are fairly large—for example, firms that manufacture fabricated metal products, explosives, clothing, wood products, and electronics.

Brigham Young University, with its enormous student body and staff, is of inestimable worth to the county's economy. Not only does the university contribute millions of dollars in salary income to county residents, but its operations affect such other economic activities as construction, trade, finance, transportation, communications, services and government.

Tour No. 5A - Utah Valley and Wasatch Mountain Drives

At a junction 2 m. south of Point of the Mountain, turn east from I-15 on State 80 to Alpine, American Fork Canyon, Timpanogos Cave National Monument, and Alpine Scenic Drive.

ALPINE (4,950 alt. 2,649 pop.) is a residential and farming community nestled in a coved corner of Utah Valley. Soaring 6,000 precipitous feet above the town on two sides are giant massifs of the Wasatch Range, supplying to Alpine an environment that resembles parts of Switzerland. The gaping maw of American Fork Canyon opens a mile away to the southeast. The town's inspirational setting is a beacon for esthetes, resulting in the founding of a resident art colony known as North Mountain in recent years *(see The Arts)*. A sculpture garden is under development, and an art center is being constructed. Contemporary structures built by a growing populace overshadow in sheer quantity Alpine's 19th century architecture, but some interesting early examples can still be seen. Among these are a number of antique homes (Alpine was settled in 1850). The **Relic Hall** of the Daughters of Utah Pioneers dates from 1857-63, a venerable building that has served as a chapel, school, recreation and civic center, city hall, and museum *(Historic register listing)*. Also listed on a historic register is the **Moyle Home and Tower** (800 North and 600 East on Grove Drive). The home was built of stone about 1858 with subsequent modification. Nearby is a ruined stone tower, built by the Moyle family in early days as a defense against Indians but never used for that purpose.

Trails lead from Alpine to **Lone Peak** and other lofty summits at 11,000 feet and more, as well as over a shoulder of **Box Elder Peak** (11,101 alt.) into American Fork Canyon. These trails provide some of the sublimest views in Utah. Wasatch peaks of the Utah Valley area—as those in Salt Lake Valley and northward—are becoming

Wasatch peaks from Alpine.

WARD ROYLANCE

American Fork Canyon from the trail to Timpanogos Cave.

increasingly popular for recreational hiking and serious climbing. Most summits are attainable by persons in good health, in a single day or two at most, and well-worn trails lead to the better-known heights. There are many trail possibilities and combinations. Hikers are advised to make use of detailed forest maps or trail guidebooks, such as the trail series issued by Wasatch Publishers of Salt Lake City.

AMERICAN FORK CANYON is a profound gorge separating Mount Timpanogos from the Box Elder Peak massif. A true chasm, it ranks with Big and Little Cottonwood canyons in awesome grandeur and depth. For several miles, walls rise steeply on either side for thousands of feet. The Visitor Center of **Timpanogos Cave National Monument** is located beside State 80 in the depths of the canyon, 3 m. east of its mouth (4 m. from Alpine Junction). The cave itself requires a steep 1½-mile climb by foot trail to the cave entrance. *See Timpanogos Cave National Monument.* Refreshments are available at the lower parking area during summer months, and a number of sites for camping and picnicking have been developed along the road by Uinta National Forest.

The road forks 7 m. east of Alpine Junction, about 3 m. from the Monument Visitor Center. Turn left (north) along the main canyon to **Tibble Fork Reservoir** and summer home area. At the reservoir *(trout fishing)* the road forks again. One paved spur (left) leads to **Granite Flat Campground** of Uinta National Forest, in a superlative forest setting overlooked by soaring peaks. An unpaved spur of this side-road winds in dizzy switchbacks to the **Silver Flat Reservoir** and summer home area, from which foot trails lead to **Silver Lake** and high peaks behind Alta. Alpine views from this road—especially of the majestic northeast face of Mount Timpanogos and American Fork Canyon—are indescribably grand, but this drive is not recommended for the timid. The main canyon road continues from Tibble Fork Reservoir along the bottom of American Fork Canyon, becoming rougher as it proceeds. About 5 m. from the reservoir is **Dutchman Flat**, in the 1870s and 1880s the site of **Forest City** mining camp. Only foundations and dumps remind visitors that several hundred people once lived here, and that mines continued to operate in the area until recent decades. A fork of this road to Dutchman Flat—negotiable by vehicles with adequate clearance—climbs eastward over a high ridge to **Snake Creek Canyon, Wasatch Mountain State Park, Cascade Springs, Midway, and Heber City.** *See Tour No. 5B.*

The main **ALPINE SCENIC DRIVE** (State 80) bears right (south) from the canyon junction several miles east of the cave Visitor Center. This paved but narrow

Northeast face of Mount Timpanogos from Alpine Scenic Drive.

road is normally open from May to late October. It climbs, dips and winds in sharp curves as it circles the east shoulder of **Mount Timpanogos** (11,750 alt.). Here the great mountain presents a complex facade that could hardly differ more dramatically from its west face. Glaciation has gouged out huge cirques or basins rimmed by grand precipices several thousand feet high. The scene is one of alpine majesty, reminiscent of the Canadian Rockies. *Caution: Keep far right on curves. Drive with utmost care!*

Several developed camping and picnicking sites (Uinta National Forest) are beside the road between American Fork Canyon and Provo Canyon, a distance of some 12 miles. From **Timpooneke Campground** an engineered foot trail leads to the summit of Mount Timpanogos, connecting with the trail from Aspen Grove *(below)*. Also from Timpooneke a fairweather dirt road winds around the north end of the peak to spectacular overlook points above Utah Valley. The **Ridge Trail,** a popular hiking route, forks from State 80 about a mile south of Timpooneke and follows a high ridge northward to connect with a network of other trails, as shown on detailed maps of Uinta National Forest. From a junction in this vicinity, **Cascade Scenic Drive** forks east to **Cascade Springs** in Uinta National Forest, a "retreat" that "offers boardwalks and trails over and around the startlingly beautiful springs and convenient rest areas and biological and geological information designed for a self-guided tour." From Cascade Springs the sideroad continues through **Wasatch Mountain State Park** to a junction with the Snake Creek Canyon road between Midway and American Fork Canyon *(see above)*.

From **Aspen Grove** a well-worn foot trail leads 6 m. to the 11,750-foot summit of Mount Timpanogos, where the eye encompasses a full-circle aerial sweep of thousands of square miles of jumbled topography. For more than 50 years—until the ecology was seriously threatened—Brigham Young University sponsored an annual hike along this trail to the mountain's crest. As many as 4,000 hikers participated, though perhaps only half managed to attain the top. The trail passes through the 11,000-acre **Mount Timpanogos Scenic Area,** retained by Uinta National Forest in "a nearly-pristine condition for the aesthetic and spiritual satisfaction of all of us, and of generations unborn." The scenic area embraces the mountain's famed "glacier" (a perpetual snowfield) as well as waterfalls, lakes, vegetation and wildlife such as mule deer, bobcat, porcupine, rodents, and golden eagle—at least 29 species of mammals and 54 species of birds.

Sundance Resort and residential area is beside the main drive about 2 m. south of Aspen Grove. Before 1968 Sundance was known as Timp Haven Resort. In that year it was purchased by actor-director Robert Redford and associates, who since have made improvements in ski runs and facilities. Redford and others have homes in the area, making ecological balance a prime concern in development. The resort features a full-service restaurant *(open all year),* chair lifts, ski school, rentals and sales, snack bar, and general store. Limited accommodations are available on site. More than 20 ski trails have been developed for varying levels of expertise. Sundance is locally popular for summer dining and performances of the **Sundance Theater.** Held during summer evenings, plays are performed on the stage of an open-air amphi-theater, to which spectators are conveyed in groups from the parking area. The resort is also a locus for hiking trails..

Alpine Scenic Drive joins US 189 in **Provo Canyon,** 3 m. from Sundance Resort, 12 m. from Provo, and 8 m. from Orem. *See Tour No. 5B below.*

From junction with State 80 (above), continue south 1 m. on I-15 to Lehi exit:

LEHI (4,550 alt. 6,848 pop.) was named for a Book of Mormon prophet and is pronounced *Lee-high.* Lehi is an attractive residential community based largely on farming, manufacturing and trade. Many of its people also commute to work in other places. Manufactured products include fire-bricks, explosives, travel trailers, furniture, and metal products. Said the 1941 edition: "Here, in 1890 [1891], the first successful sugar beet factory in the intermountain region was put in operation, and here also Isaac Good-win planted the first alfalfa seed in Utah. Beets and alfalfa have become major crops in the state. Lehi was hit hard by polygamy persecutions of the 1870's and 1880's, and many residents were forced into hiding. A small boy of Lehi, ordered by Federal officers to point out a polygamist, led them solemnly and with much cautious circumspection to a chicken run and pointed out a rooster."

Of architectural note in Lehi is the **Thomas Cutler Mansion,** 150 E. State, an elaborate residence built in 1875 and remodeled in 1898. Builder of the house was Thomas R. Cutler, manager of the big sugar factory in Lehi. Later its second floor served as Lehi's first hospital. The **Winn Home,** 192 N. 200 West, is a two-story adobe house with stucco exterior, built in 1859-60 by William H. Winn, who was mayor of Lehi, state legislator, businessman and church leader. Both buildings are listed on historic registers.

The **John Hutchings Museum of Natural History,** 685 N. Center, was built in the 1960s—as a community project—to house the diversified collections of the late John and Eunice Hutchings and their family. Among its many outstanding exhibits are relics of pioneer days, including furnishings and firearms . . . a multitude of Indian arrowpoints, spearheads, grinding stones, tools, utensils, baskets, and other Indian artifacts, principally from Utah Valley . . . seashells from various parts of the world . . . mounted birds and eggs representing many species of western birds . . . an extensive collection of fossilized plants, insects, fish, trilobites, etc. The museum also features an excellent collection of mineral specimens. *Open to the public; admission fee.*

Turn west from Lehi via State 73 to Fairfield, 20 m., site of **Stagecoach Inn** and **Camp Floyd State Historical Monuments** *(see Tour No. 4A for description).* At junction with State 68, 4 m. west of Lehi, turn south a short distance to:

Saratoga Springs, a large amusement park and resort on the shore of Utah Lake. Known as "The family fun park," Saratoga features a midway with numerous rides and games, including a 300-foot waterslide, refreshment stands, etc. . . . four pools for bathing, swimming and diving, fed by warm mineral springs. . . . acres of lawns and picnic sites . . . campground . . . miniature golf course . . . and a boat harbor from which scenic lake cruises may be arranged. Built on the site of natural warm springs, Saratoga has been a popular resort for more than 100 years. In 1979 its management announced a five-year plan for developments costing four million dollars. *Open Easter weekend to Labor Day.*

AMERICAN FORK (4,600 alt. 12,417 pop.) had little more than a fourth of its present population in 1941, when it was described as "a community of small farms and modest homes . . . chiefly known as a poultry and egg producing center." Poultry Days of yesteryear long since gave way to an annual Steel Days celebration, recognizing the city's economic dependence on nearby Geneva Steel Works and offshoot metal industries. Though examples of contemporary architecture far outnumber those from the last century, American Fork repays a leisurely drive through the streets of its central district. The **Smith Home,** 589 E. Main, is considered notable enough—because of its typical late-Victorian design—to be listed on the National Register of Historic Places. Its builder, Warren B. Smith, was an early civic and business leader. Also of note is a pillared mansion in a park setting of lawns and garden, elaborate gazebos and towers, visible from I-15. Built many years ago and then abandoned for a time, the house was restored during the 1960s and 1970s—and the park created—by Afton and David Fitzen. American Fork's acclaimed **Utah Pageant of the Arts** has been presented annually in June and July since 1973. Termed "a new art phenomenon," the pageant recreates art masterpieces such as paintings, sculpture, tapestry, artifacts, glass and porcelain, through the use of live models, costumes, sets, lighting, music, and narration. The pageant's cast now numbers more than 200.

Turn north from American Fork on State 74 to **Alpine, American Fork Canyon, Timpanogos Cave National Monument,** and **Alpine Scenic Drive.** *See description above.*

Turn south from American Fork to Utah Lake and **American Fork Boat Harbor,** a popular launching site.

PLEASANT GROVE (4,600 alt. 10,684 pop.) has a backdrop hardly surpassed for grandeur in the state, namely the stupendous western face and buttressed foothills of **Mount Timpanogos,** rising like an immense wall for 7,000 feet. Utahns have a deep affection for "Timp," but not all of them appreciate the true magnitude of the great massif, which must be ranked among the nation's grandest peaks on the basis of bulk and absolute elevation. The peak's crest above 10,000 feet measures four miles in length, and its base covers more than 50 square miles. For the most part the peak consists of limestone laid down about 300 million years ago in Mississippian-Pennsylvanian times. People blessed with imagination have no difficulty seeing the profile of a Sleeping Princess formed by the mountain's summit ridge.

Pleasant Grove, according to the 1941 edition, was "named for the thick stands of cottonwood trees, which almost obscure the buildings. The bench lands about Pleasant Grove produce fruits and berries of excellent flavor, which are canned locally or shipped fresh, mainly to Pacific Coast markets, by refrigerator truck." The city's population has multiplied six times since 1941, and its boundaries are not as distinct as they were then, as the community becomes increasingly a part of the Utah Valley megalopolis. Pleasant Grove was settled in 1850, nostalgic reminders of its long past being evident to those who look for them.

Hauling fruit from Pleasant Grove to Salt Lake City, about 1915.

Worthy of listing on the National Register of Historic Places is the **Old Bell School** in Memorial Park, a quaint structure dating originally from 1861 with additions in 1880 and 1887. Now a museum operated by Daughters of the Utah Pioneers, the venerable building is reputed to be one of the oldest remaining pioneer schools in the state. Another registered site is the **Benjamin W. Driggs Home,** 119 E. Battle Creek Drive, a two-story house built of stone in Greek Revival style. Dating from the 1880s, the house has been restored. Other noteworthy structures include the **Clark Home,** 50 W. Center, built of clapboard in 1869-70 . . . **Fugal Blacksmith Shop,** 436 E. 700 North, dating from 1896, "a rare example of early blacksmith shops with much of the original equipment still in occasional use" . . . **Town Hall,** 107 S. 100 East, built of stone in 1886 . . . **Olpin Home,** 510 S. Locust, built of rock about 1875 with brick addition about 1895. The home of the family of the musical King Sisters has been restored (corner 100 East and 200 South).

Turn north from Pleasant Grove on State 146 to **American Fork Canyon, Timpanogos Cave National Monument,** and **Alpine Scenic Drive.** *See above for description.* State 146 passes through a pleasant rural landscape at the foot of Mount Timpanogos, with several parking turnoffs affording vistas of valley, lake, and mountains.

OREM (4,800 alt. 52,399 pop.) had a population of 1,915 in 1940 and was described in one sentence in the 1941 edition: "Orem . . . incorporated in [1919], produces garden stuff, much of which is canned at the Pleasant Grove Canning Plant in Orem, one of the largest tomato canneries in the Intermountain West." Today most of the truck gardens and many of the orchards have given way to residential areas, commercial developments, parks, schools, and industrial sites. Orem, in fact, is the largest and one of the youngest of Utah's "new cities," a product almost entirely of the second half of this century. As such it reflects the physical and cultural values of its time and locale—in particular those peculiar to Utah Valley and the State of Utah. While there is little of early historical interest in Orem, the city merits serious touring for no reason other than its status as a truly contemporary Utah community. Orem, Provo and county environs form a metropolitan area which ranks among the fastest-growing such areas in the nation. Orem is notable for the length of its main street—US Highway 91-89 (State Street)—which extends for five miles through the center of the city.

Orem's economy has a diversified base of manufacturing, trade, education, etc. Numerous industrial firms have located in the city. Geneva Works of U.S. Steel Corporation has been the foundation manufacturing industry for almost 40 years, not only providing direct employment for some 5,000 workers but also supporting a host of satellite industrial and commercial activities. Brigham Young University also is essential to Orem's economic stability, as it is to that of Provo.

Turn west from Orem to **GENEVA WORKS** of United States Steel Corporation, a behemoth industrial plant on the shore of Utah Lake. Geneva ranks next below Kennecott's Utah Copper operations in industrial employment in Utah, employing about 5,000 workers in its multiple steel and mining operations. Its annual payroll totals approximately 150 million dollars. Geneva Works is a fully integrated steel plant which processes iron ore, scrap metal, coal, and limestone through complex steps resulting in products such as pig iron, steel plates, sheets and coils; structural shapes; pipe; coal chemicals; and nitrogen products. Coal is shipped to the plant from mines in Colorado and Utah *(see Tour No. 10D)*. Most of the iron ore comes from company operations near Lander, Wyoming, with smaller quantities from open-pit mines near Cedar City *(see Tour No. 8A)*. Limestone and dolomite are mined at the Keigley Quarry near Payson for use in the blast furnace and open-hearth operations. During the steel-making process at Geneva, coal is converted to coke and gases by baking in ovens at 2150 degrees F. for about 16 hours. Some of the resulting coke is sold to the chemical industry, while byproducts of the coking process are separated and refined into coal tar chemicals and nitrogen products. The remaining coke and byproduct gas are utilized to fire the furnaces. In the blast furnaces, iron is separated from slag impurities. In the open-hearth furnaces, many kinds of steel are produced from pig iron. Steel is then processed at Geneva's rolling and structural mills into a wide range of specialized products, or some of the plant's iron and steel may be shipped to U.S. Steel plants in California for processing, or sold commercially.

Geneva Works was constructed by the federal government between the years 1942 and 1944, a result of World War II's industrial demands. Total cost approached 200 million dollars. After the war the plant was sold to United States Steel, its designer. While the plant's economic contribution to Utah Valley, Carbon County, Iron County, and the state in general cannot be denied—or even calculated

Donny and Marie Osmond
on stage, Osmond Studios,
Orem.

OSMOND STUDIOS

accurately—many Utahns consider it a mixed blessing. Emissions from the plant provided the basis for lawsuits filed by local farmers some years ago. Despite the expenditure of millions of dollars for controls, plant emissions continue to be a source of air contamination.

This condition generated debate in the late 1970s when the Environmental Protection Agency announced that additional emission controls costing more than 100 million dollars would be required. Company officials countered that EPA's control standards were unnecessarily stringent, prohibitively high in cost, and would force closure of the plant if insisted upon. Many local residents as well as state officials and congressional representatives were united in their support of the company's stand. A compromise plan of controls finally was adopted, and it is likely that the plant will continue to play an important role in the state's economy.

Drive southeast from Orem on 1200 South Street to **Brigham Young University** *(see Provo, below).*

Near the 1200 South (BYU) offramp of I-15 is the new **Orem Campus, Utah Technical College,** a product of the 1970s.

Utah Technical College is a state-supported institution of higher learning having an enrollment of about 4,000 students on the Orem and Provo campuses. The college emphasizes vocational, technical, business, health, and paraprofessional training, and also offers programs in general education. Credits may be transferred to other schools in the state's Higher Education system. Recently completed at the impressive new Orem campus are facilities for business, mechanical and electrical, automotive and trades training, as well as a learning resource center. Future construction is to include an auditorium, physical education building, technology building, and a complex for administration and health occupations.

Drive east toward the mountains on 800 North Street to Osmond Studios and Provo Canyon. *(For Provo Canyon—US 189, see Tour No. 5B below.)*

Osmond Studios, also known as the Osmond Entertainment Center, were built during the late 1970s as a technical center for the production of television and movie features. Principal sponsors were the well-known Osmond family, native Utahns who now reside in the Provo-Orem area. Among the center's initial productions were the "Donny and Marie Show" and the "Donna Fargo Show," as well as other television features and a theater film. Its facilities include areas for set design and construction, sound stage, and rehearsal halls. *Studio tours may be arranged.*

PROVO (4,550 alt. 73,907 pop.) became Utah's second-largest city during the 1970s, surpassing Ogden in that period. During the decade its population increased by 40 per cent, while Orem's doubled, helping to catapult Utah County into the position of 9th fastest-growing metropolitan statistical area in the nation. Provo is the Utah County seat, and the site of Brigham Young University, largest church-related college in the world. Its setting was described in the 1941 edition:

> The city huddles at the base of the precipitous Wasatch Range, the western face of which is an almost perpendicular fault scarp. Provo Peak, rising to an altitude of [11,068] feet due east of the city, extends sharply above the jagged ridge of the Wasatch Range. On the base of the peak, about 2,000 feet above the upper level of the city, is the white block-letter "Y," 300 feet tall, which is newly whitewashed each year by freshmen of Brigham Young University. Northward there rises the long bulk of Mount Timpanogos, [11,750] feet high. The Provo area slopes gently westward, and beyond the city limits are farmlands and pastures, and broad, fresh-water Utah Lake, which can be seen only from the upper streets of the city. Across the lake rises the low range of the Lake Mountains, and other mountains are visible in every direction.

As the largest city in the state south of Salt Lake City, Provo is a commercial magnet for a vast area; and the presence of Brigham Young University has made it an important cultural center as well. The university is the city's largest industry. Students, faculty, staff and their families comprise a significant part of the city's population. The local economy is diversified, being based on trade, manufacturing, services (including private education), government, and other industries. Manufactured products include apparel (several large firms), metal products, books, dolls, and industrial valves.

"The town centers about the intersection of University Avenue and Center Street," said the 1941 edition. At that time its population was 18,000. "Within a four-block radius are the principal stores and most of the public buildings, mainly two- and three-story structures of the architectural style popular soon after the turn of the century." This downtown core has changed remarkably little since that was written, though plans have been laid for extensive downtown redevelopment, including a large shopping mall. "Like other Mormon-built towns, Provo has wide streets laid out in the four cardinal compass directions. There is a profusion of shade trees, mostly Lombardy and Carolina poplars, Norway maple, box elder, elm, and walnut. In the [older] residential sections the houses are set well back in spacious green lawns, which must be watered every day; and in the backyards there are usually vegetable and flower gardens." This description of Provo in 1941 would be fairly accurate in 1981, insofar as the long-established central part of the city is concerned. Provo's historical background was summarized in the 1941 edition:

> In March, 1849, John S. Higbee, at the head of thirty families, took wagons, horses, cattle, farming implements, and household equipment, and left Great Salt Lake City to establish a Mormon colony on the Provo River. The place chosen was a favorite Indian fishing ground, where the Utes held a fish carnival at the

time of the spring spawning. Within a few miles of their goal the settlers were confronted by a band of Ute Indians. After solemnly promising not to drive the Indians from their lands, they were allowed to continue. Fording Provo River, the settlers established themselves on the south bank. Farming and building were begun and within a few weeks they had constructed a fort, plowed 225 acres of land, and planted rye, wheat, and corn.

In 1858 the population of Provo was temporarily increased by the arrival of 30,000 Mormons from Great Salt Lake City and other northern Utah settlements who feared the advance of Colonel Albert Sidney Johnston's army *(see History)*. When the Federal force molested no property, Brigham Young announced that he was preparing to return to Great Salt Lake City. Within a few hours all of the settlers had begun their homeward journey.

The Utah Southern Railroad, now a part of the Union Pacific System, was completed from Salt Lake City to Provo in 1873. The Utah and Pleasant Valley Railroad, built by Milan Packard to transport coal from the mines near Scofield, was extended north from Springville to Provo in 1878. It was known as the "Calico Road" because the workmen who graded the roadbed were paid mainly in general merchandise from Packard's store in Springville. In 1881 The Calico Road was sold to the predecessor of the Denver & Rio Grande Western Railroad, and Provo obtained its first trunk line service. Completion of the railroad gave new impetus to the city's industrial growth, and was followed by installation of the city's electric service (1890) and a waterworks system (1892). Culturally and commercially, the town forged steadily ahead. . . .

The construction of Geneva Steel Works in World War II was a catalyst for industrial and population growth, contributing to a 60 per cent jump in population during the 1940s. The phenomenal expansion of Brigham Young University—from a student body of 2,800 in 1940 to approximately ten times that many in 1980—also has been a crucial factor in the city's growth.

Being one of Utah's venerable and relatively conservative communities, not prone to discard or replace the old merely for the sake of change, Provo still exhibits many interesting structures from its 19th century and turn-of-the-century past. As stated above, the central business center displays the architectural styles of the early years of this century or even before. Side-street cruising is rewarded by fascinating discoveries of quaint or unusual architecture. In Provo, as a rule, functional older buildings are cherished and maintained. Dilapidated or derelict structures are the exception.

Among Provo's many distinctive buildings listed on historic registers are the following: **Knight Block,** 20-24 N. University, a three-story brick and stone commercial building erected about 1900 for Jesse Knight, prominent mining figure and philanthropist of that period . . . **Provo Third Ward Chapel,** 200 N. 500 West, English parish gothic style, dedicated in 1903 . . . **Lower BYU Campus,** 500 North and University, an imposing cluster of six distinctive buildings comprising the first campus, built between 1884 and 1912, now being adapted to commercial use as a center known as Academy Square . . . **Provo LDS Tabernacle,** 50 S. University, a formidable steepled building of red brick, dating from 1885 and still used for church meetings . . . **Hotel Roberts,** 192 S. University, originally built in 1882 and remodeled in 1926, the oldest operating hotel in Provo. Numerous private homes are listed on historic registers. Among these might be mentioned the following: **Beebe House,** 489 W. 100 South, with Queen Anne tower, built around the turn of the century by a Provo businessman . . . **Talmage Home,** 345 E. 400 North, built in 1874 and associated with brothers James E. and Albert Talmage, prominent Utah educators . . . **Smith Home,** 315 E. Center, built for a wife of George Albert Smith, Mormon apostle of early days . . . **Eggertsen Home,** 390 S. 500 West, dating from 1876 when it was built by S. P. Eggertsen, founder of an influential local family . . . **Beesley Home,** 210 S. 500 West, an adobe structure built in the 1860s . . . **Allen Home and Carriage House,** 135 E. 200 North, large brick Victorian house dating from the 1890s when it was built by Dr. Samuel H. Allen, a physician, and subsequently the home of other prominent residents . . . **Clark-Taylor Home,** 306 N. 500 West, an adobe house of very early vintage. "One of the first homes erected after pioneers of Provo moved out of the fort in 1852-53. A consecration deed to Brigham Young in 1855 indicated that the home was already built by that year . . . one of the oldest and best preserved pioneer homes in Utah." . . . **Reed Smoot Home,** 183 E. 100 South, the Utah residence of Senator Reed Smoot, advisor to five Mormon Church presidents and apostle in the church. "His house, built in 1892, reeks with the history of presidential visits, senatorial conferences, political intrigue, and religious persecution." . . . **Brereton Home,** 112 E. 300 South, a two-story adobe structure built about 1860, now adapted to office use . . . **Jesse Knight Home,** a distinguished residence built in 1905 for one of early Utah's most prominent industrialists and financiers. There are many other notable buildings in Provo, too numerous for listing here. *Visitors may obtain a historic tour guide from the Chamber of Commerce, 10 E. 300 North.*

Other attractions in Provo include the following:
Utah County Building, Center and University, "a classic structure of white oolite stone on a base of Utah granite." A Bicentennial fountain is a recent addition. **Sowiette Park and Pioneer Museum,** 500 West and 600 North, which occupies the site of the second fort built at Provo. According to the 1941 edition, the park "was named for the principal war chief of the Utes, who tried to protect the settlers from the warlike followers of Chief Walker. The latter, in the 1850's, camped near the fort planning to attack the small group of pioneers. Chief Sowiette moved his warriors into the fort and prepared to defend his white friends. Walker and his braves whooped around the stockade all night, but finally withdrew. The walls and clearing of the old fort have been replaced by trees, tennis courts, a swimming pool, a baseball field, and tourist grounds . . . The **Pioneer Memorial Building** . . . contains a collection of pioneer relics and Indian artifacts [open during summer months] . . . The **Pioneer Cabin,** north of the Memorial Building, is a replica of an early Utah cabin, furnished with authentic pioneer furniture." **McCurdy Historical Doll Museum,** 246 N. 100 East, which displays hundreds of dolls of varying vintage and origin. The dolls illustrate fashions in dress, including folk and Spanish provincial dress; episodes of history and historical personages; Indian culture; etc. Categories include boy dolls, wax dolls, antique dolls, and First Ladies of America. Curio shop. *Open to the public.* **Old Fort Utah,** 200 N. 2050 West (Geneva Road), is a log replica of the pioneer fort of 1849 which housed the first residents of Provo. In Fort Utah (Lions Club) Park. **Mormon Temple,** on a hillside above Brigham Young University, is an architecturally striking building faced with white cast stone and surmounted by a central segmented spire. The temple was completed in 1972. Visitors are welcome to tour the landscaped grounds; the building itself, however, is not open to the public.

In the mountains east of the city, behind and above the **Utah State Hospital,** was to have been an ambitious recreational development known as the **Heritage Mountain Resort.** Developers proposed a large complex in a basin at the foot of Provo Peak, to be reached by funicular railway from the valley. Facilities were to include chairlifts, lodges, cultural villages, theaters and convention facilities—all to cost more than 100 million dollars. Though necessary permits were obtained during the late 1970s, after years of preparation and despite severe opposition, anticipated financing has not been forthcoming as yet.

Utah Lake State Park, Provo.

UTAH LAKE STATE PARK/PROVO BOAT HARBOR is a developed marina and recreation site on the shore of Utah Lake, 3 m. west of Provo by way of Center Street. The 300-acre park has been developed with launching ramps, restrooms, drinking water, lawns, and extensive facilities for camping and picnicking. *Fee area.* UTAH LAKE is the state's largest natural body of fresh water, having a surface area of approximately 150 square miles. The lake drains into Great Salt Lake through the Jordan River, being replenished by Provo, Spanish Fork, and American Fork rivers, Hobble Creek, and lesser streams. The lake is extremely popular for pleasure boating, waterskiing and fishing (carp, catfish, bass, walleye pike, yellow perch); however, it can be dangerous in high winds, while submerged rocks and sandbars are other hazards that warrant caution. Utah Lake's history, insofar as water rights and fluctuations are concerned, was described on pages 222-24 of the 1941 edition.

BRIGHAM YOUNG UNIVERSITY

Known variously as BYU, the "Y", and the Mormon University, Brigham Young University occupies a compact, ultramodern campus of some 650 acres in northeast Provo. Owned and financially supported by the Latter-day Saints (Mormon) Church, BYU is recognized as the largest church-related university in the world and the largest school in Utah. In 1980 it also ranked as the nation's largest private university. Daytime and evening campus enrollment in 1980-81 totaled more than 29,000, while an additional 100,000 students were receiving instruction through the Continuing Education program.

The majority of students at BYU are members of the Mormon Church. Though church membership is not a condition of admission, all students must observe strict standards of personal conduct, including a dress code. Students also are expected to observe the Mormon Word of Wisdom, which discourages smoking, the use of illegal drugs, and the drinking of alcoholic beverages, tea and coffee. Offsetting the image of staidness engendered by its codes of personal conduct, BYU encourages student participation in a wide range of social, cultural, and athletic activities—which the school makes extraordinary efforts to support. Students come from every state and more than 70 foreign countries. Among them are some 7,000 former missionaries of youthful age, recently returned from tours in a hundred countries, thus adding special meaning to BYU's claim that "The world is our campus."

Brigham Young University offers a broad range of scholastic offerings in its colleges, which include Biological and Agricultural Sciences . . . Business . . . Engineering Sciences and Technology . . . Family, Home, and Social Sciences . . . Fine Arts and Communications . . . General Studies . . . Humanities . . . Nursing . . . Physical Education . . . Physical and Mathematical Sciences. Undergraduates may choose from a variety of religion courses, and an Honors Program has been designed to enrich the curriculum of superior students. As a church school, an active pursuit of BYU is "the synthesis of spirituality and intellectual pursuit, culminating in a refinement of character." The school's motto is a teaching of the Mormon prophet, Joseph Smith: The glory of God is intelligence.

While the educational accomplishments of BYU are hardly apparent to the casual eye, the remarkable campus is most dramatically evident. In 1941 the school's enrollment numbered less than 3,000 students, and the campus consisted of half a dozen buildings. During the 40 years since that time the enrollment has multiplied ten times, necessitating an extraordinary building program. Construction of new facilities began accelerating in the 1950s, during the 20-year administration of president Ernest L. Wilkinson. Much of the cost was borne by the church, the remainder—totaling many millions of dollars—coming from contributions. On-campus housing for thousands of students was built; a new library; student commons building; administration building; field house; science center and laboratories; Fine Arts center; and numerous instructional buildings. The result is a most attractive community of strikingly diversified contemporary architecture, every building distinctive in style, separated by landscaped open spaces that allow the eye to roam—in particular to the east, where great peaks form the skyline.

Campus tours are available on regular or arranged schedules, from the **Thomas House Hosting Center.** Among noteworthy points of interest on the campus are the following: **Franklin S. Harris Fine Arts Center,** which houses the departments of Art, Communications, Speech and Dramatic Arts, Music, and Communicative Disorders. The center features two art galleries, including a grand gallery, five theaters, radio and television complex, classrooms, and offices. It was described by architect William L. Pereira as "the most comprehensive center of its kind ever commissioned by an American university" . . . **Harold B. Lee Library** (named for the 11th president of the Mormon Church), a massive mural-faced structure, contains nearly two million volumes. Outstanding special collections include Mormon Books and Chronicles, a Victorian collection of first editions, and volumes from presses of the 15th and 16th centuries . . . **Marriott Center,** a 23,000-seat arena used for sporting events, devotionals, concerts, and other large-group events. Ten stories high, the center was named for J. Willard Marriott, philanthropist . . . **Wilkinson**

Brigham Young University, looking northeast toward Rock Canyon and Cascade Mountain (10,908 alt.).

Student Center, one of the largest union buildings on any campus, having seven levels and about 290,000 square feet of floor space . . . **Eyring Physical Science Center,** which features the Summerhays Planetarium (public lectures) . . . **Monte L. Bean Life Science Museum,** featuring numerous public exhibits. The museum provides a variety of educational services for the public as well as faculty and students, and houses extensive collections such as the largest herbarium in Utah (200,000 mounted plants), more than a million pinned and preserved insects, 45,000 amphibians and reptiles, 6,000 birds, 10,000 fish, and more than 6,000 mammals.

South of Provo, I-15 passes through the open valley between the lake and Wasatch Range, bypassing all communities. While the freeway does provide a magnificent mountain panorama as well as closeup views of intensively cultivated fields and picturesque farms, tourists who are more interested in architecture and other manifestations of long-time human occupancy are advised to travel US 91 and 89, the old highways. These roads, combined for much of the distance, generally parallel the foothills and serve as the main streets for Springville, Spanish Fork, Salem, and Payson—aged communities which were founded 130 years ago as some of the earliest white settlements in the west. Those travelers with time and inclination for leisurely exploring will be amply repaid by sidestreet probing here, as elsewhere throughout Utah.

SPRINGVILLE (4,500 alt. 12,101 pop.) is a clean and pleasant residential community, known as The Art City because of its celebrated Springville Art Museum *(below).* The city resembles other Utah Valley communities in having a long history (settled 1850). Growth during the intervening years has been orderly. Most inhabitants, being long-time or non-transient residents, have developed a pride in home and community that is evident. Visitor attractions include the following:

Civic Center Park, featuring a contemporary city building. A **Pioneer Mother Monument** and **Memorial Fountain** in the park are the work of noted sculptor Cyrus E. Dallin, Springville native. During a long and productive life, Dallin received widespread recognition for works such as *Paul Revere, Massasoit, Angel Moroni* (atop the Mormon Temple in Salt Lake City), *Brigham Young* (Brigham Young Monument in Salt Lake City), *Signal of Peace, Medicine Man,* and other sculpture creations. A number of his works are in the Springville Art Museum . . . **Daughters of the Utah Pioneers Museum,** 175 S. Main, open by arrangement . . . **Old Presbyterian Church,** 251 S. 200 East, dating from 1886 when it was built as part of the Hungerford Academy (National Historic Register) . . . **Kelsey Home,** 366 W. 300 South, built in 1889 with ornate Eastlake-style wood trim . . . **Bringhurst Home,** 306 S. 200 West, built of adobe, rock and pine about 1860. William Bringhurst, for whom it was built, was prominent in early church, civic, and business affairs. Many other older buildings of architectural distinctiveness are preserved in Springville, including a number of aged commercial buildings in the central business district.

SPRINGVILLE MUSEUM OF ART (High School Art Gallery) is housed in an attractive Spanish-style building at 126 E. 400 South. Dedicated in 1937, the building was built by the Works Progress Administration to house extensive collections of the local high school. Since then the museum's collections have been expanded greatly through gifts and a systematic purchase program. Many well known artists (painters and sculptors) are represented, including Rockwell Kent, Frederick Waugh, and a number of works by Utah natives Cyrus E. Dallin, John Hafen, and Mahonri Young, among others. The museum is especially noted for its annual month-long National Art Exhibit in April, when works from far and near are exhibited. *Open to the public.*

Beside the old highway between Springville and Provo once stood an imposing iron-reduction plant known as **Ironton,** the predecessor of Geneva Works. Operated by Columbia Steel, the Ironton Works were built in 1924 and dismantled after World War II. The plant included 56 coke ovens, a blast furnace, and by-product facilities. Neither the plant nor the adjoining village of Ironton remain today, though Pacific States Cast Iron Pipe Company nearby—first utilizing iron from Ironton, then from Geneva—is an active manufacturing installation.

Turn east from Springville to **Hobble Creek Canyon,** Uinta National Forest, and connecting roads leading to **Strawberry Reservoir, Squaw Peak Trail,** and **Diamond Fork.** Winding through gentle, wooded mountain country, the main drive and its forks offer access to a popular golf course in the canyon, excellent fishing streams, and numerous developed camping and picnic sites. The main drive and spurs are especially beautiful in late September and early October, when autumn colors are at their most glorious. *See Tour 5B below for description of Squaw Peak Trail.*

SPANISH FORK (4,550 alt. 9,825 pop.). A solid commercial and residential community, Spanish Fork lies in a productive agricultural region at the junction of I-15 and US 6-89. Traditionally, its economy has been based largely on trade and the raising of crops and livestock in the vicinity, as well as dairy and orchard production. Livestock auctions and ram sales are important economic events. Spanish Fork is noted as the home of the Utah State Junior Livestock Show, held in May, advertised as the oldest show of its kind west of the Mississippi River. Popular activities at this show include stock judging, horse pulling contests, parades, rodeo, sales, and horse show. Recent years have seen the arrival of light manufacturing industries, including three large apparel firms. The community rates itself as the "No. 1 city in the country for the variety of recreational programs and number of participants." The **Daughters of Utah Pioneers Historical Museum,** 40 S. Main, is open by arrangement.

Turn east from Spanish Fork on US 6-89 to Spanish Fork Canyon, Price, and the valleys of central Utah. *See Tours No. 7A and 10A.*

Salem (4,600 alt. 2,233 pop.) is a residential community at the base of **Loafer Mountain** and **Santaquin Peak,** twin summits of almost identical altitude (10,687 and 10,685 respectively), only a mile apart. Salem was settled in 1851 and was "first named Pond Town for the small spring-fed lake about which the town grew up." The lake remains the center of town; around it many fine new homes have been built, and on its shore is a lovely community park with picnic facilities and playground.

Between Salem and Spanish Fork can be seen a zigzag road high on the mountain to the southeast. This road gave access to the famed **Koyle Dream Mine** and, several miles beyond, to what the map refers to as "Old Spanish Mine (Inactive)." The road continues to a microwave station.

In 1894, John Koyle of Spanish Fork announced that a heavenly being had appeared to him in a dream and had shown him the location of an ancient Nephite mine. (Nephites, according to the Book of Mormon, were among the ancient inhabitants of the Americas.) He was shown the spot where he should begin excavation that would connect with the Nephite tunnel and lead to nine large rooms filled with Nephite gold. Later a Mormon bishop (1908-13), Koyle was able to attract hundreds of believers, who invested both labor and money in his mining venture over a 50-year period despite the fact that the Nephite rooms were never found and the mine failed to yield a discernible amount of precious metal. Koyle's claim that he received periodic instructions from the "Three Nephites" of Mormon legend gave hope to investors that the mine ultimately would be a success.

Relieved of his office of bishop in 1913, Koyle received continued opposition from Mormon Church leaders, who finally excommunicated him a year before his death in 1949 for insubordination. Many of his followers remained loyal, and some have continued mining operations periodically to the present time.

A large concrete flotation mill, built during the Great Depression (1932) to process platinum ore, which Koyle believed he had found, may be seen high on the mountain east of Salem—a visible reminder of the Dream Mine episode.

PAYSON (4,700 alt. 8,246 pop.) is a dignified trading and agricultural center, surrounded by rich farmlands and orchards. Settled in 1850, it is "a community of old trees and solid homes." Many of the latter are noteworthy for historical and architectural interest. Examples include the following:

John Dixon Home, 218 N. Main, the oldest of four historic homes in the vicinity of the Nebo Stake Tabernacle *(below)*. A distinguished red sandstone residence of Richardsonian Romanesque design, the house was built in 1893 for John Dixon, mayor of Payson and wealthy livestockman . . . **Nebo Stake Tabernacle** (Mormon), 300 East and 100 North, of brick, stone and wood, dates from 1906. Almost identical to the Rexburg, Idaho, tabernacle—and designed by the same architect, Otto Erlandsen—the building is of Italian Renaissance or Baroque style . . . **Community Bible Church,** 160 S. Main, is identified by a steep gabled roof, wood belfry and bell. It has served since 1882 as a Presbyterian church and community bible church . . . **Peteetneet School,** 600 East and 200 South, is an impressive structure overlooking the city from a rise. The building was the work of Richard C. Watkins, architect for more than 200 school buildings in the intermountain area. Three stories high, with bell tower and red sandstone accent on its red brick walls, the school was completed in 1901 and is still in use. Payson's **Main Street Business District** has been attractively renovated as a semi-mall, retaining the most interesting facades of its numerous old buildings.

Near Payson, in July 1853, Alexander Keele was killed by Indians and the Walker War began. Continuing for some months and costing a number of lives on both sides, Utah's first major Indian war also resulted in the evacuation of settlements, the loss of much livestock, and the need for heavily armed guards for a time. Difficulties were finally settled at a personal conference between Ute Chief Walker and Brigham Young, and a prized letter which the chief had received from the Mormon leader was buried with him at his request when he died the following year.

Turn south from Payson to **Payson Canyon** and the **NEBO SCENIC LOOP,** one of Utah's most thrilling alpine drives. The road is paved through Payson Canyon to the vicinity of Devil's Kitchen, 28 m. *(see below).* **Payson Lakes,** 12 m., are the delightful setting for large developed campgrounds of Uinta National Forest (8,000 alt.). *Group reservations should be made well in advance.* From there the road winds across high ridges and along the east shoulder of the grand Mount Nebo massif, whose multiple summits reach 11,900 feet. Vistas to the north, across Utah Valley and the Wasatch Range—and south or east across the corrugated plateau country— are breathtaking. A steep unpaved fork of the main road, about 18 m. from Payson, descends Santaquin Canyon to **Trumbolt Park** (picnicking) and **Santaquin.** The main drive continues south at altitudes exceeding 9,000 feet, in places clinging to precipitous slopes that may challenge the courage of some drivers and passengers. In places the vegetation has been closed to grazing; there the plant cover is surprisingly lush. Toward the south, overlooking Salt Creek Canyon, **Devil's Kitchen** is a brightly colored, grotesquely eroded alcove on the slopes of Mount Nebo, reached

Mount Nebo (11,900 alt.).

by short foot trail from the road. From this vicinity the road descends into **Salt Creek Canyon,** the site of several campgrounds of the Uinta National Forest, and joins State 132 east of Nephi *(see Tour No. 4B).*

SANTAQUIN (4,900 alt. 2,175 pop.) is an appealing rural community in the south end of Utah Valley, surrounded by farms and fruit orchards which produce peaches, pears, apricots, apples and cherries. The Santaquin area was settled in 1851 and first named Summit Creek, later changed to Santaquin after a local Sanpitch Indian chief who subsequently became a cattleman and farmer. Black Hawk, leader of the Utes during the Black Hawk War of the 1860s, died at Spring Lake near Santaquin in 1870 and was buried in the foothills near Santaquin. **Keigley Quarry,** a large open-pit mining operation on the mountainside, several miles north of Santaquin, furnishes limestone and dolomite for the furnaces of Geneva Works.

West of Santaquin, US 6 leads to Goshen, Elberta, Eureka, and the Tintic Mining District *(see Tour No. 4B).* **GOSHEN** (4,500 alt. 582 pop.) "is a tree-shaded livestock and farming community, settled in [1867], with a typical small-town business district, a residential section where old houses rub elbows with new, and outlying farms that crowd the city limits." In 1980 the town's population was smaller than it was in 1940. Said the 1941 edition:

> Pioneers in the valley moved from place to place to find suitable homesites. According to Solomon Hale, Brigham Young, who made a special trip from Great Salt Lake City to select this site, chided the people for their constant moving: "Your chickens have been moved so many times that every time they see a wagon they just turn over and stick their feet in the air to be tied for another moving."

Archeologists from Brigham Young University excavated a mound near Goshen in 1966, finding artifacts representing the Desert culture of 7,000 to 9,000 years ago and the Fremont culture of 800 years ago, as well as items from the historic era of the late 1800s.

Tour No. 5B - Provo River and Upper Weber Country (Provo River Canyon, Heber Valley, Kamas, Uinta Mountains, Rockport Lake)

US 189 parallels the Provo River upstream from Utah Valley to its middle reaches in Heber Valley and the vicinity of Woodland-Kamas. The river's headwater sources are in the western Uinta Mountains, in an area marked generally by Bald Mountain and Mirror Lake—a central locus from which flow four of Utah's major streams: the Provo, Weber, Bear and Duchesne. As it nears Utah Valley the Provo passes through Provo Canyon, a profound but rather open gorge formed by the tremendous walls of Mount Timpanogos on the north and Cascade Mountain on the south. The river is acknowledged, along most of its length, as one of Utah's prime trout streams—a factor of importance in road improvement deliberations.

Turn east from Orem on 800 North, or north from Provo on University Avenue, to US 189 and **PROVO CANYON.** In the mouth of the canyon is a large electric generating complex (Utah Power and Light Company): the **Hale steam plant** and an older hydro-electric plant known as **Olmstead.** The Olmstead facility originated in 1903-04 with the building of a modest generating plant (still utilized) by the newly-formed Telluride Power Company. Supervising construction were two brothers, Lucien L. and P. N. Nunn, principals in the company. This plant, and a smaller predecessor at the site, were pioneers in the industrial generation of high-voltage AC electric power and its long-distance transmission. From this site in the late 1890s a 40,000 volt transmission line was built to Mercur, about 35 miles away, which thus became one of the first mining camps in America to receive AC electric power. L. L. Nunn also established here the Telluride Institute for

Bridal Veil Falls and Skyride   Provo River in Provo Canyon.

UTAH TRAVEL COUNCIL
BUREAU OF RECLAMATION (STAN RASMUSSEN)

the training of electrical engineers. The plant was acquired by Utah Power and Light Company in 1958.

At Springdell, 2 m. up-canyon from the Orem road junction, a road forks south. This is the **SQUAW PEAK TRAIL,** which climbs high above Utah Valley atop the lofty foothill terrace that forms the base of Cascade Mountain and Provo Peak.

From the main **SQUAW PEAK TRAIL**—and from short spurs or foot trails leading to overlook points— the view encompasses the whole of Utah Valley and Utah Lake, the magnificent Wasatch mountain front, and jumbled ranges to the west. In places the road is as much as 4,000 precipitous feet above the valley, with the ledges of **Cascade Mountain** (10,908 alt.) and terraced slopes of **Provo Peak** (11,068 alt.) looming above for another half-mile or more. Foot trails spiderweb the area, leading from Provo up Rock Canyon, Slate Canyon and Slide Canyon to summits such as Buffalo Peak (8,018), Squaw Peak (7,876), Y Mountain Summit (8,568), and even higher points. (These trails and others are described in *Utah Valley Trails* by Paxman and Taylor, Wasatch Publishers.) From **Rock Canyon Campground** (Uinta National Forest), 6,800 feet altitude, 10 m. from US 189, a foot trail climbs over the Wasatch crest between Cascade Mountain and Provo Peak to join a network of trails on the east side of the high peaks. The main drive continues south from Rock Canyon, over Camel's Pass, and down into **Hobble Creek Canyon** where it joins a paved road from Springville *(see Tour 5A above).* This southern segment of road clings to the mountainside at a hair-raising height and is not recommended for the squeamish. Vistas are sublime.

Bridal Veil Falls is a lovely two-level cascade on the south side of Provo Canyon, 10 m. from Provo. The falls can be viewed from a roadside parking area or from one of the world's steepest aerial tramways, the **Skyride,** which carries passengers to a terminal on the edge of a precipice 1,228 feet above the road. Foot trails lead from here, or from the base, to vista points overlooking Provo Canyon and Utah Valley. Refreshments, food, and souvenirs are available at **Bridal Veil Falls Resort,** at the tramway's lower terminal *(spring, summer, fall).* The resort also serves as the western terminus of the **Heber Creeper Railroad,** a scenic excursion line that extends for 18 miles between the falls and Heber City. *See below.*

VIVIAN PARK, a Utah County park 2 m. east of the falls, on the south side of the river, has long been a popular outing resort, with lake, picnic areas, and playgrounds, as well as summer homes.

From **Vivian Park** a surfaced county road leads through the canyon of Provo River's South Fork to Camp Trefoil, a Girl Scout camp nestled in a majestic mountain-ringed basin formed on the west by the grand heights of Cascade Mountain, Lightning Peak and Provo Peak. To the north, the road provides a superlative view of the skyscraping south face of Mount Timpanogos, framed by the canyon walls. Here the great peak bears startling resemblance (in miniature) to Switzerland's Jungfrau as viewed from Interlaken. Trails lead from the canyon to west, south and east—to the great cirque of Cascade Mountain, the Wasatch ridge, Lightning Peak, Windy Pass, and other alpine points. Hikers may obtain trail maps from Uinta National Forest or detailed publications such as *Utah Valley Trails.*

At **Wildwood,** 1 m. east of Vivian Park, is the junction with **Alpine Scenic Drive** (State 80) leading to Sundance Resort, Aspen Grove, American Fork Canyon, and Timpanogos Cave National Monument. *See Tour No. 5A above.*

Deer Creek Dam and **Reservoir** were under construction in 1940, when the first edition of this guidebook was in preparation. Constructed between 1938 and 1941, by the U.S. Bureau of Reclamation, the dam is a massive earth-fill structure 235 feet in height and 1,304 feet in width, connecting the lower walls of Provo Canyon. The reservoir is about seven miles long and three-quarters of a mile wide, with a surface area of nearly 3,000 acres and capacity of 153,000 acre-feet. Its water is vital to urban Utah, being utilized for culinary, industrial and agricultural purposes in both Salt Lake and Utah valleys. Among its major industrial users is Geneva Steel Works at Orem. Beside US 189, on the lake's east shore, is **DEER CREEK LAKE STATE RECREATION AREA,** a boating and fishing development of the Utah State Division of Parks and Recreation. Facilities include a concrete launching ramp, docks, and a large campground with restrooms, showers, drinking water, sewage disposal. *Fee area.* Also on the lake's shore are several commercial boat camps.

HEBER VALLEY, known technically as Provo Valley, joins Ouray, Colorado, in claiming to be "The Switzerland of America." Both are justified in this comparison by their superlative alpine beauty; Heber Valley is further justified by having so many residents of Swiss descent. There are few scenes more delightful than Heber Valley in the late afternoon, near dusk, looking westward across a green expanse of scattered trees and fields with grazing sheep and cows, to shadowy ramparts of Timpanogos and Cascade Mountain. The valley is encircled by mountains, its many streams making it one of Utah's most verdant agricultural areas. Many of its people still rely—as they have since pioneer days—on farming, livestock, and dairying for their livelihoods. Trade and recreation have become more important in recent decades.

Beside US 189 near its junction with US 40 is the **Heber Valley Airport,** a base for non-powered gliders or sailplanes, which may be seen on the apron or overhead in the air. Heber Valley's air currents are considered ideal for soaring, and this unusual local sport attracts more devotees as it becomes better known. US 189 joins US 40 in Heber City, the two becoming one for ten miles to Hailstone Junction. South and east from Heber City, US 40 traverses **Daniels Canyon** and the high Strawberry Reservoir country to Uinta Basin *(see Tour No. 6).*

HEBER CITY (5,600 alt. 4,400 pop.) is the seat of Wasatch County and contains more than half the county's population. Cleanliness and an aura of serenity, the charm of new blended with old, are among its notable attributes—these in addition to beauty of physical setting. "Pioneer dwellings, built of red sandstone or gray limestone, mingle with buildings of more recent vintage."

Heber City's most distinctive edifice is the old **Wasatch Stake Tabernacle** (Mormon) in a central park setting, built during the 1880s and converted to secular use in the 1960s. On the main facade of the prominent sandstone building is a central bell tower. Windows are arched. The former tabernacle is now devoted to dramatic presentations (Pioneer Playhouse) and other cultural events. Also listed on historical registers are a number of picturesque 19th century homes, **St. Lawrence Catholic Church** (1915), 100 West and Center, and several commercial buildings of early 20th century vintage.

Watkins-Coleman Home, Midway *(above, left)*, Railroad Museum, Heber City *(above, right)*, fishing on Deer Creek Reservoir *(left)*, and dog sled racing in Wasatch Mountain State Park *(right)*.

HEBER PIONEER VILLAGE, RAILROAD MUSEUM, and **HEBER CREEPER DEPOT** are located on the west side of Heber City, beside the road to Midway (State 113). Here is Utah's largest collection of vintage steam locomotives and rolling stock . . . a museum building featuring railroad memorabilia . . . a "village" of original and replica structures from the turn of the century or before . . . and the Heber City Depot, from which the Heber Creeper tour train departs on scheduled excursions through Heber Valley and Provo Canyon.

(1) **The Railroad Museum** consists of steam and diesel locomotives, open-air and enclosed passenger cars, boxcars, cabooses, tank car, engine tender, etc.—increasingly rare mementoes of railroading in bygone years. Each example is unusual for one reason or another. For example, one passenger car was the private car of Daniel C. Jackling, "father" of the Bingham Copper Mine; another was used on the Bamberger line between Salt Lake City and Ogden; and two open-air cars once transported excursionists between Salt Lake City and Saltair Resort. Locomotives are of various types and sizes, and several are utilized on the Heber Creeper line. Also a unit of the Railroad Museum is the historic **Corinne Railroad Station,** transported by truck from its former site at Corinne, where it served as the Museum building for the Sons of Utah Pioneers. The two-story frame building displays historical and interpretive exhibits.

(2) **Pioneer Village** is a cluster of quaint wood-frame buildings of western style, some originals and some replicas, of varying age and design. They have been arranged along both sides of a street to resemble a western business district of the turn-of-the-century era. During visitor season, the buildings are occupied, serving as

shops and stores, livery stable, jail, Chinese laundry, hotel, restaurant, etc. It is anticipated that the authentic village will serve as a movie set. Many of the buildings were moved from Corinne, where they were maintained by the Sons of Utah Pioneers. Both the Railroad Museum and Pioneer Village are projects of the Timpanogos Preservation Society, a non-profit corporation. Most of the buildings, relics, and railroad rolling stock were donated to the Society by the National Society, Sons of Utah Pioneers.

(3) **Heber Creeper** is a recreational railroad, transporting passengers from the old Heber City Depot to Bridal Veil Falls and return, a distance of 18 miles each way. The route passes through the rural countryside of Heber Valley, follows the west shore of Deer Creek Reservoir, and parallels Provo River through Provo Canyon. Steam locomotives are featured, as are enclosed coaches, open-air, lounge, concession, and dining cars. Passengers are entertained with activities and events such as disco dancing and staged encounters between lawmen and outlaws. The line features night dining excursions and makes special provisions for ski parties, weddings, conventions, family night, and Christmas celebrations. Trains leave Heber City and Bridal Veil Falls twice daily between May and October, in addition to an evening dining run. Modified schedules apply during off-season months. *For details, write or phone Heber Creeper, Heber City, Utah 84032.*

The Heber Creeper dates from 1899, when it began operating as a freight, livestock and passenger carrier between Provo and Heber City. In the 1930s, it is said, more sheep were shipped from the Heber City Depot than any other depot in the nation. Changing economic and transportation patterns forced discontinuance of freight service in 1968. Three years later the line was converted to scenic excursion service; during the decade since, ridership has increased steadily to as many as 100,000 passengers annually.

Turn west from Heber City on State 113 to Midway and Wasatch Mountain State Park.

MIDWAY (5,600 alt. 1,194 pop.) has a delightful rural setting of expansive fields, dairy farms, and grazing livestock on the west edge of Heber Valley, against foothills of the Wasatch Range. Many of its native residents are descended from Mormon settlers of Swiss origin; Swiss influence can be detected in the town's architecture and neat agricultural order. Swiss Days is an annual celebration in September. Newcomers, many of them, are part-time residents, choosing the locale for weekend homes. In Midway are numerous "limestone craters [pots] . . . averaging about 20 feet in diameter, formed by deposition from springs or geysers." Limestone "pot rock" was used for buildings and fences. Water from these "hot pots" has been popular since early days for recreation and therapeutic bathing, providing the basis for several commercial resorts. **Mountain Spaa** (formerly Luke's Hot Pots) is one of the oldest of these, offering indoor and outdoor pools, bath house, riding horses, lawns and camp-picnic facilities, dance hall, cafe and dining room, and lodging. Another popular bathing and dining establishment of early days was Schneitter's Hot Pots, converted during the 1950s into a destination resort known as **The Homestead.** The Homestead has a reputation for fine quality dining and lodging, as well as fresh- and mineral-water pools, tennis, golf, horseback riding, winter sports, and facilities for weddings and receptions.

A number of Midway structures are interesting from an architectural and historical standpoint. Among these is the **Old Midway School** (National Register), 100 North and 100 West, built in 1901 of local limestone and pot rock. The school's architect was John Boss, a native Swiss. The **Watkins-Coleman Home,** 5 E. Main, is one of the most photographed residences in Utah, a charming red house with white wood trim and green roof, sheltered by evergreen trees. The home was built in 1869 by Mormon Bishop John Watkins, an English architect-builder and polygamist, for two wives. In 1903 it was purchased by Henry Coleman and has remained in the Coleman family ever since. According to the National Register, "It is a one-and-one-half story Gothic Revival residence with walls of hand-pressed brick. Sandstone quoins mark the corners, and there are lacy bargeboards in the four main gables and the central dormer, all of which are topped by pointed finials. Some additions and minor alterations have been made."

Turn south from Midway to **CHARLESTON,** a rural hamlet; to Deer Creek Reservoir; and to junction with US 189.

Turn north from Midway to Wasatch Mountain State Park and roads leading through the park to American Fork Canyon, Big Cottonwood Canyon (Brighton), and Park City.

WASATCH MOUNTAIN STATE PARK, encompassing 22,000 acres of wooded mountain slopes, is Utah's largest state park. The park features an outstanding golf course, improved camping and picnic areas, and a network of scenic mountain-canyon roads. The entrance to the park features a **Visitor Center** located 2 m. north of Midway on State 224. The beautifully landscaped championship golf course of 27 holes is set in a mountain alcove and is a complete golfing facility with cart and club rentals, club house, and restaurant. **Pine Creek Campground,** north of the golf course and adjacent to State 224, is a large and well developed camping area with more than 125 units, improved with modern restrooms, showers, electric-water-sewer hookups, and facilities for groups, campers, trailers and tents. *Fee area, reservations advised.* Other camping and picnic areas are located throughout the park. **Snake Creek Canyon** is an impressive defile—particularly scenic when autumn colors are rampant—through which a forest road climbs to Pole Line Pass, then down into American Fork Canyon *(see Tour No. 5A).* For information and reservations, contact Wasatch Mountain State Park, P.O. Box 10, Midway, Utah 84049, or call 363-3232 or 654-3961.

North of the golf course, State 224 ascends **Pine Creek Canyon** to heights overlooking Heber Valley in grand panorama. At a junction about 6 m. from the Visitor Center, the road forks: Continue north to **Park City** *(Tour No. 5C)* or turn west over **Guardsman Pass** (10,000 alt.) to Brighton and Big Cottonwood Canyon *(Tour No. 3).* At this writing, a Dutch investment firm is planning an extensive recreational development in the high country adjoining Wasatch Mountain State Park, between Park City and Heber Valley.

North of Heber City, combined US 189-40 passes across the valley floor, affording inspirational views of the Wasatch Range to the west. Within a few miles it enters the narrowing channel of Provo River, and at **HAILSTONE JUNCTION,** 8 m. from Heber City, the road forks once more— US 40 continuing north to I-80 near Park City *(see Tour No. 5C below)* and US 189 following Provo River eastward to Francis. In 1941 Hailstone was "a lumber camp where 300,000 feet of lumber, 15,000 railroad ties, and 400,000 feet of mine props are cut annually. Nobody seems to remember why the place was named Hailstone."

FRANCIS (6,500 alt. 371 pop.) is a farming and livestock hamlet beside the Provo River, in the south end of Rhodes Valley. At Francis US 189 turns north to Kamas.

State 35 forks eastward from Francis, following the river for a way, climbing gradually to **Wolf Creek Pass** (9,900 alt.), then dropping to Hanna and Duchesne in the Uinta Basin *(see Tour No. 6).* The country through which the road passes is a vast, rugged region with few all-year residents. It is mountainous, yet its topography is rolling and there are few prominent summits; even the highest rarely exceed 10,000 feet. Streams drain to the Provo and Duchesne rivers, and forest growth alternates with far-spreading expanses of open space. Hundreds of miles of fairweather roads crisscross the area, providing access for fishermen, hunters, loggers, rangers, stockmen, and summer home residents.

KAMAS (6,500 alt. 1,065 pop.) is an incorporated town in Rhodes Valley, at the mouth of Beaver Creek Canyon. Beaver Creek is a tributary of the Weber River. The town's economy is based on agriculture, logging, travel and recreation. Recent decades have seen the influx of more and more part-time summer residents in the area. Said the 1941 edition, "Thomas Rhodes, a hunter, obtained permission from Brigham Young to settle here with twenty-five others in 1857. During the hard winter of 1861-62 they ground wheat in a coffee mill, their only available machine." Of interest to visitors is the **Kamas Fish Hatchery,** 3 m. from town, where hundreds of thousands of trout are produced each year for lake and stream stocking.

Turn east from Kamas on paved State 150 to **Mirror Lake** (31 m.), the **Uinta Mountains,** and **Evanston, Wyoming** (79 m.). This drive is one of the most visually entrancing and popular mountain routes in Utah, in particular that segment from Kamas to Mirror Lake. State 150 winds and climbs through wooded terrain of remarkable vegetation variety (conifers at higher elevations), gradually gaining in elevation as it penetrates the region of lofty glaciated peaks. For much of the distance to Mirror Lake it parallels Provo River; beyond Mirror Lake, to Evanston, many miles of the road follow the route of Bear River. The region is hardly excelled in Utah for stream and lake fishing (trout), and Wasatch National Forest has provided numerous developed picnic and camping sites in secluded locations beside the road. Of special interest between Kamas and Mirror Lake are **Beaver Creek Natural Arboretum** (6 to 15 m.) . . . **Duchesne Tunnel** (18 m.), a six-mile-long conduit through a mountain, 12 years under construction, built to convey water from the Duchesne River drainage to that of Provo River . . . lovely **Upper Provo River Falls,** a series of terraced cascades, 24 m. . . . and numerous lakes near the road.

Bald Mountain Pass (10,678 alt.) provides the first stunning view of the western end of the **High Uintas Primitive Area,** here a great forested basin drained by Duchesne River, containing Mirror Lake and a multitude of other glacial lakes known generally as the Grandaddy Lakes. Looming above the basin are grand rocky peaks and ridges, in particular **Bald Mountain** (11,947), **Hayden Peak** (12,473), and **Mount Agassiz** (12,429). A foot trail known as the Bald Mountain National Scenic Trail leads from the pass to the top of Bald Mountain, from which the view is even more thrilling and expansive. **Mirror Lake** is the site of a large forest campground maintained by Wasatch National Forest. Trails lead from Mirror Lake and the highway to other lakes in the basin, as well as to other parts of the Uinta Range. *See Tour No. 6 for description of the Highline Trail and High Uintas Primitive Area.* Information and maps may be obtained from Wasatch National Forest, 125 S. State, Salt Lake City, Utah 84111. *State 150 normally is closed by snow between October and May or June, varying slightly from year to year, and with altitude or location.*

North of Kamas, US 189 passes through mountainous terrain in a wide valley filled with productive fields, between foothills of the Wasatch Range on the west, the Uinta Range on the east. At **OAKLEY** (6,400 alt. 470 pop.), a farming village, paved State 213 forks east into Weber River Canyon.

East of Oakley, State 213 traverses the flat bottom of **Upper Weber River Canyon** to **Holiday Park,** about 20 m., the site of summer homes in the river's upper reaches. From Holiday Park trails branch southward into a region of 11,000-foot

WARD ROYLANCE

UTAH TRAVEL COUNCIL

WARD ROYLANCE

Fishing near Smith and Morehouse Reservoir *(top)* and Mirror Lake *(above)*.

Upper Provo River Falls

peaks and many lakes and streams, a favorite locale for fishing and hiking. **Smith and Morehouse Reservoir** is reached by short sideroad from State 213 at a junction about 12 m. east of Oakley. This large man-made lake—popular for fishing—is in an exceptionally scenic setting of steep slopes and bald-topped peaks. Two forest campgrounds are near the lake. The Weber's canyon in this vicinity is the site of summer home developments.

ROCKPORT LAKE, formed by Wanship Dam, is an important water-control unit of the Weber Basin Project, occupying the site of the former village of Rockport *(see description in the 1941 edition)*. On the east shore of the thousand-acre reservoir is **ROCKPORT LAKE STATE RECREATION AREA** (6,000 alt.), an elaborate public resort with boat ramp, numerous camping and picnic units, restrooms, showers, drinking water, and commercial marina. The lake is exceptionally popular for powerboating, sailboating, waterskiing, swimming, and fishing, attracting 300,000 visitors in a recent year. **Wanship Dam** was constructed in the 1950s.

WANSHIP (5,900 alt.) is a roadside village at the junction of US 189 and I-80. According to the 1941 edition, Wanship was "settled in 1859 and named for a Ute chief, retain[ing] many of its original frame buildings, set close together along the highway. The houses were built of native lumber, sawed at pioneer mills in the mountains. In 1872, when the population was three times the present number [205 in 1940], Wanship was an important stage station on the Overland route."

See Tour No. 5C below for description of I-80 east of Salt Lake City.

Tour No. 5C - Interstate Highway 80 east of Salt Lake City to Park City, Coalville, Echo Canyon, and Evanston, Wyoming

I-80 leaves and enters Salt Lake Valley through **PARLEYS CANYON,** a steep and tortuous gorge named for Parley P. Pratt, Mormon pioneer and apostle who opened a toll road through the canyon in 1850. A marvelous work of highway engineering, multi-lane I-80 climbs in sweeping curves to Parleys Summit, 3,000 feet higher than the valley floor, then descends a lesser distance to Parleys Park *(see below).* **Mountain Dell Reservoir,** 10 m. from junction with I-15 in Salt Lake City, is a crucial storage unit in the city's waterworks system. The small but architecturally interesting concrete dam measures 100 feet in height, 560 feet in width, and was completed in 1924.

At a junction immediately east of the reservoir, State 65 forks north through **Mountain Dell** to a junction with a paved road from Emigration Canyon *(see Salt Lake City).* North of this latter junction, State 65 is the **Pioneer Memorial Highway,** passing up Mountain Dell Canyon and surmounting Big Mountain—a formidable obstacle for the Donner-Reed pioneers in 1846 and the Mormon pioneers who followed a year later. Beyond Big Mountain it drops into East Canyon, skirts East Canyon Reservoir, and joins I-80N at Henefer *(see Tour No. 2).*

The mountains and slopes at Parleys Summit and for several miles to the east are witnessing an extensive and expensive residential construction boom, most home owners commuting the 15 or 20 miles to Salt Lake City. One of the most ambitious developments of recent years is at the **Jeremy Ranch** near the junction of I-80 and East Canyon road. In 1978 the Summit County Planning Commission was considering 11 different residential projects between Parleys Summit and Park City, several of which involved more than 1,000 acres each. It has been estimated that the population of this area might expand from 6,000 at the present time to 25,000 or even 40,000 by 1990, due in part to voter approval of a regional sewer project.

PARLEYS SUMMIT SKI RESORT, about 2 m. east of the summit, is a modest winter sports resort, appealing especially to intermediate and beginning skiers. **Ecker Ski Hill** is famed as the "site of many record ski jumps in early years. In 1937, Alf Engen, Salt Lake City skier, leaped 245 feet to set a world's record for amateurs." **Gorgoza,** nearby, was a railroad siding in 1941. According to the 1941 edition, the siding was named for Rodriguez Velasquez de la Gorgozada, a Spaniard, "said to have invested almost a million dollars in a narrow-gauge railroad from Park City to Salt City. . . ." The railroad was built, operated for five years, then became bankrupt. "Later it was made a branch line of the Denver & Rio Grande Western Railroad."

At **KIMBALL JUNCTION,** State 248 forks south to Snyderville, Park City West, and Park City. *See Tour No. 5C(2) below for description.* **Parleys Park** has expanded here into a wide-open, fairly level intermontane valley at 6,000 to 7,000 feet in elevation, draining into Weber River by way of East Canyon Creek. Since pioneer days the park has been utilized for grazing and high altitude farming. Today, new housing developments are scattered across the floor of the park, intimating a future day (perhaps not too distant) when open space will be the exception here.

Tour No. 5C(1) - Kimball Junction to Echo Reservoir, Coalville and Evanston

I-80 crosses Parleys Park to join US 40 at Silver Creek Junction (3 m. from Kimball Junction), then descends Silver Creek Canyon to Weber River Valley at Wanship *(see Tour No. 5B above)*. Between Kimball Junction and Silver Creek Junction, to the north of the highway, is historic KIMBALL STAGE STOP. According to its National Register description:

> The Kimball Hotel-Stage Stop and Barn is one of the few remaining original stations of the Overland Stage. William H. Kimball constructed the two-story sandstone hotel in 1862. Besides the housing of overnight guests, it contained a large dining room, a bar, and a store. The hotel was well known for its food and attracted notable guests such as Walt Whitman, Mark Twain and Horace Greeley. The main structure is in good condition, and two log barns built in the early 1860's still stand across the road. Much of the integrity of the stage complex remains. . . .

Travelers with time for leisurely sightseeing will be repaid by leaving I-80 at Wanship and driving the old highway to Hoytsville and Coalville. Settlement of this area began in the 1850s; much of nostalgic interest remains. **HOYTSVILLE** (5,700 alt.) is a farming village that dates from 1859; first named Unionville, it was renamed for Samuel P. Hoyt, a prominent pioneer. During the 1860s Hoyt built a gristmill with machinery transported laboriously from the east before completion of the railroad. The mill operated only a few years because the river changed its course. Its walls still stand after more than a hundred years. Hoyt also built a massive two-story mansion of white sandstone, containing nine fireplaces and surrounded by a high rock wall. Construction occupied the years between 1863 and 1870. This remarkable building has been preserved and restored, and can be seen from the old highway. At one time it was reputed—locally, at least—to be "the finest and most expensive house in the west."

COALVILLE (5,600 alt. 1,031 pop.) is the Summit County seat, "situated on a bench of land sloping from the narrow mouth of Chalk Creek Canyon to the Weber River." Traditionally the city has been a supply center for farmers and ranchers. Even today, with Summit County's fast-developing status as a center for Overthrust Belt oil and gas production, there is little apparent physical change. Coalville's population was little more in 1980 than it was in 1940. Nevertheless, it is likely that marked changes are on the horizon. Coalville's historical background was summarized in the 1941 edition.

Summit County, with 1,849 square miles of land area, is not large as Utah's counties go. Its 1980 population of 10,227 ranks it about midway among counties on the population scale, but in percentage *rate* of population increase between 1970 and 1980 only two counties ranked higher. Most of this gain has taken place in Park City and vicinity, or in unincorporated areas of the county. By far the greater part of the county is unpopulated mountain country. Farming, livestock raising, and logging have always been the economic mainstays in the river valleys, and metal mining in the Park City area until recent years, when recreation, leisure, and attendant economic activities have become dominant. Recreation is likely to continue in this position indefinitely, but it may be challenged by mining as Summit County's part of the Overthrust Belt oil and gas field is developed.

This giant field was discovered in the 1970s through the drilling of very deep and costly wells (18,000 feet or more) and is now conceded to be one of the most significant oil and gas discoveries in North America during recent decades. Hundreds of wells have been, or are being, drilled in the Coalville-Evanston region. Ultimate production cannot even be conjectured at this time. As one example, however, Amoco estimated in 1981 that potential oil and gas reserves in its share of the Anschutz Ranch East field, astride the Utah-Wyoming border north of Coalville, may be the energy equivalent of a billion barrels of oil. Evanston, being the area's largest community, has been the local boomtown insofar as trade, construction, population increase, and related growth activities are concerned. Income to Utah and Summit County, to date at least, has come indirectly from severance and other taxes, employment of local people, etc. This imbalance may change.

Coalville's most distinctive building, the old **Summit Stake Tabernacle** (1879-86), was demolished in 1971 after heated hearings, leaving a legacy of bitterness among some church members and architectural preservationists. The **Summit County Courthouse and Jail** date from 1904-1905.

Coalville and Weber River Valley, looking southeast. The old tabernacle can be seen in this view, taken in 1966.

BUREAU OF RECLAMATION (MEL DAVIS)

Echo Dam and Reservoir, part of the Weber Basin Project, date from 1927-30 when the dam was built by the U.S. Bureau of Reclamation. The reservoir has a surface area of 1,500 acres and a capacity of 74,000 acre-feet. Its water provides supplemental irrigation water for more than 100,000 acres of land in Weber and Davis counties. The earth-fill dam, built at a cost of $1,600,000, is 158 feet high and 1,900 feet wide. On its east shore is a tree-shaded resort with campground, picnic park, and boat ramp. The lake is popular for boating and waterskiing.

ECHO (5,460 alt.) marks the junction of I-80 and I-80N; east of Echo the highways are one. Union Pacific Railroad parallels the freeway to east and west. At the junction are travel service facilities. Little remains to indicate that the population was larger in former days. In 1941 Echo was "a straggling railroad town" with "a more colorful past than present." Its past was described in the 1941 edition:

> The town lies a half mile northwest of the site of the original Weber River stagecoach station, erected in 1853. The station was eagerly hailed by travelers, who often met with a riotous reception. A group of Shoshoni who lived near by made it a habit to descend hair-raisingly on the station as the stagecoaches drew up. . . .
>
> During railroad construction in 1868, tent saloons, gambling houses, and brothels sprang up to fleece the Irish "Paddies." Men often disappeared overnight. Seven unidentified bodies were removed from one hole, under a saloon and gambling hall; it was thought that the tent covered a trap door, through which dead men and refuse were dumped. The town quieted as the rails moved west, and the old Weber Station survived long enough to become a filling station. When it was razed in 1931, its thick old walls gave up a love letter from an eastern girl to a Pony Express rider, some small change, a five dollar gold piece, a Pony Expressman's gun case, and a pair of gold-rimmed spectacles.

Listed on the State Historical Register is the **Echo Church-School** at the head of Temple Lane. This small brick structure was built in 1876 as a Presbyterian chapel and school, served as a public school from 1880 to 1913, and as a Mormon chapel from 1913 until 1963. The Echo cemetery is nearby to the north.

ECHO CANYON—"a cavernous ravine in which sounds reverberate weirdly from towering walls"—is perhaps the most historic route of travel in Utah. Describing the route of US 30S, predecessor of I-80/I-80N, through Echo and Weber canyons, the 1941 edition waxed nostalgic:

> The flavor of the years lingers especially on the eastern section of the route. The canyons have reechoed to the passage of Indians, trappers and explorers, Pacific emigrants, Mormon pioneers, wagon freighters, California gold-seekers, Pony Express riders, Overland Stage drivers, and travelers of every description. The first transcontinental railroad followed the beaten path through Echo and Weber canyons. Like dragon's teeth, railroad spikes sprouted railroad towns, which stagnated as the rails moved westward.

Several pages of the 1941 edition were devoted to a description of Echo Canyon and its history. Among its special points of interest is **Cache Cave,** about 20 miles from Echo and about a mile east of the highway via ranch road *(private property; inquire locally).* "The cave was a prominent landmark on the old Mormon Trail, and was known as a 'register of the desert,' because many early emigrants and Mormon soldiers carved their names on its walls,'' according to the 1941 edition. Mormon pioneers of the first party visited the cave in July 1847. Echo Canyon had previously served as a route of travel for fur trappers as early as the 1820s. ''The Harlan-Young party made the first wagon tracks down Echo Canyon in 1846, and were followed a week or ten days later by the tragically famous Donner-Reed party. These emigrant trains broke a road that saved the Mormons of 1847 enormous labor.''

Mormon Pioneer Wagon train in Echo Canyon. *From mural by Lynn Fausett, Pioneer Trail State Park, Salt Lake City.*

Tour No. 5C(2) - Park City and vicinity

Turn south from I-80 at Kimball Junction, following State 224 through Snyderville, past Park West, to Park City, 27 m. from Salt Lake City. **PARK WEST,** 4 m. from Park City, is a self-contained resort with townhouse condominiums, nine double-chair lifts, 44 miles of trails, suited for all levels of expertise. Condominiums are available for rental. Lodge with restaurant and lounge, ski school, sports center (rentals, sales, repairs), night skiing. Helicopter ski flights may be arranged to remote areas. Shuttle bus service to Park City. During the summer, Park West offers tennis, swimming, and a summer concert series featuring well known artists.

PARK CITY (7,000 alt., 2,823 pop.). Park City's 1980 census count of permanent residents amounted to only half of the residents and visitors who occupy its facilities at all seasons of the year. Park City is one of Utah's phenomenal boomtowns of the contemporary age. While the Old Town has been preserved more-or-less intact since recreational development began nearly 20 years ago, its surrounding environs have been completely transformed. Old Town itself, with its authentic mining background, distinctive early western architecture, and nostalgic old-time romance, has become a popular shopping district and entertainment center for visitors who come from far and near to use Park City's recreational and residential facilities. Many amenities have combined in attracting people to Park City, and neither the scope nor type of development that has taken place in the past decade (and is anticipated for the future) could have been foreseen by the planners of the early 1960s.

In 1960 Park City was a dilapidated, deteriorating town of 1,366 people, many of them unemployed, elderly or retired. Mining had long since seen its heyday, and the operations of scores of mines that once operated in the vicinity were consolidated into one firm, the United Park City Mines Company, which was finding survival difficult. Contrast that scene with 1981: The old section of town has become an important tourist attraction. Most of its aged buildings have been, or are being, restored and put to commercial or residential use. Ultramodern houses and lodges perch on the steep hillsides above the Old Town. Nearby, Park City Ski Area—which includes an imposing Resort Center complex—houses an assortment of recreation-oriented businesses. To the north are a new Holiday Inn and Holiday Village Shopping Mall. To the east of that is a large residential and commercial district, including Prospector Square convention center. On the northwest is a municipal golf course. Condominium clusters sprawl across hundreds of acres of valley floor and climb the hillsides, and new construction meets the eye in seemingly every direction. Over the mountain to the east, in Deer Valley, construction is underway on a huge 6,750-acre resort that will further expand the town's reputation as a recreation community. It is planned to include hundreds of housing and rental units in several villages, with 20 lifts servicing skiers on Bald Mountain, Bald Eagle Mountain, and Flagstaff Mountain. More than 80 designated runs are planned. The project is estimated to require 12 years and 300 million dollars for completion.

While winter sports (November-December to April-May) provide the basic bread-and-butter to many Park City businesses, the area is promoted as an all-year, four-season resort. For example, the **Park City Arts Festival,** held every August, draws more than 200,000 visitors on a two-day weekend to Historic Main Street,

Golfers and condominiums, Park City.

UTAH TRAVEL COUNCIL

Park City's Main Street during the annual Arts Festival

attracted by 150 exhibitors of arts and crafts, supplemented by performing arts and food booths. The city's 18-hole golf course is a summer attraction, as will be the Jack Nicklaus golf course in Park Meadows. Local nightlife features several dozen restaurants, bars, and nightclubs. The Egyptian Theatre, constructed in 1926, is Park City's community theatre today, the locale for musicals, dramas, and comedies. **Kimball Art Center,** acknowledged as one of the finest of its kind in the state, features a Main Gallery, gift shop, facilities for arts and crafts work, and an auditorium for musical and dramatic presentations. *Public welcome.* Numerous shops and stores offer a wide selection of goods throughout the year, and other businesses provide a full complement of services.

HISTORIC MAIN STREET DISTRICT (OLD TOWN) consists of a narrow commercial thoroughfare in the mouth of a canyon, flanked by several parallel streets at staggered elevations. Most of the buildings date from the turn-of-the-century or before, the majority having been built following the great fire of 1898. Displaying a picturesque medley of styles and building materials from the past, the Main Street District is listed on the National Register of Historic Places as a Historic Commercial District: "the best remaining metal-mining town business district in Utah." Indeed, more than 60 edifices are considered of historic and architectural interest. Many are listed on national and state historic registers.

RESORT CENTER. A monumental group of multi-storied brick buildings, the Resort Center serves as the lower terminal for Park City's complex of gondola and chair lifts, and the Alpine Slide. In the Center are shops for sales and rentals, Kinderhaus (child care center), restaurants, state liquor store, food shops, Ski Patrol, Ski School, lounges, and other facilities. Lodging referrals are available through the Park City Chamber of Commerce, phone 649-5633.

The gondola lift features four-passenger cars and extends from the Resort Center at 7,000 feet to the Summit House at 9,400 feet, a distance of 2½ miles. Ski runs descend from there. The Summit House affords a spectacular view in addition to dining service. Mid-Mountain Lodge, at the midway Angle Station, provides lodging and food service. The Snowhut at the base of the Prospector lifts is a popular lunch spot. In addition to the gondola, nine double and two triple chairlifts provide access to terrain of varying difficulty, crisscrossed by more than 68 designated ski runs, plus the wide-open Jupiter and Scotts Bowls (650 acres) serviced by the Jupiter chairlift. The *Alpine Slide* is comprised of shallow chutes on the mountainside, in which riders descend on "sleds." The top is reached by chairlift.

In 1981 construction began on **PARK CITY VILLAGE**, adjoining the Resort Center. This ambitious project—one of the largest single construction projects in Utah's history—is estimated to cost more than 100 million dollars when completed in about eight years.

LODGING AND TRANSPORTATION. Park City's hotels, lodges, apartments, chalets and condominium units are estimated to have a capacity of 8,300. This capacity is being expanded constantly with new facilities, and a wide range of lodging and package choices is available. *Write Chamber of Commerce, P.O. Box 758, Park City, Utah 84060 for details.* During peak seasons, buses from Salt Lake City provide regular scheduled service to Park City. Limousine, helicopter, taxi, and rental car services also are available. Continuous shuttle bus service connects all points within Park City. Taxi service also is available within the area.

HISTORICAL BACKGROUND. What is seen in Park City today—other than Old Town—is largely the result of activities taking place over the past 20 years. The golf course, Resort Center, ski runs and lifts, commercial centers and condominiums—all of these are recent developments. Their origin dates primarily from 1962, when United Park City Mines Company announced plans for recreational development on 10,000 acres of the company's property. With funds of approximately $3,000,000, including a federal loan of more than a million dollars, the company's Treasure Mountain Division built the gondola tramway, upper and lower terminals, golf course, and other facilities. Since then the resort operation has changed ownership more than once, and many other entrepreneurs have become involved in phases of local development. The following summary of mining days is excerpted from the 1941 edition:

In 1853 cattle were grazing in the high, cool meadows during the short summers, and the winters were locked in long, snowy silences. Then, in the winter of 1869, ore was discovered. The solitude was shattered by the tramp of prospectors' feet, by the ring of picks on hard rock, by the rumble of blasted earth, and by the laughter of hard-fighting, fast-living men.

According to General William Henry Kimball, keeper of the stage station *(see below)* a few miles from Park City, three soldiers from Colonel Patrick E. Connor's company ran across a bold outcrop of quartz about two miles south of Park City. They broke off a chunk, marked the spot with a red handkerchief, and hurried down the canyon. The assay disclosed 96 ounces of silver, 54 per cent lead, and one-tenth ounce of gold. It was not until 1870, however, that they began operation, naming the claim the Flagstaff.

The opening of the Flagstaff started a stampede. Tents and brush shanties sprang up along the canyon, followed by a boarding house, a general store, a blacksmith shop, a livery stable, a meat market, and saloons.

The Walker and Webster Gulch finds were made in the early 1870's, followed by the McHenry Gulch strike (now part of the Park Utah Consolidated), and a short time after the Jones bonanza was discovered (later known as the Daly-Judge mine). Rector Steen located ore running 400 ounces of silver in the ton in 1872, and named the claim the Ontario. Steen and his partners sold out for $27,000 that same year to a Mr. Stanley and George Hearst, father of William Randolph Hearst, chain newspaper publisher. Thomas J. Kearns, later U.S. Senator *(see Salt Lake City),* and David Keith, a large stockholder in the Silver King Coalition, got their start in Park City. Mergers later brought most of the property under the heads of two companies, the Park Utah Consolidated and the Silver King Coalition. . . .

By 1880 Park City was a good-sized town. The *Park Mining Record,* later called the *Park Record,* was established by the Raddon family, and has continued under their management. The first telegraph line was completed from Park City to Echo; a Catholic church was erected; and a water system, consisting of a small reservoir and a pipe down one street, was installed. Amusements were simple, and, as befitted the men of the district, generally muscular—boxing matches, wrestling matches, and foot or snowshoe races.

Bad luck stalked the camp in the 1890's. The panic of 1893 dealt Park City a hard blow, and a series of fires nearly wiped it off the map. The first fire broke out in a furniture store. Next to go was the sampling works, followed by the most disastrous conflagration of all, the hotel fire of 1898. It started in the kitchen, and, fanned by a canyon breeze, spread so rapidly that firemen were unable to control it. When the smoke cleared away, Park City counted a million-dollar loss. The town dug in, and within ninety days a new business district arose. There were rumors of a "fire bug." The *Park Record,* always a barometer of public opinion, wrote: ". . . should anyone be caught in the act of setting fire to a building his life would not be worth a straw. . . . Murder may be committed and the law allowed to take its course, but the line is drawn on the fire bug and God help the man. . . . A long rope and a short-shift will be his portion as sure as fate." . . .

The coming of prohibition, the World War, the slump in silver prices, the depression, labor troubles, and the death of many of the old-timers, combined to partially tame this once wide-open town. Although stills blowing up could be heard in the mountains, and the residents were able to find a species of alcoholics when they wanted to, the town never really recovered from the shock of prohibition. Beer parlors and State liquor stores replaced the palaces of drink; fighting on the streets became more scientific and less spectacular; and automobiles took the miners into towns on pay day. Gambling was carried on furtively behind closed doors, and characters like "First Class" Sickler, who thought all ore looked first class, grew scarce. Park City's light has dimmed, but there clings an aura of the past. Park City is still the slightly uncouth mining camp of yore.

Park City in 1896. *Utah Historical Society photo.*

Tour No. 6
DINOSAURLAND REGION
(Daggett, Duchesne and Uintah counties)

This tour region includes the Uintah (Uinta) Basin, much of the Uinta Mountains, Ute Indian country, Flaming Gorge Dam and Reservoir, Green River, and Dinosaur National Monument. Though citizens of the Uinta country now advertise their region as Dinosaurland, there is far more of interest in this northeastern corner of Utah than the fossils of extinct reptiles, however fascinating those may be.

Uinta Mountains in winter, as seen from the air.

In ways this is the least known part of the state. Yet its history and unique natural scene—even more, perhaps, the dramatic cultural and economic transformation now underway—merit widespread concern.

Climatically this is a harsh land, having on average the lowest mean temperatures and moisture totals of any climatic region of the state. Topographically it is forbiddingly rugged, being ringed by corrugated highlands, and even the relatively level Uinta Basin displays a badlands surface of shallow pocket valleys, broad stream channels, and flat-topped ridges or benches. Traditionally, until recent years, the bulk of its population subsisted marginally on agriculture and recreational travel. Today, mineral production provides the region's most important economic cornerstone, and this industry is likely to expand even more dramatically in the years to come.

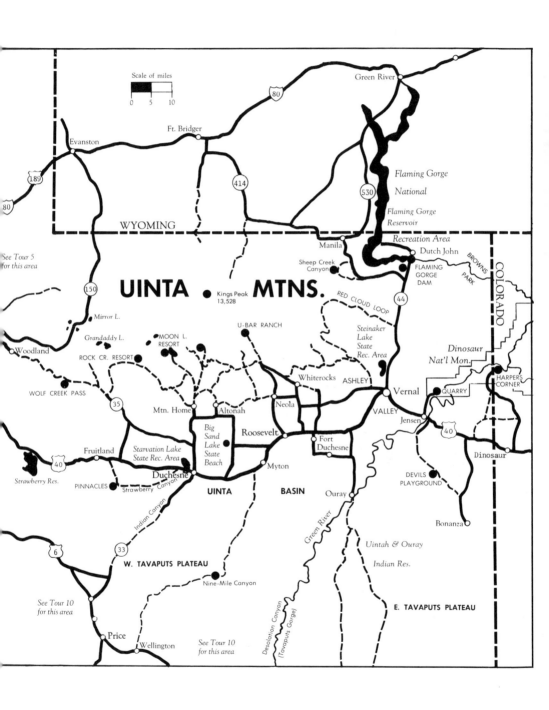

Scale of miles
0   5   10

Green River

80

Ft. Bridger

Evanston

189

80

414

530

Flaming Gorge

National

Flaming Gorge
Reservoir

WYOMING

Manila

Recreation Area

Dutch John

*See Tour 5
for this area*

Sheep Creek
Canyon

FLAMING
GORGE
DAM

BROWNS

PARK

COLORADO

UINTA   •   MTNS.

150

Kings Peak
13,528

RED CLOUD LOOP

44

Mirror L.

U-BAR RANCH

Steinaker
Lake
State
Rec. Area

Dinosaur
Nat'l Mon.

Grandaddy L.

MOON L.
RESORT

ROCK CR. RESORT

Woodland

Whiterocks

ASHLEY

Vernal

HARPERS
CORNER

QUARRY

WOLF CREEK PASS

Neola

VALLEY

Mtn. Home

Altonah

35

Jensen

40

Dinosaur

Roosevelt

Big
Sand
Lake
State
Beach

Fort
Duchesne

Fruitland

Starvation Lake
State Rec. Area

40

Myton

DEVILS
PLAYGROUND

Strawberry Res.

Duchesne

PINNACLES

Strawberry Canyon

UINTA

BASIN

Ouray

Indian Canyon

Bonanza

6

33

Green River

W. TAVAPUTS PLATEAU

Uintah & Ouray

Indian Res.

Nine-Mile Canyon

E. TAVAPUTS PLATEAU

*See Tour 10
for this area*

Desolation Canyon
(Tavaputs Gorge)

Price

Wellington

*See Tour 10
for this area*

(Regarding the spelling of Uinta: Technically, when applied to geographic features—mountains, river and basin—the formal spelling is Uinta. The form Uintah is correctly used with regard to political divisions such as Uintah County, Uintah and Ouray Indian Reservation. In practice, the Basin has long been referred to by many people—local residents in particular—as the Uintah Basin.)

Tour No. 6A — US 40 from Daniels Canyon east to Vernal, together with Uinta Mountains and sideroads in Uinta Basin

East of Heber City and Provo River Valley, US 40 enters the Uinta country through **Daniels Canyon,** a long defile with a gradual incline, a natural route of travel since time immemorial. **STRAWBERRY RESERVOIR,** at about 7,600 feet altitude, is cupped between rolling summits in a transitional montane zone between the Uinta Range and the Tavaputs/ Wasatch plateaus.

This large man-made lake has been a favorite fishing resort since original impoundment more than 60 years ago as the state's first important federal reclamation project—and the first large-scale diversion of water from the Colorado River Basin into the Great Basin. Since then it has collected Uinta drainage water for transmountain diversion to Utah Valley via Strawberry Tunnel. The original Strawberry Valley Project involved construction of roads, dam, power plant, canals, dikes, and a 20,000-foot-long concrete-lined diversion tunnel. Construction required many years, extending from 1905 to 1922. The first storage water was delivered to Utah Valley in 1915. As a crucial element in the Bonneville Unit of the Central Utah Project, the reservoir is being enlarged—by construction of Soldier Creek Dam on Strawberry River—from a capacity of 270,000 acre-feet to a capacity of more than a million acre-feet. Additional water will be brought from headwaters of the Duchesne River via 38 miles of tunnels and aqueducts. The reservoir's water flows in two directions:west via tunnels into the Great Basin, generating electricity enroute, and east to Starvation Reservoir near Duchesne.

Between Strawberry Reservoir and Fruitland the highway passes through rolling mountain country, sparsely vegetated with brush and pygmy evergreens. Near Fruitland it emerges into the vastness of Uinta Basin, and the massive bulk of the Uinta Range comes to dominate the northern horizon.

FRUITLAND (6,600 alt.) is a cluster of ranches, "settled in 1907 and named by land promoters who hoped to attract settlers." At a junction 7 m. east of Fruitland, State 208 forks north to a junction with State 35 (10 m.), which leads in one direction to Duchesne, in the other to **Hanna, Wolf Creek Pass,** and **Provo River Valley** *(see Duchesne below).* Ten miles north of Fruitland, in 1972, strip mining was begun, then halted, on a deposit estimated to contain nearly two billion tons of high quality coal.

East of the junction with State 208, US 40 passes through a dense growth of pinyon pines and junipers, claimed by local enthusiasts to be "the world's largest pinyon cedar forest"—perhaps a dubious claim. In this vicinity is Pinyon Ridge, a rural land subdivision. **Starvation Reservoir,** a major impoundment in the valley formed by the confluence of Strawberry and Duchesne rivers, is a 3,000-acre water control unit of the Central Utah Project. On its shore is **Starvation Lake State Beach,** a recreational development with boating and camping facilities.

Here the highway has descended into the Uinta (Uintah) Basin, in the words of the Utah Travel Council "a vast bowl rimmed by mountains, a peaceful valley carpeted with irrigated fields, sagebrush flats, and undulating forests of juniper and pinyon pine. Along the streams flowing down from the mountains, farmers have literally turned the valley into a land of milk and honey, for dairying is an important local industry and Basin honey is famous for its quality and flavor. In summer, thousands of sheep and cattle graze the hills and fields; in winter they feed on produce grown in the valley or graze the lower elevations. . . ." About a third of the Basin's people live in three cities on U.S. Highway 40: Duchesne, Roosevelt, and Vernal. The other two-thirds are scattered across the valley in smaller towns, villages, and ranches. Many Utes reside at Whiterocks, Fort Duchesne, Myton, and Ouray, though some have homes elsewhere.

DUCHESNE (5,500 alt. 1,677 pop.) is the seat of Duchesne County, a vast domain of more than 3,000 square miles, thinly populated over most of its extent and bounded on three sides by high mountains. The county's population increased by 70 per cent between 1970 and 1980, one of the highest growth rates among Utah's counties, with the majority of newcomers settling outside the limits of incorporated communities. Much of this growth was due to expansion of the petroleum industry, particularly in the rural Basin area to the north and east of Duchesne, which attained high ranking among Utah's oil producing regions during the 1970s and promises to boost production in the 1980s. Despite its phenomenal growth, Duchesne city remains a modest community in appearance, outwardly the least changed of the Basin's three cities.

Turn north from Duchesne via State 87 and paved sideroads to **Mountain Home, Boneta, Bluebell,** and other farming villages at the base of the Uinta Mountains. In a rare setting of rural charm, these hamlets are largely dependent on livestock and the growing of grain and feed crops. Successful oil drilling of the past decade has transformed the area in respects, bringing unforeseen wealth to some, adding new structures to the landscape. Unpaved roads lead north from Mountain Home, passing through the Indian reservation to **Ashley National Forest,** giving access to **Rock Creek Canyon, Moon Lake** (Lake Fork Canyon), and **Yellowstone Canyon.** Each of these is the site of forest campgrounds (Ashley National Forest), at the head of trails leading into the region of high peaks and the High Uintas primitive Area. Resorts in these canyons provide varying services and accommodations: **Rock Creek Resort,** about 40 m. north of Duchesne on Rock Creek (cabins, lodge, playground, campground, pack trips, trail rides, skimobiles) . . . **Yellowstone Ranch,** 38 m. north of Duchesne on Yellowstone River (cabins, lodge, campground, trail rides, pack trips) . . . **Moon Lake Lodge,** 35 m. north of Duchesne on Moon Lake (cabins, lodge, supplies, boat rentals, trail rides, pack trips).

State 87 curves eastward in a circuitous path through Altamont, Upalco and Ioka to a junction with US 40 about 5 m. west of Roosevelt.

From State 87 at a junction 7 m. north of Duchesne, State 35 forks west to **Tabiona, Hanna, Wolf Creek Pass, Woodland** and junction with US 189A at **Francis** *(see Tour No. 5).* For 30 miles State 35 parallels the Duchesne River in the pleasant valley it has carved in its journey from the High Uintas. Unpaved sideroads and trails penetrate the wild country, extending away in all directions. From **Hanna** an unpaved sideroad gives alternate access to Rock Creek Resort *(above).* Another unpaved road leads north from State 35 near Hanna into the deepening gorge of the

Duchesne to **Defa's Mountain (Dude) Ranch,** 44 m. from Duchesne, one of Utah's venerable and better known guest ranches, (cabins, cafe, lodge, horses and guides for pack trips). Trails lead from this vicinity to Grandaddy Lakes, connecting with an extensive network of high-country Uinta trails *(see Uinta Mountains below).*

Turn south from Duchesne via State 33 to **Indian Canyon** and junction with US 6 at Castlegate *(see Tour No. 10A).* This scenic 40-mile route passes through a gorge of gentle contours and soft colors, gradually ascending to a 9,100-foot pass on the summit of **West Tavaputs Plateau,** then dropping through Willow Creek Canyon to Castlegate. The road is characterized by easy grades and curves. The Indian Canyon route was an important link between the Uinta Basin and the railroad at Helper and Colton, particularly during early decades of this century, between the freighting heydays of Nine Mile Canyon and improvement of the route now followed by US 40.

East of Duchesne, US 40 traverses the broad valley of **Duchesne River** to Myton. The great **Uinta Mountain uplift** looms to the north, and though several high peaks can be glimpsed, the range's glaciated ridge of barren 13,000-foot summits is hidden from valley view. This grand spine is dramatically apparent from the north, or from the Mirror Lake highway (Tour No. 5), or from headwaters of south-flowing streams—but most comprehensively, of course, from a high-flying plane.

THE UINTA MOUNTAINS

The **Uinta Mountains,** Utah's loftiest, are unusual in more than a few respects, including the fact that they are claimed to be the largest individual mountain range in the contiguous 48 states having a distinct east-west axis. Together with the Wasatch Range, they represent the Rocky Mountains province in Utah. Nearly a dozen peaks exceed 13,000 feet in altitude, the highest being Kings Peak at 13,528 feet. As described in *The Geologic Story of the Uinta Mountains* (U.S. Geological Survey Bulletin 1291), the Uintas "have an overall length of about 150 miles and a mean width of about 35 miles. At their widest, toward the west, they are more than 45 miles across, and at their narrowest, near the center of the range, they are less than 30 miles across. The boundaries are somewhat indefinite, inasmuch as the flanks pass into bordering hogback ridges and broad sloping mesas that merge gradually with the high arid tablelands of the adjacent basins." The Uintas were further described on page 490 of the 1941 edition:

The Uinta Range, part of which is included in the Primitive Area, in general form is a broad, elongated, flat-topped arch. The culminating peaks and ridges lie for the most part along the north side of the arch. The plateau-like summit in many places is deeply dissected and eroded into jagged peaks and ridges; at their bases are immense amphitheaters, and below are deep canyons. The central part of the range, along the anticlinal crest, is formed of nearly horizontal rock strata, buried at many places beneath glacial material, which impounds numerous lakelets and ponds. A great portion of this region is occupied by grassy parks, open meadows, and heavily forested slopes, above which the barren peaks rise boldly. The northern flank of the range slopes off steeply to the undulating Green River Basin of Wyoming. The southern slopes drop more gently to an extensive plateau region and then into the Uinta Basin. These slopes are deeply incised by streams, many of them with canyon channels from 1,000 to 2,000 feet deep. In this most heavily timbered region in the state the rock coloring is delicate, ranging through the rich warm colors of the spectrum to mellow blends of green, blue, lilac, pearl, amethyst, and purple. . . .

Moon Lake and Lake Fork Canyon.

Packing into the High Uintas.

The origin and age, as mountains, of the Uinta Range is part of what geologists call the "Laramide Problem." It is supposed that they were uplifted at about the same time as the rest of the Rocky Mountains, and that the cause was the so-called Laramide Revolution, but so many complex factors are involved that there is little agreement among geologists as to what caused the stresses which forced the rocks into a great arch, or in what period it occurred. Geologists also differ as to the ice ages of this region, some claiming that there were three, while others say five. They are agreed that it was . . . covered with ice as recently as 25,000 years ago, and that some of its glaciers were twenty miles long. Glaciers carved out the great amphitheater-like cirques, their debris dammed up hundreds of lakes, and water melting from them wielded the principal erosional tools that cut scores of deep canyons.

Ute Indians hunted in the Primitive Area before the coming of the white man, following the game up the mountains in summer, drying the meat, tanning the hides, and gathering and drying berries.

The first white man known to have crossed the Uintas, in 1825, was General William H. Ashley, leader of the first trapping expedition to reach present Utah *(see History)*. A shortage of food among Mormon settlers in the fall of 1847 led to the next known penetration of the High Uintas, by Mormon hunters. "I used to be a good hunter," writes Priddy Meeks in his journal, a copy of which is in possession of the Utah Historical Records Survey, "and I believe the Lord will bless me with good luck and I will trust in him like old Lehi and try it." . . . In later years wandering prospectors, cowboys, and sheepherders penetrated the forests and climbed the peaks, leaving only burnt sticks and tin cans to mark their passing. . . . Homesteading pioneers preferred better land in lower valleys, irrigable with water from these mountains. Some logging was done, but the roads were too rough and the distance to the large centers too far to make it profitable. All things seemed to conspire to leave the High Uintas a primitive area, just as it was in the days of Ashley, Priddy Meeks, and the Swede.

According to G. E. and B. R. Untermann, "Formations in the Uinta Mountain and Basin area consist chiefly of sediments of marine and continental (lake, floodplain and eolian) origin. A few minor exposures of igneous rocks occur . . . The stratigraphic history of the region is generally one of great regularity, with deposition often being continuous and of a transitional nature . . . Formations range in age from Precambrian (Uinta Mountain group) to Cretaceous (Mesaverde), representing eight geological systems and three eras . . . Twelve of these formations are in large part of marine origin, indicating the frequency with which the area was submerged beneath the sea. Approximate maximum total deposition of known sediments . . . amounts to 45,000 feet in the eastern Uinta Mountain and Basin area and to 63,000 feet in the western part of the region . . ."

As an eloquent summary, the following is quoted from Wallace R. Hansen's *Geologic History of the Uinta Mountains* (U.S. Geological Survey Bulletin 1291), page 108:

In trying to visualize the crustal movements that produced the Rocky Mountains 60-70 million years ago, one is bemused by the magnitude of the uplifting forces that raised thousands of cubic miles of rock in the Uinta Mountains alone from a position near or even below sea level to present altitudes, thousands of feet higher. If the strata that have been eroded from the Uinta Mountains were restored in our imagination, the upper layers would be 30,000-40-000 feet above sea level. This is not to say that the mountains ever stood that high, even though some early-day geologists surmised they did. For as the mountains rose, erosion attacked and carried away the heights, and the higher the mountains rose, the more vigorous the attack. It is doubtful that the mountains were ever really much higher than now—possibly a few thousand feet higher, but never Himalayan, certainly, in size.

The upbuckling that produced the mountains was accompanied by comparable downbuckling under the basins. As the mountains rose, the basins subsided, so that deposits once near sea level throughout the region are now 12,000-13,000 feet high in the mountains but are as much as 30,000 feet below sea level beneath the Green River and Uinta Basins. Moreover, debris shed from the mountains accumulated in the adjacent basins, and its added weight further depressed the basin floors. Obviously, the crust is not unyielding; it responds to pressures directed horizontally, vertically, or obliquely. Such pressures—building up at the end of the Cretaceous Period—caused the crustal movements that produced the Uinta Mountains.

HIGH UINTAS PRIMITIVE AREA represents the remote heart of the Uinta Range. A 237,000-acre federal preserve occupying parts of Ashley and Wasatch national forests, the Primitive Area extends along both sides of the Uinta crest from Mirror Lake on the west to Kings Peak on the east, including within its boundaries many of the highest summits in Utah as well as hundreds of lakes. The following appears in the 1941 edition:

Five plant zones are represented in the Primitive Area: the Arctic, on the grassy moss- and lichen-covered but treeless peaks above 11,000 feet; the Hudsonian, marked by Engelmann spruce and alpine fir, usually from 9,000 to 11,000

High Uintas Primitive Area.

WARD ROYLANCE

feet; the Canadian, with white balsam, blue spruce, and aspen as low as 7,000 feet; the Transition between 6,000 and 7,000 feet, represented by scrub oak and yellow pine; and the Upper Sonoran, with its juniper and sage below 6,000 feet. Indigenous flora includes twenty-five genera of grasses, thirty different shrubs, and more than one hundred types of herbs and weeds. The pine, spruce and fir are varied with quaking aspen, pinon pine, mountain ash, hickory, juniper, and scrub oak. Bird life comprises all species indigenous to the western Rockies, augmented by many migrants.

Animals are abundant. Bighorn sheep roam the crags, elk browse in the valleys, bear put on fat before their long winter sleep. The most plentiful big game animal is the mule deer. Badger, porcupine, Canadian lynx, mountain lion, and coyote are numerous, and there is a great variety of smaller animals.

Access to the Primitive Area—The most convenient paved access route leading to the edge of the Primitive Area is State 150 between Kamas, Utah, and Evanston, Wyoming *(see Tour No. 5)*. Near Mirror Lake, reached by this road, the Highline Trail begins and "runs in a general east-west direction along the crest of the Uinta Mountains; it is the only feasible path through the lofty passes. There is a network of trails across the area, with the Highline Trail the trunk or main artery. Well-marked connecting trails lead to highway points of entry . . . A round trip, made as described [from Mirror Lake to Henry's Fork Park, eastern terminus of the trail, a distance of 56 m. one-way] requires several days on horseback [or foot], stopping only for meals and sleep. Food, first aid supplies, fishing equipment, warm bedding or a medium-weight sleeping bag, and warm clothing must be carried the entire trip." This trail—which affords the ultimate Uinta wilderness experience—is described in detail on pages 493-495 of the 1941 edition. Only a minority of Uinta hikers, of course, attempt such an arduous undertaking. It is hardly necessary to do so for a savoring of the Primitive Area, which may be entered from many access points around its perimeter. A number of roads lead from US 40 in the Uinta Basin to trail heads in canyons of south-flowing streams such as the Duchesne, Rock Creek, Lake Fork, Yellowstone, and Uinta. In addition, numerous trails enter the area from roads to the west, north and east. Those entering the Primitive Area should be equipped with detailed maps obtainable from Wasatch or Ashley National Forest offices, and should observe the following precautionary measures:

1. Dress warmly; use good boots; take a rain covering.
2. Carry sufficient first-aid equipment.
3. Let a responsible person know to what lake region you plan to go and when you expect to return.
4. Carry sufficient food, a warm bedroll, and a small tent.
5. Take along a shovel, axe and matches.
6. Never travel in the Primitive Area in parties of less than three people.
7. The use of horses will shorten travel time and reduce fatigue.

Turn north from Bridgeland Junction, 10 m. east of Duchesne, to **Upalco** and **Big Sand Lake State Recreation Area,** 11 m. from US 40. On this picturesque reservoir of 400 acres, the state has developed a scenic viewpoint and facilities for camping and picnicking. The lake is popular for fishing.

MYTON (5,100 alt. 500 pop.) is a quiet village in the valley of the Duchesne River, surrounded by thinly vegetated badlands. Though it has grown in the past few years, Myton has a history of still livelier days when it was a bustling trade center for prosperous farms and a stop along the Nine Mile freighting route. Before white settlers arrived in 1905 it was the site of an Indian trading post called "The Bridge." A number of Ute Indians live in the vicinity, and there are gilsonite mines and oil wells nearby. Pleasant Valley, south of Myton, contains some of the region's finest "rock writings" left by ancient Indians, as well as dinosaur fossil deposits.

Turn south from a junction 2 m. west of Myton to **NINE MILE CANYON, Wellington** and **Price** (80 m.). *See Tour No. 10-D for description.* This scenic route provides closeup viewing of numerous panels of curious petroglyphs (rock etchings), the work of prehistoric Indians, and romantic traces of turn-of-the-century years when the road was utilized for freight and traffic between Uinta Basin communities and the railroad at Price.

Also turn south from this junction (fork from Nine Mile road 2 m. from US 40) to **SAND WASH LAUNCHING SITE** on the Green River, 34 m. from US 40 via mostly unpaved road. At the north end of Desolation Canyon, this site is preferred for launching by many river runners because it shortens downstream floating distance by more than 30 miles through rather uninteresting terrain below Ouray. A ramp is maintained here by U.S. Bureau of Land Management. Some boaters arrive by plane. At the site is a monument denoting the head of Desolation Canyon as a National Historic Landmark. Boaters travel from this point downstream to takeout points near Green River, a distance of 75 to 95 miles, passing through a magnificent gorge thousands of feet deep. Rapids add a thrill of potential danger to a trip that features wilderness seclusion, historic landmarks, wildlife, undisturbed flora, and fascinating geology. Several commercial operators offer tours through Desolation Canyon.

Oil rig near Roosevelt.   *Photo by Vern Jetley, Bureau of Reclamation.*

ROOSEVELT (5,200 alt. 3,842 pop.) is the largest city and commercial capital of Duchesne County, midway between Duchesne and Vernal. It also serves as the main commercial center for members of the Ute tribe. The city lies in an open valley surrounded by flat-topped benches. Roosevelt's population almost doubled (from 2,000 to 3,800) between 1970 and 1980, a growth that continues, due largely to the area's oil boom. This growth is apparent in hundreds of new buildings and businesses of recent vintage, a new oil refinery, and a considerable increase in traffic volume.

Roosevelt was founded in 1905 at the time much of the Ute reservation was opened to homesteading, and was named after Theodore Roosevelt by its first settlers, the Harmston family. In a history written for the Roosevelt Area Chamber of Commerce, George E. Stewart described the Basin's land rush days:

> Finally, in 1905 and 1906 the Ute Reservation was opened to homesteaders. The big land rush was on! It was not like the land race along the Cimarron in Oklahoma, the government had learned its lesson there, so in the Big "U" Country the red tape made the rush much more orderly. But the homesteaders came by the hundreds.
>
> An old Ute said, "When the Americats came, they came by the many manys, they came nose to tail like a string of black ants crossing the sand." Some came from Colorado through Vernal, some through Strawberry Valley, but most came along the stage road from Price through Nine Mile Canyon.
>
> An oldtimer who lived at the Strip before and during "the opening" said it was like the touch of a fairy's wand, yesterday there was nothing but wilderness and desert, today there are fences, ditches, plowing, plantings, houses and towns; settlers were everywhere . . . it was almost magical." . . . Under the law you picked your land, paid $2.25 an acre for one hundred and sixty acres. You must move on the land, build an abode, improve it and live there five years. After you "proved up" you received title in fee simple by way of a patent from the U.S. Government . . . In the "Early Days" Roosevelt was a tent and shanty town. Even some of the businesses began in tents. But, of course, these were only temporary, lasting only until something more substantial could be built . . . There it was, it sprang up almost overnight, a town; rocky, dusty, rough and raw with a purely frontier flavor . . . Roosevelt being the hub, along with its other early advantages, quickly became the principal trading center for all the western area of Uintah Basin.

Cattle and sheep, dairying, timber, alfalfa seed, and honey—these have been bolsters of the local economy over the years, varying in relative status with changing conditions. Trade and tourist travel also have helped. In later years, exploration for and production of oil and natural gas have gained high ranking on the economic scene.

Roads lead in all directions from Roosevelt and from US 40 in the vicinity, giving access to rural towns, farms and ranches, oil fields, forests

Smith's Wells Station, old Price-Myton road.

UTAH STATE HISTORICAL SOCIETY

and canyons. Spread across the stream bottoms and benchlands, watered from flowing canals, are well-kept fields of alfalfa and grain, interspersed with drilling rigs, oil pumps and storage tanks. Cattle, sheep and horses graze serenely, and modern dwellings alternate here and there with forlorn log cabins or vacant-eyed frame homes. Many of the Basin's humble old buildings, dating in some cases from the late 1800s, in most cases from the homestead days of the early 1900s, speak eloquently of hardship—of many years when crops were poor, money scarce, and families large.

THE UTE INDIANS

UINTAH AND OURAY INDIAN RESERVATION, with headquarters at Fort Duchesne, 8 m. east of Roosevelt, occupies a considerable part of the Uinta Basin lowlands, Uinta and Tavaputs foothills, and rugged highlands of the East Tavaputs Plateau east of the Green River (Hill Creek Extension). At one time the reservation was more than four times its present size of approximately one million acres.

(Ed. note: Some of the following is taken verbatim from a booklet entitled BIG U COUNTRY, written by the Revision Editor of this guidebook for the Utah Tourist and Publicity Council.)

For untold centuries, Ute Indians lived in the valleys and roamed the mountains of Utah and western Colorado. Two Ute boys led the Dominguez-Escalante expedition of 1776 through the Uinta Basin to Utah Valley, where the party spent three days visiting the Timpanogos Utes. It was the Utes who first met the Mormon pioneers, cooperated with them, and later came into conflict with them. Many of the most noted Indian chiefs and warriors of Utah's early history were Utes or closely related Paiutes—men like Walker, Black Hawk, Sanpitch, Tintic, Kanosh, Sowiette, Tabby, Santaquin, and Arapene.

Probably the Uinta Basin was not a permanent home for many Utes before the whites established trading posts here during the 1830s, or even previously, as it seems to have been somewhat of a no-man's land or seasonal hunting grounds for several different bands. But as whites continued to settle, range and mine the best lands in Utah and Colorado, the Utes were driven from their traditional homes and hunting grounds. Isolated incidents and full-scale warfare occurred, and eventually—between 1861, when Abraham Lincoln established the first Ute reservation in "Uintah Valley," and 1883—the northern Utah (Spanish Fork or Uintah) and western Colorado (Whiteriver and Uncompahgre) Ute bands were settled on the Uintah reservation. These three bands still retain their separate identities, though individually their members are integrated to some extent.

Uprooted from their age-old homes and prevented from making a livelihood as they had traditionally done, the Utes suffered great hardship for many years. Poverty, ignorance, and apathy were widespread until the past few decades, when a marked change began to take place. Today the Ute Tribe is an excellent example of how, with leadership, planning, and financing, an underprivileged culture can radically improve many of its living patterns in a relatively short time.

The Ute Tribe. Numbering about 1,700 members, the Ute Tribe has been incorporated since 1936. It is comprised of full-blood Utes, about half of whom belong to the Uncompahgre Band. The remaining members are about equally divided between the Whiteriver and Uintah Bands. In addition there are some hundreds of mixed-blood Utes who were terminated as wards of the federal government in 1961 and do not participate in all tribal functions. Members of the tribe regulate their tribal affairs through an intricate governmental organization headed by a Tribal Council, which includes representatives of the three bands chosen by their members.

Tribal Activities. Since 1950 the Utes have prosecuted successful court cases against the federal government for the taking of their lands in Colorado and Utah during the last century. As a tribe and individually they were awarded more than 25 million dollars in judgments. Some of this money was allotted directly to individuals, the remainder used by the tribe for group betterment activities such as electrification, housing, education, purchase of cattle, development of a tribal farm, operation of youth camps, and acquisition of land for consolidation purposes. These judgment funds have been supplemented by income from royalties, bonuses, and leases of tribal and tribe-member lands for production of oil and gas. Income is received also from various grants programs and from business enterprises operated as units of the Ute Tribal Enterprise System, i.e. livestock, a culinary water system, research laboratory, service station, bowling lanes, and recreational-tourist offerings. Other economic activities include arts and crafts, logging, and licenses for fishing and hunting on tribal lands. The reservation also has tremendous undeveloped reserves of asphalt, oil shale, gilsonite, and coal.

Notable advances have been made in Ute education, housing, leadership training, land improvement and utilization, recreation and youth activities. Young people attend public schools of the area. Basketball is very popular, as are boxing and baseball. The tribe presents pageants and rodeos, and is represented at Indian events outside the state. The **Bear Dance** and the **Sun Dance** are annual events on the reservation *(dates vary from year to year; check locally for details).* A description of the dances appeared in the 1941 edition.

BOTTLE HOLLOW INN AND CONFERENCE CENTER, 7 m. east of Roosevelt beside US 40, is an architecturally distinctive, elaborate resort complex featuring a luxury motel, restaurants, lounge, conference center, service station, trailer-camper park, gift shop, Indian museum, dance plaza, swimming pool, and game room. Owned and operated by the Ute Tribe, Bottle Hollow was completed in 1971 at a cost of more than two million dollars. A nearby lake provides boating, fishing, bathing and waterskiing. A buffalo herd is maintained at the resort.

FORT DUCHESNE, 1 m. south of Bottle Hollow junction, is the site of Ute tribal offices and those of the Bureau of Indian Affairs. Little of a historic or nostalgic nature strikes the eye to denote that Fort Duchesne has been at this locale since 1886, when it was established as an army post, or that it was occupied by infantry and cavalry troops from that time until 1912, when it was abandoned as a military post. Several historic buildings remain, including a powder house, guard house, and post hospital, now occupied by Bureau of Indian Affairs. Since departure of the military, Fort Duchesne has served as headquarters for the reservation. Two companies of black cavalrymen, named "buffalo soldiers" by the Utes and other western Indians, served at the fort between its founding and 1901.

WHITEROCKS, 13 m. north of US 40, is an unassuming Ute residential community, more interesting for its history than its present-day status. Near here, meager evidence indicates, was located the **Reed Trading Post,** established perhaps as early as 1828. If that was the case, it was the first fixed trading post in Utah. Apparently this post was transferred to Antoine Robidoux in the 1830s. The exact year is uncertain, probably being 1837 but possibly dating to 1832. Thereafter known as Fort Robidoux or Fort Winty, the location served as an unsavory rendezvous, trading post, fort, and travelers' stop until 1844, when the post was burned to the ground and white males killed by enraged Utes. Only Robidoux's absence at the time saved him from the same fate. Another early post seems to have been operated by Robidoux during the 1830s at the junction of Green and White rivers.

Whiterocks was the site of an Indian Agency from 1869 until 1912, when Agency offices were moved to Fort Duchesne. In June and early July of 1869, during their epic first journey down the Green and Colorado, Major Powell and his party stopped at the mouth of the Duchesne (then called the Uinta) for a few days. At this time the Major and two of his men walked 40 miles upstream to Whiterocks. His description is a valuable portrait of early days on the Ute reservation:

July 1, [1869]. This morning, with two of the men, I start for the agency. It is a toilsome walk, 20 miles of the distance being across a sand desert. Occasionally we have to wade the river, crossing it back and forth. Toward evening we cross several beautiful streams, tributaries of the Uinta, and pass through pine groves and meadows, arriving at the reservation just at dusk. Captain Dodds, the agent, is away, having gone to Salt Lake City, but his assistants receive us very kindly. It is rather pleasant to see a house once more, and some evidences of civilization, even if it is on an Indian reservation several days' ride from the nearest home of the white man.

July 2. — I go this morning to visit Tsau-wi-at [Sowiette]. This old chief is but the wreck of a man, and no longer has influence . . . He is said to be more than 100 years old . . . His wife, "The Bishop," as she is called, is a very garrulous old woman . . . She has much to say to me concerning the condition of the people, and seems very anxious that they should learn to cultivate the soil, own farms, and live like white men. After talking a couple of hours with these old people, I go to see the farms. They are situated in a very beautiful district, where many fine streams of water meander across alluvial plains and meadows . . . It will be re-membered that irrigation is necessary in this dry climate to successful farming. Quite a number of Indians have each a patch of ground of two or three acres, on which they are raising wheat, potatoes, turnips, pumpkins, melons, and other vegetables. Most of the crops are looking well . . . This beautiful valley has been the home of a people of a higher grade of civilization than the present Utes.

Powell then described pottery fragments, foundations of "ancient houses," and "mealing-stones that were not used by nomadic people. . . ." The Utes, seeing his interest, took pains "to show me several other places where these evidences remain, and tell me that they know nothing about the people who formerly dwelt here. They further tell me that up in the canyon the rocks are covered with pictures." One of the places shown Powell by the Utes may have been **Whiterocks Village,** a prehistoric settlement excavated by the University of Utah in 1966. A number of structures were unearthed, as well as a large quantity of cultural debris. Evidence indicates occupa-tion by Fremont Indians about A.D. 850. *Historic register listing.*

The drive from US 40 to Whiterocks is interesting for no other reason than that it passes through near-virgin terrain along the Uinta River—a wild streamside landscape of willows, brush and deciduous trees, undisturbed by tilling, much the same as it might have appeared when Utes were the only inhabitants of the Basin.

The road north from Whiterocks leads to **Uinta Canyon,** where there are campgrounds **(Ashley National Forest)** and the beginning of trails to Uinta streams, lakes and high peaks. **U-Bar Ranch,** a venerable enterprise, features cabins, meals, horses and guides for pack trips, fishing and hunting excursions. Uinta Canyon is also accessible by road from Neola. This area has been the filming locale for several television and theater films in recent years.

From US 40 at a junction 16 m. east of Roosevelt (14 m. west of Vernal), State 88 forks south to Pelican Lake, Ouray National Wildlife Refuge, and the Ute settlement of Ouray.

PELICAN LAKE, 10 m. from US 40 near Leota, is an impoundment of more than a thousand acres, popular for fishing (bass and bluegill) and waterfowl hunting. A new campground and launching ramp were opened at the lake in 1981 *(carry drinking water).* **OURAY NATIONAL WILDLIFE REFUGE** extends along the Green River for about eight miles, embracing some 13,000 acres of river, sandbars, islands, bottomlands and riverbank. Beginning in 1961, the refuge has developed a system of dikes, canals, roads, and marsh habitat. More than 130 species of birds have been observed at the refuge, including Canada goose, numerous ducks and other waterfowl, hawks and eagles, owls, swallows, songbirds, pheasants and woodpeckers. Wildlife is abundant, with animals such as mule deer, coyotes, bobcats, rabbits, and an occasional mountain lion and black bear. Though the refuge lies in a desert environment with scant rainfall, the river encourages a luxuriant growth of plants—which, in combination with plentiful water, invite birds from both Pacific and Central flyways. *Visitors are welcome.* Migration seasons provide the most interesting times for birdwatching: April-May in the spring, August-November in the fall. October through November are recommended as "the best months of the year to visit the refuge if you are interested in waterfowl."

OURAY is a small settlement near the confluence of Duchesne and Green rivers, an important Ute center since early days of the reservation, named for Chief Ouray of the Uncompahgre Utes. A number of its rustic buildings date from the 1880s. Non-Indian farmers and ranchers also live in the Ouray area, and nearby at Leota and Randlett. Some of the Basin's first Mormon settlers planted their roots in this area in 1879, and across Green River near the mouth of White River. At this latter site, in 1881, **Fort Thornburgh** (predecessor of Fort Duchesne) was established, being removed within a short time to Maeser. As early as 1833 this area apparently was the site of a trading post, operated by Kit Carson. A bridge across the Green at Ouray gives access to the **White River country** and **East Tavaputs** region. Ouray is a launching and takeout site for river runners.

VERNAL (5,300 alt. 6,600 pop.), Uintah County seat, is the largest and oldest city in northeastern Utah, for which it serves as a regional capital. Population increased dramatically between 1970 and 1980, promising greater growth in the decade to come as development of fossil fuels accelerates. The bustling Vernal of today hardly resembles the slow-paced community of 1941, when it was described as "a trade center for sheepherders and cowhands; broad-brimmed Stetsons, high-heeled boots, and jangling spurs are commonplace. Approximately 200,000 sheep and 25,000 cattle are grazed in the surrounding country, and clover blossoms provide the basis for another industry—bee culture." Gone now are most of the sheep, the city's population has tripled since those days, and spurs are seldom seen. Transients far outnumber the residents.

Vernal is in the valley of Ashley Creek, a perennial stream flowing from the Uinta Mountains and emptying into Green River near Jensen. Ashley Valley was initially settled in the early 1870s, its first house being erected by Pardon Dodds, former Indian agent at Whiterocks. Other settlers began arriving soon afterwards, and by 1879—when the Meeker Massacre in Colorado stimulated building of a temporary fort—the valley's population numbered in the hundreds. Before the name Vernal became official in 1893 it was known variously as Hatchtown, Ashley Center and Ashley. Both Etienne Provost and Antoine Robidoux were in the area in 1824, and the Dominguez-Escalante expedition has passsed through in 1776. However, the name of the valley and stream commemorates the visit of General William H. Ashley and a few trapper companions who traversed Green River downstream from Wyoming to the Uinta Basin in 1825. There encountering a party of trappers from New Mexico, led by Etienne Provost, they returned to the north slope of the Uintas by a circuitous westerly route. In 1869, camped a few miles south at the mouth of the Duchesne, Major Powell wrote: "Some years ago, Captain Berthoud surveyed a stage route from Salt Lake City to Denver, and this is the place where he crossed the Green River. His party was encamped here for some time, constructing a ferry boat and opening a road."

After white settlement began during the 1870s, Vernal gradually became the trading center for ranches, farms and humble communities scattered across the eastern Basin and mountains, isolated from the rest of the state by long distances and rough roads. In early years it was easier to bring supplies over the Uintas from Wyoming than from Salt Lake City. Not until the railroad was completed through Price in the 1880s did the problem of supply become less than critical; but even with improvement of the Nine Mile road and building of the narrow-gauge "gilsonite" railroad, there remained decades of long-distance freighting and passenger travel over rough dirt roads.

Dinosaur Natural History Museum, 120 E. Main *(Open daily all year)* is for many visitors the most fascinating museum in Utah. An official Utah state park and

Dinosaur Gardens and museum interior, Dinosaur Natural History Museum.

information center, the museum dates from the 1940s, having gradually expanded its collections and exhibits until today it contains a number of halls devoted not only to natural history but also to human history, archeology and anthropology. Thousands of items are displayed. Featured are exhibits on prehistoric life of the Uinta region . . . wildlife and plants . . . geology . . . Utah's natural resources and visitor attractions . . . Ute culture and crafts . . . prehistoric Indian antiquities . . . mineral and fluorescent exhibits. Of special note are the numerous fossils on display, including lifelike models and reconstructed skeletons of vanished species; also a valuable collection of more than 100 large paintings of ancient landscapes and life forms, the work of Ernest Untermann, Sr.

Adjoining the main museum is **Dinosaur Gardens,** an open-air natural area in which are displayed life-size models of 14 strange prehistoric creatures—some of them former residents of the Uinta region. Made from fiberglass and resin, the work of Utah sculptor Elbert Porter, the models include: Tyrannosaurus Rex, largest of all man-eating dinosaurs, about 18 feet tall and 50 feet in length . . . Diplodocus, an enormous plant-eater with long tail and long neck measuring 80 feet in length and weighing as much as 30 tons . . . Triceratops and Stegosaurus, armored dinosaurs . . . flying reptiles . . . a giant woolly mammoth . . . and other strange creatures of the past. Also in the Gardens is a full-scale replica of the skeleton of "Dippy" the Diplodocus, 76 feet long, for years the museum's symbol. On the lawn in front of the museum is an impressive life-size sculpture grouping of three dinosaurs engaged in combat, the work of Utah sculptor Millard F. Malin.

Until recent years the museum was known as the Utah Fieldhouse of Natural History. It has been a commendable community and state cooperative project. Two individuals most directly responsible for the museum's growth during its first 20 years were its curators, the late G. E. and B. R. Untermann—known affectionately as Ernie and Billie—a husband and wife team, both of them nationally recognized geologist-naturalists.

Pioneer Museum (Daughters of Utah Pioneers), 5th West and 2nd South, opposite Uintah Stake Tabernacle. *Open afternoons, June to September or by appointment.* Housed in an attractive complex of rock buildings, the DUP Pioneer Museum is regarded as one of the most outstanding of its kind in the west. Its relics, numbering more than 2,000, are professionally arranged—originally under the direction of Billie Untermann, curator of the Natural History Museum. The main building itself is a relic, having been built in 1887 of native stone as the Uintah Stake Tithing Office and thereafter known as "The Little Rock House." It was moved (not quite intact) from its original site some blocks away in 1960, with annexes being added over the next decade.

Old Uintah Stake Tabernacle (Mormon), 5th West and 2nd South, is a large and distinctive brick structure with octagonal cupola. The tabernacle dates from the first decade of the present century (1907) and has functioned since then as a meetinghouse. According to description in the State Register, the tabernacle is "basically Federal in style, [and] the entire building is an expression of strength and dignity."

Bank of Vernal Building (now Zion's First National Bank), 3 W. Main. The building gained a modicum of fame as the Parcel Post Bank, so called because the bricks in its facade—four or five tons of them—were shipped from Salt Lake City by parcel post. As described in the 1941 edition, "It was erected in [1916], when freight was $2.50 a hundred pounds and parcel post only $1.05."

Postal regulations prohibited mailing more than 50 pounds in one package or more than 500 pounds in a shipment to one address. Bricks were mailed in packages of seven, addressed to a dozen different Vernal residents. The Salt Lake City, Price, and Vernal post offices were flooded with bricks. Vernal farmers, becoming parcel-post conscious, ordered tools, wagon parts, and canned goods by mail. Farm products were mailed to market; one shipment of corn required ten four-ton trucks. Mail trucks were often loaded to capacity without carrying a single letter. Federal parcel post regulations were changed shortly thereafter, preventing shipment of more than 200 pounds a day to any addressee. The Vernal star route, from Salt Lake City, [was] the longest in the United States, 188 miles, serving fifty post offices.

Old Ashley Post Office is a quaint log structure built in 1879 by Wilbur C. Britt. According to the State Register, "In 1878 [Britt] taught the first formal school in the Uintah Basin. The log cabin consisted of one large room with a partition separating the post office from a store. Mail was delivered once a week from Green River, Wyoming. In winter the carriers who normally made the trip on horseback were forced to use snowshoes. The building belongs to the Daughters of Utah Pioneers." *Private.*

Thorne Photo Studio and Museum, 18 W. Main, displays a large private collection of Indian artifacts and cultural items, as well as antique firearms, pioneer relics, and fossils. Leo Thorne, the studio's late proprietor, was a student of the area's archeology. Many of the artifacts are believed to be the work of a culture dating to the time of Christ or before, including a mummy found in a Dry Fork cave. *Open to the public during business hours.*

County Library, 155 E. Main, features a **Little Gallery of Arts** and **First Ladies of the White House Doll Collection.**

Tour No. 6B — Tours from Vernal

(1) **North through Maeser to Dry Fork and Red Cloud Loop.** Turn north in Vernal at 5th West and Main and follow State 121 (Lapoint road) to Maeser, one of the older settlements of Ashley Valley, 3 m. From a junction 1 m. west of Maeser Center, turn north to Dry Fork Canyon and Red Cloud Loop. **Uintah County Park (Merkley Park),** 3 m. from State 121, is in a verdant valley at the confluence of Dry Fork and Ashley creeks. High on a sheer cliff beside the highway is a full-color painting of the American flag, bearing inscriptions "Remember the Maine" and "Pearl Harbor." **Fort Thornburgh** was established in this vicinity in 1881, following the Meeker massacre of 1879. A humble post, the "fort" was supplied from Fort Bridger over a primitive trans-Uinta road blazed in 1881 by Judge William A. Carter, a Wyoming merchant. The road was improved by troops and used as a supply route for several years; wagon trains required three weeks each way. Fort Thornburgh was closed in 1884 and the road was gradually abandoned as the Nine Mile route to the railroad at Price was improved. **DRY FORK CANYON,** nestled between broken cliffs of sandstone, was settled in the late 1870s and at one time contained a modest village population. Few of the original buildings remain. The canyon is more renowned as the site of the famed Dry Fork petroglyphs—hundreds of carved and painted pictures on the cliffs, apparently the work of more than one ancient Indian culture. The best known panels are on the **McConkie Ranch** *(private; permission must be obtained),* 10 m. from Vernal, where the glyphs are inscribed along the north cliffs for two miles. The McConkie site is a type site for the classic Vernal style, "attributed to the Fremont Culture, but it may be pre-Fremont [more than 800-1,000 years old]. It is characterized by elaborate anthropomorphs [human figures], generally with trapezoidal bodies, headdresses, necklaces, earrings, kilts, and other decor-

ations . . . Animals are also present, but generally are insignificant as are the occasional geometric designs. The whole valley must at one time have contained several large occupation sites." *(Quotation from historic register description.)* The trails along the cliff are unimproved, steep in places, and require a degree of exertion.

Near the McConkie Ranch, in a side canyon to the south, are the **Peltier Ranch Petroglyphs,** works of different style and older vintage. Though considered to be of Basketmaker or Pueblo I age, their actual origin and age are in doubt. *Both sites are listed on historic registers.*

The Maeser-Dry Fork road continues into the Uinta Mountains as the **Red Cloud Loop,** traversing scenic canyons, passing through evergreen and aspen forests of Ashley National Forest, giving access to camp and picnic areas, overlook points, fishing streams and lakes. The drive joins State 44 about 21 m. north of Vernal and about 40 miles from Dry Fork. **Brush Creek Cave,** 6 m. west of the junction with State 44 (half-mile trail), is a limestone cavern into which Brush Creek disappears.

(2) **Northeast from Vernal** a road leads to **Rainbow Park,** 20 m. (boat launching) and **Island Park** (ranching) in Dinosaur National Monument *(see).* Another road, partly paved, leads to Diamond Mountain and Jones Hole National Fish Hatchery, 40 m. from Vernal. *(The hatchery may also be reached from State 44.)* This road climbs almost 3,000 feet to the rim of **Diamond Mountain Plateau** at nearly 8,000 feet, then drops abruptly into **Jones Hole,** a deep gorge that is tributary to Whirlpool Canyon of the Green River. Containing the only clear trout stream in Dinosaur National Monument, Jones Hole is the site of a national fish hatchery which produces trout for fishing waters in Utah, Wyoming and Colorado. *Open to visitors.* Some visitors may desire to hike the trail downstream to Green River. The drive from Vernal affords inspirational views across the Uinta-Dinosaur geological wonderland. **Diamond Mountain Plateau** was named for "one of the greatest mining swindles in American history," described by the 1941 edition and other publications. In 1871, the swindle's clever perpetrators "salted" a remote area with rough diamonds and other gemstones—previously purchased in Europe—then interested wealthy investors and absconded with hundreds of thousands of dollars of investment money. Clarence King, noted geologist and surveyor of the Uinta Mountains (after whom Kings Peak was named), "made a visit to the field. He found diamonds in tree forks and rock crevices, but none in the underlying rock." For years the "diamond field" was thought to be in Utah—hence the name of the plateau—but is now known to be across the state line in Colorado.

From the Jones Hole road, at a junction 27 m. from Vernal, turn north off the pavement on a road leading to **Crouse Reservoir** (trout fishing). The main sideroad follows Crouse Canyon to **Green River** and **Browns Park,** crossing the river on a narrow suspension bridge 50 m. from Vernal. **Browns Park** is a mountain-girt ranching valley, about 25 miles long, that extends along Green River from the Red Canyon area in the west (Utah) to Lodore Canyon on the east (Colorado). *See Flaming Gorge National Recreation Area.* Known first as Browns Hole, before renaming by Major Powell, this remote basin still remains one of the most isolated parts of

Utah and Colorado. Rustic ranches are scattered about, giving little hint of the sometimes romantic, sometimes violent events which have transpired here since trapper days of the 1800s. The fabled Wild Bunch and other outlaws used the park as a hideout and base of operations for years, and many are the tales of outlaw goings-on in the park, as well as stories about other eccentric residents—who seemed to reside here in extraordinary profusion. Geologically, Browns Park is an intermontane valley formed partly by erosion and partly by faulting. From the bridge, roads lead to Colorado, to Wyoming, and west to Dutch John, Flaming Gorge Dam, Manila, and State 44. A short distance from the road to Dutch John, near the mouth of Jesse Ewing Canyon (about 10 m. west of the bridge across Green River; watch for directional signs) is the **John Jarvie Historical Property.** A nostalgic vignette of the frontier west, preserved by the Bureau of Land Management, this rustic ranch exhibits an old stone house, a dugout, and other antique structures, as well as a small collection of western artifacts and a cemetery. The house dates from 1888. John Jarvie, who settled in Browns Park about 1878, operated a store, postoffice, and ferry at the site. He was murdered in 1909. Public campground nearby.

The circle distance from Vernal totals about 140 miles. A detailed tour guide is available from the chamber of commerce and merchants in Vernal. Carry sufficient gasoline, tools, spare tire, food, etc. No supplies or services between Vernal and Dutch John.

(3) **State 44 north from Vernal to Manila, Dutch John and Flaming Gorge National Recreation Area.** State 44 is the main paved access to the mountain, river and lake country north of Vernal. Beginning about 4 m. from Vernal, a series of 20 interpretive signs along the highway call attention to points of geological interest that can be seen enroute. Known as **Drive Through the Ages,** State 44 from Vernal to Manila passes through rocks laid down over a billion years. Much of the route is through picturesque woodlands of Ashley National Forest. Sideroads lead *east* to Diamond Mountain Plateau, connecting with roads to Jones Hole and Browns Park *(see No. 2 above); west* to Brush Creek Cave, Red Cloud Loop *(see No. 1 above),* Oaks Park and East Park reservoirs, and four forest campgrounds. Two forest campgrounds are beside State 44, 31 m. from Vernal. Greendale Junction, 35 m., marks the approximate boundary of **Flaming Gorge National Recreation Area,** which see for continuation of State 44 and State 260.

Steinaker Reservoir, visible from an overlook 4 m. north of Vernal, is an important unit of the Central Utah Project. By storing high flows of Ashley Creek (diverted via a diversion dam and feeder canal), it provides supplemental irrigation water to about 15,000 acres of land in Ashley Valley. The project also provides municipal water for the Vernal area. Steinaker Reservoir is popular for bass and trout fishing, boating and waterskiing. On its west shore is **Steinaker Lake State Recreation Area,** developed with camping and picnicking facilities, boat ramp, toilets, and swimming beach.

The **Stauffer Chemical Company** open-pit phosphate mine and processing complex can be seen from the highway about 11 m. north of Vernal. Operations began in 1959, at which time reserves of rich phosphate rock were estimated at 700 million tons. After processing at the mine, the phosphate is shipped elsewhere for use in the manufacture of fertilizer.

Red Fleet Dam and Reservoir, first known as Tyzack and only recently completed, are elements in the Jensen Unit of the Central Utah Project. Surplus flow of Big Brush Creek is stored for municipal, industrial and irrigation use, as well as for recreation, fish and wildlife, and flood control. Under development in 1980 were a boating ramp, camping and picnicking facilities, restrooms, and drinking water. Turnoff to the dam is 15 m. north of Vernal. Turnoff to the recreation area is 12 m. north of Vernal.

(4) US 40 EAST OF VERNAL. East of Vernal, US 40 traverses a thinly populated, semi-arid expanse of low ridges and open valleys, visually dominated by the tortured rock faces of Split Mountain and Blue Mountain. From the highway there is little evidence of the region's unbelievable wealth of hydrocarbon minerals, deposited by great lakes that occupied the Basin during the Eocene epoch of 50 million years ago or so.

At **JENSEN,** 14 m. from Vernal, a highway bridge crosses Green River. This imposing stream, second largest in Utah, flows down from the Wind River Mountains of Wyoming to join the Colorado River in Canyonlands National Park. Its course through Utah is largely a series of grand gorges, interrupted here and there by valleys. The Green has been both a barrier and boon to transportation. The Dominguez-Escalante party forded the Green in 1776 a few miles north of Jensen, near the present-day Quarry Visitor Center of Dinosaur National Monument. General Ashley and a few companions floated down the river from Wyoming to the Uinta Basin in 1825, introducing an age of boating that even today has hardly reached a crescendo of popularity *(see Tour No. 10-D and Dinosaur National Monu-*

Bales of alfalfa hay, near Jensen, typical of Uinta Basin agriculture.

ment). Before the first bridges were built, land travelers found it necessary to ford the river—a hazardous undertaking even in times of low water—or to ferry across. Ferries operated near Jensen until the first bridge was opened in 1911, even longer at Alhandra downstream *(see below).*

North from Jensen, State 149 leads 7 m. to the Visitor Center and Quarry of **Dinosaur National Monument** *(see parks section),* and to riverside campgrounds of the monument. This is an area of startling geological spectacle, where multi-hued strata have been broken, tilted and folded, then exposed by erosion. Across the river, a mile or so from the Quarry Visitor Center, a grove of cottonwood trees marks the campsite of the Dominguez-Escalante exploring party, who spent three nights here in September 1776. These travelers—among the first whites to enter Utah—named the river Rio de San Buenaventura. From Escalante's diary description, historian Herbert E. Bolton determined that some of the cottonwood trees which the New Mexicans found at the campsite were still standing after 175 years, though the inscription carved into one of them no longer was visible. Two buffalo were killed in the vicinity by the party. At that time the river served as a boundary between the Utes and other Indians whom they termed the Comanches.

Turn south from Jensen 2 m. to **Stewart Lake Waterfowl Management Area** near the mouth of Ashley Creek. In the vicinity is an impressive stone monument and replica of a ferryboat (Daughters of Utah Pioneers), marking the location of **Mau-be Ferry** which operated here for more than 20 years until it was destroyed by an ice jam in 1909. A fairweather road continues south along the river to the historic ruins of **Alhandra Stage Stop and Ferry,** about 7 m. from Jensen. Listed on the National Register of Historic Places, this site was located on a toll route connecting Uinta Basin communities with the narrow-gauge railroad at Watson *(see Bonanza below).* "Travelers went by stagecoach and, later, auto along the road past Jensen and south . . . to the ferry site. From the ferry the stage passed two additional toll stops . . . before reaching Watson. The ferry operated from 1906 through 1919 until the big bridge at Jensen made it obsolete . . . This was one of the last stage routes in operation in the United States. . . ." *(Register description).* The ferry's east-bank terminus is accessible by road leading south from US 40, across the bridge from Jensen.

East of the river, massive **Blue Mountain (Yampa Plateau)** looms ever closer, an enchanting skyline. The uplift's steep flanks are most intriguing, especially those curved monoclinal slopes overlooking the highway, known as Cliff Ridge or Stuntz Ridge, which are the result of folding or flexing of the earth's crust. Blue Mountain is the southeasternmost extension of the Uintas. Near **Dinosaur, Colorado,** 3 m. east of the Utah line, is head-quarters of Dinosaur National Monument. From here a paved road climbs and winds across the heights of Blue Mountain to **Harpers Corner** in the monument, affording some of the most soul-stirring panoramic views in either Utah or Colorado *(see Dinosaur National Monument).*

Turn south from US 40 at a junction 11 m. east of the Green River to the gil-sonite mining town of **Bonanza** and the **Red Wash Oil Field** in a weird badlands region of colorful desolation, drained by White River. Bonanza and Red Wash have yielded immense wealth from hydrocarbons. Red Wash has been one of Utah's major producers of crude oil for decades, and Bonanza is the state's gilsonite capital. The area also symbolizes the Basin's potential future in the production of oil from immense deposits of oil shale and tar sands, which abound throughout the Basin—in Utah and across the state line in Colorado—in untold richness. Utah contains nearly all tar sands in the nation. For example, Asphalt Ridge near Vernal alone is estimated to contain two billion barrels of oil. Developments underway at this writing include plans for a dam and reservoir on White River, a new coal-fired power plant, intensive exploration, and perfecting of shale oil processing technology. Government planners anticipate that large-scale development of oil shale in this area will bring thousands of new residents to the Basin and necessitate greatly expanded community facilities—or even the establishment of one or two large new cities. Site preparation for the power plant of **Deseret Generating and Transmission Cooperative** began in July 1981. Located 30 miles southeast of Vernal, near Bonanza, the first unit of the huge installation will generate 400 megawatts of power. Coal is to be hauled 32 miles from a mine near Dinosaur, Colorado, and water piped 19 miles from Green River. Initial cost of the project is estimated at more than a billion dollars.

In contrast to oil shale and tar sands, which only now are on the threshold of development, gilsonite has been mined in the Basin for 80 years or more. The versatile mineral was described in the 1941 edition:

> Gilsonite, sometimes called uintaite, is a black, lustrous, brittle asphalt. It resembles glossy coal and melts at 325 degrees, but will not burn. Gilsonite is resistant to acids and alkalies and is used in the manufacture of varnishes, paints, rotogravure ink, waterproofing compounds, electrical insulation, telephone mouthpieces, roofing materials, and floor coverings. The Uintah Basin deposit was discovered in 1885 by Samuel H. Gilson, prospector, Indian scout, and Pony Express rider.

Though gilsonite occurs along a narrow belt for more than 60 miles (into Colorado) and has been mined at several sites, greatest production by far has been from the mines and plants of American Gilsonite Company at Bonanza and nearby. Its uses at present are much more varied than those indicated above; for example, the mineral is processed for gasoline, metallurgical coke, pavement asphalt, and insulation for underground pipes. Though some gilsonite is mined, prepared and shipped by traditional methods, the largest share of production comes from deep shafts and tunnels, where water is ejected from jets under high pressure to cut the gilsonite into small pieces. These are pumped to the surface and processed on-site into slurry consistency. This slurry then travels through a pipeline to a refinery near Grand Junction, 72 miles away. When the line was completed in 1957, such pipeline transport of solid materials was a new and revolutionary technique, but it has proved successful despite initial engineering problems. Much of the pipeline route follows the roadbed of the old **Uintah Railway,** a narrow-gauge rail line built primarily to haul gilsonite between the mines at **Watson, Dragon and Rainbow** (now ghost-towns, located 16 to 20 miles south of Bonanza) and the main railroad at Mack, Colorado, 50 or more miles away. But it served as well to carry commercial freight and passengers. The line was an important link between Basin communities and the outside world between completion in 1904 and abandonment in the late 1930s. *(See Alhandra Stage Stop and Ferry above.)*

According to George E. Long, as quoted in *Tales from the High Country:*

> The line boasted the steepest grades of any slick track railroad in the world, along with some of the sharpest curves known to railroading. The Uintah consisted of strange looking cabooses and motor rail cars along with several other unique features not found in other early historic railroads. The most outstanding item in the line's rolling stock was her famous Mallet (pronounced Malley) type engines. The Company had two of these locomotives built to negotiate the steep and sharp curves of Baxter Pass. They were designed so they swiveled in the middle, giving them an articulated action . . . They were the largest narrow gauge locomotives ever built, weighing 123 tons each . . . After the abandonment of the line in 1939 these famous engines went on to make history in Oregon and later to Central America. Aside from this historic episode, the Uintah Basin never got a railroad as was the talk for many years. . . .

Tour No. 7
PANORAMALAND—EAST
(Piute, Sanpete, Sevier and Wayne counties)

This tour region extends through Sanpete and Sevier valleys, and eastward through the High Plateaus to Capitol Reef National Park, Utah's Painted Desert, the Henry Mountains, Lake Powell and the remote Junction country now included in Canyonlands National Park and Glen Canyon National Recreation Area. Also described are a number of central Utah's panoramic mountain drives.

Centerfield-Gunnison, northern Sevier Valley.

Tour No. 7A — US Highway 89 from Thistle south to Circleville

Southbound US 89 separates from US 6 in Spanish Fork Canyon at the hamlet of **Thistle,** formerly an important railroad point. Geologically the Thistle area is significant, marking a transition between the Rocky Mountain Province (Wasatch Range) and Colorado Plateau Province (High Plateaus). Rock formations are dramatically deformed in this vicinity.

US 89 follows Thistle Creek southward between high mountains on either side. Tiny **BIRDSEYE** was named for a local deposit of Birdseye marble, a beautiful decorative stone. **Loafer Mountain** (10,687 alt.) looms above the town and valley.

Indianola Valley, high and cold (6,000 alt.) was settled in 1864. One mile north of the Indianola turnoff a marker beside the highway tells of the massacre of six members of the Given family in 1865 during the Black Hawk Indian War. Much of the valley is devoted to grain and alfalfa and livestock production.

South of Indianola Valley the highway passes over a ridge marking the divide between Thistle Creek drainage (emptying into Great Salt Lake) and Sanpitch River drainage (emptying into Sevier Lake).

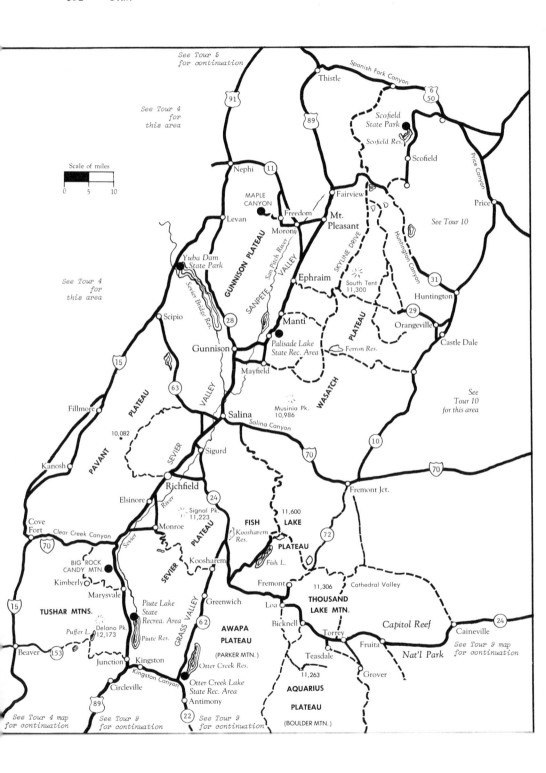

See Tour 5
for continuation

Spanish Fork Canyon

Thistle

6
50

Scofield
State Park

Scofield Res.

91

See Tour 4
for
this area

89

Scofield

Price Canyon

Nephi   11

MAPLE
CANYON

Fairview

Price

Freedom

Mt.
Pleasant

See Tour 10

Levan

Moroni

Yuba Dam
State Park

GUNNISON PLATEAU

San Pitch River

VALLEY

SKYLINE DRIVE

Huntington Canyon

31

See Tour 4
for
this area

Ephraim

South Tent
11,300

Huntington

Sevier Bridge Res.

29

Scipio

SANPETE

28

Manti

PLATEAU

Orangeville

Gunnison

Palisade Lake
State Rec. Area

Ferron Res.

Castle Dale

15

PAVANT

63

VALLEY

Mayfield

WASATCH

See
Tour 10
for this area

Fillmore

PLATEAU

10,082

Musinia Pk.
10,986

Salina

SEVIER

Salina Canyon

Kanosh

Sigurd

70

10

70

Cove
Fort

70

Clear Creek Canyon

Richfield

24

Fremont Jct.

Elsinore

River

Signal Pk.
11,223

FISH   LAKE

Monroe

Koosharem
Res.

11,600

72

BIG ROCK
CANDY MTN.

SEVIER

Sevier

PLATEAU

Koosharem

PLATEAU

Fish L.

Kimberly

Marysvale

Fremont

11,306

Cathedral Valley

15

Piute Lake
State
Recrea. Area

Greenwich

Loa

THOUSAND
LAKE MTN.

Beaver   153

Delano Pk.
12,173

Puffer L.

Piute Res.

GRASS VALLEY

62

AWAPA

PLATEAU

(PARKER MTN.)

Bicknell

Torrey

Capitol Reef

Fruita

24

Caineville

Junction   Kingston

Kingston Canyon

Otter Creek Res.

Teasdale

Nat'l Park

See Tour 9
map
for continuation

Circleville

Otter Creek Lake
State Rec. Area

11,263

Grover

89

Antimony

AQUARIUS

See Tour 4 map
for continuation

See Tour 9
for continuation

22

See Tour 9
for continuation

PLATEAU

(BOULDER MTN.)

Scale of miles

0   5   10

SANPETE VALLEY, route of US 89 for 50 miles, is one of Utah's prime agricultural regions. More than any part of the state, perhaps, it retains a flavor of the pioneer past in its tree-shaded towns, quaint old houses, crumbling outbuildings, and pastoral landscape. The valley received its first white settlers in 1849 (at Manti), two years after the first Mormon pioneers arrived in Utah. Settlement continued through the 1850s, thus making the valley one of the earliest Mormon colonies in the state. Scandinavian surnames, abundant here, reveal the nationality origin of many of its first settlers.

Cradled between mountains to east and west, Sanpete Valley widens out south of Fairview, then narrows again near Sterling where the Sanpitch River departs Sanpete and enters the valley of the Sevier. The great **Wasatch Plateau,** known locally as Manti Mountain, forms the eastern horizon, rising in points to more than 11,000 feet; streams flowing through deep canyons in this mighty uplift provide water for most of the valley's communities. Sanpete is a corruption of Sanpitch (Sampitches, Sampichya, Sanpuchi), original name of the native Utes.

FAIRVIEW (6,000 alt. 916 pop.), a farming and commercial center in the upper valley, was settled in 1859 by pioneers from Mt. Pleasant, attracted by meadows of wild hay. Fairview contains more quaintly picturesque early-day barns and outbuildings, probably, than any other town in Utah, as well as numerous 19th century houses. Some of these are historically and architecturally noteworthy.

Fairview Museum of History and Arts, housed in a former school house built of stone and dating from 1900, features historical relics, Indian artifacts, local craftwork and art. Originally this visitor attraction was conceived as a "national shrine to love and devotion," honoring in particular the late Peter and Celestia Peterson of Fairview, who were married for more than 80 years and lived to be centenarians. The museum displays sculptures and sculpture models by noted Utahn Avard Fairbanks, including one that honors the Petersons. Also of note are miniature hand-carved models of exceptional quality, created by local artist Lyndon Graham.

Turn east from Fairview on State 31 to **Fairview Canyon, Skyline Drive, Huntington Canyon,** and **Huntington** in Castle Valley *(see Tour No. 10).* This scenic mountain-canyon drive crosses the spine of **Wasatch Plateau,** a highland often described as a southern extension of the Wasatch Range. Technically it is not. The massive uplift is a monoclinal flexure, differing in structure from the Wasatch Range and being a part of the High Plateaus subdivision of the Colorado Plateau Province. The plateau's western side is a great sloping whaleback, plunging beneath Sanpete and Sevier valleys; its eastern face overlooks Castle Valley in one of western America's grandest escarpments.

Skyline Drive intersects State 31 near the head of Fairview Canyon, extending north to Tucker on US 6 and south to Mayfield, Ferron and Salina Canyon. The drive is within the boundaries of the Manti-La Sal National Forest for nearly its entire length. For much of this distance it winds along the plateau's summit at elevations of 9,000 to 11,000 feet, skirting glacial basins and deep canyons, passing through aspen and evergreen groves and grassy meadows that flaunt displays of wildflowers in late spring and summer. Views sweep thousands of dizzy feet downward onto the farms and towns of Sanpete Valley, then beyond to the west over marching

Turkey growing is a major industry in Sanpete Valley.

ranks of mountain ranges. Eastward the alpine panorama consists of deep canyons, cliffs, and forested mountain slopes, with here and there the blue of a lake as accent. The road is unpaved, rough in spots, and open along its full length of more than 100 miles for only a few months (July to early October). Access, however, is convenient, with a number of transmountain roads crossing the drive from west to east, connecting Sanpete towns with communities in Emery County.

MT. PLEASANT (5,900 alt. 2,049 pop.), a spacious community of unusually broad streets, has an economy based primarily on agriculture, commerce and education. Mt. Pleasant dates from the late 1850s when settlers from Ephraim established a new community on the site. Most of these people were of Danish origin, yet the original colonists included not only Danes but Americans, Canadians, English, Scots, Swedes and Norwegians as well. The town contains a number of 19th century buildings of note, and some later ones of interest. In 1979 the commercial district of 44 buildings was listed in the National Register of Historic places because of well-preserved architectural and commercial significance, and because it is "a fascinating documentary record of the commercial vigor of rural Utah in the decades from 1890 to 1910." Some of these buildings date from the 1870s.

Older homes with archeological and historical significance include the **Morten Rasmussen House,** 417 W. Main, built in 1875 (Federal style) . . . **Alma Staker House,** 81 E. 300 South, "one of the two best extant examples of Greek Revival-inspired 'temple form' vernacular house type in Utah" . . . **William Seely Home,** 150 S. State, built in 1861, a two-story stuccoed adobe residence with 12 rooms and basement . . . **James Hansen Home,** 382 W. Main, built in 1861-62. **Old Pioneer Museum** (Daughters of Utah Pioneers), 150 S. State, displays historic relics.

In Mt. Pleasant is **WASATCH ACADEMY,** a private school founded in 1875, today the oldest continuously operating secondary school in the state. Its founder, Dr. Duncan J. McMillan, was a Presbyterian minister who had come west in ill health and arrived in Mt. Pleasant as one of the first non-Mormon residents. The academy is an interdenominational, non-profit, coeducational, boarding and day school, offering a wide range of courses and activities for grades 9 through 12. It has both state and national listing as an outstanding historical site.

Turn west from Mt. Pleasant 7 m. to **MORONI** (5,500 alt. 1,086 pop.), in the widespreading expanse of the northern valley. Mt. Nebo looms to the north. The town was named for the angel Moroni, a Book of Mormon prophet whose golden image caps the highest tower of the Salt Lake Temple. Moroni is said to have revealed to Joseph Smith the golden plates, bearing the characters from which Smith translated the Book of Mormon *(see Mormon Church)*. The town was settled as a farming community in 1859 and has been a major turkey raising, processing and feed milling center for more than 50 years. Moroni exhibits several venerable and distinctive structures from the past century, including (at least temporarily) the **Moroni Tithing Office** on the southwest corner of Town Square. Built of oolitic rock, the historic building dates from the 1880s. The majority of Moroni's historic public, commercial and religious buildings have been replaced.

Turn north from Moroni 8 m. via State 132 to **FOUNTAIN GREEN** (6,000 alt. 578 pop.), an agricultural community founded in 1859 and at one time widely recognized for its long-fiber wool. Previous to America's entry into World War I, the quantity produced here, with the high price of wool, made Fountain Green one of the wealthiest towns per capita in the nation. It is known also as the native home of the late LeRoy Robertson of Brigham Young University and University of Utah, one of Utah's most honored musical composers. Chief Sanpitch was killed by settlers in this vicinity in 1866.

Turn west from Moroni several miles to **WALES** and **FREEDOM,** hamlets on the foothills of the **Gunnison Plateau** (Sanpitch Mountains). Wales is noteworthy as Utah's first coal mining colony, settled in 1859 by Welsh converts to the Mormon Church. Several miles north from Freedom a steep, unpaved road climbs into **Maple Canyon.** This narrow gorge is formed in massive conglomerate (cemented rocks and gravel) and is luxuriantly wooded with maples. *(Public campground.)* The canyon's most unusual feature is a natural curiosity known as **Box Canyon,** a dead-end gorge from 500 to 700 feet deep, half a mile long, and so narrow that in places a person can touch both walls at the same time. The walls overhang in places, blocking out the sky and giving a dungeon-like effect. *Caution: falling rocks are a possible hazard.* Indians are said to have had legends concerning this forbidding gorge, which resembles in narrowness, depth and sheerness of its walls many canyons in the red sandstone country.

Turn south from Mt. Pleasant 4 m. to **SPRING CITY** (5,700 alt. 671 pop.), a bucolic village 4 m. east of US 89. Spring City was settled and resettled during the 1850s and 1860s, its people having been forced to move during the Indian wars of that period. Leader of the first two groups of settlers was James Allred, a bodyguard of Joseph Smith, and the town's first name was Allred's Settlement. At one time it was on the main highway and a busy railroad, and prosperity was its lot—hence the town's unusual number of impressive buildings. Today the town has a reputation for pastoral, nostalgic charm—the beauty of its historic buildings and the aura of bygone years that distinguishes it from other "more progressive" places. Many of its older buildings are being preserved and restored, some by people who have moved there from other places. An unusual number, in fact, are listed on historic registers.

"Many examples of log, adobe, frame, and stone buildings of vernacular styling exist in their original settings, original landscape elements, including dirt streets, irrigation ditches, rows of Lombardy poplars, stone and picket fences, log barns and stone outbuildings, remain intact." *(National Register description.)* The **Mormon Ward Chapel,** strikingly original in design, dates from 1902 and is still used for religious services. **City Hall,** built in 1893 of oolitic limestone, served initially as a school. The **Orson Hyde Home,** Main and C streets, dates from the 1850s. Of oolitic limestone, two stories high, the house was the residence of Orson Hyde, Mormon apostle and pioneer leader of Sanpete Valley. It is estimated that a third of Spring City's homes exhibit folk-house architecture of the 1865-90 period, and another third display pattern-book styles of the period from 1880 to 1910. The **Old Schoolhouse,** dating from 1899 (National Register), was converted to a museum in 1981 by the Daughters of Utah Pioneers.

East from Spring City an unpaved road climbs steeply to the top of Wasatch Plateau, intersecting **Skyline Drive** not far from **South Tent** (11,300 ft.), highest point on the plateau.

EPHRAIM (5,500 alt. 2,810 pop.) is an educational, agricultural and commercial center. It is the home of **Snow College,** a state institution having an enrollment of about 1,000 students and offering lower division college and technical courses. Founded in the 1880s as a Mormon academy, the school underwent successive stages as a private junior college, state junior college, branch of the state Agricultural College, and finally its present status. In addition to education, Snow College serves as an intellectual, artistic and musical center for central Utah.

Ephraim dates from 1854, when it was settled by families from nearby Manti who built a fort and lived in it until 1860. Their first years were made difficult by hardships such as killing frosts and grasshoppers. Later years brought bountiful harvests of grain and wealth in the form of sheep, cattle, turkeys and other agricultural products.

Recent decades have seen beginnings as an industrial center with several manufacturing firms in the town. In 1979 Sperry Univac announced plans to manufacture computer subassemblies in a new 20,000 square foot building at the Ephraim Industrial Park.

Ephraim is notable, with Manti, Spring City and other Sanpete Valley communities, for its distinctive 19th century architecture. Visitors should drive the side streets to view the older homes, uncommon in style, made of stone, logs, adobe and frame, with some dating back more than a century. On Main Street (which is listed as a Historic District on the National Register of Historic Places) is a large two-story stone structure known as the **United Order Co-op Mercantile Institution,** now being restored. This building dates from 1864 and served as a co-op, grocery store, social hall, movie house, garage, Sanpete Academy (1888), and the first home of Snow College. The Main Street Historic District also features about 30 other buildings of architectural and historic significance, which together "trace the steps of Ephraim's journey from Farm Village to Commercial City" during the late 19th and early 20th centuries. Side streets display a fascinating array of architecture from long-gone years. **Ephraim Town Hall and Jail (Old Jail House),** 38 E. Center, was built about 1875 and served many functions during the intervening years; it is now a private residence. **Canute Peterson**

Home, 10 N. Main, dates from about 1869. **Hansen Sparks Home,** 75 W. 1st North, is a two-story eight-room house, built in 1862 of rock and adobe (now stuccoed).

Turn east from Ephraim on State 29 *(improved but not fully paved),* which winds steeply to the summit of Wasatch Plateau, where it intersects **Skyline Drive** at about 10,000 feet altitude. **Lake Hill Campground** (8,500 alt. Manti-La Sal National Forest) has improved facilities for camping and picnicking. East of Skyline Drive the road descends through valleys and canyons past Joes Valley Reservoir to Orangeville (see Tour No. 10). State 29 is paved from the reservoir to Orangeville.

SPERRY UNIVAC

The expansion of manufacturing to rural areas is an important state goal. Sperry Univac is a recent arrival in Ephraim.

MANTI (5,500 alt. 2,080 pop.), Sanpete County seat, is one of the oldest Mormon settlements in Utah, having been settled in November 1849. In 1851 Manti was among the first five settlements to be incorporated by the State of Deseret. Many people lived in dugouts in Temple Hill during the first winter, while men on snowshoes brought handsleds loaded with supplies from wagons which could not break through the heavy snows to the village. Next spring those settlers living in the hill found themselves competing for space with hordes of rattlesnakes, but not a person was bitten. Brigham Young visited in 1850, at that time changing the name of the valley from Sanpitch to Sanpete and naming the village Manti from a city mentioned in the Book of Mormon. Subsequent years brought anxiety, hardship and some deaths from Indian conflicts.

The **Manti Temple** (Mormon), of cream-colored oolitic limestone, occupies a commanding position overlooking the valley from a low hill. Of strikingly unusual architecture, the temple is central Utah's dominant man-made landmark. Construction began in 1877 on a site dedicated by Brigham Young a few months before his death and was completed in 1888 at a cost of

Sanpete County Fair in Manti, 1926. Mormon Temple can be seen behind the horse-powered carousel.

more than a million dollars. Architect was William H. Folsom. The temple is used for sacred ordinance work and ceremonies; only Mormons in good standing are admitted, but a Visitors Center is open to the public.

Manti, like Ephraim, has built a modest industrial base, though its economy is diversified with agriculture, trade and tourism. In recent years the popular **Mormon Miracle Pageant**—a religious drama held on the temple grounds in July—attracts more than a hundred thousand visitors during its run. In 1980, 113,000 people came from every state and 40 foreign countries, with as many as 30,000 attending on weekend nights. The pageant's cast in 1981 numbered 400.

Manti's buildings are exceptionally interesting, both architecturally and historically, featuring numerous well preserved edifices from the 19th century—homes, churches, public and commercial buildings—most of them tastefully maintained and usefully occupied. Visitors should make a point of driving the side streets, for in few parts of western America is there such a display of original early-day architecture of distinctive styling. Many of the buildings are listed on national and state historic registers.

Turn east from Manti through **Manti Canyon** on an improved but not fully paved road to the summit of Wasatch Plateau and junction with **Skyline Drive** at more than 10,000 feet altitude (Manti-La Sal National Forest). Enroute, 5 m. from Manti at 7,400 feet, is **Manti Community Camp,** open June-September, with camping and picnic facilities, trailer spaces.

STERLING (199 pop.) is a pleasantly open town at the mouth of Six-mile Canyon in the narrowing southern end of Sanpete Valley.

Turn east from Sterling to **Palisade Lake State Recreation Area** (2 m.), a recreational development on the shore of a picturesque reservoir. *Drinking water, 71 campsites, restrooms with hot showers, fishing, swimming, boating (no motors),*

9-hole golf course. Fee area. Today's development is reminiscent of pioneer beginnings, when a blossoming resort was created at the lake by Daniel Funk and his family. An original settler of Manti, Funk became friendly with Ute chief Arrapeen, whose band wintered in the Sterling vicinity. During the 1860s Funk acquired from the Indians a deed to the small valley east of Sterling, and during ensuing years he and his family arduously built a dam and a canal. Eventually a reservoir formed in the valley. Gradually, during the 1870s and 1880s, the reservoir became a popular resort with rowboating, bathing, fishing, picnicking, refreshment booths, a dance pavilion, and even a steam-powered sightseeing boat. Daniel Funk died in 1887; future years brought sporadic attempts at commercial and public recreation, but none matched the comparative glory of the youthful period. **Cedar Crest Lodge,** an attractive complex of timbered buildings on the crest of a ridge overlooking the lake and Sterling Valley, offers lodging, dining, and reception facilities.

East of Palisade Lake, the road (unpaved beyond the resort) continues up **Sixmile Canyon** to the Wasatch Plateau.

South of Sterling 6 m. via US 89 and State 137 is **MAYFIELD** (5,500 alt. 397 pop.), a secluded village on Twelvemile Creek, surrounded by tall trees, mountains and hills.

East of Mayfield an improved but unpaved road climbs through **Twelvemile Canyon** to heights of Wasatch Plateau, Skyline Drive, Ferron Reservoir and Ferron in Castle Valley *(see Tour No. 10).* Mayfield is the most convenient southern terminus of **Skyline Drive,** though a network of fairweather forest roads crisscrosses the southern plateau, connecting the drive with Salina Canyon and Emery. In the Mt. Baldy area, in the upper reaches of Twelvemile, is **Aspen Giants Scenic Area** where some of the largest known quaking aspen grow. This is a region of great white cliffs, culminating in the prominent white knob known as **Musinia** (11,000 feet).

GUNNISON (5,200 alt. 1,255 pop.), a commercial and agricultural center near the confluence of Sanpitch and Sevier rivers, was founded in 1860 and named for Captain John W. Gunnison, United States topographical engineer who gained popularity with the Mormons by writing a book about them which they considered more unbiased than most. After passing through this area on a railroad survey in 1853, Captain Gunnison and others of his survey party were massacred by Indians near Sevier Lake.

Musinia Peak (10,986 alt.) is a regional landmark. Here it is seen from the south end of Skyline Drive.

WARD ROYLANCE

Northwest from Gunnison, State 28 passes through semi-arid valleys and forests of pygmy evergreens to US 91-Interstate 15 at Levan *(see Tour No. 4-B)*. At 5 m., just off the highway, is the village of **FAYETTE,** (165 pop.) named after Fayette, New York, where the Mormon Church was founded by Joseph Smith in 1830. The town's abandoned meetinghouse (Mormon) "stands as a pristine example of rural town ecclesiastical architecture of pioneer Utah." The quaint sandstone building served for church meetings and as a schoolhouse and town hall between 1875 and 1932.

CENTERFIELD (5,100 alt. 653 pop.) is a farming community noted for the length of its main street (US 89), along which the town stretches for three or four miles. Until recent years, when the processing of sugar beets became uneconomical here, it was an important sugar center, being the site of the largest sugar refinery in central Utah. The refinery, long abandoned, was demolished during the 1970s.

Four miles west of Centerfield, near Sevier River, is the former site of a cooperative Jewish colony known as **CLARION.** Beginning in 1911, about 75 Jewish families from eastern states moved into the valley, each acquiring 40 irrigated acres around a central commissary, schoolhouse and community well. Crops were bountiful the first year or two, but harvests began to decline and financial problems developed. It is said that local advice about insulating the wood houses was ignored, resulting in freezing cold in winter and sweltering heat in summer. Many of the colonists were cultured people who could not adapt to the handling of farm animals and the problems of cultivation and irrigation. Gradually the settlers drifted away, and by 1920 nothing remained of the Jewish experiment.

South of Gunnison-Centerfield the highway follows the eastern foothills of Sevier Valley. The Wasatch Plateau, so omnipresent above Sanpete Valley, retreats to the east and finally terminates at Salina Canyon. On the west, subdued and ordinary earth colors give way to the glorious vermilions and pastels of the **Aurora Cliffs (Pavant Plateau),** surmounted by a great cone known as the **Red Pyramid.** Beyond Salina to the south is a cluster of weird badland cones or gypsum hills, and rising behind these the dark and massive hulks of other high plateaus—the Sevier, Fishlake and Tushar—all reaching summits of more than 11,000 feet. Through the valley, in lazy meanders, flows **Sevier River,** a murky stream of a modest size that belies its importance to thousands of people.

SEVIER RIVER, one of Utah's most vital and thoroughly utilized streams, arises in the southern High Plateaus near Cedar Breaks and Bryce Canyon and expires more than 200 miles downstream in the Sevier Desert southwest of Delta. Most of central Utah's settlements are in the valley of the Sevier and its northern tributary, the Sanpitch, which flows through Sanpete Valley. These valleys are heavily cultivated, supporting a diverse agricultural economy. In places the Sevier and its forks have cut their way through mountain obstructions, forming very impressive gorges. Sevier as a name was applied first to the river by early travelers from New Mexico, who named it "Rio Seviro," probably meaning severe. Anglos changed the Spanish name to Sevier, applying that anglicism to other features such as county, valley, plateau and town.

SALINA *(Spanish for salt; pron. suh-LINE-uh.* 5,200 alt. 1,992 pop.). Salina is a commercial center for livestock, farm produce, coal, salt and highway travel. It is strategically situated in Sevier Valley at the mouth of Salina Canyon, at the junction of US 89 with Interstate 70 ("the Main

Street of America''), which connects Denver and points east with Las Vegas and Los Angeles. Salina was first settled in 1864, vacated during Indian troubles of the 1860s, and resettled in 1871. Scattered about the city are a number of structures of historical and architectural interest, including an **old rock meetinghouse-schoolhouse** (1864), and a steepled **Presbyterian church** (1884) now used as a residence.

Turn east from Salina to **SALINA CANYON**, route of Interstate 70. Salina Canyon is one of the oldest routes of travel in historic times, being an important transmountain link in the famed **Spanish Trail**, followed not only by trading and slave caravans of New Mexicans from about 1830 or earlier years—prior to Mormon settlement—but also by mountain men, government surveyors such as Gunnison, and military troops. The trail had various branches in Utah, but the main through-route between Santa Fe and Los Angeles apparently followed Salina Canyon into Sevier Valley, thence southward along the Sevier River to the low divide (Bear Valley) between the Tushar Plateau and Markagunt Plateau, where it veered westward into the Great Basin. *(See final paragraphs of this tour.)* Another branch appears to have left Salina Canyon in its upper reaches, passing by Fish Lake into Grass Valley, down Grass Valley to East Fork Canyon, then to Sevier Valley near Junction and Circleville, where it joined the main trail.

Salina Canyon's rock formations contain immense deposits of bituminous coal, which has been mined since early days. In 1973 the Southern Utah Fuel Company's mine, about 30 miles east of Salina, was purchased by Coastal States Energy Co. of Houston, Texas. This firm increased production to more than a million tons a year, making it in 1978 the largest and one of the most efficient underground coal mines west of the Mississippi River. Coal is transported by truck to railroad loading sites at Salina and Levan, or directly by truck to consumers.

The canyon and surrounding highlands also serve as summer range for cattle and sheep. Roads lead north and south into Fishlake and Manti-La Sal national forests, giving access to stockmen, rangers and recreationists. State 72, an unpaved but maintained route, offers high-level panoramic views across the eastern desert and provides access to Thousand Lake Mountain and Cathedral Valley *(see Tour No. 7B).*

North of Salina a few miles is **REDMOND** (5,100 alt. 619 pop.), formerly on US 89 but isolated by highway realignment. It is most noted for being the site of a large salt mining operation north of town where a reddish-brown rock salt is quarried from an open pit and sold in blocks or smaller sizes. The salt contains valuable nutritional elements and is used primarily as a livestock feeding supplement, as a component of turkey feed, as road salt, etc. Halite crystals, valued by rock collectors, also come from the mine. West of town is a deposit of bentonite clay, an unusual mineral having a variety of uses such as oil well drilling, forest fire control, stucco mixing, laundry use, and even as a waterproofing for roofs.

Turn west from Salina via US 50 through open valleys to Scipio and junction with US 91-Interstate 15 *(see Tour No. 4B).* Eight miles west of Salina, forking from US 50, an unpaved but maintained forest road climbs onto the **Pavant Range (Plateau)** and winds southward along the plateau's summit through Fishlake National Forest. This is a scenically outstanding mountain-forest drive at 8,000 to nearly 10,000 feet, resembling in scenic impact the better known and longer Skyline Drive *(see above).* Rocks of the Pavant are the most colorful in central Utah, and the drive affords thrilling glimpses downward over Sevier Valley and into a network of deep canyons opening out into the valley. Viewpoints also afford panoramic glimpses of Pahvant Valley and the Sevier Desert to the west. The road skirts the base of Red Pyramid, Mt. Catherine, White Pine and Sunset peaks, which are among the highest summits on the plateau at more than 10,000 feet. Toward the south, forks descend to Richfield and Elsinore; more primitive spurs lead off to the west and south. Condition of this road, as with all unpaved mountain drives, may change from time to time. It is advisable to check in advance with offices of Fishlake National Forest in Richfield.

SIGURD (5,300 alt. 386 pop.) is a small village about 12 miles south of Salina, several miles east of the highway. It is the site of two gypsum-processing mills which utilize local deposits in the manufacture of plasterboard and other building products.

Turn east from Sigurd Junction via State 24 to Fish Lake, Wayne County, Capitol Reef National Park, Hanksville, Lake Powell and other points in east-central Utah *See Tour No. 7B.*

RICHFIELD (5,300 alt. 5,482 pop.) is the seat of Sevier County and the commercial capital of a vast mountain-valley region. Agriculture is the region's main enterprise (livestock, alfalfa, grain, etc.) but Richfield's economy receives important support also from trade, manufacturing, mining and other industries. It is a major highway stop, the site of federal and state government offices, and the home of Sevier Valley Tech, a state vocational school.

Richfield was first settled in January 1864 by people who spent their first winter in a "hole in the ground." The first name was Omni, for a Book of Mormon character, and Fort Omni was built of rock in 1865. Site of this fort is marked by a bell campanile at First North and Second West.

Architecturally, little of an outstanding nature remains in Richfield to witness its pioneer past. The imposing county courthouse, built in 1892, was demolished in 1975 despite organized efforts to save it. And the first Sevier Stake Tabernacle—a majestic structure of Gothic Revival style—was razed in 1923 after being damaged by an earthquake some years earlier. In its day this building was one of the noblest religious edifices in Utah, but it served a useful life of only 15 years and its history was one of misfortune, as told by Pearl F. Jacobson in *Sevier County Historic Sites (1978).* The **Ralph**

Glenwood, Sevier Valley, and Sevier Plateau.

WARD ROYLANCE

Ramsay Home, 57 E. 200 North (just east of the County Courthouse), dates from 1873-74. Its builder, Ralph Ramsay, carved the original eagle for Salt Lake City's famed Eagle Gate. Ramsay also was noted as one of the most proficient wood carvers of 19th century Utah, creating furniture used in homes of Brigham Young and other dignitaries. The **Young Block,** at the corner of Center and Main streets, is termed "the most architecturally significant commercial building in Sevier County." It dates from 1907. Both the Ramsay Home and Young Block are listed on the National Register of Historic Places. The **Daughters of Utah Pioneers Relic Hall,** 340 W. 500 North, exhibits pioneer relics and artifacts.

Turn east from Richfield via State 119 to Glenwood and junction with State 24 leading to Capitol Reef National Park *(see Tour No. 7B).* Enroute, climbing the valley's eastern slopes, the road passes through prismatic **Rainbow Hills,** which display a spectrum of bright and varied colors and from their heights provide a delightful panorama of Sevier Valley and the mountains surrounding it.

GLENWOOD (5,300 alt. 447 pop.) is a quiet, sleepy village—a mixture of the old and new. In respects its pioneer history is most unusual. Like a number of other Mormon communities in the 1870s, the village at least partially experimented with President Brigham Young's United Order. *(See also Orderville in Tour No. 9A and Kingston below.)* Livestock herds were cooperative, as were grain fields and industries such as the sawmill, woolen mill, grist mill, tannery, lumber finishing mill, molasses mill, and so on. Each worker, despite the kind of work performed, received the same pay; and at the end of the year all debts and accounts receivable were cancelled. Unlike Orderville, the community did not operate a common kitchen and dining room. The Glenwood experiment is supposed to have been successful in many ways, but like that in Orderville it was broken up mainly by outside influences and internal friction.

The **Joseph Wall Gristmill,** a fortress-like building with mansard roof and sturdy walls of black lava rock and brick, was added to the National Register of Historic Places in 1980. A relic of United Order days, the mill was built about 1874 and saw continued use for some 75 years.

THE HIGH PLATEAUS

From Richfield, in the words of scientist-explorer Clarence E. Dutton, the Sevier Plateau may be beheld in "all its grandeur, rising 5,800 feet above the plain below; its upper third a sheer precipice, the lower two-thirds plunging down in steep buttresses which thrust their bases beneath the level floor. Its aspect is dark and gloomy from the dark gray dolerites and trachytes which make up its whole mass."

The Sevier Plateau is only one of the High Plateaus visible from the Richfield vicinity. In every direction the view encompasses a spectacle of tabular highlands, from the Wasatch on the northeast, clockwise to the Fishlake, then the mighty Sevier (close to Richfield and therefore the dominating mass), on to the hoary summits of the Tushar in the southwest, and finally the Pavant's rainbow-hued slopes on the west. Other High Plateaus are out of view: the grand Aquarius (Boulder Mountain), Thousand Lake Mountain, the Paunsaugunt and Markagunt, and the rugged, remote Kaiparowits.

All of the plateaus are based on sedimentary deposits which have been raised and lowered over millions of years by crustal forces, and the precipitous edges of some are the result of great faults or breaks in the earth's surface.

In addition to faulting, the plateau province has been molded to an important extent by extensive volcanic activity over ages of time. Nearly every form of volcanic eruption is exhibited in this region, including trachyte, rhyolite, and basalt, and some lavas have issued from the earth in very recent times. Taken altogether, the vast erosion, faulting, and volcanic factors operating on this region have made it of fascinating interest to the geologist.

MONROE (5,400 alt. 1,476 pop.), several miles east of US 89, nestles in a secluded cove at the southern end of the valley. Behind it loom the Sevier Plateau's highest peaks, 6,000 feet above. Unlike many communities in central Utah, Monroe has managed to maintain a fairly constant population for 60 years or so, even expanding in recent years. This is due to a diversified economy. In latter years it is becoming increasingly a residential area for commuters and retired people.

Monroe is one of Utah's showplaces for attractive, distinctive 19th century and early 20th century architecture, numerous older buildings having been thoughtfully restored, maintained, and still in functional use. Community and individual pride are apparent. On Main Street a restored log cabin built in 1866-67 serves as a **pioneer relic hall.** An old **Presbyterian church** built of stone in the 1880s, has been preserved as a home. The **Old Monroe City Hall,** a square structure of stone blocks, still stands, as does (1979) an old steepled **Methodist church** of frame construction. These are only a few of Monroe's aged buildings, many of distinguished Victorian architecture, others of more humble logs, stone and frame.

Since early days **Monroe Hot Springs,** southeast of town, have provided bathing in what is reputed to be the only natural non-sulphurous body of hot water in the state. These springs are a result of the Sevier Fault, a major break in the earth's crust, still active and the cause of earthquakes in historic times. During the late 1970s a pilot project was conducted to determine the feasibility of tapping natural hot water to heat the community's homes. Several wells were sunk and engineering studies made. Mounting costs and other factors forced cessation of the project in 1980, after $400,000 had been expended from a federal grant.

Monroe Canyon, between castellated walls southeast of town, is the site of **Monrovian Park,** an improved picnic area and playground (Fishlake National Forest). Beyond the park the unpaved road climbs steeply in zigzags up the mountain side to the summit of **Sevier Plateau** at 10,000 feet or more, affording sublime views over Sevier Valley, the Tushar peaks, and seemingly a good part of central and southern Utah. The fairweather road is impassable in wet weather; rutted and rough in spots. It continues through Fishlake National Forest, across open alpine meadows and through groves of aspen and evergreens, finally descending to Koosharem in Grass Valley *(see Tour No. 7B).* Summit peaks rise above the drive to more than 11,000 feet. This route, as with most of the area's alpine drives, is particularly dramatic in late September-early October, before first snowfall, when autumn colors are at their scenic climax.

ELSINORE (5,300 alt. 612 pop.). Elsinore is a farming and trading community located in the midst of fields of alfalfa and grain. It was settled in 1874-75 and named by Danish colonists for the site of Hamlet's castle in Denmark; for a time its founders lived communally in the United Order experiment of that period. A pioneer log cabin dating from 1876 is preserved on the church lot. Other distinctive buildings include a number of early rock structures and the two-story **White Rock School,** built in 1897-98 and restored as a Bicentennial Project in 1976.

WARD ROYLANCE

Bald peaks of the Tushar Range (12,000 alt.) loom above the Sevier River trough, as viewed from the Sevier Plateau near Monroe.

JOSEPH and **SEVIER** are small highway villages at the south end of the valley, near the US 89-Interstate 70 junction. Both date from pioneer days, and several aged buildings attest to their antiquity. Other structures, not so old but of architectural interest, include the **old Joseph Schoolhouse** (1894-1904) and **Sevier LDS Chapel** (1928-33), a quaint rock structure now privately owned. Still standing in Joseph in 1979 was an adobe house dating back more than a hundred years, said to have been used as a communal home during the United Order period of the 1870s. Two miles north of Joseph, beside the highway, the **Parker home** is a distinguished residence of stone blocks with dormer windows and tower, stained glass windows, large porch, and ornate wood decoration. Built about 1910, this appealing house is of interest to highway travelers, many of whom stop to take photographs. It is included on state and national registers of historic places.

Turn west from Sevier Junction via Interstate 70 through **Clear Creek Canyon** to Interstate 15 at Cove Fort *(see Tour No. 8)*. Clear Creek Canyon is a narrow pass between the Tushar and Pavant mountains, requiring great expense and engineering ingenuity in the construction of I-70 during the 1970s and 1980s. Four huge support structures alone cost more than $17,000,000. The canyon setting is imposing, with jagged, curiously eroded palisades of igneous rock. Prehistoric people left artistic evidence of their presence on its rocks.

From exit 5 m. west of Sevier Junction, an unpaved, steep and winding forest road meanders southward along the canyon of Mill Creek, climbing to the site of **Old Kimberly,** 8 m., nestled in an evergreen forest at 9,000 feet, beneath majestic peaks of the Tushar. The road continues on through dense aspen and evergreen growth of

Fishlake National Forest to Marysvale, 16 m. from Kimberly, climbing to 10,000 feet or so. A lusty turn-of-the-century mining town, Kimberly today exhibits little to testify of its heyday of vibrancy: a few crumbled or crumbling buildings, waste deposits, and new mining buildings. Kimberly, center of the Gold Mountain Mining District, dates from 1888, when gold was discovered in the area. Shafts were sunk and mills built during the 1890s, but the real boom began about 1899 when Peter Kimberly of Chicago and associates acquired the Annie Laurie group and other claims, built a cyanide mill, and employed 300 men. More men were employed at the Sevier and other mines, and by 1907 nearly $3,000,000 in gold and silver had been produced. There was little production after 1907, though a revival in the mid-1930s furnished employment for about 50 families. Since then, most of the buildings have been removed or have collapsed. *Respect private property.*

In 1981, highway construction obscured the turnoff from I-70. This unpaved loop drive from I-70 to Marysvale, though usually well maintained, is steep and narrow, clinging to precipitous mountainsides thousands of feet above the canyon floor. It should be avoided by those afraid of heights. Inquire locally or at Fishlake National Forest offices as to road condition. *Good brakes are a necessity.*

Marysvale Canyon, route of US 89 between Sevier Junction and Marysvale, cuts through masses of igneous rock, twisting and turning in tight curves south of Sevier, then opening and straightening somewhat near **Big Rock Candy Mountain.** This brightly colored hill, painted in vivid yellow and chocolate hues, was the inspiration for America's popular folk song *The Big Rock Candy Mountain.* Resorts in the vicinity provide lodging, food, fuel and souvenirs.

MARYSVALE (5,900 alt. 359 pop.) is a picturesque town in the canyon of Pine Creek, overshadowed by peaks of the Tushar and Sevier plateaus. Its size gives little indication of the fact that in the great mountains nearby are rich mineral deposits—that in 100 square miles of mountainous country near Marysvale are supposed to be concentrated more pay bodies of gold, copper, silver and lead ores—as well as uranium and alunite—than most other known regions of equal size. Vagaries of market, remoteness, technical problems, and frustrating geology have combined to prevent full development.

Despite these handicaps, mines near Marysvale have produced large quantities of valuable minerals. Gold was discovered in Bullion Canyon in 1854, though isolation of the mines proved a serious drawback to exploitation. Other rich mineral deposits were found thereafter; and it is reported that the Deer Trail Mine, discovered in 1878, yielded in one year (1919) some 16,000 tons of ore containing 4,344 ounces of gold, 26,107 ounces of silver, 332,092 pounds of lead, and 3,136 pounds of copper. In 1911 was discovered near here a large body of pure alunite—a mineral which has been used for its potash content as well as for metallic aluminum.

A spiderweb of roads on the barren hillsides northeast of Marysvale mark what was a major producer of uranium ore during the 1950s and 1960s. Shafts went as deep as 900 feet, and though government officials knew of the health dangers from radiation, no agency accepted responsibility for precautions. The result, which began receiving publicity in 1979, was that an abnormally large proportion of Marysvale uranium miners had died, or were expected to die, of lung cancer caused by radioactive radon gas.

West from Marysvale, unpaved but maintained roads climb steeply into the **Tushar Mountains,** giving access to mine workings, the site of Old Kimberly *(see above),* and heights of more than 10,000 feet in the area of the loftiest peaks. Panoramic views are superb, but these roads are not for the timid. Inquire locally about condition, or at Fishlake National Forest in Richfield or Beaver, where maps are available.

Tushar Plateau is more commonly known as the Tushar or Beaver Mountains and contains the highest peaks in Utah with the exception of a few in the Uinta and La Sal ranges. In Dutton's words the plateau is a composite structure, "its northern half being a wild bristling cordillera of grand dimensions and altitudes, crowned with snowy peaks, while the southern half is conspicuously tabular." Although several of its highest peaks are pleasingly symmetrical in shape, they are not the remains of volcanic craters. Nevertheless, the plateau was formed to a large extent by volcanic activity on a grand scale, with the subterranean materials issuing through huge fissures in the earth. This extensive volcanic activity has formed deposits of valuable ores, but most of these have not been easy to extract. The name Tushar is derived from T'shar (Paiute), meaning "white" and referring to the plateau's light-colored peaks.

South of Marysvale US 89 follows the Tushar foothills, some hundreds of feet above the trough of Sevier River to the east. Peaks loom overhead to 12,000 feet and more, and across the valley the imposing **Sevier Plateau** stretches in massive grandeur from north to south. That great tabular uplift is perhaps 70 or 80 miles in length but only 10 to 20 in width. Its highest summits are near Monroe and Richfield. Much of the Sevier's bulk is igneous trachyte, erupting through huge earth fissures over long periods of time.

Piute Reservoir, one of central Utah's largest bodies of water, backs up behind a dam on the river east of the highway. **Piute Lake State Beach,** on its shore, offers facilities for boating, camping and picnicking. The reservoir is open to all-year fishing.

JUNCTION (6,250 alt. 151 pop.), seat of Piute County, near the confluence of the south and east forks of Sevier River, is the political center of a little-populated farming and livestock region. Piute County is one of Utah's smallest, least populated and most mountainous, with an economy based

View eastward from State 153 between Junction and Beaver. Sevier River Valley, Sevier Plateau, and East Fork Canyon in distance.

WARD ROYLANCE

largely on agriculture, trade and mining. The **Piute County Courthouse** in Junction dates from 1902-03; it is a picturesque towered building of red bricks, made on the site and laid seven layers thick on a foundation of granitic rocks. Other singular buildings of early vintage may be seen by driving the side streets.

Turn west from Junction via State 153 to the **Tushar Plateau, Puffer Lake,** and **Beaver.** The road is unpaved but well graded for about half the distance to Beaver; parts of it, particularly east of Mt. Holly Resort, are closed in winter. From Junction it climbs steeply up **City Creek Canyon** to expansive flats (10,000 feet) near the plateau's highest summits. Views from this road are among Utah's best for panoramic grandeur, and it offers convenient hiking access to the naked Tushar spine, highest in southern Utah. Climbing these summits is not particularly difficult, though loose rock may be hazardous. A. G. MacKenzie, in a newspaper article *(Salt Lake Tribune, August 13, 1922),* described his ascent of **Mount Belknap** (12,139 alt.) in the company of Josiah F. Gibbs of Marysvale, then 77 years of age. The ascent was made in one day, "a job of work and pleasure." In his opinion the peak offered a more comprehensive view of Southern Utah than any other point, extending more than a hundred miles in most directions. *(See Tour No. 8 for further details of this drive.)*

South of Junction 2 m., turn east on State 62 to **Kingston, Otter Creek Lake, Antimony** and **Grass Valley.**

KINGSTON (146 pop.) 2 m. east of US 89 via State 62 at the mouth of East Fork Canyon, displays little of its historic past. The community from which the present town took its name was located a mile or so to the west, receiving its name from the King family of Fillmore who led its founding as a communal settlement in the 1870s. For a number of years the community practiced the Mormon United Order *(see Glenwood above; also Orderville in Tour No. 9A).* There was a community dining hall, community cattle, community fields, community grist mill, woolen factory and tannery. The experiment was poignantly described in Phil Robinson's classic *Sinners and Saints,* a tale of travel through early Utah (London 1883). Descendants of the Kingston pioneers still live in the vicinity.

State 62 passes through **East Fork (Kingston) Canyon,** a scenic gorge confined between volcanic battlements eroded into exotic shapes. **Otter Creek Lake State Beach** is popular for boating, fishing and camping.

ANTIMONY (6,500 alt. 94 pop.) is an agricultural village named for a nearby deposit of antimony ore; originally it was known as Coyote. State 22, unpaved part of the distance south of Antimony, connects with State 12 near Bryce Canyon *(see Tour No. 9C).*

State 62 veers northward from **Otter Creek Junction,** passing through the spacious expanse of **Grass Valley** to Greenwich, Koosharem and Burrville *(see Tour No. 7B).* This is wide-open ranching country, cupped between the grand Sevier and Aquarius uplifts, the home of eagles, ravens and hordes of jackrabbits. In the vicinity of present-day Antimony, in 1873, occurred an incident which threatened to renew earlier hostilities between the Navajo nation and Mormon settlers of Utah. At that time the valley was open range with a few scattered ranches. The 1860s had witnessed warfare between white settlers and Ute and Navajo raiders, who drove off livestock, killed herders and travelers, and forced temporary abandonment of many settlements. Peace had come before 1873, however, and in that year three young Navajo braves had traveled north from Arizona to trade with Mormons in central Utah. In Grass Valley they were caught in a storm and took shelter in a cabin belonging to the McCarty family (several members of which later became notorious outlaws). Being hungry, they killed a calf. A confrontation with the McCartys (and, it is said, Orrin Porter Rockwell) ensued and two of the Indians were slain. The third, badly wounded, escaped and made his way back to his people, reporting that the Mormons had attacked his party and killed his companions. (The McCartys were not Mormons.) The Navajos then threatened renewed hostilities, which were only averted through peacemaking efforts of Jacob Hamblin and Mormon leaders. Hamblin later recalled that his all-night peace conference with angry Navajos, who threatened his life, was the nearest he had ever come to being killed by Indians.

CIRCLEVILLE (6,100 alt. 445 pop.) lies in Circle Valley, almost surrounded by rugged and massive plateaus towering to more than 11,000 feet. Agriculture is the main industry, as it has been since the first days of settlement, though highway travel and trade support the economy.

Circleville's main claim to fame (and one which irritates some local people) is its having been the boyhood home of Robert LeRoy Parker, better known as Butch Cassidy the outlaw. Butch was one of the west's most "celebrated" badmen around the turn of the century when he and the Wild Bunch carried on lucrative activities such as robbing trains and banks and rustling cattle. Although one of their most publicized hideouts was in the wild and almost inaccessible canyon country near Hanksville *(see Tour No. 7B),* Butch and the Wild Bunch operated over much of the west. Cassidy's exploits have been told and retold in books and articles, and in a fictional film starring Robert Redford and Paul Newman. Some members of the Parker family, who continued to reside in the Circleville vicinity, insisted that Butch was not killed in South America as reported but returned to visit the home of his youth and died in the Northwest, after "going straight," changing his name and living to a good age. The old Parker homestead, marked by a log house where Butch visited his family in later years, is beside the highway about 2 m. south of town.

South of Circleville, US 89 again plunges into a narrow canyon formed in volcanic rock of somber hue and known as **Circleville** or **Panguitch Canyon.** This was the route for some decades before 1850 of the **Old Spanish Trail** between Santa Fe and Los Angeles *(see Salina Canyon above).* Of more immediate interest was the journey of John Charles Fremont and his suffering fellows, who passed through this canyon in the winter of 1853-54. This was during Fremont's ill-fated Fifth Expedition, and at that time he and his party were in desperate straits after a terrible journey across the Green River desert and through Grass, Sevier and Circle valleys. When they reached the Tushars, deep in snow, none of the men possessed any shoes, wearing instead only stockings or moccasins of rawhide—and their food supply was almost exhausted. Their journey was described by S. N. Carvalho, a member of the party, in *Incidents of Travel and Adventure in the Far West* (New York 1857). By the time they finally reached Parowan, on the west side of the plateaus, the men had lived on horse meat for more than 50 days, had been without food of any kind for two days, and one of their number had perished from exposure.

The southern end of Panguitch Canyon opens into upper Sevier Valley. *See Tour No. 9A for continuation.*

Tour No. 7B — State Highway 24 east from US 89/I-70 to Hanksville and vicinity; also State Highway 95 east from Hanksville

State 24 branches southeast from US 89/I-70 near Sigurd, entering mountainous terrain of the High Plateaus through which it passes for 60 miles. From an altitude of 5,300 feet at Sigurd it climbs gradually through canyons and vales to Grass Valley at 7,000 feet, surmounts Fish Lake Pass at 8,400 feet, then descends to 7,000 feet again in Rabbit Valley and parallels the Fremont River along its winding course to Hanksville at 4,300 feet. Scenically it is one of the choicest routes in the state, providing—with a network of sideroads—those delightful views that inspired the name Panoramaland. Sideroads penetrate the High Plateaus and red-rock wilderness of Canyonlands.

State 119, east from Richfield, is an alternate approach to State 24. Passing near Glenwood *(see Tour No. 7A),* this route ascends by switchbacks into the brightly colored **Rainbow Hills,** giving high-level overviews of Sevier Valley, the Tushar peaks, and the prismatic Pavant front across the valley.

About 20 m. from US 89/I-70 the highway enters **Grass Valley,** a deep and narrow mountain-girt basin. Only a few hundred people live in this almost treeless valley bottom that stretches for more than 30 miles; it is ranching country for the most part, and at nearly 7,000 feet is too high for most crops. **Koosharem Reservoir,** formed along Otter Creek by a low dam, is popular for trout fishing.

On the west side of the highway, 1 m. south of Koosharem Reservoir, is a **stone monument** and bronze marker commemorating a peace treaty of 1873 that ended long-lasting hostilities between whites and local Indians. Actual site of the treaty conference—a large grove of red cedar trees—stands beside State 62 about midway between Burrville and Koosharem. Known ever since as **Cedar Grove,** this historic spot has been a favorite locale for picnics and celebrations. It can be seen from the monument, several miles away to the south.

State 62 branches southward not far from the monument, leading to **BURR-VILLE, KOOSHAREM** and **GREENWICH,** the upper valley's communities. These villages typify the rural isolation of Utah's yesterday, still retaining an atmosphere of frontier rusticity. Until recent years the Greenwich-Koosharem area was the home of a small group of Paiute Indians, remnants of a community who claimed the Fish Lake-Aquarius country as their homeland when whites first arrived. White settlement began in earnest after the peace treaty of 1873, and local Indians congregated at the **Koosharem Indian Reservation,** eking out a livelihood from farming, hunting, and sale of pine nuts, buckskin gloves and moccasins. By 1980, few if any remained in the vicinity. Interesting points include early structures of logs, bricks and frame, some dating from the 1870s and 1880s, as well as a youth camp development of modern vintage. The **Amusement Hall** in Koosharem, built in 1914, has served as a community center ever since. In Greenwich, a **picturesque brick building** beside the highway, complete with bell and belfry, was dedicated in 1906 and has served as schoolhouse, Mormon chapel and Relief Society meetinghouse, and tourist information center. *See Tour No. 7A for south valley.*

State 24 leaves Grass Valley by way of the "Fish Lake grade," a climb of more than 1,500 feet that resulted in countless boiling radiators before the era of highpowered engines and highway realignment. **Fish Lake Pass or Summit** (8,400 alt.) marks the division between Piute and Wayne counties, and also the approximate separation between **Fish Lake Plateau,** looming two thousand feet higher to the north, and **Parker Mountain (Awapa Plateau)** which stretches away in heaving swells toward the south. This latter is a shoulder terrace of the Aquarius, and is uncommonly free of extensive forest growth because of rainshadow (higher mountains to the west capture incoming moisture). Primarily it is grazing country, the home of numerous pronghorn antelope.

Two miles west of Fish Lake Summit, State 25 branches from the main highway and climbs to **FISH LAKE** (7 m.), one of Utah's most popular fishing and outdoor recreation areas. *State 25 is closed to highway vehicles in winter but is popular for snowmobiling.*

Public facilities at Fish Lake include lodges, cabins, meals, groceries and supplies, boat rentals and docks, horses, guides, public campgrounds and picnic areas. Numerous summer homes are clustered near the lake.

In a volcanic basin caused by faulting, Fish Lake is a scenic jewel measuring five miles in length, nearly a mile in width, at about 8,800 feet altitude. On either side steep slopes rise more than 2,000 feet to summits of 11,000 feet or more. Luxuriant vegetation of Fishlake National Forest surrounds the lake, which is fed by half a dozen streams; its overflow water drains into **Johnson Valley Reservoir** at the north, thence becoming the source of the Fremont River. Autumn foliage is spectacular in the fullest sense.

Fish Lake has been a popular resort area ever since arrival of the whites, and was a source of food for Indians since time immemorial. The lake was a rest stop on a main branch of the Old Spanish Trail during the first half of the 19th century, and perhaps was visited by New Mexicans even prior to that time. Legend handed down

Fish Lake.

Fremont River headwaters near Fish Lake.

from local Indians to the area's first white settlers tells of Spanish/Mexican silver mining in Sevenmile Canyon to the north of Fish Lake, ended by massacre of the white intruders. Fruitless searches have been made for these ancient mine workings, known as the Lost Josephine.

Rainbow trout are the principal game fish here, but large-size catches are not as common as in past years. Mackinaw trout, while larger and more exciting, comprise only a fraction of the total harvest. Problems that frustrate Wildlife personnel in their efforts to keep the lake a prime harvest area include moss, chubs, short season, fishing pressures, pollution, lake depth, and unfavorable growth conditions for young rainbows.

As described on page 346 of the 1941 edition, Fish Lake was the scene of a treaty with the Fishlake (Paiute) Indians in June 1873, preliminary to another treaty in July of that year at Cedar Grove *(see above).*

Fish Lake Plateau, of which the "Hightop Plateau" containing Fish Lake is but a part, is a rugged lava-covered highland measuring some 30 by 25 miles in extent, heavily utilized for livestock grazing. Much of it is forested with evergreens and aspen. Numerous lakes, reservoirs and streams provide good fishing, and the plateau is noted as a productive deer hunting area. Roads and trails allow convenient access to most parts of the plateau. On the crest west of Fish Lake is the plateau's highest point (11,613 alt.). Other summits, however, appearing as isolated peaks, are almost as lofty: **Mt. Marvine** (11,600), **Mt. Terrel** (11,531); and **Hilgard Mountain** (10,855). In the region of Utah's High Plateaus these elevations make the Fish Lake highland second only to the Tushars in altitude.

Fish Lake Pass provides the first bird's-eye view of Wayne Wonderland to the east—tantalizing glimpses of rainbow colors, far-off peaks, and strange rock forms. Majestic uplifts loom in the distance: Thousand Lake Mountain on the north, the grand Aquarius on the south, Utah's classic table-top plateaus. State 24 dips and climbs across the almost treeless Awapa, finally dropping more than a thousand feet into Rabbit Valley.

Rabbit Valley is a circular basin at 7,000 feet, surrounded by four plateaus, each with its distinctive personality and all the scene of igneous activity over ages of time. The valley was settled by whites during the 1870s, following the peace treaty at Cedar Grove. Wayne County's oldest towns are in the valley, which is so high and has such a short growing season that agriculture is limited mainly to livestock raising, garden vegetables, potatoes, some dairying, and feed crops such as alfalfa and barley. Water, being comparatively plentiful, allows the irrigation of thousands of acres by sprinklers.

LOA (7,000 alt. 364 pop.), a pleasantly open, dignified community, is Wayne County seat. Its name was suggested by Franklin B. Young, early settler and formerly a Mormon missionary to Hawaii. Most houses in Loa, as in many other rural Utah towns, are corner houses—or, it should be noted, this was the case until the subdividing trend of recent years. The remainder of each block, here as elsewhere, is devoted to gardens, corrals and outbuildings, pastures and vehicle parking.

Loa was settled in the mid-1870s and organized as a townsite about ten years later. Its landmark building, an attractive rock structure with terraced steeple, is the *Wayne Stake Tabernacle,* built between 1906 and 1909. In the 1940s a large amusement hall wing was added. Across the street is a white brick building, built about 1898 and used as a tithing and church office, more recently as a Daughters of Utah Pioneers meetinghouse and relic hall. The Wayne County Courthouse, dating from 1938-39, displays a collection of polished rocks, the work of Dr. A. L. Inglesby of Fruita.

Turn north 5 m. to **FREMONT** (7,200 alt.), named for the Fremont River which flows nearby. The Fremont area was first to be settled by whites in Rabbit Valley during the 1870s, and despite the changes of passing years the town retains an aura of rural quaintness. Meriting an off-highway drive is **Worthen's Merc,** an old-fashioned country store (now closed) built of more than 70 varieties of rock. Known as the **Store of 10,000 Stones** or **House of Rocks,** the building was constructed during the 1940s of rocks gathered over a period of years by the store's proprietor, J. Worthen Jackson. Included are stones from 31 states and several foreign countries. Its builder, the late Worthen Jackson, gained a measure of renown as a scenic and hunting guide when the region to the east was wild and little known to the outside world. He and his brother Perry were credited with "discovering" Goblin and Cathedral valleys as tourist attractions.

Of historic interest is the old **Fremont church house,** built of local volcanic rock about 1902-07 and restored in the 1970s for public functions. A marker commemorates the ill-fated 5th expedition of John Charles Fremont, after whom the town and river were named. Fremont and a party of fellow explorers passed through this general area during the winter of 1853-54, suffering from cold and hunger. Having been forced to eat most of their animals, they cached scientific instruments and equipment in the vicinity. Later, it is said, this cache was stolen by Indians. Apparently Fremont's name was first applied to the river by the Powell Survey in the early 1870s, though Fremont's exact route in this area is uncertain. White settlement followed this expedition by 20 years.

Northwest of Fremont, at Brian Springs, is the **Loa Fish Hatchery,** a state installation which produces fingerling trout for transplanting to fishing waters throughout Utah. *Open to visitors.*

Turn north from Fremont via State 72 *(improved but unpaved)* to the heights of **Fish Lake Plateau** and **Thousand Lake Mountain.** Sideroads give access to productive fishing spots such as Mill Meadow, Forsyth and Johnson Valley reservoirs, Fish Lake, Fremont River and smaller streams. Seven miles from Fremont a sideroad climbs eastward between high peaks to the eastern shoulder of **THOUSAND LAKE MOUNTAIN,** to **Elkhorn Guard Station and Campground** at 9,300 feet (Fishlake National Forest; camping and picnicking facilities). Scenic views from this road, encompassing a wild panorama of Canyonlands and Utah's Painted Desert to the east, are superlative. As described on page 347 of the first edition, the view "is best in early morning, when the sunlight, casting shadows from cliff to cliff, combines with the haze of dawn to produce a constantly-changing color screen over the landscape." Front lighting is best in afternoon, however. **Cathedral Valley** and **South Desert** (Capitol Reef National Park) occupy the middle ground beyond a plunging foreground of brush-covered meadows interspersed with groves of aspen and evergreens. From near to far away, rank after rank of cliffs and canyons, mesas, buttes, mountain ranges and other works of nature run the gamut of geological form. As far as the eye can see spreads Canyonlands, displaying in aerial perspective the results of ages of erosion and crustal deformation. Laccolithic uplifts, swells, monoclines, anticlines, synclines, igneous dikes and sills—all can be seen from here. Peaks of the Henrys loom above all, but the San Rafael Swell is in plain view, as are the Caineville mesas and Factory Butte, Black Mountain, and Wasatch cliffs of Emery. Waterpocket Fold stretches away to the south from beneath one's feet, extending far beyond the sandstone maze of Capitol Reef. Even the Flat-top buttes can be seen, guarding the entrance to Robber's Roost, with hazy intimations of the Junction country beyond—and on a clear day the La Sals rise stark against the horizon more than a hundred miles away.

Several miles before Elkhorn is reached, unpaved branch roads drop from the mountain into **Cathedral Valley** and to Baker Ranch, joining eventually with I-70 at Fremont Junction, or with State 24 east of Fruita *(see Capitol Reef National Park)*.

State 72 continues across rolling highlands to I-70 at **Fremont Junction,** with panoramic glimpses to the east resembling those from the Elkhorn road.

Thousand Lake Mountain is a classic tabular uplift, a miniature of the much larger Aquarius but equally as high (11,306 alt.). The name is a misnomer, as the plateau bears only a dozen or so small lakes and ponds. Local old-timers believe its name was intended to apply to the Aquarius.

BICKNELL (7,200 alt. 296 pop.), on a bench at the base of Thousand Lake Mountain and painted cliffs, overlooks an expanse of Fremont River marshes in the valley below. The southern view is dominated by the hulking mass of Aquarius Plateau (Boulder Mountain). An attractive community with obvious civic pride, Bicknell has blossomed with new homes and commercial buildings, leaving limited testaments of its 19th century past. Among those that remain are the old brick (now stuccoed) **Mormon Relief Society Building** (1897-99) and a quaint two-story stone building across the street, built about 1900, which served for many years as a store.

Bicknell was settled during the 1870s, its first location being several miles south in the valley, near the river. For 40 years or so the town bore the name Thurber, after a pioneer leader, taking the name Bicknell in 1916 in return for a library offered by Thomas Bicknell, an easterner, to any Utah town that would take his name. Thurber, and Grayson in San Juan County, accepted. Thurber got half of the library and the name Bicknell; Grayson got the other half and became Blanding, the maiden name of Mrs. Bicknell.

Bicknell has a diversified economy based on farming and livestock, trade, lumbering and government employment. Two public schools are in town, pupils being bused daily from distant parts of the county, including Hanksville nearly 60 miles away. A number of residents are retired couples, and many have moved to Bicknell from other places.

Turn east from State 24, 1 m. south of Bicknell to **Sunglow Recreation Area** (Fishlake National Forest), a camping and picnic area secluded 1 m. from the highway in a circular amphitheater formed by high red cliffs. Those with knowledge of geology are sure to be entranced with the area's broken and deformed rocks, situated on the **Thousand Lake Fault** and marking an abrupt transition between surface rocks of the High Plateaus and Canyonlands. While the surrounding uplifts are blanketed with a thick layer of somber-hued igneous rock that largely conceals colorful sedimentary rocks forming their base, here a great fault or break in the earth's crust has raised upwards into view, beneath Thousand Lake Mountain, those brightly painted, very ancient rocks that continue east and south throughout the Canyonlands region for tens of thousands of square miles. This same fault has dropped, at least relatively, the mountainous terrain to the west, resulting in a strata offset of several thousand feet.

From State 24, 3 m. south of Bicknell, near the Fremont River, a road forks to the south.

Drive on this road (paved for several miles) to **Bicknell Bottoms** of the Fremont River, marshy lowlands that are popular for waterfowl shooting (the Bottoms are a waterfowl management area). The river in this vicinity provides good fishing. Near the road is the **J. Perry Egan Fish Hatchery** *(open to visitors),* a state Wildlife unit that has been in operation since the early 1970s. Known formally as a fish cultural station, the hatchery serves as an important egg producer, shipping more than 20 million trout eggs annually to other fish producing stations. It also produces large numbers of fish for the stocking of lakes and streams.

The sideroad continues across almost treeless expanses of Parker Mountain and eventually drops down through forests and canyons to **Escalante,** about 50 m. from Bicknell. Enroute, sideroads lead onto the heights of Parker Mountain, to Posey Lake, Hell's Backbone, and the 11,000 foot summit of **AQUARIUS PLATEAU,** more commonly referred to as **BOULDER MOUNTAIN** *(see also Tour No. 9C).* The first edition's description of this majestic tabular uplift, in respects the grandest of Utah's high plateaus, is not too accurate today. No longer is it little explored, nor is it necessary to arrange for horses and guides. Roads give fairly adequate (albeit rocky and rough) access to most parts of the mountain, supplemented with a network of short foot trails. Stockmen, lumbermen and forest rangers know the plateau well. Yet it remains wild enough for popular tastes. The plateau's remarkably flat summit, known as **Boulder Top,** is a rolling tableland of perhaps 50 square miles, formed of dark lava and rimmed by steep cliffs that make of it a battlemented natural fortress. Views from the edge of this escarpment are sublime. In the words of a local lumberman, "You can see around the world."

Most of Boulder Top exceeds 10,000 feet in elevation, with summits in excess of 11,000 feet; **Bluebell Knoll,** highest of all, is 11,328 feet. Lava boulders are scattered everywhere. Stands of Engelmann spruce and fir cloak much of the summit, interspersed with meadows of arctic tundra (used for grazing) and numerous small lakes and ponds, the latter being remnants of the most recent glacial age. Extensive evergreen growth is very unusual for such an altitude, and it is said that the Aquarius bears one of the highest forests in the world. Boulder Top's waters are too shallow and cold for dependably good fishing, but some lakes avoid severe winterkill and are kept stocked well enough to offer some challenge. Though the Aquarius has been the habitat of bear and cougar, large carnivores are rare today. Even deer are not as plentiful as in former times.

The junction of State 24 with the aforementioned sideroad coincides with a narrow gateway between Thousand Lake Mountain and the Aquar-

Red Gate of the Fremont River between Bicknell and Torrey, as seen from the Velvet Ridge.

WARD ROYLANCE

ius, carved by the Fremont River. Explorer-scientists of the 1870s applied the name **Red Gate** to this colorful portal between the High Plateaus and Canyonlands. Within the Red Gate, on the west bank of the river near the bridge, stands an aged two-story **gristmill** of frame construction, built in 1890 and serving an active life for 50 years until about 1940. Backed by spectacular red cliffs known as **The Fluted Wall,** the photogenic old mill is listed on state and national historic registers. Nearby is the Navajo Trails youth camp.

The **FREMONT RIVER,** named for explorer John C. Fremont *(see Fremont above),* issues from Fish Lake. It is a modest stream, only about 150 miles from head to mouth, but the terrain through which it flows is among the most wonderfully diversified in the west. In its upper reaches, west of Capitol Reef, the river is clear and cold, a habitat of trout; after reaching the younger, softer rock formations east of the Reef, however, it becomes a muddy carrier of sediment and meanders lazily through broad floodplains of mud and sand. At Hanksville it combines with Muddy River; from there downstream it takes the name **Dirty Devil,** entering a forbidding gorge and finally emptying into Lake Powell near Hite. The Fremont and its tributaries support nearly the entire population of Wayne County, but the river's water is efficiently utilized only in the upper valleys. Downstream, floods have traditionally wrought periodic devastation because of ineffective flow controls.

In a delightful setting is **TEASDALE** (7,000 alt.), 1 m. south from State 24, cradled in a cove of the forested Aquarius, looking out over brilliant cliffs and green fields. Here are well-preserved older homes, graceful reminders of a bygone era when some local residents gained wealth from large flocks of sheep. The white steepled Mormon chapel is a landmark. Nearby, on a side street, is a curious "**bottle house**" built by Tora Nelson, world traveler who moved her art and antique collection to Teasdale in 1956 and installed it in an abandoned schoolhouse as a museum. Afterwards she built, almost singlehandedly, a two-story building of peaked design, utilizing glass bottles for some of the walls. This served for years as a public museum displaying her collection of cultural objects. By 1979 ill health had forced Mrs. Nelson to halt museum showings.

Today's population includes retirees and summer residents, migrants attracted by Teasdale's bucolic aura and its natural setting. Here is located the district ranger for Boulder Mountain (Dixie National Forest). Roads in the vicinity climb the north slope of Boulder Mountain to fishing lakes and streams, and an unpaved but improved road (an old highway) follows the geologically interesting Teasdale Fault eastward past serrated Cockscomb Ridge and picturesque ranches to a junction with the Grover-Boulder road *(see below).*

Northward from the highway between Teasdale and State 24 looms one of the awesome sights of western America: the full southern face of **THOUSAND LAKE MOUNTAIN,** a stupendous frontal exposure of rainbow cliffs and mountain slopes rising 4,000 feet in terraced steps from the Fremont River to the mountain's tabular crest. The effect is stunning, involving a rare combination of prismatic color, stately forms, and grand scale. Revealed in a single visual sweep are 200 million years of earth's history, tilting upwards from the brownish-red Moenkopi of the Fluted Wall

South face of Thousand Lake Mountain from the Teasdale road.

through buff-colored Shinarump, varicolored Chinle, orange-red Wingate, beige Navajo, and finally the greens and blacks of the mountain's forests and cloaking lava flows.

All of these colorful rock types are found to the east, descending in elevation from the mountain and paralleling the highway into the park.

TORREY (6,800 alt. 140 pop.) lies on a sloping bench, the townsite marked by large cottonwood and poplar trees. Open valley and the hulk of the Aquarius form its southern environs; close by on the north loom red cliffs, citadel buttes and temples of multicolored rocks, and above all the brooding heights of Thousand Lake Mountain. Overgrown lots and tumble-down buildings bespeak decades of out-migration, neglect and economic difficulties. Civic pride and community enterprise so apparent in towns to the west is less evident here. In contrast, Torrey reflects individuality—an independent casualness not overly common in rural Utah—and therein lies much of the peculiar charm that entices travelers from the highway onto the town's streets.

Turn north from State 24 at Torrey's western outskirts to **Sand Creek, Velvet Ridge, Holt Draw** and panoramic viewpoints high on the eastern shoulder of **THOUSAND LAKE MOUNTAIN.** This drive and its branches, extremely rough and steep in places, and perhaps requiring the fording of shallow streams, penetrate a handsome region of red Wingate cliffs, pastel Chinle hills, and gently contoured Navajo slopes and ledges. Most of the area is within the boundaries of Fishlake National Forest. One fork winds westward across the **Velvet Ridge,** an intermediate bench atop the Fluted Wall, overlooking Fremont River and Teasdale, named for the ridge's fluorescent Chinle mounds. Another fork enters **Hells Hole,** a deep, vari-colored, cliff-encircled basin—a miniature Zion Canyon—passing at the foot of Wingate-Chinle cliffs where petrified wood can still be found in fragmented pieces. The route up the mountain through Holt Draw is steep and rough, but its higher reaches above **Sand** and **Paradise flats** offer a soul-stirring overview of Capitol Reef, the northern Waterpocket Fold, Cathedral Valley and South Desert, the Caineville country, Henry Mountains and San Rafael Swell—in other words, a variation of views from the Elkhorn road *(see above).* This road also provides hiker access to **Water Canyon, Deep Creek** and other parts of the little-known, extremely rugged **Waterpocket Fold** where it emerges from the mountain. *Hikers should obtain information regarding this area from Capitol Reef National Park.*

Turn south from State 24, 1 m. east of Torrey, to **GROVER,** the **AQUARIUS PLATEAU (BOULDER MOUNTAIN),** and **BOULDER.** Grover, in a secluded valley between Miners Mountain and Boulder Mountain, is a ranching hamlet, in recent years the homesite for summer residents. During the 1970s and early 1980s the old schoolhouse was used as an extraordinary "in the round" theater known as the Grover Playhouse, scene each July of lively dramatic productions attracting crowds of local residents and visitors. These were the work of Ruth and Nathan Hale, members of the related Dietlein family, and friends. Summer residents of Grover, the Hales and Dietleins were involved professionally with the Glendale Community Theater in California.

The road continues over the east and south shoulders of Boulder Mountain, climbing to more than 9,000 feet. The road is paved for several miles south of Grover, graded and widened for most of the remaining distance. Within a few years the entire 30-odd miles between Grover and Boulder will be hard-surfaced, but at this writing the road is closed during winter months and drivers are cautioned to watch for other vehicles, including logging trucks. Enroute to Boulder the road passes through aspen, ponderosa pine, pinyon and juniper of Dixie National Forest, affording aerial views of the painted, corrugated wonderland to the east and south *(see Tour No. 9C for description).* Along the way are three improved forest campgrounds.

From the western outskirts of Grover, about 7 m. from State 24, an unpaved road forks south. Known as the **North Slope road,** this forest route (Dixie National Forest) climbs steeply up the shoulder of Boulder Mountain through pygmy evergreens, ponderosa pine, fir and spruce to elevations approaching 10,000 feet. Four-wheel-drive is recommended for those attempting its upper reaches. The road gives hiking and jeeping access to Donkey and Fish Creek reservoirs, Blind Lake, etc. For spectacle, views from this drive rival those of Thousand Lake Mountain and the Grover-Boulder road. Marvelous views are obtainable as well from a steep, rough road that climbs the north slope of Boulder Mountain from the vicinity of Teasdale, giving access to Donkey Lake, Coleman Reservoir, and other waters.

About 2 m. east of Torrey, State 24 curves northward and drops into the valley of Sand and Sulphur creeks, then follows the base of brightly colored cliffs and slopes to Fruita and **CAPITOL REEF NATIONAL PARK** *(see parks chapter).* Though not included within the park, the "breaks" of Thousand Lake Mountain near Torrey are worthy of inclusion among the foremost scenic wonders of Utah. Here the grand uplift has erupted into a complex of yawning canyons, stepped cliffs and ledges, great buttes and mesas. Cliffs of brown-red Moenkopi formation at the bottom are sculptured into flying buttresses and fluted columns, giving the effect of cathedrals in places, or of Egyptian temples, or mile after mile of upright mummy figures. Seemingly every color of the rainbow is represented here in this kaleidoscopic area known as **Torrey Breaks.**

The 15 miles of State 24 east of Torrey Breaks are included within Capitol Reef National Park, described in the parks chapter.

East of the park, State 24 enters a landscape like no other in Utah or perhaps in America. Colors have changed from vivid shades of red to rusts, buffs, tans, and shades of bluish gray and purple. This is **Utah's Painted Desert.** In place of the ancient rocks of Jurassic and Triassic age that form the sheer cliffs and domed slopes of Capitol Reef, younger and softer rocks appear, and these crumble more easily to mud, clay or low cliffs and ledges. And yet this rule is violated in the vicinity of Caineville where the youngest layered rocks of all—massive Cretaceous formations a thousand feet thick

South Caineville Mesa and Blue Valley near Caineville.

or more—appear in majestic buttressed cliffs, the disintegrating faces of the great Caineville mesas and Factory Butte. Erosional sculpturing here differs completely from that of the park, giving an effect of pleated drapery with contours that change dramatically with time of day and become truly exquisite when accented by the highlights and shadows of late afternoon, or by sun and clouds.

Sideroads just east of the park give access to scenic areas north and south of the highway. The **South (Notom) Road** branches from State 24 9 m. east of the park visitor center at Fruita, paralleling the east flank of the Waterpocket Fold and providing access to the park's southern extension *(see Capitol Reef National Park).*

The **River Ford (North) Road** branches from State 24 12 m. east of Fruita *(3 m. east of the Notom turnoff),* crossing the Fremont River in a normally shallow ford *(if unsure, test it by wading!)* then winding through rugged canyons and across widespreading flats to **Cathedral Valley** and northern reaches of **Capitol Reef National Park** *(which see for additional details).*

CAINEVILLE (4,600 alt.) is a ranching and farming hamlet stretching for several miles between the Fremont River and highway. A larger village existed here for several decades in the late 1800s and early years of this century. The climate is agreeable and the soil productive, but the river is uncooperative and has a discouraging tendency to wash away fields and orchards with little warning. Because of this, most residents moved elsewhere after a particularly disastrous flood in 1909 (vividly described by a witness, Evangeline Godby, in the *Deseret News* issue of July 17, 1981). At this writing, Bud and Peggy Garver—transplanted Californians and modern pioneers—operate an atmospheric restaurant and store known as Buena Vida Cantina and Trading Post. The **old Mormon church house,** a vacant frame structure, is prominent from the highway. South 1 m. from this chapel, hidden behind dense canal vegetation, is the **Elijah Cutler Behunin Cabin,** a dilapidated log structure built about 1883 as the first building in Caineville. This unpaved sideroad, formerly the main highway, winds along the fantastically sculptured, tilting whaleback slope of

Caineville Reef, overlooking the river and stately palisades of **South Caineville Mesa,** and eventually meeting the paved highway 3 m. west of Caineville.

Turn north from State 24 on the western outskirts of Caineville to **Capitol Reef National Park (Cathedral Valley)** and other points of unusual scenic and geologic interest. *(See Capitol Reef National Park; also see River Ford road above.)*

East of Caineville, State 24 passes through a desolate, haunting landscape of clays, muds, and "pinto" hills, mostly colored in pastel shades. As described in the first edition, crumbling "spires and monuments have fallen; broken and buried, they make softly-clothed mounds in a wasteland . . . The late afternoon sun paints the dunes, mesas, and mountain walls in delicate mirage-like pastels." Known generally as **Blue Valley,** the river valley between Caineville and Hanksville has witnessed attempts at settlement, and several modest communities actually survived for a few years until floods and other factors proved fatal. One of these, known as **GILES,** is marked by a ruined rock structure beside the highway about 12 m. east of Caineville. In 1941, according to the first edition, "the recreational hall, the school house, and scattered dwelling ruins remain to tell the story of dirty work by the Dirty Devil (Fremont River)." Only vestiges of these remain today, south of the highway.

Near **Factory Butte,** one of Utah's grandest butte-forms and a regional landmark —at junction about 10 m. west of Hanksville—an unpaved sideroad leads north to Salt Wash on the flank of the San Rafael Swell. Here was to have been the proposed **Intermountain Power Project.** During the 1970s this site was intensively studied for its coal and water resources and proposed as the location for America's largest coal-fired power generating installation—of magnitude equal to that of the proposed Kaiparowits plant *(see Tour No. 9B).* Though coal, water and other physical assets were favorable, the site was on federal lands only a few miles from Capitol Reef National Park. Because of this proximity and the possibility of occasional air quality deterioration in the park, Secretary of the Interior Cecil Andrus looked upon the site with disfavor. An alternative location for the plant, near Delta, was approved in 1979. *See Tour No. 4B(1).*

Fairweather roads continue through a tortured landscape of weird rock erosion, into **Muddy River Canyon,** and along the south flank of San Rafael Reef to **Wild Horse Butte, Goblin Valley** and State 24 north of Hanksville. *Inquire locally as to passability.*

Fremont River *(left)* and Factory Butte *(right)* in the Painted Desert east of Capitol Reef National Park.

HANKSVILLE (4,300 alt. 350 pop.) was long one of Utah's most isolated communities, not seeing the first paved access road until 1959. Today, though Hanksville is the hub of highways leading in three directions, it remains physically remote from large centers of population. But the town's economy, for decades based on farming and ranching and sporadic small-scale mining, has expanded to include recreational travel, government employment, and large-scale mining.

Quoting from page 349 of the first edition, Hanksville "was used, in the eighties and nineties, as a rendezvous for the Robber's Roost gang. The gang held sway over all the territory south and east of Hanksville; some people welcomed them in the small settlements, perhaps because the outlaws were good spenders. The large cattle companies were their chief victims." Since that was written, numerous books, articles and a major Hollywood film production have described Butch Cassidy, Robber's Roost, and the Wild Bunch. Cassidy would hardly recognize the "boomtown" Hanksville of today, with its mobile homes, auto service stations, motels and diverse other new structures. Charley Gibbons' old store building remains (unrecognizable today)—also the quaint Mormon church house, built of stone in 1890, and a few original homes.

Hanksville was settled in the early 1880s and named for one of its founders, Ebenezer Hanks. It witnessed gold mining days of the Colorado River and Henry Mountains *(see Glen Canyon National Recreation Area; also Henry Mountains and Hite below)*. Freighting was an occupation of earlier days. The town has seen uranium booms and busts, oil drilling, sporadic coal mining, and broken dreams of prosperity from the Intermountain Power Project. As an economic factor, tourism has grown over the years, slowly but steadily, until travel to and from Lake Powell now equals or surpasses uranium production in importance.

North from Hanksville, State 24 crosses wide-open sandy desert to I-70 and Green River *(see Tour No. 10)*. At **Temple Mountain Junction,** 21 m. from Hanksville, a sideroad forks west and another to the east. The west fork (paved for several miles) leads to Goblin Valley State Reserve, Temple Mountain and the interior of San Rafael Swell *(see Tour No. 10 for description)*. The east fork leads to Robber's Roost, Horseshoe Canyon and the Maze District of Canyonlands National Park.

This latter route—unpaved, rough and sandy in spots—gives access to one of Utah's least known, least visited, and most rugged canyon regions. Though it has been fabled as **Robber's Roost** for nearly a hundred years and has been utilized as a cattle range for much of that time, the area is only recently becoming known for the grandeur of its scenery and its fascinating archeological treasure: the ancient Indian rock art of **Horseshoe Canyon.**

This vast wedge between the Green and Dirty Devil rivers is rather gently contoured for the most part, its gorges not being too apparent from the road. Close to the rivers, however, where **Lands End Plateau** breaks away in a sinuous vertical wall known as the **Orange Cliffs,** gentle contours dissolve into a confusing maze of steep-walled canyons, cliffs, buttes, and numberless smaller erosional forms. In erosional complexity and red-rock grandeur, this region matches any other part of Canyonlands. Part of the area is the weird **Land of Standing Rocks,** western counterpart of the Needles, which together form one of the world's strangest landscapes: the inner Junction country where the Green and upper Colorado rivers join near the

Overlooking the Land of Standing Rocks (Canyonlands National Park) from Lands End *(left)*. Sign is at Temple Mountain Junction north of Hanksville.

head of Cataract Canyon. *See also Glen Canyon National Recreation Area and Canyonlands National Park.*

STATE 95 AND 276 SOUTH FROM HANKSVILLE TO LAKE POWELL

State 95, Utah's Bicentennial Highway, connects Hanksville on the west with Blanding on the east, 126 miles away, passing through an isolated, little populated region that long represented Utah's last frontier. The highway provides easy, convenient access to the marinas of upper Lake Powell, as well as to Natural Bridges National Monument, Grand Gulch, and other points in southeastern Utah described in Tour No. 11.

Between Hanksville and the junction with State 276, unpaved sideroads branch eastward from State 95 into a labyrinth of canyons formed by the **Dirty Devil River** and its tributaries, as well as to cliff-edge observation viewpoints. Other roads fork westward into the Henry Mountains.

At 16 m. from Hanksville, turn east on an unpaved, fairweather road which winds laboriously across a corrugated wilderness of sand and bare rock to **Burr Point (Dirty Devil Overlook)** 11 m., atop a thousand-foot cliff. The point overlooks the gorge of Dirty Devil River, set in an unreal world of grand cliffs and canyons.

At 16.5 m. from Hanksville, turn east into **Poison Spring Canyon** on an unpaved, fairweather road leading to a shallow ford of the Dirty Devil River *(avoid in inclement weather!),* then through North Hatch Canyon to Sunset Pass and junction with the main access road between State 24 and the Standing Rocks-Maze District of Canyonlands National Park. A fork of this road climbs the Orange Cliffs in switchbacks to the top of Big Ridge, thence to Lands End, the head of Flint Trail, and Hans Flat Ranger Station *(see Glen Canyon National Recreation Area).* Poison Spring Canyon deepens to a thousand feet at the river. Beyond, the Hatch Canyon system is a network of deep gorges, formed by sheer Wingate cliffs based on Chinle slopes; they bear the marks of uranium mining and prospecting, and petrified wood is (or was) abundant. The **Big Ridge** forms the northern rampart; roads and trails on top are reached from Robber's Roost or by switchback road from North Hatch Canyon, mentioned above, This area is ideal for exploring in four-wheel-drive vehicles, but it is isolated and remote, and floods may wash out sections of road. Precautionary measures should be standard procedure, including the obtaining of information in advance from local sources (such as Bureau of Land Management office in Hanksville). *See Off-road Travel Suggestions.*

THE HENRY MOUNTAINS. At junction 9 m. south of Hanksville, turn west on unpaved road toward the Henry Mountains, past Fairview Ranch. The road climbs steeply into deep canyons on the east slope of **Mt. Ellen** (11,615 alt.), highest and largest of the Henry peaks. In midsummer it may be possible to cross Mt. Ellen, over a high pass, via the right-hand road; otherwise it is necessary to follow a lower route around the peak to Penellen Pass, where the main east-west route connects State 95 with the Waterpocket Fold road.

Many miles of fairweather roads crisscross the Henrys, connecting the three northern peaks, giving access to Bromide Basin, the site of old Eagle City, Wolverton millsite, Starr Springs, etc. Detailed maps should be obtained (for example, from Bureau of Land Management office in Hanksville).

The Henrys consist of five isolated peaks: Mt. Ellen (11,615 alt.), Mt. Pennell (11,371), Mt. Hillers (10,723), Mt. Holmes (7,930) and Mt. Ellsworth (8,235), all named by the Powell surveys. Known as the **Little Rockies,** the latter two peaks stand prominently beside the Bullfrog highway; the others are much higher and more massive. The Henrys are noted as the last mountains in the 48 contiguous states to be formally named and placed on official maps. They were "discovered" in 1869 by the river party led by Major John W. Powell, who called them initially the Unknown Mountains, later applying the name of Prof. Joseph Henry of the Smithsonian Institution. (New Mexican travelers, Mormon explorers, fur trappers and others surely knew of them before that—they are prominent landmarks visible for a hundred miles.) Geologically the range is unusual, having an uncommon structure recognized by Powell and geologists of subsequent surveys. Basically the present mountains are composed of igneous material; but they are not volcanoes and originally this igneous material was buried under sedimentary rocks, into which it had intruded as magma (molten lava), pushing up as "laccolithic" uplifts. During the intervening 60 or 70 million years since this process began, the overlying sedimentary formations have been removed from most of the higher elevations, but they still encircle the peaks, in places as deformed, contorted beds that are clearly visible.

Since at least the 1870s the Henrys have been known to contain gold deposits, and the peaks have been intensively prospected. But they are stubborn yielders, and apparently few if any gold miners ever struck it rich. The peaks were considered a source of the fine gold in the sandbars of Glen Canyon; their creekbeds have been placered and their orebeds mined and probed for a hundred years or more. **Eagle City** was their principal boomtown, but it survived only a few years during the 1890s and is hardly evident today.

In more recent years the Henry area is proving to be the repository of rich deposits of uranium and vanadium ore. Coal, silver and copper are present, and commercial oil production may lie in the future. And the mountains have been a prime range for cattle and sheep since pioneer days, having supported a number of large livestock operations. Some of these were preyed upon by outlaws of Robber's Roost. Deer hunting is popular, and the area has been home for a large herd of bison since the 1940s. Desert bighorn sheep roam the Little Rockies. Smaller animals and birds abound, and cougar are present.

About 20 m. south of Hanksville, State 95 enters the shallow upper end of a deepening gorge known as **North Wash,** an historic route of travel between Hanksville and Hite (Dandy Crossing) since the 1880s. Until the years following World War II the road was only a wagon trail; but even after the first "improved" road was constructed in 1946 by Art Chaffin and a small crew it remained a fairweather route for another 15 years or more, featuring pockets of deep sand, fording the stream 50 times in a distance of 15 miles, and becoming impassable in times of flood. The road was brought to modern standards during the 1960s. Before Lake Powell rose and inundated old Hite in 1964, the road followed the west bank of the Colorado River downstream for six miles from the mouth of North Wash to the ferry site. Today it follows the lake's west shore northward to a bridge crossing of Dirty Devil Bay, then to a bridge crossing of Narrow Canyon, and thence to a bridge crossing of White Canyon—these bridges and highway construction, performed during the 1960s at great cost, representing a triumph of engineering. Two of the bridges (White Canyon and the Colorado River) received national design citations in 1965-66.

The **Hite Marina** of today lies on the east side of the lake, opposite the location of old Hite and the first ferry site. The ferry was moved up-canyon after Hite was inundated in 1964, to the mouth of North Wash, where it remained until the highway and bridges were completed shortly thereafter. The first Hite marina also was located here until moved to the east bank a few years ago. As described in the 1941 edition, **HITE** was:

a "town" on the Colorado River with two stone buildings and a population of one! Cass Hite, supposed renegade and former member of Quantrill's Civil War guerillas, built a rock hovel here in the early [1880s]. For years he existed by washing out "flour" gold from the sandbars of the Colorado. In 1893, when in one of the larger settlements for supplies, he was diligently questioned about gold on the Colorado. Whether to keep prospectors away from his hideout, or in sincerity, he said that the coarse gold had washed down to the riffles and sandbars at the foot of Navaho Mountain *(see Rainbow Bridge National Monument)*. A gold rush was started, ferries were built, and great dredges were hauled to the Colorado, where they still lie, twisted and rusting. Finding no gold, disappointed prospectors "went after" Hite, intending to kill him. The resourceful isolationist went into hiding for two years until the incident blew over. Hite's crossing, which he called "Dandy Crossing," was consistently used by the Indians. It is one of four and perhaps the best natural crossing of the Colorado.

State Highway 95 crosses the gorge of Dirty Devil River on a high bridge. Photograph was taken in 1967 before Lake Powell flooded the canyon.

BUREAU OF RECLAMATION (MEL DAVIS)

After Cass Hite died his ranch was abandoned for many years and the crossing was little used until the ranch was revived in 1934 by Arthur and Della Chaffin. Art Chaffin was a man of many talents, ambitious and energetic: miner, farmer, rancher, Indian trader, roadbuilder, mechanic, ferry operator, river guide. Up to the time of his death in 1979 at an advanced age, he was planning a new real estate project in his beloved red-rock country on the flanks of the Henrys. Chaffin's prompting of state officials was responsible for the first improved road through North Wash to Hite and across the river in White Canyon, a total distance of 70 miles, which he and a small crew of men bulldozed in a short time and at an unbelievably small cost. Chaffin himself built the first motorized ferry, dedicated with the new road in September 1946. When that ferry was destroyed by a flood the following year, he built another, providing the only vehicular crossing of the Colorado for 300 miles. The Chaffin name was synonymous with Hite for more than 20 years.

Regarding the North Wash road of 1946, C. W. McCullough wrote in the *Deseret News* (December 6, 1947), "Let us use that term *road* with tongue in cheek . . . It is a road that calls out 'Good luck: you'll need it!' when you leave the pavement at either end. An adventure trail, the Hite road writhes and twists through boulder strewn washes, shifting sands and dry creek beds that carry a constant potential of debris-choked floods. It calls for a cool head, a stout heart and a car not too underslung." Yet those very qualities made it memorable in the lives of thousands of sightseers and river-bound boaters who traversed it during the first 15 years or so before improvements diminished its appeal as an adventure route.

In the upper reaches of North Wash, 26 m. south of Hanksville, **State 276** branches from State 95 and leads southward to **Bullfrog Marina-Resort** and **Lake Powell** (42 m.). **Mt. Hillers** looms high to the west, and the two cameo peaks of the **Little Rockies** (Mt. Holmes and Mt. Ellsworth) are geological and scenic curiosities beside the highway on the east. The landscape is a colorful tangle of steep-walled gorges, slickrock slopes, distorted strata, and picturesque erosional forms.

At 19 m. from North Wash Junction a sign marks the turnoff to **Starr Spring Recreation Site,** 3 m., a shady BLM campground on the historic site of Starr Ranch, which flourished as a major cattle operation for some years after its founding in the 1890s. Interesting ruins remain in a verdant setting.

About 12 m. north of Bullfrog, beside the highway, is the new community of **TICABOO,** Utah's "most totally planned" community of recent times. At present an elaborate mobile home park with attractive new lodge and store, Ticaboo came into being during the late 1970s and early 1980s. Uranium on which the town is based is mined nearby in Shootamaring (Shoot-a-Ring) Canyon and processed in a new $40,000,000 mill located several miles north of Ticaboo. *Lodging, food, fuel.*

From a junction about 5 m. north of Bullfrog Marina, an unpaved road forks west. This exceptionally scenic route (washboardy, dusty and rough in places) threads its way along the rims of yawning gorges and across far-spreading flats to Grand Gulch (Hall's Creek Canyon), Waterpocket Fold, Burr Trail, Circle Cliffs, State 24 and Capitol Reef National Park. *See Capitol Reef National Park and Tour 9C.*

BULLFROG MARINA-RESORT is the largest recreation development on the north end of Lake Powell. *See Glen Canyon National Recreation Area.* It features launching ramp, campground, stores and service station, boating services and supplies, lodging and meals, airport, boat tours, boat and houseboat rentals.

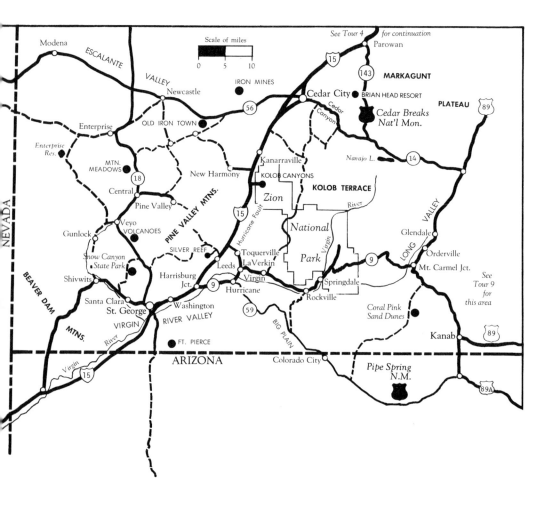

Scale of miles

0   5   10

See Tour 4   *for continuation*
Parowan

Modena

ESCALANTE

VALLEY

IRON MINES

Newcastle

15

143   **MARKAGUNT**

56

Cedar City   ● BRIAN HEAD RESORT

PLATEAU

89

Enterprise

OLD IRON TOWN

Cedar Canyon

Cedar Breaks Nat'l Mon.

Enterprise Res.

MTN. MEADOWS

New Harmony

Kanarraville

Navajo L.

14

18

Central

KOLOB CANYONS

KOLOB TERRACE

Pine Valley

Zion

River

NEVADA

Veyo

VOLCANOES

PINE VALLEY MTNS.

15

Hurricane Fault

National

Virgin

Glendale

LONG VALLEY

Gunlock

SILVER REEF

Toquerville

Orderville

Snow Canyon State Park

Leeds

LaVerkin

Park

9

Mt. Carmel Jct.

Shivwits

Harrisburg Jct.

Virgin

Springdale

See Tour 9 for this area

BEAVER DAM

Santa Clara

9

Hurricane

Rockville

Washington

St. George

59

Coral Pink Sand Dunes

MTNS.

VIRGIN

RIVER VALLEY

Kanab

89

River

FT. PIERCE

BIG PLAIN

Virgin

15

ARIZONA

Colorado City

Pipe Spring N.M.

89A

Tour No. 8
COLOR COUNTRY—WEST
(Beaver, Iron and Washington counties)

This tour features the Great Basin and High Plateaus in Beaver, Iron, and Washington counties, from Cove Fort on the north to Beaver, Cedar City, and St. George on the south. The principal artery is Interstate 15. From this major north-south thoroughfare, connecting roads branch in all directions, giving access to a trove of historical, cultural, and natural curiosities.

Tour No. 8A — Interstate Highway 15 from Cove Fort south to the Arizona line, with sideroads branching from Beaver, Cedar City, St. George, etc.

The 1941 edition describes the route between Cove Fort and Beaver as traversing "rolling wastes of sage and juniper, punctuated by scattered wind- and sun-beaten ranchhouses between the towering forested crags of the Tushar Mountains (L) and castellated ridges of the Mineral Mountains (R). This is the region of the 'Utah mile', which, in the way of distance, may be anything from a half-hour to an all-day hike. Speech becomes more languid, the western drawl begins to appear, and the main topics of conversation are the lack of rain, crops, and politics. Families are larger; there are few diversions except in . . . larger towns." That description could apply almost as well today as 40 years ago.

BEAVER (6,000 alt. 1,792 pop.), now bypassed by the highway, is the center of a farming, ranching, and mining district and the seat of Beaver County. In recent years it has attracted as residents a significant number of retired people.

Mormons settled Beaver in 1856, beginning to raise large herds of sheep and soon establishing a big woolen mill. About 1870 the discovery of rich mineral deposits in the San Francisco Mountains west of Beaver started to bring hordes of miners and camp-followers into the district; and by 1871 friction between Mormon and non-Mormon, coupled with fear of Indians and the precarious standing of law and order, caused both sides to ask for federal troops. Pursuant to this request, four companies of soldiers camped in tents on Beaver River from May 1872 until the following year, when a number of black rock buildings were erected at the mouth of Beaver Canyon, two miles east of the city. In 1874 this post was named **Fort Cameron** in honor of Colonel James Cameron, hero of Bull Run, and for years its 250 soldiers maintained the peace in Beaver County and brought added prosperity to the region.

General Philip Sheridan visited Fort Cameron in 1882, being met with all the pomp and ceremony Beaver's people could muster; but he saw that the post no longer served a necessary purpose, and the next year it was evacuated by the army and sold to the Mormon Church and private parties for $4,800 (it had cost $200,000). Later the buildings were used by one of southern Utah's famous old schools, Beaver (later Murdock) Academy, which finally closed its doors in 1922. Only one or two of the original buildings remain, and today the area of the old fort/academy is occupied by homes, farms, the racetrack, and playgrounds.

Beaver is a showplace of early Utah architecture—a frozen moment in time, as it were—so rich in unusual and distinctive buildings that it is considered a Historic District. According to a National Register of Historic Places description, ". . . the history of the town depicts an interesting story of Mormon-Gentile accommodation. Beaver has enjoyed a rich architectural development and contains over 300 structures of significance. Early pioneer types and styles are particularly well represented. Log cabins, early frame buildings, and an excellent collection of brick structures are extant. Most apparent, however, are the many fine black rock and pink rock homes built by Thomas Frazer and the Boyters. Built between 1868 and the 1890s, these rock homes document the outstanding design and building accomplishments of some of Utah's finest pioneer master craftsmen.''

Most noteworthy of all is the **Old Beaver County Courthouse,** a towered structure with clock and bell, built of brick on a massive lava-rock foundation. The building dates from the 1870s and 1880s and was used as a public office and court building for almost a hundred years. It was saved and restored through the combined efforts of many individuals and organizations, who devoted thousands of hours to its rehabilitation. Today the Courthouse functions as a **Pioneer Museum,** Art Gallery and auditorium for live theater. Its windowless, stone-walled basement was used as Beaver County's jail; well-traveled visitors cannot ignore the sobering resemblance to Old World dungeons.

Turn east from Beaver via State 153 into **Beaver Canyon** and onto the heights of the **TUSHAR MOUNTAINS.** Enroute, at the mouth of the canyon, the road threads through an attractive area of new housing, past the municipal golf course and the well-kept racetrack. Here, every summer since 1939, has been held the Dairy District Derby, Utah's largest thoroughbred horse races. For many decades Beaver Canyon and the Tushars (also known as the Beaver Mountains) have been one of southern Utah's favorite fishing, hunting and camping regions. Recent years have seen the introduction of a winter sports and homesite development known as Mt. Holly *(see below).* Fishlake National Forest has developed a number of camping and picnicking facilities at Kent's Lake, City Creek, Mahogany Cove, Anderson Meadow, and other alpine sites. Mountain-girded **Puffer Lake** *(privately owned)* is popular for fishing; **Otter Creek Resort** is nearby. Densely wooded except for rocky peaks and crests, this mountain region is the highest and most rugged in southern Utah, with several summits exceeding 12,000 feet. *See also Tour No. 7A.* The spectacular alpine terrain, while not particularly challenging for serious climbers, does offer exciting choices for hiking and scrambling, and for horseback riding. Because of their ruggedness—particularly in the north—the Tushars might be termed southern Utah's equivalent of the Wasatch Mountains. East of Puffer Lake, State 153 *(now unpaved)* passes over the high **Big Flat** crest at more than 10,000 feet, then soon drops in tight turns to Junction and US 89 *(Tour No. 7A).* Here, as described in the 1941 edition, the road affords "a sweeping view of the Sevier Valley far below, with its towns of Junction and Circleville . . . The road, descending by switchbacks to the valley floor, looks like a twisted tape flung out from the mountainside. A hair-

Tushar ridge (12,000 alt.) from Big John Flat near Mt. Holly resort.

pin turn . . . brings the glistening hay-look of Piute Reservoir into view below. This very steep grade should not be attempted by timorous drivers.''

Mt. Holly is a winter sports and residential development located 20 paved miles east of Beaver, nestled in a canyon beneath the 12,000-foot ridge of **Mt. Holly-Delano Peak.** Originating in the early 1970s on land leased from the state, in the midst of Fishlake National Forest, Mt. Holly was envisioned by its developers as a ski resort with numerous lifts and runs, lodges, shops and hotels, surrounded by private homes and condominiums. At this writing, facilities include a double chairlift, T-bar, day lodge, motel, ski rentals, and dining facilities. A number of condominium units and private homes have been built in the area. The project has been the subject of acrimonious debate between proponents and opponents.

Turn west from Beaver via State 21 to Minersville, Milford, Old Frisco, Pahvant Valley, Lehman Caves National Monument, and other Great Basin points. *Below, excerpts from the 1941 edition appear in quotation marks.* The road passes through the lush bottomlands along the valley of Beaver River, which forms a divide between the Mineral Range (north) and Black Mountains (south).

Minersville Reservoir, also known as Rocky Ford Reservoir, impounds water of Beaver River for irrigation. The Beaver River, originating in the high Tushars, formerly meandered far northward and emptied into the Sevier Lake sink, but its water is so thoroughly utilized for agriculture that little if any reaches its original destination. On the shore of Minersville Reservoir is **MINERSVILLE LAKE STATE RECREATION AREA,** a boating park with campground and launching facilities. The lake is popular for both boating and fishing.

MINERSVILLE (5,600 alt. 552 pop.) is the "center of a small but rich agricultural district, where four crops of alfalfa are harvested annually; other parts of the state usually get only three cuttings. Corn, fruits, and early garden vegetables are supplementary products. Pioneer adobe and log houses stand among more recent frame and brick structures." *From Minersville, State 130 winds south through the rugged Black Mountains, foothills and open valleys to junction with I-15 near Cedar City.*

MILFORD (4,966 alt. 1,293 pop.) is a division point for the Union Pacific Railroad, an important farming center, and a trading and supply center for far-flung mines and ranches. Its population has remained nearly constant for many decades, numbering 1,500 in 1930 and remaining within 200 or 300 of that figure through the intervening years. Isolation and a fairly stable population and economic base—with no dramatic booms or busts for decades—have combined to lend Milford a nostalgic aura of timelessness. This may be due for a change in the near future. Milford's historical background was summarized in the 1941 edition:

> For several years after its settlement in 1870, Milford was a straggling frontier town, its business section consisting mostly of mine supply stores, dependent entirely upon the mines at Frisco and Newhouse. Ore seekers traveling to and from the "diggin's" in 1880 forded the Beaver River below a stamp mill. The crossing, known as the "mill ford," suggested a name for the town. When ore production fell off in the eighties, Milford lost heavily. Agriculture and railroading gradually took up the slack.

East of Milford several miles is a major geothermal field which promises to become an important source of electrical and industrial energy in the future. During the 1970s a number of firms drilled exploration wells in the area, to depths as great as 13,000 feet; the majority of these were successful in tapping water with sufficient flow, pressure, heat and steam for commercial use. In September 1980 announcement was made of a contract between Utah Power and Light Company and one of the well developers, Phillips Petroleum Company, calling for construction of an experimental 20-megawatt power generating plant that will utilize steam from Phillips's wells. If this plant proves successful, it is anticipated that additional development will occur. The Milford installation is the first such geothermal development in the United States outside of California, and one of few in the world.

West of Milford, State 21 enters a mountainous region dominated by the lofty dome of **Frisco Peak** (9,700 alt.). This has been the scene of mining activity for more than a hundred years, primarily from mines at old Frisco and Newhouse which are reputed to have yielded ores with a value in excess of $60,000,000. The most profitable ores were gold, silver, copper, lead and zinc with some tungsten; but the richer ores have been mined, and changing conditions have discouraged large-scale production of most minerals for some time. What the future may hold is conjectural. Copper has been mined by open-pit methods near Milford, and milled in the vicinity. Iron, manganese, mercury, molybdenum, uranium, alunite and many other minerals —in addition to those mentioned above—are known in Beaver County. Future conditions may favor development.

The MX Missile. The valleys of western Utah, and many others in Nevada, were proposed as sites for the cluster-basing of the MX intercontinental ballistics missile. Milford and Delta were considered as locales for important system bases. If the MX basing mode—or even a modified version of the plan under consideration—had been approved by President Reagan, developments of a magnitude hard to imagine would soon have been underway in this vicinity. *See Tour No. 4B(1) for fuller details.*

OLD FRISCO (6,600 alt.), a ghost town site 15 m. west of Milford, is marked by a few ruins, old charcoal ovens, a cemetery, and mine dumps. There is not much visible to the eye to indicate that several thousand people lived here during the 1880s in one of Utah's largest, rowdiest mining towns. Then there were hundreds of buildings, including stores, saloons, hotel, schoolhouse, and even a hospital. Little has changed since the 1941 edition's description of Frisco:

> . . . Frisco is little more than a cross that marks the spot. "Desert amethysts" —bits of broken glass—are scattered through the old town, remnants of miners' whoopee and headaches long past.

Discovered accidentally in 1875 by two prospectors, James Ryan and Samuel Hawkes of Pioche, Nevada, the Horn Silver Mine, on the hill a mile west of Frisco, was the richest silver producer in Utah. From a hole 900 feet long, 400 feet wide, and 900 feet deep, more than $54,000,000 was taken in ten years.

In a copyrighted article published (1936) in the *Salt Lake Mining Review* (partially reproduced by special permission), Murray Schick wrote:

How many, for instance, know that the Horn Silver put a celebrated financier on his feet after he had lost his fortune trying to finance the building of the Northern Pacific railroad. That the first promoter of the Horn Silver died on a train as he was taking the financier to look at the mine. That Jay Gould, personally, had a hand in extending the first railroad to the mine. . . . Jay Cooke was the J. Pierpont Morgan of his day. His fame rested chiefly on his success in selling United States government bonds to finance the Civil War. . . . 'Solid as Cooke's bank' was a popular metaphor. . .

Lycurgus Edgerton . . . associated with Jay Cooke in the Northern Pacific promotion . . . had . . . heard of the marvelous mine development in Utah [Schick continues]. On a visit to the East he told Cooke about the mine. . . . Cooke . . . started for Utah with Edgerton. Cooke arrived, but Edgerton died enroute from a heart attack.

Jay Cooke bought the property for $5,000,000 in 1879.

By this time, Frisco was booming. From Alta and Ophir, Utah, and from Colorado, Nevada, and Arizona came "boomers"—miners, gamblers, gunmen, and dance hall girls. A sheriff—Pearson, first name forgotten—who came from Pioche, was elected to clean up the town. With the simple philosophy that dead men give no trouble, he put on a law enforcement campaign; there were no fines to be paid, no jail sentences to serve, and burial expenses were not excessive. Pearson gave a man his choice—shoot it out, or leave town. Many tried to shoot it out, but Pearson had strong nerves and a quick trigger-finger. He was known to have killed as many as six men in one night, and it finally became necessary to hire a "body mover" to clean up after him. The "wagon" made the rounds every morning and hauled away one or two corpses; they were buried without questions or funeral announcements. Frisco acquired a reputation as the wildest camp in Utah. Each of the twenty-one saloons had its stories of killings. In one place two men were killed over fifty cents in a faro game.

Jay Cooke was not concerned with the morals of the town. He wanted a railroad to the place.

At Salt Lake City [Schick writes], Cooke interested the heads of the Mormon Church in extending the railroad they already owned to the new mining district and they took a quarter interest in the railroad. Then Cooke was in a position to ask the Union Pacific company for the rest. Sidney Dillon was president of the railroad. Though Cooke had forgotten it, he had once loaned Dillon $20,000 to tide him over. When Dillon heard what Cooke wanted he stepped out of the room, and brought back a short man with a black beard. It was Jay Gould. Gould looked at his maps. . . . Before the end of the conference Gould and Dillon consented to supply the money for the construction and the building of the Horn Silver railroad was assured. [The railroad was completed to 'Frisco in 1880.]

From 1880 to 1885 the mine produced heavily. Men dropped in heat sometimes at 108 degrees, and dust from the ore sent as many as forty men a month to hospitals with "miner's con." The owners, feverish for more wealth, disregarded all mining tenets, and the "glory hole" caved in to the seventh level, taking the shaft with it. The night shift came off work and the day men were lined up at the hoist house waiting their turn to go down. Mine officials stopped them, saying that there had been a trembling in the shaft. While the miners were standing around, the whole mine caved in with a crash that broke windows in Milford, fifteen miles away. A new shaft, 910 feet deep, was sunk through rhyolite at a cost of $26 a foot. Meantime, most of the miners moved out, taking their houses with them, and leaving residential Grasshopper Street a pile of ruins.

A company was organized in 1928 to take over the old interests, and since then the mine has been producing 10,000 tons a year. Frisco never had running water. Its water was hauled seven miles and sold for four cents a gallon. For that reason, old-timers say, Frisco will never live again.

Several miles west of the Frisco turnoff, State 21 leaves the **San Francisco Mountains** and enters the open expanse of **Wah Wah Valley,** a typical Great Basin depression. The lonely ruins of old **NEWHOUSE** sprawl along the eastern slopes of the valley, 2 m. north of the highway from a turnoff 5 m. west of Frisco. Foundations, rubble and mine dumps are the sole reminders of the town that existed here some 70 years ago.

Right on this road to NEWHOUSE, 2.2 *m.* (5,250 alt.), an abandoned mining community with only a few rock formations to prove it ever existed. In its boom days, 1905 to 1910, Newhouse was a model mining camp. Miners' houses were comfortable, clubs and cafes were well furnished, and gun-play was not too frequent. The mine is about a mile east of the old townsite. Discovered in 1870, it was filed on as the Cactus. From its discovery until 1900 many unprofitable attempts were made to operate it. At that time it was acquired by Samuel Newhouse, who operated it from 1905 to 1910, when the ore body ran out. In that period the mine produced $3,500,000. The Newhouse Building, the Newhouse Hotel, and other buildings in Salt Lake City were built with profits from this mine.

The route of State 21 west of Newhouse Junction is described in the 1941 edition, as excerpted below. Mileages shown are approximate distances from Beaver:

Between Newhouse Junction and the Wah Wah Range, the highway winds through **Wah Wah Valley,** spotted with white alkali flats, tumbleweeds, and stunted sage.

The summit, 66.1 *m.,* of the **WAH WAH RANGE** is bordered by a thick growth of tall juniper trees interspersed with pinon pines. The mountains, with a north-south trend, are barren and dry.

At 70.1 *m.* the highway crosses the east border of **Pine Valley,** a wide desert area overgrown with sagebrush and cactus.

At 75.4 *m.* is the junction with a dirt road.

Left on this road to **Indian Peak Reservation,** *5 m.,* a 10,240-acre tract, created a reservation by President Wilson in 1915 for two bands of Paiute Indians. Patches of potatoes, corn, and alfalfa are grown, but farming is

Union Pacific Station, Milford.

Frisco Peak (9,660 alt.), looking east from Wah Wah Valley.

hampered by lack of water. The gathering of pine nuts is the chief source of income. The reservation is heavily wooded with pinon pine, and several thousand pounds of nuts are picked in a good season.

At 82.4 *m.* is the junction with a dirt road.

Right on this road to the **Desert Range Experiment Station,** 3.4 *m.,* a U.S. Department of Agriculture project for experimentation with desert plants. The station, a cluster of green-roofed white buildings in the center of Pine Valley, is surrounded by twenty-four paddocks used for grazing experiments. The paddocks are observed before and after grazing for the effect on various types of desert forage.

GARRISON, 113.9 *m.* (5,000 alt., 127 pop.), a ranching community with windmills and tar-papered shacks, was settled in the 1850's by cattle rustlers, who corralled their stolen stock at a ranch hereabouts. They harvested hay along a near-by stream, and when pursued slipped from one State to another. The outlaws departed in the eighties, after a mining boom drew prospectors into the region. Garrison Ranch was established after the mine boom waned.

The motion picture, *Covered Wagon,* was filmed on the rolling hills and plains of this area in 1922. The picture was directed by James Cruze, and the female lead role was played by Betty Compson; both are natives of Utah.

State 21 crosses the **Nevada Line,** 115.3 *m.*

South of Beaver, I-15 traverses "sagebrush flats, across sage- and juniper-clad foothills, and, through wide windswept valleys, descends into Parowan Valley between the timbered Black Mountains and the dry bed of Little Salt Lake." The Old Spanish Trail entered Parowan Valley (or departed from, depending on direction of travel) several miles south of the Beaver-Iron county line. Along this old trail, Fremont's starving and freezing band of explorers came to Parowan in February 1854.

State Highway 20 forks east from I-15 at a junction 17 m. south of Beaver, threading a broken region of canyons, valleys and low mountains, connecting with US 89 near Panguitch *(see Tour No. 7A).*

LITTLE SALT LAKE, west of the highway, is hardly more than a dry playa, yet it appears from a distance as a large body of water. The lake was known by Paiute Indians as Parowan, a name meaning "evil water"—not salt or bad-smelling water, but "wicked" water. The reason for this, it seems, was an Indian legend in which the lake waters once rushed up suddenly and "stole a man." Indian tradition claims that the lake bottom had holes in it and that the water sometimes "jumped up high." Residents of towns to the east used the lake as a source of salt and also as an ice skating rink. When pioneers arrived it was fed by springs and runoff water. Since then, agricultural use and wells have cut off its supply sources.

PARAGONAH *(Indian, meaning "many springs" or "marshes"; pron. pare-uh-GO-nuh or pare-uh-GOO-nuh)*—6,000 alt. 310 pop. Paragonah is an agricultural town between red and brown cliffs on one side and Parowan Valley on the other. Its people grow alfalfa and grain, raise sheep and cattle. The town was settled in 1852. Archeologists have explored local Pueblo remains at various times for decades. During the 1950s and 1960s a series of excavations were conducted by the University of California (Los Angeles) in collaboration with Southern Utah State College. Numerous pit-houses and granaries were uncovered and myriad artifacts found, including tools, weapons and pottery, but only a few human remains. Some of these items are on display at SUSC in Cedar City. SUSC also has excavated at Summit, a few miles south of Parowan. The area's Pueblo culture flourished between 700 and 1150 A.D.

PAROWAN (6,000 alt. 1,836 pop.), county seat of Iron County, now bypassed by the main highway, is known as "Mother of the South," southern Utah's oldest permanent settlement. Visitors see it as an attractively sited, clean city of new homes and many old ones, situated at the base of junipered red cliffs and overlooking broad Parowan Valley. It is the center of a large livestock and farming industry; some of its people also commute to Cedar City. "Houses range from primitive pink adobe structures to modern firebrick houses, their colors cooled by the blue shadows of trees." Parowan's early history was summarized in the 1941 edition:

> The Iron County Mission to Parowan and Cedar City was the first great Mormon colonizing expedition in Utah. Led by George A. Smith, it left Fort Provo in December, 1850, and consisted of 119 men, 310 women over fourteen years of age, and 18 children under fourteen. "I hope our ears will not be saluted," he admonished his followers, "with any profanity, swearing of blasphemous words, or taking the name of the Lord in vain. . . . We are going to build up the Kingdom of God." The 129 wagons contained, besides the colonists, pioneer armament, saddles, "lights of Glass," carpenter and blacksmith tools, various kinds of seeds, "pitt saws," plows, "syths and cradles," mill irons, cats, dogs, and chickens. Milk cows, beef cattle, oxen, mules and horses served as draft animals. The Parowan site, Smith found, had "red sandy soil covered with bunch grass, sage and rabbit brush, and grease wood. . . . My wicky-up is a very important establishment, composed of brush, a few slabs and 3 wagons."

> It was the business of the Parowan colonists to put in crops, so that following immigrants could open up the coal and iron deposits. Cedar City was the second settlement made. Two colonies so close together, at such a distance from Great Salt Lake City, stifled each other's growth after the iron manufacturing enterprise failed. Jules Remy, who passed through Parowan in 1855, found it "nothing more than a poor straggling village, built of wood and adobes of red earth."

However poor it might have been, and despite failure of the Iron Mission, Parowan remained an important settlement in the south, furnishing a high percentage of colonists for other parts of the country.

Parowan displays some noteworthy buildings of architectural and historical value, including the following Historic Register sites: (1) **Rock Church,** erected in 1862 and now one of Utah's oldest extant chapels, used as a relic hall; (2) **Third Ward Meeting House (Mormon),** built in 1915-16 in Prairie School styling; (3) **Jesse Smith Home,** just west of Main on First South, built of adobe in 1856-57 with additions in 1865.

Turn east from Parowan via State 143 to **Parowan Canyon, Brian Head Resort, Cedar Breaks National Monument,** and junction with State 14. Parowan Canyon is a colorful alternate route to Cedar Breaks, Brian Head and other points on the lofty, forested Markagunt Plateau *(for details regarding these points see State 14 under Cedar City below).* It winds through lovely forests and red rocks to 10,000-foot heights of the plateau. Enroute is **Vermillion Castle Forest Campground** *(Dixie National Forest)* with improved facilities for camping, picnicking and trailer parking. Sideroads lead to Yankee Meadows Reservoir, Panguitch Lake, and numerous smaller lakes on the plateau.

Turn west from Parowan via improved road to **Parowan Gap,** a deep, narrow gorge cut through the Red Hills. Geologically the area is of more than ordinary interest because of its diversified rock formations, distorted by faulting and folding on an unusual scale. But Parowan Gap has wider renown as the site of remarkable Indian petroglyphs or "rock writings," incised on its walls. Here, over what is surmised to have been a long period of time, prehistoric Indians told on the rocks a conjectural story of long journeys, perils, religious beliefs, and daily life—or at least the writings are believed by some students to represent such things. Others are convinced, rather, that they were part of a religious ritual, intended to insure good hunting. Parowan Gap is listed in the National Register of Historic Places. *Antiquities are protected by law.*

CEDAR CITY (5,800 alt. 10,972 pop.) is a regional capital, until the 1970s the largest city in the state south of Utah Valley, and one of the oldest. An attractive community, Cedar City has a diversified economy based on travel, tourism and recreation, trade, agriculture, manufacturing, mining, education, government, etc. The 1970s witnessed the largest ten-year growth in the city's history. Its early background was summarized in the 1941 edition:

[Cedar City] was settled in 1851 by English, Scotch, and Welsh "miners and manufacturers" to open up the coal and iron deposits. In 1852 a hundred families of skilled Mormon converts were named to strengthen the "iron mission."

A multiplicity of difficulties finally doomed the iron manufacturing venture: There was trouble fluxing the ore; trouble finding sufficiently skilled workmen; trouble with floods, hard winters, and crop devastation; and, finally, iron brought in by Johnston's army and the trans-continental railroad made native production unprofitable. Cedar City grew, however, in consequence of extensive stock-raising in the area. Since the 1920's interest in scenic wonders has drawn outside people to the city, which is in easy reach of Cedar Breaks, Bryce Canyon, and Zion Canyon. The Dixie National Forest, to the east and west, annually attracts hundreds of deer hunters, fishermen, and vacationists.

Iron mines to the west provided a major economic boost to the city for decades following World War II, though production has fallen gradually

Cedar City is at the western base of the Markagunt Plateau (11,000 alt.) in distance. Cedar Breaks stretches along the plateau's summit ridge.

WARD ROYLANCE

since 1961. Tourism and recreation have been important to Cedar City since the 1920s, not only from the standpoint of highway travel but because for decades the city was a center to which thousands of tourists would come by rail each year, then board motor buses for tours of the area's national parks and monuments. With the advent of better roads and the demise of rail passenger travel, this industry has expired, though tourist travel by other means remains of importance. Still standing is the historic **Union Pacific Railroad Depot** on Main Street, built in 1922-23 as the end of a spur line from Lund. Among the first passengers to disembark at the new depot was President Warren G. Harding, a sightseeing tourist.

Cedar City's pioneer history is not as apparent in its architecture as that of certain other places in southern Utah; however, some early structures do remain. Among its distinctive buildings are: (1) **Union Pacific Railroad Depot,** noted above . . . (2) **Hunter Home,** 76 E. Center, a two-story red brick house built in sections from 1866 to 1924 . . . (3)**Old Main** and **Old Administration Building,** Southern Utah State College, dating from 1898 and 1904 respectively . . . (4) **George L. Wood Cabin,** built in 1851 by an original settler and reputed to be the first log cabin erected in southwestern Utah . . . (5) **Mormon First Ward Chapel (Old Rock Church),** near the corner of Main and Center, an imposing steepled building of varicolored native stone. Probably the most striking building in Cedar City, this religious edifice was built during the 1930s, years of the Great Depression, its rocks being gathered locally by church members. Local red cedar was used for interior finishing, local wool for rugs and draperies. Its rocks include iron and copper ore, gold ore, petrified wood, limestone, sandstone, and different varieties of quartz. Cedar City's old town clock is in the tower, and many salvaged items—including brick—were utilized from an earlier Mormon tabernacle, razed to make way for a federal building. *Open to the public by means of conducted tours.*

SOUTHERN UTAH STATE COLLEGE, on a tree-shaded campus of 100 acres in the heart of the city, is a four-year institution of higher learning. SUSC was founded in 1897, existing under various names as a branch of the University of Utah and Utah State University until 1965, when it became an independent degree-granting school. Bachelor degrees are offered in numerous fields, with certificates in many others; special emphasis is placed on vocational programs. The college owns and operates a 1,000-acre farm west of Cedar City and a 3,700-acre ranch in the mountains to the east. Of particular interest on the main campus are the **Library** (featuring the Palmer Room of Western History and John Seymour Special Collections) . . . **William R. Palmer Indian Museum** . . . **geological exhibit** in the Science Building . . . **Braithwaite Fine Arts Gallery,** and the **Adams Memorial Theatre.** The latter is an authentic full-size replica of an Elizabethan playhouse, used for productions of the nationally-noted **Utah Shakespearean Festival** and named in honor of Fred Adams, founder and long-time director of the Festival. Held every year since 1962, and supported by the entire community, the Festival is scheduled daily except Sundays over a period of five weeks or more in July and August. Three Shakespeare plans are presented, rotating on different nights, produced by a company of 150 actors, musicians, dancers, costumers, stage personnel, etc., recruited from many states. Offered in connection with the Shakespeare plays are seminars, backstage tours, Renaissance concerts, Elizabethan dancing and music, art exhibits, and other activities. Attendance has grown to the tens of thousands, with people coming from many states and foreign countries. In 1981 the Royal Shakespeare Company and other theatrical dignitaries from England—convinced that the Adams Theatre was most authentically suitable—staged Shakespeare segments for a Masterpiece Theater series, filmed on site by British Broadcasting Corporation.

Iron Mission State Historical Monument, located on north Main (US 91) near City Park, is a museum featuring myriad artifacts documenting the history of southern Utah in general and the Cedar City area in particular. Included is a diorama of the original iron foundry built by the Iron Mission colonists of the 1850s, as well as relics of that period. Of dominant interest is the museum's superb collection of more than 100 horsedrawn vehicles, such as wagons, coaches, buggies, surreys, carts, farm machinery, and sleighs. Most of these vintage vehicles were collected by the late Gronway Parry, a Cedar City resident and pioneer of southern Utah's tourist transportation industry. Mr. Parry began his collection 50 years ago or more. In the process of restoring his vehicles, Mr. Parry found it necessary to rediscover forgotten techniques of wheelwrighting, finishing, woodworking, etc.

SUSC PHOTOS

Southern Utah State College: campus scene *(above, left)* and Shakespearean Festival *(above, right.)* Iron Mission State Historical Monument *(below)* exhibits antique buildings, early vehicles, and painting of pioneer iron foundry.

STATE PARKS DIVISION   SUSC

WEST OF CEDAR CITY

Roads west of Cedar City lead into the flat vastness of Escalante Desert and Escalante Valley, southernmost bay of ancient Lake Bonneville . . . to Iron Mountain, Desert Mound and Iron Springs, site of Utah's famed iron mines . . . to Lund on the mainline Union Pacific Railroad . . . to Minersville-Milford . . . and to the

Nevada line. Most of this region is arid Great Basin terrain of valleys and mountains, but thousands of acres in the vicinity of Enterprise, Newcastle and Beryl have been turned into green fields through utilization of Escalante Valley's great underground reservoir—Utah's largest. (At one time the reservoir was estimated to contain as much water as Lake Mead.) The valley and desert were named for Father Escalante, scribe of the Dominguez-Escalante expedition which passed through the area in October 1776 *(see also Tour No. 4B).* By that time winter was approaching and snow had fallen in the mountains. They were very cold, food was low, and the priests were fearful of what might happen to the party if they continued through unknown country toward California so late in the season. Others not agreeing with them, lots were cast to decide whether they should continue toward Monterey or return to New Mexico. This event took place on October 11 at a spot some 10 miles northeast of Lund. The decision, as recorded by Escalante and history, was that they should return to New Mexico. Thereafter, their trail led south to the Arizona Strip, east to Glen Canyon and Crossing of the Fathers, thence south and east to New Mexico.

State 56 is the main access highway. From this route, several miles west of Cedar City, paved roads fork northwest to **Iron Springs** and **Desert Mound,** sites of large open-pit iron mine operations. According to the 1941 edition, the Iron Springs area is "where *Union Pacific* was filmed among the rolling sage plains and desert buttes. Many another picture, in whole or in part, has been filmed in this vicinity, including *Ramona, The Good Earth,* and *The Bad Man of Brimstone.*" From this area, also, the original Iron Mission obtained its ore.

West of the Iron Springs turnoff, State 56 continues through low iron-rich hills to Newcastle. **Iron Mountain** is on the immediate north, the locale of large open-pit iron mines, and south of the highway in the vicinity of the Columbia mine entrance is **Old Irontown.** All of these operations—Old Irontown, Iron Mountain, Iron Springs (Three Peaks), and Desert Mound (Granite Mountain)—are located along a narrow iron-ore zone stretching 20 miles from southwest to northeast. The zone has been estimated to contain more than 100 million tons of economically recoverable ore containing 45 per cent iron or more. Several hundred million additional tons are buried at depths up to 3,000 or 4,000 feet. Intensive mining in this century began in the 1920s, when Columbia Steel Corporation began shipments to the Ironton plant near Springville. World War II brought demand from steel plants at Geneva, Fontana and Pueblo, resulting in tremendously increased production. This continued at

Iron Mountain Mine, Columbia Iron Mining Company

a high level for some years, rising from 300,000 tons in 1940 to 3,000,000 tons in 1950 and 4,000,000 tons in 1957, the year of greatest production. From that high point, annual production has dropped steadily. Geneva Works now obtains most of its ore from Wyoming, and Utah Construction recently announced closure of its iron operations here. Largest producers over the years were Columbia, shipping to Geneva, and Utah Construction, shipping to Kaiser Steel in California and to Colorado Fuel & Iron in Colorado.

OLD IRONTOWN, about 22 m. west of Cedar City and 3 m. south of State 56, displays a few visible signs of the modest community that existed here during the 1870s and 1880s. Known as Iron City, the settlement was built on iron production and manufacturing. Iron ore was brought from rich deposits nearby, and a railroad was built to coal mines east of Cedar City. When the local coal proved unsuitable for coking, charcoal was substituted, and for several years an iron manufacturing industry flourished. A combination of adverse circumstances defeated the enterprise within a decade or so. Only a beehive charcoal oven, a few ruins and foundations remain. The site is listed in the National Register of Historic Places.

NEWCASTLE (5,300 alt.) is a farming community "defended from the desert by castellated rock formations." Recently, traditional agriculture based on wells and reservoirs has been supplemented by greenhouse hydroponics gardening, involving heated water from geothermal wells. The Christensen family, builders of four greenhouses in 1979, were pioneers in utilizing hot water coming from a well at 220 degrees F. Formerly the water was used to irrigate 200 acres, but only after being cooled in a series of ponds. At present the greenhouses are devoted to the growing of tomatoes.

State 18 forks south from State 56 at a junction 6 m. west of Newcastle, leading to **ENTERPRISE** (5,300 alt. 905 pop.). Enterprise is a farming and ranching community at the extreme southern tip of Escalante Valley. Mountains and foothills form its horizon in three directions. In the highlands to the south, Enterprise Reservoir is a popular fishing spot and recreation area. Enterprise's background was described in the 1941 edition.

From Enterprise, State 18 continues south to Mountain Meadows, Pine Valley, Veyo and St. George. *For tour description see St. George area below.*

North of State 56 from junction with State 18, a paved county road leads across the flat valley floor to **BERYL** (5,100 alt.), a center of irrigated fields which are watered from wells. Large-scale agriculture began in **Escalante Valley** in the years following World War II, and by 1960 more than 200 wells were watering about 20,000 acres in this vicinity. Alfalfa, barley and potatoes have been principal crops. Excessive water pumping in the 1940s and 1950s resulted in a rapidly lowering water table and in limitations on the amount utilized by individual farmers.

MODENA (5,500 alt.), on State 56, "exists as a Union Pacific flag-stop on the southwestern edge of the Escalante Desert." That notation as well as the following is from the 1941 edition:

> State 56 here turns sharply southwest toward the Nevada Line, recalling its early importance as an arterial support of Pioche and Panaca, Nevada mining camps. Among the freighters who hauled supplies to Pioche in the seventies there grew up a legend that a rocky gorge near the Nevada Line was haunted by the Gadianton robbers, a terroristic brotherhood which the Book of Mormon explains as having sprung up among the Nephites and Lamanites in the century before Christ. Wide-eyed freighters told tales of rocks closing the way, and of the canyon folding up to entrap them.

West of Modena, State 56 parallels the railroad to the Utah-Nevada state line and continues from there as Nevada 25 to Panaca.

EAST OF CEDAR CITY

State 14 forks east from downtown Cedar City, climbing between the steep walls of **Cedar (Coal Creek) Canyon** to Dixie National Forest and heights of the **MARKA-GUNT PLATEAU (CEDAR MOUNTAIN)**. State 14 joins US 89 at Long Valley Junction 41 m. from Cedar City *(see Tour No. 9A)*.

The Markagunt (Indian, "highland of trees") is one of the highest and most massive of southern Utah's High Plateaus. Less rugged than most highlands, blessed with lakes and streams, and clothed with pleasant, open forests of aspen and ever-greens, the Markagunt is a favorite retreat for lovers of the outdoors. Private home-site developments have multiplied in recent decades, as have short-term visitors inter-ested in sightseeing, camping, fishing, hunting, skiing, picnicking, hiking, snow-mobiling, horseback riding, or other outdoor activities. "Nature is here in her gentle mood," wrote Clarence E. Dutton a hundred years ago, "neither wild nor inanimate, neither grand nor trivial, but genial, temperate, and mildly suggestive. A few canyons which it is a pleasure to cross; long grassy slopes which seem to ask to be climbed; hill tops giving charming pictures of shaded dells and sloping banks. . . ." These attributes are appreciated just as much today. Yet the Markagunt does possess aspects of grandeur, for its high rim breaks off into the stupendous rainbow amphi-theater of Cedar Breaks, and provides in dizzy overview some tantalizing glimpses of the temples and towers of Zion National Park.

State 14 and sideroads such as State 143 (north to Parowan) give access to the following points of interest, among others:

Zion Overlook is a parking area beside State 14 in the upper reaches of Cedar (Coal Creek) Canyon. Below, in stirring panorama, spreads the forested Kolob Ter-race, an intermediate platform into which the canyons of Zion National Park have been cut. West Temple and other buttes in the park loom majestically in the dis-tance, and there are enticing hints of narrow, bottomless gorges in the middle-ground. More spectacular than usual is the view from Zion Overlook in late Sep-tember-early October, at the height of fall color season, when aspen glorify the Kolob panorama with gold.

Cedar Breaks National Monument, at 10,000 feet altitude, is one of the nation's highest national parks or monuments. *See National Parks chapter for description.*

Brian Head Ski and Summer Resort is near Cedar Breaks, 29 m. from Cedar City via State 14/State 143, or 12 m. from Parowan via State 143. At an altitude of 10,000 to 11,000 feet, with plentiful winter snow and varied slopes, Brian Head developed originally as a ski resort with miles of ski trails and runs, chairlifts and tows, ski and snowmobile rentals, but has transformed into an all-year recreation center offering a variety of lodging and dining facilities, shops and store, horseback riding, and other amenities. The resort appeals in particular to winter sports enthusiasts from southern California and Las Vegas.

Brian Head Peak (11,315 alt.) is one of the highest points in Utah that can be reached by passenger car. Formed of volcanic material (common on most of the Markagunt), the peak's summit overlooks Cedar Breaks, Brian Head resort, and much of southern and western Utah, with distant glimpses of Nevada and Arizona. Shelter and restrooms. Accessible (usually) from July to October or November.

Lava Beds add a somber but intriguing touch to much of the Markagunt land-scape. As noted elsewhere, the dramatic evidence of igneous activity is apparent throughout much of southern and western Utah, and this area is no exception. Of special interest are fields of broken black basalt lava in which trees have established their roots. It is probable that some of the plateau's lava welled onto the surface as recently as 1,000 or 2,000 years ago.

Navajo Lake from overlook beside State 14. *Hal Rumel photo.*

Navajo Lake (9,250 alt.) is a favorite photographic subject of highway travelers, and also a favorite fishing, camping and picnicking spot. The lake is fairly large, measuring 3½ m. in length. Dixie National Forest maintains a campground on the south shore, where boats, lodging, fuel and limited supplies are provided by a private resort. The lake is drained in two directions by sink holes: to the Pacific Ocean via Cascade Falls and the Virgin River, and to the Great Basin via Duck Creek Spring and the Sevier River. **Cascade Falls,** a picturesque waterfall, can be reached by road and short nature trail from Navajo Lake or State 14 near Duck Creek.

Duck Creek Pond and Campground (Dixie National Forest) are in a delightful forest of aspen and evergreens beside the highway several miles east of Navajo Lake. The pond is a popular fishing spot. A summer home area known as **Movie Ranch,** 2 m. east of Duck Creek, was the shooting locale for several pre-World War II movies, including *My Friend Flicka,* and television series of more recent years.

Strawberry Point is an overview atop the Pink Cliffs rim, reached by driving 9 m. of unpaved road from a junction 5 m. east of Duck Creek pond. From here the vista extends across a broken landscape of cliffs and profound canyons, far south into the Arizona Strip and westward to the grand forms of Zion National Park. A remarkable natural bridge is just below the point.

SOUTH OF CEDAR CITY (INTERSTATE 15)

South of Cedar City, I-15 ascends a gradual slope of the valley to an almost imperceptible drainage divide marking the south rim of the Great Basin in this vicinity, and the north rim of the Virgin River system. Said the 1941 edition: "Mormon colonization south of this point in early times was characterized as 'going over the Rim,' and in colloquial usage the same phrase came to connote violent death." The mountain front on the east becomes more precipitous as the highway proceeds south into the Virgin River Valley, changing rapidly into a great cliff near Pintura. This front marks the **Hurricane Fault,** a 200-mile break in the earth's crust, which has upraised the strata to the east and down-dropped corresponding rocks to the west, forming a strata offset of thousands of feet—perhaps as much as 14,000 feet in places. To the west, the dark volcanic mass of the **Pine Valley Mountains** looms ever higher, to summits of more than 10,000 feet elevation. The hamlets of Hamilton Fort, Kanarraville and New Harmony are near the highway.

HAMILTON FORT (5,600 alt.) displays a few very old houses as evidence of its being one of the oldest inhabited sites in this region. Settled in 1852, the village has had at least four different names: Shirts Fort, Fort Walker, Sidon, and Fort Hamilton.

KANNARAVILLE (5,500 alt.) nestles against colorful red and gray cliffs, commanding a fine view of valleys and mountains to the west. It was founded during the early 1860s and named after local Paiute chief Kanarra. Cattlemen here organized the Kanarra Cattle Company, a huge cooperative which ranged its livestock over a remote and far-flung empire embracing much of southern Utah.

NEW HARMONY (5,200 alt. 117 pop.) is an attractive farming village cupped in a mountain-girt valley. Its spectacular eastern horizon is formed by the Hurricane fault scarp and **Finger Canyons** of Zion National Park's Kolob section. The site of New Harmony's predecessor, Fort Harmony—marked by foundation stones—lies two hundred yards south of State 144 to New Harmony, one mile west of I-15. The site is listed on the National Register of Historic Places. Fort Harmony's poignant early history was summarized in the 1941 edition:

John D. Lee established Fort Harmony, first settlement "over the Rim," in 1852. The settlement, four miles southeast, was abandoned because of the Walker War *(see History),* but Lee returned two years later and built a new fort. As "Indian farmer," Lee was living here at the time of the Mountain Meadows Massacre *(see below)* in 1857, at a point twenty miles west. Lee organized Washington County and for a while he was probate judge, clerk, assessor, and collector.

"Harmony No. 2," as Lee called it, was demolished in 1862 by a rainstorm that continued unceasingly for twenty-eight days. Lee did not remove his wet clothing for eight days and nights. Two of his children were killed when the walls of his home gave way. The Harmony colonists buried their dead and moved to the head of Ash Creek, where New Harmony was built to endure to the present.

Two miles south of the New Harmony turnoff is junction with paved sideroad leading east into the **Kolob Canyons (Finger Canyons)** section of **ZION NATIONAL PARK** *(see).* Climbing and winding, this road leads to high viewpoints overlooking giant red cliffs and grand gorges. *Developed rest areas. Closed in winter.*

I-15 in this vicinity traverses the upper slopes of **Ash Creek Canyon,** between the Hurricane Fault scarp and Pine Valley Mountains. Before the era of paved roads, broken lava made this area (known as the **Black Ridge)** one of the roughest stretches of road between north and south. In 1856 Peter Shirts surveyed a road south from Fort Harmony, through the forbidding Black Ridge area and down Ash Creek Canyon. Leap Creek, near Pintura, was an especially serious obstacle because of its depth and steep

Kolob Canyons from the air *(above)*.

Virgin River Valley from the air, at dusk *(top left)*.

Pine Valley Mountains from the southeast *(left)*.

walls. Shirts jokingly proposed to "leap across," and forever afterward the crossing has been known as Peter's Leap. For several years Dixie pioneers traveled the Shirts route, and portions may still be followed on foot. The route is listed on the state historic register. Eighty years before Shirts, the Dominguez-Escalante party had followed roughly the same route, applying the name Rio del Pilar to Ash Creek. In Ash Creek Canyon—a "stony cut" —they were deserted by their Indian guides. They continued without a guide and "traveled with great difficulty over the many stones for a league to the south."

At **PINTURA,** a fruit-growing village, the altitude is 4,000 feet—much lower than Cedar City's 5,800 feet, yet higher than the 2,800 feet of St. George. Pintura, a Spanish word meaning picture or painting, was applied to the town in 1925. Before that, since 1868, the village had been known as Belleview—and for some years before 1868 it was called Ashton.

Four miles south of Pintura, at **Anderson Junction** (formerly Andersons Ranch), State 17 forks south to Toquerville, LaVerkin, and a junction with State 9 leading to Hurricane and to Zion National Park.

TOQUERVILLE (3,200 alt. 277 pop.) is an attractive, tree-shaded community in which the new and old contrast in pleasing dignity. Above it looms the rocky bulk of Hurricane Ledge. Not many decades ago, like other communities in Dixie, Toquerville was a dying village. This trend has been reversed as "outsiders" have discovered the area's residential and climatic advantages. Toquerville was settled in 1858 as one of the first settlements south of Cedar City, and named for Toquer, friendly chief of local Paiutes. For years the town prospered, free from disastrous floods, enjoying a benign climate. Incidents from its early history are told in the 1941 edition.

Among Toquerville's interesting old buildings are the following, all listed on historic registers: **Naegle Winery,** a massive two-story structure built of stone in 1866, used as a residence for a large polygamous family (upper floors) and winery (basement.) Its masonry is said to have been the work of Frederick Foremaster, builder of Fort Pearce *(see Tour No. 8A)* . . . **Old Mormon Church and Tithing Office,** a combined meetinghouse, school and social hall dating from the years between 1866 and 1879 . . . **Spilsbury Home,** a "lovely home constructed in the 1880s by George Spilsbury for his son, David, of stuccoed adobe."

Four miles south of Anderson Junction is the turnoff to Leeds, Silver Reef, and Red Cliffs Recreation Site.

LEEDS (3,500 alt. 218 pop.) is an unassuming town beside the highway, claimed to have the longest growing season in southern Utah. Known for several years in early days as Bennington, Leeds has a wild and romantic past which it has managed to outlive and tell about. Only a mile from old Silver Reef *(see below),* the village received an invigorating shot in the arm for many years; it was a trade center and host for hundreds of miners during the boom years of the 1870s and 80s, providing them incidentally with a powerful beverage called Dixie Wine. These prosperous days, however, passed away with the ore deposits at Silver Reef; and today only some aged red houses commemorate them. It is said that many of these old buildings in Leeds would assay high in silver, since they were built of silver-bearing sandstone taken from the reef.

West of Leeds 1.5 m. is **SILVER REEF,** now a place of ruins and empty foundations, complemented in recent years by a number of new homes. In its 19th century heyday, Silver Reef was one of Utah's prosperous mining camps. Two remaining antique buildings are of special note: the **Rice Bank** and the **Wells Fargo & Company Express Building.** The latter was built in 1877 of red sandstone, ashlar blocks and rubble. It has been in use as an office and residence during most of its existence and is listed on the National Register of Historic Places. Silver Reef's story was told in the 1941 edition:

Right on this road to the junction, 1.2 m., with a dirt road; L. at the base of a red reef to **SILVER REEF,** 0.3 m., where, brooding and vacant-eyed, an old bank building watches over the grave of a once-famous silver mining camp. The nature-paved streets—huge boulders indifferently leveled—still wind along the ridge, but rattlesnakes, Gila monsters, tarantulas, and centipedes slither along where once hard men tramped. The ruined foundations of churches, saloons, dance halls, gambling dens, schools, and homes are weed-covered and tumbled-in, and brush-choked cellars gape lazily in the hot sun. . . .

The first recorded mine location in the district was that of John Kemple, who explored the area in 1866 and returned in 1870 or 1871 to file his first claim. He established the district, naming it the Harrisburg Mining District, and appointed a recorder. A few miners and prospectors came during the next two years, but it was not until 1874, when Elijah Thomas sent a sample of horn silver to Walker Brothers, Salt Lake City bankers, that any real interest was aroused. Walker Brothers dispatched William T. Barbee, Thomas McNally, and Ed Maynard, assayer, to the spot. Barbee became so enthused when he found horn silver even in petrified wood, that he located twenty-two claims on Tecumseh Ridge and hurried to Salt Lake City for supplies. Returning with a blacksmith, tools, and other mining supplies, he established "Bonanza City."

Although many Mormons resented the intrusion of miners in the territory, Apostle Erastus Snow thanked God for sending Brother Barbee to alleviate the hard times under which the settlers were struggling. Barbee's letters, published in the *Salt Lake Tribune,* brought thousands of miners into the district, and the boom was on. Pioche, Nevada, was almost deserted by miners rushing to Silver Reef in buckboards, wagons, carts, on horses, mules and burros. Among the new arrivals was Hyrum Jacobs, merchant, who set up his camp in the center of a ridge and named it Silver Reef. Between 1877 and 1903 more than 9,000,000 ounces of silver were removed from the reefs and sold for an average price of $1.15 an ounce.

By 1880, the big ore producers were consolidated under various companies, each with its own amalgam stamp mill. Watson N. Nesbitt pioneered a hyposodium leaching plant in the Leeds mill, but the method was too expensive. The Buckeye mine in 1877 was turning out a thousand-ounce brick every day with an average purity of 990 (out of 1000). The Christy mill in 1878 reported milling 10,249 tons valued at $302,597 or $29.17 a ton. The price of silver fell, the ore became less rich, and water in the mines added to production costs. Wages were cut in 1881, and there was a strike. The strike leaders were jailed, but the loss to credit-burdened stores forced many shops to close. Silver prices continued downward, the old-timers left, newer men did not understand the mines or the men, and the companies ceased operations in 1891.

The following year there was a revival of mining that lasted until silver dropped to 65 cents in 1903. The camp was deserted until 1916, when Alex Colbath raised $160,000 and organized the Silver Reef Consolidated Mines Company. The rise in silver prices during the World War induced a New York company to lease the property in 1920, but a sharp decline in price prevented the construction of a large mill. Samuel M. Silverman of New York purchased the properties in 1928, and in the spring of that year the American Smelting and Refining Company purchased 51 per cent of the stock and sank a 541-foot shaft. When the price of silver dropped to 25 cents, all development stopped, and in 1940 the Reef was just a ghost town, with more past than future.

[Mr. and Mrs. Colbath were residents of Silver Reef for more than 30 years until the 1950s, residing for much of that time in the Wells Fargo building. Uranium was produced at Silver Reef during the 1950s and 1960s.]

At Leeds, a freeway turnoff gives access to **RED CLIFFS RECREATION SITE** (U.S. Bureau of Land Management), a camping and picnicking area with restrooms, water and fireplaces. The site is at 3,200 feet altitude, at the base of red cliffs known as Silver Reef, and is a choice place for the observation of unusual geology as well as diversified plant life representing a botanical/climatic transition zone. From the campground a half-mile **Desert Wilderness Trail** introduces visitors to cacti, juniper, shrubs, pinyon pine, mesquite, yucca, and numerous other plants. Interesting birds and animals also may be seen.

I-15 has now descended into the Virgin River Valley, known more commonly as **"Dixie"**—that part of Utah having the lowest altitude. The name Dixie was applied because of the region's warm climate, suitable for growing cotton, and does not hint at the fact that it encompasses one of the most

BUREAU OF RECLAMATION (W. L. RUSHO)

Old Cotton Factory in Washington *(left)*, and rock ruins at Silver Reef *(below)*.

DEPT. OF TRANSPORTATION (CAL BRIGGS)

geologically interesting and scenically marvelous parts of the world. Here is Zion Canyon and tributary gorges . . . rainbow cliffs of startling beauty . . . great faults and volcanic cones . . . frozen streams of lava, geologic anticlines, warm springs and vast sand dunes . . . mesas, buttes, plateaus and mountain ranges. For the most part it is a harsh land of dead rocks, wonderful to behold; but for human beings, trying to wrest a bare existence from its sterile soil, it is not a pleasant land. Except for scenery and climate, usable resources are few, and Dixie was never able to hold its youth or maintain a stable population until recent years. Tillable farmland is strictly limited, and violent floods have washed away much of it. Mining has been sporadic at best. For nearly a hundred years agriculture and livestock were the most important economic factors in Dixie. These have gradually given way in relative ranking to tourism, recreation, manufacturing, trade, and retirement industries of more recent years.

At **Harrisburg Junction,** 7 m. south of Leeds, State 9 (formerly State 15) forks east to Hurricane, LaVerkin and Zion National Park. *See Tour No. 8B.* The junction was named for HARRISBURG, an agricultural town which existed between the junction and Leeds for about 40 years—from the 1860s to the end of the century. Though long abandoned, a number of Harrisburg's enduring rock buildings still stand, in remarkably good condition. These and the former settlement's old rock fences can be viewed from US 91 and the interstate highway.

WASHINGTON (2,800 alt. 3,092 pop.) no longer is the "leisurely group of red adobe and red brick houses" described in the 1941 edition. From I-15 it resembles a sprawling mobile home annex of nearby St. George, its population having quadrupled in the decade between 1970 and 1980. Washington's pioneer heritage is apparent from side streets and old US 91, now a frontage road which passes through the town as Telegraph Street. The most imposing structure is the **Old Cotton Factory,** a massive three-story stone building dating from the 1860s.

Unused for its original purpose since the early years of this century, the factory served for 50 years as a symbol of hope and industry for struggling Dixie pioneers. Construction on the building was begun in 1865 as a project of Mormon Church president Brigham Young, who sold it within a few years to a public cooperative known as the Rio Virgen Manufacturing Company. For thirty years the factory managed to continue operations, surviving crisis after crisis, processing locally-produced cotton and wool into batting, textiles and manufactured goods such as clothing and blankets. Consistent operations ended about the turn of the century, due to lack of raw materials, though sporadic activities continued for several more years. Machinery was sold about 1910, and the building has been used for storage and other diverse purposes since then. It is listed on the National Register of Historic Places.

Washington was settled in 1857 by Mormons—most of them natives of the South—"called" by church authorities to grow cotton in the warm climate of the Virgin River Valley. Subsequent years witnessed unbelievable hardships and discouragements, including malaria, frequent floods which washed out dams and irrigation works, alkali, heat, and near starvation at times.

ST. GEORGE (2,800 alt. 11,350 pop.) "stands at the heart of Utah's Dixie, and is known for its long hot summers and mild winters." As in 1941, it is marked by the white Mormon Temple, "which rises dazzlingly above red soil, green trees and lawns, and trim red houses of adobe and brick." But today the great temple competes for attention with a forest of skyscraping advertising signs, and "trim red houses of adobe and brick" are much less apparent in contemporary St. George than they were in 1941 —or even 10 or 20 years ago. The city's popoulation was 3,600 in 1940 and 7,100 in 1970. In 1980 it had grown to 11,350 and is increasing at a rapid rate.

The county seat of Washington County, St. George is a regional capital —the largest city along the route of I-15 between Utah Valley on the north and Las Vegas on the south, a distance of nearly 400 miles. Growth until the past decade or two was slow, the local economy being inadequate to support even the natural increase in population. Then, during the 1960s and 1970s, a number of factors combined to stimulate in-migration, doubling the county's population between 1970 and 1980, and encouraging a general pattern of growth that shows no sign of diminishing. In the forefront of these factors is Dixie's climate, the mildest in Utah during winter months, attracting myriad tourists and many part-time and full-time residents. These migrant residents come not only from other parts of Utah but also from Las Vegas, southern California, and elsewhere. (St. George's long-time advertising theme has been "Where the summer sun spends the winter." Now gaining popularity is the Hilton Inn's slogan, "The *other* Palm Springs.") Dixie's climate is hardly a new phenomenon, of course, but it is probably the chief reason for the phenomenal growth of recent years, *in combination with* a superlative scenic setting, relative affluence, ease of transportation, a mobile population and numerous sightseeing tourists, a larger retired population, higher retirement incomes, and the preference of many urban

Mormon Temple, St. George

WARD ROYLANCE

dwellers for a less stressful living environment. Not to be discounted is the influence of the Mormon Temple in St. George, which attracts thousands of Latter-day Saints as a religious magnet. The most apparent result of all these factors is an explosion of St. George's commercial district and new residential suburbs in nearly every direction. Condominium townhouses are popular. Less visible than new construction is the replacement of a traditional way of life with another that is less distinctive, an occurrence that is deplored by many long-time residents. St. George and sister communities of the Virgin River Valley no longer doze lazily in the Dixie sun and dream of their rural pioneer past. They have been yanked rudely into the hectic current of mainstream America, and in the process their characteristic local color is being overwhelmed by the contemporary culture of the region and the nation, or more particularly that of the region's large urban centers. To marked degree they have become—or are becoming—miniature models of Las Vegas, Los Angeles, or even Salt Lake City. At the same time it must be acknowledged that deliberate effort has been made to keep some development as architecturally attractive and environmentally compatible as possible.

"The story of St. George's founding has an epic character," said the 1941 edition, continuing as follows:

The success of cotton-raising experiments induced Church authorities in 1861 to undertake large-scale colonization of extreme southern Utah. Even then the area had a reputation as a hard place to live, and those "called" to the Dixie mission "to sustain Israel in the mountains," in many instances were not happy about it.

By December [1861] more than two hundred wagons were on the site of St. George, and the "town" was two long rows of wagons facing each other, with a ditch between. Before there was a single house in it, St. George was an incorporated town. Crops failed year after year, while heat, sand, and wind rasped at the nerves of the colonists. Visiting St. George in 1870, Orson Huntsman observed, "I believe we were close to hell, for Dixie is the hottest place I ever was in." A Dixie poet sang:
The wind like fury here does blow that when we plant or sow, sir,
We place one foot upon the seed and hold it till it grows, sir.
The colonists, however, stuck to their task, growing cotton and fruit and, in the seventies, experimenting with silk. Erastus Snow was the apostle designated to build up Dixie, and if life was hard for him and the other men, it was heartbreaking for some of the women. David Cannon's young wife, living in a willow lean-to in place of the luxury she had known, told her husband that if he could find just one flower fit to pin on a lady's dress, she would try to be satisfied. In the spring he presented her with a bouquet of orchid-colored sego-lilies, and she thought them as beautiful as any flower she had ever seen. . . .
The difficulties over polygamy passed in the nineties, and St. George settled down to agricultural development. The lack of railroad facilities made high freight rates a serious handicap, but the improvement of US 91 as an arterial highway opened truck routes to Salt Lake City and the Pacific Coast. With the rise of tourism, St. George's position half-way between Salt Lake City and Los Angeles, and as a point of departure for near-by scenic wonders, revitalized the town. In 1940 it is a brisk town, flavored by its romantic past, sitting warm under the sun. The large white "D" on a black ridge flanking the town is emblematic of Dixie Junior College, founded in 1911 as the L.D.S. Dixie Normal College, and given to the State as a junior college in 1933. . . .

DIXIE SUGAR LOAF (R), in view north of the town, is a capstone of solid rock surmounting vermillion bluffs—"as bald as the head of the prophet Elisha," George Washington Brimhall said of it in 1864.

Architectural buffs can discover numerous quaint and curious structures by driving or walking the side streets. A number of these are listed on historic registers. Available from the chamber of commerce is a published "Walking Tour" guide describing many interesting historical buildings. The modern campus of Dixie College *(below)* also is of interest. **Ancestor Square** in downtown St. George is a restoration and recreation of 19th century architecture of local western style, landscaped attractively and housing restaurants and shops. Comprehensive convention and entertainment facilities are offered by the Hilton Inn, Four Seasons and other entrepreneurs. Golf courses, swimming pools, tennis courts, and other recreational attractions appeal to residents and visitors alike.

The **MORMON TEMPLE** *(visitor center and grounds open to non-Mormons)* is one of Utah's truly distinguished and most photogenic buildings. "Resting on a slight elevation" in a residential area several blocks south of the business district, the temple "is visible for miles." Its visual beauty, however, is only one of the sacred edifice's attributes: since completion more than a hundred years ago it has been the goal of countless faithful Mormons—many of them in the waning years of life—who have spent days, months or even years in St. George, acting as proxies in temple ordinance work. Thousands of others have been married in the temple. In this respect, the St. George Temple has served as an economic mainstay for the city. The 1941 edition described it thus:

> The squarely built white stucco temple (L) has three tiers of tall round-arched windows, surmounted by a row of oval windows. It has a well-proportioned cupola with a weather vane, and covers nearly an acre within a ten-acre tract. Spacious green lawns, bordered with a profusion of colorful plants, accent the snowy exterior of the structure and tend to magnify its size. Completed in 1877, this was the first Mormon Temple erected in Utah. At night, floodlights on the building produce a cameo-like effect. Built on swampy ground, the foundations consist of hundreds of tons of black volcanic rock, beaten down by an old cannon used as a horse-power pile driver.

To that account should be added the comment that construction of the temple was a work of sacrifice requiring six years of great hardship and devotion. Saints from northern Utah were called on 40-day missions to work on the temple, while those in the south gave one day in ten as tithing labor. 17,000 tons of rock were quarried by hand and hauled by ox team; large timbers were freighted overland some 80 miles and seven days from Mount Trumbull near Grand Canyon. Church members contributed food, made the carpets, did the decorating. The temple was dedicated five months before the death of President Brigham Young, who had overseen much of its construction.

The **MORMON TABERNACLE,** Main and Tabernacle Streets, is a handsome steepled edifice built of red sandstone, designed "in the simple proportions of a New England meeting house. It has a four-faced clock on a square tower, surmounted with a slender white wooden steeple. The small-paned windows form a pattern characteristic of the days when glass had to be shipped long distances in less breakable sizes." The steeple rises 140 feet. Features inside are ornate plaster cornices and ceiling ornaments, locally crafted, as well as two self-supporting, circular staircases and a gallery. Large timbers were hewn by hand. Construction occupied more than ten years, beginning in 1863, most of the expense being covered by tithes. The first meetings were held in the building in 1869. Glass was shipped from New York City to southern California by boat, then brought to St. George by wagon. The clock and bell were purchased by public subscription and served the entire town thereafter. Considered to be one of the most beautiful of Utah's older buildings, the tabernacle is listed on historic registers.

OLD WASHINGTON COUNTY COURTHOUSE, 85 E. 100 North, "is a square two-story red brick building of Colonial design with a classical portico enclosing an iron-railed balcony at the second-floor level." Construction extended over a period of years from 1867 into the 1870s. Basalt lava rock forms the foundation, and in the cupola which tops the structure were included a scaffold and trapdoor, to serve as a gallows if needed. Prisoners occupied dungeon-like cells in the basement. In 1960 county offices were removed from the building, after which it housed other agencies including the chamber of commerce.

BRIGHAM YOUNG WINTER HOME and **OFFICE,** 200 North and 100 West, is a "rectangular two-story buff adobe building with a porch, standing behind a wooden pale fence and shaded by tall trees. A white-plastered one-story building at the east end of the house was used by Brigham Young as an office when he wintered in 'Dixie.' The house . . . was a center for social and religious gatherings during the winter." The house was constructed between 1869 and 1873 and used as a winter residence by the Mormon Church president until his death in 1877. Between 1959 and 1975 it was a Utah State historical monument, but in recent years it has been maintained by the Mormon Church, with public tours being conducted by missionaries. Listed on historical registers.

Dixie College, St. George

DIXIE COLLEGE is a two-year community college, state supported, under direction of the State Board of Regents. Associate degrees and certificates are awarded. The attractive campus, with more than 20 modern buildings, serves a student body of approximately 1,500 and is located only a few blocks from downtown St. George. Dixie College offers a diversified program in the fields of humanities and social sciences, business and trades (including vocational-technical), natural sciences, and the arts. The college was born in 1911 as a church institution, the St. George Stake Academy, later being renamed Dixie Normal School and Dixie Junior College. Its present name became official in 1970. Control passed from the LDS Church to the state in 1933.

McQUARRIE MEMORIAL HALL (PIONEER MUSEUM), adjoining the Old Courthouse to the north, is a comprehensive exhibit of early-day relics of the Dixie region. The red brick building, completed in 1938, is a gift of Mrs. Hortense McQuarrie Odlum.

TOURS FROM ST. GEORGE

(1) Old US 91 west to Santa Clara, Utah Hill, Arizona and Las Vegas

Until the opening of I-15 through the Virgin River gorge in 1973, this was the main route between Utah and Las Vegas/southern California. The highway now gives access to a fast-spreading complex of new housing subdivisions between St. George and Santa Clara.

SANTA CLARA (2,600 alt. 1,091 pop.) has multiplied four times in population in only ten years, between 1970 and 1980, participating with other Dixie communities in the residential boom of recent times, and in effect becoming a suburb of St. George. Its historical heritage remains evident in the older part of town, described by the 1941 edition as "a clustering group of light brown adobe, red sandstone, and modern brick houses shaded by green trees." The description continued as follows:

> Long orchards stretch away over the red earth at the edge of town. Jacob Hamblin and others settled here in 1854. Seven years later the colony was strengthened by Swiss settlers sent to the Dixie Mission. The Swiss were industrious, and despite the catastrophic flood of 1862, which all but destroyed the town, Santa Clara prospered. There was, however, some sense of differentiation between the Anglo-Saxon settlers of St. George and the Swiss of Santa Clara; only in recent decades has this antagonism modified.

The **Jacob Hamblin House** in Santa Clara is a quaint "two-story structure of random stone masonry, with a shingle roof and brick chimney. Built in 1862, the house was sturdy enough to withstand Indian attack [if necessary], and a large upstairs room was used for social occasions." Jacob Hamblin—renowned as the Mormon Leatherstocking or missionary to the Indians—was among the first whites to settle this part of Utah during the 1850s. He and his family lived in this rock dwelling for about seven years during the 1860s. It was restored and operated by the Utah State Park and Recreation Division as a state historical monument for some years after 1959, then was purchased by the Mormon Church. *Open to the public.* Listed on historical registers.

The following is quoted from the 1941 edition:

> Jacob Hamblin, an active force in the settlement of southern Utah, dedicated himself to the promotion and maintenance of peace between white settlers and Indians. Born at Salem, Ohio, in 1819, he emigrated to Utah in 1850. Four years later he was sent on a mission to the Indians of southern Utah, where he spent most of his remaining busy years, befriending the Indians of southern Utah and northern Arizona. Major J. W. Powell, explorer of the Colorado River, leaves a description of Hamblin in a familiar situation—around an Indian campfire: "He is a silent, reserved man, and when he speaks, it is in a slow, quiet way, that inspires great awe. His talk is so low that they must listen attentively to hear, and they sit around him in a death-like silence. When he finishes a measured sentence, the chief repeats it, and they all give a solemn grunt. . . ."
>
> Hamblin is buried in Alpine, Arizona, where he died August 21, 1886, while in hiding from "polyg hunters."

Turn north from a junction immediately west of Santa Clara to the hamlet of **IVINS** and **SNOW CANYON STATE PARK,** an area of intricately sculptured, beautifully colored sandstone cliffs, curious volcanic phenomena, dunes of fine red sand, Indian rock art, and other interesting features. Snow Canyon measures about three miles in length. A scenic cameo, it is one of Dixie's most charming attractions, popular for camping, hiking and photography. It has served as locale for several motion pictures. In ancient and recent times, great streams of black lava cascaded over the canyon's sedimentary rim and solidified into picturesque falls. This lava

Snow Canyon from highway overlook north of St. George

covered the floor of the canyon from wall to wall and half-buried a few red and rounded sandstone islands. The access road connects with State 18 north of St. George *(see below),* forming a loop. Improved campground and picnic area with tables, drinking water, toilets. *Open all year.*

Old US 91 continues west through the Shivwits-Shebit Indian Reservation (Paiute), described in the 1941 edition as follows:

The **SHIVWITS-SHEBIT INDIAN RESERVATION** . . . covers an area of about 27,000 acres. Its eighty-odd Indian inhabitants are the sole remnant of numerous tribes of southern Utah, northern Arizona, and eastern Nevada. The Indians rely for a livelihood upon Government work and the sale of baskets, gloves, purses, belts, and moccasins. Food supplies are purchased in St. George, and the Indian children attend white schools. Willow-covered summer sheds and one-room winter houses of frame or rock have replaced the old brush tepees. There are four graduates of Carlisle College on the reservation, Thomas Mayo, Tony Tillohash, Brig. George, and Foster Charles Toab, all members of Glenn S. (Pop) Warner's famous football teams of the nineties. Tillohash worked with Dr. Edward Sapir in assembling a Government bulletin on American Indians.

Since that account was written, the reservation has declined in size. The Shivwits (Shivwitz) and four other Paiute bands were terminated as a tribe in 1954 in the hope that members could be assimilated into the general culture more rapidly. This did not occur as planned, however, and tribal status was reestablished in 1980.

North of Shivwits an improved road traverses the narrow valley of Santa Clara River to **Gunlock Lake State Recreation Area** (boating, camping, fishing, water sports). The road continues through Gunlock to junction with State 18 at Veyo *(see below).* **GUNLOCK** is a farming and ranching village named for "Gunlock Bill" Hamblin, sharpshooting brother of Jacob Hamblin *(above).* Santa Clara River Valley was the route of the Old Spanish Trail, south from Mountain Meadows, and of later travelers enroute to and from southern California. After the Mountain Meadows massacre in 1857, alternate routes of travel were developed. Brightly colored rocks, lava-capped cliffs and odd-shaped peaks enhance the valley's rustic charm.

Old US 91 crosses the **Beaver Dam Mountains** over a 4,600-foot summit, then descends to Arizona over the steep Utah Grade—a long, sustained incline which was a formidable obstacle to heavy trucks and cars for many years. The lowest point in Utah, at 2,100 feet above sea level, is on **Beaver Dam Wash** just west of the highway where it crosses the Arizona line. In 1980 the Beaver Dam slopes became a focus of bitter controversy caused by federal classification of the area's desert tortoise as an endangered species, thus restricting livestock grazing. Though the desert tortoise is found elsewhere, this is its only habitat in Utah.

(2) State 18 north to Pine Valley, Mountain Meadows, Enterprise and State 56

North from St. George, State 18 skirts the upper edge of **SNOW CANYON STATE PARK,** a deep, sculptured sandstone gorge accessible by circular road between State 18 and Old US 91 near Santa Clara *(see above).* Short spurs from State 18 give dramatic overviews of the canyon. Near the north end of Snow Canyon, the highway passes between two of three imposing, symmetrical volcanic cinder cones known as the **Diamond (Dameron) Valley Volcanoes**—igneous phenomena of youthful age, geologically speaking. They are related to extensive lava flows of the area—some of which are prominently visible at Snow Canyon—and perhaps to the hot springs at **VEYO,** the site of a bathing/health resort. These natural curiosities are products of tremendous igneous activity that has taken place over ages of time in the area of the **PINE VALLEY MOUNTAINS,** a borderland region of crustal weakness between the Basin & Range and Colorado Plateau provinces. Volcanic cones and lava flows of varying age abound in the Virgin River Valley, while the Pine Valley Mountains themselves are composed of igneous material which was deposited much earlier. Though now exposed, this immense mass of igneous rock was intruded as molten magma (laccolithic intrusion) into surface rocks which have since eroded away, and the Pine Valley Mountains are believed to be the largest known example of a laccolith. This uncommon type of uplift also is represented by the Henry, La Sal and Abajo mountain groups in eastern Utah.

From Veyo, State 18 climbs north between the Pine Valley and Bull Valley mountains to Enterprise and an eventual junction with State 56. At **Central,** 6 m. north of Veyo, is junction with sideroad leading east into a mountain-girt basin known as Pine Valley. The name of the entire mountain range came from this alpine paradise at the headwaters of Santa Clara River, as did that of the hamlet of **Pine Valley.** Steep slopes, clothed with evergreens, loom high above to crests of 10,000 feet and more. **PINE VALLEY** (6,600 alt.) is a charming cluster of rustic dwellings, some of which date from pioneer days when the mountains produced timber for the settlements of southern Utah as well as selected wood for the great tabernacle organ at Salt Lake City. Also, the area has long been a livestock and recreation center. Pine Valley's lovely wooden chapel is one of Utah's oldest church buildings in continuous use, having been built in 1868 by Ebenezer Bryce, a former shipwright and the person for whom Bryce Canyon was named. The chapel is listed on the National Register of Historic Places. Nearby is **Pine Valley Lake,** popular for fishing, the site of an improved campground maintained by Dixie National Forest. Other national forest picnicking-camping developments are in the vicinity.

MOUNTAIN MEADOWS is a pleasant, open valley about half a dozen miles north of the turnoff to Pine Valley. Originally much lusher than today, the Meadows were a well known stop on the Old Spanish and California trails for decades between the 1820s and 1850s, a place where southbound caravans would make final preparations for the long desert trek ahead and northbound trains would rest and recuperate. The Spanish called them Las Vegas de la Santa Clara, and Fremont described the spot as "all refreshing and delightful to look upon." Their fame (or infamy) derived from the slaughter in 1857 of about 120 men, women and children—eastern emigrants traveling to California— by some 50 local white men and Indians. The massacre was prompted, in the words of the National Register description, by a combination of "Mormon-Indian alliances, Mormon emotionalism, fear of an impending invasion, Mormon hatred for Missourians, and an inadequate communication system. . . ." Despite uncounted books and articles on the subject, some details of the massacre are controversial and likely will always remain so. The account in the 1941 edition gave undue emphasis, perhaps, to the role of John D. Lee. Subsequently, a thorough and much more comprehensive examination of the tragic incident—a volume authored by historian Juanita Brooks—appeared under the title *The Mountain Meadows Massacre*. The following, it is believed, is an accurate recounting of the massacre and its causes:

Fear of an invading army was the primary cause of this tragic occurrence (September 7-11, 1857). At about the same time that word was received in the small southern Utah settlements of the approach of the United States Army *(see History),* the Fancher Train—a party of California-bound emigrants, composed of several families from Arkansas and a group of horsemen who called themselves the "Missouri Wildcats"—made their way through central Utah following the southern route to California because of the lateness of the season. Unwise action by members of the party, including failure to keep their animals under control while going through Mormon communities and the expression of anti-Mormon sentiments, antagonized the settlers, who had been stirred to a war hysteria by the fiery preaching of Apostle George A. Smith and others. The climax of this bad feeling was reached at Cedar City when the local citizens, who had been ordered to husband their supplies because of the threatening war situation, refused to sell food to the Fancher train. The angry emigrants expressed hope that the invading army would punish the Mormons and threatened to raise another military force when they arrived in California. Leaving Cedar City, they travelled to Mountain Meadows, where they stopped to rest their livestock before the long, hard journey across the Nevada-California desert.

A meeting was held in Cedar City under the leadership of Stake President Isaac C. Haight, and proposals were made to wipe out the emigrants before they could get to California and carry out their threats. Calmer heads prevailed, and a rider was sent to Salt Lake City to obtain Brigham Young's advice. His written instructions to let the emigrants pass were received late.

A band of Indians, attracted by the herds of cattle, and apparently encouraged by some Mormons, had been following the train and decided to attack the emigrants in their Mountain Meadows encampment. The attack failed. The Indians then turned to their erstwhile friends and allies, the Mormons, demanding help in overcoming the beleaguered camp. John D. Lee, the Mormon in charge of Indian Affairs in southern Utah, became involved and ultimately played a major role in carrying out the plan of the massacre, although he later claimed that he had opposed the whole scheme and had acted only under duress when three men who had escaped from the besieged camp to seek aid were killed by Mormons and Indians. The local Mormon leaders decided that they could not wait for Brigham Young's advice: it would be too dangerous to let the Fancher party spread the word in California that the Mormons were aiding the Indians in attacking emigrant trains. Under a flag of truce, Lee was able to convince the emigrants to lay down their arms with a promise of safe conduct back to Cedar City. The Mormon militia, acting under military orders, killed the disarmed emigrant men, while the Indians were permitted to kill the women and older children, apparently because the Mormons were concerned about the "shedding of innocent blood." Seventeen small children were spared and ultimately, with government help, returned to relatives in Arkansas.

Federal government attempts to apprehend and punish the participants resulted in failure as the tight-knit Mormon society closed ranks and protected its members. John D. Lee was apprehended almost 20 years after the massacre. Following two trials, he was executed by a firing squad at the scene of the crime. Other leaders involved, such as Stake President Haight, experienced much community disapproval; Haight was disfellowshipped and spent much of his life hiding from federal officials. William H. Dame, however, was able to convince both Mormons and non-Mormon officials of his innocence and continued to serve in important church positions.

This tragic massacre increased the Mormon reputation of fanaticism and made relationships with federal officials more difficult.

(3) Highway I-15 south to Arizona and Nevada

Interstate Highway 15 south of St. George, within Utah, measures only nine spectacular miles. From there to Las Vegas, a distance of slightly more than 100 miles, the terrain consists of profound gorges, rugged mountain ranges, and one of America's most forbidding deserts. Only a few hundred people live in the vicinity of the highway between Utah and Las Vegas. The highway parallels the Virgin River for about 40 miles south of St. George, following that temperamental stream through the chasm it has cut through the Virgin Range. Almost all of this canyon route is in Arizona and represents one of the lengthiest (nearly ten years) and most challenging feats of road construction in the history of the rural interstate system. Numerous bridges and trestles were required, as well as earth movement on an enormous scale and 2,000 tons of explosives. Quicksand and falling rocks were serious hazards. Total cost of the 30 miles of I-15 in Arizona—the most difficult stretch—approached 50 million dollars, with one four-mile segment costing about 15 million dollars. Fewer than 100 people reside along the Arizona portion of I-15, and therefore the road was of little direct consequence to Arizona. However, it was of crucial importance to Utah because its more direct routing cut 20 miles and 30 minutes of driving time between Utah and Las Vegas/southern California. For that reason, Utah consented to the temporary diversion to Arizona of ten million dollars of federal highway funds from Utah's entitlement.

BLOOMINGTON, several miles south of St. George via I-15, is Utah's first planned resort community, the product of commercial enterprise. Its basic concept —that of townhome condominiums and individual residences clustered around common facilities such as golf course, clubhouse, swimming pools, stable, playgrounds, lakes and lawns—was formed in the 1960s by a group of land planners and developers who incorporated under the name Terracor. The community has grown at a steady if not phenomenal rate since beginnings of the golf course-country club in 1968, to more than 500 individual homes and about 200 townhouse units in 1980. Architecture is subject to strict controls. In the hills east of Bloomington, across the highway, is a younger planned community known as **Bloomington Hills,** while still other residential suburbs such as **Tonaquint** are being developed in the vicinity.

Pine Valley in February

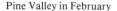

WARD ROYLANCE

Tour No. 8B - State Highway 9 from Harrisburg Junction (I-15) to Hurricane, LaVerkin, Rockville, Springdale, Zion National Park and US 89

At Harrisburg Junction on I-15, take Zion National Park/Hurricane exit. The road soon cuts through a rocky ridge, the **Virgin Anticline,** and drops down to a crossing of the Virgin River. All around is a geological wonderland of cliffs and mesas, volcanic cones, buttes and mountains. The rise of **Red Sand Mountain** fills the southern view. **Dixie Springs,** a private homesite development—recently annexed by Hurricane City—occupies much of the land south of the highway.

HURRICANE (3,200 alt. 2,361 pop.) is a boomtown of sorts, hardly recognizable with so many new houses and business buildings. Youthful when compared with other Dixie towns, Hurricane dates from 1906, two years after irrigation water first became available from the Hurricane Canal. The Hurricane bench had been recognized since the 1860s as having farming value, if water were available; but not until the 1890s—after pressures of growing population and loss of lands to floods in older towns of the area had generated enough interest—were steps taken to bring water to the bench. The story of the **Hurricane Canal** is an epic in Utah history. Beginning in 1893 and not finishing for 11 years, Dixie people dug and blasted from the Virgin River's cliffs a canal eight feet wide, four feet deep, and nearly eight miles long. Using nothing more complicated than a wheelbarrow, they built dams (two of which were destroyed by floods), trestles to support high flumes, and nine tunnels through solid rock. The first water flowed through the canal in 1904, making possible in subsequent years a Garden of Eden where crops include fine orchard fruits of many varieties, grapes, figs, nuts, berries, melons, alfalfa, grain, etc. The canal is listed on the National Register of Historic Sites. Much of Hurricane's growth in recent years is due to the influx of part-time residents and retirees, who enjoy the benign climate. In the late 1970s the city's boundaries were enlarged several times by the annexation of 6,400 acres to the west, known as **Dixie Springs.**

Hurricane received its name from an episode of the early 1860s when Erastus Snow and others, descending the steep fault scarp on a makeshift road, were assaulted by a fierce wind. Snow exclaimed, "Well, that was a hurricane! We'll call this place Hurricane Hill." Wrote Andrew Karl Larson, "So it was that the hill, the fault, the bench, the town, and the canal got their names; at least tradition has it that way." Here in 1776 the Dominguez-Escalante expedition crossed the Virgin River, naming it Rio Sulfureo because it consisted "in great part of hot and sulphurous water." Apparently they did not realize that this condition was very local. From this vicinity the expedition traveled south along the cliff, then eastward through the Arizona Strip to the Colorado River.

East from Hurricane, State 59 climbs **Hurricane Ledge** and passes through open country near the foot of the Vermilion Cliffs to Colorado City (formerly known as Short Creek), Pipe Spring National Monument, Fredonia and US 89-A. Before the late 1950s and early 1960s this was an unpaved road. Improvement was accelerated by the building of Glen Canyon Dam and the need for a new route from Los Angeles that would alleviate heavy truck traffic through Zion National Park. As described in Tour No. 9, "from time immemorial" the route has been used as a highway by Indians and more recently by both Indians and whites. Portions of it were paralleled by the Dominguez-Escalante expedition of 1776. After the settlement of Dixie in the 1850s and 1860s, until completion of the Zion-Mt. Carmel highway in 1930, it was the only feasible all-year route from east to west in this region. It was the general route of travel for great herds of sheep and cattle, which formerly grazed by the tens of thousands in the vast Arizona Strip. Colonists of Kane County traveled to and from St. George over the route, including newlyweds (hence the name "Honeymoon Trail"). Navajo raiders followed the route during the 1860s, and government map-makers a decade or so later. In more recent years it has been the access route for polygamous residents of Colorado City.

South from Hurricane, an unpaved road winds along the foot of Hurricane Ledge into Arizona. From this road, about 8 m. south of Hurricane, a sideroad forks west to **Warner Valley, Fort Pearce Wash,** and **Old Fort Pearce.** *(These points also may be reached from St. George and Washington. Refer to detailed road map.)* **Old Fort Pearce** exhibits the walls of a rock fort built in 1866-67 by Mormons, during the Black Hawk Indian War when Navajos from east of the Colorado were causing serious loss to southern Utah's pioneer community through raids on their livestock. **Fort Pearce Wash** and springs near the fort were used by white travelers of that time, and by Indian raiders as well. The fort was never used for battle, though for decades it served as a watering and roundup center for livestock. For ages the area had been an Indian campsite; Indian artifacts were common at one time. **Warner Valley** is the proposed site for a large coal-fired power plant that would utilize water from the Virgin River and coal from the Alton coal field north of Kanab.

Between Hurricane and LaVerkin, State 9 crosses the entrenched **VIRGIN RIVER** over a high bridge. Directly to the east is the yawning mouth of **Timpoweap Canyon,** by which the river has cut through the Hurricane Fault (Ledge). Far down in the canyon's mouth is a popular bathing resort which utilizes water from hot mineral springs. The Virgin is the normally shallow, muddy sculptor of Zion, giving little hint that such a puny stream could be the architect of such geological grandeur. Dixie's pioneers, however, knew what it could do in raging flood. The Virgin rises principally in the upper reaches of the Markagunt Plateau—Kolob Terrace and empties into Lake Mead near Overton, Nevada, after passing through one of the nation's dreariest deserts. It drains an area of about 11,000 square miles, with a total length of possibly 150 miles. The name apparently is a corruption of the Spanish **Rio Virgen.**

LA VERKIN (3,300 alt. 1,174 pop.), like neighboring Hurricane, is nestled beneath the crumbling ledges of Hurricane Fault. LaVerkin was settled in 1898 after a canal across the canyon from the Hurricane Canal was completed. Though this canal was built in much less time than Hurri-cane's, and with less labor and expense, a tunnel 900 feet long was required and serious leaking occurred for years. This problem eventually was remedied by the building of flumes and extensive use of concrete. As at Hurricane, water made the LaVerkin bench blossom with orchards, vine-yards, and fields. The name La Verkin derives from the Spanish La Virgen (Virgin). The town's population has increased dramatically during the past decade.

State 9 east of LaVerkin winds in switchbacks up the Hurricane Ledge, and "tops out" at the foot of **Hurricane Mesa,** an imposing tableland to the north. Between 1954 and 1962 this flat-topped mesa was the scene of Air Force experiments designed to test the effectiveness of ejection seats in jet aircraft. Aircraft conditions were simulated by attaching dummies to sleds and ejecting them at supersonic speeds from the edge of the mesa. Lava flows, cinder cones and other volcanic remnants accent a dramatic landscape of brightly colored sedimentary rocks.

VIRGIN (3,400 alt. 169 pop.) is a small farming village, one of the oldest in this part of Utah. Virgin dates from 1858, when it was settled by a group under young Nephi Johnson. Nephi, several months earlier, had been the first white man to enter and explore the depths of Zion Canyon. Like its neighbors in this region, Virgin City suffered terribly from disease, raging floods, and crop failures. The following is excerpted from the 1941 edition:

> Settlers came into the valley in the middle 1850's, when the Mormon Church sent colonies into "Dixie" to establish cotton plantations, sugar-cane fields, vineyards, orchards, and silk culture. Malaria swept the camps, crops were discouraging, and it was years before the orchards would bear profitably.

> Sylvester Earl, in an interview with Louise Slack, tells of the Virgin oil boom in 1907, following the original discovery of oil in 1903:

> > They drilled the well and struck oil on the fourteenth day of July in 1907. This was the first oil producing well in the State of Utah. It caused great excitement and a boom in Virgin City. We couldn't even feed the people who came there, there were so many. In a few months there were seventeen oil rigs. . . . There were tent towns with two big tent hotels and saloons, but the money panic of 1907 came and knocked the bottom out of the whole proposition.

North from Virgin a partially paved road climbs up the canyon of North Creek to the **Kolob Section** of **ZION NATIONAL PARK** *(see),* and onto the 8,000-foot heights of **Kolob Terrace,** exiting on US 91 near Cedar City, or climbing to State 14 on the Markagunt Plateau. The route is outstandingly scenic, with inspirational views of giant cliffs, buttes and gorges—in particular the tremendous face of West Temple, Great West Canyon, Spendlove Knoll, and the red-walled mesas of the Kolob Canyons area. Sideroads and trails lead east and west into the park, and—

Crags at the mouth of Zion Canyon *(right).*

Sculptured sandstone in the Zion-Mt. Carmel district *(below),* typical as well of the Kolob area north of Virgin.

WARD ROYLANCE PHOTOS

farther north—to headwaters of the park's great canyons. This road is the main access to summer homes and ranches on the Kolob.

Between Virgin and Rockville several hamlets known as Dalton and Duncan's Retreat existed for a while during the 1860s.

ROCKVILLE (3,700 alt.) is a tree-shaded riverside village under the jagged rocky peaks and thirsty talus slopes of lower Zion Canyon, its residents tending fruit orchards and a few sandy fields along the valley floor. Rockville is an old settlement, dating from 1862. For several decades between 1880 and 1900 the village prospered, and today it is still one of the most substantial communities in the area. In early days the people grew cotton, made sorghum from cane, and produced silk. On the main street (State 9) is a historic building known as the **Deseret Telegraph and Post Office.** The diminutive wood frame structure was built in the 1870s and served for years as an office of the church-owned Deseret Telegraph Company which linked all of Utah and Mormon settlements in nearby states over 1,000 miles of wire. Adjoining the frame building is a red sandstone house, built by Edward Huber in 1864 as a residence of the postmaster and telegraph operator. *Listed on National Register of Historic Places.*

Some Rockville people dry-farm the Big Plain south of Smithsonian Butte and Zion Canyon—part of a vast rolling mesa which extends from the Zion region far south to the breaks of Grand Canyon. The graded road leading to this picturesque tableland is very steep, but it affords magnificent views of the cliffs and temples of Zion. At Big Plain Junction the road joins State 59 from Hurricane *(see above).*

Forking from this road, across the river bridge, is a 3-mile spur leading west to the well-known ghost town of **GRAFTON** *(privately owned).* Here a photogenic brick church and several distinctive old houses stir memories of the past. Grafton was settled in the 1860s and managed to overcome floods and other difficulties through the years, surviving until the 1920s. Because of its striking location and quaint buildings, Grafton has been a locale for western movies, including *Butch Cassidy and the Sundance Kid* starring Robert Redford and Paul Newman. The church, built in the 1880s, is a registered historic site. Vandalism in recent years threatens the town's existence.

Across the river from Rockville, in the mouth of East Fork (Parunuweap) Canyon, was **SHUNESBURG.** A farming community of pioneer days, Shunesburg exhibits little except ruins and foundations to indicate its location. *Private; no admittance.*

SPRINGDALE (3,900 alt. 258 pop.) is closest of all Dixie settlements to Zion Canyon, being within its towering walls a mile from the entrance to Zion National Park. Springdale's long-time agricultural status is hardly apparent today, having largely been replaced by the tourist industry. The main street is lined with motels, service stations, restaurants, stores and shops; and new homes have appeared on the valley floor where crops once grew and livestock grazed. The 1941 edition said:

See Zion National Park for description of State 9 within the park. East of the park the highway crosses the **Kolob Terrace,** densely wooded with pygmy evergreens, to US 89 at **Mt. Carmel Junction.** The forbidding gorge of Parunuweap (East Fork) Canyon—or, more accurately, its upper walls— can be glimpsed to the south. Far above, on the north, is the brooding rim of the Markagunt.

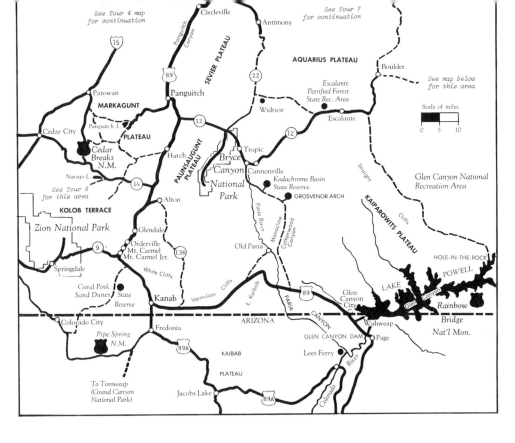

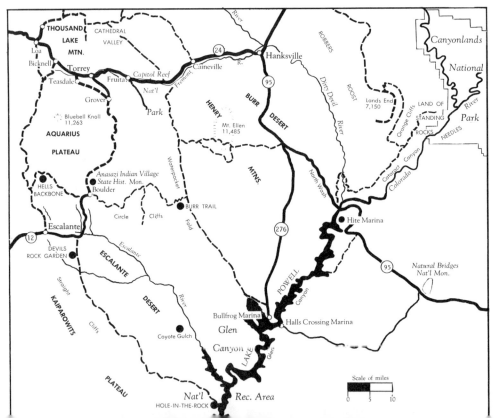

Tour No. 9
COLOR COUNTRY — EAST
(Garfield and Kane counties)

This tour region extends from the upper Sevier River Valley of the High Plateaus, eastward into the brilliantly colored, unbelievably rugged Canyonlands region. Included are renowned parks, vast expanses of forest and red-rock desert, Lake Powell, Utah's "Little Hollywood" (Kanab), and one of the world's highest concrete dams.

Tour No. 9A - US Highway 89 from Circleville south to Kanab

South of Circleville, US 89 follows the narrow canyon of Sevier River, cut through an incredible mass of igneous rock. Colors and erosional designs of the rocks are most intriguing. This was the route followed in pre-Mormon years by travelers along the Old Spanish Trail between New Mexico and California, and in the fierce winter of 1853-54 by the exhausted exploring party of John Charles Fremont *(see Tour No. 7A)*. Emerging from the canyon's confines, the old trail curved westward through low passes toward Paragonah and the Great Basin, leaving the High Plateaus through which it had passed for many miles.

About 15 miles north of Panguitch the highway enters the widespreading expanse of upper Sevier River Valley. Hayfields carpet the valley floor, where livestock seemingly outnumber the human population. Toward the west, the grand Tushar mass has given way to low open valleys and isolated peaks, which blend southward into the bulky highlands of the Markagunt Plateau. On the east, the Sevier Plateau's volcanic crest has been eroded into a jagged profile not ordinarily seen in the plateau country. This imposing ruggedness is succeeded, gradually, east of Panguitch, by the brilliant sedimentary coloring of the Paunsagunt Plateau, mother of Bryce.

This high valley, and its extension southward beyond Hatch, were settled by Mormon pioneers in the 1860s. The Black Hawk Indian troubles caused abandonment of the first settlements between 1866 and 1871. Since then the area's economy has been based largely on stockraising and feed crops, lumbering, highway travel, and seasonal recreation. Altitude and a short growing season limit crop production. In recent decades there has been a moderate growth in summer resident population.

PANGUITCH (6,600 alt., 1,343 pop.), seat of Garfield County, bustles in summer with local industry and highway traffic. Tourism supports a number of motels, restaurants, and service stations. In winter, commercial activity slows considerably. Panguitch is noted for the distinctive brick architecture of its early homes and outbuildings, and for the original facades of some of its turn-of-the-century Main Street commercial structures.

Panguitch *(an Indian word meaning big or heavy fish)* was not settled until 1864, although an exploring party from Parowan, across a mountain

Sevier River Valley north of Panguitch.

ridge to the west, had visited the site in 1852. The original founders, a few families from Parowan and Beaver, were snowbound the first winter, keeping themselves alive on frost-nipped wheat, beef, potatoes, and what meager supplies could be packed in from across the mountains. The settlement expanded to about 70 families in 1865. The following year Indian troubles resulted in the building of a fort and, in the same year, abandonment of the valley, not to be resettled for another five years. The new settlers found the fort and original buildings intact.

Turn west from Panguitch to **Panguitch Lake** (21 m.), a popular fishing and summer home site. Private resorts and a public campground support fishing, boating, camping, riding and other outdoor activities. On the Markagunt Plateau at an elevation of more than 8,000 feet, the lake measures about one square mile in area. It fills a volcanic basin, and surrounding it are forbidding beds of black lava, rough and jagged and of fairly recent origin. The source of the more recent lava flows apparently was about three miles southwest, with more ancient fields to the southwest and southeast. Unpaved roads lead from the lake to Yankee Meadows Reservoir, Cedar Breaks, Mammoth Creek and State Highway 14. **Panguitch Lake Campground** (Dixie National Forest) is open from June to October. Located there are 69 camping and picnicking units.

South of Panguitch, US 89 continues along **Sevier Valley,** which narrows somewhat and increases rapidly in elevation. At 8 miles from Panguitch is the junction with State 12, leading to Bryce Canyon National Park, Escalante, Boulder, the Circle Cliffs, Hole-in-the-Rock, Lake Powell and other relatively isolated parts of Color Country *(see Tour No. 9C).*

HATCH (6,900 alt., 121 pop.), a pleasant community overlooking the river bottoms and the pink Sunset Cliffs of Paunsagunt Plateau. Straddling the highway, Hatch was settled in the early 1870s as a ranch and named for the founding family. The village grew into Hatch Town within a few years. A disastrous flood in 1900 washed out a dam nearby, causing resettlement on a new site. Another flood, in 1914, destroyed a newer, even more costly dam, resulting in great damage to sites downstream. Hatch is a tourist center with motels, cafes, service stations and stores.

Upper Sevier Valley from Hatch to Long Valley Junction is alpine country, with ponderosa pines at higher levels, sagebrush and pygmy evergreens at intermediate elevations. The valley is cupped between lofty plateau highlands. Long Valley Junction marks the drainage divide between the Sevier system, which drains north and then west into the Great Basin, and the Virgin, which drains into the Colorado River (Lake Mead) and finally the Gulf of California. The Sevier and its headwater streams such as **Asay** and **Mammoth creeks** provide adequate water for the valley. In the late 1800s there was a fairly large population. However, problems of water control and the severe climate caused many settlers to move away. Scattered buildings, most of them ramshackle and abandoned, are vestige reminders of settlement clusters that once dotted this area.

LONG VALLEY JUNCTION (7,200 alt.) is marked by a store and service station. Turn west from here on State 14 to **Cedar City** (40 m.), **Cedar Breaks National Monument** *(see in Parks Section),* and **Brian Head Resort.** The highway crosses the forested summit of the **Markagunt Plateau,** a popular recreation locale offering diversified choices such as fishing, hunting, skiing, camping, and superb panoramic views. *See Tour No. 8 and Cedar Breaks National Monument for details of the plateau's attractions.*

South of Long Valley Junction, US 89 descends into **Long Valley** through forested, gently contoured terrain, the headwaters of Virgin River's East Fork. Marked sideroads lead several miles east to **ALTON** (6,875 alt., 75 pop.), in a valley cleared of trees, with houses clustered at the foot of pink and white cliffs. Laid out in 1907 near the abandoned site of an older settlement known as Upper Kanab, the town devotes itself mainly to agriculture. In the vicinity are immense coal deposits. Serious consideration has been given to strip mining 10 million tons of coal annually from this area for proposed power plants near St. George and Las Vegas. Long Valley is formed along a great break in the earth's crust known as the Sevier Fault. Strata on the east side of the valley are higher than corresponding rocks on the west. This displacement is very apparent in the lower valley.

GLENDALE (5,824 alt., 237 pop.) is a pleasant community strung out along the highway in the narrow upper valley. Its people farm, raise livestock, mine coal, and provide services to highway travelers (lodging, food, gasoline). The little town has a history dating from 1864, when it was founded as Berryville by Mormon settlers from northern towns. It was fortified as a stockade and used for protection by Long Valley residents during the Navajo Indian troubles of 1865 and 1866. In the spring of 1866 two young men named Berry and the wife of one, all from Berryville, were killed by Indians near Pipe Spring (apparently in retaliation for whites having killed some Indians not long before), and soon afterward all the area's settlers abandoned their homes and fields. In 1871 the region was resettled by old residents of the area and evacuees from Moapa Valley, Nevada; Berryville was renamed that year as Glendale after Glendale, Scotland, former home of Bishop James Leithead.

ORDERVILLE (5,250 alt., 423 pop.), largest of the Long Valley communities, has a claim to historical fame as one of the principal sites of the Mormon United Order experiment *(see History),* though few physical evidences of this period remain. Today its economy relies primarily on agriculture and highway travel (lodging, food, gasoline, large rock shop, pioneer relic hall).

Orderville's people today are as individualistic as other Americans, but their ancestors lived for 11 or 12 unusually successful years in an idealistic communal society created "to insure unity in moral, material, and spiritual life." After the disastrous financial crisis of 1873, a number of Mormon communities followed the advice of their leaders in establishing cooperative "in common" societies. Orderville became the United Order center for Long Valley, and at least partly because of its geographic isolation from larger and older centers of population, continued the experiment longer than any other Mormon community. From 1875 to about 1886, its people (who numbered 543 in 1877) worked cooperative farms, orchards, dairies, stockyards and sheep herds, blacksmith and carpenter shops, bakery, sawmill, gristmill, molasses mill, silk industry, bucket factory, woolen factory, cooper shop, and tannery. The members pooled their wealth, ate at a common table, and met morning and evening for worship. All proceeds were turned into a common storehouse and shared by everyone according to need.

Abandonment of the venture was the result of cumulative difficulties. Young men and other new members could not obtain stock. Anti-polygamy legislation made refugees of leaders. The death of Brigham Young in 1877 weakened the church's resolve with respect to the program. Booming mines brought prosperity to other towns in southern Utah, causing dissatisfaction among envious Orderville youth. An illegal charter, high taxes, internal contention, jealousy and ridicule—all these factors gradually undermined the Order. Finally the church leaders advised that the Orderville program be disbanded, and between 1884 and 1889 its property was transferred to private ownership. Thus ended more than a decade of trial in applied idealism. Only from a limited perspective could it be termed a failure.

MT. CARMEL (5,200 alt.) is an agricultural village situated beneath a majestic white rampart known as the Elkhart Cliffs, on the east. Called Winsor when the first house was built in 1865, the hamlet was abandoned in 1866 and resettled during 1871 by people from Nevada's Muddy River towns who renamed it Mt. Carmel after a mountain in Palestine. Some of these first settlers removed to Orderville in 1875 to participate in the United Order there. The famous western painter, Maynard Dixon, lived at Mt. Carmel for several years during the early 1940s before his death, and his remains are buried there.

MT. CARMEL JUNCTION *(motels, restaurant, service station)* is at the junction of US 89 with State Highway 15, which gives access to **Zion National Park** via the Zion-Mt. Carmel tunnel *(see Zion National Park)*. South and west of here the **Virgin River's East Fork,** a modest stream, enters a deep and narrow gorge known formally as **Parunuweap Canyon.** In its lower reaches east of Rockville the canyon approaches 2,000 feet in depth, rivaling in grandeur its sister gorge, Zion (Mukuntuweap) Canyon.

South of Mt. Carmel Junction, US 89 ascends a high bench at the base of beautiful White Cliffs. Grand vistas stretch in all directions, particularly westward to the towers and temples of Zion National Park.

At 4 miles an unpaved but improved road leads south to **CORAL PINK SAND DUNES STATE RESERVE** (11 miles), a colorful basin filled with dunes of fine pink sand eroded from the surrounding cliffs and ridges. This is a popular area for color photography, picnicking, camping and dunebuggying. Movie makers have used the area as a filming location. The sideroad continues south across the state line into the Arizona Strip, connecting with the highway between Kanab and Hurricane. *Improved camp units; restrooms; water; camper and trailer loops.*

US 89 descends into the picturesque canyon of **Kanab Creek,** known here as Three Lake Canyon, with its colored cliffs and intriguing displays of crossbedded sandstone, remnants of ancient desert dunes. A roadside lake has been featured in numerous films, and Moki Caverns (commercial) exhibits extensive rock and black-light displays.

At sign marked "Robinson's Ranch," an unpaved side road follows Kanab Creek upstream (north) to a guest ranch operation, an old movie site, underground lake, and the legendary hiding place of Montezuma's Aztec treasure. *Private property in this area; inquire locally to avoid trespass.* Kanab Creek begins in the southern reaches of the Paunsaugunt Plateau, beneath the Pink Cliffs of Bryce, gradually increasing its canyon in depth until it joins the Colorado through one of the most profound tributary gorges of Grand Canyon. Side canyons in this area contain interesting cliff dwellings and rock art.

KANAB (5,000 alt., 2,148 pop.), is the seat of Kane County and the commercial center of a vast farming, livestock, lumbering, movie-making, and recreation area. In recent years a number of retirement and vacation homes have been built in the vicinity. The city is a major highway stop and contains excellent motels, cafes, shops and other services.

Pinnacles and ranch, Long Valley near Glendale *(left)*.

Coral Pink Sand Dunes near Kanab *(below, left)*.

Panguitch Lake *(below, right)*.

WARD ROYLANCE PHOTOS

Kanab *(pron. Kuh-NAB)* is a Paiute word meaning "place of the willows." In the vicinity are sand dunes, prehistoric Indian sites, volcanic craters and lava flows, majestic cliffs and canyons, mountains, valleys, forests, deserts, and far-spreading plains. The wide variety of natural scenery is ideal for outdoor movie-making, and the Kanab area—known as Little Hollywood—has served since the 1920s as locale for several hundred motion picture and television productions. Film-making over the years, primarily during the 1940s and 1950s, has brought a great deal of money into the community; however, changing trends make this industry an undependable source of employment and industry.

For decades the picturesque white buildings of **Parry's Lodge** on Kanab's main street have been a romantic beacon for knowledgeable movie-goers. There they might reasonably expect to meet a star face-to-face, and on its walls they could inspect a multitude of autographed photos of Hollywood greats who had headquartered there. Among them: Robert Taylor, Frank Sinatra, Dean Martin, Sammy Davis Jr., Maureen O'Hara, Deanna Durbin, Roddy McDowell, Victor Mature, Yvonne DeCarlo, James Arness, Rhonda Fleming, Ava Gardner, Howard Keel, Wallace Beery, etc.

Kanab dates from the mid-1860s. In 1867-68 a "fort" was built, and by 1870 some ten families were living there. Brigham Young visited the settlement twice during 1870, making suggestions and supervising the town planning. There was not enough water for much farming, however; local people depended for the most part on livestock grazing. During two days of terrific floods in 1883 the bed of Kanab Canyon was lowered a record 40 feet. Kanab served as field headquarters for the Powell-Thompson topographic survey of northern Arizona and Utah which lasted six years from 1871, and Zane Grey lived here in 1912 while writing his *Riders of the Purple Sage.* For long years Kanab was perhaps the most isolated town in America. Cut off from the east by gorges of the Colorado, it could be reached with difficulty from the west only by a rough dirt road from the Virgin River settlements. The 23-mile journey from Orderville on the north required four harrowing days; and north of Orderville the mountain passes were closed by snow for almost half the year.

Side streets in Kanab reveal interesting examples of 19th century architecture, some humbly rustic, others indicating relative prosperity. Of special note, having historic register listings, are: **Heritage House Museum** (Bowman-Chamberlain Home), 14 E. 1st South, a red brick residence in Queen Anne Victorian style, built in 1892 by Henry Bowman and later sold to Thomas Chamberlain, prominent early leader. The house was purchased by Kanab in 1974, then restored by local citizens to serve as a community museum. Dr. George R. Aiken, physician and civic leader, received a state award in 1980 for his efforts in the restoration. *Open to the public.* . . . **Lundquist Home,** 200 West and Center, a white brick structure dating from 1890, combining "the grace of 19th century French provincial architecture with a flair and style that expresses the best of today's contemporary living." Restored 1962. . . . **James A. Little Home,** 247 N. 100 West, built in 1873. "The adobe structure typifies the migrant, polygamist, pioneer's struggle to house his families."

South of Kanab, **Alternate US 89** leads to Fredonia and other points in Arizona including Grand Canyon's North Rim, the vast Arizona Strip, Kaibab Forest, House Rock Valley, Marble Canyon (Navajo) Bridge, and Lees Ferry.

FREDONIA (4,900 alt.) is located in Arizona's Coconino County, second largest county in the 48 contiguous states. Its name derives from "free dona" or free women, applied because Mormon refugees from federal anti-polygamy laws were among its first settlers during the 1880s.

From Fredonia, roads give access to the **ARIZONA STRIP,** that little-populated part of Arizona lying between the Utah line and Grand Canyon. From time immemorial, the Strip has been used as a highway by Indians and more recently by both Indians and whites. Ranchers have grazed their cattle there since the 1860s, and during the great cattle days from 1900 to 1914 as many as 20,000 head of cattle were counted at the roundups held at Pipe Spring and Canaan Ranch. Today stockmen use the depleted ranges for much smaller herds. **PIPE SPRING NATIONAL MONUMENT** features a frontier rock fort dating from the 1870s, when it was built to safeguard an important source of water. Arizona 389 crosses the Arizona Strip along the majestic Vermilion Cliffs, becoming Utah 59 at the state line. *See Tour 8.*

Tour No. 9B - US 89 from Kanab to Page, Arizona

East of Kanab, US 89 follows the stately **Vermilion Cliffs** through open country. Northward through occasional breaks in the red rampart the eye catches glimpses of other cliffs, a **Grand Staircase** rising in giant steps of white, gray and finally pink—the Pink Cliffs of Bryce Canyon National Park. Southward the hulk of Kaibab Plateau (Buckskin Mountain in this vicinity) becomes lost in distance toward the invisible North Rim of Grand Canyon. Here and there strange buttes and promontories appear. US 89 from Kanab to Page and south into Arizona is relatively new, dating only from the late 1950s when it was built to connect Glen Canyon damsite with centers of population. The stretch east of Kanab in Utah was completed in 1958 at a cost of nearly six million dollars; sections in Arizona were completed at a later date. In 1959 it was designated as US 89, while the highway south of Kanab—the original US 89—was redesignated as Alternate US 89.

North from US 89 (8 m. east of Kanab) is **Johnson Canyon,** a low-walled valley which, because of plentiful water, has been used for more than a hundred years as a stock range. A spiderweb of fair-weather dirt roads branch off to penetrate the broken land between Paunsaugunt Plateau, Paria River and the Vermilion Cliffs; the main road continues on to **Alton.** Among the canyon's attractions are ranch buildings (the valley was settled during the 1870s), an old western movie set, and Eagle Arch, an unusual natural formation. The cliffs east of here have been a fruitful source of petrified wood.

Turn north from US 89 (about 35 m. east of Kanab) to **OLD PARIA TOWN-SITE,** reached by six-mile dirt road *(slick when wet; do not attempt in stormy weather).* Here, in a basin formed by Chinle formation—among the most brilliantly colored of rocks—Mormon pioneers established a farming community in the late 1860s and early 1870s. Known first as Pahreah (muddy water), after the normally small stream from which water was taken, the town prospered for a decade or so, and many buildings were built. Crops were good; fruit and nuts were grown; livestock grazed the countryside. Then a series of floods in the 1880s and later years proved disastrous, most people gradually left, and by the turn of the century only a handful remained. A few ruins, several old houses, and a forlorn cemetery are all that remind one of the original settlement. Modern moviemakers constructed a false-front western "town" near the old town; this was used as a set for such films as "Sergeants Three," starring Frank Sinatra and Sammy Davis, Jr.

Forming the eastern skyline in this vicinity is a high, north-south trending ridge known as **The Cockscomb (Coxcomb).** Builders of US 89 encountered a formidable challenge in cutting a roadway through the ridge several miles southeast of the Old Paria turnoff, where it is more than a thousand feet high. Technically The Cockscomb is but one section of a giant earth flexure or fold known as the **East Kaibab Monocline,** which extends about 150 miles from the vicinity of Bryce Canyon southward into Arizona. Scenically the monocline is a spectacular feature, with its sawtooth crest visible for many miles from US 89, and beautifully colored, tilted rocks sculptured into strange shapes and intriguing erosional designs.

The Cockscomb as seen from US 89.

WARD ROYLANCE

A particularly interesting part of the monocline is **Cottonwood Canyon,** formed along the uptilted layers of the flexure; the road between Cannonville and US 89 follows this canyon *(see below).* Near Old Paria, the Paria River cuts through the uplift from west to east in Shurtz Gorge, a chasm 900 feet deep, less than 100 feet in width, and only a mile in length.

Five miles south of the Old Paria turnoff, where US 89 begins to ascend the west slope of The Cockscomb in Fivemile Valley, an unpaved road leads southward into upper **House Rock Valley.** At four and eight miles from the highway, trails lead from this unpaved road into the western arm of **PARIA CANYON PRIMITIVE AREA** *(see also Paria Canyon below).* Details and maps should be obtained from, and hikers should register with, the Office of U.S. Bureau of Land Management in Kanab. Wilderness hiking routes here feature narrow passageways, natural windows and dramatic erosional forms in the **East Kaibab Monocline.** The most challenging and exciting of all is **Buckskin Gulch,** an exceptionally narrow, 400-foot-deep tributary of the Paria, which can be hiked its 12-mile course from **The Dive** to its confluence with the Paria, seven miles downstream from the Paria trailhead. Average width of the gulch is less than 15 feet, and ropes are necessary to descend two 20 to

30-foot drops caused by rock falls. In only one spot is it possible to climb out of the canyon. Floods are a hazard and mud is a problem; hikers must not fail to register and obtain latest weather information from rangers before attempting the Buckskin hike.

East of The Cockscomb, the highway descends into the valley of Paria River, an area of sand and wild rock erosion. Hardly a sign indicates that, a hundred years ago, a fair-sized community existed here. This was **ADAIRVILLE,** founded in the 1870s but gradually abandoned because of flooding.

Turn south from US 89 at sign *(east of Paria River crossing, 43 m. from Kanab)* to **PARIA CANYON PRIMITIVE AREA** *(U.S. Bureau of Land Management).* Drive 3 m. over unpaved road to White House Ruins, site of an old homestead, where cars may be parked and visitors must register. *Hiking permits are required; see below.* From this point hikers descend the awesome **gorge of Paria River** to Lees Ferry, Arizona. The 35-mile route follows the river, and frequent wading is necessary; one five-mile stretch known as The Narrows has such precipitous walls that there is no escape route in case of flash flood, hence the requirement for last-minute weather checking with rangers. From four to six days are recommended for the hike. Rewards: spectacular red-rock scenery, wilderness seclusion, adventure experiences such as wading, quicksand, danger of flash floods, summer heat. Interesting features include natural arches; Indian antiquities; springs, seeps and pools; rock slides; narrow side canyons; old ruins and ranches. *Season and permits:* Warmer months most comfortable; winter is too cold for wading. Danger of floods from upstream rain is most acute in July, August and September. At any time, obtain permits not more than 24 hours in advance from BLM District Office in Kanab (this may be done by telephone), or from on-site ranger during high-use season.

Three miles east of Paria River crossing, an unpaved road leads north to Cannonville, Kodachrome Basin and Bryce Canyon National Park. Turn north on this road through the rugged, colorful, lonely **Paria River-Cottonwood Canyon country.** See *Tour No. 9C for description.*

GLEN CANYON CITY (4,200 alt.) is a rather nondescript settlement of mobile homes, trailers, frame buildings, and other more-or-less permanent structures. The town dates from the late 1950s, the beginnings of Glen Canyon Dam, when land speculation in the area was rampant. The dreams of its founders were not realized. Glen Canyon City gained unwelcome notoriety in recent years as the home of a polygamist cult.

North from Glen Canyon City, an unpaved road crosses Wahweap Creek and ascends Lone Rock Canyon to **Nipple Bench.** This desolate flat, surrounded by canyons and cliffs, symbolizes the "battle" of Kaiparowits—a struggle of ideas, values, emotions, theories and hypotheses, involving legions of engineers, financiers, planners and specialists, America's most powerful environmental organizations, government officials, and numbers of ordinary citizens, all concerned about the proposed construction of a large coal-fired power plant and its potential effects on the environment.

The corrugated **KAIPAROWITS PLATEAU** *(pron. Kuh-PARE-owits),* north of Glen Canyon City, has long been regarded as one of Utah's last wilderness frontiers, though a network of fairweather dirt roads makes much of it reasonably accessible; stockmen have used it as rangeland for a hundred years; oil is produced in quantity; and it is known to contain immense reserves of coal. Despite local familiarity, the 1500-square-mile region is noteworthy as a wilderness because of its complete lack of permanent inhabitants; its labyrinthine system of steep-walled canyons;

The Kaiparowits Plateau from the south, looking north toward the Henry Mountains. In this vicinity was to have been the proposed Kaiparowits power plant.

and its formidable cliffs. Much of the plateau can be seen in overview from the rim of Bryce Canyon, its surface appearing deceptively unbroken from that distant vantage point.

The plateau is described in the guidebook's first edition, especially on pages 340 and 342: "Among its wilderness of stark rocks . . . are cliff dwellings, flaming monoliths, strange fossils, dinosaur tracks, slashed canyons, inaccessible tablelands, sand dunes, small lakes, cave dwellings, burial mounds, and petroglyphs." **Smoky Mountain** "is accessible through a canyon containing more than three hundred caves, once inhabited by prehistoric peoples. Millions of tons of material have issued forth from the side of this mountain . . ."

Gradually, beginning in 1964, the name Kaiparowits became known outside Utah. In that year a consortium of California and Arizona power companies announced plans to build a behemoth coal-fired electric generating plant on the plateau, utilizing some of its coal reserves, as well as water from Lake Powell. Planning and water rights were the main concerns during initial years.

Opinions were formed, studies conducted, and statements issued on the basis of the consortium's announced *plans,* which by the mid-1970s called for a new city of 15,000 to 20,000 residents; a generating capacity of 3,000 megawatts; four underground coal mines producing more than 400 million tons of coal over the installation's 35-year life expectancy; new transmission lines totaling 1,400 miles or more; and a total estimated cost which had risen to 1½ billion dollars in 1971, 3½ billion dollars in 1976. The power plant would require 2,500 workers for construction and 500 for operation, and the four mines would employ 2,000 miners.

Early in 1976 the final environmental impact statement was issued by the Department of the Interior. In six bound volumes, the statement totaled more than 3,000 pages. Among the effects listed: stack emissions would cause a reduction in air quality, and there likely would be earth subsidence from mining; dust from excavation; adverse effects on wildlife, vegetation, archeological and historical values, and scenic esthetics; socioeconomic concerns; and problems of solid waste disposal—in addition to use of considerable water. These effects had already been publicized and thoroughly discussed. While there was disagreement as to the actual extent of negative impacts, most of the emotions were generated by *pros* and *cons*—by *values*. The ire of environmental groups and many individuals was aroused primarily by the fact that the plant would be located in a wilderness area within a few miles of Lake Powell and Glen Canyon National Recreation Area, and within 100 miles of numerous national parks, national monuments, national forests, and other public recreation areas. On the other hand, state and local government, and most of Utah's people (according to a survey), favored the project if appropriate environmental safeguards were observed.

All the furor, the studies, debates, hearings and impact statements were for naught, in a direct sense. While awaiting final decision of the Secretary of the Interior in April 1976, the power firms announced abandonment of the project on the grounds that costs had become prohibitive, and because of government delays and the threat of environmental lawsuits.

As US 89 approaches the Utah-Arizona line, the country becomes more ruggedly spectacular. Grand buttes and lines of cliffs appear, and looming over all is the huge rounded hulk of **Navajo Mountain** (10,388 alt.), a regional landmark, sacred to the Indians of the region. Finally the waters of Lake Powell come into view, set in an unearthly landscape of bright color and weird rock forms. This is Glen Canyon country, gouged out over countless centuries by the Colorado River and its tributaries. Twenty-odd years ago it was an almost inaccessible wildland; today it is visited by millions of recreationists and highway travelers.

GLEN CANYON DAM, BRIDGE, VISITOR CENTER and LAKE POWELL *(see parks chapter for Glen Canyon National Recreation Area).* **Dam, bridge, visitor center, and Page are in Arizona, most of Lake Powell is in Utah.**

Truly a monument to engineering prowess, this giant water storage and power generating development became a reality in the decade between 1956 and 1966. Construction began in 1956, shortly after Congress passed the Colorado River Storage Project. Its purpose: maximum utilization of the river's water through large-volume storage (to compensate for cyclical changes in flow); generating of electric power to pay for the project; recreation; and other reasons. Total cost of construction, including the town of Page, amounted to more than 250 million dollars.

The dam, bridge and visitor center are startling sights when first viewed; so is the blue lake stretching away to the northward in a weird landscape of bare rock. They seem inappropriate—out of place—in this strangest of wildlands, hundreds of miles from the nearest metropolitan area. Statistics alone are imposing:

THE DAM—710 feet high above bedrock, 583 feet above the original riverbed; maximum thickness 350 feet; crest length 1,560 feet; volume of concrete, 5 million cubic yards; cost $145,000,000. Construction (blasting) began in October 1956; the last bucket of concrete was placed in September 1963; and water storage began in March 1963. Construction involved coffer dams and huge diversion tunnels; a service road tunnel through solid rock measuring 30 feet in diameter and 10,000 feet long; 29 million pounds of reinforcing steel; 10 million tons of aggregate for the concrete; a huge 4-inch steel cable a mile long, for hoisting; and footbridges across the canyon. Thousands of construction workers were needed; a completely new city (Page) came into existence; a new highway costing nearly $6,000,000 was extended from Kanab, and another was built from Flagstaff. The entire project was dedicated September 22, 1966.

THE POWERPLANT—Cost $70,000,000. Contains eight generating units with a peak capacity of nearly a million kilowatts (one-third that of the proposed Kaiparowits coal-fired plant). The eighth and final generator was placed on line in 1966.

THE BRIDGE—World's highest steel-arch bridge, 700 feet above the river at base of dam. Span 1,028 feet; length of deck 1,271 feet; 30-foot roadway with sidewalks; cost $4,000,000. The bridge was begun in 1958, opened to traffic in January 1959 and dedicated the following month. Two footbridges were used before completion of the vehicle bridge; one, of steel mesh and cable, crossing the canyon 700 feet above the river, was built in 60 days during 1957 at a cost of $200,000.

CARL HAYDEN VISITOR CENTER, perched on the west rim of the canyon, above the dam, was dedicated in September 1968 and named in honor of Arizona Senator Carl Hayden. It provides exhibits, an information desk, and self-guided tours through the dam and powerplant.

LAKE POWELL *(see also Glen Canyon National Recreation Area in parks section)* is the huge body of water impounded behind Glen Canyon Dam. Whereas the dam is in Arizona, the greater part of the lake is in Utah. The lake was named for Major John Wesley Powell, who led the first exploratory expeditions through canyons of the Colorado River system in 1869 and 1871 and applied names to many

Glen Canyon Dam, Lake Powell, and the Colorado River, looking north toward Wahweap Bay and the Kaiparowits Plateau.

BUREAU OF RECLAMATION (STAN RASMUSSEN)

of its landscape features, including Glen Canyon. Major Powell also was a pioneer of federal reclamation activities. The lake measures 186 miles in length, filling almost the entire Glen Canyon basin upstream into Cataract Canyon. Its incredibly indented shoreline totals about 2,000 miles. On the lake are several major marina-resort developments (Wahweap, Bullfrog, Hall's Crossing and Hite) and a smaller marina near Rainbow Bridge; all of these except Wahweap are in Utah.

PAGE, ARIZONA, on a bench overlooking the damsite from the east, was built by the federal government as a construction town. In 1956, when project construction began, the nearest community of moderate size was Kanab, 76 miles away; the closest major cities were Salt Lake City, 400 miles, and Phoenix, about 300 miles. Within two or three years hundreds of new homes had been built, as well as a sewer and water system, paved streets and sidewalks, schools and a hospital. By 1959 the town had about 5,000 residents, with several thousand more being added before completion of the dam and powerplant. A number of motels, restaurants, shops and services make it the largest highway center between Flagstaff and Kanab, a distance of 200 miles.

Tour No. 9C - State Highway 12 from US 89 east to Escalante and Boulder; also points enroute and beyond

From junction with US 89 seven miles south of Panguitch, Utah Highway 12 crosses Sevier Valley and enters lovely **Red Canyon,** a miniature of Bryce with similar erosional forms and the same exquisite colors. Red Canyon is cut into the Paunsaugunt Plateau, the gentle highland whose battlement flanks are known as the Sunset Cliffs where they overlook Sevier Valley, and as the Pink Cliffs where included in Bryce Canyon National Park. Bristly ponderosa pines complete the perfect scene.

Emerging from Red Canyon after a few miles, the highway enters a broad upland known variously as Panguitch Hayfield, Emery Valley and John's Valley. Unpaved sideroads lead north and south into little-visited parts of Dixie National Forest. At 14 m. is **BRYCE JUNCTION,** a center of motels, stores, service stations and Bryce Canyon Airport (7,600 alt.).

Turn south to **Ruby's Inn Lodge and Resort** (1 m.), a tourist complex offering lodging, meals, supplies, fuel; also, in season, horseback rides, lectures, scenic flights. Almost immediately thereafter the road enters **BRYCE CANYON NATIONAL PARK** *(see parks chapter).*

Turn north on State 22 through the broad valley of Sevier River's East Fork to **Widtsoe, Antimony** and **Otter Creek Lake State Beach** *(see also Tour No. 7).* This partly paved, improved road offers far-reaching vistas of southern Utah's plateau country, displaying an exotic blend of openness and gentle contours, contrasted startlingly with massive bulk, precipitous cliffs, yawning canyons, and delightful combinations of color. Contradictions in alpine form loom high on either side.

At 11 m. from Bryce Junction, an unpaved road climbs east to **Pine Lake** in Dixie National Forest, a popular recreation area; forest campground nearby. Rough road continues about 4 m. to the upper levels of **Table Cliff Plateau** (10,300 alt.), an extension of the Aquarius. A short trail leads from road's end to **Powell's Pink Point** at the plateau's southern tip, where a sweeping panorama unfolds—a view extending on a clear day into surrounding states. Of this noble promontory, so visible against the eastern skyline from Bryce Canyon, Clarence E. Dutton wrote in his *Geology of the High Plateaus of Utah* (1880):

. . . it presents the aspect of a vast Acropolis crowned with a Parthenon. It is hard to dispel the fancy that this is a work of some intelligence and design akin to that of humanity, but far grander. Such glorious tints, such keen contrasts of light and shade, such profusion of sculptured forms, can never be forgotten by him who has once beheld it. This is one of the grand panoramas of the Plateau Country . . . to the mind which has grown into sympathy with such scenes it conveys a sense of power and grandeur and a fullness of meaning which lay hold of the sensibilities more forcibly than tropical verdure or snow-clad Alps or Arcadian valleys.

Pink Cliffs sculpture in Red Canyon *(left)*, Pine Lake and Table Cliff Plateau *(right)*.

A few miles south of Antimony the valley of East Fork pinches into narrows known as **Black Canyon,** cut through ancient lava, stark and forbidding, a reminder that so much of the plateau country—despite the prismatic colors of its sedimentary rocks—has seen immense outpourings from volcanic vents.

WIDTSOE (7,600 alt.) marks the junction of an unpaved road leading east through Dixie National Forest, climbing over a 9,000-foot pass and joining State 12 near Escalante. Until the early 1950s or so this was the main route between Bryce Canyon and Escalante. Widtsoe today is no more than a small collection of ramshackle buildings and foundations, but 50 and 60 years ago it was a modest community built on dry-farm agriculture. Its origins as a town date from 1910, and the town existed until the mid-1930s, growing in that period to more than 1,000 in 1920, then declining to only a few families in 1935.

State 12 continues eastward from Bryce Junction, dropping from the plateau at 7,600 feet into **Bryce (Paria) Valley** more than a thousand feet lower. Enroute it passes through outriggers of the park's colorful rock formations. In Bryce Valley are the attractive communities of Tropic, Cannonville and Henrieville, as well as memories of several other settlements now defunct. **TROPIC** (6,300 alt. 338 pop.), largest and youngest of the valley's towns, is nestled beneath the pink cliffs of Bryce. It was settled in 1891, during construction of Tropic Reservoir and canal. Residents are farmers and stockraisers; lumbering and coal mining also offer employment, as do the park and the tourist industry. **CANNONVILLE** (6,000 alt., 134 pop.), settled in 1876, was named for early Mormon leader George Q. Cannon; a sister community nearby, Georgetown (abandoned many years ago), also was named in honor of this prominent man. Cannonville was locally known as Gunshot, the settlers maintaining that it was not large enough to be called a cannon.

HENRIEVILLE (6,000 alt. 167 pop.) is a farming community in a small valley, strung along the highway like a necklace. For some years, beginning in the 1930s, scientists made this town a base for expeditions into the Kaiparowits Plateau. At that time it was necessary to explore the remote plateau with pack animals, over a period of several weeks *(see page 342 of the 1941 edition);* since then much of the region has been opened up with a network of roads, though hiking and riding still are required for close-up viewing. Henrieville's people, as those of Tropic and Cannonville, engage in livestock raising, the growing of hay, grain, corn and fruit. The town was settled during the 1870s and named for James Henrie of Panguitch.

South from Cannonville a road *(unpaved for the most part)* leads to **Kodachrome Basin State Reserve, Grosvenor Arch** and **Cottonwood Canyon,** joining US 89 about 47 m. east of Kanab *(see Tour No. 9B).* From this maintained route other unpaved roads give access to **Bull Valley Gorge** and other remarkable points in the rugged **Paria River Valley,** as well as to canyons and broken slopes of the **Kaiparowits Plateau.** During the early 1970s, when the Kaiparowits power project was being considered, study was devoted to improving much of this road, and extending it as a main access between the power development, Glen Canyon City, and northern Utah. The route was first improved for passenger vehicles in 1957, local citizens bearing the cost in an attempt to influence the state to see its advantages as a major highway between northern Utah and the Glen Canyon damsite *(see Tour No. 9B).*

KODACHROME BASIN STATE RESERVE, 8 m. from Cannonville, was established to preserve an area of unique geological phenomena, erosional forms and color combinations. Its most unusual features are a group of upright, cylindrical spires or "chimneys," of different color and material than the rock from which they project. Their origin is uncertain; one explanation is that they were geyser plugs— tubes filled with more resistant material than the encasing rock, remaining behind when the surrounding matrix eroded away. However formed, they are distinctive geological features; but they represent only a part of the basin's weird erosional forms and picturesque cliffs, all painted in a spectrum of soft and vivid colors. In 1979 an impressive natural arch was discovered by park superintendent Tom Shakespeare, about 2 m. east of the park. A contest the following year named the arch for its discoverer. Rangers reside at the park. Improved campground: water, tables, restrooms.

This area was described and pictured by the *National Geographic Magazine* in its issue of September 1949 ("Motoring into Escalante Land" by Jack Breed), which applied the name Kodachrome Flat to the area formerly known locally as Thorny Pasture. The National Geographic Society's expedition also applied the name Grosvenor—in honor of the society's president, Dr. Gilbert Grosvenor—to a superb double arch "discovered" by the expedition in the same general area. Kodachrome Basin, Grosvenor Arch, the Paria basin, old Paria, Bull Valley Gorge, Kaiparowits Plateau, Crossing of the Fathers and other interesting points are pictured and described in this article, which remains more than 30 years later the definitive illustrated travelog on the region.

Grosvenor Arch is sculptured from a cream-colored cliff, standing as a superb buttress. In design and the beauty of its pastel coloring, the arch is one of Utah's most delightful works of natural artistry. Secluded in a small cove, the great arch lies about a mile from the main sideroad, about 10 miles east of the Kodachrome Basin

Strange rock forms are found in Kodachrome Basin *(left)* and in Cottonwood Canyon *(right)*, a few miles to the south.

turnoff. Stylistically and esthetically it is in a class by itself. The top of the arch is 152 feet above the ground and 99 feet in width. For a number of years Grosvenor Arch was included as part of the Kodachrome Basin State Reserve.

A mile south of the Grosvenor Arch turnoff, just east of the main road, is a grouping of large alabaster stones known as **Gilgal.** Superficially a Stonehenge in miniature, the stones are arranged systematically and purposefully in two concentric circles of 12 stones each, one within the other, with a center stone or "altar table" in the exact center. Stones of the outer ring symbolize the 12 Tribes of Israel; those of the inner ring symbolize the 12 Apostles. Mathematical distances and placement of the stones are precise, according to Biblical numerology, and are symbolic of the second coming of Christ. The monument was created in 1978 under the supervision of Dallas J. Anderson, a professor of art at Brigham Young University, who was its originator.

South of the Gilgal turnoff the road descends into **COTTONWOOD CANYON,** a highly scenic gorge which it follows for the next 15 miles or so. Cottonwood Canyon, the route of Cottonwood Creek, parallels the axis of the **East Kaibab Monocline** (Cockscomb), a major flexure or fold in the earth's crust *(see Tour No. 9B);* in fact, the canyon is formed between the broken, tilted edges of rock layers that were uplifted along the great fold. Rock forms, designs and colors are outstandingly scenic, making this one of southern Utah's choicest vehicle drives. Cottonwood Creek empties into Paria River near the lower end of **Shurtz Gorge,** a deep and narrow chasm where Paria River cuts through the monocline; from that point the road parallels the river for most of the remaining distance to US 89, which it meets some 47 m. from Cannonville and about the same distance east of Kanab.

State 12 continues from Cannonville to Henrieville through picturesque Bryce (Paria) Valley. East of Henrieville it enters the canyon of Henrieville Creek, ascending rather gently to a summit (about 7,400 feet) marking the divide between Paria and Escalante drainage. Along the way there are breathtaking views of **Table Cliff Plateau** and the weird badland "breaks" known as **The Blues,** that fan out from beneath its upper ramparts. Beyond the drainage divide, which also marks the general separation between Aquarius and Kaiparowits plateaus, State 12 descends Upper Valley. Here in the headwaters of Escalante River, the terrain opens up, expanding at Escalante town into the desert vastness of the Escalante River Basin.

7 m. west of Escalante, a cluster of petroleum tanks marks the turnoff of an unpaved road leading south into **Upper Valley Oil Field,** a moderate oil producer.

BUREAU OF RECLAMATION (W. L. RUSHO)

Grosvenor Arch, near Kodachrome Basin and Cottonwood Canyon.

The road continues south through the broken **Kaiparowits Plateau,** skirting the eastern slopes of **Canaan Peak** (9,196 alt.) and threading the upper ends of deep canyons. Branches of the increasingly rough road lead to Grosvenor Arch and Cannonville; Collett Canyon; Glen Canyon City and US 89 *(see Tour No. 9B);* and other parts of the corrugated highland. *Detailed maps and prior consultation with knowledgeable authorities are wise precautions before attempting these roads; an area office of U. S. Bureau of Land Management is located in Escalante.*

5 m. west of Escalante, two roads lead northward from the highway: one follows **Birch Creek,** then passes across the summit of Escalante Mountains to Widtsoe *(see);* the other leads to **Barker Reservoir** (public campground), in Dixie National Forest.

2 m. west of Escalante, turn north a short distance to **ESCALANTE PETRI-FIED FOREST STATE RESERVE,** a thousand-acre preserve displaying the fossilized remnants of ancient trees. This is one of Utah's most accessible and impressive natural exhibits of petrified wood, in a setting of multicolored Chinle (Sleeping Rainbow) rocks. Beside **Wide Hollow Reservoir** is a public campground *(restrooms, water, fishing, boating).*

ESCALANTE (5,300 alt. 652 pop.), 47 m. from Bryce Junction, 61 m. from US 89. No longer the "horse town" described on page 340 of the first edition, where "people ride on horseback from one part of town to another, and newsboys deliver papers on horseback," Escalante does retain an aura of frontier isolation and old-fashioned rusticity—though these attributes are not as apparent as they were only a few years ago. The town was settled in 1875 by Mormon pioneers and called Potato Valley for a species of wild potato. It was named after the river, which in turn was named by one of the Powell expeditions in honor of Francisco Silvestre Velez de Escalante, Spanish Catholic priest, who explored portions of Utah in 1776 but came no nearer this spot than 65 miles or so.

Until recent decades Escalante was very isolated by poor roads and its people relied primarily on farming, stockraising and lumbering for economic support. These activities remain important, but highway travel, tourism, modest oil production, and government employment have diversified the economic base. The region contains immense quantities of bituminous coal, and plans have been announced for a large coal-fired power plant; also there is promise of increased petroleum production. But because of Escalante's location near Glen Canyon National Recreation Area and the Escalante and Kaiparowits wildlands, development proposals that might have an adverse effect on the pristine environment have met resistance from powerful conservation groups and many individuals; these in turn have been verbally assailed by local people.

Escalante displays numerous structures of early vintage, some dating from the 1880s and 1890s, or even the late 1870s. Their antiquity is not always apparent, as adobe or log construction may have been camouflaged with plaster or wood. Many of the town's red brick homes were built before the turn of the century. Sidestreet driving rewards the effort with architectural discovery.

Turn south from Escalante on an unpaved road into **Alvey Wash,** a deep canyon, the road eventually climbing to high benches and ridges of the Kaiparowits Plateau at 6,000 and 7,000 feet. In every direction from the road are arroyos and deepening canyons, which become tremendous steep-walled gorges as the road continues south toward the Glen Canyon breaks. Sideroads exit through the forks of Collett Canyon to the east, and lead off to the left and right; the main road meanders south over Smoky Mountain, offering overviews of the Lake Powell country, then descending into Warm Creek Canyon and finally exiting at Glen Canyon City on US 89 *(see Tour 9B). Obtain maps and road information from BLM area offices in Escalante or Kanab.*

Turn north from Escalante into Dixie National Forest and the canyon of Pine Creek, paralleling the tilted, eroded flanks of the **Escalante Anticline,** through which the Escalante River has carved a narrow channel. This river canyon is popular for scenic hiking. The main road *(unpaved and rough in spots but maintained; closed in winter)* continues north across a 10,000-foot terrace of the **Aquarius Plateau** to Bicknell and Loa *(see Tour No. 7B).* At 15 m. is **Posey Lake,** a popular fishing and camping spot surrounded by forested mountain slopes; public camping units. At 14 miles (one mile east of Posey Lake) a sideroad leads east to Hells Backbone and Boulder. This also is an unpaved forest road, closed in winter, steep in places, perhaps rutted and corrugated in places, but generally suitable for passenger cars. As described on page 340 of the book's first edition, **Hells Backbone** "is a knife-edged ridge with a bridge on top spanning a streamless crevice no wider than the bridge itself. On both sides are precipitous walls that drop hundreds of feet, with Death Hollow on one side and Sand Creek Canyon on the other. For years the residents of Boulder carried mail and packed provisions along this ridge.'' To this should be added mention of the remarkable erosional artistry and delicate coloring of the canyon walls, contrasting with the massive, evergreen-clad slopes of the plateau. Hardy hikers may traverse **Death Hollow** downstream to the Escalante River (22 m.), then upstream to Escalante (8 m.) or downstream to State 12 (7 m.). This is a strenuous adventure, passing through deep pools and forbidding narrows, requiring ropes or swimming in places. *Obtain details from BLM office, Escalante.*

State 12 east of Escalante passes across undulating flats that afford exciting views south and east across the Escalante River Basin. The basin's entrenched canyons are not visible, but the grand dome of **Navajo Mountain** can be seen through the haze, 70 miles or so to the south, at the far end of the majestic east face of **Kaiparowits Plateau.** This 2,000 to 3,500-foot rampart, its front almost unbroken, is known as Fifty-Mile Mountain or the Straight Cliffs; also as the Escalante Rim. Though only 50 miles long between Escalante and the plateau's southeastern point opposite Navajo Mountain, the giant palisade actually extends perhaps twice that distance around the plateau's southern front, where it is much more incised and sinuous.

5 m. east of Escalante, an unpaved but maintained road forks south to **Hole-in-the-Rock,** the **Escalante Canyons** (Glen Canyon National Recreation Area), **Devils Rock Garden, Collett Canyon,** and other points. *It is recommended that maps and information be obtained from offices of BLM and Glen Canyon National Recreation Area, in Escalante or elsewhere. Hikers in particular should obtain advance information.*

Escalante River labyrinth from the air, looking northwest toward the Aquarius Plateau. Stevens Arch appears as a lighted keyhole in the large foreground shadow.

BUREAU OF RECLAMATION (MEL DAVIS)

The road parallels the **Straight Cliffs** of Kaiparowits, which loom overhead for almost the entire distance. Not apparent is the true ruggedness of the sunken canyon system to the east; an overview or entry into the canyons are necessary for this. But the landscape is intriguing. This is the general route of the Hole-in-the-Rock pioneers of 1879 *(see below)*.

At 9 m. a road leads eastward to **Harris Wash,** giving trail access to Escalante River Canyon, George Hobbs Historical Site, Baker Bench petroglyphs, Silver Falls Canyon, and an intricate network of Escalante side canyons.

At 12 m. or so, just off the road to the west, is **Devils Rock Garden,** a compact but remarkable area of exotic rock erosion, including Metate Arch and a group of picturesque standing rocks. A short distance beyond, a dirt road leads west into **Collett Canyon** and the interior of Kaiparowits Plateau.

At 34 m. a water tank marks a trailhead; from here a trail leads down **Hurricane Wash** into **Coyote Gulch,** a spectacular gorge emptying into **Escalante River Canyon.** In Coyote Gulch are located **Jacob Hamblin Arch** and **Coyote Bridge,** two of the area's most impressive natural rock spans. At the gulch's mouth, atop the Escalante's rim, is **Stevens Arch**—perched hundreds of feet above the canyon floor.

West from here a rough dirt road climbs part way up the face of the Straight Cliffs and winds southward for about 13 miles, providing enroute some bird's-eye views over the unbelievably rugged country to the east and south. A branch of this road descends to the main road eight miles south of Hurricane Wash, providing a circular loop.

In 1963, at **Carcass Wash,** 45 m. south of Escalante, occurred a modern-day tragedy. A group of Boy Scouts from northern Utah, accompanied by adults, were enroute to Hole-in-the-Rock in an open truck. As the driver tried to shift gears on a grade, the brakes failed. The truck rolled backward for more than 100 feet, then dropped over a high bank. Of the group, 13 were killed and twice that number injured.

South from Hurricane Wash for 15 miles or so, trails from the main road give access to gorges of the lower Escalante system, a bewildering labyrinth of deep, narrow chasms offering challenges for every degree of hiking and climbing expertise. Most of the canyon area is a part of **Glen Canyon National Recreation Area** *(see).* There are numerous natural arches in this area, including Broken Bow, LaGorce, Bement, and Nemo arches. The latter is a reminder of Everett Ruess, a romantic young wanderer-poet from California who vanished in this region in the 1930s. Though his pack animal was found, and the inscribed word "Nemo," Everett had disappeared without further trace. Many local people attributed his disappearance to foul play.

At about 37 m. **Dance Hall Rock** appears nearby toward the east. A spacious amphitheater carved out of smooth sandstone, it served the Hole-in-the-Rock pioneers of a century ago as an ideal dance floor.

HOLE-IN-THE-ROCK, 52 m. from State 12, one of Utah's most historic and scenically noteworthy natural sites, is a slot or break in the wall of Glen Canyon, through which Mormon pioneers in 1879 and 1880 lowered their wagons to the river far below, then ferried them across to an even more forbidding country beyond. Even on foot, today, it is a strenuous endeavor to negotiate the narrow, precipitous passageway; and the lower reaches of the "hole" are now beneath Lake Powell.

The epic crossing through Hole-in-the-Rock was but an episode in a journey that holds an honored place in the annals of the early west. Only an outline can be given in this book, and most of this appears in Tour No. 11. Suffice to say here that, in 1879, 230 members of the Mormon Church from southwestern Utah were "called" to colonize the southeastern corner of the state. An advance party had been to that

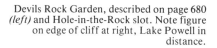

Devils Rock Garden, described on page 680
(left) and Hole-in-the-Rock slot. Note figure
on edge of cliff at right, Lake Powell in
distance.

UTAH TRAVEL COUNCIL

region by a circuitous route but knew next to nothing about the wild country along
the more direct route chosen for the main trek. The journey began in November 1879
with more than 80 wagons and a thousand head of cattle. The colonists had already
passed through the new settlement of Escalante and were encamped on the desert
near Dance Hall Rock when their fearful predicament became apparent: they were
blocked ahead by the sheer wall of Glen Canyon, and they could not retreat to the
settlements of central Utah because of mountain snow. They chose to go on. Their
full story is told in David E. Miller's book *Hole-in-the-Rock*. The following
summary is paraphrased or quoted from Miller's account:

The road to Escalante was over a well established route. South of Escalante
the route dropped into the desert and proceeded to Forty Miles Spring, which was
known by Mormon cattlemen. Expedition headquarters was established here for
more than three weeks, the water supply being the best between Escalante and the
river. Here was the assembly point for wagons gathering from various points in
southwestern Utah. "Forty Miles Spring and camp," wrote Miller, "were located
a short distance down the wash from Dance Hall Rock. This huge sandstone
formation was so constructed as to constitute a large amphitheater with a relatively smooth floor. Pioneers of the Forty Miles camp held dances at the 'Hall'
and thus gave it its name." Most members indulged enthusiastically in song and
dance, and religious services were an important part of camp life.

At Fifty Miles Spring it was decided that the company should be divided
until a road could be completed through the Hole and out of the river gorge to the
east. Half of the wagons and people settled down at Fifty Miles Spring while the
remainder moved to the rim in the vicinity of Hole-in-the-Rock. Below the Hole
the sandstone sloped at a 45-degree angle. Here the workers blasted, chiseled, and
picked out a narrow dugway on a grade that would not be too steep for wagons.
Because the natural slot was too narrow for a wagon, an artificial platform to
accommodate one set of wheels was built by driving wooden pegs into holes in the
cliff, then piling brush and rock on the pegs. Cuts were made in places to provide
footholds. Finally, in Miller's words, wagons were prepared "by rough-locking
the hind wheels. In addition to this, long ropes and chains were attached to the

rear axle or some other part of the running gears so that a dozen or more men could hang on behind the wagon to help slow it down.'' Wagons were driven with horses or oxen hitched to the front, a driver on the seat, and as many people holding from the rear as could find footing. Women and children made the passage on foot, even walking becoming difficult after a time. This episode was vividly described by Hoffman Birney in *Zealots of Zion,* as quoted in the 1941 edition:

> After two weeks of hard work on the trail, an effort was made to move some of the horses down from the plateau to a bench above the Colorado. . . . The majority of the animals made the treacherous descent without mishap, but nine horses were unable to keep their footing on the glassy rocks. They slipped, slid over the smooth slope to the rim of the cliffs, and crashed down to death. After considerable more work the first wagon began the descent through the Hole-in-the-Rock. The wheels were locked and men, hanging back on long rope, checked its speed until it had been guided around the turn below the cleft and headed for the dugways. . . . The wagon struck the built trail, bounced over the rocky barrier, gained momentum on the steep grade, and reached the bottom riding on the crest of a miniature landslide of its own making. By the time the last of the eighty-odd vehicles had made the descent, the roadway was as bare of loose rock as it had been before the work began.

By January 26, 1880, all the wagons had been driven down to the river and ferried across on a boat built and designed by Charles Hall. The cattle and horses were made to swim across. But many more miles remained before the indomitable pioneers reached the San Juan, as described in Tour No. 11.

State 12 continues east and north, descending steep curves to the **Escalante River,** a modest stream which flows between magnificent walls to Lake Powell, about 70 sinuous miles to the southeast. From the bridge a foot trail leads upstream to **Escalante Natural Bridge** (2 m.), a picturesque arch cut from the south wall. The trail continues upstream to a northside tributary known as **Death Hollow** (7 m. from the bridge), an extremely deep and narrow gorge extending northward from the river for more than 20 miles to the Hells Backbone road (see above). Death Hollow offers special hiking rewards; check with BLM office for details. Hikers also have a choice of routes through wild canyons downstream from the bridge.

CALF CREEK RECREATION AREA (BLM), a mile north of the river bridge via State 12, is in an oasis setting beside the clear water of little **Calf Creek.** Colored cliffs loom overhead. *Tables, firepits, drinking water, toilets, playground.* Upstream (north) from the campground, a sandy foot trail leads along the canyon floor to **Lower Calf Creek Falls** (2¾ m.), formed by a 126-foot dropoff in the streambed. Native vegetation along the trail is intriguing *(a trail guide is available from BLM);* also to be seen are ruins of small Indian structures and examples of Indian rock art; a pioneer fence; miniature natural arch; etc. **Upper Calf Creek Falls,** 5½ m. upstream from the parking area, can only be reached by a hike over slickrock from State 12 *(inquire locally).*

State 12 climbs out of Calf Creek Canyon in a series of steep curves, "topping out" on a razorback ridge between profound canyons on either side. The full circle view is literally breathtaking, and in fact some people—especially the drivers—prefer to keep their eyes on the road. Painted mostly in delicate shades of white, buff and cream, the truly stunning panorama encompasses a chaotic expanse of bare rock, which has been molded into the soft contours characteristic of Navajo sandstone. The landscape for miles around is formed of this marvelous rock, so very lovely to look at. No sharp angles here: this is an exquisite display of roundness—of curves, arcs and sweeps, bowls, mounds, basins, and arching slopes.

This special beauty of soft, curving contours and gentle colors continues to Boulder and beyond. Three miles west of town is the junction with the mountain road to Escalante via **Hells Backbone** *(see above).*

BOULDER (6,000 alt. 113 pop.), 29 m. from Escalante, is nestled serenely on a sloping shoulder of the Aquarius in an idyllic setting. The community is less a town in the usual sense than a loose grouping of farms and houses. Pride is evident. Fields and buildings blend in harmony with the valley's delightful erosional forms—round dome-buttes and curving, swirling rock faces, their whiteness an ideal complement to the green vegetation and blue sky.

Boulder was settled in 1894 and named for the dark volcanic boulders that litter the slopes of lava-capped Boulder Mountain (Aquarius Plateau). The first edition (page 340) described an interesting segment of its history:

> For years after settlement the tiny town was isolated from the world by towering walls of solid rock, 35 miles by pack train from Escalante. A man packed in a pick-up truck, in pieces, reassembled it, and ran it eight years without a license; gasoline, also "imported" on pack horses cost seventy-five cents a gallon. In 1923, President Harding set aside 130 acres of public domain for a townsite, but a survey was neglected, and for nearly ten years the residents were legally squatters," immune from taxation.

Visitor facilities include several modest motels, gasoline, groceries and limited supplies. Also in Boulder is a popular visitor attraction:

ANASAZI INDIAN VILLAGE STATE HISTORICAL MONUMENT, an attractive visitor center-museum and the reconstruction of a prehistoric Indian dwelling. It occupies the site of what once was a large frontier community of Anasazi (pueblo) Indians, who probably migrated to the area from northeastern Arizona

Visitor Center-Museum, Anasazi Indian Village State Historical Monument.

about 1050 A.D. and remained for about 150 years. A relative abundance of water and game, and a fairly benign climate, made this a favored location; but the village seems to have been abandoned about the same time as most other Anasazi and Fremont communities throughout the Four Corners region. (The contemporary Fremont culture, which bore resemblance to the Anasazi but was distinct in many ways, flourished 30 miles to the north along the Fremont River. *See Tour No. 7B.)*

Built in 1970, the visitor center-museum contains historical and cultural displays; information and publications; restrooms. Most of the former village, excavated in 1958-59 by the University of Utah and reburied for protection, is not visible. In 1978 a reconstruction of a typical Anasazi dwelling was built near the museum.

NORTH OF BOULDER

Paved State 12 ends at Boulder (1981). Grading and surfacing have been underway for several years on the road between Boulder and Grover/ Torrey/State 24 to the north, but it is likely that this route will remain closed during winter months for some time to come. The **Boulder-Grover road** crosses the eastern shoulder of **Aquarius Plateau (Boulder Mountain),** reaching 9,200 feet altitude and affording soul-stirring views across a corrugated, rainbow-hued landscape that has few equals for rugged grandeur.

The road's immediate environment is a delight—a landscape *(Dixie National Forest)* of evergreens and aspen, with expansive meadows and picturesque groves, gurgling streams, and the blue of **Lower Bown's Reservoir** serving as orientation. Above all looms the brow of the Aquarius, a dark volcanic rampart surrounding the 11,000-foot table known as **Boulder Top**—an alpine region of numerous small lakes and one of America's highest evergreen forests. Along the road are three excellent public campgrounds: Oak Creek, Pleasant Creek and Singletree, each featuring tables, firepits, toilets, drinking water. Primitive facilities are found at Lower Bown's Reservoir, a popular fishing spot. Rough sideroads approach **Boulder Top,** the plateau's table summit, from this side; they may not be passable at times. Foot trails also lead to the top. *See Tour No. 7B.*

No writer has described the Aquarius and its views better than Captain Clarence E. Dutton, geologist-explorer of the Powell Survey, who wrote in the classic *Report on the Geology of the High Plateaus of Utah (1880):*

> The Aquarius should be described in blank verse and illustrated upon canvas. The explorer who sits upon the brink of its parapet looking off into the southern and eastern haze, who skirts its lava-cap or clambers up and down its vast ravines, who builds his camp-fire by the borders of its snow-fed lakes or stretches himself beneath its giant pines and spruces, forgets that he is a geologist and feels himself a poet . . . we are among forests of rare beauty and luxuriance; the air is moist and cool, the grasses are green and rank, and hosts of flowers deck the turf like the hues of a Persian carpet. The forest opens in wide parks and winding avenues, which the fancy can easily people with fays and woodland nymphs. . . Upon the broad summit are numerous lakes—not the little morainal pools, but broad sheets of water a mile or two in length. Their basins were formed by glaciers, and since the ice-cap which once covered the whole plateau has disappeared they continue to fill with water from the melting snows.
>
> . . . The plateau is simply a remnant left by the erosion of the country around its southern and eastern flanks . . . We may gain some notion of the stupendous work which has accomplished this result by taking our position upon the southeastern salient at the verge of the upper platform.

It is a sublime panorama. The heart of the inner Plateau Country is spread out before us in a bird's-eye view. It is a maze of cliffs and terraces lined off with stratification, of crumbling buttes, red and white domes, rock platforms gashed with profound canyons, burning plains barren even of sage—all glowing with bright color and flooded with blazing sunlight. Everything visible tells of ruin and decay. It is the extreme of desolation, the blankest solitude, a superlative desert . . . The view to the south and southeast is dismal and suggestive of the terrible. It is almost unique even in the category of plateau scenery . . . The rocks are swept bare of soil and show the naked edges of the strata. Nature has here made a geological map of the country and colored it so that we may read and copy it miles away . . . Far to the southeastward, upon the horizon, rises a gigantic dome of wonderfully symmetric and simple form. It is the Navajo Mountain.

EAST OF BOULDER

An unpaved but well graded road from Boulder gives access to the **Circle Cliffs, Burr Trail** and lower **Waterpocket Fold (Capitol Reef National Park), Henry Mountains,** and **Bullfrog Marina-Resort (Lake Powell).** Extremely scenic, this road is passable most of the year by ordinary cars, but it is dusty and may be rough in spots; the cramped and very steep switchback turns of **Burr Trail** make it impractical for large motorhomes or vehicles towing large trailers or large boats.

The road enters **Circle Cliffs** through picturesque Navajo buttes and mesas, eventually passing into a deep, narrow chasm known as **Long Canyon,** which extends for about seven miles through a highland of red Wingate sandstone. Through this same cliff-forming sandstone, which forms a rim around the Circle Cliffs amphitheater, other canyons of the Escalante River and Halls Creek systems have been gouged out by nature; they are popular for hiking and backpacking.

In the interior of the amphitheater, sideroads lead to abandoned uranium workings, scenic points, grazing lands, and rainbow-hued Chinle slopes where petrified wood was abundant in former years, often in the form of giant logs. This popular fossil may still be collected *(government regulations apply; inquire at BLM offices),* but most of the gem quality material and larger pieces have been taken. At the **Wolverine Petrified Wood Area,** a fence protects some choice specimens from collecting

Burr Trail (35 m. from Boulder) is a break or notch in the steep face of Waterpocket Fold. The road descends in tight switchbacks *(too angular for large vehicles or long multiple-vehicle combinations),* dropping about 800 feet in little more than a mile. From the heights west of the trail, views are truly breathtaking, encompassing a brilliant multicolored landscape of cliffs and canyons, buttes, mesas, plateaus and mountain peaks, crustal deformations, and an assortment of erosional forms that defy description. Extending north and south from the area at the top of the trail are **Upper** and **Lower Muley Twist Canyons,** exceptionally scenic gorges that are popular for jeeping and hiking *(see Capitol Reef National Park).*

From the bottom (east end) of the Burr Trail, the main **Waterpocket Fold road** extends north along the Fold to State 24, south to park over-looks, the Henry Mountains, and Bullfrog Resort-Marina (Lake Powell). In either direction the road is suitable for passenger cars but may be rough in spots and should be avoided in wet weather.

Escalante-Boulder canyons *(right)* from
State 12, looking southwest toward the
Kaiparowits Plateau.

WARD ROYLANCE PHOTOS

Left. Looking east toward the Henry Mountains
and head of Burr Trail from the interior of the
Circle Cliffs.

Below left. Switchbacks of the Burr Trail.

Below, right. View east from the Boulder-
Grover road across Aquarius Plateau (Boulder
Mountain).

Tour No. 10
CASTLE COUNTRY
(Carbon and Emery counties)

This tour region is one of great topographic contrast, extending from Utah Valley (the Great Basin) on the west to Castle Valley and Green River on the east (Canyonlands), with lofty plateaus between. It includes Utah's coal country and a cultural amalgam of diverse nationality backgrounds.

Tour No. 10A - US Highway 6 from Utah Valley to Price

Between the mouth of Spanish Fork Canyon at Moark Junction, on the southeastern curve of Utah Valley, and Price some 65 miles away, US 6 passes through one of the longest sustained stretches of canyon and mountain terrain traversed by any highway in Utah. No longer, however, are travelers beset by steep grades, sharp curves and the narrow roadbed that frustrated drivers of yesterday. Today's highway is designed for speed and ease of driving.

Spanish Fork Canyon in its lower reaches was the route of the Spanish Dominguez-Escalante exploring party of 1776; hence its name. The canyon extends from Utah Valley to rolling plateau summits of the Soldier Summit-Colton area, a distance of some 30 miles. It is a scenic defile, providing ever-changing vistas of natural beauty. Historically the canyon has uncounted tales to tell. It has been a key route of travel for more than a hundred years and has harbored a number of communities during those years. The majority of these were transitory, related to the railroad, and little remains to tell that they ever existed.

About 4 m. east of Moark Junction, a pond of water on the north side of the highway marks the site of **Castilla Hot Springs,** for nearly 50 years (between the 1880s and 1930s) a very popular resort. Here was a large indoor pool of warm mineral water as well as private baths (the water was considered therapeutic), lawns and groves, a game field, dance pavilion, restaurant, and hotel. Special excursion trains brought happy crowds from Utah Valley. A decline began in the 1930s and the hotel was gutted by fire in the 1940s. Holding a financial interest for some years was Cyrus E. Dallin, noted sculptor.

One mile east of Castilla, turn north into the canyon of **Diamond Fork,** an important tributary of Spanish Fork. Unpaved roads give access to forest campgrounds and popular fishing waters, one branch leading to Springville via the forks of Hobble Creek Canyon, another fork leading to Strawberry Reservoir. The Diamond Fork of today carries more water than in pioneer years, having been made a unit in the diversion of water from Strawberry Reservoir (Uinta Basin drainage) across a divide via Strawberry Tunnel into Diamond Fork drainage (Utah Lake). Diamond Fork Canyon was on the route of travel followed by the Dominguez-Escalante party of 1776 *(see History),* and thereafter by trappers, explorers and settlers.

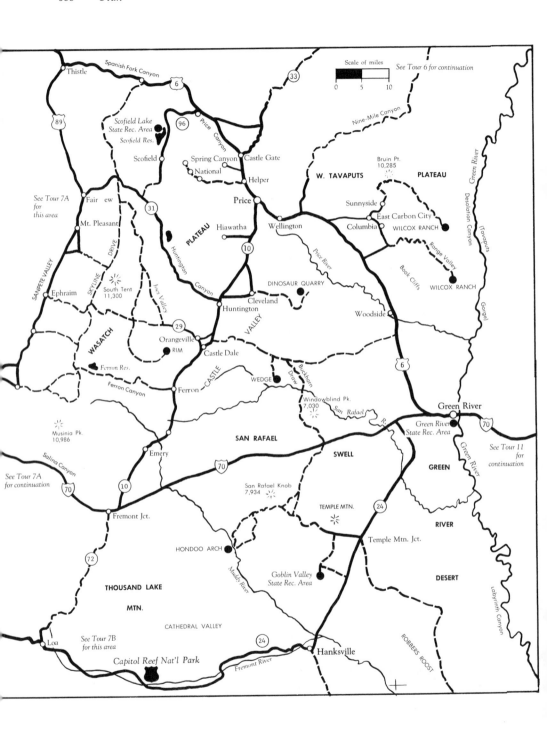

Scale of miles

See Tour 6 for continuation

0   5   10

Thistle

Spanish Fork Canyon

6

33

89

Scofield Lake
State Rec. Area
Scofield Res.

96

Price Canyon

Spring Canyon   Castle Gate

Scofield

National   Helper

W. TAVAPUTS   PLATEAU

Bruin Pt.
10,285

Nine-Mile Canyon

Green River

Desolation Canyon

*See Tour 7A
for
this area*

Fairview

31

PLATEAU

Price

Sunnyside

East Carbon City

Columbia   WILCOX RANCH

Mt. Pleasant

Hiawatha   Wellington

SKYLINE DRIVE

SANPETE VALLEY

WASATCH

Ephraim

South Tent
11,300

Ines Valley

Huntington Canyon

10

Range Valley

(Tavaputs)

Gorge)

Book Cliffs

WILCOX RANCH

DINOSAUR QUARRY

Price River

Cleveland

Huntington   VALLEY

Woodside

29

Orangeville

RIM   Castle Dale

CASTLE

6

Ferron Res.

Ferron Canyon

Ferron

WEDGE

Buckhorn Draw

Windowblind Pk.
7,030   San Rafael R.

Green River

Green River
State Rec. Area

70

Musinia Pk.
10,986

Emery

SAN RAFAEL

SWELL

GREEN

*See Tour 11
for
continuation*

Salina Canyon

70

*See Tour 7A
for continuation*

70

10

San Rafael Knob
7,934

TEMPLE MTN.

RIVER

Fremont Jct.

24

Temple Mtn. Jct.

DESERT

72

HONDOO ARCH

Muddy River

Goblin Valley
State Rec. Area

Labyrinth Canyon

THOUSAND LAKE

MTN.

CATHEDRAL VALLEY

24

ROBBERS ROOST

Loa

*See Tour 7B
for this area*

Hanksville

Capitol Reef Nat'l Park

Fremont River

At Thistle Junction, US 89 branches south to Sanpete and Sevier valleys, Kanab and Glen Canyon Dam *(see Tours No. 7A and 9A)*.

THISTLE (5,000 alt.), now but a roadside hamlet of nondescript buildings, gives little hint of having been a bustling community during the era of steam railroading, prior to World War II. Its origins as a ranching site date back more than a hundred years; then, gradually, coincident with the growth of railroading in the 1880s, and 1890s and later, Thistle developed into a key rail junction with roundhouse, water towers, switchyards, maintenance buildings, facilities for lodging and eating, homes, etc. At Thistle was the northern terminus of the railroad serving central Utah to the south, and being on the main line of the east-west D&RGW Railroad, it served as a natural division or turnaround point for helper engines required to assist heavy trains across the mountains to the east. With the advent of the diesel engine and other changes in transportation, Thistle's function as a rail center declined. Most evidences of its railroading heydays were long ago removed.

At 18 m. from Thistle (6 m. west of Soldier Summit), where Clear Creek and Soldier Creek join the main canyon, a roadside park marks the site of a former railroad settlement known as **TUCKER**. Tucker originated during the 1870s and 1880s as a railroad camp serving first a narrow gauge rail system known as the Pleasant Valley Railroad, then later the Denver & Rio Grande Western when it built its new main line through the canyon. In early years Tucker was a booming construction town, and for years thereafter it was a rail station—a point where cattle and sheep were shipped to market. Track realignments and other changes caused eventual abandonment of the station site, leaving nothing in the way of original buildings.

South from the roadside park at Tucker an unpaved road winds up canyons, through verdant forests and across alpine meadows, climbing to heights of 9,000 to nearly 11,000 feet. This is Utah's famed **Skyline Drive** *(see also Tour No. 7A)*, which traverses the heights of Wasatch Plateau for a hundred miles or so, from Tucker on the north to Mayfield on the south. Considering sustained elevation combined with great length, Skyline Drive may well lead the nation in its road class. Scenic views are superb. The drive's full length can be driven for only a few months during late summer and fall; however, a number of east-west transmountain roads between Sanpete and Castle valleys provide easy access and egress at various points, enabling the drive to be traversed in segments. Portions of the drive are popular for winter snowmobiling.

SOLDIER SUMMIT (7,440 alt.), a motley cluster of roadside businesses, marks the highest point on US 6 in Utah, and also the highest mainline railroad pass in the state. It received its name from the fact that several soldiers were buried there; who the soldiers were or when they died is not certain, although it seems probable that they were members of a military party enroute from Utah to the east at the beginning of the Civil War.

Despite its unimpressive appearance today, Soldier Summit at one time was an important railroad center with several hundred year-round residents, a roundhouse, train yards, shops, hotel, stores, schoolhouse and other facilities. At the height of population, during the 1920s, it was a railroad division point, servicing transmountain trains with helper engines. The town's decline began in 1930, leaving little to tell of its railroading past.

Streams flowing westward from this area drain into the Great Basin, those flowing east into the Green and Colorado rivers.

Colton Junction (7,200 alt.) lies in a broad summit valley in the headwaters area of Price River. Technically the area is a zone of transition between the Wasatch Plateau, rolling away to the south, and the Roan or Tavaputs Plateau stretching off toward Colorado on the east; the distinction, however, is not apparent to the eye. This grand highland, formed of somber-hued Cretaceous rocks, contains Utah's richest, most accessible, and most heavily utilized coal deposits. Since the 1870s this coal has been mined and shipped away by the millions of tons. Coal of the Wasatch and Tavaputs was the base on which most cities and towns of Carbon County were founded and flourished; changes in the use of coal were the reason why many of them declined.

COLTON, known first as Pleasant Valley Junction, was born during the 1880s as a railroad camp. Several buildings are all that remain to mark the site of a town that existed for more than 60 years. At one time it contained a depot, roundhouse and turntable, facilities for servicing helper locomotives, bunkhouses, and a full-scale community of several hundred residents. The decline of Colton—like that of Soldier Summit and Thistle—was hastened by the advent of diesel locomotives, which did not require the assistance of helper engines.

Turn south from Colton Junction to Scofield Reservoir (12 m.) and Scofield town (16 m.).

Scofield Reservoir, formed by headwaters of Price River, lies in an alpine bowl known as Pleasant Valley at 7,600 ft. altitude. It is a popular fishing and boating lake, its shores lined with cabins, resorts and campgrounds. **Scofield Lake State Recreation Area** (open May-October) is a developed area with camping, picnicking and boat-launching facilities. The lake is also designated as Carbon County Recreation Area.

SCOFIELD (7,700 alt. 105 pop.), 17 m. from US 6, is an old coal mining community shut in by mountain slopes. Scofield was a near-ghost town several years ago, but with renewed activity in coal mining may once more resemble the bustling town that prospered between its birth in 1879 and the 1920s, when decline began. At one time its population approached 2,000, with a number of large coal mines in the vicinity providing employment. Several thousand other people lived nearby in Clear Creek, Winter Quarters and throughout the valley. John Henry Evans wrote in **The Story of Utah** that "At one of the mines belonging to this company [Pleasant Valley Coal Company] a gang of Chinese was employed [1880]. They used no powder, but only picks and shovels. And the work on the sides and over-head is described as 'The most beautiful one could wish to see.'"

At Winter Quarters, a mile or so from Scofield, was what is reputed to be Utah's first commercial coal mine, opened in 1877; this provided the base for a community that thrived for several decades. It was the site, also, of Utah's worst mine disaster, in 1900. As reported on page 407 of the 1941 edition:

The Daily Tribune of Salt Lake City reports Utah's worst mine disaster:

At Winterquarters mine near Scofield at 10:25 on the morning of May first 1900. From outside the mine a low thud was heard, and experienced miners knew that there had been an explosion. They didn't know . . . that of the 310 men working in the . . . mines . . . only 104 would escape alive. The others were entrapped in a lethal chamber which did an efficient job, leaving 199 dead, no

Winter Quarters as it appeared about 1900.

injured. . . . It is reasonably certain that a dynamite explosion . . . ignited the coal dust in the air, and that like oiled lightning the explosion spread to every part of the mine. . . . The Pleasant Valley Coal Co. had orders for 2,000 tons of coal a day, so the mines were worked day and night. . . . In some places the miners worked in dust ankle deep. . . . The bodies as they were brought out were placed in company buildings, boarding houses, the Mormon Church, the school house, and all available buildings. . . . 105 widows . . . visited the places . . . and there were 270 children whose fathers were laid out. . . . Coffins came to Scofield by the car loads, and as the supply in Utah ran short, some were sent from Denver. At nearly every home caskets could be seen, either on the porch, or through the open door, sometimes one, sometimes several. . . . President McKinley expressed his condolence, and President Loubet of France sent a message of sympathy.

The Scofield Cemetery, a registered historic site, contains the bodies of 149 of the 199 who died—the greatest loss of life, to that time, in the history of coal mining in the United States.

South of Scofield is **CLEAR CREEK,** 5 m., where coal mine workings and a few buildings mark the site of a town that once boasted a population of more than 500. Founded in 1900 as a company town, Clear Creek contained numerous homes, a large hotel, school, churches, mine and business buildings. Its decline began in the 1930s and 1940s with increased mining costs and lessening demand for coal. There has been coal production on a more or less continuing basis to the present time, and plans were announced in recent years for long-term development of several large new mines west of Clear Creek, with potential annual production of five million tons. The general area of Clear Creek also is the site of one of Utah's most productive natural gas fields. A winding mountain road continues from Clear Creek to Huntington Canyon.

East of Colton Junction, US 6 dips and climbs across the **Roan (Tavaputs) Plateau,** following Price River to the head of Price Canyon and thence down that imposing gorge to its mouth in Castle Valley. Six miles from Colton Junction a paved sideroad forks off to the east, connecting US 6 with State 33 at Bamberger Monument *(see Castlegate below).*

PRICE CANYON drops 2,000 feet in about ten miles, serving as an effective divide between Wasatch Plateau to the south and Roan (Tavaputs) Plateau to the east. The canyon has long served, also, as a divide of sorts between different cultural and geographical worlds—between the mountain-valley-basin region of northern and central Utah, which had been undergoing settlement and development since 1847, and Castle Valley of the Canyonlands region, a frontier that did not attract settlers until the 1870s. The canyon has been a forbidding barrier to transportation from beginnings of settlement. Despite its natural disadvantages for travel, Price Canyon has been the route of transport for most of Utah's coal production since the early 1880s, when the D&RGW mainline was completed. During that century, hundreds of millions of tons of coal have passed through the canyon by train and truck, enroute to homes and industries throughout Utah and the Pacific west.

In the canyon's upper reaches a sideroad forks west and south from US 6 to **Price Canyon Recreation Site** (BLM), 4 m., a developed area with picnicking and camping facilities.

The site of **ROYAL (ROLAPP)**, 6,344 alt., formerly a coal mining community of several hundred inhabitants, also marks the location of Castle Rock, one of two prominent battlements on either side of the canyon, together forming **Castle Gate,** a famed landmark until highway construction in the 1960s destroyed some of Castle Rock and the original gate effect.

CASTLEGATE or **CASTLE GATE** (6,150 alt.), named for the castellated formations originally guarding the entrance to the valley, survived floods, explosions and an historic outlaw raid to become what was once an outstanding coal mining camp. Nothing is left of yesterday's bustling town, but coal mining operations in the vicinity are among the largest of their type in Utah, with promise of becoming even larger. Occupying much of the former townsite is a large steam electric plant, which utilizes local coal for generating power. The plant is a unit of Utah Power and Light Company.

As described in the 1941 edition, Castlegate's "red-roofed frame houses seem to remember the turbulent days of the 1890s. They stand a little pathetically against the rising red cliffs, and keep watch down the winding street." On pages 405 and 406 were described several episodes in Castlegate's history. One of those was a daring payroll robbery by Butch Cassidy and his Robbers Roost gang in 1897.

This was Castlegate's only contact with the gang that terrorized the country from Canada to Mexico and from Nebraska to the Pacific Coast, between 1870 and 1904. . . . The worst flood in the history of the county hit Castlegate in 1917. Water poured through the narrow canyon, washing houses and bridges before it, twisting steel rails like pretzels. Debris covered the territory for miles, and for ten days no trains passed through the city. Strangely, only one life was lost.

Early in the morning of March 8, 1924, three terrific explosions shook the town. Accumulated gas and coal dust ignited at the No. 2 mine and took the lives of 173 men. The force of the explosions tossed water pipes like jackstraws, steel rods as large as a man's forearm were blown to bits, and the heavy timbers in the main haulageway were hurled to the opposite side of the canyon, a mile away. Debris, water, fire, and gas hindered the rescue work, and it was nearly ten days before all of the bodies were removed. Every canary bird in Carbon County was brought into service in the rescue work, since the birds die from slight traces of gas, long before man is aware of its presence. In a number of homes every male member of the family was lost. In seven instances, both father and son were killed. Wholesale funerals were held in all churches, and many of the victims are buried in the small cemetery atop the workings in which they met their death.

North from Castlegate, State 33 climbs over the Roan Plateau, then between colored cliffs of **Indian Canyon** to Duchesne (44 m.). The route, which ascends to 9,100 feet and may be closed at times in winter, is notable for its alpine and canyon scenery. About 7 m. from Castlegate, at the junction with cutoff road from the head of Price Canyon *(see above),* is **Bamberger Monument.** Listed on the state historical register, this unusual marker was erected about 1917 by convicts from the state prison who had worked on construction of State 33 in return for reduced sentences and/or other benefits. The monument was named for Simon Bamberger, state governor at the time. It has been renovated in recent years by local citizens.

Across the river from the highway port of entry/checking station, 2 m. south of Castlegate, is Panther Canyon, once the site of the town of **HEINER.** Named for a coal company official, Heiner was established about 1912 and grew to a population of 500 or 600 within the next decade or so. As with many other coal towns, it survived into the 1940s and 1950s, then was gradually abandoned as coal production fell after World War II. Only foundations remain today.

Turn west from the vicinity of Helper to the **SPRING CANYON** group of coal mining towns. Here, forming the largest concentration of ghost towns in Utah, are the remains of **PEERLESS, SPRING CANYON (STORRS), STANDARDVILLE, LATUDA, RAINS, MUTUAL,** and **LITTLE STANDARD.** These communities waxed and waned between years of World War I and the 1950s and 1960s, at times having a total population of several thousand. Several were notable as distinctive planned communities with modern utilities, well-built houses and commercial buildings, lawns and trees, schools and churches. Mines on which they were based produced record quantities of coal, some reaching 2,000 tons per day. The capsule histories of these towns and others which have died are given by Stephen L. Carr in *Historical Guide to Utah Ghost Towns.*

HELPER (5,800 alt. 2,724 pop.), at the mouth of Price Canyon where lines of great terraced cliffs stretch away to either side, was fortunate in being one of the few coal country communities that managed to survive the coal depression years in relatively intact condition. Having a more diversified economic base than neighboring communities, and being a regional center of sorts, Helper retained a measure of vitality and in more prosperous recent years has recouped the lost population of former times.

In the edition of 1941, Helper was described as overflowing "on both sides of Price Canyon. Houses cling precariously to the steep walls, barely keeping their feet out of the street and Price River. The narrow street is crowded with American, Italian, Greek, Austrian, Japanese, and Chinese miners, who depend upon the 28 mines in the area for a livelihood. Railroad men mingle with the crowd, and there is a sort of an armed neutrality between them and the miners." This is no longer an accurate description; the town has changed and mellowed with time, though mining and railroading have remained important economic supports. The following excerpt from the 1941 edition is still appropriate:

Teancum Pratt brought his two wives here in 1870 while he prospected for coal. For many years the family lived in a dugout, but eventually Pratt acquired nearly the whole district. Helper is platted according to his original survey. He sold his property to the Denver & Rio Grande Western in 1883, and a narrow-gauge railroad was brought in. Standard gauge replaced the narrow gauge in 1890, and two years later a depot, roundhouse, oilhouse, coal chute, and hotel for trainmen were erected. The town became known as Helper in 1892 because extra engines or "helpers" were kept here to push trains up the heavy grade to Soldier Summit.

Helper went through a period of outlawry, gambling and killings when gunfights were too common to attract any attention, and the Robbers Roost gang . . . visited the town.

Helper's **Civic Auditorium** on Main Street was the only building of its kind in Utah when dedicated in 1937. An attractive brick structure, it was designed as an unusually functional civic center with auditorium, meeting-rooms, card-rooms and library. In the auditorium are the City Library and Bicentennial Mining Museum *(next below)*.

Bicentennial Mining Museum, in the Civic Auditorium on North Main, is marked by a monumental statue of a coal miner, made of plate steel. Expertise and dedication are apparent in the museum's exhibits, which feature the history of coal mining, railroading, and local culture in the Carbon-Emery area over a hundred-year period. About 700 photographs line the walls in company with posters, murals, paintings, and maps. Cases display myriad cultural and industrial artifacts. Coal mining machinery and techniques of the past are illustrated in a full-size model of a coal mine. Created in the 1970s, the museum is the result of a cooperative effort between the Helper Municipal Corporation and the state Bicentennial Commission. Its first curator, Fred Voll—former railroad mechanic, artist, and local historian—is most responsible for its excellence.

Turn east from Helper to **KENILWORTH** (6,600 alt.), a mining camp on a high bench at the base of a cliff. In 1941 Kenilworth's population was "almost entirely American . . . rare in this district. Heber J. Stowell discovered the first vein of coal here in 1904, and the mine was a big producer during and after the World War."

Just east of the highway, 2 m. south of Helper, is **SPRING GLEN,** a residential and farming village. Soon after the turn of the century Spring Glen became a center for Carbon County's Slavic population.

In this vicinity also is the **Carbon Country Club and Golf Course.**

Turn west from US 6, 2 m. south of Helper, to the abandoned but historically interesting and photogenic coal mining towns of **COAL CITY, NATIONAL** and **CONSUMERS.** Fairly intact buildings and mine workings mark the sites of communities which once housed several hundred residents and flourished during the 1920s and 1930s. Consumers in 1941 was a model mining camp with the largest coal mine in the district. "A. E. Gibson, with his partner, located a nine-foot coal seam in 1920, and, though hampered by snowdrifts, crude machinery, and lack of food, shipped 34 carloads the first winter. Outside interests later purchased the mine, and built up the town."

PRICE (5,600 alt. 9,086 pop.), Carbon County seat, is the largest city in southeastern Utah. Price has seen both good times and bad during its hundred-year history: more often than not they have been good. According to the 1941 edition, Price was "a moneyed town, with modern buildings, numerous cafes, saloons, and behind-the-scenes gambling houses. If there is a touch of coal dust in the air, it is a dust that means cash, and local people do not give it too much time to settle." The same description could apply today with little change, except that today there is more "coal dust" in the air than ever before, and promise of even greater amounts in future. Many new buildings have been added, including schools, an enlarged college campus, hospital, county building, numerous new homes, motels and other business buildings.

Price has been the coal capital of Utah since the 1890s or thereabouts; and for much of that time it was also the coal capital of the western United States. During the past hundred years scores of mines within 50 miles of Price have yielded about 400 million tons of "black diamonds" totaling more than a billion dollars in value. The number of miners actually engaged in the area's coal industry has fluctuated through the years, sometimes wildly. Annual production has varied from three to ten million tons or more; at the same time the number of working mines rose from 22 in 1910 to 69 in 1949, then dropped to less than a third that many in recent years. Yet most trends of the past decade or so have been upward—in employment, tonnages and (most striking of all) in monetary value: $30 or so per ton in late years compared with little more than $1 per ton in 1900. Price, as the regional capital, has profited economically from these trends.

Caleb Rhodes saw farming possibilities in the Price vicinity when he passed through in 1877. Two years later he and others began farming along

Allosaurus dinosaur, Prehistoric Museum.

the Price River, but large-scale settlement was delayed until the coming of the railroad in the 1880s. A post office was established in 1883 and the city was organized in 1892, becoming the seat of newly formed Carbon County in 1894. The name was taken from the river, which was named by William Price, Mormon bishop of Goshen, Utah Valley, who had explored the river's headwaters during the 1860s.

Price was originally settled as an agricultural community by Mormons; therefore, in its first beginnings, it resembled most other Utah communities of the 19th century. However, whereas most others remained predominantly Mormon and agricultural for some decades after founding—as, for example, the Emery County communities south of Price—Price began to change its cultural identity within a relatively few years. As coal mining operations expanded following completion of the mainline railroad between Colorado and Salt Lake City in 1883 (and in fact during rail construction), new residents of differing cultural and racial background began to settle in the region, not only in Price but in coal and construction camps for miles around. By the time of World War I Price had become the residential or trading capital for thousands of Utah's "new immigrants" representing diverse nationalities and races. Over a period of several decades Utahns of native or long-term residency—primarily Mormons of old-line American and northern European descent—were joined by non-Mormon Anglos, Japanese, Chinese, Finns, Italians, Greeks and southern Slavs (Serbs, Croats, Slovenes). Syro-Lebanese and Armenians came, as did Mexicans, blacks, native Indians, and others. It is reported that a WPA survey of the 1930s found, as patrons of one poolhall in Helper, former residents of 32 different nations.

The experiences of these "new immigrants" in Utah were similar in respects to those of millions of others who were plunged into America's great melting pot. Their coal country vicissitudes cannot be detailed here; suffice to say that these included exploitation, prejudice and discrimination, mine tragedies, brutality, and economic hardship—treatment looked upon with shame by later generations. The new immigrant episode in Utah's history is described in numerous works, the most comprehensive of which is *The Peoples of Utah,* edited by Helen Z. Papanikolas.

Since those early years, here as elsewhere in the state, there has been a continuing process of mingling, acceptance, assimilation—of general cultural leveling—so that today the differences that were such powerful emotional catalysts in bygone days have changed their connotations.

ATTRACTIONS OF NOTE

Price Municipal Building, 200 E. Main, constructed in 1938-39 as one of the largest buildings in Utah built with WPA funds *(listed on National Historic Register).* The main lobby is encircled on all four walls by an epic mural depicting scenes from the history of Carbon County, including 82 figures in lifelike representations. Dedicated in 1941, the huge canvas was the work of Lynn Fausett (1894-1977), a native of Price and one of Utah's most respected painters. According to Robert S. Olpin in *Dictionary of Utah Arts,* the mural represents "possibly the most totally successful of his large scale creations."

College of Eastern Utah, 451 E. 400 North, is a state supported, two-year community college, offering a broad selection of courses. Founded in 1938 as Carbon College, it shared at that time the same building as the local high school. Since then its enrollment has grown from 146 to about 1,000, and its campus has become an attractive complex of modern buildings. The present name was adopted in 1965.

Prehistoric Museum (College of Eastern Utah) is located on the north side of the Price Municipal Building *(above)*. Opened in 1961 as a modest community venture, the museum now has a reputation as one of the finest of its kind in the west. Outside the entrance is a sculpture in steel of a ferocious Allosaurus dinosaur preying upon a smaller reptile. Inside, the most imposing exhibit is the mounted skeleton of a giant Allosaurus known as "Al," the fossil bones of which were taken from the Cleveland-Lloyd Dinosaur Quarry south of Price *(see Tour No. 10-B)*. The museum is a trove of prehistoric artifacts, including cultural relics of the Fremont Indians who inhabited eastern Utah about 700 years ago. Among these are the famed Pilling Figurines, a set of 11 small clay figures discovered in 1950 in the Range Creek area by Clarence Pilling of Price, dating probably to the 11th century. According to the museum, the figurines "are considered in archeological literature to excel both in beauty and technical construction any other like find of comparative age in the American Southwest." Another notable exhibit is a large mural depicting full-size a portion of the Barrier Canyon (Horseshoe Canyon) pictographs of Canyonlands National Park.

Hellenic Orthodox Church, 61 S. 200 East. This unusual church building, dating originally to 1916, is considered "a monument to the faith, culture, and industry of the early Greek immigrants in the West." Though subject in intervening years to remodelings and renovation, the "basic integrity" of the traditional Byzantine construction has been maintained. "Beautiful icons, stained glass windows, and a massive brass and crystal chandelier enhance the interior of the church." *(Listed on the National Register of Historic Places; quotations from the register description.)*

Notre Dame De Lourdes Catholic Church, 200 N. Carbon Avenue. Constructed under the leadership of Father Alfred F. Giovannoni and dedicated in 1923, the church "stands as a monument to [Father Giovannoni's] work in Utah: a native of Italy, he volunteered to come to the United States in 1911 when the large Italian migration to the U. S. created a dire need for Italian-speaking priests. The church played a significant role in uniting the various groups of the county as the Italians, Slovenians, Croatians, French, Basque, Northern European and American Catholics found a common bond in the church." *(Listed on the National Register of Historic Places; quotation is from the register description.)*

Coal Mines of the Area—Coal mining in the Carbon-Emery area was described on page 404 of the 1941 edition. Since that time, mining equipment and techniques have changed to the extent that much more coal can be mined by fewer miners than previously. One dramatic example: in the late 1970s a long-wall mining machine costing $8,000,000 was installed in the Deer Creek Mine, which provides coal for the Huntington power plant. This awesome machine, having a 32-inch shearing blade, proceeded to set an underground world record by cutting 15,000 tons of coal from a wall in one 24-hour period. Fifty years ago it was considered phenomenal for a local coal mine with a large crew to produce 2,000 tons of coal in one day. Though most mines in the area continue to utilize less expensive equipment than the long-wall machine, and more traditional methods, competitive pressures are stimulating continual change.

Tour No. 10B - State 10 through Castle Valley, south from Price to I-70 (Fremont Junction)

Castle Valley is that vast basin extending east and south from the mouth of Price Canyon, cupped between cliff-faced highlands on the west and north, and the domed uplift of San Rafael Swell on the east. South of Price, State 10 winds at the base of great cliffs, enormously rich in coal and gashed by profound canyons. Promontories and free-standing buttes testify to the aptness of Castle Valley's name. State 10 connects most of the valley's communities. Sideroads lead west to coal camps, coal mines and power plants, mountain lakes and streams, forests, and eventually Sanpete Valley. Other roads lead east from State 10 to desert farms and villages, Cleveland-Lloyd Dinosaur Quarry, and rocky fastnesses of the San Rafael Swell.

Turn west on State 122, 6 m. south of Price, to **HIAWATHA, WATTIS** and **MOHRLAND,** important coal mining centers. Wattis and Mohrland are largely deserted as communities, though they flourished for 40 years or so from the World War I period into the 1950s and 1960s. Hiawatha in the 1940s is said to have had a population of 1,500. Mohrland in 1929 had 1,000 in town or nearby. **HIAWATHA** (249 pop.) remains a functioning, viable community, perhaps Utah's least changed and best preserved example of a coal mining town of World War I vintage. Homes, buildings and yards are maintained with care. The external coal operations of U. S. Fuel Company ("King Coal") provide an impressive industrial exhibit. Since 1916 the firm has produced almost 60 million tons of coal from mines in the vicinity, advertising itself as the "largest producer of commercial coal in Utah."

HUNTINGTON (5,700 alt. 2,316 pop.) was for nearly a hundred years, until the 1970s, a quiet town dependent on agriculture and to some extent on coal mining. Founded in the late 1870s by Mormons, Huntington and other Emery County communities to the south remained rural "cowtowns" with a predominantly Mormon population until energy developments of the past decade brought profound social and economic changes. Chief among these was construction of the area's first huge coal-fired electric generating plant, built in Huntington Canyon by Utah Power and Light Company *(see below).* This brought hundreds of engineering and construction workers into Castle Valley, beginning in 1970 and continuing for years thereafter, followed by plant personnel and several hundred miners. Local government officials and residents were not unanimous in welcoming the economic and social impacts of the plant and mine, the main consensus being that the development was a mixed blessing.

Also nearby is **Huntington Lake State Recreation Area,** a 200-acre reservoir beside State 10, 2 m. north of Huntington, with facilities for camping and picnicking, toilets, boating ramp and dock, swimming, water-skiing. Open April to November.

Turn west via State 31 to **HUNTINGTON CANYON,** site of a large electric generating complex, recreation areas, streams, lakes and forests. State 31 climbs through Huntington Canyon, an imposing gorge enclosed between tremendous cliffs, to the summit of Wasatch Plateau at 9,000 feet, where it intersects Skyline Drive *(see Tour No. 7A and 10A),* then descends to Fairview in Sanpete Valley. Most of the route is through Manti-La Sal National Forest. The **Huntington Canyon Power Complex,** 9 m. west of Huntington, was built during the 1970s as the first of its magnitude in Utah, costing well over a hundred million dollars. The complex consists of two large 430-megawatt generating units together with coal processing facilities and nearby Deer Creek coal mine. Nearly 200 miners are employed in producing the thousands of tons of coal used each day, or more than two million tons per year. Water is provided by **Electric Lake,** 26 m. from Huntington near the head of the canyon, created especially for the power complex. Beside the lake is the reconstruction of a coke oven similar to several original ovens used during the 1870s at **Connellsville,** a site now under the lake.

Turn east from State 10 via State 155 to **CLEVELAND, ELMO, DESERT LAKE WATERFOWL RESERVE,** and **CLEVELAND-LLOYD DINOSAUR QUARRY** (18 m.). At the quarry, on the rocky, barren slopes of the San Rafael Swell, the Bureau of Land Management maintains interpretive and picnicking facilities at the site of what is claimed to be the nation's largest known dinosaur graveyard. The quarry is in the Morrison formation of Jurassic age (about 140 million years ago), similar to that at Dinosaur National Monument. Beginning in the 1920s, fossil bones have been removed by the thousands, most of them during the 1960s under a cooperative scientific program headed by Professor W. Lee Stokes of the University of Utah, a native of nearby Cleveland and nationally-known paleontologist/geologist. The quarry was dedicated as a visitor attraction in 1967, development work having been performed by the Castle Valley Job Corps Center at Price. Up to that time 15,000 bones had been removed, furnishing material for 25 dinosaur reconstructions in various parts of the U. S., Canada, Europe and Japan. The quarry is noted for having yielded a remarkable quantity of Allosaurus remains, the Allosaurus being an earlier version of the gigantic, carnivorous Tyrannosaurus Rex.

CASTLE DALE (5,800 alt. 1,910 pop.), seat of Emery County, is a solid town with prosperous farms and fat livestock, named for castlelike rock formations in the vicinity. Orange Seely (Seeley) first entered this section in 1875, bringing herds for grazing. It was settled several years later, and for the next 90 years remained a quiet Mormon community based largely on agriculture. For Castle Dale, as well as for Huntington, the 1970s

Hunter plant near Castle Dale.

Trucking coal from the mine.

and 1980s marked a decided change in history as Utah Power and Light Company built the state's largest complex of coal-fired electric generating plants, fueled by some of its largest coal mining operations. Within a few years Castle Valley's population increased dramatically (and traumatically), as hundreds of construction workers, operating personnel, and miners arrived with their families. Emery County's assessed valuation increased more than 20 times in a decade, and it was necessary to spend millions of dollars for new school buildings, additions to the county courthouse, and expanded community services and facilities.

Despite profound social change and great population growth in recent years, Castle Dale has managed somehow to maintain a degree of traditional charm, grace, and dignity.

The **Castle Dale Power Complex (Hunter Plant)** is located two miles south of town, near the highway. When finally completed it will consist of four main generating units, each of 430 megawatts maximum capacity. The first unit, costing more than 200 million dollars, was placed on line in 1978; the second unit in 1980; and the final two units are expected to be completed by the mid-1980s. The entire complex will have a total cost of more than a billion dollars and, together with the Huntington complex nearby, will have a generating capacity of about 2,600 megawatts, or almost as much as the huge Intermountain Power Project near Delta—itself the largest coal-fired power plant in the nation. When all units are completed, five million tons of coal will be required every year, brought by conveyor and truck from the Wilberg mine in Straight Canyon. Water is provided from Millsite Reservoir near Ferron. Projected plant life is 35 years, by which time it is expected that new methods of producing electric energy will have been developed.

Emery County Museum is located in the old Castle Dale School *(below),* one block north of the county courthouse. A cooperative local undertaking, the remarkable museum features noteworthy collections of Indian artifacts, historic relics, minerals and rocks, photographs and paintings of persons and events, fossils, etc. A full-size mounted skeleton of a meat-eating Allosaurus dinosaur greets visitors. One room has been designed to resemble an old-time country general store.

Turn west from Castle Dale via State 29 to **ORANGEVILLE** (5,800 alt. 1,309 pop.), a farming and residential community at the mouth of Straight Canyon. The town was settled in 1877 and named for Orange Seely (Seeley), a man who weighed more than 320 pounds. According to the 1941 edition, "His feet were only number five in length but were almost as wide as they were long." The account continued: "A Utah Historical Records Survey manuscript says: 'People came from thirty to fifty miles for him to set broken bones and pull teeth, or if they could not come to him he set out cheerfully on horseback to go to them.' Mrs. Seely is quoted as saying, 'The first time I ever swore was when we arrived in Emery County and I said 'Damn a man who would bring a woman to such a God Forsaken country!'"

State 29 continues up Straight Canyon to **Joe's Valley,** a mountain basin ringed by forested slopes, containing **Joe's Valley Reservoir.** At 7,000 feet this large lake is popular for fishing and boating. Manti-La Sal National Forest maintains an improved campground at the lake and the area is popular in winter for snowmobiling. From the lake an unpaved road leads north to Huntington and Cleveland reservoirs and Huntington Canyon. Another road winds south and east from the lake onto **North Horn Mountain** (9,610 alt.), described in the 1941 edition as "looming skyward through a tangle of pines and aspens. In the summer of 1937, remains of a fossil titanosaur, never before found in North America, were uncovered on this mountain by George B. Barnes of an exploring party from the Smithsonian Institution. The animal was about 15 feet tall and had a 50-foot tail." The North Horn road ends at **The Rim**, a dizzy cliff-edge viewpoint nearly 3,000 feet above Orangeville. The panorama from this bird's-eye overlook is superlative, encompassing much of Castle Valley, the San Rafael Swell, and the great cliff front which extends 200 miles in a grand semicircle from Emery northward to the Price area, and then eastward into Colorado. Apparent from here is the relative simplicity of the corrugated region's geological structure. It can be seen how the Wasatch and Tavaputs plateaus, faced by cliffs and composed of relatively youthful Cretaceous rocks, represent a retreating erosional front. Rocks of the highlands once extended over the entire region to the east and south, burying under thousands of feet those older formations that now are visible in the San Rafael Swell uplift. The Swell, it will be noted, is somewhat of a structural or central core which, through doming ages ago, accelerated the erosional processes, this resulting eventually in removal of the overlying Cretaceous and younger rocks from above the Swell, as well as older rocks from the Swell's interior.

From Joe's Valley, State 29 continues westward, crossing the plateau's summit at Skyline Drive (10,200 feet), then switchbacking down to Ephraim.

Turn east from State 10, 2 m. north of Castle Dale, to the **SAN RAFAEL SWELL** *(see Tour No. 10C below)*. The road is unpaved but maintained; avoid if wet.

State 10 continues southward through Castle Valley to Ferron, Emery and a junction with I-70 at Fremont Junction.

FERRON (5,900 alt. 1,718 pop.) is a pleasant, tree-shaded agricultural community. Like its neighbors to north and south, Ferron was settled by Mormons. Massive construction and mining expansion of recent years has brought profound change to the community. Naked desert spreads away toward the San Rafael Swell on the east; Ferron Canyon's broad mouth yawns to the west. Millsite Reservoir nearby provides water for irrigation as well as for the huge Hunter power complex near Castle Dale. Of special historic interest is the former **Presbyterian Church and "Cottage,"** dating from 1907-08, which served until 1942 as a church school, parsonage and dormitory *(listed on National Historic Register)*.

Turn west from Ferron through Ferron Canyon to **Ferron Reservoir** (9,600 feet), 25 m., a modest lake in a setting of alpine beauty, popular for fishing. Manti-La Sal National Forest provides a large campground, boat launching. Beyond the reservoir the road continues to an intersection with Skyline Drive, thence to Mayfield *(see Tour No. 7A)*.

EMERY (6,247 alt. 372 pop.) still retains a picturesque "cowtown" atmosphere of rustic homes, rows of Lombardy poplars, and dirt streets—increasingly rare even in rural Utah. For many years some of its citizens obtained an income from "county banks" or small coal mines, operated by residents who trucked the coal to market. The town was settled in 1881 and pioneers bored a 1,240-foot tunnel to tap Muddy Creek for irrigation water.

FREMONT JUNCTION, 74 m. from Price, marks the intersection of I-70, State 10, State 72 and an unnumbered, unpaved road leading into

Capitol Reef National Park (Cathedral Valley). *See Tour No. 7B.* Back-country roads lead from this latter route into the labyrinthine "Behind the Cliffs" country on the southwestern slopes of San Rafael Swell, a desolate and little visited area that offers intriguing opportunities for scenic discovery.

Tour No. 10C - San Rafael Swell

A classic geological phenomenon, the **SAN RAFAEL SWELL** is an oval-shaped uplift that has been so severely eroded over eons of time that its inclined flanks form a saw-toothed ridge or "reef" completely encircling a central elevated core known by early geologists as Red Amphitheater but called Sinbad Country today. Nature has sculptured the Swell's multi-colored rocks into an infinitude of strange forms of every dimension and shape. The Swell is remarkable, also, because it exhibits within a compact area many of the landscape and structural characteristics typical of the much larger Canyonlands region.

In 1941 the interior of the Swell was isolated and remote, little visited by anyone other than stockmen. Since then I-70 has been built, crossing the Swell from east to west, cutting it almost exactly in half. Yet much of it, away from the highway, remains almost as unknown to the public at large as in 1941.

1. **Off-highway attractions in the northern part of the Swell, accessible from Castle Dale on the north or I-70 (Sinbad Interchange) on the south**

a. **Buckhorn Flat,** an expansive flat lying between Red Plateau (Cedar Mountain) and the San Rafael River-Buckhorn breaks, is traversed by the access road from Castle Dale. The flat is notable for having been a route of transport for 150 years—first as a section of the Old Spanish Trail *(see also Tour No. 7A and 9A)* and the route of American explorers following that trail . . . as a freighting and mail route between Colorado, Green River and Castle Valley towns . . . as the original railbed route of the D&RGW Railroad west from Green River in the early 1880s (more than $200,000 were expended in surveying and grading in the vicinity before the route was abandoned) . . . as the escape route of Butch Cassidy and Elza Lay after the Castlegate robbery of 1897 . . . and in later years as the main route of travel from Castle Dale into the interior of the Swell.

b. **The Wedge Overlook** (junction 13 m. along main road east of Castle Dale, then 8 m. south from junction), affords a series of panoramic views from the upper edge of the spectacular San Rafael gorge, 600 feet above the winding river. The topography is one of naked rock, painted in shades of red, carved into a maze of steep-walled canyons, cliffs, and some of Utah's most splendid free-standing buttes. For visual impact The Wedge affords one of Utah's choice experiences.

c. **Buckhorn Draw or Wash** is a deep red-rock gorge cut into the northern flank of the Swell. The draw extends some ten miles from Buckhorn Flat (15 m. east of Castle Dale) southeastward to its mouth in the interior of the Swell, at the San Rafael River. In its upper reaches the draw is shallow, but it deepens rapidly and its walls grow higher until they exceed a thousand feet at the river. In its ten-mile course the draw descends through 75 million years of geological history, from late Jurassic rocks at the upper end to early Triassic at the river. In rock structure and erosional characteristics, Buckhorn resembles numberless other gorges of Canyonlands, but it is more easily accessible than most, marvelous by any standards, a cameo master-piece that more than repays visitation .

GREEN RIVER CUT-OFF
HIWAY 50 and 6 .... 44 →
BUCKHORN WEDGE..22 →
BUCKHORN WASH...16 →
Indian Pictographs ___ 22 →
GOBLIN VALLEY.___74 →
U-24 and TEMPLE JCT.88 →
HANKSVILLE _____100 →
TAN SEEPS_____ 60 →
HIDDEN SPLENDOR....89 →
GRADED ROAD
Carry Adequate Gas & Water

Rock sculptures in Goblin Valley *(above)*.

San Rafael River Canyon as seen from The Wedge Overlook *(upper right)*.

This sign near Castle Dale greeted travelers entering the San Rafael Swell in the 1950s and 1960s *(right)*.

Beside the road, about halfway through the draw, is a badly vandalized panel of prehistoric Indian cliff-art known as petroglyphs (incised "rock writing"). Mingled with and at times superimposed upon the Indian art are the names of travelers of historic times. The canyon also contains pictographs (painted rock art) as well as a cave that served as shelter for prehistoric peoples. Buckhorn's antiquities are listed on the National Historic Register.

In its issue of July 20, 1952, the *Salt Lake Tribune* contained a description of explosives tests conducted near the head of Buckhorn Draw in the summer of 1952. One of a series of scientific experiments conducted at different sites by the U. S. Army Corps of Engineers to determine the characteristics of rocks when subjected to explosives, the Buckhorn test involved elaborate preparations and equipment,

Clustered at the mouth of Buckhorn is a majestic group of sandstone buttes, a miniature Monument Valley. These include **Windowblind Peak,** stateliest of all at more than 1,500 feet, as well as **Assembly Hall** and **Bottleneck** peaks. The river is crossed by a picturesque suspension bridge, and on the south bank of the river is an improved campground developed by BLM. *Poisonous snakes are not a serious hazard in Utah, but here as elsewhere it is wise to be alert for rattlesnakes.*

The **San Rafael River,** a modest stream named by New Mexicans traveling the Old Spanish Trail, is the combined product of Huntington, Cottonwood, Ferron and smaller streams. It empties into Green River after slicing a series of deep and narrow canyons through the Swell. West of the mouth of Buckhorn its gorge can be viewed in overview from The Wedge *(see above)*. East of the mouth of Buckhorn it flows alternately through open country and entrenched chasms, one of which—the Black Box—is hundreds of feet deep and very narrow with almost sheer walls. Here the river cuts through the Swell's most ancient rocks, corresponding to those found at upper levels of Arizona's Grand Canyon. The San Rafael has been traversed by those finding excitement in unusual challenge; it is too shallow for boats, however, and travel requires frequent immersion as well as scrambling over obstacles. East of Buckhorn a primitive road follows the river along its north bank, leading to the Red Canyon and Spring Canyon labyrinth of cliffs and canyons. The road also gives access to the rim of **Black Box.**

South of Buckhorn the road continues through high, open grazing country with widespreading vistas across a broken wonderland, finally joining I-70 at Sinbad Interchange some 44 miles from Castle Dale. Rough sideroads lead off toward the Black Box, Mexican Mountain and other parts of the Swell's corrugated interior, known generally as Sinbad (Sindbad) country. South of I-70 the main access road continues on to Temple Mountain, Hondoo (Muddy River) country, and State 24 *(next below).*

2. **Off-highway attractions in the southern part of the Swell, conveniently accessible from State 24 (Temple Mountain Junction) or I-70 (Sinbad Interchange).**

a. **San Rafael Reef** is prominently visible from the east—from I-70, US 6, or from State 24, which parallels the reef between I-70 and Temple Mountain Junction. The reef is a monoclinal flexure consisting of steeply tilted rocks of ancient Jurassic-Triassic origin, gashed by short but very deep and narrow canyons. Its incised whaleback slope is toward the east; high cliffs form its broken western face inside the Swell. The reef's crest is a jagged sawtooth skyline accented with buttes and pinnacles that suggest the local name **"Silent City."** I-70 passes through one of the reef's canyons just south of the canyon of the San Rafael River, and the road to Temple Mountain passes through another. Some of the reef's canyons harbor excellent examples of prehistoric Indian rock art. *See also Tour No. 10D.*

b. **Goblin Valley State Reserve,** on the eastern outer flanks of the Swell, was created to protect one of the most extraordinary concentrations of eroded rocks in America. The "valley"—actually a long, narrow, shallow basin enclosed between low but fantastically sculptured cliffs extending for miles—contains literally countless chocolate-colored "goblin" rocks of varying size. Many of the rocks are inviting objects for vandalism, being free-standing and precariously balanced, and the valley floor consists of soft mudstone and sand that retain the impressions of feet and tires. The valley's rock designs are unique in Utah, stimulating uninhibited imagination and providing beguiling subjects for photographic experimentation. The area is especially dramatic in late afternoon and near dusk, when shadows are long and silhouetting accents the infinitude of strange and exotic profile designs. Then, truly, it becomes an enchanted valley of "goblins" and there is no doubt whatsoever about the appropriateness of its name. *Open all year.* State ranger on duty. Picnicking and camping facilities; drinking water (canteen advised in hot weather). Carry food; no supplies available on site. Wear appropriate clothing and hiking shoes; hot in summer, cold in winter. Goblin Valley is 21 m. north of Hanksville via State 24, then 5 m. west on Temple Mountain road, then 8 m. south.

c. **Temple Mountain,** a prominent and distinctive butte visible for many miles, juts high above the crest of San Rafael Reef. The reason for its name is plain to see. Temple Mountain has been known since early years of the century as a rich repository of vanadium and uranium. It is said that uranium used in the first atomic bomb came from there, and it was the scene of extensive mining during the "uranium rush" of the 1950s. Today the butte and abutting cliffs are pocked with tunnels and shallow caves *(danger, use care!);* these and assorted ruins attest to former glory days. The area is reached by short paved road from State 24 from junction 21 m. north of Hanksville, the sideroad passing through San Rafael Reef in a short but narrow gash of a canyon. In this canyon, high on the north wall and visible from the road, is a small panel of prehistoric Indian pictographs, somewhat vandalized but still of interest.

d. **Sinbad Country.** The main sideroad continues north from Temple Mountain, rising with a bulge of the Swell's cliff-ringed interior. This great amphitheater, 30 miles long from north to south and 15 miles wide, has long been known locally as Sinbad (Sindbad) country, though the name's origin is unknown. Since pioneer days it has been utilized for stock grazing, and until recent years it was not uncommon to see wild horses in the area. High points within the Swell provide aerial panoramas of a colorful, broken landscape extending far beyond the reef surrounding Sinbad.

e. **Hondoo-Muddy River Country** is easy of access from I-70 (Sinbad Interchange) or State 24 (Temple Mountain), the unpaved road being suitable for passenger cars in dry weather. In general the area resembles that at the mouth of Buckhorn *(above),* consisting of giant cliffs, deep canyons, and great buttes. Yet it differs in erosional design and coloring, and perhaps exhibits a wider variety of natural forms. The access road forms a loop, beginning near **Family Butte,** which may be traveled in either direction, in both cases descending rather precipitously from the heights of Sinbad country into the drainage maze of Muddy River (more technically Muddy Creek). Scenic views along the way are superb. About halfway along the loop, at imposing **Tomsich Butte**—the site of sporadic uranium mining dating from "rush" years of the 1950s to the present time—the Muddy enters the interior of the Swell through a deep canyon. Cliffs here are a thousand feet high or more, beautifully sculptured, and painted in subdued hues. **Hondoo Arch,** at the top of a skyscraping cliff across the river from Tomsich Butte, is the dominant feature because of its uniqueness: a rectangular slot in the rock, in shape resembling the loop *(hondoo, hondo)* in the end of a lariat, through which the other end is threaded to form a running noose.

A southern extension of the loop road leads to the fabled **Hidden Splendor** uranium mine (originally the Delta), discovered in 1952 by Vernon Pick and sold by him to Atlas Corporation for nine million dollars. The mine has been worked sporadically since its discovery, but production values are reported to be much less than the purchase price. Stories about Pick appeared in *Life, Readers Digest,* and other national publications. More primitive roads fork from the Hondoo loop road in its higher reaches, leading to wild canyon breaks of Temple Mountain. The main Sinbad road continues north from Family Butte to I-70, 28 m. from Temple Mountain Junction on State 24. A dominant landmark north of Family Butte is **San Rafael Knob** (7,921 alt.), highest point in the Swell.

f. **Interstate Highway 70.** Known as the "Main Street of America," I-70 was almost an afterthought in planning the interstate highway system in Utah. The highway bisects the nation in an east-west line from Washington D.C. to Cove Fort, Utah, where it joins I-15 and continues to southern California.

In this tour section I-70 enters Utah from Colorado in Grand River Valley and parallels the Book Cliffs to Green River. Several miles west of Green River the cliffs veer away toward the northwest while the highway continues westward, bisecting the rocky fastnesses of the San Rafael Swell, a wild and broken country hardly known to the outside world before the highway came. Initial construction of the San Rafael segment began in the 1960s, with formal opening of 70 miles of two east-west lanes in late 1970. At that time the state Department of Highways proclaimed it the "longest section of new interstate through previously untouched territory to be opened in this century." In 1981 there were no service stations, motels or restaurants in the 110 miles between Green River and Salina.

Tour No. 10D - US 6, Price to Green River

Southeast of Price, US 6 traverses an arid region of low bluffs and shallow washes, its drab desolation relieved here and there by the greenery of farms, streamside vegetation and a scattering of pygmy evergreens. Even the great Book Cliffs, looming to the north as a facade for high plateaus, do little to break the monotony of wasteland; despite their magnitude, they are but bare rock of somber hue. Yet the impression for many travelers is one of grandeur, conveying a powerful sense of the inconceivable ages involved in the building up and tearing down of earth's crust in this region.

The Book and Roan cliffs to the north and east give not a hint to the traveler of the mineral wealth they contain. These great ramparts form one of the most impressive series of escarpments in America, extending in a 200-mile semicircle from Emery to Price to Colorado. Buried in the cliffs are layer upon layer of bituminous coal, rock asphalt and oil shale. Farther north, their rocks contain tar sands, gilsonite, and liquid petroleum.

WELLINGTON (5,600 alt. 1,406 pop.) is a farming, trade and residential center. Turn south from Wellington a short distance to wells that have produced most of Utah's natural carbon dioxide gas for many years. Carbon dioxide is used in the manufacture of dry ice and carbonic gas for refrigeration and beverages. Before mechanical stokers came into common use, when lump coal was in demand, liquid carbon dioxide was used for blasting coal. Put up in cartridges, it was electrically detonated.

Also near Wellington is a multi-million-dollar, 13-story plant built in 1958 to blend and wash coal mined at U. S. Steel's mines in Colorado and at Horse Canyon, destined for the coke ovens at Geneva Works in Utah Valley.

North from US 6, at a junction 3 m. east of Wellington, a paved road leads 13 m. to the modern coal mining complex of Soldier Creek Mining Company. North from the mine, the road (now unpaved but suitable for passenger cars) continues over a summit into **NINE MILE CANYON,** the cliff-walled channel of Minnie Maud Creek. Winding along the canyon bottom for some 20 miles, the main road exits Nine Mile through Gate Canyon. Eventually it enters the grand expanse of Uinta Basin, crossing 20 miles or so of open badlands before joining US 40 two miles west of Myton and about 70 miles from its southern terminus at US 6. Surmounted here and there by snowcapped peaks that hint of others not seen, the bulk of the Uinta Mountains stretches across the northern horizon for a hundred visible miles.

This route is one of Utah's fascinating sideroad drives, not only because of exceptional scenery but for its glimpses into the romantic past. Picturesque old ranch buildings, corrals, and farm equipment are scattered along the valley floor. Cattle graze by the hundreds in fields of alfalfa. This was the main route of travel for 40 years between the Uinta Basin and the railroad at Price, a lifeline over which wagons, stages, buggies, mounted riders, and myriad livestock traveled in endless parade. Most of the land-rush settlers of 1905-06 used this route. First improved as a main road during the 1880s by army troops from Fort Duchesne, the route was only gradually replaced in early decades of this century by the Uintah Railway and improved roads through Indian Canyon and Daniels Canyon. Few original mementos of early freighting days have been preserved—yet nostalgia is provided by foundation ruins, old log cabins, a few tumbledown frame buildings, and other quaint structures of a bygone era. Nine Mile Canyon also is the headquarters for the vast Nutter ranch, which dates in this vicinity from the 1890s, one of Utah's largest and longest-continuing livestock operations. Preston Nutter, its founder, became somewhat of a legend in his time as one of the state's true cattle barons. In 1981 it passed from family ownership to a Texas mineral corporation.

Of special interest to visitors are the canyon's Indian antiquities, more particularly its numerous petroglyphs or rock etchings, which can be seen on smooth rock faces beside and near the road for 20 miles or more. *A detailed folder describing the location of points of interest in the canyon is available from Castle Country, P.O. Box 1037, Price, Utah 84501.* Remember: *Antiquities are protected by federal and state laws.* The canyon is listed on the state Register of Historic Places because of its outstanding Indian antiquities. As described by the register:

Other archeological details about Nine Mile Canyon appear in the 1941 edition (page 401). Many of the sites are located on private land; if in doubt, obtain permission locally.

At **Sunnyside Junction,** 17 m. from Price, turn east on State 123 to East Carbon City and Sunnyside.

Soldier Station, a stop along the Nine Mile road, as it appeared about 1900 *(left).*

Building coke ovens at Sunnyside about 1900 *(below).*

G. E. ANDERSON PHOTOS

EAST CARBON CITY (6,000 alt. 1,942 pop.), formerly known as Dragerton, is a commercial and residential center for large coal mines operated at Sunnyside by Kaiser Steel Corporation, and at Horse Canyon by U. S. Steel. The community flows imperceptibly into **SUNNYSIDE** (611 pop.). In earlier years, many of the area's miners and their families lived within Whitmore Canyon at old Sunnyside, but this was gradually replaced by newer communities outside the canyon at Dragerton and new Sunnyside, as well as Columbia.

The Sunnyside area originally was part of the vast Whitmore cattle ranch. Two Whitmore employees, Jefferson and John Tidwell, found a seam of coal in 1898 and sold it to the Utah Fuel Company for $250. As described in the 1941 edition, "A year later more than 1,200 men were employed in the mines at Sunnyside. Coke made here was shipped to Castlegate for use in smelting. In 1902-03 more than 400 coke ovens were burning at Sunnyside. It boomed as a coke town until 1929, when other products were introduced for smelting. Of the 816 coke ovens once in use [during World War I], only six were operating in 1940." World War II brought reactivation of about 300 ovens, which continued until Kaiser closed the last oven in 1958. They have since been removed. Several miles from Sunnyside is a deposit of rock asphalt. Here, according to the 1941 edition, there is "enough oil-impregnated sandstone to pave everything in sight. The deposit was first utilized in 1892, but serious development waited until 1928. The stone is quarried here, trucked to a mill, and crushed to the consistency of coarse sand. It can be laid cold." Quarrying operations were conducted until the early 1950s, when competition from manufactured petroleum asphalt forced cessation of mining—this despite acknowledged superiority of the rock asphalt.

Since they opened 80 years ago, the Sunnyside mines have produced more than 50 million tons of coal. Kaiser Steel now owns the mine complex, having become a lessee operator in 1942, during World War II, and later purchasing the local mines. Coal production is destined primarily for Kaiser's steel plant at Fontana, California. Up-canyon from Sunnyside the road continues in steep switchbacks onto upper levels of the **West Tavaputs (Roan) Plateau,** with lush alpine meadows and forests, entering private lands and terminating at the dizzy rim of a gorge that plunges 5,000 feet into Desolation Canyon. Perched on the rim is the lodge of the **Tavaputs Plateau Ranch,** a working ranch and hunting guide-guest lodge operation founded and operated by Don and Jeannette Wilcox and family of Green River *(see below).*

Turn south from East Carbon City via State 124 to **COLUMBIA** (6,400 alt.), a tree-shrouded village of modest cottages, high on a hillside, built in the early 1920s as a model town to house miners supplying coking coal to the Columbia Steel Plant at Ironton. For governmental purposes it is now a part of East Carbon City. Nearby, from 1923 until closure in the late 1960s, Columbia Steel (a subsidiary of United States Steel) operated the Columbia mine, which produced a total of 20 million tons or so of coal during an active life of 44 years. From the Columbia turnoff, State 124 continues five miles to the **Horse Canyon (Geneva) Mine** of U. S. Steel Corporation. Dating from 1942-43, during World War II, the Geneva mine was developed to provide coking coal for the huge Geneva Works at Orem, as well as other markets. Within a few years it had become the largest producing coal mine west of the Mississippi River, having a total production to date of more than 30 million tons. Beyond the mine an unpaved road climbs steeply up Horse Canyon and over a shoulder of imposing Patmos Head (9,851 alt.) into **Range Valley,** one of the deepest and most spectacular side gorges of Green River's Desolation Canyon. The road continues through locked gates *(private)* to **Range Valley Ranch,** a working cattle/hunting guide/guest lodge operation. In a Shangri-la setting of enormous cliffs and verdant bottoms, the ranch is operated by Waldo and Julie Wilcox of Green River.

In even earlier times, Tavaputs livestock operations of the Whitmores and Preston Nutter of Nine Mile Canyon were the stuff from which legends are made. Space does not permit recital, but mention should be made, at least, of **Big Springs Ranch** in the East Carbon area during the 1880s and 1890s. The ranch and its somewhat mysterious builder, Lord Scott Elliott, were described by C. W. McCullough in the *Deseret News* of August 15, 1948. McCullough wrote: "The history of Utah is primarily a story of its waterholes. To conquer a world of desert, man established life, settlement and agriculture close to streams, lakes, gushing springs and brackish alkali seeps." Lord Elliott, an Englishman, "appeared out of nowhere, fabricated briefly a great empire, and faded out into nowhere again." The "empire" consisted, it is said, of 30,000 head of sheep, as well as horses and cattle, and a model ranch with a 14-room house, well kept grounds, barns, corrals and stackyards. Elliott prospered for years. Then drouth and severe winters, depression and finally the death of his wife were blows from which he did not recover.

WOODSIDE (4,600 alt.) is but a stop on the highway beside Price River. Originally Woodside was a farming community known as Lower Crossing, first settled in the 1880s. According to Stephen L. Carr, there were vegetable and turkey farms, and it was a center for cattlemen, sheepmen and railroaders. By World War I it had become a modest community with shops and a school; then, with drouth, changes in railroad operations, and the fading of livestock operations, the town disappeared. For some years, until about 1970, a tourist center and several service stations managed to survive because of tourist interest in the local "geyser." This curiosity resulted when the railroad drilled for water in 1910 and, in words of the first edition, "got it, but it was so vile nothing could be done with it. The well spouted 75 feet in the air and refused to be capped. Humans avoided the poisonous water, but cattle died from drinking it." The geyser erupted at frequent intervals thereafter but gradually dwindled in volume until it barely rose above the ground (at least for a time).

South of Woodside the Book Cliffs pinch closer to the rise of San Rafael Swell, with Beckwith Plateau looming high above, an aerial island enclosed by canyons and cliffs. The Book Cliffs apparently had received their name sometime before Gunnison's passage in 1853, for Beckwith, his chronicler, wrote: "The Little mountain, sometimes from the regular appearance and variegated color of its strata, like the Roan, called the Book mountain, lay during to-day's march plainly in view from Green river north and west, to where it apparently joins the first range of the Wahsatch." He described this imposing escarpment and the countryside roundabout in fitting eloquence:

> This mountain wall . . . is very irregular; deep ravines and gorges extend back into it, giving it . . . the appearance of an unfinished fortification, on a scale which is pleasing to the imagination, and contrasts the works of men strongly with those of nature. . . . Desolate as is the country over which we have just passed, and around us, the view is still one of the most beautiful and pleasing I remember to have seen. As we approached the river yesterday, the ridges on either of its banks to the west appeared broken into a thousand forms—columns, shafts, temples, buildings, and ruined cities could be seen, or imagined, from the high points along our route.

Four miles from Woodside a dirt road forks west, winding through the northern breaks of the Swell to Buckhorn Flat and Castle Dale *(see Tour No. 10C above),* paralleling closely in places the route of the Old Spanish Trail, the trail of later explorers, and the original D&RGW railroad grade. The route was used, also, as a

Book Cliffs near Green River *(above)*.

San Rafael River as it emerges from San Rafael Reef
(right).

cutoff for considerable travel between Castle Valley and central Utah and points east, even after the railroad was built to Price. Orville Pratt, who traversed the Spanish Trail from Santa Fe to Los Angeles in 1848, wrote as follows of the country west of the Green River crossing: "The country continues as almost all the way heretofore, sandy, hilly & utterly barren. Water is also scarce, & if there is no mineral wealth in these mountains I can hardly conceive of what earthly use a large proportion of this country was designed for!" (Quoted by LeRoy Hafen in *The Old Spanish Trail.)*

From junction with I-70, turn west on I-70 to junction with State 24 (9 m.), then south on State 24 to **Hanksville, Bullfrog Resort and Lake Powell, Capitol Reef National Park and other points** *(see Tour No. 7B).*

State 24 parallels **San Rafael Reef,** marking the eastern boundary of San Rafael Swell, a strikingly eroded monoclinal ridge of steeply inclined rocks of Jurassic age. All around is the sandy **San Rafael Desert,** apparently a wasteland but long used for cattle grazing. At **Temple Mountain Junction** (24 m. from I-70), roads fork west to Goblin Valley and Sinbad-Hondoo country *(see Tour No. 10C above),* east to Robbers Roost, Glen Canyon National Recreation Area and Canyonlands National Park *(see Tour No. 7B).* **Robbers Roost** has gained widespread notoriety from legend, myth and the writings of such authors as Zane Grey, Charles Kelly, Pearl Baker and even Robert Redford the actor. Its history is summarized in the files of the National Register of Historic Places, in which it is described as follows:

This area was the fourth stop along the famous "Outlaw Trail" . . . Numerous outlaws both visited here and made this their headquarters. Some of them were Butch Cassidy (Robert Leroy Parker), the Sundance Kid (Harry Longabaugh), Kid Curry, Harvey Logan, Bill Carver, Matt Warner, Elza Lay, Tom and Bill McCarty, Ben Kilpatrick, John Carter (C. L. "Gunplay" Maxwell), "Blue John" (John Griffith), and "Silver Tip" (James F. Howells). These and others used this area as a hideout while evading the law. The area was used for this purpose from 1875 until 1905. This particular spot afforded excellent protection from surprise as well as providing good potable water. Many of the horses rustled by the outlaws were held here until they could safely be sold in Grand Junction or Durango, Colorado. The cattle that were rustled were held up on Roost Flats until they too could be sold. Not a single lawman entered the Roost to capture any of the outlaws.

Since its outlaw days the Roost has been used as a cattle range, in particular by the Biddlecome family (of which writer Pearl Baker was a member) and the Ekker family, related to the Biddlecomes by marriage.

From a base south of Temple Mountain Junction and east of Gilson buttes, army missile tests were conducted during the 1960s. A temporary camp was occupied by hundreds of artillery troops training in the firing of solid-propellant Pershing missiles from Utah to White Sands Missile Range in New Mexico, 400 miles away *(see Green River below)*.

GREEN RIVER (4,100 alt. 1,048 pop.), also known as Greenriver, occupies both banks of the stream from which its name derived. Today it is a sprawling, bustling, growing community, but its people are realistic about future prospects because the town's hundred-year history has been one of alternating growth and decline—growth from railroading, cattle and sheep, farming, uranium and oil, highway construction, land development, a missile base, tourism and river recreation—contrasted with the bust when boom conditions changed.

New Mexicans, traveling the Old Spanish Trail in the 1830s and 1840s, crossed Green River at a ford several miles north of the present highway. Their ford, an Indian crossing, was used in ensuing years by the Gunnison survey party (giving birth to the name Gunnison's Crossing, used for many years thereafter), and by countless other travelers until the railroad was completed in the early 1880s.

The town's history to 1940 was summarized in the first edition:

> Settled in 1878, the town was a mail relay station between Salina, Utah, and Ouray, Colorado, until the Rio Grande Western Railroad entered in 1882. With the coming of the railroad, a short-lived land boom hit the little settlement. In an interview Chris Halverson stated that he and his brother caught 180 beaver the first winter, selling the hides for 50¢ to $1.50. Prospectors found gold in the region, but it was "flour" gold, too fine to sift out. Eastern farmers tried to irrigate with water from the Green River. The river was hard to handle—it still is—and crop after crop flooded out. The few who succeeded took land along small streams that could be controlled. Melon-growing began in 1917, but it was not until 1926 that local melons reached New York City, where they have since commanded premium prices.

The town's melons have been appreciated by epicures ever since and may still be obtained from roadside stands in season.

On the east side of the river, between 1963 and 1979, when it was put on temporary caretaker status until 1981, a large missile testing operation was active at the **Utah Launch Complex.** Employing hundreds of workers at times, the complex was the principal off-range facility of the White Sands Missile Range. During its operational life it supervised the assembly, testing and firing of several hundred Athena and Pershing missiles between Green River and White Sands, 400 miles away. The Athena was a test vehicle, designed to develop data having to do with atmospheric re-entry of military missiles, in particular the ICBM. Though each Athena test firing cost nearly a million dollars, this was less than half the cost of using an Atlas rocket for the same test. One of the missiles tested, an Athena H, measured 60 feet in length and weighed 30,000 pounds—twice that of a standard Athena. The Athena H traveled at 17,000 miles per hour, attained a high point of more than 100 miles, and reached target 400 miles away about five minutes after liftoff. In 1980 plans were announced for use of the base in test firing of a third-generation Pershing artillery missile. Tests were scheduled for 1982 or 1983.

As a stream, **GREEN RIVER** is one of Utah's two largest. It originates in the Wind River Mountains of Wyoming and joins the Colorado more than 100 miles below the town. "Beckoning with one hand and thumbing its nose with the other, [Green River] lures the riverman," says the 1941 edition. "It is a wolf in sheep's clothing, hiding behind a bland and limpid surface its turbulent upstream past, and giving no hint of its crashing, thrusting, downstream future." With several clarifying notations, the account continues:

> Trappers used sections of the river in the 1820's, but if they reached the junction of the two rivers, it has not been recorded. The first man to attempt the Green appears to be General William H. Ashley, who went downstream almost to Greenriver, Utah, in 1825. The name, "D. Julien," with the date 1836, appears several times on the walls of the canyons of the Green River, but little else is known of his trip.
>
> The one-armed Major John Wesley Powell may not have been a good manager, but there can be no question of his daring. He made two assaults upon the rivers, one in 1869, the other in 1871. Without maps or charts Powell made his way along the Green and Colorado to Grand Canyon. Leaving Green River, Wyoming, May 24, 1869, Powell set out with four boats and a crew of nine. The boats passed uneventfully through U-shaped Horseshoe Canyon, and Kingfisher Canyon. . . .
>
> In Lodore Canyon, Powell had his first accident, resulting in the loss of a boat. The men were saved, but it was thought that all the barometers, which were on this boat, had been lost. Powell sent two men through the rapids to the still intact cabin the next day, and they returned triumphantly with the barometers and a three-gallon keg of whisky. Powell, because he had only one arm, almost lost his life in Split Rock Canyon *(see Dinosaur National Monument).*
>
> At the junction of the Uinta, Powell went to visit the Indian reservation— located in [1869] at Whiterocks—and Frank Goodman left the party. He had been on the boat that was lost, and Powell intimates that he had lost his nerve, but the Major was not always fair to the men who left him. Above Stillwater Powell gazed upon "a strange, weird, grand region. The landscape every-where, away from the river, is of rock—cliffs of rock; tables of rock; plateaus of rock; terraces of rock; crags of rock—ten thousand strangely carved forms. Rocks everywhere, and no vegetation, no soil, no sand . . . a whole land of naked rock, with giant forms carved on it; cathedral shaped buttes, towering hundreds or thousands of feet; cliffs that cannot be scaled, and canon walls that shrink the river into insignificance, with vast, hollow domes, and tall pinnacles, and shafts set on the verge overhead, and all highly colored—buff, gray, red, brown, and chocolate; never lichened; never moss-covered; but bare, and often polished."
>
> Between Lees Ferry and the [lower end of] Grand Canyon, three of his men, thoroughly fed up with the management of the party, with the roar of water, with high enclosing walls, and fearing great rapids below, left the expe-

dition. Shivwits Indians, refusing to believe their story that they came from the river, killed them [apparently as innocent pawns in an act of revenge].

Powell seems to have taken his second expedition lightly. According to the journal of William Clement Powell, his nephew, dissension began early. The party left Green River, Wyoming, May 22, 1871, and by June 11, Frank Richardson was ready to leave the party, "at the Maj. request." F. S. Dellenbaugh, expedition artist, was only 17 at the time, but from young Powell's account he was quite a man.

Nate Galloway, a trapper, was probably the first man to run the rivers alone. In 1895, he made the trip from Green River, Wyoming, to Jensen, Utah, where he meant to disembark a load of beaver pelts. However, he preferred river hazards to officers looking for beaver poachers, and continued on to Lees Ferry, Arizona, by himself. He made repeated trips through Cataract Canyon and Grand Canyon before leading the Julius F. Stone expedition. Charles S. Russell, E. R. Monnette, and Bert Loper started from Greenriver, Utah, in 1907 in steel boats. Loper laid up at Hite to repair his boat, and the others reached Needles, California, in February, 1908.

The Julius F. Stone expedition of 1909 left Green River, Wyoming, in September, with four boats designed by Nate Galloway, and reached Needles in November, bringing two boats through without a spill. Stone gives the story in *Canyon Country*. He returned to the river in 1939 at the age of 83, and with boats furnished by Dr. A. L. Inglesby made another trip with Charles Kelly, Dr. Inglesby, Dr. R. G. Frazier, now (1940) with Admiral Byrd in the Antarctic, William A. Chryst, who helped Kettering develop the automobile self-starter, and George Stone, son of Julius. The party found a carved date, "1642," not yet identified, and an "1837" with some unintelligible lettering.

Emery C. Kolb, James Fagin, and Ellsworth Kolb, with two flat-boats designed by Nate Galloway, left Green River, Wyoming, in September, 1911, and arrived at the Bright Angel Trail in November. The brothers resumed their trip, and arrived at Needles in January, 1912. Ellsworth went on alone to the Gulf of California, in May, 1913, making the run in eight days. A record of their trip, *Through the Grand Canyon from Wyoming to Mexico*, was written by Ellsworth.

Boyhood dreams were realized by Clyde Eddy when in 1927 he made the trip from Greenriver, Utah, to Needles. Eddy made another trip in 1934,

Boaters in Gray Canyon, north of Green River.

F. A. BARNES

accompanied by Dr. R. G. Frazier, Bill Fahrni of Bingham, and three men from Vernal. They made a complete photographic record of the river from Lees Ferry to Boulder Dam.

The next trip to attract public attention was the "lone wolf" voyage of Buzz Holmstrom, who left Green River, Wyoming, in October, 1937. Buzz studied each rapid before attempting it, and more than once had to portage or line his boat over the rocks. He emerged at Boulder Dam, fifty-two days later.

Since that account was written, countless thousands have followed Clyde Eddy, Buzz Holmstrom and their predecessors through the canyons. Among these was Senator Barry Goldwater, who later wrote and illustrated a book about his experience. *See also Glen Canyon National Recreation Area.*

The 1941 account neglected to include Powell's passage through Desolation Canyon, north of town, where the Green has cut one of the deepest and most magnificent river canyons in America, and where river travelers encounter numerous rapids. This stretch of the Green has gained increasing popularity with boaters. The canyon is included in the National Register of Historic Places, which describes it as follows:

> . . . The 1869 expedition of 11 men and four boats started from the point on the Green River where it is crossed by the Union Pacific Railroad [Wyoming]. In Desolation Canyon the men saw a heretofore unexplored area of the United States and were confronted by dangers and natural wonders, frightening and at the same time awe-inspiring. Here the men gave enduring names to mountains, rapids, streams, and other natural landmarks that never before had been seen by white men. Except for an occasional abandoned ranch, Desolation Canyon is virtually unchanged from its appearance in 1869. There are no permanent residents of the canyon.

Arrangements may be made at Green River for boating expeditions through Desolation Canyon. These may involve an air flight from Green River to embarkation point in the Uinta Basin, making possible an 80-mile downstream floating experience.

GREEN RIVER STATE RECREATION AREA, on the west bank of the river, is a 50-acre public development featuring camping facilities, toilets, showers, water, fireplaces, boat ramp and dock. *Open April to October.* This unusual park is the starting point for private and commercial boating tours through canyons of the Green and rapids of Cataract Canyon below confluence with the Colorado, exiting at Hite Marina on Lake Powell. The park also is embarkation point for an adventure boating event of national reputation known as the annual **Friendship Cruise,** sponsored cooperatively by Green River and Moab. Inaugurated as a river marathon in 1958 by boating enthusiasts, the cruise was an annual event every Memorial Day weekend until 1980, involving in some years as many as 400 powerboats. The two-day cruise route takes boats through a spectacular series of cliff-walled, red-rock canyons, extending 118 miles down the Green to its confluence with the Colorado, then 65 miles up the Colorado to Moab. No real rapids are encountered and there are no serious dangers, but the cruise is considered an exhilarating adventure by participants because of the wilderness environment, sandbars, driftwood and other potential hazards. *Write Friendship Cruise, Green River, Utah 84525 for details.* The cruise was cancelled in 1981, and at this writing its future is uncertain.

Tour No. 11
CANYONLANDS
(Grand and San Juan counties)

This tour region encompasses more than 11,000 square miles of that central, corrugated part of the Colorado Plateau known as Canyonlands. Formed largely of bare rock and sand of bright and startling hues, the Canyonlands region—in a technical sense—incorporates a much larger area than Grand and San Juan counties. But these two counties have adopted that name as a symbol to denote their unique landscape

Interstate Highway 70, still uncompleted at the time of this writing, parallels the Book Cliffs between Green River and Grand Junction. The highway topography of low ridges and barren, undulating plains is visually monotonous, affording but tantalizing glimpses of fantastic red "breaks" to the south. Formidable ramparts, broken by yawning gorges, loom to the north. Almost the only signs of human habitation are at Crescent Junction, Thompson and Cisco.

CRESCENT JUNCTION (4,800 alt.) is at the junction of I-70 with US 163, which leads south to Moab *(see Tour No. 11A below)*. Service station, restaurant.

Canyons of the lower Green River.

F. A. BARNES

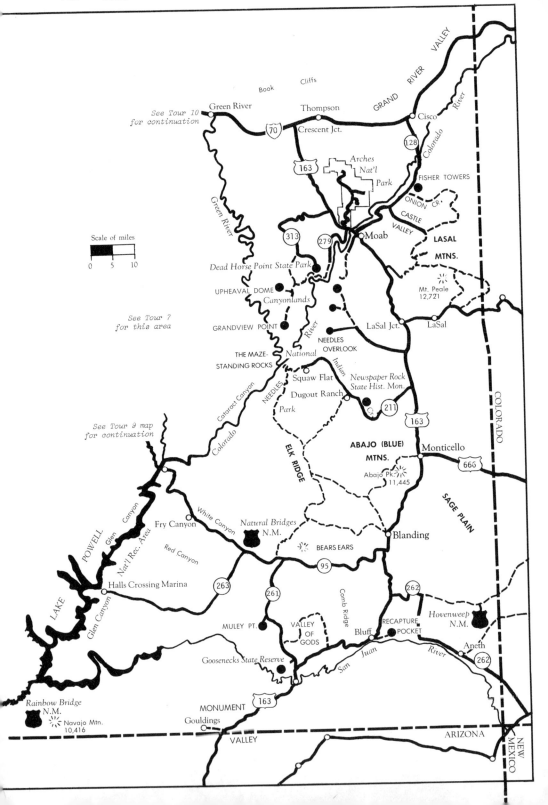

Book   Cliffs

See Tour 10
for continuation

Green River

Thompson

GRAND RIVER VALLEY

Cisco

70

Crescent Jct.

128

Colorado River

Arches
Nat'l
Park

FISHER TOWERS

163

ONION CR.

CASTLE VALLEY

Green River

313   279

Moab

LASAL MTNS.

Dead Horse Point State Park

Mt. Peale
12,721

UPHEAVAL DOME

Canyonlands

See Tour 7
for this area

GRANDVIEW POINT

National

Colorado River

LaSal Jct.

LaSal

NEEDLES OVERLOOK

THE MAZE-
STANDING ROCKS

Squaw Flat

Newspaper Rock
State Hist. Mon.

Cataract Canyon

NEEDLES

Dugout Ranch

211

163

Park

See Tour 9 map
for continuation

Colorado

ELK RIDGE

ABAJO (BLUE)
MTNS.

Monticello

666

Abajo Pk.
11,445

SAGE PLAIN

COLORADO

Glen Canyon Nat'l Rec. Area

White Canyon

Fry Canyon

Natural Bridges
N.M.

Blanding

POWELL

Glen Canyon

Red Canyon

BEARS EARS

95

LAKE

Halls Crossing Marina

263

261

262

MULEY PT.

VALLEY
OF
GODS

Comb Ridge

RECAPTURE
POCKET

Hovenweep
N.M.

Bluff

Aneth

262

Gooseneck State Reserve

San Juan River

Rainbow Bridge
N.M.

Navajo Mtn.
10,416

MONUMENT

163

Gouldings

VALLEY

ARIZONA

NEW MEXICO

Scale of miles
0   5   10

THOMPSON (5,100 alt.), now located away from the highway, is a small ranching center, formerly a railroad watering point and highway stop.

Turn north from Thompson to **Sego Canyon Indian Writings** (3 m.) and the ghost town of **SEGO** (5 m.). A group of prehistoric Indian pictographs and petroglyphs, badly vandalized, are on the cliffs beside the road. Sego, a coal mining town that is now deserted, had a population of 200 in 1940 and more than twice that many in prior decades. Coal was discovered in the vicinity shortly after the turn of the century by Harry Ballard, a local rancher, and subsequent years brought voluminous production that continued until the 1940s and 1950s. Most of the valuable buildings were removed in that latter decade, only a few dilapidated ruins remaining today. As described in the 1941 edition, mine officials sent two huge dinosaur tracks to eastern museums in 1931, one measuring 53½ by 32 inches in size, the other 44 by 32 inches. The American Museum of Natural History "sent an expedition to the region in 1937, and Barnum Brown, curator of fossil reptiles, reported in the March 1938 issue of *Natural History* that 'Footprints of a giant with a 15-foot stride, and estimated to tower 35 feet, are among the valuable specimens brought back'."

South of I-70 between Thompson and Cisco, in the rugged painted desert north of Arches National Park, is the **Yellowcat Mining District.** This area has been an important and historic producer of vanadium and uranium for decades, as evidenced by excavations, shafts, ruins and dumps. The area is accessible from several directions, including I-70, the Thompson cutoff road north of Moab, and State 128 south of Cisco, but a confusing network of roads makes it advisable to carry detailed maps and/or guidebooks such as those by F. A. Barnes.

CISCO (4,400 alt.), now bypassed by the highway, consists of a few houses and corrals. According to the 1941 edition, Cisco "was built in the center of a red mesa by the Denver & Rio Grande Western Railroad to serve sheep and cattle ranchers. The barrenness of the region is deceptive, for a variety of hardy plants make it important for grazing. Rich deposits of vanadium, uranium, and copper have been found in the hills . . . The Colorado Museum of Natural History sent an expedition into the Book Cliffs near Cisco in 1939 to excavate cliff dwellings." Among its findings were a series of curved, unconnected walls and "A new type of fire pit, circular in form and of material baked to a bricklike consistency."

Cisco was the temporary home of Charles A. Steen, the storied uranium millionaire, and his family when he first hit "paydirt" at the Mi Vida mine south of Moab. At that time (1952) the Steens were flat broke, living in a tarpaper shack and ready to call it quits. *See Moab below; also Mi Vida in Tour No. 11C.*

In the general vicinity of Cisco is one of Utah's most interesting historical inscriptions, carved on a smooth rock face in 1837 by Antoine Robidoux, a trapper-trader who was enroute to the Uinta Basin to establish the first permanent settlement by whites in Utah. The translated inscription (written in French) reads: "Antoine Robidoux passed here 13 November 1837 to establish a trading house on the Vert [Green] or Winte [Uinta] River."

South from Cisco, State 128 descends to the canyon of the Colorado River, which it follows to Moab *(see Tour No. 11B below).* This route provides views of some of the most stirring river/red rock/mountain scenery in Utah, and is the longest riverside scenic drive along the Colorado for hundreds of miles.

Harley Dome, 6 m. west of the Colorado line, takes its name from a geological structure which contains natural gas having a rich helium content. The wells were capped in the 1920s and set aside in a federal reserve, and though regulations now allow commercial production, this has not taken place. Helium also has been found near Woodside, west of Green River. A road leads south from Harley Dome to the embarkation area of Westwater Canyon, where boaters launch their rafts or other craft for downstream expeditions through a series of exciting rapids. BLM rangers are on duty from spring to fall. *See Tour No. 11B below.*

Tour No. 11A - US 163 south from Crescent Junction to Moab

Exquisitely designed peaks of the La Sals loom ever higher as the Colorado River is approached. Immediately to the east, ragged slopes of Salt Valley Anticline form a dramatic horizon, breaking away in places to reveal the multitudinous rock sculptures of Arches National Park. Drab, monotonous plains on the west become transformed, almost imperceptibly, into a shattered region of blocky buttes and mesas, and grand cliffs painted in rainbow colors. Here, for the first time in this area, the unique personality of Canyonlands—that central core of the vast Colorado Plateau Province—becomes apparent.

West of the highway, connecting with it and with State 313 leading to Dead Horse Point and Canyonlands National Park *(below),* is a complex of fairweather dirt roads giving access to dizzy cliff-edge viewpoints, profound gorges, and a marvelous world of red-rock forms—of natural bridges and arches, buttes and pinnacles, spires, goblin rocks, and other erosional curiosities of wide variety. This strange region—a rugged peninsula formed between the Green and Colorado rivers—attracts increasing numbers of off-road vehicles as its adventure opportunities become better known. Many miles of the area's dirt roads may be negotiated by ordinary pickup trucks, or even passenger cars. The most challenging, however, and those offering some of the choicest views, are suitable only for trail bikes or vehicles with four-wheel drive. Hiking possibilities are unlimited. Among the remarkable features that can be reached by vehicle (and in some cases by short hike) are overlook points along the east rim of Green River's Labyrinth and Stillwater canyons . . . tributary gorges such as Mineral and Spring canyons . . . Blue Hills . . . Monitor and Merrimac buttes . . . Bartlett Rim . . . Gold Bar Rim . . . Little Canyon and Bull Canyon . . . Poison Spider Mesa . . . and Gemini twin natural bridges. Detailed guidebooks and maps of the roads and trails are available locally, among them the works of Moab writer F. A. Barnes.

State 313 forks west from US 163 at a point 21 m. south of Crescent Junction and 13 m. north of Moab. This hard-surfaced, all-weather road climbs through Sevenmile Canyon to open flats at nearly 6,000 feet altitude, leading to Dead Horse Point State Park and Island in the Sky, the north district of Canyonlands National Park, both 20-odd miles from US 163.

DEAD HORSE POINT STATE PARK perches atop the rim of the Orange Cliffs escarpment, a magnificent line of sheer Wingate sandstone cliffs which trace a serpentine boundary of perhaps 500 miles around the inner Junction Country where the Green and upper Colorado rivers merge. The edition of 1941 described Dead Horse Point well *(below).* At that time the Point was on the edge of a "howling wilderness," hardly marked by man and little known even to natives. Today it is a state park with visitor center and improved campground. The river below is traversed by hundreds of boats, the roads by thousands of vehicles, and the eastern foreground includes some large mineral evaporation ponds. Despite intrusion by the works of men, the view from Dead Horse Point remains one of Utah's soul-stirring erosional panoramas. As described in the 1941 edition:

> The main side road ends . . . in a grove of green cedars growing out of red sandstone, and a short trail leads to DEAD HORSE POINT. The point is shaped like a blunt arrowhead, 30 yards wide at the neck and 400 yards at its greatest width. It is, by western standards, "sorta level," which means that there are no deep gullies. The trail crosses the neck, a narrow strip of land separating two yawning gorges each more than a thousand feet deep. These gorges dwindle into insignificance when the trail comes to a dizzy, teetering halt at the rim of the UPPER GRAND CANYON OF THE COLORADO. Here the face of the earth breaks away into a [2,000]-foot chasm, offering perhaps the most sensational canyon panorama in Utah.

> The point overlooks 5,000 square miles of the red and rugged Colorado Plateau. The view sweeps east to the La Sal Mountains, south to the Abajo Mountains, southwest to the Henry Mountains, west to the Aquarius Plateau, and down into a tremendous gorge, at the bottom of which, in a canyon within a canyon, the silt-laden Colorado River flows through a maze of buttes and mesas. The river is visible in a dozen places as it winds sinuously from the east, makes a great loop toward the point, doubles back on itself, and finally meanders off to the south.

> The origin of the name of Dead Horse Point is probably a better index to its character than any description yet written. A band of wild desert ponies was herded onto the point, the best of the "broomtails" were culled for "cow service," and the rest were left to return to the range. Confused by the peculiar topography of the point, the horses wandered around in circles, and eventually died of thirst in full view of the Colorado River, half a mile away—straight down.

In September 1978 Dead Horse Point was the site of the first Moab World Invitational Hang Gliding Tournament, which attracted glider pilots from many states and several foreign countries. Weather and adverse winds prevented complete success, but the event introduced the Point to thousands of spectators and newspaper readers. "It's that first step that gets you . . . one minute solid rock and the next, for the first 1,000 feet anyway, nothing but a breeze climbing up the face of the rock

Views from Dead Horse Point.

WARD ROYLANCE PHOTOS

cliff to shake your eyelashes," wrote Ray Grass, *Deseret News* sports writer. Visitors are sternly cautioned to keep back from the rim, only partially fenced. Several persons have been killed by falling over the edge—a vertical drop of 400 feet or so.

Turn south from State 313, 8 m. north of Dead Horse Point, to **Island in the Sky,** the north district of **CANYONLANDS NATIONAL PARK,** separated from other sections of the park by fearsomely rugged terrain that necessitates many miles of travel to visit the other two districts by vehicle. Island in the Sky is an irregular mesa or "island" bounded by sheer cliffs and connected to **Big Flat** (the "mainland") by **The Neck.** At The Neck, according to the 1941 edition, "a tributary gorge of the Colorado River (L) and a tributary gorge of the Green River (R) are separated by a narrow ridge less than 40 feet wide, which constitutes the only passageway to a 40,000-acre mesa—a 'peninsula' surrounded by air and depth. Steep cliffs form the sides of the mesa, which could be fenced with a forty-foot fence." The road continues southward from The Neck to **Grand View Point,** overlooking the Junction Country and Monument Basin. Side spurs lead to **Green River Overlook** and **Upheaval Dome.** *See Canyonlands National Park chapter for further details.*

South of the junction with State 313, US 163 continues toward Moab through a region of high red cliffs and breaks. It is paralleled on the west by the "Potash Railroad," a spur of the D&RGW Railroad, especially built in the 1960s to service the potash mine of Texasgulf Inc., downriver from Moab *(see Tour No. 11B(2) below).* Toward the east are the weird rock forms of Arches National Park, and remnants of the old highway can be seen nearby, more closely following the route of Moab's pioneers through Moab Canyon.

Moab Canyon is formed along a prominent fault, or break in the earth's crust, which raised the rock formations on the west and lowered the corresponding strata on the east, separating identical rocks on either side of the canyon by 2,000 feet or more. This tremendous displacement is very apparent from the Arches switchbacks *(below).* From this viewpoint, with the aid of mental gymnastics, rocks in the bottom of the canyon at the Visitor Center (Navajo sandstone) may be placed in their original position atop the more ancient rocks in the opposite (western) cliff, carrying along on top of the Navajo all the hundreds of feet of even younger rocks in which the strange forms of Arches National Park have been carved.

The entrance to **Arches National Park** is near the south end of Moab Canyon, 5 m. north of Moab, marked by a Visitor Center and other park buildings. *See Arches National Park in parks section for details.* The park's main attractions are above and behind the east wall of the canyon, reached by a steeply switchbacking access road which affords choice overviews of the Colorado River, the greenery of Moab, Spanish Valley and the La Sals.

One mile south of the park entrance is junction with State 279, a paved highway traversing the north bank of Colorado River downstream to Texasgulf's potash mine, and from there as an unpaved road to White Rim Drive, Shafer Trail, and Canyonlands National Park. *See Tour No. 11B(2) below.* The large industrial plant near the junction is the **uranium reduction plant** of Atlas Corporation, which has processed much of the area's uranium production since the mid-1950s. The mill was built at a cost of eight million dollars by Charles A. Steen, the "uranium king," to process ore from his Mi Vida mine; later it was purchased by Atlas Corporation.

The **Colorado River** is crossed by a long highway bridge, built in 1954 to replace a one-lane bridge completed in 1912. This in turn replaced ferryboats operated since the 1880s. Travelers on the Old Spanish Trail, and others before the ferry was built, crossed the river several hundred yards downstream (west) from the bridge. This was a hazardous, sometimes fatal undertaking.

From the south end of the bridge, State 128 leads upstream to Castle Valley, Fisher Towers, Dewey Bridge, and I-70 at Cisco interchange. *See Tour No. 11B(1) below.*

MOAB (4,000 alt. 5,333 pop.), seat of Grand County, is the commercial center of an extensive mining and livestock country. Since 1930 or so, Moab has achieved considerable importance as a visitor center for scenic and recreational attractions, as well as a reputation for being a regional cultural center (the visual and performing arts, crafts, museum, etc.). For 30 years it has been the uranium capital of Utah, being the one-time home of Charles A. Steen, noted "Uranium King," whose mansion home can be seen from the highway north of town, atop a knoll *(see below).*

In the 1941 edition, Moab was described as having "a small business district, selling everything from hay and gasoline to malted milk and liquor —the only 'legal' liquor in the county. Squat red adobe houses stand neighbor to more pretentious firebrick houses. In the evening neon lights illuminate the business district, but after midnight, except on Saturdays, the town does a complete 'blackout'." Since that was written the city's business district has expanded greatly, sprawling mainly along the highway to north and south; and residential areas have sprouted across the valley floor. Much of this expansion dates from the 1950s when Moab became a uranium boomtown. Charlie Steen *(see below)* was not the first prospector to find uranium in the Moab vicinity, by any means, nor the only large operator. The "uranium rush" following World War II had been gaining momentum throughout the entire Four Corners region for several years before his bonanza strike. But the Mi Vida find was of such magnitude that it drew worldwide attention, serving as a beacon for thousands of hopeful prospectors and tens of thousands of "penny stock" speculators. Moab rode the uranium wave to its crest in the late 1950s, then descended to more stable levels in the 1960s. The city never has returned to anything resembling its pre-uranium rusticity. Uranium mining and processing remain an important economic base, complemented by tourism, recreational boating, potash mining, petroleum and regional trade. Movie making has brought money and publicity. *See Color Section for view of Moab and its setting.*

Tourism as an industry was stimulated by the creation of Canyonlands National Park and the advancement of Arches from national monument to national park. River boating has increased in popularity over the years, given particular impetus by the annual Friendship Cruise in May *(see Green River above).* Several commercial tour operations are based in Moab, offering tours by boat, four-wheel-drive vehicles, and airplane. Moab advertises itself as a jeeping capital. The Chamber of Commerce sponsors an annual Jeep Safari on Easter weekend, which attracts as many as 200 jeeps, and also a Four Wheeler Campout on Labor Day.

WARD ROYLANCE

Castle Valley as seen from Porcupine Rim *(left)* and uranium reduction plant of Atlas Minerals near Moab.

Ascending the broken sandstone ledges east of Moab are several popular trails suitable for trail bikes and other off-road vehicles. Passing through scenic red-rock terrain, high above Moab, they provide spectacular views of valleys, river, canyons and myriad exotic erosional forms. One branch tops out on Porcupine Rim, 2,000 feet above Castle Valley. Another spur is the Moab Slickrock Bike Trail, a ten-mile marked route across exhilarating stretches of naked slickrock to bird's-eye overlooks. This trail is administered by the U. S. Bureau of Land Management.

Charles A. "Charlie" Steen and the Steen Mansion — High on a red hill beside the highway north of town is the modernistic mansion built by Charlie Steen, uranium multimillionaire, whose "rags-to-riches and back-again" story has been the stuff of legend for three decades. The home was built by Steen and his wife M. L. in the mid-1950s, shortly after Charlie's discovery of the Mi Vida bonanza 30 miles south of Moab *(see Tour No. 11C)*. He and his family resided there for about ten years until moving to Nevada and building an elaborate mansion near Reno. During their residence in Moab the Steens hosted lavish parties at the mansion, often attended by Hollywood celebrities and other dignitaries. Also, for several years, they sponsored an annual Discovery Party for the general public; nearly 9,000 guests attended the 1956 event. The Steens were noted as public and private benefactors, being especially generous with those who had helped them during their years of hardship.

Moab Museum, 125 E. Center, contains a number of exhibits having to do with the history, archeology, geology, and economy of the area. Among its permanent exhibits are Indian artifacts, mineral specimens, gemstones, and a black light display. Of special note is an exhibit telling the story of uranium mining and milling. The museum is supported by the Southeastern Utah Society of Arts and Science.

Moab's historical background was summarized in the 1941 edition, as follows:

The first attempt to settle Moab Valley came in 1855, with establishment of a mission in the Elk Mountains (now the La Sals). Advance preparations were made in 1854, when five wagon-loads of provisions were cached in the valley. The following spring, the Church called forty-one men to establish the mission. The group left Great Salt Lake City in May, taking with them fifteen wagons, thirteen horses, sixty-five oxen, sixteen cows, two bulls, one calf, two pigs, twelve chickens, four dogs, flour, wheat, oats, corn, potatoes, peas, five plows, twenty-two axes, and other tools. . .

By mid-July the men had planted crops and built a stone fort. They held friendly meetings with the Indians, converted and baptized some of them.

During late September, in a sudden series of attacks, Indians killed three of the Mormons and set fire to haystacks and log fences. The missionaries abandoned the fort the next morning "without eating breakfast." They departed so hurriedly that water was left running in the irrigation canal from Mill Creek. Water continued to run through this ditch, year after year, until eventually it carved an arroyo twenty-five feet deep.

The next settlers were probably two brothers, George and Silas Green, who brought 400 cattle into the valley about 1875. They were apparently killed by Indians. In the summer of 1877 two prospectors, William "Nigger Bill" Granstaff, a mulatto, and a French-Canadian known only as "Frenchie" took possession of the fort, and laid claim to the valley. In 1878 A. G. Wilson made a trade with "Frenchie" for his land, but when he returned with his family the following spring the Frenchman had traded the same land to Walter Moore, and had left the valley. The mulatto, however, remained until 1881. In that year the settlers had their last trouble with the Indians. . . .

A post office was established in 1879, and a committee chose the Biblical name Moab for the town. Grand County was created in 1890, and Moab was named the county seat.

Tour No. 11B - Colorado River and La Sal Mountain Drives

The Colorado River originates in the Rockies of Colorado and flows 1,400 miles before discharging into the Gulf of California, an arm of the Pacific Ocean. It is the second longest river in the 48 contiguous states outside the Mississippi River system; the Rio Grande is longer but carries less water. The Colorado River and its tributaries drain parts of seven western states—one-twelfth of the area of the 48 states or 242,000 square miles (almost three times the area of Utah). Its drainage basin measures 900 miles in length and from 300 to 500 miles in width. If the drainage basin were not so arid, the river would have a much greater volume.

In Utah, with very few exceptions, the main Green and Colorado rivers are almost completely entrenched in deep, steep-walled canyons, their water therefore being of little direct use for agriculture. This is the most important reason why, though the Colorado-Green river system drains almost half of the entire state, less than ten per cent of Utah's people reside within its basin.

The Colorado above its junction with the Green was known as the Grand until 1921, when the name was changed. From Moab downstream to the junction, a distance of 68 miles, the river's flow is almost unobstructed, making it navigable (usually) by powered craft during spring runoff months. At other times it is more suited to rafts or jet-powered craft. Upstream the river is popular for pleasure boating in rafts, canoes or kayaks. Over the years various entrepreneurs have launched commercial craft on the river at Moab, including Tex McClatchy's 93-foot double-deck sternwheel excursion boat, launched in 1972 and later moved to Lake Powell. Advertised as the only excursion boat of its kind west of the Rockies, McClatchy's *Canyon King* was designed to carry 150 passengers on five-hour runs in airconditioned comfort. Having a much longer life at

Moab is the *Canyonlands by Night* open barge, which carries as many as 80 passengers on a two-hour after-dark excursion upstream, with a narrator giving verbal interpretation of the area's geological and historical background, while powerful lights illuminate the sculptured cliffs.

Much farther upstream, just west of the Utah-Colorado line, **Westwater Canyon** offers a challenging whitewater experience. Here in this 17-mile canyon there are nearly a dozen rapids, several of which compare with the most dangerous cataracts of Grand or Cataract canyons. Cliffs of Westwater Canyon are partially formed of dark metamorphic gneisses, nearly two billion years in age, the oldest exposed rocks in eastern Utah. They represent the exposed Precambrian spine of the ancient Uncompahgre Uplift. BLM rangers are on duty at the canyon's launch point south of Harley Dome from April through October. Permits and reservations are required; these and boating information may be obtained at BLM offices in Moab.

The following history is quoted from pages 425 and 427-28 of the 1941 edition:

> Almost without exception, explorations of the Colorado River by boat have started at some point on the Green. In 1889, however, Frank M. Brown led a party down the upper Colorado River to make a preliminary survey for a "water-level" railroad route from Colorado to California. The party set out from Grand Junction, Colorado, and reached the confluence of the Colorado and the Green without mishaps. Below the junction, Brown was swept to his death in the Soap Creek Rapids. The reorganized party continued to Needles, California, reporting the route impractical because of periodic floods. . . .
>
> Beginning with the launching of the *Major Powell* in 1891, unsuccessful attempts were made to establish navigation service between Moab and Greenriver. Improved overland highways ended these experiments, and today (1940) navigation is mostly confined to sight-seeing trips. In 1923 Ross Thomson and Mike O'Neil made the 65-mile trip from Moab to the junction in a 16-foot canoe, covering the distance in 10 hours and 21 minutes. The following year William Tibbetts and Tom Perkins also made haste down the river. Escaping

Boarding rafts on the Colorado River upstream from Moab.

from the Moab county jail, where they were being held for cattle theft, they started in a rowboat. They were pursued by officers in a motorboat. Almost overtaken, they landed and escaped into the adjacent canyon country. They were never recaptured.

(1) Up-river scenic drive (State 128) to Castle Valley, Onion Creek, Fisher Towers, Dewey Bridge and Cisco, with La Sal Mountain Scenic Loop and other side tours.

State 128 forks from US 163 at the river, 3 m. north of Moab. Scenically, this paved drive is one of the choicest in Utah, winding beside the Colorado for more than 30 miles, providing an ever-changing visual feast of painted cliffs, great buttes and spires, green valleys, lofty peaks, and a cluster of most unusual pinnacles known as Fisher Towers. In places the road is confined between the river on one side and a high cliff on the other.

At junction 16 m. from US 163, turn south on paved road into **Castle Valley,** a scenically outstanding pastoral basin cupped between high cliffs on two sides, the river and La Sal Mountains on the other two. Until recent years it was wide-open ranching country, signs of human occupancy being scattered and scarce. The 1970s brought changes in the form of systematic land sales in small parcels, and through transfer of 7,200 acres of federal land to state ownership. The conspicuous landmark which gave the valley its name is **Castle Rock,** also known as Castleton Tower, a lofty finger of red sandstone rising from a large ridge which displays on its opposite end a group of spires known—for obvious reasons—as the Priest and Nuns. Castle Rock has gained national attention from its star billing in General Motors network television commercials featuring an automobile atop the pinnacle's skyscraping summit platform. In 1980 it was scaled in 90 minutes by George Willig and a companion. Willig had previously climbed the World Trade Center in New York City and Angels Landing in Zion National Park. Their encounter with Castle Rock was filmed by ABC News, which utilized a crew of 60 for the filming.

In the valley's high southern end, 10 m. from State 128, was a community of former times known as **Castleton** (6,750 alt.). In the 1941 edition it was described as ''a cluster of weathered log houses occupied in summer by bachelor sheepherders who graze their flocks in the La Sal Mountains.'' Only a few years previously, in the 1930s, Lyman Duncan of Moab wrote that ''the hotel, post office and the old general store and saloon buildings still stand, surrounded by a number of log cabin dwellings that have withstood the elements.'' Even less remains today to identify the site of the former mining boomtown.

Just beyond the remnants of Castleton the road divides into two forks. One leads eastward across the high slopes of the La Sals and drops into the Dolores River gorge enroute to the historic mining town of Gateway, Colorado. The other road winds across the range's western shoulder to US 163 and Moab as the **La Sal Mountain Scenic Loop.** Both drives offer superb alpine scenery and stirring panoramic views across the corrugated red wonderland of Canyonlands. From the Gateway road—which is graveled over most of its length but may be unsuitable for conventional autos at times—fairweather dirt spurs *(recommended for off-road vehicles or pickup trucks)* lead to Adobe and Fisher mesas, which provide bird's-eye views of Castle Valley, Richardson Amphitheater and Fisher Valley. Another sideroad leads to Polar Mesa, connecting through Thompson Canyon with Fisher Valley and points beyond *(see continuation of State 128 river drive below).* Still other forks from the Gateway road lead into Beaver Basin and across Taylor Flat to a junction with the Geyser Pass Trail *(below).* It is recommended that detailed maps and guidebooks be obtained before traveling this sometimes confusing network of La Sal roads.

The **La Sal Mountain Scenic Loop** (partially paved) switchbacks south from Castleton to Harpole Mesa, overlooking Pinhook Valley, Castle Valley, the Colorado's gorge, and Arches National Park in one of the region's most breathtaking panoramas. Lyman Duncan wrote that "historic old Pinhook was the last battleground of Indians and whites [in the area] and still later the site of a mining boomtown. To the east winds the buggy road and trail leading into a beautiful little mountain retreat known as Miners Basin, the last holdout of miners and prospectors in the La Sal Mountains. To the west, valley-like Pinhook is enclosed by a long sharp ridge known as Harpole Mesa, where Indians ambushed the posse of whites in 1881, killing ten men in the battle that followed." The road to Pinhook, very rough at this writing, is scheduled for future improvement.

Miners Basin was the site of frenetic activity during turn-of-the-century years, when it is said that as many as 200 persons resided there during summer months. The Basin had a post office, restaurants and saloons, store and other establishments. Gold was found, but not in bonanza quantities, and the town was short-lived. Sporadic mining activity still continues.

Other sideroads lead from the main Loop drive to **Warner** and **Oowah Lakes** *(forest campgrounds, fishing)* . . . **Sand Flats Trail** leading back to Moab . . . **Geyser Pass** (10,600 alt.) between Haystack Mountain and Mount Mellenthin, leading to State 46 and Paradox, Colorado . . . and **La Sal Pass.** The main road eventually joins US 163 south of Moab. The main Loop road—open only from spring to late fall—usually is suitable for ordinary passenger cars (much of it is paved), but vehicles with high clearance and/or four-wheel-drive are recommended for sideroad travel.

From the Castle Valley turnoff, State 128 continues upstream along the Colorado's canyon, which widens out into Professor Valley, with a serpentine alcove on the south known as Richardson Amphitheater. **Fisher Towers** are visible for miles, a cluster of dark red corrugated spires rising from the soaring 2,000-foot-high south wall of the valley. Also known as the Colorado River Organs, these uniquely sculptured formations were featured in the November 1962 issue of *National Geographic.* Titan, tallest of the towers (900 feet), has been climbed several times.

Just west of the short spur leading to the base of Fisher Towers (22 m. from US 163) another unpaved sideroad winds south into the forbidding gorge of **Onion Creek,** following the creek along its tortuous path through one of the most fantastic areas of rock erosion in Utah. The route is described in the 1941 edition:

> At 1 *m.* the road reaches ONION CREEK *(poisonous water; contains arsenic),* a small, deceitfully clear stream of water. Sheepherders, driving their flocks through this region, lose many sheep from drinking this water. For nine miles the route is along the [channel] of this stream, winding between red sandstone bluffs; the clear water, splashing on fenders or windshields, leaves albuminous splotches. The TOTEM POLE, 5 *m.,* is a tall pinnacle on the edge of a cliff. At THE NARROWS, 6 *m.,* the gorge is squeezed to a width of 10 feet by sandstone walls 400 feet high. For a mile the passageway twists between these walls, permitting a view of only a few feet forward or backward. GAUDY GARDEN, 8 *m.,* is a conglomeration of fantastic formations and bizarre colors. The road winds through a succession of shale hills—yellow, brown, gray, green, and purple, against a background of red towers. FISHER VALLEY, 14 *m.,* locally known as "Forbidden Valley" because of its inaccessibility, is a green farmland at the base of the La Sal Mountains. Three miles wide and eight miles long, it is surrounded by pink sandstone cliffs..

Travelers with time and appropriate vehicles (conventional autos are not recommended) may continue through Fisher Valley to a complex of backcountry roads leading onto the La Sals in one direction, or in the other direction to Dolores River Overlook, Top-of-the-World Overlook, Powerpole Rim and State 128 at Dewey *(see below).*

Warner Lake and peaks of the La Sal Range *(top)*.

Priest and Nuns and Castle Rock *(above)*.

Entrance to Onion Creek Canyon *(left)*.

Colorado River, Fisher Towers, and La Sal Mountains from State 128 *(below)*.

Onion Creek's weird forms are carved from the Moenkopi and Cutler formations. Its rainbow colors are found mainly in exposed gypsum deposits. Vast quantities of gypsum and other "salts" were laid down millions of years ago in the Paradox Basin surrounding Moab, then covered by thousands of feet of younger deposits. Underground movement of these fluid minerals, including potash, was responsible for much of the Moab area's tortured terrain, being instrumental in creating, or encouraging the creation of, faults, anticlines, synclines, grabens, valleys and canyons. Fisher Valley, Castle Valley, the anticlines of Arches National Park, Spanish and Moab valleys, Paradox Valley, Upheaval Dome, and the sunken "valleys" (grabens) of the Needles—all these and more are the result of crustal deformation caused by movement of subterranean salt.

Beyond Fisher Towers State 128 continues along the river to **DEWEY**, 31 m. from US 163, a rustic old ranching hamlet, where the road crosses the Colorado on a narrow, one-lane suspension bridge. Upstream is **Westwater Canyon** *(see above),* where whitewater enthusiasts enjoy a short but thrilling stretch of rapids. At Dewey the Colorado is joined by the Dolores River, which winds its tortuous way to the mother stream through deep and scenic canyons. Downstream to Moab the Colorado is relatively placid, becoming increasingly popular for float-boating in recent years.

A fairweather sideroad from Dewey climbs southeast into a rugged area known as Entrada Bluffs. The road crosses ridges and mesas, with a network of forks leading to the Dolores canyon and Gateway, Colorado; to canyon overviews; Fisher Valley; Polar Mesa; the La Sal Mountains; and other points. It is possible to circle around through Fisher Valley and Onion Creek Canyon, emerging on State 128 at Fisher Towers *(see above).* Of special note are two panoramic overview points not far from Dewey, reached from the Entrada Bluffs road. One tops out on **Powerpole Rim,** more than a thousand feet above the Colorado River and about 7 m. from Dewey. The other, known as **Top-of-the-World Trail,** leaves the main sideroad about 5 m. from Dewey and ascends another 5 m. to a high rim at 6,800 alt., nearly 3,000 feet above the Colorado. This viewpoint, as described by F. A. Barnes, is outstanding. Fisher Valley and "its gigantic exposure of gypsum and the Onion Creek maze lie below the cliffs. The cliffs to the west blend into the soaring, dark red Fisher Towers. Beyond these spires, to the north and west, are the broad river valley of Richardson Amphitheater and the cliffs of Dome Plateau, while the soaring walls of Fisher Mesa and the peaks of the La Sal Mountains dominate the western skyline. Since the viewpoint is high, the different but highly scenic terrain to the north can also be seen, making Top-of-the-World a full-circle panoramic viewpoint." Detailed guidebooks and maps, such as those by Barnes, available locally, are recommended.

State 128 continues north from Dewey, leaving the canyons and joining I-70 near Cisco, 47 m. from US 163. Enroute, a sideroad forks west into the Yellowcat mining district.

(2) Downriver from US 163 via State 279 to Potash, Shafer Trail and White Rim Trail (north bank of the river).

State 279 forks from US 163 near the Atlas Uranium Mill and follows the north bank of the winding Colorado to Texasgulf's potash mining operation, 15 m. from US 163. Enroute it is paralleled by a railroad spur built at great cost by the D&RGW Railroad in the 1960s to service the mine. The route is highly scenic, in respects similar to the up-river drive *(State 128 above)* from US 163 to Castle Valley. Hikes may be taken into secluded side canyons and to picturesque natural arches, several of which can be seen from the road. Other attractions include dinosaur tracks and prehistoric Indian rock writings (petroglyphs). The pavement ends at the potash opera-

Colorado River gorge and State 279 (Potash-White Rim road) downstream from US 163. *Photo by F. A. Barnes.*

tion; this is the recommended road terminus for passenger cars. However, the dirt road beyond may be passable by ordinary vehicles for some miles further, as it climbs higher above the river. *(See Canyonlands National Park.)* This unpaved extension is not without its hazards. Some years ago newspapers reported the tragic death of a woman who, after dark, had stepped from her car and immediately dropped over the edge of a high cliff.

Texasgulf Inc. Potash Complex, sprawling across hundreds of acres of benchland between the river and the Orange Cliffs, was developed to utilize underground deposits of potash far beneath the river, the potash to be used primarily as fertilizer. The complex involves a huge vertical shaft reaching to a depth of 2,800 feet, miles of underground chambers and tunnels, a headframe (hoist tower) 185 feet high, screening building, storage building, and vast evaporation ponds beneath Dead Horse Point. Mining began in 1965 with machines cutting the mineral from beds 3,000 feet underground, in a conventional mining operation. This would have permitted continuous production of 4,000 tons of ore every day. However, it soon became apparent that exploratory drilling had failed to reveal the fact that the potash beds were not uniformly horizontal but had, instead, the distressing habit of undulating. This characteristic, as well as flooding, market conditions, and other problems, forced eventual change from conventional to solution mining of the potash. Conversion expenses brought total project costs to nearly $50,000,000, exclusive of the railroad spur, which had cost about $5,000,000. Though the two-year conversion process was essentially completed by 1972, more years were required to refine the solution process, which involves flooding underground tunnels with water, dissolving the salts (not pure potash), pumping the solution back up and into evaporation ponds, waiting for solar processing, and finally harvesting, mechanical processing and shipping. A bothersome byproduct is common salt—millions of tons of it—which is discarded.

(3) Downriver from Moab to Cane (Kane) Creek Canyon with sideroads leading to Moab Rim, Hurrah Pass, Land Behind the Rocks, Lockhart Basin, etc.

West from US 163 in Moab, the Cane (Kane) Creek access road leads through the river canyon's Portal, then downstream along the Colorado's south bank, giving access to dramatically scenic cliff and canyon country. This is a popular area for off-road vehicles because roads are unpaved beyond the first four miles or so. Shallow streams must be forded; there are steep grades in places; and road surfaces may not be suitable at times for passenger car use. Normally, however, ordinary cars may be driven to Hurrah Pass, or almost that far.

At the **Portal,** quoting the 1941 edition, "the Colorado pierces towering cliffs that surround the valley, and begins its long imprisoned journey through canyons thousands of feet deep. Along the route are natural bridges, arches, windows, buttes, pinnacles, monuments—a continuous, constantly-changing display of strange and remarkable formations carved in naked red rock."

About one mile inside the canyon's Portal, a very steep and rough sideroad (suitable only for off-road vehicles) winds up the cliff, topping out in **Land Behind the Rocks** *(also see below),* with grand rim views of the river and its gorge, Moab and Spanish Valley, the La Sal Mountains, Arches, rims and mesas to the north, and the unearthly landscape of Behind the Rocks. Though relatively short (up to six miles one way), the drive is exceptionally rewarding in scenic thrills.

The 1941 edition describes one of Utah's unusual—and puzzling—mysteries, as follows:

[From the road] a foot trail (L) leads up the side of the cliff, through a cleft in the sandstone walls, then follows the canyon rim for a short distance, and descends to the PETROGLYPH OF THE MASTODON, the "riddle of the Colorado." The "mastodon" is an ancient drawing chipped in red sandstone. It measured 42 inches from snout to rump, and is 14 inches high at the shoulders. The upturned trunk is shorter than that of an elephant. The petroglyph was discovered in 1924 by John Bristol, Moab newspaperman, but little information regarding the strange carving was circulated until 1933, when Dr. Lawrence M. Gould, geologist-geographer on Byrd's first Antarctic Expedition, visited and photographed it. Weathering of the sandstone in which the drawing is cut proves that it is very old. It is 300 feet above the present river bed—far above other petroglyphs along the stream. Scientists are generally agreed that early man carved only images of what he actually saw, but the mastodon is said to have been extinct for 30,000 years—15,000 years before the supposed advent of man. This gives rise to speculation as to whether man was here 30,000 years ago, or whether the mastodon survived until 15,000 years ago. The Mastodon petroglyph remains the "riddle of the Colorado."

About 4 m. from US 163 the pavement ends as the road leaves the river gorge and turns south into Cane (Kane) Creek Canyon.

Near this point, **Pritchett Canyon** enters from the southeast. This narrow, highly scenic gorge is the route of an off-road vehicle trail leading into **Land Behind the Rocks,** a compact but exceptionally rugged region of slickrock fins and domes and labyrinthine drainage channels, a maze of strange and beautiful erosional forms. Much of the area is difficult or impossible of access even to hikers. So rugged is it that one of its largest known arches was not discovered until 1970, and then only through aerial sighting. Behind the Rocks is bounded on the east by the sheer line of cliffs forming Spanish Valley's western face; on the other side its boundary is the gorge of Cane Creek. The area contains a dozen or so impressive natural arches and bridges, best known of which is **Pritchett Arch.** Somewhat resembling the famous Rainbow Bridge in form, though much smaller, this symmetrical opening was pictured in *National Geographic* in its issue of February 1910. Dimensions of the opening are approximately 100 feet in width and 70 feet in height. Easiest access to Behind the Rocks is from US 163, 13 m. south of Moab. From that point the main access road and several spurs give hiking access to the "slickrock jungle," arches and bridges, and to vehicle overlook points along the rim of spectacular Cane Creek Canyon. Detailed maps and guidebooks, available in Moab are recommended.

The main Cane Creek drive continues through a deep, serpentine gorge which is narrowly confined for the first few miles, then widens out. Uranium workings can be seen in the cliffs, and countless erosional forms. Spur roads lead to **Hurrah Pass,** a high ridge between Cane Creek Canyon and that of the Colorado; to **Amasa Back, Chicken Corners,** and **Jackson Hole**—all of which are outstanding for marvelous red-rock terrain, and each offering something special in the way of excitement for backcountry travelers. Two longer trails extend southward from the Cane Creek Drive. One traverses the length of **Cane Creek Canyon** to US 163, at Kane Springs rest area, 15 m. south of Moab. This is a distance of about 13 m. from the Hurrah Pass Junction. The other, much longer road (about 50 m. in length), known as **Lockhart Basin Trail,** loops around from Hurrah Pass to the south, following a broad terrace between the Colorado and a long line of towering cliffs, finally joining State 211 (the Needles access road) near the Sixshooter Peaks. The road passes beneath overlook points on the rim of Hatch Point, from a thousand to two thousand feet above the trail *(see Tour No. 11C below)*. Features of this drive include endless panoramic views of the Orange Cliffs and the corrugated Junction-Needles country; erosional phenomena beyond description; and intimate personal contact with the red-rock wilderness.

Tour No. 11C - Moab to Blanding via US 163 with side tours to Canyon Rims Overlooks, Indian Creek, Canyonlands National Park and Abajo Mountains

South of Moab, US 163 traverses **Spanish Valley,** a semiarid "graben" or sunken basin thinly vegetated with brush and prickly pear. The valley's name signifies its use as a segment of the Old Spanish Trail from the 1830s to 1850s, and perhaps even earlier. East of the highway loom superb peaks of the **LA SAL MOUNTAINS,** second highest range in the state, which rank in sheer beauty among the loveliest alpine groups of America. The La Sals *(Spanish, meaning salt, and long known as the Salt Mountains)* were formed by laccolithic doming, caused by intrusion of igneous rock between the underlying sedimentary beds. In this structural respect they resemble other "island ranges" of the Colorado Plateau: the Abajos, Henrys, Navajo Mountain (probably), and Ute Mountain in Colorado. The range is roughly 15 miles long and six miles wide, and high mesas radiating from the main mass cover a much larger area. Mount Peale, the highest peak, has an elevation of 12,721 feet, but this lofty summit, lying to the east, is not too apparent from the valley. Half a dozen peaks exceed 12,000 feet, and several others are only slightly lower. Forests of pine, fir and aspen cover the higher slopes; juniper (cedar), scrub oak and brush grow on the lower slopes. The greater part of the range is included in Manti-La Sal National Forest, which supervises the grazing of thousands of sheep and cattle. Streams from the La Sals provide Moab with some of its agricultural water.

About 8 m. south of Moab a sideroad forks east into the mountains as the **La Sal Mountain Scenic Loop** *(see Tour No. 11B above).* Continuing its climb southward out of Spanish Valley, US 163 enters a zone of pygmy evergreens. Toward the north, the jagged Moab Rim, the La Sals above their brightly colored shoulders, and the weird skyline of far-off Arches all combine for powerful emotional impact.

About 13 m. south of Moab, an unpaved road forks west to rugged, little-known **Land Behind the Rocks**—to panoramic overlooks along the rim of Cane Creek Canyon, Pritchett Canyon, and eventual junction with the Colorado River drive *(see Tour No. 11B(3) above).*

About 16 m. south of Moab is **Kane Springs Rest Area** and **Picnic Ground** *(drinking water, tables, restrooms),* a shady oasis in a red-rock alcove. Kane Springs has been a welcome stop for white travelers in this arid country for 150 years or longer, and from time immemorial for Indians.

Several hundred yards along the highway from Kane Springs is an attraction known as **Hole 'N the Rock.** Here, in the side of a great sandstone bluff, sculptor A. L. Christensen undertook the herculean task, almost singlehandedly—beginning in 1945—of excavating 50,000 cubic feet of rock to create a cavern home and business establishment with 5,000 square feet of floor space. After his death in 1957, Mrs. Christensen (Gladys) and other family members continued to exhibit the "mansion" as a visitor attraction and memorial. Both A. L. and Gladys are buried nearby. Open all year. Gift and rock shop, snack bar, tours.

Across the highway from Hole 'N the Rock, a rough four-wheel-drive road enters Cane (Kane) Creek Canyon and follows that grand gorge northward to the Colorado River, thence to Moab *(see Tour No. 11B(3) above)*.

Between Hole 'N the Rock and La Sal Junction, on a rise beside the highway, is the **Moab Compressor Station** of Northwest Pipeline Corporation. The station services a buried 26-inch pipeline, 1,400 miles long, which conveys natural gas between the Four Corners and Pacific Northwest. The line was built in the 1950s at a cost of approximately 200 million dollars.

LA SAL JUNCTION, 22 m. from Moab, marks the junction of US 163 with paved State 46 leading east to Naturita and other points in Colorado. The junction is a popular wayside dining and service stop for ranchers, miners and truckers.

Turn right on State 46 to **LA SAL** (7,125 alt.), a small ranching community settled in the 1930s when Old La Sal, 12 m. east, was abandoned because of frequent floods. La Sal is headquarters for Redd Ranches, a vast livestock operation that ranges thousands of sheep and cattle over a huge expanse of public and private land in Utah and Colorado. For years the town was almost synonymous with Charlie Redd, more than any other person its founder and vital spark for decades. La Sal, Charlie Redd, his family and his ranching empire were public news over a period of years, the subject of numerous journalistic articles. Four lengthy articles about Redd appeared in Salt Lake City newspapers in 1947 and 1948 alone. One of these, by Tom Mathews, in the *Salt Lake Tribune* issue of October 3, 1948, described him as "A Big Man—just as big as the country which produced him." At that time, Mathews wrote, "His holdings include 35,000 acres of deeded land, 250,000 acres of permit range land and 2,000 acres of cultivated land. He runs 18,000 head of breeding ewes on the Redd ranch and just to keep them company another 2,500 head of cattle. Of the latter 500 are registered Herefords. On the Kansas wheat stubble he grazes as many as 40,000 head of lambs . . . He is not a resident of La Sal. He is La Sal.

South of La Sal Junction 1 m. is junction with unpaved road leading to **Looking Glass Rock,** a large opening in a rock dome (2 m. from US 163). **Wilson Arch,** 3 m. south of La Sal Junction, beside the highway, also is a salmon-colored sandstone wall through which a large opening has been eroded.

About 5 m. south of La Sal Junction, the highway crosses **Hatch Wash.** In 1941, when the highway followed a different alignment, there was no bridge. Then, "in wet weather Hatch Wash crosses US 160 . . . The wash comes out of a deep rocky gorge (L), crosses the highway, and drops a sheer 150 feet into another gorge (R). Near the road (R) the torrential flood waters have gouged a 'well', 75 feet deep."

In **Dry Valley,** at a junction 11 m. south of La Sal Junction (33 m. south of Moab, 22 m. north of Monticello), a paved road leads westward across a wide expanse of gradually rising "flats" to the **CANYON RIMS RECREATION AREA** (U. S. Bureau of Land Management). The access road is paved for the 22 mile distance to **Needles Overlook,** graded and maintained to two other developed areas to the north: **Hatch Point Campground** and **Anticline Overlook.**

The Canyon Rims area features aerial observation points along the rim of **HATCH POINT,** a great peninsula with ragged edges, about 20 miles long but only a few miles wide. Circumscribed by precipitous cliffs up to 2,000 feet high, the Point is one among several "islands" of the Junction Country—rock platforms jutting from the "mainland," connected only by narrow causeways and surrounded by thin air. The Point's eastern rim overlooks Hatch Wash and Cane Creek Canyon, while its southern rim is formed by a chasm known as Hart's Draw. Its western edge, affording the grandest panorama, is a sinuous escarpment that serves as an outer wall of the Colorado's inner basin.

Viewpoints from the rim of Hatch Point are limited only by personal inclination, hiking ability, and time. Needles Overlook and other spots along the west rim overlook the heart of **CANYONLANDS NATIONAL PARK,** that unbelievably rugged Junction Country where the Green and Colorado rivers meet, a weird region of naked rock where seeing is not necessarily believing. Superlatives applied to the views from Dead Horse Point and Grand View Point are just as appropriate here. The eye sweeps across a corrugated maze of cliffs, canyons, remarkable crustal deformations, and erosional forms that bewilder with their strangeness. The latter range from grand buttes to the exquisite sculptures of Monument Basin and the Needles-Salt Creek-Standing Rocks country *(see Canyonlands National Park).*

A stirring verbal description was penned more than a century ago by geologist John Newberry, who accompanied the Macomb Expedition to this region in 1859. From a base camp at Ojo Verde, in Hatch Wash on the Old Spanish Trail, a squad from the main exploring party traveled southwest across Hatch Point to the edge of "a magnificent canyon 1200 feet in depth" [probably Harts Draw] into which "with great difficulty" they descended. Speaking of the panorama to the west, as seen from the rim, Newberry wrote:

> From this point the view swept westward over a wide extent of country, in its general aspects a plain, but everywhere deeply cut by a tangled maze of canons, and thickly set with towers, castles, and spires of most varied and striking forms; the most wonderful monuments of erosion which our eyes, already experienced in objects of this kind, had beheld. . . . Toward the west the view reached some thirty miles, there bounded by long lines and bold angles of mesa walls similar to those behind us, while in the intervening space the surface was diversified by columns, spires, castles, and battlemented towers of colossal but often beautiful proportions, closely resembling elaborate structures of art, but in effect far surpassing the most imposing monuments of human skill. In the southwest was a long line of spires of white stone, standing on red bases, thousands in number, but so slender as to recall the most delicate carving in ivory or the fairy architecture of some Gothic cathedral; yet many, perhaps most, were over five hundred feet in height, and thickly set in a narrow belt or series some miles in length. Their appearance was so strange and beautiful as to call out exclamations of delight from all our party.

The Bureau of Land Management has developed a campground at **WIND-WHISTLE,** beside the main sideroad 5 m. from US 163. At **Needles Overlook** are picnic tables. There are camping units and a nature trail at **Hatch Point Campground.** Picnic tables, interpretive exhibits and trails have been provided at **Anticline Overlook,** which some believe affords the most wonderful overview of any rim point in the Canyonlands region.

East from US 163 in the vicinity of the Canyon Rims junction, other sideroads lead to **Lisbon Valley** and **Big Indian mining districts,** the location of enormously rich uranium mines, also the site of oil wells and copper deposits.

In 1952, at **Big Indian,** Charlie Steen found the bonanza uranium lode (**Mi Vida** - "My Life") that made him a multimillionaire. Other uranium mines, such as that of Rio Algom, began operations in the vicinity, making this Utah's single most productive uranium district over a period of decades. From this area in 1958 Lisbon

Cane Creek Canyon, Land Behind the Rocks *(atop the cliffs)*, and La Sal Mountains, looking east from Anticline Overlook in Canyon Rims Recreation Area. *F. A. Barnes Photo.*

Uranium Corporation delivered "the richest single truck load of uranium ore in the history of the American mining industry"—20 tons of ore averaging nearly 22 per cent U308, with a value of about $30,000. In 1979 Atlas Corporation announced that a drilling program in the south end of **Lisbon Valley** had delineated an ore body containing more than four million pounds of economically recoverable U308, worth several hundred million dollars at prevailing prices. The district became a significant oil producer starting in 1960 with the successful drilling of Pure Oil Company's Northwest Lisbon No. 1 USA well. This discovery was designated as "the discovery of the year" by the national petroleum industry, recognizing the size of the field and overcoming of its reputation as a poor prospect. Lisbon Valley's oil production is piped south to the Greater Aneth complex, whence it is distributed by a major pipeline system.

In the south end of Dry Valley, at the junction of US 163 and State 211 (13 m. north of Monticello), the bulbous, symmetrical dome of **Church Rock** flanks the highway on the east, **Sugar Loaf** mound on the west. The latter, according to the 1941 edition, resembles a "gigantic loaf of bread. Its top is hollowed out by erosion, and in pioneer days teamsters stretched tarpaulins inside the depression to catch rain water for their horses."

Paved State 211, main access to the south district of Canyonlands National Park, leads westward through a gap in a ridge, down into Indian Creek Canyon, past Newspaper Rock, Dugout Ranch and the Sixshooter peaks, to pavement's end in The Needles. The decrepit wooden buildings beside State 211 in the vicinity of the main highway are remnants of the former **Home of Truth Colony,** a religious community founded in 1933 by Mrs. Marie M. Ogden. Long defunct, the community was described in the 1941 edition, and in more detail by Wallace Stegner in *Mormon Country.* Relics of the Home of Truth are displayed in the Monticello Museum.

West of Photograph Gap, 3 m. from US 163, State 211 descends into **Indian Creek Canyon,** a grandly scenic sandstone gorge. Its sculptured walls, beautifully colored and surmounted by wondrous erosional forms, enclose an oasis of lush streamside vegetation and alfalfa fields. Indian Creek flows from the Abajo Mountains, a perennial stream that provides water for ranches along its course—and, incidentally, for Blanding in the other direction far to the south, via a long diversion tunnel. Walls of the canyon are festooned with well-preserved petroglyphs and pictographs of varying antiquity, the most notable of which are displayed at **Newspaper Rock State Historical Monument** (11 m. from US 163). Newspaper Rock is a smooth rock face under a protective overhang, bearing at least 350 distinct Indian "glyphs," some of them superimposed on others of earlier vintage. These are of differing age and cultural origin, ranging apparently from the Anasazi period of 800 years ago or more to the Ute era of the past century. Additions by whites also are present, but remoteness has prevented serious vandalism, and Newspaper Rock ranks among the state's archeological treasures. Nearby is a modest campground with toilets. Carry drinking water.

About 8 m. farther along the canyon appear the green fields and shady groves of **Dugout Ranch,** nestled in a superlative setting of red cliffs and finger buttes. Dugout Ranch for many years was the headquarters of S&S (Scorup-Sommerville) Cattle Company, one of Utah's largest cattle empires, whose Canyonlands stock range surely ranks among the most fearsomely rugged and forbidding parts of America. The life of J. A. "Al" Scorup—who purchased the ranch in 1919, in partnership with others—became the stuff of legend before his death in 1959 at the age of 87. He and his brother Jim, natives of Sevier Valley, migrated to southeastern Utah as young men before the turn of the century, being among the first non-Indians to see the White Canyon bridges *(see Natural Bridges National Monument).* Working with Jim and others, overcoming heartbreaking obstacles, Al Scorup gradually built a large cattle operation in the labyrinthine breaks of San Juan County. (A short biography, by David Lavender, appeared in *Desert Magazine* for October 1940.) Though cattle ranching was his first love, Scorup engaged also in banking, civic, grazing and livestock association activities. Scorup was responsible for bulldozing the first vehicle road from Dugout Ranch into The Needles, including—in the late 1940s—the famed Elephant Hill jeep road which still remains a vehicle challenge more than 30 years later. Cave Spring, now a park attraction, was a Scorup cowboy camp. *See Canyonlands National Park.*

South from Dugout Ranch an unpaved road climbs through **Cottonwood Canyon** to the 9,000-foot forested heights of Elk Ridge, providing bird's-eye overviews of the sublime **Salt Creek-Lavender Canyon-Needles maze.** The road connects with other unpaved roads leading to Beef Basin, Dark Canyon Primitive Area, the Abajos, Kigalia Ranger Station, Bears Ears, State 95, Blanding and Monticello. *See Tour No. 11E and Canyonlands National Park.* From this sideroad a short spur forks north from Cathedral Butte on Salt Creek Mesa to **Big Pocket Overlook,** 3 m., atop an aerial peninsula jutting high above an exquisite labyrinth of naked rock—a tangled complex of ridges and slopes, canyons and flats, spires, turrets, and other superlative erosional forms—all carved in elegant contours and painted in eyesoothing pastels.

In the vicinity of Dugout Ranch and the Sixshooter peaks, two other canyons are accessible from State 211. These are **Lavender** and **Davis canyons,** respectively about 3.5 and 7 miles from the ranch junction. Paralleling Cottonwood Canyon on the

Indian Creek Canyon, enroute to The Needles.

west, these gorges feature natural arches and other curious erosional phenomena as well as prehistoric Indian ruins, all in a cloistered setting of near-pristine wilderness.

The west wall of Indian Creek Canyon breaks away to the north of Dugout Ranch and a widespreading expanse opens out, with a long line of great Orange Cliffs and blocky buttes forming the distant horizon. A peculiar spell overwhelms many visitors at this magic portal, marked by the symmetrical twin fingers known as **South** and **North Sixshooter Peaks,** distinctive buttes that rise more than a thousand feet above their bases. Several miles beyond North Sixshooter, where State 211 turns west, an unpaved sideroad forks northward and goes through **Lockhart Basin,** a great rock-walled amphitheater formed by the escarpment of Hatch Point, to Hurrah Pass, Cane Creek Canyon, and Moab *(see Tour No. 11B).*

(Passenger cars are not very suitable for the sideroads described above, which are rough, rocky, sandy and subject to washouts—at least in spots. However, four-wheel-drive is not necessarily required. If in doubt, inquire locally or from rangers. Detailed guidebooks and maps, such as F. A. Barnes' Canyon Country series, are advisable for back-country travel.)

State 211 continues westward from the Lockhart Basin turnoff into the rock jungle of Canyonlands National Park. *See park section for details.*

South of its junction with State 211, US 163 soon leaves Dry Valley and climbs to higher levels near 7,000 feet where Sage Plain merges into the foothills of the Abajos. **SAGE PLAIN,** more than a thousand square miles in extent, sweeps eastward into Colorado to Mesa Verde and the peaks of the San Miguel, La Plata and Ute mountains. Monotonously level and gently rolling to the eye, the vast plain is incised by a network of shallow to deepening channels draining into the canyons of Montezuma, McElmo and Recapture creeks, and thence into the San Juan River. It is used as winter range for livestock, and much of it is dry-farmed, with pinto beans and grains being important crops.

Dominating the landscape near Monticello are the **ABAJO MOUNTAINS,** known more commonly—since pioneer days—as the Blues or Blue Mountains. The formal name, originally applied by New Mexicans before Anglo settlement, is pronounced "uh-BAH-hoe," meaning "low" or "low down" in Spanish. Their "lowness' is deceiving, for Abajo Peak, the highest summit, has an altitude of 11,360 feet and several other points approach or exceed 10,000 feet. Like the La Sals and Henrys, the Abajos are of laccolithic origin, and almost the entire range is included in the Manti-La Sal National Forest.

MONTICELLO (7,050 alt. 1,929 pop.), seat of San Juan County (Utah's largest county), is a cool green city on the east slope of the Abajos, at the headwaters of Montezuma Creek. It was named for Thomas Jefferson's home in Virginia, but the name is pronounced "mon-ti-SELL-o" instead of "mon-ti-CHELL-o" as in the East. Because of altitude, temperatures rarely reach 90 degrees, but winters can be very cold and the growing season is short. In 1941 the community derived its livelihood principally from sheep and cattle and its population totaled 665. Since then its economic base has been considerably broadened to include large-scale farming, vanadium mining and processing during World War II, and then uranium, oil, highway travel, and recreational tourism. Energy minerals— uranium, oil and gas—have been the main source of the county's wealth for nearly 30 years. Mineral value totaling more than a billion dollars during that time has given San Juan County one of the highest tax bases of any rural county in Utah. Several wealthy residents of Monticello have made their money largely from uranium, but wealth is not flaunted ostentatiously.

A more numerous and affluent population, compared with that of 40 years ago, is indicated by expanding business and residential sections, a golf course, museum, airport, indoor swimming pool, etc. Yet Monticello remains, comparatively, a quiet rural community.

Monticello Museum, 80 N. Main. contains exhibits of early Indian cultural artifacts and historical relics of San Juan pioneers. Among these are

Sage Plain between Monticello and Blanding.

WARD ROYLANCE

items brought to the area through Hole-in-the-Rock. Also featured are articles having to do with the Home of Truth religious colony *(see above)*.

Other details concerning Monticello appear in the 1941 edition.

Turn west from Monticello on a paved road into the **Abajo Mountains** *(see above)* and **Manti-La Sal National Forest.** The pavement ends 5 m. from US 163 at **Dalton Springs Forest Campground** (8,200 feet). *Tables, toilets, drinking water, trailer spaces; open June to October.* About 2 m. beyond is **Buckboard Forest Campground** (8,600 feet) with similar facilities and season. Reached by the same road are **Lake Monticello** (fishing, camping) and **Blue Mountain Ski Area,** a modest winter sports development (2 lifts, good cross-country skiing terrain). The Abajos also are popular for snowmobiling. A network of unpaved roads crisscrosses the Abajos from this main access road, one looping to the right and back to US 163 north of Monticello. Another climbs high through Cooley Pass between 11,000-foot peaks and descends the south slope to Blanding. Additional vehicle routes, ranging from rough to primitive, give access to other parts of the range, while many miles of trails invite the hiker and snowmobiler. Inquire locally about details.

East from Monticello, US 666 crosses sparsely-populated **Sage Plain** into Colorado—to Cortez, Mesa Verde and Durango.

Between Monticello and Blanding, US 163 drops nearly a thousand feet as it crosses the rollercoaster foothills of the Abajos and headwater tributaries of Montezuma-Recapture creeks.

VERDURE, 7 m. (6,900 alt.) is a cluster of houses huddled in a green pocket enclosed by mountainous slopes. The San Juan pioneers, who first came north from Bluff in search of new and less grudging farmland, settled at Verdure and Monticello in 1887 and 1888.

US 163 descends into **Devil's Canyon,** a tributary gorge of Montezuma Canyon, where Manti-La Sal National Forest maintains a public campground and picnic area. According to the 1941 edition, "For much of the year the stream-bed is dry, but after a rainstorm it is swept by a swift, roaring torrent. Before the creek was bridged, heavily-laden freight wagons were occasionally trapped by unexpected flood-waters and dashed to pieces against the canyon walls." Devil's Canyon is described by the U. S. Bureau of Land Management as an "ecologically unique area," habitat for animals such as the Abert squirrel and cougar.

Turn east from Devil's Canyon, and from Recapture Canyon *(below)*, to **Alkali Ridge Historical Landmark** (10 m. by unpaved road), where archeologists excavated 13 prehistoric Indian sites in the early 1930s. Here, nearly a thousand years ago, was a long-lived community of pueblo Indians. Scientists excavated a complex of more than 200 connected rooms, then refilled their diggings to prevent deterioration and vandalism. The site is marked by a stone monument dedicated in 1965.

Recapture Canyon, 4 m. north of Blanding, is a broad, deep valley through which can be seen the Abajos in an impressive view. A sawmill operation flourished for years near the highway. Reputedly, the canyon was named by Peter Shirts, an oft-moving pioneer of southern Utah who settled in the San Juan country in the 1870s. According to Albert R. Lyman, Shirts "was reading a story of Hernando Cortes, and he got a strange idea that Montezuma escaped from Cortes and was recaptured at the creek which he named Recapture. He also named Montezuma Creek with the same idea in mind." If this was true, Shirts had applied the names prior to 1877, when they appeared in a published report of the Hayden Survey. Another explanation is that government surveyors of 1875 applied the name when they "recaptured" some horses stolen by Indians.

BLANDING (6,100 alt. 3,118 pop.), on White Mesa, is an attractive, stable community, the largest in San Juan County, surrounded by fields of hay and grain. Its residents in 1941 derived their livelihood mainly from sheep and cattle. As with Monticello, this is no longer the case. The discovery of uranium, oil and natural gas in the 1950s, at Aneth and other locations throughout the Four Corners region, transformed Blanding and Monticello in particular, and San Juan County in general. Wealth from minerals, though hardly distributed on an equitable individual basis and of a somewhat undependable nature, did raise the general tax base astronomically, as well as the *per capita* income level. The county's significant Indian population—previously among the most economically deprived groups in the nation, and amounting to nearly half the total population of San Juan County—also benefited from the new economic climate. In addition, the county's economy has been influenced by tribal, state and federal expenditures on behalf of Indian residents—primarily Navajo and Ute—who numbered 5,600 in 1980 (total county population was 12,253).

Increased wealth is evidenced by new dwellings, new schools, new businesses and industrial developments, etc. Surprisingly, Blanding exhibits few of the usual signs of extreme growth; it remains a rather quiet, orderly community, obviously home-oriented and conservative, resistant to change merely for the sake of change.

Wrote Albert R. Lyman, Blanding's "Old Settler": "This town was begun on the 2nd of April 1905 when I landed here with my wife and 1st child. I was the first settler." Years before, his uncle Walter Lyman had seen a large city on White Mesa in a forceful vision, which he remembered through life. Albert R. Lyman gained note as a writer of local history and devoted most of his long career to education. During the last 30 years or so of his life, he and his wife Gladys—with community and LDS Church support—dedicated their educational efforts toward Navajo and Paiute youth.

The following is excerpted from the 1941 edition:

> "Blanding," [said Herbert E. Gregory], "owes its existence to . . . Walter C. Lyman, the father of the irrigation project that brought the waters of the Abajo Mountains to some 3,000 acres of favorably lying land. . . . In 1905 the first settlers arrived—chiefly those whose farms had been ruined by the San Juan River at Bluff and those driven from Mexico by political and religious persecution." Blanding stands on land once occupied by prehistoric Indians, and ruins of adobe and rock were used in constructing some of the older buildings. The town was first named Grayson, but was renamed in 1915 when Thomas W. Bicknell, an Easterner, offered a library to any Utah town that would take his name. Two towns, Grayson and Thurber, accepted. A compromise was arranged whereby Thurber became Bicknell and Grayson became Blanding, taking the maiden name of Mrs. Bicknell; the library was divided between them.

Edge of the Cedars Museum in Blanding. *F. A. Barnes photo.*

Edge of the Cedars State Historical Monument is located in Blanding at 660 W. 400 North, on the east rim of Westwater Canyon. It consists of two units: a strikingly attractive museum facility, built of native stone, and the ruins of a pre- historic Anasazi village adjacent to the museum. The village, accessible by marked trail, was occupied from about 750 to 1220 A.D. and consists of six residential- ceremonial complexes. Formal excavation was begun in the 1960s by Weber State College, but much remains to be done and a continuing excavation-stabilization pro- gram is underway. The ruins are listed on both state and national historic registers. **Edge of the Cedars Museum,** dedicated in 1978, was constructed by the Utah State Division of Parks and Recreation with the objective of preserving and interpreting the cultural history of the Anasazi, Ute and Navajo Indians, as well as early white pioneers and settlers—all residents of the San Juan area at different times over a period of 2,000 years or more. The museum features an information lobby, interpre- tive exhibits, auditorium, research and work rooms, Indian crafts demonstration area, and sales shop. Open daily except for major holidays.

Tour No. 11D - Blanding to Monument Valley (Arizona line) via US 163

Three miles south of Blanding, west of the highway, is **Five Kiva Ruin** in Westwater Canyon, badly vandalized over the years but recently the subject of technical excavation and reconstruction by the Division of State History. The site was occupied for more than 1,200 years from the early Basket- maker era near the time of Christ to about 1250 A.D. when it was aban- doned by the Anasazi people.

Four miles south of Blanding is junction with **State Highway 95,** Utah's Bicentennial Highway, leading west to Natural Bridges National Monument, Lake Powell and Hanksville. *See Tour No. 11E for details.*

Five miles south of Blanding, beside the highway, is the brightly colored uranium mill and ore buying station of **Energy Fuels Nuclear Inc.** of Denver. Costing several tens of millions of dollars, the complex began milling operations in 1980, processing not only the ore deposits owned by Energy Fuels but also those of numerous other mining operations throughout the vast Four Corners region. Cooperative services include surveying, financing and development assistance.

Beside the highway in this vicinity, about 5 m. south of Blanding on the east side of the highway, is **Posey Monument.** The monument was erected by the Boy Scouts of Blanding in recognition of the Paiute Indian War of 1923, said to be the last Indian war in the nation. *See Bluff below.*

In 1941, along more than 80 miles of highway south of Blanding to Arizona, the total white population was less than 100. Excepting a few families at Mexican Hat, nearly all of those people lived at Bluff. Population has increased since then, of course—for Indians as well as whites—but the region still has one of the smallest population densities in the nation. South of Blanding the highway runs along a flat divide between **Cottonwood Canyon** on the west and **Recapture Canyon** on the east. "The canyons are not always visible from the road, but at one place they are less than thirty feet apart. The road traverses the southwest corner of Sage Plain, running through miles of gently rolling sagebrush, greasewood, and rabbitbrush. . . ." Distant views are tantalizing. Island peaks appear in every direction, some dim with distance. Strange buttes and crags are interspersed between the peaks, barely hinting at the broken wilderness of rock not yet too apparent, appetizers promising a feast yet to come: hazy Shiprock and the mystic forms of Monument Valley . . . the corrugated summit of Comb Ridge . . . Bears Ears buttes . . . and assorted smaller forms scattered about.

State 262 forks east from a junction 15 m. south of Blanding (11 m. north of Bluff), leading to **Hovenweep National Monument, Greater Aneth Oil Field, Montezuma Creek,** and **Four Corners Monument.**

Paved State 262 was built in 1958-59 to allow access from Utah to the newly-developed **Greater Aneth Oil Field,** which had been discovered two years previously. Before the new highway was built, oil workers found it more convenient to trade and live in Colorado; afterwards, Utah communities received a larger share of economic benefits. The route passes through a rugged landscape adjoining Montezuma Canyon, into which it descends near the settlement of **Montezuma Creek,** 23 m. from US 163. The highway continues from Montezuma Creek through Aneth to the Colorado border, connecting thence with US 160 (Navajo Route 1) which gives access to **Four Corners Monument,** marking the only site in the nation where four states meet in a common point (Utah, Colorado, New Mexico and Arizona).

Though the frenetic oil boom days of the 1950s are history, it is a memorable experience to travel this seemingly empty land for miles without seeing a sign of human occupancy, then topping a rise or rounding a curve and abruptly entering a landscape dotted with hundreds of oil well pumps, some in rhythmic motion, others stationary. Standing as a prominent landmark—almost as a mirage—south of the

Oil pump in the
Aneth Oil Field.

DEPT. OF TRANSPORTATION
(GERALD PETERSON)

San Juan River on the Navajo Reservation, is southeastern Utah's largest industrial installation. This is the imposing extraction and pumping complex of **El Paso Natural Gas Company,** known informally as El Paso, Utah. Construction was begun in 1958 and continued over several years, the work not progressing fast enough to prevent the loss of great quantities of gas by flaring from the hundreds of oil wells that had been completed before gas collection facilities were available. The multi-million-dollar complex includes large compressor buildings, storage buildings, dehydration plant, and gasoline extraction facilities. Also at the site are about 60 modern residences. The plant services all the area's wells in gathering and processing natural gas.

To make the complex and wells on the south side of the river accessible from Utah, a million-dollar bridge was constructed across the San Juan. Before the bridge was completed in the late 1950s, several years after discovery of the first Aneth well, it was necessary to drive more than 150 miles by rough and circuitous roads to get vehicles and equipment from one side of the river to the other.

The **Greater Aneth Oil Field** saw its beginning in January 1956 when The Texas Company brought in a deep well at high production, followed shortly by a confirmation well sunk by Superior Oil. Within the next two or three years about 500 wells were in production, and Greater Aneth was renowned as the largest new United States petroleum discovery in years. The field immediately rocketed San Juan to No. 2 ranking in total value of mineral production among Utah's counties, where it remained for about 15 years until Duchesne County surpassed it in the early 1970s. The field's crude oil is not used within Utah but is transported out of state via pipelines to southern California and the Gulf states. Much of the natural gas, however, is accessible to Utah's metropolitan areas, via Northwest Pipeline's transmission system.

About 8 m. along State 262 from US 163 is junction with unpaved road leading east to **HOVENWEEP NATIONAL MONUMENT,** Utah's best-known prehistoric Anasazi ruins *(see Hovenweep National Monument).* This region is occupied by **MONTEZUMA CANYON** and its extensive tributary system, as well as the related **Recapture-McElmo** systems, which drain Sage Plain into the San Juan River—an area of more than 1,000 square miles measuring some 40 by 40 miles in extent. Though not as deeply incised as canyon country to the west, nor scenically as dramatic, these systems are relatively wild. **Montezuma Canyon** has been identified by the Bureau of Land Management "as a unique area with outstanding archeological, geological, historical and scenic values." The main canyon itself, and some of the side canyons, are traversed by fairweather dirt roads. Parts of the area are habitat for golden and bald eagles, despite several decades of uranium-vanadium development and canyon ranching. The Montezuma-McElmo-Recapture area was much more densely populated 800 years ago than it is today, having been the home for a large population of Anasazi Indians, including those at Hovenweep and Alkali Ridge. Many specimens of prehistoric rock art and numerous ruins may be seen. A description of the Montezuma Canyon area is contained in *Canyon Country Hiking* by F. A. Barnes.

South of the junction with State 262, US 163 descends from Bluff Bench to the valley of the **SAN JUAN RIVER** and the rustic frontier village of **Bluff**. In this descent it leaves the drab, relatively youthful Cretaceous rocks of Sage Plain and enters the more brightly colored, older formations typical of the broken Canyonlands country.

BLUFF (4,300 alt.) dates from 1880 when it was settled by the Hole-in-the-Rock pioneers *(see below)*. Its history since then has been a poignant one of hardship and anguish, poverty and riches, growth and decline, then growth again. The latter period marks Bluff today, as evidenced by a lengthened main street and a motley assortment of modern structures mixed with those of more aged vintage.

In 1941 Bluff consisted of "a score of dusty red houses, built of the soil on which they stand. Five artesian wells provide water for an oasis-like growth of shade trees and fruit orchards. Bluff has an Indian trading post where Navajos are frequent visitors, bringing wool, silver work, goat meat, and hand-woven rugs to trade for groceries and clothing." The red brick (and stone) houses remain as do the Navajos and the lush vegetation. The trading post, when operating, is utilized more by visitors than by the Indians, who prefer the local stores and restaurants. But local color is still a trait of Bluff, including as it does the **Navajo Twins** buttes at the mouth of Cow Canyon; the Episcopal Mission *(below);* quaint pioneer buildings and dusty streets; Indians in their distinctive dress (less so today than formerly, however); guides offering vehicle and boating tours; roadside "trading posts" and eating places.

Cemetery Hill is a nostalgic point of interest. "Located in the classic western manner on a bleak gravel hill above our town," Mary Foushee wrote, the cemetery "offers to history and nostalgia buffs a glimpse of the past."

Locomotive Rock, as described by Marian Crawford in the *Deseret News* of March 13, 1948 "stands watch over the first of the brave Hole-in-the-Rock pioneers to die. She lies beneath the rocks and the wind whispers in the willows and down from San Juan hill. It seems to chant a melody—the San Juan song. 'It's far off the beaten track . . . And we never will come back . . . But we'll find our El Dorado . . . In San Juan'."

The Mormons of 1880 were not Bluff's only pioneers. Others came years later. Among these was Father Harold B. Liebler, revered "priest with the long hair," who established **St. Christopher's Episcopal Mission to the Navajo Indians** in 1943. Against great odds, relying mainly on volunteer help and contributions, Father Liebler and a small staff gradually built the mission into an attractive tree-shrouded complex that includes a school, a hogan-shaped chapel, fields, dwellings, kitchen, dining hall, and other facilities. The mission is located on the north bank of the river, two miles east of Bluff via paved road. Visitors are welcome.

Joining both banks of the river a mile east of the mission is a picturesque "hanging" cable-supported footbridge. Several miles beyond the mission and bridge is **Recapture Pocket,** an area of strange goblin rock forms.

Bluff's **Indian Day Celebration** is a colorful happening each year in June, featuring Navajo games, horse races, and other events.

Bluff was founded in 1880 by Mormon colonists called by their church to establish a colony on the San Juan River. Their epic journey through the Hole-in-the-Rock, across the Colorado River, and through the slickrock country between the river and Bluff is one of the most amazing episodes in Mormon colonizing history. That tale has been told many times by many writers, but in fullest detail by Dr. David E. Miller in *Hole-in-the-Rock.*

The major objective of the San Juan settlement was cultivation of better relations with the Indians, together with the laying of foundations for future permanent Mormon settlements before non-Mormons secured a foothold in the region. There was also the desire for more and better land and the hope that Mormons from the southern states would find the climate more to their liking. Because little was known about the San Juan area, an exploring party was sent out in the spring of 1879 from Paragonah to pioneer a wagon road and determine the feasibility of settlement. Crossing the Colorado at Lees Ferry, the party traveled to Moenkopi and from there to the mouth of Montezuma Creek on the San Juan River. Every piece of potential farmland was searched out and claimed, and a few houses were built. Scouts were sent to explore the surrounding country, some going as far north as the Blue Mountains where excellent range was noted.

The time soon came for most of the company to return to western Utah. Finding the new land satisfactory, they planned to return with families and possessions. Two families remained at Montezuma while the remainder of the company returned to the Utah settlements by a northern route believed to be more practical. Striking the Old Spanish Trail near the La Sal Mountains, they crossed the Colorado at Moab and the Green at Gunnison Crossing, then followed the old trail to Sevier Valley. It was mid-September when they reached Paragonah. They had made a great circuit of a thousand miles, and had marked hundreds of miles of road through desolate, little-known terrain.

Though this exploring expedition had located the site for the San Juan Mission settlement, their southern route was not satisfactory for a large company. Water was scarce and the Indians, while not actively hostile, were not friendly. The northern route was more practical as a trail, but it was deemed too circuitous, requiring more than 200 miles of extra travel compared with a direct route, if one could be found. Captain Silas Smith sent a report of the exploration to Church authorities at Salt Lake City, recommending that a San Juan settlement was feasible. As a result of this report, settlers were called by the Church to make a permanent settlement on the San Juan River. In his report, Smith had suggested that a shorter, more direct route be located. Because of the lateness of the season, time was a critical concern. Therefore a more direct and shorter route was chosen, east of Panguitch and south of Escalante, a result of preliminary exploration and favorable report by Charles Hall, an early settler of Escalante. Hall had explored along the brink of the Colorado River gorge, noting a narrow cleft in the canyon wall through which he could see the river and the sandstone knobs that marked the head of Cottonwood Canyon on the east side of the river. Hall concluded that it would be difficult, but possible, to lower wagons down to the river through the narrow "hole in the rock," but once across it should be easy to move the company to the San Juan River and the Montezuma settlement. Unfortunately, Hall's report was much too optimistic and the estimated six weeks for the journey became almost six months. Either of the rejected routes would have been much shorter in time, requiring far less energy to reach the goal.

That part of the journey to Escalante, and from there through Hole-in-the-Rock and across the river, is described in Tour No. 9C. However formidable the obstacles encountered during that stage of the trek, those faced on the east side were just as forbidding, if not moreso. While the roadway through the Hole was being prepared, scouts were sent across the river to survey the terrain between Cottonwood Canyon and the Montezuma settlement. Their ordeal, and that of the main party after crossing the Colorado, was recounted in the 1941 edition (quoted material is from Hoffman Birney's *Zealots of Zion):*

Four men, sent ahead [from Hole-in-the-Rock] to find the best route, returned in twenty-five days, a month before the crossing of the Colorado was completed. On the second day they came to the Slick Rocks, an area of steeply sloped sandstone, impossible to avoid and apparently impossible to descend; a scout followed a herd of mountain sheep across it.

They were forced many miles to the north by rough terrain . . . and the necessity for discovering a pass through the Clay Hills [Birney continues]. They found that pass, the only one in the range, by following another dim trail made by the ancient inhabitants of the land. . . . East of the Clay Hills . . . lay a many-branched gorge so vast that they christened it the Grand Gulch. . . . On Christmas Day . . . they cooked the last of their food. That Christmas dinner was "a slapjack of flour and water baked in a frying-pan."

Late in the eleventh day, after four days without food, the men staggered into a cabin on the present site of Bluff. The following morning they continued to the settlement at Montezuma, and after a single day's rest began the return trip, with a forty-eight-pound sack of flour for food. When they got to the Colorado River they were tired and discouraged. The company, however, had no choice but to move forward: Heavy snows made it impossible to return; lack of forage made it impossible to remain. They hauled lumber 60 miles from Escalante to build a ferryboat, and blasted a road in the east wall of the canyon. . . . *(See Tour No. 9C.)* . . .

To tell of the journey of that caravan [writes Hoffman Birney], would be virtually to repeat the tale of the sufferings of the four pathfinders and to multiply five-fold the labor that had been necessary to descend through the dreaded Hole to the river. . . . The Hobbs party made the trip in eleven days; to cover the same ground with heavily-laden wagons took just five times as long—a daily average of less than three miles. . . .

East of Elk Ridge the company descended into the canyon of Comb Wash and turned south to the San Juan River, reaching the mouth of Cottonwood Creek in April, 1880 [but not before surmounting one of the most formidable obstacles they had yet encountered—"San Juan Hill"—the almost sheer, unbroken face of Comb Ridge. "They left their blood there," wrote Marian Crawford, "and bits of their clothes, and a wagon or two and horses too weary to make the last hard pull."] Still 15 miles from the Montezuma settlement, [Bluff] was "the first place they had found to stop and also the first place from which they had no strength to go on." Exhaustion had halted the company at the most suitable site on the San Juan River.

This trail, or sections of it, was used for some years afterward for communication between the isolated new community and populated Utah but gradually was abandoned as easier routes were developed. In this century many people have traversed the trail, or portions of it, by jeep, on foot or horseback. Sections of the trail are paralleled today by State 95 and State 263. In 1980, the Centennial of San Juan, jeep tours to Hole-in-the-Rock and San Juan Hill were conducted during the year, and commercial guides have offered jeep tours along the pioneer trail for years. The 1941 edition's account continued:

Hoffman Birney evaluates the journey thus: "It was labor beside which the toil of the emigrant trains that crossed the entire continent to California and Oregon was child's play. . . . Nowhere in the history of America is there a more impressive example of the power of a creed, of the faith that moveth mountains, than in the conquest of the Hole-in-the-Rock and the story of the Saints of the San Juan."

An act of the Territorial legislature created San Juan County in February, 1880, when it had no permanent inhabitants, and leaders of the Mormon company were appointed its officials while still struggling eastward from the Colorado River crossing. Bluff became the county seat and remained so until 1895, when it was removed to Monticello. . . [A few years later, around the turn of the century, it is claimed that those remaining in Bluff had the highest family income of any town in the world. This was a result of boom conditions in nearby Colorado and demand for their livestock.] During the first year "about half the population moved away." Yet as the manuscript "San Juan Stake History" records, "somehow, in this wonderful colony which had come through from Escalante whether it could or not, there remained a splendid element of invincibility. When the dissatisfied and disheartened ones moved on to the east, and back to the west, that invincible spirit clenched its jaws the tighter. . . ."

With the nearest white settlement more than seventy miles away, the colonists had difficulty with the Paiutes and Navahos. A fort was built to protect women and children, but when Indians stole cattle and horses, the settlers dared do little about it. The most they usually accomplished was to retake the stock. The settlement was not entirely free from Indian trouble until 1923, when Old Posey, chief of the dispossessed Paiutes, died. For twenty years he had done almost everything to make himself unpopular. His career came to an end when he and his band assisted in the escape of two Paiutes who had been arrested for robbing a sheep camp. A posse pursued the Indians for several days, killed one of them, wounded Old Posey, and captured the rest. Old Posey escaped to an abandoned cave in Comb Wash, where he died, his wounds stuffed with weeds, his lifeless face toward the approaching enemy.

More serious were the vagaries of the San Juan River. Time after time the settlers attempted to divert water from the river, but each time the stream rose unexpectedly and flooded the fields. The Church sent Francis A. Hammond to act as president of the San Juan Stake. He moved most of the people to Monticello, and stock-raising replaced farming as the primary industry. By 1935 the twenty miles of farmland that existed along the San Juan River in 1880 had been reduced by floods to 200 acres at Bluff. By that time, however, the townspeople had begun to irrigate with water from artesian wells.

Three miles west of Bluff is a junction leading to **Sand Island** and a **Public Campground** (BLM), used by river boaters for launching and disembarking. From this junction the road forks south to **Sik-Is Bridge (Bridge of Friendship).** The bridge was dedicated in 1971, replacing a heavily-used footbridge destroyed in 1970 by floods. Between the campground and bridge, beside the river, a low bluff displays a large panel of **petroglyphs.**

Turn southward via this bridge to **NAVAJO INDIAN RESERVATION,** where as many as 150,000 Navajos reside in one of the harshest, least productive environments in the country. The three-state reservation embraces about 25,000 square miles of red-rock desert, high mesas, plateaus and mountains, dissected for the most part by stream channels which—most of them—are dry except for intermittent runoff. Utah's part of the reservation, more than a million acres, amounts to less than ten per cent of the entire reservation; yet it comprises a fourth of San Juan County's area. About 40 per cent of the county's people are Navajos (in 1980 they numbered about 5,000). An article in the *Ogden Standard-Examiner* of November 23, 1967 summarized the Navajo predicament. Written by Tom Tiede and entitled "Vast Navajo Lands Form Nation's Largest Ghetto," the article stated the following:

> The Navajo Indian Reservation . . . It's 25,000 square miles of privation. It's 16 million acres of despair. It's 100,000 faces of poverty. It's an area the size of West Virginia . . . and the median income of a family of five is $580 a year. At its extremity it reaches a distance from Boston to Washington . . . and 75 per cent of the homes are at least a mile from any source of water. It's a day's crossing in a fast automobile . . . and 60 per cent of the people are unemployed, while another 20 per cent work only now and then . . . Nearly everyone has it hard in Navajoland, for this is the most backward, least productive region of its size in the country. As one Indian puts it: "This is the place God and the government forgot."
>
> That opinion isn't altogether fair, of course . . . any of a thousand government officials insist that they, at least, have not forgotten the woeful misfortune of the 120,000-strong Navajo nation . . . BIA people can tick off a long list of aid programs . . . "In the past six years," says one official, "we've spent over $1.5 billion on the Indians. Tell me, what more do they want?" The answer is simple. They want progress. In the hundred years since the Navajos were herded into this desert region (1868), they've experienced a lot of programs but little progress. In fact, they've slipped backward in some aspects of living . . . The United States has provided widespread welfare service, but the result has been to foster dependency, apathy and a lack of motivation . . . In sum, the total effect is nearly total failure. . . .
>
> But the Navajo is also guilty. Inertia is almost a tribal custom . . . Stubbornness is deep-seated . . . Initiative is dreary . . . Tribal direction is slim . . . Of course, Navajos won't admit that these faults hinder their progress. Nor will Washington admit it is bureaucratically blind. The two sides have bickered thus since this whole poverty pocket originated. And so it stands, the status quo.

Another writer points out the fear by older Navajos of culture loss, which explains to a degree the so-called Navajo "faults" listed above. Like the nation's other Indians, the Navajo "are faced with the troublesome choice of embracing the material good that 'progress' can bring or of clinging fast to their old ways. The former could mean cultural destruction. The latter would surely mean continuing, grinding poverty . . . the great mass of Navajo [are] caught in the midstream of acculturation and unsure of which shore to swim to."

Improvement has come since Tiede's article was written, particularly in areas of education and individual transportation. Yet a 1980 survey of the reservation in Utah showed that much of the housing remains substandard. The great majority of reservation residents in Utah must haul water, and only a fourth of the homes have indoor flush toilets or refrigeration.

PONCHO HOUSE RUIN, one of Utah's oldest, most photogenic, impressively situated and least-known cliff dwellings, is on the Chinle Wash just north of the Utah-Arizona line. It is reached by rough and circuitous dirt roads from Bluff, Mexican Hat or Montezuma Creek, but can only be visited by tribal permit or with authorized guides. According to the 1941 edition, "This ancient ruin, one of the largest in the Southwest, is four stories high, 600 feet long, and contains 125 rooms." It is estimated that Poncho House once had 300 rooms.

West of Bluff the highway ascends steep-sided **Comb Ridge** and crosses its summit in an easy pass. In 1941 the much more primitive road climbed the ridge "by a series of switchbacks" and wound over the summit through a rocky pass. At that time, on the other side, "for a mile the road weaves through **Snake Canyon** . . . where some of the curves are so sharp that a motorist almost collides with his own tail light. The canyon winds through red eroded hills, and is said to have received its name when an unfortunate snake broke his back trying to crawl through it."

Comb Ridge may be viewed in its precipitous grandeur from the highway on the heights of **Lime Ridge** to the west, extending far northward as a great escarpment toward the Abajos and Elk Ridge. Both Comb Ridge and Lime Ridge are flexures in the earth's crust, Lime Ridge being an anticline (two-sided slope) and Comb Ridge a monocline (one-sided slope). Comb Ridge is a flexure of major dimensions, its slope on the east, a high cliff face on the west, and a jagged crest.

Comb Ridge monocline is about 80 miles in length and forms the eastern margin of the great **MONUMENT UPWARP,** a major crustal uplift that extends from the vicinity of Kayenta, Arizona, northward to the Junction Country. Comb Ridge resembles in respects the Waterpocket Fold and San Rafael Reef, its rocks being identical to the rocks of those monoclines (that is, of Triassic and Jurassic age, and similar formations). However, most of the exposed rocks in the central part of the gouged-out Monument Upwarp are older than those around its perimeter, being mainly of ancient Permian origin. In fact, a greater area of Permian rocks is exposed in this immense uplift than anyplace else in Utah, and the dramatic erosional and crustal

Aerial view of Comb Ridge and Comb Wash, looking north to the Abajo Mountains.

BUREAU OF RECLAMATION

features described hereafter, from Bluff to Monument Valley, are in Permian rocks. This country is an ideal illustration of why the **Colorado Plateau** is regarded so highly by geologists as an outdoor classroom. G. K. Gilbert described these attributes of the Colorado Plateau in Volume III of the Wheeler Survey reports (1875):

> The simplicity of its [the Plateau's] structure, the thoroughness of its drainage, which rarely permits detritus to accumulate in its valleys, its barrenness, and the wonderful natural sections exposed in its canons, conspire to render it indeed "the paradise of the geologist." There he can trace the slow lithological mutations of strata continuously visible for hundreds of miles; can examine, in visible contact, the strata of nearly the entire geological series, and detect every nonconformity, however slight, and can study the simpler initiatory phases of an embryo mountain system.

From the heights of **Lime Ridge** the fantastic pinnacles and buttes of Monument Valley loom ever more dramatic. These splendid forms are beacons for the remaining distance to Kayenta. About 12 m. from Bluff, an unpaved sideroad forks northwest into **VALLEY OF THE GODS,** Utah's miniature Monument Valley, the 17-mile drive exiting at State 261 north of Mexican Hat.

Here in a basin between Cedar Mesa and the gorge of the San Juan is a red fairyland of blocky buttes and slender spires. In general these forms resemble those in the valley's more famous neighbor to the south, yet here they are more intricately sculptured and on a smaller, more intimate scale. Local guides apply such names as "Lady in a Bathtub," "Five Sailors," "Santa Claus and Rudolph," "The Turbaned Indian Prince," and other fanciful terms. Others see visions such as "The Southern Belle." For decades the area was the specialty of Jim and Emery Hunt, operators of a tour service from their lodge at Mexican Hat; but the valley is relatively unvisited, relegated to the scenic backburner because of better-known attractions in the vicinity. Still standing in the valley is the ruin of an imposing ranch house built by Clarence and William "Buck" Lee in the 1920s. The rock mansion contained nine rooms, four of them with fireplaces. Water was piped from a spring. In the 1941 edition a full page was devoted to Buck Lee and his operation, describing him as an artist and a teller of marvelous tales who provided guided tours to area attractions.

From the Valley of the Gods turnoff, US 163 continues its descent into the basin of the San Juan River, known formally as the Mexican Hat syncline. Panoramic views extend across a forest of weird standing rocks, mesas, cliffs, canyons and tortured earth. Ahead is the **Raplee Anticline,** known to every geologist as a superb crustal flexure, displaying its classic, eroded curve in such clarity that even the most innocent layman cannot resist geologic enlightenment.

State 261 forks north from US 163 at junction 4 m. north of Mexican Hat, giving access to Goosenecks State Reserve, Moki Dugway and Cedar Mesa, Muley Point Overlook, Grand Gulch Primitive Area, State Highway 95, and Natural Bridges National Monument:

1. **GOOSENECKS STATE RESERVE** is 4 m. by paved road (State 316) from State 261 at junction 5 m. north of Mexican Hat. The reserve is an overlook point on the rim of the San Juan River canyon, "one of the world's most magnificent examples of an entrenched meander." According to the 1941 edition, "Here, in a mud-gray canyon [about 1,000 feet] deep, the San Juan makes a series of symmetrical bends, around which it flows six miles to travel an airline distance of

[1½]. The river is viewed from the north rim as it flows north, then south, then north again, and finally south again, in a series of close-set curves. The center bend is three miles around, but the dividing ridge, at its narrowest point, is less than 100 yards wide. According to geologists the San Juan once meandered over the surface of a level plain; a slow regional uplift forced the stream to cut deeper and deeper into the plain. Eventually, eons hence, the meanders may cut through, leaving a series of gigantic natural bridges. . . ."

The canyon's rocks were formed in shallow waters some 300 million years ago in Pennsylvanian time, being laid down over a period of about 40 million years and consisting mainly of limestone, shale and sandstone. Fossils are common. Thousands of feet of younger rocks were laid down atop those in the walls of today's canyon, but these were removed by erosion as the land rose. The reserve features an observation shelter, several camp sites, toilets. No water or firewood.

2. **MOKI DUGWAY** and **CEDAR MESA**. Moki Dugway refers to the steep switchbacks of State 261 where it climbs the thousand-foot face of **Cedar Mesa**. The Dugway has been improved since it was bulldozed out of the cliff during the uranium boom of the 1950s but still provides aerial thrills sufficient for most drivers. Views enroute are spectacular, sweeping downward into the San Juan canyons and Valley of the Gods, and southward to the jagged skyline of Monument Valley. The rim of Cedar Mesa, at 6,000 feet, is a thousand feet higher than the terrace forming the floor of Valley of the Gods, which in turn is a thousand feet higher than the river.

3. **MULEY POINT OVERLOOK,** a panoramic viewpoint, ranks for visual impact with better-known Canyonlands overlooks to the north. On the high rim of Cedar Mesa, reached by unpaved road leading about 5 m. from State 261 at junction near the top of Moki Dugway, Muley Point offers a geological and scenic spectacle,

Great Goosenecks of the San Juan River and Monument Valley as seen from Muley Point Overlook.

a bird's-eye sweep across hundreds of millions of years of earth's crustal history, revealed in bare-bones stratigraphic clarity. Whereas the Canyonlands viewpoints are situated on middle-aged Mesozoic rocks (Jurassic-Triassic) looking down on older Permian rocks, Muley Point is situated on Permian rocks looking down onto even older Pennsylvanian rocks in the walls of the San Juan's canyons. In other words, Goosenecks State Reserve (No. 1 above) could be considered the lowest step in southeastern Utah's Grand Staircase; Muley Point the next higher step; and Canyon Rims, Dead Horse Point and Grand View Point the third step. Suitable viewpoints on the summit of the Henry Mountains, Caineville mesas, or the Roan and Book Cliffs—overlooking relatively youthful Cretaceous formations—might well serve as the top of the Grand Staircase. Muley Point affords an easily accessible, comprehensive overview of the San Juan's gooseneck canyons (entrenched meanders) as well as a superb panoramic sweep across Monument Valley. The point is located in Glen Canyon National Recreation Area.

4. **GRAND GULCH PRIMITIVE AREA** is a natural-archeological preserve of the U.S. Bureau of Land Management, limited to travel on foot or horseback. As described in the 1941 edition, Grand Gulch is "the tremendous box canyon that forced Bluff colonists far off their course. Here are several hundred cliff-dwellings, few of them fully explored and many of them entirely untouched since they were abandoned centuries ago. Existence of the Basket Maker culture was first substantiated by T. M. Prudden as the result of collections made in Grand Gulch in the 1890's." A tributary of the San Juan, Grand Gulch extends about 50 miles northward from its mouth. Its steep or overhanging walls are impassable to humans except in a few places; countless ledges and crevices contain what is said to be the nation's largest concentration of prehistoric Basketmaker and Pueblo dwellings and storage structures outside of Mesa Verde. The Gulch also is rich in rock art. Grand Gulch's culture covered a tremendous time span of 1,300 years, from 2,000 to 700 years ago. Scenically the Gulch is outstanding, remaining virtually a wilderness because of remoteness and difficulty of access. It is becoming increasing popular for backpacking, the study of archeology and nature. Travel is controlled from Kane Gulch Ranger Station of the BLM, four miles south of State 95, beside State 261 (about 33 miles north of Mexican Hat). Permits are required; strict regulations apply.

5. **STATE HIGHWAY 95.** *See Tour No. 11E below.*

6. **NATURAL BRIDGES NATIONAL MONUMENT.** *See description in parks section.*

US 163 continues to Mexican Hat, the splendid spectacle of **Raplee Anticline** (known also as the **Navajo Rug**) dominating the landscape. This remarkable structure is "an upfold or arch of stratified rock," so symmetrical and picturesquely eroded that photographs of it are used in geology texts around the world. The anticline is 15 miles long and 1,500 feet high at its crest. **Mexican Hat Rock** comes into view, resembling an enormous Mexican sombrero balanced precariously on a tapered base.

The settlement of **MEXICAN HAT** (4,200 alt.) is perched on the north bank of the San Juan River where it emerges from the Raplee Anticline and begins a longer entrenchment downstream through the Goosenecks and other deep gorges to Lake Powell. In 1941 the settlement amounted to little more than the Mexican Hat Lodge, where Norman Nevills had begun in 1937 to offer adventure trips on the San Juan and Colorado. Nevills continued these offerings until he and his wife were killed in the crash of their small plane in 1949. During his years at Mexican Hat, Nevills became perhaps the most noted of all river guides, not only specializing in boating on the San Juan and in Glen Canyon, but also guiding parties through the fearsome rapids of Grand Canyon and the Green. Neil M. Clark described his exploits in a major feature in *The Saturday Evening Post* of May 18, 1946.

From the nature of his offerings, Nevills gained a degree of fame in his brief years at Mexican Hat. But Jim and Emery Hunt were local tour operators of much longer residence. Their lodge and trading post, tucked on a narrow ledge between the river and a vertical cliff, beside the bridge, represented Mexican Hat for many visitors until expansion of the town along the highway in recent decades. Specialties of the Hunts were tours of Monument Valley and Valley of the Gods. The Hunts were Mexican Hat's only citizens for years, and for many more they comprised half of the community's total population. After World War II, however, uranium and oil finds, better roads, and tourism changed this situation. The Mexican Hat of today bears little resemblance to that of the 1930s and 1940s. The area's early background was summarized in the 1941 edition:

> The muddy SAN JUAN RIVER, 78.1 *m.,* is spanned by a suspension bridge. The river rises in the San Juan Mountains of southern Colorado, flows into New Mexico, back into Colorado, enters Utah near the Four Corners, and flows westward to its junction with the Colorado River near the Arizona Line. Discovery of gold along the upper tributaries of the San Juan led E. L. Goodridge to make the first known boat trip down the river in 1879. He found only minor quantities of flake gold, but "little streams of oil coming from loose boulders" induced him to seek funds for development of an oil claim near the present San Juan bridge. The venture was eventually financed in 1907, and the following spring, Goodridge brought in "a gusher, throwing oil to a height of 70 feet." By 1911 there were twenty-seven drilling rigs in the field, a small town had sprung into existence at Goodridge (now Mexican Hat), and a bridge was constructed over the San Juan River. Most of the wells produced only a little oil and gas, and many were "dry holes." None produced oil in commercial quantities.
>
> In 1891 rumors began to circulate that San Juan sands were rich in gold. The "gold rush" of 1892-93 followed, bringing almost 2,000 men into the region. A few prospectors recovered enough gold to make day wages. Many prospectors drifted north to the Abajo Mountains *(see above)* but found only added disappointment.
>
> From the Colorado Line to a point midway between Bluff and Mexican Hat the river occupies a flood plain half a mile to a mile wide, bordered by low walls. West of Bluff the river follows a meandering canyon to the Colorado River. The airline distance from the head of the canyon to the Colorado is only 63 miles, but the distance by stream is 133 miles. The most closely spaced bends are the Goosenecks *(see above),* but at the GREAT BEND the river makes a nine-mile loop and returns to within half a mile of its starting point. At the west end of this loop the Colorado is only 5 miles away, but the San Juan travels 34 miles before the two streams meet. The depth of the canyon varies from a few hundred feet to half a mile.

South of the San Juan River, US 163 traverses the **NAVAJO INDIAN RESERVATION** *(see Bluff above).* "Only one automobile crossed this strip before 1921," said the 1941 edition. Since then the majestic beauty of **MONUMENT VALLEY,** straddling the state line ahead, has become known the world over and countless thousands have come to see it. Many more would have come if the valley were not so remote.

Alhambra Rock, 2 m. south of the river, is a jagged black volcanic mass, contrasting with the red of the surrounding country. **Monument Pass,** 17 m.

south of the river, marks the north entrance to **Monument Valley,** "where maroon buttes and pinnacles rise, like skyscrapers, out of the red desert, and tower nearly a thousand feet [and more] above the valley floor. Between the monuments, distant ranges in Colorado, New Mexico, and Arizona can be seen. Agathlan Peak, a metallic blue volcanic spire, stands out in the red Arizona desert . . ." *(1941 edition).* US 163 in Monument Pass is flanked by giant fingers and buttes on either side. Beyond is a forest of other enchanted standing rocks. Only a sampling of their names can be given here: Buttes and fingers known as *The Eagle, Brigham's Tomb, Natanni Tso, Castle Butte, Big Indian, The Mittens, Mitchell and Merrick, Grey Whiskers, Elephant, Camel, Totem Pole, Three Sisters, Yei-Bichei, Sun's Eye,* and *Big Hogan* . . . Mesas by the name of *Oljeto, Sentinel, Eagle, Old Baldy, Pueblo, Wetherill, Spearhead and Hunt* . . . Valleys called *Windmill, Primrose and Mystery* . . . Canyons and washes named *Rock Door, Stagecoach, Eagle Rock, Train Rock, Monument.*

John Ford, the Hollywood director famed for his action westerns, is most responsible—at the urging of Harry Goulding—for bringing the beauties of Monument Valley to the attention of the general public, at least in earlier years. Beginning in 1938 with his classic *Stagecoach,* Ford subsequently filmed *My Darling Clementine, War Party,* and *She Wore a Yellow Ribbon*—all in the 1940s. Other films were shot at least partially in the valley. These included *Billy the Kid, Kit Carson, Fort Apache, How the West Was Won, The Living Desert, The Searchers,* and *Cheyenne Autumn.* A false-front Tombstone was built for *My Darling Clementine.*

Monument Valley has been a **Navajo Tribal Park** since 1959. The following year saw dedication of an attractive **Visitor Center-Observatory** located four miles east of Goulding's Junction and US 163, at the entrance to a 14-mile scenic tour route. Visitors desiring to tour the valley's off-highway attractions must register at the Visitor Center or obtain the services of an authorized guide. Native subjects expect a photographic fee for posing. *Do not photograph Navajos without their permission.*

For many, Monument Valley has always been associated with **Goulding's Trading Post-Lodge-Tours.** The trading post was established by Harry and Mike Goulding in 1923 and is now listed on the National Register of Historic Places. The Gouldings have been the valley's best-known residents, not only offering crucial trading post services to the Navajos in 30-odd years of dirt-road isolation, but also providing lodging and tours for travelers, assistance and comfort to the Navajos in cases of illness and distress, boosterism in promoting the valley's attractions, local color and authentic information for uncounted writers and photographers. According to the 1941 edition, Harry Goulding was called T'pay-eh-nez or Long Sheep by the Navajos, "either because he is tall, and owned sheep, when he came into the valley, or because he had many sheep." Adjoining the lodge is **Monument Valley Hospital,** in Rock Door Canyon, standing on land donated by the Gouldings. Its origins date from 1950, when Marvin and Gwen Walter, Seventh-day Adventist missionaries, established a modest clinic there. In the years since, with assistance from the Tribal Council, the church, and others, the original traveling clinic has grown into a full-fledged hospital with physicians, nurses and modern equipment.

Monument Valley, looking north.

West from Goulding's a paved road leads 10 m. to **OLJETO,** a Navajo center with trading post, primary school, church, and housing. The **Oljeto Trading Post,** established by the Wetherill family many years ago and operated since the late 1940s by Ed and Virginia Smith, is interesting for its old-time, rustic authenticity. In a back room the Smiths display a valuable collection of Navajo craftwork such as baskets and beadwork; old guns; and other relics.

Tour No. 11E - Blanding to Natural Bridges and Lake Powell via State 95; also State 263

State 95, Utah's Bicentennial Highway (paving was completed in 1976), connects US 163 near Blanding with State 24 at Hanksville, more than 125 miles away. In all this distance there is no town, and no services except at Fry Canyon and marinas on Lake Powell. The terrain is wild, an almost pristine landscape of pygmy evergreens, beacon buttes, island ranges, cliff-faced mesas, and seemingly bottomless gorges.

State 95 was one of the last highways in Utah to be completely paved, its construction having taken place in stages over a period of 70 years or more, from first primitive beginnings as trail segments. Sections near the Colorado River did not see much improvement until after World War II, when much of southeastern Utah was opened by a network of uranium access roads. Originally the route between Blanding and Natural Bridges passed over Elk Ridge near Bears Ears. Segments of the present highway, and State 263 to Halls Crossing, parallel sections of the route traversed by the Hole-in-the-Rock pioneers *(see Bluff)*. It is estimated that construction costs during the final two decades of roadbuilding totaled 20 million dollars.

Special attractions along U95, traveling west from US 163 near Blanding, include the following *(mileages are approximate):*

1. **Butler Wash View Area,** 11 m., marks the general locality of an armed encounter between a local white posse and a party of Paiute Indians led by Posey. Posey was shot and later died from the wound, but most of his party escaped. This was in 1923. In the vicinity are prehistoric Indian ruins. A rough, fairweather road extends south through Butler Wash to US 163 near Bluff.

2. **Comb Ridge,** 14 m., has been a formidable natural barrier since pioneer days. The ridge is a long, narrow monoclinal uplift, sloping on the east, cliff-faced on the west, through which builders of U95 cut a deep notch for the highway. *See Tour No. 11D above for fuller description.* Looking north along the west face, the steep dugway of the old highway can be seen several miles away. Comb Ridge was a serious obstacle to the Hole-in-the-Rock pioneers, who were almost completely exhausted by the time they reached it *(see story under Bluff, above).*

3. **Mule Canyon Rest Area,** 22 m., is at the site of a partially restored prehistoric settlement complex. A tower and kiva are accessible for public inspection. In the vicinity are seven round towers, known as Cave Towers, which date from late Pueblo times of 1050 to 1150 A.D. *Indian antiquities are a priceless national heritage; severe penalties for unauthorized excavation or damage.*

4. **Salvation Knoll,** 30 m., was named by four Mormon scouts who had left the main pioneer party at Hole-in-the-Rock to search out a route to the San Juan River. On Christmas Day, 1879, lost and hungry, they climbed this knoll to survey the terrain. Successful in gaining their bearings, they attached the name Salvation Knoll.

5. **Junction with U261,** 35 m., which leads south to Grand Gulch Primitive area, Muley Point, Moki Dugway and Mexican Hat *(see Tour No. 11D above).* All around is a dense forest of pinyon pine and juniper (cedar) trees. Looming 2,000 feet above the highway on the north is Elk Ridge, surmounted by the landmark twin buttes or knolls known as Bears Ears (9,060 alt.). Their name is an Americanization of the Spanish term Orejas del Oso meaning "ears of the bear," applied by early New Mexican travelers.

6. **Junction with U275,** 37 m. U275 leads 4 m. to Natural Bridges National Monument *(see national parks).* A short distance along U275 is junction with unpaved route (old U95) leading to the heights of **Elk Ridge** and a network of high-country forest roads in Manti-La Sal National Forest. These pleasant alpine roads fork variously to Dark Canyon Primitive Area, Canyonlands National Park, the Abajo Mountains, Blanding and Monticello, providing access for a motley assortment of stockmen, lumbermen, miners, rangers, hunters, hikers, and off-highway tourists. Spectacular views are commonplace here: down into the depths of steep-walled box canyons, across mesas and plateaus of the Four Corners region to the south and east, and over the marvelous slickrock erosional wonders of Canyonlands. For full enjoyment, a detailed map is a requirement. Most roads are passable only during summer months, and even then they may be rutted, muddy and generally rough. **Dark Canyon Primitive Area** (Bureau of Land Management) incorporates the main gorges and side-canyons of three major tributaries of Cataract Canyon, namely Dark, Bowdie and Gypsum canyons—grandly imposing gorges that are deep and narrow with unscalable walls for much of their length. The primitive area is popular as a destination for wilderness backpackers.

7. **Junction with U263,** 43 m., leading to **Halls Crossing Marina** on Lake Powell (40 m. from U95). This exceptionally scenic paved road parallels the route of the old Hole-in-the-Rock Trail for much of its distance, along the **Red House Cliffs** and through the **Clay Hills** via Clay Hills Divide. Rough sideroads branch west into the vast reaches of **Red Canyon** and south to the **San Juan arm of Lake Powell.** About

15 miles from the lake, the original pioneer trail *(traversable by jeep, or partly so)* branches off to **Cottonwood Canyon,** on the opposite side of the lake from Hole-in-the-Rock. Other trails probe the Clay Hills, Moki Canyon, Lake Canyon, and tributary gorges of the San Juan. **HALLS CROSSING MARINA** is a major facility on Lake Powell, across the lake from Bullfrog Marina. First developed by San Juan County financial interests, it is now a unit of Del Webb enterprises, who operate other marinas on the lake. Available: comprehensive boating services such as fuel, repairs, storage, slips and buoys, boat and motor rentals, boating tours. Food, accommodations, supplies. Airstrip.

   8. **U95 west of U263** traverses a bench between entrenched White Canyon and a red rampart of precipitous Wingate cliffs. Buttes, curious erosional forms, and distant peaks of the Henrys accent the broken skyline. Points of interest include **Fry Canyon Store and Motel,** an oasis since uranium boom years of the 1950s *(food, fuel, limited supplies, accommodations)* . . . **Jacob's Chair** butte, named for Jacob Adams, a cowboy who was drowned in a local flash flood . . . **Soldiers' Grave,** containing the remains of two soldiers killed during the unsuccessful pursuit of raiding Utes in 1884 . . . and the site of **Happy Jack Mine** (few indications except dangerous haulage roads). Happy Jack began as a modest copper mine; then, from about 1949 to 1963, it was one of the most productive uranium mines in Utah, being the source of about 600,000 tons of uranium ore and making a fortune for its owners. Its ore was a complex mixture of pitchblende, iron, copper, aluminum, sulphur, silver and coal. Uranium content was high. Happy Jack ore, and that of other White Canyon producers, was upgraded at a processing mill near the mouth of White Canyon, across the Colorado River (east bank) from the original settlement and ferry at Hite. Both sites—formerly on old U95—are now under water. Built in 1949 by the Vanadium Corporation of America, the mill operated for a decade or so during the first uranium boom of the 1950s. Living conditions were difficult during the first few years, food and supplies being hauled in from Blanding and Hanksville, each a hundred miles or so away over rough roads.

   9. **LAKE POWELL** (north end) is serviced as a boating recreation area by **HITE MARINA,** located on the lake's east bank several miles south of U95. The marina is named for the original settlement and ferry of Hite, now under water, situated on the west side of the lake (formerly the Colorado River). Hite Marina was relocated periodically as the lake rose, being situated first on the west shore at the mouth of North Wash, then later moved to the east shore. It features boating ramp, docking and storage, fuel, boating and fishing supplies, boat rentals, store, airstrip. Lake Powell is crossed in this vicinity over **three high bridges,** namely White Canyon and Colorado River (cited in 1965 and 1966, the years of completion, as the most beautiful bridges of their class in the nation), and the Dirty Devil bridge. *U95 west of the lake is described in Tour No. 7B.*

F. A. BARNES

Halls Crossing on Lake Powell, Henry Mountains in distance.

Index

Asterisk (*) beside a page number indicates that an illustration accompanies the test. See respective cities and parks for features not listed here.

Part A — General Index
(See Part B for index to The Arts Section—pages 201-268)

Kilpatrick, Ben 710
Kimball Art Center 565
Kimball: Heber C. 83, 87*, 470; Junction
   560-61; Stage Stop 561
Kimberly 605-06, 607
King, Clarence 89, 586
King family 608
King, William H. 103, 109
Kings Peak 11
Kingston 608; Canyon 608
Kingston, Ray 201
Kirtland, Ohio 70
Knight, Jesse 99, 102, 513
Knightsville 512
Knowles, Emery 372
Kodachrome Basin State Reserve 76*, 675
Kolb: Ellsworth 713; Emery C. 713
Kolob: Canyons 642, 643*, 658; Terrace
   658-59; also see Zion National Park
Koosharem 610; Indian Reservation 610;
   Reservoir 610
Koyle: Dream Mine 549-50; John 549-50

Labyrinth Canyon 718
Lagoon Amusement Park 433; color section*
Lake Bonneville: see Bonneville, Lake
Lake Fork Canyon 572, 574*
Lake Point Junction 485, 495
Lake Powell: see Powell, Lake
Laketown 407, 420
Lambourne, Alfred 294-95
Land, Air and Water 37-45
Land Behind the Rocks 730-31, 732, 735*
Land of Standing Rocks 321-22
Land resources 38-40
Lands End Plateau 621-22
Larkin, Melvin A. 400
Larson, Andrew Karl 656
La Sal Junction 733
La Sal Mountain Scenic Loop 725-26
La Sal Mountains 22, 718, 719, 720, 722,
   725-28, 732, 735*, color section*
Latuda 693
Lavender: Canyon 736; David 736
La Verkin 657
Lay, Elza 710
Layton 428, 429
LDS Business College 194
Lead-zinc mining 135
Leamington 515
Lee: Clarence 750; John D. 642, 654;
   William "Buck" 750
Leeds 644
Lees Ferry, Arizona 357, 360, 669
Lehi 537; Co-op 91*
Leithead, James 663
Leonard, Glen M. 178
Lester, Margaret x
Levan 524; Ridge 523
Lewiston 397

Liberal Party 89, 94
Liberty 425
Libraries 199-200
Liebler, Father Harold B. 744
Leinhard party 69, 426
Life zones: see Plant Life
Lightning Peak 553
Lime Ridge 749
Linwood 347
Lion House 446-48
Lisbon Valley 734-35
Little: Cottonwood Canyon 26, 151, 478-83*;
   Mountain Industrial Area 424; Rockies
   623, 625; Sahara Recreation Area 514;
   Salt Lake 633; Standard 693; Valley 298,
   414; Yellowstone 507
Litton Industries 472
Livestock: see Agriculture
Loa 612; Fish Hatchery 613
Loafer Mountain 549, 591
Local government finance 166
Local government land 39-40
Lockhart Basin 731, 737
Locomotive Springs State Wildlife Manage-
   ment Area 413
Lodore Canyon 338-39
Logan 398-403; Mormon Temple — color
   section*
Logan: Canyon 150*, 399*, 403-05; Harvey
   710; River 405*
Long, George E. 590
Long Valley 663, 665*; Junction 663
Longabaugh, Harry 710
Looking Glass Rock 733
Loper, Bert 713
Lost Creek Dam-Reservoir-State Beach 427
Lower Sonoran zone: see Plant Life
Lucerne Valley 347, 348
Lucin Cutoff 298, 362
Lutheran Church 178
Lyman, Albert R. 739, 740
Lyman, Walter 740
Lynndyl 515
Lyon, T. Edgar 178

Mabey, Charles R. 109
Macomb, J. N. 89; Expedition 734
Madsen, Brigham D. 414
Madsen, David B. 61
Maseser 585; Karl G. 191, 195*
Magazine publishing industry 199
Magna 473-74
Magna copper complex 473-74, 477*
Malad Valley 412
Malin, Millard F. 584
Malmquist, O. N. 99
Mammoth 512, 513; Creek 663
Man and His Bread Museum 395
Manifesto 93
Manila 347

Part B — Index to The Arts Section (pages 201-268)

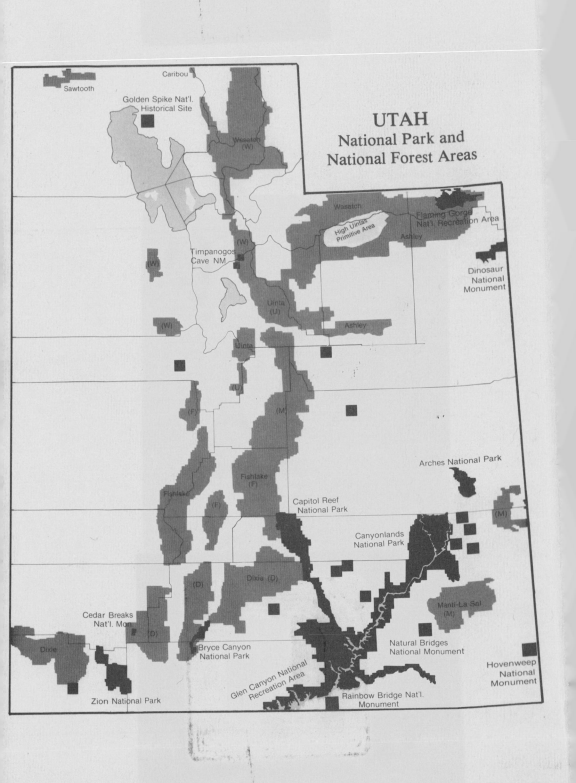

UTAH
National Park and
National Forest Areas

Sawtooth

Caribou

Golden Spike Nat'l.
Historical Site

Wasatch
(W)

Wasatch

High Uintas
Primitive Area

Flaming Gorge
Nat'l. Recreation Area

Ashley

Dinosaur
National
Monument

Timpanogos
Cave NM

(W)

(W)

(W)

Uinta
(U)

Ashley

Uinta

(U)

(M)

Arches National Park

(M)

(F)

Fishlake
(F)

Fishlake

(F)

Capitol Reef
National Park

Canyonlands
National Park

Dixie (D)

Manti-La Sal
(M)

(D)

Cedar Breaks
Nat'l. Mon.

(D)

Dixie

Bryce Canyon
National Park

Natural Bridges
National Monument

Hovenweep
National
Monument

Glen Canyon National
Recreation Area

Zion National Park

Rainbow Bridge Nat'l.
Monument